hodie
Scio
Chius
Ery-
thra
Cla...
ve
I.

IONII...

Leuconium

Lebedos
Ephesus
Phaneæ
Teos
Myus

Arginusæ I.

Æ-GÆ-U-M

Samus
I.
Samus
Heraclea
Miletus

Mare
Icari-
=um

Trogylium Pr.
Eleus I.

Icarus I.
Mindus
CARIA

Myconus
I.

Myconus

Lada I.

Mare
Myrtoum

SPORA=

Delos I.
nonnullis

Borgylia

Patmos I.
Ptolemeo

Gyarus

Lerus I.

...us
...s I.

Paros I.

Cos
sagra

Halicarn...

=DE'S I.

Asty
palea

DORIS
Cressa

Strongyle I.

Clarus I.

Cos I.

Cnidus

Mare
Ialyssus

Nisyris quæ
et Porphyris I.

Nisy
ris

Rhodium

Rh...
Rh

cesine
Mynia

Zinara
I.

Teughssa
I.

Chalce I.

Lind
dus

Oliaros I.

Astypalea I.

Pylus

Astypalea

Gira I.

Camy

Telus I.

Anaphe I.

=TUM

I.

=ERRANEUM

THE LANDMARK
XENOPHON'S *HELLENIKA*

THE LANDMARK
XENOPHON'S
HELLENIKA

A New Translation by John Marincola
with Maps, Annotations, Appendices, and Encyclopedic Index

Edited by Robert B. Strassler

With an Introduction by David Thomas

PANTHEON BOOKS · NEW YORK

Library of Congress Cataloging-in-Publication Data

Xenophon.
[History. English]
The Landmark Xenophon's Hellenika : a new translation / by John Marincola ; with maps, annotations, appendices, and encyclopedic index edited by Robert B. Strassler ; with an introduction by David Thomas.
    p. cm.
Includes bibliographical references and index.
ISBN 978-0-375-42255-3
1. Greece—History—To 146 B.C.E. 2. Greece—History—Peloponnesian War, 431–404 B.C.E.
I. Marincola, John. II. Strassler, Robert B., 1937– III. Title.
DF214.X4613 2009   938´.06—dc22   2009020970

Designed by Kim Llewellyn
Maps by Beehive Mapping
Index by Margot Levy
Photo research by Ingrid MacGillis

www.pantheonbooks.com

Printed in the United States of America

First Edition

9 8 7 6 5 4 3 2 1

TO
TONI, MATT, KAREN,
DAVE, LEO, AND CALEB

CONTENTS

INTRODUCTION

David Thomas

Introduction

§1.1. In his *Hellenika*, Xenophon of Athens gave his version of the events of the half century that had just passed when he wrote it, the years between 411 and 362.[a] That was a dramatic period in the history of Greece, in which the fortunes of the leading Greek city-states rose and fell disconcertingly as they repeatedly fought one another in shifting combinations. It was also a period that was vital in the development of our own culture. The citizens of Athens overcame problems in reconciling law and popular government and so produced a stable democracy. Much of what was written then continues to inspire philosophers and historians today.

§1.2. *Hellenika* largely concentrates on the relations between the two leading Greek city-states, Athens and Sparta, which were at war with each other for about half this period but were allies at its end. Xenophon had been a young man in Athens in the 400s, served in the Spartan army in early middle age, and later lived as a dependent of Sparta, so he knew what he was writing about. He finished the work only about five years or so after 362, when his narrative ends, and had in mind an audience that also knew a great deal about his subject matter—a fact that can create difficulties for the modern reader. Xenophon intended to tell his readers some new things, but he mostly aimed to give them his own slant on what was for them a familiar story. He wanted to make clear the messages he thought he found in the recent past. At the same time, he was almost as much concerned to make the past live again for his audience.

What Happened Before

§2.1. The very first sentence presupposes knowledge that the first readers all had but that is not so familiar today. It starts disconcertingly with the words "And after these things...."[a] The reader is evidently expected to know what happened earlier.

Intro.1.1a All dates in this edition of Xenophon's
Hellenika and its supporting materials are
B.C.E. (Before the Common Era), unless
otherwise specified.

Intro.2.1a In the Introduction and appendices, the
authors may have used their own or other
translations.

§2.2. At *Hellenika*'s opening, in 411, the Athenians[a] are fighting the Spartans,[b] with the Persians[c] intermittently supporting the latter. The story of the shifting relationships of these three powers had been a large part of the history of Greece throughout the fifth century, as it was to continue to be throughout the period that Xenophon covers.

§2.3. In 480 the Great King of Persia, Xerxes, had mounted a huge expedition against continental Greece. Then as later, Sparta and Athens were the two most militarily powerful city-states in Greece: the Spartans on land and through the system of alliances by which they controlled almost all of the Peloponnese;[a] the Athenians at sea, through their fleet, the largest of any Greek state. The two cities stood together against the Persians, and many of the other Greeks joined them, though Sparta's traditional rival in the Peloponnese, Argos,[b] stayed neutral and Athens' northern neighbor Thebes[c] ended up fighting on the Persian side. A small Spartan-led force heroically but unsuccessfully resisted the Persian advance at Thermopylae.[d] Not long after, the Persians were ignominiously defeated at sea at the battle of Salamis[e] and the following year on land at the battle of Plataea.[f] The Greeks' stand against the mighty Persians was a formative experience, recounted for us with great literary skill half a century later by Herodotus, "the father of history." The threat of a Persian conquest of mainland Greece fell away and was never revived.

§2.4. The Athenians went on to liberate the Greek cities of the islands of the Aegean Sea[a] and the western shore of Asia Minor[b] from their Persian overlords. But then they converted the cross-Aegean naval confederacy created to counter the Persians into an Athenian empire. It was not long before Athens and Sparta were bitterly hostile to each other. They fought one inconclusive war, about which we know little, in the 450s, and then in 431 they began what is known to us as the Peloponnesian War. The first two decades of this conflict were chronicled by a contemporary, the Athenian Thucydides, one of the greatest historians of all time. Thucydides' narrative breaks off in the autumn of 411, and Xenophon's history begins at roughly the same point. A little earlier, the Persians reappeared in the story, trying to use the Greek conflict and Athens' difficulties to their advantage in reasserting their position over the Greeks of Asia Minor. That is the situation on the first page of *Hellenika*, where the Spartans are being supported in their struggle against Athens by Pharnabazos, the Persian satrap (governor) of Hellespontine Phrygia[c] in northwest Asia Minor.

§2.5. Much of the hostility between Athens and Sparta might be described as great-power rivalry, but there was also an ideological element. Athens was a direct democracy: important policy decisions were taken by an assembly in which all citizens could readily participate, and those citizens made up a large majority of the adult Greek males living in Attica.[a] Athens had been a democracy since the end of

---

Intro.2.2a Athens: Intro. Map 3.2. See Appendix B, The Athenian Government and the Oligarchy of the Thirty.
Intro.2.2b Sparta: Intro. Map 3.2. See Appendix E, Spartan Government and Society.
Intro.2.2c Persia: Intro. Map 3.2, locator. See Appendix D, Persia in Xenophon's *Hellenika*.
Intro.2.3a Peloponnese: Intro. Map 3.2.
Intro.2.3b Argos: Intro. Map 3.2.
Intro.2.3c Thebes: Intro. Map 3.2, inset.
Intro.2.3d Thermopylae: Intro. Map 3.2.
Intro.2.3e Salamis: Intro. Map 3.2, inset.
Intro.2.3f Plataea: Intro. Map 3.2, inset.
Intro.2.4a Islands of the Aegean Sea: Intro. Map 3.2.
Intro.2.4b Asia (Asia Minor): Intro. Map 3.2, locator.
Intro.2.4c Hellespontine Phrygia: Intro. Map 3.2.
Intro.2.5a Attica: Intro. Map 3.2, inset.

the sixth century. During the fifth century Athenian institutions had become yet more democratic, the active politicians had been drawn from widening social circles, and enthusiasm for democracy had led Athens to proselytize among Athenian subjects and allies (though cities ruled by traditional aristocracies were not forced to become democracies unless they had rebelled).

§2.6. The Spartans, by contrast, tended to support oligarchies, both among their neighboring allies (the Peloponnesian League) and elsewhere. Sparta's own constitution is difficult to characterize succinctly, but it was not a classic oligarchy. For one thing, there were two hereditary kings who retained quite a lot of power and acted as the principal generals. For another, the citizen-body was reasonably numerous and had the right to attend an assembly, which elected various officials and voted on whether or not to go to war. But more steadily influential than the assembly was a small council, largely elected for life, which was a typically oligarchic feature. Moreover, the number of citizens was smaller than in Athens, and the number was constantly shrinking, principally because of the way in which the Spartan system of land tenure interacted with qualifications for full citizenship. Most important of all, Sparta's citizens were a small segment of the Greek adult males in Laconia[a] and Messenia,[b] the two territories the Spartans directly controlled. The majority of the inhabitants, though Greeks like the Spartans, were unfree—the so-called helots,[c] who were tied to the land in a special form of state serfdom. A sizeable number of the free Greeks did not have full citizens' rights. So Sparta had good reasons for not encouraging the extension of political power to the poorer classes in neighboring states; and conversely, aristocrats and others among the rich even in Athens had some reason to look favorably on the methods by which the Spartan elite stayed in control.

§2.7. According to Thucydides, the Peloponnesian War that had broken out in 431 was caused by Sparta's fear and jealousy of Athens' growing power. But after a decade of fighting, the parties concluded a stalemate peace, the Peace of Nikias (named for the Athenian general who led the negotiations). It was an uneasy truce, punctuated by military activity on both sides that fell short of full-scale war. In 415 the Athenians sent a massive expedition against the Sicilian city of Syracuse[a] in an attempt to ensure, among other things, that Syracuse's resources could not be used to support Sparta in any further conflict. However, the expedition was crippled shortly after it began when Alcibiades, one of the three generals in command and the venture's principal proponent, was forced to flee into exile as a result of accusations of impiety. In 413 the expedition was totally destroyed, with a huge loss of ships and men. By this time, the Spartans had revived their war effort, and they redoubled it the following year as many Athenian subject-allies in the Aegean, emboldened by Athens' defeat in Sicily, revolted. The Persians now began to fish in these troubled waters, and before long formally reached agreement with the Spar-

Intro.2.6a   Laconia: Intro. Map 3.2.
Intro.2.6b   Messenia: Intro. Map 3.2.
Intro.2.6c   Helots: see Appendix E, §11–12, and Appen
             dix F, The Spartan Army (and the Battle of
             Leuctra), §6.
Intro.2.7a   Syracuse, Sicily: Intro. Map 3.2, locator.

tans on the terms of an alliance against Athens, under which it was envisaged that the Persians were to control the Greek cities of Asia Minor. In 411, the strain of the war led to a temporary collapse of democratic self-confidence in Athens and the imposition of an oligarchic regime known as the Four Hundred. The oligarchs, however, fell out among themselves about whether to surrender to Sparta. The extreme oligarchs, who wanted to capitulate, lost out to a more moderate group led by one Theramenes; the Four Hundred were then replaced by a wider oligarchy, the Five Thousand, which later slid back into a full democratic regime. In the meantime, the Athenian fleet based on the east Aegean island of Samos[b] had remained true to the democracy throughout and had won a famous victory against the Spartan fleet in the Hellespont at the battle of Kynossema[c] (summer 411), thanks to a decisive intervention by none other than Alcibiades, whom the fleet had recalled from exile. It is shortly after this battle that Thucydides breaks off his narrative, and not long thereafter, Xenophon takes up the tale.

What Happened Next

§3.1. So now we have come to the period that this book covers, and one might hope to leave it to Xenophon to tell the story. But, as we said earlier, he presupposes a lot of knowledge on the part of his readers, and it is one of his most striking characteristics as a historian that he leaves out many things that in any conventional view would count among the most important events of the period he covers. So an opening sketch may help orient the modern reader.

§3.2. We saw that, shortly before *Hellenika* begins, the Spartans and the Persians had become allies. But while Persia's satrap in the north of western Asia Minor, Pharnabazos, lived up to the agreement, the southern satrap, Tissaphernes, temporized about fulfilling Persia's treaty obligations to maintain the Spartan fleet. Partly because of this, Athens succeeded in holding out for a further six and a half years. To start with, the Athenians obtained notable successes under the leadership of Alcibiades (in particular the battle of Cyzicus[a] in early 410). But the Athenians dismissed him again, and Cyrus, the younger son of Daruis II, the Great King of Persia, brought the full extent of Persia's vast financial resources to bear in support of Sparta. Eventually, in 405, the canny Spartan admiral Lysander won a decisive victory at the battle of Aigospotamoi,[b] where he captured almost the entire Athenian fleet. In the spring of 404, after a long siege, he forced Athens to capitulate. The Athenians then suffered a more violent period of oligarchy when Lysander compelled them to subject themselves to a group of thirty men, called the Thirty by contemporaries but known to later generations as the Thirty Tyrants. The Thirty included Theramenes, and, as he had with the Four Hundred seven years earlier, he tried to moderate their course. But this time he lost to the extremists, who were led by an embittered former exile, Kritias. Theramenes was executed, and something of a reign of terror ensued until the Spartan government, fed up for many reasons with

Intro.2.7b Samos: Intro. Map 3.2.
Intro.2.7c Kynossema, Hellespont: Intro. Map 3.2.
Intro.3.2a Cyzicus: Intro. Map 3.2.

Intro.3.2b Aigospotamoi (Aigospotamos): Intro. Map 3.2.

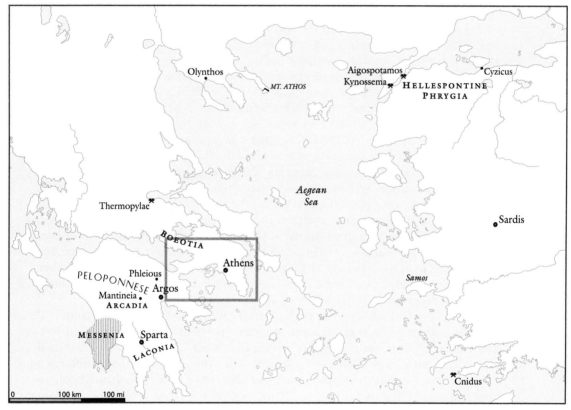

*See the Editor's Preface and the Key to Maps for an explanation of map layout, symbols, and typography.

INTRO. MAP 3.2

Lysander and his cronies, switched course and forced a reconciliation between the oligarchic regime in the city and an armed band under an Athenian named Thrasyboulos that had taken over Athens' port, Peiraieus.[c] In 403 the democracy was restored.

§3.3. Although it was only for a short period after her victory over Athens that Sparta engaged in or winked at atrocities in Athens and in several other cities, Spartan domination of Greece was quickly resented not only by Athens but also by Sparta's previous allies Corinth[a] and Thebes. Sparta also forfeited the support of Persia, now under a new Great King, Artaxerxes II. Having defeated a rebellion by Sparta's friend Cyrus at the battle of Cunaxa[b] (401), Artaxerxes set about restoring Persia's former control of the Greek cities of Asia Minor. Although the Spartans had agreed to Persian control of these cities a decade earlier, now they sent troops to Asia Minor to resist the Persians, climaxing in 396 with the dispatch of one of their two kings, Agesilaos, to lead their forces there. But after a striking success at the battle of Sardis,[c] his expedition was cut short. Sparta had to recall him to deal with a renewed outbreak of war in continental Greece when Corinth, Thebes, and Athens joined together to fight Sparta in what we know as the Corinthian War (395–86). Persia this time financed a fleet on the anti-Spartan side, and under Pharnabazos and the Athenian Konon it won a decisive victory at the battle of Cnidus[d] (394). Although the war in Greece and, to a degree, in the East Aegean sputtered on for years, the Spartans had to abandon their attempt to free the Greek cities of Asia from Persia. The Asian Greeks gained nothing, even when King Artaxerxes switched his support back to Sparta in exasperation at Athenian attempts to revive their interests along the coast of Asia Minor and to dabble in Cyprus[e] and Egypt.[f] Persian control over the Asia Minor seaboard was reaffirmed by the peace terms that Artaxerxes successfully dictated in 386 (the so-called King's Peace). Artaxerxes, revealed as the arbiter of the Greek world, had achieved even more power in the West than his early-fifth-century predecessors had won with their direct imperialism.

§3.4. Through the King's Peace, the Spartans were again dominant in continental Greece. Their position might seem even more powerful than it had been in 404. They broke up the Arcadian city of Mantineia[a] into four villages and intervened successfully in nearby Phleious.[b] Outside the Peloponnese, they conquered Olynthos[c] on the North Aegean coast and also assisted one Theban faction to power against its rival, occupying the Theban citadel with their own troops (382)— something that even sympathetic contemporaries such as Xenophon regarded as shocking. But the wheel of fortune turned. A tiny band of exiles succeeded in liberating Thebes in midwinter 379/8, and Athens and Thebes once again stood together against Sparta in the Boeotian[d] War (378–371, with a brief interval of peace in 375/4). Two factors were crucial to the revival of Athenian fortunes: the Athenians managed to induce some of their former Aegean allies to join them once

Intro.3.2c Peiraieus: Intro. Map 3.2, inset.	Intro.3.3e Cyprus: Intro. Map 3.2, locator.
Intro.3.3a Corinth: Intro. Map 3.2, inset.	Intro.3.3f Egypt: Intro. Map 3.2, locator.
Intro.3.3b Cunaxa (Mesopotamia): Intro. Map 3.2, locator.	Intro.3.4a Mantineia, Arcadia: Intro. Map 3.2.
	Intro.3.4b Phleious: Intro. Map 3.2.
Intro.3.3c Sardis: Intro. Map 3.2.	Intro.3.4c Olynthos: Intro. Map 3.2.
Intro.3.3d Cnidus: Intro. Map 3.2.	Intro.3.4d Boeotia: Intro. Map 3.2.

again in a naval alliance (the Second Athenian League), with greater safeguards against Athenian misuse of the position of alliance leaders, and they also persuaded Artaxerxes to stand aside and even to press Sparta to accept the new situation. The Thebans were successful as well, reuniting Boeotia under their control, though their methods ultimately so alienated the Athenians that they deserted Thebes and agreed to the Peace of 372/1, when Artaxerxes seems to have once again tilted in the Spartan direction. But the reunited Boeotians astonished the whole Greek world when, led by the intelligent and charismatic Theban Epaminondas, they crushed the Spartan army under King Kleombrotos at Leuctra[c] in midsummer 371, the first defeat of the Spartans by other Greeks in a full-blown pitched battle for well over 150 years.

§3.5. Thus ended the Spartan hegemony over Greece. And very shortly afterward the Thebans ended Sparta's older hegemony over the Peloponnese and even Spartan control of Messenia[a] in the southwest of the Peloponnese. At one time the Messenians had been independent of Sparta, but they had been conquered centuries earlier. Now, in 369, Messenia was restored to independence by an invading army under Epaminondas. Five times in the 360s Theban armies penetrated the Peloponnese; as a consequence, it became obvious to all but the Spartans themselves and a few of their diehard supporters that Messenia was destined to remain independent. The Theban expeditions also ensured that Megalopolis,[b] a city near Sparta's northern border, founded by the Arcadians after Leuctra and fortified over the following years, would also remain as a check on Spartan ambitions, even though Arcadia itself had since split into pro- and anti-Theban elements. To the indignation of Sparta's supporters, in 367 the Theban Pelopidas persuaded the Persians to accept the situation brought about by Leuctra and the liberation of Messenia and switch away from the Spartans again, recognizing Thebes as the leading state in Greece. This diplomatic effort misfired at first, partly because Thebes and Persia did not initially appreciate that a stable settlement required them to make concessions to Athens; but in 366 most Greek states other than Sparta recognized the liberation of Messenia.

§3.6. Meanwhile, the Athenians, though impelled during 369–366 by distrust of Thebes to act in alliance with Sparta within the Peloponnese, were more concerned with reviving the Aegean empire they had created in the fifth century. Although the Athenians seem to have conducted themselves within or fairly close to the letter of their commitments to the members of the Second Athenian League, they did not over time remain true to the promises to the Aegean islanders that they had proclaimed in the 370s. Athens used League resources on long-running campaigns of little benefit to the allies, mostly in attempts to conquer the city of Amphipolis[a] (from 368) and the Thracian Chersonese[b] (from 365). Slightly earlier in 365, the Athenian general Timotheos had retaken the island of Samos[c] from the control of a Persian interloper; Athens then expelled the Samians and assigned their lands to

Intro.3.4f   Leuctra: Intro. Map 3.2, inset.
Intro.3.5a   Messenia: Intro. Map 4.2, BX.
Intro.3.5b   Megalopolis: Intro. Map 4.2, BX.
Intro.3.6a   Amphipolis: Intro. Map 4.2, AX.
Intro.3.6b   Thracian Chersonese (peninsula): Intro. Map 4.2, AY.

Intro.3.6c   Samos: Intro. Map 4.2, BY.

colonies of Athenian citizens. The same hard-nosed attitude prevailed in Athenian attitudes toward Sparta. In 366 the Athenians were persuaded by Persian concessions on Athens' role in the Aegean to leave Sparta out in the cold and sign up for the general peace that recognized the independence of Messenia.[d] Admittedly, Athens and Sparta once again fought on the same side in 364–62, but the Athenians were not motivated by love of Sparta but, rather, by the desire to substitute Athenian influence for that of Thebes in Arcadia. In 362 after the battle of Mantineia (in effect a draw, as Epaminondas, though victorious, was killed in the hour of victory), Athens and all the other mainland Greek states except Sparta entered into another common peace to which Messenia was admitted as a party.

§3.7. Xenophon breaks off his work with the death of Epaminondas on the battlefield of Mantineia. The subsequent common peace confirmed Sparta's fall from dominance. Greece south of Thessaly[a] was now widely governed by democracies, and it was possible to imagine that the region might enter an era of comparative peace and stability—though that is emphatically not the way that Xenophon presents it, nor is it the view adopted by those many modern historians who follow his lead here.

§3.8. We need to continue the story a little further, because though the events retailed in *Hellenika* end in 362, Xenophon's account naturally took time to write and was finished a little later. It can be shown that the passage on Thessaly at 6.4.33–37 must have been written between 357 and 353. Within that period, winter 356/5 is to my mind the likeliest date for the final composition. So Xenophon completed his work, and expected his first audience to read it, in the knowledge of a further six years of events.

§3.9. There were two key developments in 357, both of which crucially destabilized Greece and opened the way for the extinction of the liberty of the city-states in the following decades. In that year, Athens' most powerful Aegean allies rebelled, spurred on by the representative of the Persian empire in Caria,[a] the satrap Mausolus. The consequent war, known to us as the Social War, was still ongoing when Xenophon wrote, if he was doing so in winter 356/5. The war ended in mid-355 when a virtually bankrupt Athens had to let the rebels secede after the Great King of Persia (now no longer Artaxerxes II but his son, Artaxerxes III Ochus) threatened to intervene on their side—a threat that had become a familiar motif of fourth-century history to date. Also in 357, the Thebans felt strong enough to push for the final ruin of both Sparta and Phocis,[b] Boeotia's neighbor and an even older enemy of Thebes. Thebes manipulated the Amphiktyonic League, the international body that controlled the sacred shrine and oracle of Apollo at Delphi,[c] into imposing massive fines on the Phocians for cultivating sacred land and on Sparta for having occupied the Theban citadel in 382, more than twenty years earlier. But this Theban skullduggery lit the fuse that ultimately ended the power, and even existence, of the state of Thebes and destroyed the liberty of Greece. The Phocians did not take their punishment lying down. Encouraged by King Archidamos III of Sparta, they seized

Intro.3.6d It is highly controversial whether Athens and Persia were part of the peace accords in this year, as Xenophon's silence implies the opposite: for the evidence, see n. 7.4.10b. Persia's role in the Peaces of 375/4 and

372/1 is also somewhat controversial.
Intro.3.7a Thessaly: Intro. Map 4.2, AX.
Intro.3.9a Caria: Intro. Map 4.2, BY.
Intro.3.9b Phocis: Intro. Map 4.2, AX.
Intro.3.9c Delphi: Intro. Map 4.2, AX.

Delphi; in late 356, when Xenophon was probably putting the final touches to his work, they were nerving themselves to finance their defense against the outraged Amphiktyonic League by appropriating the huge wealth that the pious had given to the Delphic shrine over the centuries. It must have been a time of anguish for Xenophon, a deeply religious supporter of Delphi (see, e.g., 7.1.27), who, though he strongly disapproved of Sparta's treatment of Thebes in 382–379, still greatly preferred his former patrons at Sparta to their enemy Thebes.

§3.10. The ultimate victor in the fourth century was not Sparta, Athens, or Thebes or even Persia but Macedon,[a] a state almost unmentioned in *Hellenika* for the good reason that it kept falling to pieces until Philip II succeeded to power there in 360/59. Philip then set out, by astute and cynical diplomacy and above all by the creation of a formidable fighting machine, to unify his realm, to deter the aggressors on its borders, and to dominate Greece. The Sacred War between the Amphiktyonic League and the Phocians gave him crucial opportunities, of which he took prompt advantage. But even before it broke out he had captured Amphipolis and Pydna:[b] Philip's looming shadow may perhaps help explain why Xenophon gives so much space to the opportunities and threats presented to Sparta (and hence to Greece) in the north, first by the Olynthians[c] (5.2.11–19) and then by Jason of Pherai,[d] whose dominance in Thessaly in the late 370s Xenophon deals with at length at 6.1.4–19, 6.4.27–32.

§3.11. As indicated above, Xenophon's first readers would not have needed *Hellenika* to tell them about the main facts in this sketch—for example, they would all have heard about the Thirty, the battle of Leuctra, and the Second Athenian League. There are two other topics that most of the initial audience would have borne in mind when reading the work but that readers today need to be told about: Xenophon's life and Xenophon's other works.

Xenophon's Life

§4.1. Xenophon was probably born around 430 or a little later,[a] just after the beginning of the Peloponnesian War, into an Athenian family that was rich enough to own horses but was perhaps not quite the cream of the aristocracy. On reaching manhood, he no doubt fought for Athens in the last decade of the fifth century, and he almost certainly served in the cavalry, an elite corps that gave especially strong support to the Thirty. Most of his first audience would have been well aware of this even before starting to read *Hellenika*.

§4.2. Moreover, probably every reader would have known that in 401, two years after the restoration of democracy, Xenophon embarked on a great adventure: he joined the forces being raised by Artaxerxes II's brother Cyrus, who, as mentioned above (3.3), was making a bid for the Persian throne. It had been the sixteen-year-old Cyrus who had thrown the full weight of Persian money behind the Spartans

---

Intro.3.10a   Macedon: Intro. Map 4.2, AX.
Intro.3.10b   Pydna: Intro. Map 4.2, AX.
Intro.3.10c   Olynthos: Intro. Map 4.2, AX.
Intro.3.10d   Pherai (Thessaly): Intro. Map 4.2, AX.
Intro.4.1a   The direct evidence is actually that he was

born ten years earlier than this, but in most scholars' view indirect evidence from his *Anabasis* outweighs it.

and against the Athenians. But when his father, Darius, died, it was not Cyrus but his elder brother, Artaxerxes, who had succeeded to the throne. Cyrus, with ten thousand Greek troops and about twice as many from Asia, marched from Sardis[a] in western Asia Minor further inland to Mesopotamia, where he fell at the battle of Cunaxa.[b] His Greek troops had to make their own way back to the Greek world, their difficulties increased because the Persians treacherously arrested and executed all but one of their most senior officers. The Ten Thousand fought their way northward, harassed by native tribes and enduring harsh weather conditions, until they came to the Black Sea[c] coast and ultimately to the Hellespont.[d] Now led by Xenophon, they eventually joined up with the Spartan army, then on its anti-Persian campaign in Asia Minor. The story became common knowledge in Greece, being grist to the mill of people like the Athenian orator, teacher, and pamphleteer Isocrates, who in his *Panegyricus* of 380 argued that it all showed what a pushover the Persians would be if the Greeks launched a crusade against them.[e] Most of the first readers of *Hellenika* would also have known about the episode from Xenophon's own account, *Anabasis* ("The March Up-Country"),[f] which made so much of his part in the proceedings that he found it prudent to put it out under the pseudonym of Themistogenes of Syracuse, to whom he attributes it at 3.1.2.

§4.3. Readers of *Anabasis* and probably most Athenians would have been aware of what followed. Xenophon joined the Spartan expeditions to Asia in the early years of the fourth century, and thus in 396–394 he served under the Spartan king Agesilaos when the latter came out to crusade in person. When the Corinthian War broke out in 395 and Agesilaos was recalled to mainland Greece, Xenophon accompanied him and so would have been present at the battle of Coronea,[a] where Athens was among the cities whose troops were ranged against the returning Spartan force. Through an adverse judgment by the Athenians, Xenophon found himself formally an exile from Athens. It is not clear to us now exactly when this happened, but it occurred between 399 and 394, in my (minority) view most likely in 396; it is interesting to note that Xenophon never expresses bitterness about his exile, so presumably he accepted that he had done something to deserve it. Anyway, he could not go back to Athens, and so at some point after 394, though perhaps not immediately, he was settled by the Spartans in the northwest Peloponnese on an estate at Skillous,[b] near Olympia,[c] as he tells us at *Anabasis* 5.3.7, on territory previously owned by Elis,[d] the city-state to the north of Skillous. There he lived as a country gentleman for about twenty years, until he lost the estate after the battle of Leuctra, when the Eleians forcibly repossessed their outlying lands. Shortly thereafter, he took up residence in Corinth.[e]

§4.4. Whether Xenophon ever came back to live in Athens is a controversial question today. His first readers obviously knew one way or the other, and they

Intro.4.2a Sardis: Intro. Map 4.2, AY.
Intro.4.2b Cunaxa: Intro. Map 3.2, locator.
Intro.4.2c Black Sea: Intro. Map 4.2, AY.
Intro.4.2d Hellespont: Intro. Map 4.2, AY.
Intro.4.2e Isocrates (436–338) was perhaps the most influential rhetorician of his time. For more on Isocrates, see Ancient Sources.
Intro.4.2f See §5.2 for a discussion of the possible sequence and dates of publication for Xenophon's other works.
Intro.4.3a Coronea, Boeotia: Intro. Map 4.2, BX.
Intro.4.3b Skillous: Intro. Map 4.2, BX.
Intro.4.3c Olympia: Intro. Map 4.2, BX.
Intro.4.3d Elis: Intro. Map 4.2, BX.
Intro.4.3e Corinth: Intro. Map 4.2, BX.

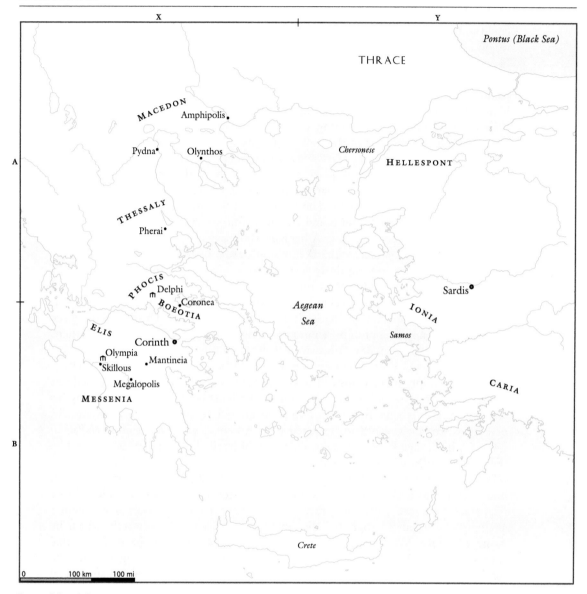

Intro. Map 4.2

could judge the tone of his references to Athens accordingly, but we do not. What we do know, and what every Athenian reader in the 350s would have known, is that he was the father of a great Athenian hero, the cavalryman Gryllos, whose gallant exploits against the Thebans at the battle of Mantineia[a] in 362 were depicted by the painter Euphranor in one of Athens' chief public buildings, the Painted Stoa. So high was Gryllos' reputation that subsequent generations of Athenians came to believe that Euphranor's painting depicted Gryllos slaying the Theban general Epaminondas, but no one in the 350s would have made that mistake. They would have recognized that when, at *Hellenika* 7.5.17, Xenophon describes in some detail a cavalry engagement that took place on the day before the main battle in which Epaminondas was killed, and remarks that good men were killed on both sides, he is commemorating his son's death. The memorial is the more fitting for Xenophon's air of impartial objectivity; he doesn't even mention Gryllos' name (also carefully suppressing the names of all other Athenians who participated in the battle).

§4.5. Most scholars believe that Xenophon's exile was revoked in the 360s: they point to the facts that during those years his sons fought for Athens and he himself wrote his *Hipparchicus* ("On the Command of Cavalry"), a work directed in detail at an Athenian audience and seeking to help the Athenian military effort. Many, but not all, of those scholars think he went back to live in Athens. This is not the place for detailed argument, but in my (minority) view Xenophon's right to live in Athens had been reinstated in 386, since it is likely that the King's Peace of that year prescribed that all exiles except murderers should be restored in all relevant cities. However, Xenophon chose instead to stay in Skillous, and when he was turned out of there, he chose to try his luck in Corinth. That must be significant in assessing his attitude toward Athens. But Xenophon probably did go back to Athens eventually, perhaps when the Corinthians expelled their Athenian garrison in 366 (*Hellenika* 7.4.4–5). If so, then it was just a coincidence that he died in Corinth, as reported by the late writer Diogenes Laertius.[a]

§4.6. Other details of Xenophon's life, such as the date of his marriage, are yet more obscure to us and were not necessarily clear to many of his first readers. More important than the truth of various other scraps from late sources is whether anything else about Xenophon's life can be recovered from the way in which he wrote *Hellenika*. Where it is vivid and detailed, does this show he was an actual witness, or is it the art of the writer? Sometimes it is very tempting to infer the former. At 1.2.1–13 he tells us about a campaign in Ionia[a] by the Athenian general Thrasyllos in extraordinary detail to no obvious point. That suggests that he may be giving us his memories of his own first serious military campaign. Similarly, when Xenophon seems to see the rule of the Thirty from the point of view of a member of their cavalry, this is likely to be because he himself served in that capacity, although he does not say so explicitly. That is in any case likely from his age at the time and the abundant evidence of his horsemanship. But vividness is a dangerous criterion by

Intro.4.4a Mantineia: Intro. Map 4.2, BX.
Intro.4.5a Diogenes Laertius, *Lives and Opinions of Eminent Philosophers* 2.6.56. This work is a compilation of varying worth, usually thought to date from around 225 C.E.

Unfortunately, the date Diogenes gives for Xenophon's death (360/59) is false, as *Hellenika* and at least one other of his works refer to later events.
Intro.4.6a Ionia (in Asia Minor): Intro. Map 4.2, BY.

which to infer personal witness, since Xenophon can also write vividly about events at which he was not present, for example events in Europe when he was in Asia.

§4.7. One other fact about Xenophon is known and will certainly have been in the minds of his first readers; perhaps he would have said it was the most important thing in his life. He was a devoted admirer of the notorious wise man and mystic Socrates, who was put to death by the Athenians in 399 ostensibly for introducing new gods and corrupting the city's youth. Despite Xenophon's devotion, he had sidestepped Socrates' efforts to persuade him not to go on Cyrus' expedition, as is recounted in *Anabasis* (3.1.4–8), but Xenophon's subsequent difficulties confirmed to him how wise Socrates had been, and he later wrote four works in which Socrates is the main character. Socrates denied that he was truly wise and said he was merely a lover of wisdom, a philosopher. He himself wrote nothing, but his numerous disciples in the next generation were prolific, especially Plato, of whom it has been said that the whole of Western philosophy since consists of footnotes to his dialogues. The differences between Xenophon's portrait of Socrates and that in Plato's dialogues (and between both of them and the Socrates who appears in the comic dramatist Aristophanes' play *Clouds*) constitute one of the great problems of classical scholarship. Plato's Socrates is very interested in metaphysics and epistemology, he is shown frequently engaging in destructive cross-examination of opponents, and he espouses some peculiar and distinctive views (in particular, that the good man never harms anyone, even his enemies). Xenophon's Socrates often concerns himself with practical matters, is shown acting as a sort of therapist to his friends, and apparently has much more conventional views. But Socrates makes only a brief appearance in *Hellenika*, when, presiding by chance over the Athenian assembly in 406, he defies the mob that is howling for the blood of six Athenian generals (1.7.15). Xenophon had said what he had to say about Socrates elsewhere and saw no reason to repeat himself. Perhaps he means to imply that *Hellenika*'s world of politics, war, and diplomacy benefits from prudence but has no place for true wisdom.

Other Works by Xenophon

§5.1. Fifteen works were transmitted through antiquity under Xenophon's name, and fortunately all fifteen have come down to us. However, almost all modern scholars agree on stylistic grounds that what has been transmitted to us as *Constitution of the Athenians* is not by Xenophon. Indeed, most scholars believe that one particular observation in it predates 424, so the work was therefore written before Xenophon reached adulthood. There is some ancient evidence to support the modern view, for Diogenes Laertius tells us that the first-century scholar Demetrius of Magnesia denied the authenticity of a work to which he gives the title *Constitution of the Athenians and of the Lacedaemonians*.[a] Scholars in the last two centuries have raised doubts about several of the other fourteen works, especially two of them

---

Intro.5.1a Lacedaemonians: for practical purposes, the term may be regarded as equivalent to "Spartans," but strictly speaking, it also covers free men in Laconia who were not citizens of Sparta, such as the *perioikoi*, on whom see Appendix E, §10.

(*Constitution of the Lacedaemonians* and *Cynegeticus*), but the general, although not universal, consensus today is that all fourteen are genuine.

§5.2. The order and date of the fourteen works are much debated. It would take us too far away from *Hellenika* to do justice to the arguments, so I will state my own views briskly. Xenophon's first publication was probably *Cynegeticus*, dating perhaps from around 390. The work gives advice on hunting, especially on Athenian methods of what we know today as beagling, that is, hunting hares on foot with hounds that track their prey by scent. Then there was a long gap in publication, but not necessarily in writing, perhaps broken in the late 370s with *Socrates' Apology*, an account of Socrates' defense speech to the jury, in 399. Xenophon wrote this after, and presumably in rivalry with, one of Plato's most famous works, his version of Socrates' speech (which Plato, unlike Xenophon, was there to hear). Probably in the early 360s Xenophon brought out *Anabasis*, telling of his part in Cyrus' expedition, the return of the Ten Thousand Greek mercenaries in Cyrus' army, and their subsequent adventures until just before they joined the Spartan forces in Asia Minor. At about this time, Xenophon also published *Memorabilia*, an extended defense of Socrates' virtues as a teacher and a citizen, followed by two further Socratic works: *Symposium*, a portrait of a more playful Socrates at a fictional dinner party given by the young Kallias, an Athenian aristocrat who turns up in *Hellenika* in his old age, making a pompous speech (6.3.4–6); and *Oeconomicus*, a Socratic dialogue on the principles of household and estate management, which contains a hidden message that the life of members of the landed gentry, such as Xenophon himself, is second best to the life of Socrates. Another dialogue, *Hiero* (perhaps not written until the following decade), also features a "wise man"—not Xenophon's hero, Socrates, but the less savory fifth-century poet Simonides, who tries to show Hiero, the autocrat of Syracuse, how he could live in happiness if he adopted less arbitrary and more beneficial policies toward his subjects. Very probably in 365 Xenophon put out *Hipparchicus*, a useful manual of advice for Athenian cavalry commanders, followed (how much later is unclear) by another manual, *On Horsemanship*, on how to look after horses. At the end of this prolific decade, he published his most technically innovative work, *Cyropaedia*, or *Education of Cyrus*, a cross between a historical novel about the sixth-century founder of the Persian Empire, Cyrus the Elder, a technical military manual, and a politico-moral treatise (although modern scholars disagree about what the moral is supposed to be). After 360 came *Agesilaos*, a laudatory memorial to the Spartan king with whom Xenophon served in 396–394. And despite much dispute, *Hellenika* itself, incontrovertibly finished in the 350s, should also largely be regarded as a work of this late period—although, as we shall see, the beginning (1.1 to around 2.2.23) was written much earlier. Most likely in the summer of 355, as the Social War came to its unfortunate end, and thus probably after the completion of *Hellenika*, Xenophon wrote *Poroi* (*Ways and Means*), a short treatise on how Athens could recover from war by developing existing economic resources. Finally, *Constitution of the Lacedaemonians* seems to have been found among Xenophon's papers after his death, presumably alongside the non-Xenophontic *Constitution of the Athenians*, having been put aside by him unfinished. He probably wrote it in 378–377.[a]

§5.3. If one surveys this body of work as a whole, it becomes apparent that Xenophon was interested in experimenting with the structure of his works and with developing new genres of writing. He kept tight control over his material, much more than first appears, and enjoyed playing with the expectations of his readers. Although his works cover many different genres, his style is generally consistent (*Cynegeticus* and the beginning of *Hellenika* are comparative exceptions, as to a lesser extent is *Constitution of the Lacedaemonians*), and many themes surface in several works, especially the desirability of physical toil and self-control and the importance of good leadership for states and especially for armies.

§5.4. Two of these works deserve more comment here. *Constitution of the Lacedaemonians* is a problematic piece, and much about it is controversial. The work is ostensibly written to show how Sparta's success is built on the Spartans' civil and military institutions, including their bizarre educational practice of encouraging teenage boys to learn how to steal, and in all but one of its chapters Sparta appears to be an object of praise; but the penultimate chapter is a strong denunciation of the contemporary Spartans for being untrue to their own ideals. Despite a number of apparent contradictions between this chapter and the preceding ones, on close reading most contradictions disappear; but the work is still inconsistent on the central point of whether the Spartans obey their ancestral laws. Probably this is because the draft is not in final form. Xenophon could hardly have written a denunciation of Sparta while he was on campaign with the Spartan army or published it while he was still a Spartan dependent in Skillous, but his complaints presuppose a continuing background of Spartan governors (harmosts) abroad, and this was not the case after Leuctra in 371. Thus we see that already in the 370s Xenophon was of two minds about the Sparta for whose service he had deserted his native city, to such an extent that he could not get his exposition of his position to come out right, and so put it aside.

§5.5. The second work requiring further comment here is *Agesilaos*, in some ways a much shorter companion piece to *Hellenika*. As befits an encomium, *Agesilaos* depicts a virtually flawless king, whereas, as we shall see, *Hellenika* shows him with blemishes, if not "warts and all." The description of Agesilaos' Asian expedition of 396–394 is very similar in the two works, but the precise wording differs: Xenophon evidently took the earlier version and went over it with considerable care to produce the later one. Unfortunately, it is difficult to tell whether he toned down the expansive and confident remarks and the elevated vocabulary of *Agesilaos* to produce the more measured, objective, and (in terms of Athenian dialect) strictly correct *Hellenika*, or whether he started with the apparently straightforward account

Intro.5.2a For a different view, see Paul Cartledge in
            Appendix E, §5, where the work is assigned
            to the 350s.

in *Hellenika* and both expurgated it and pepped it up to produce a more fitting obituary notice for his dead leader. The changes in vocabulary and emphasis can be used to argue in either direction. But there is one point, less often emphasized, that shows that *Agesilaos* was written before at least the second half of *Hellenika*. At *Agesilaos* 2.20, Xenophon briefly describes a campaign by Agesilaos during the early 380s against the Acarnanians,[a] who lived to the northwest of the Corinthian Gulf.[b] According to the manuscript text (which there is no intrinsic reason to doubt, although determined agnostics have done so), Agesilaos dislodged the enemy from the hilltops by sending up light-armed men, the type of troops better suited to difficult terrain. Xenophon relates the same incident at greater length at *Hellenika* 4.6.4–12, but here it is charges uphill by heavy infantry that dislodge the Acarnanians, a much more striking feat. Nowhere does it seem likely that Xenophon simply made up his stories (although he may have twisted some of them in the telling), so it appears that the circumstantial detail in the *Hellenika* version broadly represents the truth. If that is so, we can deduce that the version in *Agesilaos* is a garbled account from limited information, and Xenophon learned the details of what really happened between the two works.

Herodotus and Thucydides

§6.1. Before taking up *Hellenika*, most of the first readers would have read earlier historians, and this would have conditioned what they expected from a work of history. Xenophon will have borne this in mind in what he wrote. Indeed, he invites comparison with predecessors explicitly at 7.2.1, when he says that other writers concentrate on big cities, but he will also write of the deeds of a small one, Phleious. Implicitly, too, at 5.1.4, he contrasts his history, which tells how the Spartan admiral Teleutias inspired his men, with other histories, which pass over that sort of thing and deal instead with money, danger, and stratagems.

§6.2. Some Greek historians who had published before 356 are just names to us, and from others we have only a few lines. But luckily the two most important, Herodotus and Thucydides, have come down to us in full. Herodotus wrote in the 430s and 420s about the great Persian expedition against Greece of 480–479 (and much else besides). Thucydides took the history of the Peloponnesian War as his subject, but although he mentions its end in 404, he did not write a narrative of the last seven years of the war, ending instead in autumn 411. The last sentence of his history leaves the Persian satrap Tissaphernes in midjourney from Aspendos[a] in the south to the Hellespont[b] via Ephesus,[c] and manifestly marks the work as unfinished. Thucydides evidently left it incomplete at his death, probably in the 390s.

§6.3. Thucydides and Herodotus approached historical narrative in different ways, leaving Xenophon with a choice as to which to follow. Xenophon in *Hellenika* scarcely ever echoes Herodotus, or tries to bring his history directly to mind, but the general flavor of Xenophon's work has seemed to many people to be closer to

Intro.5.5a   Acarnania: Intro. Map 8.6.
Intro.5.5b   Corinthian Gulf: Intro. Map 8.6, inset.
Intro.6.2a   Aspendos: Intro. Map 12.12.

Intro.6.2b   Hellespont region: Intro. Map 8.6.
Intro.6.2c   Ephesus: Intro. Map 8.6.

Herodotus than to Thucydides. Herodotus writes in a simple and engaging style; his work is replete with anecdotes and suffused by divine intervention. Thucydides writes in a highly contorted way, with many abstract nouns; he is an austere narrator of military and diplomatic events, and he never evinces belief in the gods, let alone in their intervention in human affairs. In these three respects, Xenophon is much more like Herodotus.

§6.4. However, Herodotus and Thucydides offered Xenophon a choice of models in other ways, and in these respects he seems to have favored Thucydides. While the underlying movement of Herodotus' history is chronological, progressing through the history of the Persian empire from the 550s to 479, he is constantly flying off on a tangent to other places, peoples, and periods. By contrast, after Thucydides' first book and once his narrative reaches the outbreak of the Peloponnesian War, he writes in strict annalistic form with few digressions. Herodotus constantly assigns stories to sources and often gives rival versions of events, with discussion as to what we are to make of it all. Thucydides never names his sources, and it is rare for him to discuss them and their disagreements, although he does make a couple of methodological pronouncements (e.g., 1.22.2–3) that show that he was fully aware of the difficulties of reconciling evidence and separating the true from the false. Herodotus is always at the reader's side, giving his opinions and filling his history with his chatty and curious personality. Thucydides, by contrast, derives authority from creating the impression of magisterial objectivity and refers to himself in the third person when he has to narrate his own actions as an Athenian general. Finally, although Herodotus no doubt winnowed and selected from the various reports he gathered, his work gives the impression that he has tried to find a place for all sorts of information, whether or not relevant to his main theme, and that when he fails to tell us things we would like to know, this is usually not because he is withholding information (aside from a few religiously minded suppressions of taboo topics) but because he has been unable to find out the relevant facts. Thucydides, however, must have struck contemporaries as selective in his approach. For example, his account of the run-up to the Peloponnesian War almost completely omits material that later historians emphasized in their rival analyses of the war's causes; he gives us full speeches on both sides on just two of the hundreds of occasions when Athenian orators clashed in the assembly; and he largely ignores Persia's role in the war before 412.

§6.5. In all these respects, Xenophon is more like Thucydides than he is like Herodotus. As regards chronology, he is not as strict as Thucydides, but he does proceed more or less chronologically, and he almost always signals his departures from chronological order. He is almost as austere in not indicating his sources as Thucydides, and on the other two points he actually outdoes him: he is cavalier with omissions, and he keeps his own name altogether out of his work, even where he plays a part in events (so at *Hellenika* 3.2.7 the leader of the mercenaries who had been with Cyrus speaks, but we are not told that this is in fact Xenophon himself).

Hellenica Oxyrhynchia, Ephorus, and Diodorus Siculus

§7.1. There is one final piece of background we need to fill in. Xenophon's first readers could compare the first half of *Hellenika* to another history of the 400s and 390s, known to us today as the *Hellenica Oxyrhynchia*, and this Landmark edition contains substantial extracts from it as Appendix P.[a]

§7.2. The text of the *Hellenica Oxyrhynchia* was lost in late antiquity, and scholars had no knowledge of it until 1906, when an extensive papyrus fragment was found in the preserved rubbish heap of the ancient Egyptian town of Oxyrhynchus (hence its modern name). The fragment gave a detailed account of the mid-390s that, although confirming Xenophon's narrative in very broad outline, both adds significantly to it and is at variance with it in important particulars. It does not name its author, but it is likely that he was an Athenian called Cratippus, who is known to have produced a history beginning around 411 and carrying on into the late 390s if not further. However, because this point is not universally agreed upon, the author —the Oxyrhynchus Historian—is conventionally referred to as P (from "papyrus"). The fragment found in 1906 is known as the London Fragment, because it is now kept in London. Later in the last century, two shorter fragments were found that evidently belonged to the same history. As the three fragments came from three different copies, we can gather that the book was fairly popular. The second fragment found is known as the Florentine Fragment and gives a similarly detailed account of some incidents in the last decade of the Peloponnesian War, including the battle of Notion,[a] which was responsible for Alcibiades' losing his command for the second time. The Cairo Fragment, the shortest of the three, covers an Athenian campaign in western Asia Minor that took place a little earlier, in fact the very campaign of Thrasyllos that, as we said above (§4.6), may well have been Xenophon's first campaign. The whole work seems to have started in 412, shortly before Thucydides ends, at a more natural break in events. There is a little evidence that it was published in two parts, with a break in 403. We can see that it continued to at least 395, and it probably ended with the King's Peace of 386.

§7.3. Whether or not its author was Cratippus, *Hellenica Oxyrhynchia* was written in the first half of the fourth century. It contains a passage about the Phocians that must have been written before the destruction of Phocis in 346 and appears to precede the outbreak of the Sacred War of 356–346 which centered on Phocis (Fragment 21.3).[a] Probably it was written a good deal earlier than 356, since the degree of detail included in it must have been collected soon after the events it covers. A date well before Xenophon finished *Hellenika* would be beyond doubt if we could prove that *Hellenica Oxyrhynchia* was by Cratippus, since we know that he belonged to Thucydides' generation. So it is likely that while Xenophon was the first historian of the period 386–362, for the earlier period 411–386 he would have been able to read *Hellenica Oxyrhynchia*. If *Hellenica Oxyrhynchia* was available to be

Intro.7.1a   Appendix P, Selected Fragments of the *Hellenica Oxyrhynchia* Relevant to Xenophon's *Hellenika*, translated by John Marincola.

Intro.7.2a   Notion: Intro. Map 8.6.

Intro.7.3a   *Hellenica Oxyrhynchia* is here cited in accordance with the numeration of the fragments in M. Chambers, ed., *Hellenica Oxyrhynchia* (Stuttgart: Teubner 1993).

read before Xenophon wrote *Hellenika*, Xenophon would surely have taken the opportunity to read it. He was far from ignoring what other people had written, since his other works often start from another writer's book or carry on a dialogue with a predecessor in the relevant field. But if he did read *Hellenica Oxyrhynchia*, as I believe he did, he evidently did not think much of it, for the two works frequently disagree in emphasis and judgment and on occasion directly contradict each other on factual matters.

§7.4. These disagreements are the more striking because *Hellenica Oxyrhynchia* seems to be a very professional piece of work. It has a plain, dry style, sparer than Xenophon's and without Xenophon's occasional vivid images and high-flown words. It incorporates a great deal of detail, such as the names of minor individuals and places, and seems to keep close to the hard facts. It appears to aim at a consistent level of treatment throughout the period it covers. In the fragments we have, there are no long speeches, and it is known that Cratippus objected to Thucydides' inclusion of speeches, which he considered boring and a distraction from the action. But this is not to say that P wrote a bare chronicle. On the contrary, he analyzes political groups and includes arguments about the causes of events. He is more candid than Thucydides (at least in the latter's main narrative) in acknowledging other views, and more specific in setting out his own reasoning. He displays an interest in political institutions when he describes the workings of the Boeotian Federation. Such an interest is foreign to Herodotus, Thucydides, and Xenophon. One's natural first thought on reading this serious and careful work is that if Xenophon disagrees with it, so much the worse for Xenophon.

§7.5. Some say that P's austerity and serious-mindedness is a façade, that he slanted his narrative unfairly to convey his own views, and that he even made up incidents when he had insufficient evidence with which to fill out his account. Certainly P, in the words of McKechnie and Kern in their commentary, "knew how to use a plain style to suggest and convince,"[a] and when he tells us (in Fragment 23)[b] how the Athenian general Konon suppressed a mutiny among his fleet at Caunus[c] in 395, we can see that his narrative technique supports his thesis that Konon was brave, prudent, and resourceful—as he surely was. And no doubt P did not get everything right. But it is quite a different matter to allege that he made things up, and not only out of political bias but sometimes from the frivolous desire to pad out his history. Plainly P wishes to convey the impression that he is diligent in collecting evidence and careful in evaluating it, and he would hardly achieve this aim if still-living eyewitnesses, of whatever political persuasion, would flatly contradict him.

§7.6. Appendices to this Landmark edition include passages translated not only from *Hellenica Oxyrhynchia* but also from a much later writer, Diodorus Siculus.[a] His work is a very different kettle of fish. Diodorus lived in the first century and wrote a universal history of the world in forty books from its beginnings to his own day. The books that cover the Xenophontic period are Books 13, 14, and 15, which

Intro.7.5a *Hellenica Oxyrhynchia*, edited with translation and commentary by P. R. McKechnie and S. J. Kern (Warminster: Aris & Philips, 1988).
Intro.7.5b See this passage in Appendix P.
Intro.7.5c Caunus: Intro. Map 8.6.
Intro.7.6a See Appendix O, Selections from the *Histories* of Diodorus Siculus Relevant to Xenophon's *Hellenika*, translated by Peter Green.

FIGURE INTRO.7.2. A DETAIL OF THE LONDON PAPYRUS FRAGMENT FROM THE *HELLENICA OXYRHYNCHIA*, DESCRIBING THE BATTLE OF SARDIS.

ends in 361. Within those books, about half the narrative concerns Sicily (with a little on Italy), the rest being about Greece and to some extent Persia. Although some recent scholars have discerned some signs of intelligence in Diodorus, it has long been recognized that he was a wretched historian, who created his narrative largely if not exclusively by paraphrasing chunks of his predecessors' works in the most careless way. Generally, at least when dealing with mainland Greece, he followed one narrative source for a long period before switching over to another. He often botched this process by muddling names that the source gave correctly and by getting confused between his source's main narrative and introductions, digressions, or recapitulations. He tried to fit his sources' narratives into a chronological framework drawn from a separate handbook, but he made astonishing mistakes in correlating the two. He kills off the fifth-century Spartan king Archidamos II and the fourth-century Athenian general Chabrias prematurely, and then refers to them as alive at a later date. One wonders whether he ever read his history all the way through again after writing his first draft.[b] However, the sources that Diodorus mangled were generally good ones, not because he could judge their quality but because he chose the best-known works in the field, provided they were reasonably easy to read. Therefore, if one can filter out his characteristic blunders, his history can be extremely important in reconstructing events, and hence in evaluating other historians, such as Xenophon.

§7.7. For mainland Greece in the Xenophontic period, Diodorus used an important fourth-century historian called Ephorus, who wrote throughout the period 360–330 and composed the first universal history. This covered the whole Greek world from the mythical period to his own times, although it survives only in short extracts, usually referred to by the numbers assigned by the great German historian Felix Jacoby in his compilation of all surviving fragments of Greek historians.[a] One of the things we are told about Ephorus is that he did not write annalistically, dealing with each year in turn, but habitually pursued different subjects beyond their strict chronological place. This is part of the evidence that Diodorus depended on him, because it explains why Diodorus had particular difficulty aligning his main narrative source for these years with the chronological handbook he used for his skeleton of dates. Diodorus did a much better job in his account of the very end of the fourth century, when he was following a different and presumably more straightforward source. It may be that Ephorus is not the source for absolutely everything in Diodorus' narrative of the Xenophontic period (some people think that he lifted his account of the battle of Leuctra from another source). But almost all of it must derive from Ephorus.

§7.8. Now, when the London Fragment of *Hellenica Oxyrhynchia* was found, scholars immediately inferred that what it said (in Fragments 14 and 15)[a] about the battle of Sardis in 395 was the ultimate source for Diodorus' version (14.80),[b] which

Intro.7.6b This Introduction is in line with what until recently has been the general consensus about Diodorus' competence. But it is only fair to point out that Peter Green, the translator of the Diodorus passages in Appendix O, maintains a much less dismissive view of Diodorus' methods and capacities.

Intro.7.7a F. Jacoby, *Die Fragmente der griechischen Historiker*, 15 vols. (Berlin, 1923–30; Leipzig, 1940–58). Ephorus is historian number 70.

Intro.7.8a See Appendix P for Fragments 14.3–6 and 15.

Intro.7.8b See Appendix O.

scholars had previously spurned because it contradicted what is probably an eyewitness account in Xenophon (*Hellenika* 3.4.21–24). Study of the second, Florentine Fragment (Fragment 8ᶜ) likewise suggested that Diodorus' account of the battle of Notion in 406 (Diodorus 13.71.2–4ᵈ) was derived from it. But this was not because Diodorus was using P's work directly. *Hellenica Oxyrhynchia* is an annalistic history, and if Diodorus had had it in front of him, his chronology of the period around the end of the Peloponnesian War would not have been the mess that it is. Rather, Diodorus was abridging Ephorus, and Ephorus was in turn making use of P. Ephorus was a serious historian, unlike Diodorus, and he would not have simply paraphrased P. Indeed, we can see that throughout his work he tried hard, sometimes too hard, to supplement the best primary source with other evidence. So presumably there are some things in Diodorus' account of mainland Greece in 412–386 that do not derive from P. But most of it surely does, although this valuable material is mixed up with Diodorus' blunders. Accordingly, since the discovery of the London papyrus in 1906, historians generally have given more weight to what Diodorus says about the first half of the fourth century than they did before; this is true not only for the period that P covered but also for the years after 386.

The Opening of *Hellenika*

§8.1. Thus prepared, let us return to the opening words of *Hellenika*, "And after these things, not many days later."

§8.2. Xenophon begins this way, expecting the reader to recognize that he is picking up roughly where Thucydides left off. The fit is not in fact watertight, but Thucydides stops and Xenophon starts in the autumn of 411, which is by no means a natural breaking point. So Xenophon is evidently continuing Thucydides' work and is in some sense claiming to be a historian who can be compared with Thucydides. That was bold and probably unwise, as Thucydides set formidable standards of research and penetration. Presumably because he saw himself as continuing Thucydides, Xenophon did not follow his predecessors and provide a preface setting out the scope and methods of his work. It seems that he thought that this would be obvious.

§8.3. That was perhaps not so unreasonable for the narrative of the Peloponnesian War and, even beyond that, down to the overthrow of the Thirty at the end of our Book 2. Like Thucydides, Xenophon here proceeds year by year, although the modern reader has to be warned that this would not have been as clear in the original text of *Hellenika* as it is in the version that has come down to us, because later in antiquity copyists added annalistic material from other sources.ᵃ Xenophon describes all the major battles that Athens fought in the East Aegean. He recounts at length only one debate in the Assembly (1.7), when Socrates obstructed, and one Euryptolemos spoke at length against, a vote to condemn *en bloc* six Athenian

---

Intro.7.8c See Appendix P.
Intro.7.8d See Appendix O.
Intro.8.3a For more on the extent of these interpolations and the difficulties they create for modern reconstructions of events, see

Appendix C, Chronological Problems in the Continuation (1.1.1–2.3.10) of Xenophon's *Hellenika*.

generals for not rescuing shipwrecked Athenian sailors after the battle of Arginousai[b] (they were condemned all the same). But singling this debate out is not particularly surprising, since Thucydides had also chosen only a few specimen debates from the many possibilities. Thucydides was obviously a great researcher, and Xenophon too must have talked to other people to produce his account of these years: he certainly wasn't at the first two battles he describes, his account of Arginousai draws on information from both sides of the battle, and he often updates us on the number of ships on one or both sides. Also like Thucydides, Xenophon in this section doesn't display obvious bias against either Athens or Sparta, and indeed he recounts what happened under the Thirty in a way that shows he recognizes that he was wrong to have supported them and wrong to have resisted the return of the democracy. So he makes an effort to be objective, and his choice of things to write about is fairly straightforward, although the amount of detail varies disconcertingly from incident to incident.

§8.4. When we turn to Diodorus for comparison, we get some surprises. On every one of the battles they both describe, their accounts seem remarkably different—sometimes so different that they seem to be writing about quite different battles, although at least the same side wins. Now one of the things that study of the Florentine Fragment of *Hellenica Oxyrhynchia* has shown is that this is misleading. The point is obscured a little because the papyrus is in tatters, but we can see that P's account of the battle of Notion in 406 (Fragment 8) was, as one would expect, fuller than both Xenophon's (1.5.12–14) and Diodorus' (13.71.2–4), and it makes sense of the apparently contradictory reports they give about the numbers of ships involved.[a] Xenophon and Diodorus do not really disagree about the essentials, but they both select from the facts in such a way as to suggest a contradiction when there is only a difference in emphasis. This point applies generally. For most of these battles, the apparently contradictory accounts of Xenophon and Diodorus are more likely to be complementary. In the first battle that Xenophon describes at length in *Hellenika*, that of Dardanos/Abydos[b] (*Hellenika* 1.1.2–7, Diodorus 13.45.1–47.2[c]), there is an apparent discrepancy, but it could arise because Xenophon's version may rely on information from Dorieus the Rhodian, one of the main participants on the anti-Athenian side whom Xenophon presumably met later, after Dorieus was, as Xenophon tells us, captured by the Athenians. In his second battle account, that of Cyzicus[d] (*Hellenika* 1.1.14–19, Diodorus 13.49.2–51.8[e]) it is impossible to square the two accounts on the issue of whether the Athenians caught the Spartan navy at sea unawares or whether they lured it out of port; but if we could read what P had to say, we might see something that makes sense of both. Perhaps the Athenians set out intending to lure the Spartans out of port, as Diodorus says, but then found they didn't need to, because the Spartans were already at sea and so were caught unawares, just as Xenophon describes. What Diodorus shows is not that Xenophon is wrong but that he is selective, whether

---

Intro.8.3b Arginousai Islands: Intro. Map 8.6.
Intro.8.4a See, together with the relevant passages in
    Hellenika and in Appendices O and P,
    A. Andrewes, "Notion and Kyzikos: The Sources
    Compared," *Journal of Hellenic Studies* 102

(1982): 15–25 (not universally accepted).
Intro.8.4b Dardanos and Abydos: Intro. Map 8.6.
Intro.8.4c See Appendix O.
Intro.8.4d Cyzicus: Intro. Map 8.6.
Intro.8.4e See Appendix O.

because he believes he has got hold of a trustworthy witness and looks no further or because there is a particular point he wants to make about the battle (in the case of Cyzicus, it would be that the Athenian commander Alcibiades, at least at this stage in his career, had luck on his side).

§8.5. But after the end of the war, and especially after the fall of the Thirty, Xenophon's selectivity, as revealed by Diodorus' rival account, grows more and more quirky. There is less reassuring detail, such as the numbers of ships. There are more departures from strict chronological order. Xenophon's narrative in Books 1 and 2 is a lot sketchier than Thucydides' and does not inspire the confidence that Thucydides, rightly or wrongly, arouses in virtually all readers; but after Book 2 it looks as if he wasn't even trying to write the same sort of history. One example of this is the treatment of the animal sacrifices that Greek armies and navies made before they set out from base and immediately before battle. Thucydides, a confirmed rationalist, hardly ever mentions them, and neither does Xenophon up to the end of the Peloponnesian War. Thereafter, however, they are a recurring feature of Xenophon's military narratives, especially where the Spartans are concerned. Thus Xenophon follows Thucydides' precedent at the beginning of *Hellenika* but subsequently reverts to a more traditional attitude to Greek religious practices.

§8.6. Xenophon's account of the Peloponnesian War differs from the rest of *Hellenika* in another respect. There is a marked difference in one point of Greek style, which unfortunately cannot be conveyed in a translation. Greek is a language rich in words that connect words and sentences and shade their meaning, and in almost all his work, including most of *Hellenika*, Xenophon makes frequent use of these little words, including some favorites that are characteristic of his style. However, the special favorites are absent from his account of the war; indeed, few of the shading words are found there at all. (It may occur to you that when he writes about the war, Xenophon is perhaps imitating Thucydides' style; but this explanation doesn't work, because Thucydides' style is very distinctive, rich in abstract nouns and full of highly contorted sentences, and is quite unlike this, or any, part of Xenophon.) In the later books of *Hellenika*, including the account of the Thirty, Xenophon's writing is full of flavor; his style is flexible, subtle, and on occasion rich; and the speeches he writes are individual and almost always strongly differentiated from the surrounding narrative. But in his account of the Peloponnesian War Xenophon writes with a flatter style, not differentiating between narrative and the principal speech, that of Euryptolemos in the debate on the six generals. Sometimes Xenophon's narrative is abbreviated and thin in detail, and in such cases pepping it up with connecting and shading words might have been inappropriate or even incongruous. But some parts of the war narrative are quite full, and yet they employ very few connecting and shading words; it has been suggested that Euryptolemos' speech is written this way in order to make him sound sweetly reasonable, but there is no lack of connecting and shading words in other speeches from this period where the speechwriter wants to achieve this effect.

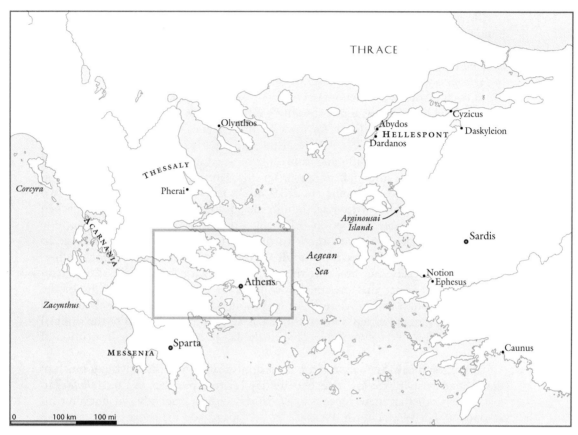

INTRO. MAP 8.6

§8.7. The explanation, long known although not universally accepted, is that Xenophon wrote the first part of *Hellenika* much earlier than the rest. His account of the final years of the Peloponnesian War dates probably from the mid-380s, just after he wrote *Cynegeticus*, which varies even more from his mature style. The rest of *Hellenika* was written years later, some say over a long period but more probably in roughly one go sometime between 362 and 356. The dividing line between the early and late sections is not absolutely clear, because the stylistic argument is a statistical one and not reliable for drawing precise lines. Before 2.2.23 we are in the early section; after 2.3.11 we are in the late one. It is certain that the ancient division into books was different from the one used in medieval manuscripts and modern texts, and the indications from the late lexicographer Harpocration suggest that the end of summer in 2.3.9 marks the original end of the first two books.[a] But 2.3.9 is not written as though the author is about to put down his pen for years, so probably Xenophon originally stopped at 2.2.23 with the bitterly ironic remark that the fall of Athens to the Spartans was believed at the time to herald the beginning of freedom for all Greece. That would be a strong ending. Roughly thirty years later he wrote the rest, starting with the account of the dictatorship of the Thirty that presumably constituted Book 3 in the scheme of the work as Xenophon left it. When he came to join what he had written earlier with the new material, he added a short bridge passage, forming the end of the original Book 2, to fill in the few months between the fall of Athens and the institution of the Thirty.

§8.8. Presumably Xenophon did not mean his readers to make anything much of the change in style. We saw that he carefully rewrote passages of the *Agesilaos* to make them suit their new context in *Hellenika*, but he evidently did not alter his account of the Peloponnesian War, except perhaps to add the short bridge passage. He must have been satisfied with his original opening and thought it comparable in its aims and methods with the work of his old age. We may feel that his selection and handling of material has moved further away from Thucydidean principles, but it seems that Xenophon did not sense any incongruity.[a]

The Organization of *Hellenika* after 2.3.10

§9.1. After 2.3.10, *Hellenika* continues to be organized chronologically for the most part, rather than thematically or geographically. But it ceases to proceed annalistically, and it is often difficult to tell which year the narrative has reached.

§9.2. Xenophon deals at length with the deterioration and fall of the Thirty, which he himself witnessed, but passes over what was happening outside Athens at

Intro.8.7a   Most of 2.3.9 and all of 2.3.10 are due to
             the interpolators: see Appendix C.
Intro.8.8a   For a review of other theories, see Appendix
             N, Compositional Theories of Xenophon's
             Hellenika.

the time. Then the narrative shifts to Asia Minor and the fortunes of the Spartan army there, in effect following Xenophon's own life story, before doubling back at 3.2.21 to fill in some incidents from the Peloponnese. He reverts to chronological order again for 396–394 but cuts back and forth between continental Greece and the Spartans in Asia Minor. Xenophon then gives the history of the Corinthian War in two separate chronological narratives: the first follows the war on the mainland (though after the outbreak of the war he is virtually silent about its progress on Thebes' northern frontier), and the second describes the war at sea, which eventually becomes the sole narrative thread. There is in the main a single chronological line from 5.1.25 (387, the lead-in to the King's Peace) to 7.1.32 (368, in the middle of the war in the Peloponnese that broke out after the battle of Leuctra), although at two points Xenophon signals digressions in which he jumps forward in time to cover the history of Thessaly[a] (6.1.18–19, 6.4.27–37). Once we get to 7.4.1, there is again a single chronological line from there to the end, tightly focused on the Peloponnese to the exclusion of important events in the Aegean and in Thessaly.

§9.3. Between 7.1.32 and 7.4.1, the narrative is more complicated. From 7.1.33 to 7.1.40, it follows the Theban Pelopidas to Asia and back again to tell the story of how he and Artaxerxes failed in their attempt to force peace terms on the warring Greeks in 367/6. Then 7.1.41–43 recounts a campaign by Epaminondas in the Peloponnese that was in fact simultaneous with Pelopidas' negotiations, although Xenophon does not make this clear.[a] At 7.1.44 Xenophon begins the story of Euphron, the autocrat of Sicyon,[b] and, although he doesn't say so, he has once again tacked backward in time, by about eighteen months.[c] According to Xenophon, Euphron was a traitor successively to both Sparta[d] and Thebes,[e] and loyal to no one. Into the middle of his story Xenophon inserts, obviously as a deliberate contrast, a section (7.2) on the noble exploits of Phleious,[f] a small city-state in the northeast Peloponnese that he depicts as outstandingly loyal to the Spartans. Section 7.2 recapitulates from the Phleiasian point of view the whole of the first phase of the war in the Peloponnese (370–366), so it is a thematic insertion, even though its internal arrangement is chronological. Then Xenophon returns to Euphron, and he tells us expressly (7.3.4, 7.4.1) that he is allowing the end of Euphron's story to run on out of chronological order.

§9.4. In quite a few places Xenophon's narrative does not provide enough information for us now to be sure exactly where we stand chronologically. But while this imprecision is irritating for historians today, it does not show that Xenophon had failed to work out the chronology for himself or to impose order over his material. Rather, although he uses chronology as his main organizational principle,

Intro.9.2a Thessaly: Intro. Map 8.6.
Intro.9.3a The view taken here is that Epaminondas'
            third Peloponnesian expedition is simultane-
            ous with Pelopidas' mission to Asia; other-
            wise there seem to be too many events to fit
            between Pelopidas' departure for Asia and
            the Theban capture of Oropos, on Thebes'
            border with Athens. But note that most
            scholars disagree, including *The Cambridge*

Ancient History, whose chronological scheme
has been used in the side notes to this trans-
lation.
Intro.9.3b Sicyon: Intro. Map 8.6, inset.
Intro.9.3c Most but not all scholars think that Euphron's
            coup happened in 368.
Intro.9.3d Sparta: Intro. Map 8.6.
Intro.9.3e Thebes: Intro. Map 8.6, inset.
Intro.9.3f Phleious: Intro. Map 8.6, inset.

he is not greatly interested in it, nor does he expect his readers to care about it. Even in the confusing passage 7.1.32–7.3.12, we should not imagine that Xenophon lost the plot. He recounts at length at 7.1.32–7.40 how Thebes and Persia failed to drive a wedge between the Spartans and their allies in 367/6. Then he tries, by using all the narrative tricks he can, to distract us from the fact that this failure was negated only a year later by the great diplomatic success the Thebans had with the Peace of 366/5, which he eventually and grudgingly reports at 7.4.6–10. Even then, he leaves out the Persian involvement in this peace, just as in other places he minimizes the success of Persian influence over events in mainland Greece—for example, he omits the Persian role in promoting the Peace of 375/4. Similarly, he leaves out Athenian participation in the Peace of 366/5, presumably because he wanted to give the impression that the independence of Messenia[a] could still be an open question for the Athenians even in the 350s. Thus he suppressed mention of the two occasions (366 and 362) when they had formally recognized the new state. To make his case, he manipulates his narrative and omits information one might reasonably expect him to provide. As we shall see, he is often tendentious in this way.

§9.5. Xenophon is well in control of the overall shape of his work. For example, he imposed a rigorous discipline upon himself for the years 365–362, narrowing the focus of the tale to the Peloponnese to make it natural to end with the battle of Mantineia[a] in which his son died. In so doing, he ignored sequences of events, such as the history of the Persian front, which would leave loose ends if truncated in 362, and both then and earlier he carefully excluded almost all overt references to subsequent events.[b] True, *Hellenika* may seem to end arbitrarily: "To this point, then, let it be written by me. Perhaps someone else will make subsequent events his concern." But in fact Xenophon has worked hard to create a sense of closure to his narrative.

An Episodic and Anecdotal History

§10.1. Within Xenophon's basically chronological framework, however, *Hellenika* does not give the impression of taut construction. On the contrary, the work is episodic. Much of it is written as a series of anecdotes, and conventional expectations of history do not explain why we are told a great deal about some incidents and little or nothing about others. For example, we have a long section (3.1.16–3.2.1) about Derkylidas, the second Spartan general who campaigned in Asia in the 390s. We read how he cleverly played with a nasty piece of work called Meidias, and how he took nine cities (although villages might be more accurate) in eight days. This campaign had little influence on the outcome of events yet is described in greater detail than anything else that the Spartan army did in Asia Minor in these years. Again, we are told at considerable length at 6.2.27–32 about the training methods

Intro.9.4a   Messenia: Intro. Map 8.6.
Intro.9.5a   Mantineia: Intro. Map 8.6, inset.
Intro.9.5b   The only exception is the murder of Alexander of Pherai at 6.4.35–37, in the course of the second digression on Thessaly. But there are some covert references to more recent events, for example a hidden dig at 5.4.64 at the Athenian general Chares' behavior in Corcyra in 361.

that the Athenian general Iphikrates employed as he sailed his fleet toward Corcyra.[a] The detail is piled on even though Xenophon makes clear that the good training of Iphikrates' sailors made no difference to the result of his campaign, because the crucial Athenian success happened before he arrived. But we are told nothing at all about Iphikrates' other technical military innovations, nor about the campaigns he undertook, during the period covered by *Hellenika*, in Egypt,[b] the Aegean,[c] and Thrace.[d] The anecdotes are, by and large, arranged chronologically, not just jumbled together, but they fall short of a narrative that has been drawn up on consistent historical principles and that seeks to reveal the connections between different events and the factors that lead to historical change.

§10.2. Was Xenophon then just incompetent? Three observations show he was not.

§10.3. First, Xenophon casts his history predominantly in the form of anecdotes to re-create the past vividly and to bring the dead to life for future ages. This is one of the main purposes of the work. He is a master of dropping in a single concrete detail that calls up a whole scene to our eyes. One example occurs at 4.4.5, when the young Corinthian aristocrats have taken refuge in a temple on a hill above the city[a] as their elders are massacred, and as they deliberate about what to do next, the capital from a column in the temple falls. We can imagine how startled the young men are in their overwrought condition. Again, at 6.4.36 we learn about the murder of Alexander of Pherai,[b] which was organized by his wife. Xenophon conjures up the scene of the murder for us through the detail that while the assassins set about their work, his wife kept the door shut, gripping the handle. Elsewhere, to speed up his narrative, Xenophon uses fictional techniques, such as conversation between people who were actually in two different places, as at 3.4.5, where the Spartan king Agesilaos and the Persian satrap Tissaphernes appear to talk to each other when they were in fact communicating from their respective bases; or at 5.4.26, where another Spartan, Kleonymos, is depicted as talking to his father, Sphodrias, although the latter, as has just been made clear, has fled from Sparta to avoid being punished for treason. Similarly, Xenophon makes longer stretches of narrative come alive by making us see events through the reactions of the individuals involved in them. The most elaborate example concerns a Spartan disaster in 390 at Lechaion,[c] near Corinth. A Spartan detachment of heavily armed soldiers was caught in the open without any cavalry support and largely wiped out by Athenian light-armed troops and horsemen. The news of this defeat led Agesilaos, in command of the main Spartan army, to retreat to Sparta on the double even though he had just captured the district of Peiraion[d] to the north of Corinth. Xenophon's narrative (4.5.6–17) first concentrates on Agesilaos, his pleasure in his initial victory, his handling of some ambassadors from his Boeotian[e] enemies who have come to see him. Then a messenger arrives. His distraught state is painted in a few telling words, but we are kept in suspense as to the nature of his bad tidings until we have observed Agesilaos' reaction to the disaster and how he now deals with the ambassadors.

Intro.10.1a Corcyra: Intro. Map 8.6.
Intro.10.1b Egypt: Intro. Map 3.2, locator.
Intro.10.1c Aegean Sea: Intro. Map 8.6.
Intro.10.1d Thrace: Intro. Map 8.6.
Intro.10.3a Acrocorinth and Corinth: Intro. Map 8.6, inset.

Intro.10.3b Pherai (Thessaly): Intro. Map 8.6.
Intro.10.3c Lechaion: Intro. Map 8.6, inset.
Intro.10.3d Peiraion: Intro. Map 8.6, inset.
Intro.10.3e Boeotia: Intro. Map 8.6, inset.

§10.4. However, Xenophon does not recount this incident in this way solely to maintain our suspense and enliven his narrative. We are also meant to note the uncertainty of fortune and how Agesilaos' reaction to it varies in appropriateness. Here, as elsewhere, Agesilaos comes across as too pleased with himself in the hour of victory and perhaps as arrogant toward the Boeotians, but he is also shown to react swiftly, decisively, and with ready wit when there are problems. It is a less eulogistic portrait than that given in Xenophon's *Agesilaos*, which is virtually nothing but praise, but unlike *Agesilaos*, *Hellenika* makes the king live for us even now, more than two thousand years later. Xenophon is also making historical points with a wider application—when he shows us here Agesilaos' hatred of Thebes and his tendencies to overreach in times of success but to be able to retrieve the situation in times of difficulty.

§10.5. The historical points embedded in this lively passage illustrate the second of the three observations I offer in defense of Xenophon's competence. He often implicitly makes what one might call a historian's point, but he usually does so quietly and indirectly. There is an uncontroversial instance of this in another of his works, *Anabasis*. At *Anabasis* 2.1.7, we learn how, in the aftermath of the battle of Cunaxa,[a] King Artaxerxes sent a Greek in his service called Phalinus to negotiate with the Greek mercenaries, including Xenophon, who had just fought against him. An earlier historian, Ktesias, who was present at the battle as Artaxerxes' doctor, had written of how he accompanied Phalinus on this mission. Xenophon writes that Phalinus came alone. He does not directly call Ktesias a liar, but as he earlier cited Ktesias' account of how the rebel leader Cyrus died (Xenophon himself being on another part of the battlefield), he is not writing in ignorance of Ktesias' claim, and he does not expect his readers to be ignorant of it either. He is putting Ktesias down quietly but effectively. The point was not lost on attentive readers in antiquity.

§10.6. Instances in *Hellenika* are more controversial but also more important. In 395 Agesilaos marched east through Anatolia as far as Paphlagonia[a] and then turned back westward to the seat of the Persian satrap of Hellespontine Phrygia at Daskyleion.[b] We have P's account of this as well as Xenophon's. As so often, the two seem to be writing about two different sets of events, although in this case they don't actually contradict each other (except trivially, in that Xenophon calls the Paphlagonian king Otys and P calls him Gyes). P's account (Fragments 24–25)[c] includes many military details and bristles with names of strongholds that Agesilaos failed to capture. By contrast, Xenophon (4.1.1–15) tells charming and instructive stories of Agesilaos' relations with King Otys and with a rebellious local Persian nobleman, Spithridates, who married his daughter to Otys as a result of Agesilaos' machinations.

One suggested explanation of this difference in treatment is to say that P is hostile to Agesilaos and thus tells of his failures, while Xenophon's account is overly kind to him and concentrates on his successes. But P usually, although not always, refers to Agesilaos' expeditionary force as "the Greeks," thus implying that Agesi-

Intro.10.5a   Cunaxa: Intro. Map 3.2, locator.
Intro.10.6a   Paphlagonia: Intro. Map 3.2, locator.
Intro.10.6b   Daskyleion: Intro. Map 8.6.
Intro.10.6c   See Appendix P.

laos' cause is the cause of Greece and not just of Sparta. Conversely, Xenophon shows how Agesilaos' diplomatic efforts ended in failure, for although he successfully brought Spithridates and Otys together, this triumph led soon after to their jointly deserting Agesilaos when his chosen lieutenant, Herippidas, managed to anger both of them by his officiousness (*Hellenika* 4.1.26–27).

Nor should we think that Xenophon prefers to give us childish yarns rather than hard facts, thus displaying a distorted sense of what truly causes events, while P austerely ignores such nonsense. Perhaps P always preferred to concentrate on hard facts, but he would surely have had something to say about Otys' marriage to Spithridates' daughter had he known about it. So it would seem that Xenophon has used personal knowledge to fill in, at perhaps excessive length but certainly in engaging style, a gap in P's research. It is also of historical interest to show how Agesilaos manipulated people. More important still, by ignoring Agesilaos' attempts to storm minor fortresses, and by writing at length about his relations with Spithridates and Otys, Xenophon implicitly suggests to readers who have digested P's work that he thought Agesilaos' crusade against King Artaxerxes was better pursued by diplomacy among the native princes rather than by purely military means, even if faults in execution meant that the diplomatic effort eventually failed. After Xenophon's death, things were different, but he was surely right to prefer the diplomatic approach in his own time.

§10.7. Agesilaos' most notable success in Asia, the battle of Sardis,[a] is another instance in which modern scholars have accused Xenophon of an inconsistent and slipshod approach when in my view he was implicitly, and perhaps validly, challenging P's judgment of priorities. The battle was fought between Agesilaos and the troops of the Persian satrap Tissaphernes near the Persian city of Sardis in the summer of 395. According to P (Fragment 14),[b] Agesilaos achieved victory in battle by means of a cunning infantry ambush. Some of the details are obscure because the papyrus of P is in tatters in parts of this section, but to judge from the parallel passage of Diodorus (14.80.2–3),[c] P placed this ambush after Agesilaos had ravaged the suburbs of Sardis, although it is not clear whether it was set up to the west of Sardis or to the east. Xenophon, who was probably present at the battle and certainly in the general vicinity, instead writes at length (3.4.21–24) about a cavalry encounter in the open near the banks of the Pactolus River before Agesilaos reached the suburbs of Sardis. Xenophon and P seem to be totally at odds, and it has been thought that their disagreement also extends to the routes followed by Agesilaos and the Persians into the plain of Sardis.

Some of the explanation may be that we can read only part of P's account, because there are forty lines a little earlier in the relevant area of the papyrus where only a strip about eight letters wide survives. But the stray words that have been preserved in this strip suggest it was about how Tissaphernes and Agesilaos were maneuvering their armies. If P did not think the cavalry battle by the Pactolus River was important, his account of it may have been brief and could have fit into this

Intro.10.7a   Sardis: Intro. Map 8.6.
Intro.10.7b   See Appendix P.
Intro.10.7c   See Appendix O.

space. Indeed, there is a scrap of evidence that this is so, for we can work out that the Greek word for "river" was written in the appropriate place.[d] We are, however, still left with the fact that Xenophon does not tell us about the battle with the ambush, although that is what takes up most space in P. Some modern scholars say P made it up, but he gives the impression of being a conscientious and painstaking historian (as discussed in §7.5). Others say that Xenophon was a forgetful old man when he wrote his account of the campaign, or that he was absent and had not done his research properly, or even that he was sour about the great victory for one reason or another. But to my mind it was not for any of these reasons that he was silent about the later battle with the ambush. Rather, it was because P had made so much of it in comparison with the earlier battle, and Xenophon wanted to redress the balance. As a cavalryman, what interested him was the performance of the cavalry, and the first battle demonstrated the vital point that Greeks could defeat Persian cavalry, the enemy's strongest arm; furthermore, that battle gave Agesilaos temporary control of the plain of Sardis. The cavalry played no part in the second battle, and although perhaps more people died in that battle and the Greeks gained as much or even more booty from it, it merely cleared the way for Agesilaos' return march; it was less strategically significant and held less of a lesson for the future. Xenophon disagrees with P not about the facts, really, but about what mattered more—and again on this occasion Xenophon's point seems to have been a good one.

§10.8. Not just in these two cases but in all the incidents he recounts, Xenophon has some point or other in mind, at least after the great divide at 2.3.10. But my third observation about his anecdotes is that although the point is sometimes what we might expect from a historian, sometimes it is more like what one finds in a novel. To react appropriately, we need to be alert to the kinds of complexity that we more readily associate with novels.

§10.9. At 7.2.1, Xenophon tells us he wishes to display noble deeds and there-upon launches into a long passage on the courage and loyalty of the Phleiasians, knights, it appears, of simple heroism. But Xenophon recognizes that nobility of character is often more complex. Take the story of Anaxibios, the Spartan governor of Abydos[a] in 389, who was killed in an ambush (4.8.35–39). There are many aspects to this anecdote. Xenophon shows that Anaxibios was careless about recon-noitering on the march, so one lesson is the need to take appropriate military precautions—a common Xenophontic theme. A second lesson concerns the Greek custom whereby, when an army marched out, sheep and other animals were sacri-ficed to read the future from the state of their innards. Xenophon emphasizes that Anaxibios ignored the omens of disaster revealed by the entrails of the animals he sacrificed. So the story shows the importance of having due respect for sacrificial omens—another common theme, in fact rather a fixation, for Xenophon. Third, it is an episode in a feud, since in *Anabasis* Xenophon presents Anaxibios as having wronged him when they met in and around Byzantium in 400 when Anaxibios was

Intro.10.7d   See Appendix P, Fragment 14.3, which translates the final words of the tattered passage.

Intro.10.9a   Abydos: Intro. Map 8.6.

navarch (admiral) of the Spartan navy. It is also a brief polemic on Spartan politics, since Xenophon has just told us (4.8.32) that it was as a result of improper, or at least undue, influence that Anaxibios obtained his command at Abydos, at the expense of Xenophon's admired old commander Derkylidas. Xenophon intended us to find Anaxibios lacking in all these respects. But he also, and perhaps primarily, aimed to portray a brave man who inspired loyalty in his friends. When Anaxibios realizes he has been trapped by the enemy, he fully accepts his responsibility and the dictates of the Spartan code of honor, which required him not to turn in flight. At the same time, he tries to spare his friends by ordering them to leave him and get away safely. They disobeyed, and all fought and died together. So the story does not preach a simple moral lesson. Rather, it reveals that the final judgment on Anaxibios has to be a complex one.

§10.10. The most notorious instance in which Xenophon (apparently) treats his readers to a simple moral lesson is at 5.3.3–7, where the Spartan commander Teleutias, stepbrother to King Agesilaos, is killed during the siege of Olynthos[a] because he loses his temper and chases the enemy cavalry too far. Xenophon then gives a short lecture on the importance of not losing one's temper, a point he pursues tastelessly, preaching at us over Teleutias' corpse. Undoubtedly, he underlines the message about anger too vigorously here (an unusual fault for him—usually he does not state his views explicitly but lets them emerge in his narrative or puts them into the mouth of a character). But the passage should be seen in context. Teleutias has hitherto appeared to be a paragon of military virtue. His attention to morale, accessibility to his men, and sharing of their privations are emphasized at 5.1.13–17, preceded by another rather over-the-top passage, at 5.1.3–4, in which morale building is declared to be worthier of note than resources, danger, and stratagems. Precisely because Xenophon has praised Teleutias' good qualities so strongly, he is emphatic about his one weakness. Xenophon is trying to make clear that Teleutias' anger was not a unique slip by an otherwise ideal leader but a serious flaw. Anger is a common trait among the senior Spartans whom Xenophon depicts. At 6.2.19 the Spartan Mnasippos foolishly beats up his junior officers, and so his troops go into battle in a poor state of mind. Again, in the latter stages of the Peloponnesian War, Kallikratidas overreacts to being kept waiting by the Persian Cyrus (1.6.6–7). Xenophon could be hinting at 5.3.7 that the reason Spartans are addicted to outbursts of temper may be the high proportion of unfree people within Spartan society, whom upper-class Spartans can attack without restraint.

§10.11. Despite the fact that, when praising Teleutias at 5.1.3–4, Xenophon appears to deny that control of resources, personal courage, and tactical skill are important topics, he incorporates all three in his work. Perhaps he writes less about resource management in *Hellenika* than about the other two, but there are several references to Athenian generals' problems in finding money to pay rowers (e.g., 5.4.66, of Timotheos; 6.2.37, Iphikrates' solution). To illustrate how courage is a theme in *Hellenika*, one need only to refer again to the Phleiasians and to Anaxibios.

Intro.10.10a   Olynthos: Intro. Map 8.6.

Outside battle, courage is shown by Socrates and, in his last hour, by Theramenes (2.3.56). As for tactical skill, good army leaders are masters of stratagems and know how to get out of difficulties, even those they have created themselves. At 6.5.16–21, Agesilaos skillfully extracts his army from a dangerous cul-de-sac into which he has unwittingly marched them. Although the original slip proves he is fallible, the main point of the story is his presence of mind and tactical ingenuity. Xenophon also underlines Epaminondas' novel tactics at the battle of Mantineia as noteworthy (7.5.21). But while Xenophon rates tactical ability more highly than 5.1.3–4 might suggest, he is consistent in regarding it as less important than creating good morale in the troops. Already in his *Memorabilia* (3.1) he had stressed the unimportance of tactics as compared to morale. This is also one of the lessons of the tale of Mnasippos, whose violent anger so damaged his troops' morale that although he gave orders for a technical maneuver to enable them to deal with an unexpected attack, they could not carry it out and lost the battle (6.2.21). So Mnasippos, like Teleutias, came to disaster because he could not control his passions. The place of psychology in changing the course of battles is a central preoccupation for Xenophon, and something he emphasizes far more than do other ancient historians, perhaps because his personal military experience was especially great and varied.

§10.12. One of the main concerns of the anecdotes in *Hellenika* is leadership, as with the bad leader Mnasippos and the good but imperfect leader Teleutias. It is also one of the main concerns throughout much of Xenophon's other writings. In *Anabasis* (1.9) Cyrus receives a long and glowing obituary notice emphasizing his positive qualities as a leader, although the preceding narrative is more ambivalent, not disguising his carelessness before the battle of Cunaxa and his rashness during it. In *Cyropaedia* Xenophon shows us one very good leader, in the person of Cyrus' namesake, the sixth-century Persian King Cyrus the Elder. Some modern scholars see Xenophon as aiming to create a model of ideal leadership. But even Cyrus the Elder is not shown as the ideal leader. He is not quite free from blemish militarily and, what is more important, cannot be intended as a model for Greeks in the civic institutions he sets up or maintains, such as the use of eunuchs. Nor can Xenophon have meant us to see his old general and patron Agesilaos as an ideal leader, for in *Hellenika* Agesilaos makes the occasional slip, he is liable to be too pleased with himself, and he displays an element of humbug in his makeup. The reason there is only praise for him in *Agesilaos* is not that Xenophon thought there was nothing to blame but only that he was writing an encomium. And leadership itself is not a problem-free concept. Jason of Pherai is declared at *Hellenika* 6.1.5–6 and 6.1.15–16 to be an excellent military leader, dedicated to training his men and replete with ascetic virtues. He is also shown as gifted with diplomatic skill, and he does not exhibit either anger or the lusts of the flesh. Some scholars who see Xenophon as focused on ideal leadership take Jason to be one of his ideal or near-ideal leaders. However, Jason is not a model people should imitate generally but, rather, a scoundrel who is struck down by the gods in his pride because of his impious intentions toward the wealth of the temple at Delphi[a] (6.4.29–32). Nor is it necessary for a military force or a city to have a single leader. No one is named as the leader of the heroic Phleiasians, and by nesting their story within the tale of Euphron of Sicyon, Xenophon implicitly contrasts their collective civic virtue with the way in which the people of Sicyon gladly accepted as their leader, and after his death honored as their second founder, a man who in Xenophon's eyes was a mean-spirited traitor. Despite noting some of the advantages (and disadvantages) of rule by strongman in *Cyropaedia*, Xenophon did not believe it to be the solution to the problems of Sparta, Athens, or the Greek states collectively.

Speech in *Hellenika*

§11.1. Casting his narrative in the form of anecdotes is not the only way in which Xenophon enlivens it. The speeches he writes also have that effect. Although Cratippus was an exception (see §7.4 above), composing extended speeches for historical figures was a standard technique among historians throughout antiquity. The speeches in Thucydides had served largely as vehicles for the author's own analysis, and hence the speakers in his work, though differentiated to some extent, all tend to speak in a style characteristic of Thucydides himself and unlikely to accurately reflect how they had really phrased their speeches. The function of speeches in *Hellenika* is quite different: Xenophon aimed to depict the character of his speakers, partly by what they say, partly by skillfully differentiating the style in which they say it.

§11.2. Here are two examples of the technique. At 7.1.12 Kephisodotos takes the floor in the Athenian assembly. He is full of suspicion. He speaks in short, aggressive sentences. His dramatic presentation dominates the assembly. Also emphatic and aggressive is the extreme oligarch Kritias, whose denunciation of his rival Theramenes at 2.3.24–34 bursts with forcefulness. "Bear this in mind!" he instructs the council brusquely. But Kritias' speech is more complex than that of Kephisodotos. There is a much wider variety of sentence structures, some of them quite unusual, with inversions in the natural order of clauses. In order to emphasize Kritias' passion, on occasion beginning a sentence in one construction, another is substituted as it proceeds (as in the sentence you have just read, which I have written to exemplify the phenomenon it describes, since translators tend to smooth out such awkwardnesses). Metaphors, poeticisms, unusual words, dignity-enhancing plural forms, and other devices of rhetoric heighten the solemnity and stateliness of the speech's richly wrought style, as from his vertiginous eyrie the proud eagle suddenly swoops down on his prey. It has been shown to correspond exactly to what ancient critics said was characteristic of Kritias' style in works now lost. This is a bravura performance by Xenophon.

§11.3. Just as masterly is the trio of speeches at 6.3.3–17 from the Athenian envoys to Sparta in 371. First comes the pompous Kallias. He was hereditary torchbearer at the Eleusinian Mysteries, which were prestigious throughout Greece, so it

Intro.10.12a Delphi: Intro. Map 8.6, inset.

is natural that he should try to impress the Spartans by referring to them, but he bungles his diplomatic effort by laying a too-heavy emphasis on Athens as the universal source for Greece's seed corn. Next we hear the pungent Autokles, who seems to think insulting his hosts is the way to influence them and cannot even make his insults accurate, since he misdescribes how the Peloponnesian League worked and harks back to the way the Spartans had run their empire more than thirty years earlier. Finally, despite these two false starts, the wily Kallistratos smoothes everything over and ingeniously puts the best possible gloss on what was actually a tricky strategic position for Athens. The most austere historian might have given space to two of these people. Kallistratos was a figure of the first importance, and there is reason to suppose he and Xenophon thought alike on many subjects; Autokles no doubt represented an important strand in Athenian opinion, besides being a foil to point up Kallistratos' diplomatic skill. But it is tempting to suggest that the portrait of Kallias was developed mainly for its own sake, and to record for future Athenians the humorous aspects of Kallias more precisely, if now in a less kindly manner, than Xenophon had done in his earlier work *Symposium*. In at least Kallias' case, the depiction of character is an end in itself.

§11.4. But speech is not just a tool in Xenophon's box of tricks. It is also itself a topic. Speech is slippery. Even in good causes, facts and arguments are liable to be twisted. Xenophon himself in *Anabasis* (3.2.24–26) had dazzled the demoralized troops after Cunaxa with improbable comfort, saying they should hurry home and tell their mates of the riches of Persia and the ease with which they could be obtained. An instance in *Hellenika* is the sophistry of the speech in which the assassin of the traitor Euphron defends himself (7.3.7–11). Indeed, one might, with a little ingenuity, suggest that there is only one speech of any length in the whole of *Hellenika* that does not contain at least one misstatement of fact or erroneous argument—and that is the Spartan prince Archidamos' exhortation to his troops before he leads them into battle in 368 (7.1.30), which does not contain any assertions of fact or argumentation at all! So at 6.3.7–17 the apparently blunt and frank Autokles argues from partly false and partly anachronistic premises about Sparta's relations with her allies, while the excellent Kallistratos pretends that Athens feels under no pressure from the Great King when in fact, as usual, Artaxerxes has indicated what he wanted and, no doubt, threatened to intervene if he does not obtain it. The theme starts even before the Great Divide at 2.3.10, with the debate after the battle of Arginousai in which Euryptolemos argues that the assembly should arrange for the six Athenian generals before it to be tried individually by a regular procedure rather than moving immediately to a vote covering all of them (1.7.16–33). Undoubtedly we are supposed to root for Euryptolemos in this debate almost as strongly as the Athenian mob clamored against him, but that does not stop Xenophon from depicting him as trying to manipulate the crowd with misleading or disingenuous arguments, even going so far as to say that twelve Athenian ships were lost in the battle (1.7.30) when the narrative has given the figure as twenty-five (1.6.34). It is another instance where Xenophon's message is not black and white.

§11.5. The archetypal tricky speaker was Theramenes, Kritias' opponent in the time of the Thirty. Kritias taunts him for this and other double-dealing by throwing in his face his nickname, The Slipper (because it fits both feet). In this crisis, Theramenes behaved heroically and met his death with spirit (2.3.56). But, according to Xenophon, he had previously been a villain, plotting the downfall of the generals after the battle of Arginousai. Now, in his final hour of heroic resistance, Xenophon has Theramenes give a version of the Arginousai affair (2.3.35) that is at odds with Xenophon's own narrative of it at 1.7.3–6. Many have claimed that this shows that Xenophon separates the different scenes of his work in his own mind and colors each for maximum effect without regard to consequent contradictions. Now, Xenophon has probably exaggerated Theramenes' previous villainy, ignoring the role of misunderstanding and fearful self-defense in the Arginousai tragedy, and it may even be that the version of the affair that Theramenes gives here is closer to the truth than Xenophon's narrative, the latter being flawed by Xenophon's closeness to the situation and the passions it evoked. But it is one thing to criticize Xenophon's accuracy and quite another to claim that his work is incoherent. Xenophon was not such an incompetent storyteller as to fail to see that his audience would remember when they read Book 2 what they had been told in Book 1. His point, right or wrong, is that even in Theramenes' most heroic hour, a genuinely heroic hour, he told lies.

§11.6. The thought occurs: If speech is slippery and Xenophon depicts his younger self as speaking disingenuously, then what of the speech represented by *Hellenika* itself? I doubt that Xenophon means to give us a subliminal warning about his own work, but *Hellenika* is certainly slippery. For example, Xenophon makes a number of pronouncements through the work that apparently give his views on the scope and methods of history, thus to some extent making up for the absence of a formal preface—but there is something fishy in each case. At 2.3.56 he records the dying witticism of Theramenes and then adds, "Now, I am not unaware that these remarks are not worthy of record." It is a paradoxical way of giving emphasis. Perhaps P in his austerity omitted the remarks, and this is a dig at him. Then again at 7.2.1 Xenophon expressly contrasts his account of the Phleiasians with how earlier historians have passed over the deeds of small cities, but in fact earlier historians had generally not ignored small cities, and elsewhere Xenophon focuses rather relentlessly on Sparta and Athens, other states appearing by and large only in relation to those two. Xenophon sounds as though he is announcing a new conception of history, but really he is justifying a digression. Similarly, when at 4.8.1 he claims he will report only the important events in the (Corinthian) war at sea and pass over the rest, he is not signaling any great change in the criteria he had used in narrating the war on land but is, rather, trying to head off criticism of the balance of his narrative. Perhaps he fears it will be judged to give undue space to just one of the Spartan commanders, Teleutias. A similar motive may be a factor behind the emphatic way in which at 5.1.4 he downgrades money, danger, and stratagems as compared to morale building. As we have seen, the point is a genuine one, but it is being used as a smokescreen to deflect attention from the lack of proportion in the way he plugs Teleutias while telling us much less than he might have about the deeds of other naval commanders.

The Grinding of Axes?

§12.1. It is not just in relation to these apparent methodological pronouncements that Xenophon may be seen as slippery. Indeed, while in antiquity Xenophon was considered a particularly fair-minded writer (e.g., see Lucian, *How to Write History* 39; Agatharchides, *Die Fragmente der griechischen Historiker* 86, Fragment 19.37), moderns have generally taken the opposite view: that he is peculiarly prone to political bias. The sound of axes being ground is perceived throughout the narrative. It is therefore time to move away from Xenophon's general themes and to consider whether he pushes any partisan theses on us. I shall review in turn Xenophon's dislike of Thebes, ambivalent stance toward Sparta and Athens, support of their so-called dual hegemony, and attitude toward the Great Panhellenic Crusade against Persia. But first something he cared about more than any of them: the cavalry.

§12.2. As a cavalryman himself, Xenophon is a partisan of the cavalry, and he repeatedly emphasizes its role. Thus we are told several times (at 3.1.5, 3.2.15–18, 3.4.13–15) that superiority in cavalry was vitally important to Persian control of the plains of Asia Minor and that the Greeks would have to do better in this sphere if they were to prevail. Cavalry plays a major role in the triumphs of Agesilaos in Asia (3.4.22–24) and in Thessaly[a] (4.3.4–9): here, especially when recounting the Thessalian skirmish, Xenophon writes as if he has something to be personally proud about, and we may infer that he had trained Agesilaos' cavalry himself. Xenophon goes on to stress the place of cavalry in Teleutias' early successes against Olynthos[b] (5.2.40–42, 5.3.1–2), and although he generally plays down Theban successes where he can, he gives us details of a Theban cavalry victory in 378 (5.4.44). Xenophon emphasizes the usefulness of cavalry against light-armed troops (5.4.54), he applauds the prowess of Syracusan cavalrymen who come to help Sparta in the 360s (7.1.21), and of course he praises the role of the Athenian cavalry at Mantineia[c] (7.5.15–17). It is no accident that the heroic Phleiasians are cavalrymen. He also stresses the evil consequences that follow when commanders mismanage the cavalry, as did the Spartan commander at Lechaion[d] (4.5.16) and the Athenian Iphikrates near Oneon[e] in 369 (6.5.52), and he claims that having defective cavalry was a main cause of the overwhelming Spartan defeat at Leuktra[f] (6.4.10–11). Much more than any political or even moral thesis, if there is a single lesson Xenophon would like us to take away from his work, it is the value of good cavalry.

§12.3. Almost as strong and undiluted as his advocacy of the cavalry is his dislike

Intro.12.2a   Thessaly: Intro. Map 12.12.
Intro.12.2b   Olynthos: Intro. Map 12.12.
Intro.12.2c   Mantineia: Intro. Map 12.12, inset.
Intro.12.2d   Lechaion: Intro. Map 12.12, inset.

Intro.12.2e   Oneon (Mount Oneon in the *Barrington Atlas*): Intro. Map 12.12, inset.
Intro.12.2f   Leuktra: Intro. Map 12.12, inset.

of Thebans, especially successful anti-Spartan Thebans. At 7.5.12 his dislike bursts out openly when, describing a minor setback the Thebans suffered in 362, he sarcastically refers to "these breathers of fire, these soldiers who had already defeated the Spartans." His bias appears also at 3.5.8–15, where he shows the Theban envoys to Athens in 395 to be deeply unpleasant people. They reveal their shiftiness by distorting the recent past when they imply that Sparta still maintains the oppressive garrisons and close oligarchies that Lysander installed around the Aegean in 404–403: Xenophon had pointed out at 3.4.2 that the Spartans had dissolved the close oligarchies, something that probably happened years earlier, around the time they withdrew support from the oligarchs at Athens. The only arguments the Thebans use are open appeals to naked self-interest, without any attempt to show the justice of their case. They are so selfish that they do not realize that the Athenians might be, or at least might like to be thought to be, concerned with what is right. Xenophon's dislike of Thebans can be seen again in the opening campaigns of the Corinthian War. He draws a picture of the Thebans as swinging foolishly between extremes of hope and fear on the battlefield of Haliartos[a] in 395 (3.5.20–24), and he insinuates that they showed cowardliness in their troop dispositions and timing the following year at the battle of the Nemea River[b] (4.2.18). Bias has also been seen in the fact that Xenophon does not name the Theban leaders Epaminondas and Pelopidas at the battle of Leuctra, although this may be to stress the role of the gods in Sparta's defeat rather than to denigrate the men through whom they worked. According to other sources, Pelopidas was a principal figure in the Liberation of Thebes[c] (although propaganda and hindsight may have inflated his role), but Xenophon does not name him; he also suppresses Pelopidas' success against a detachment of Spartans at a battle near Tegyra,[d] in north Boeotia, in the mid-370s. It can hardly be a coincidence that when Pelopidas is first named, at 7.1.33, he is toadying to the Great King; similarly we are not given Epaminondas' name until 7.1.41, when his third expedition to the Peloponnese backfires (although not really through his fault). Xenophon appears to treat Epaminondas more fairly in his account of the Mantineia campaign, when he praises his military preparations, boldness, training methods, and tactics (7.5.8, 7.5.19–20). But the portrait is not quite as fair as it looks: Xenophon suggests that only desperate ambition made Epaminondas bring the enemy to battle at Mantineia, but as he outnumbered his opponents roughly two to one, his conduct does not require a psychological explanation.

§12.4. However, Xenophon's bias against the Thebans is not as ubiquitous as his advocacy of cavalry. While he shows bias against the Thebans when he has cause to mention them, he does not look for occasions to castigate them, indeed passes over some obvious opportunities. He omits various disaster-prone campaigns that Pelopidas waged in Thessaly in the 360s, which could have been used to make Pelopidas, and Thebes in general, look stupid. Xenophon gives minimal details of Thebes' harsh treatment of Plataea[a] and Thespiai[b] in 373 in the course of the unification of

Intro.12.3a Haliartos: Intro. Map 12.12, inset.	Intro.12.4a Plataea: Intro. Map 12.12, inset.
Intro.12.3b Nemea River: Intro. Map 12.12, inset.	Intro.12.4b Thespiai: Intro. Map 12.12, inset.
Intro.12.3c Thebes (Boeotia): Intro. Map 12.12, inset.	
Intro.12.3d Tegyra: Intro. Map 12.12, inset.	

Boeotia, and he does not even mention the destruction of Thebes' ancient Boeotian rival Orchomenus[c] in 363, when he could easily have shown the Thebans as hateful. And it is clear that Xenophon had not always hated all Thebans, for in his youth he had a great friend, Proxenus, who was a Theban (*Anabasis* 2.1.10). It was this man whom he had followed into Cyrus' service in 401 and whom he commemorated in a dedication to Apollo at Delphi.[d] Xenophon's bias against Thebes therefore arose, or at least grew, after 401, presumably as a result of Thebes' actions in 395 against Sparta and in 371–362 against Sparta and its Peloponnesian supporters.

§12.5. Xenophon's bias against Thebes thus implies that he was biased in favor of Sparta, and such a bias is what we might expect from someone who had fought for Sparta against his own city, who lived for twenty years as a Spartan client, and who wrote an encomium on a Spartan king. And he certainly displays straightforward support for other Spartan sympathizers and agents within the Peloponnese, men such as the Phleiasian aristocrats and both Pasimelos of Corinth and Alkimenes, the men who let the Spartans into the Long Walls between Corinth and Lechaion in 392 (4.4.7). Open bias is on display in Book 7 when Xenophon refers to the Peloponnesian opponents of Thebes as "those who wanted what was best for the Peloponnese" (7.4.35, see also 7.5.1).

§12.6. But of the Spartans themselves Xenophon writes less wholeheartedly. We saw that he was ambivalent about them at the time when he drafted, and then laid aside, his *Constitution of the Lacedaemonians*, probably in the 370s. That was shortly after Sparta had occupied the Theban citadel in 382, an act that in *Hellenika* (5.4.1) Xenophon denounces as impious and wicked. *Constitution of the Lacedaemonians* complains about the behavior of Spartan governors abroad. One recent example was that in 378 the Spartan governor of Thespiai, in Boeotia, the rash and incompetent Sphodrias, had made a sudden march on Athens at a time when the Athenians believed they were at peace with Sparta. In *Hellenika* (5.4.24) Xenophon represents the subsequent acquittal of Sphodrias by the Spartan council as totally unjust.

Throughout *Hellenika* unsatisfactory Spartans pop up. Xenophon could hardly have avoided mentioning some of them, such as Sphodrias and King Kleombrotos, the loser at Leuctra, who is portrayed as generally useless throughout his Boeotian campaigns, but there are many others, such as Anaxibios and Mnasippos, whom he could easily have left out or whose stories he could have told less garishly. An extreme example is his treatment of Thibron, twice sent out to Asia in the 390s. Xenophon depicts him as incompetent (3.1.7, 3.2.1, 3.2.7, 4.8.18–19, 4.8.22) and implies that he was the passive homosexual partner of the strong flautist Thersander[a] (4.8.18, 4.8.22). Even Xenophon's patron Agesilaos and Agesilaos' half brother Teleutias do not get unblemished write-ups, as we have already seen. Spartan error, unpopularity, and occasional disgrace are often on view, helping to give *Hellenika* a sour tone, which Xenophon perhaps regarded as called for by the conventions of history.

§12.7. Still, the point can be overdone. Some modern scholars think that Xenophon

Intro.12.4c   Orchomenus: Intro. Map 12.12, inset.   Intro.12.6a   See n. 4.8.18b.
Intro.12.4d   Delphi: Intro. Map 12.12, inset.

not only objected to the Spartan occupation of the Theban citadel but, in common with many Greeks, also disapproved of Sparta's general behavior in the late 380s. In fact, Xenophon's criticisms were restricted to the occupation of the Theban citadel. According to him (5.4.1), the divine plan behind what happened to Sparta in 371 and thereafter is revealed partly by the fact that Sparta's wickedness was punished by, and only by, the very people against whom it had been perpetrated, that is, the Thebans. By the logic of this argument, the Spartans had not been wicked in their actions during the 380s against Mantineia, Phleious (at that stage a democracy), and Olynthos. And although plenty of people did think those actions had been wicked, at least in the first two cases, Xenophon's account shows he meant exactly what he wrote at 5.4.1. It is true that he does not give us reasons against the view, common in his day, that the attack on Mantineia in 385 was a disgraceful breach of the just-concluded King's Peace, and ingenuity is required to imagine what defense he thought the Spartans had. But note his satisfied report at 5.2.7 of the consequences of splitting the city into its component villages, and his seeming astonishment at 6.5.3 that the Mantineians supposed that the terms of the general peace that Sparta agreed to in 371/70 after Leuctra meant that they were now to be in every way autonomous: Xenophon thought the Spartans had acted perfectly appropriately in attacking Mantineia in 385 and splitting the city up. It is plain, too, that Xenophon shared the view he attributes to the Spartan magistrates at 5.3.10–13 that the Phleiasian democrats had been acting "brazenly" when they compelled their former exiles to litigate in the state's own courts, that the juries in those courts were composed of "those who had committed the crimes," and that, all in all, the Phleiasians were behaving "outrageously." Modern scholars have found it difficult to square Spartan intervention with the autonomy clause of the King's Peace, but Xenophon did not. We may well shudder to be told that after the taking of Phleious, Sparta organized a court to decide who should live and who should die (5.3.25), but Xenophon regards it as an appropriate step in creating the splendidly loyal Phleious of the 360s, and holds it up as an example of the Spartans' restraint and law-abiding nature that when they packed the tribunal with their supporters, they did not choose only the former exiles. In the same way, he accepts at face value the justice of the show trial that convicted the Theban Ismenias (5.2.35–36), writing as though it was significant that Ismenias failed to make any impression on the kangaroo court that the Spartans had assembled to gain their revenge for his part in the outbreak of the Corinthian War thirteen years earlier.

§12.8. However, Xenophon's bias toward Sparta becomes even clearer if we consider what he omitted from *Hellenika*, even when it lay fair and square in the path of the narrative. There are only faint glimmers of the ruthlessness and cruelty with which the Spartans behaved across the Aegean at the end of the Peloponnesian War. It is striking that Ephorus (*Die Fragmente der griechischen Historiker* 70, Fragment 71) reported that Xenophon's old commander Derkylidas was a man of bestial savagery, something one could not guess from Xenophon's report of his activities.

Characteristically, Xenophon does not defend Derkylidas against the accusation by argument or counterexample but merely ignores the charge. Furthermore, except in the case of the Thirty at Athens, Xenophon glosses over the evil of the narrow oligarchies and Spartan governorships that Lysander set up around 405–404. He mentions them only after they are over (3.4.2, 3.5.13), giving no details, and the reason he introduces them is to demonstrate the unreliability of the Thebans, who tendentiously argue as if these repressive institutions are still continuing in 395. Xenophon docs not hide the fact that Spartan led troops actively assisted the Thirty in their depredations (2.3.13–14), nor does he conceal that these troops also proved inadequate when put to the test against the rebel democrats (2.4.4–7). Nevertheless he obscures Lysander's key role in setting up the Thirty in the first place. Most modern scholars agree that after Athens surrendered to the Spartans and began to tear down the Long Walls (2.2.23), three or four months passed before Lysander completed the work of destruction and forced the appointment of the Thirty, but this would not be guessed from *Hellenika*. Contrary to the impression Xenophon gives, Athenian democracy was not the immediate casualty of military defeat: Lysander had to go out of his way to bring it to an end (see for example Diodorus 14.3.6).[a] Xenophon's obfuscation here is particularly noteworthy, as he could have used the Spartan role to absolve himself by making out that the moderate Athenian oligarchs were under duress from the outset.

§12.9. Even more significant, Xenophon repeatedly avoids revealing the attitude of other Greeks to the liberation of Messenia[a] from Spartan control in 369. He has to bend his narrative in striking ways to achieve this. At 6.5.51, he actually passes over the fact that when Epaminondas left Laconia[b] during his first intervention in the Peloponnese, he went on to Messenia and freed it. Xenophon cannot have hoped to persuade readers then or later to forget the liberation, and indeed we subsequently do hear of Messenians independent of Sparta (7.1.27, 7.1.36, 7.4.9, 7.4.27, 7.5.5). But by omitting the liberation in its proper place, he can avoid showing how most non-Spartan Peloponnesians gleefully assisted the Thebans in this task, and also how the Athenians, despite their alliance with the Spartans, stood back and let it happen. Xenophon, while not making clear what was going on in the south of the Peloponnese, complains at 6.5.51 about the fact that the Athenian commander Iphikrates did not advance farther than Corinth. Xenophon pretends that his complaint is on military grounds, implying that Iphikrates was not carrying out his instructions, but Iphikrates' inaction did him no harm at all in the eyes of the Athenian people, as soon afterward they gave him the plum command in the North Aegean. Later, Xenophon fails to tell us about Athenian involvement in the Peace of 366/5 and brings his work to a close just short of the Peace of 362/1. These failures are for the same reason as the omission at 6.5.51. In both peaces the Athenians, along with the Greeks generally, acknowledged the independence of Messenia. But the Spartans clung to the foolish hope that they could recover Messenia, and so, evidently, did Xenophon. It seems that he had little sympathy for the

Intro.12.8a   See Appendix O.
Intro.12.9a   Messenia: Intro. Map 12.12.

Intro.12.9b   Laconia: Intro. Map 12.12.

Messenian (and Laconian) helots, just as he regards as almost incomprehensible the veneration the serfs of Sicyon felt for Euphron, who liberated them a year or so later (7.3.12). From what he says approvingly in *Cyropaedia* about the opportunities that, according to him, Cyrus the Elder gave to the Persian peasantry, Xenophon thought that the Spartans mishandled their own lower orders, but he shows more fellow feeling for the aspirations of Kinadon (*Hellenika* 3.3.4–11), who was only just the wrong side of the criteria for full citizenship at Sparta, than he does for the truly oppressed.

§12.10. Xenophon does recount some Spartan failures, such as the battle of Leuctra, and some unsatisfactory successes, such as the King's Peace. That was unavoidable if the story of these years was to be told at all and does not show that he was being impartial. It is true that he could have avoided recounting the misdeeds of so many individual Spartans, but note that Xenophon tends to tell us about incompetence and personal weakness rather than about cruelty and financial dishonesty, the complaints we find in other sources. His criticisms of Spartans are those of an insider, the kind that the Spartans themselves would make of their fellows, and they are often presented so as to deflect criticism from the state of Sparta onto individual Spartans. For example, in recounting the acquittal of Sphodrias for his attack on Athens, Xenophon emphasizes a personal motive, namely, Agesilaos' wish to further his own son's love affair with Sphodrias' son. We are not exposed to the Spartan government's reasons for thinking it was now useless to try to conciliate Athens by punishing Sphodrias. So pro-Spartan bias has indeed affected Xenophon's account of the period. Despite his criticisms of Spartan individuals, in his eyes the Spartans collectively were the good guys.

§12.11. Occasionally Xenophon seems to be so pro-Spartan as to rejoice in Sparta's successes against Athens, his native city. With evident glee he describes a surprise raid by Teleutias' ships on the Athenian port of Peiraieus[a] during the Corinthian War (5.1.19–24). It is hardly surprising to find Xenophon ambivalent about democratic Athens, especially when recounting a war between Athens and Sparta. After all, he had been a cavalryman in the service of an oligarchy in 404–3 and was in arms against Athens in 394. However, Xenophon, whether or not he returned to Athens in the 360s, did still think of himself as an Athenian, as he shows both in *Hipparchicus* and throughout *Poroi*. Nor was he a diehard oligarch. In *Memorabilia* (3.5) Xenophon's Socrates argues against the younger Pericles' pessimism about Athens, saying that with various reforms the city can again obtain the premier rank in Greece. The reforms he advocates do not include a change of regime, and he says nothing to imply that a democracy cannot achieve greatness. Indeed, in Xenophon's account of the events of 403 he shows that Thrasyboulos and his democratic followers were right in their resistance to the Thirty and in their subsequent struggle with the moderate oligarchs who, backed by Xenophon's younger self, took power in the city of Athens when most of the Thirty retired a few miles away to Eleusis.[b] He handsomely acknowledges at 2.4.43 that the democrats kept their word not to

Intro.12.11a Peiraieus: Intro. Map 12.12, inset.
Intro.12.11b Eleusis: Intro. Map 12.12, inset.

engage in reprisals after 403 (although he does take a bit of the shine off this by remarking at 3.1.4 that they were glad enough in the winter of 400/399 to send off the cavalry to Asia with Thibron and rather hoped they would never return). It is true that he tries to show us that the city oligarchs had reasons for rejecting democracy and the democratic leaders, and he distances his youthful self from oligarchic atrocities, but he intends this to be taken not as an argument for the course of action he and the other moderate oligarchs pursued, but as an apologia for having made a mistake.

§12.12. Xenophon's treatment of Athens contains an omission that is almost as startling as his suppression of the Liberation of Messenia. He says nothing about the foundation of the Second Athenian League in 378 and studiously avoids a direct mention of it at 5.4.34. Indeed it hardly appears as such thereafter. (It is named at 6.3.19 and 6.5.2, hinted at in 6.1.12 and 7.1.36, and referred to with studied vagueness at 5.4.64.)[a] Although the league was consensual at the outset, Athens' most powerful allies came to regard it as oppressive, and so Xenophon's silence about it has been interpreted as a sign that he disapproved of Athenian imperialism, a parallel to his disapproving silence about the liberation of Messenia. Indeed, some see it as part of a more general case against imperialism, whoever the empire builders may be—Athens, Sparta, Thebes, or any other state. But this is to overread, even though it is true that in 355, probably a year later than *Hellenika*, his *Poroi* condemned the Athenians' imperialistic ways and argued that they should try to lead the other Greeks not by the exercise of power but through consensus building. By that time Athens' collapse at the end of the Social War (§3.9 above) meant that the game was up. One could be against imperialism in 355 without having opposed it a year earlier—this was probably true of most Athenians. Xenophon cannot have intended *Hellenika* to be building a case against Athenian imperialism, for silence does not build a case. There was plenty he could have said about Athenian imperialism in the 360s had he wanted to argue that such ventures always go wrong and lead to oppression and waste, but he conspicuously fails to mention the prime examples of Samos[b] and Amphipolis[c] (the latter is named only once, at 4.3.1, in a context irrelevant in this connection).

§12.13. The one time when Xenophon shows an Athenian trying actively to build a trans-Aegean empire is the account at 4.8.25–34 of the final expedition of the Athenian general Thrasyboulos (probably in 390). We learn from other sources that this was a bit of a shambles: much of the fleet suffered a shipwreck in a storm,

---

Intro.12.12a For the Second Athenian League, see Appendix H, Political Leagues (Other Than Sparta's) in Xenophon's *Hellenika*, §9. The exact date of its founding is controversial. *The Cambridge Ancient History*, the chronology used as the basis for this edition, places it in spring 379/8. Other scholars have placed it a few months later, and in Appendix H, §9, Peter Rhodes dates it to 378/7.
  Also controversial is the exact meaning of 6.3.19 and 6.5.2, where Xenophon refers to "the Athenians and their allies." This phrase appears from inscriptional

evidence to have been the official name of the Second Athenian League, and the view taken in the text here is that Xenophon is using it in that sense. But some scholars say that 6.3.19 should not count as a use of the official name, as Xenophon is talking about all allies of Athens, a few of whom at this point were probably not members of the league. Another view is that at 6.5.2 he is referring to all participants in the Peace of 371/70, at least some of whom did not join the League.

Intro.12.12b Samos: Intro. Map 12.12.
Intro.12.12c Amphipolis: Intro. Map 12.12.

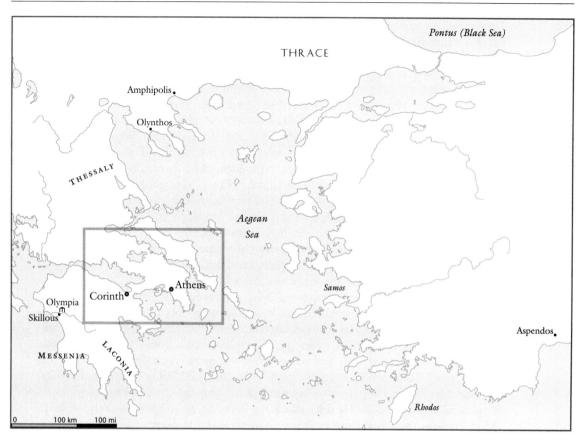

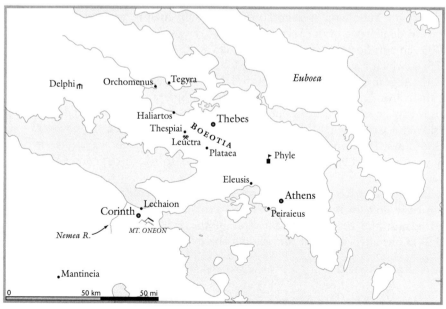

INTRO. MAP 12.12

Thrasyboulos seems to have imprudently allowed the enemy to gain the initiative on Rhodos,[a] and there is evidence that his colleagues used strong-arm tactics on allied cities for personal gain. By the end, his colleagues were talking treasonably about resisting attempts to recall them to Athens to face trial. But from Xenophon we hear only of Thrasyboulos' successes until, out of the blue, disaster strikes at Aspendos,[b] in southern Asia Minor, and he is killed in a skirmish. Xenophon then comments that Thrasyboulos had the reputation of being a good man (4.8.31), an odd obituary notice if Xenophon's real attitude was that Thrasyboulos' imperialism was wicked and/or unwise. Admittedly, Xenophon does not say that Thrasyboulos actually was a good man, only that he had the reputation of being one, but this need not hint at any doubt about the man's imperialistic policies. Xenophon may be reluctant to assert without qualification that Thrasyboulos was good because the gods are not supposed to let good men down, so Thrasyboulos' unhappy end raises the question of whether, despite appearances, he had some hidden defect. It follows from Xenophon's treatment of Thrasyboulos and his imperial venture that Xenophon cannot have been a principled anti-imperialist, and principled anti-imperialism is not the reason he has little to say about the Second Athenian League.

§12.14. This conclusion is supported if we turn from this Athenian attempt at empire building to the more successful imperialistic efforts of Sparta. Xenophon never breathes a word against Spartan control of the Peloponnese, nor, as we have said, does he draw conclusions from Sparta's violence and cruelty in the late 400s. At least in *Hellenika*, he does not write about the moral corruption that Ephorus and others in the fourth century saw as flowing from the influx of imperial profits into Laconia. He attacks particular instances of Spartan aggression rather than Sparta's general aggressiveness. He does attack the belligerence of Sparta's enemies, such as the Thebans, but this is not evidence of generalized anti-imperialism, as distinct from antipathy to aggression from the "wrong" side.

§12.15. Though Xenophon was not opposed to imperialism as such, he had other reasons to disapprove of the Second Athenian League: it was expressly advertised in 377 as an anti-Spartan league; its resources were key to bringing about the Peace of 375/4, which was a diplomatic defeat for Sparta; and the Athenians' preoccupation with Aegean affairs in the 360s will have been seen by Xenophon as distracting them from their proper task of bolstering Sparta in the Peloponnese. Perhaps this is why he says so little about it. That Athens and Sparta had fought the Peloponnesian and Corinthian Wars against each other could not be passed over, but from 386 onward Xenophon emphasizes as much as possible the occasions on which they worked together and plays down the extent to which their long-term interests were opposed.

§12.16. Hence the space given to two speeches allegedly made by Prokles the Phleiasian in early 369. In the first (6.5.38–48) Prokles urges Athens to come to Sparta's aid against the first Theban invasion of the Peloponnese, while in the second (7.1.2–11) he advocates that they should share the command, Sparta to lead

Intro.12.13a Rhodos: Intro. Map 12.12.   Intro.12.13b Aspendos: Intro. Map 12.12.

by land and Athens by sea. This has rightly suggested to many that Xenophon favored what is sometimes called dual hegemony, in which the leadership of Greece was to be shared by the two cities between which he had split his loyalties, with Sparta dominant on land and Athens at sea. But it is not all plain sailing here. Prokles is perhaps somewhat naive; and if Xenophon were wholehearted about the second speech, it is odd that no harm is shown to come from its rejection in favor of a seemingly impracticable notion of combining the command of both land and sea forces but then alternating it between the two powers every five days. Something does indeed go wrong—the Thebans are let through the pass at Oneon by Spartan carelessness and pusillanimity (7.1.15–17). However, the alternating command had nothing to do with this lapse; and as it was, according to Xenophon, entirely the Spartans' fault, it hardly supports giving Sparta permanent overall command on land. Furthermore, Xenophon is distinctly sour about the Peace of 375/4, though, as we are told by a Roman author (Cornelius Nepos, *Life of Timotheos* 2.2; see also Diodorus 15.38.4[a]) whose work often follows Ephorus, this peace expressly incorporated dual hegemony. It would seem that any sentiments Xenophon had in favor of joint Spartan–Athenian leadership were outweighed here by his dislike of the benefits that the peace brought for Thebes, and possibly by distaste for the Persians' role in promoting the peace, a role suppressed by Xenophon at 6.2.1 but revealed by the Ephoran sources, such as Diodorus 15.38.1.[b] Xenophon is much more enthusiastic about the Peace of 372/1, where Sparta was again clearly in control but, instead of the harsh settlements imposed in 404 and 386, now sought Athenian cooperation. Still, Xenophon would doubtless have voted for dual hegemony in the 350s if it could have been achieved (by then, of course, it was a pipe dream). But he hardly wrote *Hellenika* as a tract to advocate it.

§12.17. There was a related notion that the Greeks, united under their leaders, should embark on a Great Panhellenic Crusade against Persia, a theme on which the tiresome Isocrates preached interminably for half a century. It is natural to think that Xenophon, an old campaigner against Artaxerxes, would favor this idea and would draw the same lesson as did Isocrates from the march of the Ten Thousand and the Asian expedition of Agesilaos: that it would be a piece of cake to defeat the Persians and wrest Asia Minor away from them. Xenophon shows clear hostility to the Persians, and to Artaxerxes in particular, in *Agesilaos* and in the last chapter of *Cyropaedia*; and in *Hellenika* he is gleeful at the humiliating, if probably temporary, failure of Artaxerxes' diplomacy in 367/6 (7.1.37–40). However, Xenophon cannot have been completely antipathetic to Persians, for much of *Cyropaedia* advocates (alleged) Persian practices, and plenty of passages elsewhere show some sympathy for Persian ways and for individual Persians. The Persians were, after all, fine cavalrymen. Although Xenophon fought against the Persian Pharnabazos both when he was in the Athenian army and when he was in the Spartan army, he consistently depicts him favorably, offering at 1.1.6 a heroic vignette of him riding his horse into the sea to support his allies and describing at length at 4.1.29–38 how he remon-

Intro.12.16a See Appendix O.   Intro.12.16b See Appendix O.

strated with Agesilaos for ingratitude in a story that shows Pharnabazos in the best possible light.

§12.18. It is in fact remarkably difficult to find passages unambiguously showing Xenophon in tune with Isocrates' tub-thumping for the great crusade against Persia. Xenophon does bang the drum in *Agesilaos*, but if Agesilaos hated barbarians and longed for the great crusade, or even if that was merely what the Greek world thought he should have done, then his encomiast had to follow suit. So *Agesilaos* proves nothing about Xenophon's personal convictions. In *Hellenika*, Jason of Pherai hints at 6.1.12 that he intends to go on the crusade, but what one thinks of these hints depends upon what one thinks of Jason. Xenophon plays down Persia's ability to exert pressure on the mainland Greek states, omitting or minimizing it in his accounts of at least three multiparty peaces (those of 375/4, 372/1, and 366/5), probably in part because he was ashamed of Persia's dominating role. But that does not show that he wanted the Greeks to retaliate aggressively. At *Anabasis* 3.2.24–26 Xenophon depicts himself bucking up the spirits of the troops after Cunaxa by stressing Persian weakness; but as we saw (§11.4 above), this seems as much designed to show Xenophon's facility in argument as to convince the reader. The best evidence for Xenophon's crusading spirit is that he shows not only Agesilaos (4.1.41, 4.2.3) but also his opponent Tithraustes (3.5.1) as believing that Agesilaos had excellent prospects in Asia had he not been stabbed in the back by the Thebans; but even here Xenophon does not absolutely commit himself to agreeing. Still, probably he did think that victory in the great crusade was achievable, if only Greece were united behind the effort.

The Role of the Gods

§13.1. In five of the six cases we have just examined, Xenophon proves on close examination to be less of a vigorous partisan for a simplistic view than has some-times been supposed. There was, however, one dearly held thesis that Xenophon is keen to press upon us in *Hellenika*: the belief that, despite the misfortunes of good people, the gods are just and beneficent.

§13.2. For many religious-minded Greeks, the misfortunes of good people did not create a great problem, because they saw the gods as arbitrary and prone to envy, as they often appear, for example, in Herodotus. There were also a few ratio-nalists, such as Thucydides, who did not regard the injustice of fortune as a prob-lem, because for them there were no gods, or none that respond to human affairs. But Xenophon's attitude differed from both groups. He was imbued with religious rationalism, shared, by his own account, with Socrates. This led him to believe in the divine ordering of this world according to just principles—a bleak creed for all but the most successful, and a difficult challenge when one's heroes fail. So it had been a great problem for Xenophon that Socrates came to a bad end, condemned to death by the Athenian courts and made to drink poisonous hemlock like a criminal.

He succeeded in solving the problem to his own satisfaction in Socrates' case, but only by stretching the truth (common enough in Socratic writings). Plato's *Apology* showed Socrates as prepared to risk irritating his jury and as refusing to compromise his beliefs and integrity, but Xenophon's *Apology* went further. Xenophon's Socrates decides before the trial starts that death is preferable to old age (a view Plato's Socrates also reaches, but only once his execution has become inevitable), and Xenophon implausibly depicts him as in effect provoking the court to convict him and sentence him to death. Thus, according to Xenophon, the gods gave Socrates what he wanted all along.

§13.3. But only a few years after Xenophon composed the *Apology*, his problem recurred. As we saw earlier (§12.10 above), despite faults in individuals, the Spartans were collectively the good guys in his eyes, but at the battle of Leuctra they suffered a grievous fall. Xenophon had to find reasons why the gods let Sparta down. He identifies two—and only two—key Spartan sins. First, at 5.4.1, he denounces the treachery involved in Sparta's occupation of the Theban Kadmeia[a] in 382. Subsequently, at 6.4.2–3, he complains that after Sparta had neutralized Thebes' former ally Athens in the Peace of 372/1, the Spartan assembly decided to proceed directly against Thebes without going through the rigmarole of disbanding the army and repeating for form's sake the demand that Thebes should respect the autonomy of the other Boeotian cities. Xenophon implies that this was a breach of Sparta's oaths under the peace treaty. But while others besides Xenophon were indignant about the events of 382, his protestations at 6.4.2–3 are artificial, for Sparta's behavior in 371 was perfectly reasonable and no doubt anticipated among all those who had sworn to the peace. Most people would not have needed recourse to the assembly meeting just before Leuctra to find plenty of instances of Spartan injustice, arrogance, and disregard for oaths in the preceding thirty or so years. To make such a fuss about this final incident showed the strength of Xenophon's devotion to Sparta and of his rather odd brand of legalistic piety. He was finding excuses for the gods.

§13.4. Although Xenophon gives the gods an important role in his history, he does not allow his belief in divine causation to stop him from exploring the human causes of the same events. On the theological level, the sins of the Spartans are the cause of their defeat at Leuctra; but he still explains to us that the Spartans were defeated because their commander was overly hasty, their officers were drunk, and their cavalry was in very bad shape (6.4.6, 6.4.8, 6.4.10–11). One can argue about whether Xenophon was right to suggest that the Corinthian War was caused by Persian gold, Theban plots, and Spartan errors of judgment (3.5.1–16), but these causes are secular and reasonable enough. Herodotus tells many tales of the gods' miraculous intervention in human affairs, but for Xenophon there are no clear instances of this. At most, the gods inflame the courage of one set of soldiers (7.4.32) or achieve the results they want by operating on the morale of both sides (7.5.12–13). They act through human psychology and natural processes, such as the clap of thunder just before a notable Spartan victory against odds in 368 (7.1.31).

Intro.13.3a Kadmeia: the acropolis of Thebes. It was named after Kadmos, the founder of the city, and is thought to have been the site for meetings of its senate and Assembly.

No supernatural event is needed for the gods to exact retribution for the impious murder of pro-Spartan Corinthians. Justice is done when the killers are bloodily slaughtered in their turn by the sons of those they have slain (4.4.3, 4.4.12). The gods do not have to intervene miraculously to punish Anaxibios: the same careless attitude that led him to ignore bad sacrificial omens also leads him to take inadequate military precautions (4.8.35–39). But it is not just on rare and marginal occasions that the gods show their concern for the righteous. Xenophon sees them as actively shaping the balance of forces within the Peloponnese throughout the 360s, from which he implicitly draws comfort at 7.5.13 that they regard themselves as having punished Sparta enough. At any rate, it is not for human beings to presume to act in the gods' stead—as the Delphic Oracle informs inquirers worried about the plans of Jason of Pherai, the god can look after himself (6.4.30). This revelation is surely included in *Hellenika* to warn people who shared Xenophon's distaste for the events of 382 not to react by supporting the Thebans' use of religious charges against Sparta in 357, the fuse that led to the explosion of the Sacred War.

§13.5. As was mentioned earlier in connection with Anaxibios (§10.9 above), the Greeks were accustomed to offering animal sacrifices before leading the army into action and to inspecting the victims' internal organs, especially the liver, by the state of which they thought one could tell whether it was right to proceed. Xenophon was a firm believer in this practice, so fecklessly scorned by Anaxibios, and used it as an example of the gods' beneficence toward humankind. Greeks might also carry out such divinatory sacrifices on other occasions when seeking counsel; for example, on the long march of the Ten Thousand, Xenophon sacrificed to seek the gods' opinion on whether he should stand for election as supreme army commander, and also on whether he should persuade the army to establish a permanent settlement on the coast of the Black Sea.ᵃ This practice should have challenged reflective believers, for when two Greek armies prepared to do battle, both performed animal sacrifices and generally both received good omens (at any rate if the commanders continued sacrificing long enough), yet one side went on to lose the battle. Xenophon is eager to tell us of the many occasions when the gods correctly predicted the outcome, usually giving good omens to Spartan victors, occasionally giving bad omens that were ignored at the commander's peril (as they were by Anaxibios). Xenophon underscores the Spartan's piety by persistently reporting the sacrifices they offered before crossing their frontiers, a Spartan practice that Thucydides had simply ignored. But Xenophon never shows an army sacrificing successfully before a battle they proceed to lose—the Spartans are not shown sacrificing before Leuctra (although presumably they did, otherwise surely Xenophon would have made Kleombrotos' impious arrogance as plain as he had Anaxibios'), and Xenophon strongly insinuates that the Thebans were lying about their sacrifices before their defeat at the Nemea River in 394 (4.2.18). There is only one apparent exception to the rule that sacrifices, if reported, are always shown as revealing the truth: we are told at 3.5.7 of the favorable omens the Spartan king Pausanias

Intro.13.5a   Pontus (Black Sea): Intro.Map 12.12.

received on crossing the frontier in 395 on his way to join Lysander at Haliartos; yet the upshot was that Lysander was killed and King Pausanias was blamed for this and banished. Against the background of Xenophon's pious fiction that sacrifice never produces error, this cannot be meant to be an exception. Rather, it confirms the impression we get from the narrative of the failed campaign, that Lysander was responsible for his own mishap (note that the sacrifices he no doubt made are not recorded) and that King Pausanias was harshly treated by the Spartan authorities. Xenophon's handling of the topic says much for his piety and his subtlety as a narrator; it says little, however, for his intellectual honesty. Although he avoids outright lies, this is another instance of slipperiness.

Xenophon's Sources

§14.1. Herodotus and Thucydides spent many years traveling the Greek world searching out accounts of the events they wished to record. Not so Xenophon. He followed Thucydides rather than Herodotus in virtually abstaining from discussion of his sources, but he did not develop the habit of research that justified Thucydides' air of authority. That does not mean his work is all hearsay at third or fourth hand, though a likely example of this is his account of the murder of Alexander of Pherai (6.4.25–37) in the course of a digression on Thessaly. In general, Xenophon probably reported the tales of eyewitnesses directly or at only one remove. But it looks as though he usually waited until testimony on an incident presented itself and did not cross-check it with other witnesses, much less try to integrate competing accounts of the same event.

§14.2. Among Xenophon's main sources were, of course, his own memories. That is obvious for the story of the Spartans in Asia in the early 390s and their return to mainland Greece, although even here what he tells us may go beyond what he himself saw and take in what fellow soldiers told him at the time. His own memories were no doubt also the main source for his account of the Thirty, with its special emphasis on the role of the cavalry in which Xenophon must have served. We said earlier (§4.6) that the overly detailed narrative of Thrasyllos' expedition to western Asia Minor in the latter years of the Peloponnesian War probably reflects Xenophon's participation in it and his vivid memories of his own first campaign. There may well be other examples where *Hellenika* is reporting events at which Xenophon himself was present. But we should not see *Hellenika* as a disguised form of autobiography, as *Anabasis* had been. Xenophon conspicuously fails to tell us about his expulsion from Skillous,[a] dramatic and emblematic though it would have been in the telling. And conversely he recounts many things that he cannot possibly have seen himself: not only events in Europe when he was in Asia but also naval campaigns in the Corinthian War, Athenian expeditions to the west, and so on. So he must have used stories from other people, too, but he did not need to go looking for them. Skillous was a convenient rendezvous close to Olympia,[b] where Panhellenic Games were celebrated every four

Intro.14.2a   Skillous: Intro.Map 12.12.
Intro.14.2b   Olympia: Intro.Map 12.12.

years and the temple precinct was a constant magnet for tourists. There would be a steady flow of reminiscing friends to receive Xenophon's hospitality.

§14.3. Several people are named or given space in *Hellenika* beyond the needs of either a lively narrative or a measured history. Some of these citations seem to be Xenophon's way of thanking his friends, perhaps specifically for their information. Although Pasimelos of Corinth's adventures in 392, recounted at 4.4.4–12, were objectively important, that Xenophon troubles to tell us at 7.3.2 that Pasimelos witnessed Euphron's machinations at Sicyon seems more like an acknowledgment. Prokles of Phleious was probably another close associate of Xenophon's; that would explain why he is given not just one but two speeches in favor of cooperation between Athens and Sparta (see §12.16 above), among the many that must have been made on those occasions. Although Prokles is named only once in connection with events at Phleious (5.3.13), he might well be the origin of much or all of the praise of the Phleiasians at 7.2. But the most striking example of giving a friend a lot of space comes at 1.3.13, when Xenophon tells us about an Athenian embassy to Persia with an amount of detail that is excessive against the general scale of the narrative, given that the embassy was completely abortive. This is reminiscent of the detail he gives about Thrasyllos' expedition, and it suggests that Xenophon included it out of personal regard for the source, who is often thought to be Euryptolemos, one of the ambassadors. For it is probably this same Euryptolemos[a] who is mentioned as having welcomed his kinsman Alcibiades on his return to Athens from exile, flush with the laurels of victory (1.4.19), and whose brave speech gets so much space in the account of the six generals arrested after Arginousai (1.7.12–34).

§14.4. These three friends may have contributed even where not named. For example, it could have been Euryptolemos who told Xenophon about the battle of Cyzicus. It is also easy to suggest other personal connections behind stories. We said earlier that Xenophon's slant on the battle of Dardanus/Abydos (1.1.2–7) may have come from Dorieus, one of the participants, or from someone in his squadron; and Xenophon's version of the battle of Aigospotamoi (2.1.20–32) sounds suspiciously like what would have been said in his own defense by Adeimantos, an Athenian general who was captured by the enemy during the battle but, unlike his fellow generals, was released unharmed. But using friends as sources should not be dismissed as mere chumminess. Xenophon recognized that historians should report only what they had good evidence for, and perhaps for that very reason he confined himself to what he had been told by witnesses he had personal reasons to trust. In the absence of a great deal of work (by the 350s, when *Hellenika* was written, unfair to demand of a man probably in his seventies), he could hardly have avoided this restriction. Unfortunately, however, even eyewitness evidence is problematic, as Xenophon should have learned from Thucydides (1.22.2–3). Eyewitnesses may have limited perspectives (like Dorieus) or reasons for deceit (like Adeimantos), and trusting his friends sometimes led Xenophon into error.

Intro.14.3a That Euryptolemos the Athenian envoy at 1.3.13 is the same person as Euryptolemos the son of Peisanax, who appears at 1.4.19 and 1.7.12–34, has been disputed and requires the text to be emended at 1.4.7 (see note on this passage). However, the emenda-tion is probable on other grounds, and it could well be that Xenophon wanted to stress Euryptolemos' family affiliations in the later two passages but to avoid introducing them in the first one.

§14.5. An example of this is the account at 6.2.3 of the events that followed the Peace of 375/4. On his way home after the peace has been declared, the Athenian general in the west, Timotheos, intervenes on Zacynthus[a] in what, according to Xenophon, the Spartans immediately determined was a provocation. Xenophon says that the Spartans then prepared a fleet and sent it out under Mnasippos. But no one now questions that Diodorus was right (15.45.4, 46.2)[b] to say that first the Spartans had sent two smaller naval expeditions to the west under Aristokrates and Alkidas. Xenophon has left out a year. Diodorus goes on to say (15.47.2)[c] that Mnasippos sailed out only after the Spartans had observed that Athens' response in the west had gone adrift, since Timotheos, although instructed to return there, had instead sailed around the North Aegean looking for money and men. Xenophon's account is again different (6.2.11–13). He has Mnasippos set out before Timotheos, and thus makes Timotheos out to be a fool who sailed northeast when he knew that the enemy fleet had sailed west. Here too (although now we are entering the realm of controversy again) it seems—both from what is likely in itself and from other evidence—that Xenophon is wrong. In what follows, however, Xenophon is accurate enough: Timotheos was deposed from command, and his fellow Athenian politicians Iphikrates and Kallistratos took over the fleet and sailed to the west, only to find that Mnasippos had already been defeated and killed.

§14.6. It is instructive to ponder the probable origin of these errors, which are unlikely to be innocent slips. Someone tendentiously abbreviated the events of 375–373 and placed some of them in the wrong order. But it probably was not Xenophon himself, for his story runs counter to his natural bias. In his account, the Spartans seem to react hastily and aggressively to the initial alleged provocation in 375/4. In fact, their initial response, although bad-tempered, was proportionate. Mnasippos' subsequent expedition, however badly implemented, could have been presented as a sensible reaction to the developing situation in 373, when the Spartans recognized they had a narrow window of opportunity to strike in the west before Timotheos could get his fleet together. But it is not difficult to identify the sort of person who would have had a motive to bend the facts as *Hellenika* does, namely someone interested in blackening Timotheos' reputation. Thus Xenophon's source made out that the collapse of the Peace of 375/4 was simply due to Timotheos' actions on Zacynthus in winter 375/4 and that his preparations in 373 to meet the Spartan reaction were not merely prolonged but totally inept. And something else seems fishy around here, for despite the impression that Xenophon gives (6.2.14, 6.2.27), Iphikrates and Kallistratos had not been speedy to discharge their commission, and, again contrary to Xenophon (6.2.39), their joint voyage was not a striking example of enemies sinking their differences—they had kept the fleet in Athens while they together prosecuted Timotheos (who was acquitted). All in all, it seems likely that someone motivated by Athenian internal politics told Xenophon a deceitful tale. It is of less significance to give a name to this deceitful source, but the

Intro.14.5a   Zacynthus: Intro. Map 8.6.
Intro.14.5b   See Appendix O.
Intro.14.5c   See Appendix O.

excellent (if wily) Kallistratos himself seems as good a suspect as any. Into this Athenian material Xenophon inserted what he had learned about the faults of Mnasippos, presumably from Spartan acquaintances. But it seems he failed to cross-check his sources by questioning his Spartan friends further about the background, as they would then have been bound to tell him about Aristokrates and Alkidas, and one supposes Xenophon would not then have implied that Mnasippos was sent out immediately after Timotheos' act of provocation. So what we have here is not research, but uncritical interweaving of tales from two sets of friends.

§14.7. Still, it is possible to go too far on how little research Xenophon did and how inadequately he responded to evidence or the lack of it. He claims at 6.4.13 that the Spartans held their own for some time in the battle of Leuctra, but he does not assert this as plain fact: he gives a ground for it, that they managed to carry off the dead body of King Kleombrotos, thus showing that it is an inference. That suggests that elsewhere, where he does not give grounds, he believes he has direct evidence. We said earlier (§5.5 above) that at *Hellenika* 4.6.4–12 Xenophon corrected the version of Agesilaos' Acarnanian campaign of 389 that he had given in *Agesilaos* (2.20), presumably because an early reader told him he was wrong and supplied the relevant detail. He gives many numbers for the size of fleets in the Peloponnesian War, and these inspire confidence—the variations with Diodorus' numbers show Xenophon did not derive them from P, and on the whole they seem more satisfactory than those in Diodorus. Conceivably, Xenophon may have consulted only one eyewitness, perhaps Euryptolemos, to get these numbers, but as Euryptolemos (or whoever it was) had no need to include them to make a good story, Xenophon presumably had to question him further to elicit them. Likewise, there are details in the account of Thrasyboulos' last expedition in 390 (4.8.25–30) that go far beyond the needs of the story.

§14.8. Furthermore, it seems likely that Xenophon made a special effort to find out what really happened when his son died at the battle of Mantineia (7.5.15–17) and, up to a point, to give the enemy his due. His account is clearly superior to that of Kallisthenes, the next historian to describe the events of 386–362, whose version of Epaminondas' marches to and from Sparta before the battle is logistically impossible. Nor, to judge from Diodorus 15.82–87,[a] was Ephorus' subsequent account much better (though, as often, Diodorus seems to have added blunders of his own). For instance, Ephorus seems to have taken Kallisthenes' account of Epaminondas' march and modified it only to the minimum extent required to make it barely feasible. The great second-century historian Polybius tells us that Ephorus was wholly inexperienced in land battles, and in particular had written nonsense about Leuctra and Mantineia. Polybius, by contrast, was a soldier—as, of course, was Xenophon.

Intro.14.8a   See Appendix O.

Xenophon's Trustworthiness

§15.1. Though Xenophon, as we have seen, sometimes makes mistakes, and sometimes those mistakes may be due to the deceitfulness of his sources, there is no clear instance where *Hellenika* makes a direct assertion that is not true and that Xenophon must have known was not true. It seems safe to say that Xenophon did not tell outright lies.

§15.2. If we accept this principle, the consequences are important. Starting at 2.3.11, Xenophon tells the story of the Thirty from the time of their installation. According to his account, near the beginning of their rule a Spartan garrison came to Athens; then Kritias arranged for the judicial murder of his rival Theramenes; and after that Thrasyboulos, at this point an exile from the Thirty, raised the standard of democracy at the fortress of Phyle[a] in the Athenian countryside. But these events are placed in the reverse sequence by the *Constitution of Athens* written later in the fourth century within the school of the philosopher Aristotle.[b] However, Xenophon surely would have remembered these harrowing events from his youth correctly. Major error here would have to be put down as lies on his part. Conversely, if we accept from his record elsewhere that he does not tell lies, he must be right here. And fortunately other evidence bears this out. For once, Diodorus (14.4–6, 14.32)[c] and the other Ephoran sources support him on the main points after the Thirty have come to power, although not on every detail. Since Ephorus was mostly following P in these years, P too probably placed these three events in the same order as did Xenophon. As for the author of the Aristotelian *Constitution of Athens*, although he has modern supporters on this and other historical points,[d] he was a legalistic pedant with no sense of historical reality, liable to be duped by forged documents and propaganda shams. Furthermore, he was so biased in favor of moderate oligarchs that he fails to mention that their hero Theramenes was himself a member of the Thirty. Xenophon is not only the liveliest and most atmospheric historian of the Thirty; we can largely trust him on these events.

§15.3. However, while Xenophon does not tell outright lies, he can deliberately mislead, for example in the way he makes use of references to the destruction of the Long Walls in Athens in 404 to slide over the Spartans' second intervention there, specifically to force the Thirty on the Athenians (see §12.8 above). Similarly misleading is 3.2.21, a famous chronological crux where Xenophon appears to synchronize at least some part of the Spartan Derkylidas' campaigns in Asia (399–397), which he has just described, with at least some part of the Spartan war against Elis, which he goes on to describe. One would naturally infer that they either both started at much the same time or that he recounted Derkylidas' campaigns first because they started first. But other implications of Xenophon's narrative virtually require that the Eleian War broke out before Derkylidas went to Asia. Furthermore, the slightest overlap between

Intro.15.2a Phyle: Intro. Map 12.12.
Intro.15.2b This Aristotelian *Constitution of Athens* of the 320s is a different work from the *Constitution of the Athenians*, probably written a century earlier, that was mentioned in §5.1 as being wrongly included among Xenophon's works. It should be noted that the negative view

taken here about its historical section does not apply to the second half, where the author describes contemporary Athenian institutions.
Intro.15.2c See Appendix O.
Intro.15.2d In Appendix B, §17, Peter Krentz supports the Aristotelian *Constitution of Athens* against Xenophon on the Thirty.

the Eleian War and the Spartans' campaigns is incompatible with what the learned biographer Plutarch had to say five hundred years later about the length of the reign of King Agesilaos, who came to power after the Eleian War had ended. A few scholars have thought that Xenophon is right and Plutarch is wrong. Most have supposed that Plutarch is right and Xenophon was careless or in error. But in fact Xenophon is again being deliberately misleading, for he takes care only to imply this synchronization and not to assert it, since at this point what he writes is not a complete sentence. One can only speculate as to the reasons, but it seems a fair bet that there was something about the course of Spartan policy in these years that he wanted to obscure.

§15.4. It can be difficult to draw a line between deceitfulness and merely putting a spin on the facts. At 4.4.6, Xenophon apparently asserts that the Argives extinguished the independence of Corinth immediately after the Corinthian aristocrats were massacred in February 392. However, it appears from the mention of Corinthian ambassadors at a peace congress in Sardis a little later (4.8.13) that this is not so. And later still, there was another peace congress at Sparta (unmentioned by Xenophon), the fruits of which were unsuccessfully commended to the Athenians by the politician Andocides, and it seems from his speech (Andocides, *On the Peace with Sparta*, 3.24–27)[a] that Corinth was then still a sovereign state. The truth seems to be that in 392 Argos and Corinth entered into a close association allowing the citizens of each state rights to own land and attend the assembly of the other state. It seems that the final move to full union came only in 390, around the time that Iphikrates is recorded as having shed pro-Argive Corinthian blood (4.8.34). A closer look at 4.4.6 shows that Xenophon uses verb forms there that are appropriate for a union in progress rather than consummated. So he was aware of the truth but adopted the perspective of his Corinthian friend Pasimelos, who doubtless thought that the arrangements of 392 as good as extinguished the state of Corinth. Xenophon would presumably say that was a legitimate interpretation of events.

§15.5. This same speech of Andocides reveals another piece of spin by Xenophon. According to Xenophon (4.8.12–16), Athens had selfishly broken up the earlier Congress of Sardis after failing to obtain from it three particular islands in the Aegean. From Andocides 3.12, 3.14 we learn that the Congress of Sparta permitted Athens to retain the three islands, but the Athenians still rejected the peace terms. There is good evidence that they did so because the proposed agreement ceded the Greeks of Asia to continuing Persian control, a motive on Athens' part that does not seem so selfish. So can Xenophon escape the charge that he has suppressed the Congress of Sparta because of bias against Athens? Perhaps he would respond that he was making the legitimate point that the Athenians were indeed selfish throughout, not concerning themselves with the Greeks of Asia from disinterested motives but only for what they could get out of them. We would still prefer him to have said so explicitly.

§15.6. Similarly, where Xenophon downplays successful Persian involvement in mainland Greek affairs in the years 376–366, he might make a case that the impetus for the peace agreements concluded in these years came from mainland Greece; he

Intro.15.4a   For further discussion of this speech, see
              n. 4.8.15c.

might argue that after 386 the Persians served merely as a rubber stamp, except in the unsuccessful intervention of 367 that he does narrate at length. That would be a thin excuse even if true (and in fact, it seems more likely that the Persians actively shaped the outcomes of these peace negotiations), but perhaps it brings Xenophon's omissions on this topic within the bounds of legitimate interpretation. It would be like his leaving out various events during Agesilaos' 395 campaign in Asia (see §10.6–7 above), by which he is not suggesting that these events did not occur but implying, rather, that they were not important.

§15.7. Some of Xenophon's omissions are startling indeed—the Liberation of Messenia; the foundation, extent, and importance of the Second Athenian League; the Athenian war for Amphipolis; the capture of Samos and its aftermath; the foundation of Megalopolis. But he can't have intended to deceive in these cases. Perhaps he did hope to extinguish the memory of the Theban Pelopidas' victory at the battle of Tegyra in the mid-370s, but in general, when he omitted such major events, he can't have imagined that people would not know of them or that he could make readers forget they ever happened. He intended his audience to think of him as a historian but not to assume he was providing a full chronicle. Most of the omissions that astonish us now must have seemed pretty odd to Xenophon's first audience. Presumably he anticipated that reaction and even intended it as part of the literary effect. "With what ingenuity," he might hope his friends would say approvingly, "does old Xenophon avoid specifying Epaminondas' appalling actions in Messenia, and how fitting that the unspeakable should remain unspoken!" It is not so much that these omissions undermine his trustworthiness as that they raise doubts about his comprehension of his time, if the reading he presents fails to accommodate much of what seems obviously important to us.

Xenophon's Interpretation of the Xenophontic Period

§16.1. To come to a judgment on Xenophon's interpretation of the events of this half century is not an easy task. First one has to make Xenophon's interpretation explicit; then one has to develop one's own interpretation in order to set Xenophon's against it. Both steps are fraught with problems. For example, some scholars praise Xenophon for showing that the Greek city-state system was bankrupt: in their view, constant internecine strife rendered Greece ripe for inevitable takeover by a power under the control of a single directing mind, like Macedon. But both this reading of Xenophon and this view of Greek history are dubious. Xenophon stresses the unexpected continuance of disorder in Greece because the battle of Mantineia proved indecisive, but this does not mean he despairs of order ever being achieved: for him, the outcome is in the hands of the gods, whom he did not cease to think of as beneficent, if inscrutable. Indeed, his main point here is more likely to be that since everything is still up for grabs, pro-Spartans need not despair of seeing the developments of the 360s reversed. But if he had concluded that

Sparta, Athens, and Thebes were already doomed in 362 to come under some other power's control, he would surely have been wrong. Macedon's rise after 362 was by no means inevitable; there was no historical law compelling the Thebans, Athenians, and Spartans to make Philip's triumph easier by various and repeated errors of judgment. And there are two similar reasons why it would be inappropriate to praise Xenophon for hankering after the rule of a strongman. First, such a desire would not have been praiseworthy—Athens and Sparta both drew strength and stability from their collective institutions, which meant they were not dependent on the continued life and good fortune of any individual. Second, he is not arguing for autocracy or something close to it, in preference to the traditional constitutions of the Greek cities. If he has a message about autocrats in *Hellenika*, it is that the wrath of the gods is liable to descend on them, bringing them to a sticky end.

§16.2. Historians who prefer to find deep causes for political and diplomatic change will see Xenophon as superficial, when not superstitious, about the downfall of Sparta. Others later in the fourth century offered economic causes for the catastrophe. Ephorus, and other scholars both ancient and modern, argued that it was the inevitable result of a destabilizing and demoralizing influx of wealth at the end of the Peloponnesian War, a view advanced less frequently now that it has become clear that the citizen-body of fifth-century Sparta already displayed significant inequalities of wealth. The philosopher Aristotle attributed Sparta's collapse to a growing shortage of manpower produced by her land-tenure arrangements, and modern studies have shown that Sparta's land-tenure arrangements and her citizenship rules would together lead to a fall in the number of Spartan citizens. But the suggested links between these factors and Sparta's loss of control over the Peloponnese in these years are not beyond doubt. Fewer citizens did not have to mean fewer soldiers. At least as potent may have been changes in military technique and avoidable errors of judgment—that is, the type of cause that Xenophon writes about (when he is not theologizing).

§16.3. However, this much at least must be said against Xenophon as a man of insight into his contemporary world: he failed to recognize that the Spartans could never recover Messenia. That was a key error in judgment, although perhaps hard for Spartans and their fellow travelers like Xenophon to avoid. The refusal to come to terms with the loss of Messenia prevented Sparta from reaching a stable accommodation with the other Peloponnesian states. That helped let Philip of Macedon into Greece, which Xenophon would surely have deplored. Still, had he lived, it would have been some consolation to him that Philip's success laid the groundwork for the Greeks at last to launch the great crusade against Persia and to triumph under Philip's son Alexander.

David Thomas
Hertfordshire, UK

EDITOR'S PREFACE

Robert B. Strassler

This Landmark edition of Xenophon's *Hellenika* follows the publication of two other Landmark editions, Thucydides' *The History of the Peloponnesian War* in 1996 and Herodotus' *Histories* in 2007. One might, therefore, expect that many readers of the *Hellenika* would be familiar with the Landmark format and features, However, since it cannot be assumed that all readers will be thus informed, and because there are a couple of new wrinkles in the features of this volume not found in the others, I shall give a full explanation of them in this preface.

Because this is the third Landmark edition of an ancient historian, I don't feel the same need to explain why we create these editions that I did with the earlier two books. Suffice it to say that general readers (and some scholars) find the ancient texts difficult to follow for a variety of reasons, and it seems that good, clear maps, an Introduction rich in background information, helpful explanatory notes, and appendices on subjects in the text that are particularly difficult for modern readers to understand all prove useful and effective for keeping the reader oriented and interested. I will not discuss the significance of Xenophon himself, because that subject has been very competently covered by David Thomas in his Introduction. It has to be admitted that Xenophon is not a great historian like either Herodotus or Thucydides, but he is a good writer with much to say that should interest anyone curious about the end of the Peloponnesian War and what followed during the next forty years in Greece. Without the *Hellenika*, we would know nothing or very little of many events and developments of that dynamic period. The *Hellenika*, which is sometimes so episodic and anecdotal as to resemble a memoir, is yet a history, and I believe it lends itself very well to the regular features of the Landmark format.

One new feature of this Landmark volume, which for lack of alternate contemporary sources could not be developed for Herodotus or Thucydides, is that we include significant material from two other historians who were more or less contemporaries of Xenophon and who, in part, wrote about the same events. Thus, if the readers follow a footnote's suggestion to turn to Appendix O (selections from the work of Ephorus as transcribed by Diodorus Siculus in his *Histories*) or Appendix P (relevant text from papyrus fragments of the *Hellenica Oxyrhynchia*), they will be able to compare and contrast for themselves diverse accounts of historical events. I am certain that these comparisons will enrich their understanding of the period, their grasp of the problems faced by historians dealing with these events, and their assessment of the virtues and failings of Xenophon as a historian. To assist the readers in identifying these accounts, a **Cross-Reference Table** of Related Passages in Xenophon's *Hellenika*, Diodorus' *Histories*, and the *Hellenica Oxyrhynchia* is included in the backmatter of this book.

Another unique element of *The Landmark Xenophon's Hellenika* concerns the difficulties faced when determining the dates and sometimes the sequence in which the events described take place. There are many problems of chronology that the reader of Herodotus and Thucydides will encounter, but they are not as central to the main sequence of events that form the heart of those narratives. For Xenophon's period, however, the very interpretation of some elements of the source text provoke and require particular chronological schemes in an attempt to make sense of them. So we deal with a variety of plausible schemes supported by different scholars, each one leading to a particular explanation of the sources and often differing in the timing and/or sequence of events as well as the significance of particular events. For this reason, any dating scheme for the half-century from 411 to 362 is immediately controversial among scholars.

As a result of this chronological muddle, we decided that all dates in this volume, unless otherwise noted, would be based on a single source, *The Cambridge Ancient History*.[a] Therefore, for the years 411–404 we followed the scheme championed by David Lewis and A. Andrewes found in volume 5 (pages 503–5, 512), and from 404 to 362 we used the chronological indications in the table at the back of volume 6 (the full table is on pages 882–901, though it reaches the year 362 on page 889); where that didn't specify what we needed, other chronological indications were ferreted out from the main text of Volume 6. By relying on this one common and easily located source, I hope to provide a chronological anchor for the general reader who might otherwise despair of mastering the large and often confusing material of the scholarly discussion of fourth-century dates. However, since I do want the reader to know that there are other respectable chronological schemes advocated by scholars that differ in part—and sometimes in large or crucial parts—from the one chosen for this volume, the more important and attractive of these alternate dates are mentioned in the footnotes. Also to that purpose is Appendix C, which provides a close look at problems plaguing the chronological connection between Thucydides' text and Xenophon's account to the end of the Peloponnesian

EP.a   *The Cambridge Ancient History* (Cambridge and
       New York: Cambridge University Press, vol. 5,
       1992; vol. 6, 1994).

War. The appendix describes the strengths and weaknesses of several dating schemes for this seven- or eight-year interval, and it does so in sufficient detail to give the reader a taste of the nature and depth of the chronological problems that arise when one attempts to determine correct dates of (and sometimes sequence of) events in this period.

In addition to these two notable and unique resources, this edition of the *Hellenika* contains a full and, to some readers by now, familiar array of features: Introduction, maps, side notes, footnotes, explanatory appendices, tables, illustrations, glossary, bibliography, and a thorough index.

First and foremost among those features are the maps. This edition contains forty-eight maps designed to support every episode of the narrative, with each map located amid or adjacent to the text it supports. Every city, town, shrine, river, mountain, or other geographic feature that is mentioned in the text is referenced by a footnote to a nearby map. Those maps that display many labels employ a simple coordinate system to help readers search for a particular site, and with a few exceptions in the interest of clarity, each map displays the names of only those features that appear in the surrounding text. If the location of a place is unknown, the footnote says so. If we moderns are not sure of a site's location, our uncertainty is mentioned in the footnote and indicated on the map with a question mark.

Although a number of maps are single images, most are double and a few are triple, arranged in overlapping format from small scale (wide scope) to large scale (detailed scope). On the page, the reader will find that if there is more than one map, the scale of the maps increases from the top down. The first and topmost map is usually called a **locator map**, covering the widest and most easily recognized area. It is framed by a thin black border. Within the locator map a dark and slightly thicker rectangular outline may identify the location and boundaries of the **main map**. Occasionally, when the main map is of sufficient scope to be easily recognizable itself, the locator map is dispensed with, and the main map becomes the topmost map. A few of the main maps contain a thick, light gray rectangular outline indicating, in turn, the location and edges of larger-scale **inset maps**. These maps (always with light gray borders) show areas of particular narrative interest in greater detail. All maps display simple distance scales in miles and kilometers at the bottom left corner.

Locating the correct map from the rectangular outlines is facilitated by map shape, common major sites labeled, prominent physical features (islands or coastlines), and border frame characteristics.

Following cartographic convention, water and other natural features such as islands and peninsulas are labeled with italics to distinguish them from cultural features, labeled with roman type. Centers of population are indicated using small dots and uppercase lettering designed to approximate their relative sizes and degrees of importance at the time. A **Key to Maps**,[b] located just before the beginning of Xenophon's text, contains a complete legend of typography and symbols used, and an illustration of the map border-frame system.

Take, for example, the sample map to the right (Map 5.1.17, which means it is located in Book 5 in Chapter 1, at or near Section 17). The locator map at the top stretches over 1,500 miles, from Italy to the eastern coast of the Mediterranean. The main map in the center extends some 600 miles, centered on the Aegean Sea. And the inset map covers one hundred miles, from Argos in the northeastern Peloponnese to Attica.

Footnotes that cite labels found on the locator map show the word "locator." Those footnotes citing labels on main maps will show no other designation except for the coordinates (if the map has coordinates) indicating the quadrant of the map in which the reader will find the site. All footnotes referring to a site located on an inset map will use the word "inset." Sample footnotes referring to Map 5.1.17 illustrate those rules below.

> 5.1.5a   Rhodos: Map 5.1.17, locator.
> 5.1.6a   Ephesus: Map 5.1.17, BY.
> 5.1.1b   Aegina: Map 5.1.17, inset.

To assist the reader who wishes to rapidly locate a particular place, a **Reference Maps** section with a place-name **Directory** listing all sites that appear on the maps in this book can be found in the final pages of this volume, along with five reference maps. The Directory shows the reference map by number and the coordinates on that map by which the site can be located. Even minor sites mentioned only once in the text are included in the directory, but if they are not shown on the Reference Maps for reasons of clarity and lack of space, the reader will instead be referred to a map within the text. The sites mentioned in the texts of Appendices O and P are not referred to any maps of this volume as the maps were prepared to support Xenophon's text and not the texts of other historians.

The authority for all the maps in this volume is the *Barrington Atlas of the Greek and Roman World*, edited by Richard J. Talbert and published by Princeton University Press in 2000. Readers who would seek larger, more precise, and more detailed maps of any regions depicted in this edition should seek them in that atlas. In order to help those readers who do turn to the *Barrington Atlas*, all labels that appear on the maps of this volume are spelled exactly as they are in the atlas, so that no one seeking to find Cyme or Chalcidice in one volume will be confronted by Kyme or Khalkidike in the index of the other. Since the *Barrington Atlas* covers both the Greek and Roman periods, it employs an orthographic system in which place-names are transliterated into either Greek or Latin, and this apparently inconsistent set of transliterations is carried over into the maps of this volume. Some people may be bothered by this seemingly arbitrary bilingual labeling

EP.b   See Key to Maps, page lxxxii.

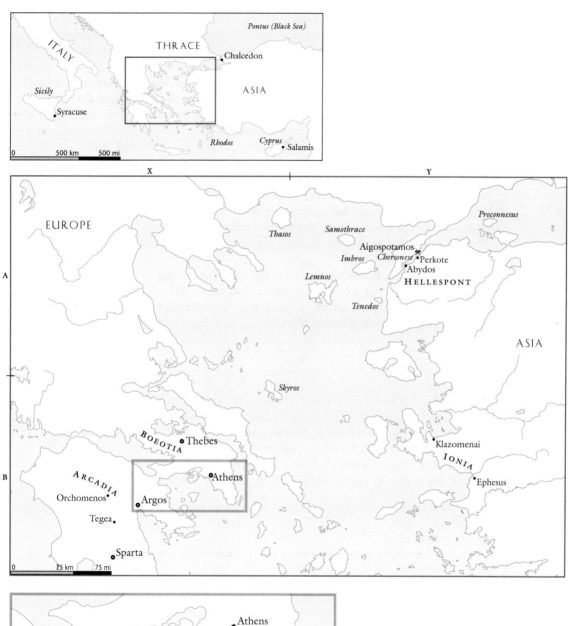

SAMPLE MAP 5.1.17

(although I don't believe it will disturb the general reader). Anyone who wishes to pursue questions of map-label orthography in this edition should consult Professor Talbert's discussion of ancient names presented on page xxv of the Introduction to the *Barrington Atlas*.

For all other names—that is, for names of sites whose locations are unknown and therefore do not appear on any maps, or for names of people, and for Greek or foreign nouns for which there is no commonly accepted English spelling—I have attempted to use only Greek transliterations, not Latin or English ones. In the few cases where an object, person, or country is particularly well known in an alternate transliteration—Pericles, Persia, trireme, and so forth—I have employed that common English spelling.[c]

For easy reference, this volume provides a **Chronological Outline of Text**, which lists the main events and episodes of the narrative by book and location, and applies dates to the entries where applicable (and known).

In the usual Landmark format, dates appear on every page in at least two locations.

First, the **running heads** are found on the top of each page of text. They provide at a glance the dates and locations (if known and applicable) of the action found in the first complete chapter on the page, and a brief description of that action. A sample running head below is typical.

BOOK FIVE   512?   ATHENS   *Prokles says Athens should command at sea*

Side notes are found on the outside page margin at the beginning of the chapters into which the text was divided long ago by Alexandrian scholars. The first line of the side note display the book, chapter, and section number (or numbers if the paragraph covers more than one section, which many of them do). The second line shows the year in our calendar B.C.E. in which the events described take place,[d] and the third line shows in capital letters the location of where the action takes place.

4.2.20–22	Book/Chapter/Section(s)
394	Date
NEMEA RIVER	Location
The Spartan allies are defeated by	Summary of action
the enemy, but the Spartans defeat	
the Athenians opposing them and	
turn to inflict heavy losses on the	
enemy contingents as they return	
from their initial pursuit.	

EP.c There are a few exceptions. The *Barrington Atlas* uses Latin "Mare" and "Lacus" for "Sea" and "Lake," and in those cases I have used the English equivalents. Another exception occurs in the few instances where the *Barrington Atlas* uses a Greek name for a place or country that is very well known by its English equivalent. For example, where it uses "Persis," this edition uses the common "Persia." There are also four or five unimportant sites located on one or two maps that are not found in the *Barrington Atlas*, and they are identified as such in the footnote that references them.

EP.d All dates found in this volume refer to the period B.C.E unless otherwise stipulated.

Finally, there is a brief description of the contents of the chapter. The two side notes below, both drawn from Book 4, are typical.

Footnotes not only refer place-names in the text to nearby maps, as mentioned above, but they may also serve to connect certain points in the text to other relevant sections, or to the work of other ancient writers and poets; in this volume in particular, they may cite relevant text of Diodorus Siculus' *Histories* from Appendix O and/or relevant text from surviving fragments of the *Hellenica Oxyrhynchia* in Appendix P. They may also refer to particular paragraphs in the Introduction or in one or more of the other appendices where the reader will find discussion of the topics or events footnoted. On occasion, they may provide background information that does not appear in any of the appendices, and they may also point out and briefly describe some of the major scholarly controversies about interpretation, translation, chronology, or corruption of the text.[e] A few explanatory footnotes are quite long and detailed, but they contain important information that could not be further condensed. Footnotes and map references are repeated throughout the work to assist those who will read only selections from it, or whose reading of the text is discontinuous.

At the translator's request, and at variance with the earlier Landmark volumes, the original Greek **units of distance** (stade, plethron, foot, etc.) have been left in the text and footnotes used to translate these units into common English miles and feet. All conversion calculations assume that Xenophon's intended "stade" was the Attic stade of 583 modern feet and his "foot" the more or less standard foot of about eleven and a half modern inches. The reader should know, however, that we are not sure of the precise value for many of the ancient units cited, that there were different "standard" stade and cubit units in use in the ancient Greek world, and that Xenophon may well have intended one of these "others" when he generically names one. Finally, we cannot know how carefully and precisely he arrived at some of his measurements—many were clearly estimates, some were probably calculated guesses. I would advise any reader with further questions concerning these matters to consult Thomas Martin's excellent Appendix I in this volume, "Units of Distance, Currency, and Capacity in Xenophon's *Hellenika*."

This edition of the *Hellenika* begins with an excellent and informative **Introduction** by David Thomas, in which he describes not only the history of the period in which Xenophon lived but what is known of Xenophon himself, his other works, and the earlier histories that we know were available to him (Herodotus and Thucydides) and that may have served, in one respect or another, as models to follow. Thomas also explores what is known of two other fourth-century historians, some of whose work is included in this volume as Appendices O and P. He then focuses on the *Hellenika*, its composition, style, and literary devices. Finally he deals with Xenophon as a historian, his virtues and faults, his sources, his attitude toward reli-

EP.e   In the Introduction and appendices, the authors
      may have used their own or other translations.

gion, his obvious biases, his reliability, and his own interpretation of the time in which he lived and wrote. It is a skillful and thorough job.

The volume's twelve **Appendices**, by a number of scholars, cover a lot of ground, from the standard subjects on ancient Greece—units of currency and distance, elements of land and naval warfare, characteristics of Greek religion—to the more particular discussions of Athenian and Spartan government in Xenophon's life, political leagues in the fourth century, theories on the dates and sequence in which Xenophon composed the various parts of the *Hellenika*. One appendix is devoted to a biography of Agesilaos, perhaps the most important single figure in the book. Another gives brief biographies of other people mentioned in the *Hellenika* who either played significant roles in the book or, if not, then in the history of the period. It is hoped that these appendices will provide a sufficient minimum of explanatory and/or background information to help a general reader understand and relate to the text. As was mentioned above, relevant paragraphs in the introduction and the individual appendices are cited by footnote throughout the text, so that the reader will know where to look for explanation or further information.

To assist the reader who wishes to locate passages or subjects within the text, this edition offers the most thorough and complete **Index** that can be found in any English translation of the text. There is, in addition, a **Glossary** of terms and a short **Bibliography** of both ancient sources and modern works, which is specifically designed for that general reader who might wish to read more about Xenophon or his world. The **Translator's Notes** supply the necessary scholarly clarifications and attributions to the translation of this text; and for readers of the Greek, the words and phrases are listed in that appendix. Note that all text enclosed by square brackets in this volume is believed to be an interpolation (added material) by a later author.

Finally, the book contains a number of **illustrations**. These are not intended to be just attractive ornaments; they have been chosen specifically to enhance the reader's sense of the historicity of the text. For example, at 2.4.33 Xenophon writes of a skirmish between Athenians and Spartans: "in this encounter Chairon and Thibrakos, both polemarchs, were killed, as was Lakrates, an Olympian victor, and others who are now all buried in the Kerameikos, in front of the city gates." Figure 2.4.33 shows the remains of a tomb in the Athenian Kerameikos district near the city gates, which has been identified as the tomb of these Spartans.

ACKNOWLEDGMENTS

I must acknowledge that I received a great deal of assistance in editing this volume. So many people provided material and scholarly support that it was indeed a collegial effort, and I am most grateful to all of those who contributed to it.

John Marincola, who translated the text, is among the first and foremost of those to whom I must record my gratitude. He spent long hours and much e-mail traffic dealing with my endless suggestions and criticisms of his drafts as we struggled to make the final English version clear and fluent within the constraints of fidelity to the Greek text. He even remained calm and accommodating when David Thomas sent him comments and queries concerning the translation of certain passages. John was extraordinarily patient and accommodating, and we were always able to find a reasonable and pleasant solution. I want also to mention that John provided this volume with the translation of the relevant texts of the *Hellenica Oxyrhynchia*. Despite commitments to many other projects, he never failed to deliver what he had promised in good time, or to provide important assistance upon request.

For the clear and simple maps of this edition, I must thank Jonathan Wyss and Kelly Sandefer, the professional cartographers who staff Beehive Mapping. They produced the maps for *The Landmark Herodotus* also, and once again we worked together very well. No feature of the Landmark editions has received more praise than the maps. They provide geographic orientation for the reader, which is essential to his or her comprehension and enjoyment of the ancient text. I must also thank Jonathan and Kelly for their endless patience with me and my numerous requests for changes, many of them picayune, and for the correction of errors that were mostly caused by me. My debt to them is indeed great.

The maps are beautiful, but when I speak of good design, I must in the same breath express my profound gratitude to the book designer, Kim Llewellyn. Kim has now designed every page of all three Landmark editions, somehow juggling maps, illustrations, footnotes, and side notes and always producing a page where all the elements fit together attractively. These pages invite the reader into the book, where he or she may be captivated by the text. This is no trivial capability for a work of ancient history directed toward general readers. I remain in awe of Kim's ability to solve what seem to be intractable design problems with agility and ease. And it should be mentioned that she designed the jacket cover of this edition as well as that of Herodotus. I believe that whatever success the Landmark editions have received, her efforts are responsible for a significant portion of it. I cannot thank her enough.

In the same vein, it is difficult for me to imagine how the book would have turned out if I had not been able to draw upon the skills and talents of David Thomas. David brought to it his thorough knowledge of fourth-century Greece, his familiarity with Xenophon's other works, his command of a large number of ancient sources, and his acquaintance with recent scholarly literature on the period. He is the author of the excellent and comprehensive Introduction to this edition, and he wrote two of its appendices: Appendix C, which discusses chronological problems in Xenophon's narrative of the final years of the Peloponnesian War, and Appendix N, which describes various theories about the timing, sequence, and manner in which Xenophon wrote his text. He also made significant contributions to Appendix M, the series of brief biographies of important persons who appear in the *Hellenika*. He compiled this edition's bibliography. And in addition to these most valuable direct contributions, he voluntarily reviewed and checked just about every other element of the work, from the text's translation and all the other appendices to the substantial index. His constructive comments, criticisms, and suggestions were always valuable. Indeed, it is fair to say that this edition bears his stamp as much as it might that of anyone else, and is so greatly improved by his efforts as to be very much the product of his energy and erudition. I am profoundly grateful to him for all that he has done, a sentiment that I believe should be shared by any and all who draw pleasure and instruction from reading this volume.

I want of course to thank George L. Cawkwell, who served as a mentor to me throughout this and the two earlier books. His sound advice never failed to stand me in good stead, and he remains, as he approaches ninety years of age, a very accomplished and sharp scholar who still knows his stuff. Perhaps the most significant service he performed for me on this book was to recommend and introduce me to David Thomas, who had been a student of his many years ago. Beyond all that, George's good company and hospitality and that of his wife, Pat, who sadly died last year, was a great comfort to me at all times. I cannot thank him enough for all his help over the twenty-five years or so that I have known him.

I must also thank Paul Cartledge, who was extremely helpful in sharing his expertise on Sparta in the time of Agesilaos and Xenophon. He wrote three excellent appendices and contributed much helpful advice and counsel. He has been a supporter of these Landmark editions from the very beginning, and as we have worked together, we have become good friends. It is always a pleasure to see him, which I do more frequently these days, since his position at New York University brings him to America on a fairly regular basis.

I would also like to thank the other scholars who contributed appendices to this edition. I have not yet had the good fortune to meet Peter Krentz, P. J. Rhodes, or Christopher Blackwell in person, but I feel that I know them all from the extensive and interesting exchange of e-mails between us. All of them are highly competent historians and very pleasant to work with. They accepted the constraints of Landmark appendix writing with good grace and never expressed annoyance or pique about the many questions, comments, and suggestions with which I greeted their drafts. I do hope to meet them all someday and to thank them in person.

I am grateful as well to Christopher Tuplin for his excellent appendix on the Persians in *Hellenika*. I particularly appreciated his unfailing good humor in response to my many questions, comments, and suggestions, and I owe him a special thanks for agreeing to compose and add a significant amount of material that we decided, rather late in the game, had to be included in his essay. I enjoyed working with him.

Tom Martin, Nicole Hirschfeld, and John W. I. Lee are by now experienced hands at writing Landmark appendices, having written them for the edition of Herodotus, and in the case of the first two, for *The Landmark Thucydides* as well. They do it with great skill and apparent ease. I am very happy to have them as collaborators, and I thank them once again for their efforts.

Margot Levy is responsible for the extensive and rich index. I feel that it is important for the reader to be able to recall and find sometimes disparate elements of a book, and the ability to do so for general readers will depend in great measure on the quality and fullness of the index. Margot's index for Xenophon's *Hellenika* suits our purpose admirably. I am profoundly grateful to her, and I hope she may be enticed to do more indexes for future Landmark books.

My old friend Ingrid MacGillis once again worked to locate and secure rights to publish many of the photographs that illustrate this volume. Anyone who has tried to do this can tell you how frustrating and difficult the task can be. But Ingrid keeps her cool and uses many wiles and all of her languages to mollify the most recalcitrant museum staff. The result is that she almost always gets her photo license in the end. I am very happy and grateful that she undertakes this labor with such success. It is fun to work with her, and I hope we continue to work together.

Some of the excellent photographs of sites were provided by Professor John Buckler who offered them to us without charge. We turned to him when we could not otherwise find photographs of such high quality that depicted the desired subjects as well. I want to publicly express my gratitude to him for all his friendly help, cooperation, and generosity.

I am grateful also to another old friend, Lorna Greenberg, for her insightful and very useful editorial assistance and counsel. She is a professional editor and brought a professional thoroughness to our work together. After so many years as a friend, it was a unique pleasure to work with her as a colleague. And my thanks also go to Skyler Balbus, one of my brightest Simon's Rock students, who provided some very fine research and writing for the biographies of Appendix M.

I must also thank my editor, Edward Kastenmeier, who provides a ready and steady connection between the publisher and myself. A book like this, with an editor, a translator, a cartographic firm, an indexer, and ten additional contributors, can be a difficult handful to manage. Although I always tried to spare him from the many scheduling and other problems of organizing so many people, it was very nice to know that Edward was behind me, ready to help if I stumbled or ran into problems I could not handle. Thanks also go to the rest of the crew at Pantheon Books who worked on this project: Altie Karper, Lydia Buechler, Candy Gianetti (who did such a fine job of copyediting), and Chris Jerome and Rita Madrigal (the proofreaders), as well as Andy Hughes and Lisa Montebello of the Production Department. All of them helped produce the book and deserve our thanks.

Finally, I would like to express my gratitude and appreciation for all the extra hours and assistance that I received from Peter Green, the translator of the large selection of excerpts taken from Diodorus Siculus. This process turned out to be more complex and difficult than I had envisioned. Peter was patient and kind enough to revise footnotes more than once for me, and to add new sections to Appendix O as the need for them was perceived. I'm not sure that we could ever have organized those selections or provided the reader with necessary ancillary information about them without Peter's assistance.

And last but not least, I want to thank my family for their support and forbearance of the many problems and difficulties that weigh me down during the years while I labor on these Landmark editions. I know they have to put up with a great deal from me, and I am grateful for their patient tolerance. I specifically want to thank my son-in-law, David Herbstman, who helped me through the transition from one word-processing software system to the next (which I found particularly annoying and harrowing). My brother and business partner, David Strassler, remained permissive and even supportive of my efforts to work on ancient Greeks rather than current business problems. My children, Matthew and Karen, helped when they could spare time from their own careers as professors and, in my daughter's case, as a parent. Finally, I must thank my wife, Toni, who continues to put up with it all and help when she can. She provides the domestic tranquility without which I fear I could not edit a rhyming couplet.

R.B.S.
June 2009

CHRONOLOGICAL OUTLINE OF TEXT
by Book/Chapter/Section in Xenophon's *Hellenika*

BOOK 1: The Final Years of the Peloponnesian War, 411–406

411–409	HELLESPONT	1.1	Fighting in the Hellespont.
409	IONIA	1.2	Thrasyllos' expedition to Ionia.
408	HELLESPONT	1.3	More Athenian victories; Byzantium.
407	ASIA-ATHENS	1.4	Alcibiades at his zenith.
407–406	IONIA-ATHENS	1.5	Fall of Alcibiades; Notion.
406	AEOLIS-IONIA	1.6	Athens' victory at the Arginousai Islands.
406	ATHENS	1.7	Trial of the generals.

BOOK 2: Aigospotamoi; The Thirty at Athens, 406–403

406–405	HELLESPONT	2.1	Athens decisively defeated by Lysander at Aigospotamoi.
405–404	ATHENS	2.2	Athens accepts Spartan surrender terms.
404	ATHENS	2.3	Reign of the Thirty; Theramenes executed.
404–403	ATHENS	2.4	Thrasyboulos and allies restore democracy to Athens.

BOOK 3: Spartan Military Operations in Asia, 401–395

402?–400	ELIS	*3.2.21–31*	War between Sparta and Elis.
401–400	ASIA-BLACK SEA	3.1.1	Xenophon and Cyrus' Greek mercenaries return.
400?	SPARTA	*3.3.1–4*	Agis dies. Leotychidas and Agesilaos contend. Agesilaos becomes king.
400–399	IONIA-AEOLIS	3.1.3–7	Sparta sends Thibron to defend Asian Greeks against Tissaphernes.
399	AEOLIS-BITHYNIA	3.1.8–3.2.5	Derkylidas campaigns in Aeolis and Bithynia.
flashback	AEOLIS	3.1.10–15	Xenophon digresses: the story of Mania and Meidias.
399?	SPARTA	3.3.4–11	Conspiracy of Kinadon is discovered and thwarted.

NOTE: Italic type indicates where Xenophon's sequence by book/chapter does not follow chronological sequence.

Key to Maps

Map Configurations

- Locator map
- Main map
- Inset map

Typography

ASIA	Continent
AEOLIS	Region
Athens	Large city
Megara	Town, village, or other location
Kadousians	People, tribe
Eurotas R.	Body of water; island; promontory
MT. OLYMPUS	Mountain

Cultural Features

- Settlement
- Deme
- Fortified place
- Temple
- Battle site
- Road
- City walls and fortifications

Natural Features

- Mountain
  Mountain range
- Cliff or escarpment
- River
- Marsh
- Sea or lake
  (approximate extent in Classical Period)

Distance Conversions
See Appendix I, Units of Distance, Currency, and Capacity in Xenophon's *Hellenika,* §13.

Dates
All dates in this volume are B.C.E. (Before the Common Era) unless otherwise specified.

BOOK ONE

$\mathbf{A}$nd after this,[a] not many days later, Thymochares came from Athens,[b] in command of a few ships. And the Spartans[c] and Athenians immediately fought a sea battle again,[d] and the Spartans, with Agesandridas as their commander, were victorious.

[2] A little later, at the beginning of winter, Dorieus son of Diagoros sailed from Rhodos[a] into the Hellespont[b] at dawn with fourteen ships. They were spotted by the Athenian lookout, who informed the generals of their presence. The generals then sailed out against Dorieus with twenty ships, but he escaped from them, and as he got away he attempted to beach his triremes[c] in the area around Rhoiteion.[d] [3] When the Athenians drew near, they fought from the ships and the land, until the Athenians, having accomplished nothing, sailed away to Madytos[a] to join the rest of their forces.

[4] Mindaros, watching the fight from Ilion,[a] where he was sacrificing to Athena,[b] set out to help by sea and, launching his own ships, sailed off so that he might pick up those of Dorieus. [5] But the Athenians, putting out to sea against him, engaged him along the shore near Abydos,[a] fighting

1.1.1
411
?
Spartans defeat the Athenians in a sea battle.

1.1.2–3
411
HELLESPONT
Dorieus defends his ships from shore against Athenian attack.

1.1.4–7
411
HELLESPONT
Mindaros engages the Athenians in an attempt to help Dorieus, but after some battle, the Spartans flee when Alcibiades and his squadron arrive.

1.1.1a Xenophon envisions his work as a continuation of Thucydides' history, which breaks off in 411. Nonetheless, there is a gap between the last events in Thucydides and the beginning here: Thucydides (8.84) left Dorieus at Miletus, and he now arrives from Rhodos. Miletus and Rhodos: Map 1.1.22. The Peloponnesian fleet, which was last reported at Elaious (Thucydides 8.107), is now at Troy (Ilion), and the Athenians are at Madytos, although Thucydides (8.107) left them at Cyzicus; all locations: Map 1.1.22, inset.

1.1.1b Athens: Map 1.1.22. According to Thucydides 8.95, Thymochares had commanded some of the Athenian ships that were recently defeated off Eretria, Euboea: Map 1.1.22.

1.1.1c Sparta: Map 1.1.22.

1.1.1d Scholars are not certain where this battle took place. Agesandridas, who had commanded the Spartan flotilla that earlier defeated the Athenians off Eretria, is not known at this time to have commanded ships for Sparta in the Hellespont (Map 1.1.22), where Mindaros was in command.

1.1.2a Rhodos: Map 1.1.22. Dorieus and his ships were of course a Peloponnesian flotilla.

1.1.2b Hellespont: Map 1.1.22.

1.1.2c Triremes: see Appendix K, Trireme Warfare in Xenophon's *Hellenika*, §2.

1.1.2d Rhoiteion: Map 1.1.22, inset.

1.1.3a Madytos: Map 1.1.22, inset.

1.1.4a Mindaros had taken command of the Peloponnesian fleet earlier in the year (Thucydides 8.85) and successfully sailed it past the Athenian fleet at Lesbos (Map 1.1.22) to the Hellespont (Thucydides 8.101).

1.1.4b Sacrificing to Athena: see Appendix J, Ancient Greek Religion in the Time of Xenophon, §4, 5, 8.

1.1.5a Abydos: Map 1.1.22, inset.

from morning until evening. The Athenians had been victorious in some places and defeated in others when Alcibiades[b] sailed up to join in the attack with eighteen ships. [6] At this, the Peloponnesians[a] fled to Abydos. Pharnabazos[b] brought his forces up to help them and, driving his horse into the sea as far as he could, he took part in the battle and urged on the rest of his cavalry and infantry. [7] The Peloponnesians fought by forming their ships in close order and arranging them parallel to the shore. Finally, the Athenians sailed off to Sestos,[a] taking with them thirty of the enemy ships without crews and recovering the ones that they themselves had lost.[b]

[8] From there all the ships, except for forty of them, sailed out from the Hellespont to different places, in order to collect money.[a] Thrasyllos,[b] who was one of the generals,[c] sailed to Athens in order to announce what had taken place and to request that the Athenians send an army and more ships.

[9] And after this, when Tissaphernes[a] came to the Hellespont, Alcibiades went to see him. And although Alcibiades had come in a single ship, bringing tokens of friendship and gifts, Tissaphernes seized and imprisoned him in Sardis,[b] saying that the King[c] had ordered him to make war on Athenians. [10] Thirty days later, Alcibiades, together with Mantitheos (who had been captured in Caria),[a] procured horses and escaped by night from Sardis to Klazomenai.[b]

[11] The Athenians at Sestos, learning that Mindaros intended to sail against them with sixty ships, slipped away by night to Kardia.[a] Alcibiades, too, went there from Klazomenai with five triremes and a skiff. Learning that the Peloponnesian ships had set sail from Abydos to Cyzicus,[b] Alcibiades himself went on foot to Sestos and ordered the ships to sail around and rendezvous there. [12] When they had arrived and were just about to put out to sea to fight a naval engagement, Theramenes[a] sailed in with

1.1.8–10
411
HELLESPONT
Tissaphernes comes to the Hellespont and, when visited by Alcibiades, imprisons him at Sardis. Alcibiades escapes.

1.1.11–15
410
HELLESPONT
The Athenian fleet under Alcibiades concentrates at Sestos and, learning that the Peloponnesian navy is at Cyzicus, prepares for battle.

1.1.5b Alcibiades, Athenian general: see Appendix M, Brief Biographies of Important Characters in Xenophon's *Hellenika*, §3.

1.1.6a Peloponnese: Map 1.1.22.

1.1.6b Pharnabazos, Persian satrap: see Appendix M, §21; and Appendix D, Persia in Xenophon's *Hellenika*, §3–5, 7–10.

1.1.7a Sestos: Map 1.1.22, inset.

1.1.7b Diodorus gives a parallel account of this battle (see Appendix O, Selections from the *Histories* of Diodorus Siculus Relevant to Xenophon's *Hellenika*, 13.45–47.2). Some scholars think the two historians strongly disagree. Others think they can be largely reconciled. See the Introduction, §8.4.

1.1.8a Collecting money: see Appendix B, The Athenian Government and the Oligarchy of the Thirty, §14. The Athenian government extracted annual tribute (*phoros*) from subject states of its empire in the fifth century. While a few of the larger subject states paid in kind—contributing their own

military forces—the vast majority contributed money, which was used by Athens to support its own large standing military forces (mostly its fleet) and for other purposes the Athenian Assembly might approve.

1.1.8b See "Thrasyllos" in Appendix M, §27.

1.1.8c Athenian generals: see Appendix A, The Arginousai Affair, §2, 3, 5, 6.

1.1.9a Tissaphernes, Persian satrap: see Appendix M, §29.

1.1.9b Sardis: Map 1.1.22.

1.1.9c In this volume, when the word *King* is capitalized, it refers to the Great King of Persia. The King at this time was Darius II.

1.1.10a Caria: Map 1.1.22.

1.1.10b Klazomenai: Map 1.1.22.

1.1.11a Kardia: Map 1.1.22.

1.1.11b Cyzicus Map 1.1.22, inset.

1.1.12a Theramenes, Athenian general: see Appendix M, §24.

FIGURE 1.1.9.
COIN OF THE SATRAPAL
GOVERNMENT OF TISSAPHERNES
FROM THE BEGINNING OF THE
FOURTH CENTURY. IT MAY
ACTUALLY BE HIS LIKENESS.

twenty ships from Macedon,[b] and simultaneously Thrasyboulos[c] with twenty others from Thasos.[d] (Both had been out collecting money.) [13] Alcibiades ordered these also to remove their mainsails[a] and follow him, and he himself sailed to Parium.[b] The total number of ships that gathered there was eighty-six. On the following night they set out and arrived at Proconnesus[c] the next day around breakfast time. [14] There they discovered that Mindaros was in Cyzicus, as was Pharnabazos with the infantry. So they remained there that day, but the next day Alcibiades, summoning an assembly, exhorted them that it was necessary to fight on sea and land and at the very walls. "For we do not have money," he said, "while our enemies have unlimited resources from the King." [15] On the previous day, when they had anchored at Proconnesus, Alcibiades had kept all the boats with himself, even the small craft, so that no one might inform the enemy of the number of Athenian ships, and he proclaimed death as the penalty for anyone caught sailing to the other side of the strait.

1.1.12b Macedon: Map 1.1.22.
1.1.12c Thrasyboulos (of Steiria): an Athenian general in the Ionian War and the leader of the democrats in the civil war of 403. Xenophon consistently refers to him as plain Thrasyboulos, yet at 4.8.25 calls him Thrasyboulos of Steiria (an Attic deme, Map 4.6.1, AY) in order to avoid confusion with Thrasyboulos of Kollytos, who was in command not long after (5.1.26) and was presumably an important politician already in the late 390s. Xenophon evidently thought it was self-evident that

it was Thrasyboulos of Steiria who was being talked about in the Ionian War and the liberation from the Thirty unless one actually specified Thrasyboulos of Kollytos. See "Thrasyboulos" in Appendix M, §26.
1.1.12d Thasos: Map 1.1.22.
1.1.13a The sails and any other superfluous weighty items were removed from triremes before battle: see 6.2.27 and Appendix K, §2.
1.1.13b Parium: Map 1.1.22, inset.
1.1.13c Proconnesus: Map 1.1.22, inset.

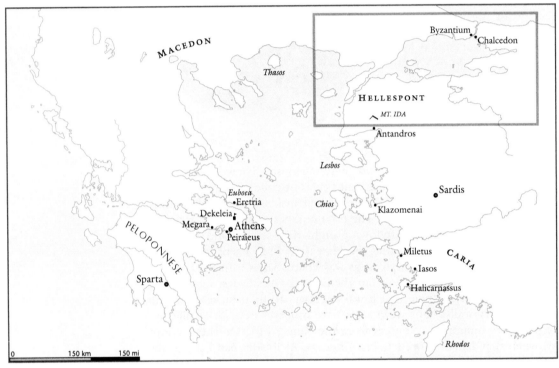

MAP 1.1.22

[16] After the assembly, he made preparations for a sea battle and set out for Cyzicus as a heavy rain was falling. But as he approached Cyzicus the rain stopped, the sun came out, and Alcibiades spied the ships of Mindaros, sixty in number, practicing their maneuvers far from the harbor and cut off from it by his own fleet.[a] [17] The Peloponnesians, seeing that the Athenian ships were more numerous than before and were nearer the harbor, fled to the shore. Beaching their ships, they fought against the Athenian ships that were sailing in against them. [18] Alcibiades, taking twenty of his ships, sailed around and disembarked onto the land. When Mindaros saw this, he himself likewise disembarked and was killed while fighting on the shore; his men took to flight. The Athenians then went to Proconnesus, taking with them all of the ships except those of the Syracusans[a] (which the Syracusans themselves had burned), and on the next day they sailed from Proconnesus to Cyzicus.

[19] The people of Cyzicus received the Athenians, since the Peloponnesians and Pharnabazos had left the city. [20] Alcibiades, remaining there twenty days, took much money from the people of Cyzicus but did their city no other harm and finally returned to Proconnesus. From there he sailed to Perinthus[a] and Selymbria.[b] [21] The Perinthians received the army into the city, while the Selymbrians gave them money but did not admit them inside their walls. [22] From there, the Athenians went to Chrysopolis[a] in Chalcedon[b] and fortified it. They established a custom-house[c] in that city, and they began to collect a ten percent tax on all vessels sailing from the Black Sea.[d] They left behind as a guard thirty ships and two generals, Theramenes and Eumachos, to watch over the land and the ships sailing out and to do any damage they could to the enemy if some opportunity presented itself. The rest of the generals departed for the Hellespont.[e]

[23] A letter that had been sent to Lacedaemon[a] by Hippokrates, Mindaros' vice-admiral, was captured and brought to Athens.[b] It said, "Ships gone, Mindaros dead, men starving; don't know what to do."[c] [24] But Pharnabazos exhorted the whole Peloponnesian army and their allies not to lose heart over timber as long as they themselves were alive, for there was much more timber in the King's lands. He gave each man a cloak and money for two months' rations, and arming the soldiers, he established them as guardians over his own territory on the coast. [25] Calling

1.1.16–22
410
CYZICUS
The Athenian fleet sails to Cyzicus and defeats the enemy on land and sea, taking Cyzicus itself and obtaining much money. Establishing a fort to tax shipping through the Pontus, the Athenian fleet returns to the Hellespont.

1.1.23–26
410
ANTANDROS
Mindaros' famous dispatch is captured by the Athenians. Pharnabazos encourages the Spartans to rebuild their fleet and finances the rebuilding.

1.1.16a   Xenophon and Diodorus (see Appendix O, 13.50) disagree about why Mindaros was cut off from the harbor. For a discussion of such differences between their accounts, see the Introduction, §8.4.
1.1.18a   Syracuse, Sicily: Map 1.1.22, locator.
1.1.20a   Perinthus: Map 1.1.22, inset.
1.1.20b   Selymbria: Map 1.1.22, inset.
1.1.22a   Chrysopolis: Map 1.1.22, inset. Chrysopolis is located near the city of Chalcedon in a district referred to as Chalcedon.
1.1.22b   Chalcedon: Map 1.1.22, inset.
1.1.22c   The Greek term is *dekateutērion,* literally "tithed at a tenth," a term used when

property is confiscated and one-tenth is dedicated to the god.
1.1.22d   Pontus (Black Sea): Map 1.1.22, inset. For more on taxes on trade, see Appendix B, §14.
1.1.22e   Hellespont: Map 1.1.22, inset.
1.1.23a   Lacedaemon (Sparta): Map 1.1.22. The terms *Sparta* and *Lacedaemon* are used almost interchangeably throughout this book; for distinctions, see Appendix E, Spartan Government and Society, §7.
1.1.23b   Athens: Map 1.1.22.
1.1.23c   This brief missive is in the Doric dialect, that used by the Lacedaemonians.

together the generals and the trierarchs[a] from the cities, he ordered them to build triremes in Antandros[b] to the number that each of them had lost, and he gave them money and told them to bring the wood from Mount Ida.[c] [26] While they were building the ships, the Syracusans, together with the Antandrians, completed a part of the wall. In addition, the Syracusans were the most highly regarded of all those performing guard duty. Because of this, the Syracusans have the title of "benefactor" and the privileges of citizenship at Antandros. Now Pharnabazos, when he had arranged these matters, immediately set out to bring help to Chalcedon.

[27] During this time there came an announcement from home to the Syracusan generals that a sentence of exile had been passed against them by the people.[a] The generals called together their own men, and Hermokrates, their spokesman, bemoaning their misfortune, said that they had all been exiled unjustly, contrary to the law. The generals encouraged their troops to remain zealous in the future, as they had been in the past, and to show themselves brave men in carrying out the commands they received on each occasion, and they ordered them to choose men who would command them until those who had been chosen in place of themselves should arrive from Syracuse.

[28] But the Syracusans, especially the trierarchs, marines, and helmsmen,[a] shouted that the generals should continue in command. The generals, however, said that they would not engage in civil strife against their own city, but if anyone had an accusation to make against them, it was right that they should render an account of their actions; and they spoke to the men, saying, "Remember how many sea battles you yourselves have won through your own efforts, and how many ships you have captured, and how often you, with your allies, have been undefeated under our command, holding the position of honor[b] on land and sea through our courage in commanding and your skill in obeying." [29] No one could find any fault with the generals, and since their men requested it, they agreed to remain in command until those chosen to take their place—Demarchos son of Epikydos, Myskon son of Menekrates, and Potamis son of Gnosias—arrived. The majority of the trierarchs swore that when they returned to Syracuse, they would bring about the return of the generals from exile; praising all of them, the generals sent them off to wherever they wished to go.

[30] Those who had been in close contact with Hermokrates especially missed his care, his eagerness, and his affability. For each day, both in the morning and in the evening, he would call to his own tent the most capable of the trierarchs, helmsmen, and marines whom he had come to know over

1.1.25a Trierarchs: trireme captains. See Appendix K, §11.
1.1.25b Antandros: Map 1.1.22.
1.1.25c Mount Ida: Map 1.1.22, inset.
1.1.27a The generals were not connected with the popular party at Syracuse. This probably took place in 410, although some scholars prefer 411. For further discussion of the date, see Appendix C, Chronological Problems in the Continuation (1.1.1–2.3.10) of

Xenophon's *Hellenika*, §3.
1.1.28a Marines were soldiers whose mission was to board enemy ships or to repel enemy boarders. Some were hoplites (armored foot soldiers) and some were archers. They were distinct from the crew of sailors who sailed the ship, among whom was the helmsman who directed it with the steering oar. See Appendix K, §2, 11.
1.1.28b Literally, "the strongest formation."

time; there he would share with them what he intended to say or do, and he would instruct them and ask them for their advice, either on the spot or after they had considered the matter.

[31] It was due to this that Hermokrates was especially well regarded in the council, where he had the reputation of being the best speaker and the best adviser. Because he had in the past brought accusations against Tissaphernes in Sparta and because he was thought to speak the truth (Astyochos[a] having served as his witness), it happened that when he went to Pharnabazos, he received money even before asking for it, and with this he prepared mercenaries and triremes for his return to Syracuse. While he was doing this, those chosen to succeed the Syracusan generals arrived in Miletus[b] and took over the ships and the army.

[32] At this same time civil strife broke out in Thasos,[a] and those who supported Sparta, together with the Spartan garrison commander Eteonikos,[b] were expelled. The Spartan Pasippidas was charged with plotting this revolt together with Tissaphernes and was consequently exiled from Sparta. Kratesippidas was sent out to lead the fleet that Pasippidas had assembled from the allies, and he took over command of it in Chios.[c]

[33] Around this time, while Thrasyllos was in Athens,[a] Agis[b] made a foray from Dekeleia[c] up to the very walls of Athens. Thrasyllos, leading out the Athenians and all the others who were in the city, marshaled them by the Lykeion gymnasium,[d] intending to fight if the Spartans should attack them. [34] But when Agis saw this, he swiftly retreated, and a few of those in the rear were killed by the light-armed troops. So because of this, the Athenians became even more enthusiastic about giving Thrasyllos what he had come for, and they voted that he should enroll a thousand hoplites,[a] a hundred cavalry, and fifty triremes.

[35] Agis, however, when he saw many grain boats sailing into the Peiraieus,[a] remarked that it was useless for his men to have long prevented the Athenians from tilling their land if they could not stop the grain that was coming to them by sea. He said also that it would be best to send

1.1.32
409
THASOS
Revolution at Thasos drives out the Spartan governor.

1.1.33–34
410
ATTICA
A raid by Agis from Dekeleia is turned back by the Athenians under Thrasyllos.

1.1.35–36
410
ATTICA-HELLESPONT
Agis sends Klearchos with fifteen ships to attack the Athenians in the Hellespont.

1.1.31a Astyochos had commanded the Spartan fleet before Mindaros, in 412–411.
1.1.31b Miletus: Map 1.1.22.
1.1.32a Thasos: Map 1.1.22. Some scholars, suspecting the involvement of Tissaphernes, accept Kahrstedt's emendation from "Thasos" to "Iasos," a small town in Asia about twenty miles north of Halicarnassus (Map 1.1.22). (John Marincola)
1.1.32b Eteonikos: a Spartan naval commander.
1.1.32c Chios: Map 1.1.22. The side note date 409 refers only to the revolution at Thasos. Kratesippidas' command took place almost entirely in 408.
1.1.33a Athens: Map 1.1.22. To recall what Thrasyllos had come for, see n. 1.1.8a.
1.1.33b Agis, king of Sparta 427–400: see Appendix M, §2.
1.1.33c Dekeleia: Map 1.1.22. Dekeleia was in Athenian territory but had been turned into a Spartan stronghold during the

Peloponnesian War (around 413). The Spartans held it till the end of the war, in 404, to control rural Attica (Map 1.2.10, inset) and to prevent land communication between Athens and Euboea (Map 1.1.22).
1.1.33d Lykeion gymnasium was outside Athens' walls (Map 2.4.30, inset).
1.1.34a Hoplites: heavily armored infantry, often equipped with helmet, breastplate, and greaves but always carrying a large round shield, a thrusting spear, and a short sword. See Appendix L, Land Warfare in Xenophon's *Hellenika*, §3.
1.1.35a Peiraieus, the port of Athens: Map 1.1.22. For many years now, Athens had depended upon grain imported by ship from elsewhere; most of it came from the Black Sea regions through the Hellespont. Control or at least freedom of the sealanes was thus of vital strategic importance to Athens.

Klearchos son of Ramphias and *proxenos* of the Byzantines,[b] to Chalcedon and Byzantium.[c] [36] When this was agreed upon, fifteen ships (troop transports rather than fast ships)[a] set sail, manned by the Megarians[b] and the rest of the allies. Three of these were destroyed in the Hellespont[c] by the nine Athenian ships that were always keeping watch there over the merchantmen, but the rest escaped to Sestos[d] and from there got safely to Byzantium.

[37] And this year ended, [the one in which the Carthaginians,[a] with Hannibal as their leader, made an expedition against Sicily[b] with 100,000 men and in three months captured two Greek cities, Selinus[c] and Himera.][d]

[1] In the next year[a] [the one in which the ninety-third Olympiad occurred, where Euagoras of Elis[b] won the two-horse race (a new event added that

1.1.37
409
SICILY
The year ends.
Carthaginians capture
Selinus and Himera.

1.2.1–3
409
PYGELA
The Athenians under
Thrasyllos ravage the land
around Pygela and defeat
a unit of Milesians sent
out to help the Pygelaians.

1.1.35b Klearchos was very important in Xenophon's life as the principal leader of the Ten Thousand until his execution by the Persians just after the battle of Cunaxa. (See the Introduction, §4.2, which mentions the treacherous execution by the Persians of all but one of the Greek generals.) A *proxenos* was the citizen of a city who looked out for the interests of another city and would assist the citizens of that city when they were visiting. Klearchos was *proxenos* of the Byzantines at Sparta.

1.1.35c Byzantium: Map 1.1.22.

1.1.36a For more on ancient ships, see Appendix K, §2.

1.1.36b Megara: Map 1.1.22. Byzantium was a colony of Megara, supposed to have been founded in 667.

1.1.36c Hellespont: Map 1.1.22 and inset.

1.1.36d Sestos: Map 1.1.22, inset. Because Sestos was in Athenian hands (1.1.11), this is possibly a manuscript error. Breitenbach conjectured "Abydos."

1.1.37a Carthage: Map 1.1.22, locator.

1.1.37b Sicily: Map 1.1.22, locator.

1.1.37c Selinus: Map 1.1.22, locator.

1.1.37d Himera: Map 1.1.22, locator. The narrative since 1.1.11 has been mostly concerned with events of 410, with arguably some events of 411 mixed in, so one would naturally think that the destruction of Selinus and Himera also belongs in 410, or possibly in the winter months of 410/9. But in fact (or, at any rate, in accordance with *The Cambridge Ancient History*), the two cities were destroyed during the campaigning season of 409. Most modern scholars believe that the explanation for the confusion is that this and similar passages that set up synchronisms or enumerate the years of the war are later interpolations into Xenophon's text: see Appendix C, §5–9. Note that all text enclosed by square brackets in this volume is believed to be an interpolation (added material) by a later author. For the Greek, see Translator's Notes.

1.2.1a The narrative has reached the year 409

according to the chronology used in this edition, which is that argued for by David Lewis and A. Andrewes in *The Cambridge Ancient History*, 2nd edition, vol. 5 (Cambridge: Cambridge University Press, 1992), pp. 503–5 (see especially p. 512), though some scholars believe the year is actually 410. But the direct dating indications in this sentence are to 408. Of course, the ancients did not date with reference to the (assumed) birth date of Jesus Christ, as we do, but had many different local systems.

The first direct dating indication is a reference to a celebration of the Olympic Games (see Appendix J, §10–11). In ancient times as today, these happened every four years; 408 is the correct year in the ongoing sequence and, according to the system of the ancient chronographers, marks the ninety-third set of games. The second direct dating indication is a reference to the ephorate at Sparta, a magistracy that changed every year in the early autumn (for the ephorate, see Appendix E, §11, 14–17). One of the five ephors, the eponymous ephor, gave his name to the year, and the rest of our evidence suggests that Euarchippos was eponymous ephor for 408/7. The third direct dating indication is a reference to the archonship at Athens, a magistracy that changed every year in midsummer (for the archonship, see Appendix B, §6). One of the ten archons, the eponymous archon, gave his name to the year, and Euktemon is known to have been eponymous archon for 408/7.

Most modern scholars believe that the part of the sentence containing these three references to 408 is an interpolation by a later author, and likewise that the references to the ephor and archon at 1.3.1, 1.6.1, and 2.1.10 and to Olympiad, ephor, and archon at 2.3.1 have been interpolated (and that the references to the ephor and archon at 1.3.1 are again a year out). See further Appendix C, §5–9.

1.2.1b Elis: Map 1.2.10, BX.

year) and Eubotas of Cyrene[c] won the *stadion*][d] when Euarchippos was ephor at Sparta[e] and Euktemon was archon at Athens,[f] the Athenians fortified Thorikos.[g] Thrasyllos, taking the boats that had been voted him and making leather shields for 5,000 of the sailors so that they could serve together with the regular peltasts,[h] sailed out for Samos[i] at the beginning of summer. [2] Remaining there for three days, he sailed to Pygela[a] and there set about ravaging the land and attacking the wall. Some men of Miletus[b] brought help to the Pygelaians and pursued some of the light-armed Athenian troops who were scattered about. [3] But the peltasts and two regiments of hoplites brought help to their own light-armed troops and killed all those who had come from Miletus, except for a few; they also captured about two hundred shields and set up a trophy.[a]

[4] On the next day the Athenians sailed into Notion[a] and, after making suitable preparations, sailed from there to Colophon,[b] whereupon the people of Colophon came over to their side. On the following night they made a raid into Lydia[c] at that time of year when the grain is at its height: they set fire to many villages and took money, slaves, and much other plunder. [5] The Persian Stages was in the area, and when he saw that the Athenians had scattered from their camp pursuing individual plunder, he attacked them. And even though the Athenian cavalry came to help their men, Stages managed to capture one Athenian alive and kill seven others. [6] After this, Thrasyllos led the army back to the sea, intending to sail to Ephesus.[a] Tissaphernes, however, perceiving Thrasyllos' goal, gathered together a large army and dispatched cavalry, announcing to all that they must bring help at Ephesus to Artemis.[b]

[7] On the seventeenth day after the incursion into Ephesus, Thrasyllos sailed off and disembarked his fleet's hoplites[a] around Koressos,[b] while he

1.2.4–6
409
LYDIA
The Athenians win Colophon over and raid Lydia. The Persians attack their raiders with some success. Thrasyllos heads for Ephesus, where Tissaphernes has gathered a large force.

1.2.7–10
409
EPHESUS
The Athenians are routed with heavy losses in an assault on Ephesus.

1.2.1c   Cyrene: Map 1.2.10, locator.
1.2.1d   The two-hundred-yard footrace.
1.2.1e   Sparta: Map 1.2.10, BX. For Spartan ephorate, see Appendix E, §11, 14–17. For the ephor here, see n. 1.2.1a.
1.2.1f   Athens: Map 1.2.10, BX and inset. See n. 1.1.37d. For the archon here, see n. 1.2.1a.
1.2.1g   Thorikos: Map 1.2.10, inset.
1.2.1h   Accepting here the reading of the manuscripts. (John Marincola) For the Greek, see Translator's Notes. Peltasts were troops armed only with a small, light shield, a javelin, and a short sword. Unhindered by body armor, they could move much more quickly than the fully armed hoplite, whose equipment was both far heavier and far more expensive than theirs. See Appendix L, §3–8.
1.2.1i   Samos: Map 1.2.10, BY.
1.2.2a   Pygela: Map 1.2.10, BY. Listed as P(h)ygela in the *Barrington Atlas*.
1.2.2b   Miletus: Map 1.2.10, BY.
1.2.3a   Trophy: After a battle in ancient Greece, the victors would gather up their dead,

strip those of the enemy, and raise a trophy. The defeated would collect the bodies of their fallen during a truce that they would explicitly request and be granted for that purpose. In this way, appropriate reverence was shown and proper burial was accorded to all war dead. See Appendix L, §13.
1.2.4a   Notion: Map 1.2.10, BY.
1.2.4b   Colophon: Map 1.2.10, BY.
1.2.4c   Lydia: Map 1.2.10, BY.
1.2.6a   Ephesus: Map 1.2.10, BY.
1.2.6b   Artemis was the main goddess of Ephesus. The reference here is to the famous temple of Artemis at Ephesus.
1.2.7a   Each trireme normally carried a complement of ten hoplites and sometimes more. See Appendix K, §2.
1.2.7b   The Oxyrhynchus Historian says that Koressos was the name of the harbor of Ephesus (see Appendix P, Selected Fragments of the *Hellenica Oxyrhynchia* Relevant to Xenophon's *Hellenika*, Fragment 1). The *Barrington Atlas* shows a Mount Kores(s)os: Map 1.2.10, BY.

stationed the cavalry, slingers,[c] marines, and all the rest around the marsh on the other side of the city. At dawn he led both units forward. [8] The Ephesians[a] from the city advanced to meet him, as did the allies whom Tissaphernes had brought there, and the Syracusans[b]—both those from the earlier group of twenty ships and those from the later group of five (who happened to be present there, having recently come with Eucles the son of Hippon and Herakleides the son of Aristogenes)—and the men from the two ships from Selinus.[c] [9] These all at first attacked the hoplites in Koressos, routed them, and killed about a hundred of them, pursuing them down to the sea. Then they turned to assault those alongside the marsh. There, too, the Athenians were put to flight, and about three hundred of them were killed. [10] The Ephesians set up a trophy there and another one at Koressos. To the Syracusans and Selinuntians who had shown themselves the bravest they gave the prizes for valor, both to the groups as a whole and to many of the individuals; they also gave to anyone who wished it the right to reside in Ephesus tax-free. To the Selinuntians, since their city had been destroyed,[a] they gave the additional right of citizenship.

[11] The Athenians, taking up the corpses under truce, sailed away to Notion; and after they had buried them there, they sailed immediately for Lesbos[a] and the Hellespont.[b] [12] When they were anchored at Methymna,[a] on Lesbos, they saw the twenty-five Syracusan ships from Ephesus sailing by. Putting out to sea against them, the Athenians captured four of the ships with their crews, and they pursued the rest back to Ephesus. [13] Thrasyllos sent all the prisoners back to Athens, except for Alcibiades, an Athenian who was a cousin and fellow exile of Alcibiades, whom Thrasyllos ordered to be stoned to death.[a] From there Thrasyllos sailed to Sestos[b] to join the rest of the army, and from there the entire force crossed over to Lampsacus.[c]

[14] Winter was now coming on, the winter in the course of which the Syracusan prisoners who were held in the quarries at the Peiraieus[a] tunneled through the rock and escaped by night, some to Dekeleia,[b] some to Megara.[c]

[15] In Lampsacus, where Alcibiades was gathering together the entire army, the veteran soldiers refused to be marshaled with the more recent ones under the command of Thrasyllos, on the grounds that, whereas they

1.2.7c Slingers were troops armed with slings that hurled round stones or cast round lead bullets before the battle opened or in support of the battle line. The missiles traveled with such force that they could kill or cause serious injury to those who were struck.

1.2.8a Ephesians: accepting Sauppe's emendation *Ephesioi* in place of the manuscripts' *sphisin*. (John Marincola) For the Greek, see Translator's Notes.

1.2.8b Syracuse: Map 1.2.10, locator.

1.2.8c Selinus: Map 1.2.10, locator.

1.2.10a Selinus had been destroyed by the Carthaginians (Carthage: Map 1.2.10,

locator) shortly before the events here narrated (409). See 1.1.37.

1.2.11a Lesbos: Map 1.2.10, AY.

1.2.11b Hellespont: Map 1.2.10, AY.

1.2.12a Methymna: Map 1.2.10, AY.

1.2.13a Some have found this incredible and emended the text from *kateleusen* ("stoned") to *epelusen* ("released"). (John Marincola)

1.2.13b Sestos: Map 1.2.10, AY.

1.2.13c Lampsacus: Map 1.2.10, AY.

1.2.14a Peiraieus: Map 1.2.10, inset.

1.2.14b Dekeleia: Map 1.2.10, inset.

1.2.14c Megara: Map 1.2.10, inset.

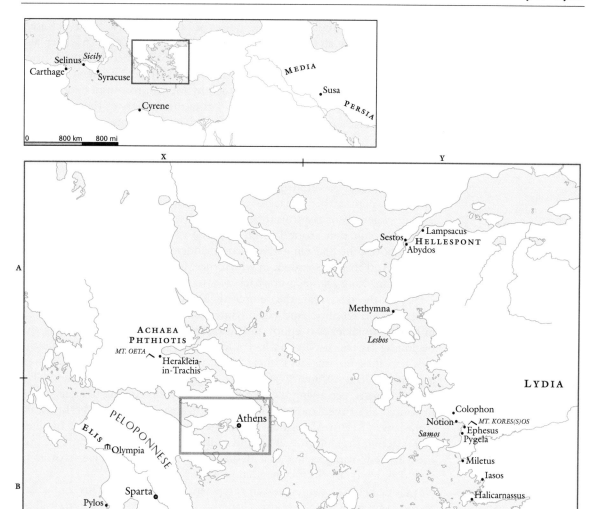

MAP 1.2.10

themselves were undefeated, the newer soldiers had just been defeated. Nonetheless, they all wintered there, fortifying Lampsacus. [16] They also made an expedition against Abydos,ᵃ and Pharnabazos met them with many cavalry, but he was defeated in battle and fled. Alcibiades pursued him with the cavalry and 120 hoplites commanded by Menandros, until darkness put an end to it. [17] On account of this battle, the soldiers of their own volition came together and welcomed the men who had come with Thrasyllos. During the winter, the troops went into the mainland by different routes and repeatedly plundered the Persian King's territory.

[18] At this same time, the Spartans released under treaty those of the helotsᵃ who had revolted from Maleaᵇ and fled to Koryphasion.ᶜ During this same period the Achaeansᵈ betrayed the colonists of Herakleia-in-Trachisᵉ when all of them were arrayed against the Oetaeans,ᶠ their enemy, with the result that around seven hundred of them were killed, together with Labotes, the Spartan garrison commander.

[19] And this year ended, in which the Medes,ᵃ who had revolted from the Persianᵇ King Darius, went back over to him.

[1] In the next year, the temple of Athena in Phocaeaᵃ was struck by lightning and set afire. And when winter came to an end [this was the year in which Pantakles was ephor and Antigenes was archon]ᵇ and spring was beginning (twenty-two years had now elapsed in this war), the Athenians sailed to Proconnesusᶜ with their whole force. [2] Setting out from there against Chalcedonᵃ and Byzantium,ᵇ they camped near Chalcedon. The Chalcedonians, perceiving that the Athenians were preparing to attack them, deposited all of their movable property with their neighbors, the Bithynian Thracians.ᶜ [3] But Alcibiades, taking the cavalry and a few of the hoplites, and ordering the ships to sail around to Bithynia, demanded the property of the Chalcedonians, saying that if the Bithynians did not give it over, he would attack them. So they handed it over.

[4] Alcibiades, having made an agreement with the Bithynians, came back to the camp bringing the booty. Using his whole force, he began to wall off Chalcedon from sea to sea, including as much of the river as possible, with

---

1.2.18
409
HERAKLEIA
Spartans release helots. Colonists of Herakleia-in-Trachis are heavily defeated.

1.2.19
409/8
MEDIA
The year ends. Medes subjected.

1.3.1–3
408
HELLESPONT
Athenian operations against Chalcedon and Byzantium.

1.3.4–7
408
CHALCEDON
Alcibiades besieges Chalcedon, defeating the Spartan-led garrison and the Persians when they attempt to drive him off.

1.2.16a Abydos: Map 1.2.10, AY.
1.2.18a Helots: Spartan serfs. See Appendix E, 12.
1.2.18b Cape Malea, Peloponnese: Map 1.2.10, BX.
1.2.18c Koryphasion: Thucydides 4.3.2 explains that this is the Spartan name for Pylos (Messenia): Map 1.2.10, BX. See Appendix E, §12. He also says that many helots fled to Pylos/Koryphasion during the period 425–409, when it was occupied by the Athenians (Thucydides 4.41.3, 5.35.6).
1.2.18d Achaea Phthiotis: Map 1.2.10, AX.
1.2.18e Herakleia-in-Trachis: Map 1.2.10, AX.
1.2.18f Mount Oeta: Map 1.2.10, AX.
1.2.19a Media: Map 1.2.10, locator.
1.2.19b Persia: Map 1.2.10, locator.
1.3.1a Phocaea: Map 1.3.12, BY.

1.3.1b For ephors and archons, and the use of them for dating events, see n. 1.2.1a and Appendix C, §5–9. As explained there, the direct dating indications here have been interpolated and are out by a year, Antigenes being in reality the archon for 407/6. For the Greek, see Translator's Notes.
1.3.1c Proconnesus: Map 1.3.12, AY.
1.3.2a Chalcedon: Map 1.3.12, inset.
1.3.2b Byzantium: Map 1.3.12, AY, inset.
1.3.2c Bithynian Thrace: Map 1.3.12, AY. It is assumed that Xenophon is referring throughout this episode to Bithynian Thracians but, having first identified them as such, he calls them just Bithynians afterward. Bithynia and Bithynian Thrace are otherwise quite separate and distinct regions.

a wooden wall.[a] [5] Then Hippokrates, the Spartan garrison commander, led his army out from the city, intending to give battle. The Athenians lined up opposite him, and Pharnabazos, from outside the encircling wall, brought help with his army and many cavalry. [6] The hoplites of Hippokrates and Thrasyllos fought for a long time, until Alcibiades brought assistance with some hoplites and his cavalry. Hippokrates was killed, while those with him fled into the city. [7] At the same time Pharnabazos, who had not been able to join up with Hippokrates because of the narrowness of the land (since the river and the fortifications were not much distant from each other), retreated to the Herakleion[a] of the Chalcedonians, where he had his camp.

[8] After this, Alcibiades went to the Hellespont[a] and the Chersonese[b] in order to demand money.[c] In his absence, the remaining generals came to an agreement with Pharnabazos about Chalcedon, namely, that Pharnabazos would give twenty talents[d] to the Athenians and would escort Athenian ambassadors to the King. [9] Oaths were also exchanged with Pharnabazos that the Chalcedonians would pay the Athenians the tribute[a] they had been accustomed to paying previously and any arrears of payments owed, and that the Athenians would not make war on the Chalcedonians until the envoys should come back from the King. [10] Alcibiades was not present at the oath-taking, but he was in the area of Selymbria.[a] He captured this city and then went to Byzantium, bringing with him the entire force from the Chersonese, along with soldiers from Thrace[b] and more than three hundred cavalry. [11] Pharnabazos, thinking that Alcibiades, too, should take the oaths, was waiting in Chalcedon until Alcibiades should come there from Byzantium. But when Alcibiades arrived, he refused to swear unless Pharnabazos should swear to him also. [12] After this Alcibiades took the oath at Chrysopolis,[a] in the presence of Mitrobates and Arnapes (the representatives sent by Pharnabazos), and Pharnabazos swore in Chalcedon before Euryptolemos and Diotimos (the representatives sent by Alcibiades). They swore to the general agreement and also made agreements with each other in private.

[13] Pharnabazos then immediately departed and ordered the envoys who were making their way to the King to meet him at Cyzicus.[a] The

1.3.8–12
408
CHALCEDON
Alcibiades goes to the Hellespont to raise funds. Other generals reach agreement with Chalcedon and Pharnabazos. Alcibiades returns and also exchanges oaths to ratify the pact.

1.3.13
408
CYZICUS
Pharnabazos assembles the envoys from the Greeks to the King.

1.3.4a   "From sea to sea": from the Bosporus to Propontis. The "river": there are river mouths on each side of the peninsula on which the city stands, and one of them apparently broke the line of the stockade, which was carried as near as possible to each bank of the river. Chalcedon: Map 1.3.12, inset.
1.3.7a   A shrine to Herakles, presumably near the city of Chalcedon.
1.3.8a   Hellespont: Map 1.3.12, AY.
1.3.8b   Chersonese: Map 1.3.12, AY.
1.3.8c   Collecting money: see Appendix B, §14.
1.3.8d   The talent is a unit of weight whose value varied over time and place between 55 and 80 pounds. The Attic talent weighed about 57 pounds; the Aeginetan, about 82. We cannot be sure which

one Xenophon refers to here. See Appendix I, Units of Distance, Currency, and Capacity in Xenophon's *Hellenika*, §8, 10, 13.
1.3.9a   Tribute: annual amount levied by Athens on the cities it dominated in the fifth century. See n. 1.1.8a and Appendix B, §14.
1.3.10a   Selymbria: Map 1.3.12, AY.
1.3.10b   Thrace: Map 1.3.12, AY.
1.3.12a   Chrysopolis: Map 1.3.12, inset.
1.3.13a   Cyzicus: Map 1.3.12, AY.

Athenian[b] envoys sent were Dorotheos, Philocydes, Theogenes, Euryptolemos, and Mantitheos, and with them went the Argives[c] Cleostratus and Pyrrolochos. Envoys from the Spartans also went, Pasippidas and others, and with them also Hermokrates (now in exile from Syracuse[d]) and his brother Proxenos.

[14] While Pharnabazos was escorting these men, the Athenians conducted a siege of Byzantium by building an encircling wall; and around the city wall they made assaults, both from a distance and from close in. [15] Inside Byzantium were Klearchos, the Lacedaemonian garrison commander, and with him some of the *perioikoi* and a few of the *neodamōdeis*,[a] as well as Megarians[b] (whose commander was the Megarian Helixus) and Boeotians[c] (commanded by Coiratadas). [16] The Athenians, when they could not accomplish anything by force, persuaded some of the Byzantines to betray the city. [17] Klearchos, the garrison commander, thinking that no one would do this, had arranged everything as best he could and, entrusting matters in the city to Coiratadas and Helixus, crossed over the straits[a] to Pharnabazos to get pay for the soldiers from him. He also wished to gather together the ships that were in the Hellespont, some of which had been left as guards by Pasippidas, others in Antandros,[b] and others that Agesandridas (who was Mindaros' junior officer[c]) commanded in Thrace. Moreover, Klearchos wanted to build additional ships so that, with an expanded fleet, he might attack the allies of Athens and thus compel the Athenians to withdraw their forces, and so lift the siege of Byzantium.

[18] But when Klearchos sailed out, those Byzantines who would betray the city—Cydon, Ariston, Anaxikrates, Lykurgos, and Anaxilaos—set to work. [19] Anaxilaos was later tried at Sparta[a] because of his betrayal but escaped the penalty of death: he defended himself by saying that he was a Byzantine, not a Spartan, and that he did not betray the city but, rather, saved it, for he saw the women and children perishing by famine, since Klearchos gave all food in the city to the Spartan soldiers; and so it was for this, not for gain or from hatred of the Spartans, that he had let the enemy into the city. [20] When the conspirators had made their preparations, they opened the so-called Thracian gates during the night and brought in the army and Alcibiades. [21] Helixus and Coiratadas, knowing nothing of this plan, went out with their full force to meet the enemy in

1.3.13b   Athens: Map 1.3.12, BX.
1.3.13c   Argos: Map 1.3.12, BX. Argos was a long-standing enemy of Sparta and had been allied with Athens for most of the time since 420.
1.3.13d   Syracuse: Map 1.2.10, locator.
1.3.15a   *Perioikoi* and *neodamōdeis*: different classes of Spartans. For *perioikoi*, see Appendix E, §10. For *neodamōdeis*, see Appendix E, §9, 12, and Appendix F, §6.

1.3.15b   Megara: Map 1.3.12, BX.
1.3.15c   Boeotia: Map 1.3.12, BX.
1.3.17a   Straits: the Hellespont.
1.3.17b   Antandros: Map 1.3.12, AY.
1.3.17c   It is not clear what actual position an *epibates* (Xenophon's word here) held; the term is used at Thucydides 8.61.2, where it seems to mean a detachable officer. (John Marincola)
1.3.19a   Sparta: Map 1.3.12, BX.

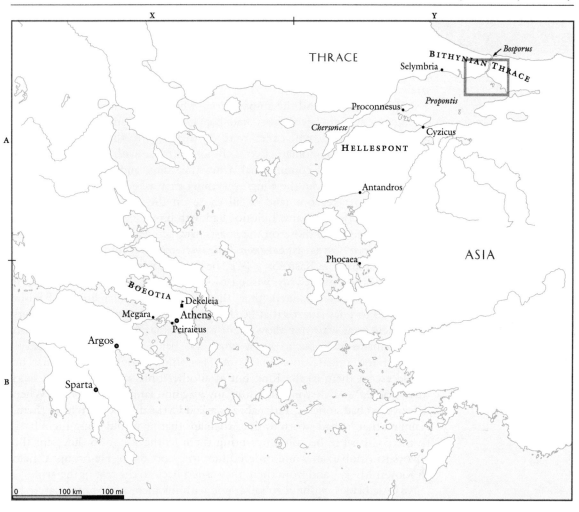

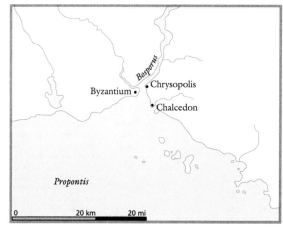

MAP 1.3.12

the agora.ᵃ But since the Athenians were in control everywhere in the city and there was nothing they could do, they surrendered themselves. [22] They were then sent to Athens,ᵃ but Coiratadas managed to escape notice in the crowd of those disembarking at the Peiraieus,ᵇ and he got himself safely to Dekeleia.ᶜ

1.4.1–7
407
ASIA
Athenian envoys en route to the King meet Spartan ambassadors who have just won his support. Cyrus is appointed Persian commander in the area. Under orders, Pharnabazos detains the Athenian envoys for three years before letting them return home.

[1] Pharnabazos and the ambassadors, who were in Gordion in Phrygiaᵃ during the winter, heard what had happened at Byzantium.ᵇ [2] At the beginning of spring, when they were on their way to the King, they were met by the Lacedaemonian envoys (Boiotios, those with him, and the rest of the ambassadors) coming back from the King, and they said that the Spartans had won from the King everything they asked for; [3] in addition, Cyrus was to take command of all those on the coast who would fight together with the Spartans. Boiotios had with him a letter bearing the royal seal, addressed to all those on the coast, in which was the following: "I am sending down Cyrus as *karanon* (*karanon* means "commander") of all those who muster at Kastolos."ᵃ [4] The Athenian envoys, when they heard these things and saw Cyrus, wished to see the King more than ever, but if that could not be arranged, then they wished to return home. [5] But Cyrus said to Pharnabazos that he should either hand over the ambassadors to himself or at least not allow them to go home, for Cyrus did not wish the Athenians at home to know what was being done. [6] Pharnabazos detained the ambassadors for a time, asserting at one moment that he would escort them to the King but at another time saying he would send them home, "so that you will not in any way find fault with me." [7] When three yearsᵃ had gone by, Pharnabazos asked Cyrus if he could release them, claiming that he had sworn to the Athenians that he would bring them back to the coast, since he could not bring them to the King. So they sent the envoys to Ariobarzanes and ordered him to escort them. He brought them to Kios in Mysia,ᵇ and from there they sailed back to the rest of the army.

1.4.8–9
407
CARIA-THRACE
Alcibiades collects one hundred talents from the Kerameios region. Thrasyboulos subdues Thrace.

[8] Alcibiades, wishing to sail home with his men, went immediately to Samos.ᵃ Taking twenty of the ships there, he sailed to the Kerameios Gulf ᵇ in Caria,ᶜ [9] from which, after collecting a hundred talents, he sailed back

1.3.21a   Agora: the central market square of any ancient Greek city, where all business and much politics and social life took place. There is a parallel passage in Diodorus (Appendix O, 13.66–67).
1.3.22a   Athens: Map 1.3.12, BX.
1.3.22b   Peiraieus: Map 1.3.12, BX.
1.3.22c   Dekeleia: Map 1.3.12, BX.
1.4.1a   Gordion, Phrygia: Map 1.4.9.
1.4.1b   Byzantium: Map 1.4.9.
1.4.3a   Kastolos (Kastolou Pedion): Map 1.4.9. Cyrus was the King's second son by his principal wife, Parysatis. He had been appointed commander of the maritime provinces of Asia Minor and ordered to take command of Persian forces mustering at Kastolos and to support the Spartans in their war against the Athenians.

See Appendix D, §2, 3. See also the Introduction, §3.2–3.4.2. For more on Cyrus the Younger, see Appendix M, §7.
1.4.7a   Many have found "three years" a pointlessly long time, and it is incompatible with the chronology from *The Cambridge Ancient History*, which is followed in this book. Andrewes emended "years" to "months," which also allows the ambassador Euryptolemos to be identified with Euryptolemos the son of Peisanax, who plays a big part in the story later. See Appendix C, §14, and Appendix A, §9, 10.
1.4.7b   Kios, Mysia: Map 1.4.9.
1.4.8a   Samos: Map 1.4.9.
1.4.8b   Kerameios Gulf: Map 1.4.9.
1.4.8c   Caria: Map 1.4.9.

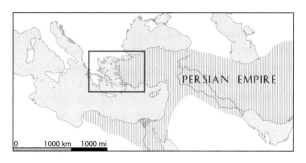

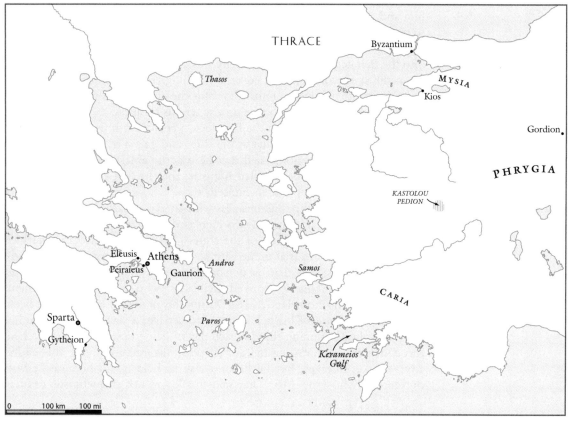

MAP 1.4.9

to Samos. Thrasyboulos went with thirty ships to Thrace,[a] where he subdued all the lands there that had gone over to the side of the Spartans, including Thasos,[b] which was suffering badly from wars, civil strife, and famine.

[10] Thrasyllos sailed home to Athens[a] with the rest of the army. Before he arrived there, the Athenians had chosen as generals Alcibiades (who was still in exile), Thrasyboulos (who was abroad), and from those present at Athens, Konon.[b] [11] Alcibiades, in possession of the money from Samos, sailed back to Paros[a] with twenty ships; from there he went directly to Gytheion[b] to spy on the thirty triremes that he had learned were being outfitted there by the Spartans, and also to find out how the city felt toward him and the possibility of his returning home. [12] When he saw that they were favorably inclined toward him, since they had after all chosen him to be a general, and that his close friends were sending for him in private, he sailed into the Peiraieus,[a] on the day the city was celebrating the Plynteria festival,[b] when the statue of Athena is covered—a thing that some divined was of ill omen, both for Alcibiades himself and for the city. For on that day none of the Athenians would dare to take up any serious business.

[13] When he sailed into the Peiraieus, a crowd both from the Peiraieus and the city[a] gathered together at the ships and gazed in amazement, wishing to see Alcibiades. Some said that he was the ablest of the citizens and the only one to have been exiled unjustly; that he had been slandered by those who were less able than himself, those who gave the people wicked advice and conducted public business with an eye toward their own private gain, whereas Alcibiades had always increased the state's wealth, from both his own resources and those of the state. [14] They recalled that he had been willing to go on trial immediately when he was charged with profaning the Mysteries,[a] but that his personal enemies, by postponing what was considered a just request, deprived Alcibiades (who was away from Athens at the time) of his homeland.[b] [15] During this period of exile, he had been compelled, because of his helplessness, to act like a slave and to serve his enemies,[a] always running the risk each day of being destroyed. He watched those dearest to him—his fellow citizens, his relatives, and the entire city[b]—make mistakes, but he had no way to help them, because he was prevented by his exile. [16] They said that it was not characteristic of men

1.4.10–12
407
SAMOS-PEIRAIEUS
Alcibiades is elected a general. On the basis of that indication of acceptance, he returns to Athens, but on a day of ill omen.

1.4.13–16
407
ATHENS
Alcibiades is welcomed back when he lands at the Peiraieus. People laud his abilities and regret his exile, blaming former demagogues for destroying Athens' best men.

1.4.9a   Thrace: Map 1.4.9.
1.4.9b   Thasos: Map 1.4.9.
1.4.10a Athens: Map 1.4.9.
1.4.10b See "Konon" in Appendix M, §16.
1.4.11a Paros: Map 1.4.9.
1.4.11b Gytheion: Map 1.4.9.
1.4.12a Peiraieus: Map 1.4.9.
1.4.12b Plynteria: the festival in which the garments of the statue of Athena were taken off and washed.
1.4.13a The city in this case was Athens itself, located about four and a half miles from its port at Peiraieus.
1.4.14a "Mysteries" refers to the Eleusinian Mysteries: see Appendix J, §9, 11.
1.4.14b In 415, when Alcibiades was accused of

what amounts to blasphemy, he requested an immediate trial, but his opponents succeeded in having the trial postponed. Shortly afterward, when the Athenian expedition to Sicily departed, he, as one of its generals, had to leave Athens without a trial and was away when the Athenians—now convinced of his guilt—summoned him home for trial and, as Thucydides says, for execution. Instead of returning home, he fled to Sparta. See Thucydides 6.27–29, 6.53, 6.60–61.
1.4.15a The Spartans and the Persians.
1.4.15b The city of Athens.

such as Alcibiades to want a change in the political order or a revolution, since he had won more distinction from the people than his contemporaries and had not been considered inferior to his elders. His enemies, on the other hand, were exactly the same men they had been before his exile: the difference was that once they gained power they destroyed the best men, and since they themselves were the only ones left, the citizens favored them because they did not have other, better ones whom they could employ.[a]

[17] Others said that Alcibiades alone had been responsible for their past evils, and there was the danger that he alone would be the author of future evils that they feared would befall the state.[a]

[18] Alcibiades anchored near the shore and did not immediately disembark, fearing his enemies. Instead, standing on deck, he kept looking to see if his relations were there. [19] Only when he saw his cousin Euryptolemos the son of Peisanax and the rest of his household and friends with them did he disembark and go up to the city, accompanied by men who were prepared to stop anyone from laying hands on him. [20] In the Council and Assembly, he defended himself, saying that he had not committed impiety but that he had been treated unjustly. Other things of that sort were said, and no one spoke in opposition, because the Assembly would not have tolerated it. Alcibiades was chosen general with supreme authority over the other generals, on the grounds that he was the man to restore the former power of Athens. Although the celebration of the Mysteries had been previously conducted by sea on account of the war, Alcibiades conducted the procession to Eleusis[a] over land, leading out all the soldiers.

[21] After this he enrolled an army of 1,500 hoplites, 150 horsemen, and 100 ships. Two months after his return home, he sailed for Andros,[a] which had revolted from the Athenians, and with him were sent Aristokrates[b] and Adeimantos the son of Leukolophides, who had been chosen as generals to operate on land. [22] Alcibiades disembarked the army at Gaurion,[a] in the territory of the Andrians. They routed those Andrians who came out to oppose them, and they shut them up inside the city and killed a few of them as well as the Laconians[b] who were there. [23] Alcibiades then set up a trophy and, after remaining there for a few days, sailed for Samos, making this his base of operations for conducting the war.

1.4.17–20
407
ATHENS
Some Athenians blame Alcibiades. He defends himself before the Assembly and is granted supreme power over the other generals. He leads the procession on land to celebrate the Mysteries at Eleusis.

1.4.21–23
407
ANDROS
Alcibiades leads an expedition to Andros, lays siege to the city, and sails to Samos, his future base.

1.4.16a   The text here is difficult, and the sense is somewhat uncertain. I have accepted the manuscript reading as it stands. (John Marincola) For the Greek, see Translator's Notes.

1.4.17a   It is striking that the pro-Alcibiades arguments are given in much more detail than the anti-Alcibiades ones.

1.4.20a   Eleusis: Map 1.4.9. The celebration of the Eleusinian Mysteries included a procession from Athens to Eleusis. Since the occupation of Dekeleia by the Spartans in 414, the overland route was not considered safe. There is also some irony here, in that Alcibiades fled Athens after being accused of mocking or blaspheming the

Mystery ceremonies. See Appendix J, §9, and Figure 1.4.20.

1.4.21a   Andros: Map 1.4.9.

1.4.21b   Aristokrates helped Theramenes overthrow the Four Hundred, of which he had been a member. Elected general in 407 after the battle of Notion, he participated in the battle of Arginousai in 406 and was one of the generals who were executed.

1.4.22a   Gaurion: Map 1.4.9.

1.4.22b   By Laconians, Xenophon means Spartans and *perioikoi*.

FIGURE 1.4.20. THE SACRED WAY AT ELEUSIS, WHERE ALCIBIADES LED THE ATHENIANS TO CELEBRATE THE MYSTERIES IN 407.

[1] The Spartans, not much before this, had sent out Lysander[a] as the naval commander to replace Kratesippidas, whose term in command had expired. Lysander went first to Rhodos[b] and, taking ships from there, sailed for Cos[c] and Miletus,[d] and from there to Ephesus,[e] where he remained with seventy ships until Cyrus arrived at Sardis.[f] [2] When Cyrus arrived, Lysander went to meet him with the envoys from Sparta.[a] There Lysander spoke against Tissaphernes, revealing what he had done, and asked Cyrus to be as zealous as he could in prosecuting the war. [3] Cyrus said that his father had ordered him to do just that, that he himself was of the same opinion and was determined to do everything he could. He said that he had come with 500 talents, and if this was not enough, he would use his own funds, which his father had given to him. And if even these were insufficient, he would mint coins using the throne on which he sat—which was made entirely of silver and gold. [4] They praised him for speaking thus and asked him to provide for each sailor the pay of one Attic drachma[a] per day, informing him that if this was the wage, the crews of the Athenians would desert and he would thus spend less money.[b] [5] Though Cyrus praised their speech, he said it was not possible for him to do anything beyond what the King had ordered, and the treaty[a] stipulated that he give thirty minae[b] per month to each ship that the Spartans wished to maintain. [6] Lysander said nothing at that time, but after dinner, when Cyrus, while drinking to his health, asked Lysander what he could do to please him most, Lysander said, "You could add one obol to the pay for each sailor." [7] Because of this, the daily wage was now raised to four obols, from the previous three. Cyrus, in addition, paid the back pay of the sailors and advanced them a month's pay, with the result that they became much more enthusiastic.

[8] The Athenians, hearing of this, were discouraged and sent envoys to Cyrus through Tissaphernes. [9] But he would not receive them, even though Tissaphernes beseeched him. Tissaphernes said that the King should do exactly as he himself was doing, namely, see to it that no Greek state be allowed to become strong but, rather, that all should be kept weak by fighting among themselves (he had been persuaded by Alcibiades[a] to follow this course of action).

[10] Lysander, when he had drawn up his naval forces, beached the

1.5.1–7
407
RHODOS-SARDIS
Lysander takes command of the Peloponnesian fleet in place of Kratesippidas. Cyrus promises generous financial support and, for Lysander, increases the sailors' daily wage.

1.5.8–9
407
SARDIS
The Athenians try to see Cyrus, but he refuses them and Tissaphernes' advice.

1.5.10
407
EPHESUS
Lysander rests and repairs his fleet.

1.5.1a   This is Xenophon's first mention of Lysander. See Appendix M, §18.
1.5.1b   Rhodos: Map 1.5.13.
1.5.1c   Cos: Map 1.5.13.
1.5.1d   Miletus: Map 1.5.13.
1.5.1e   Ephesus: Map 1.5.13.
1.5.1f   Sardis: Map 1.5.13.
1.5.2a   Sparta: Map 1.5.13.
1.5.4a   The Attic drachma, which contained six obols, was the average wage of an ordinary worker at Athens. Normal pay for sailors who rowed the triremes was three obols per day. See Appendix I, §10, 13, and Appendix K, §8.
1.5.4b   Cyrus would spend less because the war would end sooner if the Athenian sailors

deserted in order to receive higher pay from the Spartans.
1.5.5a   Presumably the treaty or agreement made by the Spartan envoys in 407. See 1.4.2.
1.5.5b   Minae: a unit of weight and currency. One hundred drachmas equals 1 mina and 60 minae equals 1 talent. Since each trireme had a crew of 200, a daily wage of 3 obols (half a drachma) meant that half a talent was required to support a trireme at sea for two months. See Appendix I, §7–8, 13, and Appendix K, §2.
1.5.9a   For Alcibiades' advice to Tissaphernes, see Thucydides 8.46.1–5; and Appendix D, §4 and n. D.4b.

ninety ships that were at Ephesus, repairing them and drying them out,[a] but but did not initiate action.

[11] Alcibiades, hearing that Thrasyboulos had come out of the Hellespont[a] and was fortifying Phocaea,[b] sailed toward him, leaving behind Antiochos, his helmsman, in command of the ships and ordering him not to attack the fleet of Lysander. [12] Antiochos, with his own and one other ship, sailed out from Notion[a] into the harbor of the Ephesians, and he passed by the very prows of the ships of Lysander. [13] Lysander, launching at first a few of his ships, pursued Antiochos, but when the Athenians went to assist Antiochos with more triremes, Lysander then drew up his entire fleet in order and turned to the attack. After this the Athenians mobilized their remaining triremes from Notion, launching their ships one at a time as each got clear of land. [14] They then fought a sea battle, the Spartans in proper formation, the Athenians with their ships scattered, until the latter fled, having lost fifteen triremes. The majority of the men got away, though some were captured. Lysander, after taking up the ships and setting up a trophy at Notion, sailed to Ephesus, and the Athenians sailed to Samos.[a]

[15] After these events, Alcibiades arrived back at Samos and with all the ships set out for the port of the Ephesians, and he stationed them at the mouth of the harbor, waiting to see if anyone was willing to fight. When Lysander did not put out against him, because his ships were greatly inferior in number, Alcibiades sailed back to Samos. The Spartans, a little after this, took Delphinion[a] and Eion.[b]

[16] When the news of the sea battle was brought to the Athenians back home, they were angry with Alcibiades, because they thought the ships had been lost through negligence and lack of control on Alcibiades' part, and they elected a different group of ten as their generals: Konon, Diomedos, Leon, Pericles,[a] Erasinides, Aristokrates, Archestratos, Protomachos, Thrasyl-

---

1.5.10a   On the need to periodically dry out trireme hulls, see Appendix K, §2.

1.5.11a   Hellespont: Map 1.5.13.

1.5.11b   Phocaea: Map 1.5.13. There is a problem with this remark. Phocaea was in Spartan hands in 412 (Thucydides 8.31), and later in Book 1 the Spartans flee there after their defeat at the Arginousai Islands (see 1.6.33). This suggests that Phocaea at this time was not on Athens' side, and it is therefore curious that Thrasyboulos would be fortifying it. Some scholars have suggested that "fortifying" (*teichizein*) should be emended to "walling off" (*apoteichizein*) or "circumvallating" (*periteichizein*), either of which would suggest a hostile action appropriate against an enemy territory. (John Marincola) For the Greek, see Translator's Notes. Diodorus (Appendix O, 13.73) has Alcibiades sail to Klazomenai, while Plutarch (*Parallel Lives*, "Alcibi-

ades" 35.4) has him make for Caria.

1.5.12a   Notion: Map 1.5.13. Diodorus has a more extensive and quite different account of the ensuing battle at Notion. See Appendix O, 13.70–72.2. For the account of the Oxyrhynchus Historian, see Appendix P, Fragment 8.1–4. Some scholars try to reconcile these accounts: see the Introduction, §8.4.

1.5.14a   Samos: Map 1.5.13.

1.5.15a   Delphinion: Map 1.5.13.

1.5.15b   No site called Eion is known in Phocaea. There is a city called Eion at the mouth of the Strymon River in the north Aegean (Map 1.5.13). It is likely that the text here is corrupt, and Schneider, noting that Diodorus (Appendix O, 13.76) writes "Teïans" (citizens of Teos) here, emended "Eion" to "Teos." (John Marincola) Teos: Map 1.5.13.

1.5.16a   Pericles, the son of the great Pericles who led Athens into the war with Sparta.

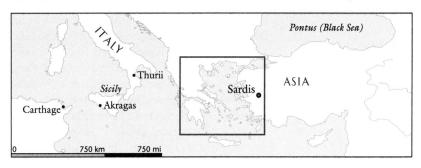

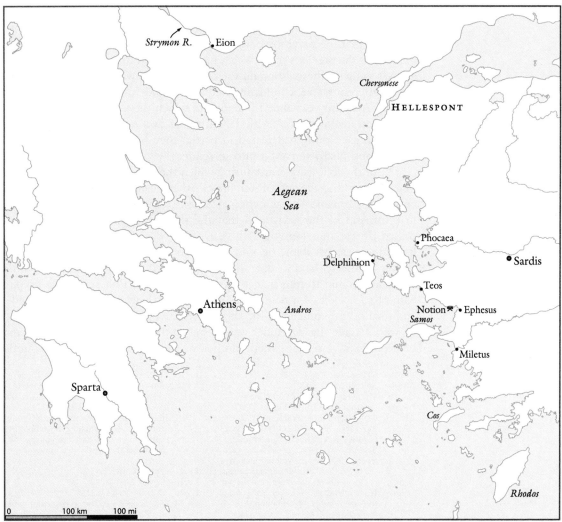

MAP 1.5.13

los, and Aristogenes. [17] Alcibiades was in disfavor even among the troops; taking a single trireme, he sailed off to the Chersonese,[a] to his own castle.

[18] After this Konon sailed from Andros[a] with the twenty ships he had there to command the fleet at Samos (for so the Athenians had voted). To replace Konon at Andros, they sent Phanosthenes, with four ships. [19] Phanosthenes happened upon two triremes from Thurii[a] and captured them, together with their crews. The Athenians put these men into prison, except for their commander Dorieus: he was a Rhodian by birth, but long before this he had been exiled from Athens and Rhodos; the Athenians had condemned him and all his family to death, and he was now a citizen of Thurii. But at this time the Athenians took pity on him, and they released him without even demanding a ransom. [20] When Konon came to Samos, he found that the naval force was despondent; he fitted out seventy triremes in place of the previous ones (which had numbered more than one hundred) and set sail with these, bringing the other generals with him and disembarking at different places, conducting raids and plundering the enemy's territory.

[21] And this year ended [the one in which the Carthaginians[a] made an expedition against Sicily[b] with 120 triremes and an army of 120,000 and took Akragas[c]: though defeated in battle, they besieged the city for seven months and finally starved it into surrender].[d]

[1] In the following year,[a] during which there was an eclipse of the moon one evening[b] and the ancient temple of Athena caught fire, [when Pityas was ephor at Sparta and Kallias archon at Athens,][c] the Spartans sent Kallikratidas in command of the navy, now that the time of Lysander's command had passed [it was the twenty-fourth year of the war]. [2] When Lysander was handing over the ships, he said to Kallikratidas that he was doing so as master of the sea and as one who had defeated the enemy in a sea battle. Kallikratidas said to him that if he should sail from Ephesus[a] while keeping Samos[b] to his left—for Samos was where the Athenian fleet was stationed— and turn over command of the ships after arriving at Miletus;[c] then, he said, he would agree that Lysander was master of the sea.[d] [3] Lysander said that he would not interfere when another was in command, and Kallikratidas

1.5.17a Chersonese: Map 1.5.13.
1.5.18a Andros: Map 1.5.13.
1.5.19a Thurii (in Italy): Map 1.5.13, locator.
1.5.21a Carthage: Map 1.5.13, locator.
1.5.21b Sicily: Map 1.5.13, locator.
1.5.21c Akragas (in Sicily): Map 1.5.13, locator.
1.5.21d For the Greek, see Translator's Notes.
1.5.21a Because the interpolater at 1.5.21 made an error in dating the year in which Akragas fell to the Carthaginians, and because of the significant difference between our Julian calendar's December year-end and the calendrical point Xenophon chose to mark the end of his year (there were many such points used in the ancient world), all the events cited in chapters 1.5.18–1.6.3 are correctly dated in *The Cambridge Ancient History* chronology as having taken place in the year 406.

1.6.1b This eclipse took place on April 15, 406.
1.6.1c For ephors and archons and the use of them for dating events, see n. 1.2.1a and Appendix C, §5–9. As explained there, though the year indicated here (406) is correct, the direct dating indications by ephor and archon have been interpolated. For the Greek, see Translator's Notes.
1.6.2a Ephesus: Map 1.6.22.
1.6.2b Samos: Map 1.6.22.
1.6.2c Miletus: Map 1.6.22.
1.6.2d See Appendix F, The Spartan Army (and the Battle of Leuctra), §13, which sheds light on the contention between the opportunistic and imperialist Lysander and the panhellenist Kallikratidas, who hated working with the Persians.

himself, in addition to the ships he took from Lysander, fitted out fifty more with men from Chios[a] and Rhodos,[b] and from the allies elsewhere. Bringing all these together—they were 140 in all—he prepared to meet the enemy.

[4] Kallikratidas soon learned, however, that he was being slandered by the friends of Lysander, who were not only doing their tasks without enthusiasm but were also spreading the report among the allies that the Spartans blundered most seriously by changing naval commanders, adding that because of this, unsuitable men were often in charge, men who were barely familiar with naval matters and who did not know[a] how to get the most out of their men; and that by sending commanders who were without experience of the sea and not known by the men serving, the Spartans were running the risk of suffering some calamity. Because of this, Kallikratidas called together the Spartans who were there and said to them the following: [5] "I am content to stay at home, and if Lysander or some other man wishes to claim to be more experienced in naval affairs, I for my part will not stand in his way. But since I was sent out by the city to command the ships, I am not able to do anything other than to carry out my orders in the best way that I can. What you can do is this: consider these issues of my ambition and the blame that is laid against Sparta, our city, and—since you know about these things as well as I do—tell me what seems best to you: should I remain here, or should I sail back home to report on the state of things here?"

[6] When no one dared to say anything other than that he should obey the commands from those at home and should do what he had been sent to do, Kallikratidas went to Cyrus and demanded money to pay the sailors. Cyrus said to wait for two days. [7] Kallikratidas, annoyed by the delay and angered by his unsuccessful visits to Cyrus, said that the Greeks were most wretched, since they flattered barbarians for the sake of money; and that if he got home safely, he would, to the extent he was able, attempt to reconcile Athenians and Spartans. He then sailed back to Miletus, [8] and from there sent triremes to Sparta[a] for money. Then, calling an assembly of the Milesians, he spoke as follows: "For me, men of Miletus, it is necessary to obey those at home. But I think it is appropriate that you be most avid in prosecuting the war, since you live among the barbarians and have already suffered the greatest evils from them. [9] You must show the rest of the allies the way that we can most swiftly and effectively harm the enemy, until the Spartans whom I sent for funds return to us, [10] since Lysander, before he departed, gave back to Cyrus the money already here as if it were extra. And Cyrus, when I went to him, kept postponing our conference, and I could not convince myself to be constantly hanging about his door. [11] I promise you that I will give you a worthy recompense for any services you render to us during the time that we await the funds from home. But with the gods' help, let us show the barbarians that even without attending on them we may take vengeance on our enemies."

1.6.4–5
406
EPHESUS
Lysander's friends complain that an experienced and competent commander was being replaced by one who lacked these qualities. Kallikratidas tells them that he and they must follow orders.

1.6.6–11
406
MILETUS
The critics are silenced. Cyrus puts off Kallikratidas when he requests funds. Angered by Cyrus' refusal and Lysander's designs, Kallikratidas asks Sparta to send funds, and meanwhile turns to the Milesians for support.

1.6.3a   Chios: Map 1.6.22.
1.6.3b   Rhodos: Map 1.6.22.

1.6.4a   For the Greek, see Translator's Notes.
1.6.8a   Sparta: Map 1.6.22.

1.6.12–18
406
LESBOS
The Milesians and Chians
contribute funds to
Kallikratidas. He sails to
Methymna and takes it,
dividing the booty among
his sailors and selling the
captured slaves and Athe-
nians. He then pursues
the Athenian fleet to
Mytilene, defeats it, and
besieges it there. Cyrus
sends money.

[12] When Kallikratidas had said these things, many arose, especially those who had been accused of opposing him, and were in fear, and proposed a grant of money, and they themselves even offered private contributions. He took this money and, after procuring from Chios a payment of five drachmas for each of the sailors, sailed to Methymna in Lesbos,[a] which was controlled by the enemy.[b] [13] The Methymnaians refused to go over to the Spartan side, since there was a garrison of Athenians[a] there and those in charge of affairs were pro-Athenian. So Kallikratidas made an assault against the city and took it by force. [14] Now the soldiers divided up all the movable property, but Kallikratidas gathered all the captives into the agora. The allies pressed him to sell even the Methymnaians, but he said that at least while he was commander, not one of the Hellenes would be enslaved if he had anything to do with it. [15] On the next day, he released the free-born, but he sold the Athenians who made up the garrison and all the prisoners who were slaves. To Konon he sent word that he would put an end to his illicit love affair with the sea.[a] And when Kallikratidas saw Konon putting out to sea at dawn, he set off in pursuit, trying to cut off his route to Samos to prevent him from fleeing there. [16] But Konon got away with his fastest sailing ships, since he had chosen from among the many ships of his fleet the best rowers for the few triremes he was taking with him, and he got away to Mytilene in Lesbos[a] and with him two of the ten generals, Leon and Erasinides. Kallikratidas sailed with Konon into the harbor, pursuing with his 170 ships. [17] Konon, as he got there first . . . prevented by the citizens . . . (?),[a] he was forced to fight near the harbor, and he lost thirty ships, although the men escaped to land. The rest of his ships, forty in number, he beached beneath the wall. [18] Kallikratidas, coming to anchor in the harbor, began to besiege the city, cutting off the way out to the sea. He sent by land for the entire force of the Methymnaians, and he disembarked his army from Chios. And now Cyrus sent him the money.

1.6.19–21
406
LESBOS
Konon is blockaded by
land and sea. To alert the
Athenians to his plight,
he sends out two triremes;
one to the Hellespont,
the other to the open sea.
The surprised enemy pur-
sues and captures the one
heading for the open sea.

[19] Konon found himself besieged by land and sea, with no place from which he could easily procure food; there were many men shut up in the city, and the Athenians at home did not send help because they knew nothing of what had happened. Konon, therefore, picked two of his best sailing

---

1.6.12a Methymna, Lesbos: Map 1.6.22. For a
         much less dramatic account (Diodorus') of
         Kallikratidas' assumption of his command,
         see Appendix O, §13.76.
1.6.13a Athens: Map 1.6.22.
1.6.15a The verb *moicheuō* used here means to
         have sexual relations with another man's
         wife. Kallikratidas is thus warning the
         Athenian that the sea rightly belongs to
         himself.
1.6.16a Mytilene, Lesbos: Map 1.6.22.
1.6.17a The text here seems to be corrupt, and
         certain emendations have been proposed.
         It is just possible that the received text
         means something like "As Konon was
         prevented beforehand [from beaching his
         ships?] by the citizens, he was forced. . . ."

But if this is so, it suggests that Mytilene
was no longer an ally of the Athenians. To
eliminate that discrepancy, the text must
then be emended to read "enemy"
(*polemiōn*) rather than "citizens" (*politōn*).
But even so, "prevented beforehand by the
enemy" is ambiguous, and it may be
preferable to suppose that something has
fallen out of the text. (John Marincola)
For the Greek, see Translator's Notes.
Diodorus seems to contradict Xenophon
here about whether there was one battle
near the harbor entrance or two (one just
outside, the second inside) on successive
days. Diodorus provides an interesting
account of this fighting at Mytilene; see
Appendix O, 13.77–79.7.

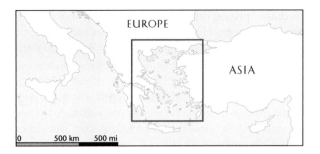

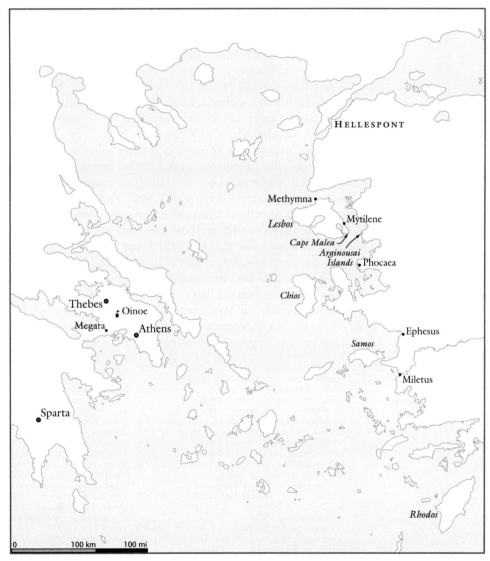

Map 1.6.22

ships and, before dawn, placed crews on them comprising the best rowers from all the ships of the fleet. He placed marines in the hold of the ships and spread the screens over each side.[a] [20] They remained like this for the day, but in the evening, when it was dark, he brought the crews ashore, so that the enemy would not know what they were doing. On the fifth day they put on a moderate supply of food, and when it was midday and those guarding them were careless (and some were even resting), they sailed out from the harbor; one ship headed for the Hellespont,[a] the other for the open sea. [21] Since the men in charge of the blockade happened to be taking their meal on land,[a] they all tried to put to sea as best they could to bring assistance, cutting their anchor lines and hurrying out[b] in disarray. Finally on board, they pursued the ship that had set out for the open sea, and at sunset they overtook it, defeated it in battle, and taking it in tow, brought it back with all its crew to their camp.

[22] But the ship making for the Hellespont got away and, arriving at Athens, informed the Athenians about the siege. In the meantime, Diomedon[a] had brought aid with twelve ships to the besieged Konon, anchoring in the strait of Mytilene. [23] Kallikratidas immediately sailed against him and took ten of his ships, but Diomedon got away with his own and one other ship. [24] When the Athenians learned of the events at Mytilene and the siege, they voted to bring help with 110 ships, manning them with everyone—both slave and free[a]—who was of age. The ships were manned and departed in thirty days. Even many of the Knights[b] went on board. [25] The ships made for Samos,[a] and from there they took ten Samian ships. They also collected other ships, more than thirty, from the rest of their allies, compelling all of them to serve on board, as well as any of their own ships that happened to be abroad. The total fleet they amassed numbered more than 150 ships.

[26] Kallikratidas, hearing that the relief force was already at Samos, left behind fifty of his ships at Mytilene, with Eteonikos as commander, and put to sea with 120. The Peloponnesians stopped for their meal[a] at Cape Malea on Lesbos[b] [which is opposite Mytilene]. [27] On the same day the Atheni-

1.6.22–25
406
ATHENS
The ship that sailed for the Hellespont brings word of the siege to Athens. The Athenians vote to prepare an emergency relief fleet that, with others collected from allies, totals 150 triremes.

1.6.26–28
406
CAPE MALEA, LESBOS
Learning of the approach of the relief fleet, Kallikratidas sails to meet it. He sees the Athenian fleet's campfires at night but cannot attack because of bad weather.

1.6.19a Marines: the ten hoplites that formed part of the normal crew of a trireme. By placing them in the hold, Konon might have lowered the center of gravity of the ship and thereby increased its speed, but also might have tried to fool the enemy, who would not see them and would assume that no trireme would leave in the enemy's presence without its hoplites to defend it. Side screens, which primarily protected the crew from enemy missiles, also hid the crewmen from enemy eyes. For trireme marines, see n. 1.1.28a and Appendix K, §2, 7.
1.6.20a Hellespont: Map 1.6.22.
1.6.21a It was not possible to prepare and serve meals to a crew of two hundred men on a trireme, so meals were normally taken on land. See Appendix K, §2, 7.
1.6.21b Reading Göller's *epeigomenoi* for the manu-

scripts' *epeiromenoi*. (John Marincola) For the Greek, see Translator's Notes.
1.6.22a Diomedon: Athenian general who defended Ionia after the disaster in Sicily. He took part in the battle of Arginousai in 406 and was among the generals executed at Athens.
1.6.24a Athens would use slaves in its military forces only in times of great emergency.
1.6.24b Knights were Athens' richest citizens, who could afford to maintain horses and serve in the cavalry. They normally did not serve in the fleet, so it is indicative of the severity of the crisis that Knights would now serve at sea. See Appendix A, §7.
1.6.25a Samos: Map 1.6.22.
1.6.26a For more on the feeding of ship's crews, see n. 1.6.21a and Appendix K, §7.
1.6.26b Cape Malea, Lesbos: Map 1.6.22.

ans happened to be taking their meal on the Arginousai Islands.[a] These are [opposite Cape Malea on Lesbos] across from Mytilene. [28] Kallikratidas saw their fires at night and was informed that they were the campfires of the Athenians. He tried to put to sea in the middle of the night so as to fall upon them unawares, but a heavy rain and lightning prevented this. When the rain let up, he sailed at dawn to the Arginousai Islands.

[29] The Athenians sailed out to meet him, with their left wing extended into the open sea. They were arranged as follows: Aristokrates, holding the left wing, commanded fifteen ships, and next to these was Diomedon with a further fifteen. Stationed behind Aristokrates was Pericles, and behind Diomedon was Erasinides. Next to Diomedon were the ten Samian ships in a single line (their commander was a Samian named Hippeus). Next to these were the ten ships of the taxiarchs,[a] also deployed in a single line. Behind these were the three ships of the naval commanders and whatever other allied ships there were. [30] Protomachos held the right wing with fifteen ships; next to him was Thrasyllos with another fifteen. Behind Protomachos was Lysias,[a] holding an equal number of ships, and behind Thrasyllos was Aristogenes. [31] They were so arranged in order to prevent the enemy from breaking their line, since the Athenian ships were in poor condition. Because the Lacedaemonian ships were in better condition, they were all arrayed against the enemy in a single line, prepared for either a breakthrough or encirclement maneuver.[a] Kallikratidas held the right wing. [32] Hermon of Megara,[a] the helmsman for Kallikratidas, said to him that it would be a good idea to sail away, for the triremes of the Athenians were much more numerous. But Kallikratidas replied that Sparta would conduct herself[b] no worse if he were to die, but it would be shameful to flee.[c]

[33] After this they fought, and the battle lasted a long time, first with the ships all crowded together, then with them scattered. When Kallikratidas' ship rammed another ship, he himself fell into the sea and disappeared and was not seen again; then the Athenian Protomachos and those

1.6.29–32
406
ARGINOUSAI ISLANDS
The two fleets engage. The Athenians take a formation that exploits their larger numbers and compensates for their lack of skill. The Peloponnesians attack in line, prepared for both encirclement and breakthrough maneuvers.

1.6.33
406
ARGINOUSAI ISLANDS
The battle of the Arginousai Islands. The Athenians are victorious.

1.6.27a   Arginousai Islands: Map 1.6.22. They lie between Lesbos and the mainland of Asia Minor.
1.6.29a   The Athenian citizen body was divided into ten tribes. Each tribe contributed one regiment to the armed forces, and each regiment was commanded by an officer called a taxiarch, so there were ten of them. See Appendix B, §7.
1.6.30a   It has been noted that Lysias wasn't one of the generals named at 1.5.16. With less certainty, it has been suggested that Leon, who was listed, isn't mentioned now, implying that he may have been on the other ship dispatched by Konon at 1.6.22 and was therefore captured. Lysias would then have been elected as a substitute for Leon.
1.6.31a   The breakthrough maneuver (*diekplous*) was accomplished by rowing between the

ships of the enemy line and then turning to ram the sterns or sides of the enemy's triremes. In the encirclement (*periplous*), one rowed around the end of the enemy's fleet and then turned to ram its ships' sides or sterns.
1.6.32a   Megara: Map 1.6.22.
1.6.32b   Reading Breitenbach's *oikesai* for the manuscripts' *oikeitai*. (John Marincola) For the Greek, see Translator's Notes.
1.6.32c   Contrast this attitude with that of Phrynichus, the Athenian commander who in 412 said that "he would never allow the reproach of disgrace to drive him into a risk that was unreasonable. It was no disgrace for an Athenian fleet to retreat, . . . it would be more disgraceful to be defeated, and to expose the city not only to disgrace but to . . . danger." (Thucydides 8.27.2)

with him on the right wing defeated the Lacedaemonian left, after which there was a general flight of the Spartans to Chios,[a] although most of them went to Phocaea.[b] The Athenians sailed back to the Arginousai Islands.

1.6.34–35
406
ARGINOUSAI ISLANDS
Losses on both sides are tallied. The Athenians have won a great victory but are unable to rescue the crews of their disabled ships because of a storm.

[34] The Athenians lost twenty-five ships together with their crews, except for a few who made their way to shore; the Spartans lost nine of the ten Spartan ships that were engaged, as well as sixty ships of their allies. [35] The Athenian generals decided that Theramenes and Thrasyboulos (who were trierarchs) and some of the taxiarchs should sail with forty-seven ships to help the disabled ships and their crews, while the other generals, with the rest of the fleet, should attack the enemy ships under Eteonikos, which were conducting the siege at Mytilene.[a] Although they wished to carry out these plans, the wind got up, and a great storm arose and prevented them. So they set up a trophy and camped there.

1.6.36–38
406
LESBOS-CHIOS
When Eteonikos learns of the Peloponnesian fleet's defeat, he quickly and quietly breaks the siege and sails off from Mytilene to Chios. The Athenians join with Konon and follow the enemy.

[36] A dispatch boat met Eteonikos and informed him of everything that had happened in the sea battle. He sent out the boat again, ordering those on board to keep silent and to tell no one what had happened but, rather, to sail back immediately to their own camp garlanded and crying out that Kallikratidas had won the sea battle and that the ships of the Athenians were destroyed, all of them. [37] This they did, and he himself, when those sailed back, made a sacrifice of thanksgiving for good news. He ordered the soldiers to take their meal and the traders to load their goods on board the merchant ships in silence and to sail to Chios (for the wind was favorable), and he ordered the triremes to sail likewise to Chios with all speed. [38] He burned the camp and then led the infantry to Methymna.[a] Meanwhile, Konon launched his ships (for the enemy had run off and the wind had become more favorable) and went to meet the Athenians who now arrived from the Arginousai Islands. He told them of Eteonikos' actions, so the Athenians sailed back to Mytilene and from there sailed out for Chios. They did not accomplish anything there, however, and sailed back to Samos.

1.7.1–2
406
ATHENS
The Athenian generals are accused of having abandoned the men in the wrecked triremes.

[1] The Athenians at home deposed all the generals except Konon, and in addition to Konon they chose Adeimantos and Philokles. [2] Of the generals who had fought in the sea battle, Protomachos and Aristogenes did not return to Athens, but the other six—Pericles, Diomedon, Lysias, Aristokrates, Thrasyllos, and Erasinides—sailed back. Archedamos, who at the time was the leader of the people in Athens and had charge of the two-obol allowance,[a] imposed a fine on Erasinides and accused him in court, claiming that he had funds from the Hellespont[b] that rightly belonged to the people; Archidamos made accusations as well about Erasinides' generalship. The court decided that Erasinides should be put

---

1.6.33a   Chios: Map 1.6.22.
1.6.33b   Phocaea: Map 1.6.22.
1.6.35a   Mytilene: Map 1.6.22.
1.6.38a   Methymna: Map 1.6.22.
1.7.2a   Reading Dindorf's *diobelias* for the

manuscripts' *diokelias*. (John Marincola)
The two-obol fund was intended to relieve wartime poverty and hardship.
See Appendix B, §8.
1.7.2b   Hellespont: Map 1.6.22.

in prison. [3] After this the generals spoke at length in the Council[a] about the battle and the magnitude of the storm. When Timokrates proposed that the rest of the generals should also be imprisoned and handed over to the people for trial, the Council imprisoned them. [4] Then there was a session of the Assembly in which some men, and Theramenes[a] especially, denounced the generals, saying that they should give some explanation as to why they did not rescue the shipwrecked men. To show that the generals blamed no one else, he displayed as evidence a letter that the generals had sent to the Council and the People in which they stated that nothing other than the storm was responsible. [5] After this, each of the generals defended himself briefly (for they were not permitted enough time for a proper speech in accordance with the law), narrating what had happened, namely, that they themselves sailed against the enemy and that they had entrusted the taking up of the shipwrecked to suitable men from among the trierarchs and those who had previously been generals, Theramenes and Thrasyboulos, and such others. [6] And if anyone had to be blamed in the matter of the failure to rescue the shipwrecked men, it should be none other than those to whom the task had been entrusted. "And yet simply because they accuse us," they said, "we will not falsely accuse them by saying that they are guilty but, rather, it was the magnitude of the storm that prevented the rescue of the shipwrecked." They furnished as witnesses of these facts the helmsmen and many others who had sailed with them. And their statements began to convince the people. [7] Many private citizens rose and said they were willing to offer themselves as sureties for the generals. But it was resolved that the matter be postponed to another assembly (for it was then late in the day and they would not be able to see the show of hands), and that in the meantime, the Council should prepare a measure for the Assembly as to how the men should be tried.[a]

[8] After this came the feast of the Apatouria, in which fathers and their relatives meet together. Now Theramenes and his followers suborned many men to wear black cloaks and have their hair shorn close[a] during the festival so that, when they went to the Assembly, it might appear that they were relatives of the men who had died; they also persuaded Kallixenos[b] to accuse the generals in the Council. [9] They then held an assembly in which the Council introduced its resolution, which had been proposed by Kallixenos as follows: "Since the Athenians have heard in the previous assembly both those accusing the generals and the generals' own defense of

1.7.3–6
406
ATHENS
The Athenian generals defend themselves, saying the storm was responsible, and refuse to condemn those who had been assigned to rescue the shipwrecked, saying that the storm prevented them from carrying out the task. Because it was late, the matter was postponed until the Council could prepare a trial procedure for the Assembly.

1.7.8–10
406
ATHENS
Theramenes and his followers wear black cloaks and cut their hair short. They persuade the Council and Assembly to vote immediately on whether or not the generals are guilty of failing to rescue their shipwrecked compatriots and to condemn them to death if found guilty.

1.7.3a   For a description of the roles of the Athenian Council and Assembly, see Appendix B, §5, 8.
1.7.4a   See "Theramenes" in Appendix M, §24. Xenophon's account, and the part played in it by Theramenes, should be compared with that of Diodorus (Appendix O, 13.101–103.2). Many scholars think that Theramenes' attack on the generals was not as unprovoked as Xenophon makes it seem: see Appendix A, especially §8.
1.7.7a   Normally at Athens the Council considered all matters first. Its resolution of the issue was then turned over to the Assembly for final deliberation. See Appendix B, §5. Diodorus' account of these proceedings (Appendix O, 13.101–103.2) is quite different from Xenophon's.
1.7.8a   Traditional indications of mourning.
1.7.8b   Nothing else is known of Kallixenos. The scholiast to Aristophanes' *Frogs* says that the two people responsible for this were Kallixenos and Diomedon of the deme Cholargos.

themselves, they should now all vote according to tribes;[a] for each tribe two urns should be set up, and a herald should announce to each that those who thought the generals were guilty of not rescuing the victors in the sea battle should place their ballot in the first urn, and those who thought they were not guilty should place theirs in the second urn; [10] and if they are judged to be guilty, they should be sentenced to death and handed over to the Eleven,[a] and their property should be confiscated, and a tenth should be given over to the goddess."[b]

1.7.11–15
406
ATHENS
Those who try to defend the generals are shouted down by the crowd, determined that the people should have their way. Of the presiding committee, only Socrates objects to putting the matter to a vote.

[11] Then someone stood up in the Assembly and claimed that after the sea battle, he had been saved by clinging to a grain barrel, and that those who were drowning commanded him, if he should be saved, to make known to the Athenian people that the generals failed to rescue those men who had fought bravely on behalf of their country. [12] Euryptolemos the son of Peisanax and some others served a summons against Kallixenos, claiming that he had written an illegal proposal. While some citizens praised this action, the multitude shouted out that it was a terrible thing if someone prevented the people from doing whatever they wished. [13] And when, on the strength of these shouts, Lykiskos said that the ones who served the summons should themselves be judged by the same vote as the generals unless they withdrew it, the mob again shouted so furiously that those men were forced to withdraw their summonses. [14] Then, when some of the presiding committee[a] refused to allow the motion to come to a vote on the grounds that it was contrary to the law, Kallixenos again mounted the platform and accused them on the same charge as he had Euryptolemos. And the crowd shouted to him to serve a summons against the presiding committeemen who had refused to allow a vote. [15] This so frightened the presiding committee that they now agreed to put the matter to a vote, all of them except one—Socrates son of Sophroniskos, who said he would do nothing except in accordance with the law.[a]

1.7.16–19
406
ATHENS
Euryptolemos speaks to the Assembly, asking that each of the accused generals be granted one more day to prepare his own defense.

[16] After this, Euryptolemos mounted the platform and spoke the following words on behalf of the generals:[a] "I have come up here, men of Athens, to make some accusations against Pericles, although he is my relation, and against Diomedon, although he is my friend, but also to defend them in some matters, and at the same time to give my advice about what seems best to me for the entire city. [17] Now, then, I accuse these two because they changed the minds of their fellow generals who had wanted to write a letter to the Council and to you, the people, stating that they had

1.7.9a   All Athenian citizens were members of one of ten tribes.
1.7.10a   The "Eleven" took custody of condemned prisoners and carried out executions.
1.7.10b   The goddess, of course, was Athena, Athens' titular deity.
1.7.14a   Presiding committee: a committee of the Council that ran the meetings of the Assembly. See Appendix A, §3.
1.7.15a   For other versions of Socrates' role here,

see Plato, *Apology* 32b, and Xenophon, *Memorabilia* 1.1.18, 4.4.2. See also Appendix A, §7–9, and the Introduction, §4.7.
1.7.16a   For a discussion of Euryptolemos' speech, see Appendix A, §10–11.

ordered Theramenes and Thrasyboulos to rescue the shipwrecks with forty-seven triremes, but that these two did not take them up. [18] So now are they to be blamed in the same way as those who failed to do their individual duty, and in place of their generosity then, are they now to be intrigued against by others and to run the risk of being destroyed? [19] That will not occur if you are persuaded by me to do what is just and lawful, and if you will learn well the truth and not, changing your minds later, find out that you have erred most severely against the gods and yourselves. I advise you in those matters to follow a course whereby you cannot be deceived—either by me or by anyone else—and whereby, with full knowledge of the facts, you may punish the wrongdoers (either all together or each one separately), by any penalty you wish to inflict: namely, to give them at least one day, if not more, for them to make their defense, not trusting in any others but yourselves.

[20] "For all of you, men of Athens, know that the decree of Kannonos is very harsh: it orders that if anyone should harm the people of Athens, he should make his defense in chains in front of the people, and if he is adjudged guilty, he is to be executed by being thrown into the pit, and his property is to be confiscated and a tenth dedicated to the goddess. [21] It is by this decree that I urge you to judge the generals, and by god if you so decide, my kinsman Pericles will go first. For I would think it shameful for me to place more value on him than on the whole city. [22] Or, if you wish, judge them according to the law that is set up for sacrilegious people and traitors, which states that if someone betrays the city or steals sacred property, he is to be judged in court, and if he is found guilty, his property is to be confiscated and he is not to be buried in Attica.[a] [23] By whichever of these laws you choose, men of Athens, let these men be judged, each one individually,[a] with the day for each divided into three parts, one in which you will gather together and vote [whether or not they are innocent or guilty], one for the prosecution, and one for the defense. [24] If things are done in this way, the guilty will pay the greatest penalty, and the innocent will be set free by you, men of Athens, and they will not be unjustly[a] destroyed. [25] You will judge them with reverence for the law and in keeping with your oaths and you will not be fighting on the same side as the Spartans by destroying these men, who captured seventy ships and were victorious in battle, without a trial, and contrary to the law.

1.7.22a   Attica: Map 1.2.10, inset. Euryptolemos doesn't say it, but if found guilty under this law, the traitor is certainly executed also.
1.7.23a   Individual trials, before a court or in some cases by the Assembly, were the norm at Athens, so Kallixenos' proposal for a decision on all the generals by one vote without hearing them further was contrary to accepted standards; but it

was probably not ruled out by a specific law in the fifth century. Some scholars think that the Decree of Kannonos referred to at 1.7.20 itself provided for individual trials, but even if it did, it probably did not actually outlaw collective verdicts.
1.7.24a   Reading Leonclavius' *adikōs* for the manuscripts' *adikountes*. (John Marincola) For the Greek, see Translator's Notes.

Euryptolemos entreats the Athenians to stand by their laws and recapitulates the events, arguing that what the generals planned for the rescue was competent and that the facts of the storm are not in dispute. He points out the absurdity of trying one of the generals who himself was rescued from a sinking ship and therefore could not bear responsibility for the failure to rescue others.

[26] "For what is it that you fear that leads you to act in such haste? Is it that you fear you might not be able to punish or acquit someone as you wish if you judge according to the law, but that you would be able to do so if you act contrary to the law? That is precisely the way that Kallixenos persuaded the Council to introduce the decree about the single vote to the Assembly. [27] But then perhaps if you execute an innocent man, you will regret it later. And consider how painful and injurious regret is, even more so when you have been mistaken in a case where a man's life is at stake.[a] [28] You gave to Aristarchos, who previously tried to destroy the democracy and then betrayed Oinoe to the Thebans your enemies,[a] a day to defend himself in whatever manner he wished, and you did everything else in his trial according to the law: you would be doing a terrible injustice if you deprived these generals—who did everything for you in accordance with your order and who conquered the enemy—of these same privileges with which to defend themselves. [29] Do not do this, men of Athens. Observe your laws, through which especially you have become great, and do not attempt to do anything contrary to them. Consider again the events themselves in which the failings of the generals are supposed to have occurred. For when they had won the battle and were sailing to land, Diomedon ordered all of them to put out to sea in column and to take up the shipwrecked men and boats, but Erasinides said they should all sail as swiftly as they could against the enemy who were at Mytilene.[a] Thrasyllos said they could do both if they left some ships there and went against the enemy with the rest. [30] If this were approved, he said that each of the eight generals should leave behind three ships from his company, and these, together with the ten ships of the taxiarchs, the ten ships of the Samians, and the three of the commanders would total forty-seven ships, four for each of the twelve ships that had been disabled.[a]

[31] "Among the trierarchs left behind were Thrasyboulos and Theramenes, the latter being the same one who in the previous assembly accused the generals.[a] And the other generals with the rest of the ships sailed against the enemy. What in all this was done inappropriately or badly? Is it not right that just as those who were ordered to go against the enemy should give an account if they failed to accomplish this, so those who did not follow the

---

1.7.27a   There are several difficulties in the Greek here, but I accept the emendations proposed by Hatzfeld. (John Marincola) For the Greek, see Translator's Notes.
1.7.28a   Oinoe (Attica) and Thebes: Map 1.6.22. Euryptolemos refers here to an infamous betrayal by an Athenian of an Athenian fortress on the frontier with Thebes, which is described in Thucydides 8.98.
1.7.29a   Mytilene: Map 1.6.22.
1.7.30a   Xenophon said in 1.6.34 that twenty-five Athenian ships had been lost. Even if the number were twelve, the number of men lost would have been above two thou-

sand, which would have been a substantial number of casualties for Athens, and we might recall that wealthy and influential men served in the ships of this fleet. Diodorus (Appendix O, 13.100.3) agrees with the figure of twenty-five. Xenophon could be showing that Euryptolemos, though generally in the right, stretched his case in places. Alternatively, perhaps the crews of thirteen of the ships were rescued during the battle, though if so, it is strange that we don't hear more about it.
1.7.31a   Theramenes made this accusation at 1.7.4.

generals' orders to rescue the shipwrecked should be put on trial, since they did not carry out these orders? [32] I can say so much for both, that the storm prevented them from doing anything the generals ordered. There are witnesses to this, those rescued by chance, including one of your generals, who was saved from a sinking ship and who himself needed rescuing—and yet he is among those whom the accusers now order to be judged by the same vote as those who did not do what they had been ordered.

[33] "Do not, men of Athens, in the face of victory and good fortune, act as if you had been defeated and met with disaster; and do not be cruel in condemning these men for treason instead of recognizing their helplessness when confronted by what were acts of god. These were men who could not carry out their orders because of the storm. It would be more just to crown these men as victors with garlands than to punish them with death because you have been persuaded by wicked men."

[34] When he finished speaking, Euryptolemos made a motion in accordance with the decree of Kannonos that the men should be judged separately. (The motion of the Council was that all should be judged together.) When these motions were put to a vote, they at first decided for the motion of Euryptolemos. Menekles made an objection on oath,[a] and when they voted for a second time, they chose the motion of the Council. After this they found the eight generals who took part in the sea battle guilty. The generals who were present, six in number, were put to death.[b]

[35] Not much later the Athenians had a change of heart, and they voted that those who had deceived the people should have complaints lodged against them and should give sureties until they could stand trial, and that Kallixenos should be one of these men. Four others were indicted and were held in confinement by those who had given sureties for them. Later, during the civil strife in which Kleophon[a] was killed, these men escaped before being brought to trial. Kallixenos returned to Athens when the men of the Peiraieus came back to the city,[b] but he was hated by all and died of starvation.

1.7.33
406
ATHENS
Euryptolemos finishes his defense of the generals.

1.7.34
406
ATHENS
The motion to judge the men separately is voted down. Instead the generals are immediately found guilty and executed.

1.7.35
406
ATHENS
The Athenians repent their decision and lodge complaints against "those who had deceived the people."

1.7.34a   The nature of Menekles' objection is unclear. One view is that he was impugning the legality of Euryptolemos' proposal. Under the law, it seems that such an objection should have suspended the consideration of the matter before the Assembly, but Xenophon's narrative does not convey that impression. Hence, it has been suggested that Menekles complained that the presiding committee had falsely reported the vote, that a second vote was necessary.

1.7.34b   They were possibly executed by drinking the poison hemlock, but we cannot be sure. See Appendix B, §11.

1.7.35a   Kleophon was a leader of the "popular" (democratic as opposed to oligarchical) party. A prominent politician, he was executed in 404, not long after the battle of Aigospotamoi and while Theramenes was negotiating with the Spartans (Lysias 13.12). For Lysias, see Appendix B, §17 and Ancient Sources.

1.7.35b   In the autumn of 403, when, following the overthrow of the Thirty a few months earlier, the democracy was restored. See 2.4.39–43.

BOOK TWO

For as long as it was summer, the soldiers who were with Eteonikos[a] at Chios[b] subsisted on the produce of the land and by working the land for a price. But when winter came and they had no food and they were in addition poorly clad and barefoot, they joined together and plotted to attack the city of Chios. They agreed that those among them who found this plan appealing should carry a reed so that they might know how many they were. [2] When Eteonikos learned of the plan, he was uncertain what to do because of the large number of men he saw carrying reeds. He thought it would be dangerous to try to stop them openly, fearing they might react hastily, take up arms, and capture the city. And once they had gained the upper hand in this way, they would become hostile to the Spartans and would ruin all his plans. On the other hand, it would clearly be terrible if in attempting to thwart them, he had to kill many men who were allies. If he did that, he would ensure that Sparta[a] would get a bad reputation among the other Greeks and many of his soldiers would become disaffected. [3] So he took fifteen men with him, each of them armed with daggers, and went through the city. There they came upon a man with an eye disease just coming out from a visit to his doctor. Since the man was holding a reed, Eteonikos killed him. [4] A commotion arose, and people asked why he had killed the man, and Eteonikos replied that it was because he was carrying the reed. When this response became known, every man who had been holding a reed got rid of it, fearing the consequences of being seen holding one.

[5] After this, Eteonikos called together the Chians and ordered them to contribute money with which he could pay the soldiers so that they would not continue to form conspiracies. The Chians did as he requested. Eteonikos at the same time commanded the men to board their ships; going in turn to each ship, he fervently encouraged and exhorted the men, and, acting as if he knew nothing of the conspiracy, gave each of them a

2.1.1–4
406
CHIOS
Eteonikos cleverly thwarts a dangerous plot among his hungry men to capture the city of Chios.

2.1.5
406
CHIOS
Eteonikos pays his men with money demanded from and given by the Chians.

2.1.1a   Eteonikos: see 1.6.36ff.
2.1.1b   Chios: Map 2.1.16, BY.

2.1.2a   Sparta: Map 2.1.16, BX.

2.1.6–7
406
EPHESUS
Sparta's allies send envoys
to Sparta to ask that
Lysander be reappointed.
Cyrus makes the same
request. Lysander is sent
as vice-admiral.

2.1.8–9
406
SARDIS*
Cyrus executes two of
Darius' nephews.

2.1.10–12
405
EPHESUS-SARDIS
Lysander takes command
and receives money from
Cyrus with which to pay
the sailors.

month's pay. [6] After this, the Chians and the rest of the allies gathered together at Ephesus[a] and discussed the events that had transpired, and they decided to send ambassadors to Sparta to report on the situation and to demand that Lysander be reappointed to command the fleet, since he enjoyed a good reputation among the allies because of his earlier command when he won the sea battle at Notion.[b] [7] The ambassadors were sent, and with them also went messengers from Cyrus, who made the same request. The Spartans dispatched Lysander as vice-admiral and Arakos as admiral, for it was their law that no one could be admiral more than once; but in fact they gave command over the ships to Lysander [and these events occurred when twenty-five years of the war had elapsed].

[8] In this year, Cyrus executed Autoboisakes and Mitraios, sons of the sister of Dareiaios [who was the daughter of Xerxes, Darius' father],[a] because when they met with him, they did not thrust their arms into their *korē*. Now, this is a mark of respect that Persians make only for the King; the *korē* is longer than a regular sleeve, and when one's hands are thrust into it, they are thereby rendered harmless.[b] [9] Hieramenes and his wife then said to Dareiaios that it would be terrible for him to ignore the excessive haughtiness of Cyrus. So Dareiaios, pretending that he was ill, sent messengers to bring Cyrus to him.

[10] In the following year [when Archytas was ephor at Sparta and Alexios was archon at Athens],[a] Lysander arrived in Ephesus and sent for Eteonikos in Chios with his fleet. He gathered together all the rest of the ships, no matter where they were at the time, and while they were being repaired, he ordered other ships to be built in Antandros.[b] [11] He went to Cyrus to ask for money, but Cyrus told him that all the money from the King had been spent—indeed much more than the King had given; he also indicated to him what had been provided to each of the previous Spartan admirals. In spite of this, Cyrus gave the money to Lysander. [12] He took the funds, established commanders for the triremes, and paid the soldiers their back pay.

Meanwhile, at Samos,[a] the generals of the Athenians were also preparing their navy for battle.

2.1.6a   Ephesus: Map 2.1.16, BY.
2.1.6b   Notion: Map 2.1.16, BY. On the battle, see 1.5.11–14.
2.1.8*   Sardis: Map 2.1.16, locator and inset.
2.1.8a   Two things are unusual about this passage: (1) Darius' father was Artaxerxes, not Xerxes; and (2) in this section (and only here) we find the form of Darius' name, Dareiaios, that is used by the historian Ktesias in his narrative. It is additionally odd that the form Dareiaios should be found in the same text with the more commonly used Dareios. Some scholars think that all of sections 8 and 9 is spurious.
2.1.8b   Rendered harmless in the sense that they

cannot hold or reach for weapons.
2.1.10a   For ephors, archons, and the use of them for dating events, see n. 1.2.1a and Appendix C, Chronological Problems in the Continuation (1.1.1–2.3.10) of Xenophon's *Hellenika*, §5–9. As explained there, though the year indicated here (405) is correct, the direct dating indications by ephor and archon have been interpolated.
2.1.10b   Antandros: Map 2.1.16, AY.
2.1.12a   Samos: Map 2.1.16, BY.

[13] Then Cyrus sent for Lysander because a messenger had come from his father, saying that his father was sick and was summoning him to his side; he was currently at Thamneria, in Media near where the Kadousians[a] live. (His father had marched against these Kadousians because they were in revolt.) [14] When Lysander arrived, Cyrus forbade him to fight a battle against the Athenians until he had many more ships at his disposal. He pointed out that since he and his father both had a great deal of money, they could use it to outfit many more ships. He assigned to Lysander all the tribute from the cities which was considered his personal property,[a] and he gave him in addition surplus money from his treasury. Reminding him that he was a friend of both the city of Sparta and Lysander personally, Cyrus then departed on his journey inland to see his father.[b]

[15] After Cyrus had given Lysander all his funds and had been summoned and had gone to see his father, Lysander distributed the pay to the army and set sail for the Kerameios Gulf[a] in Caria.[b] Once there, he made an assault against the town of Kedreai,[c] which was an ally of the Athenians, and on the second day's assault he captured the town by force and enslaved its inhabitants, who are a people of mixed heritage, part Greek and part non-Greek. From there, Lysander sailed on to Rhodos.[d]

[16] The Athenians, using Samos as their base, raided the King's territory and then sailed against Chios and Ephesus, preparing for a sea battle. They chose as generals Menandros, Tydeus, and Kephisodotos in addition to the ones they already had.

[17] Lysander sailed from Rhodos along the coast of Ionia[a] to the Hellespont,[b] to keep watch over the merchant boats sailing out of the Hellespont and to be near those cities that had revolted from the Spartan alliance. The Athenians, for their part, sailed to Chios, but they kept to the open sea as they sailed by Chios, since the mainland of Asia[c] was now hostile to them. [18] Lysander sailed along the coast from Abydos[a] and headed for Lampsacus,[b] a city then allied with the Athenians. He found the people of Abydos and other cities there with their land forces; their leader was Thorax, a Spartan. [19] They attacked Lampsacus and captured it by force, and the soldiers plundered the city, which was rich

2.1.13–14
405
SARDIS
Cyrus gives Lysander money and instructs him to avoid battle until he can man many more ships. He leaves to join his father in Media.

2.1.15
405
KEDREAI
Lysander assaults Kedreai and captures it, enslaving the inhabitants.

2.1.16
SAMOS
405
The Athenians raid Persian territory, choose new generals, and sail toward the enemy, preparing for battle.

2.1.17–21
405
HELLESPONT
Lysander attacks and captures Lampsacus, which is plundered. The Athenians arrive at the Hellespont shortly afterward and camp at Aigospotamoi, opposite the enemy fleet at Lampsacus.

2.1.13a Thamneria, Media: location unknown. Kadousians (Kadousioi), location of territory: Map 2.1.16, locator.
2.1.14a The tribute that Cyrus assigned to Lysander was that portion of the revenue received from the cities under his control that was allocated to him personally and thus considered his personal property. Presumably, the rest of the revenue from those cities belonged to the government and was designated to cover administrative expenses.
2.1.14b For more on Cyrus the Younger, see Appendix M, Brief Biographies of Important Characters in Xenophon's *Hellenika*, §7, the Introduction, §4.2,

and Appendix D, Persia in Xenophon's *Hellenika*, §3–5, 8–9.
2.1.15a Kerameios Gulf: Map 2.1.16, BY.
2.1.15b Caria: Map 2.1.16, BY.
2.1.15c Kedreai: Map 2.1.16, BY.
2.1.15d Rhodos: Map 2.1.16, BY.
2.1.17a Ionia: Map 2.1.16, BY.
2.1.17b Hellespont: Map 2.1.16, inset.
2.1.17c Asia (Asia Minor): Map 2.1.16, AY. They sailed through the open sea rather than along the nearby coast, which was a much more normal and convenient course for triremes. See Appendix K, Trireme Warfare in Xenophon's *Hellenika*, §5.
2.1.18a Abydos: Map 2.1.16, inset.
2.1.18b Lampsacus: Map 2.1.16, inset.

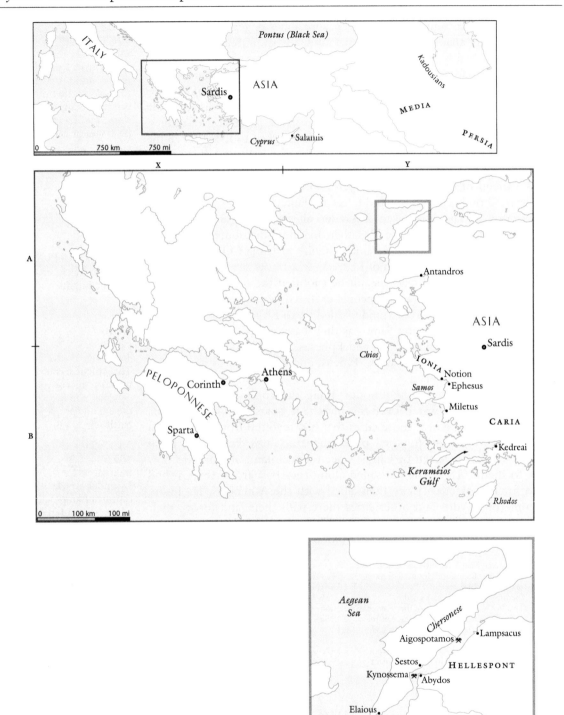

MAP 2.1.16

with wine and grain and full of all the other necessities. Lysander released those inhabitants taken captive who were freeborn. [20] Now the Athenians, who had been sailing on the heels of the Spartans, anchored at Elaious[a] in the Chersonese[b] with 180 ships. While the soldiers were taking their morning meal, they learned of the fall of Lampsacus, and they immediately sailed to Sestos.[c] [21] There they loaded provisions on board and sailed for Aigospotamoi,[a] opposite Lampsacus, where they took their evening meal. At Aigospotamoi, the Hellespont is about fifteen stades[b] wide.

[22] Night came, and just before dawn Lysander signaled to his men to take their morning meal and go on board the ships. He prepared everything for a sea battle and had the screens placed on the ships,[a] and then directed his men neither to move from their arrangement nor to put out to sea. [23] The Athenians also, when the sun was rising, arranged their ships in line in front of the harbor to offer battle. But when Lysander did not sail out against them and the hour grew late, they sailed back to Aigospotamoi. [24] Lysander ordered his swiftest ships to follow the Athenians, to watch what they did when they disembarked, and to report back to him. He did not, however, allow his own sailors to disembark until these ships returned. He repeated this procedure for four days, and each day the Athenians put out against him, offering battle, which he refused.

[25] Alcibiades had been watching all this maneuvering from his castle,[a] and he saw that when the Athenians were at anchor on the shore they were not near a city, and so they had to go for their supplies to Sestos, which was fifteen stades[b] distant from the ships; while on the other side the enemy was in the harbor of the city of Lampsacus and had everything it needed. He went down and told the Athenians that they were not anchored in a good place and urged them to move their camp to Sestos, where there was a harbor and a city. "For if you are there," he said, "you can fight a sea battle at any time of your own choosing." [26] But the Athenian generals, especially Tydeus and Menandros, ordered him to depart, for they said that they were now generals, not he. So he left.[a]

2.1.22–24
405
AIGOSPOTAMOI
For four days the Athenians offer battle, but Lysander refuses to engage.

2.1.25–26
405
AIGOSPOTAMOI
Alcibiades points out the disadvantages of the Athenian camp's location but is told to go away.

2.1.20a   Elaious: Map 2.1.16, inset.
2.1.20b   Chersonese: Map 2.1.16, inset.
2.1.20c   Sestos: Map 2.1.16, inset.
2.1.21a   Aigospotamoi (Aigospotamos): Map 2.1.16, inset. Aigospotamos means "goat's river."
2.1.21b   If Xenophon meant 15 Attic stades, which were 583 feet long, that distance is more than one and a half miles. In fact, the Hellespont is wider than 15 stades at all locations that modern scholars have proposed for the beach where the Athenian fleet was drawn up.
2.1.22a   These were temporary screens set up along the bulwarks in preparation for battle, to serve as protection against missiles. Screens of this type on triremes

were mentioned in 1.6.19. See Appendix K, §5.
2.1.25a   The location of Alcibiades' castle is not known, but it was obviously nearby.
2.1.25b   Fifteen Attic stades of 583 feet would be a distance of a little more than one and a half miles. However, the true distance between Sestos and Aigospotamoi (Aigospotamos) is a good deal greater than that; scholars have proposed various explanations for the error.
2.1.26a   Diodorus' account of the exchange between Alcibiades and the Athenian generals is different and interesting; see Appendix O, Selections from the *Histories* of Diodorus Siculus Relevant to Xenophon's *Hellenika*, 13.105.3–4.

[27] But Lysander, when it was now the fifth day and the Athenians sailed out against him and returned as before, ordered those assigned to follow them that whenever they should see that the Athenians had disembarked and were scattered throughout the Chersonese—and this they were doing much more each day, for they had to get their food from afar, and they had grown contemptuous of Lysander, since he consistently refused to do battle with them—they should sail back toward the Spartan fleet and raise a shield as a signal to him when they were in the middle of their return journey. And they did as they had been ordered.

[28] Lysander, when he saw the signal, immediately ordered his fleet to row toward the Athenians at full speed. Thorax, in command of the foot soldiers, went along with him. The Athenian general Konon, aware that Lysander's forces were approaching, signaled to all the other Athenians to get on board their ships and prepare for action as quickly as possible. But because the men were scattered, they only managed to fill some of the ships with two banks of rowers instead of three, and some indeed with only one, while others were completely without rowers. Konon's ship and seven others put to sea with him with their full complement of rowers (and also with its full complement was the *Paralos*[a]), but Lysander captured all the rest of the Athenian fleet on the shore. He also took prisoner the majority of the enemy soldiers on land, although some managed to flee into small fortresses in the area.[b]

[29] Konon, now in flight with the nine ships, realized that the entire Athenian cause was lost and put in at Abarnis,[a] a headland of Lampsacus, and there captured the main sails of Lysander's ships.[b] Then he himself with eight ships sailed to Euagoras in Cyprus,[c] while the *Paralos* went to Athens[d] to announce what had happened.

[30] Lysander brought everything he had captured, all the ships and the prisoners, including the generals, especially Philokles and Adeimantos, to Lampsacus. On the very day he accomplished these things, he sent Theopompos, a Milesian[a] pirate, to Sparta[b] to announce the news of what had happened, which he did, arriving there two days later.

2.1.28a	The *Paralos* was a special Athenian state trireme used on sacred embassies and other public or official missions.	2.1.29c	Euagoras was the ruler of the city of Salamis on Cyprus (Map 2.1.16, locator). For many years he was independent of Persian power and, as a friend of Athens, gave refuge to Athenian émigrés, especially Konon. After ten years of battling the Persians, he was finally defeated by them in 381 or 380 and given not ungenerous terms. He was assassinated in a palace intrigue in 374.
2.1.28b	For Diodorus' account of the fighting at Aigospotamoi (Aigospotamos), see Appendix O, 13.105–106.1–6.		
2.1.29a	Abarnis: precise location of this promontory unknown.		
2.1.29b	By capturing the sails of Lysander's fleet, Konon reduced their ability to pursue him. The sails were left on shore with other tackle so as to lighten the triremes and make them faster and more maneuverable in battle. See Appendix K, §5.	2.1.29d	Athens: Map 2.1.16, BX.
		2.1.30a	Miletus: Map 2.1.16, BY.
		2.1.30b	Sparta: Map 2.1.16, BX.

[31] After this, Lysander gathered the allies together and told them to consult about the fate of the prisoners. In that discussion, many accusations were made against the Athenians, both the many deeds they had already done that were contrary to custom and law, and the many resolutions they had passed in their Assembly concerning how they would treat their enemies if they had won the battle—in particular, the vote to cut off the right hands of those they captured. It was also noted that the Athenians, when they had captured a Corinthian[a] and an Andrian[b] trireme, had thrown all the men on those ships overboard. (Philokles was the Athenian general who had sent these men to their deaths.) [32] Many other accusations were made against the Athenians, and it was finally decided to kill all those of the prisoners who were Athenians, with the exception of Adeimantos, who alone had attacked the decree in the Assembly about the cutting off of hands. He was, however, charged by some with betraying the ships.[a] Philokles, who had thrown overboard the Corinthians and the Andrians, was first asked by Lysander what he thought he deserved for having begun uncustomary and illegal actions against the Greeks, and then had his throat cut.[b]

[1] When Lysander had organized affairs in Lampsacus,[a] he then sailed for Byzantium[b] and Chalcedon.[c] The people there opened their gates to him, allowing their Athenian guards to depart under the terms of a formal truce. Those Byzantines who had betrayed their city to Alcibiades[d] fled at that time to the Black Sea,[e] and from there they later went to Athens[f] and were granted Athenian citizenship. [2] Lysander dispatched the Athenian garrison to Athens, and he did the same for any Athenians he found elsewhere, giving them all a safe-conduct to sail there but not to any other place. He did this knowing that the more people who were gathered into the city of Athens and Peiraieus,[a] the sooner they would suffer from a general lack of provisions there. Leaving behind Sthenelaos, a Spartan, as harmost[b] of Byzantium and Chalcedon, he himself sailed to Lampsacus and began to repair his ships.

[3] The *Paralos* arrived at Athens[a] during the night, bringing news of the disaster at Aigospotamoi,[b] and a cry arose in the Peiraieus and ran up

The Spartans and their allies decide to execute the Athenian prisoners as punishment for their crimes at sea and for the cruel resolutions they passed in the Assembly concerning the treatment of prisoners.

2.2.1–2
405
HELLESPONT
Lysander is admitted to Byzantium and Chalcedon. Intending to soon blockade Athens, he sends all Athenians back to their city to aggravate its future lack of provisions.

2.2.3–4
405
ATHENS
The *Paralos* brings the news of Aigospotamoi to Athens. There is much grief for the losses and fear for the future. The Athenians vote to prepare the city for a siege.

2.1.31a Corinth: Map 2.2.5, BX.
2.1.31b Andros: Map 2.2.5, BX.
2.1.32a Demosthenes (19.191) reports that when Konon returned to Athens, he accused Adeimantos of treason.
2.1.32b Plutarch, in his *Parallel Lives* ("Lysander" 13.1–2, "Alcibiades" 37.4), says that the number of Athenians killed was three thousand. Pausanias (9.32.9), a second-century C.E. travel writer who wrote detailed descriptions of many places in Greece, writes that their number was four thousand. But some scholars have doubted that this mass execution ever occurred.

2.2.1a Lampsacus: Map 2.2.5, AY.
2.2.1b Byzantium: Map 2.2.5, AY.
2.2.1c Chalcedon: Map 2.2.5, AY.
2.2.1d For the betrayal of Byzantium to the Athenians under Alcibiades, see 1.3.16–21.
2.2.1e Pontus (Black Sea): Map 2.2.5, AY.
2.2.1f Athens: Map 2.2.5, inset.
2.2.2a Peiraieus: Map 2.2.5, inset.
2.2.2b The harmost is usually (as here) a garrison commander.
2.2.3a Really Peiraieus, the port of Athens.
2.2.3b Aigospotamoi (Aigospotamos): Map 2.2.5, AY.

through the Long Walls[c] and into the city itself as one man imparted the calamitous news to the next. As a result, no one slept that night as they mourned not only for the men destroyed but even more for themselves, thinking they would suffer the same catastrophes they had inflicted on others—the Melians[d] (colonists of the Spartans[e] whom the Athenians had defeated by siege), Histiaians,[f] Skionaians,[g] Toronaians,[h] Aeginetans,[i] and many other Greeks. [4] On the next day they held an assembly in which they resolved to block up all the harbors except for one, to repair the walls and place guards on all of them, and to prepare the city in every other way for a siege. They then occupied themselves with carrying out these tasks.

[5] Lysander meanwhile sailed out of the Hellespont[a] with two hundred triremes. He first went to Lesbos,[b] where he ordered the affairs of the cities there, especially those of Mytilene.[c] He sent Eteonikos in command of ten triremes to the lands around Thrace,[d] and Eteonikos brought all the settlements there over to the side of the Spartans. [6] Immediately after the sea battle of Aigospotamoi, all the Greeks who were still subject to the Athenians revolted from them, all except the Samians.[a] At Samos, the people had slaughtered the aristocrats and were in control of the city. [7] After this, Lysander sent word to Agis[a] at Dekeleia[b] and to Sparta that he was going to sail against Athens with his two hundred ships.[c] The Spartans and the rest of the Peloponnesians,[d] except for the Argives,[e] marched out in full force with Pausanias, the other of the two Spartan kings,[f] as their commander. [8] When all of these forces were concentrated together, he marched them to Athens and camped in the Academy[a] [that is the name of a gymnasium]. [9] Lysander sailed to Aegina and gave the city back to the Aegine-

2.2.5–9
405
LESBOS-THRACE-AEGINA-
PEIRAIEUS
Lysander orders the
affairs of the cities of
Lesbos. All the Greeks
and Thracians subject to
Athens revolt. Lysander
restores several cities to
their original inhabitants.
His fleet blockades the
Peiraieus.

2.2.3c　Long Walls of Athens: Map 2.2.5, inset; also Map 2.4.30, inset. The Long Walls connected the city wall with the walls of its port, the Peiraieus. They, together with the Phaleron Wall (which connected the city to the beach at Phaleron), made Athens impervious to a siege during the city's naval supremacy. One of the terms of peace imposed on Athens by the victorious Spartans in 404 was that substantial sections of these walls be torn down.

2.2.3d　Melos: Map 2.2.5, BX. After capturing Melos in 416, the Athenians put the Melian men to death and sold the women and children into slavery (Thucydides 5.116.4).

2.2.3e　Sparta: Map 2.2.5, BX.

2.2.3f　Histiaia: Map 2.2.5, AX. The Athenians expelled the Histiaians and occupied their territory in 446 (Thucydides 1.114.3).

2.2.3g　Skione: Map 2.2.5, AX. In 421, the Athenians captured Skione, executed the adult males, sold the women and children into slavery, and gave the land to the homeless Plataeans to live in (Thucydides 5.32.1).

2.2.3h　Torone: Map 2.2.5, AX. In 422, the Athenians captured Torone, enslaved the women and children, and sent the adult men to Athens, from which they subsequently returned after being exchanged for

other prisoners held by the enemy after the peace treaty was concluded (Thucydides 5.3.4).

2.2.3i　Aegina: Map 2.2.5, inset. The Aeginetans were expelled from their island in 431; seven years later, a large number of them were captured in their place of refuge, in the Peloponnese, and put to death (Thucydides 2.27.1, 4.57).

2.2.5a　Hellespont: Map 2.2.5, AY.

2.2.5b　Lesbos: Map 2.2.5, AY.

2.2.5c　Mytilene: Map 2.2.5, AY.

2.2.5d　Thrace: Map 2.2.5, AY.

2.2.6a　Samos: Map 2.2.5, BY.

2.2.7a　Agis, king of Sparta 427–400: see Appendix M, §2.

2.2.7b　Dekeleia: Map 2.2.5, BX.

2.2.7c　See Figure 2.2.7 of the modern trireme *Olympias*, designed by scholars and marine architects. The ship is on permanent display at the Hellenic Navy Museum, near the Peiraieus. See also Figures K.1, K.2, and K.3 and n. K.4b.

2.2.7d　Peloponnese: Map 2.1.16, BX.

2.2.7e　Argos: Map 2.2.5, BX.

2.2.7f　For the two kings of Sparta, see Appendix E, Spartan Government and Society, §12, 14. See "Pausanias" in Appendix M, §19.

2.2.8a　Academy, Athens: Map 2.4.30, inset.

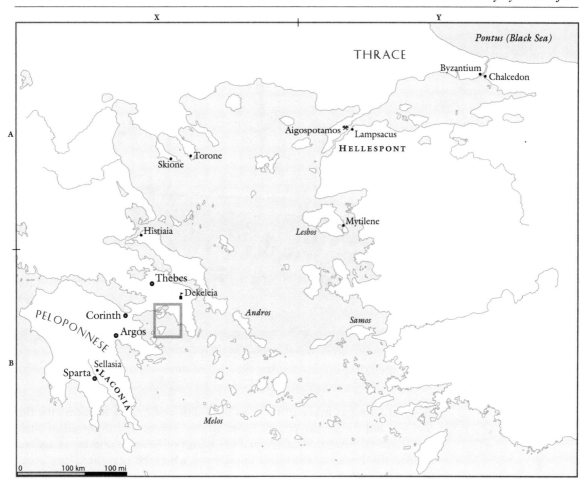

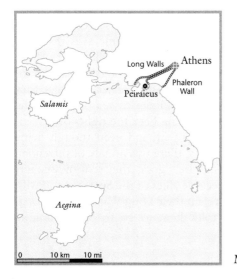

MAP 2.2.5

FIGURE 2.2.7. THE MODERN TRIREME *OLYMPIAS*, LAUNCHED IN 1987, HERE SHOWN WITH A STUDENT CREW AT ROWING TRIALS.

tans, gathering as many of these as he could, and he did the same for the Melians and for all the rest of those whom Athens had deprived of their own country. After this he ravaged the island of Salamis[a] and lay at anchor outside the Peiraieus with 150 ships, from where he prevented any boats from sailing in.

[10] The Athenians, now besieged by land and sea, were at a loss about what to do, for they had no ships, allies, or grain. They feared that there was nothing that could save them from suffering the same evils that they themselves had unjustly inflicted against the citizens of smaller states. They had done these things not for the sake of avenging wrongs but simply to display their arrogance, for the only offense of these states was that they had allied themselves with the Spartans. [11] For this reason, then, the Athenians tried to strengthen their city by giving back the rights of citizenship to those whom they had deprived of them, and even though many were dying of starvation throughout the city, there was no talk of surrender. But finally, when their grain supply was entirely gone, they sent messengers to Agis to say that they were ready to become allies of the Spartans and willing to make a treaty if only they could retain their Long Walls and the fortifications of the Peiraieus. [12] Agis told them to go to Sparta, for he

2.2.10–12
405
ATHENS
The Athenians, lacking any means to resist, finally send to Agis to ask if they can become allies of the Spartans, if only they can retain their Long Walls and the fortifications of the Peiraieus. Agis refers them to Sparta to discuss the issue of alliance.

2.2.9a   Salamis (in Attica): Map 2.2.5, inset.

himself did not have the power to make a treaty. When the ambassadors informed the Athenians of his reply, they sent them to Sparta.

[13] But when the ambassadors on their way were passing through Sellasia[a] [which is near Laconia[b]] and the ephors learned that they were going to make the same offer they had previously made to Agis, they stopped them on the spot and ordered them to depart, telling them that if the Athenians really desired peace, they should come back with a better proposal. [14] When the ambassadors returned home and announced this to the city, a great despondency fell upon all the Athenians. For they thought they would be enslaved and that in the time it would take to send other messengers, many in the city would die of starvation. [15] Still, no one proposed that they should even debate the tearing-down of their Long Walls: for indeed Archestratos, who had said in the Council that it would be best to make peace with the Spartans on the terms they offered—that is, to tear down some ten stades[a] of each of the Long Walls—was thrown into prison. And a decree was passed that it was not permitted to debate such ideas.

[16] This was how opinion stood in Athens[a] when Theramenes spoke to the Assembly. He said that if they would send him to Lysander, he would find out and tell them when he returned whether the Spartans demanded the destruction of the walls in order to enslave the Athenians or simply because they wanted assurance of Athenian good faith. But when they sent him to Lysander, he wasted more than three months there, waiting for the moment when the Athenians would agree to any proposal because their entire supply of grain would have been consumed. [17] When he finally returned, three months later, he announced to the Assembly that Lysander had detained him for some time and then had ordered him to go to Sparta,[a] saying that he had no power to grant what the Athenians wished and only the ephors[b] there could do that. So the Athenians chose Theramenes and nine others to go as ambassadors with full power[c] to Sparta. [18] Meanwhile, Lysander sent some Spartans and an Athenian exile named Aristoteles[a] to the ephors in order to inform them of what he had told Theramenes—namely, that they alone had full power in the matter of war and peace. [19] So when Theramenes and the other ambassadors arrived at Sellasia and were asked why they had come there, they replied that they had full powers from the Athenians to make peace; after hearing this, the ephors ordered the ambassadors to come before them.

When the ambassadors arrived at Sparta, the ephors called an assembly, at which the Corinthians[a] and Thebans[b] especially, but also many other

2.2.13–15
405
ATHENS-SELLASIA
The Athenian envoys are stopped by the ephors at Sellasia and told to come back with a better offer. But in Athens, no one is allowed to even mention a breach in the Long Walls.

2.2.16–19
405–404
PEIRAIEUS-SPARTA
Theramenes, sent to Lysander to find out his intentions, delays until the Athenians have exhausted their food supplies, then returns, saying they must apply to the ephors at Sparta for peace. The Athenians send him and other envoys with full powers to deal with the ephors.

2.2.13a Sellasia: Map 2.2.5, BX.
2.2.13b Laconia: Map 2.2.5, BX.
2.2.15a Ten Attic stades would convert to about 5,830 feet, a bit more than a mile.
2.2.16a Athens: Map 2.2.5, inset.
2.2.17a Sparta: Map 2.2.5, BX.
2.2.17b Ephors at Sparta: see Appendix E, §16.
2.2.17c Ambassadors with "full power" were able to make a binding agreement without

referring back to the Athenian Assembly for approval or ratification.
2.2.18a In 405, Aristoteles was in exile in Sparta. He assisted Lysander during the siege of Athens and became one of the Thirty Tyrants.
2.2.19a Corinth: Map 2.2.5, BX.
2.2.19b Thebes: Map 2.2.5, BX.

Greeks, urged the Spartans not to make peace with the Athenians but, rather, to destroy them. [20] The Spartans, however, said they would not enslave a Greek city that had accomplished so much good for Greece during the time of its greatest dangers;[a] they preferred, rather, to offer peace to Athens upon the following conditions: that the Athenians take down their Long Walls[b] and the fortifications of the Peiraieus;[c] that they hand over all of their ships except twelve; that they allow their exiles to return to Athens; that they have the same friends and enemies as the Spartans; and that they be willing to follow the Spartans as their leaders on land or sea, on whatever campaign the Spartans should order them.

[21] Theramenes and the ambassadors who were with him brought these terms back to Athens. When they entered the city, a large crowd gathered around them, afraid that they had returned without having accomplished anything. For it was no longer possible to delay further, since a large number of Athenians were already perishing every day from starvation. [22] On the following day, the ambassadors announced the terms under which the Spartans would make peace. Theramenes addressed the Athenians, saying that they had no choice but to obey the Spartans and accept their terms, including taking down the walls of the city and the Peiraieus. Some people spoke in opposition, but many more approved, and in the end they voted to accept the peace. [23] After this, Lysander sailed into the harbor of the Peiraieus, and the exiles returned. With great zeal they dismantled the walls, to the accompaniment of music provided by flute girls,[a] and they believed that that day would be the beginning of freedom for all of Greece.

[24] And thus the year ended. [In the middle of this year, Dionysios son of Hermokrates, a Syracusan,[a] became tyrant of Syracuse when the Syracusans defeated the Carthaginians[b] in battle, although the Carthaginians had taken Akragas[c] when its supply of food was exhausted and the Siceliots had to abandon their city.]

[1] In the following year, [the Olympiad[a] in which Krokinas of Thessaly[b] won the *stadion* race, when Eudios was ephor at Sparta[c] and Pythodorus archon at Athens[d]—although the Athenians do not put him on their official list, because he was chosen during the reign of the oligarchy; instead, they refer to it as "the year without an archon." The rule of the oligarchy at Athens

2.2.20a   A reference to Athens' leadership and bravery during the Persian Wars (490, 480–479).
2.2.20b   Long Walls of Athens: Map 2.2.5, inset; also Map 2.4.30, inset.
2.2.20c   Peiraieus: Map 2.2.5, inset.
2.2.23a   Flute girls at Athens were courtesans who entertained men at their symposia, or wine-drinking parties.
2.2.24a   Syracuse: Map 2.3.4, inset.
2.2.24b   Carthage: Map 2.3.4.
2.2.24c   Akragas: Map 2.3.4, inset.
2.3.1a   Olympia: Map 2.3.4. For Olympiads, ephors, archons, and the use of them for

dating events, see n. 1.2.1a and Appendix C, Chronological Problems in the Continuation (1.1.1–2.3.10) of Xenophon's *Hellenika*, §5–9. As explained there, though the year indicated here (404) is correct, the direct dating indications by ephor and archon have been interpolated. On the Olympic Games, see Appendix J, Ancient Greek Religion in the Time of Xenophon, §10–11.
2.3.1b   Thessaly: Map 2.3.4.
2.3.1c   Sparta: Map 2.3.4.
2.3.1d   Athens: Map 2.3.4.

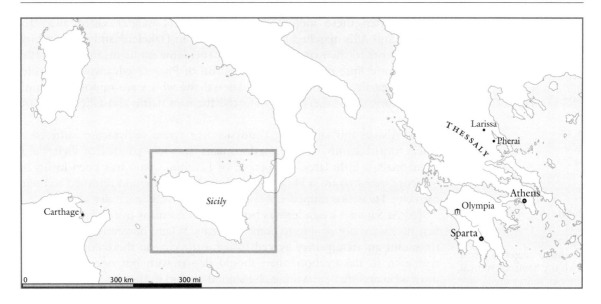

MAP 2.3.4

came about in the following way:] [2] it was decided by the people in the Assembly to choose thirty men who would be responsible for writing down the ancestral laws, according to which the government would be run. The following men were chosen: Polychares, Kritias,[a] Melobios, Hippolochos, Eucleides, Hieron, Mnesilochos, Chremon, Theramenes,[b] Aresias, Diokles, Phaedrias, Chaireleos, Anaitios, Peison, Sophocles, Eratosthenes, Charicles, Onomacles, Theognis, Aeschines, Theogenes, Cleomedes, Erasistratos, Pheidon, Dracontides, Eumathes, Aristoteles, Hippomachos, Mnesitheides.[c]

2.3.2a   See "Kritias" in Appendix M, §17.
2.3.2b   See "Theramenes" in Appendix M, §24.
2.3.2c   This is the full list of the Thirty, but it has been suspected of being an interpolation by some. For the figures mentioned here (some of whom play prominent roles in the narrative to follow), see R. Develin,

Athenian Officials 684–321 B.C. (Cambridge, 1989), pp. 184–5; for full treatment, see P. Krentz, *The Thirty at Athens* (Ithaca: Cornell University Press, 1982). See Appendix B, The Athenian Government and the Oligarchy of the Thirty, §12–21.

2.3.3–4
404
ATHENS-THESSALY
The Spartans leave Athens. Eclipse of the sun. Lykophron of Pherai tries to conquer Thessaly.

2.3.5
404
SICILY
The year's events in Sicily.

2.3.6–10
404
SAMOS-SPARTA
Lysander comes to terms with the Samians, returns the city to its exiled citizens, and sails home in triumph to Sparta, turning over trophies, garlands, and an immense sum of money. The war is over. A list is given (probably by an interpolator) of the twenty-nine eponymous ephors who served during this long war.

[3] When these men had been chosen, Lysander sailed away to Samos,[a] and Agis marched the army away from Dekeleia[b] and dispersed its detachments to their own cities. [4] At this same moment, just about the time of an eclipse of the sun,[a] Lykophron of Pherai,[b] who wished to rule all of Thessaly, conquered those Thessalians who were opposed to him (Larissaeans[c] and others). He defeated them in battle and killed many of them.

[5] Also at this same time Dionysios, the tyrant of Syracuse, suffered a defeat at the hands of the Carthaginians and lost control of Gela[a] and Camarina.[b] A little later, the people of Leontini,[c] who had been living at Syracuse, revolted from Dionysios and the Syracusans and returned to their own city. Dionysios immediately ordered the Syracusan cavalry to Katane.[d]

[6] At Samos,[a] Lysander was besieging the Samians from all sides, but at first they were not willing to come to terms. When, however, he was about to mount an assault, they agreed to leave the city on the following terms: that each of the freeborn men should depart with but one cloak in his possession and that everything else should remain in the city and be handed over. Under these terms they departed. [7] Lysander then gave control of the city and everything in it to the citizens who had been exiled, and he established a group of ten magistrates to watch over it. He then dismissed the various naval contingents of the allies, which returned to their individual cities, [8] and he sailed back to Sparta[a] with the Spartan ships. He brought with him the prows of all the ships that he had captured, plus the triremes from Peiraieus[b] (except for twelve), the garlands he had received as gifts for himself from the cities, some 470 talents[c] of silver (which was the amount that remained from the funds that Cyrus[d] had assigned to him for prosecuting the war), and anything else that he had acquired in the course of the war. [9] He gave all these things to the Spartans just as the summer was ending. At this point, the war was over, having lasted twenty-eight and a half years.[a] During those years, the following men served as eponymous ephors:[b] Aenesias was the first, and in his term the war began, in the fifteenth year after the Thirty Years Peace was established following the capture of Euboea.[c] After

---

2.3.3a Samos: Map 2.2.5, BY, and Map 2.4.3.
2.3.3b Dekeleia: Map 2.2.5, BX.
2.3.4a This eclipse took place September 3, 404.
2.3.4b Pherai: Map 2.3.4.
2.3.4c Larissa: Map 2.3.4.
2.3.5a Gela: Map 2.3.4, inset.
2.3.5b Camarina: Map 2.3.4, inset.
2.3.5c Leontini: Map 2.3.4, inset.
2.3.5d Katane: Map 2.3.4, inset.
2.3.8a Sparta: Map 2.4.3.
2.3.8b Peiraieus: Map 2.4.3.
2.3.8c The talent was a unit of weight, whose value varied over time and place between 55 and 80 pounds. See Appendix I, Units of Distance, Currency, and Capacity in Xenophon's *Hellenika*, §8, 10, 13.
2.3.8d See 2.1.14 for when Cyrus gave Lysander money.

2.3.9a The war in fact lasted twenty-seven and a half years, from 431 to 404.
2.3.9b Xenophon (or an interpolator, since some scholars believe this list is an interpolation) here gives the list of eponymous ephors (the ephor whose name was used to identify the year or years) for each year of the war. On the ephors, see Appendix E, §16.
2.3.9c Euboea: Map 2.4.3, inset. In spring or summer 446, Euboea revolted from the Athenian empire, but it was eventually recaptured that same year by Pericles. Shortly thereafter, the Spartans and Athenians made a Thirty Years Peace, which lasted but fifteen years, hostilities breaking out in spring 431.

him there were the following: [10] Brasidas, Isanor, Sostratidas, Exarchos, Agesistratos, Aggenidas, Onomacles, Zeuxippos, Pityas, Pleistolas, Kleino-machos, Ilarchos, Leon, Chairilas, Patesiadas, Kleosthenes, Lukarios, Eper-atos, Onomantios, Alexippidas, Misgolaïdas, Isias, Arakos, Euarchippos, Pantacles, Pituas, Archytas, and Eudios, in whose term Lysander did the aforementioned deeds and sailed home to Sparta.[a]

[11] At Athens, the Thirty were chosen as soon as the Long Walls and the walls of Peiraieus had been destroyed.[a] Although they were charged with writing up the laws according to which the city would be governed, they continually postponed writing the laws down and publishing them for all to see. Instead, they established a Council and other offices in an arbitrary manner, as it seemed best to them. [12] At first they arrested and executed those who everyone knew had made their living, during the time of the democracy, by being informers and who had caused much trouble for the noblemen.[a] The Council condemned these men with plea-sure, and the rest of the citizens, conscious that they were not at all like these men, were indeed not sorry to see them go. [13] But then the Thirty began to scheme about what steps they might take that would permit them to run the city however they liked. They first sent Aeschines and Aristoteles to Sparta, and once there, these men persuaded Lysander to send a garrison to protect and assist the Thirty until, so they said, they could do away with the wicked and establish the new constitution. More-over, the Thirty offered to furnish the garrison's pay themselves. [14] Lysander agreed and arranged for troops to be sent to them with Kalli-bios as their commander. When the Thirty had received the garrison, they fawned over Kallibios in every way so that he would approve of all the steps they wished to take. When Kallibios gave them the men they required, the Thirty then no longer arrested only the wicked and those of little worth; instead they now seized those whom they considered least likely to accept being pushed aside and kept out of public life and also those who would be able to mobilize large numbers of citizens in opposi-tion to the Thirty.

[15] Now, in that first period Kritias and Theramenes had the same views and were friends. But when Kritias proved to be keen on putting many men to death (for in fact he had been exiled by the people under the democracy), Theramenes opposed him, saying that it was not reason-able to execute men who had done no harm to the upper class simply because they were honored by the people. "Even you and I," he said, "have said and done many things in order to gain favor with the people."

2.3.11–14
404
ATHENS
The Thirty delay publica-tion of new laws and set up their own interim regime. They ask for and are given a Spartan garri-son by Lysander. With this protection, they begin to seize not just the obvious criminals but men of stature who might successfully oppose them.

2.3.15–16
404
ATHENS
As the Thirty put more and more men to death, Theramenes begins to oppose Kritias' policy.

2.3.10a Here is the break in the narrative described in the Introduction, §8.6–8.
2.3.11a Xenophon omits Lysander's active role in this, made clear in Lysias 12.71–8 and Diodorus (see Appendix O, 14.3.4–7). Lysias makes Theramenes a prime mover with Lysander in the installation of the Thirty, and Diodorus instead shows him overborne by Lysander. Probably but not certainly Lysias is correct and Diodorus is reporting a piece of playact-ing that he has misunderstood. But both agree that Spartan force was required. See the Introduction, §12.8.
2.3.12a Literally, "the good and fair" (*kaloi k'agathoi*). (John Marincola)

2.3.17–19
404
Athens
When Kritias and the other oligarchs draw up a list of three thousand to share in the government, Theramenes denounces it as both arbitrary and dangerous.

2.3.20
404
Athens
The Thirty disarms the citizenry except for their chosen body of three thousand citizens.

2.3.21–23
404
Athens
In order to raise money to pay the garrison, each of the Thirty is required to select one resident alien and have him put to death so that his property could be confiscated. Theramenes objects to this policy, and the rest of the Thirty begin to plot against him.

[16] However, Kritias, who at that point continued to treat Theramenes as a friend, replied that men who wanted more power for themselves could not avoid doing away with those who were most able to stop them. "And if you think that because we are thirty and not one we can take less care to protect our rule than if we were simply a tyranny, then you are a simpleton."

[17] Later, when the Thirty continued to put many people to death unjustly and many citizens were openly joining together wondering what would become of the state, Theramenes again spoke out, warning the Thirty that unless they brought in additional suitable men to share in the government, the oligarchy could not possibly survive. [18] In response to this, Kritias and the rest of the Thirty, who already feared that opposition might form, especially around Theramenes, drew up a list of three thousand men who, they said, would share in governing the city. [19] But Theramenes opposed this scheme, saying that it seemed ridiculous to him on two counts: first, that they should arbitrarily limit the number of "good" men with whom they wished to share the rule of the city to no more than three thousand, as if that number must of necessity include all of the city's noblemen, and that there would be no good men left outside this group, nor scoundrels within it; and second, he said, "I see us pursuing two contrary and opposed policies: establishing our own rule by force while rendering it weaker than the people we are governing." These then were his opinions.

[20] The Thirty, however, conducted a review of the Three Thousand in the agora,[a] while other citizens, those who were not on the list, were reviewed at different places throughout the city. These others were ordered to ... arms ... when those were gone,[b] the Thirty ordered the soldiers of the garrison and some citizens who were partisans of the Thirty to remove all the arms, except those of the Three Thousand, and so they took the confiscated weapons to the Acropolis and deposited them there in the temple.[c] [21] When this had been accomplished, the Thirty began to put many men to death simply out of personal enmity or because of their wealth, believing that they could now do anything they wanted. Indeed, in order to raise money to pay the garrison, the Thirty even decided that each one of them should seize one resident alien,[a] execute him, and confiscate his property. [22] But when they ordered Theramenes to seize someone of his own choosing, he answered, "But it doesn't seem respectable to me for people

2.3.20a Agora: the central market square of any ancient Greek city, where all business and much politics and social life took place. For the location of the Athenian agora, see Map 2.4.30, inset.
2.3.20b There is a gap in the text here; the general sense is clear—that the Thirty disarmed all the citizens except the Three Thousand—but the details are not.
2.3.20c The temple Xenophon refers to here is the

Parthenon, the temple to Athena on the Acropolis of Athens: Map 2.4.30, inset.
2.3.21a The resident aliens (metics) were particularly numerous in Athens, and a few of them were among the wealthiest people in the city. Most, however, were poor, if not poorer than the average Athenian. For Diodorus' account of the excesses and crimes of the Thirty, see Appendix O, 14.5.5–14.6.3.

who claim to be the best men to actually behave more unjustly than the informers. For those men at least allowed those from whom they extorted money to go on living, whereas we kill men who have done nothing wrong just so we may take their money and property. How is this not in every way more unjust than what the informers did?" [23] The Thirty, however, considering that Theramenes was attempting to prevent them from doing what they wished, began to plot against him and slander him in private, one man talking to another and saying that he was spoiling the government they had established. They ordered some young men who had a reputation for the greatest audaciousness to furnish themselves with daggers hidden under their armpits and to present themselves before them. They then called together the Council.

[24] When Theramenes arrived, Kritias stood up and made the following speech: "Men of the Council, if any one of you believes that more men are being put to death than the occasion warrants, let him consider that executions always occur everywhere whenever constitutions are changed. It is necessarily the case that a large number of citizens are and will remain hostile to anyone who establishes an oligarchy here, since this city is the most populous of all Greek cities, and since the people have been nurtured in freedom for the longest time. [25] We established this constitution with the approval of the Spartans because we know from personal experience how harsh democracy as a form of government can be to men such as yourselves and us; we are aware also that the common people will never be friendly toward the Spartans who preserve us, while for us the aristocracy will always be trustworthy. [26] And if we learn of someone who opposes oligarchy, we do away with him insofar as we can. And it seems particularly just to us that if one of our own people seeks to damage this established order of ours, he must pay the penalty.

[27] "Now, it is our judgment that Theramenes here is trying by whatever means he can to destroy both us and you. If you examine the facts, you will find that I speak the truth when I say that no one has found greater fault with our present state of affairs or has more vigorously opposed us when we wished to do away with one of the popular leaders than Theramenes here. Now, indeed, if he had thought this way from the beginning, he would have been our enemy, but we would not rightly have considered him a wicked man. [28] But as it is, it was he who began to trust and treat the Spartans as friends, and it was he who began the effort to overthrow the democracy, and it was he who especially advocated punishment for those who were first brought before you for trial; but now that you and we are open enemies of the people, our present state of affairs is no longer pleasing to him, and he is trying to make himself safe while leaving us to pay the penalty for what we have all done.

2.3.24–26
404
ATHENS
Kritias makes a speech to the Council attacking Theramenes.

2.3.27–34
404
ATHENS
The rest of Kritias' speech attacking Theramenes and accusing him of treason. He argues that Theramenes is dangerous and must be executed.

[29] "And so it is fitting that he pay the penalty, on the grounds that he is not only an enemy but also a traitor to both of us,[a] and treason is more fearful than war in the same measure as the invisible is more difficult to guard against than the visible; it is more hateful by virtue of the fact that although men will make treaties with their enemies and even become their friends, no one ever makes peace with a man who is once detected as a traitor: no one can ever trust him again. [30] So that you may realize that this man is a traitor by nature and that what he does is not recent, I will remind you of some of his previous actions. Although from the beginning of his career he was honored by the people, just like his father Hagnon,[a] he was nevertheless most eager to overthrow that democracy and establish the oligarchical rule of the Four Hundred,[b] and he was a leader in that body. But when he perceived that some opposition had arisen to that oligarchy, he became in turn the first leader of the people against the Four Hundred. [31] From this turnabout you know, of course, that he has been called The Slipper.[a] (For the slipper is suitable to fit both feet, and he faces both directions.) But I say to you, Theramenes, that a man worthy to stay alive is not one who with cunning leads his associates into dangers and, when some opposition arises, immediately change sides; no, he must, like a ship, work steadily through a storm until he finds himself with a favorable wind. Otherwise, how would sailors ever arrive at their destination if, whenever the wind or current opposed them, they immediately turned and sailed in the opposite direction?

[32] "Now, all changes of government no doubt bring death in their train, but you, Theramenes, because of how easily you change sides, are responsible for the deaths of most of the oligarchs who died at the hands of the people and most of the democrats who were killed by the better men.[a] Theramenes here is the very same man, I tell you, who, although ordered by the generals to take up those of the Athenians who were drowning in the sea battle off Lesbos,[b] did not himself save them but then nevertheless accused the generals and had them executed in order to ensure his own survival. [33] Now, any man who manifestly works only for his own advantage and who has no regard for honor or friendship—how can it ever be right to spare such a man? Must we not be on guard against him and act to protect ourselves, knowing as we do how he has changed from side to side in the past, lest he do this very same thing against us in the future?

"So, then, we bring this man before you for trial as one who plotted the

---

2.3.29a By "both of us," Kritias refers to the Thirty, of which he is a member, and the Council, to which he is speaking.

2.3.30a Hagnon: a famous Athenian general; he was responsible for the Athenian colonization of the strategic city of Amphipolis (Map 3.2.11, AX) in 437/6. In 413 he was chosen by the Four Hundred, of which he was a member, as one of the advisors to draw up a new constitution (Lysias 12.65) after the Athenian forces in Sicily had been annihilated.

2.3.30b The Four Hundred: a short-lived oligarchy

that lasted several months in the year 411. See Thucydides 8.67.3–97.1 and Appendix B, §12.

2.3.31a He is actually called *kothornos*, the boot used in tragedy, which could be worn on either foot. I have tried to get the podiatric pun in my translation. (John Marincola) For the Greek, see Translator's Notes.

2.3.32a Kritias refers here to the battle of Arginousai (Map 2.4.3). Xenophon's account of the battle is at 1.6.29–35.

2.3.32b Lesbos: Map 2.4.3.

ruin and betrayal of both of us. And to convince you that we are behaving reasonably, keep this in mind. [34] The finest constitution is reputed to be, I suppose, that of the city of Sparta. Now, if one of the ephors tried to attack that constitution, if instead of obeying the majority he found fault with the way the government had been set up and opposed its magistrates, don't you think that he would be found to deserve the greatest punishment, both by his fellow ephors and by the entire city? By this same logic, if you are wise, you will not spare this man but protect yourselves, for his safety will encourage many of those who hold political opinions opposed to our own to believe they can accomplish great deeds, whereas his death will cut off the hopes of all those who oppose us both within the city and outside it."

[35] When Kritias had finished his speech, he sat down, and Theramenes arose and responded with the following: "I will begin, gentlemen, by recalling the last thing Kritias said against me, namely, that I was responsible for the death of the generals because of my accusation against them. But certainly I did not begin by accusing anyone; it was they, rather, who said that I had not carried out their orders to go to the rescue of those unfortunate men in the sea battle off Lesbos. I defended myself by saying that because of the storm, it was not possible to sail at all, much less to take up the men, and I was thought by the city to have spoken reasonably. The generals, on the other hand, appeared to be accusing themselves, for they claimed that it was possible to save the men but that they had sailed off and left them to die.[a] [36] Yet I am not surprised that Kritias has been misinformed[a] about this, for at the time he was not here but off, rather, in Thessaly[b] with Prometheus, establishing a democracy and arming the serfs[c] against their masters. [37] Let us hope that nothing like that happens here!

"In one thing, however, I do agree with Kritias: if someone is trying to remove you from power and by his action is strengthening those who are plotting against you, it is certainly just that he should receive the greatest punishment. But you will be able, I think, to judge best who it is who is actually doing that after you have considered what each of us has done and what each is now doing. [38] Now, we were all in agreement when we established our power and designated the magistrates and brought to trial the men who were commonly agreed to be informers. But when these Thirty began to arrest the noblemen, at that point I began to hold opposing views. [39] For when Leon of Salamis[a]—a man who was both thought

2.3.35–39
404
ATHENS
Theramenes gives a speech in his own defense. He answers the charges of Kritias one by one and attacks Kritias as the instigator of policies that are alienating the government's friends and strengthening its enemies.

2.3.35a What the generals are reported by Xenophon to have said to the Assembly can be found at 1.7.5–7.

2.3.36a "Misinformed": reading Wolf's *paranenoēkenai* for the manuscripts' *paranenomēkenai*. (John Marincola) For the Greek, see Translator's Notes.

2.3.36b Thessaly: Map 2.3.4.

2.3.36c The *penestai* of Thessaly were a hereditary class of dependents, often compared with Spartan helots (for example, see Dionysius of Halicarnassus,

Roman Antiquities 2.9). *Penestai* may be etymologically connected with *penēs*, "poor man."

2.3.39a Salamis: Map 2.4.3. A Leon mentioned at 1.5.16 and 1.6.16 may be the same man; from his actions there in putting down the oligarchical coup on Samos in 411, he would certainly have been suspect to the Thirty. This is the Leon whom Socrates refused to summon before the Thirty (Plato, *Apology* 32c–d).

to be and actually was meritorious, and one who was completely innocent of any wrongdoing—was put to death, I knew that those like him would grow fearful and become hostile to this government. And I knew, too, that when Nikeratos son of Nikias[b] was apprehended—a wealthy man and one who, like his father, had never displayed any populist leanings—that this would lead men like him to become our enemies.

[40] "And when Antiphon[a]—a man who during the war furnished the city with two swift triremes[b]—was executed by us, I knew that all those who had the city's best interests at heart would now hold you in suspicion.

[41] "I also spoke against the order of the Thirty that each one of us should seize one resident alien, for it was plainly obvious that if we destroyed these men, all the resident aliens would become enemies of our government. I spoke against taking away the weapons of the majority, since I did not think that it was right to make the city weak. For I recognized that the Spartans had not permitted the city to survive in order to become so feeble that we would not be able to assist them; if they had wanted such a situation, they could have simply let the famine go on a little longer, and none of us would have survived.

[42] "Nor did it please me that a garrison of foreign troops was hired to support us until we could gain control over those we rule, when we could have formed such a force from our own citizens. But when I saw that many in the city were becoming our enemies or going into exile, I did not approve the decision to banish Thrasyboulos, Anytos, and Alcibiades.[a] For I knew that this step would only strengthen the elements opposed to us if such men could serve as effective leaders for the masses, and it would show those wishing to lead that they clearly had many allies.

[43] "Well, then, is it right to consider someone who openly gives such advice a supporter or a traitor? Our enemies are not strengthened, Kritias, by those of us who try to prevent our government from making more enemies, or those who try to advise us how to acquire more allies; it is, rather, those of us who unjustly deprive people of their property or who put to death people who have done no wrong: these are the ones who in

---

2.3.39b Nikias was the general of the Athenians during the Sicilian expedition, although he was opposed to it. See Thucydides Book 6; on his relationship to the democracy, see Plutarch, *Parallel Lives,* "Nicias."

2.3.40a This Antiphon is not the orator who died in 411 but probably Antiphon son of Lysonides, mentioned by the comic poet Cratinus and by Pseudo-Plutarch in *Lives of the Ten Orators* (Plutarch, *Moralia* 833A).

2.3.40b The war he refers to is the Peloponnesian War. Wealthy citizens of Athens were often obliged to undertake "liturgies," that is, works done at their own expense that benefited the public. The liturgy mentioned in this case was probably not compulsory, as that would have indicated

only that he was very rich, not very civic minded.

2.3.42a Anytos had been a general in 409, when he was responsible for the loss of Pylos and was brought to trial for it. He is said to have been the first person to bribe his way to acquittal (Diodorus: see Appendix O, 13.64.6). Just after the trial of Theramenes here, Anytos was one of the exiles who joined Thrasyboulos in raising the standard of democracy at Phyle, and he became an important figure in the restored democracy after 403, down to at least 396. In general, he seems to have played a moderate part, but he was one of the prosecutors of Socrates in 399. See Appendix M, "Alcibiades," §3, and "Thrasyboulos," §26.

fact make enemies for us; they betray not only their friends but also themselves, and all because of their shameless love of gain. [44] If you still do not understand the truth of what I say, consider the following: do you think that Thrasyboulos, Anytos, and the rest of the exiles would rather have us here at Athens do what I am advising or what the Thirty are doing? For I believe that the exiles now think that they have allies for their cause in every district of the city. But I know that if the strongest elements in the city were friendly to us, the exiles would find it difficult to even contemplate setting foot in our land.

[45] "Now let me address the charge that I am the kind of man who always changes sides. Remember that it was the people themselves, as you well know, who voted for the constitution of the Four Hundred[a] when they had been told that the Spartans would negotiate with any government except a democracy. [46] But the Spartans did not in any way reduce their prosecution of the war, and the time came when Aristoteles, Melanthios, and Aristarchos with their fellow generals were openly building fortifications on the promontory of Peiraieus, by which they wished to admit the enemy and make the city subject to them and their friends. If I at that moment perceived this and prevented it from happening, was this being a traitor to one's friends?[a] [47] He calls me The Slipper on the grounds that I try to accommodate both sides. But what, by God, shall we call Kritias, who is pleasing to neither side? For you, Kritias, were well-known as one who hated the people in the time of the democracy, and now under an aristocracy you are the one who most of all hates the best men among us.

[48] "But I always do battle with extremists, Kritias, whether they are men who think that a good democracy must allow slaves and those so poor they would betray the state for a drachma to have a share in government,[a] or whether they are men who think you cannot have a good oligarchy unless you bring the state under the tyranny of a few men. I thought in the past that the state was best served by those who could offer their abilities, be it with horses or with shields,[b] and on that point I do not change my mind even now. [49] If you, Kritias, can point to a time when I tried to deprive the state of the services of the noblemen, whether under the democracy or the oligarchy, then tell us when it was. For if I am found guilty of doing this now or of ever having done it, then I agree that I would justly deserve to suffer the ultimate punishment."

2.3.45a In Thucydides' detailed and authoritative account of the murky background to the installation of the Four Hundred (8.70, 8.86.9), improving Athens' chance of negotiations with the Spartans does not appear as a reason given in public for turning to oligarchy, though the Four Hundred did try to open negotiations with Sparta as soon as they were installed. It is unclear whether Xenophon has made a mistake or whether he means us to take Theramenes as lying here.

2.3.46a See Thucydides 8.90.5–92.11 for a description of this incident and Theramenes' role in it.

2.3.48a "Share in government": reading Wyttenbach's *archēs* for the manuscripts' *drachmēs*. (John Marincola) For the Greek, see Translator's Notes.

2.3.48b With horses or shields refers to cavalry and armored infantry (hoplites), which would exclude the poorer citizens, who would serve as light-armed infantry or rowers in the fleet.

[50] When Theramenes had finished speaking, the Council indicated its goodwill toward him by shouts of support, but Kritias, realizing that Theramenes would be acquitted if the Council were allowed to vote on his fate and considering this intolerable, approached the Thirty, said something to them, and then went outside. He ordered the young men with the daggers to approach the railing[a] so that they would be in full view of the members of the Council. [51] He then went back in[a] and said, "Men of the Council, I think it is the duty of a leader not to look on idly when he sees his friends being deceived. And that is what I shall do. Now, these young men who are standing around us say they will not permit us to acquit a man who is so clearly harmful to the oligarchy. And since one of the new laws states that no man on the list of the Three Thousand may be put to death without an affirmative vote by you, but that the Thirty are empowered to put to death those citizens not on the list, I, then, with all my colleagues concurring, strike off the name of Theramenes here from the list, and we condemn him to death."

[52] Upon hearing this, Theramenes ran to the hearth[a] and said, "I implore you, men of the Council, to see that I receive a minimum of justice, that it should not be in Kritias' power to do away with me or any one of you whom he wishes to erase but, rather, that such judgments be rendered against you and me in accord with whatever law the Thirty enacted about those on the list. [53] And by god I am aware that this altar will not help me in any way, but I come to it to demonstrate that the Thirty here are not only the most unjust in their dealings with men but also the most impious in their respect for the gods. I am amazed that those of you, gentlemen, who are noblemen are not defending yourselves, for you must surely know that my name is not more easily erased than any of yours."

[54] Then the herald of the Thirty ordered the Eleven[a] to seize Theramenes. They went in with their assistants, Satyros, the boldest and most shameless of them, leading the way. Kritias said, "We hand over Theramenes here to you; he has been condemned in accordance with the law. [55] You, the Eleven, are to take him and bring him to the place where you are to do what follows from this, our sentence."[a] When he said this, Satyros, with the help of his assistants, began to drag Theramenes from the altar. Theramenes, as one might expect, called continuously upon both gods and men to witness what was happening. But the Council did nothing, since they saw that the

---

2.3.50a   There was probably an outer barrier at the entrance to the Council House that separated members from nonmembers (the *kigklis* referred to by Aristophanes), but what is meant here is probably the barriers known as *dryphaktoi* that separated the seats of the Council members at the front of the chamber. See P. J. Rhodes, *The Athenian Boule* (Oxford University Press, 1972), pp. 29–30; for a plan of the Council Chamber at this time, see p. 301.

2.3.51a   "Back in" to the Bouleuterion—the Council Chamber, in which the Council had its meetings. The Council at this time consisted of five hundred men chosen by the Thirty: see 2.3.2, 2.3.11.

2.3.52a   To seek the protection of the gods as a suppliant. See Appendix J, §12.

2.3.54a   The Eleven were officials who were responsible for the incarceration of condemned prisoners and for carrying out executions.

2.3.55a   A euphemism of a sort frequently found in Greek society. Kritias wishes to avoid saying, "And you are to execute him."

men at the railposts were men like Satyros, and noticed, too, that the area in front of the Council House was full of soldiers from the garrison, and they were also mindful of the fact that these men were armed with daggers.

[56] So as they dragged Theramenes away through the agora, he continued to protest the injustice done to him in a clear and loud voice. It is said that when Satyros told him that he would be sorry if he did not keep quiet, Theramenes answered, "And if I keep silent, will I not be just as sorry?" And when he was compelled to die by drinking the hemlock,[a] they say that he cast the dregs out of the cup as if he were playing the *kottabos*,[b] and he said as he threw it, "Here's to the beautiful Kritias." Now, I am not unaware that these remarks might not be considered worthy of record, but I think it admirable in the man that even when his death was at hand, his mind lost neither its sense nor its sense of humor.

[1] That is the way Theramenes died. And the Thirty, thinking they could now act as tyrants without fear, proclaimed that all citizens who were not on the list of the Three Thousand were not only forbidden to enter the city proper but were to be evicted from their estates, so that the Thirty and their friends could take possession of the lands. Those thus evicted fled to the Peiraieus,[a] but the Thirty evicted many from there too, and so both nearby Megara[b] and Thebes[c] were full of refugees.

[2] After this, Thrasyboulos set out from Thebes with about seventy men and seized Phyle,[a] a fortress with a commanding position. The Thirty set out from the city to retake the place, and they brought with them the Three Thousand and the cavalry. It was an especially fine day, and when they arrived, some of the boldest young men attacked the fortification, but they accomplished nothing and retreated when some of them were wounded. [3] The Thirty wanted to wall off the place in order to cut off the access routes by which the enemy could obtain supplies, and to lay siege to the place. It snowed heavily during the night, however, and it continued into the next day. Thus prevented by the snowstorm from carrying out their plan, the Thirty returned to the city, having lost very many of their baggage carriers to the men at Phyle. [4] Aware that the men at Phyle would plunder the country estates unless they were guarded, the Thirty sent the Spartan[a] garrison troops (except for a few) and two divisions of cavalry to the border, about fifteen stades[b] from Phyle. There they camped in rough terrain and kept watch over Phyle.

2.3.56
404
ATHENS
Xenophon justifies repeating Theramenes' last remarks as indicating his admirable spirit.

2.4.1
404
ATHENS
The Thirty evict from Athens those not on the list of three thousand and confiscate their property.

2.4.2–4
403
PHYLE
Thrasyboulos and seventy followers occupy the fort of Phyle. The Thirty make an expedition to drive them out but are thwarted by a snowstorm and forced to return to Athens. They send troops to watch the fort.

2.3.56a Being made to drink hemlock (a poison whose precise composition is unknown) was the standard Athenian method of administering the death penalty after trial.

2.3.56b The game of *kottabos* was played at the symposiums (drinking parties). A drinker threw the dregs from his wine cup into a bowl, or at a disk that was set atop a pole, and at the same time spoke the name of his beloved. He would then divine from the clanging sound made by the bowl or disk his chances for success in love. As Peter Krentz points out, Theramenes' line to the "beautiful" (*kalos*) Kritias may allude to Kritias' claim to be one of the "good and

fair" (*kaloi k'agathoi*), or it may be a curse, since Theramenes dedicated to Kritias his drink not of wine (the usual beverage) but of the poisonous hemlock.

2.4.1a Peiraieus: Map 2.4.3, inset.
2.4.1b Megara: Map 2.4.3, inset.
2.4.1c Thebes: Map 2.4.3, inset.
2.4.2a Phyle: Map 2.4.3, inset. This fortress was near the border between Attica and Boeotia.
2.4.4a Sparta: Map 2.4.3.
2.4.4b The Attic stade was 583 feet long, so 15 Attic stades would convert to 1.63 miles. See Appendix I, §4–5, 13.

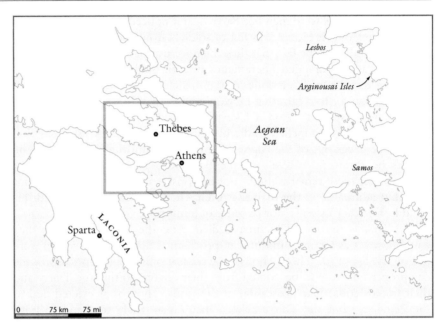

MAP 2.4.3

2.4.5–7
403
PHYLE
Thrasyboulos, now
with seven hundred
men, makes a successful
dawn attack on the
enemy camp near Phyle,
routing the enemy.

[5] By now there were around seven hundred men gathered at Phyle. One night, Thrasyboulos marched these men down from Phyle to a position about three or four stades[a] from the enemy's position, where he halted and waited. [6] Just before dawn, there was a point when the enemy troops were off their guard, each one going about his business (and away from his weapons), and the grooms were noisily rubbing down their horses. At this moment Thrasyboulos' men took up their arms and attacked on the run.

2.4.5a The Attic stade was 583 feet; so 3.5 Attic
        stades would convert to about 2,000 feet.

FIGURE 2.4.8. AT ELEUSIS, A SEGMENT OF A CYCLOPEAN WALL, BUILT WITH LARGE, IRREGULAR BLOCKS THAT ARE FITTED TOGETHER.

They struck down some of the enemy and, routing the rest, pursued them for six or seven stades,[a] killing more than 120 of the hoplites and three of the cavalrymen—Nikostratos (whose nickname was "Handsome") and two others, who were killed while still in their beds. [7] They then set up a trophy,[a] packed up all the arms they had taken, and went back to Phyle. When the reinforcements of horsemen from the city arrived to bring help, they found that the enemy was no longer there, so they waited until the relatives of the slain took up the bodies, and then returned to the city.

[8] After this defeat, the Thirty no longer considered their rule secure, and so they decided to make the town of Eleusis[a] into their own private possession for just themselves, so that they would have a place of refuge if they needed it. And so Kritias and the rest of the Thirty went to Eleusis, ordering the cavalry to accompany them. Upon their arrival, they held a review of the Eleusinians. They claimed that they wanted to know how many

2.4.8
403
ELEUSIS
The Thirty decide to make Eleusis a safe haven. They march there with the cavalry and take possession of the city, sending its citizens to Athens.

2.4.6a Six or seven stades was not a long pursuit, about 1,400 yards at most, assuming Attic stades of 583 feet, but a good distance for men in full armor.

2.4.7a After a battle in ancient Greece, the victors would gather up their dead, strip those of the enemy, and raise a trophy. The defeated would collect the bodies of their fallen during a truce that they would explicitly request and be granted for that purpose. In this way, appropriate reverence was shown, and proper burial was accorded to all war dead. See Appendix L, Land Warfare in Xenophon's *Hellenika*, §13.

2.4.8a Reading Classen's *Eleusiniois* for the manuscripts' *hippeusin* (John Marincola). For the Greek see Translator's Notes. Eleusis: Map 2.4.3. See Figure 2.4.8, a scene of Eleusis.

men of military age there were, so that they could figure out how many additional men would be needed for a garrison, and to this end, they ordered each man's name to be recorded. After his name was recorded, each individual was ordered to go through the town gate in the direction of the sea. The cavalry of the Thirty were stationed on either side of the gates, and as each man came through them, the cavalry attendants tied him up. When all of them had been thus bound, the Thirty ordered Lysimachos, the commander of the cavalry, to lead them back to Athens and there hand them over to the Eleven.[b]

[9] On the next day, the Thirty called the hoplites on the list and the rest of the cavalrymen into the Odeion,[a] and Kritias stood up and addressed them: "No less for you, gentlemen, than for ourselves are we establishing this government, and so it is necessary for you to share in the dangers, just as you share in the benefits. The Eleusinians captured here must be condemned, so that both you and we may take confidence in, and draw fear from, the same deeds."[b] He then pointed out a spot and ordered them to go there and render their vote for all to see. [10] Half of the Odeion was occupied by the Spartan garrison troops in their full armor. Only those citizens who thought solely of their own gain were pleased by these proceedings.

After this, Thrasyboulos mustered about a thousand of the men assembled at Phyle[a] and arrived during the night at the Peiraieus.[b] When the Thirty learned of their presence there, they immediately set out for the place, taking with them the Spartan garrison troops, the cavalry, and the hoplites. As they marched along the wagon road that leads from Athens to Peiraieus, [11] the men from Phyle for a time tried to prevent them from advancing along the road. But when they realized that they were not sufficiently numerous to man and defend the extensive circle of the town's wall, they retired in close order to the Hill of Mounichia.[a] The troops who had come from Athens went into the Hippodameian agora[b] and there formed into battle line, such that they filled the road that leads to the temple of Mounichian Artemis[c] and the shrine of Bendis.[d] The depth of their line was not less than fifty men.[e] Arrayed thus, they moved upward toward the enemy. [12] The men from Phyle on their side also filled the road, but they were not more than ten men deep. Stationed behind them, however, were

2.4.9
403
ATHENS
Kritias and armed men force the Three Thousand to vote to execute the men from Eleusis, making them confederates in crime.

2.4.10–12
403
PEIRAIEUS
Thrasyboulos marches to the Peiraieus with one thousand troops and prepares to defend the Hill of Mounichia. The Thirty march on them from Athens with the Spartan garrison, the cavalry, and the hoplites.

2.4.8b   The Eleven were the men charged with carrying out executions, although Xenophon does not say explicitly that the men taken to Athens were in fact executed.

2.4.9a   An odeion was a building designed for musical performances. This one, just to the southeast of the Acropolis, was built by Pericles. See Map 2.4.30, inset.

2.4.9b   Kritias is saying that if the hoplites and cavalrymen share in the deed, there will be less likelihood that they will in the future either inform on the Thirty or bring some legal action against them.

2.4.10a   Phyle: Map 2.4.3, inset.
2.4.10b   Peiraieus: Map 2.4.3, inset.
2.4.11a   Mounichia Hill, inside the walls of the Peiraieus: Map 2.4.30, inset.

2.4.11b   Agora in Peiraieus: Map 2.4.30, inset. Called "Hippodamian" after the famous town planner Hippodamos of Miletus.

2.4.11c   Temple of Mounichian Artemis: Map 2.4.30, inset.

2.4.11d   Bendis, a Thracian goddess whose cult had been accepted at Peiraieus for the resident Thracians there.

2.4.11e   A battle line fifty men deep is extraordinary; hoplite battle formations were usually not deeper than eight to twelve men. It means the width of the front available on that road was quite narrow, which of course favored Thrasyboulos and his men from Phyle. See Appendix L, §6, 7.

peltasts and light-armed javelin throwers,[a] and behind these were rock throwers. And there were many of the latter, since they came from the local neighborhood. As the enemy approached, Thrasyboulos ordered his men to lower their shields (he set down his own as well) but to keep the rest of their weapons at the ready. Then, standing in the middle of them, he addressed them:

[13] "Fellow citizens, I want to inform some of you and to remind others of you about what sort of men these are who are coming against us. Those on the right wing are the ones whom you yourselves routed and pursued four days ago. Those stationed at the end of their line on the left are the very Thirty who have deprived us of our city, although we had committed no wrong. These are the men who drove us from our houses and who condemned our dearest relatives and friends. Now the opportunity has come that they thought would never occur but for which we have continuously prayed: [14] we now stand opposed to them with arms. And because these men seized us when we were eating or sleeping or in the marketplace, and some of us were banished not only when we had done nothing wrong but when we were not even at Athens, the gods are now our allies for all to see: remember that they sent a snowstorm upon these men in the midst of good weather, which greatly benefited us; and whenever we go into battle, they grant us the right to set up trophies of victory, even though we are few and our opponents many. [15] Even now the gods have brought us to a place of battle where our enemies will not be able to throw their spears or javelins over the heads of those in front of them because of the steep ascent; while we, throwing spears and javelins and rocks downhill, will reach them and wound many of them severely. [16] Now someone might suppose that it will be necessary for the men in our front lines to fight on equal terms with the enemy; yet if you do what you should and enthusiastically discharge your weapons, none of you will miss hitting our opponents, for the simple fact that the road is completely filled up with them, and thus they will have to defend themselves by skulking under their shields. So we will be able to strike them wherever we wish, just as if they were blind men, and to spring upon them and rout them. [17] But it is necessary, men, that you behave in such a way that each one of you will feel himself to be most responsible for gaining the victory. If god wills, this victory will restore to us our country, our homes, our freedom, and honors, and, if we have them, our wives and children. Those of us are truly blessed who as victors will see this sweetest of days. Even one who dies fighting here will be fortunate, for no one, however wealthy, could procure for himself so fine a monument. When it is the right moment, I shall begin the *paean*.[a]

2.4.13–17
403
PEIRAIEUS
Thrasyboulos speaks to his men, reminding them of what they have suffered at the hands of the Thirty, of their past miraculous victories, and of their strong tactical position on the Hill of Mounichia.

2.4.12a Peltasts and light-armed javelin throwers were troops armed only with a small, light shield, a javelin, and a short sword. Unhindered by body armor, they could move much more quickly than the fully armed hoplite, whose equipment was both far heavier and far more expensive than theirs. See Appendix L, §7.

2.4.17a The *paean* was the war chant sung by ancient Greek troops going into battle.

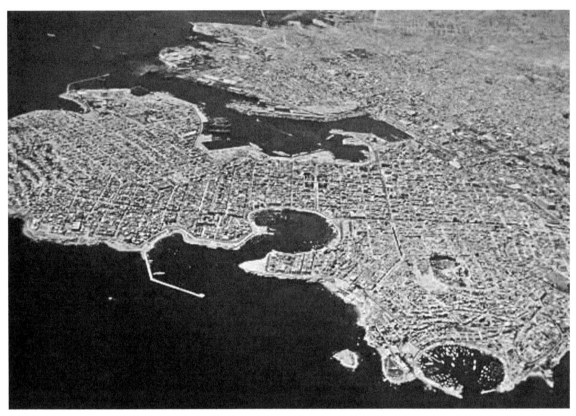

FIGURE 2.4.10. THE TOPOGRAPHY OF THE PEIRAIEUS TODAY (SHOWN IN AN AERIAL PHOTOGRAPH, ABOVE) IS REMARK-ABLY SIMILAR TO THAT IN XENOPHON'S DAY, AS SEEN IN A MAP OF THE SAME AREA (OPPOSITE PAGE) SHOWING LAND-MARKS MENTIONED IN HIS ACCOUNT OF THE FIGHTING BETWEEN THE ATHENIANS UNDER THRASYBOULOS AND THE SPARTANS UNDER PAUSANIAS.

2.4.18–19
403
PEIRAIEUS
The seer who instructed
Thrasyboulos to wait
until someone is killed
or wounded moves to
the front and is killed,
fulfilling his own prophecy.
The men of Phyle do win
the battle.

When we call upon Enyalios,[b] then let us all with one and the same spirit have our vengeance upon these men, in requital for all the wanton outrages we have endured at their hands."

[18] Finishing his speech with these words, he turned toward the enemy and waited, for he had been informed by his seer that he must not attack before one of his own men was either killed or wounded. "When this happens," the seer had said, "I shall lead you, and there will be victory for you and your men, but for me, I think, death." [19] And he was not wrong, for when they took up their arms, he himself, as if led on by some fate, leaped out in front, fell upon the enemy, and was killed. (He is buried at the ford of the Kephisos River.[a]) The rest of the men from Phyle gained the victory and pursued the enemy all the way down to the level ground. Of the Thirty, Kritias and Hippomachos were killed, and of the Ten who ruled in the Peiraieus, Charmides son of Glaucon and about seventy others also

2.4.17b   Enyalios: an ancient name for Ares, god   2.4.19a   Kephisos River: Map 2.4.30, inset.
of war.

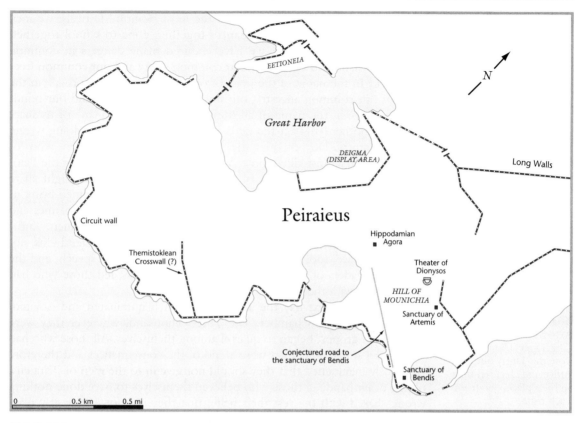

EETIONEIA

Great Harbor

N

DEIGMA (DISPLAY AREA)

Long Walls

Circuit wall

Peiraieus

Hippodamian
Agora

Themistoklean
Crosswall (?)

Theater of
Dionysos

*HILL OF
MOUNICHIA*

Sanctuary of
Artemis

Conjectured road to
the sanctuary of Bendis

Sanctuary of
Bendis

0   0.5 km   0.5 mi

Map 2.4.10.

died. They gathered up the arms of the dead men but did not remove the tunic of a single citizen. When this had been completed and they were giving back the dead under truce,[b] many of the men approached one another and began to speak together.

[20] Kleokritos, the herald of the Mystery Initiates[a] and a man with an especially beautiful voice, called for silence and then spoke: "Fellow citizens, why do you drive us out? Why do you wish to put us to death? For we have done you no wrong ever, and we have shared with you the most

2.4.20
403
PEIRAIEUS
Kleokritos, a herald with a beautiful voice, gives a moving speech emphasizing the common experience of them all as Athenian citizens.

2.4.19b Xenophon mentions as a significant indication of fraternal feeling here that the victors in this case did not strip the dead, and he makes no mention of their raising a trophy in honor of their victory. Traditionally, after a battle in ancient Greece, the victors would gather up their dead, strip those of the enemy, and raise a trophy. The defeated would collect the bodies of their fallen during a truce that

they would explicitly request and be granted for that purpose. In this way, appropriate reverence was shown and proper burial was accorded to all war dead. See Appendix L, §13.

2.4.20a Kleokritos belonged to the family of heralds (Kerukes), one of two families associated with the Mysteries of Demeter (see Appendix J, §9), whose office was hereditary.

solemn sacred rites and sacrifices and the most beautiful festivals; we men from both sides have joined in dances together, gone to school together, served as soldiers together; we have endured many dangers in common with you by land and by sea, for our common safety and our common freedom. [21] In the name of the gods of our fathers and our mothers, in the name of our common ancestry, our links through marriage and our bonds of friendship—in the name of all these things, which so many of us share with one another—respect the gods and men and cease from doing wrong to your country. Do not obey the Thirty, the unholiest of men, who for their own gain almost killed more Athenians in eight months than the Peloponnesians killed in ten years of war.[a] [22] Even though we might share with you in the government in peace as fellow citizens, these men bring us to a war against each other that is the most shameful, burdensome, and impious of all wars, and one that is hateful to both gods and men. Know well, however, that even for these men who have just been killed by us, not only you but we, too, have wept many tears." This was his speech, and the remaining leaders of the Thirty, affected by his words, led those who had marched out with them back to the city.

[23] On the next day the Thirty, very much humiliated and isolated, met in the Council Chamber. The Three Thousand, wherever they were stationed in groups, began to quarrel among themselves. All those who had committed some violent act were afraid of the consequences and therefore vigorously maintained that they should not give in to the men of Peiraieus; on the other hand, all those who believed themselves to have done nothing wrong shared with the rest their belief that they did not in any way need these evils that had come upon them. They said that it was not right to obey the Thirty, nor to permit them to destroy the city. Finally, they voted to remove them from office[a] and to choose others to rule in their place; they chose ten men, one from each tribe.[b]

[24] The Thirty then left Athens and went to Eleusis.[a] The newly elected Ten, with the help of the cavalry commanders, gave their attention to matters in the city, which was in a very agitated state, as there was still a high level of mutual distrust among the citizens. The cavalrymen were in fact sleeping in the Odeion with their horses and shields, and because of the prevailing suspicion, they patrolled continually in the evening with their shields along the walls, and toward dawn with their horses; they lived in constant fear that some men from Peiraieus[b] would attack them. [25] And the exiles there were now numerous indeed, and made up of men of every station. They were

making arms for themselves, some of wood, some of wickerwork, and they were painting them for battle. Before ten days had passed, they had exchanged oaths that whoever fought with them, even if they were not Athenians, would have the right of equal taxation with that of citizens.[a] When they marched out, they advanced with many hoplites and light-armed troops, and they even had about seventy horsemen. They made forays into the countryside, gathering wood and the fruit that was in season, and then returned to Peiraieus to sleep. [26] Not one of the men in the city went out in arms, but the cavalry sometimes harassed those who were foraging and managed to harm some of the men in their phalanx.[a] Once they chanced to meet some men from the deme of Aixone,[b] who were going to their own properties for provisions. Lysimachos the cavalry commander cut their throats, even though the men from Aixone entreated him repeatedly not to do it and many of his own cavalrymen were opposed to the deed. [27] Then the men in Peiraieus captured Kallistratos of the tribe of Leontis in the countryside and killed him in retaliation. And indeed the men of Peiraieus had now grown so confident that they made attacks even on the wall of Athens.

Perhaps it might be appropriate here to mention what the engineer of the city did when he learned that the men of Peiraieus were intending to bring siege engines up along the Lykeion Racetrack.[a] He gave orders that oxen should be yoked together and large blocks of stone should be hauled in wagons and then deposited in the roadway wherever each driver wished. They did as he instructed, and each of these stones caused many problems for those attempting to bring up the siege engines.

[28] From Eleusis, the Thirty sent ambassadors to the Spartans,[a] as did the men from the city who were on the list, and they asked for help on the grounds that the people had revolted from their Spartan alliance. Lysander thought that he could quickly bring the men of Peiraieus to terms if he besieged them by land and sea and cut them off from their supplies, so he arranged with the Thirty and the men of the city that they be given a loan of one hundred talents,[b] and he managed also to have himself sent out as governor, together with his brother Libys, who was to hold the office of admiral. [29] Lysander himself marched by land to Eleusis and gathered many Peloponnesian[a] hoplites on the way. The admiral kept watch by sea to prevent any supplies from reaching the men of the Peiraieus by ship. Indeed, within a short period of time, the men of Peiraieus became despondent about their situation, while the men of the city once again were confident, thanks to the presence of Lysander.

2.4.28
403
ATHENS
Both sides appeal to Sparta for help. Lysander comes by land to Eleusis while his brother blockades Peiraieus from the sea. The men of Peiraieus are soon despondent.

2.4.29–31
403
SPARTA-ATHENS
With support of the Ephor-ate, Pausanias brings a Spartan and allied army to Athens to keep Lysander from gaining too much individual power. Pausanias demonstrates against the walls, accomplishing nothing.

2.4.25a The right of *isoteleia* ensured that resident aliens to whom it was granted would be allowed to pay taxes at the lower citizen rate rather than the usual (and higher) metic tax.
2.4.26a These would have been the armed men guarding the others who were foraging.
2.4.26b Aixone: Map 2.4.30. Reading *Aixoneon* (Palmer) for the manuscripts' meaningless *exo neon* ("outside of ships"). (John Marincola) On Athenian demes, see

Appendix B, §3.
2.4.27a This *dromos* for horse races apparently ran through the site of the Lykeion and would have provided a pathway for the approach of siege machinery. Lykeion: Map 2.4.30, inset.
2.4.28a Sparta: Map 2.4.30.
2.4.28b One hundred talents was a sum sufficient to hire an army of mercenaries. See Appendix I, §8, 10, 13.
2.4.29a Peloponnese: Map 2.4.30.

When things were progressing in this way, the Spartan king Pausanias grew suspicious that if Lysander should accomplish his goal, he would not only win great repute but would also gain complete control over Athens. He persuaded three of the five ephors,[b] and with their approval he led out an army from Sparta to Athens. [30] All of Sparta's allies joined in the expedition, except the Boeotians[a] and the Corinthians:[b] these said that they could not consider themselves to be abiding by the treaty if they should send troops against the Athenians, who had in no way violated the treaty. In fact, they refused to participate because they thought that the Spartans wanted to make Athens their own secure possession.[c]

When Pausanias arrived, he had his army set up camp in the so-called Halipedon[d] near the Peiraieus. He commanded the right wing while Lysander, with his mercenaries, held the left. [31] Pausanias sent heralds to the men of Peiraieus, ordering them to depart, each to his own home. When they did not obey him, he attacked them, and so that it would not be evident that he was favorably inclined toward them, he kept his forces well away from the wall, about the distance from which the battle cry is raised. When this assault accomplished nothing, however, he led his troops back to camp.

On the next day, taking two regiments of the Spartans and three squadrons of the Athenian cavalry, he marched to the Quiet Harbor,[a] so as to examine where and how Peiraieus could most easily be walled off. [32] As he was departing, some men attacked him and harassed his troops. Pausanias became annoyed and gave orders to the cavalry to attack the men at a gallop, while he ordered the ten-year troops[a] to follow them. He himself followed at the head of the rest of his forces. They killed about thirty of the enemy's light-armed troops and pursued the rest to the Theater of Peiraieus.[b] [33] It so happened, however, that all the peltasts and the hoplites of the men from Peiraieus were arming themselves at the theater. Thus the light-armed men were able to immediately run out and hurl their javelins, spears, arrows, and slings. These missiles wounded many of the Spartans, who, being thus hard pressed, started to retreat slowly backwards. Their withdrawal encouraged their opponents to attack them with more vigor, and in this encounter Chairon and Thibrakos, both polemarchs,[a] were killed, as was Lakrates, an Olympian victor, and others who are now all buried in the Kerameikos,[b] in

2.4.32–34
403
ATHENS
While examining the ground, Pausanias' troops are harassed by some from Peiraieus, and a full-scale battle develops from initial skirmishes as each side throws in reinforcements. Finally, the Athenians are thrown back and defeated.

2.4.29b   Ephors: see Appendix E, §16.
2.4.30a   Boeotia: Map 2.4.30.
2.4.30b   Corinth: Map 2.4.30.
2.4.30c   The Greek is ambiguous here and could mean that the Spartans wished the Athenians to be their loyal allies, or (less likely) that they themselves wanted to possess the actual city-state. (John Marincola)
2.4.30d   Halipedon, a salt marsh: Map 2.4.30, inset.
2.4.31a   The Quiet Harbor is thought to be a small bay lying just to the west of the Great Harbor: Map 2.4.30, inset.
2.4.32a   Ten-year troops were the men who had served in the army no longer than ten years, approximately from the ages of

twenty to twenty-nine. They were thus the youngest and quickest soldiers in the Spartan army. See Appendix F, The Spartan Army (and the Battle of Leuctra), §11.
2.4.32b   Theater of Dionysos (Peiraieus): Map 2.4.10 and Map 2.4.30, inset.
2.4.33a   Spartan polemarchs (high military officers): see Appendix F, §5.
2.4.33b   The Kerameikos was a district of Athens (where the clay for famous Athenian pottery came from). It had workshops, a famous gate (Kerameikos Gate: Map 2.4.30, inset), and a famous cemetery. See Figure 2.4.33 of the grave of Spartan troops found at Kerameikos near the city gates.

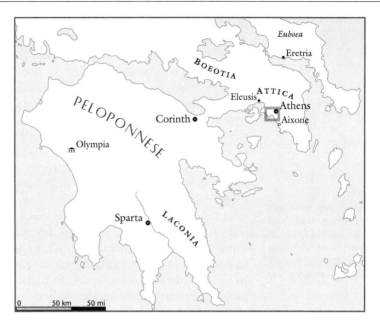

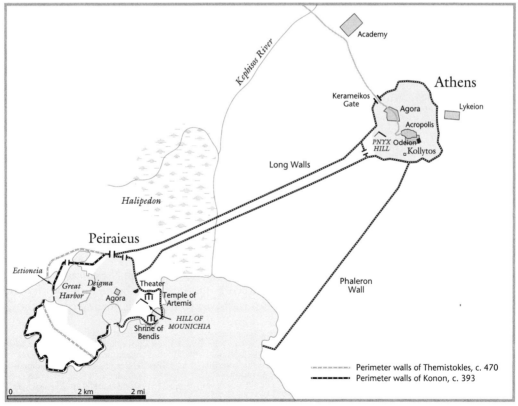

MAP 2.4.30

front of the city gates. [34] Thrasyboulos and the rest of the hoplites, seeing them fall, brought up reinforcements and quickly deployed themselves in a line eight men deep in front of the marshes.[a] Pausanias was now greatly pressed and retreated about four or five stades[b] toward a hill. As he withdrew, he ordered the rest of the Spartan and allied units to march to his position. There he arranged the troops into a very deep phalanx and led them against the Athenians, who received them in hand-to-hand combat. Some of the Athenians were pushed back into the mud of the marshes, while others gave way, and about 150 of them were killed.

[35] Pausanias then erected a trophy and returned to his camp. He was not at all angry with the men of Peiraieus; indeed, he sent a message to them in secret, instructing them to send heralds to himself and the ephors who were with him, and even informing them of exactly what they should request; and the men of Peiraieus did as he ordered. He was also trying to cause dissension within Athens itself, so he ordered the men in charge there to send to him and the ephors as many men as they could, instructing them to say that there was no reason to make war against the men of Peiraieus but, rather, that both sides should be reconciled and both should be friends of the Spartans.

[36] Now, it is customary for two ephors to march out with the king,[a] and Naucleidas, who was one of the two present at that moment with Pausanias, was delighted with Pausanias' plan, and in fact, both ephors inclined much more to the thinking of Pausanias than to that of Lysander. Because of this, they eagerly sent to Sparta both the men from Peiraieus (who were prepared to offer a treaty to the Spartans) and some private individuals who had come to them from the city, namely Kephisophon and Meletos. [37] After these men had departed for Sparta, however, some official representatives of the men holding office in the city came to the Spartans and announced that they were handing over to the Spartans both the walls of the city and their own persons, for the Spartans to do with as they wished.[a] They said that they thought the men of the Peiraieus should do likewise and hand over the Peiraieus and Mounichia[b] if they were really, as they claimed, friends of the Spartans.

[38] When the ephors and the Spartan Assembly had heard these proposals, they decided to send fifteen men to Athens,[a] and they charged them, working together with Pausanias, to reconcile the parties as best they could. And they did make a reconciliation agreement on the following terms: that there was to be peace between both sides; that the men of the city and the men of Peiraieus were each to depart to his own home, except for the Thirty

---

2.4.34a   Marshes: reading Madvig's emendation *Halōn* for the manuscripts' *allōn*. (John Marincola) For the Greek, see Translator's Notes. These marshes are probably the Halipedon, the salt marshes north of Peiraieus.

2.4.34b   If Xenophon measures by the Attic stade of 583 feet, then 4 or 5 stades would convert to 800 to 1,000 yards.

2.4.36a   For ephors accompanying the king on campaign, see Appendix F, §14.

2.4.37a   This is a formula of unconditional surrender.

2.4.37b   Mounichia Hill at Peiraieus: Map 2.4.30, inset.

2.4.38a   Athens: Map 2.4.30.

FIGURE 2.4.33.
THE TOMB OF THE LACEDAIMONIANS
IN THE BURIAL GROUNDS OF THE
KERAMEIKOS OUTSIDE THE CITY WALLS
AT ATHENS. FIRST EXCAVATED IN 1930,
THE POLYANDREION (COMMUNAL TOMB)
SHOWS EVIDENCE OF XENOPHON'S
ACCOUNT AT 2.4.33 OF THE SPARTAN
SOLDIERS WHO DIED IN THE BATTLE. AN
INSCRIPTION THAT RAN ALONG THE TOP
OF THE TOMB (NOW IN THE KERAMEIKOS
MUSEUM) WAS CARVED WITH THE
LETTERS "LA . . ." (FOR "LAKEDAIMO-
NION") AND THE NAMES OF THE TWO
POLEMARCHS CHAIRON AND THIBRAKOS.
IT WAS WRITTEN IN LACONIAN RATHER
THAN ATHENIAN, WITH THE LETTERS
RUNNING FROM RIGHT TO LEFT SO THE
INSCRIPTION COULD BE READ BY THOSE
APPROACHING THE CITY. THIRTEEN OR
FOURTEEN SKELETONS WITH SPEAR AND
ARROW WOUNDS WERE FOUND CARE-
FULLY LAID OUT IN THREE CHAMBERS.
ACCOMMODATING SPARTAN TRADITION,
THE WARRIORS WERE BURIED WITHOUT
GRAVE GOODS.

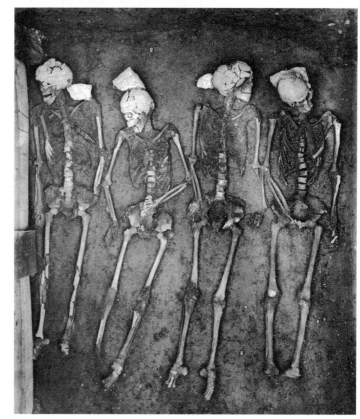

and the Eleven and the Ten who had ruled in Peiraieus.[b] If some men of the city feared for their safety, it was decided that they might go and live at Eleusis.

[39] When these arrangements were completed, Pausanias dismissed the army, and the men from Peiraieus went up to the Acropolis[a] carrying their weapons and sacrificed to Athena. When they came down, the generals called an assembly,[b] and there Thrasyboulos rose to speak. [40] "Men of the city," he said, "I advise you to know yourselves. And you would especially know yourselves if you attempted to define those qualities on which you pride yourselves so much that you would attempt to rule over us. Do you believe you are more righteous than we are? Well, the common people are poorer than you, but they have never acted unjustly against you for the sake of money. Whereas you, on the other hand, who are the wealthiest of us all, have committed many shameful crimes just for the sake of personal gain. But since you lack all concern for justice, perhaps you are so confident because of your bravery. [41] And yet what better way could there be of determining who is braver than by considering what happened when we fought against each other? But you might insist that you are superior in judgment—you who had a walled city and weapons and money and the Spartans as allies and were yet defeated by men who possessed none of these things. Do you base your pride on the friendship of the Spartans? How can that be now, when they have handed you over, just as people collar and hand over vicious dogs, to the common people here, whom you have wronged—and having done that, they then turned and went home? [42] Yet despite all that, I do not think that you, gentlemen, are men who will transgress any oaths you swore to observe; I trust, rather, that you will demonstrate, in addition to the rest of the good deeds that you have recently displayed, that you are men who abide by their oaths and are pious." Speaking in this manner, and adding more to the same effect, namely that there should be no disorder but that they should continue to obey the laws of old, he dismissed the Assembly.

[43] Then they established magistrates and formed a government. Later, when they heard that the men at Eleusis were trying to hire foreign soldiers, the entire citizen body marched out. And when the generals of the men from Eleusis came to a conference, they killed them, and they then sent men who were friends and relatives of the rest at Eleusis to persuade them to come to an agreement. Both parties then swore oaths not to remember past wrongdoings,[a] and to this day they live as fellow citizens and the people abide by their oaths.

2.4.39–42
403
ATHENS
Pausanias and his army leave Athens. The men from Peiraieus go to Athens and sacrifice to Athena. Thrasyboulos addresses the Assembly and reproves the oligarchs for their arrogance. Then, saying they must obey the old laws, he dismisses the Assembly.

2.4.43
403
ATHENS
Democratic government is established at Athens, and after some fighting, peace is made.

2.4.38b The members of the Thirty, the Eleven, and the Ten remained liable to prosecution for their earlier misdeeds, whereas their followers did not. Consequently, almost all of the leaders did not go home but remained in Eleusis (Map 2.4.30). However, we know from Lysias' speech against Eratosthenes (Lysias 12.54–55) that two members of the Thirty, Pheidon and Eratosthenes, had not gone to Eleusis in the first place. Eratosthenes stood trial and may well have been acquitted.

2.4.39a Acropolis of Athens: Map 2.4.30, inset.

2.4.39b The phrase "called an assembly" is not in the manuscripts but was added by Cobet to make up for the lack of connection between the two incidents. (John Marincola) For the Greek, see Translator's Notes.

2.4.43a These oaths were taken in the year 401 (Aristotelian *Constitution of Athens* 40.2).

BOOK THREE

So in this way, then, the civil strife at Athens[a] came to an end. After this, Cyrus sent messengers into Sparta,[b] asking that they should now reciprocate the friendship he had shown to them during their war with the Athenians.[c] The ephors,[d] thinking his request was just, ordered Samios, who was navarch[e] at the time, to provide Cyrus with anything he needed. And Samios indeed zealously carried out whatever tasks Cyrus requested of him. Adding his own fleet to that of Cyrus, he accompanied him in his voyage to Cilicia,[f] where he prevented Syenessis, the ruler of Cilicia, from opposing Cyrus on land when Cyrus was marching against the King.[g] [2] The story of how Cyrus gathered an army and with it marched up-country against his brother, how the battle between them turned out, how Cyrus himself was killed, and how after this the Greeks made their way safely back to the sea[a]—all this has been written by Themistogenes of Syracuse.[b]

[3] Now when Tissaphernes,[a] who had given much valuable service to King Artaxerxes in the war against his brother, was sent to the coast of Asia Minor[b] to be satrap over those he had previously ruled and those whom Cyrus had ruled as well, he immediately demanded that the Ionian cities[c]

3.1.1a Athens: Map 2.4.30.
3.1.1b Sparta: Map 2.4.30.
3.1.1c For Cyrus' services to the Spartans, see 1.5.2–9, 1.6.18, 2.1.11–14.
3.1.1d Ephors: a council of five officials of the Spartan government, elected annually. See Appendix E, Spartan Government and Society, §16.
3.1.1e Navarch: Spartan commander of the Peloponnesian fleet.
3.1.1f Cilicia: Map 3.1.13, locator.
3.1.1g The previous King of Persia, Darius II (last mentioned at 2.1.14), had died in the meantime, so this was really a succession contest in which Cyrus attempted to depose his elder brother, who was crowned as Artaxerxes II in 404. See Appendix D, Persia in Xenophon's Hellenika, §3.
3.1.2a The battle's precise location is unknown, but it took place near Cunaxa: Map 3.1.13, locator. The Greek army then marched

north from Cunaxa to the city of Trapezus on the Black Sea: Map 3.1.13, locator.
3.1.2b This sentence summarizes the story of Xenophon's book Anabasis. Nothing is known of Themistogenes, and it is generally believed that the name is a pseudonym of Xenophon himself. Certainly Plutarch took it that way: see "On the Glory of Athens" 345E.
3.1.3a See "Tissaphernes" in Appendix M, Brief Biographies of Important Characters in Xenophon's Hellenika, §29, and Appendix D, §2, 3, 6.
3.1.3b Asia Minor (Asia): Map 3.1.13, locator.
3.1.3c Ionia was a region on the central west coast of Asia Minor, including nearby islands, that was colonized by the Greeks around 1000 B.C.E. The twelve Ionian cities were Lebedos, Teos, Klazomenai, Erythrai, Samos, Phocaea, Chios: Map 3.1.13, BX; and Miletus, Myous, Priene, Ephesus, Colophon: Map 3.1.13, BY.

3.1.1–2
401
ASIA
Cyrus asks the Spartans for help and receives it from the Spartan fleet. Xenophon mentions the saga of the Greek army that assisted Cyrus and that had to make the long march (which he describes in his book *Anabasis*) from Mesopotamia to the Black Sea.

3.1.3
400
ASIA
Tissaphernes, made satrap of his own and Cyrus's former cities, demands that the Ionian cities subject themselves to him. They refuse and ask Sparta to protect them.

recognize his rule. The cities, however, would not receive him, because they wished to be free and because they feared Tissaphernes' wrath, since when Cyrus was alive, they had preferred him to Tissaphernes. They therefore sent ambassadors to Sparta, asking the Spartans, since they were now the leaders of all Greece, to protect them, the Greeks in Asia, so that their land would not be ravaged and they themselves would be free men.

[4] So the Spartans sent Thibron^a to them as governor,^b giving him about a thousand of the freed helots^c as soldiers and about four thousand of the rest of the Peloponnesians.^d Thibron also demanded three hundred cavalry from the Athenians, promising that he himself would provide for their upkeep. The Athenians sent those who had served in the cavalry under the Thirty, for they thought that it would be advantageous to the people if these men went abroad and died there.^e

[5] When they arrived in Asia,^a Thibron gathered additional soldiers from the Greek cities on the mainland, since at that time all the Greeks of Asia obeyed any order that a Spartan might give them.^b Thibron at this time did not bring his cavalry down into the plain but kept a close watch on the enemy and was content to keep their forces from ravaging the land near whatever position he happened to be holding. [6] When, however, those Greeks who had gone into the interior with Cyrus had returned safely and joined his army,^a he arrayed his forces in the plain, so as to confront those of Tissaphernes.

In addition, he captured the cities of Pergamum^b (which came over of its own free will), Teuthrania,^c and Halisarna.^d These last two cities were ruled by Eurystheus and Prokles, who were both descended from Demaratos the Spartan; these cities had been given to Demaratos by King Xerxes in exchange for his having accompanied Xerxes in his invasion of Greece.^e Also coming over to Thibron's side were the brothers Gorgion and Gongylos; the former ruled over Gambreion^f and Palaiagambreion, the latter over Myrina^g and Gryneion.^h These cities had been given by the King to Gongy-

---

Left margin notes:

3.1.4
400/399
SPARTA-ASIA
The Spartans send troops and Thibron to take command as harmost.

3.1.5–7
399
ASIA
Thibron stays on the defensive until his army is reinforced, then he confronts the enemy in the plain. Several cities go over to his side, and he captures other, weaker ones, but his siege of Larisa fails, and he is directed to march against Caria.

3.1.4a   Thibron: Xenophon mentions him in the last sentence of the *Anabasis*. See Appendix M, §25.
3.1.4b   Xenophon uses the term *harmost* here: see Appendix E, §19 and the Glossary.
3.1.4c   These were the *neodamōdeis*, helots (serfs) who had been freed, usually for some great service to Sparta and her allies. Their rights and/or privileges are unknown. See Appendix E, §9, 12; Appendix F, The Spartan Army (and the Battle of Leuctra), §6; and Thucydides 5.34.1.
3.1.4d   Peloponnese: Map 2.4.30.
3.1.4e   For the Knights' support of the Thirty at Athens, see 2.4.1–10.
3.1.5a   In the winter of the year 400. For Diodorus' account of this campaign in Asia by Thibron, see Appendix O, Selections from the *Histories* of Diodorus Siculus Relevant to Xenophon's *Hellenika*, 14.35–36.4.
3.1.5b   Xenophon is contrasting the situation in 400 with that of later times, when the

Spartans had lost the moral authority they exercised in the immediate aftermath of the Peloponnesian War. A similar sentiment can be found at *Anabasis* 6.6.9–12.
3.1.6a   This is the action with which Xenophon's account, the *Anabasis*, ends: see *Anabasis* 7.8.24. Thus Xenophon, as a commander of this force (see Appendix O, 14.37.1), joined the Spartan army at this point. See the Introduction, §4.2–3.
3.1.6b   Pergamum: Map 3.1.13, AY.
3.1.6c   Teuthrania: Map 3.1.13, AX.
3.1.6d   Halisarna: Map 3.1.13, AY.
3.1.6e   For more information about the deposed Spartan king Demaratos, who accompanied Xerxes in 480, see Herodotus, *Histories* 6.61–70, 7.3, 7.101–5.
3.1.6f   Gambreion: Map 3.1.13, AY. The precise location of Palaigambreion is unknown.
3.1.6g   Myrina: Map 3.1.13, BX.
3.1.6h   Gryneion: Map 3.1.13, BY.

los, the brothers' ancestor, in recognition of the fact that Gongylos alone of all the Eretrians[i] had taken the Persian side against the Greeks and fled as an exile to the Persian court.[j]

[7] There were in addition some weak cities that Thibron took by force. Thibron also besieged Larisa[a] (the one called Egyptian Larisa), encircling it with an army after his attempts at persuasion had failed. When he could not take it by any other means, he attempted to cut a shaft and dig a conduit that would cut off the city's water supply. The Larisaians, however, would run out from the wall and throw wood and stones into the shaft. When Thibron, in response, made a wooden covering over it, the Larisaians countered by attacking at night and setting the cover on fire. Since it seemed that he was having no success, the ephors ordered him to leave Larisa and campaign instead against Caria.[b]

[8] While Thibron was in Ephesus planning his march to Caria, the man who was to succeed him as commander, Derkylidas,[a] arrived; Derkylidas had such a reputation for shrewdness that his nickname was "Sisyphus."[b] So Thibron departed for home, where he was fined and sent into exile, because the Spartan allies had brought a charge against him that he had allowed his army to plunder the friends of the Spartans. [9] As for Derkylidas, when he took over the army, he realized that Tissaphernes and Pharnabazos[a] viewed each other with suspicion, so after conferring with Tissaphernes, he led his army into the territory of Pharnabazos, choosing to fight one rather than both of them at the same time. Now even before this, Derkylidas was hostile to Pharnabazos, for when he was harmost of Abydos[b] (in the time when Lysander was admiral),[c] he was slandered by Pharnabazos and punished by being made to stand holding his shield, which is considered a grave dishonor by Spartans of quality, since it is normally inflicted on those who fail to maintain formation. This former insult made Derkylidas all the happier to invade the territory of Phar-

3.1.8–9
399
EPHESUS
Derkylidas arrives to take command and, realizing that the two satraps in the area are rivals, directs his force against Pharnabazos.

3.1.6i   Eretria, Euboea: Map 2.4.30.
3.1.6j   This Gongylos was probably the grandfather of Gorgion and Gongylos; for his exploits after the Persian defeat in 479, see Thucydides 1.128.6.
3.1.7a   Laris(s)a? (in Aeolis): Map 3.1.13, BX. Perhaps Xenophon says this is called "Egyptian" Larisa to distinguish it from Larisa in the Troad (the region around Troy): Map 3.1.13, AX, and from Larissa, Thessaly: Map 2.3.4.
3.1.7b   Caria: Map 3.1.13, BY.
3.1.8a   See "Derkylidas" in Appendix M, §8.
3.1.8b   Sisyphus: the mythical figure from Corinth, who was noted for his cunning. He was skilled in wiles and, in fact, knew so much about them that he could not be deceived. The ancient historian Ephoros (F. Jacoby, *Die Fragmente der griechischen Historiker* 70 F 71, Berlin, 1923–30; Leipzig, 1940–58) wrote that Derkylidas was called Sisyphus because

he could not be deceived.
3.1.9a   Pharnabazos, a Persian satrap of the Dardanelles and Bosporus area and a longtime rival of Tissaphernes: see Appendix M, §21, Thucydides 8.6, and passim.
3.1.9b   Abydos: Map 3.1.13, AX. The harmost is usually (as here) a garrison commander.
3.1.9c   In 407 or possibly 405. Although in the latter year the command belonged nominally to Arakos, this was merely a device to get around the Spartan law stipulating that a man could be a naval commander only once; there can be no doubt that Lysander, though nominally Arakos' second-in-command, was actually in charge.

3.1.10
?–399
AEOLIS
Flashback of the story of
Mania from Aeolis.
Derkylidas is very different from Thibon. He
does not allow the army
to plunder allied territory.
Mania, wife of the
deceased subsatrap, brings
gifts to Pharnabazos.

3.1.11–12
?–399
AEOLIS
Flashback on the story of
Mania from Aeolis
continues. How Mania
takes the place of her
dead husband as a
subsatrap in Aeolis under
Pharnabazos.

3.1.13
?–399
AEOLIS
Flashback on the story
of Mania from Aeolis
continues. Mania rules as
a faithful servant of
Pharnabazos.

3.1.14–15
399
AEOLIS
When Mania is murdered
by Meidias, her son-in-
law, Pharnabazos swears
to avenge her.

nabazos. [10] And even at the very outset he differed greatly in his command from Thibron in that he did not allow his army to harm his allies as it marched through friendly territory up to Aeolis,[a] an area controlled by Pharnabazos.

Now this section of Aeolis was part of the satrapy ruled by Pharnabazos, but Zenis of Dardanos,[b] for as long as he was alive, administered this land for Pharnabazos. When he died of an illness and Pharnabazos was preparing to give the territory to someone else, Mania, the wife of Zenis and herself a Dardanian, organized an expedition and went to meet Pharnabazos, taking gifts both for Pharnabazos himself and for his concubines and those men who had the greatest influence with him, hoping thus to win them over.

[11] When they finally met to speak together, Mania said, "Pharnabazos, my husband was your friend in every way, and he was especially careful to pay over to you all the tribute that was yours, so much so that you praised and honored him. Now if I serve you as well as he did, why should you appoint someone else as your deputy? Of course, if I should fail to please you in any way, you can certainly remove me from the office and give the rule to someone else in my place." [12] Upon hearing this, Pharnabazos decided that the woman should be made satrap. And when she had taken charge of the land, she paid over the tribute no less scrupulously than her husband had done. In addition, Mania always brought gifts to Pharnabazos whenever she went to meet him, and whenever he visited her land, he found that her hospitality was much finer and more enjoyable than that of all his other subordinates.

[13] And she carefully guarded those cities that she ruled for him, and she added to his domain some cities that had not been subject to him previously—namely, the coastal cities Larisa,[a] Hamaxitos,[b] and Kolonai.[c] She conquered them by using a Greek mercenary force to attack their walls while she herself looked on from her carriage. She gave gifts unstintingly to anyone who gained her admiration, and her mercenary force was most splendidly equipped. She also campaigned alongside Pharnabazos whenever he attacked the Mysians[d] or Pisidians,[e] since these regularly plundered the King's land. And so Pharnabazos honored her handsomely and at times even called upon her for advice.

[14] She had passed the age of forty when her son-in-law Meidias was stirred up by some men who said that it was shameful for a woman to rule while he himself was but a private citizen. Now Mania, as befits a sole ruler, was particularly guarded in her dealings with everyone else, but she trusted her daughter's husband and treated him just as any woman would her son-

3.1.10a   Aeolis: Map 3.1.13, AX.
3.1.10b   Dardanos: Map 3.1.13, AX.
3.1.13a   Larisa (in the Troad): Map 3.1.13, AX.
    For other cities in this volume with the
    same name, see n. 3.1.7a.
3.1.13b   Hamaxitos: Map 3.1.13, AX.
3.1.13c   Kolonai: Map 3.1.13, AX.
3.1.13d   Mysia: Map 3.1.13, AY.
3.1.13e   Pisidia: Map 3.1.13, locator.

MAP 3.1.13

in-law. And it was he, they say, who approached her at one point and stran-gled her. He also killed her son, an exceedingly handsome young man about seventeen years old. [15] After he did this, he took possession of Skepsis[a] and Gergis,[b] strongholds where Mania had kept most of her wealth. All the other cities refused to receive him, as their garrisons chose to keep them safe for Pharnabazos. After this, Meidias sent gifts to Pharnabazos, requesting that he be permitted to rule over the same territory that Mania had held. Pharnabazos replied that Meidias should watch over those things until he himself came to take the gifts, together with Meidias himself. For he declared that he did not wish to live unless he could avenge the death of Mania.

[16] It was at this moment that Derkylidas arrived,[a] and immediately, in just one day, the coastal cities of Larisa, Hamaxitos, and Kolonai all came over to him of their own accord. He also sent word to the cities of Aeolis and asked them to free themselves and to receive him within their walls, becoming allies of the Spartans. The citizens of Neandria,[b] Ilion,[c] and Kokylion[d] obeyed him, since the Greek garrisons in these towns had been very badly treated after the death of Mania. [17] The garrison commander in the well-fortified city of Kebren,[a] however, would not receive Derkylidas, for he thought that he would be rewarded by Pharnabazos if he should retain the city for him. This angered Derkylidas, and he prepared to attack the city, but the sacrifices were not favorable on the first day, so he put it off to the next.[b] On the next day, however, they were similarly unfavorable, and he postponed it again to the third day. For four days he continued sacrificing, becoming very annoyed indeed, since he wanted to become master of all of Aeolis quickly, before Pharnabazos could intervene. [18] Now a certain Athenadas, a Sicyonian[a] company commander, thought that Derkylidas was blustering and wasting time and said that he himself could interrupt the water supply to the people of Kebren. Running forward with his own unit, he tried to block up the spring, but those inside the town came running out, wounding Athenadas and killing two others while driving the rest to flight with blows and missiles. This incident annoyed Derkylidas, who feared that any attack he might launch would now be less spirited, when at that moment there came out from the wall heralds from the Greek citizens announcing that the actions of the commander did not please them and that they themselves wished to ally with the Greeks, rather than the barbarians. [19] While they were still speaking, a messenger arrived

3.1.16–17
399
AEOLIS-KEBREN
With Derkylidas in command, more cities desert the Persians and go over to the Greeks. The commander of Kebren holds out against them, while Derkylidas delays his attack due to unfavor-able sacrifices.

3.1.18–19
399
KEBREN
Finally the Greek townspeople and the commander of Kebren go over to the Greek side.

3.1.15a   Skepsis: Map 3.1.13, AX.
3.1.15b   Gergis: Map 3.1.13, AX.
3.1.16a   Xenophon here picks up the campaign of Derkylidas from where he left it at 3.1.9. Diodorus' version of Derkylidas' campaign in Aeolis and the Troad can be found in Appendix O, 14.38.2–3.
3.1.16b   Neandria: Map 3.1.13, AX.
3.1.16c   Ilion (Troy): Map 3.1.13, AX.
3.1.16d   Kokylion, possible location: Map 3.1.13, AX.

3.1.17a   Kebren: Map 3.1.13, AX.
3.1.17b   Religious custom demanded that commanders make sacrifice and review omens before initiating such an assault. See Appendix L, Land Warfare in Xenophon's *Hellenika*, §13. See also n. 3.2.10b.
3.1.18a   Sicyon: Map 3.2.11, BX.

from their commander, announcing that he was in complete agreement with those who had just spoken. So Derkylidas, since it happened that on this day the sacrifices now proved favorable,[a] immediately took up his weapons and led the army to the gates. The men within opened them and permitted Derkylidas to enter. After he established a garrison there, he immediately marched against Skepsis and Gergis.

[20] Meanwhile, Meidias awaited the arrival of Pharnabazos, and as he was now afraid of his own citizens, he sent to Derkylidas, saying that he wished to negotiate with him on condition that Meidias could first take hostages from him. Derkylidas sent him one man from each of the cities and told him to select whichever ones and however many that he wished. Meidias took ten of them and then emerged from the city. In conversation with Derkylidas, he asked him on what conditions he might become an ally, and Derkylidas said on condition that he allow the citizens under his control to be free and autonomous. And as he said this, Derkylidas started to move toward Skepsis. [21] Meidias, knowing that he could not now rely upon his citizens to help him prevent Derkylidas' advance, allowed him to enter the city. Derkylidas sacrificed to Athena on the acropolis of Skepsis and then led out Meidias' garrison. He handed over the city to the citizens, and he exhorted them to conduct its affairs in a manner consistent with being Greeks and free men. He then departed and led his army toward Gergis as many of the people of Skepsis accompanied him along the way, honoring him and expressing their delight at what he had done.

[22] Meidias followed along, asking that Derkylidas leave him in control of the city of Gergis, and Derkylidas replied that Meidias would not fail to receive whatever was just. And as he said this he was moving toward the gates of Gergis with Meidias in tow, and the army followed peacefully, with the men walking two by two.[a] Those who were on the lookout from the towers (which were quite high) hurled no missiles when they saw that Meidias was with Derkylidas. Derkylidas then said, "Give the order, Meidias, to open the gates, so that you may lead and I may go with you to the temple and there sacrifice to Athena." Meidias hesitated to have the gates opened, fearing that he would be immediately taken prisoner, but he nevertheless gave the order to open them. [23] When Derkylidas entered, he went straight to the acropolis, keeping Meidias in tow. He ordered the rest of his soldiers to take positions around the walls, and he himself with the men around him sacrificed to Athena. When that was done, he ordered the bodyguards of Meidias to ground their arms in front of his own army, because, he said, they would now be his mercenaries and Meidias did not need to be afraid any longer. [24] Meidias, however, being at a loss as to what to do, said, "I will depart, so that I may prepare the rites of hospitality for you." But Derkylidas said, "No, by Zeus, do not leave, since it would be

3.1.20–21
399
SKEPSIS
Meidias, fearful now of his own citizens, asks Derkylidas the conditions under which they could become allies. Bowing to pressure from Derkylidas, he surrenders the city of Skepsis.

3.1.22–24
399
GERGIS
Derkylidas forces Meidias to order the gates of Gergis to open for him and enters the city peacefully. He promises to treat Meidias fairly.

3.1.19a   Favorable sacrifices: see Appendix J, Ancient Greek Religion in the Time of Xenophon, §2, 5, 12.

3.1.22a   An army moving forward in a two-by-two formation could hardly be deployed for battle.

shameful if you prepared hospitality for me after I have just sacrificed, rather than that I entertained you. Wait here with us, and while dinner is being prepared, let's you and I consider how we can act justly toward each other."

[25] When they had sat down, Derkylidas said, "Meidias, tell me, did your father leave you in charge of his house?" and Meidias replied that indeed he had done so. "And how many properties were there? How many estates? How many pastures?" Meidias began to list them, but the Skepsians who were present said, "He is lying, Derkylidas." [26] To which Derkylidas answered, "Well, don't worry about the little details." When Meidias had finished making his list, Derkylidas said, "Now tell me to whom did Mania belong?" and they all said that she belonged to Pharnabazos. "Well, then," he continued, "is it not the case that all of her property also belonged to Pharnabazos?" and they all replied that that was indeed the case. Derkylidas then said, "Well, then, those possessions would now belong to us, since we now are in control of them and Pharnabazos is our enemy. So let someone bring us to where the wealth of Mania and Pharnabazos has been stored."

[27] All the rest then led the way to Mania's house (the one that Meidias had taken for himself), and Meidias followed with them. Derkylidas went in and then summoned the treasurers, ordering his own servants to seize them. He warned them that if they were caught stealing any of Mania's property, they would immediately have their throats cut. So the treasurers showed him everything that was there, and when he had seen it all, he shut it up, placed a seal on the building, and placed guards in front of it. [28] He then went out and said to the squadron commanders and company commanders whom he found at the door: "We have acquired enough wealth to pay an army of eight thousand men for a year, and if we acquire anything more, we will add it to this fund." He said this because he knew that when the soldiers had heard it, they would conduct themselves in a more orderly and obedient manner.

But then Meidias asked, "And what about me? Where am I to live, Derkylidas?" He replied, "In that very place where it is most just for you to live, Meidias—in your hometown of Skepsis and in your father's house."

[1] After Derkylidas had made these arrangements and had captured nine cities in eight days, he considered how he could pass the winter in friendly territory without his army becoming a burden to his allies (as the troops under Thibron had been), and also how he might keep Pharnabazos from feeling superior enough to harm the Greek cities with his cavalry. So he sent a message to Pharnabazos and asked him whether he wanted peace or war. Pharnabazos was worried that the fortification of Aeolis[a] was done to attack his own homeland, Phrygia,[b] and so he chose to make a truce.

3.2.1a Aeolis: Map 3.1.13, AX.
3.2.1b There were two Phrygias in the ancient world: one in central Anatolia, southwest of Lydia, which was called Phrygia (Map 1.4.9; Ref. Map 2, CZ), and the other, near the Hellespont, called Hellespontine Phrygia (Map 3.1.13, AY). Pharnabazos' estates that were being plundered were in the vicinity of Daskyleion: Map 3.1.13, AY.

[2] After this, Derkylidas went to Bithynian Thrace,[a] where he wintered, and this choice of location did not at all displease Pharnabazos, since the Bithynians had often gone to war against him. Now for a time Derkylidas was able to plunder Bithynia safely and thereby provide what he needed for his troops; but then some allies from Seuthes[b] came to him from across the strait:[c] these numbered about two hundred cavalry and three hundred peltasts.[d] They made their camp about twenty stades[e] from the Greek one, and they built a stockade around it. They then asked Derkylidas to provide some hoplites[f] as guards for the camp and, going out for plunder, they managed to take many slaves and much booty. [3] Their camp was now full of prisoners, and the Bithynians, learning how many of the Thracians went out to raid for plunder and how many Greeks stayed behind as guards, gathered together a great number of peltasts and cavalry and at dawn fell upon the hoplites, about two hundred in all. When they came to close quarters, they began to hurl their missiles and javelins at them, so that many of the hoplites were killed or wounded. The hoplites, on the other hand, could not harm their antagonists, because the stockade (which was about the height of a man) prevented them from coming to close quarters. Finally, they broke through their own fortifications and went at the Bithynians, [4] but the Bithynians gave way wherever the hoplites tried to close, and since they were peltasts, they could easily outrun the pursuing hoplites[a] and still keep throwing their javelins at them, now from one side, now from another, and in this way they struck down many of the hoplites on each of their advances. Finally, as if confined in a pen, the hoplites were all shot down by the javelins. Only about fifteen of them made it back safe to the Greek camp, and these did so by retreating as soon as they perceived what was happening, running off during the battle, since the Bithynians took no notice of them. [5] All this was accomplished by the Bithynians quite quickly, and when they had killed the Odrysian Thracians who were guarding the tents, they took all the plunder and departed. So when the Greeks learned about this assault and brought assistance, they found nothing in the camp but naked corpses. When the Odrysians came back, they buried their dead, drank a great deal of wine in their honor, and held a horse race.[a] For the rest of the time they remained there, they camped together with the Greeks and continued to conduct raids for plunder throughout Bithynia.[b]

3.2.2–3
399
BITHYNIAN THRACE
Derkylidas winters in Bithynian Thrace, and his allies from Odrysian Thrace raid the country and gather much plunder and many captives in their camp. The Bithynians attack the camp at dawn.

3.2.4–5
399
BITHYNIAN THRACE
The Greek hoplites cannot harm the swift Bithynian peltasts, who shoot down all their opponents with missiles, then escape, taking with them the camp's accumulated plunder and captives.

3.2.2a   Bithynian Thrace: Map 3.2.11, AY.
3.2.2b   Seuthes, king of the Odrysians, not the King Seuthes who reigned from 425 to 415 and was mentioned by Thucydides at 2.97.3, 2.101.5–6, and 4.101.5.
3.2.2c   From Odrysian Thrace they crossed the Bosporus to reach Derkylidas. Map 3.2.11, AY.
3.2.2d   Peltasts: lightly armored infantry, originating in Thrace.
3.2.2e   If the 20 stades were Attic stades of 583 feet, they would convert to a little over 2 miles. See Appendix I, Units of Distance,

Currency, and Capacity in Xenophon's *Hellenika*, §4–5, 13.
3.2.2f   Hoplites: heavily armored infantry, often equipped with helmet, breastplate, and greaves, but always carrying a large round shield, a thrusting spear, and a short sword.
3.2.4a   The peltasts were not encumbered by the heavy bronze armor and shields carried by the hoplites.
3.2.5a   Herodotus (*Histories* 5.8) notes that the Thracians put on athletic contests as part of their burial rites.
3.2.5b   Bithynia: Map 3.2.11, AY.

[6] When spring came, Derkylidas marched from Bithynian Thrace to Lampsacus.[a] While he was there, the Spartan government sent three commissioners from home, Arakos, Naubates, and Antisthenes, whose orders were to examine the situation in Asia[b] in general, and specifically to tell Derkylidas to remain in office and retain his command for the coming year. They had also been ordered by the ephors to address the soldiers and tell them that the ephors[c] condemned their previous conduct[d] but praised their recent behavior, since they no longer acted unjustly. If, then, in the future the soldiers acted unjustly, the ephors would not tolerate it, but if they behaved with justice toward their allies, they would commend them. [7] Yet when the commissioners said these things to the soldiers in assembly, the leader of the men who had fought with Cyrus[a] said, "See here, Spartans, we are the same men now as we were last year. But there is a different commander now from the one we had before. You yourselves, therefore, can figure out quite easily why we do not now act unjustly, whereas back then we did."

[8] The commissioners from home and Derkylidas were sharing a tent; one of the men with Arakos noted that they had left behind in Sparta[a] some envoys from the Chersonese,[b] who had reported that they could not now cultivate the Chersonese because of the constant plundering raids of the Thracians.[c] But they asserted that if a wall were constructed across the peninsula from sea to sea, it would protect much good agricultural land, both for themselves and for as many other Spartans as would wish to join them. And so the man with Arakos said that he would not be surprised if some Spartan were sent with a force from the city to build such a wall.

[9] Derkylidas listened to them but did not reveal his own idea. Instead, he sent the commissioners off to Ephesus[a] via the Greek cities, delighted that they were going to see the cities in a state of peace and prosperity. So they set out, and Derkylidas, knowing now that he would remain in command, again sent to Pharnabazos and asked him whether he wanted war or a truce, such as had been in force during the winter. Pharnabazos again chose a truce, and so Derkylidas left Pharnabazos' cities in peace and crossed over the Hellespont[b] with his army into Europe.[c] He traveled through that part of Thrace with which he had established friendly relations, was hosted by Seuthes,[d] and finally reached the Chersonese. [10] He learned that there were eleven or twelve cities there, and that the land was excellent and extremely fertile, but that it had been laid waste by the Thracians, just as he had been told. When he found that the isthmus was only

3.2.6a   Lampsacus: Map 3.2.11, AY.
3.2.6b   Asia (Asia Minor): Map 3.2.11, AY.
3.2.6c   Ephors: a body of five powerful magis-
         trates at Sparta. See Appendix E, §16.
3.2.6d   In the previous year under the command
         of Thibron.
3.2.7a   The men who fought with Cyrus: see
         3.1.1–2. This speaker is undoubtedly
         Xenophon himself. Why he does not
         name himself here is unclear. See the

Introduction, §6.5.
3.2.8a   Sparta: Map 3.2.11, BX.
3.2.8b   Chersonese: Map 3.2.11, AY.
3.2.8c   Some manuscripts read "of the Persians,"
         not "of the Thracians." (John Marincola)
         Thrace: Map 3.2.11, AY.
3.2.9a   Ephesus: Map 3.2.11, BY.
3.2.9b   Hellespont: Map 3.2.11, AY.
3.2.9c   Europe: Map 3.2.11, AX.
3.2.9d   Seuthes, king of Odrysian Thrace.

thirty-seven stades wide,[a] he did not delay but sacrificed[b] and immediately began to build the wall, parceling out individual portions of the work to the soldiers. He promised he would give prizes to the first men to complete their portion and also to the others, each according to his merits. With such incentives, he completed the wall before late summer, although he had only begun it in the spring. It enclosed and protected eleven cities, many harbors, much good land for sowing, much cultivated land, and many very beautiful pasturelands, fit for all types of animals.[c]

[11] Having built this wall, Derkylidas crossed back again to Asia. Reviewing the state of the cities there, he found that all were doing well but that there were exiles from Chios[a] who had seized Atarneus,[b] a fortified city. These exiles were using Atarneus as a base from which to launch plundering raids throughout Ionia,[c] and they were living off this plunder. Learning that there was a great deal of grain within Atarneus, Derkylidas made camp there and began to lay siege to the city. He brought it to terms in eight months and set Drakon of Pellene[d] in charge of affairs there. Then he filled the city with all sorts of provisions, so that it would be his own secure base whenever he came there. Having accomplished all this, he departed for Ephesus, which is three days' march from Sardis.[e]

[12] Now up to this time Tissaphernes and Derkylidas continued to live in peace, as did the Greeks in Asia with the Persians. But now ambassadors from the Ionian cities[a] came to Sparta and told them that it was in Tissaphernes' power to permit the Greek cities to live autonomously if he so wished. They said that if Caria,[b] where Tissaphernes resided, were to suffer damage, they believed that he would quickly agree to allow the Greek cities to be autonomous. Upon hearing this, the ephors sent orders to Derkylidas to cross over into Caria with his army; they also ordered Pharax, the navarch, to sail alongside and support the army with his ships. Both men carried out their orders.

[13] Just at this time Pharnabazos happened to be visiting Tissaphernes. He had come for two reasons: first, because Tissaphernes had been appointed supreme commander, and second, because he wished to affirm that he was ready to join forces with him to make war on the Greeks so as to drive them from the King's territory. Pharnabazos was jealous of Tissaphernes' supreme command, and he especially resented that he himself had been deprived of his rule over Aeolis.[a] Tissaphernes allowed Pharnabazos to speak and then said, "The first thing for you to do is to cross over the Maeander River[b] to Caria with me, and there we will discuss these issues."

3.2.11
398
ATARNEUS
Derkylidas crosses back to Asia and besieges Atarneus, which had been seized by Chian exiles. After taking it, he makes of it a secure base.

3.2.12
397
SPARTA
In order to force the Persians to free the Ionian cities, Sparta orders its army and navy to attack Tissaphernes in Caria.

3.2.13–14
397
CARIA-IONIA
The two Persian satraps join forces to attack Ionia, and Derkylidas follows them to protect the Greek cities there.

3.2.10a Thirty-seven Attic stades, each 583 feet long, would convert to a little over 4 miles.
3.2.10b In ancient Greece, one sacrificed before all great undertakings, battles, and/or construction projects. See Appendix J, §4, 5.
3.2.10c For Diodorus' account of this wall, see Appendix O, 14.38.6–7.
3.2.11a Chios: Map 3.2.11, BY.

3.2.11b Atarneus: Map 3.2.11, AY.
3.2.11c Ionia: Map 3.2.11, BY.
3.2.11d Pellene: Map 3.2.11, BX.
3.2.11e Sardis: Map 3.2.11, BY.
3.2.12a For a list of the twelve Ionian cities, see n. 3.1.3c.
3.2.12b Caria: Map 3.2.11, BY.
3.2.13a Aeolis: Map 3.2.11, AY.
3.2.13b Maeander River: Map 3.2.11, BY.

3.2.15
397
IONIA
The Greeks are surprised on the march to find the enemy forces in front of them, deployed for battle.

3.2.16–17
397
IONIA
Derkylidas deploys his troops for battle, but only the Peloponnesians stand firm. The rest run away or make clear that they won't stay long.

3.2.18–20
397
IONIA
Although Pharnabazos wishes to give battle, Tissaphernes refuses to do so, remembering how well the Greeks fought against Persians at Cunaxa. He offers to parley, and Derkylidas accepts. They agree that the Persians will grant autonomy to the Greek cities provided that Derkylidas' army leaves Persian territory and the Spartan harmosts leave the cities.

[14] When they arrived in Caria, they agreed that they should establish suitable garrisons for the strongholds in that region and then return to Ionia.

When Derkylidas learned that the two men had crossed back over the Maeander, he told Pharax that he feared that the Persians would plunder the region once they saw that it was undefended, and so he, too, crossed back over the Maeander. His forces advanced into Ionia in no particular order, as they thought the enemy had already proceeded far into the countryside around Ephesus. Suddenly, however, they spotted in front of them several scouts watching them from the top of some burial mounds.ª [15] Derkylidas and Pharax ordered some of their men to climb up the mounds and towers nearby, and the men who did so saw the enemy army deployed across the road on which they were advancing: there were Carians with their whitened shields, and as many of the Persians as happened to be present, and all the Greek forces that both Tissaphernes and Pharnabazos commanded, as well as quite a good-sized force of cavalry—those of Tissaphernes on the right wing, those of Pharnabazos on the left.

[16] When Derkylidas learned of the enemy's presence, he ordered the regiment and company commanders to deploy their men into battle order eight ranks deep as quickly as possible. He stationed the peltasts on the wings, and he did the same with the cavalry, all that he had with him, which were of variable quality. He himself then attended to the sacrifice.ª [17] Now all the Peloponnesiansª in his army remained quiet and prepared for battle, but those troops who came from Priene,ᵇ Achilleion,ᶜ the islands, and the Ionian cities either abandoned their arms in the high grain of the Maeander plain and ran away or remained at their positions but clearly showed that they did not intend to stand and fight.

[18] It was reported to Derkylidas that counsel among the Persians was divided, Pharnabazos wishing to attack but Tissaphernes refusing to give the order, for he remembered how the Greek army of Cyrus' supporters had fought with and defeated the Persians, and he believed that all Greek forces were similar to those. Instead, he sent a message to Derkylidas that he wished to have a conference with him. Derkylidas, taking the best-looking infantry and cavalrymen he had, went forward toward the messengers and said to them, "Well, now, as you can see, I was planning to fight, but since Tissaphernes wishes to confer, I will not oppose him in this. If we parley, however, we must exchange pledges and hostages." [19] When these terms had been decided and executed, the two armies separated, the Persian force into Trallesª in Caria and the Greek force into Leukophrys,ᵇ where there was a very sacred temple of Artemis and a lake. This lake is more than a stade wide;ᶜ its bottom is

3.2.14a These would have been tombs on top of which had been set lofty burial mounds. The mounds would have made ideal observation posts.
3.2.16a For ritual sacrifices before battle, see n. 3.1.17b.

3.2.17a Peloponnese: Map 3.2.11, BX.
3.2.17b Priene: Map 3.2.11, BY.
3.2.17c Achilleion: Map 3.2.11, AY.
3.2.19a Tralles: Map 3.2.11, AX.
3.2.19b Leukophrys: Map 3.2.11, BY.
3.2.19c An Attic stade is 583 feet.

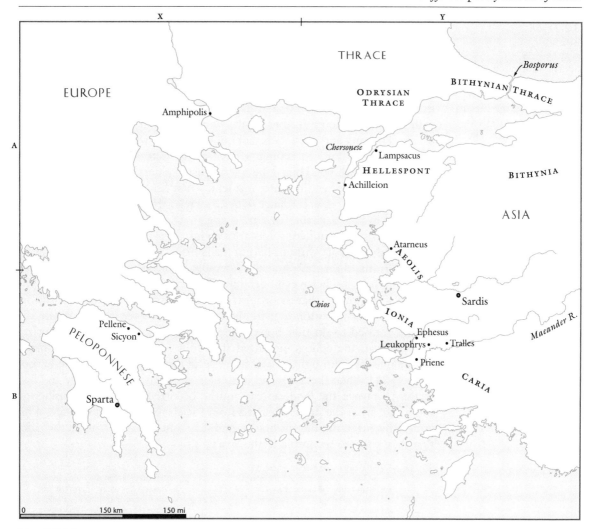

MAP 3.2.11

sandy, its waters are warm and potable, and it never runs dry. This, then, is
what they did on that day.

On the next day, they met at an agreed-upon place, and they decided
to learn from each other what each side might accept as terms for peace.
[20] Derkylidas demanded that the King allow the Greek cities to be
autonomous, and Tissaphernes and Pharnabazos said they could accept this
if the Greek army were to leave their territory and the Spartan harmosts
were removed from the cities. After this discussion they made a truce with
each other until these proposals could be reported back to Sparta[a] by
Derkylidas and to the King by Tissaphernes.

3.2.20a   Sparta: Map 3.2.26.

3.2.21–24
402?
SPARTA-ELIS
Sparta, motivated by many grievances, decides to chastise Elis, and so demands that the Eleians give autonomy to their subject territories. The Eleians refuse. King Agis leads an army into Eleian territory but turns back after an earthquake. This makes the Eleians bolder in their hostility to Sparta.

[21] While these things were being accomplished in Asia under Derkylidas' command, this is what the Spartans were doing.[a] They had long been angry with the Eleians[b] because the latter had made an alliance[c] with the Athenians,[d] Argives,[e] and Mantineians.[f] In addition, the Eleians, alleging that they had obtained a judgment against the Spartans, had forbidden them from taking part in the horse races and the athletic contests.[g] Not content with this, they offered further insult: when Lichas[h] handed over his chariot to the Thebans and they were announced as the winners of the race, he entered the stadium[i] intending to crown the victors. But the Eleians set upon him and whipped him—he was a Spartan elder[j]—and drove him from the games. [22] Then, in a later incident, when King Agis[a] had been sent to sacrifice to Zeus[b] in accordance with an oracle, the Eleians prohibited him from praying for a victory in war, saying that it had long been established that Greeks should not consult oracles about a war against other Greeks. He was forced to depart without having made his sacrifice.[c] [23] Angered by all these affronts, the ephors and the assembly resolved to teach the Eleians a lesson in how to behave moderately. They therefore sent envoys to the Eleians to announce that the magistrates of the Spartans thought it just that the Eleians grant autonomy to their surrounding territories. When the Eleians refused to do this, however, regarding their subject cities as prizes taken in war, the ephors mobilized the army. Agis was sent in command, and he marched through Achaea[a] into Eleian territory, following the Larisos River.[b] [24] When the army had just entered the enemy's territory and had begun to ravage the land, an earthquake occurred, and Agis, considering this a sign from the gods, departed from Eleian territory and disbanded his army. This made the Eleians bolder, and they sent out envoys to all the cities that they knew to be hostile to the Spartans.

3.2.21a   About February or March. There is a chronological problem here. Scholars usually put this war in the years 402–400 and assume Xenophon's chronological sequence is wrong here.
3.2.21b   Elis: Map 3.2.26.
3.2.21c   This alliance was formed in 420: see Thucydides 5.31, 5.47.
3.2.21d   Athens: Map 3.2.26.
3.2.21e   Argos: Map 3.2.26.
3.2.21f   Mantineia: Map 3.2.26.
3.2.21g   The Spartans were forbidden from participating in these contests in the Olympic Games that year: for details see Thucydides 5.49. The Eleians had condemned the Spartans for violating the truce that always accompanied the Olympic festival, and when the Spartans did not pay a fine, they were not allowed to compete in the games of 420. See Appendix J, §10–11, for ancient religious festivals. Olympia (Map 3.2.26 and inset) was in Eleian territory, and its temple and festival were normally under Eleian control. See *Hellenika* 7.4.28–32, for an an exceptional episode in which Arcadians and Pisans seized Olympia and conducted the

festival. The Eleians attacked them and a battle took place in the shrine itself.
3.2.21h   Lichas was a prominent Spartan. He handed his team over to the Thebans because at that time the Eleians, who controlled the games, had forbidden the Spartans from participating in them; see Thucydides 5.50.4, Pausanias 6.2.2.
3.2.21i   The stadium at Olympia: for a closeup of the stadium, see Map 7.4.29, inset.
3.2.21j   Xenophon uses the noun *geron*, which may mean either that Lichas was (simply) an old man or that he was a member of the Spartan Gerousia, the Council of Elders, which advised the king and ephors; see Appendix E, §15.
3.2.22a   King Agis of Sparta.
3.2.22b   Agis went to make the sacrifice at the great temple to Zeus at Olympia. See Appendix J, §3–4, 10.
3.2.22c   The date of this incident is not known.
3.2.23a   Achaea: Map 3.2.26. Presumably on this campaign Agis was attacking Elis from the north.
3.2.23b   Larisos River: Map 3.2.26. The river forms the boundary between Achaea and Elis.

FIGURE 3.2.21. AN ATTIC
CERAMIC STAMNOS, C. 510,
DEPICTING A FOUR-HORSE
CHARIOT RACE.

[25] As the year drew to a close,[a] the ephors again mobilized the army against Elis, and all the allies (excepting only the Boeotians[b] and the Corinthians[c]), as well as the Athenians, joined the army under Agis' command. As Agis was invading through Aulon,[d] the Lepreans[e] immediately revolted from the Eleians and went over to his side, as did the Makistians[f] and their neighbors the Epitalians.[g] And when Agis was about to cross the river,[h] the Letrinoi[i] and the Amphidoloi[j] and the Marganeis[k] also came over to join him. [26] Then Agis went to Olympia and there sacrificed to Olympian Zeus, and no one any longer tried to prevent him from sacrificing. Those rites completed, he advanced toward the city proper of Elis, devastating and burning the land and capturing a great number of cattle and prisoners on the way from the surrounding countryside. When others, especially many of

3.2.25–26
401?
ELIS
A second expedition against Elis led by Agis reinforced by allies leads to many defections from the Eleians to his side. He sacrifices at Olympia and takes much plunder and many prisoners from Eleian lands. Even the Achaeans and Arcadians join to share in the spoils.

3.2.25a Diodorus (Appendix O, 14.17.4–12, 14.34.1) gives a slightly different account of the Spartan-Eleian war.
3.2.25b Boeotia: Map 3.2.26.
3.2.25c Corinth: Map 3.2.26.
3.2.25d Aulon: Map 3.2.26.
3.2.25e Lepreon: Map 3.2.26.
3.2.25f Makistos: Map 3.2.26, inset.
3.2.25g Epitalion: Map 3.2.26, inset.
3.2.25h Alpheios River: Map 3.2.26 and inset.
3.2.25i Letrinoi: Map 3.2.26, inset.
3.2.25j Amphidolia: Map 3.2.26, inset.
3.2.25k Margana (Marganeis), possible location: Map 3.2.26, inset.

the Arcadians[a] and Achaeans, heard of this, they willingly joined him and received a share of the plunder. Indeed, this campaign became in essence a great provisioning for the Peloponnese.[b]

[27] When Agis came to the city, he devastated the beautiful suburbs and gymnasia; but he did not attempt to take the city itself, although it was thought that he was unwilling rather than unable to do so, particularly since it was unwalled.

When the army, which continued to plunder the land, had reached the vicinity of Kyllene,[a] an Eleian named Xenias (the one who was said to have measured the silver he inherited from his father with a bushel[b]), and his followers wished the city to go over to the Spartan side through their agency.[c] So they rushed from their houses with swords in hand and began to slaughter many of their fellow citizens, including one man who so closely resembled Thrasydaios, the leader of the common people, that they believed they had in fact killed Thrasydaios. Thinking their leader dead, the commons completely lost heart and took no action against the Spartan partisans. [28] Now the killers thought they had accomplished everything, and those of the same opinion began to bring their weapons into the agora,[a] but Thrasydaios was not dead: he had fallen asleep in the very place where he had gotten drunk. And when the people discovered that he was still alive, they flocked to his house from all sides, just as the leader of bees will be surrounded by his swarm.[b] [29] After Thrasydaios had gathered up the people, he led them into battle, in which they proved to be victorious, and when this happened, those who had committed the earlier slaughters rushed out of the city to join the Spartans.

Agis in turn departed and crossed back over the Alpheios River; he left guards behind in Epitalion near the Alpheios, and he also left there Lysippos as harmost and the exiles from Elis. When he had done these things, he disbanded the army, and he himself returned home.

[30] For the rest of the summer and the following winter, the land of the Eleians was plundered by Lysippos and those with him. The following summer Thrasydaios opened talks with Sparta and came to an agreement to destroy the walls of Pheia[a] and Kyllene[b] and to try to give up the Tryphylian cities Phrixa[c] and Epitalion and leave independent the Letrinoi, the Amphidolians, and the Marganeis; and in addition to these the Acroreians[d] and

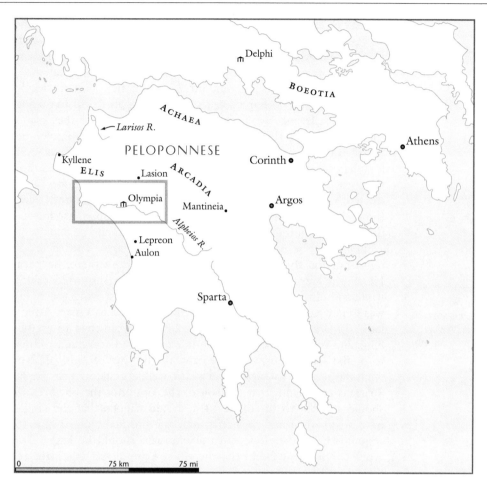

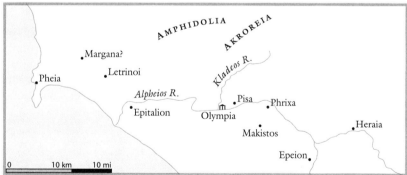

MAP 3.2.26

the city of Lasion,^e which had been claimed by the Arcadians. The Eleians, however, demanded that they be allowed to keep Epeion,^f a city between Heraia^g and Makistos, for they said they had agreed to purchase all that land from its inhabitants at the time for a price of thirty talents;^h and that they had already paid this amount. [31] But the Spartans decided that it was no more just to purchase land by force than it was to take it by force when the seller was weaker than the purchaser, and so they compelled the Eleians to give up this city also. The Spartans did not, however, deprive the Eleians of their supervision of the temple of Olympian Zeus, even though long ago it had not belonged to the Eleians; for the Spartans thought that the men who were claiming it from the Eleians were boors and were not suitable to oversee the temple.^a When these things had been agreed upon, the Eleians made peace and an alliance with the Spartans, and in this way, then, the war of the Spartans and the Eleians came to an end.

[1] With the war ended, Agis went to Delphi^a and there sacrificed a tenth portion to the god.^b After departing from there, he became ill in Heraia (he was now an old man), and he was transported back to Sparta while still alive, although he died shortly after arriving there. His funeral was somewhat grander than that usually accorded to a man. After the stipulated days of purification had passed, the Spartans had to establish a new king, and two men were claiming the kingship: Leotychidas, who professed to be the son of Agis, and Agesilaos, the brother of Agis. [2] Now Leotychidas argued as follows: "You know well, Agesilaos, that the law of the Spartans commands that the son of the king, not the brother of the king, should succeed to the office. If it should happen that the king does not have a son, then and only then may the brother succeed him." Agesilaos responded, "I, therefore, am the one who should be king." Leotychidas replied, "But how could that be when I am alive?" Agesilaos responded, "Because Agis, the one whom you call father, said that you were not his son."^a To which Leotychidas replied, "But my mother, who knows far better than he ever did, claimed and still claims that I am his." And Agesilaos said, "But Poseidon revealed quite clearly the error of your claim when, by means of an earthquake, he drove from the bedroom the man who was really your father.^b Time, which is said to be most truthful, provided additional evidence: for you were born in the tenth month after that man who sired you was seen to be in your mother's bedroom." In this way the two men disputed the succession.

3.3.1–2
400?
SPARTA
Agis dies shortly after the war with Elis ends. Leotychidas, his son, and Agesilaos, his brother, contend to succeed him, Agesilaos claiming that Leotychidas was not really a son of Agis.

3.2.30e   Lasion: Map 3.2.26.
3.2.30f   Epeion: Map 3.2.26, inset.
3.2.30g   Heraia: Map 3.2.26, inset.
3.2.30h   The talent was a unit of weight whose value varied over time and place between 55 and 80 pounds. See Appendix I, §8, 10, 13.
3.2.31a   These "boors" were the Pisans (Pisa: Map 3.2.26, inset), who claimed to have run the Festival of Zeus at Olympia (Map 3.2.26, inset) in the distant past.
3.3.1a   Delphi: Map 3.2.26.
3.3.1b   A tenth portion of spoils of victory was the

traditional dedication to the gods. See Appendix J, §6.
3.3.2a   Plutarch in his *Parallel Lives* ("Alcibiades" 23.7–8, "Agesilaos" 3.1–2) says that Leotychidas was considered to be the son of Alcibiades, who had had an affair with Timaea, the wife of Agis.
3.3.2b   Plutarch mentions this earthquake (*Parallel Lives*, "Alcibiades" 23.7) as keeping Agis out of the bedroom rather than, as here, the alleged adulterer, and this may be the same tremor that Thucydides records at 8.6.5.

[3] Now Diopeithes, who was a very good interpreter of oracles, supported Leotychidas and said that there was an oracle of Apollo that had been given to the Spartans that warned them to guard against "the lame kingship."[a] Lysander, however, spoke on behalf of Agesilaos and said that he did not think that the god was saying that the "lame kingship" referred to someone who stumbled and limped but, rather, that they should ensure that no one was king who was not genuinely born of the Herakleidai. For indeed the kingship would be lame unless those from the stock of Herakles led the city.[b] [4] The Spartans, after hearing the arguments on both sides, chose Agesilaos as their king.

Agesilaos had not even completed the first year of his reign as king when, in the course of conducting one of the customary sacrifices on behalf of the city, he was told by his seer[a] that the gods were revealing a most frightening plot. When he sacrificed a second time, the seer said that these sacrifices warned of the plot even more strongly than the first. When Agesilaos sacrificed a third time, the seer said, "Agesilaos, the god is giving us the same sign that he would if we were in the midst of the enemy." After this they sacrificed both to the apotropaic gods and to the savior gods,[b] and only with difficulty did they finally obtain good omens, at which point they ceased sacrificing.

Within five days after these sacrifices, someone went to the ephors and informed about a plot and the ringleader of the plot—a man named Kinadon. [5] He was a young man who was fine in body and brave in spirit, but he was not one of the Equals.[a] When the ephors asked how the plot was intended to proceed, the informer said that Kinadon had led him to the border of the agora and there asked him to count how many Spartiates were present in the agora. "And," he said, "I counted the king and the ephors and the members of the Council[b] and a few others, and I told him that I had counted about forty. Then I asked Kinadon, 'Why did you order me to count them?' To which he replied, 'Consider these few men that you counted as your enemies, and all the rest of the people in the agora, who number more than four thousand, to be your allies.'" The informer continued, saying Kinadon then pointed out to him one or two men here and there whom he designated as enemies while all the rest were allies. Kinadon also remarked that on every estate of the Spartiates there was but one man who was their enemy—the master—and many allies.

3.3.3
400?
SPARTA
Agesilaos convinces the Spartans that he and not Leotychidas should be king, and he wins their vote.

3.3.4–5
399?
SPARTA
Religious sacrifices predict evil for Sparta, and a few days later a plot by a man named Kinadon is exposed by an informer, who says that Kinadon hoped to succeed because of the tremendous disparity in numbers between the Spartiates and their domestic enemies.

3.3.3a Agesilaos was lame. Plutarch mentions this oracle at *Parallel Lives*, "Agesilaos" 3.4–5. See Appendix G, Agesilaos, §3.
3.3.3b Lysander and Agesilaos were former lovers. See Appendix G, §3.
3.3.4a Apparently the king had an official seer for these official sacrifices. See Appendix J, §2, 4.
3.3.4b Apotropaic gods are those who avert evil, and savior gods are those who protect and save.
3.3.5a Spartiates, those Spartans who enjoyed

full citizenship rights, were also called Equals (*homoioi*). See Appendix E, §§7, 9, 11, 17.
3.3.5b The Council in this case is the Gerousia, the Council of Elders. See Appendix E, §15.

3.3.6–7
399?
SPARTA
The ephors obtain the
details of the plot from
the informer.

[6] The ephors then asked the informer how many men were involved in the plot, and he said Kinadon had told him that the leaders of the conspiracy were few in number but that they were all trustworthy men. But the leaders of the plot themselves said that everyone was in on it with them— helots, newly freed citizens, lower-grade citizens, and the peoples of the surrounding towns.[a] For whenever they conversed with such men about the Spartiates, they said that not even one of the men in those groups could hide how bitterly he felt toward the Spartans, going so far as to say that they would even eat them raw. [7] When the ephors then asked them where they intended to obtain weapons, they said that Kinadon had told them, "Those of us who have served with the Spartans in battle are already in possession of weapons," and as for arming the mass of conspirators, Kinadon had led the informer into a warehouse,[a] where he showed him the many daggers, swords, and iron spits, as well as numerous axes, axe-heads, and scythes that could be found there. He said that all these things were weapons for men who were farmers or carpenters or stonemasons, and each of the other crafts as well had their weapons, which would be sufficient, especially against men who were unarmed. Finally, the ephors asked when these things were going to take place, and the informer replied only that he had been ordered to remain in the city.

3.3.8–10
399?
SPARTA
Believing the informer's
story to be credible, the
alarmed ephors send for
Kinadon and order him
to go to Aulon to carry
out a mission. Their real
intent is to arrest and
interrogate him away from
the city so as to capture
the other conspirators
before they know the plot
has been betrayed.

[8] When the ephors had heard all this, they determined that the man had described a very deliberate plot, and they were greatly troubled. Indeed, they were so disturbed that they did not even bother to summon the so-called Little Assembly;[a] instead they gathered together as many members of the Council as they could find then and there, and they resolved to send Kinadon into Aulon[b] with some of the younger men and to order him to bring back certain Aulonians and those helots whose names were written on the *skytale*.[c] They also ordered him to bring back a woman who was reputed to be the most beautiful woman there and who had continually corrupted the Spartans who went there, whether young or old. [9] Now Kinadon had done tasks like this for the ephors previously, so when they gave him the *skytale* on which were written the names of the men to be apprehended, Kinadon asked which of the young men he should take with him. The ephors responded, "Go tell the eldest of the bodyguard

3.3.6a   This list includes respectively helots (serfs), *neodamōdeis*, *hypomeiones*, and *perioikoi*. For more on these various grades see Appendix E, §9–12.

3.3.7a   A warehouse or store of iron agricultural equipment or other tools.

3.3.8a   The Little Assembly was possibly an assembly of Spartiates who could easily be summoned, but this is only speculation. This may be the only time the Little Assembly is mentioned in all extant Greek literature: see Appendix E, §17.

3.3.8b   Aulon: Map 3.2.26.

3.3.8c   The *skytale* was a rudimentary Spartan device for encoding messages. A leather

strap was wound around a dowel of a given diameter, and the message was written on the strap down the dowel and across the individual turns of the strap. When unwrapped, the strap would seem to have a series of random letters. The recipient of the message was given or equipped with a dowel of the same diameter as the first one. When the strap was wrapped around it, the letters could be seen to form words written in lines down the dowel's length. Plutarch in *Parallel Lives* ("Lysander" 19.4–5) describes how these secret dispatches of the Spartans worked.

officers[a] to send with you six or seven of those who happen to be present."
(The ephors had, of course, taken care that the commander should know
which ones to send, as well as the fact that Kinadon himself was to be
arrested.) In addition, they told Kinadon that they would send three wagons
so that he would not have to lead the prisoners back on foot, all the while
concealing, as best they could, that they were really sending for one man
only—Kinadon himself. [10] They chose not to arrest him in the city, because
they did not know the extent of the conspiracy and they wished first to hear
from Kinadon who his accomplices were before the latter were aware that
they had been denounced and before they might attempt to run away. Those
who were to arrest him were supposed to keep him in custody but try to
learn from him the names of all those who had participated in the conspiracy,
and they were instructed to write down the names and send them as quickly
as they could to the ephors. The ephors considered the threat so serious that
they also sent a squadron of cavalry to accompany the men to Aulon.

[11] When Kinadon had been arrested, a horseman came from Aulon to
the ephors, bearing the names of those whom Kinadon had identified, and
they immediately arrested Teisamenos, the seer, as well as the most prominent of the rest of the conspirators. Kinadon was brought back to Sparta
and interrogated; he confessed everything and gave them the names of all
those in on the plot. When the ephors at last asked him why and to what
purpose he had formed this plot, he replied that he had done it so that he
would not be inferior to anyone at Sparta. His hands were then bound and
a collar was placed on his neck, and he and those with him were led around
the city, struck with whips and goads as they went. In this way these men
received their punishment.[a]

[1] After this, a man from Syracuse[a] named Herodas, who was in
Phoenicia[b] with a certain shipowner, observed there a number of Phoenician triremes, some of which were being fitted out, others that were already
manned and prepared for sea, and still others that were sailing in from elsewhere. When he heard that three hundred triremes in all were being
prepared, he went on board the first ship making for Greece and reported
to the Spartans that the Persian King and Tissaphernes were fitting out this
large naval force. But he knew nothing about where it was to sail. [2] The
Spartans were alarmed and called together their allies in order to confer on
what should be done. Lysander believed the Greek fleet to be far superior;
recalling that the Greek army that had marched up-country[a] had managed

3.3.11
399?
SPARTA
Kinadon is arrested and
reveals the names of the
other conspirators. All are
publicly punished.

3.4.1–2
396
PHOENICIA-SPARTA
Receiving news from
Phoenicia that the Persians
were preparing a large
fleet, Lysander persuades
the Spartans to organize
an army under Agesilaos
to attack the Persians in
Asia by land. He hopes
to restore the dekarchies
that he had established
but the ephors had abol-
ished.

3.3.9a   These officers, the *hippagretai*, were three
          in number, and they chose the Horsemen
          (*hippeis*), the elite body of troops three
          hundred strong who were selected, upon
          completion of the normal Spartiate train-
          ing, to accompany the king. For the
          Horsemen, see Appendix F, §7.
3.3.11a   Though Xenophon does not mention it,
          the men were surely executed thereafter.
3.4.1a   Syracuse, Sicily: Map 3.4.12, locator.

3.4.1b   Phoenicia: Map 3.4.12, locator. The
          Persian fleet consisted mainly of the fleets
          of the Phoenician cities that Persia ruled.
3.4.2a   Yet another reference to the forces that
          went with Cyrus and of which Xenophon
          had eventually become a leader and the
          chronicler. See 3.1.1–2 and notes.

to return home safely, he persuaded Agesilaos to promise to lead a campaign against Asia,[b] if the authorities would place thirty Spartiates, about two thousand newly freed helots,[c] and a force of about six thousand of the allies under his command. For among his objectives in doing this, Lysander hoped to accompany Agesilaos in the campaign so that he could, with Agesilaos' help, reestablish the dekarchies[d] that he himself had set up earlier in the cities but that the ephors had eliminated when they decreed that the cities should be governed instead by their own ancestral laws.

3.4.3–4
396
AULIS
Agesilaos' request for troops is granted. He sends for allies and leaves for Aulis, where his attempt to sacrifice before leaving for Asia is thwarted by the Boeotarchs. Furious at this, Agesilaos sails for Asia.

[3] When Agesilaos agreed to assemble and lead such a force, the Spartans gave him everything he asked for and a six-month supply of grain. He then performed the necessary sacrifices, the border-crossing sacrifices[a] as well as the others, and, marching out from Sparta, he sent messengers to all the cities, announcing how many men each city should send to him and where they should muster. For his own part, he wished to go to Aulis[b] to sacrifice there, as it was the very place where Agamemnon had sacrificed before sailing to Troy.[c] [4] While he was there, the Boeotarchs[a] learned that he was sacrificing, and they sent horsemen to him to declare that he was not to sacrifice there in the future; they also took whatever remained of the sacrifices that had already been completed and threw them away from the altar. Agesilaos became furious at this conduct; he called upon the gods to witness what had been done,[b] and, boarding his trireme, he sailed away. After arriving at Geraistos[c] and gathering there as much of the army as he could, he then made an expedition to Ephesus.[d]

3.4.5
396
EPHESUS
Agesilaos demands autonomy for the Greek cities but grants Tissaphernes a truce while he transmits these demands to the King.

[5] When Agesilaos arrived at Ephesus, Tissaphernes sent a messenger to ask him why he had come, and Agesilaos responded, "So that the cities in Asia might be autonomous, just as the cities are in our part of Greece." To which Tissaphernes replied, "If you are willing to make a truce while I send to the King for approval, then I think you can sail away having accomplished this much, if that would satisfy you."

3.4.2b   Asia (Asia Minor): Map 3.4.12, AY.
3.4.2c   They are called *neodamōdeis* in the text: former helots who had been freed, usually for some great service to Sparta and her allies, and who were now armed as hoplites and serving in the Spartan army. See Appendix E, §9, 12; Appendix F, §6; and the Glossary.
3.4.2d   Dekarchies: when Lysander and the Peloponnesian fleet liberated the cities of the Aegean from Athenian rule in 405–404, he set up new governments (dekarchies) ruled by ten men—local, pro-oligarchic citizens, usually selected by Lysander—but later these governments proved unpopular, and Sparta abolished them. For the roles of ephors, navarchs (*nauarch/nauarchos*), and harmosts in the Spartan empire, see Appendix E, §16 (ephors), 19 (harmosts), and Appendix K, Trireme Warfare in Xenophon's *Hellenika*, §11.
3.4.3a   These sacrifices were a traditional requirement for all Spartan commanders before crossing the Spartan frontier.
3.4.3b   Aulis: Map 3.4.12, BX. Aulis was in Boeotian

(Boeotia: Map 3.2.26) territory.
3.4.3c   Troy (Ilion): Map 3.4.12, AY. Sacrificing at Aulis was intended to recall and imitate the famous assault of the Greeks against the city of Troy. This was the subject of epic poetry, of which Homer's *Iliad* and *Odyssey* are two works that have come down to us intact. For Agesilaos, it was an act of traditional piety or a good publicity stunt proclaiming a retaliatory attack on the east. Perhaps it was both.
3.4.4a   Boeotarchs: chief magistrates of the Boeotian government. For more on them and the Boeotian Council, see Appendix H, Political Leagues (Other Than Sparta's) in Xenophon's *Hellenika*, §6, and Appendix P, Selected Fragments of the *Hellenica Oxyrhynchia* Relevant to Xenophon's *Hellenika*, 19.2–4, describing the Boeotian government of the fourth century.
3.4.4b   It was an act of sacrilege to disturb the remains of a sacrifice to the gods. See Appendix J, §7, 11, 12.
3.4.4c   Geraistos: Map 3.4.12, BX.
3.4.4d   Ephesus: Map 3.4.12, BY.

FIGURE 3.4.4. AN ATHENIAN RED-FIGURE BELL KRATER OF THE THIRD QUARTER OF THE FIFTH CENTURY. THE ALTAR IS BEING SPRINKLED WITH BLOOD IN PREPARATION FOR ROASTING THE ENTRAILS OF THE SACRIFICIAL VICTIM, WHICH ARE SKEWERED ON THE STICK CARRIED BY THE NAKED YOUTH.

"Indeed I would be happy with that outcome if I believed that you would not deceive me."

"But it is possible for you to get a pledge from me [a pledge not to behave deceitfully.]"

"And you can get from me a pledge that if you do these things without deceit]ᵃ we will do no harm to the territory that you govern during the time of the truce."

[6] On these conditions, and in the presence of the commissioners whom Agesilaos had sent to him—Herippidas,ᵃ Derkylidas, and Megillos—Tissaphernes swore an oath that he would abide by the truce without deceit. The three emissaries then swore in the presence of Tissaphernes and on behalf of Agesilaos that if he kept his word, they would observe the terms of the truce in force.ᵇ But Tissaphernes immediately proved false to his oath, for instead of requesting peace from the King, he asked for a large force to be sent to him in addition to the one he already had. Yet even

3.4.6
396
SARDIS
Tissaphernes swears to observe the truce, but his oath is belied by the real nature of his request to the King. Agesilaos is aware of this betrayal, but abides by the truce.

3.4.5a   The words in square brackets are not in the Greek text; they have been supplied to make sense of the passage. (John Marincola) For the Greek, see Translator's Notes.

3.4.6a   Herippidas, Spartan general: see Appendix M, §11.
3.4.6b   According to Xenophon (*Agesilaos* 1.10), the treaty was for three months.

though Agesilaos knew Tissaphernes was playing him false, he nevertheless observed the truce.

[7] Since there was peace and he had leisure, Agesilaos spent his time at Ephesus. The governments of the cities had been greatly disturbed since there were neither democracies, as there had been in the time of the Athenians,[a] nor were there dekarchies, as there had been in the time of Lysander. But since everyone knew Lysander, they would all apply through him to obtain their requests from Agesilaos. The result was that a huge mob was always paying court to Lysander and following him around, so much so that it seemed as if Agesilaos was but a private citizen and Lysander the king. [8] Agesilaos later made it very clear that he, too, was unhappy with this state of affairs, but at this time, it was the other members of the thirty[a] who, motivated by envy, were not silent. Indeed, they said to Agesilaos that Lysander was behaving contrary to the law, conducting himself more regally than even a king was entitled to do. After this, when Lysander brought people to the king, Agesilaos would always send them away without giving them what he knew they wanted. And when Lysander perceived that every time his wishes were made known, Agesilaos decided just the opposite, he understood what was happening. So he ceased to allow a crowd to follow him around, and he said openly to those who wished to obtain some favor from the king that they would actually achieve less if he himself were a party to the request.

[9] Lysander was distressed by this dishonor, and so he went to the king and said, "Now I see, Agesilaos, that you know very well how to diminish your friends."

"Yes, by Zeus," Agesilaos replied, "at least those who wish to appear greater than me. As for those who increase my honor, well, I would be ashamed of myself if I did not know how to honor them in return."

"Well," said Lysander, "perhaps you are behaving now more sensibly than I did in the past. Do me one favor at the very least—send me away from here so that I might not be ashamed by being here and having no influence with you, and also so that I might not be in your way. Wherever I go, I shall attempt to always conduct myself so as to be of some advantage to you."

[10] Agesilaos agreed with what Lysander had said, and so he sent him off to the Hellespont.[a] When Lysander arrived there, he learned that the Persian Spithridates had been slighted in some way by Pharnabazos, and so he talked with the man and persuaded him to leave the King's service, along with his children, his possessions, and about two hundred of his horsemen. Lysander left everything else behind in Cyzicus[b] but put Spithridates and his son on board ship and brought them to Agesilaos.[c] When Agesilaos saw

---

3.4.7a   The Athenians had often installed democracies on the Athenian model in their subject cities.

3.4.8a   The "thirty" in this instance were a group of thirty Spartiate officers who were sent out with Lysander to accompany King Agesilaos on this campaign.

3.4.10a   Hellespont: Map 3.4.12, AY.
3.4.10b   Cyzicus: Map 3.4.12, AY.
3.4.10c   The Oxyrhynchus Historian's account of how Spithridates came to Agesilaos does not mention Lysander at all. See Appendix P, Fragment 24.3.

them, he was pleased by what Lysander had done, and he began to question Spithridates about the territory under the control of Pharnabazos.

[11] Tissaphernes, for his part, was feeling confident because of the troops that had been sent down from the King, and so he demanded that Agesilaos withdraw from Asia, saying that he would declare war on him should he fail to do so. The Spartans who were there, and the rest of the allies, were quite openly troubled, because in their judgment the current force presently at Agesilaos' disposal was very inferior to the resources of the King; but Agesilaos, beaming with joy, told the envoys to announce to Tissaphernes that he was quite grateful, because Tissaphernes, by violating his oaths, now had the gods as his enemies and he had also, by this same action, made the gods the allies of the Greeks. After this Agesilaos immediately ordered the soldiers there to provision themselves for a campaign, and he sent word to the cities that he would have to pass through on his march to Caria,[a] that they should prepare to set up marketplaces for his army.[b] He ordered the Ionians,[c] Aeolians,[d] and Hellespontines to send to him there at Ephesus troops that would accompany him on the campaign.

[12] Tissaphernes' strategy was to exploit his superiority in cavalry, as Agesilaos had none; and since Caria was unsuitable terrain for cavalry and he believed also that Agesilaos would be furious at his deceit and thus would, in fact, attempt to take Tissaphernes' own estate in Caria, he marched his entire infantry to Caria, leading the cavalry to the Maeandrian River valley,[a] because he thought the plain there would permit his cavalry to overrun the Greeks before they could reach terrain that was unsuitable for horses. But Agesilaos, instead of going to Caria, immediately turned in the opposite direction and marched toward Phrygia,[b] subduing the cities he came to on his march; by falling upon them unexpectedly, he managed to take an enormous amount of booty.[c]

[13] Now with one exception, Agesilaos marched safely through the country, but not far from Daskyleion,[a] as he advanced, his horsemen ascended a hill so that they might see what lay ahead. By some coincidence there was also a company of horse there under the command of Rathine and Bagaios, Pharnabazos' bastard brother. This squad was approximately equal in number to that of the Greeks and had been sent ahead by Pharnabazos to this very same hill. When the horsemen spotted each other, there was only about four plethra [b] between them, and at first both parties stood their ground and made no move forward. The Greeks were deployed in a

3.4.11
396
SARDIS-EPHESUS
Encouraged by reinforcements sent by the King, Tissaphernes declares war. Some in the Spartan camp are anxious, but Agesilaos rejoices that his enemy has violated his oaths.

3.4.12
396
PHYRGIA
Tissaphernes plans to lure the Greeks toward Caria and attack with his cavalry in the Maeander plain, but Agesilaos marches to Phrygia, capturing many cities and amassing much booty.

3.4.13–14
396
DASKYLEION
Agesilaos' advance is halted when his cavalry is defeated by a unit of enemy horsemen whose spears are superior to those of the Greeks.

3.4.11a Caria: Map 3.4.12, BY.
3.4.11b Ancient Greek soldiers and sailors were expected to purchase their food from local markets with their own money, which made prompt and adequate military pay quite important. For a city to offer a special market at a convenient location for foreign military personnel was a polite and presumably profitable amenity; it also helped to keep such visitors out of the city.

3.4.11c Ionia: Map 3.4.12, BY.
3.4.11d Aeolis: Map 3.4.12, AY.
3.4.12a Maeander River: Map 3.4.12, BY.
3.4.12b Phrygia (Hellespontine Phrygia): Map 3.4.12, AY.
3.4.12c Diodorus gives an account of Agesilaos' first campaign in Asia. See Appendix O, 14.79.1–3.
3.4.13a Daskyleion: Map 3.4.12, AY.
3.4.13b Plethra: a plethron equaled 100 feet. See Appendix I, §4, 13.

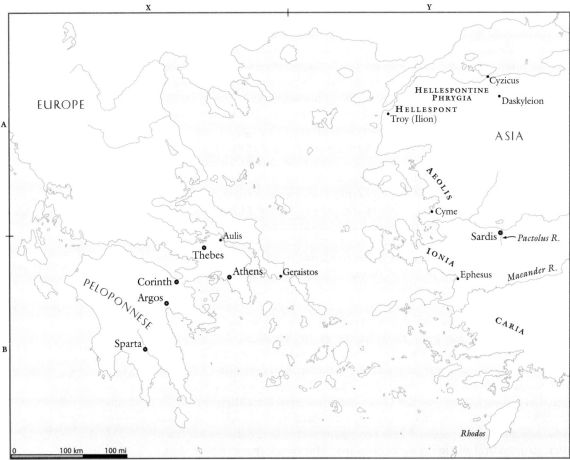

MAP 3.4.12

line like a phalanx four rows deep, while the Persians formed a narrow front rank not more than twelve cavalrymen across but many horsemen deep, and they were first to charge. [14] When they came to close quarters, those Greeks who struck one of the enemy found that their spears shattered, while the Persians, who were using light spears[a] made of cornel wood, managed to kill twelve men and two horses. Because of this, the Greek horsemen turned and fled. When Agesilaos brought his hoplites to their assistance, the Persians retreated, and one of them was killed. [15] On the day after this cavalry engagement, when Agesilaos was sacrificing so as to determine whether or not he should go forward, the liver of the sacrificial victim was seen to have no lobe,[a] and at the appearance of this sign, he turned around and began to march back to the sea.

From this encounter Agesilaos realized that unless he could acquire a sufficient cavalry, he would never be able to offer battle in the plain, and so he decided that he must establish a corps of horsemen or be compelled always to fight on the run. He compiled a list of the wealthiest men in the cities there, whom he ordered to provide horses; and by announcing that whoever furnished a horse, weapons, and a suitable man for service would not himself have to serve in the army, Agesilaos brought it about that his requirements for cavalry were swiftly met, since, of course, any man would eagerly seek to find someone else to die in his place.

[16] After this, just as spring was beginning, he gathered the army together at Ephesus.[a] As he wished to train the army, he set up prizes among the hoplites for the one who was found to be in the best physical condition, and among the cavalry for the one who exhibited the best horsemanship. He set up prizes for the peltasts[b] and the archers also, to go to those who excelled at their particular skills. Because of this policy, one could see all the gymnasia full of men exercising, the horse track full of men practicing their horsemanship, and the javelin throwers and archers working at their tasks. [17] Indeed Agesilaos made the whole city where they were stationed a marvel to look at; the agora was full of all sorts of horses and weapons for sale, and the coppersmiths, joiners, smiths, leather workers, and painters were all fashioning weapons for war in such profusion that one would have thought the whole city was really a workshop for war. [18] One would have been encouraged, too, by the sight of Agesilaos in the lead and the rest of the soldiers garlanded as they went from the gymnasia to dedicate their garlands to Artemis.[a] For whenever men honor the gods, prepare themselves vigorously for war, and take care to obey their commanders, it is reasonable for everyone to be full of high hopes. In

3.4.15
396
DASKYLEION
After sacrifices prove unfavorable, Agesilaos returns to the sea. Realizing that he must add a cavalry arm to his forces, he orders the wealthy men of his cities to each supply a mounted and equipped cavalryman, adding that those who do so will not have to serve in the army.

3.4.16–19
395
EPHESUS
Agesilaos mobilizes his army in early spring, offering prizes to those who excel and rewarding hard training. All Ephesus becomes a workshop of war. He orders that the captured barbarians be sold naked so his men will see their white skin and flabby muscles and come to despise their enemy.

3.4.14a   The Persian cavalry used the *palton*, a
            light spear something like the *jereed* of
            the Moors: see Appendix D, Persia in
            Xenophon's *Hellenika*, §8.
3.4.15a   The lack of a lobe in a sacrificial victim's
            liver was a particularly bad omen. See

Appendix J, §2. See Figure 3.4.15.
3.4.16a   Ephesus: Map 3.4.12, BY.
3.4.16b   Peltast: an infantryman usually equipped
            only with a javelin, a short sword, and a
            small wicker shield. See Appendix L, §7.
3.4.18a   Artemis was the patron deity of Ephesus.

FIGURE 3.4.15.
VASE, C. 525, BY THE
ANTIMENES PAINTER,
DEPICTING A DIVINATION
SCENE OF THE PRESENTA-
TION AND EXAMINATION
OF A LIVER.

addition, believing that contempt for the enemy would impart strength to
his men for the battle, Agesilaos ordered the heralds to sell naked those
barbarians who had been captured in the plundering raids. When the
soldiers saw the skin of these captives, which was white because they never
took their clothes off, and when they saw, too, that these men were soft
and unused to toil because they were accustomed to ride in carriages, they
concluded that fighting such men would be no more difficult than fighting
women.

[20] It was now about a year since Agesilaos had sailed out, and so Lysander and the thirty who had been sent with Agesilaos to accompany him sailed home to Sparta, and officers led by Herippidas acted as their replacements. From these, Agesilaos put Xenokles and one other man[a] in charge of the cavalry, Scythes in charge of the newly freed helot hoplites, Herippidas in charge of the men who had served with Cyrus,[b] and Mygdon in charge of the soldiers from the allied cities. To all of them he said that he was going to lead them immediately against the choicest portions of the land by the shortest route possible, so that they should immediately prepare their minds and bodies for combat. [21] Once again Tissaphernes thought that Agesilaos said this in order to deceive him and conceal the fact that he was really going to march against Caria,[a] so just as he had done before, Tissaphernes crossed his infantry over into Caria and stationed his cavalry in the plain of the Maeander.[b] But Agesilaos had not lied, and just as he had announced, he led his army to the area around Sardis.[c]

For three days, as he marched through the land, he was able to find ample provisions for the army, since none of the enemy were present, but on the fourth day the Persian cavalry finally appeared. [22] [Their commander][a] ordered the man in charge of the Persian baggage train to cross over the Pactolus River[b] and to set up camp there, while the horsemen themselves, seeing the Greek camp followers scattered over the countryside seeking plunder, attacked and killed many of them. Agesilaos, when he realized what was happening, ordered his horsemen to go to their aid. The Persians on their side saw the Greek cavalry coming to give assistance, so they drew themselves together and deployed themselves into a formation many rows deep.

[23] At this point Agesilaos, who knew that all of his forces were with him, whereas the enemy's infantry had not yet arrived, decided that it was the right moment to attack if he could do it. Having sacrificed, he immediately led his phalanx against the enemy horse that had deployed; he ordered the hoplites from the ten-year class[a] to close with the enemy, and the peltasts to lead the way at a run. He also gave the order for his cavalry to attack as he was following with the entire army. [24] Now the Persians had withstood the charge of the Greek horse, but as soon as all the formidable units of

3.4.20–22
395
SARDIS
Lysander and his group of Spartiates are replaced by another group of thirty. Agesilaos marches on Sardis. Persian cavalry attacks the Greek foragers scattered over the plain. The Greek cavalry attacks to protect the foragers.

3.4.23–24
395
VICINITY OF SARDIS
Agesilaos attacks with his infantry, aware that the enemy infantry is not yet present. The Persian cavalry flees and is pursued. Its camp is taken, yielding immense booty, including camels.

3.4.20a   Some scholars have suggested that this "one other man" who is not named is none other than Xenophon himself, but that is inconsistent with the generally held opinion that the thirty referred to here were all Spartiates.

3.4.20b   These were Greek troops who had served under Cyrus, marched to the Tigris to fight at Cunaxa, and returned on an arduous and adventurous journey recounted by Xenophon in his work *Anabasis*. They had been made a separate unit within Thibron and Derkylidas' army and were now integrated into the Spartan command structure by the appointment of Herippidas, a Spartiate, to lead them. See 3.1.1–2.

3.4.21a   Caria: Map 3.4.12, BY.
3.4.21b   Maeander River: Map 3.4.12, BY.
3.4.21c   Sardis: Map 3.4.12, AY.
3.4.22a   No subject for the verb is given here by Xenophon, and "their commander" has been supplied from his work the *Agesilaos* (1.30), where these same events are narrated. (John Marincola) For the Greek, see Translator's Notes.
3.4.22b   Pactolus River: Map 3.4.12, BY.
3.4.23a   The ten-year class consisted of the youngest men in the army, those serving their first decade of service, aged twenty to twenty-nine. It was standard Spartan practice to organize the army by age groups.

the Greek army were upon them, they gave way.[a] Some of them immediately fell into the river, while the rest fled. The Greeks pursued them and even captured the Persian camp. The peltasts, as one would expect, turned to plundering, while Agesilaos made his own camp in a circle that included both his own and the enemy's possessions. Not only was a large amount of money captured (more than seventy talents'[b] worth), but Agesilaos also at that time captured the camels that he later brought back to Greece.[c]

[25] Tissaphernes happened to be in Sardis while the battle was taking place, and so the Persians charged that he had betrayed them. And the Persian King, knowing that Tissaphernes was to blame for this disastrous turn in his affairs, sent to Sardis a man named Tithraustes, who beheaded Tissaphernes.[a] Then Tithraustes sent ambassadors to Agesilaos with the following message: "Agesilaos, the man responsible for your and our troubles has now received his due. The King thinks that you should now sail home to Sparta and that the cities of Asia should be autonomous and pay to the King the tribute they paid as of old." [26] Agesilaos answered that he could not do this without first consulting the authorities in Sparta, to which Tithraustes said, "Well, then, until you hear from the authorities in your city, go to the territory of Pharnabazos,[a] since I have taken vengeance on your enemy." "Before I set out for that place," Agesilaos replied, "you must supply my army with provisions." And so Tithraustes gave him thirty talents; Agesilaos took them and then departed for Phrygia,[b] which was in Pharnabazos' territory.

[27] When Agesilaos was in the plain above Cyme,[a] there came a message from the authorities at home that he should command the fleet as well and that he should appoint whomever he wished to be admiral. The Spartans had made this decision in the belief that if Agesilaos was commander of both, his army would be much stronger, since the manpower of both forces could be combined into one, and the navy, too, would be stronger, since the army could be present wherever it needed support. [28] When Agesilaos heard this, he ordered the cities of the islands and the coast to build as many triremes as each was willing to man. These new triremes, some of which were promised by the cities and others by individuals who wished to gratify Agesilaos, numbered in all about 120. [29] Agesilaos selected Peisander, his wife's brother, as admiral; he was an ambitious man, strong in spirit, but a bit too inexperienced in the matter of building and equipping ships. So Peisander departed and began to attend to naval matters, while Agesilaos, just as he had originally intended, marched off toward Phrygia.

3.4.25–26
395
SARDIS
The Persian King sends Tithraustes to kill Tissaphernes and to tell Agesilaos that he will give autonomy to the cities if they will pay tribute as of old. Agesilaos asks for time to consult Sparta. Tithraustes tells him to attack Pharnabazos' territory.

3.4.27–29
395
CYME
Word comes from Sparta that Agesilaos is to be commander of both the army and the navy. He appoints Peisander to lead the fleet and orders the island and coastal cities to build triremes while he resumes his march to Phrygia.

3.4.24a   For different accounts of this battle, see those of Diodorus (Appendix O, 14.80.1–8) and the Oxyrhynchus Historian (Appendix P, Fragments 14, 15). See also the Introduction, §10.7.

3.4.24b   Seventy talents was a huge sum. The talent was a unit of weight whose value varied over time and place between 55 and 80 pounds. See Appendix I, §8, 10, 13.

3.4.24c   Xenophon speaks of this as a well-known event.

3.4.25a   Diodorus gives a fuller account of the

downfall of Tissaphernes; see Appendix O, 14.80.6–8.

3.4.26a   The territory of Pharnabazos, who had been Tissaphernes' and was now Tithraustes' fellow Persian satrap, was located in northwestern Asia, including the Hellespont, Hellespontine Phrygia, and Aeolis (Map 3.4.12, AY). See Appendix D, §1.

3.4.26b   Phrygia (Hellespontine Phrygia): Map 3.4.12, AY.

3.4.27a   Cyme: Map 3.4.12, AY.

FIGURE 3.4.23. MID-FIFTH-CENTURY CALYX-
KRATER (TOP) DEPICTING A GREEK HOPLITE AS
HE KILLS A PERSIAN ARCHER. FOURTH-CENTURY
VASE (RIGHT) DEPICTING COMBAT BETWEEN A
PERSIAN INFANTRYMAN AND A GREEK HOPLITE,
THOUGHT TO HAVE BEEN INSPIRED BY THE WAR
FOUGHT IN 390 BETWEEN PERSIA AND SPARTA.

FIGURE 3.4.24. AN IMPRESSION TAKEN FROM A LATE-FIFTH-CENTURY GRECO-PERSIAN CYLINDER SEAL DEPICTING COMBAT BETWEEN A PERSIAN CAVALRYMAN AND A GREEK HOPLITE.

3.5.1–2
395
GREECE
Tithraustes sends an envoy to Greece with money to bribe leading Greeks to persuade their cities to attack Sparta. Men of Thebes, Corinth, and Argos accept the money. Athenians refuse it but are eager to fight Sparta to recover their hegemony over Greece.

[1] Tithraustes, for his part, believed that Agesilaos disdained the King's power and that Agesilaos was not at all intending to leave Asia but, rather, had grand hopes that he could subjugate the King; as he was unsure what to do in the current state of affairs, Tithraustes sent Timokrates of Rhodos[a] to Greece, giving him gold equivalent to the value of fifty talents of silver and ordering him, after he had obtained the firmest pledges of good faith, to give the money to the leading men in the cities there on condition that they agree to make war against the Spartans.[b] Timokrates went to Greece and gave the money to Androkleidas, Ismenias, and Galaxidoros in Thebes,[c] to Timolaus and Polyanthos in Corinth,[d] and to Kylon and his party in Argos.[e] [2] The Athenians[a] would not accept the money, but they were nevertheless eager to wage war against Sparta,[b] thinking that they would again acquire an empire.[c]

3.5.1a　Rhodos: Map 3.4.12, BY.
3.5.1b　See Appendix D, §3, on this example of Persian strategy to use gold to keep Greece disunited.
3.5.1c　Thebes: Map 3.4.12, BX; and Map 3.5.9, AY.
3.5.1d　Corinth: Map 3.4.12, BX; and Map 3.5.9, AY.
3.5.1e　Argos: Map 3.4.12, BX; and Map 3.5.9, BY.
3.5.2a　Athens: Map 3.5.9, AY.
3.5.2b　Sparta: Map 3.5.9, BX.
3.5.2c　The text is corrupt here. (John Marincola) For the Greek, see Translator's Notes.

110

The others took the money and began to slander the Spartans, each in his own city, and when they had brought their individual cities to hate the Spartans, they then allied the greatest cities with one another.

[3] The leading men in Thebes knew that unless someone found a means to begin a war, the Spartans would not break their treaties with their allies, and so they persuaded the Opuntian Locrians[a] to levy a tax on land that was disputed by these Locrians and the Phocians,[b] for they believed that the Phocians would respond to any Locrian move like this by invading Locris.[c] They were not disappointed in their expectations, for the Phocians immediately invaded Locris and captured a great deal of booty. [4] Androkleidas and his faction quickly persuaded the Thebans to provide assistance to the Locrians, arguing that the Phocians had not invaded the disputed territory but, rather, Locris itself, which was recognized as being a friendly and allied state of the Thebans. When the Thebans in their turn invaded Phocis and began to ravage the land, the Phocians, just as the Thebans had hoped, immediately sent envoys to Sparta and asked for assistance, stating that they were not the aggressors but, rather, had invaded Locris in an attempt to defend themselves.[a]

[5] The Spartans for their part were eager to exploit these events as a pretext for attacking Thebes. They had grown increasingly angry with the Thebans over a long period for many reasons. First of all, at Dekeleia[a] the Thebans had claimed for themselves the tenth-part tithe that was due to Apollo at Delphi.[b] In addition, the Thebans had refused to follow the Spartans when the latter marched against the Peiraieus.[c] The Spartans also accused the Thebans of having persuaded the Corinthians not to march with the Spartans on that occasion,[d] and they remembered as well that the Thebans would not allow Agesilaos to sacrifice at Aulis and had even thrown from the altar the sacrifices that had already been made upon it.[e] Finally, they resented the Thebans for not having accompanied Agesilaos on his campaign into Asia.[f] So the Spartans reckoned that it was a very good occasion to lead an army against the Thebans and to stop their insulting behavior toward themselves. Moreover, they felt the moment to be especially opportune, since their activities in Asia, given Agesilaos' victories, were meeting with such success; and they had no other war on their hands in Greece that might otherwise impede them from attacking Thebes.

3.5.3–4
395
THEBES-PHOCIS-LOCRIS
The Thebans bring on a war by persuading the Opuntian Locrians to tax land in dispute between themselves and Phocis. When the Phocians invade Locris in response, Thebes assists her allies by invading Phocis, which leads the Phocians to ask Sparta for help.

3.5.5
395
SPARTA
The Spartans are pleased to use the invasion of Phocis as an excuse to attack the Boeotians. For a long time they have been disturbed by the Boeotian lack of cooperation and disdain for Spartan policies. They hope to teach Thebes a lesson in how to behave.

3.5.3a Locris (Opuntian): Map 3.5.9, AY. See
        Appendix P, Fragment 21, for a different
        account of the immediate origins of the war.
3.5.3b Phocis: Map 3.5.9, AX.
3.5.3c Locris: this refers to Opuntian (not
        Ozolian) Locris.
3.5.4a The Oxyrhynchus Historian gives a more
        detailed account of this Theban faction's
        plotting; see Appendix P, Fragment 21.1–5.
3.5.5a Dekeleia: Map 3.5.9, AY. Dekeleia was
        used as a base by the Spartans and Thebans
        in the Peloponnesian War for their plun-
        dering depredations in Attica.
3.5.5b Apollo's tenth refers to ten percent of the
        spoils taken from Attica during the Pelo-
        ponnesian War (the war against Athens,

which ended in 404), which the Spartans
had promised, in the event of victory, to
dedicate to Apollo at Delphi. See Plutarch,
Parallel Lives, "Lysander" 27.2.
3.5.5c Peiraieus, the port of Athens: Map 3.5.9,
        AY. Pausanias' march took place in 403.
3.5.5d See 2.4.29–38.
3.5.5d See 2.4.30 for the refusal of the Thebans
        and Corinthians to join this campaign.
3.5.5e See 3.4.4 for the Theban response to
        Agesilaos' attempt to sacrifice at Aulis
        (Map 3.5.9, AY).
3.5.5f Asia (Asia Minor): Map 3.4.12, AY. See
        3.4.3, although Xenophon did not there
        mention the Thebans' absence from the
        campaign.

3.5.6–7
395
SPARTA-PHOCIS
The Spartans are united in their decision to go to war. They call out their army and instruct their allies to send contingents to meet them on the march. The Thebans send envoys to Athens.

[6] Since the city of Sparta had firmly decided on this policy, the ephors mobilized the army and sent Lysander to Phocis, instructing him to gather together the Phocians themselves, the Oetaeans,[a] the Herakleiots,[b] the Malians,[c] and the Ainianians[d] and to lead them all to Haliartos.[e] Pausanias was to command the expedition and had agreed to meet Lysander at Haliartos on an appointed day, bringing there the Spartans and the rest of the Peloponnesians under his command. Lysander did everything he was assigned to do, and in addition persuaded the Orchomenians[f] to revolt from Thebes. [7] The border-crossing sacrifices of Pausanias proved favorable, and he stopped at Tegea,[a] sending out the officers[b] for the allied troops and awaiting the soldiers from the *perioikic* cities.[c] When it was obvious to the Thebans that the Spartans were going to invade their territory, they sent envoys to Athens to say the following:

3.5.8–9
395
ATHENS
The Theban envoys speak to the Athenian Assembly, requesting assistance and giving reasons why the Athenians should provide help and hate the Spartans.

[8] "Men of Athens, you found fault with us when we voted to impose harsh terms on you at the conclusion of the war,[a] but you were not right to blame us all for this. It was not our *city* that voted thus but one man only, who happened at that time to be serving on the board of the allies. On the other hand, when the Spartans called on us to march with them against the Peiraieus, then our whole city voted to refuse the Spartan demand to march out with them. So, then, since it is not least on your account that the Spartans are angry with us, we consider it just for you to assist our city now. [9] We consider it even more incumbent on all those of you who belonged to the men of the city[a] to mobilize eagerly against the Spartans, since they set you up in an oligarchy and made you hateful to the people; and although they came with a great force as your allies, they later handed you over to the multitude.[b] For all they cared, you would have perished; but it was the common people of Athens here who saved you.

3.5.10–13
395
ATHENS
The speech of the Theban envoys to the Athenian Assembly continues. They explain why the Athenians need not fear the Spartans and should willingly ally with Thebes in battle against them.

[10] "Men of Athens, everyone knows that you would like once again to have the empire that you formerly possessed. And how better could you accomplish this than by providing assistance to people who have been treated unjustly by the Spartans? Do not fear them because they rule many people; on the contrary, that fact should give you even greater confidence, considering that when you ruled the greatest number of people, you then had the greatest number of enemies. As long as those enemies had no state that would support them if they revolted, they concealed their hatred of you, but as soon as the Spartans became leaders against you, then those enemies displayed their true feelings toward you. [11] This is what will now happen to the Spartans if both of us fight side by side against them in

3.5.6a   Mount Oeta: Map 3.5.9, AX.
3.5.6b   Herakleia (also known as Herakleia-in-
             Trachis): Map 3.5.9, AX.
3.5.6c   Malis: Map 3.5.9, AX.
3.5.6d   Ainiania (Ainis): Map 3.5.9, AX.
3.5.6e   Haliartos: Map 3.5.9, AY.
3.5.6f   Orchomenus, Boeotia: Map 3.5.9, AY.
3.5.7a   Tegea: Map 3.5.9, BX.
3.5.7b   The *xenagoi*, Spartan citizens who were
             responsible for gathering the allies from

the other Peloponnesian states.
3.5.7c   *Perioikic* cities: communities surrounding
             Sparta that were nominally independent
             but that followed Sparta's lead in foreign
             policy. See Appendix E, §10.
3.5.8a   The Thebans argued that Athens should
             be destroyed. See 2.2.19.
3.5.9a   The men of the city were pro-oligarchy;
             those in the Peiraieus were pro-democracy.
3.5.9b   See 2.4.28 for further.

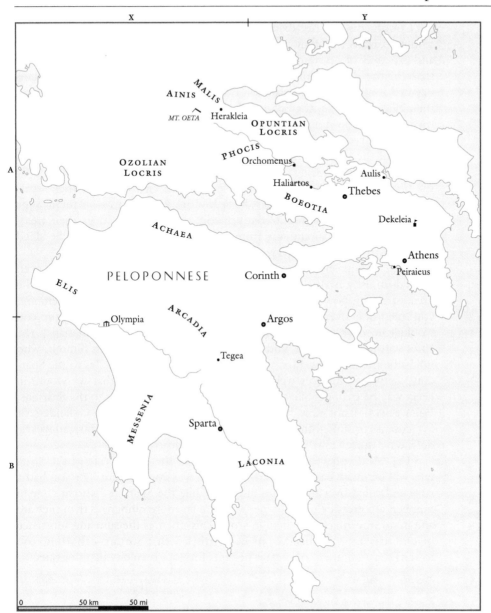

MAP 3.5.9

battle: the many who hate them will reveal themselves. If you will intelligently consider the situation, you will recognize immediately the truth of
our argument; for who now do the Spartans have left as friends? Surely not
the Argives, who have always been hostile to them. [12] The Eleians,[a] too,
who have been deprived by the Spartans of much territory and many
subject cities, are certainly now their enemies. Do we even need mention

3.5.12a Elis: Map 3.5.9, AX

the Corinthians, the Arcadians,[b] and the Achaeans,[c] who so greatly protested to the Spartans that they had sustained a full share in all the toils, dangers, and expenses of the war against you—and yet after the victory received no share in the distribution of honors, rule, or booty? Indeed, the Spartans deemed it appropriate to establish even helots as harmosts,[d] and, although their allies were free, the Spartans, when fortune smiled on them, revealed themselves to be not allies but despots over them. [13] For they in fact openly deceived the cities that they had persuaded to revolt from your rule. Instead of the freedom they had promised, the Spartans imposed a twofold slavery on them: for they are being tyrannized both by the harmosts and by the boards of ten[a] that Lysander set up in each city. Consider their treatment even of the King of Asia:[b] he spared no expense to help them wage that war so that they might conquer you, and now how does their treatment of him differ in any way from what it would have been had he allied himself with you and waged war against *them*?

[14] "If you should now lead those states who have so clearly been treated unjustly by the Spartans, is it not likely that you will be by far the greatest ruling power of all time? For when you had your former empire, you ruled only over those cities located on the coast, but in the future you would rule over everyone—including ourselves, the Peloponnesians,[a] the cities you formerly ruled, and even the territory of the King himself, who holds the greatest power. As for us, we were very valuable allies to the Spartans,[b] as you yourselves well know, but now it is likely that we would in every way be stronger allies to you than we were in the past to the Spartans. For we would not now be attempting to bring assistance to islanders or Syracusans[c] or some other foreign people as we did then, but instead will be defending ourselves who have been treated unjustly.

[15] "And you should also know well that the greedy rule of the Spartans will be much easier to overthrow than was your empire. For you had a navy and ruled over those who did not, while the Spartans, who are few in number, are greedily robbing men who are far more numerous than they are and in no way inferior to them in arms. This, then, is the sum and substance of our message. We believe, men of Athens, that we are exhorting you toward the attainment of greater benefits for your own city than for ours."

3.5.14
395
ATHENS
The speech of the Theban envoys to the Athenian Assembly continues. They assert that by joining them against Sparta, Athens will recover her former empire and become the strongest power of all time.

3.5.15
395
ATHENS
The Thebans conclude their speech, saying that Athens will gain much more than Thebes.

3.5.12b   Arcadia, Map 3.5.9, BX.
3.5.12c   Achaea: Map 3.5.9, AX.
3.5.12d   This assertion can hardly be true. No helot (serf) would have been given the office of harmost. Xenophon may be assuming that his contemporary readers would understand that the Thebans, whom he considers unpleasant spin doctors, would be exaggerating here. Helots were the lowest class of Spartan serfs in Laconia and Messenia (Map 3.5.9, BX). See Appendix E, §11–12. Harmosts were the chief magistrates and/or garrison commanders appointed by the Spartans to govern the cities that

they had occupied. They were usually resented by the natives. See Appendix E, §19.
3.5.13a   Boards of ten: the dekarchies, or ruling oligarchies, established in cities by Sparta (really by Lysander) after the Peloponnesian War. Since Sparta had abolished them at least one year earlier than this (see 3.4.2), we must assume that this is one more instance of Xenophon's anti-Theban spin. See Appendix E, §19.
3.5.13b   King of Asia: King of Persia.
3.5.14a   Peloponnese: Map 3.5.9, AX.
3.5.14b   Sparta: Map 3.5.9, BX.
3.5.14c   Syracuse, Sicily: Map 3.4.12, locator.

[16] The Thebans concluded their speech at this point, and very many Athenians spoke in their support. The Athenian Assembly then unanimously voted to bring assistance to the Thebans. Thrasyboulos[a] announced the decision to the Thebans, pointing out also that, although the Peiraieus[b] was unwalled, the Athenians would nevertheless run the risk of paying back to the Thebans a greater gift than they had received. "For whereas you did not join in their attack against us, we shall actively fight together with you if you are attacked by them." [17] The Thebans then departed and prepared to defend themselves, while the Athenians made arrangements to go to their assistance.

Now the Spartans no longer delayed, but Pausanias the king set out for Boeotia[a] in command of the army of Sparta and of the Peloponnesian allies, except for the Corinthians, who refused to accompany him. Lysander, who was leading the contingents from Phocis,[b] Orchomenus,[c] and the territories in that area, arrived at Haliartos[d] ahead of Pausanias. [18] Once there, he neither remained inactive nor awaited the army from Sparta, but with just the men he had, he went up to the wall of the Haliartans. At first he was making headway in persuading them to revolt from Thebes and be autonomous. But when some of the Thebans who were stationed on the wall prevented the Haliartans from defecting, Lysander began to attack the wall. [19] The Thebans, upon learning of his arrival and assault, marched on the double to Haliartos from their territory with both their infantry and their cavalry. It is unclear whether Lysander failed to notice them as they approached and attacked him, or whether he did see them coming but held his ground in the belief that he would be able to defeat them. But it is clear that a battle took place at the wall; a trophy now stands witness to it at the gates of Haliartos. Lysander[a] was killed, and the rest of his men fled to the mountains, with the Thebans in hot pursuit.

[20] The Thebans pursued them up the mountainside, but then the difficult nature of the terrain and the narrow paths checked their pursuit, at which point Lysander's hoplites faced about and began to pelt them with javelins and stones. Two or three in the front rank were killed, and the hoplites then rolled stones downhill and in high spirits counterattacked the Thebans and drove them down the slope, killing more than two hundred of them. [21] The Thebans thus ended the day quite crestfallen, thinking they had suffered as many losses as they had inflicted.

On the next day they learned that the Phocians and all the rest of the individual contingents with the Spartans had departed during the night, which raised their spirits. But when in turn Pausanias arrived leading the army from Sparta, they once again felt themselves to be in great danger, and

---

3.5.16
395
ATHENS
The Athenians vote to assist the Thebans if they should be attacked by the Spartans.

3.5.17–19
395
HALIARTOS
The Spartans advance from the Peloponnese under King Pausanias and from Phocis and Orchomenus under Lysander. Lysander arrives at Haliartos first and attacks the walls of the city. The Theban army arrives in time to intervene. In the ensuing battle at the wall, Lysander is killed, and his army is forced to flee.

3.5.20–22
395
HALIARTOS
The Theban pursuit is stopped by difficult ground, and when the enemy counterattacks, the Thebans are driven back with substantial losses. Their spirits rise and fall as reinforcements arrive to both sides. Instead of attacking, Pausanias calls a council to discuss whether to attack or ask for a truce to recover their dead, who lie by the walls.

3.5.16a	Thrasyboulos, an important Athenian last seen at the end of Book 2: see Appendix M, §26.		Theban hegemony throughout this period. See Appendix H, §6.
3.5.16b	Peiraieus: Map 3.5.9, AY.	3.5.17b	Phocis: Map 3.5.9, AX.
3.5.17a	Boeotia: Map 3.5.9, AY. Thebes was the leading city of the Boeotian Federation, although some Boeotian cities resisted	3.5.17c	Orchomenus, Boeotia: Map 3.5.9, AY.
		3.5.17d	Haliartos: Map 3.5.9, AY.
		3.5.19a	For a brief sketch of Lysander's career, see Appendix M, §18.

it is said that there was much silence and dejection in their army. [22] On the next day, however, the Athenians arrived and deployed in the field with the Thebans; this reinforcement, combined with the fact that Pausanias did not lead his army forward to battle, greatly increased their morale.

Pausanias, meanwhile, called together the regimental commanders and the captains of fifty in order to take counsel with them about whether they should join battle immediately or ask for a truce in order to recover the bodies of Lysander and of those who had died with him.

[23] Pausanias and the other Spartan officials weighed the following facts: Lysander was dead, his army defeated and scattered; the Corinthians[a] had completely refused to join their expedition; and the men who were present were not eager for battle. They considered, too, that the enemy's cavalry force was large while their own was small, and—the greatest difficulty—that the corpses they wished to recover were lying beneath the city wall, where it would not be easy to retrieve them, even if they had a stronger force, because of the opposition from the enemy's troops on the wall.[b] For all these reasons, then, they concluded that it would be best to seek a truce for recovering the corpses.[c]

[24] The Thebans, however, refused to grant a truce to give back the bodies unless the Spartans agreed to leave their territory. The Spartans for their part were only too glad to make such a promise, and so they took up the bodies and left Boeotia. Because of these events, the Spartans departed with downcast spirits, but the Thebans became quite insolent, striking anyone who set foot on even the edge of their land[a] and driving them back onto the roads. In such a manner did this Spartan campaign came to an end.

[25] Pausanias, however, when he arrived home, was charged with having committed a capital offense. He was accused of having arrived at Haliartos later than Lysander, whereas he had agreed to arrive there on the same day; of having taken up the bodies under truce, rather than trying to get them back by fighting; and of having set free the democratic faction of the Athenians when he had captured them in the Peiraieus.[a] And since on top of all this, he failed to show up at his trial, he was convicted in his absence and condemned to death. He fled to Tegea[b] and died there from some illness. These, then, were the events that took place in Greece.

3.5.23–24
395
HALIARTOS
Weighing all the factors militating against an attack, the Spartans decide to ask for a truce to recover their dead. The Thebans grant it but demand that the Spartans leave their territory, which the Spartans are only too happy to do. These events leave the Spartans downcast and the Thebans insolent.

3.5.25
394
SPARTA
Pausanias is accused of capital crimes and sentenced to death. He flees to Tegea and dies there, probably in the 370s.

3.5.23a Corinth: Map 3.5.9, AY.
3.5.23b From their position on the wall, the enemy could threaten any who approached the corpses by shooting arrows or throwing javelins, spears, and stones on them from above.
3.5.23c To ask for a truce in order to retrieve one's dead was to admit defeat—that is, that one's own side did not control the field after the battle. The Spartans were accustomed to granting truces to their opponents, not to asking for such a truce.
3.5.24a This striking and driving back probably refers to any of the Spartan soldiers who stepped off the road on the retreat and were pushed roughly back onto it. Presumably, by the terms of the truce, the Spartan

soldiers were to keep only to the road and not touch Theban territory in any way. The Thebans seem to have interpreted this most literally.
3.5.25a For Xenophon's own account of this latter charge, see 2.4.39. The second-century C.E. travel writer Pausanias (3.5.6) says that King Pausanias was tried for this charge as soon as he returned from Athens. Most scholars believe Pausanias was tried twice for the same offense, so that Xenophon's and Pausanias' account do not contradict each other. Diodorus mentions the banishment of King Pausanias; see Appendix O, 14.89.1.
3.5.25b Tegea: Map 3.5.9, BX.

BOOK FOUR

At the beginning of fall, Agesilaos arrived in Phrygia,[a] a territory belonging to Pharnabazos.[b] Here he burned and plundered the land, taking some cities by force while others submitted to him of their own accord. [2] Spithridates[a] told him that if he would come with him to Paphlagonia,[b] he would arrange a conference for him with the king of the Paphlagonians and make him the ally of this king. Agesilaos set out eagerly, since he had for a long time wanted to induce some nation to revolt from the Persian King. [3] When he arrived at Paphlagonia, Otys[a] came and concluded an alliance with Agesilaos, since in fact Otys had failed to go to see the King when the latter had summoned him. On the advice of Spithridates, Otys left behind one thousand horses and two thousand peltasts[b] for Agesilaos.

[4] Agesilaos was grateful to Spithridates for having made these arrangements and asked him, "Spithridates, tell me: would you not give your daughter to Otys?" "I would give her more eagerly than he would take her," Spithridates replied, "for she is the daughter of a man in exile, while he is a king who has a large territory and many resources." For the time being this was all that was said about the marriage. [5] But just as Otys was about to depart and had come to Agesilaos to make his farewells, Agesilaos had Spithridates removed from the room, keeping only the thirty[a] with him, [6] and he began a conversation with Otys by asking, "Tell me, Otys, what kind of family does Spithridates come from?"

4.1.1–3
395
PHRYGIA-PAPHLAGONIA
Agesilaos plunders Phrygia and concludes an alliance with Otys, king of Paphlagonia.

4.1.4–6
395
PAPHLAGONIA
Agesilaos tries to bring about a marriage between the daughter of Spithridates and Otys.

4.1.1a   The narrative picks up from 3.4.29, where Agesilaos was marching to Hellespontine Phrygia: Map 4.1.31.

4.1.1b   Pharnabazos, Persian satrap: see Appendix M, Brief Biographies of Important Characters in Xenophon's *Hellenika*, §21.

4.1.2a   Spithridates, a Persian nobleman who, slighted by Pharnabazos, was persuaded by Lysander to leave the King's service and join the Spartans: see 3.4.10.

4.1.2b   Paphlagonia: Map 4.1.31, locator.

4.1.3a   Otys, king of Paphlagonia, is called Cotys in Plutarch (*Parallel Lives*, "Agesilaos" 11.1–2). The Oxyrhynchus Historian calls him Gyes; see Appendix P, Selected Fragments of the *Hellenica Oxyrhynchia* Relevant to Xenophon's *Hellenika*, Fragment 25.1–2.

4.1.3b   Peltasts: troops armed only with a small, light shield, a javelin, and a short sword. Unhindered by body armor, they could move much more quickly than the fully armed hoplite, whose equipment was both far heavier and far more expensive than theirs. See Appendix L, Land Warfare in Xenophon's *Hellenika*, §7.

4.1.5a   The thirty annually selected Spartan commissioners who accompanied Agesilaos on this campaign: see 3.4.20 and Appendix E, Spartan Government and Society, §14.

"He is not inferior to any of the Persians," he replied.

"You have seen how handsome his son is?"

"Yes, indeed. In fact, I dined with him last evening."

"And yet[a] they say that Spithridates' daughter is even more attractive than his son."

"Yes, by Zeus," said Otys, "she is beautiful indeed."

4.1.7–9
395
PAPHLAGONIA
Agesilaos continues
to arrange a marriage
between the daughter of
Spithridates and Otys.

[7] Agesilaos continued: "Now since you have become our friend, I would like to advise you to take this man's daughter as your wife. She is after all very beautiful—and what is sweeter for a man than that? In addition, she is the child of an extremely well-born father, one who holds such power that when he was injured by Pharnabazos, he so avenged himself on that man as to make him an exile from his entire kingdom, as you yourself can see.[a] [8] Know well, then, that just as he can avenge himself on one who is his enemy, in the same way he could do good to the man who is his friend. And consider also that if you married this woman, you would have not only Spithridates as your kinsman but also me and the rest of the Spartans;[a] and since we Spartans are the leaders of Greece, you would also have the rest of Greece. [9] Were you to agree, you would have a more splendid wedding than anyone: has any bride ever had so many horsemen, peltasts, and hoplites[a] as she would have, were we to escort her to your house?"

4.1.10
395
PAPHLAGONIA
Agesilaos assures Otys
that the marriage was
his own idea.

[10] Otys replied, "Do you say these things because it is what Spithridates wants?"

"By the gods, I swear that he did not ask me to say any of these things. It is I, rather, who desire to say this: for although I am exceedingly happy when I avenge myself on an enemy, I think I am much happier still when I can devise something good for my friends."

4.1.11–13
395
PAPHLAGONIA
Spithridates says he will
do whatever Agesilaos
thinks best.

[11] "Well, then, why don't you see whether Spithridates would go along with this?"

Agesilaos turned to the thirty and said, "Herippidas,[a] I want you all to go and instruct our friend that he should want the same things that we want."

[12] They got up and went out to discuss the matter with Spithridates, and when they had been gone for a time, Agesilaos said to Otys, "Would you like us to call Spithridates here?"

Otys replied, "I think he would be much more persuaded by you to follow this plan than by all the rest of them."

4.1.6a   See Translator's Notes.
4.1.7a   Agesilaos' remark here refers to Spithridates' cooperation with the Spartans, by which he (and they) were able to plunder Pharnabazos' territory and cause him much pain. Perhaps Pharnabazos temporarily left his satrapy of Hellespontine Phrygia for a while, but as Agesilaos is speaking with rhetorical exaggeration, this may not be true.
4.1.8a   Sparta: Map 4.2.16, BY. This statement is a bit exaggerated, since the Spartans present would not really be his kinsmen.

4.1.9a   Hoplites: heavily armored infantry, often equipped with helmet, breastplate, and greaves but always carrying a large round shield, a thrusting spear, and a short sword. See Appendix L, §3–8.
4.1.11a   Herippidas was a leading member of the thirty Spartiates who accompanied Agesilaos on this campaign: see n. 3.4.8a, 3.4.20, and Appendix M, §11.

So Agesilaos called Spithridates and the others. [13] As soon as they entered, Herippidas said, "No need, Agesilaos, to make a long speech about all the other things that we said to each other. To get to the point, Spithridates says that he would happily do all that you thought best."

[14] "Well, I think it best," said Agesilaos, "for you, Spithridates, to give your daughter to Otys—and may good fortune attend such a marriage— and for you, Otys, to take her as your wife. But naturally we could not get her here before spring, if we were to bring her by land."

"Yes, but by Zeus," said Otys, "with your permission she could be sent for immediately by sea." [15] Shaking their right hands as a pledge of their word, they agreed to these terms and sent Otys away. And since Agesilaos knew that Otys was eager for the marriage, he immediately fitted out a trireme and gave orders to Kallias, a Spartan, to bring the girl back.

Agesilaos himself set out for Daskyleion,[a] where Pharnabazos had his royal residence. In the area around the residence, he found many large villages, which supplied provisions in abundance, and wild animals as well, exceptionally fine ones, some of them kept in enclosed parks,[b] others roaming in the open spaces. [16] A river full of all sorts of fish flowed near the place, and there were unlimited numbers of birds for those who were able to capture them. It was in this place, then, that Agesilaos wintered, and he managed to obtain provisions for his army both from that location and from foraging expeditions.

[17] One day, while the Greek soldiers were getting their provisions in a contemptuous and careless way (for they had never previously encountered any danger while obtaining what they wanted), Pharnabazos came upon them while they were scattered throughout the plain. He had with him two scythed chariots[a] and about four hundred horsemen. [18] When the Greeks saw him advancing to attack them, about seven hundred of them gathered into a tight formation. Pharnabazos, however, without delay placed the chariots in front of him and his cavalry and gave the order to attack the Greeks immediately. [19] The chariots bore down on them, scattering the compact mass of the soldiers, and the cavalry swiftly cut down about one hundred of the Greeks. The rest fled to Agesilaos, who happened to be nearby with the hoplites.

[20] Two or three days later, Spithridates learned that Pharnabazos' camp was located at Kaue,[a] a large village about 160 stades[b] away, and he immediately informed Herippidas of this. [21] Herippidas, who was eager

4.1.14–16
395
PAPHLAGONIA-DASKYLEION
The marriage is approved, and Agesilaos sends a ship to bring the girl to Otys quickly. He winters in the region of Daskyleion, where he finds provisions for the army.

4.1.17–19
395
DASKYLEION
Pharnabazos, with chariots and cavalry, surprises the disorganized Greek foragers, killing about one hundred of them.

4.1.20–25
395
KAUE
Based on information supplied by Spithridates about the location of Pharnabazos' camp, Herippidas attacks it at dawn with cavalry and infantry, killing many Mysians and capturing much booty. Pharnabazos escapes.

4.1.15a Daskyleion: Map 4.1.31. The Oxyrhynchus Historian has an account of Agesilaos at Daskyleion (see Appendix P, Fragment 25.3–4).

4.1.15b Xenophon refers to these gardens, where the Persians kept wild animals for hunting, in two of his other works, the *Anabasis* 1.2.7 and the *Cyropaedia* 1.4.11. See Appendix D, Persia in Xenophon's *Hellenika*, §5.

4.1.17a Xenophon describes these chariots in the *Anabasis* 1.8.10: "The chariots had scythes placed sideways from the axles

and also beneath the chariot facing the ground, so that they might slice through anything with which they made contact." The Persians regularly used these chariots in battles. See further Appendix D, §10.

4.1.20a Kaue: site unknown.

4.1.20b Assuming Xenophon's 160 stades were Attic stades, each of 583 feet, the distance would convert to 93,280 feet, or about 18 miles. See Appendix I, Units of Distance, Currency, and Capacity in Xenophon's *Hellenika*, §4–5, 13.

to accomplish some brilliant achievement, asked Agesilaos for two thousand hoplites, the same number of peltasts, and the horsemen of both Spithridates and the Paphlagonians; in addition, he asked for as many of the Greeks as he could persuade to accompany him. [22] Agesilaos granted all this to him, and Herippidas began to sacrifice.[a] When he finally obtained good omens late in the day, he stopped sacrificing and ordered the men to take their meal and present themselves in front of the camp. When darkness fell, however, he found that not even half the men of each contingent were present. [23] Fearing that if he failed to carry out his proposed march, he would be mocked by the other members of the thirty, Herippidas set out with the force that he had. [24] At dawn he fell upon the camp of Pharnabazos and slew many of the Mysians[a] who were Pharnabazos' advance guard. Pharnabazos and his men escaped, but the camp was captured. Many drinking cups and other possessions of the sort that Pharnabazos could be expected to have were taken, as well as much baggage and many pack animals. [25] Indeed, the amount of booty taken was inordinately large because Pharnabazos feared that if he set up permanent camp somewhere, he would be encircled and besieged; so just like a nomad, he kept always on the move, from one part of his territory to another, and he was careful to conceal his camps.

[26] When Spithridates and the Paphlagonians brought back the booty they had captured, Herippidas positioned his company and division commanders[a] so as to intercept them and take everything they had captured away from them in order that he might bring back as much booty as possible to the men in charge of selling it. [27] Spithridates and the Paphlagonians, however, would not stand for this; believing themselves unjustly treated and dishonored, they gathered together at night and departed for Sardis,[a] to Ariaios,[b] whom they trusted because Ariaios too had revolted against the King and been at war with him. [28] This defection of Spithridates, Megabates,[a] and the Paphlagonians caused Agesilaos more grief than anything else that happened in this campaign.

[29] There was a man of Cyzicus,[a] Apollophanes, who happened to have been for a long time the guest-friend[b] of Pharnabazos and who had recently become a guest-friend of Agesilaos also. He told Agesilaos that he thought

4.1.26–28
395
DASKYLEION
Herippidas strips Spithridates and the Paphlagonians of their share of the booty, and they, thus insulted, leave the Greek army, which distresses Agesilaos.

4.1.29–30
395
VICINITY OF DASKYLEION
A mutual friend of Agesilaos and Pharnabazos arranges a meeting between them.

4.1.22a He sacrificed in order to learn the gods' will. See Appendix J, Ancient Greek Religion in the Time of Xenophon, §2–4.
4.1.24a Mysia: Map 4.1.31.
4.1.26a The taxiarchs and *lokhagoi*: see Appendix F, The Spartan Army (and the Battle of Leuctra), §10, and Appendix B, The Athenian Government and the Oligarchy of the Thirty, §7.
4.1.27a Sardis: Map 4.1.31.
4.1.27b Ariaios: this may be the same Ariaios whom Xenophon knew well as the lieutenant of Cyrus the Younger during his campaign against his brother the King, which Xenophon described in his *Anaba-*

sis. After Cyrus' death, Ariaios gained a pardon from the King, broke his oath of fidelity to the Greeks in the army, and helped Tissaphernes accomplish his arrest of the Greek generals.
4.1.28a Megabates was Spithridates' son and is named only here in the *Hellenika*. Plutarch (*Parallel Lives*, "Agesilaos" 11.2) leaves no doubt that Agesilaos was attracted by youths' good looks.
4.1.29a Cyzicus: Map 4.1.31.
4.1.29b Guest-friend: a formal type of reciprocal-hospitality relationship between men from different states.

FIGURE 4.1.31.
COIN ISSUED BY THE SATRAPAL
GOVERNMENT OF PHARNABAZOS
AT THE END OF THE FIFTH
CENTURY. IT MAY BE A LIKENESS
OF PHARNABAZOS.

he could convince Pharnabazos to confer with him about a treaty of friendship. [30] When Agesilaos responded positively, Apollophanes procured a truce and pledges and brought Pharnabazos to an agreed-upon place where Agesilaos, with the thirty around him, was stretched out on a grassy part of the land and awaiting him. Pharnabazos arrived wearing clothing that was worth a great deal of gold, and as his servants placed embroidered carpets beneath him, on which the Persians, with their soft style of living, are accustomed to sit, Pharnabazos noticed the spare and simple outfit of Agesilaos. Ashamed of indulging in such luxury, he lay down just as he was next to him on the ground.

[31] First the two men greeted each other, and then Pharnabazos stretched out his right hand, as did Agesilaos in return. After that, Pharnabazos (for he was the older of the two) began the conversation: [32] "Agesilaos and all you Spartans who are here present, I was your friend and ally when you were at war with the Athenians, and by giving you funds, I made your navy strong, and at the same time I myself on horseback fought with your army and drove the enemy into the sea.[a] Nor could you accuse me, as you did Tissaphernes,[b] of ever having said or done anything duplicitous toward you. [33] Yet although I behaved like that, I now am treated by you in such a way that I cannot even find food in my own land unless, like the wild beasts, I gather up what you yourselves have left behind. When I look at what my father left to me, those things in which I used to take pleasure—the fine dwellings, and parks full of trees and wild animals—I find that some have been cut down while others have been burned to the ground. So then if I am ignorant of what is holy and just, explain to me how these actions of yours are those of men who know how to show gratitude."

4.1.31–33
395
VICINITY OF DASKYLEION
At the meeting between Pharnabazos and Agesilaos, the Persian speaks first, recalling his good service to the Spartans in their war with Athens, and asking how it is just that they repay him by destroying and plundering his property.

4.1.32a See 1.1.6 for the event described by Pharnabazos here.

4.1.32b Tissaphernes, Persian satrap: see Appendix M, §29.

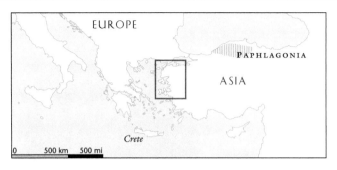

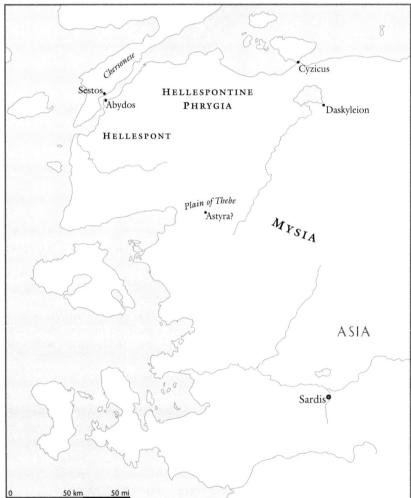

MAP 4.1.31

[34] So he spoke, and all the thirty felt ashamed before him and were silent. Agesilaos, however, eventually said, "Well, Pharnabazos, I think you know that even in the cities of Greece men become guest-friends with one another, but when their cities become enemies, men fight with their fatherlands against even their guest-friends, and if they happen to meet, they sometimes kill one another. Now we are at war with your King, and we are therefore compelled to consider all that he possesses as hostile to us. It would, however, be worth everything to us if you would be our friend. [35] Now if it were simply a matter of your exchanging one master for another—the King for us Spartans, I mean—I would not advise you to do this. But as it is, there is the possibility for you to be our ally and to bow before no one—to have no master but, rather, to live enjoying the fruits of what is yours. And let me say that I think that being free is equal to any amount of money. [36] But we are not asking you to be free and poor but, rather, that by using us as your allies, you may increase not the King's empire but your own, conquering those who are your fellow slaves and thereby making them subject to you. And if you were at the same time wealthy and free, would there be anything missing to prevent you from being fortunate in every way?"

[37] To this Pharnabazos replied, "Shall I tell you in fact what I am going to do?" When Agesilaos said that this would be most fitting, Pharnabazos continued: "Well, now, if the King sends another commander and makes me subject to him, I will choose to be your friend and ally. If, however, he appoints me to be in charge of this realm (so great a thing, it seems, is the desire for honor), know that I shall fight against you to the best of my ability." [38] Agesilaos took his hand upon hearing this and said, "You are a man of honor, and since you are such, I would very much wish that you were our friend. But in any case you may rest assured on one count: I will now depart from your land as swiftly as I can, and in the future, even if there is a state of war between us, we shall keep away from you and your territory, at least as long as we have someone else against whom we can campaign."

[39] With these words, the meeting ended. Pharnabazos mounted his horse and departed, but his son by Parapita, a boy still in the handsomeness of youth, remained behind and ran up to Agesilaos. "Agesilaos," he said, "I make you my guest-friend." To which Agesilaos responded, "I, for my part, accept it." "Don't forget this," said the young man, and he immediately gave the beautiful spear[a] that he had to Agesilaos. The latter accepted it and gave the boy in exchange a very beautiful collar, which he took from the neck of the horse that Idaeus, his secretary, was riding. Then the boy mounted his horse and went on after his father. [40] Later on, however, during the absence of Pharnabazos,[a] this son of Parapita was deprived of his

4.1.34–36
395
VICINITY OF DASKYLEION
Agesilaos tries to persuade Pharnabazos to rebel against the King and to ally with the Spartans.

4.1.37–38
395
VICINITY OF DASKYLEION
Pharnabazos replies that he will remain loyal to the King as long as he is not made subject to another commander. Agesilaos vows to leave Phrygia and not to disturb Pharnabazos' property again.

4.1.39–40
395
VICINITY OF DASKYLEION
Pharnabazos' son and Agesilaos exchange gifts and pledge to be guest-friends.

4.1.39a   This spear was a *palton*, a Persian light
          javelin.
4.1.40a   Pharnabazos was absent from his satrapy

during 394–393 and 388–387 (probably
at court after his marriage) and in Egypt
in 374/3.

FIGURE 4.1.40. REMAINS OF THE STADIUM SEATS AT OLYMPIA. STARTING BLOCKS FOR THE RACERS ARE AT THE LOWER LEFT.

rule by his brother[b] and went into exile. At that time, Agesilaos looked after him in every way, and when the boy fell in love with the son of Eualkes, an Athenian, Agesilaos did everything to bring it about that Eualkes' son, who was the tallest of the boys, was judged eligible to take part in the *stadion*[c] race at Olympia.[d]

[41] Agesilaos then immediately departed from Pharnabazos' territory, just as he had said he would. Spring was now just beginning, and Agesilaos came into the plain of Thebe, where he camped around the temple of Artemis Astyrene.[a] There he concentrated his entire force, adding to those troops that he had with him upon arrival all his other units from wherever they happened to be stationed. The reason for this was that Agesilaos was

4.1.41
394
THEBE
Agesilaos leaves Phrygia and camps at Thebe, planning to march inland toward the King.

4.1.40b　It is not clear from the Greek here whether the brother of Pharnabazos is meant or the brother of this boy (that is, a half brother, Pharnabazos' son by a woman other than Parapita). Plutarch's *Parallel Lives*, "Agesilaos" 13.2, seems to understand it as the latter.
4.1.40c　*Stadion*: a 200-yard footrace.
4.1.40d　Olympia: Map 3.5.9. Plutarch (*Parallel*

Lives, "Agesilaos" 13.1–3) explains that Agesilaos got the boy accepted into the boy's rather than the men's footrace, where his size would almost guarantee his victory. See Appendix J, §10.
4.1.41a　Plain of Thebe (Thebe Pedion) and Astyra, possible location: Map 4.1.31.

now preparing to march inland[b] as far as he could; he was intending to deprive the King of all those nations he would leave behind him as he advanced on his way toward the King.[c]

[1] While Agesilaos was occupied with these plans, the Spartans at home, having learned of the funds that had come into Greece[a] and that the greatest cities had allied to make war against them,[b] decided that their city was in danger and that it was necessary to mount an expedition. [2] And as they themselves began preparations for this, they sent Epikydidas right away to Agesilaos. Upon his arrival in Asia,[a] he went to Agesilaos and described the entire situation, explaining how things stood and informing him that the city had ordered Agesilaos to return and to bring help as quickly as possible to his country. [3] Agesilaos was quite distressed at these orders, thinking of how many honors and hopes he would now be deprived of. Nevertheless, he called his allies together and revealed to them what the city had ordered, explaining that it was necessary for him to bring help to his country and promising, "if this expedition turns out well, I want you, my allies, to know that I shall not forget you but shall return to accomplish what you desire." [4] When they heard this, many of the allies began to weep, and all of them voted to send help with Agesilaos to Sparta, determined, if everything went well in Greece, to bring him back to Asia.

[5] They all then set about making their preparations to accompany Agesilaos. Agesilaos, for his part, left behind in Asia Euxenos as harmost[a] and with him a garrison of not less than four thousand men, so that he might be able to protect the cities and keep them safe. Seeing that many of the soldiers were eager to remain rather than join an expedition against Greeks, and wanting to take with him as many of the best soldiers as he could, he offered prizes to the city that would send the best army, and to each commander of mercenaries who would best fit out a company of hoplites, archers, and peltasts. He also informed the commanders of the cavalry that he intended to give a prize to whichever of them should furnish the regiment with the best horses and cavalrymen. [6] He said that he would make his decision about all the prizes in the Chersonese[a] after they had crossed from Asia into Europe,[b] so that the commanders might know that it was their duty to keep their men on the march in good order.[c]

4.2.1–4
394
SPARTA-THEBE
Sparta, assailed by a Persian-financed alliance of Greek enemies, orders Agesilaos to return home to help his mother country.

4.2.5–6
394
THEBE
Agesilaos offers prizes to the best units to induce more soldiers to accompany him to Greece. The prizes are to be awarded after they cross over to Europe.

4.1.41b Xenophon uses the word *anabasis* here and elsewhere in the *Hellenika*, which is usually translated as an expedition "up-country," but here it is rendered as a march "inland," for Greeks always used it to indicate "away from the sea."

4.1.41c For more on Agesilaos' planned *anabasis* against Persia in 394, see Appendix G, §5.

4.2.1a In 3.5.1, Xenophon writes that funds distributed by the Persian Tithraustes were accepted by Theban, Corinthian, and Argive recipients on condition that they promise to persuade their cities to make war on Sparta.

4.2.1b Diodorus describes the foundation of this anti-Sparta alliance; see Appendix O,

Selections from the *Histories* of Diodorus Siculus Relevant to Xenophon's *Hellenika*, 14.82.1–4.

4.2.2a Asia (Asia Minor): Map 4.1.31, locator.

4.2.5a As Sparta took over foreign cities from the defeated Athenian empire, harmosts served as Spartan governors of those cities and as garrison and military commanders of the forces in them: see Appendix E, §19.

4.2.6a Chersonese: Map 4.1.31.

4.2.6b Europe: Map 4.1.31, locator.

4.2.6c The translator follows here the interpretation of Underhill; the verb used by Xenophon, *eukrinein*, does not occur elsewhere. (John Marincola)

4.2.7–8
394
HELLESPONT
Agesilaos leaves a force
to protect the cities and
marches his army to and
across the Hellespont.

[7] The prizes consisted for the most part of exquisitely crafted hoplite and cavalry arms, and there were also gold crowns. The cost of all the prizes was not less than four talents.[a] Despite the fact that so great a sum was spent on the prizes, enough money was found to provide costly weapons for the expedition. [8] When Agesilaos crossed the Hellespont,[a] the Spartans Menaskos, Herippidas, and Orsippos and one man from each of the allied contingents were chosen to be judges for the competition. After the decision was made, Agesilaos took the army and set out by the same road that the King had traveled when he invaded Greece.[b]

4.2.9–13
394
CORINTH
The Spartans mobilize
their army and march to
Sicyon, joined along the
way by the forces of Tegea
and Mantineia. The allies
decide to meet the Spar-
tans as early as possible
and debate how deep
their phalanx should be.

[9] During this time, the ephors[a] mobilized the army, and since Agesipolis was still a boy,[b] the city ordered Aristodemos, who was of the royal family and the boy's guardian, to lead it. [10] As they marched out from Sparta,[a] their opponents, who had already mustered their forces, came together and deliberated on the most advantageous strategy for themselves in the coming campaign. [11] Timolaos of Corinth[a] spoke to the allies as follows: "It seems to me that the Spartans are like rivers. For rivers at their sources are not large, but easy to cross; yet as they go farther, other rivers empty into them and make their current flow more powerfully. [12] So it is with the Spartans: in the place from which they start out they are alone, but as they move forward they add the forces of more cities to their own and become more numerous and difficult to defeat in battle. Likewise, I see that those who wish to get rid of wasps are stung by many of them if they try to destroy them when the wasps are rushing out of their hives; but if one sets the hive on fire while the wasps are within, one suffers no harm and gets the better of the wasps. Considering these factors, I conclude that it would be best for us to fight our battle in Sparta itself, but if not there, then as close to Sparta as possible." [13] Since Timolaos was thought to have given good advice, the allies voted in favor of it.

While they were deliberating about the leadership of their army and trying to come to an agreement as to the number of ranks in which the army should be deployed (for they did not want, by forming their ranks too deep, to provide the enemy with an opportunity to encircle them), the Spartans, having already united with the Tegeans[a] and the Mantineians,[b] marched out, taking the road that runs by the sea.[c]

4.2.7a The talent was a unit of weight whose value varied over time and place between 55 and 80 pounds. See Appendix I, §8, 10, 13.

4.2.8a Hellespont: Map 4.1.31. Pausanias, the second-century C.E. travel writer, says (Pausanias 3.9.12) that Agesilaos crossed from Abydos to Sestos (Map 4.1.31).

4.2.8b The reference is to Xerxes in 480; the route is recounted by Herodotus at *Histories* 7.105–132, 7.179–201 passim.

4.2.9a Ephors: a council of five officials of the Spartan government, elected annually. See Appendix E, §16.

4.2.9b Agesipolis had succeeded his father Pausa-

nias as king of Sparta when the latter was condemned to death in absentia in 395. See Appendix M, §1.

4.2.10a Sparta: Map 4.2.16, BX.

4.2.11a Corinth: Map 4.2.16, AY.

4.2.13a Tegea: Map 4.2.16, BY.

4.2.13b Mantineia: Map 4.2.16, BX.

4.2.13c The last phrase is most uncertain; the manuscripts' reading *amphialon* is a poetic word that means "sea-girt," such that one might assume the word "road" would be understood, but many scholars have found this unlikely. (John Marincola)

[14] The Corinthians and their allies, in the course of their march, were in the area around the Nemea River[a] at nearly the same time as the Spartans and their allies were near Sicyon.[b] As the Spartans invaded by way of Epieikeia,[c] the light-armed troops of the enemy at first were able to hurl javelins and shoot arrows at them from above, and in this way did great harm to them. [15] But when the Spartans descended to the coast,[a] they advanced through the plain there, destroying and burning the land. At this their opponents kept away and made their camp, keeping the riverbed[b] in front of them. And when in their forward march the Spartans had advanced to within ten stades[c] of the enemy, they too made their camp and remained quiet.

[16] I will now enumerate the forces on each side. Around 6,000 Spartan hoplites had been gathered together, along with nearly 3,000 hoplites from Elis,[a] Triphylia,[b] Akroreia,[c] and Lasion;[d] 1,500 from Sicyon; and not less than 3,000 from Epidauros,[e] Troizen,[f] Hermione,[g] and Halieis.[h] In addition to these there were about 600 Spartan horse, accompanied by about 300 Cretan[i] archers and not less than 400 slingers[j] from Marganeis,[k] Letrinoi,[l] and Amphidolia.[m] The Phleiasians,[n] however, did not accompany the expedition, for they claimed they were observing a truce.[o] This then was the force with the Spartans.[p]

[17] On the enemy's side were gathered about 6,000 Athenian[a] hoplites, Argives[b] that were said to be 7,000 in number, about 5,000 Boeotians[c] (since the Orchomenians[d] were not present), about 3,000 Corinthians, and in addition not less than 3,000 from all of Euboea.[e] So great was their hoplite force. The cavalry consisted of about 800 Boeotians, around 600 Athenians, about 100 Chalcidians[f] from Euboea, and about 50 from the Opuntian Locrians.[g] There was a greater number of light-armed troops with the Corinthian forces, since the Ozolian Locrians,[h] Malians,[i] and Acarnanians[j] were with them.

4.2.14–15 394 NEMEA RIVER The Spartans invade Corinthian territory by the sea road. The Corinthians and their allies prepare for battle near the Nemea River.	
4.2.16 394 NEMEA RIVER Xenophon enumerates the forces on the Spartan side.	
4.2.17 394 NEMEA RIVER Xenophon enumerates the forces on the side of the Corinthian-Boeotian-Athenian-Argive alliance.	

4.2.14a   Nemea River: Map 4.2.16, AY.
4.2.14b   Sicyon: Map 4.2.16, AY.
4.2.14c   Epieikeia: site unknown.
4.2.15a   The coast of the Corinthian Gulf: Map 4.2.16, AY.
4.2.15b   The bed of the Nemea River. See Diodorus' account of the battle in Appendix O, 14.83.1–2.
4.2.15c   If Xenophon's 10 stades were Attic stades, each of 583 feet, the distance would be a little over a mile.
4.2.16a   Elis: Map 4.2.16, AX.
4.2.16b   Triphylia: Map 4.2.16, BX.
4.2.16c   Akroreia: Map 4.2.16, AX.
4.2.16d   Lasion: Map 4.2.16, AX.
4.2.16e   Epidauros: Map 4.2.16, BY.
4.2.16f   Troizen: Map 4.2.16, BY.
4.2.16g   Hermione: Map 4.2.16, BY.
4.2.16h   Halieis: Map 4.2.16, BY.
4.2.16i   Crete: Map 4.1.31, locator.
4.2.16j   Slingers were troops armed with slings that hurled stones or lead bullets.
4.2.16k   Margana (Marganeis), possible location: Map 4.2.16, BX.
4.2.16l   Letrinoi: Map 4.2.16, BX.
4.2.16m   Amphidolia: Map 4.2.16, AX.

4.2.16n   Phleious: Map 4.2.16, AY.
4.2.16o   The truce was probably connected to some religious celebration, although at 4.4.15 Xenophon says that the people of Phleious feared that the Spartans would try to repatriate Phleiasian exiles.
4.2.16p   Xenophon has forgotten to include the Tegeans and Mantineians here, although both are mentioned at 4.2.13 and the Tegeans at 4.2.19 and 4.2.21. This error makes it impossible for us to estimate the relative size of the two opposing armies by simply adding up the figures he gives at 4.2.16–17.
4.2.17a   Athens: Map 4.2.16, AY.
4.2.17b   Argos: Map 4.2.16, BY.
4.2.17c   Boeotia: Map 4.2.16, AY.
4.2.17d   Orchomenus (in Boeotia): Map 4.2.16, AY. See 3.5.6 for the reason behind their absence from the army.
4.2.17e   Euboea: Map 4.2.16, AY.
4.2.17f   Chalcis (in Euboea): Map 4.2.16, AY.
4.2.17g   Opuntian Locris: Map 4.2.16, AY.
4.2.17h   Ozolian Locris: Map 4.2.16, AX.
4.2.17i   Malis: Map 4.2.16, AX.
4.2.17j   Acarnania: Map 4.2.16, AX.

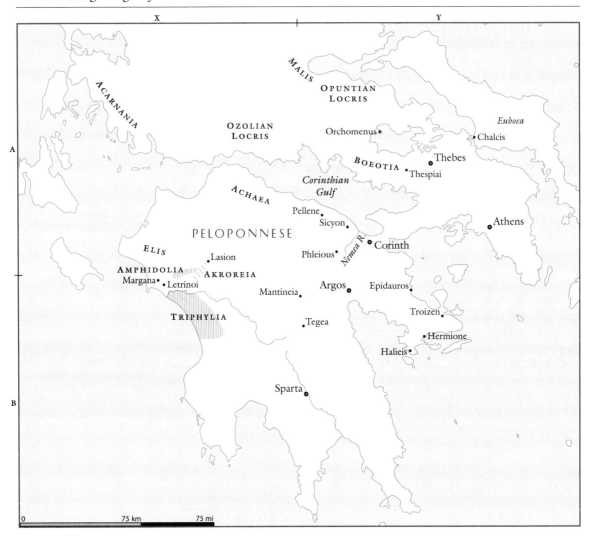

Map 4.2.16

4.2.18
394
NEMEA RIVER
The Boeotians change
wings to face the Achaeans
instead of the Spartans,
and initiate the battle. But
they drift off to the right,
forcing the Athenians on
their left to do the same.

[18] This then was the strength of each side. Now the Boeotians, as long as they held the left wing, were in no way eager to join battle.[a] But when the Athenians were stationed opposite the Spartans, and the Boeotians took over the right wing and were stationed against the Achaeans,[b] the Boeotians

4.2.18a The inference is that the Thebans on their left wing would be reluctant to fight the Spartans, who would be opposite them on the right wing of their own line. This is another example of Xenophon's constant denigration of the Thebans throughout the *Hellenika*: he implies that the extremely deep phalanx of the Thebans here reveals

their desire to avoid combat, rather than that they were developing a new and successful tactical battle formation, which they had used previously at the battle of Delium (Thucydides 4.93.4) and later at the battle of Leuctra (6.4.6–15). See the Introduction, §12.3; and Appendix L, §6.
4.2.18b Achaea: Map 4.2.16, AX.

straightaway said that the omens[c] were favorable and announced that the troops should prepare themselves, for the battle would soon take place. First they failed to adopt the sixteen-deep formation[d] but instead made their phalanx excessively deep; then in addition they wandered to the right[e] so that they might overextend the enemy with their wing. The Athenians had to follow so as not to be separated from the line, even though they knew that there was a danger that they themselves might be outflanked and encircled.

[19] Now for a time the Spartans did not realize that the enemy was marching toward them, because the ground was heavily overgrown. But when their enemy struck up the *paean*,[a] then indeed they realized what was happening and immediately gave the order that everyone should arrange themselves for battle. After they were deployed in the way that the allied commanders had assigned to each unit, they passed the word along the line that everyone should follow the lead company. In this way, then, the Spartans too led their phalanx to the right, and they stretched their wing past the enemy to such an extent that there were but six tribes of the Athenians arrayed against the Spartans, while the remaining four found themselves opposite the Tegeans.[b]

[20] When the armies were less than a stade[a] apart, the Spartans, as is their custom, sacrificed a she-goat to Artemis Agrotera[b] and then charged their enemy, curving their line around that part of the enemy wing that their line extended beyond, so as to outflank it. When the forces made contact, all the rest of the Spartan allies were defeated by those opposed to them, but both the men of Pellene[c] and the Thespians[d] arrayed against them fought and fell on the spot where they stood. [21] The Spartans themselves were victorious over that portion of the Athenian army that they covered,[a] and by encircling the part of the Athenian wing that their line overlapped, they killed many of them. And since they themselves were unharmed, they were able to advance with their own lines unbroken. They passed by the four tribes of the Athenians before the latter had returned from their pursuit,[b] with the result that the only losses that these Athenians suffered were the ones that occurred in their original encounter with the Tegeans.[c] [22] The

4.2.19
394
NEMEA RIVER
Surprised by the enemy advance, the Spartans quickly deploy into line with their allies and advance to their right, overlapping the Athenians on the enemy's left.

4.2.20–22
394
NEMEA RIVER
The Spartan allies are defeated, but the Spartans defeat the Athenians opposing them and turn to inflict heavy losses on the enemy contingents as they return from their initial pursuit.

4.2.18c Religious custom demanded that commanders perform a sacrifice and review omens before entering battle. See n. 3.2.10b; the Introduction, §8.5; Appendix E, §2, 21; Appendix F, §1; Appendix J, §2, 12; Appendix L, §13; and Figure 4.2.23b.
4.2.18d Presumably the sixteen-rank depth here was agreed on at 4.2.13; the ordinary Greek phalanx was eight ranks deep (Thucydides 5.68). See Appendix L, §4–6.
4.2.18e Thucydides (5.71.1) observes that this was a universal tendency of hoplite armies, since the men moved to the right to protect their unprotected side. See further Appendix L, §5.
4.2.19a The *paean* was a ritual chant that classical Greek soldiers and sailors sang as they advanced into battle, rallied, or celebrated victory.
4.2.19b Athenians were divided into ten tribes and

were mustered by tribes in the phalanx. Given that the Spartan and Athenian hoplite numbers were about equal (six thousand for each, as enumerated above), the Spartans ought to have been opposite all ten of the tribes.
4.2.20a If it was an Attic stade, that would be about 583 feet. See Appendix I, §4–5, 13.
4.2.20b Artemis Agrotera: goddess of the hunt.
4.2.20c Pellene: Map 4.2.16, AY.
4.2.20d Thespiai: Map 4.2.16, AY.
4.2.21a That is, the six tribes.
4.2.21b These four Athenian tribes had conquered the men opposed to them; having broken the line, they then went in pursuit of the fleeing hoplites.
4.2.21c That is, in the opening phase of the battle, due to the two antagonists' positions in the battle lines.

Spartans, for their part, attacked the Argives when the latter were returning from their pursuit; when the first polemarch[a] was intending to attack them in the front, someone, it is said, shouted out that they should allow the Argive front to pass by. When they had done this, the Spartans were then able to strike those running past them on their unprotected[b] side, and in so doing killed many of them. Then the Spartans set upon the Corinthians and some Thebans,[c] who were also returning from their initial pursuit, and they killed quite a number of these.

[23] After all this had occurred, the defeated at first fled toward the walls of Corinth;[a] but when the Corinthians shut the gates against them,[b] they again made their camp on the ground they had used before. The Spartans then marched to the place where they had first fought the enemy and there set up a trophy.[c] That, then, is how this battle turned out.

[1] Agesilaos, meanwhile, was hurrying from Asia to bring assistance to the Spartans. When he had reached Amphipolis,[a] however, Derkylidas met him there and reported that the Spartans had gained a victory, and that while only eight of the Spartans had died, the enemy had lost a very great number. He also revealed that losses among the Spartan allies had been substantial.[b] [2] Agesilaos asked Derkylidas, "Would this be the right time for those cities that have contributed soldiers to our campaign to learn as quickly as possible of our victory?"

Derkylidas replied, "Yes, for when they hear of this, it is likely that they will be even more enthusiastic."

"Wouldn't you be the best person to announce this to them, since you yourself were present at the battle?"

To which Derkylidas, who was delighted to hear this, since he was always fond of travel, replied, "I would, if you order me to do so."

"Well, then, I give the order, and I command this besides: that you announce to them that if our Spartan affairs come out favorably, we shall be together again, just as we said."[a]

[3] So Derkylidas set out for the Hellespont.[a] Agesilaos, for his part, with his troops, passed through Macedon[b] and advanced into Thessaly.[c]

4.2.23
394
NEMEA RIVER
The alliance forces flee to Corinth. The Spartans set up a trophy.

4.3.1–2
394
AMPHIPOLIS
Agesilaos on his way to Greece is informed at Amphipolis that the Spartans have won the battle. He asks Derkylidas, who brought him the news, to announce the victory to the allied cities in Asia.

4.3.3–6
394
THESSALY
Marching through Thessaly, Agesilaos is opposed by Thessalians allied to Boeotia. He deploys his troops into a hollow square.

4.2.22a First polemarch: Spartan military officer. See Appendix F, §5.
4.2.22b The unprotected side was the right side, as the shield was carried on the left arm.
4.2.22c Thebes: Map 4.2.16, AY.
4.2.23a Corinth: Map 4.2.16, AY.
4.2.23b Xenophon's manner of expression here suggests that the first men who fled to the city walls were admitted and the gates were only closed later. Demosthenes 20.53 suggests the opposite, that the walls were at first closed against them but that the anti-Spartan faction in the city then opened them.
4.2.23c After a battle in ancient Greece, the victors would gather up their dead, strip those of the enemy, and raise a trophy,

usually a set of captured armor raised on a pole. The defeated would collect the bodies of their fallen during a truce that they would explicitly request and be granted for that purpose. In this way, appropriate reverence was shown and proper burial was accorded to all war dead. See Appendix L, §13..
4.3.1a Amphipolis: Map 4.3.9, locator.
4.3.1b Diodorus (Appendix O, 14.83) gives the casualty numbers as 1,100 for the Spartans and their allies and 2,800 for their opponents.
4.3.2a For Agesilaos' farewell promise, see 4.2.3.
4.3.3a Hellespont: Map 4.3.9, locator.
4.3.3b Macedon: Map 4.3.9, locator.
4.3.3c Thessaly: Map 4.3.9, AX.

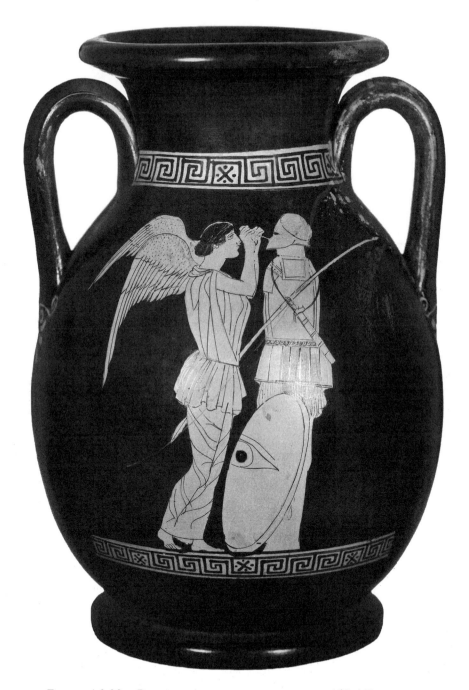

FIGURE 4.2.23A. RED-FIGURED TWO-HANDLED JAR, C. 450–440, DEPICTING
NIKE, GODDESS OF VICTORY, ATTACHING A CAPTURED SET OF ARMS TO A TREE
STUMP OR A POLE—AN EARLY REPRESENTATION OF A BATTLE TROPHY.

FIGURE 4.2.23B.
FRAGMENT OF A TERRA-COTTA
ATTIC KYLIX C. 490–480,
DEPICTING A HOPLITE SACRIFIC-
ING A RAM BEFORE BATTLE.

There his troops were pursued and harassed by allies of the Boeotians[d]—
the Larissaeans, Krannonians, Skotoussaians, Pharsalians[e]—and all of the
other Thessalians save those who at that time happened to be exiles. [4]
Agesilaos for a time led the army in a hollow square, placing half of the
cavalry in the front and half in the rear. But when the Thessalians tried to
hinder his progress by attacking the men in the rear, Agesilaos sent to their
aid the cavalry that he had stationed in front, all except the horsemen he
kept with himself. [5] When both armies had set themselves in formation,
the Thessalians turned about and began to retreat slowly, thinking that it
was not advantageous to fight a cavalry battle against hoplites. The Greeks
followed them quite cautiously. [6] Agesilaos, however, who realized what
mistakes each side was making, sent his own cavalry escort—men who were
particularly stalwart—to give orders to the rest of the cavalry that all of
them together would charge the Thessalians as swiftly as possible, and to
carry on the pursuit so as not to give them the possibility of returning

4.3.3d   Boeotia: Map 4.3.9, BX.
4.3.3e   Larissa, Krannon, Skotoussa, and
         Pharsalus, Thessaly: Map 4.3.9, AX.

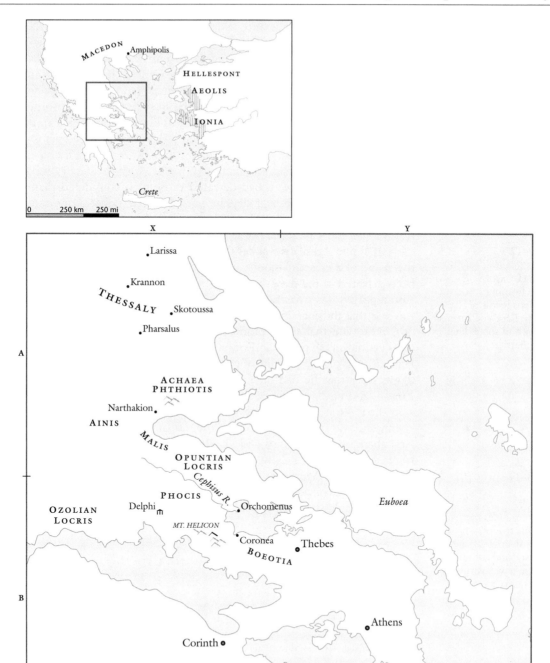

MAP 4.3.9

135

4.3.7–9
394
THESSALY
Agesilaos surprises the
Thessalians with a sudden
cavalry attack and routs
them.

again. [7] The Thessalians were taken completely by surprise when they saw the enemy horse bearing down on them; some of them fled while others turned about, and still others, trying to turn around, exposed the flanks of their horses to the Spartans and were thus captured. [8] Polemarchos, the Pharsalian hipparch,[a] did turn about and was killed fighting with his men around him. After this, the Thessalians fled in such panic and disorder that some were killed and others captured, nor did they stop fleeing until they came to the mountain called Narthakion.[b] [9] At that time Agesilaos set up a trophy between Pras[a] and Narthakion, and he remained there, greatly pleased with what he had accomplished: for he, with the cavalry force that he himself had assembled, had defeated those who considered themselves best in cavalry. On the next day, he passed by the Achaean mountains of Phthia,[b] and for the remainder of his journey he passed through friendly territory, all the way to the borders of Boeotia.

4.3.10–12
394
BOEOTIA-CNIDUS
At the border of Boeotia,
Agesilaos learns of the
Spartan fleet's defeat near
Cnidus and some details
of the battle.

[10] While Agesilaos was on the border of Boeotia, the sun appeared in the shape of a crescent moon,[a] and the news arrived that the Spartans had been defeated in the naval battle[b] and that the admiral Peisander[c] had died. Also reported was a description of how the sea battle was conducted. [11] It was said that the encounter between the fleets had taken place in the vicinity of Cnidus[a] and that the Persian Pharnabazos was the admiral commanding the Phoenician[b] ships, while Konon,[c] who led the Greek contingent for the Persians, was placed in front of him. [12] When Peisander arrayed his ships, it was clear that he had far fewer ships than the Greek contingent under Konon, and in the ensuing battle, the allied ships on his left wing immediately fled. While Peisander was attacking, his trireme was struck by the enemy and was forced to land. Now the rest of those who were driven to the land abandoned their ships and saved themselves as best they could, trying to reach Cnidus, but Peisander himself was killed while fighting on his ship.[a]

4.3.13–14
394
BOEOTIA
Agesilaos hides the truth
from his troops, whose
loyalty in adversity he
distrusts, and announces
that the naval battle was
a Spartan victory.

[13] When Agesilaos learned of the defeat, he was at first very distressed. He considered, however, the character of his army: the majority, he knew, would share happily in good news, but there was no need to share adverse tidings with them;[a] so in the end, he decided to alter the report, and ordered that an announcement be made that Peisander had died, but

4.3.8a   Hipparch: a commander of cavalry.
4.3.8b   The precise location of Mount Narthakion
          is unknown, but presumably it is near the
          city of Narthakion in Malis: Map 4.3.9, AX.
4.3.9a   Pras: site unknown.
4.3.9b   Achaean mountains of Phthia (Achaea
          Phthiotis): Map 4.3.9, AX.
4.3.10a   That is, the sun was eclipsed by the moon
          until only a crescent appeared (like that of
          the moon). This eclipse took place on
          August 14, 394.
4.3.10b   The definite article indicates that Xenophon
          assumed his audience would know of this
          famous sea battle, the defeat of the Spartans
          at Cnidus by the forces led by Konon the
          Athenian and the forces of Pharnabazos.
4.3.10c   For Peisander's selection to lead the fleet,
          see 3.4.29.

4.3.11a   Cnidus: Map 4.8.27.
4.3.11b   Phoenicia: Map 3.4.12, locator.
4.3.11c   This is the first mention of Konon since
          his flight after the battle of Aigospotamoi
          at 2.1.29. For information on what Konon
          had done since that battle, see Appendix
          M, §16.
4.3.12a   For Diodorus' version of the battle of
          Cnidus, see Appendix O, 14.83.4–7.
4.3.13a   Because many of his men were allied or
          mercenary troops and would, unlike citi-
          zens, not wish to stay if they had no
          prospects for success. The loss of
          command of the sea might endanger the
          Spartans' ability to return home to Asia. It
          certainly threatened Agesilaos' plan to
          return and attack the King.

that he had been victorious in the naval battle. [14] At the same time that the announcement was made, he sacrificed as if for a victory, and he sent around to many of the troops portions of the sacrificial victims. The result was that when a skirmish ensued against their enemies, the troops of Agesilaos fought well and were victorious because of the report that the Spartans had won the naval battle.

[15] The forces that were now drawn up against Agesilaos were the following: the Boeotians, Athenians,[a] Argives,[b] Corinthians,[c] Ainianians,[d] Euboeans,[e] and both Opuntian and Ozolian Locrians.[f] With Agesilaos were the Spartan regiment that had crossed over from Corinth, half of the regiment from Orchomenus,[g] the newly freed helots[h] from Sparta who had campaigned with him, and, in addition, the foreign contingent that Herippidas, commanded; there were also those from the Greek cities in Asia and as many troops as had joined Agesilaos as he marched through Europe. From the immediate environs there were Orchomenian and Phocian[i] hoplites. Agesilaos had many more peltasts than his opponents, but the number of horse was about equal for both sides. [16] These then were the forces on each side, and I shall now describe how the battle turned out—a battle quite unlike any other in our time.

The opponents came together in the plain of Coronea,[a] Agesilaos and his troops advancing from the Cephisus River,[b] while the Boeotians and theirs marched from Mount Helicon.[c] Agesilaos held the right wing of his troops; the Orchomenians were farthest away from him on the left. On the other side, the Thebans themselves held the right wing, while the Argives held the left.

[17] As they were coming together there was for a time great silence on both sides. But when they were distant from each other about a stade,[a] the Thebans[b] raised their war cry[c] and came to close quarters on the run. And when there were about three plethra[d] between them, the troops commanded by Herippidas, and along with them the Ionians,[e] Aeolians,[f] and Hellespontines,[g] ran out from Agesilaos' phalanx and advanced together on the run; when they came within spear-thrusting distance, they routed their opponents. The Argives, however, did not even await the charge of Agesilaos and

4.3.15–16
394
CORONEA
The forces of each side are identified. Each side has the same number of cavalry, but Agesilaos' force has more peltasts.

4.3.17
394
CORONEA
The battle is described. The Thebans rout their opponents and advance to attack the Spartan baggage train.

4.3.15a   Athens: Map 4.3.9, BY.
4.3.15b   Argos: Map 4.3.9, BX.
4.3.15c   Corinth: Map 4.3.9, BX.
4.3.15d   Ainianians (Ainis): Map 4.3.9, AX.
4.3.15e   Euboea: Map 4.3.9, BY.
4.3.15f   Opuntian Locris: Map 4.3.9, AX. Ozolian Locris: Map 4.3.9, BX.
4.3.15g   Orchomenus (in Boeotia): Map 4.3.9, BX.
4.3.15h   The *neodamōdeis*: see Appendix E, §9, 12, and Appendix F, §6.
4.3.15i   Phocis: Map 4.3.9, BX.
4.3.16a   Coronea: Map 4.3.9, BX.
4.3.16b   Cephisus River: Map 4.3.9, BX.
4.3.16c   Mount Helicon: Map 4.3.9, BX.
4.3.17a   The Attic stade was 583 feet, the Olympic stade 630.8 feet. We cannot be sure which Xenophon is referring to

here. See Appendix I, §4–5, 13.
4.3.17b   Thebes (Boeotia): Map 4.3.9, BY.
4.3.17c   The war cry was the *paean*, chanted or sung by ancient Greek troops going into battle. See Appendix L, §13.
4.3.17d   Three plethra equals one half of a stade, or about 300 feet. See Appendix I, §4–5, 13.
4.3.17e   Ionia: Map 4.3.9, locator.
4.3.17f   Aeolis: Map 4.3.9, locator.
4.3.17g   Hellespont: Map 4.3.9, locator.

4.3.18–19
394
CORONEA
The allied left flees Agesilaos' forces before contact is made. Agesilaos wheels his troops to face the Thebans and forces them to fight head-on through the Spartans to join their allies. Some break through and escape, but many are killed.

4.3.20
394
CORONEA
His victory complete, Agesilaos spares some of the enemy who have taken refuge in a temple.

4.3.21
394
CORONEA-DELPHI
Agesilaos sets up a trophy and grants a truce to the Thebans to collect their dead. At Delphi he dedicates a tenth to the god.

4.3.22–23
394
PHOCIS-LOCRIS
Gylis the polemarch commands the army in an attack through Phocis to Locris and plunders the villages but toward evening is attacked by the Locrians. The Spartans drive them back but suffer casualties on difficult ground. Gylis is killed.

his men but instead fled immediately toward Mount Helicon. [18] Then, while some of the foreigners were trying to crown Agesilaos,[a] someone reported to him that the Thebans had routed the Orchomenians and were now attacking the baggage train. Agesilaos immediately wheeled his phalanx around and led it against the Thebans. Now the Thebans on their part, when they saw that their allies had fled toward Helicon, wanted to break through to the body of their own men and so massed themselves and approached boldly. [19] And it was here, one may say, that Agesilaos proved his courage beyond a doubt: for he did not choose what would have been the safest course for himself and his men, which would have been to let the troops marching against him pass through and then attack them from behind; instead he met and came to blows with the Thebans head-on. Crashing together their shields, they shoved, they fought, they killed and were killed, and finally, although some of the Thebans broke through to Mount Helicon, many were killed as they tried to retreat there.

[20] When Agesilaos' victory was complete, he himself was carried toward the phalanx—for he had been wounded—and some horsemen told him that about eighty of the enemy, with their arms, had taken refuge in the temple, and they asked him what they should do about them. And he, though suffering from many wounds, did not forget the divine power[a] but gave orders to his soldiers that they were not to harm these men but to allow them to depart wherever they wished. So then, since it was now late in the day, they took their evening meal and retired.

[21] In the morning, he ordered Gylis the polemarch to assemble the troops and to set up a trophy, adding that they should all be garlanded for the god and that all the flute players should play. These orders were carried out, and when the Thebans sent heralds asking permission to take up the bodies for burial under truce, their request was granted.[a] And Agesilaos went to Delphi,[b] where he dedicated a tenth of the spoils to the god, a dedication that amounted to not less than a hundred talents.[c]

Gylis the polemarch, who was put in command of the army, departed for Phocis, and from there invaded Locris.[d] [22] Once there, the soldiers carried off from the villages both goods and food. They did this for the whole day, but toward evening, when the Spartans in the rear were departing, the Locrians followed them, throwing missiles and javelins. The Spartans turned, pursued them, and struck some of them down. After this, they no longer followed from behind but instead pelted them only from higher ground. [23] The Spartans attempted to pursue them by going up the

---

4.3.18a To crown him as the victor, believing that the battle was over.

4.3.20a For the characterization of Agesilaos, and especially his piety, see Appendix G, §4.

4.3.21a After a battle in ancient Greece, the victors would gather up their dead, strip those of the enemy, and raise a trophy. The defeated would acknowledge their defeat by requesting a truce under which they could collect the bodies of their fallen, which lay on the field occupied by the enemy. This truce

would be granted by the victors, and in this way, appropriate reverence would be shown and proper burial was accorded to all war dead. See Appendix L, §13.

4.3.21b Delphi: Map 4.3.9, BX. Delphi was the site of the great oracular shrine of Apollo.

4.3.21c One hundred talents was an immense sum. See Appendix I, §8, 10, 13.

4.3.21d These are the Ozolian Locrians, whom Gylis wished to punish for their support of the Thebans at Coronea: see 4.3.15.

hills, but darkness came on and some of them, while pursuing, fell down because of the difficult terrain; others fell because they could not see what was in front of them, and still others because they were struck by missiles. It was here that the polemarch Gylis and one of his comrades, Pelles, were killed; all told, about eighteen Spartiates died, some struck dead by stones, others wounded by javelins. Indeed, if those who were taking their dinner at the camp had not come to their assistance, all might have been killed.

[1] After this, the rest of the army was disbanded, the men going each to their own cities, and Agesilaos sailed home. From that time on the Athenians,[a] Boeotians,[b] Argives,[c] and their allies continued their war against the Spartans,[d] using Corinth[e] as their base, while the Spartans and their allies made Sicyon[f] theirs. Now the Corinthians saw that with the enemy so near, it was their own land that was always being ravaged and many of their citizens who were being killed, while the rest of their allies could live in peace and enjoy the produce of their lands undisturbed. Because of this, the majority and the best[g] of the Corinthians began to desire peace, and gathering together, they encouraged one another to advocate for it. [2] The Argives, Athenians, Boeotians, and those Corinthians who had taken bribes from the King and were most responsible for the war realized that unless they did away with those who were supporting peace, there was a danger that the whole city might ally itself again with the Spartans. So for this reason they tried to engineer a plot to kill them. Their first plan was the most impious of all, given that all men refrain from killing during a festival, even if someone has been condemned under the law: those men, however, chose the last day of the Eucleia festival,[a] when they thought they could capture more men in the agora,[b] so as to more easily facilitate their destruction.

[3] And so, upon a given signal, those who had the responsibility for killing the selected victims unsheathed their swords and struck: they attacked one man who was standing among a circle of his friends, another was slain while seated, someone else was killed in the theater, and they even struck down one man who was sitting as a judge. When people recognized what was happening, the best men immediately took flight; some ran toward the statues of the gods in the agora, others to the altars. And it was there that both the men giving the orders and those obeying them—these most unholy men who had no regard whatever for what was lawful—slaughtered even those at the altars, acting in such a way that

4.4.1–2
393
CORINTH
The war continues, the allies based at Corinth, the Spartans at Sicyon. Since the land that was being ravaged and most of those killed were Corinthian, a faction for peace forms in Corinth and gains support. But those who support the war plot to massacre the peace seekers during a religious festival.

4.4.3
392
CORINTH
The conspirators carry out the massacre in the agora, even going so far as to impiously slay victims at the very altars of the gods, which causes good men to recoil in horror.

4.4.1a Athens: Map 4.4.12.
4.4.1b Boeotia: Map 4.4.12.
4.4.1c Argos: Map 4.4.12.
4.4.1d Sparta: Map 4.4.12.
4.4.1e Corinth: Map 4.4.12 and inset.
4.4.1f Sicyon: Map 4.4.12, inset.
4.4.1g The terminology suggests the aristocratic or wealthy citizens, often in Greek called "the best."
4.4.2a The festival of Artemis Eucleia. See Appendix J, §8–12, for more on festivals and Greek attitudes, particularly regarding respecting truces.
4.4.2b Agora: the central market square of any ancient Greek city, where all business and much politics and social life took place.

some of those who were not the object of attack but were men nevertheless respectful of law and custom felt despair in their hearts when they witnessed such impiety.

[4] In this way many of the older men died, for a great number of them happened to be in the agora. The younger men, on the other hand, since Pasimelos[a] had suspected what was going to happen, remained quiet in the Craneion.[b] When they heard the clamor, however, and some men who were fleeing their killers arrived where they were, they ran up to the Acrocorinth,[c] beating back the Argives and any others who attacked them on the way. [5] While they were discussing what to do, a capital fell down from the top of a column, though there had been no earthquake and not even a wind was blowing. And when they sacrificed, the seers who examined the victims said that it would be better for them to go down from the citadel than to stay. So they descended and fled beyond the territory of Corinth, intending at first simply to stay in exile; but when their friends urged them not to go and their mothers and siblings went to them with the same appeal, and when some of the men in power swore that they would suffer no harm, some of them returned home to Corinth.

[6] Yet when they went home, they saw things that made some of them feel that their life was not worth living: the rulers of the city were acting like tyrants, and their city was disappearing, since its boundary stones had been removed, and it was now being called Argos instead of Corinth; in addition, they found themselves compelled to share in Argive citizenship, although they did not want it at all, and they realized that they themselves had less influence in the city than did mere metics.[a] They decided then that it would be a worthy accomplishment to try to make their city Corinth once again[b]—as it had been from the beginning—to make it free and purified of murderers, and to allow it to enjoy good government; and they thought that if they could accomplish these objectives, they would be the saviors of their city, but that even if they failed, they would obtain a death most worthy of praise, since they would have died striving for the highest and most honorable goals.[c]

[7] With this in mind, two men, named Pasimelos and Alkimenes, swam across a swollen river to meet with Praxitas, the Spartan polemarch who happened to be on guard in Sicyon with his own regiment. They told him

---

4.4.4–5
392
CORINTH
Many older Corinthians die, but the younger men escape to the Acrocorinth, from which many leave for exile, although some are persuaded to return home.

4.4.6
392
CORINTH
Those young men who do return find life in Corinth intolerable, and some decide to overthrow the current regime or die honorably in the attempt.

4.4.7–8
392
CORINTH
Two Corinthians decide to open a gate in the walls connecting the city with its port so that the current pro-war government will be defeated in the field.

4.4.4a Pasimelos: a Corinthian not previously mentioned by Xenophon as one of the "best." He reappears at 4.4.7–8 and 7.3.2.

4.4.4b According to Pausanias 2.2.4, the Craneion was a grove of cypresses in front of the city.

4.4.4c Acrocorinth: Map 4.4.12, inset. The Acrocorinth was a steep, high hill near the city of Corinth on which was situated an ancient walled citadel. See Figure 4.4.5, two views of the Acrocorinth.

4.4.6a The metics of an ancient Greek city were resident aliens who usually had no rights of citizenship.

4.4.6b Corinth separate and independent again, instead of united with Argos.

4.4.6c Many, though not all, scholars think that the events of 392 described here did not amount to a full union whereby there ceased to be a separate Corinthian state (that followed a couple of years later; see 4.5.1). In 392 there were probably only arrangements whereby Argive residents in Corinth (and vice versa) could exercise rights of citizenship instead of merely being resident aliens. See the Introduction, §15.4.

FIGURE 4.4.5. THE ACROCORINTH (ACROPOLIS OF CORINTH) AS SEEN FROM THE LECHAION ROAD IN THE AGORA OF CORINTH (LEFT) AND THROUGH THE COLUMNS OF THE TEMPLE OF APOLLO ADJACENT TO THE AGORA (BELOW).

that they could provide him an entrance into the walls that stretched down to Lechaion.[a] Praxitas for his part believed them, because he knew from before that they were trustworthy. So, having arranged that the regiment that had planned to depart from Sicyon should remain there, he prepared for the attempt to gain entrance. [8] When Pasimelos and Alkimenes, by chance and by contrivance, had been assigned to guard those gates where the trophy stands,[a] Praxitas arrived, in command of the Spartan regiment as well as Sicyonian troops and all the Corinthian exiles who happened to be present. But when he got to the gates, he was afraid of entering, and so he sent one of his trusted men to see what things were like inside. Pasimelos and Alkimenes took the man around and showed him everything in so open a manner that when he returned to Praxitas, he told him everything had been just as the two men said, with no deceit on their part

[9] So then Praxitas and his men managed to get inside the walls. Since, however, there was a good distance between the two walls, the men when they deployed into line seemed to themselves to be too few,[a] so they made a stockade and a ditch in front of themselves as best they could and waited for their allies to bring up reinforcements. A hostile garrison of Boeotians was stationed behind them at the harbor. They were not challenged on the next day (the day, that is, after the night on which they entered), but on the following day the Argives came with all haste to bring assistance. They found a battle line arrayed against them, with the Spartans on its right wing, the Sicyonians next to the Spartans, and the Corinthian exiles, to the number of about 150, next to the eastern wall. The mercenaries under Iphikrates[b] arrayed themselves near the eastern wall, and next to them were the Argives, while the Corinthians from the city held the left wing. [10] And it was these Corinthians, made contemptuous by their superior numbers, who immediately attacked. They routed the Sicyonians[a] and, shattering their stockade, pursued them to the sea, where they killed many of them. Pasimachus, the Spartan commander of the cavalry, had a few horses with him, and when he saw the Sicyonians being hard pressed, he ordered his men to tie their horses to trees and, picking up the shields of the Sicyonians, led a group of volunteers against

4.4.9–10
392
CORINTH
The Spartans under Praxitas enter the walls through the gate opened by the two Corinthian defectors and establish a palisaded camp as they wait for reinforcements. After one day the allies attack the Spartan camp. The Corinthians rout the Sicyonians in the center, killing many and pursuing the rest. Some dismounted Spartan cavalry try to stem the rout but are too few.

4.4.7a Lechaion, the port of Corinth: Map 4.4.12, inset. Like a number of other ancient Greek cities, Corinth was situated several miles from the coast and in this period had constructed two Long Walls to provide a secure connection between it and its port, thus preventing the city from being cut off from the sea. Athens' three Long Walls to the Peiraieus (Map 2.4.30, inset) are the most famous example.

4.4.8a This trophy had been set up by the Spartans after their earlier victory: see 4.2.23.

4.4.9a There were probably too few to anchor both flanks of their battle line on the two walls, and so a battle line formation would leave one flank dangerously unprotected.

4.4.9b Iphikrates: an Athenian general famous for his successful use of peltasts against hoplites. See Appendix M, §12.

4.4.10a Apparently, the Argives did not stretch out their line as the Spartans had done, with the result that their left struck the easy target of the Sicyonians, who were deployed to the left of the Spartans. Xenophon assumes that his readers will be able to work all this out, given the prior knowledge he imagines they will have of the bravery or otherwise of the various contingents, as soon as they are told that the Corinthians on the left routed the Sicyonians.

FIGURE 4.4.7A. AN ARTIST'S
CONCEPTION OF ATHENIAN
TRIREME SHIP SHEDS, BASED ON
FOUNDATION REMAINS FOUND
AT THE PEIRAIEUS IN THE LATE
NINETEENTH CENTURY.

FIGURE 4.4.7B. THE MODERN TRIREME *OLYMPIAS*, LAUNCHED IN 1987, RESTING AT DRY DOCK IN ITS
SHIP SHED.

the Argives. The Argives, seeing the sigma[b] on the shields, thought they were Sicyonians, and were in no way frightened. It is said that at this point Pasimachus uttered the remark, "By the twin gods, you Argives, these sigmas will deceive you,"[c] and came to close quarters with them. And fighting with his few troops against many, he was killed, as were others who fought with him.

[11] The Corinthian exiles, however, defeated those who were stationed opposite to them, slipped through, and advanced away from the harbor, moving forward to a position near the city wall. The Spartans, for their part, seeing that the troops opposing the Sicyonians had defeated them, went out to help them, keeping the stockade on their left side. But when the Argives perceived that the Spartans were moving behind them, they turned back on the double and ran from the stockade. Some of them, who had been stationed farthest out on the right wing, were struck by the Spartans on their unprotected side and killed, while those who were stationed nearest the wall crowded together and began to retreat toward the city in a large, disordered mass. But when these came upon the Corinthian exiles and recognized them as enemies, they turned back again. Some of them climbed up the steps to the top of the wall, from which they threw themselves down and were killed, while others, being pushed together around the steps, were struck and killed there. Still others were trodden under foot by one another and suffocated.[a] [12] The Spartans were not at a loss whom to kill, for the god had given them at that time at least an opportunity that they never could have prayed for: a petrified multitude of their enemy had been handed over to them, stupefied and offering their unprotected side, with not one of them intent on defending himself; indeed, they were all assisting in their own utter destruction. How could one believe this to be anything but a divine occurrence? At any rate, so many fell in such a short time that the inhabitants, who were used to seeing heaps of grain, wood, and stones, saw instead on that day heaps of corpses. Even the Boeotian guards at the harbor[a] were killed, some on the walls and others while climbing up on the roofs of the ship sheds.[b]

4.4.11
392
CORINTH
The Corinthian exiles defeat their opponents and advance toward Corinth. The Spartans come to the assistance of the Sicyonians, and the enemy, seeing the Spartans between them and the city, try to run past them, losing all cohesion.

4.4.12
392
CORINTH
Finding the exiles in front of them, the troops form a disorganized mob, and the Spartans slaughter many of them as they mill around, no longer defending themselves, seeking in vain for some way to escape.

4.4.10b   Sigma: the Greek letter "S" (Σ) for Sicyon. Spartan shields that displayed the Greek letter lambda (Λ), or "L," standing for Lacedaemon, would have received more respect.

4.4.10c   The twin gods are Kastor and Polydeukes. The remark is given in the Doric dialect that was used by the Spartans.

4.4.11a   The Corinthians from the city, on the Argive left wing, seem to have disappeared. One commentator suggests that Xenophon simply assumes that the reader will realize they were defeated by the Spartans, who held their side's right wing. But that cannot be right, as Xenophon expressly says that these Corinthians attacked and defeated the Sicyonians in the center, so it

appears that the Argive forces must have lined up across a less broad front than their opponents, leaving the Spartans unchallenged in their sector. The explanation for the "disappearance" of the Corinthians from the city may be that Xenophon wishes to convey that after the events of 4.4.6, there was no real distinction to be made between them and the Argives; or it may be that he wanted to avoid making clear that the enemies whom the Corinthian exiles gleefully proceeded to slaughter were fellow Corinthians; or perhaps both.

4.4.12a   The port (harbor) of Corinth was Lechaion.

4.4.12b   See Figures 4.4.7a and b for views of trireme ship sheds.

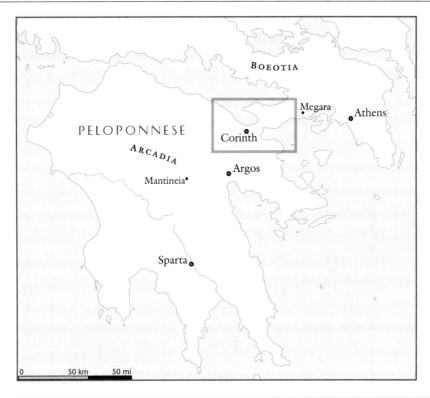

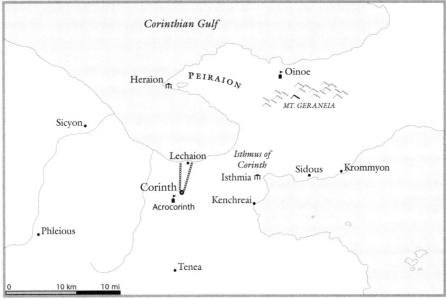

MAP 4.4.12

4.4.13
392
CORINTH
After the battle, the Corinthians and Argives under truce gather their dead. Praxitas tears down a section of the wall, marches north, and captures Sidous and Krommyon.

4.4.14
391
CORINTH
War continues without citizen armies.

4.4.15
391
PHLEIOUS
Iphikrates the Athenian inflicts such a defeat on the Phleiasians that the latter call in the Spartans to garrison their walls and citadel, despite their fear that they will bring back their pro-Spartan exiles. Later the Spartans turn the city back over to its citizens.

4.4.16–18
391
ARCADIA-CORINTH
Iphikrates invades and plunders Arcadia without hindrance from Arcadian hoplites. His troops fear the Spartan hoplites, who despise their allies because of a defeat they suffered. The Athenians rebuild the walls between Corinth and Lechaion.

[13] After the battle was over, the Corinthians and the Argives took away the bodies of the dead under truce. The allies of the Spartans now arrived, bringing reinforcements, and when all the troops were gathered together, Praxitas decided first to take down a section of the walls[a] large enough to provide a sufficiently wide opening for an army to pass through. Next, leading his army in the direction of Megara,[b] he attacked and captured both Sidous[c] and Krommyon[d] and placed garrisons within the walls of both these places. Then, turning back, he walled Epieikeia[e] so that it might be a protection for his allies[f] in front of a friendly territory, and he then disbanded the army and himself went back to Sparta.[g]

[14] After this battle, both sides ceased to mobilize large armies of citizens. Instead, they sent garrisons, some to Corinth,[a] others to Sicyon, and these kept watch over the walls of those cities. Each side did, however, employ mercenaries and energetically continued to prosecute the war with these.

[15] It was at this time that Iphikrates invaded the territory of Phleious[a] and set up an ambush. With a few men he set out to plunder the area, and when the Phleiasians from the city came to the rescue in an unguarded manner, he managed to kill so many of them that the Phleiasians, thoroughly frightened by this force from Corinth, sent for the Spartans and handed the citadel and the city over to them to guard.[b] And they did this even though previously they had been unwilling to admit the Spartans inside the walls, because they feared that the Spartans would bring back with them the Phleiasian exiles who claimed that they had been driven into exile on account of their pro-Spartan sympathies. The Spartans, however, for as much time as they had control of the city, did not once mention a restoration of exiles, even though the Spartans were favorably inclined toward them. Instead, when they thought the city had recovered its confidence, they withdrew from the place, handing back to the Phleiasians their city and its laws in the very same condition as when it had been turned over to them.

[16] Iphikrates and his men for their part continued to invade many places in Arcadia,[a] plundering the land and even making assaults on the walls. They continued to do this because the Arcadian hoplites completely refused to come out against them, so greatly did they fear Iphikrates' peltasts. But the peltasts in their turn were so frightened of the Spartans that they would not approach within a spear-cast of the hoplites, because once on a previous occasion the younger Spartans, even from that distance, had managed to capture and kill some of them. [17] Yet if the Spartans

4.4.13a   Praxitas was destroying sections of Corinth's Long Walls, which connected it with its port of Lechaion.
4.4.13b   Megara: Map 4.4.12.
4.4.13c   Sidous: Map 4.4.12, inset.
4.4.13d   Krommyon: Map 4.4.12, inset.
4.4.13e   Epieikeia: site unknown.
4.4.13f   The ally in this case is Sicyon: Map 4.4.12, inset.

4.4.13g   Sparta: Map 4.4.12.
4.4.14a   Corinth: Map 4.4.12 and inset.
4.4.15a   Phleious: Map 4.4.12, inset.
4.4.15b   Iphikrates' success at Phleious is also mentioned by Diodorus; see Appendix O, 14.91.3.
4.4.16a   Arcadia: Map 4.4.12.

looked down on the peltasts, they were even more contemptuous of their own allies. For once before, when the Mantineians[a] had gone to the Spartans' assistance, they came up against[b] some peltasts who had run out from the wall that stretches toward Lechaion;[c] but because of the javelins thrown by the peltasts, the Mantineian hoplite line gave way, and some of them were killed when they fled. As a result, the Spartans even dared to mock them, saying that their allies feared peltasts the way children fear the bogeyman.

The Spartans themselves marched a regiment out from Lechaion that, with the Corinthian exiles, made camp in a circle around the wall of Corinth.[d] [18] Now the Athenians in their turn were also intimidated by the strength of the Spartan force. They were quite concerned that the Spartans, having torn apart the Long Walls of the Corinthians, would then directly attack themselves, and so they thought it best to re-erect the walls that Praxitas had torn down. With this as their objective, they marched out with all their force and, with stonemasons and carpenters, rebuilt in just a few days (and very handsomely) the wall that extended toward Sicyon and the west. They then refurbished the eastern wall in a more leisurely manner.

[19] The Spartans now attacked Argos,[a] because they saw the Argives enjoying the fruits of their lands and taking pleasure in the war.[b] Agesilaos led the expedition, and after he ravaged all of their territory, he immediately marched to Corinth, going by way of Tenea;[c] when he arrived, he captured the walls that had been rebuilt by the Athenians. His brother Teleutias[d] supported him by sea, leading there a squadron of about twelve triremes. And so their mother could call herself fortunate, since on the same day one of her sons captured the walls of the enemy while the other, attacking by sea, seized the ships and the dockyards. Having accomplished these things, Agesilaos disbanded the army of the allies and led his citizen army back home to Sparta.

[1] After this, the Spartans heard from the Corinthian exiles that the men in the city had placed all their cattle safely in Peiraion[a] and that many were receiving their sustenance from these animals. And so, with Agesilaos in command again, they turned around on the spot and marched back toward Corinth.[b] The first place he came to was the Isthmus,[c] and since it

4.4.19
391
ARGOS
Agesilaos lays waste the territory of Argos and returns to Corinth, now assisted by a fleet commanded by his brother. Finally he returns home.

4.5.1–2
390
ISTHMUS
Learning that the Corinthians have taken their cattle to safety, Agesilaos and his Spartans march back and, coming to the Isthmus, complete the sacrifices and games that the Argives began but that his advance interrupted.

4.4.17a   Mantineia: Map 4.4.12.
4.4.17b   Reading Madvig's *ep' ekdramontas* for the manuscripts' *epekdramontas*. (John Marincola) For the Greek, see Translator's Notes.
4.4.17c   Lechaion, the port of Corinth: Map 4.4.12, inset.
4.4.17d   Corinth: Map 4.4.12, and inset.
4.4.19a   Argos: Map 4.4.12.
4.4.19b   Because they themselves were not involved and were not suffering losses of any kind.
4.4.19c   Tenea: Map 4.4.12, inset.
4.4.19d   See "Teleutias" in Appendix M, §23.
4.5.1a   Peiraion: Map 4.4.12, inset. From Strabo 8.6.22, we learn that Peiraion is the area

on the northwest side of the Isthmus of Corinth (Map 4.4.12, inset)—the narrowest part of the neck of land that linked the Peloponnese to northern Greece—terminating in the promontory where the sanctuary of Hera, the Heraion, stood.
4.5.1b   In his *Agesilaos* 2.18, Xenophon gives as additional motives for the expedition that (a) the Corinthians had sown the entire district and were enjoying its produce, and (b) Agesilaos thought that from there he could make it difficult for the Boeotians to join up with and support the Corinthians.
4.5.1c   The Isthmus of Corinth.

was in fact the month in which the Isthmian Games[d] are held, the Argives happened to be there, and they were conducting the sacrifice to Poseidon on the grounds that Argos and Corinth were now one city.[e] But when the Argives realized that Agesilaos was advancing against them, they returned to their city in great fear, taking the road that runs by Kenchreai[f] and leaving behind in their haste both the sacrificial victims and the meal that they had prepared. [2] Although Agesilaos saw them go, he did not pursue them but, rather, set up his camp in the sacred area and sacrificed to the god. He then delayed his departure until the Corinthian exiles had conducted the sacrifice and the contest in honor of Poseidon. After Agesilaos had left, however, the Argives returned and conducted the games all over again from the beginning, so that for some of the contests in that year, the same person was twice beaten, while in other contests the same person was twice proclaimed victor.

[3] Three days later Agesilaos led the army toward Peiraion, but seeing that it was guarded by a large force, he withdrew after breakfast toward Acrocorinth[a] and acted as if the city were being betrayed to him. The result was that the Corinthians, fearing that someone actually was betraying the city, summoned Iphikrates and the majority of the peltasts to their assistance. Agesilaos, however, perceiving that these peltasts had actually advanced past his own during the night, wheeled around and marched to Peiraion, arriving there at dawn. He himself marched on the road running by the hot springs,[b] while he ordered a regiment to march along the crest of the ridge. He camped this night by the springs, while the regiment spent the night in possession of the heights.

[4] And it was here that Agesilaos won great renown by a small but very timely bit of thoughtfulness. None of the men who were carrying provisions to the regiment had brought fire, and because the men were up so high, the night was cold. In the evening it rained and hailed, and the men, who were dressed for summer, were shivering in the dark and had no heart for their dinner. It was then that Agesilaos sent up to them at least ten men carrying fire in pots. Since the men went up by different pathways, the fires that were made were many and large ones, especially since there was a lot of wood available up there. Then all the men anointed themselves,[a] and many of them began their dinner all over again from the beginning. It was on this night too that the temple of Poseidon[b] was seen in flames, but no one knows who set it on fire.

4.5.1d Isthmian Games: this passage and Thucydides 8.10.1 are the main pieces of evidence for when the Isthmian Games fell in the year. Celebrated at the sanctuary to Poseidon at Isthmia (Map 4.4.12, inset), these games would have been held in late June or July 390. On Greek religious festivals, see Appendix J, §10.
4.5.1e For the Argive treatment of Corinth, see 4.4.6.
4.5.1f Kenchreai: Map 4.4.12, inset.
4.5.3a Acrocorinth: Map 4.4.12, inset.
4.5.3b These springs were located by the shore, near the modern town of Loutraki, at the

foot of a southwest spur of Mount Geraneia: Map 4.4.12, inset.
4.5.4a They anointed themselves with oil, which acts as an insulator and helps to keep the body warm.
4.5.4b Xenophon here means one of two temples: either the great temple of Poseidon at Isthmia, the shrine on the Isthmus of Corinth, near which the Isthmian Games were held, or possibly a small temple in Peiraion, not far from the promontory where the Heraion (Map 4.4.12, inset) stood.

[5] When those in Peiraion realized that the heights were being held by the Spartans, they no longer thought to defend themselves but instead all fled to the temple of Hera[a]—men and women, slaves and free, and even the majority of the cattle. Agesilaos with his army advanced by way of the sea, and at the same time the regiment on the the heights descended and seized Oinoe (which was a walled fort).[b] And here they took whatever they found inside, so that on that day all the soldiers had plenty of provisions from the villages. Those who had taken refuge in the temple of Hera came out, intending to allow Agesilaos to do whatever he wished with them. He decided that those who had taken part in the slaughter[c] should be handed over to the Corinthian exiles, while everything else should be sold. [6] At that point very many prisoners came out from the temple.

Many embassies were also present there, especially that of the Boeotians,[a] who had come to ask what they must do to obtain peace. But Agesilaos, in a very disdainful manner, pretended not to see them, even though Pharax, the man who looked after Theban interests at Sparta,[b] was standing next to them so that he could present them to Agesilaos. Agesilaos merely sat on the circular structure near the lake[c] and watched the abundance of goods that were being brought out. Some Spartans from the camp, holding their spears, were following as guards, and they were being closely watched by those present, for those who are fortunate and victorious always seem for some reason to be worth looking at.

[7] While Agesilaos was sitting there, looking like a man who delighted in what was going on, a horseman, his horse sweating profusely, was speeding toward him. Many people kept asking the horseman what he had come to announce, but he would not answer any of them; finally, as he neared Agesilaos, he leapt down from his horse and ran toward him. With an exceedingly downcast look, he told Agesilaos of the disaster that had befallen the regiment at Lechaion.[a] Upon hearing this, Agesilaos immediately jumped up from his seat, grabbed his spear, and ordered the herald to call together the polemarchs, the captains of fifty, and the commanders of foreign troops. [8] When these men had hastened to him, he told them to eat whatever they could (since they had not yet taken their morning meal) and then muster their men as swiftly as possible, while he himself, taking no meal, led out his headquarters staff.[a] The spear-bearers, with their weapons

4.5.5–6
390
PEIRAION
As the Spartans advance, the enemy retires into the temple of Hera and surrenders. Much booty is taken. Agesilaos ignores the presence of the Boeotian embassy.

4.5.7–8
390
PEIRAION
Agesilaos is informed of a disastrous defeat of the troops at Lechaion. He immediately marches to the scene but, learning that all the dead have been recovered, returns to the temple of Hera. Everything they captured there is sold.

4.5.5a   The temple of Hera, the Heraion, is located on the point of the Peiraion Peninsula.
4.5.5b   Oinoe (in Peiraion): Map 4.4.12, inset.
4.5.5c   The massacre referred to here is the slaughter of the peace-seekers by the anti-Spartan faction during the religious ceremony in 392. See 4.4.2–4.
4.5.6a   Boeotia: Map 4.6.1, AY.
4.5.6b   He was the Theban *proxenos* at Sparta. A *proxenos*, although a citizen and resident of his own state, served as a "friend or representative" (much like a modern honorary consul) of a foreign state.

4.5.6c   See Figure 4.5.6a for a view of what may be the ruins of this structure, as John Buckler, who took this picture, asserts that it is the only circular structure in the area.
4.5.7a   Lechaion: Map 4.6.1, inset. Xenophon describes this event at 4.5.11.
4.5.8a   Headquarters staff: Xenophon says in *Constitution of the Lacedaemonians* 13.1 that in addition to the polemarchs, three other Spartiates who were responsible for provisioning for the army dined in the King's tent on campaign. These are probably the people referred to here. See Appendix E, §13, and Appendix F, §5.

FIGURE 4.5.6A. REMAINS OF THE TEMPLE OF HERA (HERAION) IN PEIRAION. THE CIRCULAR STRUCTURE IN THE UPPER CENTER MAY BE THE ONE XENOPHON MENTIONS, WHERE AGESILAOS WAS RUDE TO THE AMBASSADORS.

4.5.9–10
390
CORINTH
Agesilaos marches to Corinth and cuts down all the trees he comes across, proving that the enemy, despite its earlier success, still refuses to face the Spartan army in battle.

in hand, came in haste, Agesilaos leading and they following. When they had passed by the hot springs and entered into the plain of Lechaion, three horsemen came toward him and announced that the bodies of the dead in the battle had been recovered. When Agesilaos heard this, he gave the order to ground arms and he halted for a while. Then he led the army back toward the temple of Hera. On the next day everything they had captured was sold.

[9] The Boeotian ambassadors were now summoned and asked why they had come. This time, however, they made no mention of peace but said instead that, unless Agesilaos prevented them, they wished to be allowed to enter the city to join their own soldiers. He smiled and said, "Ah, but I am well aware that you do not wish to see your soldiers but, rather, to behold how great was the success that your friends have achieved. So wait here for a while, and I myself will take you there: for in my presence you will learn even better how great it has proved to be." [10] Agesilaos was true to his word, and on the next day, after offering sacrifice, he led his army toward the city. When he arrived there, he did not throw down the Corinthian trophy,[a] but

4.5.10a   The trophy that the Corinthians set up
          after their victory. See Appendix L, §13.
          For a depiction of a trophy, see Figure
          4.2.23a.

FIGURE 4.5.6B. THE PEIRAION PENINSULA, IN THE DISTANCE BEYOND THE COLUMNS OF THE TEMPLE OF APOLLO, AS SEEN FROM THE CITY OF CORINTH.

instead, by cutting down and burning whatever tree he came across, he showed that no Corinthian dared to come out of the city to oppose him. After this, he set up his camp at Lechaion and refused to allow the ambassadors to go into the city, sending them off instead by sea to Kreusis.[b]

Now inasmuch as such a defeat was most unusual for the Spartans, there was much grieving throughout the army—except for those whose sons, fathers, or brothers had died in that battle: *these* men went around with beaming faces, delighting in their personal misfortune, as if they had been victors.

[11] The regiment's disaster at Lechaion came about in the following way. It is the custom of the Amyklaians,[a] no matter where they find themselves, whether on campaign or away from their city for any other reason, always to leave for home at the time of the festival of the Hyakinthia, so that they may participate in the festival and sing the *paean* to Apollo.[b] At the time of which we are speaking, Agesilaos had left all the Amyklaians in the army back in Lechaion. The polemarch who was in command of the garrison there directed the garrison troops of the allies to guard the wall,

4.5.11–12
390
LECHAION
The Spartan regiment from Lechaion accompanies the Amyklaians past the city of Corinth. After leaving them, they return, marching by Corinth.

4.5.10b Kreusis: Map 4.6.1, AY; a Boeotian port on the Corinthian Gulf, and the nearest seaport to Thebes.
4.5.11a Amyklai: Map 4.6.1, BX.
4.5.11b The festival of the Hyakinthia took place

in early summer and lasted three days. It was celebrated in the village of Amyklai and was held in honor of Apollo and the youth Hyakinthos, whom he had loved.

151

while he himself, with the regiment of hoplites and that of cavalry, accompanied the Amyklaians as they marched past the city of Corinth[c] on their way home. [12] When he was about twenty or thirty stades[a] distant from Sicyon,[c] the polemarch returned to Lechaion with the hoplites (who numbered about six hundred) and ordered the cavalry commander to follow him once he had escorted the Amyklaians as far as they wished. Now everyone well knew that there were many enemy peltasts and hoplites in Corinth, but because of their previous successes against these men, they disregarded the possibility that they might be attacked. [13] But the hoplite commander Kallias son of Hipponikos and Iphikrates, the leader of the cavalry, looking down from the walls of the city of Corinth, could see that the Spartans were not numerous and were unaccompanied by peltasts or cavalry, and so the commanders determined that it would be safe to attack them with the peltasts, for if the Spartans should march by the road, they knew that the peltasts would be able to hit them on their unprotected side[a] and thus destroy them; and even if the Spartan hoplites should try to pursue the peltasts, it would be an easy matter for exceedingly light-armed peltasts to flee from hoplites. Having calculated all this, the commanders led the men out from the city.

[14] Kallias stationed the hoplites not far from the city while Iphikrates led the peltasts in an attack against the regiment. As the Spartans were under attack, some of them were wounded while others fell. The shield-bearers[a] were ordered to take up these men and carry them to Lechaion. These men alone of the regiment can be truly said to have been saved.[b] The polemarch then ordered the first ten-year class[c] to chase away the assailants, [15] but when these men pursued, they could capture no one, since they were hoplites pursuing peltasts and could not come within a spear's throw of them. (Iphikrates had ordered the peltasts to retreat before the hoplites could come to close quarters with them.) When the Spartan hoplites retired from the pursuit, however, they were scattered about, since each man had individually pursued his target as swiftly as he could, and at this point Iphikrates' men would wheel around and again throw their javelins at the hoplites from in front of them, while other peltasts would run alongside the hoplites and throw javelins at their unprotected side. At the first attack the slingers quickly laid low nine or ten Spartans, and because of this they attacked much more boldly thereafter.

4.5.11c   Corinth: Map 4.6.1, AY, and inset.
4.5.12a   If Xenophon meant 20 or 30 Attic stades of 583 feet, the distance would be 2 to 3 miles.
4.5.12b   Sicyon: Map 4.6.1, AY, and inset.
4.5.13a   The hoplite's unprotected side was his right side, as the shield was carried on the left arm.
4.5.14a   These Spartan shield-bearers were helots, who carried the hoplites' shields when not in battle. For more on helots, see Appendix E, §11–12, and Appendix F, §6.

4.5.14b   What Xenophon means is that only those who were actually following orders could be said to have survived honorably; the others did so by fleeing, and so incurred great disgrace.
4.5.14c   Ten-year class: these were all the younger men whose time in military service was ten years or less. Assuming that they entered military service at the age of twenty, these would be the youngest cadre in the force, aged twenty through twenty-nine. Spartiates served in the army till they reached the age of sixty.

[16] While the effects of this attack were being gravely felt by the hoplites, the Spartan polemarch ordered the fifteen-year class[a] to charge and pursue the slingers. But when these hoplites retreated after the pursuit, even more of them were killed. And now when the best men had already perished, the cavalry[b] joined them, and with the cavalry's support the Spartans again attempted to pursue the peltasts. Yet when the peltasts gave way, the cavalry bungled the attack: for they did not pursue the enemy until they had killed some of them but, rather, kept an even pace with the hoplites in both their attack and their retreat. Since this action continued in the same way, the result continued to be the same, and the Spartans were diminishing in both number and resolution while their enemy became bolder and their attackers more numerous. [17] Finally, not knowing what to do, the Spartans gathered together on a small hill about two stades[a] distant from the sea and about sixteen or seventeen stades[b] from Lechaion. When the Spartans in Lechaion realized what was happening, they got into boats and sailed alongside the shore until they were opposite the hill. The men on the hill were now at a loss as to what to do: they were suffering dreadfully and enduring wretched deaths while unable to harm the enemy in any way, and in addition they now saw the Athenian hoplites coming at them. At this point they gave way and fled, some throwing themselves into the sea, while a few made it safely to Lechaion with the cavalry. The total dead from all the skirmishes and the flight was around 250. [18] That, then, is the story of how the disaster at Lechaion occurred.

After this, Agesilaos took the defeated regiment with him and departed, leaving a different one behind in Lechaion. On his journey home, he led his men into each city as late as he possibly could and departed the next morning as early as possible. He set out from Orchomenos[a] before dawn[b] and passed by Mantineia[c] while it was still dark,[d] for he thought the Spar-

4.5.16–18
390
LECHAION
The Spartan regiment attempts to counterattack, but its cavalry is handled badly, and the attack fails. Then, under pressure, it withdraws to a hill, where the soldiers are struck by missiles and suffer losses. Finally they break all formation and flee. Losses are heavy.

4.5.16a Fifteen-year class: men inducted into the army fifteen years earlier, now experienced soldiers. Assuming that they began their military service at twenty, this was the cadre of men between the ages of twenty and thirty-four. It is not clear whether, by calling out the fifteen-year class, the polemarch meant all the men who had served fifteen years or less (which in these circumstances would make the most sense) or whether, having already called out the ten-year class, he meant only those with eleven to fifteen years of service.

4.5.16b This is the cavalry that had originally escorted them.

4.5.17a Two Attic stades of 583 feet each would convert to 388 yards.

4.5.17b Xenophon's 16 or 17 stades, if they were Attic stades of 583 feet, would convert to 1.7 or 1.9 miles.

4.5.18a Orchomenos (in Arcadia): Map 4.6.1, AX.

4.5.18b Reading Büchsenschütz's *pro orthrou* for the manuscripts' *orthrou*. (John Marincola) For the Greek, see Translator's Notes.

4.5.18c Mantineia: Map 4.6.1, BX. Along with the other Arcadians, Mantineia had probably

been a Spartan ally since the sixth century. The Mantineians were the only Arcadians not to appear in arms against Sparta at the battle of Dipaia, sometime in the 470s or 460s (Herodotus, *Histories* 9.35.2). But Mantineia had deserted and fought against Sparta in the confused period 420–418, and although the Mantineians fought on the side of the Spartans in the Corinthian War (4.4.17), they remained disaffected, as is shown by this passage and even more by the Spartans' subsequent charges at 5.2.2. Thucydides (5.29) attributes their behavior in 420–418 to fear (justified in the event) that Sparta would try to undo the local hegemony they had established in the 420s over neighboring Arcadian states; he also mentions that Mantineia was by this time a democracy, which was unusual among Sparta's Peloponnesian allies. It seems to have remained a democracy down to Sparta's intervention in 385/4. For more on the relationship between Sparta and Mantineia, see the Introduction, §12.7.

4.5.18d The distance between the two cities is about 8 miles.

tans would be mortified if they saw the Mantineians rejoicing at their misfortune.

4.5.19
390
CORINTH
Iphikrates captures Sidous, Krommyon, and Peiraion, but the Spartans hold on to Lechaion.

[19] As for Iphikrates, he had great success in his battles after this action. For example, the Spartan Praxitas had established garrisons in Sidous[a] and Krommyon[b] when he captured these fortifications, and Agesilaos had done the same in Oinoe[c] when he captured Peiraion:[d] Iphikrates now captured all these places. The Spartans and their allies held on to Lechaion,[e] however, but the Corinthian exiles no longer went forth by foot from Sicyon[f] because of the disaster that had happened to the Spartan regiment. Instead, they sailed along the coast to Lechaion and, making this their base, harassed the men in the city and were themselves in turn harassed.

4.6.1–2
389
CALYDON
Calydon, now part of Achaea, is attacked by the Acarnanians and their allies. The Achaeans send ambassadors to Sparta to ask for help.

[1] After this, the Achaeans[a] who held Calydon[b] (which was long ago a part of Aetolia[c]) and had made the Calydonians citizens of Achaea were compelled to place a garrison in the city, because the Acarnanians,[d] assisted by their allies, the Athenians[e] and Boeotians,[f] had attacked it. And so the Achaeans, being pressed by these forces, sent ambassadors to Sparta.[g] When they arrived, the ambassadors said that they were not receiving equitable treatment from the Spartans. [2] "For we," they said, "join you, men of Sparta, on campaigns however you direct us and we follow you wherever you lead us. But you, on the other hand, seem not to care at all that we are being besieged by the Acarnanians and their allies, the Athenians and Boeotians. And it is hardly possible that we can hold out should things remain as they are. We must either abandon the war here in the Peloponnese and cross over[a] with all our forces to wage war on the Acarnanians and their allies, or we Achaeans will have to make peace with them on whatever terms that we can."

4.6.3–4
389
ACARNANIA
The Spartans decide to assist the Achaeans and send an army under Agesilaos to attack the Acarnanians and their Athenian and Boeotian allies.

[3] They said these things as a way of threatening to defect from their alliance with the Spartans if the latter failed to bring them assistance. After they had spoken in this manner, the ephors and the assembly resolved that it was necessary to wage war with the Achaeans against the Acarnanians. Accordingly, they sent out Agesilaos in command of two regiments and a corresponding portion of the allies, and the Achaeans, for their part, joined them with their entire army. [4] When Agesilaos crossed over,[a] all the Acarnanians who lived in the countryside fled to the city, while all the cattle were driven off far away so that they would not be captured by the enemy. When Agesilaos arrived at the borders of the enemy's territory, he sent a message to the Acarnanian League[b] at Stratos,[c] informing them that unless

4.5.19a   Sidous: Map 4.6.1, inset.
4.5.19b   Krommyon: Map 4.6.1, inset.
4.5.19c   Oinoe (in Peiraion): Map 4.6.1, inset.
4.5.19d   Peiraion: Map 4.6.1, inset.
4.5.19e   Lechaion: Map 4.6.1, inset.
4.5.19f   Sicyon: Map 4.6.1, AY, and inset.
4.6.1a   Achaea: Map 4.6.1, AX.
4.6.1b   Calydon: Map 4.6.1, AX.
4.6.1c   Aetolia: Map 4.6.1, AX.
4.6.1d   Acarnania: Map 4.6.1, AX.
4.6.1e   Athens: Map 4.6.1, AY.
4.6.1f   Boeotia: Map 4.6.1, AY.
4.6.1g   Sparta: Map 4.6.1, BX.

4.6.2a   Cross over the north side of the Corinthian Gulf (Map 4.6.1, AX) from their positions in front of Corinth.
4.6.4a   Crossed over the Corinthian Gulf.
4.6.4b   Acarnanian League: on these federations or leagues, many of which formed in the fourth century, see Appendix H, Political Leagues (Other Than Sparta's) in Xenophon's *Hellenika*, §2.
4.6.4c   Stratos: Map 4.6.1, AX. Stratos was the largest city in Acarnania. See Figure 4.6.4.

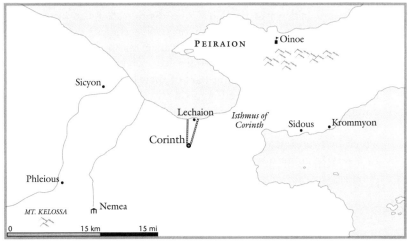

Map 4.6.1

FIGURE 4.6.4. THE VIEW FROM THE ACROPOLIS OF STRATOS, SHOWING THE TEMPLE REMAINS AND THE VALLEY BELOW.

4.6.5–7
389
ACARNANIA
Agesilaos lays waste the
Acarnanian territories
and captures much cattle,
horses, other livestock,
and slaves, which he sells.

they withdrew from their alliance with the Boeotians and Athenians and chose instead to ally with the Spartans and the Achaeans,[d] he would ravage their entire territory, one district after another, and he would spare nothing. [5] When they failed to be persuaded by his words, he made good on his threats and laid waste the land, one district after the next. He advanced each day a little more than ten or twelve stades,[a] and the Acarnanians, seeing the slowness of the army's advance, thought they could safely bring their cattle down from the mountains (which they did), and they even continued to work the greater part of their land. [6] This seemed to Agesilaos to be quite bold indeed, and on the fifteenth or sixteenth day after he entered the country, he sacrificed early in the morning and set off, marching a distance of 160 stades[a] before evening and arriving at a lake around which he found nearly all the cattle of the Acarnanians. These he captured to a very large number, and took as well troops of horses, all kinds of live-

4.6.4d   Reading *Achaious*, which was added by
          Simon. (John Marincola) For the Greek,
          see Translator's Notes.
4.6.5a   Ten or twelve Attic stades of 583

feet would convert to 2,000 or 2,300
yards.
4.6.6a   One hundred sixty Attic stades would
          convert to almost 18 miles.

156

stock, and many slaves. After he had seized all this, he remained on the spot, and the next day he conducted a sale of the booty. [7] At this point many Acarnanian peltasts arrived; since Agesilaos had made his camp by the side of a mountain, these peltasts were able, from the heights, and without any loss to their own men, to shower the Spartans with stones and to use their slings to such good effect that they forced the Spartans, even though they were in the middle of preparing dinner, to withdraw down into the plain. The Acarnanians departed during the night, while the Spartans, setting a guard, lay down and took their rest.

[8] On the next day Agesilaos led his army back. Now the road that went out from the meadow and plain around the lake was narrow because it ran between mountains. The Acarnanians, in possession of the heights of the mountains, threw javelins and stones down at the soldiers as they marched by, and then, by sneaking down to the skirts of the mountains, pressed the Spartans hard and caused them such great difficulties that the army could finally no longer move forward. [9] Although the hoplites and the cavalry moved out from the phalanx and chased these men, they were unable to do the slightest bit of damage to their attackers, for the Acarnanians would move off swiftly and find safe places. Agesilaos, realizing that it would be difficult to advance the army through the narrow path while it was suffering in this way, decided instead to pursue those who were attacking from the left because, even though they were indeed numerous, the mountain on that side was more accessible to hoplites and cavalry. [10] While he was making the sacrifice, the Acarnanians pressed his forces quite strongly with their stones and javelins and, coming up close to them, succeeded in wounding many of them. But when Agesilaos gave the order, the first fifteen-year class[a] ran out and the cavalry charged, and Agesilaos followed with the rest. [11] Those of the Acarnanians who had descended from the mountaintop and were discharging their weapons quickly retreated and in their flight up the mountain were killed. On the top of the mountain, however, the Acarnanian hoplites and the majority of the peltasts were stationed, and they held their ground there, and by discharging their missiles and hurling their spears, they wounded some of the Spartan cavalrymen and killed some of the horses. Yet just before the Spartans came to close quarters with them, these men gave way, and on that day around three hundred of them were killed. [12] After the fighting ended in this manner, Agesilaos set up a trophy[a] and thereafter laid waste the countryside, slashing and burning. At the insistence of the Achaeans, he also made assaults against some of the Acarnanian cities, but he failed to take a single one of them.

4.6.8–10
389
ACARNANIA
As Agesilaos advances through a pass beyond the lake, his forces are attacked in the mountains and sorely pressed.

4.6.11–12
389
ACARNANIA
By a stout counterattack Agesilaos skillfully routs the enemy. Thereafter, he lays waste the land and unsuccessfully assaults some Acarnanian cities. In the autumn he departs.

4.6.10a   See n. 4.5.16a on the "fifteen-year class."
4.6.12a   After a battle in ancient Greece, the victors would raise a trophy, usually a set of armor stripped from enemy dead and raised on a pole as an offering to the gods who had given them the victory. See Appendix L, §13.

Autumn was now coming on, and Agesilaos was making plans to depart from the country. [13] The Achaeans, however, believing that he had accomplished nothing because he had not been able to capture a single city, either by consent or by force, asked him, even if he did nothing else, to at least remain in the area long enough to prevent the Acarnanians from sowing the seed for next year's crop. He answered that what they proposed was precisely the opposite of what would be to their benefit: "For I will lead an expedition back here next summer, and the more these people sow, the more they will desire peace." [14] Having said this, he departed overland through Aetolia,[a] taking such roads as neither many nor few could travel against the will of the Aetolians, but they allowed him to pass through their country, for they were hoping that he would help them take back the port city of Naupactus.[b] When he came to Rhion,[c] however, he crossed over the gulf and went home. He crossed in this spot because the Athenian triremes based at Oiniadai[d] prevented him from sailing across via Calydon[e] to the Peloponnese.[f]

[1] As the winter ended and spring began, Agesilaos fulfilled his promise to the Achaeans[a] and mobilized the army against the Acarnanians.[b] The Acarnanians, however, learned of his plan to invade their land and realized that, because their cities were sited inland, they would be as much besieged by the destruction of their grain as they would be from having an army camped round their city. So they sent ambassadors to Sparta,[c] who made an alliance with the Achaeans and peace with the Spartans. This is how matters turned out with Acarnania.

[2] After this the Spartans decided that it would not be safe to lead a campaign against the Athenians[a] or Boeotians[b] so long as they had Argos[c] in their rear, for Argos bordered their own territory, and it was a large city and hostile toward Sparta. So they decided to mobilize their army against Argos. Agesipolis[d] was given the command, and when he learned of his appointment and that the sacrifices at the frontier[e] had proved favorable, he went to Olympia and there consulted the god,[f] asking whether his refusal to accept the Argives' claim of a holy truce would be impious, for the Argives had declared the sacred months not at the usual time but at the moment that the Spartans were about to invade. The god indicated to Agesipolis that it would

4.6.14a	Aetolia: Map 4.6.1, AX.	4.7.2a	Athens: Map 4.6.1, AY.
4.6.14b	Naupactus: Map 4.6.1, AX. A port city on the north coast of the Corinthian Gulf.	4.7.2b	Boeotia: Map 4.6.1, AY.
		4.7.2c	Argos: Map 4.6.1, BY.
4.6.14c	Cape Rhion (also called Rhion): Map 4.6.1, AX. A strategic site on the south shore of the Corinthian Gulf, just opposite Cape Antirhion at the narrowest point (2,000 yards) between the Peloponnese and the northern shore.	4.7.2d	Agesipolis, king of Sparta, was still a boy in 394 (4.2.9) but is no longer too young, six years later, to be given this command.
		4.7.2e	These sacrifices were traditional augury requirements for all Spartan commanders before crossing the Spartan frontier. If they proved unfavorable, the frontier could not be crossed.
4.6.14d	Oiniadai: Map 4.6.1, AX.		
4.6.14e	Calydon: Map 4.6.1, AX.		
4.6.14f	Peloponnese: Map 4.6.1, AX.		
4.7.1a	Achaea: Map 4.6.1, AX.	4.7.2f	Olympia: Map 4.6.1, BX. The main god worshiped at Olympia was Zeus, whose oracle was located there.
4.7.1b	Acarnania: Map 4.6.1, AX.		
4.7.1c	Sparta: Map 4.6.1, BX.		

be considered in accord with piety to reject a proclamation of a holy truce when it had been unjustly declared. From there Agesipolis went to Delphi[g] and in turn asked Apollo if he felt the same way about the truce as did his father,[h] and Apollo replied that his opinion was very much the same.

[3] Having done these things, then, Agesipolis joined the army at Phleious,[a] where it had been mustering for him until he returned from consulting the oracles, and from there he marched on Argos by way of Nemea.[b] The Argives, when they realized that they would not be able to halt the advance, sent two heralds (as is usual for them), who wore garlands and claimed that a holy truce was in force. But Agesipolis answered that it did not seem to the gods that the Argives were justly proclaiming this truce, and so he refused to honor it; instead, he invaded Argive territory and, by so doing, caused much perplexity and shock in the city and the countryside.

[4] On the very first evening that they were in Argive territory, while the men were taking their dinner and had just poured the libations, the god sent an earthquake. All the Spartans, beginning with the royal tent, then sang the *paean* to Poseidon.[a] The soldiers thought that the army would be brought back from Argos, since once before, when an earthquake had occurred, Agis had led his army back from Elis.[b] But Agesipolis said that if the god had sent the earthquake when their army was on the point of invading, he would have thought they were being warned to go back; but by sending the quake when they had already invaded, he thought the god was ordering them to continue on. [5] And so on the next day he offered sacrifice to Poseidon and advanced the army farther[a] into Argive territory. Now Agesilaos had recently invaded Argos,[b] and Agesipolis found out from the soldiers how far Agesilaos had led them toward the wall of the city and how much of the Argive territory they had ravaged. So, like an athlete in the pentathlon, he strove to outdo Agesilaos in every way. [6] Once he crossed the ditches in front of the wall, and only when pressed by the men on the towers who were hurling missiles down, he led his men back across the ditches. There was also an occasion on which, when most of the Argives had gone to "the Laconian,"[a] Agesipolis came so near the gates that the Argives in charge of them, greatly fearing that the Spartans would fall upon

4.7.3
388
ARGOS
As Agesipolis advances on Argos, the Argives send heralds proclaiming the holy truce, but he refuses to honor it and lays waste their territory.

4.7.4–6
388
ARGOS
Agesipolis is not deterred from Argos by an earthquake but advances farther into Argive territory and spoils more of it than Agesilaos had done earlier.

4.7.2g Delphi: Map 4.6.1, AY.
4.7.2h Zeus was believed to be the father of Apollo.
4.7.3a Phleious: Map 4.6.1, inset.
4.7.3b Nemea: Map 4.6.1, inset.
4.7.4a Poseidon, the god of the sea, was also known as the "earth shaker," the god of earthquakes.
4.7.4b Elis: Map 4.6.1, AX. For King Agis' return from Elis, see 3.2.24.
4.7.5a Reading Tillmanns's *au porro* in place of the manuscripts' *ou porro* ("not far"). (John Marincola) For the Greek, see Translator's Notes.
4.7.5b For Agesilaos' invasion of Argos, see 4.4.19.

4.7.6a Laconia: Map 4.6.1, BY. It is not clear to what place Xenophon is referring when he says "the Laconian." Since the city is under siege, it is inconceivable that the Argives could have left and gone to Laconia (that is, Sparta), and it is therefore supposed that this refers to someplace in or adjacent to the city of Argos. It is also possible that the Greek text is corrupt. (John Marincola)

them at the gates, shut out Boeotian horsemen who wished to enter the city. And so the Boeotian horsemen were compelled, like bats, to cling closely by the walls beneath the battlements. And if the Cretans[b] had not happened to be away ravaging Nauplia[c] at the time, many men and horses would have been shot down by their arrows.[d] [7] After this, while Agesipolis was camped around the enclosed space,[a] a thunderbolt fell upon the camp. Some men died from having been struck by the thunderbolt, and others from the shock itself. After this Agesipolis wanted to construct a fort at the entrances to Argive territory around Mount Kelossa,[b] and so he offered sacrifice, but the livers of the victims were found to be lacking a lobe.[c] When this happened, he led the army away and disbanded it, having done a great deal of damage to the Argives because he had attacked them unexpectedly.

[1] That was the way the war on land was fought. Now I shall relate the events that happened at sea and to the cities on the coast; these actions occurred while all the things just narrated were taking place on land. I shall record those deeds that were most worthy of remembrance while omitting those not worthy of account.

First, then, when Pharnabazos and Konon had conquered the Spartans in the sea battle,[a] they sailed both to the islands and to the coastal cities, expelling the harmosts[b] installed by the Spartans and promising the cities that they would not fortify the citadels within their walls but would leave the cities to be autonomous. [2] The inhabitants of the cities were delighted to hear this; they heartily approved of this action and sent gifts of friendship to Pharnabazos. It was Konon who instructed Pharnabazos that by acting in this way he would make the cities his allies, whereas if he were viewed as wanting to enslave them, each city would be quite capable of making a good deal of trouble for him; and there was the additional danger that the Greeks, when they perceived what he was doing, would unite together against him. [3] Pharnabazos was persuaded to follow this advice, and he then disembarked at Ephesus,[a] where, entrusting the command of forty triremes to Konon, he told the Athenian to meet him at Sestos[b] while he himself went off by land to his own satrapy.[c] He did this because Derkylidas, who from long ago had been his enemy,[d] happened to be in

4.7.7
388
ARGOS
When lightning strikes Agesipolis' camp, killing some men, and sacrificial animals' livers are found to lack a lobe, he disbands the army.

4.8.1–3
394
AEGEAN COASTAL CITIES
After defeating the Spartan fleet at Cnidus, Konon persuades Pharnabazos to allow the coastal cities to be autonomous, which pleases them greatly. Then Pharnabazos sends Konon by sea to Sestos while he goes on foot to his satrapy to capture Abydos from Derkylidas, an old enemy.

4.7.6b Crete: Map 4.1.31, locator.
4.7.6c Nauplia: Map 4.6.1, BY.
4.7.6d Cretan archers were Spartan allies and had fought with them at Corinth: see 4.2.16.
4.7.7a This "enclosed space" is unknown. Pausanias, the second-century C.E. travel writer, says that the thunderbolt fell on Agesipolis when he was camped beneath the Argive wall (Pausanias 3.5.9).
4.7.7b Mount Kelossa: Map 4.6.1, inset.
4.7.7c To find that the liver of a sacrificial animal lacked a lobe was the most disturbing and ill-omened of signs. See Appendix J, §2, and Figure 3.4.15.
4.8.1a This reference is to the battle of Cnidus

(Map 4.8.27), which took place in 394. Agesilaos was informed of this battle at 4.3.10–12.
4.8.1b Harmosts (governors) were officers installed in conquered cities by Sparta to rule over them; see 3.5.12–13, and also 2.2.2, 2.4.28, 3.1.4, 3.1.9, 3.2.20, 3.2.29, 4.2.5.
4.8.3a Ephesus: Map 4.8.7, BY.
4.8.3b Sestos: Map 4.8.7, AY.
4.8.3c Pharnabazos' own satrapy was Hellespontine Phrygia, and his capital was at Daskyleion: Map 4.1.31.
4.8.3d For the origins of the enmity between Derkylidas and Pharnabazos, see 3.1.9.

Abydos[c] when the naval battle was fought, but unlike the other harmosts, Derkylidas did not withdraw from his city and instead kept control of Abydos and preserved it as an ally of the Spartans. For he had called together the citizens of Abydos and had spoken to them as follows:

[4] "Men of Abydos, now it is possible for you, who were even before this friendly to our city,[a] to make clear that you are benefactors of the Spartans. For there is nothing amazing in demonstrating trustworthiness in good times; but when people show themselves to be firm in their support when their friends are in misfortune, such conduct is remembered for all time. It is not the case that we are no longer of any account because we have been defeated in battle. On the contrary, even in the past, when the Athenians had command of the sea,[b] our city was always capable of helping its friends and harming its enemies. And the more that the rest of the cities and fortune turn away from us, the more one will be able to see how remarkable your loyalty actually is. And if someone among you is afraid that we will be besieged here by land and sea, let him know that there is not yet a Greek fleet at sea, and if the barbarians should attempt to rule the sea, Greece will not allow it; and so by helping herself, Greece will also be your ally."

[5] When they had heard this, the people of Abydos obeyed him, not grudgingly but enthusiastically. They received in a friendly manner the harmosts who had come to Abydos[a] and sent for those who were not there. When many experienced men were gathered together in the city, Derkylidas crossed over into Sestos (which is opposite Abydos and not more than eight stades[b] distant) and brought together all those who held land in the Chersonese[c] through the agency of the Spartans,[d] and he also received all the harmosts of the European cities who had fled into exile. He told these men that they should not lose heart, knowing that even in Asia, which from the beginning had been the King's territory, there were still Aegae[e] and the small city of Temnos[f] and other places where they could live and not be subject to the King. "Moreover," he said, "what place could you find that is stronger than Sestos, what city would be more difficult to take by siege? For those who would besiege it would need to employ both a navy and an army." By talking to them in this and similar ways, he prevented them from being overly frightened.

4.8.4
394
ABYDOS
Derkylidas speaks to the men of Abydos, exhorting them to remain loyal to Sparta despite the recent defeat of her fleet.

4.8.5
394
ABYDOS
The people of Abydos enthusiastically join Derkylidas, who crosses to Sestos and gathers all Spartan harmosts and sympathizers in the Chersonese, encouraging them to resist the Persians.

4.8.3c   Abydos: Map 4.8.7, AY.
4.8.4a   "Our city" here refers to Sparta: Map
          4.8.7, BX.
4.8.4b   The reference is to Athens' naval empire
          that began shortly after the Persian Wars
          (480) and extended throughout most of
          the fifth century until destroyed by the
          Spartans in 405.
4.8.5a   These were the harmosts who had been
          driven out of their individual cities by
          Konon and Pharnabazos.
4.8.5b   Eight Attic stades of 583 feet would
          convert to about 0.9 mile.
4.8.5c   Chersonese: Map 4.8.7, AY.
4.8.5d   "Through the agency of the Spartans," a

reference to Derkylidas' walling off the isthmus of the Chersonese against the Thracians: see 3.2.10.
4.8.5e   Aegae: Map 4.8.7, AY.
4.8.5f   Temnos: Map 4.8.7, AY.

4.8.6
394
ABYDOS-SESTOS
Pharnabazos orders
Konon to blockade these
cities from the sea while
he begins to lay waste the
territory of Abydos.

4.8.7
393
MELOS-LACONIA-CYTHERA
In spring, Pharnabazos
and Konon sail to
Lacedaemon via Melos
and, after laying waste
Lacedaemonian territory,
go on to Cythera.

4.8.8
393
CYTHERA-CORINTH
After fortifying the city
on Cythera, Pharnabazos
encourages the allies at
Corinth to continue the
war against Sparta,
distributing money before
leaving for home.

4.8.9–10
393
ATHENS
Pharnabazos agrees to let
Konon take the fleet to
Athens to assist the Athenians in rebuilding their
fortifications on whose
destruction the Spartans
had previously expended
so much effort.

[6] When Pharnabazos discovered what was happening in Abydos and Sestos, he announced to the cities that unless they expelled the Spartans, he would declare war on them. When they ignored his order, he directed Konon to prevent their ships from going to sea while he himself began to lay waste the territory of the Abydaians. But when he failed to subjugate them, he departed for home after ordering Konon to win over the other cities of the Hellespont so that he might muster as large a fleet as possible in the spring. He was angry with the Spartans because of what he had suffered at their hands, and he therefore made it his highest priority to enter their land and take there what vengeance he could.[a]

[7] And so they spent the winter engaged in such activities. At the beginning of spring, having fitted out many ships and hired mercenaries, Pharnabazos, together with Konon, sailed though the islands to Melos,[a] and from there sailed on to Lacedaemon.[b] Landing first at Pherai,[c] Pharnabazos laid waste the surrounding territory; then, going ashore at various places along the coast, he did whatever damage he could. But fearful of the lack of harbors in this area, the prospect of help coming from the Spartans, and the scarcity of provisions in that territory, he quickly turned about and sailed for Phoenicus on the island of Cythera.[d]

[8] Here the men in possession of the city of the Cytherans abandoned their walls, fearing that they might be captured if there was a siege, and Pharnabazos allowed them to depart under truce to Sparta while he himself repaired the wall, and he left behind among the Cytherans a garrison with Nikophemos, an Athenian, as its commander. Having done this, he sailed for the Isthmus of Corinth,[a] where he exhorted the allies to carry on the war against Sparta with vigor and to show themselves trustworthy men to the King. After leaving them as much money as he had with him, he sailed home.

[9] Konon, however, said to Pharnabazos that if he, Konon, should be allowed to keep the fleet, he would support it by raising funds from the islands and would in addition sail to his own city[a] and assist the Athenians in rebuilding their Long Walls and the wall around the Peiraieus, "for nothing," he said, "would be more grievous to the Spartans than this. By doing this, you will at once gratify the Athenians and have your vengeance on the Spartans: for you will have brought to nought what they had created with the greatest of effort."[b] Hearing this, Pharnabazos not only eagerly dispatched Konon to the Athenians but also furnished him with funds for the rebuilding.

4.8.6a   For the attacks on Pharnabazos' territory by Derkylidas and Agesilaos, see 3.4.12ff. and 4.1.1ff. Hellespont: Map 4.8.7, AY.
4.8.7a   Melos: Map 4.8.7, BX.
4.8.7b   Lacedaemon, the territory of the Spartan state within the region of Laconia. Sparta itself was too far inland to be directly attacked by Pharnabazos' fleet. For a discussion of the terms Sparta, Laconia (Map 4.8.7, BX), and Lacedaemon, see Appendix E, §7–8.
4.8.7c   Pherai (Peloponnese): Map 4.8.7, BX.
4.8.7d   Phoenicus: location unknown. Cythera: Map 4.8.7, BX.

4.8.8a   Isthmus of Corinth: Map 4.8.7, inset.
4.8.9a   Of course Konon's own city was Athens: Map 4.8.7, BX.
4.8.9b   The Long Walls of Athens, which connected Athens' city wall with the walls of its port, the Peiraieus (Map 4.8.7, BX), and made Athens impervious to a siege during the city's naval supremacy, had been torn down in 404 in fulfillment of one of the terms imposed on the defeated city by the victorious Spartans (see 2.2.20–23). Diodorus also describes Konon's reconstruction of Athens' walls; see Appendix O, 14.85.2–3. See also Figure 4.8.10.

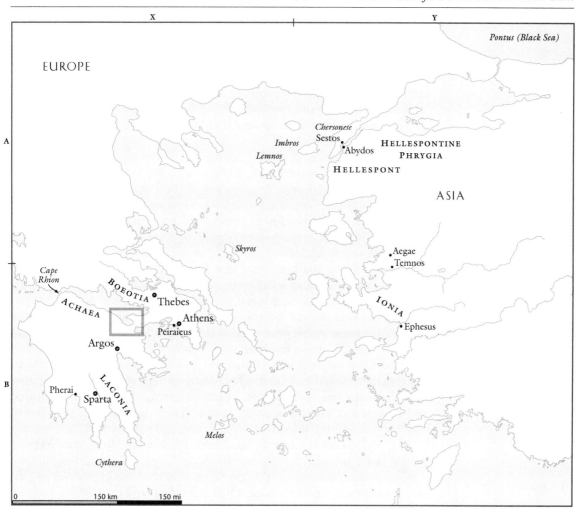

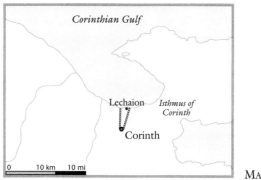

MAP 4.8.7

[10] When he arrived, Konon erected a large portion of the wall, offering his own men for the task, and paying for carpenters and stonecutters and any additional work that was necessary. There was, however, a part of the wall that the Athenians themselves, assisted by the Boeotians[a] as well as other cities that had volunteered, had rebuilt. The Corinthians,[b] meanwhile, appointed Agathinos to command the ships that they had fitted out with the money that Pharnabazos had left them, and they used them to maintain control of the gulf[c] around Achaca[d] and Lechaion.[e] The Spartans also fitted out ships, and Podanemos was their commander. [11] He, however was killed in an attack, and when his vice-admiral Pollis was also wounded and had to depart, command of these ships fell to Herippidas.[a] Then Proainos the Corinthian took over command of the Corinthian ships from Agathinos and abandoned Rhion,[b] which the Spartans then occupied. After this, Teleutias[c] went to take over Herippidas' ships, and he now took control of the gulf again.

[12] When the Spartans heard that Konon was using the King's money to rebuild the Athenians' walls, to maintain his fleet, and to win over to the Athenian side both the islands and the cities on the mainland, they decided to inform Tiribazos,[a] the King's general, of these things, thinking that he would then either come over to their side or put an end to the support of Konon's navy. Having resolved to do this, they sent Antalkidas[b] with instructions to tell Tiribazos of what was going on and to try to make peace between Sparta and the King. [13] When the Athenians learned of this, they too sent some ambassadors, namely Hermogenes, Dion, Kallisthenes, and Kallimedon, accompanied by Konon. They also invited their allies to send envoys, and the Boeotians, Corinthians, and Argives[a] did so.

[14] When they reached Tiribazos, Antalkidas said that he had come to ask for peace between his city and the King, a peace that the King himself desired: for the Spartans would now lay no claim to the Greek cities in Asia[a] but would be content if the King left all the islands and the rest of the Greek city-states autonomous. "And if we," he said, "would accept such terms, why should the King continue to make war against us or spend his money? For the Athenians could not possibly make war against the King if we did not take the lead, nor would it be possible for us to do that if the cities were

4.8.10a Boeotia: Map 4.8.7, BX.
4.8.10b Corinth: Map 4.8.7, inset.
4.8.10c Corinthian Gulf: Map 4.8.7, inset.
4.8.10d Achaea: Map 4.8.7, BX.
4.8.10e Lechaion: Map 4.8.7, inset.
4.8.11a Herippidas was last mentioned at 4.3.17.
4.8.11b Cape Rhion: Map 4.8.7, BX. A strategic site at the narrowest point of the Corinthian Gulf.
4.8.11c Teleutias, brother of Agesilaos, was last mentioned at 4.4.19.
4.8.12a According to Xenophon in the *Anabasis* (4.4.4), Tiribazos was the satrap of western Armenia when the army of ten thousand Greeks who had accompanied Cyrus the Younger

retreated through that satrapy to the North Sea. He seems to have succeeded Tithraustes as satrap of Ionia (Map 4.8.7, BY).
4.8.12b Antalkidas, Spartan statesman: see Appendix M, §4.
4.8.13a Argos: Map 4.8.7, BX. The Persians have here used their gold very effectively to achieve their ends in Greece. See Appendix D, §2 and n. D.2a.
4.8.14a Asia (Asia Minor): Map 4.8.7, AY.

FIGURE 4.8.10. A SECTION OF THE THEMISTOKLEAN WALL OF THE PEIRAIEUS. THE BRICKS LAID ABOVE THE LARGE LOWER BLOCKS ARE PART OF KONON'S REPAIRS.

autonomous." [15] Tiribazos was very pleased at the words of Antalkidas, but to those delegates not from Sparta, these were merely empty words, since the Athenians would not agree that all the cities and the islands should be autonomous, fearing that they might thereby be deprived of Lemnos, Imbros, and Skyros;[a] the Thebans[b] were alarmed that such an agreement would compel them to allow the Boeotian cities to be autonomous; and the Argives thought they could not then hold on to Corinth as though it were Argive territory (which they very much wanted to maintain). So no peace agreement could be reached, and each of the parties returned home.[c]

4.8.15a Lemnos, Imbros, Skyros: Map 4.8.7, AX. These three islands had been acquired early on in the fifth century for the Athenians by Miltiades and Kimon. See Herodotus, *Histories* 6.140 (conquest of Lemnos), and Thucydides 1.98 (conquest of Skyros).
4.8.15b Thebes: Map 4.8.7, BX.
4.8.15c Xenophon here omits the further negotiations at Sparta that almost all scholars agree are proven from Andocides 3.33 (doubts about the speech's authenticity are implausible). At these the Spartans after all conceded Lemnos, Imbros, and Skyros to Athens, and Boeotia (other than Orchomenus) to Thebes, but to no avail, as Athens, and presumably Thebes, rejected the

proposed terms. *The Cambridge Ancient History* and many scholars also believe that two surviving passages from the third-century historian Philochoros of Athens refer to these talks (F. Jacoby, *Die Fragmente der griechischen Historiker*, 15 vols., Berlin, 1923–30, Leipzig, 1940–58, 328 F 149), and that Sparta continued throughout them to concede the Greeks of Asia to the Persians. This is, however, disputed, for example, in the full treatment of C. D. Hamilton, *Sparta's Bitter Victories* (Ithaca: Cornell University Press, 1979), pp. 249–59. For a brief discussion of Xenophon's spin on this episode, see the Introduction, §15.5. (David Thomas)

4.8.16
392
SUSA? PERSEPOLIS?
Tiribazos goes to the King
to report on these matters
and to ask what further
moves he should make.

[16] Tiribazos, however, did not think it was safe for him to support the Spartans without the King's approval, so he gave funds to Antalkidas in secret so that the Spartans, by maintaining a fleet, would induce the Athenians and their allies to desire peace more strongly. He imprisoned Konon on the grounds that the Spartan accusations were true and that he had wronged the King.[a] Having taken these steps, Tiribazos then went to the King in order to report what the Spartans had said, to tell him that he had imprisoned Konon as having wronged the King, and to ask the King what further steps he should take in all these matters.

4.8.17
391
IONIA–MAEANDER VALLEY
Tiribazos is replaced by
the pro-Athenian
Strouthas, so Sparta sends
Thibron to wage war
against the King.

[17] While Tiribazos was meeting with the King in the interior, the King sent Strouthas to take charge of affairs on the coast. Strouthas, however, was strongly inclined to the Athenians' side, because he remembered how much harm the King's lands had suffered at the hands of Agesilaos. When the Spartans saw that Strouthas was hostile to them and friendly toward the Athenians, they sent Thibron[a] to wage war against him. Thibron crossed over into Asia, and using Ephesus[b] along with Priene,[c] Leukophrys,[d] and Achilleion[e] (these are cities in the plain of the Maeander[f]) as his base, he raided and plundered the territory of the King.

4.8.18–19
391
IONIA–MAEANDER VALLEY
Strouthas—noticing
that the Spartans make
their raids without order,
contemptuous of their
foes—attacks them unex-
pectedly, kills Thibron
and his companion
Thersander, and routs
the rest, killing many.

[18] As time went by, however, Strouthas came to realize that every time Thibron made his expeditions, he failed to maintain proper formation but instead proceeded as if contemptuous of the Persians. And so Strouthas sent horsemen into the plain and ordered them to charge and encircle Thibron's forces and to carry off whatever they could.[a] It so happened that after breakfast Thibron and Thersander the flute player were spending time in the tent together. Thersander was not only a fine flute player, but he also claimed to be very strong, since he was a great imitator of Spartan ways.[b] [19] Strouthas, seeing that the enemy was bringing assistance without order and that the men in front were few, suddenly appeared at the head of many cavalry drawn up in proper battle formation. They first killed Thibron and Thersander; once these fell, the rest of the Spartans took flight, and the Persian cavalry pursued them and struck down many of them.[a] Some escaped safely to friendly cities, while more had in fact been left behind in camp, since they found out too late that a raiding party had gone out. For

4.8.16a   According to one tradition, Konon was executed by the Persian King, but the more likely tradition suggests that he escaped to Cyprus, where shortly afterward he died: see Lysias 19.39, 19.41; Isocrates 4.154.
4.8.17a   Thibron, Spartan general: see Appendix M, §25.
4.8.17b   Ephesus: Map 4.8.27.
4.8.17c   Priene: Map 4.8.27.
4.8.17d   Leukophrys: Map 4.8.27.
4.8.17e   Achilleion: Map 4.8.27, inset. This city is located in the Troad, far to the north of the Maeander River plain. No city of that name is known to have been in the valley. The geographic error is Xenophon's.

4.8.17f   Maeander River: Map 4.8.27.
4.8.18a   An example of superior Persian generalship and use of cavalry.
4.8.18b   In Xenophon's time, the statement that Thersander was a great admirer of Spartan ways would be a double entendre, referring to homosexual practices. The description of Thersander as "very strong" would imply that he was thought to be the active partner and, therefore, Thibron the passive one.
4.8.19a   Another description of the death of Thibron is given by Diodorus; see Appendix O, 14.99.1–3. For Xenophon's evaluation of Thibron, see the Introduction, §12.6.

as so often was the case, Thibron made his sorties without even announcing them. That was how this campaign ended.

[20] When the men from Rhodos[a] who had been driven out by the democratic faction arrived in Sparta,[b] they explained to the Spartans that it was unworthy of them to allow the Athenians to conquer Rhodos and in so doing add such a great power to the one they already had. The Spartans realized that if the common people at Rhodos had their way, all of Rhodos would be added to the Athenians' power, while if the wealthier citizens prevailed, then the Spartans themselves would have control of the island. The Spartans then manned eight ships for the Rhodian exiles and put Ekdikos in command of them. [21] They sent Diphridas out with him on these ships, and they ordered Diphridas to cross over into Asia[a] and to preserve Spartan rule over the cities that had accepted Thibron; furthermore, he was instructed to take command of that part of Thibron's army that had escaped destruction and collect any other soldiers that he could, and with these men wage war against Strouthas. Diphridas did these things and in addition managed to capture Tigranes, the man who was married to Strouthas' daughter, together with the daughter herself, as they were on their way to Sardis.[b] He ransomed them for a great deal of money, and with this money he was immediately able to hire mercenaries. [22] Diphridas was no less gracious than Thibron, but in his capacity as general he was more resolute and more enterprising, since pleasures of the body did not master him, and he always accomplished whatever task he set himself.

Ekdikos sailed to Cnidus[a] and learned there that the commons in Rhodos were in complete control of both land and sea and that they had twice the number of ships that he himself had, so he remained quiet at Cnidus.

[23] When the Spartans realized that Ekdikos had an insufficient force to help their friends, they ordered Teleutias to sail to Ekdikos, taking with him the twelve ships that he commanded in the gulf[a] around Achaea[b] and Lechaion.[c] Teleutias was also instructed to send Ekdikos home, to take care of the cities that wished to be friends of the Spartans and to do whatever harm he could to Sparta's enemies. When Teleutias arrived at Samos,[d] he took the ships that were there and sailed to Cnidus, while Ekdikos sailed home.

[24] By the time Teleutias sailed into Rhodos, he had twenty-seven ships with him. On his voyage there he encountered ten Athenian triremes commanded by Philokrates son of Ephialtes, which had sailed from Athens[a] and were making for Cyprus[b] in order to bring help to Euagoras.[c] Teleutias

Margin notes:

4.8.20–22
391
RHODOS-SPARTA-CNIDUS
Rhodians driven out by the democratic faction appeal to Sparta for help. Sparta sends ships and instructs Diphridas to rally Spartan forces against the Persians. Diphridas captures Strouthas' daughter and ransoms her for enough money to hire mercenaries.

4.8.23–24
390
SAMOS-RHODOS
The Spartans send Teleutias with more ships to help restore Rhodos to a Spartan alliance, and as he gathers more ships and captures ten Athenian ships on their way to Cyprus, he finally arrives at Rhodos to assist Spartan partisans there. Xenophon points out that both sides were acting contrary to their best interests.

4.8.20a Rhodos: Map 4.8.27.
4.8.20b Sparta: Map 4.8.27. Xenophon has not previously given any information about this situation. See Diodorus (Appendix O, 14.79, 14.97) for the background and a slightly different account of events. The men named Ekdikos and Diphridas in the *Hellenika* are called Eudokimos and Diphilas in Diodorus.
4.8.21a Asia (Asia Minor): Map 4.8.27 and inset.
4.8.21b Sardis: Map 4.8.27.
4.8.22a Cnidus: Map 4.8.27.
4.8.23a Corinthian Gulf: Map 4.8.7, inset.
4.8.23b Achaea: Map 4.8.27.
4.8.23c Lechaion: Map 4.8.7, inset.
4.8.23d Samos: Map 4.8.27.
4.8.24a Athens: Map 4.8.27.
4.8.24b Cyprus: Map 5.1.17, locator.
4.8.24c Euagoras was the ruler of the city of Salamis (Map 5.1.17, locator) on Cyprus and a friend of Athens. See n. 2.1.29c.

captured all of them. In all this, however, both sides were acting in a way most opposed to their best interests, for the Athenians, who considered the King a friend, were making an alliance with Euagoras, who was fighting against the King, and Teleutias, even though the Spartans were at war with the King, was destroying those who were also sailing to wage war against him. Teleutias then, after sailing to Cnidus and disposing of everything he had captured, came back again to Rhodos and brought assistance to those who were on the side of the Spartans.

[25] The Athenians for their part now realized that the Spartans were again deploying a naval force, so they sent out Thrasyboulos of Steiria[a] with forty ships. Having set sail, he made no attempt to help Rhodos, because he thought that it would prove difficult for him to take vengeance on the friends of the Spartans there, since they held a fortress and were assisted by Teleutias with his fleet. At the same time Thrasyboulos thought that the Rhodians who were friendly to the Athenians could not be defeated by their enemies, since they not only controlled the cities but were also more numerous than the enemy and had actually been victorious in battle. [26] So he sailed to the Hellespont,[a] and even though he found no opponent there, he still thought that he could do something useful for his city. He learned that Amedokos, the king of the Odrysians,[b] was in conflict with Seuthes,[c] the ruler of the coast, and so he reconciled them to each other and also made both of them friends and allies of Athens. He thought that the Greek cities on the coast of Thrace would be more likely to side with the Athenians if these two rulers were friends. [27] This proved favorable to the Athenians, as did the situation of the cities in Asia, since the King was now the friend of the Athenians.[a] Thrasyboulos, realizing this, sailed to Byzantium[b] and there let out contracts for the collection of the one-tenth tax[c] for ships sailing in from the Black Sea.[d] He also changed the government of Byzantium from an oligarchy to a democracy, with the result that

---

4.8.25a Steiria (Attic deme): Map 5.1.17, inset. Xenophon calls him just Thrasyboulos up to this point in the manuscript, then adds "of Steiria" in order to avoid confusion with Thrasyboulos of Kollytos (Map 2.4.30, inset). See n. 1.1.12a for further. For more on Thrasyboulos of Steiria, see Appendix M, §26.
4.8.26a Hellespont: Map 4.8.27 and inset.
4.8.26b Odrysian Thrace: Map 4.8.27, inset.
4.8.26c The chronology and succession of Thracian kings is uncertain. There were many disputes and periods in which more than one person claimed the kingdom. That seems to be the case with Amedokos king of Thrace and Seuthes ruler of the coast. This Seuthes may be the same as the one mentioned at 3.2.2 but is certainly too late to be the one mentioned by Thucydides. He is thought to have grown up at the court of Medokos and to have taken over the remnants of Xenophon's Ten Thousand in order to win back the king-

dom of his father Maisades. In 398 he had supported Derkylidas (see 3.2.2–9).
4.8.27a The Persian King had become friendly toward the Athenians mainly because of the aggressive actions and successes of the Spartan king Agesilaos in Asia Minor and his determination to liberate those cities from Persian sovereignty.
4.8.27b Byzantium: Map 4.8.27 and inset.
4.8.27c This tax is described at 1.1.22. Xenophon omits most of the achievements of Thrasyboulos in restoring Athenian dominion in the Aegean, as well as the problems he encountered in the same period: he won over to the Athenian alliance Thasos and Samothrace (Map 4.8.27), as well as the Chersonese, Byzantium, and Chalcedon (Map 4.8.27, inset); he killed the Spartan harmost at Lesbos (Map 4.8.27, inset); and he conquered the town of Klazomenai (Map 4.8.27).
4.8.27d Pontus (Black Sea): Map 4.8.27, inset.

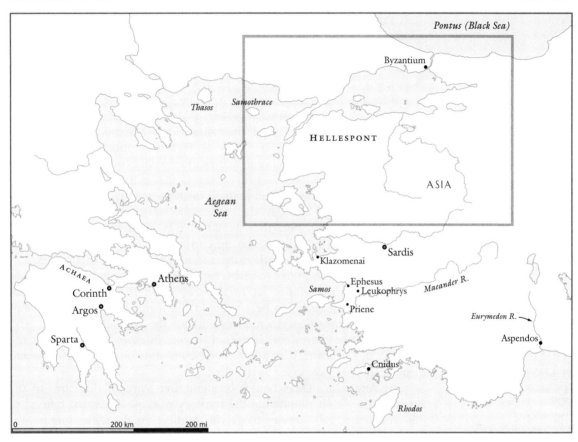

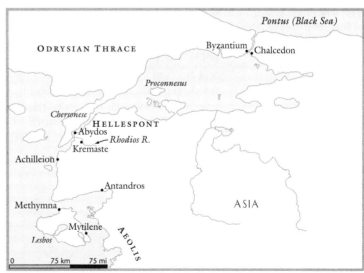

MAP 4.8.27

the commons of Byzantium were delighted to see as many Athenians as possible present in their city.

[28] When he had accomplished all these things and in addition had made the Chalcedonians[a] allies of the Athenians, he departed from the Hellespont. Arriving at Lesbos,[b] he discovered that all the cities there except for Mytilene[c] supported the Spartans, but he delayed attacking any of them until he could gather together at Mytilene all of the four hundred marines[d] from his own ships, all the exiles who had fled into Mytilene, and the strongest of the Mytilenaian citizens. To this last group he held out the hope that if he should capture the cities, they would become the leaders of all Lesbos; while to the exiles he promised that if they stayed united and attacked the cities one by one, then all of them would, in time, be able to return to their own cities; to the marines he said that by bringing Lesbos over to the Athenian side, they would have brought about a great abundance of revenue for Athens. Having encouraged each of them with these promises, he put them in battle order and led them against Methymna.[e]

[29] Therimachos, however, who happened to be the garrison commander of the Spartan soldiers at Methymna, heard that Thrasyboulos was coming to attack them, so he combined the marines from his own ships with the Methymnaians themselves and all the Mytilenaian exiles who happened to be there, and he marched out to meet the enemy at the borders. In the battle that followed, Therimachos died on the spot, and many of the rest were killed as they fled.

[30] After this, Thrasyboulos brought over some of the cities to the Athenian side while plundering the territory of those cities that refused to join in order to raise money to pay his soldiers. At the same time he was eager to sail to Rhodos,[a] so in order to make his army as strong as possible for an expedition there, he raised money from other cities and then went to Aspendos,[b] anchoring in the Eurymedon River.[c] He had already received funds from the Aspendians, but when his soldiers wrongfully pillaged their fields, the people of Aspendos were infuriated and fell upon him at night and cut him down in his tent. [31] So that is how Thrasyboulos, who had a strong reputation for being a good man, died. The Athenians chose Agyrrios to replace him and sent him to the fleet.

The Spartans now took stock of the situation in the Hellespont: in Byzantium the Athenians had contracted out the collection of the ten

4.8.28a   Chalcedon: Map 4.8.27, inset.
4.8.28b   Lesbos: Map 4.8.27, inset.
4.8.28c   Mytilene: Map 4.8.27, inset.
4.8.28d   Marines were soldiers whose mission was to board enemy ships or to repel enemy boarders. Some were hoplites (armored foot soldiers), and some were archers. They were distinct from the crew of sailors who sailed the ship. Usually, each trireme carried a complement of ten marines armed as hoplites and four archers. See Appendix K, Trireme Warfare in Xenophon's *Hellenika*, §2, 11.

4.8.28e   Methymna: Map 4.8.27, inset.
4.8.30a   Rhodos: Map 4.8.27.
4.8.30b   Aspendos: Map 4.8.27. This is a puzzling sentence. Thrasyboulos on Lesbos seeks, for some reason not explained to us, to sail to Rhodos. But he sails several hundred miles past Rhodos to arrive at Aspendos! Diodorus (Appendix O, 14.99.4) writes that he made for Aspendos and received payment from the city before being killed.
4.8.30c   Eurymedon River: Map 4.8.27.

percent tax; in addition, they were in possession of Chalcedon; and, more-over, the rest of the cities in the Hellespont were favorable to the Athenians because Pharnabazos was now their friend. And so the Spartans decided that all this must now be their concern.

[32] Although they did not find fault at all with Derkylidas, they sent out Anaxibios[a]—who was friends with the ephors[b] and who had arranged that just this thing should happen—to serve as governor at Abydos.[c] He promised that if he obtained money and ships, he would wage war against the Athenians and make the situation in the Hellespont unfavorable for them. [33] The ephors therefore gave him three triremes and an amount of money sufficient to hire a thousand mercenaries and sent him off. When he reached Abydos and had gathered a mercenary force, he detached some of the Aeolian[a] cities from Pharnabazos and conducted retaliatory campaigns against those cities that had attacked Abydos, invading and ravaging their territories. He also fitted out three more ships from Abydos in addition to those that had originally sailed with him, and he tried to capture any boat of the Athenians or their allies.

[34] When the Athenians learned of Anaxibios' activity, they became concerned that all of Thrasyboulos' arrangements in the Hellespont would be undone, so they sent out Iphikrates in command of eight ships and twelve hundred peltasts,[a] the majority of whom were men Iphikrates had commanded at Corinth.[b] Iphikrates and these troops happened to be in Athens[c] at the time because, when the Argives had made Corinth a part of Argos,[d] they had said that they no longer needed the peltasts, and indeed, some of those Corinthians who had sided with Argos had been killed by Iphikrates, so he had departed for Athens.

[35] When he arrived at the Chersonese,[a] he and Anaxibios initially fought with each other by sending out plundering raids. But later on, Iphikrates learned that Anaxibios had marched off to Antandros,[b] taking his mercenaries, the Spartans who were with him, and two hundred hoplites from Abydos, and with this force he had won over Antandros to the Spartan side. Suspecting that after Anaxibios established a garrison there, he would then bring the troops from Abydos back home, Iphikrates crossed over during the night to the most deserted part of the territory of Abydos and marched up into the mountains to set an ambush. He ordered the triremes that had brought him across the strait[c] to sail at dawn up the coast

4.8.32–33
389
ABYDOS
The Spartans send Anaxibios to the Hellespont to contend with the Athenians there. He has some success.

4.8.34–36
389
ABYDOS
To counter Anaxibios, the Athenians send a force under Iphikrates to challenge the Spartans in the Hellespont. After a period of mutual raids, Anaxibios takes his force to Antandros and persuades it to join the Spartan side. Learning of this, and predicting that Anaxibios will return to Abydos, Iphikrates takes his forces to an ambush position in the hills on the way to Abydos.

4.8.32a   For Xenophon's earlier encounters with
          Anaxibios in 400, see *Anabasis* 7.1–2 and
          the Introduction, §10.9.
4.8.32b   Ephors: a body of five magistrates with
          great power at Sparta. See Appendix E,
          §16.
4.8.32c   Abydos: Map 4.8.27, inset.
4.8.33a   Aeolis: Map 4.8.27, inset.
4.8.34a   Peltasts were troops armed only with a
          small, light shield, a javelin, and a short
          sword. Unhindered by body armor, they
          could move much more quickly than the
          fully armed hoplite, whose equipment

was both far heavier and far more expensive than theirs. See Appendix L, §7.
4.8.34b   Corinth: Map 4.8.27. For the exploits of
          Iphikrates and these peltasts at Corinth,
          see 4.4.9, 4.4.15–16, and 4.5.16–18.
4.8.34c   Athens: Map 4.8.27.
4.8.34d   Argos: Map 4.8.27. For the uniting of
          Corinth and Argos, see n. 4.4.6c.
4.8.35a   Chersonese: Map 4.8.27, inset.
4.8.35b   Antandros: Map 4.8.27, inset.
4.8.35c   The narrow channel of the Hellespont:
          Map 4.8.27 and inset.

of the Chersonese, so that it would seem that he had left on a voyage to gather money, as he had often done before. [36] And in all his planning he was not to be disappointed. For Anaxibios did return, even though his sacrifices that day (so it was said) were not favorable; yet he disregarded the sacrifice, since he considered that he would be marching through friendly territory to a friendly city, and also because he heard from the men who came to meet him that Iphikrates was sailing up to Proconnesus.[a] So for all these reasons, he conducted his march with insufficient care.

[37] Now Iphikrates and his men remained hidden for as long as Anaxibios' army was on level ground; but when the men of Abydos in the van were in the plain around Kremaste[a] (where their gold mines are),[b] the rest of the army in the rear was making the descent, and Anaxibios himself with his Spartans was just beginning the descent, then at that moment Iphikrates jumped up and attacked them at a run. [38] Anaxibios knew immediately that there was no hope of safety. He saw his army stretched out over a long and narrow track, and he realized that those who had gone ahead would not be able to climb back up to assist him; he saw as well that all the men were thoroughly frightened when they saw the ambush. He thus said to those with him: "Men, it is a fine thing for me to die here, but you must hasten to safety before the enemy is upon us." [39] As he said this he took his shield from his shield-bearer and died fighting at his station. The young man who was his lover remained by his side, and about twelve of the Spartan governors who had come from their cities to join Anaxibios also died fighting along with him. The rest tried to flee but were slain in their flight as Iphikrates' men pursued them right up to the city. About two hundred of these men died and about fifty of the Abydaian hoplites. After this action, Iphikrates returned again to the Chersonese.

4.8.37–39
389
ABYDOS
The Spartans are taken by surprise in the ambush, which Iphikrates springs at the right moment. Spartan casualties, including Anaxibios, are high as a result of Iphikrates' pursuit.

4.8.36a   Proconnesus: Map 4.8.27, inset.
4.8.37a   Kremaste: Map 4.8.27, inset.
4.8.37b   These gold mines were on the Rhodius

River (Map 4.8.27, inset), about 9 miles southeast of Abydos. For the gold mines, see Strabo 13.1.23, 14.5.28.

BOOK FIVE

These, then, were the activities of the Athenians[a] and the Spartans[b] in the area of the Hellespont.[c] During this period, Eteonikos returned once again to Aegina.[d] Previous to this, the Aeginetans had maintained commercial relations with the Athenians, but when the struggle at sea broke out into open warfare, Eteonikos, with the agreement of the ephors,[e] encouraged anyone who was willing to make raids on Attica.[f] [2] And so the Athenians, who were being plundered by these men, sent hoplites[a] under the command of Pamphilos to build a fort on Aegina from which to harass the Aeginetans by land, and also ten triremes to do the same by sea. Teleutias happened to have just arrived at one of the islands in search of revenues when he heard of these events at Aegina, so he came to the aid of the Aeginetans and drove off the naval squadron, although Pamphilos did manage to hold on to the fortification.

[3] After this, Hierax, the new admiral,[a] arrived from Sparta and took over the fleet. Teleutias sailed back home with the most splendid good fortune, for as he was going down to the sea for his journey home, not one soldier failed to shake his hand, and one of them even put a garland on his head, while another placed a fillet[b] there, and still others who arrived too late (Teleutias having already hoisted sail) threw garlands into the sea and prayed that many blessings would attend him. [4] Now I well know that in narrating these events, I do not record anything about funds expended,

5.1.1–2
389?
AEGINA
After Eteonikos uses Aegina as a base from which to plunder Attica, the Athenians establish a fortified post on the island and hold it.

5.1.3–4
389
AEGINA
Teleutias is relieved by Hierax. He is lauded and garlanded by his troops. Xenophon defends taking the time to describe this.

5.1.1a   Athens: Map 5.1.17, BX, and inset.
5.1.1b   Sparta: Map 5.1.17, BX.
5.1.1c   Hellespont: Map 5.1.17, AY.
5.1.1d   Aegina: Map 5.1.17, BX. Xenophon has not previously mentioned that the Spartan garrison commander Eteonikos was in Aegina. For more about Eteonikos, see Appendix M, Brief Biographies of Important Characters in Xenophon's *Hellenika*, §10.
5.1.1e   Ephors: a council of five officials of the Spartan government, elected annually. See Appendix E, Spartan Government and Society, §16.
5.1.1f   Attica: Map 5.1.17, inset.
5.1.2a   Hoplites: heavily armored infantry, often equipped with helmet, breastplate, and greaves but always carrying a large round shield, a thrusting spear, and a short sword. See Appendix L, Land Warfare in Xenophon's *Hellenika*, §3–8.
5.1.3a   It is generally believed that Spartan "admirals" were appointed for one-year terms, at least after the year 410, but the evidence is not conclusive.
5.1.3b   A fillet was a woolen band that, like a garland, was customarily placed on the head of a victorious athlete.

dangers confronted, or stratagems employed. And yet, by Zeus, I think it worthwhile for a man to consider what it was that Teleutias had done that so disposed the men he commanded to behave like that. For this is truly an achievement for a man, more worthy of being recorded than spending a great deal of money or encountering many dangers.[a]

[5] Hierax for his part took the rest of the ships and sailed again to Rhodos,[a] leaving behind at Aegina twelve triremes under the command of Gorgopas, his vice admiral. After this, the Athenians in their fortress were more besieged than the Aeginetans in their city, with the result that a decree was passed at Athens to fit out a large number of ships, and with these, four months later, they brought back the Athenians from the fortress. After they had done this, the Athenians found themselves again assaulted by bands of raiders and the ships of Gorgopas, so they fitted out thirteen ships and chose Eunomos as their commander.

[6] While Hierax was at Rhodos, the Spartans sent out Antalkidas[a] as admiral, thinking that by doing so, they would greatly please Tiribazos. Antalkidas went first to Aegina so that he could take Gorgopas and his ships with him on his way to Ephesus.[b] Later, however, he sent Gorgopas and his twelve triremes back to Aegina and entrusted his vice-admiral Nikolochos with the command of the rest of his force.[c] Nikolochos at first sailed toward Abydos,[d] wishing to assist the people of that city, but on the way he turned aside to Tenedos,[e] where he ravaged the countryside and exacted money, and then sailed on to Abydos. [7] The Athenian generals who were gathered together on Samothrace,[a] Thasos,[b] and the other territories in that area sailed out to bring help to the people of Tenedos; but when they learned that Nikolochos had put in at Abydos, they blockaded him and his twenty-five ships with the thirty-two they had, using the Chersonese[c] as their base.

In the meantime, while Gorgopas was sailing from Ephesus, he happened to encounter the ships of Eunomos, but he was able to reach Aegina and take refuge there, arriving a little before sunset. He immediately disembarked his men and gave them dinner.

[8] Eunomos, for his part, waited a little while and then sailed away. When night fell, he hoisted sail and with his ship led the way, carrying a light (as is customary) so that the rest of his ships, which were following, would not wander off course. At that moment, Gorgopas immediately embarked his men and followed Eunomos, watching the light but keeping a bit behind so that Eunomos' men would not see or notice them. His

5.1.5
389
AEGINA
Hierax sails to Rhodos. The Spartans and Athenians fight for supremacy at Aegina; the Athenians evacuate their fort on the island.

5.1.6–7
388
TENEDOS-ABYDOS
Antalkidas is sent from Sparta as admiral. His vice-admiral Nikolochos raids Tenedos. The Athenians blockade Nikolochos' ships at Abydos.

5.1.8–9
388
AEGINA-ATTICA
At Aegina, the Spartan ships under Gorgopas follow an Athenian flotilla at night as it returns to port and attack the ships successfully as they land near Cape Zoster in Attica.

5.1.4a This is one of the few methodological statements made by Xenophon, and many scholars have placed great weight on it: it is discussed further in the Introduction, §10.10–11, 11.7.
5.1.5a Rhodos: Map 5.1.17, locator.
5.1.6a Antalkidas, Spartan statesman: see Appendix M, §4.
5.1.6b Ephesus: Map 5.1.17, BY.
5.1.6c Xenophon does not explain why Antalkidas would leave his command of the fleet in

the hands of a deputy, but it is made clear later that he went to see Tiribazos to take advantage of the good relationship between them just alluded to, and that he went as far as the Great King's court in the heart of the Persian empire (5.1.25).
5.1.6d Abydos: Map 5.1.17, AY.
5.1.6e Tenedos: Map 5.1.17, AY.
5.1.7a Samothrace: Map 5.1.17, AY.
5.1.7b Thasos: Map 5.1.17, AX.
5.1.7c Chersonese: Map 5.1.17, AY.

boatswains kept time by clicking stones together instead of using their voices, and the men made a slicing motion with their oars.[a] [9] When Eunomos' ships approached the shore around Zoster[a] in Attica, Gorgopas, by means of the trumpet, gave the command to attack. Now the men on some of Eunomos' ships were just disembarking, other ships were still coming to anchor, while yet other ships were making their way to shore. A sea battle by moonlight took place in which Gorgopas captured four ships, which he put in tow and carried off with him to Aegina. The rest of the Athenian ships escaped and made their way to the Peiraieus.[b]

[10] After this Chabrias[a] sailed off to Cyprus[b] in order to assist Euagoras.[c] He had eight hundred peltasts[d] and ten triremes under his command, and he took additional ships and hoplites with him from Athens. At night he himself, together with the peltasts, disembarked at Aegina and set an ambush in a hollow a little beyond the Herakleion.[e] At daybreak, as had been agreed upon beforehand, the Athenian hoplites arrived with Demainetos in command. They ascended to a spot about sixteen stades[f] beyond the Herakleion, where the so-called Tripyrgia[g] stands. [11] When Gorgopas heard this, he set out to bring assistance, taking with him the Aeginetans, the marines[a] from the ships, and eight Spartiates[b] who happened to be there. He also made a proclamation that all the free men from the crews of the ships should come with him, with the result that many of them came also, each man arming himself as best he could.[c] [12] When those in the front of Gorgopas' forces had passed by the ambush, Chabrias and his men jumped up and immediately began to attack the enemy with javelins and stones, while the hoplites who had come from the ships also advanced against them. Those in the van, since they were not massed together,[a] were swiftly killed, and among these were Gorgopas and the eight Spartans. Once these had fallen, the rest turned and fled. About 150 of the Aegine-

5.1.10–12
388
AEGINA
Chabrias sets up an ambush on Aegina. He lures the Spartans out to defend against a threat and surprises and defeats them, killing many.

5.1.8a   That is, they angled their oars into the water rather than striking the water at right angles so as to make less noise. Xenophon doesn't say so, but perhaps he was also aware that splashes and foam at sea can give off a visible phosphorescent light, which this maneuver would minimize. This chapter uniquely mentions some important details of ancient trireme military practices.

5.1.9a   Cape Zoster: Map 5.1.17, inset.

5.1.9b   Peiraieus: Map 5.1.17, inset.

5.1.10a Chabrias: a competent and prominent professional soldier who served thirteen terms as general for Athens. See Appendix M, §6.

5.1.10b Cyprus: Map 5.1.17, locator.

5.1.10c Euagoras: ruler of Salamis on Cyprus who was friendly to Athens. See 2.1.29, 4.8.24.

5.1.10d Peltasts were troops armed only with a small, light shield, a javelin, and a short sword. Unhindered by body armor, they could move much more quickly than the fully armed hoplite, whose equipment was both heavier and far more expensive than theirs. As a type, they seem to have originated in Thrace. See Appendix L, §7.

5.1.10e Herakleion (temple of Herakles), at Aegina: site unknown.

5.1.10f Sixteen Attic stades at 583 feet each would convert to 1.75 miles. See Appendix I, Units of Distance, Currency, and Capacity in Xenophon's *Hellenika*, §4–5, 13.

5.1.10g Tripyrgia: this marker is unknown. It is presumably a hill of some sort.

5.1.11a Marines: each trireme normally carried a complement of ten marines armed as hoplites. See Appendix K, Trireme Warfare in Xenophon's *Hellenika*, §2.

5.1.11b Spartiates: those Spartans enjoying full citizenship rights. See Appendix E, §7, 9, 17, 19.

5.1.11c Note that not all the sailors in the Spartan fleet were free men. See Appendix K, §8.

5.1.12a Since they were not expecting a battle there, they were not in battle formation and thus fell easy prey to Chabrias' men.

5.1.13
388
AEGINA
Sparta sends Teleutias to take over the command as Eteonikos is unable to get his sailors to put to sea.

5.1.14–17
387
AEGINA
Teleutias speaks to the sailors to encourage them. He appeals to their pride and promises booty from the enemy.

tans perished; the combined total for the foreigners, resident aliens,[b] and sailors who had run ashore to give assistance was more than 200. [13] After this victory, the Athenians sailed the seas just as if it had been peacetime, since the Spartan sailors refused to row for Eteonikos—even though he tried to compel them to get on board the ships—because he would not give them their pay.[a]

After this, the Spartans sent out Teleutias to be an independent commander of these ships,[b] and the sailors were overjoyed at his arrival. Calling them together, Teleutias spoke to them as follows:

[14] "Soldiers, I have arrived here without money. If, however, God wills and you are eager, I will try to furnish you with provisions in great abundance. And know well that whenever I am your commander, I pray for your lives no less than for my own; and you might be amazed if I told you that I wish for you to have provisions more than I do for myself. Indeed, by the gods, I would prefer to go without food for two days rather than have any of you go without for one. Now, just as my door was, as you know, always open to you before,[a] so that anyone who had some request might visit me, so, too, will it be open to you now. [15] So whenever you have abundant provisions, then you will see me living with greater abundance. But if you see me enduring cold and heat and night watches, you will know that you, too, must persevere in all these things. For I do not order you to your tasks in order to tax you but, rather, so that you might gain some advantage from them. [16] And know well, my men, that this city of ours, which has a reputation for being blessed, acquired its fairness and goodness not by being lazy but by being willing to accept toils and dangers whenever it was necessary. I know well that in former time you were brave men; but you must now strive to become even braver so that, just as we gladly toil together, so, too, we will gladly enjoy prosperity together. [17] For what can be more pleasurable than not having to flatter any man, Greek or barbarian, for the sake of pay but, rather, being able to provide what is necessary for ourselves by ourselves, and moreover from the most honorable source?[a] Know well that in war the abundance acquired from the enemy furnishes both necessary sustenance for oneself and good repute among mankind."

5.1.18
387
AEGINA
The sailors respond to Teleutias with enthusiasm.

[18] So he spoke, and all the men shouted out that he should command them to do whatever was necessary, since they were ready to obey him. As he had just happened to finish sacrificing, he said, "Come now, men, have your dinner just as you were intending, and then please provide yourselves

---

5.1.12b   Resident aliens (metics) were found in many Greek states. Those in Athens are the best known. They were not citizens, could not own houses or land, and were subject to special taxes. But they had rights, and they served in both the army and the fleet and filled commercial roles. Some became quite wealthy.

5.1.13a   For more on issues of pay and provisions, see Appendix K, §7–8.

5.1.13b   Because Antalkidas when he reenters the narrative operates as overall commander

of the fleet, the translator has here adopted an emendation that would distinguish Teleutias' command as special and applying only to these particular ships. For the Greek, see Translator's Notes.

5.1.14a   As was his practice during his previous command, in 391–390: see 4.4.19–4.8.25, passim.

5.1.17a   He means by honorable military means, rather than being supported by the Persian King.

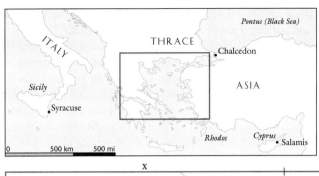

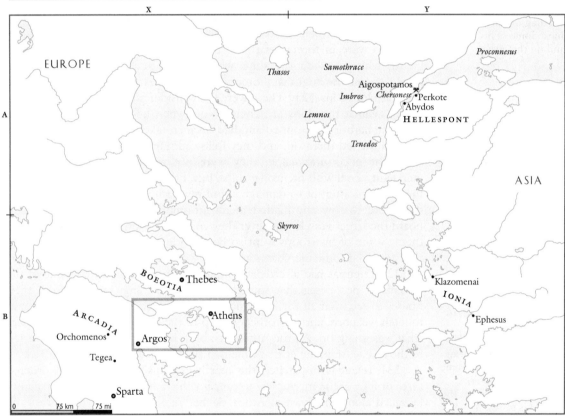

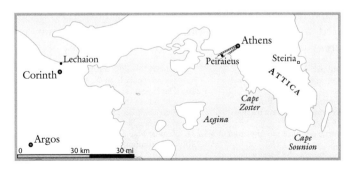

MAP 5.1.17

179

with one day's worth of rations.[a] Then go straightaway to the ships so that we may sail where God wills and arrive at an opportune moment."

5.1.19–21
387
PEIRAIEUS
Teleutias, thinking to take the Athenians by surprise, raids the Peiraieus at dawn, instructing his men to damage triremes at anchor but to capture and drag off merchant ships. Some of his men land on the quay.

[19] When they came to the ships, he put them on board and sailed by night right into the Athenians' harbor.[a] While sailing there, he at times had the men rest and even sleep and at other times set them to the oars.[b] Now if someone were to think that Teleutias was foolhardy to sail with twelve ships against the many that the Athenians possessed, let him consider the man's calculation, which went as follows. [20] He thought that the Athenians would be more careless about their fleet when it was in their harbor, since Gorgopas was now dead. He also thought that even if there were triremes at anchor in the Athenian harbor, it would be safer to sail against twenty ships at Athens than against ten elsewhere, for he knew that when the ships were in foreign harbors, the sailors would spend the night on board, whereas when the ships were in port at Athens, the trierarchs[a] would spend the night at home and the sailors would be quartered in disparate locations. [21] These were the considerations behind his decision to sail against the ships at Athens. Now when he was five or six stades[a] from the harbor, he stopped and had his men take their rest; but when day dawned, he led them on, and they followed. He commanded his men that when the encounter came, they were not to sink or incapacitate any merchant vessel with their own ships, but if they saw any trireme at anchor, they were to attempt to damage it and render it unseaworthy; in addition, they were to tow any loaded merchant ships out of the harbor and to board the larger vessels whenever they could and capture the men on board them. Some of his troops went so far as to leap onto the Deigma,[b] where they captured some merchants and shipowners and carried them away.

5.1.22–24
387
PEIRAIEUS
As the Athenians rush to rescue the Peiraieus, Teleutias sails down the coast of Attica, capturing many boats and even some corn ships at Sounion. With the money from the sale of his prizes, he gives his men one month's pay.

[22] Teleutias had already accomplished these things when some of the Athenians, perceiving that something was happening, ran out from their houses to see what all the shouting was about. Others ran into their homes to fetch weapons, and still others ran up to the city to tell the citizens there what was going on. All the Athenians, both hoplites and horsemen, rushed to the rescue, thinking at that time that the Peiraieus had been captured.

[23] Teleutias dispatched the merchant ships to Aegina[a] and ordered three or four of the triremes to accompany them; with the rest of the triremes he sailed along the coast of Attica. As he was sailing out of the harbor, he captured many fishing boats and ferries that were sailing for the Peiraieus from the islands, and these were full of people. He went next to Sounion,[b] where he captured merchant vessels, some fully loaded with grain and others with different wares. [24] And after he had done all this, he sailed

5.1.18a The ritual of animal sacrifice included feasting on most of the remains from the roasted animals.
5.1.19a The harbor of Athens was the Peiraieus.
5.1.19b Sleeping and resting of crews on triremes: see Appendix K, §7, 11.
5.1.20a Trierarchs: trireme captains: see Appendix K, §8–11.
5.1.21a Five or six Attic stades of 583 feet would

convert to a little more than half a mile. See Appendix I, §4–5, 13.
5.1.21b The Deigma was an area in the middle of the quayside in the commercial quarter of the Peiraieus where merchants displayed their wares. See Maps 2.4.10 and 2.4.30, inset.
5.1.23a Aegina: Map 5.1.17, inset.
5.1.23b Cape Sounion: Map 5.1.17, inset. See Figure 5.1.23 for two views of Sounion.

FIGURE 5.1.23. REMAINS OF THE TEMPLE OF POSEIDON AT SOUNION AS SEEN FROM THE WATER (TOP). A VIEW FROM
THE TEMPLE LOOKING SOUTH OVER THE ISLANDS OF THE SARONIC GULF (BOTTOM).

back to Aegina, where he sold the booty and from the proceeds was able to give the soldiers one month's advance pay. Thereafter he continued to sail around these waters and seize whatever he could, and by this means, he kept his ships fully manned and his soldiers happy and ready to do whatever he ordered.

[25] Antalkidas now came down to the coast with Tiribazos. Antalkidas had successfully secured the King's consent to become an ally of the Spartans in the war if the Athenians and their allies refused to accept the peace on the terms the King was proclaiming.[a] When he heard that Nikolochos with his ships was being besieged in Abydos[b] by Iphikrates and Diotimos, he marched overland to that city, and taking the ships that were there, he sailed out from Abydos at night. He had spread a rumor to the effect that the men of Chalcedon[c] had requested his presence, but he anchored near Perkote[d] and remained there, for the moment taking no action. [26] The Athenians, under the command of generals Demainetos, Dionysios, Leontinos, and Phanias, learned of his departure and pursued him in the direction of Proconnesus.[a] But Antalkidas, when they had sailed past him, turned about and returned to Abydos, because he had received word that Polyxeinos was leading twenty ships from Syracuse[b] and Italy[c] so that he might add these also to his fleet. Then Thrasyboulos, an Athenian from the deme of Kolly-tos,[d] sailed by from Thrace[e] in command of eight ships, wishing to join up with the rest of the Athenian fleet. [27] Antalkidas' lookouts signaled to him that these eight ships were approaching, and so he manned his twelve best ships, ordering, too, that if any ship lacked its full complement of men, it should be completed from the crews of the ships that were left behind.[a] With these he lay in wait as inconspicuously as he could, and once the eight ships had passed by, he pursued them and they, seeing him coming, fled. Antalki-das quickly overtook the slowest of the Athenian ships with his own fastest ones, but he ordered the ships in front not to attack these slowest ships but instead to pursue the ships of the enemy that were in the lead. When he had captured these, the men in the ships behind, seeing their fastest vessels captured, became disheartened, and they were then taken by Antalkidas' slower ships,[b] so that the entire squadron of eight ships was captured.[c]

5.1.25a Xenophon writes at 5.1.6 that Antalkidas sailed to Ephesus but has never told us, till now, that Antalkidas and Tiribazos went inland, presumably to the King at Susa (Map 1.2.10, locator) to try to arrange a Spartan-Persian alliance. For the issues surrounding this Peace of Antalkidas (also called the King's Peace), see Appendix E, §19; see also the Introduction, §3.3–4.
5.1.25b Abydos: Map 5.1.17, AY.
5.1.25c Chalcedon: Map 5.1.17, locator.
5.1.25d Perkote: Map 5.1.17, AY.
5.1.26a Proconnesus: Map 5.1.17, AY.
5.1.26b Syracuse: Map 5.1.17, locator. These ships were sent by the Syracusan tyrant Diony-sios I; the Spartans had assisted him in

404 to consolidate his hold on power.
5.1.26c Italy: Map 5.1.17, locator.
5.1.26d Kollytos (Attic deme): Map 2.4.30, inset. This Thrasyboulos must be distinguished from the earlier Thrasyboulos, of the deme of Steiria, who fought against the Four Hundred. See n. 1.1.12b.
5.1.26e Thrace: Map 5.1.17, AY.
5.1.27a It is interesting to note here that not all triremes were in equal condition or could attain equal speeds. Moreover, not all the ships of Antalkidas' fleet had full crews. See Appendix K, §2.
5.1.27b The reading here is uncertain. (John Marincola) For the Greek, see Translator's Notes.
5.1.27c Naval battle tactics: see Appendix K, §2–4.

[28] After this, Antalkidas was joined by the twenty ships from Syracuse and also by ships from that part of Ionia[a] controlled by Tiribazos, as well as ships from the areas ruled by Ariobarzanes. Ariobarzanes was Antalkidas' guest-friend[b] from long ago, and Pharnabazos, having been summoned by the King, had at that time already departed for the Persian court, for it was on this occasion that he married the King's daughter.[c] With these reinforcements, Antalkidas' fleet now numbered more than eighty triremes, and his mastery of the sea was so complete that he could even prevent the ships sailing down from the Pontus[d] from making for Athens[e] and diverted them instead to the cities of his own allies.

[29] The Athenians saw that the enemy's ships were numerous, and they began to fear that they would be conquered as completely as they had been before;[a] they also saw that the King was now an ally of the Spartans,[b] and they were still being harassed by plundering raids from Aegina.[c] For all these reasons, they now strongly desired peace. The Spartans, for their part, were also finding the war onerous: they had to maintain garrisons of one regiment in Lechaion[d] and one in Orchomenos;[e] they were forced to keep watch over the cities, both those they trusted (so as to protect them from being destroyed) and those they distrusted (to prevent them from revolting); and at Corinth[f] they experienced now successes, now setbacks. The Argives,[g] too, were eager for peace, because they saw that an expedition against them had been ordered by the Spartans and they knew they could no longer derive any advantage from claiming that a sacred truce was in effect.[h] [30] And so when Tiribazos ordered that any of those who wished to hear the peace declared by the King should present themselves, all of them swiftly gathered together. When they had done so, Tiribazos showed them the treaty with the King's seal and then read out what was written, which was as follows:

[31] "King Artaxerxes believes it to be just that the cities in Asia[a] should be his, as also the islands Klazomenai[b] and Cyprus,[c] but that the rest of the

5.1.28
387
ABYDOS
Ships from Syracuse and Ionia join Antalkidas. His fleet, now eighty ships strong, controls the sea, preventing corn ships from sailing through to Athens.

5.1.29–30
387
GREECE
Athens grows weary of the war and desires peace for many reasons. And since all desire peace, Tiribazos calls them to Sardis (?) to read them the King's terms.

5.1.31
387
SARDIS?
The terms of the King's Peace.

5.1.28a   Ionia: Map 5.1.17, BY.
5.1.28b   Guest-friendship: a formal relationship, usually formed between eminent citizens of different states but sometimes between an individual and a whole state. The parties committed themselves to profound mutual obligations, including hospitality, advice, and support, which were not taken lightly. These commitments could pass to succeeding generations.
5.1.28c   The daughter he married was named Apame: see Plutarch, *Parallel Lives*, "Artaxerxes" 27.4.
5.1.28d   Pontus (Black Sea): Map 5.1.17, locator. These ships from the Pontus would have been grain transports from the Black Sea area, which were absolutely essential for Athens. Any blocking of the ships would raise the specter of starvation for the Athenians.
5.1.28e   Athens: Map 5.1.17, BX.
5.1.29a   The reference is to Lysander's capture of the Athenian fleet in 405 at Aigospotamoi (Aigospotamos) (Map 5.1.17, AY) and his

subsequent blockade of Athens, which resulted the following spring in Athens' capitulation to Sparta and the end of the Peloponnesian War.
5.1.29b   Sparta: Map 5.1.17, BX.
5.1.29c   Aegina: Map 5.1.17, inset.
5.1.29d   Lechaion: Map 5.1.17, inset. A Spartan regiment: see Appendix F, The Spartan Army (and the Battle of Leuctra), §4–5.
5.1.29e   Orchomenos (in Arcadia): Map 5.1.17, BX.
5.1.29f   Corinth: Map 5.1.17, inset.
5.1.29g   Argos: Map 5.1.17, inset.
5.1.29h   See 4.7.2–3 on the attempt of the Argives to delay the Spartan attack by declaring a sacred truce, and the Spartan response. See also Appendix J, Ancient Greek Religion in the Time of Xenophon, §11–12.
5.1.31a   Asia (Asia Minor): Map 5.1.17, AY.
5.1.31b   Klazomenai: Map 5.1.17, BY. The city of Klazomenai was on an island so close to the mainland that it was connected to it by a causeway.
5.1.31c   Cyprus: Map 5.1.17, locator.

Figure 5.1.29. Funerary monument of Dexileos, who the inscription says was killed in the Corinthian War, c. 394. It was found in Athens' Kerameikos Cemetery, set up by his family to commemorate him; his body would have been buried elsewhere with other war dead.

Greek cities, both small and large, should be autonomous, except for Lemnos,[d] Imbros,[e] and Skyros,[f] which should, as of old, belong to the Athenians.[g] Whichever of the two parties[h] does not accept this peace, I will wage war against them by land and by sea, with ships and money, taking with me those who accept my views."[i]

[32] After hearing these words, each of the ambassadors returned to announce them to their own cities. And all the cities swore that they would observe the articles of the peace except the Thebans,[a] who demanded that they be allowed to swear on behalf of all the Boeotians.[b] Agesilaos replied that he would not accept their oaths unless they swore that both small and large cities should be autonomous, precisely as the King's proclamation had declared.[c] When the Theban ambassadors said that they had no instructions about how to deal with this, Agesilaos replied, "Well, then, go back and ask for them and tell the Thebans that if they do not comply with this stipulation, they will be excluded from the treaty." [33] The Theban ambassadors then departed.

Agesilaos, however, because of his hatred for the Thebans, was not willing to delay; instead, having won over the ephors, he immediately performed the border-crossing sacrifices.[a] When these proved favorable and he arrived at Tegea,[b] he dispatched horsemen to mobilize the *perioikoi*,[c] and he also sent officers to muster the allied troops from their cities.[d] But before he set out from Tegea, Theban envoys arrived and said that they would allow the cities to be autonomous. So the Spartans returned home, and the Thebans were compelled to join in the treaty and to allow the cities of Boeotia to be autonomous.

5.1.32–34
386
SPARTA-TEGEA-THEBES
When these terms are reported to the various states, the Thebans wish to sign on behalf of all the Boeotians, and the Corinthians and Argives wish to maintain their garrison in Corinth. But Agesilaos demands strict adherence to the terms— that all the cities be independent. When he threatens war if they refuse, they accept the terms.

5.1.31d   Lemnos: Map 5.1.17, AX.
5.1.31e   Imbros: Map 5.1.17, AY.
5.1.31f   Skyros: Map 5.1.17, AX.
5.1.31g   For the Athenian control of these islands, see 4.8.15 and n. 4.8.15a.
5.1.31h   The "two parties" here means the two opposing sides in general, not any particular two cities.
5.1.31i   This peace was known as the King's Peace because of Artaxerxes' role in setting the terms for it and his threat to enforce it. It was also called the Peace of Antalkidas for his role in seeking and achieving it. See "Antalkidas" in Appendix M, §4.
5.1.32a   Thebes: Map 5.1.17, BX.
5.1.32b   Boeotia: Map 5.1.17, BX. From well into the fifth century, the Thebans had considered themselves to be the leaders of Boeotia and had wished all the cities in Boeotia to acknowledge them as supreme. This had led to constant friction, and it was common for cities such as Athens and Sparta, as a way of keeping Theban ambitions in check, to encourage individual cities not to accept the leadership of Thebes.
5.1.32c   After the initial meeting of ambassadors in the presence of Tiribazos, there is evidently a second meeting at Sparta, though Xenophon does not say so explicitly. Nor

does he make clear why it is Agesilaos who is deciding whose oaths to accept and whom to exclude from the peace. Scholars disagree about whether there was an express clause in the treaty appointing Sparta to an official position as its guardian, or whether it was simply that the Persians had made clear that they would back Sparta against any state that held out against its interpretation.
5.1.33a   Agesilaos immediately performed these sacrifices because he wished to advance against the Thebans without delay. Spartan military expeditions did not cross their frontier without favorable sacrifices. For more on border-crossing sacrifices, see Appendix J, §2, 5, and the Introduction, §13.5.
5.1.33b   Tegea: Map 5.1.17, BX.
5.1.33c   *Perioikoi* were full citizens of towns in Laconia that the Spartans had left in possession of their territories. They enjoyed some freedom to conduct their own internal affairs but were without a voice in foreign affairs and were compelled to follow the Spartan lead in war. See Appendix E, §10.
5.1.33d   For the mustering officers and the *perioikic* cities, see 3.5.7 and nn. 3.5.7b and c.

[34] The Corinthians, however, did not dismiss the garrison of the Argives.[a] Agesilaos then announced to the respective parties that if the Corinthians did not dismiss the Argives and the Argives did not depart from Corinth, he would wage war against them. As this threat frightened both parties, the Argives left Corinth, which once again became an independent city.[b] The men who had actually committed the massacre[c] and those who had had some responsibility for it departed from Corinth of their own accord. The rest of the citizens willingly received back those who were in exile.

[35] When all these matters had been accomplished, and when the cities had sworn to abide by the peace that the King had proclaimed, the various armies and navies were disbanded. For the Spartans and the Athenians and the allies, this was the first peace after the war following the destruction of the walls of Athens.[a] [36] Although the Spartans during this war had been rather evenly matched with their opponents, they nevertheless gained a much more eminent position from this so-called Peace of Antalkidas:[a] for they had become champions of the peace that had been sent down by the King; they had gained autonomy for the Greek cities; they had added Corinth as their ally and made the cities of Boeotia independent from Thebes,[b] something they had long desired to do; and they had stopped the Argives from making Corinth their own by threatening to go to war with them if they did not depart from Corinth.

[1] Since these matters had progressed as the Spartans had wished, they decided to punish all their allies who during the war had been hostile to them and more favorable to their enemies than to themselves, and to deal with them in such a way that they could not be disloyal in the future. First, then, they sent to the Mantineians[a] and ordered them to tear down their wall, saying that otherwise they could not be confident that they would not take the enemy's side. [2] They brought the following charges against them: first, that they had learned that the Mantineians had been sending grain to the Argives[a] even while the Spartans were at war with them; second, that the Mantineians had occasionally failed to send their military

---

5.1.35–36
386
GREECE
Thus peace is established in Greece. Sparta gains the most from its terms, as she becomes the guardian of the King's Peace, and other states are weakened by the requirement that all cities be independent.

5.2.1–2
385/4
MANTINEIA
The Spartans decide to punish those allies who were were hostile to them in the recent war. They demand that Mantineia tear down its city wall to ensure loyalty and list many reasons for this.

5.1.34a For this garrison, see 4.4.6 and 4.5.1. Maintenance of the garrison would be a violation of the peace, for it would be an infringement of the autonomy clause.

5.1.34b The political union between Corinth and Argos (4.4.6) was dissolved.

5.1.34c The massacre of those who had favored Corinthian independence by those who favored its union with Argos. See 4.4.2.

5.1.35a There had been war since 395, when the Corinthian War broke out; see 3.5.3ff.

5.1.36a Xenophon never calls this treaty the King's Peace, as it was generally known; rather, he calls it the Peace of Antalkidas, for the Spartan who estab-

lished the treaty between Sparta and Persia that permitted the Persians to intimidate Athens and force her adherence to a general peace. Throughout, Xenophon downplays the role of the Persian King in Greek politics, which leads him to omit or at least deprecate Persian power to order Greek affairs.

5.1.36b Making the cities of Boeotia independent of Thebes greatly reduced that city's power.

5.2.1a Mantineia: Map 5.2.13, BY.

5.2.2a Argos: Map 5.2.13, BY.

forces to serve with those of Sparta on the pretext that a sacred truce was then in effect; and finally they charged that whenever the Mantineians did accompany the Spartan forces, they served with them badly. The Spartans also said that they were aware that the Mantineians were resentful whenever anything good happened to the Spartans and, conversely, were delighted when some misfortune overtook them. It was also said that the Thirty Years Peace between Sparta and Mantineia, which had been made after the battle at Mantineia,[b] expired in this year.

[3] When the Mantineians refused to take down their wall, the Spartans declared war on them. Now Agesilaos requested that Sparta relieve him of the command against Mantineia, saying that the Mantineians had rendered many services to his father in the wars with Messenia.[a] And so Agesipolis[b] led out the army, even though his father Pausanias[c] had been very friendly with the leaders of the popular party at Mantineia. [4] When Agesipolis entered Mantineian territory, he first began to ravage the countryside. When, despite this damage, the Mantineians still refused to take down their wall, Agesipolis next dug a trench in a circle around the city, using half of the soldiers to do the digging and the other half to stand guard in arms in front of them. After the trench was completed, Agesipolis could safely build a wall around the city.[a] But he learned that there was a large amount of grain within the city (there had been an excellent harvest the year before), and he became concerned that it would be burdensome to wear out Sparta and her allies with a long siege, so he proceeded to dam up the river, which was quite a good-sized one, that flowed through the city.[b]

[5] Once he had done this, the river could not flow out from the city, and the water began to rise above not only the foundations of the houses but also the foundations of the city's wall. The bricks at the bottom of the wall became soaked with water and failed to support the bricks above, so that the wall at first cracked and then began to sag. The Mantineians for a time tried to prop up the wall with timbers and to attempt by various means to keep the tower[a] from falling; but they were defeated by the water and, fearing that if the wall fell at any place they would all become

5.2.3–5
385/4
MANTINEIA
When the Mantineians refuse to destroy their wall, Agesipolis leads the army against them. Finding the enemy well prepared for a siege, he secures their surrender by damming the river and flooding the city. Sparta demands as a condition for peace that the Mantineians abandon their city and live in villages instead.

5.2.2b According to Thucydides (5.81.2), the treaty had been made in 418/7, so it would have expired in 388/7, a few years before this. Either Xenophon or the Spartans have made a mistake.

5.2.3a Messenia: Map 5.2.13, BX. The wars referred to here are the series of campaigns normally called the Third Messenian War, c. 464.

5.2.3b Agesipolis: Spartan king. See Appendix M, §1.

5.2.3c The Spartan king Pausanias had been exiled ten years earlier (3.5.25) and was still alive in exile (5.2.6). In fact, we know from inscriptional evidence that he outlived Agesipolis. For more on Pausanias, see Appendix M, §19.

5.2.4a Such a fortification, called a wall of circumvallation, was built outside and around the city's defensive wall. This made it easier for a besieging party to reduce its forces yet still prevent breakouts from the city and keep supplies from being brought in.

5.2.4b Diodorus (Appendix O, Selections from the *Histories* of Diodorus Siculus Relevant to Xenophon's *Hellenika*, Fragment 15.12) and the second-century C.E. travel writer Pausanias (8.8.7) say that the river flowed past the town, but they perhaps based this on Mantineia as it was rebuilt in 370 (see 6.5.3).

5.2.5a The tower must have been on that part of the wall that threatened to collapse.

prisoners of war, they now agreed to take down their wall. But the Spartans then said they would conclude no formal peace with them unless they also agreed to leave their city and to dwell instead in villages. The Mantineians, considering that it was a matter of dire necessity, agreed to do this, too.[b]

5.2.6
385/4
MANTINEIA
The leaders of the popular party are allowed to depart without harm.

[6] Those in the city who had been supporters of Argos and those who were the leaders of the popular party thought that they would be put to death by the Spartans, but Agesipolis' father had persuaded his son that these men should be permitted to depart from the city in safety (there were sixty of them). The Spartan soldiers lined both sides of the road, beginning at the city gates, and watched these men as they were leaving. And although they hated them, they nevertheless kept their hands off them—more easily, in fact, than did the Mantineians of the aristocratic party. Let this be on record, then, as a great example of obedience to authority.

5.2.7
384
MANTINEIA
The Mantineians are split into four separate villages as of old. The wealthy citizens are pleased with the new political arrangement.

[7] After this, the city wall was taken down and the Mantineians were settled into four villages,[a] dwelling just as they had in ancient times. At first they were distressed that they had been forced to take down the houses they already had and build others in their place; but later the wealthy were pleased with what had been done, because they now dwelt nearer to their estates (which were located around the villages), they now had an aristocratic government, and they were freed from the burden of demagogues. After this, the Spartans sent not one mustering officer but four, one to each of the villages, and the Mantineians now served much more enthusiastically than when they had lived under a democratic government. This is how matters turned out at Mantineia, and men became wiser from this incident in one way at least: that one should not have a river flow between one's walls.[b]

5.2.8–10
384
SPARTA-PHLEIOUS
Exiles from Phleious appeal to Sparta for help, and when the Spartans ask the Phleiasians to voluntarily accept the exiles' restoration, the Phleiasians vote to take the exiles back and restore their property.

[8] When the exiles from Phleious[a] learned that the Spartans were investigating the conduct toward Sparta of each of their allies during the war, they went to Sparta, thinking the time was now right, and reminded the Spartans that as long as they had been in charge at Phleious, the city had received the Spartans within its walls and had gone on campaign wherever the Spartans had led them. But when they were in exile, the people of Phleious did not at all follow the Spartans' lead and in fact refused to allow

5.2.5b Agesilaos' demand that the Mantineians leave the city to live in villages could have been based on a strict interpretation of the autonomy clause of the King's Peace, but it more likely reflects Sparta's concern that a centralized Mantineian state on her northern border would be much more difficult for Sparta to control than a number of separate and independent villages; see Appendix H, Political Leagues (Other Than Sparta's) in Xenophon's *Hellenika*, §8. One of the key steps taken by the Theban general Epaminondas in the 360s was to assist in the construction of a fortified central

Arcadian city, Megalopolis, to serve as a capital for the new Arcadian Federation, which could effectively close Sparta's access to the north and limit her power. See n. 7.5.5d and Appendix H, §1.
5.2.7a Diodorus (Appendix O, 15.5.4) says it was five villages.
5.2.7b On Sparta's methods to control her allies, see Appendix E, §18–19.
5.2.8a Phleious: Map 5.2.13, BY. These were the pro-Spartan oligarchic exiles mentioned last at 4.4.15 (391) as having been driven out previously by the Phleiasians.

the Spartans—and *only* the Spartans—to enter their city. [9] When the ephors heard this, they thought it merited attention. So they sent to the city of the Phleiasians and they stated that the exiles were friends of the Spartan state and that they had been driven into exile although they had committed no crimes. The Spartans said further that they wished to bring about the return of the exiles to their city not by compulsion but with the willingness of the Phleiasians themselves. When the Phleiasians heard this, they became afraid that in the event of a Spartan attack, some of their own citizens might let the exiles into the city, because there were, after all, many kinsmen of the exiles still in the city, and other people who were well disposed toward the exiles for other reasons. In addition, as is common in many Greek cities, they were concerned that there were some men in their city who desired a change of government and would wish to bring back the exiled group. [10] Fearing such possibilities, the Phleiasians voted to receive back the exiles, to return any undisputed property, and to compensate from the public treasury any of those who had previously purchased the exiles' property. And if a dispute were to arise between the two parties, the matter would be decided in court. These then were the steps that were at that time taken concerning the Phleiasian exiles.

[11] Then ambassadors came to Sparta from Akanthos and Apollonia, the two largest cities in the vicinity of Olynthos,[a] and when the ephors heard why they had come, they brought them into the assembly of the Spartans and the allies.[b] [12] There Kleigenes of Akanthos addressed them:

"Men of Sparta and of her allies, we think that a great danger is growing in Hellas,[a] one of which you are not yet aware of. Nearly all of you know, of course, that Olynthos is the greatest city of all those in Thrace.[b] Now these Olynthians have won over some of the neighboring cities on the basis that they would all use the same laws and become fellow citizens. Then they proceeded to take over some of the larger cities in the region. After this, they even tried to liberate some of the cities of Macedon[c] from the rule of Amyntas, the Macedonian king.[d] [13] And when the Macedonian cities nearest Olynthos did go over to their side, the Olynthians swiftly marched against other cities that were farther away and larger. When we left, they

5.2.11–13
382
SPARTA
Envoys from Akanthos and Apollonia arrive to complain and warn the Spartans of the expansion of Olynthos, which had taken over many neighboring cities and was driving King Amyntas of Macedon from his cities.

5.2.11a Akanthos, Apollonia, Olynthos (all in Chalcidice): Map 5.2.13, AY. The Akanthians are really warning Sparta of the newly powerful Chalcidian League. This league was formed in 432/1 and by now included many of the major cities of Chalcidice. Its headquarters were at Olynthos and, as we learn here, its people shared a common citizenship and common laws. See Appendix H, §7.
5.2.11b Diodorus (Appendix O, 15.19) writes that King Amyntas of Macedon made a direct appeal for assistance to the Spartans. See also Appendix E, §18, for Pelo-
ponnesian League procedures.
5.2.12a Hellas (the Greek name for Greece): Map 5.2.13, BX.
5.2.12b Thrace: Map 5.2.13, AY.
5.2.12c Macedon: Map 5.2.13, AY.
5.2.12d Amyntas had taken the Macedonian throne in the late 390s but was expelled by the Illyrians (Illyria: Map 5.2.13, AX) in the mid-380s. Then the Chalcidian League took over Macedonian cities and refused to restore them to Macedon a year or two later when Amyntas was restored to his throne by the Thessalians (Thessaly: Map 5.2.13, AY).

were already holding many other cities, and especially Pella,[a] which is the greatest of all Macedonian cities. We learned, too, that Amyntas had withdrawn from his cities and was already all but expelled from Macedon. Moreover, the Olynthians sent to us and to the people of Apollonia, telling us that unless we presented ourselves to campaign together with them, they would march against us.

5.2.14–19
382
SPARTA
The envoys ask Sparta to help them maintain their independence from Olynthos, pointing out the many ways that Olynthos can and may increase its power, and the inconsistency of allowing Olynthos to absorb other cities while preventing Thebes from doing so in Boeotia and Arcadia. They add that Olynthos is not yet formidable but might soon become so.

[14] "But we, men of Sparta, wish to follow our ancestral laws and to be an independent city. If, however, someone does not come to our assistance, we too will have to join the Olynthians' side. And yet they now have more than eight hundred[a] hoplites and even more peltasts. And their cavalry, if we join them, will number more than one thousand. [15] When we left, there were also Athenian[a] and Boeotian[b] ambassadors there. We were told that the Olynthians had already voted to send their own ambassadors to Athens and Thebes[c] to discuss an alliance. Now if Olynthian forces are to be added to those of the Athenians and Boeotians, you should be aware that it may no longer be so easy to deal with them. You must realize that because they hold Poteidaia,[d] which is on the Isthmus of Pallene,[e] the cities farther down that peninsula[f] will also be subject to them. And although these cities hate the Olynthians, nevertheless they did not dare to send ambassadors with us who would inform you about the state of affairs there—and you should interpret their absence as yet another piece of evidence that these cities are in a state of utmost fear. [16] Consider this, too: how is it reasonable for you to take great care to prevent Boeotia from uniting and yet ignore a much greater power that is being consolidated, one that is beginning strong not only by land but also by sea? For what stands in their way? They have good timber in their own land for building ships, revenues from many harbors and trading posts, and an abundant food supply that supports a large population. [17] And then one should also consider their neighbors—those Thracians who are not ruled by a king[a] and who have for a long time now been paying court to the Olynthians. And if the Thracians should come under the control of the Olynthians, they would be a great force added to the Olynthians' own. Indeed, if the Thracians were to follow the Olynthians' lead, the Olynthians would immediately stretch their hands to the gold mines in Mount Pangaion.[b] And we are not saying anything here that has not already been discussed a thousand times by the Olynthian people. [18] And how would one then describe the Olynthians' haughtiness? God, I suppose, ordained it such that as a people's power increases, so too does their pride.

5.2.13a	Pella: Map 5.2.13, AY. The capital city of Macedon.	5.2.15e	Pallene Peninsula: Map 5.2.13, AY.
5.2.14a	This number is thought to be corrupt, since it seems far too small.	5.2.15f	This would include Mende and Skione: Map 5.2.13, AY.
5.2.15a	Athens: Map 5.2.13, BY.	5.2.17a	These are the Chalcidian Thracians, as distinct from the Thracians of northeast Thrace: see 3.2.9, 4.8.26, and Map 5.3.13, AY.
5.2.15b	Boeotia: Map 5.2.13, BY.		
5.2.15c	Thebes: Map 5.2.13, BY.		
5.2.15d	Poteidaia (in Chalcidice): Map 5.2.13, AY.	5.2.17b	Mount Pangaion: Map 5.2.13, AY.

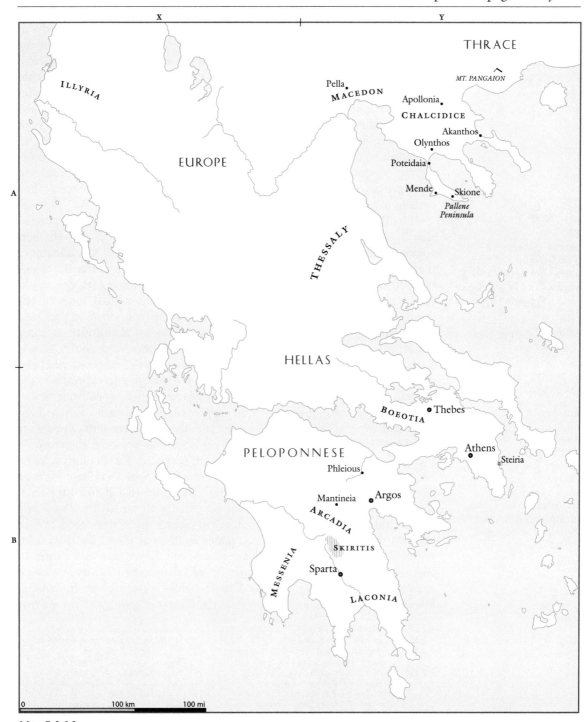

X   Y

THRACE

MT. PANGAION

ILLYRIA

Pella
MACEDON

Apollonia
CHALCIDICE

Akanthos

Olynthos

EUROPE

Poteidaia

A

Mende   Skione

*Pallene
Peninsula*

THESSALY

HELLAS

BOEOTIA Thebes

PELOPONNESE

Athens

Steiria

Phleious

Mantineia Argos

ARCADIA

B

SKIRITIS

MESSENIA

Sparta

LACONIA

0   100 km   100 mi

MAP 5.2.13

"So, then, men of Sparta and of the allied states, we have informed you of how matters stand there. Discuss these affairs if they seem to you to be worthy of your concern. But you must know this also: that the Olynthians' power, although great, is not yet one that is difficult to wrestle with, because those cities that now, against their will, have a common citizenship with the Olynthians will swiftly revolt from them if they see a substantial power standing up to them. [19] If, however, over time they become joined by rights of intermarriage and property among themselves—things that they have already voted for—and if they realize that they may profit from following the conqueror (just as the Arcadians,[a] when they join your expeditions, both preserve their own possessions and acquire those of others), then perhaps it will no longer be so easy for you to dissolve their union."

[20] When this speech was finished, the Spartans gave the allies permission to speak, and they asked them to give what they thought was the best advice for the Peloponnese[a] as a whole and for all the allies.[b] And many of them, especially those who wished to curry favor with the Spartans, recommended that an army be raised, and so it was resolved that each city would send a proportionate contingent sufficient to make a total force of ten thousand men. [21] There were also proposals that any city that preferred to contribute money in place of men could do so at the rate of three Aeginetan obols per man;[a] and that if a city usually furnished cavalry, then it should provide the pay of four hoplites in place of each horseman; [22] and if any of the cities should not contribute its share to the expedition, the Spartans were permitted to fine that city one stater[a] per day per man.

[23] After these proposals were approved, the Akanthians stood up again and tried to show that, although the decisions were good ones, they could not be quickly implemented. They said that it would therefore be preferable, while this main force was being prepared, for a commander to be sent out immediately and with him a force from Sparta (as large as could be mobilized) and the rest of the cities. They said that if this happened, those cities in the north that had not yet allied with the Olynthians would remain independent, while those that had already been compelled to join the Olynthians would become less reliable to them as allies. [24] This resolution also was passed, and the Spartans sent out Eudamidas with a force of around two thousand troops, made up of emancipated helots[a] and men drawn from the *perioikoi* and the Skiritai.[b] Before marching out, Eudamidas asked the ephors to allow his brother Phoibidas to gather the troops that

5.2.20–22
382
SPARTA-CHALCIDICE
The Spartans and their allies vote to raise and send a force of ten thousand to oppose Olynthos.

5.2.23–24
382
SPARTA-CHALCIDICE
At the urging of the envoys, the Spartans decide to immediately send a force of two thousand, made up of emancipated helots, *perioikoi*, and Skiritai, with Eudamidas in command.

5.2.19a Arcadia: Map 5.2.13, BY.
5.2.20a Peloponnese: Map 5.2.13, BX.
5.2.20b See Appendix E, §18, for powers granted to Sparta's Peloponnesian League allies.
5.2.21a Three Aeginetan obols per day. This was the equivalent of about 4.3 Attic obols (Attic coins were about seventy percent by weight of their Aeginetan counterparts). See Appendix I, §9, 13.
5.2.22a Stater: in this case probably a coin on the

Aeginetan standard, which would make its weight that of 2 drachmas, or 12.2 grams. See Appendix I, §7, 9, 13.
5.2.24a Helots: serfs tied to the land and forced to cultivate it for the Spartans. See Appendix E, §12, and Appendix F, §6.
5.2.24b Skiritai: the people of Skiritis (Map 5.2.13, BY), on the northern frontier of Spartan territory. See Appendix F, §9, and n. O.15.32.1a.

had been assigned to him but had been left behind and to bring them after him. He himself, when he came to the neighborhood of Thrace, sent garrisons to those cities that requested them and won over willingly the city of Poteidaia, even though that city was already an ally of the Olynthians. Using Poteidaia as his base, Eudamidas carried on the war as best he could, given that he had a force inferior to that of the enemy.

[25] When Phoibidas had gathered together the remaining troops assigned to Eudamidas, he marched out with them from Sparta.[a] When he arrived at Thebes,[b] he camped outside the city near the gymnasium. The Thebans at that time were split into warring factions. Ismenias and Leontiades happened to be the polemarchs;[c] they were at odds with each other, and each of them was the leader of a political club. Now Ismenias would not even approach Phoibidas because of his hatred of the Spartans, but Leontiades paid court to him and, when he had gotten on intimate terms with him, spoke as follows:

[26] "Phoibidas, you can on this day accomplish for your country the greatest good. For if you will follow me with your hoplites, I will lead you onto the acropolis. And if that happens, you may assume that Thebes will fall wholly under the power of Sparta and those of us who are Sparta's friends. [27] Now, as you can see, it has been proclaimed that no Theban shall go with you in your expedition against the Olynthians.[a] But if you join with us to accomplish what I have suggested, we Thebans will immediately send many hoplites and cavalrymen with you. And so you will assist your brother with a great force, and while he is intending to subdue Olynthos, you will have subdued Thebes, a much greater city than Olynthos."

[28] When Phoibidas heard this, his spirits were raised, since he had in fact a much greater passion for accomplishing some great deed than he did for life itself; he was not, however, considered a man who thought things through or possessed a high degree of intelligence. In any case, he agreed to this plan, and Leontiades ordered him to march out as if he were preparing to depart from Theban territory. "But when the right time comes," said Leontiades, "I will come to you and I myself will direct you."

[29] At this time the Theban Council was meeting in the portico in the marketplace, because the women of Thebes were celebrating the Thesmophoria[a] on the Kadmeia.[b] It was midday during the summer, the streets were completely deserted, and it was at this point that Leontiades went out on his horse, turned Phoibidas around,[c] and led him straight to the acropolis. He stationed Phoibidas and his men within the acropolis and gave him

5.2.25–27
382
THEBES
After Phoibidas and his troops camp near Thebes, a city faction led by Leontiades tries to persuade the unwise and ambitious Spartan commander to seize the Theban acropolis in order to take control of the city and to support the rule of the pro-Spartan faction.

5.2.28
382
THEBES
Phoibidas, who is ambitious but not very bright, agrees to the plan.

5.2.29
382
THEBES
At noon, with the streets deserted, Leontiades leads the Spartans to the acropolis, which they occupy.

5.2.25a Sparta: Map 5.3.14.
5.2.25b Thebes: Map 5.3.14, inset.
5.2.25c These polemarchs were the chief magistrates of the city of Thebes, not Spartan military commanders.
5.2.27a Olynthos: Map 5.3.14.
5.2.29a Thesmophoria: a three-day festival celebrated by women only, in honor of Demeter and Persephone. See Appendix J, §8.

5.2.29b Kadmeia: the acropolis of Thebes. It was named after Kadmos, the founder of the city, and is thought to have been the site for meetings of its senate and Assembly.
5.2.29c Phoibidas was pretending to be leaving Theban territory, so Leontiades redirects him toward Thebes.

the key to the gates,[d] instructing him to let no one into the place unless he himself should order them to do so, and he then went directly to the meeting of the Council.

[30] When he arrived there, he made the following speech: "Gentlemen, do not in any way lose heart because the Spartans now possess our citadel, for they say that they have come as enemies only to those who are eager for war. Now since the law provides that the polemarch may arrest anyone who seems to be committing acts punishable by death, I arrest Ismenias here, on the grounds that he is inciting people to war. You captains and those mustered with you, stand up and arrest this man and take him to the stipulated place." [31] Now those who were privy to the plan were at hand, and they obeyed and arrested Ismenias. As for those who did not know of the plan and were members of the faction opposed to Leontiades, some of them immediately fled from the city, fearing that they would be killed, while others went first to their homes, but on learning that Ismenias had been imprisoned in the Kadmeia, they departed for Athens.[a] They were men of the faction of Androkleidas[b] and Ismenias, and there were about three hundred of them.

[32] After this, the Thebans chose another polemarch in place of Ismenias, and Leontiades immediately went to Sparta. He discovered there that the ephors and the majority of the citizens were angry with Phoibidas because he had acted without authorization from Sparta. Agesilaos, however, said that if Phoibidas had harmed Sparta, then he should by right be punished, but if he had benefited Sparta, then it had long been the custom at Sparta that a commander in the field was permitted to act on the spot by himself to effect this. And so, he said, what they should examine was whether Phoibidas' actions had benefited or harmed the Spartans.[a]

[33] Then Leontiades went before the assembly and spoke as follows: "Men of Sparta, before the events that have just happened, you yourselves used to say that the Thebans were hostile to you, because you would see them acting as friends toward your enemies and as enemies to your friends. Did they not refuse to campaign with you against the popular party in the Peiraieus[a] who were your most bitter enemies? And did they not go to war with the Phocians[b] when they saw that you were friendly to those people? [34] Then again, knowing that you were at war with the Olynthians, they tried to make an alliance with them. And you for your part in those days were always on the alert for news that the Thebans were trying to compel all of Boeotia[a] to submit to their rule. But now, given what has happened, you need not fear the Thebans at all. Instead, a brief message will be enough for you to accomplish there as much as you desire,

5.2.30–31
382
THEBES
Leontiades announces the Spartan occupation of the Kadmeia, the acropolis, to the Theban Council and, acting as polemarch, arrests his rival Ismenias. Three hundred Thebans opposed to this coup flee to Athens.

5.2.32
382
SPARTA
Many Spartans condemn Phoibidas for acting without authorization, but Agesilaos says the issue is whether he has harmed or benefited Sparta.

5.2.33–34
382
SPARTA
Leontiades speaks to the Spartan Assembly, defending the seizure of the Theban acropolis as advantageous to Sparta.

5.2.29d The key to the gates to the citadel, not to the city walls.
5.2.31a Athens: Map 5.3.14 and inset.
5.2.31b Androkleidas and Ismenias led an anti-Spartan faction at Thebes. They schemed to initiate a war between Sparta and Thebes in 395–394, thirteen years earlier. See 3.5.4.
5.2.32a For Agesilaos' attitude here, see Appen-

dix G, Agesilaos, §9. See also Appendix E, §18, concerning Sparta's imperial policy.
5.2.33a Peiraieus: Map 5.3.14, inset. The refusal referred to occurred in 403 and is described by Xenophon at 2.4.30.
5.2.33b Phocis: Map 5.3.14.
5.2.34a Boeotia: Map 5.3.14, inset.

provided that just as we have taken your interests to heart, so you, too, take to heart ours."

[35] Upon hearing all this, the Spartans resolved that they would maintain the garrison on the Theban acropolis, inasmuch as it had been seized, and that Ismenias should be put on trial. They then sent out three judges from Sparta and one each from the allied cities, large and small alike. And only after the judges had taken their seats were the charges against Ismenias announced: namely, that he had taken the side of the barbarian; that he had become a guest-friend of Persia with the goal of harming Greece; that he had received some of the money sent by the Persian King;[a] and that he, together with Androkleidas, was most responsible for all the upheaval throughout Greece. [36] Ismenias defended himself against all these charges, but he failed to persuade the judges that he had not engaged in great and evil schemes. He was condemned and put to death. Leontiades and his men were now in charge of the city, and they rendered even more services to the Spartans than the latter required of them.

[37] After all these matters had been accomplished, the Spartans were much more eager to dispatch the joint force against Olynthos. They sent out Teleutias as governor, and with him the full Spartan proportion of the ten-thousand-man force.[a] To the allied cities they sent word that they were to follow Teleutias' orders in accordance with the resolution voted previously by the allies. Not only did all the rest of the allies enthusiastically support Teleutias (since he had a reputation for showing gratitude to those who helped him), but the Thebans were also particularly eager to send hoplites and cavalry, because Agesilaos was Teleutias' brother.[b]

[38] Teleutias then marched out and proceeded deliberately, without haste, taking care not to harm any of Sparta's friends on his advance and wanting also to accumulate as great a force as he could. He sent a messenger on ahead to Amyntas[a] to tell him that if in fact he wished to recover his kingdom, he should hire mercenaries and give money to the neighboring kings so that they would become his allies. He also sent word to Derdas, the ruler of Elimeia,[b] informing him that the Olynthians had already conquered the greater power of Macedon and they would not fail to come against his lesser power unless someone put a stop to their insolent behavior. [39] By such means, he commanded a much larger force when he arrived in allied territory. When he came to Poteidaia,[a] he put his men in battle order and advanced from there into the enemy's lands. On his way to Olynthos he did no burning or cutting down, reasoning that any destruction of that sort would obstruct his moving forward and backward while he

5.2.35–36
382
SPARTA-THEBES
The Spartans vote to garrison the Theban acropolis and to send judges to Thebes to try Ismenias. He is condemned to death. Leontiades and his faction rule Thebes and support Sparta.

5.2.37–39
382
THESSALY-MACEDON
Teleutias advances on Olynthos carefully, avoiding any harm to friendly states and gathering a great army, including a large contingent of Thebans, as he advances. He sends ahead to Amyntas to recruit mercenaries.

5.2.35a   The Persian gold referred to here is mentioned at 3.5.1.
5.2.37a   That is, they sent all the men whom Sparta was required proportionately to contribute to the force at 5.2.20.
5.2.37b   The pro-Spartan quisling government in Thebes was particularly eager to support an expedition led by Teleutias because, as he was Agesilaos' half brother, a good

word from him would have especially great weight with Agesilaos, on whose continued favor Leontiades and the other quislings were totally dependent.
5.2.38a   Amyntas, king of Macedon: Map 5.3.14.
5.2.38b   Elimeia: Map 5.3.14.
5.2.39a   Poteidaia: Map 5.3.14.

was there, whereas, upon his departure from the city, it would be advantageous to fell the trees and lay them down in such a way that they would form an obstacle to any attack from the rear.

[40] When he was not even ten stades[a] from the city, Teleutias halted the army and took command of the left wing, for it happened that in this way he himself would advance toward the gates from which the enemy came out. The rest of the line of allies stretched away from him to his right. On the far right he stationed the cavalry made up of Laconians,[b] Thebans, and as many of the Macedonians as were present, while next to himself on the left he stationed Derdas and his cavalry, about four hundred in number. He did this both because he admired this cavalry unit and because he wished to honor Derdas, so that he would be glad he had joined the expedition.

[41] When the enemy came out, they formed an opposing line beneath the wall and, deploying themselves in close order, charged Teleutias' line at the point where the Laconians and Boeotians were stationed. They struck Polycharmus, the Spartan cavalry commander, from his horse and wounded him many times as he lay on the ground; they killed others as well, until finally they put the cavalry stationed on the right wing to flight. As these fled, the part of the army next to them also began to give way, and the entire force would probably have been defeated if Derdas had not immediately advanced toward the gates of the city with his entire cavalry force. Teleutias, with the forces stationed around him, also marched toward the city. [42] The Olynthian cavalry realized what was happening and, becoming afraid that they would be cut off from the gates, turned about and returned to the city in great haste. And that is where Derdas killed a great number of the cavalry as they attempted to pass by him. The Olynthian infantry also retreated into the city, but not many of them were killed, since they had remained close to the wall. [43] When Teleutias had gained the victory and a trophy had been set up,[a] he departed, and as he marched back, he cut down the trees. He campaigned there throughout this summer, after which he disbanded the Macedonian force and the cavalry of Derdas. The Olynthians, however, continued to raid the territory of the cities allied with Sparta, taking booty and killing men.

[1] At the beginning of the following spring, about six hundred Olynthian horsemen made a raid into Apollonia[a] at midday. As they went about plundering they were scattered in many different places. Derdas with his cavalry happened to have arrived this day and was at that time taking his morning meal in Apollonia. When he saw the raid, he took no action, though he kept the horses saddled and their riders fully armed. But when the

5.2.40–43
382
OLYNTHOS
In a battle before the city walls, the Olynthians gain an initial success, but finally an advance by Derdas forces them, with some loss, to retreat within their walls. The Spartans and their allies remain there throughout the summer but then disperse. The Olynthians raid the lands of cities allied with Sparta.

5.3.1–2
381
OLYNTHOS
Derdas repels an Olynthian raid on Apollonia, driving the invaders back to the gates of their city and killing many of them.

5.2.40a   Something less than 10 Attic stades of 583 feet each would convert to about a mile. See Appendix I, §4–5, 13.
5.2.40b   Laconia: Map 5.3.14.
5.2.43a   On trophies in hoplite warfare, see Appendix L, §13.
5.3.1a   Apollonia: Map 5.3.14.

Olynthians, with complete disdain, came into the suburbs and indeed up to the very gates of the city, then he rushed out, keeping his men in good battle order. [2] When the Olynthians saw him, they began to flee, but Derdas did not let up once he had routed them but instead pursued them for more than ninety stades,[a] killing them as he went along, until he drove them back to the very wall of Olynthos. Derdas was said to have killed around eighty horsemen in this action. From that day on, the enemy remained closer to their walls, and they worked only a very small portion of their land.

[3] Later, Teleutias moved his army toward the city of Olynthos so that he might destroy any tree or anything else that the enemy might try to cultivate. As he was approaching, the Olynthian horsemen quietly came out from the walls and calmly advanced across the river that flowed past the city. They were going toward the opposing army, but when Teleutias saw them, he became annoyed at their audacity and immediately ordered Tlemonidas, the commander of the peltasts,[a] to attack the enemy at a run. [4] When the Olynthians saw the peltasts charging forward, they turned about and quietly retreated back across the river. The peltasts, however, pursued them very boldly, in the belief that they were in flight, and they crossed over the river. At that point the Olynthian horsemen saw that the men who had crossed the river were now in a place where they would be easy to handle, so they turned and attacked them, killing Tlemonidas and more than a hundred of the others.

[5] Teleutias grew angry when he saw this happening and, taking up his weapons, he led his hoplites swiftly against the enemy. He ordered the peltasts and his own cavalry to pursue the enemy and not let up. Now many others in this situation have pursued their antagonists too close to their own walls, only to be forced to make a costly retreat; and these men, too, when they were pelted from the towers, were compelled to protect themselves from the missiles and to retreat in complete disarray. [6] It was at this point that the Olynthians sent out more of their cavalry, with the peltasts in support. Finally the hoplites also rushed out and fell upon a Spartan line now in disarray. Teleutias fell fighting there, and when this happened, those around him immediately gave way, and no one any longer stood his ground, but every one of them fled. Some went toward Spartolos,[a] others toward Akanthos[b] or Apollonia, but the majority headed for Poteidaia. And as they fled in different directions, so, too, the enemy pursued in different directions and killed very many men, including the part of the army that was especially valuable.[c]

[7] Now I claim that men can learn from such experiences, and they can

5.3.3–4
381
OLYNTHOS
Teleutias orders his peltasts out to drive back the Olynthian cavalry. They do so but rashly cross a river to extend their advance and are attacked and driven back in turn, with great losses.

5.3.5–6
381
OLYNTHOS
Angry at this repulse, Teleutias attacks with all his forces, but as his troops come near the city walls, they are driven back in disarray. When suddenly attacked by the Olynthians, they break and flee in all directions. Teleutias and many other Spartans are killed.

5.3.7
Xenophon lectures against anger in general, especially when it occurs in generals.

5.3.2a   Ninety Attic stades of 583 feet each would convert to almost 10 miles.
5.3.3a   Peltasts were troops armed only with a small, light shield, a javelin, and a short sword. Unhindered by body armor, they could move much more quickly than the fully armed hoplite, whose equipment was both far heavier and far more expensive

than theirs. As a type, they seem to have originated in Thrace. See Appendix L, §7.
5.3.6a   Spartolos: Map 5.3.14.
5.3.6b   Akanthos: Map 5.3.14.
5.3.6c   Diodorus (Appendix O, 15.21.2) says that more than 1,200 men on the Spartan side were slain.

learn especially that it is not right to punish anyone in anger—even a slave, since masters who are angry often themselves suffer greater evils than they inflict on their servants. And it is a complete and utter mistake to attack an enemy with anger rather than with judgment. For anger acts without foresight, whereas judgment has in view a way to harm one's enemy without suffering any hurt from him in return.[a]

5.3.8–9
381
OLYNTHOS
In response to the defeat of Teleutias, the Spartans organize a larger expedition against Olynthos led by Agesipolis.

[8] When the Spartans heard about this event, they held a council and decided that they must send a force that was at least equal to or greater than the one they had already sent, so that they might dampen the pride of the victors and ensure that their own previous actions were not in vain. Having decided this, they sent out Agesipolis their king as commander, and with him thirty Spartiates, just as they had for Agesilaos in his expedition to Asia.[a] [9] Many *perioikoi*[a] of the upper class volunteered to go with Agesipolis, as did foreigners trained in the Spartan system;[b] and there were also the bastard sons of Spartiates, who were a fine body of men and were quite familiar with the good things in the city.[c] Also joining the expedition were volunteers from the allied cities and cavalrymen from Thessaly,[d] wishing to become known to Agesipolis; and Amyntas and Derdas took part even more zealously than before. It was under these circumstances, then, that Agesipolis set out for Olynthos.

5.3.10–12
381
PHLEIOUS-SPARTA
The men of Phleious refuse to restore rights to the exiles, who then seek aid and redress in Sparta.

[10] Meanwhile, the people of Phleious[a] were rather brazenly failing to give any justice to the returned exiles.[b] They thought that they could get away with doing nothing because they had been commended by Agesipolis for having quickly given him so much in the way of supplies for his army.[c] They thought, too, that with Agesipolis away from Sparta, Agesilaos would not march against them, supposing that the Spartans would not allow both kings to be away from Sparta at the same time.[d] The exiles had demanded that any disputed matters be resolved before an impartial court, but the men in control of the city compelled them to have their cases decided in the city itself, where they paid no attention to the complaints of the returned exiles, who wondered what sort of justice could result where those who had committed the crimes were sitting in judgment. [11] The result was that the

5.3.7a   For Xenophon's advice on the qualities of a good general, see the Introduction, §10.10–12.
5.3.8a   For the "thirty" who had accompanied Agesilaos on his campaign in Asia (Asia Minor), see 3.4.2.
5.3.9a   *Perioikoi*: Spartans from cities around Sparta who served in the army but who did not have the full citizenship rights and privileges of Spartiates. Xenophon's comment about the "upper class" shows that although all *perioikoi* were dependent on Sparta, there was class and wealth stratification among them. See Appendix E, §10.
5.3.9b   The so-called *trophimoi xenoi*. Diogenes Laertius (2.54) says that Xenophon's own sons went through this training. See Appendix E, §20.

5.3.9c   The "good things in the city" refers to the Spartan training and upbringing, comprising not only the values it brought to men who had experienced it (honor, courage, good order, for example) but also the practices (the ascetic way of life, the training, and the competition) that fostered such values. For this system see Appendix E, §5, 20.
5.3.9d   Thessaly: Map 5.3.14.
5.3.10a   Phleious: Map 5.3.14, inset.
5.3.10b   For the Phleiasian exiles referred to here, see 5.2.10.
5.3.10c   Possibly according to the terms cited at 5.2.21.
5.3.10d   Herodotus (*Histories* 5.75) says that only one king at a time could command any Spartan or allied army or force. See Appendix E, §14.

exiles came to Sparta to make accusations against those in control of Phleious, and they were accompanied by some additional men from the city who testified that many of the citizens there also felt that the exiles were not receiving justice. Now those in charge of Phleious were furious with these men, and they imposed fines on all those who had gone to Sparta without the city's permission. [12] Those fined were reluctant to return home and remained there; they complained to the Spartans, saying that the men in the city who were now acting high-handedly were the very ones who had driven out the exiles, closed their gates to the Spartans, and acquired the exiles' property and were now impudently refusing to give it up. They were the same men who had been responsible just now for fining those who had traveled to Sparta, inflicting this penalty so that no one in the future would dare go to Sparta and report what was happening in Phleious.

[13] Now since it seemed that the Phleiasians were in fact acting outrageously, the ephors declared war on them. This did not at all displease Agesilaos, since Podanemos and his party (who at that time were members of the restored exiles) were friends of his father Archidamos; moreover, Prokles son of Hipponikos and his party were friends of Agesilaos himself.[a] [14] Agesilaos did not delay but, once the border-crossing sacrifices proved favorable, marched out immediately. Many embassies came to meet him, offering money in an attempt to persuade him not to invade Phleious. He responded to them by saying that his expedition was not undertaken to injure anyone but, rather, to bring assistance to those who had been injured. [15] They said finally that they would do anything he wished, and they begged him not to invade. But he answered in turn that he could not trust their words, since they had proved false to them before; they must instead perform some trustworthy action. When they asked what this might be, he answered, "That which you did before: when you did that, you suffered no harm at our hands." He was referring to when they had handed over their acropolis.[a] [16] They refused to do this, however, and so he invaded their land and began to lay siege to the city, quickly building an encircling wall.

Many Spartans complained that for the sake of a few people, they were incurring the hatred of a city of more than five thousand men. Indeed, the Phleiasians, in order to demonstrate their number, would conduct their assemblies in a location visible to the Spartans from outside the city. Agesilaos, however, in response to this action of the Phleiasians, contrived the following stratagem. [17] He instructed the exiles to set up a common dining area[a] for themselves and any of their friends or kin who came out from the city to visit them and who were willing to take part in the army's

5.3.13–15
381
PHLEIOUS
Agesilaos leads the army against Phleious to force the Phleiasians to treat the former exiles fairly. When Phleiasian embassies implore him not to invade, he demands that they surrender their acropolis to him.

5.3.16–17
381
PHLEIOUS
Agesilaos besieges the city and quiets Spartan grumbling by instructing the exiles to arm and support any from the city who join them. Soon they have a fine force of a thousand men.

5.3.13a   For more on Prokles, see 6.5.38. Xenophon does not mention Podanemos again.
5.3.15a   Xenophon describes this event at 4.4.15, when in 391 the Phleiasians, severely pressured by the Athenians (Athens: Map 5.3.14, inset) led by Iphikrates,

allowed the Spartans to occupy their acropolis.
5.3.17a   This refers to the famous Spartan institution of the common messes. See Appendix E, §20, and Xenophon's *Constitution of the Lacedaemonians* 3.5.

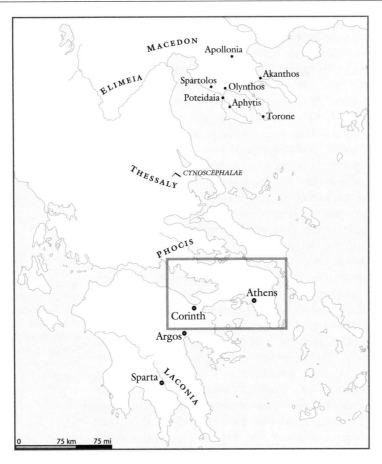

MAP 5.3.14

training; moreover, he ordered the exiles to furnish arms to these men and not to hesitate to borrow money for this purpose. They did as they were told and could soon point to more than a thousand men of splendid physique, well disciplined and extremely well armed. When the Spartans observed these men, they finally agreed that these were just the sort of men they wished to have as fellow soldiers.

[18] While Agesilaos was busy with these affairs, Agesipolis immediately set out from Macedon and advanced on Olynthos,[a] halting his army near the city. When no one came out from the city to oppose him, he laid waste any parts of the land that were still intact and invaded the territories of the allies of Olynthos and devastated their crops. He advanced on Torone[b] and took that city by force. [19] But while he was engaged in these activities, just around the height of summer, he was seized by a burning fever. And since he had previously visited the temple of Dionysos at Aphytis,[a] he now experienced a desire to visit again its shady buildings and its bright, cold waters. He was carried there still alive, but six days after he contracted the fever, he died outside the temple.[b] His body was preserved in honey and brought home to Sparta, and was given the funeral reserved for kings.[c]

[20] When Agesilaos heard what had happened to Agesipolis, he did not rejoice as one might have thought he would at the death of a rival; rather, he burst into tears and began to long for Agesipolis' company. The kings, you see, share the same lodging when they are in Sparta, and Agesilaos was the perfect companion to Agesipolis for sharing in conversations about youthful pursuits, hunting, horsemanship, and boyfriends. In addition to these things, Agesipolis showed respect for Agesilaos in their quarters, as was proper, since Agesilaos was the elder.[a] To replace Agesipolis, the Spartans sent out Polybiades as governor for Olynthos.

[21] Agesilaos' siege of Phleious had now gone on for a longer time than was thought possible in view of the grain supply in the city. The control of one's appetite makes a great difference, however, and in the Phleiasians' case, they had voted to provide the citizens with only half of the grain ration that they had given out previously, and this enabled them to withstand a siege twice as long as anyone could have reasonably expected. [22] And daring, too, sometimes differs a great deal from passivity: a certain Delphion, a man with a reputation for brilliance, gathered to himself three hundred Phleiasians, and with them he was able to prevent those who wished to make peace from doing so; he could also restrain and keep under guard those whom he distrusted. He was even able to compel the commons to take their turn at guard duty and be reliable in making their rounds. Often he and his men would run out from the city and beat

5.3.18–19
381
CHALCIDICE
Agesipolis lays waste the territory of Olynthos, captures Torone by storm, but then dies of a fever at the sanctuary of Dionysos at Aphytis.

5.3.20
381
PHLEIOUS
Agesilaos mourns the loss of a companion. Polybiades is sent out as governor of Olynthos.

5.3.21–23
379
PHLEIOUS
Despite the tenacity of the Phleiasians and the exploits of a leader of the resistance named Delphion, Phleious runs out of food and surrenders to the government of Sparta.

5.3.18a   Olynthos: Map 5.3.14.
5.3.18b   Torone: Map 5.3.14.
5.3.19a   Aphytis: Map 5.3.14.
5.3.19b   His body would have been moved out of the temple when death was imminent so as not to pollute the shrine.
5.3.19c   For Spartan royal funerals, see 3.3.1; Herodotus, *Histories* 6.58.2–3; and Plutarch, *Parallel Lives*, "Agesilaos" 40.3. See also Appendix E, §13.
5.3.20a   See Appendix E, §13.

back the men who were protecting one or another part of the wall around the city.

[23] When, however, even these picked men could no longer find food in the city although they had searched everywhere, they sent to Agesilaos and asked for a truce so that they could send an embassy to Sparta,[a] saying that they had decided to surrender the city unconditionally to those in power at Sparta. [24] This angered Agesilaos, because he was being treated as if he did not have full powers,[a] and so he sent to his friends at Sparta, telling them to arrange it so that all matters concerning the Phleiasians should be entrusted to himself; and then he allowed the embassy to proceed on its way. And although he now guarded the city even more carefully than before so that none of those in the city should escape, yet Delphion and with him another person, a branded slave who had successfully stolen many weapons from the besiegers, escaped from the city by night.

[25] When the embassy returned from Sparta and announced that the Spartans had entrusted all affairs at Phleious to Agesilaos for him to decide as he saw fit, Agesilaos rendered the following judgment. He ordered that a commission of one hundred men—fifty from the exiles, fifty from those in the city—should be established first to determine who should be allowed to live and who should justly be put to death, and then to establish a constitution by which to govern their city. He left behind a garrison with pay for six months until all these matters were accomplished. Then he dismissed the allied contingents and led the citizen part of his army home, and in this way the affair of Phleious ended, having taken one year and eight months from start to finish.

[26] Meanwhile Polybiades compelled the Olynthians to send an embassy to Sparta to discuss peace: the Olynthians had been hard pressed by famine, since food could not be brought into their city by either land or sea. The ambassadors sent by the Olynthians were fully empowered, and they agreed to a treaty stipulating that the Olynthians would have the same friends and enemies as the Spartans, that they would take part in all campaigns wherever the Spartans would lead them, and that they would be their allies. After swearing to abide by these terms, they returned home.

[27] Matters had now come to a point that was very favorable for the Spartans: the Thebans[a] and the rest of the Boeotians[b] were now wholly under Spartan control; the Corinthians[c] had become completely reliable; the Argives[d] had been humbled, since their claims to the sacred months were no longer useful to them; the Athenians[e] were isolated, with no allies at all; and all of Sparta's allies who had been hostile to her were now

5.3.23a   Sparta: Map 5.3.14.
5.3.24a   Normally, a king in the field had full powers to make all decisions. But his authority must have been tempered, at least, by the presence of two ephors on campaign with him, as Xenophon reports at 2.4.36, and would certainly have been inhibited by a "supervisory" commission of thirty Spartiates specially appointed to

accompany him, as Agesilaos had with him in Asia (3.4.2, 3.4.8, 3.4.20). See Appendix E, §14.
5.3.27a   Thebes: Map 5.3.14, inset.
5.3.27b   Boeotia: Map 5.3.14, inset.
5.3.27c   Corinth: Map 5.3.14 and inset.
5.3.27d   Argos: Map 5.3.14.
5.3.27e   Athens: Map 5.3.14 and inset.

punished.[f] In every way it seemed that Sparta had arranged her rule to be strong and secure.

[1] One might tell of many events, both Greek and non-Greek, that demonstrate that the gods are not indifferent to the impious and those who do wicked things, but for now I will keep my remarks to the matters at hand, namely the actions of the Spartans. They had sworn to allow the cities to be autonomous, yet were occupying the acropolis at Thebes; and indeed they were punished by the men who had been wronged and by them alone, even though before this time the Spartans had never been conquered by anyone. And as for the Theban citizens who wished to enslave the city to Sparta so that they themselves might rule as tyrants, it needed but seven of the exiles to bring down their power. I will now narrate how this happened.[a]

[2] There was a man named Phillidas, secretary to Archias and the other polemarchs, and he served them excellently in all matters, or so it seemed. Phillidas went to Athens on some business or other, and he there encountered Melon, one of the Theban exiles who had fled to Athens, whom he had known even before this. Melon learned from Phillidas about Archias the polemarch and the tyranny of Philippos,[a] and he realized that Phillidas hated what was happening back home in Thebes even more than he did. They therefore exchanged pledges and arrived at an agreement as to how everything should be arranged. [3] After this, Melon took the six most suitable exiles with him, armed only with daggers, and by night entered Theban territory. They spent the next day in some deserted place and then went to the city and, pretending that they were coming in from the fields, they passed through the gates of the city just at the time when the last returning laborers came in. After they entered the city, they spent that night and the following day at the home of a man named Charon.

[4] Phillidas for his part attended the polemarchs in all their affairs, and at that moment he was especially taking care of the arrangements for the feast of Aphrodite, which the polemarchs always celebrate at the end of their year in office.[a] Phillidas had long ago promised that he would bring the polemarchs the most respected and beautiful women in Thebes; and the

5.4.1
379/8
SPARTA-THEBES
Xenophon describes the justice of the gods in that Thebes, which Sparta had wronged, should be the state that conquers her.

5.4.2–3
379/8
THEBES
Xenophon describes the plot of Phillidas and Melon to assassinate the polemarchs as they celebrate the end of their terms at a banquet.

5.4.4–6
379/8
THEBES
Phillidas brings in conspirators, disguised as women and their servants, who carry daggers with which to kill the three polemarchs.

5.3.27f For the events mentioned here: Thebes and Boeotia, 5.2.36; Corinth, 5.1.34; Argos, 5.1.29, 5.1.34; Athens, 5.1.29, 5.1.35; allies punished, 5.2.1–7 (Mantineia) and 5.2.8–10 and 5.3.10–25 (Phleious).

5.4.1a For similar sentiments, see Diodorus (Appendix O, 15.1). Xenophon's narration of the liberation of Thebes that follows is especially notable for the complete omission of the activities of Pelopidas, whom both Diodorus and Plutarch (*Parallel Lives*, "Pelopidas" 7) present as the leading figure of the whole episode. For more on Pelopidas, see Appendix M, §20. For more on Xenophon's prejudice against Pelopidas, see the Introduction, §12.3–4.

5.4.2a The distinction between the two men is strangely worded; it seems as if Xenophon did not consider Philippos to be polemarch at this time. Plutarch refers to him throughout his "Pelopidas" as polemarch. Xenophon is inconsistent in his naming of these polemarchs, but it seems as if there were three: Archias, Philippos, and Hypates. According to Plutarch (*Parallel Lives*, "Pelopidas" 11.5–6), Hypates was killed immediately after Leontiades; Xenophon says nothing here about that but assumes it later in the work (7.3.7).

5.4.4a Most scholars believe that the Boeotian year began with the new moon after the winter solstice.

polemarchs—for they were that sort of men—were expecting to spend the night most pleasurably. [5] They feasted and, with Phillidas' assistance, quickly became drunk. And after much time had passed, during which they had pressed Phillidas to bring in the courtesans, he went out and brought in with him Melon and his men, three of them disguised as ladies and the rest as their maids.

[6] He brought them all into the anteroom of the treasury in the polemarchs' quarters and then himself went in and reported to the men that the women said they refused to enter the room if any of the polemarchs' servants were present there. The polemarchs then quickly ordered all their servants to depart, and Phillidas gave these men some wine and sent them off to the house of one of their number. Then he brought in the supposed courtesans and placed one next to each of the polemarchs. By prior agreement, the young men had agreed to throw off their disguise and strike as soon as they were seated. [7] This is the way, then, that some say the polemarchs died, but others say that it was as ordinary revelers that Melon and his men entered the room and killed the polemarchs.

After this, Phillidas took three of the men and went to the house of Leontiades. He knocked at the door and said that he wished to deliver a message from the polemarchs. Leontiades happened to have dined alone that evening, and he was still reclining at his table while his wife sat beside him weaving wool, and since he considered Phillidas trustworthy, he invited him in. After they entered, the men killed Leontiades and terrified his wife into silence. As they departed they told her to lock the door, adding the threat that if they found the door unlocked, they would kill everyone in the household.

[8] After these deeds were carried out, Phillidas took two men and went to the prison. He told the guard that he was bringing in a man whom the polemarchs had ordered confined. When the guard opened the door, the men immediately killed him and then set all the prisoners free. They then quickly armed these men, taking down the weapons from the stoa;[a] and leading them to the Amphieion,[b] they ordered them to remain under arms there. [9] They then immediately proclaimed to the Thebans that every one of them, both cavalry and hoplites,[a] should come out from their houses, since the tyrants were now dead. The citizens, however, as long as it was nighttime, distrusted them and did not stir; but when day came and it was evident what had happened, then all of them, hoplites and cavalry, immediately came out to help, bearing their arms. The exiles then sent horsemen

5.4.8a   It is not clear what stoa or building Xenophon is referring to here. Although it seems likely that each citizen of Thebes (and Athens) was normally responsible for his own arms and kept them in his home, presumably in these years the quisling government deprived the bulk of the Thebans of their weapons (as happened to the citizens of Athens under the rule of the

Thirty Tyrants at 2.3.20) so that they would not pose a threat to the regime.
5.4.8b   The shrine of the local hero Amphion, probably located just to the north of the Kadmeia, the acropolis of Thebes.
5.4.9a   The men who made up a city's cavalry and hoplite forces came from the two wealthiest classes of the citizenry.

to two Athenian generals stationed on the frontier.[b] And the Athenians, knowing why the men had been sent to them. . . .[c]

[10] Back on the Theban acropolis, the Spartan governor, as soon as he learned of the nighttime proclamation, sent to Plataea[a] and Thespiai[b] for help. When the Theban horsemen discovered that the Plataeans were approaching, they went out to oppose them and killed more than twenty of them. They then turned back into the city, where the Athenians, who had started from the border, had now arrived, so they launched an assault on the acropolis. [11] The men on the acropolis, realizing that they were themselves few, seeing the zeal of all the men attacking them, and learning that great rewards were being offered to the first ones to ascend the acropolis, grew fearful and said that they would be willing to depart if they were given a guarantee of safe conduct with their weapons. The Thebans granted this gladly; they made a truce and exchanged oaths, after which they dismissed the Spartans on the terms stated. [12] But as the Spartans departed, the Thebans seized any whom they recognized as their enemies and put them to death. There were some who were carried off secretly and saved by Athenians who had come from the frontier to help. But the Thebans seized all the children of the men they had put to death and slaughtered even these.

[13] When the Spartans learned what had happened, they put to death the governor,[a] who had abandoned the acropolis instead of waiting for assistance, and they declared war on the Thebans. Now Agesilaos said that he would not lead out the army: he asserted that he had begun military service more than forty years previously, and he claimed that just as other men of his age were not required to serve outside their country, so the same law also applied to the kings. But this was not in fact the reason he remained behind; rather, it was because he knew well that if he were the commander, the citizens of Sparta would accuse him of bringing troubles

5.4.10–12
379/8
THEBES
Assaulted by numerous foes, the Spartans and their allies on the Theban acropolis offer to leave if given safe conduct, which is granted. However, as they depart, the Thebans kill those whom they recognize as their political foes, and even kill their children.

5.4.13–14
378
SPARTA
When the Spartans hear of the loss of the Theban acropolis, they mobilize the army against Thebes. Agesilaos, pleading age, avoids the command, and Kleombrotos is selected instead. He marches into Theban territory but causes a minimum of damage.

5.4.9b   Xenophon seems here to be describing help from Athens that, while provided by two generals, was unofficial in nature, hence the generals could be punished subsequently (5.4.19). But according to Diodorus (Appendix O, 15.25–26), the Athenian help was voted by the Assembly and was on a large scale (five thousand hoplites and five hundred cavalry). Diodorus' account is supported by the late-fourth-century orator Deinarchos (1.39), who cites what he says was the Assembly decree and names its proposer. This apparent discrepancy between Xenophon and Diodorus has been the cause of much scholarly dispute, many scholars regarding Diodorus' version as having been inflated by patriotic exaggeration. Alternatively, the unofficial help Xenophon describes here may be separate from the official help that Diodorus mentions, which perhaps came a day or so later, and which (in this view) Xenophon has characteristically omitted.

5.4.9c   There is a gap of unknown size in the Greek text here. In the gap Xenophon probably explained how these two Athenian generals came to be at the frontier. Diodorus (Appendix O, 15.25.2–15.26.4) also gives an account of this episode, but as stated in n. 5.4.9b, it is at odds with Xenophon's version and cannot help to resolve what would have been in Xenophon's text.

5.4.10a   Plataea: Map 5.3.14, inset.
5.4.10b   Thespiai: Map 5.3.14, inset.
5.4.13a   Xenophon does not name him, no doubt because of his shameful behavior. Plutarch (*Parallel Lives*, "Pelopidas" 13.1–2) and Diodorus (Appendix O, 15.27) say that the Spartans put two of the commanders, Herippidas and Arkissos, to death and fined and exiled a third, Lysanoridas. This Herippidas is presumably the same Herippidas who accompanied Agesilaos to Asia and who was mentioned several times by Xenophon in that connection. See "Herippidas" in Appendix M, §11.

upon his country in order to give assistance to tyrants. And so he allowed his fellow citizens to make whatever other arrangements they wanted for this expedition.

[14] The ephors[a] were informed of what had happened at Thebes[b] by those who had gotten away after the slaughter there. And even though it was in the middle of winter, they sent out Kleombrotos on this, his first command.[c] Now Chabrias,[d] in command of the Athenian peltasts, was guarding the road that led through Eleutherai,[e] but Kleombrotos made his ascent[f] by the road that leads to Plataea. His peltasts went ahead of the army and encountered men on guard at the summit (these were the men who had been released from the prison at Thebes), about 150 in number, and the peltasts killed all of them, except for a few who may have escaped. Kleombrotos himself then descended to Plataea, a city that was still friendly to Sparta,[g] [15] after which he marched to Thespiai. From there he advanced to Cynoscephalae[a] in Theban territory, where he made camp and remained for about sixteen days before returning to Thespiai. He left Sphodrias[b] behind as governor, giving him one-third of each of the allied contingents and providing him with money that he had brought from home, ordering him to hire mercenaries with it, [16] which he did.

Kleombrotos in the meantime led his men home, taking the road that leads through Kreusis.[a] The soldiers were greatly perplexed as to whether they were really at war or at peace with Thebes, since what Kleombrotos had done was to lead his army into Theban territory and then depart after causing as little damage as possible.[b] [17] As he was making his way home he and his men encountered a strong wind, and some interpreted this as a sign of future events.[a] For the wind spent its violence in many ways against

5.4.14a   Ephors: see Appendix E, §16.
5.4.14b   Thebes: Map 5.3.14, inset.
5.4.14c   Kleombrotos had succeeded Agesipolis as king; see Appendix M, §15. Midwinter military campaigns were rare in ancient times because of the added hazards of inclement weather, and therefore it was unusual to entrust the command of such an expedition to a relatively untested general.
5.4.14d   Chabrias: a brilliant and successful Athenian general: see 5.1.10, 5.1.12, and Appendix M, §6.
5.4.14e   Eleutherai: Map 5.3.14, inset. See Figure 5.4.14 for a current view of a fourth-century tower at the Attic border fortress of Eleutherai. Scholars have questioned why Chabrias and Athenian troops were guarding this pass at this time. Some have seen it as evidence that the Athenians had sent official help to the Thebans very soon after the liberation. Others deny that, and certainly, since Athens was the location from which the liberation plot was organized, Athens had reason to fear Spartan retaliation, or at least that Sparta

might try to attack Thebes through Attica. So the Athenians might have posted Chabrias there simply as a precautionary move.
5.4.14f   His ascent over Mount Cithaeron from Megarian territory to Boeotia. All locations: Map 5.3.14, inset.
5.4.14g   Xenophon notes this friendship because within a few years (by 373) the Thebans had subjugated Plataea.
5.4.15a   Cynoscephalae (in Boeotia): location unknown. It should not be confused with Cynoscephalae, a mountain in Thessaly: Map 5.3.14.
5.4.15b   Sphodrias: see Appendix M, §22.
5.4.16a   Kreusis: Map 5.3.14, inset.
5.4.16b   At 6.4.5 this incident and another failure against Thebes at 5.4.59 are said to be used by (unnamed) critics of Kleombrotos to allege he is pro-Theban. He was no doubt less anti-Theban than Agesilaos, but matters were probably not as simple as his enemies made out: see further n. 6.4.5d.
5.4.17a   Future disasters for Sparta: see 6.4.2–15.

FIGURE 5.4.14. SEGMENT OF THE WALLS OF THE ATHENIAN BORDER FORTRESS OF ELEUTHERAI.

the soldiers, and there was one incident especially when Kleombrotos and the army had left Kreusis and were crossing the mountain ridge that runs down to the sea: at this point the wind blew so powerfully over the ridge that it snatched up many pack animals with their baggage, and all sorts of weapons, and blew them over the cliff into the sea. [18] Finally, many of the men found themselves unable to move forward with their weapons, so they left their shields behind in different places, turning them upside down and filling them with stones. They took their dinner as best they could in Aigosthena,[a] which is in Megarian[b] territory. On the next day they went back and retrieved their shields. Kleombrotos then dismissed the troops, and each of the contingents departed for their respective homes.

[19] Now the Athenians[a] saw the power of the Spartans,[b] and they saw, too, that the war was no longer being waged in Corinth[c] but that the Spartans were going right past Attica[d] and invading Theban[e] territory. All this made them so fearful that they put on trial the two generals who had been accomplices of Melon against Leontiades and his followers; one of them they put to death, while the other, who did not wait around to stand trial, they exiled.

[20] The Thebans in their turn also became frightened that no one besides themselves would be at war with the Spartans, and so they contrived the following ploy. They persuaded Sphodrias, the Spartan governor at Thespiai[a] (by giving him money, it was suspected), to invade Attica, so that he might induce the Athenians to go to war against the Spartans.[b] Sphodrias was persuaded, and he claimed that he would capture the Peiraieus, since it was still without gates.[c] He had his men take their dinner early and then led them from Thespiai, saying that he would arrive at the Peiraieus before daybreak. [21] The new day, however, found Sphodrias and his army only as far along as Thria.[a] There he made no attempt to evade detection but simply turned about and began to seize cattle and plunder houses.

Frightened by Spartan armies so close to Attica, the Athenians assail the generals who were in on Melon's plot.

The Thebans, frightened at the prospect of fighting Sparta by themselves, persuade or bribe Sphodrias to attack Athens. He does so, hoping to capture the Peiraieus, whose walls still lacked gates. Dawn finds him at Thria, however, which he plunders.

5.4.18a Aigosthena: Map 5.3.14. See 6.4.26.
5.4.18b Megara: Map 5.3.14, inset.
5.4.19a Athens: Map 5.3.14 and inset.
5.4.19b Sparta: Map 5.3.14.
5.4.19c Corinth: Map 5.3.14 and inset. The land operations of the war of 395–386 took place mainly on the territory around Corinth, although much of the war was fought at sea.
5.4.19d Attica: Map 5.3.14, inset.
5.4.19e Thebes: Map 5.3.14, inset.
5.4.20a Thespiai: Map 5.4.50, AX.
5.4.20b Did Sphodrias' raid impel Athens to form the Second Athenian League, or did the establishment of that league lead to the raid as a calculated Spartan response? We cannot determine the dates with sufficient certainty to be sure which of these events came first. Xenophon fully describes the raid but says very little about the Second Athenian League and nothing about its foundation. Plutarch (*Parallel Lives*, "Pelopidas" 14, "Agesilaos" 24) is in accord with Xenophon's

account, but Diodorus (Appendix O, 15.29) claims that King Kleombrotos was responsible for the raid, which would clearly imply a formal act of the Spartan government—a show of displeasure and perhaps even a threat. Of course, we cannot be certain that there was any causal connection at all between the two events. Scholars have explored many possibilities here and taken various positions but have not reached consensus.
5.4.20c Peiraieus: Map 5.4.50, BY. This suggests that the rebuilding of the walls (4.8.10) was not yet completed. Since the rebuilding commenced in 394, the ungated state of the Peiraieus walls has suggested to some that the gates had not been installed because of an otherwise unattested clause in the King's Peace. Others, however, think the defenses had not been completed simply because the Athenians had not gotten around to it.
5.4.21a Thria: Map 5.4.50, BY.

Meanwhile some men who had fallen in with Sphodrias' army during the night now fled to the city and announced to the Athenians that a very large army was coming against them. The Athenians, cavalry and hoplites alike, swiftly armed themselves and kept watch over the city.

[22] There happened to be in Athens three Spartan ambassadors, Etymokles, Aristolochos, and Okyllos,[a] staying at the home of Kallias,[b] the man who looked after Spartan interests at Athens. When the news about Sphodrias was announced to the Athenians, they immediately seized these men and kept them under guard, believing they were involved with the plot. The ambassadors, however, were completely baffled by what had happened and defended themselves by saying that they would never be such fools as to put themselves into the hands of the Athenians if they had known that there was a plot against the Peiraieus. Moreover, they would not have been at the house of the Athenian who looked after Spartan affairs, a place where they would most quickly be found. [23] They also said that it would soon be quite clear to the Athenians that the city of Sparta knew nothing of Sphodrias' actions, and they were confident that the Athenians would learn that Sphodrias had been put to death by the Spartans. So the Athenians released these men, judging them to have no knowledge of the plot. [24] Back at Sparta, the ephors recalled Sphodrias and indicted him on a capital charge. He, however, was afraid and did not obey the summons. Yet even though he disobeyed the summons and was not present at his trial, he was acquitted: to many this seemed to be the most unjust verdict ever rendered at Sparta. The reason for his acquittal was as follows.

[25] Sphodrias had a son Kleonymos who was just emerging from boyhood and was the handsomest and best regarded of the young men of his age; and Agesilaos' son Archidamos[a] was in love with Kleonymos. Now the allies of Kleombrotos intended to vote to acquit Sphodrias because they were his friends, but they were afraid of Agesilaos and his friends and also of those who belonged to neither side, since it seemed that Sphodrias had in fact done a dreadful deed. [26] Because of this, Sphodrias said to Kleonymos, "My son, it is in your power to save your father if you will beg Archidamos to make his father Agesilaos look favorably on me at my trial." When Kleonymos heard this, he got up his courage to go to Archidamos and beg him to be his father's savior. [27] When Archidamos saw Kleonymos weeping, he stood beside him and likewise shed tears. After the young man made his request, Archidamos answered as follows: "Kleonymos, you should know that I am unable even to look my father in the face; on the contrary, if I wish to have something done in the city, I ask anyone rather than my

5.4.22–24
378
ATHENS-SPARTA
Spartan envoys in Athens denounce Sphodrias' attempt. They declare that he is acting without legitimate authority and that he will be tried and executed.

5.4.25–27
378
SPARTA
Kleonymos, son of Sphodrias, begs his friend Archidamos, the son of Agesilaos, to intercede with his father the king to acquit Sphodrias. Archidamos promises to try.

5.4.22a It is not known why these Spartan ambassadors were in Athens at this Mtime, but possibly they were trying to dissuade the Athenians from recreating their naval alliance, which Diodorus and inscriptional evidence shows they were doing around this point, though Xenophon doesn't mention it. For this naval alliance, the Second Athenian League, see Appendix H, §9, and the Introduction, §12.12, 12.14–15.

5.4.22b Kallias was the *proxenos* of Sparta at Athens. A *proxenos*, although a citizen and resident of his own state, served as a "friend or representative" (much like a modern honorary consul) of a foreign state.

5.4.25a Archidamos son of Agesilaos, also known as Archidamos III: see Appendix M, §5.

5.4.28–31
378
SPARTA
After seeking an opportunity to talk to his father, Archidamos finally speaks with Agesilaos to ask him to acquit Sphodrias. Agesilaos replies that a man who has done what Sphodrias has done cannot be excused. Later Archidamos returns and asks that Agesilaos pardon Sphodrias. Agesilaos replies that a pardon might be granted only if it is honorable to do so.

5.4.32
378
SPARTA
Agesilaos argues that although Sphodrias is guilty, it is hard to execute him, for he has always performed all the duties of a Spartan, and Sparta needs such soldiers.

father. Nevertheless, since you bid me do this, trust me to do everything I can to accomplish this for you."

[28] Archidamos then left the mess hall[a] and went home to sleep. He rose early the next morning and kept watch to make sure that his father would not leave home without his knowledge. He saw his father leaving the house, but at first he hung back and allowed any of the citizens who were present to speak to his father; then he did the same for any foreigner; and he even gave way for any of the servants who had a request of Agesilaos. Later, when Agesilaos left the Eurotas[b] and returned home, Archidamos went away without even approaching his father. On the next day he did the same. [29] Agesilaos suspected why his son was following him like this, but he made no inquiry, preferring to let him be. Archidamos for his part was eager to see Kleonymos, as one might guess, but he could not approach him so long as he had not yet discussed Kleonymos' request with his father. Sphodrias' supporters, seeing that Archidamos no longer visited Kleonymos and remembering that he had before visited him all the time, were very anxious, since they supposed that Archidamos must have been reproached by his father. [30] Finally, however, Archidamos dared to approach his father and said, "Father, Kleonymos asks me to beg you to save his father, and I ask this same thing, if it is possible." Agesilaos answered, "I do not blame you for this request, but I do not see how I myself could avoid being blamed by the citizens if I did not condemn a man who took money to the detriment of his city." [31] Archidamos made no reply at that point but departed, defeated by the justness of his father's remarks. Later, however, either because he himself had thought of it or he had been instructed by someone else, he went to his father and said, "I know, Father, that if Sphodrias had committed no wrong, you would have acquitted him. But even if he has committed a misdeed, let him be pardoned by you for our sake." Agesilaos replied, "Well, then, if a pardon could prove honorable for us, it shall be so." When the son heard these remarks, he went away deeply despondent.

[32] After this, one of the friends of Sphodrias, while conversing with Etymokles, said, "I think that all of you who are friends of Agesilaos are going to vote to put Sphodrias to death." To this Etymokles replied, "By Zeus, if we do, we will not then be doing the same as Agesilaos, since he is repeating to everyone he talks with that although it is impossible to maintain that Sphodrias did not do wrong, nevertheless, as boy, youth, and adult, he has continually performed every service to Sparta, and thus it would be difficult to put such a man to death: for Sparta needs such soldiers."

5.4.28a   For the common messes of Sparta
          see Appendix E, §20, and Xenophon's
          Constitution of the Lacedaemonians
          3.5.
5.4.28b   The Eurotas (Map 5.4.50, locator) is
          the river that flows by Sparta. Plutarch
          (*Parallel Lives*, "Lykurgos" 12.7)

quotes a witticism implying that it was a
Spartan custom to swim in it, so
perhaps Agesilaos had a daily swim
there, or at least went down to its
banks regularly to watch the swimmers.

[33] When the friend of Sphodrias heard this, he reported it to Kleonymos, who was delighted and went to Archidamos and said, "We already were aware of your concern for us. But know well, Archidamos, that we will henceforth make it our special task to see that you never have cause to feel ashamed of our friendship." And the young man did not lie, for while he was alive he did everything he could for the benefit of Sparta, and later at Leuctra,[a] fighting in front of the king with Deinon the polemarch, he fell three times while surrounded by the enemy, and he was the first of the citizens to die there. His death, it is true, brought extreme grief to Archidamos, but Kleonymos, just as he had promised, brought no shame to Archidamos but, rather, honor. This, then, is how Sphodrias was acquitted.

[34] Back at Athens,[a] the Athenians who favored the Boeotian[b] cause pointed out to the people that the Spartans had not only failed to punish Sphodrias but had actually praised him for attacking Athens. So the Athenians began to construct gates at the Peiraieus and set about building ships and assisting the Boeotians with great enthusiasm. [35] The Spartans in turn called up the levy against the Thebans. They begged Agesilaos to lead the army, because they believed that he would show more sensible leadership than Kleombrotos. Agesilaos, saying that he would not oppose anything decided by the citizens, prepared to lead out the army.

[36] Now Agesilaos knew that it would not be easy to attack Thebes[a] unless he first gained control of the paths over Mount Cithaeron,[b] so when he learned that the Kleitorians were at war with the Orchomenians[c] and had a mercenary force serving with them, he made an agreement with the Kleitorians that their mercenary force would be available[d] to him if he needed it. [37] When the frontier sacrifices proved favorable,[a] but before he himself arrived at Tegea,[b] he sent to the commander of the mercenaries serving with the Kleitorians and, giving them a month's pay, ordered them to gain control of Mount Cithaeron. He also sent to the Orchomenians, saying that they must stop their war while his campaign was under way. And he warned, too, that if any city should campaign against another while his army was in the field, he would consider it his highest priority to make war on the aggressor in accordance with the decree of the allies.[c]

5.4.33
378
SPARTA
Kleonymos hears what Agesilaos said and thanks Archidamos, promising never to shame their friendship. True to his promise, he dies bravely and honorably in battle at Leuctra.

5.4.34–37
378
ATHENS-SPARTA
The adherents of Thebes at Athens argue that Sphodrias was not punished but actually commended for having plotted against Athens. Athens responds by aiding Thebes, and Sparta mobilizes against Thebes, choosing Agesilaos to lead it. He orders friendly forces to occupy Mount Cithaeron and warns other cities to stop their wars while his campaign is under way.

5.4.33a   Leuctra: Map 5.4.50, AX. Site of the great Theban victory over Sparta seven years later, in 371. See 6.4.14.
5.4.34a   Athens: Map 5.4.50, BY, and locator.
5.4.34b   Boeotia: Map 5.4.50, AX.
5.4.36a   Thebes: Map 5.4.50, AX.
5.4.36b   Mount Cithaeron: Map 5.4.50, AX.
5.4.36c   Kleitor and Orchomenos (in Arcadia): Map 5.4.50, locator. Since both were members of the Peloponnesian League (see Appendix E, §18), this passage shows that Sparta tolerated wars between her subsidiary allies unless they interfered with Sparta's own military plans.
5.4.36d   For the Greek, see Translator's Notes.
5.4.37a   Spartan military expeditions never crossed their frontier without favorable sacrifices.
5.4.37b   Tegea: Map 5.4.50, locator.
5.4.37c   Diodorus (Appendix O, 15.30) says that the Spartans, in view of the defection of many of their allied islands and cities to the Second Athenian League, reorganized their own league and began to treat their allies with greater consideration. See Appendix E, §18–19. For the Second Athenian League, see Appendix H, §9.

5.4.38–41
378
THEBES

Agesilaos crosses Mount Cithaeron and makes his base at Thespiai. At first he is kept from Theban lands by a stockade and trench. The Thebans launch a surprise cavalry attack that causes Spartan losses before being thrown back. He discovers that the enemy defends the stockade only after breakfast, so he attacks and lays waste the territory within the stockade up to the walls of the city. Then, after fortifying Thespiai, he returns to the Peloponnese.

[38] Agesilaos then crossed over Mount Cithaeron to Thespiai,[a] which he used as his base from which to invade Theban territory. He discovered, however, that the plain and the most valuable parts of their lands had been surrounded with a trench and a stockade.[b] He made his camp now in one place, now another, leading out his forces after breakfast to ravage the land on his side of the trench and stockade, while the enemy would move along opposite his forces within the stockade, arraying themselves to oppose Agesilaos wherever he appeared.

[39] At one point, when Agesilaos was already in the process of marching back to his camp, the Theban cavalry, which had up to that moment been invisible, suddenly burst out through the exits that had been made in the stockade and charged against Agesilaos' men. They attacked both the peltasts (some of whom were taking their dinner while others were preparing to take it) and the cavalry (some of whom were dismounting while others were just in the act of mounting). They struck down a large number of the peltasts, while of the cavalry they killed the Spartiates Kleas and Epikydidas;[a] one of the *perioikoi*;[b] Eudikos; and some Theban exiles who had not yet mounted their horses. [40] When Agesilaos and the hoplites turned about, however, and came to the rescue, his Spartan cavalry charged the Theban cavalry, and the first ten-year classes[a] of the hoplites advanced with the cavalry. The Theban cavalry, for their part, resembled men who have drunk a little too much at noon: they awaited the enemy marching against them so as to throw their spears at them, but none of their spears actually reached their target. They then turned about, and even though they were at a great distance, the Spartans killed twelve of them.

[41] Later, when Agesilaos realized that the enemy appeared only after breakfast, he sacrificed at daybreak and led his men out as quickly as he could, going in through the stockade at an unguarded point. Then he ravaged and burned the land all the way up to the city walls, and when he had done this, he went back to Thespiai and built walls for their city.[a] At Thespiai, he left behind Phoibidas[b] as governor, and he himself crossed back over Cithaeron to Megara[c] and there disbanded the allies, leading his own Spartan contingent home.

5.4.38a   Thespiai: Map 5.4.50, AX.
5.4.38b   Neither Diodorus (Appendix O, 15.32–33) nor Cornelius Nepos (Chabrias 1) mentions this trench and stockade. Here they represent Agesilaos' failure to accomplish anything as a result of the Athenian general Chabrias' effective generalship.
5.4.39a   Epikydidas was the Spartiate sent by Sparta to recall Agesilaos from Asia in 394. See 4.2.2.
5.4.39b   *Perioikoi* were citizens of towns in Laconia that the Spartans had left in possession of their territories and with some freedom to conduct their own internal affairs but without a voice in foreign affairs. They were compelled to follow

the Spartiate lead in war. See Appendix E, §10.
5.4.40a   Ten-year classes: all the younger men whose time in military service was ten years or less. Assuming that they entered military service at the age of twenty, these would be the youngest cadre in the force, aged twenty through twenty-nine. Spartiates served in the army till they reached the age of sixty.
5.4.41a   In Diodorus (Appendix O, 15.33), Agesilaos' counselors express surprise that he did not engage in battle.
5.4.41b   Phoibidas was the Spartiate who seized the acropolis of Thebes in 382. See 5.2.26ff.
5.4.41c   Megara: Map Map 5.4.50, BX.

[42] After this, Phoibidas sent out bands of robbers to plunder Theban territory while he himself also made raids and devastated their territory. The Thebans, in turn, marched out in full force against Thespiai to avenge themselves. When they came within Thespian territory, however, Phoibidas pressed them close with his peltasts and did not allow them to stray away from their phalanx. The result was that the Thebans were greatly distressed and retreated rather more quickly than they had advanced; then such a terrible fear fell upon their army that the mule drivers, in their eagerness to get back home, threw away the produce that they had seized. [43] Phoibidas pressed them boldly, keeping the peltasts around himself and ordering the hoplites to follow in battle formation, for he was hoping to effect a rout of the Thebans. With that in mind, he led his own troops on strongly and encouraged the rest of his men to attack the enemy, bidding also the Thespian hoplites to follow him. [44] But as the Theban cavalry retreated, they came to an impassable ravine; first they massed themselves together, and then, being unable to find a place at which they might cross, they turned to face Phoibidas.[a] Now the peltasts in front were few, and in fear of the horsemen they took to flight. The Theban cavalry, when they saw them running away, learned a lesson from those fleeing and attacked them. [45] Phoibidas, along with two or three others with him, fell fighting, and when this happened, all the mercenaries fled. In their flight they came to the Thespian hoplites, who earlier had boasted that they would not give way before the Thebans but who now immediately took to flight also, even though no one at all was pursuing them, since it was by now late in the day. And although only a few of them were killed, the Thespians nevertheless did not stop in their flight until they were safe inside their walls.

[46] This success ignited Theban spirits so much that they made expeditions against Thespiai and the rest of the surrounding cities.[a] The democratic factions of those cities, however, had fled from them to Thebes,[b] since the Spartans had established oligarchic governments in all of them, just as they had at Thebes.[c] As a result, the friends of the Spartans in all these cities begged them for help. After the death of Phoibidas, the Spartans sent a polemarch and one regiment by sea to Thespiai and garrisoned the city.

[47] When spring arrived, the Spartans again called out the levy against the Thebans and again asked Agesilaos to assume the command, just as before. His tactical view on how to invade Boeotia had not changed,[a] so even before he offered the frontier sacrifices, he sent to the polemarch at

5.4.42–46
378
THESPIAI
The Thebans attack the land of Thespiai in retaliation for the spoiling of their own territory, but they are forced to retire. Suddenly they rally and counterattack, routing their foes. Phoibidas is killed, and his army flees. The Thebans then mount raids against Thespiai and other cities. The oligarchic regimes left by Sparta in those cities appeal to Sparta for assistance. Sparta sends a polemarch with one regiment to garrison Thespiai.

5.4.47–48
377
BOEOTIA
Agesilaos leads the army again to Boeotia, deceiving the Thebans as to his route.

5.4.44a Polyainos, an ancient writer on military tactics and stratagems, writes (*Strategemata* 2.5.2) that Gorgidas, the Theban cavalry commander, was feigning flight so as to lure Phoibidas' troops onto level ground.
5.4.46a Plutarch (*Parallel Lives*, "Pelopidas" 15.3–4) says that the Thebans with Pelopidas in command routed the Spartan garrison at Tanagra (Map 5.4.50, AY), killing the governor Panthoidas.
5.4.46b Thebes: Map 5.4.50, AX, and locator.
5.4.46c Sparta generally sought to establish oligarchic regimes over its allies. See Appendix E, §18.
5.4.47a For his previous invasion, see 5.4.36.

Thespiai and ordered him to occupy the summit overlooking the road over Cithaeron and to hold it until he himself arrived.

[48] After he had crossed over Cithaeron and had arrived at Plataea,[a] he pretended that he would again go to Thespiai. He sent a message there ordering the Thespians to prepare a marketplace[b] and announcing that any embassies to himself should meet him there. This caused the Thebans to put a strong guard on the road that led from Thespiai to Thebes.[c] [49] But the next day Agesilaos sacrificed at dawn and marched out instead for Erythrai,[a] advancing with such speed that he made the two-day journey in just one and thus managed to get through the stockade at Skolos[b] before the Thebans had returned from guarding the site where he had entered their territory in the previous year. When he had done this, he proceeded to ravage the eastern territory of Thebes as far as the territory of Tanagra,[c] which at that time was in the control of Hypatodoros and his party, who were friendly to the Spartans. Thereafter Agesilaos departed, keeping the wall of Tanagra on his left.

[50] The Thebans, meanwhile, stole out secretly and set themselves in battle order in front of the ditch and the stockade on a hill called the Old Woman's Breast,[a] thinking that this was a good place to risk battle, because the ground was fairly narrow and difficult to cross. When Agesilaos saw this, however, he made no move against them but turned aside from his course and advanced toward Thebes itself. [51] The Thebans then, being afraid for the city (since it was without defenders), abandoned the place where they had deployed and went at a run toward Thebes, taking the road that leads past Potniai,[a] since this was the safer route. And indeed Agesilaos' plan seemed a successful one, since he led his army away from the enemy and yet made them retreat at a run. And as the Thebans rushed past them, some of the Spartan polemarchs took their regiments and charged them. [52] The Thebans, however, throwing their javelins down from the crests of the hills, struck and killed Alypetos, one of the polemarchs. Nevertheless, the Spartans succeeded in driving the Thebans even from this height. And then the Skiritai[a] and some of the cavalry came up and struck the hindmost of the Thebans as they were making for their city.

5.4.49
377
THEBES
By hard marching, his troops enter Theban territory unopposed and lay waste much Theban territory.

5.4.50–52
377
THEBES
When the Thebans deploy their army against him, Agesilaos does not give battle but marches instead toward Thebes. When the Thebans run to protect their city, the Spartans succeed in harassing and driving them as they run by.

5.4.48a Plataea: Map 5.4.50, AX.
5.4.48b Greek soldiers and sailors at this time were expected to purchase their food from local markets with their own money, which made prompt and adequate military pay quite important. It was not uncommon for a commander to order or ask friendly cities to offer a special market at a convenient location for his army. This was not unprofitable to the local citizens, and if the market was set up outside the city walls, it helped to keep such visitors out of the city.
5.4.48c Thebes: Map 5.4.50, AX, and locator.
5.4.49a Erythrai: Map 5.4.50, AX.

5.4.49b Skolos: Map 5.4.50, AX. Skolos is mentioned also by the second-century travel writer Pausanias (9.4.4), as located north of the Asopos River (Map 5.4.50, AX), 4.5 miles from the road between Thebes and Plataea.
5.4.49c Tanagra: Map 5.4.50, AY.
5.4.50a The hill is southwest of Tanagra, so called after Tanagra or Graia, the wife of Poemander, the city's founder: see Pausanias 9.20.2.
5.4.51a Potniai: Map 5.4.50, AX.
5.4.52a Skiritai: a people who lived in Skiritis (Map 5.2.13, BY), on the northern frontier of Spartan territory. See Appendix F, §9, and n. O.15.32.1a.

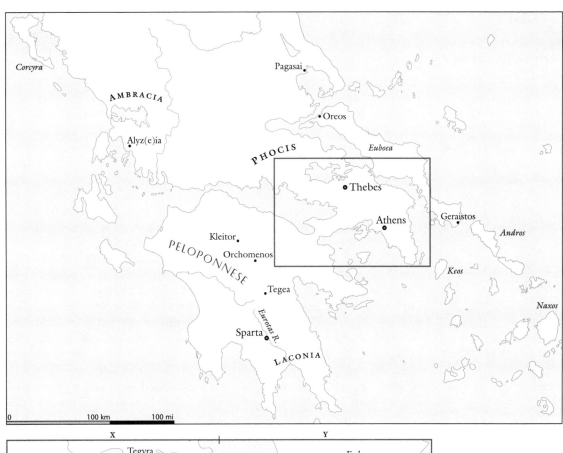

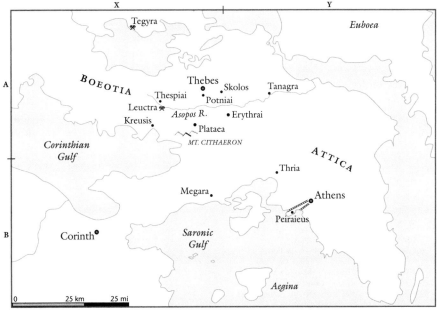

MAP 5.4.50

5.4.53–54
377
THEBES
When the Thebans reach their city wall, they re-form against the Spartans, who now retire and are harassed in turn. Finally, the Olynthian cavalry, now serving with the Spartans, attacks and kills many of the Theban peltasts.

5.4.55
377
THESPIAI
Agesilaos retires to Thespiai, where he reconciles hostile factions and then marches to Megara. There he dismisses the allies and returns home.

5.4.56–57
377
PAGASAI-OREOS
At Pagasai, the Spartan Alketas captures two triremes and much corn destined for Thebes, but on his return to Oreos, he dallies with a boy there. The prisoners seize the acropolis, and the city revolts, which permits Thebes to bring in corn easily thereafter.

[53] When they came near their wall, however, the Thebans turned around, and the Skiritai retreated when they saw this, moving at a pace somewhat faster than a walk. And although the Thebans had failed to kill a single man, they nevertheless put up a trophy, on the grounds that the Skiritai had retreated after they had climbed the hill.[a] [54] Meanwhile, when it was time, Agesilaos withdrew[a] and had his army camp in the very place where he had previously seen the enemy arrayed against him. On the next day he led the army away, taking the road that leads toward Thespiai. The peltasts who were serving as mercenaries to the Thebans pursued Agesilaos boldly and kept appealing to Chabrias for assistance, because his pursuit was not as zealous as theirs. But then the Olynthian[b] cavalry (who were now serving with the Spartans in accordance with their oaths)[c] turned around and, in the course of their pursuit of the peltasts, chased them up a hill and killed many of them, for infantry can be quickly overcome by cavalry going up a slope when the slope is easy to ascend.

[55] When Agesilaos arrived at Thespiai, he found that the citizens there were engaged in civil strife, with those who wished the city to be allied with Sparta saying that their opponents should be put to death. One of these opponents was a man named Menon. Agesilaos, however, did not allow him to be executed but instead reconciled the parties and compelled them to swear oaths to one another. Having accomplished this, he returned again, crossing over Mount Cithaeron[a] by the road that leads to Megara. There he dismissed the allies and led the Spartan army home.

[56] The Thebans were now greatly distressed by a lack of grain, since they had not been able to reap crops from their land for two years.[a] So they gave ten talents[b] to some men and sent them in two triremes to Pagasai[c] for grain. Now Alketas the Spartan was keeping guard over Oreos[d] when those men were buying the grain, and he fitted out three triremes, taking care that this preparation should remain secret. And when the shipment of the grain was under way, Alketas seized both the grain and the triremes and also captured not less than three hundred men. He placed these prisoners on the acropolis, where he himself had his camp. [57] Now rumor had it that Alketas had a boy of Oreos always following him about; he was an especially handsome and fine boy, and when Alketas went down from the acropolis, he focused all his attention on him. When the prisoners saw that he was quite

5.4.53a This is another example of Xenophon's anti-Theban prejudice. See the Introduction, §12.3. On setting up a trophy, see Appendix L, §13.
5.4.54a Agesilaos' withdrawal, according to Plutarch (*Parallel Lives*, "Agesilaos" 26.3–4), was partly due to the discontent of the Spartan allies.
5.4.54b Olynthos: Map 5.3.14.
5.4.54c For the oaths to be loyal allies of the Spartans, see 5.3.26.
5.4.55a Mount Cithaeron: Map 5.4.50, AX.
5.4.56a They could not reap their land because of the Spartan invasions and destruction wreaked during those years.

5.4.56b Ten talents was a large sum for purchasing grain in bulk. See Appendix I, §8, 10, 13.
5.4.56c Pagasai: Map 5.4.50, locator.
5.4.56d Oreos: Map 5.4.50, locator. Shortly before the events narrated here, the Spartans had assisted the people of Oreos in expelling their tyrant Neogenes, and the city had remained loyal to Sparta; it did not admit Chabrias within its walls even when all the rest of the cities of Euboea were joining the Second Athenian League: see Diodorus (Appendix O, 15.30). On the Second Athenian League, see Appendix H, §9.

careless, they seized the acropolis, and the city revolted from the Spartans. And from that point the Thebans were able to bring in grain easily.

[58] When spring again arrived, Agesilaos was sick in bed. In the previous year, after he had led the army from Thebes and had arrived in Megara, and as he was going up from the temple of Aphrodite to the residence of the magistrates,[a] some vein or other burst, and blood flowed from his body into his good leg.[b] The shin became exceedingly swollen and unbearably painful. Then a Syracusan[c] physician cut the vein along his ankle, and once the flow of blood began, it continued day and night, and although they tried everything, they could not get it to stop until Agesilaos lost consciousness; and at that point the bleeding finally ceased. He was brought to Sparta in this condition and remained ill the rest of that summer and the following winter.

[59] As spring began, the Spartans once again called out the levy against the Thebans and ordered Kleombrotos to take command. When he arrived at Mount Cithaeron with the army, he sent his peltasts on ahead in order to seize in advance the heights above the road. Now some Athenians and Thebans already held the heights, and for a while they allowed the peltasts to ascend. But when they were very close to them, the Athenians and Thebans jumped up and attacked, routed, and pursued them, killing about forty of them. Because of this, Kleombrotos concluded that it would be impossible to cross Mount Cithaeron into Theban territory, and so he returned home and disbanded the army.

[60] When the allies gathered at Sparta,[a] they made speeches in which they claimed that they were being worn out because of the Spartans' timidity. They pointed out that they could fit out more ships than the Athenians had, and with them they could reduce Athens by starvation.[b] They asserted, too, that with these same ships it was possible to send an army across the gulf[c] into Theban territory by either of two routes: via Phocis[d] or via Kreusis.[e] [61] Swayed by these arguments, the Spartans fitted out sixty triremes and chose Pollis to command them. And those who had made these criticisms were not disappointed, for the Athenians now found themselves besieged. Their grain transports went as far as Geraistos,[a] but from there they refused to sail along the coast, since the Spartan navy was around Aegina,[b] Keos,[c] and Andros.[d] The Athenians, recognizing the necessity, themselves boarded their ships and, with Chabrias as their commander,

5.4.58
376
SPARTA
Agesilaos falls ill on campaign and remains so for many months.

5.4.59
376
BOEOTIA
Sparta sends the army against Thebes under Kleombrotos. Repulsed at Cithaeron, he returns home and disbands the army.

5.4.60–61
376
AEGEAN SEA
Sparta's allies man sixty triremes and deploy them under Pollis to prevent the arrival of grain ships to Athens. The Athenians man their own fleet and defeat the Peloponnesians, so the grain passes through.

5.4.58a   According to Plutarch (*Parallel Lives*, "Agesilaos" 27.1), this "residence" was on the Megarian acropolis.

5.4.58b   Agesilaos was lame in one leg—presumably, in this case, the other one. See 3.3.3.

5.4.58c   Syracuse (in Sicily): Map 6.2.2, locator.

5.4.60a   Sparta: Map 5.4.50, locator. They met in accordance with the rules of the Peloponnesian League. See Appendix E, §18.

5.4.60b   The allies' discontent and concern were especially pronounced because of Athens' naval alliance, which was advertised to the world in March 377 though possibly established a year earlier and never

mentioned by Xenophon (see the Introduction, §12.12). The Athenians had had great success in recruiting members, including Rhodos and Byzantium (Map 6.2.2, locator), Methymna and Mytilene on Lesbos (Map 6.3.2, AY), Chios (Map 6.3.2, BY), and the cities of Euboea (Map 6.3.2, BX).

5.4.60c   Corinthian Gulf: Map 5.4.50, BX.
5.4.60d   Phocis: Map 5.4.50, locator.
5.4.60e   Kreusis: Map 5.4.50, AX. See also 4.5.10.
5.4.61a   Geraistos (in Euboea): Map 5.4.50, locator.
5.4.61b   Aegina: Map 5.4.50, BY.
5.4.61c   Keos: Map 5.4.50, locator.
5.4.61d   Andros: Map 5.4.50, locator.

fought a battle at sea[c] against Pollis and were victorious. And after that, the grain was successfully transported by ship to the Athenians.

[62] When the Spartans were preparing to send an army across the gulf to Boeotia, the Thebans begged the Athenians to send an army into the Peloponnese, believing that the Spartans could not possibly send a suitable army against the Thebans if at the same time they had to protect their own land and that of the allied cities around them. [63] The Athenians, who were angry with the Spartans because of Sphodrias' action,[a] manned sixty ships and eagerly sent them out around the Peloponnese,[b] choosing Timotheos[c] to command them. And since the enemy did not invade Thebes either in the year when Kleombrotos led the army or in the year when Timotheos sailed around the Peloponnese, the Thebans confidently attacked their neighboring cities and recovered them once more.

[64] Timotheos for his part sailed around the Peloponnese and went to Corcyra,[a] which he immediately brought under his control. He did not, however, enslave the population, nor did he send men into exile or change the laws; and because of this, the cities in that area looked upon him more favorably.[b]

[65] The Spartans manned a fleet against him, and they sent out Nikolochos, a very bold man, as its commander. When Nikolochos caught sight of the ships of Timotheos, he did not hesitate. Although the six ships from Ambracia[a] were not present, he nevertheless engaged Timotheos in a sea battle with his fifty-five ships against Timotheos' sixty. In that battle Nikolochos was defeated, and Timotheos set up a trophy in Alyzeia.[b] [66] Afterward, when the six Ambraciot ships arrived and had been added to his force, Nikolochos sailed to Alyzeia, where Timotheos was and where Timotheos' ships had been dragged up and were being repaired. Timotheos did not put to sea against Nikolochos, so the latter set up a trophy in his turn in the islands nearest Alyzeia. When Timotheos had repaired the ships he already had, his force was increased by other ships from Corcyra, and his fleet, now numbering more than seventy, now far exceeded that of the enemy. Timotheos, however, had to keep sending to Athens to ask for funds, for he had many ships under his command and required a great deal of money to maintain them.

5.4.61e   From Diodorus (Appendix O, 15.34–35) we learn that the sea battle was fought at Naxos (Map 5.4.50, locator). It was the first victory in a major sea battle for the Athenians unsupported by the Persians since the battle of Arginousai in the Peloponnesian War, thirty years earlier. After this victory many more states joined the Second Athenian League. See Appendix H, §9.

5.4.63a   Sphodrias had attempted a surprise attack on the Peiraieus; see 5.4.34.

5.4.63b   Peloponnese: Map 5.4.50, locator.

5.4.63c   Timotheos was the son of the Athenian general Konon; he himself had been general a few years before in 378. See "Timotheos" in Appendix M, §28.

5.4.64a   Corcyra: Map 5.4.50, locator.

5.4.64b   These comments on Timotheos' actions in Corcyra are perhaps better seen as a criticism of the Athenian general Chares, who fourteen years later, in 361, forcibly instituted an oligarchy on that island (see Diodorus 15.95.3, and Aeneas Tacticus, *How to Survive Under Siege* 11.13). The Athenian orator Isocrates (15.115–127) praised Timotheos for these actions. See also Ancient Sources.

5.4.65a   Ambracia: Map 5.4.50, locator.

5.4.65b   Alyzeia: Map 5.4.50, locator.

BOOK SIX

Uuring the time that the Athenians[a] and Spartans[b] were engaged in these matters, the Thebans,[c] after they had conquered the cities in Boeotia,[d] made a campaign against Phocis.[e] The Phocians for their part sent an embassy to Sparta to tell the Spartans that unless they came to their assistance, they would have to yield to the Thebans. In response, the Spartans sent Kleombrotos, the king, to Phocis by sea, accompanied by four regiments of Spartans and a corresponding proportion of the allied forces.

6.1.1–3
375
SPARTA
Polydamas of Pharsalus, Thessaly, regarded as extremely honorable, arrives at Sparta to speak to the Assembly.

[2] At just about this same time Polydamas of Pharsalus[a] also came to Sparta and appeared before the Spartan Assembly. Polydamas was very renowned in all of Thessaly[b] and in his own city especially, where he was considered to be such a noble man that when the Pharsalians were embroiled in civil war,[c] they entrusted their acropolis to him as well as the responsibility for collecting the revenues and making the expenditures on sacred matters in the amounts prescribed by law, and for conducting the rest of the municipal administration. [3] And he for his part used these revenues to guard the acropolis for them, keeping it safe, administering everything, and even giving an annual account of the finances. And whenever there was a shortfall in funds, he made it up from his own pocket, and when there was a surplus he repaid himself. He was as well a man renowned for his warm hospitality and his magnificence in the Thessalian manner.[a] Now when he arrived in Sparta, he spoke as follows:

6.1.1a Athens: Map 6.2.2, BY.
6.1.1b Sparta: Map 6.2.2, BY.
6.1.1c Thebes: Map 6.2.2, AY.
6.1.1d Boeotia: Map 6.2.2, AY. Thebes thereby reestablished her hegemony over the cities of Boeotia.
6.1.1e For the enmity between Thebes and Phocis (Map 6.2.2, AY), see 3.5.4.
6.1.2a Pharsalus: Map 6.2.2, AY.
6.1.2b Thessaly: Map 6.2.2, AX.
6.1.2c The civil war seems to have been between pro- and anti-Spartan factions. According to Diodorus (Appendix O, Selections from the *Histories* of Diodorus Siculus Relevant to Xenophon's *Hellenika*, 14.82.5), Pharsalus had had a Spartan garrison before the Corinthian War, but this was expelled by Medios, the tyrant of Larissa, Thessaly (Map 6.2.2, AY), when he captured the town.
6.1.3a For the magnificence of the Thessalians, see Athenaios 12.15.27a–b and 14.663.

6.1.4–6
375
SPARTA
The speech of Polydamas of Pharsalus. He describes how Jason of Pherai approached him and argued that Pharsalus should accept his rule, particularly because of his great force of well-trained and well-treated mercenaries, which no city can safely oppose.

6.1.7–10
375
SPARTA
Speech of Polydamas of Pharsalus continues. He describes how Jason of Pherai offered to make him the second most important man in Thessaly, and how with Pharsalus united to his forces he could become *tagos* of Thessaly and with the Thessalian cavalry, hoplites and peltasts would be a truly formidable force in Greece.

[4] "Men of Sparta, because I, like all my ancestors for as long as we can remember, am your *proxenos*[a] and benefactor,[b] I consider it appropriate, whenever I am at a loss, to come to you; or, whenever anything harmful to your interests is happening in Thessaly, to inform you of it. Now I am well aware that you have all heard the name of Jason,[c] for he is a man who holds great power and is widely known. This man, having made a truce with Pharsalus, met with me and said as follows: [5] 'Polydamas, you must know that I, given my resources, would be able to take over your city even against its will: for I possess both the majority of the cities of Thessaly and the finest of them as my allies, and I subdued them even though you were warring with them against me. You are aware, moreover, that I have in my service about six thousand foreign mercenaries that no city could easily challenge, at least in my opinion. It is possible, of course, that a greater number of men might be marshaled from elsewhere, but citizen armies include both men already advanced in age and others not yet in their prime; in addition, there are only a few men in each city who train their bodies rigorously. But in my forces there is not a single man who cannot match me in the capacity for hard work.' [6] Now Spartans, I must tell you the truth: namely, that Jason has great bodily strength, and he is especially fond of hard labor. He tests his men every day, leading them in full armor[a] both on the parade grounds and in the field during his campaigns. And he discharges those of his mercenaries whom he perceives to be cowards, while he honors those whom he sees engaging in labors and dangers when fighting the enemy by giving some double pay, some triple, and some even quadruple. He also gives them other rewards, including care when they are sick and marks of honor when they are buried. The result is that all the mercenaries in his service know well that their excellence on the battlefield brings them a life of the greatest honor and the greatest abundance.

[7] "Jason also pointed out to me (although I already knew it) that the Maracians,[a] the Dolopians,[b] and Alketas[c] the ruler in Epirus were all subject to him. 'And so,' he said, 'why would I fear that I would not easily conquer your city? Indeed, someone who didn't know me might ask why I hesitate and don't march immediately against the Pharsalians. Because, by Zeus, it seems better to me in every way that I win you over to my side willingly rather than unwillingly. If I were to win you over by force, you would be

6.1.4a   A *proxenos*, although a citizen and resident of his own city, served as a "friend or representative" (much like a modern honorary consul) of a foreign city.
6.1.4b   "Benefactor" was a formal title given to foreigners who had done a state some outstanding good service.
6.1.4c   Jason was then the tyrant of Pherai (Map 6.2.2, AY), a city in southeastern Thessaly. For more information about him, see "Jason of Pherai" in Appendix M, Brief Biographies of Important Characters in Xenophon's *Hellenika*, §13.
6.1.6a   Some scholars assert that a full set of

hoplite armor and weapons weighed as much as 70 pounds, but others dispute this, estimating that it weighed much less.
6.1.7a   Maracians: location of territory unknown. They are probably the same as Pliny's Maraces (4.2), who were a people of Aetolia: Map 6.2.2, AX.
6.1.7b   Dolopia: Map 6.2.2, AX. The Dolopians were a people of Aetolia.
6.1.7c   Alketas was king of the Molossians in Epirus (Molossia, Epirus: Map 6.2.2, AX). He joined the Second Athenian League in 375. See Diodorus 15.36.5.

plotting whatever harm you could against me, and I would want to keep you as weak as possible. But if I should persuade you to join my side, it is obvious that we would strive to make each other stronger, as best we can. [8] I know, Polydamas, that your city looks to you, and if you make her my ally, I promise you that I will make you the greatest of all men in Greece next to myself. Now hear what I am offering to you in granting you this second place, and do not simply believe what I say unless it also seems true to you after you have thought about it.

"'It is clear to us, isn't it, that if Pharsalus and the cities that are dependent upon her should come over to my side, I could easily set myself up as *tagos*[a] of all the Thessalians, and whenever Thessaly is under a *tagos*, its horsemen number about six thousand and its available hoplites number more than ten thousand. [9] And looking at their bodies and their high spirits, I think that if someone treated them properly, the Thessalians would not think it worthy of themselves to be subject to any other people. Furthermore, although Thessaly is a flat land,[a] all the peoples that encircle Thessaly become subject to her whenever a *tagos* is established, and nearly all these tribes are javelin-throwers, so it is likely that our forces would be superior in peltasts, too. [10] And I think I can say that the Boeotians and all the rest who are fighting against the Spartans are my allies. And if only I can free them from Spartan domination, they will be willing to follow me as their leader. I am certain as well that the Athenians would enthusiastically become our allies, but I do not believe it is a good idea to develop a friendship with them, since I think it would be even easier for us to acquire sea power than land power.[a]

[11] "'Consider now if I estimate rightly in these matters also. For if we possess Macedon,[a] the place from which the Athenians obtain their timber, we will be able to build many more ships than they can. And is it more likely that we, who have so many and such excellent serfs,[b] or the Athenians

6.1.11–12
375
SPARTA
Speech of Polydamas of Pharsalus continues, describing how Jason of Pherai intends to displace the Athenians as rulers of the sea.

6.1.8a The Thessalian *tagos* was neither king nor tyrant but a leader who seems to have been selected by a unanimous vote of the rulers of the four ancestral Thessalian tribal territories, which may explain why the office was only intermittently filled. (As time went by, certain of the individual cities within these territories, such as Pherai, Pharsalus, and Larissa, had come to be more important units of political organization than the territories themselves. In the early fourth century, the most statelike elements of Thessaly were the cities, the old tribal territories probably no longer having significant political existence of their own.) Much about Thessaly, including the role and the method of appointment of the *tagos*, is mysterious because of lack of evidence.

6.1.9a As a flat land eminently suited for cavalry, Thessaly produced the finest horsemen but was deficient in peltasts. Jason's point here is that since the neighboring tribes, who were adept as javelin throwers, will be

subject to him, he will have a ready supply of peltasts.

6.1.10a Since Xenophon has not informed his readers about the Second Athenian League (see the Introduction, §12.12, and Appendix H, Political Leagues [Other Than Sparta's] in Xenophon's *Hellenika*, §9), Jason's remarks seem odd here. Jason would have been reluctant to take on the Athenians because of their current strength, and in fact not long after this he seems to have become their ally (Demosthenes 49.10, 49.22).

6.1.11a Macedon: Map 6.2.2, locator.

6.1.11b Jason refers here to the Thessalian *penestai*, a hereditary class of dependents, often compared with Spartan helots (for example, in Dionysius of Halicarnassus, *Roman Antiquities* 2.9). They were mentioned earlier, at 2.3.36. Jason must have considered men of this poor and landless Thessalian class to be equivalent to the poor, landless, urban workers who manned the Athenian fleet, serving as its rowers.

could properly man these ships? And who is more likely to maintain these sailors: we, who have such abundance of grain that we export it, or the Athenians, who would not have enough grain for their people if they did not purchase it from elsewhere?[c] [12] As for money, surely it is probable that we would have greater funds, since we are not looking to little islands for tribute[a] but to peoples on the mainland. And indeed, as soon as a *tagos* is established in Thessaly, all the peoples around us will pay us tribute. You know, of course, that the King of Persia is the wealthiest of men because he receives tribute not from islands but from the mainland. Despite that, I think we could make even the King subject to us more easily than we could Greece, for I know that all the men there, with one exception, have trained for slavery rather than bravery, and I know how the King was driven to extremes by the forces both of those who went up-country with Cyrus[b] and those who marched out with Agesilaos.'[c]

[13] "When he had said these things, I answered that all his other observations were worth considering but that I found one not easy to accept: that those who were allies of the Spartans and who had no complaint against them should secede from their alliance and go over to the side of Sparta's enemies. He praised me for saying this and said that now all the more he must have me on his side, because of the sort of man I was; he then sent me off to come before you and speak the truth, that he intends to attack the Pharsalians if we do not willingly yield to him. He therefore said that I should seek your aid, remarking, 'If the gods grant that you persuade the Spartans to send suitable forces to do battle with me, well then, we shall abide by the decision of battle. But if you think they will bring you insufficient aid, would you not rightfully be blameless if you should do whatever is best for your city that honors you?'

[14] "It is about these matters that I have come to you, Spartans, and I am telling you everything that I myself have seen and what I have heard from Jason. And I think, men of Sparta, that the situation is as follows:[a] if you send assistance that will be suitable not only for the Pharsalians but for all the Thessalians to wage war on Jason, then his cities will abandon their alliance with him, for everyone is afraid of where this man's power might lead. But if you think it will be enough to send newly freed helots[b] a private citizen as their leader,[c] then I advise you to take no action. [15] For you should realize that this war will pit you against powerful forces and against a

6.1.13
375
SPARTA
Speech of Polydamas of Pharsalus continues. He says that Jason of Pherai permitted him to ask for assistance from Sparta against him and would accept the verdict of war if Sparta rendered that assistance.

6.1.14–16
375
SPARTA
Speech of Polydamas of Pharsalus continues. He says a substantial force is needed to stop Jason of Pherai, summarizes how formidable he is, and asks the Spartans what they intend to do about him.

6.1.11c Throughout the fifth and fourth centuries, Athens depended on grain imported from grain-surplus regions, particularly around the Black Sea, to support its large population.

6.1.12a This remark is probably a slight against the Second Athenian League, which had mostly islands as contributing members.

6.1.12b See 3.1.1 and "Cyrus the Younger" in Appendix M, §7. Xenophon's *Anabasis* describes this expedition. See also the Introduction, §4.2.

6.1.12c For Agesilaos' expedition against the

Persians, which was called back by Sparta, see 3.4.2–4, 3.4.11.

6.1.14a For the Greek, see Translator's Notes.

6.1.14b Newly freed helots: *neodamōdeis*, a particular class of Spartans. See Appendix E, Spartan Government and Society, §9, 12; and Appendix F, The Spartan Army (and the Battle of Leuctra), §6.

6.1.14c That is to say, if you send that kind of second-rate force instead of a proper Spartan army with Spartan hoplites and one of the kings as commander.

man who is so intelligent a general that whatever he sets out to achieve, whether by stealth, by anticipation, or by open force, he does not fail to get. He is capable of using the night as well as the day, and when he is in a hurry, he will work while simultaneously eating his breakfast or dinner. He thinks it is appropriate to rest only after he has arrived at his goal and accomplished what he has set out to accomplish. And he has made his men just like himself. At the same time he knows how to let his men have what they want whenever they have done something really good by dint of hard work, and the result is that his men have come to learn that from their hard labor will come pleasures also. [16] Moreover, of all the men I know, he is the one most able to control the desires of the body, so that he is not hindered by such things from achieving what needs to be done. Therefore, you must examine these matters carefully, Spartans, and tell me, as is proper, what you are able to do and what you intend to do."

[17] This was the speech of Polydamas. The Spartans delayed their reply for the moment and over the next two days reviewed the situation of their forces, calculating and enumerating the number of regiments that were serving abroad[a] and those that were available in and around Laconia,[b] which were being used against the Athenian fleet and in the war with their neighbors.[c] Finally they answered that at the present moment they could not send a force suitable to assist Pharsalus, and they told Polydamas, therefore, to return and arrange matters for himself and his city as best he could. [18] Polydamas praised the Spartans for their candor and departed.

Meeting afterward with Jason, Polydamas asked that he not be compelled to hand over the acropolis, since he wished to preserve it for those who had entrusted it to him. He did, however, give his own children as hostages to Jason and promised him both that he would persuade Pharsalus to willingly become Jason's ally and that he would assist him in becoming *tagos* of Thessaly. They exchanged guarantees, and Pharsalus made peace with Jason, who was then quickly established as *tagos* of the Thessalians by common consent. [19] Having become *tagos*, Jason then assessed how many horsemen and hoplites each city of Thessaly was able to contribute, and he found that he had in all more than eight thousand cavalry (including those of his allies) and more than twenty thousand hoplites. His peltasts were sufficiently numerous to array against those of the whole known world—indeed, it would be a difficult task simply to list the cities that furnished them. In addition, he ordered the surrounding peoples to pay the tribute that had been assessed in the time of Scopas.[a]

Thus matters progressed in Thessaly. I now return to the point in my narrative from which I digressed to describe the actions of Jason of Pherai.

6.1.17–19
375
Sparta
After reviewing their situation, Sparta decides that it cannot now assist Pharsalus against Jason. Polydamas returns and gives his children to Jason as hostages to ensure his submission. Jason becomes *tagos* of Thessaly. His army is large, and he imposes tribute on all the subject cities of Thessaly.

6.1.17a   They had just sent four regiments to Phocis (Map 6.2.2, AY); see 6.1.1.
6.1.17b   Laconia: Map 6.2.2, BY.
6.1.17c   These were the regiments guarding the coast of the Peloponnese (Map 6.2.2, BX) against the fleet of Timotheos (5.4.63) and conducting the war with

Sparta's neighbors, who in this case were probably the Argives (Argos: Map 6.2.2, BY).
6.1.19a   Scopas ruled the city of Krannon (Map 6.2.2, AY) and held the title of *tagos* of Thessaly in the early fifth century.

[1] While the Spartans and their allies were gathering together in Phocis,[a] the Thebans[b] returned to their own country and guarded the frontiers. The Athenians[c] now saw that although the Thebans were prospering thanks to Athenian help, they were not contributing funds to support the fleet; while the Athenians, for their part, were being worn out by the war taxes,[d] the plundering expeditions from Aegina,[e] and the cost of keeping guards posted throughout their land. They therefore became eager to put an end to the war, and so they sent ambassadors to Sparta[f] and concluded a peace.[g] [2] Two of the ambassadors then sailed immediately from Sparta to Timotheos[a] and ordered him to sail home, since there was now a peace in effect; they did this in accordance with a resolution that had been passed by the people.[b]

While Timotheos was sailing back to Athens, however, he deposited the Zacynthian[c] exiles in their native country. [3] The Zacynthians in the city then sent to the Spartans, informing them of the treatment they had suffered at Timotheos' hands, and the Spartans immediately determined that the Athenians were in the wrong. They again prepared their navy, sixty ships made up of contingents from Sparta itself, Corinth,[a] Leucas,[b] Ambracia,[c] Elis,[d] Zacynthus, Achaea,[e] Epidauros,[f] Troizen,[g] Hermione,[h] and Halieis.[i] [4] They appointed Mnasippos to command the fleet, and they ordered him to watch over all the territories in that area and to make an expedition against Corcyra.[a] They also sent to Dionysios[b] and indicated to him that it would not be to his advantage if Corcyra came under Athenian control.[c]

[5] Once his fleet had gathered together, Mnasippos set out for Corcyra. In addition to the troops from Sparta, he also had serving with him not less than 1,500 mercenaries. [6] When he disembarked at Corcyra, he was

6.2.1a Xenophon resumes the narrative here from 6.1.1.
6.2.1b Thebes: Map 6.2.2, AY.
6.2.1c Athens: Map 6.2.2, BY.
6.2.1d These special levies were imposed on income during wartime.
6.2.1e Aegina: Map 6.2.2, BY. The Athenians earlier had been subject to these raids; see 5.1.29.
6.2.1f Sparta: Map 6.2.2, BY.
6.2.1g The terms of this peace are uncertain, but other sources suggest, against Xenophon, that it was a diplomatic victory for Athens, whose claims to naval hegemony were perhaps recognized in it. Moreover, it seems that the King of Persia was involved. See Diodorus (Appendix O, 15.38). The peace provided for the autonomy of the Boeotian cities against Thebes (Isocrates 14.5) but also required Sparta to evacuate Boeotia (Map 6.2.2, AY; Diodorus 15.38.2, Isocrates 8.16), which is confirmed by the fact that there was evidently no Spartan garrison in either Thespiai or Plataea (both Map 6.3.2, inset) to protect them against the Thebans. See "Isocrates" in Ancient Sources and the Introduction, §4.2.
6.2.2a Timotheos was the Athenian general now located somewhere in the area of Acarna-

nia: Map 6.2.2, AX. See 5.4.66 and "Timotheos" in Appendix M, §28.
6.2.2b A resolution passed by the people: see Appendix B, The Athenian Government and the Oligarchy of the Thirty, §8.
6.2.2c Zacynthus: Map 6.2.2, BX.
6.2.3a Corinth: Map 6.2.2, BY.
6.2.3b Leucas: Map 6.2.2, AX.
6.2.3c Ambracia: Map 6.2.2, AX.
6.2.3d Elis: Map 6.2.2, BY.
6.2.3e Achaea: Map 6.2.2, AX.
6.2.3f Epidauros: Map 6.2.2, BY.
6.2.3g Troizen: Map 6.2.2, BY.
6.2.3h Hermione: Map 6.2.2, BY.
6.2.3i Halieis: Map 6.2.2, BY.
6.2.4a Corcyra: Map 6.2.2, AX.
6.2.4b Dionysios I, the elder, tyrant of Syracuse (Map 6.2.2, locator), whom the Spartans had helped to consolidate his power in 404 and who had sent twenty ships in 378 to assist the Spartans against Athens; see 5.1.26, 5.1.28.
6.2.4c There is a consensus among modern scholars that Xenophon has telescoped the Spartan reaction, and that before Mnasippos went out to the west he was preceded by two other Spartan admirals, Aristokrates and Alkidas. See the Introduction, §14.5, for a discussion of this episode, and Diodorus (Appendix O, 15.45.4–46.3).

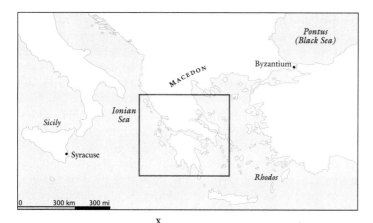

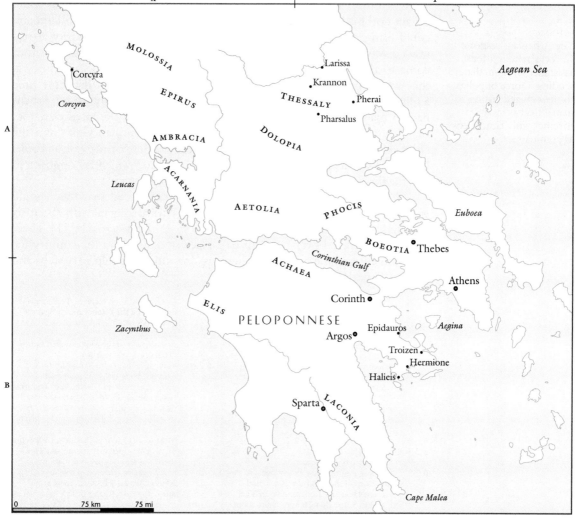

Map 6.2.2

master of the country, and he laid waste the land, which was well cultivated and most beautifully planted, destroying magnificent houses and wine cellars attached to the estates. (From this action people began to say that his soldiers had become so used to luxury that they would not drink any wine unless it had a fine bouquet.) He also captured numerous slaves and farm animals from the fields.

[7] He then made camp for his infantry on a hill about five stades[a] distant from the city and located between the city and the countryside, so that he might cut off any Corcyraean who attempted to go out to his lands. He had the navy set up its camp on the other side of the city, thinking that he would from that vantage point observe any ships that tried to sail into the city and prevent them from entering. In addition, he also blockaded the harbor except when prevented by bad weather.

[8] In this way, then, he besieged the city. The Corcyraeans, who could obtain nothing from their fields, since they were overpowered on land and could bring nothing in by ship because of the enemy's superiority at sea, saw no way out. [9] They thus sent to the Athenians and begged them to come to their aid, explaining that if the Athenians were to lose Corcyra, they would be forfeiting something of great value while at the same time adding greatly to their enemies' strength, since no other city except Athens had so many ships or such large funds available.[a] They pointed out, too, that Corcyra was well placed in respect to the Corinthian Gulf[b] and the cities on its shores, and it was well placed also to inflict damage on Laconia; best of all was its position both in respect to Epirus,[c] which lay opposite it, and for the coastal voyage from Sicily[d] to the Peloponnese.[e]

[10] When the Athenians heard this, they concluded that they should give this matter special care, so they sent Ktesikles as general with about six hundred peltasts and asked Alketas[a] to convey them across.[b] [11] These men were escorted over by night to a place somewhere in the countryside and then entered the city. The Athenians also voted to equip sixty ships and elected Timotheos to command them.[a]

6.2.8–11
374
ATHENS
The Athenians respond to Corcyra's request for assistance by immediately sending a force of peltasts to the city and voting to man a fleet of sixty triremes with Timotheos as commander.

6.2.7a   If Xenophon means 5 Attic stades of 583 feet, this would convert to a distance of about 1,000 yards. See Appendix I, Units of Distance, Currency, and Capacity in Xenophon's *Hellenika*, §4–5, 13.

6.2.9a   Although *The Cambridge Ancient History*'s chronological schema places Mnasippos' siege of Corcyra in 373, it places the Corcyraean appeal to Athens earlier, in 374, and makes this the reaction to an expedition by another Spartan, Alkidas, recounted by Diodorus (Appendix O, 15.46.2).

6.2.9b   Corinthian Gulf: Map 6.2.2, AY.
6.2.9c   Epirus: Map 6.2.2, AX.
6.2.9d   Sicily: Map 6.2.2, locator.
6.2.9e   This last argument has weight because the Athenians, if they held Corcyra, could prevent Dionysios from sending military forces to Sparta. Similar arguments about

Corcyra had been made to the Athenians right before the Peloponnesian War: see Thucydides 1.32–36. Peloponnese: Map 6.2.2, BX.

6.2.10a Alketas, king of the Molossians in Epirus (Map 6.2.2, AX); see 6.1.7.
6.2.10b To convey them across from Epirus to Corcyra. For a different and possibly preferable version of events, see Diodorus (Appendix O, 15.46–47), who suggests that the Athenians had sent Ktesikles first to Zacynthus and then (presumably from there) to Corcyra.

6.2.11a Most scholars follow Diodorus (Appendix O, 15.47.2), believing that in fact Timotheos was sent out before Mnasippos sailed west, in response to the Spartan admiral Alkidas. However, there is still much controversy over this.

[12] Timotheos, however, was unable to find enough sailors to man them in Athens, and so he made for the islands[a] and there attempted to acquire full complements, since he thought it was no small venture to sail around the Peloponnese haphazardly and against ships whose crews were well disciplined. [13] The Athenians, however, thought that Timotheos was using up that time of the year most suitable for sailing around the Peloponnese;[a] they would not excuse him but instead removed him from office and chose Iphikrates[b] in his place. [14] Once chosen commander, Iphikrates swiftly filled out his crews and compelled the trierarchs to uphold their responsibilities.[a] In addition, he took over any ship that he found in the vicinity of Athens, including the *Paralos* and the *Salaminia*,[b] saying that if things went well at Corcyra, he would send them back many ships. The total number of ships in his fleet was around seventy.[c]

[15] During this time, the Corcyraeans were so greatly suffering from hunger that some defected to the enemy, and when the number of these grew large, Mnasippos proclaimed that anyone who so defected would be sold into slavery. And when this failed to inhibit the number of defectors, Mnasippos at last drove them back by using the whip. Those inside the city refused to let the slaves inside the wall again, so that many of them died outside.

[16] When Mnasippos observed this situation, he thought he now just about had possession of the city, and he began to do something new with regard to his mercenaries. He had already dismissed some of them from service, and he now owed those who remained two months' pay; yet people said that he did not lack funds, since the majority of the cities had given him money instead of men because his was an overseas expedition.[a]

[17] Back in the city, the men on the towers of the wall noticed that Mnasippos' guards were being less careful than they had been at the outset and that some troops were scattered throughout the countryside, so they made a quick attack from the city, capturing some of the men and cutting down others. [18] When Mnasippos realized what was happening, he himself donned his armor and brought help with all the men he could assemble; he ordered the company commanders and the squadron commanders[a] to lead

6.2.12–14
373
ATHENS
When Timotheos takes too long to man his ships, the Athenians appoint Iphikrates in his place, and he, adding all the ships in Attic waters, sails with seventy triremes.

6.2.15–16
372
CORCYRA
Seeing the great hardships endured by the Corcyraeans, Mnasippos grows overconfident and withholds pay from his troops.

6.2.17–19
372
CORCYRA
When the Corcyraeans make a successful sally against some of his posts, Mnasippos orders a general counterattack, but his men are hostile to him and dispirited.

6.2.12a The islands of the Aegean Sea: Map 6.2.2, AY. See 4.8.7.

6.2.13a In winter the winds blew steadily from the west-northwest, making it very difficult for vessels to round Cape Malea (Map 6.2.2, BY) from the east.

6.2.13b Iphikrates was last mentioned at 5.1.25, when he was blockading Nikolochos at Abydos (Map 6.3.2, AY). Other evidence shows that in the meantime he had been in Thrace and Egypt. For more information on his career, see "Iphikrates" in Appendix M, §12.

6.2.14a For the trierarch's obligations, see Appendix K, Trireme Warfare in Xenophon's *Hellenika*, §11.

6.2.14b The *Paralos* and the *Salaminia* were the

two special state triremes used on sacred embassies and official business.

6.2.14c Xenophon misleads here, because there was in fact quite a long gap between Timotheos' recall from the North Aegean and Iphikrates' actually setting out for the west, necessitated by Iphikrates' part in the prosecution of Timotheos, which ended in the latter's acquittal. See the Introduction, §14.6.

6.2.16a The arrangement whereby the cities could supply money instead of men was described at 5.2.21.

6.2.18a Company commanders (*lokhagoi*) and squadron commanders (*taxiarchs*): see 3.1.28 and Appendix F, §10.

out the mercenaries. [19] But when some of the company commanders answered Mnasippos that it was not easy to furnish obedient men when they had not been given their provisions, Mnasippos struck one of them with a staff and another with the butt of his spear. Because of this, his men marched out dispirited and hating him: a state of affairs that is least helpful when men are going into battle.

6.2.20–23
372
CORCYRA
After an initial advance, the Spartans are vigorously attacked by the Corcyraeans and thrown back. Mnasippos is killed in the fighting, and the Spartan camp is almost taken.

[20] When he had deployed the men for battle, Mnasippos himself routed and pursued the Corcyraeans who had been stationed opposite the city gates. When these men came near their city walls, however, they faced about and from the tombstones[a] threw spears and javelins at the pursuers. Other Corcyraeans ran out from the different gates of the city and made an attack in mass formation on the end of the enemy's line. [21] The Spartans were arrayed eight deep, but they thought that the end of the line was too weak to hold the charge, so they attempted to wheel around[a] to support it. But when they began their backward movement, the Corcyraeans thought they were fleeing and attacked them so that the Spartans could not complete the maneuver. Then the troops next to those attempting the wheel-around movement turned to flee.

[22] Mnasippos could not bring help to those being pressed because of the attack of the enemy troops directly opposite him, and meanwhile his losses continued to mount. Finally the Corcyraeans, massing themselves together, made an attack on Mnasippos and the troops around him, who were now much diminished in number, and the citizens in the city, seeing what was happening, ran out from the gates. [23] Mnasippos himself was killed, and all the Corcyraeans swept forward in pursuit. They would have captured the camp itself, together with its stockade, had not the pursuers seen the mob of camp followers,[a] both servants and slaves, and, thinking that they would get some profit from these, turned aside after them.

6.2.24–26
372
CORCYRA
Defeated, dispirited, and worried that Iphikrates and the Athenians are about to arrive, the Spartans evacuate Corcyra and arrive safely at Leucas.

[24] The Corcyraeans then set up a trophy and gave back the dead under truce.[a] After this the men in the city felt greatly encouraged, while

6.2.20a   Cemetery tombstones and monuments were erected near ancient city gates, because no one was allowed to be buried within the walls. The retreating Corcyraeans used the tombstones for protection and to gain superior height, useful when throwing missiles.

6.2.21a   The movement that was being attempted here, the *anastrophē*, was probably a version of that described in Xenophon's *Constitution of the Lacedaemonians* 11.8; see also Appendix F, §11. The troops at the end of the line that was not under pressure would about-face and march to the rear until they cleared the last ranks; they would then turn 90 degrees and march behind their phalanx to the other end to give extra support where the enemy's attack was stronger. In this instance, as the Spartan-led troops were performing the initial countermarch, the Corcyraeans whom they had previously been facing charged forward and disrupted both the maneuver and the Spartan phalanx.

6.2.23a   Greek armies routinely got their supplies from tradesmen who followed the army, and there were probably large numbers of helots (serfs) who attended the Spartan hoplites, not to mention cooks and other noncombatant camp followers.

6.2.24a   After a battle in ancient Greece, the victors would gather up their dead, strip those of the enemy, and raise a trophy, usually a set of captured armor arrayed on a pole. The defeated would collect the bodies of their fallen during a truce that they would explicitly request and be granted for that purpose. In this way, appropriate reverence was shown and proper burial was accorded to all war dead. See Appendix L, Land Warfare in Xenophon's *Hellenika*, §13.

those outside were completely despondent. Adding to their gloom was a report that Iphikrates was almost there, and the Corcyraeans had actually begun to man their ships. [25] Then Hypermenes, who happened to be vice-admiral under Mnasippos, manned all the ships that were there and sailed around to the stockade, filled up his transport ships with the captured slaves and valuables, and dispatched them home. He himself, with the marines and those soldiers who had survived the attack, remained to guard the stockade. [26] But finally even these, greatly shaken, boarded their triremes and sailed home. They left behind a great deal of grain, wine, and slaves, as well as those soldiers who were sick or disabled. They did this because they greatly feared being caught on the island by the Athenians. These men, then, got away safely to Leucas.[a]

[27] Now when Iphikrates began his voyage around the Peloponnese,[a] he had, as he sailed, been making all preparations for a sea battle. At the outset he left behind his large sails,[b] since he expected to engage the enemy in battle, and he barely used his small sails, even when there was a favorable wind. He thought that steady rowing would put his men in better physical shape and would also increase the speed of the fleet. [28] He also devised the following strategy whenever it was time for the morning or evening meal. He would often draw back the inshore wing of the line from the land near their chosen landing spot and then arrange all the triremes prow by prow facing the shore. At a given signal they would race toward land, and it was a great victory to be the first to land, obtain water and any other provisions needed, and have one's meal. Those who arrived last incurred a significant penalty—both by virtue of the fact that they had been defeated by all the others and because, when the next signal was given to depart, they had to put to sea at the same time as the others, even though the first to arrive had been able to accomplish what they needed at leisure, while they, the last to arrive, were compelled to do everything in haste.

[29] Whenever Iphikrates was taking the midday meal in enemy territory, he not only stationed some of the guards on land, as is good practice, but he raised the masts on some of the ships and placed men at their tops to keep a lookout from there.[a] These men could thus see much farther than those on land, since they were looking down from on high. Whenever it was time for the evening meal or sleep, he would light no fire during the night inside the camp but instead kept a fire in front of the army so that no one could approach undetected. Often too, if the wind was favorable, he would have dinner and then immediately set sail: if the breeze carried them, they could relax while moving farther on; if they had to row, he would rest the crews by having groups of them row in turn. [30] When he sailed by day, he would at times lead them in columns, at times in battle formation,[a]

6.2.27–30
372
PELOPONNESE
Iphikrates, leaving behind his sails as he leads his fleet around the Peloponnese, employs many interesting techniques to train his sailors and to keep them in good shape.

6.2.26a   Leucas: Map 6.2.2, AX.
6.2.27a   Peloponnese: Map 6.2.2, BX.
6.2.27b   For more on the question of leaving sails behind, see Appendix K, §2.
6.2.29a   Masts were lowered while the ships

traveled by oar. See Appendix K, §2.
6.2.30a   They would be deployed in line, the normal formation for engaging another fleet. See Appendix K, §3.

so that as they sailed they were practicing and acquiring all the skills necessary for naval warfare; in this manner they made their way to the sea, which they thought was under the control of their enemies. And although they took morning and evening meals for the most part in their enemy's territory, Iphikrates only let the troops do what was strictly necessary, so that they always finished quickly and managed to put back out to sea before enemy troops could arrive to attack them; and in this way they quickly arrived at their destination.

6.2.31–32
372
CEPHALLANIA
Amid unconfirmed reports of Mnasippos' death, Iphikrates approaches Corcyra prepared for battle. Xenophon commends his leadership skill in keeping his men in top form over a long journey and yet arriving on time.

[31] Around the time of Mnasippos' death, Iphikrates happened to be near the Sphagiae Islands in Laconia.[a] From there he went to Elis[b] and sailed past the mouth of the Alpheios[c] River, where he anchored at a place called the Fish.[d] On the next day he set sail from there to Cephallania,[e] and he arranged his voyage in such a way that he had everything prepared for a naval battle if he had to fight one. Now he had not heard the circumstances surrounding the death of Mnasippos from any eyewitness, and he suspected that it might have been been fabricated to deceive him, so he kept up his guard. At Cephallania, however, he confirmed what had happened, and so he rested the army.

[32] Now I know, of course, that whenever men think they are going to engage in a sea battle, they make preparations and take care of their forces in all the ways I have mentioned. But what I particularly praise about Iphikrates is that when he had to bring his forces swiftly to a place where he thought he might immediately have to fight the enemy, he contrived the voyage so that his men would not be ignorant of the skills needed for a naval battle, nor would they be tardy in arriving there because they had been practicing their skills.

6.2.33–36
372
CORCYRA
At Corcyra, Iphikrates sets a watch for an approaching Syracusan flotilla. Given warning by the lookouts, he attacks and surprises the Syracusans, capturing all the ships and crews but one. The captured crewmen are ransomed against surety by the Corcyraeans.

[33] After having subdued the cities in Cephallania, Iphikrates then sailed on to Corcyra,[a] where he heard that ten triremes from Dionysios[b] were on their way in order to bring assistance to the Spartans. He then went out himself to examine the ground and select the best spot from which his men would be able to see any approaching ships and to send clear signals back to the city. There he stationed his lookouts. [34] He also arranged with them how they were to signal when the ships arrived and were dropping anchor. He also selected twenty of the trierarchs who were to follow him when the herald made the appropriate announcement. He warned them that anyone who failed to follow him must not find fault with the punishment that would be inflicted upon him. When the scouts announced that the ships were arriving and the herald made the proclama-

6.2.31a The Sphagiai (Sphacteria and other small adjacent islets) were situated off Pylos in Messenia (Map 6.3.2, BX), not Laconia (Map 6.3.2, BX), so either Xenophon has made an error or he is referring to them as off Laconia because Messenia was then controlled by Sparta and could be thought of as part of its territory.
6.2.31b Elis: Map 6.3.2, BX.

6.2.31c Alpheios River: Map 6.3.2, BX.
6.2.31d In the Greek, *ichthys*. The Ichthys Peninsula (Map 6.3.2, BX) is probably what is meant.
6.2.31e Cephallania: Map 6.3.2, BX.
6.2.33a Corcyra: Map 6.3.2, AX.
6.2.33b Dionysios, tyrant of Syracuse in Sicily (Map 6.2.2, locator.).

tion, the eagerness displayed by all was a sight worth seeing. Everyone who was about to sail went at a run to his ship. [35] When they sailed to where the enemy triremes had landed, Iphikrates captured the men who had disembarked from the ships. Only Melanippos the Rhodian, who had counseled the others not to anchor there, reembarked his men on his ship and sailed out of the harbor. And although he encountered the ships of Iphikrates and they were arrayed against him, he managed to escape them all and got away. All the ships of the Syracusans, together with their crews, were captured.

[36] Iphikrates cut the beaks off the prows of the captured triremes[a] and towed them into the Corcyraean harbor. It was agreed that each man would be ransomed for a fixed amount, except for Krinippos, the commander: he was kept under guard by Iphikrates, who intended either to sell him as a slave or to obtain a very large ransom for him.[b] Krinippos, however, because of his distress, chose to end his life himself, and Iphikrates thereafter dismissed the rest, accepting Corcyraeans as guarantors for the ransom.

[37] Iphikrates maintained his sailors for the most part by having them work the land of the Corcyraeans,[a] but he took the peltasts and the hoplites from the ships and crossed over with them into Acarnania.[b] There he gave aid to any friendly city that needed it,[c] but he made war on the people of Thyrreion,[d] who were brave fighters and possessed a strong fortress.

[38] In addition, he took over the fleet at Corcyra (around ninety ships)[a] and first sailed to Cephallania, where he collected money. Some gave voluntarily, others against their will. He then prepared to ravage the lands of the Spartans[b] and their allies, to win over any hostile cities in those parts that would consent to join him, and to make war against any that would not obey him.

[39] I think that this campaign of Iphikrates is particularly worthy of praise, and no less admirable is the fact that he asked the Athenians to choose as his colleague Kallistratos[a] the popular leader, who was in no way friendly toward him, and also Chabrias,[b] who was considered a very good general. Now if he wanted to take them because he considered them thoughtful counselors, then I think he made an intelligent move; or if he did it because he considered them to be his rivals and wanted to show

6.2.37
372
CORCYRA
Iphikrates' sailors work the land while he takes the hoplites to Acarnania.

6.2.38–39
372
PELOPONNESE
Iphikrates exacts money from Cephallania and prepares to raid Spartan territory. Xenophon again commends his generalship.

6.2.36a   The "beak" of a trireme was the cast-bronze ram at its bow. As it could weigh about a half ton, it had substantial value. See Appendix K, §6.
6.2.36b   Diodorus (Appendix O, 15.47) says that Iphikrates raised more than 60 talents and from this paid his soldiers and sailors.
6.2.37a   Eteonikos had done something similar on Chios (Map 6.3.2, BY); see 2.1.1.
6.2.37b   Acarnania: Map 6.3.2, AX.
6.2.37c   These were cities that had joined the Second Athenian League in 375.
6.2.37d   Thyrreion: Map 6.3.2, AX.

6.2.38a   If the ninety Corcyraean triremes were added to the original seventy of Iphikrates, an incredibly large fleet would have been created. The text appears to be faulty here.
6.2.38b   Sparta: Map 6.3.2, BX.
6.2.39a   Kallistratos: Athenian statesman. He is mentioned here as working with Iphikrates. A speech he gives to the Spartan Assembly is found at 6.3.10–17. See also "Kallistratos" in Appendix M, §14.
6.2.39b   The Athenian general Chabrias was last mentioned at 5.1.10ff. and 5.4.61. See Appendix M, §6.

(quite boldly) that he was neither dilatory nor careless, this seems to me the mark of a man of supreme self-confidence. Iphikrates, then, was busy with these matters.

[1] The Athenians, meanwhile, were watching events in Boeotia.[a] Their friends the Plataeans[b] had been driven out of Boeotia and had fled to Athens,[c] and the people of Thespiai[d] were begging the Athenians not to allow them to be left without a city.[e] These moves by the Thebans[f] led the Athenians to no longer approve of Thebes' actions, but they were ashamed to wage war against them, and they calculated that they would gain no benefit from it. They refused, however, to take part in any ventures with them, particularly when they saw that the Thebans were campaigning against the Phocians,[g] who were Athenian friends of old and were trying to destroy cities that had been allies of Athens in the Persian Wars.[h] [2] For these reasons, the people voted to make peace: first, they sent ambassadors to Thebes inviting them to join with Athens and, if they were willing, to go to Sparta to negotiate peace.[a] Next, they themselves sent ambassadors to Sparta; and among the men they chose were Kallias[b] son of Hipponikos, Autokles son of Strombichides, Demostratos son of Aristophon, Aristokles, Kephisodotos,[c] Melanopos, and Lykaithos. [3] Kallistratos, the popular leader, was also present, since he had promised Iphikrates that if he were allowed to return home, he would either provide money for the navy[a] or make peace: it was in this way that he was at Athens and was taking part in the efforts to achieve peace. When the Athenians came before the assembly of the Spartans and the representatives of Sparta's allies, the first of them to speak was Kallias the torch-bearer,[b] a man who delighted in being praised no less by himself as by others. He began his speech something like this:

6.3.1–3
371
ATHENS-SPARTA
The Athenians, seeing that Thebes has injured many friends of theirs, decide to leave the war and send envoys to Sparta to effect that. They also invite the Thebans to join them if they wish. Kallias, a vain man, speaks first to the Spartans.

6.3.1a Boeotia: Map 6.3.2, BX.
6.3.1b Plataea: Map 6.3.2, inset. Plataea had been a loyal friend and ally of Athens since the late sixth century.
6.3.1c Athens: Map 6.3.2, BX, and inset. Diodorus (Appendix O, 15.46.4–6) gives the details of the expulsion of the Plataeans, which took place in 373. They were intending to hand over their city to Athens when they were discovered. The Thebans captured the city while the men were away working in the fields, and they razed it, allowing the inhabitants to flee to Athens.
6.3.1d Thespiai: Map 6.3.2, inset.
6.3.1e Diodorus (Appendix O, 15.86) explains that the people of Thespiai also had their city destroyed and were forced to live in scattered villages.
6.3.1f Thebes: Map 6.3.2, inset.
6.3.1g Phocis: Map 6.3.2, inset. For Phocian friendship with Athens see Thucydides 1.108, 1.112, 3.95. When at the conclusion of the Peloponnesian War Thebes and Corinth had pressed Sparta to destroy Athens (2.2.19), it would seem that the

Phocians had opposed them (see also Plutarch, *Parallel Lives*, "Lysander" 15.3).
6.3.1h The Plataeans were at Marathon: Map 6.3.2, inset (see Herodotus, *Histories* 6.108). The Thespians were at Thermopylae: Map 6.3.2, inset (see Herodotus, *Histories* 7.222, 7.226). The Thebans, notoriously, had taken the Persian side in the war.
6.3.2a Thebes was a member of the Second Athenian League, under the terms of which the members decided on war and peace, so it is unclear why Xenophon presents the Athenians as individually going to the Thebans. For Thebes' attitude to this peace, see Diodorus (Appendix O, 15.50.4).
6.3.2b For this Kallias, see 4.5.13, 5.4.22.
6.3.2c A speech by Kephisodotos to the Athenian Assembly can be found at 7.1.12.
6.3.3a For Iphikrates' need of money, see 6.2.38.
6.3.3b "Torch-bearer" was an official title of Kallias, who was one of four officials who conducted the Eleusinian Mysteries, an office that was hereditary in his family (the Kerykes).

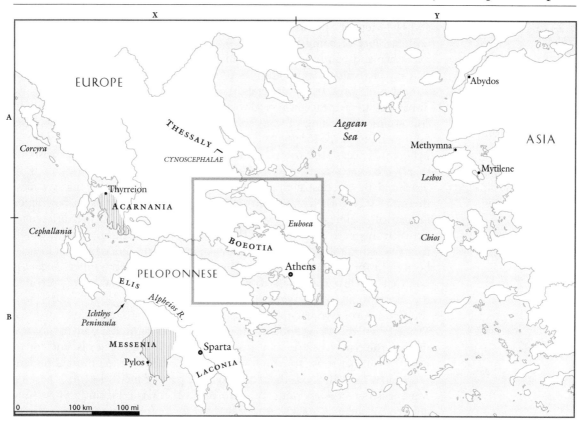

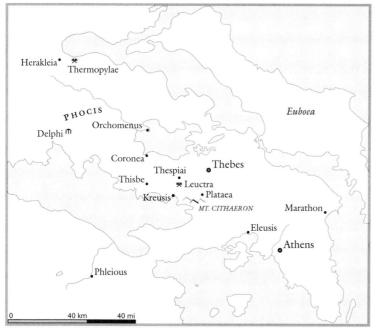

Map 6.3.2

6.3.4–6
371
SPARTA
The speech of Kallias.
He points out that he and
his father, grandfather,
and great-grandfather
have all served as *proxenos*
of Sparta at Athens.
Since Athenians and
Spartans agree on most
things, he says, they
should have no difficulty
making peace now.

[4] "Men of Sparta, I am not the only one in my family to have the responsibility of being your *proxenos*,[a] for my grandfather received it from his father and handed it down to his descendants. I want to tell you also that my city valued and continues to value my family: whenever we are at war, she chooses us as generals,[b] and whenever she desires peace, she dispatches us as peacemakers. Twice in the past I have come before you concerning the ending of war,[c] and on both those embassies I was successful in making peace for you and for us. I am now here for a third time, and I think this occasion is by far the most deserving of peace. [5] The reason is that I see that we are now of the same opinions: you and we are both distressed by the destruction of Plataea and Thespiai. Given that we have the same views, then, how can it not be reasonable for us to be friends instead of enemies? Surely wise men do not start a war if the differences between them are only slight: so then, if in fact we are in agreement, would it not be astounding if we failed to make peace? [6] Indeed, it would have been right for us not even to have begun a war against each other, since it is said that the first foreigners to whom Triptolemus, our ancestor, revealed the secret rights of Demeter and Kore[a] were Herakles, your founder, and the Dioskouroi,[b] your citizens; and he first gave the seeds of the fruit of Demeter to the Peloponnese. How, then, is it right for you to go and destroy the fruit of those men from whom you took the seeds, and for us not to wish that those to whom we gave the seeds have the most abundant crops possible?[c] If the gods have made it a part of men's lot that there be wars, it is nevertheless right for us to begin them as reluctantly as possible and to end them as quickly as we can."

6.3.7–9
371
SPARTA
Autokles, a forceful
orator, tells the Spartans
bluntly of their hypocrisy
concerning the indepen-
dence of Greek cities,
which they have prevented
more than anyone.

[7] After Kallias, Autokles, who had a reputation for being a particularly vehement speaker, addressed them as follows: "Men of Sparta, I am well aware that what I have to say will not please you. But if men wish the alliances they make to last as long as possible, they must instruct one another in the causes of the hostilities between them. Now you always say that the cities must be autonomous, but you yourselves stand most in the way of this autonomy? For you stipulate first that the allied cities must follow you wherever you lead them. [8] And yet how is this consistent with autonomy? Moreover, you decide who your enemies are without taking counsel with your allies, and then you lead your allies against those

6.3.4a   For Kallias as *proxenos* of Sparta, see
5.4.22. The office was often hereditary,
passing from father to son.
6.3.4b   Xenophon mentions only one campaign of
Kallias; he is recorded at 4.5.13 as supporting Iphikrates in a successful action in 390.
We do not know on what other occasions
he had served as general.
6.3.4c   There is no occasion other than this one in
371 for which Kallias is directly attested as
an ambassador. For one set of peace negotiations in which Kallias may well have
participated, see 6.2.1.
6.3.6a   Demeter is the goddess of grain, Kore her

daughter. Their rites were celebrated in
the secret Eleusinian Mysteries at Eleusis:
Map 6.3.2, inset. For the story of how
Demeter founded the Mysteries and
through Athens provided Greece with
corn, see Isocrates 4.28–31.
6.3.6b   The Dioskouroi were the twins Kastor
and Polydeukes, sons of Tyndareus, king
of Sparta. Dioskouroi means "sons of
Zeus."
6.3.6c   Such arguments, based on early (what we
would call mythical) actions, are a staple of
Greek diplomatic dealings.

you consider your enemies, with the result that many of these supposed autonomous states are compelled to fight against those toward whom in reality they are very friendly. And finally, you do something that is most inimical to autonomy: you establish boards of governors in the cities, a group of ten here or of thirty[a] there, and your concern in all this is not that these boards govern justly but that they hold down the cities by force. And so you resemble more those who delight in tyrannies rather than in legitimate governments. [9] When the King ordered that the cities be autonomous, you showed yourselves very much of the opinion that if the Thebans did not allow each of the cities in Boeotia to rule themselves and to use whatever laws each chose, they would not be acting in accordance with the King's orders.[a] But then you seized the Kadmeia[b] and did not thereby allow the Thebans themselves to be autonomous. Yet those who intend to be friends must not demand justice from everyone else while displaying such zeal to seize as much as they can for themselves."[c]

[10] Autokles' speech caused silence among those assembled there, although it pleased those who were angry with the Spartans.

Kallistratos[a] then spoke after him: "I do not think, men of Sparta, that I could deny that both we and you have made mistakes. I do not believe, however, that one should refuse to work with those who err, since I see that no person goes through life without making mistakes. I think, rather, that men who have made mistakes sometimes become easier to deal with, especially if they have been punished for their mistakes, as we have been. [11] And I see that at times many things have turned out badly for you, too, since you have done some arrogant deeds. One of these was your seizure of the Kadmeia in Thebes. And now, because of your unjust treatment of the Thebans, all the cities that you wished[a] so eagerly to be autonomous are once again under their control. And so I hope that now we have all learned that selfish gain will bring us no profit; we should instead be more measured in our friendships with each other. [12] As to the slander some have raised against us—namely, that we have come here not because we want friendship but because we are afraid that Antalkidas will come, bringing money from the King[a]—consider people who say this to be talking nonsense. The King, of course, has written that all the cities

6.3.10–12
371
SPARTA
Kallistratos, the popular Athenian orator, then speaks, saying that both sides have made mistakes but that friendship must surmount error, from which no one is immune. Nor is it true, he says, that the Athenians have come to Sparta out of concern for Antalkidas and the Persian King, for on the issue of independence for the cities, Athens is in agreement with the King.

6.3.8a   The most famous (or infamous) board of governors was the Thirty (later known as the Thirty Tyrants), established by threat of force in Athens after the Peloponnesian War; see the Introduction, §3.2, and Appendix O, 14.3.5–7. For boards of ten, see 3.5.13.

6.3.9a   For Agesilaos' actions while the treaty with the Persian King was being concluded, see 5.1.32. See also Appendix G, Agesilaos, §6, 9.

6.3.9b   The Kadmeia was a building on the acropolis of Thebes. For its seizure by Spartans, see 5.2.25.

6.3.9c   What Autokles says should not be automatically accepted. His remarks about the groups of ten are very out of date, and on several occasions that we know of from several sources (for example, see 5.2.11 and 5.2.37) the Spartans consult their allies and obtain their approval before going to war.

6.3.10a   For more on the Athenian statesman Kallistratos, see Appendix M, §14.

6.3.11a   Reading Breitenbach's *has* for the manuscripts' *hōs*. For the Greek, see Translator's Notes.

6.3.12a   This suggests that Antalkidas had been dispatched a second time to the Persian court for funds; see further Plutarch, *Parallel Lives*, "Artaxerxes" 22.

in Greece should be autonomous,[b] and since we have spoken and acted in accordance with his proclamation, why should we fear him? Is there anyone who thinks that the King wants to spend his money to make others powerful rather than to have his own wishes accomplished for him by others without expense?

[13] "So, then, why have we come? Well, to begin with, we are not here because we are in a difficult situation, as you could learn, if you wished, by looking at our present situation on land and sea. What, then, is the reason? Well, it is quite clear[a] . . . if some of our allies are acting in a way that does not please us but pleases you. Perhaps we may also wish to show you that you were right when you decided to save our city.[b] [14] Let me also remind you of what is advantageous and point out that, as you well know, there are states that favor you and others that favor us, and in each state some are working for Sparta's interests, some for Athens'. If, then, we become friends, from what quarter could we reasonably expect difficulties? Who would have the resources to harm us by land if you were our friends? And who could harm you by sea if we were your allies? [15] We all know that there will always be wars and attempts to end them, and that we will desire peace, if not now, then at some future time hence. Why, then, should we wait for that future time, when we will be worn out by a multitude of sufferings? Why not make peace as quickly as we can, before we suffer some irreparable blow? [16] I do not admire those athletes who have won many victories and acquired renown and yet nevertheless so love competition that they do not cease participating until they have been defeated and lost their skill. Nor do I praise a gambler who makes a winning roll and then immediately doubles his bet. I observe that the majority of such men become completely impoverished. [17] Seeing this to be the case, we must not ever enter such a contest, one where the stakes are complete success or utter failure; but while we are strong and our fortune is good, we should become friends. In this way we through you and you through us will be even greater in Greek affairs than we were in times gone by."

[18] Thinking that these words were well spoken, the Spartans voted to accept the peace, on the following terms: that the governors should be removed from the cities, infantry and naval forces should be dissolved, and the cities should be permitted to be autonomous. If anyone were to violate these terms, any state that wished could assist the city that was being treated unjustly, but any city that did not wish to do so was not obligated to

6.3.13–17
371
SPARTA
Kallistratos concludes his speech, enumerating many reasons why Sparta and Athens should become friends and be at peace.

6.3.18–20
371
SPARTA
The Spartans agree and proceed to negotiate a general peace based on the independence of all the cities. The Thebans sign, too, although later they wish to have it read "Boeotians" in place of "Thebans." Agesilaos refuses to change the agreement but offers to permit them to withdraw from it.

6.3.12b Artaxerxes had included the autonomy of Greek cities as one of the terms of the King's Peace of 387/6 (5.1.30, n. 5.1.31b), and many scholars think this is what Kallistratos/Xenophon is referring to here. However, Xenophon seems to have downplayed Persian involvement in post-386 negotiations generally (see further the Introduction, §12.18), and other sources suggest that the King directly intervened in 372/1 by sending a further rescript

(Diodorus, Appendix O, 15.50.4; Dionysius of Halicarnassus, *Lysias* 12).

6.3.13a There are several problems with the text in this paragraph. For the suggestions of Hatzfeld and Hartman in the Greek, which I have accepted here, see Translator's Notes. (John Marincola)

6.3.13b After Sparta defeated Athens in the Peloponnesian War (404), the Spartans rejected the proposal urged by some of their allies (in particular Thebes) that Athens should be completely destroyed. See 2.2.19–20.

render assistance to the injured. [19] On these terms the Spartans swore on behalf of themselves and their allies, while the Athenians and their allies each swore on behalf of themselves.[a] Thebes,[b] too, was among the cities that swore, although on the next day their ambassadors demanded that the treaty should be changed to say that "the Boeotians" rather than "the Thebans" swore.[c] Agesilaos responded to them, however, that he would change nothing that had been sworn to or written down, adding that if the Thebans did not wish to be a party to the treaty, he would remove their names: they had only to give the word. [20] In this way, then, all the rest made peace and only with the Thebans alone was there any disagreement. The Athenians were of the opinion that now there was some hope that the Thebans would, as the saying goes, be decimated.[a] The Thebans themselves departed in a state of utter despondency.[b]

[1] After this the Athenians withdrew the garrisons from the cities[a] and recalled Iphikrates[b] and the navy, compelling him to give back whatever he had acquired in the period after the oaths had been sworn at Sparta.

[2] The Spartans, however, although they withdrew the governors and the garrisons from all the other cities, did something different in regard to Kleombrotos. He was with his army in Phocis,[a] and he asked the authorities back home what he should do. Prothoos was of the opinion that they should disband the army, in accordance with the treaty they had just concluded, and should then send round to the cities to ask each to contribute whatever it wished to the temple of Apollo;[b] then if any state was unwilling to let the cities be autonomous, the Spartans would again call together volunteers who wished to defend the cities' autonomy and would lead them against the transgressor. For he said that in this way the gods

6.4.1–2
371
SPARTA
The Athenians withdraw their garrisons, fulfilling the terms of the treaty, but the Spartans disregard the warnings of the Spartan Prothoos about the appropriate diplomatic procedure to follow to keep divine favor.

6.3.19a The Athenians and their allies: this is one of Xenophon's few references in the *Hellenika* to the Second Athenian League. He also refers to it by name at 6.5.2, hints at it at 6.1.12 and 7.1.36, alludes to it with studied vagueness at 5.4.64, and studiously avoids a direct mention of it in 5.4.34. See the Introduction, §12.12.
6.3.19b Thebes: Map 6.3.2, inset.
6.3.19c Boeotia: Map 6.3.2, BX. The Thebans here demand that their hegemony or right to hegemony over Boeotia be recognized by all participants in the treaty.
6.3.20a The Greek term used here is *dekateutērion*. It literally means "tithed at a tenth," a term used when property is confiscated and one tenth is dedicated to the god. In this case the verb means that the Thebans would be punished, put in their place, isolated, and threatened by being left out of the universal peace. In any case, the English *decimate* here should not at all connote the Roman practice of punishing a military unit by executing every tenth man in it.
6.3.20b Xenophon writes this because he wants us to praise Agesilaos for isolating Thebes and to blame Kleombrotos for the subse-

quent Spartan defeat, which he regards as unforeseeable. But his bald statement must be misleading. Some, perhaps most, members of the Theban delegation may have been despondent, but its leader Epaminondas must have realized beforehand that his provocative stand would lead to war. Since he went ahead, he presumably expected that the new tactics he had developed would win the war, as in due course they did. For more on Epaminondas, see Appendix M, §9.
6.4.1a They withdrew from the cities of Cephallania (Map 6.3.2, BX) and environs: see 6.2.33, 6.2.37–38.
6.4.1b See 6.2.38.
6.4.2a Phocis: Map 6.3.2, inset. The Thebans were probably threatening the Phocians again; see 6.3.1.
6.4.2b The temple of Apollo at Delphi (Map 6.3.2, inset), presumably. It was especially suitable to make contributions to Delphi at this point as it had recently been severely damaged by an earthquake. We have the accounts of the restoration fund for years afterward. See Figure 6.4.2, a photograph of what currently remains of the temple.

FIGURE 6.4.2. REMAINS OF THE TEMPLE OF APOLLO AT DELPHI.

6.4.3
371
BOEOTIA
Sparta orders Kleombrotos
to keep his army intact
and to attack the Thebans
at once. He invades
Boeotia by a little-used
route and captures Kreusis
and twelve triremes.

would look most favorably on the Spartans, and the cities would be least
burdened. [3] The Spartan Assembly thought this proposal was nonsense,
for even at that time, it seems, the divinity[a] was leading them on. They
therefore ordered Kleombrotos not to disband his army but to lead it immediately against the Thebans unless they allowed the cities to be autonomous.
When Kleombrotos learned that the Thebans not only had failed to allow
the cities to be autonomous but had not even disbanded their army (because
they were planning to fight Kleombrotos),[b] he led his own forces into Boeotia.[c] Now Kleombrotos did not enter Boeotia from Phocis, where the Thebans expected him and where they were guarding a narrow pass,[d] but set out
from Thisbe,[e] took an unexpected, mountainous route, and arrived instead
at Kreusis,[f] where he captured the wall and twelve Theban triremes.

6.4.3a   For a discussion of Xenophon's religious
         beliefs, see the Introduction, §13.1–5.
6.4.3b   Some scholars think the words in paren-
         theses here are a gloss, that is, an explana-
         tory comment that has somehow found its
         way into the manuscript. For the Greek,
         see Translator's Notes.
6.4.3c   Diodorus (Appendix O, 15.51) says that

Kleombrotos sent envoys to Thebes, who
were rudely rebuffed.
6.4.3d   According to Diodorus (Appendix O,
         15.52), they were guarding the narrows
         near Coronea (Map 6.3.2, inset).
6.4.3e   Thisbe: Map 6.3.2, inset.
6.4.3f   Kreusis: Map 6.3.2, inset.

[4] Having done this, he marched inland and made camp at Leuctra,[a] which is in the territory of Thespiai.[b] The Thebans, having now discovered him, made their camp on the hill opposite, leaving only a small distance between them. They had no allies with them except the Boeotians. At this point Kleombrotos' friends approached him and said: [5] "Kleombrotos, if you fail to engage the Thebans in battle here, you will run the risk of suffering the greatest punishment from the Spartans. For they will remember when you were at Cynoscephalae[a] and did not harm Theban territory, and then later when you were beaten back from Theban territory, even though Agesilaos always invaded through Cithaeron.[b] So if you think of your own interests and you wish to see your country again,[c] you must lead us against these men." While his friends were saying this, his enemies said, "This man will show us now whether he really has Theban interests at heart, as people say he does."[d]

[6] These words spurred Kleombrotos into giving battle.[a] The leaders on the Theban side believed that if they did not fight it out with Kleombrotos, the cities that were their neighbors would revolt and their own city would be besieged. They also believed that if their city came under siege and failed to obtain necessary provisions, the citizens would probably turn against them; and since many of them had already been in exile before, they felt it would be better to fight it out now and die rather than to go into exile again. [7] Aside from these considerations, they were encouraged in their resolve by an oracle that had said the Spartans would be defeated near the monument to the virgins. (These virgins were said to have killed themselves because they had been violated by some Spartans.)[a] The Thebans decorated this monument before the battle. Then again, they were receiving reports from the city that the doors of the temples there had opened up of their own accord, and that the priestesses were claiming that the gods were doing this as a sign of victory; and it was also said that

6.4.4–5
371
LEUCTRA
Kleombrotos advances to Leuctra, where the Boeotians camp opposite him. He is warned by friends that this time he must give battle to the Thebans or risk being considered secretly partial to the enemy, for which he could be exiled.

6.4.6–8
371
LEUCTRA
Both Kleombrotos and the leaders of the Thebans have reasons to seek battle. Oracles and portents indicate that the Spartans this time will not be victorious, although some say these were devices of the Theban leaders.

6.4.4a   Leuctra: Map 6.3.2, inset.
6.4.4b   Thespiai: Map 6.3.2, inset.
6.4.5a   There is a well-known Cynoscephalae in Thessaly (Map 6.3.2, AX), but the location of a Cynoscephalae in Boeotia is unknown.
6.4.5b   For Xenophon's description of Kleombrotos' campaigns, see 5.4.15–16 and 5.4.59. For Agesilaos' successful penetrations via Mount Cithaeron (Map 6.3.2, inset), see 5.4.37, 5.4.47.
6.4.5c   That is, to avoid the punishment of having exile imposed against him.
6.4.5d   Perhaps the accusation that Kleombrotos was pro-Theban stems from nothing more than an inference from his withdrawal from Theban territory at 5.4.15 without harming it, but this might have been a military rather than political judgment on his part, or based on short-term considerations. However, it is quite likely that in the 370s Kleombrotos was described as pro-Theban, although probably unfairly,

because he may have wanted Sparta to focus on combating Athens. Agesilaos clearly regarded Thebes as the principal enemy, and it would not be a surprise if the long-standing rivalry between the two royal houses at Sparta meant that Kleombrotos took a different line. For more on Sparta's dual kingship, see Appendix E, §13–14.
6.4.6a   Xenophon's account of the circumstances leading up to the battle is contradicted by Diodorus' account in Appendix O, 15.54–56. Most scholars prefer Xenophon's account to that of Diodorus on most of the questions in contention.
6.4.7a   Diodorus (Appendix O, 15.54.2) says they were the daughters of Leuktros and Skedasos. The monument is mentioned also by Pausanias (9.13.6), a Greek travel writer of the second century C.E. (about five hundred years after Xenophon), who described, among other things, many battlefields and monuments.

In the battle everything goes well for the Thebans and ill for the Spartans. A Spartan thrust against the Theban baggage train results in its retreat to the main body, giving more weight to the Theban center.

The Theban cavalry is better trained than the Spartan cavalry, and while the Spartan infantry deploys into a phalanx twelve deep, the Theban phalanx is fifty men deep. The Theban strategy is to break through and over-run the Spartan line at its strongest sector, around the Spartan king.

the arms of Herakles had vanished from his temple, the reason being put forth that he had gone out for the battle to come. Now there are some who claim that all these portents were contrived by the men in control of the city. [8] Whatever was the case, in the battle itself everything went against the Spartans, while for their opponents everything went right, even what happened by chance.

Kleombrotos held his last council concerning the battle after the morning meal, and there was a rumor that because they had been drinking wine, they were somewhat spurred on. [9] Both sides were now putting on their armor, and it already had become obvious that there would be a battle. At this point, a group consisting of men who had provided the market,[a] some baggage carriers, and others who did not want to fight[b] set out from the Boeotian camp. They were attacked by the mercenaries commanded by Hieron,[c] the Phocian peltasts, and the Herakleiot[d] and Phleiasian[e] cavalry, who encircled them, routed them, and pursued them back to the Boeotian camp. In doing so, they made the Boeotian army larger and its phalanx deeper[f] than before.

[10] Then, since the two armies faced each other in a plain, the Spartans stationed their cavalry in front of their phalanx, and the Thebans placed their cavalry opposite them. But whereas the Theban cavalry was thoroughly practiced because of the wars against the Orchomenians[a] and the Thespians,[b] the Spartan cavalry at that time was in the very worst shape. [11] This was because at Sparta only the wealthiest men raised horses, and when troops were called up, each man who was selected by his officers to serve in the cavalry would come to obtain his horse and whatever arms were given to him, and immediately go to the field. Most important of all was the fact that the men riding the horses were in terrible physical shape and utterly uninterested in winning glory. [12] Such was the cavalry on each side.

The Spartan infantry, it was said, was being led into battle three files abreast for each half-unit,[a] with the result that the depth of its formation was not greater than twelve men. The Thebans, however, were arrayed not less than fifty shields deep, for they reckoned that if they defeated the bodyguard of the Spartan king,[b] the rest of the army would be very easy to handle.

6.4.9a   Greek soldiers and sailors at this time were expected to purchase their food from local markets with their own money, so merchants selling food often accompanied armies in the field.
6.4.9b   According to Polyainos 2.3.3, Epaminondas, the commander of the Thebans at this battle, had told any who were not willing to fight to depart.
6.4.9c   Hieron was a Spartan, perhaps the same one mentioned by Plutarch (*Moralia*, "On the Pythian Responses" 397b).
6.4.9d   Herakleia: Map 6.3.2, inset.
6.4.9e   Phleious: Map 6.3.2, inset.
6.4.9f   Why it would be a good thing to enlarge the army or deepen its phalanx with men

who had already shown a disinclination to fight is hard to see. Xenophon's comment here is simply odd.
6.4.10a   Orchomenus (in Boeotia): Map 6.3.2, inset. Xenophon never mentions these Theban wars against Orchomenus.
6.4.10b   Except obliquely at 6.3.1, Xenophon has not mentioned a Theban campaign against Thespiai before. For the circumstances, see Diodorus (Appendix O, 15.37).
6.4.12a   The Spartan half-unit (*enomotia*) consisted of thirty-two to thirty-six men.
6.4.12b   The Spartan king and his bodyguard were arrayed on the right wing.

FIGURE 6.4.9.
TWO VIEWS OF A FIGURINE OF A HOPLITE IN FULL
PANOPLY, C. 510–500 (ABOVE), WITH HELMET, BELL
CUIRASS, GREAVES, SHORT TUNIC, AND TYPICAL
"BOEOTIAN" SHIELD. THE WARRIOR IS IN A SIDEWAYS
COMBAT STANCE. COIN, C. 395–387 (RIGHT), DEPICT-
ING THE CHARACTERISTIC THEBAN/BOEOTIAN SHIELD.

FIGURE 6.4.15. THE BATTLEFIELD OF LEUCTRA. THE ANCIENT VICTORY MONUMENT ERECTED BY THE THEBANS CAN BE SEEN IN THE RIGHT FOREGROUND.

6.4.13–14
371
LEUCTRA
The battle begins. The Spartans have an initial advantage, as shown by their ability to take their wounded king out of the battle successfully, but after many other Spartans fall, the rest give way and withdraw to their camp, where they halt.

[13] When Kleombrotos began to lead his men toward the enemy, the first thing that happened, even before the troops with him realized that they were marching into battle, was that the cavalry of both sides engaged, and the Spartan horse were quickly defeated. In their flight, they fell upon their own hoplites at the same time that the companies of Theban troops began to attack them. Nevertheless, Kleombrotos and his troops were winning the battle at first, as one can deduce from this clear proof: his men would not have been able to take up Kleombrotos' body[a] while he was still alive and carry it off the field unless those fighting in front of them were getting the better of their opponents at the time.[b] [14] But then Deinon

6.4.13a   For another version of how the Spartans gained possession of the body of Kleombrotos, see Diodorus (Appendix O, 15.55–56.1). For details of the battle, see Appendix F, §12.
6.4.13b   It is interesting to note that Xenophon produces only a logical argument for this assertion of early Spartan ascendance; he does not allege any direct evidence for it.

One might reasonably infer that if no witness was prepared to tell Xenophon that this was what happened (so he had to resort to an indirect argument), then it was not true. However, it speaks for his good faith that when he hasn't got direct evidence for something he would very much like to believe, he doesn't claim that he has.

the polemarch,[a] along with Sphodrias, one of the king's tent companions, and Kleonymos, his son,[b] were killed, and the Horsemen[c] and the polemarch's aides-de-camp[d] (as they are called), as well as the rest, retreated under the pressure of the massed Theban attack, while the Spartan left wing, seeing the right wing being pressed, gave way. Many were killed, and others were defeated when they crossed a ditch that happened to be in front of their camp.[e] Yet, even so, they grounded arms at the camp from which they had first marched out: this had been set on ground that was not quite level, being instead on a hillside.

Some Spartans thought their misfortune unendurable; they said that they had to prevent the enemy from setting up a trophy and should try to take up the corpses by fighting for them rather than getting them back under truce. [15] The polemarchs, however, could see that nearly a thousand Spartans had died, which included about four hundred Spartiates (around seven hundred Spartiates had taken part in the battle),[a] and they realized that the Spartan allies had no heart for more fighting and that some were even pleased at what had happened. So they gathered together the ablest men and deliberated about what should be done. All of them agreed that they should ask for a truce to take up the corpses, and so they sent a herald for this purpose. The Thebans then set up a trophy and gave the bodies back under truce.

[16] When the battle was over, a messenger was sent to Sparta to announce the disaster. He arrived on the last day of the Festival of the Naked Youths,[a] during the performance of the men's chorus in the theater. When the ephors heard about the disaster, they were greatly distressed, as one would expect them to be, but they did not have the chorus leave the theater. Instead they allowed them to finish their performance, and then they revealed the names of the dead to each of the families. They ordered the women not to cry out but to bear their suffering in silence, and on the next day, one could see[b] the relatives of those who had died going around

6.4.15
371
LEUCTRA
Some Spartans wish to continue the battle, but the polemarchs decide that, given their great losses, it would be best to seek a truce to recover their dead.

6.4.16
371
SPARTA
News of the defeat arrives during a festival. The ephors, though upset, permit the chorus to finish and give out the names of the dead. They order relatives of the dead to bear it cheerfully. They do.

6.4.14a Spartan polemarchs (high military commanders): see Appendix F, §5.
6.4.14b For more on Sphodrias and his son Kleonymos, see 5.4.33 and "Sphodrias" in Appendix M, §22.
6.4.14c Accepting the emendation of Estienne of the manuscripts' *hippoi* ("horses") to *hippeis*, which means "cavalry" in general but is also the name of an elite unit that, for historical reasons, was known as the Horsemen but who fought with the king as hoplites on foot. (John Marincola, David Thomas) This makes more sense here, since Xenophon has just criticized the true cavalry. For the Greek, see Translator's Notes. See also Appendix F, §7.
6.4.14d This passage is the only ancient reference to the polemarch's aides-de-camp, whose precise functions have to be guessed at.
6.4.14e Xenophon's manner of expression suggests that this was a natural ditch, not one that had been constructed for defense.

6.4.15a For the Spartiates (Spartans with full citizen rights), see Appendix E, §17. These casualties were all the more serious because of Sparta's declining manpower; see Appendix F, §3, and the Introduction, §16.2.
6.4.16a The Festival of the Naked Youths (in the Greek, the Gymnopaidiai), translated by other scholars as the Festival of Unarmed Dancing, was one of the most important Spartan festivals, held in honor of the god Apollo. It lasted several days (perhaps five) and involved not only dancing, for which the Spartans were famous, but also singing by separate choirs of boys, young men, and old men.
6.4.16b Since non-Spartans could attend the Gymnopaidiai, this remark (literally, "it was possible to see") has sometimes been seen as evidence that Xenophon was an eyewitness. But such remarks are common in Greek historical accounts as a way to impart vividness to the narrative.

with bright and happy faces, while you would have seen on the street only a few of those whose relatives had been reported as still alive, and these few were making their way with gloomy expressions and downcast faces.[c]

[17] After this the ephors called up the two remaining regiments, taking men who were up to forty years beyond the minimum age of military service. They also called up men of the same age from the outside regiments. (Previously, for the campaign in Phocis, they had sent out men up to the thirty-five-year mark.)[a] The ephors also ordered those who had been left behind because they were then holding office to accompany these regiments. [18] Now Agesilaos had not yet recovered from his illness,[a] so the city ordered Archidamos, his son, to command the army. The men of Tegea[b] eagerly joined this force, for the followers of Stasippos[c] were still alive and were both pro-Spartan and very powerful in their city. The Mantineians from the villages also joined him in great strength, for they happened to be ruled by an aristocracy.[d] The Corinthians,[e] Sicyonians,[f] Phleiasians,[g] and Achaeans[h] also enthusiastically followed him, and other cities as well sent him troops. The Spartans themselves and the Corinthians manned triremes, and they asked the Sicyonians to sail with them, because they intended to use their ships to carry the troops across the gulf.[i] [19] Archidamos, for his part, offered the border-crossing sacrifices.[a]

The Thebans,[b] meanwhile, immediately after the battle, sent a garlanded herald to Athens,[c] both to announce the greatness of their victory and to ask the Athenians to bring assistance, saying that it was now possible to take vengeance on the Spartans for all the things they had done to them. [20] The Athenian Council happened to be meeting on the Acropolis when they heard what had happened, and it became clear to everyone that they were distressed, since they did not invite the herald to the customary meal of hospitality, nor did they give a response about assisting the Thebans. So the herald, having been treated in this manner, left Athens.

6.4.16c Spartans who survived a defeat in battle were subject to disenfranchisement (which was not always enforced). Plutarch writes that on this occasion Agesilaos had the law suspended (*Parallel Lives*, "Agesilaos" 30.4), no doubt because the Spartans were concerned about their diminishing manpower. See Appendix F, §3.

6.4.17a The minimum age of military service in Sparta was twenty, and the maximum age was sixty. See Appendix E, §15, 20. These "outside" regiments were those already outside Sparta, presumably camped before Leuctra. They had been mobilized only up to the age of fifty-five, leaving the men between fifty-five and sixty to be mobilized now.

6.4.18a For Agesilaos' illness, see 5.4.58.
6.4.18b Tegea: Map 6.4.27, BX.
6.4.18c Stasippos: this is his first mention by

Xenophon. For the Tegeans' later fate, see 6.5.6–10.

6.4.18d Mantineia: Map 6.4.27, BX. The Spartans had required that the Mantineians return to live in their villages and set up an aristocratic government; see 5.2.5–7.

6.4.18e Corinth: Map 6.4.27, BY.
6.4.18f Sicyon: Map 6.4.27, BY
6.4.18g Phleious: Map 6.4.27, BY.
6.4.18h Achaea: Map 6.4.27, AX.
6.4.18i The gulf mentioned here is the Corinthian Gulf: Map 6.4.27, AX.

6.4.19a Border-crossing sacrifices were a traditional requirement for all Spartan commanders before crossing the Spartan frontier. See Appendix J, Ancient Greek Religion in the Time of Xenophon, §2–3, and the Introduction, §13.5.

6.4.19b Thebes: Map 6.4.27, AY.
6.4.19c Athens: Map 6.4.27, BY.

[21] The Thebans sent in all haste to their ally Jason of Pherai[a] and asked him to come to their aid as they tried to consider how the future would turn out. Jason immediately manned triremes so as to bring help by sea. He gathered his mercenaries and his bodyguard of horsemen—even though at the time the Phocians were fighting him in an undeclared war[b]—and marched so quickly into Boeotia[c] that in many of the cities he appeared even before they had received news that he was on the march. Thus he arrived before any force from anywhere could be mustered against him, and he made it clear that it is often speed, not force, that accomplishes what is necessary.

[22] When Jason arrived in Boeotia, the Thebans said that now was a perfect opportunity to attack the Spartans: Jason could advance with his mercenaries from the heights while the Thebans themselves would make an assault on the Spartan front. Jason dissuaded them from this course of action, however, demonstrating to them that since they had accomplished something great, it would not be worthwhile for them to risk it all in an attempt to do something greater and perhaps be deprived of the victory they had already achieved. [23] "Do you not see," he said, "that you were victorious because you were in desperate straits? So you should think that the Spartans likewise, being in the same position, would have utter disregard for their lives and would fight it out to the death. And keep in mind that god, it seems, often delights in making the small great and the great small."[a] [24] By saying such things, he dissuaded the Thebans from risking all on another engagement.

He then counseled the Spartans, pointing out to them the difference between a defeated and a victorious army. "If you wish to forget the disaster you have suffered, my advice to you would be to catch your breath. Cease for a while from engagements, and when you have recovered your strength, then go into battle against men who have not been defeated. And know too that some of your allies are at this moment discussing treaties of friendship with your enemies. You must try, therefore, to make a truce by any means possible. I am very eager that you should do this, for I want to save you, both because of my father's friendship with you and because I am your *proxenos*."[a]

[25] In saying such things, Jason was perhaps trying to make himself indispensable to the two parties who were at war with each other. In any case, the Spartans heard him and asked him to act on their behalf in negotiating a truce.[a]

6.4.21
371
BOEOTIA
The Thebans call upon their ally Jason, who marches swiftly to Boeotia.

6.4.22–23
371
BOEOTIA
Although the Thebans are eager for another battle with the Spartans, Jason advises them against it, noting that the Spartans would now be desperate.

6.4.24
371
BOEOTIA
Jason dissuades the Thebans from continuing the fight and counsels the Spartans also to cease fighting for a time and to seek a longer truce.

6.4.25
371
BOEOTIA
Jason succeeds in negotiating a truce for the Spartans.

6.4.21a   Jason of Pherai: tyrant of Pherai (Map 6.4.27, AY), discussed at length in Polydamas' speech to the Spartan Assembly (6.1.4–16). Now also *tagos* of Thessaly (see 6.1.18 and n. 6.1.18a). See also "Jason of Pherai" in Appendix M, §13.
6.4.21b   Phocis: Map 6.4.27, AX. Because in these undeclared wars there could be no negotiations, they were often brutal and bitter.
6.4.21c   Boeotia: Map 6.4.27, AY.
6.4.23a   For a similar sentiment concerning the disposition of the god, see 7.4.32.

6.4.24a   It is not known how Jason came to be the Spartan *proxenos*. His father, whom he portrays as a friend of Sparta, was evidently not the Spartan *proxenos*, or he would have said so here. At 6.1.10, he is portrayed as hostile to the Spartans. A *proxenos*, although a citizen and resident of his own state, served as a "friend or representative" (much like a modern honorary consul) of a foreign state.
6.4.25a   Diodorus (Appendix O, 15.54.5) places Jason's negotiations on behalf of the Spartans before, not after, the battle.

When the news was brought that a successful treaty had been made, the polemarchs announced to their men that they should all be packed up after dinner, because they intended to set out during the night so that at dawn they should already be ascending Mount Cithaeron.[b] Right after the men had finished dinner, however, and before they could take any rest, the polemarchs ordered them to set out, and as soon as it was dusk they led them away, taking the road through Kreusis,[c] because they were relying more on secrecy than on the treaty.[d] [26] Their march was very difficult because they were departing at night and in fear and taking a hard road, but they eventually arrived at Aigosthena,[a] which is in the territory of Megara.[b] There they met up with the force that had been sent out with Archidamos. They waited there until all the allies had gathered together, and then the entire army marched to Corinth, where Archidamos dismissed the allied contingents and led his Spartan citizens home.

[27] Jason then departed and as he was making his way through Phocis he captured the suburbs of Hyampolis,[a] laying waste the land and killing many of its inhabitants. He went through the rest of Phocis, however, without taking any further hostile action. Arriving at Herakleia,[b] he threw down the wall of the Herakleiots.[c] It was clear that he did this not because he was afraid that once this passageway was opened up anyone could come against his realm but, rather, because he thought that by destroying Herakleia, which sits on a narrow piece of ground, he could not be prevented by anyone else from marching back into Greece whenever he wished to do so. [28] When he arrived home in Thessaly,[a] his reputation was great indeed: he had been established as *tagos*[b] according to Thessalian law and custom; he supported many mercenaries about him, both foot and horse; and he had trained these men to become their absolute best. Increasing his greatness were the many allies he already had and the many others who wished to become his allies. He was in fact the greatest man of his time, because no one could afford to treat him with contempt.

[29] The Pythian festival[a] was now approaching, and so Jason announced to the cities that they should prepare cattle, sheep, goats, and pigs for the sacrifices. And the report was that not less than a thousand cattle and more than ten thousand of the other animals were provided, even though the requisition from each city was very moderate. Jason also proclaimed that

6.4.25b Mount Cithaeron: Map 6.4.27, AY.
6.4.25c Kreusis: Map 6.4.27, AY.
6.4.25d Xenophon suggests that the polemarchs first told the men to be ready for a midnight march through Plataea (Map 6.4.27, AY) to Cithaeron but then, suspecting Theban treachery, had the men leave right after dinner and take a different route.
6.4.26a Aigosthena: Map 6.4.27, AY.
6.4.26b Megara: Map 6.4.27, BY.
6.4.27a Hyampolis: Map 6.4.27, AY.
6.4.27b Herakleia: Map 6.4.27, AX. This city controlled the only road from Thessaly

into Greece. On that road lies Thermopylae (Map 6.4.27, AX), the narrow pass where the Greeks attempted to stop the Persian invasion in 480.
6.4.27c The Herakleiots had fought for the Spartans at Leuctra: Map 6.4.27, AY. See 6.4.9.
6.4.28a Thessaly: Map 6.4.27, AX.
6.4.28b For more on the Thessalian office of *tagos*, see n. 6.1.8a.
6.4.29a The Pythian festival at Delphi (Map 6.4.27, AX) was held in August. See Appendix J, §3, 7, 10.

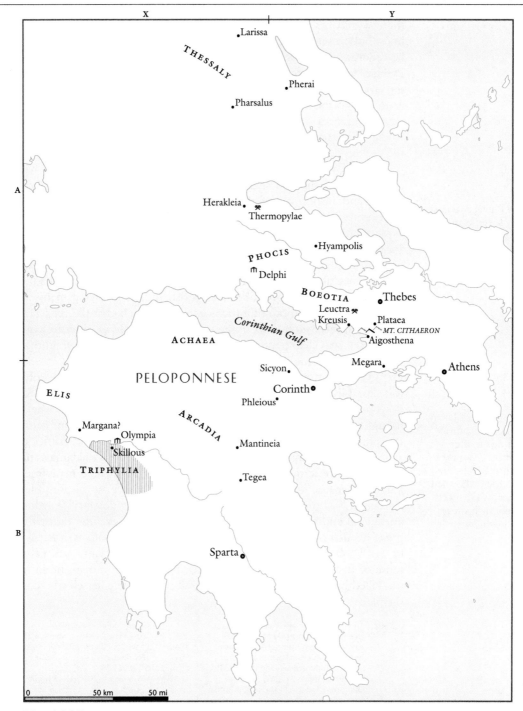

MAP 6.4.27

there would be a prize of a crown of gold for whichever city provided the finest bull to serve as leader of the herd in the god's honor. [30] In addition, he ordered the Thessalians to be prepared for battle around the time of the Pythian festival, because (it was said) he was intending to make himself director of both the festival to the god and the games in the god's honor. It is unclear to this day, however, what his real intentions were concerning the sacred treasures.[a] There is a story that when the people of Delphi asked the oracle what they should do if Jason were to lay hands on the sacred funds, the god replied that such a matter would be his business.

[31] Now to this man, who was of such eminence and who had contrived so many and such great plans, it happened that one day, after a review and inspection of the Pheraian cavalry, while he was seated and responding to anyone who came to him with a petition, he was approached by seven young men who acted as if they had some difference with one another, and these seven attacked and killed him.[a] [32] His bodyguard brought immediate and powerful aid, and they killed one of the young men with a lance as he was still striking Jason, while another, who had jumped up on his horse, was overtaken and perished after receiving many wounds. The rest, however, mounting the horses that they had at the ready, escaped. These men received honors in the majority of the Greek cities to which they fled, and it was clear from this that the Greeks were greatly afraid that Jason would have become a tyrant over their own cities.

[33] After the death of Jason, his brother Polydoros and Polyphron[a] were established as *tagoi*. While both men were on their way to Larissa,[b] Polyphron slew his brother Polydoros at night. This, at least, is what people thought, because his death was sudden and without an obvious cause. [34] Polyphron in turn ruled for a year, conducting himself in the office of *tagos* as if it were a tyranny. In Pharsalus[a] he put to death Polydamas and eight other men, those most powerful in the city, and he exiled many men from Larissa. Because of this he too was killed, the man responsible being Alexander,[b] who claimed that he was avenging the death of Polydoros and putting an end to such a tyranny. [35] But when Alexander himself became *tagos*, he also proved to be a severe ruler of the Thessalians, a harsh enemy to the Thebans[a] and Athenians,[b] and a plunderer on land and sea with no sense of justice. Having revealed himself to be such a man, he in his turn was killed by his wife's brothers, though it was the wife herself who conceived the plan.

6.4.31–32
370
PHERAI
Jason of Pherai is assassinated by seven youths. Five escape, to be treated as heroes, for many Greeks feared the tyrannical power of Jason.

6.4.33–35
370–369
THESSALY
After the death of Jason, his brother Polyphron rules for a year after killing another brother, and in turn is murdered by Alexander, who then rules harshly. He too is murdered, by his wife and her brothers.

6.4.30a   Ancient Greek temples and shrines like Delphi or Olympia (Map 6.4.27, BX) accumulated over the years substantial amounts of precious metals and other treasure from offerings and dedicated items. See Appendix J, §7.
6.4.31a   Diodorus (Appendix O, 15.60) gives the same number of assassins but somewhat different circumstances.
6.4.33a   This is oddly phrased but is exactly as Xenophon expresses it in the original

Greek. (John Marincola)
6.4.33b   Larissa (in Thessaly): Map 6.4.27, AX.
6.4.34a   Pharsalus: Map 6.4.27, AX. Polydamas ably describes Jason of Pherai at 6.1.2, 6.1.8, 6.1.18.
6.3.34b   According to Plutarch (*Parallel Lives*, "Pelopidas" 29.4), Alexander was the son of Polydoros and nephew of Polyphron.
6.4.35a   Thebes: Map 6.4.27, AY.
6.4.35b   Athens: Map 6.4.27, BY.

[36] For she had told her brothers that Alexander was plotting against them, and she hid them within her house for an entire day. When Alexander came home in a drunken state, she received him and brought him to the bedroom, but she left the light burning when he went to sleep, and she removed his sword from the room. When she realized that her brothers were hesitant to enter, she said that unless they did the deed right away she would wake Alexander. So they entered the room, and she closed the door behind them and held down the door latch until they had killed her husband. [37] The origin of her hatred for her husband was said by some to have been caused by the handsome youth who had been Alexander's favorite but whom he had placed in prison: when his wife appealed to him to release the young man, Alexander took him out and had him executed. Others say, however, that because Alexander had no children by his wife, he had sent to Thebes and proposed to marry Jason's widow. These are the reasons given for her plot against her husband. Tisiphonos, the eldest of her brothers and one of those in on the plot, became the ruler and has remained so up to the time that this narrative was written.[a]

[1] I have now treated Thessalian affairs from the time of Jason and after his death up to the rule of Tisiphonos. I now return to the point from which I began my digression.[a] The relief force that had been sent to Leuctra had been led back to Sparta[b] by Archidamos. The Athenians at that point noted that Sparta's allies[c] still felt obliged to follow the Spartans in their campaigns and also that the Spartans themselves were not yet in the condition that they had forced upon the Athenians,[d] and so they sent round to the cities to invite all those who wished to share in the peace[e] that the King had sent down to attend a congress at Athens. [2] When they had all come together, the Athenians, together with those who wished to share in it, swore the following oath: "I will abide by the treaty that the King sent down and by the resolutions passed by the Athenians and their allies. And if anyone attacks a city that has sworn to this oath, I will bring assistance to that city with all my strength." Now everyone was pleased with the oath except the Eleians,[a] who argued that the Marganeis,[b] Skillountians,[c] and Triphylians[d] ought not to be autonomous, because these cities belonged to the Eleians.[e] [3] But the Athenians and the rest had voted that all cities,

6.4.36–37
358?
THESSALY
Xenophon describes how the wife of Alexander plotted to kill her husband and the reasons why he may have incurred her hatred.

6.5.1–3
371
ATHENS
The Athenians call a conference at Athens, inviting all who wish to ratify the latest version of the King's Peace. Only the Eleians oppose it, thinking certain independent cities were really theirs to rule.

6.4.37a Because of what is known from elsewhere about the dates of Tisiphonos' tyranny at Pherai, this passage must have been written between 357 and 353, and this sets a range for the date when *Hellenika* reached final form. See Appendix O, 16.35 and n. O.16.35.1a.
6.5.1a The narrative is resumed from 6.4.26.
6.5.1b Sparta: Map 6.4.27, BX.
6.5.1c Literally, the Peloponnesians. Peloponnese: Map 6.4.27, BX.
6.5.1d That is to say, Sparta was still the leader of the Peloponnesian League, even though autonomy had been granted to all cities, large and small. For the Peloponnesian

League, see Appendix E, §18–19.
6.5.1e For this peace, see 6.3.18.
6.5.2a Elis: Map 6.4.27, BX.
6.5.2b Margana (Marganeis), possible location: Map 6.4.27, BX.
6.5.2c Skillous: Map 6.4.27, BX. Xenophon had been living at Skillous after his return from Asia until the Eleians expelled him around this time, but he has suppressed his personal misfortunes.
6.5.2d Triphylia: Map 6.4.27, BX.
6.5.2e Sparta had earlier forced Elis to recognize the independence of these cities; see 3.2.30.

both small and great, should be autonomous, just as the King had stipulated, and so they sent out men to administer the oath in each of the cities, ordering them to have the highest authorities in each city swear to its terms; and all of them did so, except the Eleians.

Because of these actions, all the Mantineians[a] thought themselves to be wholly autonomous now, so they gathered together and voted to make Mantineia one city and to encircle it with a wall.[b] [4] The Spartans, however, thought that such plans would create a troublesome state of affairs for them if it were done without their authority. They therefore sent Agesilaos as their emissary to the Mantineians, because he was thought to be their ancestral friend,[a] but when he arrived, the men in control refused to permit him to address the people. They told him to speak and to discuss whatever he wanted with them alone. Agesilaos then promised them that if they refrained for the moment from building the wall, he would see to it that the wall would be built with Spartan approval and without great expense to the Mantineians. [5] When they answered that it was impossible to delay, since the whole city had passed the resolution to construct the wall, Agesilaos departed. Although he was angry, it did not seem possible to send an army against Mantineia, because the peace had been agreed to on the assumption of autonomy for all cities. Some of the Arcadian[a] cities sent men to Mantineia to assist in constructing the wall, and the Eleians contributed three talents[b] toward the building expenses. So the Mantineians were busy with this work.

[6] In Tegea,[a] meanwhile, Kallibios and Proxenos and their followers were urging that all of Arcadia should unite[b] and that the cities should agree to abide by whatever was decided in a common assembly. But Stasippos and his followers opposed this and were urging that the city retain its territory as it was and under its ancestral laws. [7] When Proxenos and Kallibios lost the vote in the Council of the Thearoi,[a] they conceived a plan to gather the commons together, thinking that they could carry the day by their greatly superior numbers, and so they brought out the people under arms. Stasippos and his followers, upon seeing this, armed themselves also, and their party was not fewer in number. When they came to battle, Stasippos and his men managed to kill Proxenos and a few others with him, but after they had routed the rest, they did not pursue them, because Stasippos was not the sort of man who wanted to kill many of his fellow citizens.

6.5.4–5
370
MANTINEIA
The Mantineians, now feeling their independence, decide to unite in a single city again and build a wall around it. Sparta objects and sends Agesilaos to deter them, but they refuse his offer and continue to build it, aided by some other Arcadians and by funds donated by Elis.

6.5.6–8
370
TEGEA
At Tegea, two factions—one led by Kallibios and Proxenos, wanting to unite Arcadia, and the other led by Stasippos, wishing to maintain the status quo—come to blows. The partisans of Stasippos defeat their foes but do not pursue them. Kallibios' men send to Mantineia for help, which soon arrives.

6.5.3a Mantineia: Map 6.4.27, BX.
6.5.3b In 384, Sparta had divided Mantineia into four villages; see 5.2.7. Diodorus says five (Appendix O, 15.5.4).
6.5.4a At 5.2.3, Agesilaos asked not to command an army against Mantineia because of the many services the Mantineians had performed for his father in the Third Messenian War.
6.5.5a Arcadia: Map 6.4.27, BX.
6.5.5b The talent is a unit of weight whose value varied over time and place between 55 and

80 pounds. See Appendix I, §8, 10, 13.
6.5.6a Tegea: Map 6.5.23, inset.
6.5.6b Diodorus, in Appendix O, 15.59, writes that it was Lykomedes who persuaded the Arcadians to unite in a single confederacy.
6.5.7a Thearoi: other Doric cities had magistrates with this title (see also Thucydides 5.47.9), but their functions are unknown.

[8] Kallibios and his men retreated beneath the wall and the gates facing Mantineia, but when their opponents did not come after them, they remained there, gathered together, and took no further action. Now although these men had sent to Mantineia[a] long before this to ask for assistance, at this moment they entered into a discussion with Stasippos about a truce. But when the Mantineians were seen coming toward the city, some of Kallibios' men jumped onto the wall and called for them to bring help as quickly as they could, crying out to hasten them on, while others opened the gates for them. [9] When Stasippos' party saw this happening, they ran out of the city, taking the gates that lead toward Pallantion,[a] and they managed to take refuge in the temple of Artemis before their pursuers could catch them. There they locked themselves in and kept quiet, but the enemies who had pursued them climbed up onto the temple and, breaking apart its roof, began to pelt the men inside with the roof tiles. Recognizing the desperate situation they were in, the men inside told the men on the roof to stop and said that they would come out. As soon as their enemies took control of them, they bound them, threw them into a wagon, and took them back to Tegea, where, in conjunction with the Mantineians, they condemned and executed them.

[10] While this was happening, around eight hundred Tegeans of Stasippos' party managed to get away and fled to Sparta.[a] The Spartans resolved that, in accordance with the treaty,[b] they had to bring aid to the exiles and to those Tegeans who had been killed. And so they sent out a force against Mantineia, on the grounds that the Mantineians had violated the oaths by marching under arms against the Tegeans. The ephors called up the army, and the city chose Agesilaos as commander.

[11] Meanwhile all the Arcadians except the Orchomenians[a] and Mantineians had gathered at Asea.[b] The Orchomenians had not wanted to be part of an Arcadian Federation,[c] because they hated the Mantineians; they had even gone so far as to receive within their city a mercenary force that had been collected at Corinth,[d] under the leadership of Polytropos. Because of this, the Mantineians had also remained at home, in order to keep an eye on possible developments there. The Heraians[e] and Lepreans[f] however, made common cause with the Spartans in their expedition against Mantineia.

[12] When the frontier sacrifices proved favorable, Agesilaos immediately moved against Arcadia. He first occupied Eutaia,[a] a city on the border, and there he found the old men, the women, and the children in their houses, because those of military age had already left to join the Arcadian army.[b] Nonetheless, Agesilaos did no harm to the city but allowed the people there

6.5.9
370
TEGEA
When the Mantineians arrive, some of Stasippos' faction take refuge in a temple, but their pursuers, breaking through the roof, force them to surrender. They are condemned and executed.

6.5.10–11
370
SPARTA
Eight hundred Tegeans of Stasippos' faction flee to Sparta. The Spartans send an army against Tegea. The Arcadians try to unite at Asea, but they are divided by old animosities. Orchomenos gathers mercenaries to help Sparta against the Arcadian unity group.

6.5.12
370
EUTAIA
Agesilaos, leading the army, occupies Eutaia and halts, awaiting mercenary reinforcements from Orchomenos.

6.5.8a   Mantineia: Map 6.5.23, inset.
6.5.9a   Pallantion: Map 6.5.23, inset.
6.5.10a Sparta: Map 6.5.23 and inset.
6.5.10b See the oath to the peace at 6.3.18.
6.5.11a Orchomenos: Map 6.5.23, inset.
6.5.11b Asea: Map 6.5.23, inset.
6.5.11c The Arcadian Federation: see Appendix H, §8.

6.5.11d Corinth: Map 6.5.23 and inset.
6.5.11e Heraia: Map 6.5.23, inset.
6.5.11f Lepreon: Map 6.5.23, inset.
6.5.12a Eutaia: Map 6.5.23, inset. According to Pausanias (8.27.3) they had joined the Arcadian Federation. See Appendix H, §8.
6.5.12b The one being marshaled at Asea.

to remain in their houses and purchased whatever commodities he and his army needed.[c] Whenever he found something that had been taken from the people when his forces first entered the city, he ensured that it was returned to its owner. And while he was awaiting the arrival of the mercenaries under Polytropos, he repaired whatever sections of the wall that needed it.

[13] While this was going on, the Mantineians sent out an expedition against the Orchomenians; they attacked the city wall but had much the worst of it in the fighting, and some of them were killed. In their retreat they found themselves in Elymia,[a] and although the Orchomenian infantry had by this time ceased their pursuit, Polytropos and his men were pursuing them boldly. The Mantineians, realizing that if they did not defend themselves they would be shot down with javelins, turned and charged their attackers en masse. [14] In the fight that ensued, Polytropos died where he stood, and many of his men would have also perished in their flight if the Phleiasian[a] horsemen had not arrived and, by riding around the rear of the Mantineians, prevented them from continuing the pursuit. Having accomplished these things, the Mantineians went home.

[15] When Agesilaos heard what had happened at Mantineia, he realized that the mercenaries from Orchomenos could not now join him, so he resumed his march. On the first day he and his men took dinner in the territory of Tegea, and on the next day he crossed over into Mantineian territory and camped beneath the mountains to the west of the city. He then began to lay waste the land there and plundered the farms. During the night the Arcadians who had gathered together at Asea arrived at Tegea. [16] On the next day, Agesilaos camped about twenty stades[a] from Mantineia. A very large hoplite force of Arcadians from Tegea now arrived; they had come via a route that took them between the mountains of Mantineia and Tegea, and they wished to join up with the Mantineians. (The Argives[b] were also present but not with their entire contingent.) Some tried to persuade Agesilaos to attack this force separately, but he was afraid that while he was marching against the Arcadian force, the Mantineians might rush out from their city and attack him in the flank and rear. He decided, therefore, that it was best to allow the hostile forces to join up and then, if they wished to engage, to fight that battle fairly and in the open.

[17] The peltasts from Orchomenos and the cavalry of the Phleiasians with them made their way by night into Mantineia and appeared at dawn as Agesilaos was sacrificing in front of the camp. Their appearance caused the Spartans and their allies to fall quickly into line and Agesilaos himself to retire inside the camp. They were then recognized as friends, however, and afterward, when Agesilaos had obtained good omens and the army had

---

6.5.12c　Agesilaos obtained what he needed by purchase rather than demand, requisition, or plundering.

6.5.13a　Elymia: site unknown, although from the context it must be between Mantineia and Orchomenos.

6.5.14a　Phleious: Map 6.5.23, inset.

6.5.16a　Twenty Attic stades of 583 feet would convert to a little more than 2 miles. See Appendix I, §4–5, 13.

6.5.16b　Argos: Map 6.5.23, inset.

breakfasted, he led the entire force forward. When night came on, he made camp, but he failed to realize that he had done so in a valley behind Mantineia that was surrounded by mountains that were nearby and all around him.

[18] On the next day he sacrificed at dawn in front of the army; then, seeing the Mantineians coming out of the city and gathering on the hilltops at the rear of his army, he decided that he had to get out of the valley as quickly as he could. He feared, however, that if he himself led the army, the enemy would attack him from behind. He therefore took no immediate action other than to align his men so as to present an armed front to the enemy. Then he ordered the men in the rear to turn to the right and march behind the phalanx toward where he was. In this way he was able simultaneously to lead them out of the narrows and to make his phalanx continually stronger. [19] When the line had been doubled in strength in this way, he marched into the plain, maintaining his line in this formation, and he then stretched out the army back to a depth of nine or ten shields.

The Mantineians, for their part, ceased to march out from the city because their allies, the Eleians,[a] kept dissuading them from fighting a battle until the Thebans[b] arrived. The Eleians said they were sure that the Thebans would come, because they had borrowed ten talents from the Eleians to finance the expedition.[c] [20] When the Arcadians learned this, they remained quiet in Mantineia,[a] and Agesilaos, though he wished very much to lead his army back home (for it was midwinter), nevertheless remained there, not far from the city of Mantineia, for three days because he did not want his adversaries to think that he was making a rapid withdrawal out of fear. On the fourth day, the army breakfasted early and Agesilaos began to lead it back home, intending to stop at the first place he had camped when he started out from Eutaia. [21] And when no Arcadian came out against him, he led the army as quickly as he could into Eutaia, even though it was very late in the day, because he wished to lead the soldiers away before they had even seen the fires of the enemy so that no one would say that he had led them back in fear. In this way, he seemed to have brought Sparta back somewhat from its former despondency, since he had invaded Arcadia[a] and laid waste the land, and yet no one had been willing to come out and fight him. So then when he arrived in Laconia,[b] he dismissed the Spartiates and sent the *perioikic* allies[c] to their respective cities.[d]

6.5.18–19
370
MANTINEIA
Realizing his peril in the morning, Agesilaos skillfully maneuvers to withdraw his army from the valley. The Arcadians do nothing, waiting for the Thebans.

6.5.20–21
370
MANTINEIA
After several days, Agesilaos leads the army home to Sparta via Eutaia. He is not pursued. The Arcadians have now joined up with the Mantineians.

6.5.19a Elis: Map 6.5.23, inset.
6.5.19b Thebes: Map 6.5.23.
6.5.19c Xenophon has here omitted the appeal by the Arcadians to Athens in late 370. The Athenians refused the offer of alliance, after which the Arcadians turned to the Thebans (Diodorus, Appendix O, 15.62.3; Demosthenes 16.12).
6.5.20a Mantineia: Map 6.5.23, inset.

6.5.21a Arcadia: Map 6.5.23 and inset.
6.5.21b Laconia: Map 6.5.23. Diodorus gives a brief account of Agesilaos' campaign in Arcadia; see Appendix O, 15.59.3.
6.5.21c For the *perioikoi*, these neighbors of Sparta ("the dwellers around"), see Appendix E, §10.
6.5.21d The mercenaries from Orchomenos, however, remained in Sparta (Map 6.5.23 and inset); see 6.5.29.

6.5.22
370
HERAIA
With the Spartans gone, the Arcadians raid the Heraians and spoil their territory, until the Thebans arrive at Mantineia.

6.5.23
370
MANTINEIA
After Leuctra the Thebans see themselves as the foremost soldiers in Greece. Finding the Spartans not there, they prepare to return home, but the Arcadians, Argives, and Eleians beg them to invade Spartan territory.

6.5.24
370
MANTINEIA
At first the Thebans, fearing Spartan defenses, refuse to invade Spartan territory.

[22] After Agesilaos had departed and the Arcadians learned that he had disbanded his army, they themselves, who still happened to be together, made an expedition against the Heraians, not only because the Heraians had refused to join the Arcadian Federation but also because they had joined with the Spartans in invading Arcadia.[a] Entering Heraian territory, they burned down houses and cut down trees. When they received a report that the Theban force that had come to support them was now in Mantineia, they departed from Heraia and joined up with the Thebans.

[23] When the forces were united, the Thebans thought that their affairs stood in good order—they had brought assistance to the Arcadians, but no enemy was to be seen in the land—and they accordingly made plans to depart. But the Arcadians, Argives, and Eleians tried to persuade them to lead them all as quickly as possible into Laconia, pointing out the great number of their own forces[a] and praising the Theban army excessively. In fact the Boeotians,[b] basking in the glory of their victory at Leuctra,[c] were now all training at arms. Joining them were the Phocians[d] (now their subjects), all the cities of Euboea,[e] both groups of Locrians,[f] the Acarnanians,[g] the Herakleiots,[h] and the Malians,[i] not to mention the horsemen and peltasts from Thessaly.[j] So the Arcadians, seeing the whole situation and describing the shortage of manpower in Sparta, begged the Thebans not to go back until they invaded the land of the Spartans.

[24] The Thebans listened to their arguments, but they offered as counterarguments the fact that Laconia was said to be difficult to invade and their belief that garrisons had been stationed at all the locations that granted easiest entrance. As it was, a certain Ischolaos was in command of a garrison at Oion in Skiritis,[a] and he had with him emancipated helots[b] and around four hundred of the youngest Tegean[c] exiles. There was also another garrison at Leuktron,[d] above Maleatis.[e] The Thebans were also of the opinion that if they invaded, the Spartans would quickly concentrate their forces and would fight nowhere better than in their own country. In consideration

6.5.22a On the Heraian participation in that expedition, see 6.5.11.
6.5.23a According to Diodorus (15.81.2) and Plutarch (*Parallel Lives*, "Agesilaos" 31.1, "Pelopidas" 24.2), Epaminondas led an army totaling seventy thousand. Within this total, about six thousand were Thebans, according to the "Pelopidas" passage, and forty thousand were hoplites, according to the "Agesilaos" passage. The "more than fifty thousand" figure elsewhere in Diodorus (Appendix O, 15.62.5) perhaps adds cavalry and javelin throwers to the hoplites but not stone throwers and other even more lightly armed men.
6.5.23b Boeotia: Map 6.4.27, BY.
6.5.23c Leuctra: Map 6.5.23.
6.5.23d Phocis: Map 6.5.23.
6.5.23e Euboea: Map 6.5.23. Since the Euboeans

were listed as allies of the Second Athenian League, they must have defected to Thebes after the battle of Leuctra.
6.5.23f Locris, Opuntian and Ozolian: Map 6.5.23. For these Locrians, see 4.2.17.
6.5.23g Acarnania: Map 6.5.23.
6.5.23h Herakleia: Map 6.5.23.
6.5.23i Malis: Map 6.5.23.
6.5.23j Thessaly: Map 6.5.23.
6.5.24a The location of the village of Oion has not been identified. Skiritis: Map 6.5.23, inset.
6.5.24b Emancipated helots: on these *neodamōdeis*, see Appendix E, §9, 12, and Appendix F, §6.
6.5.24c Tegea: Map 6.5.23, inset.
6.5.24d Leuktron: Map 6.5.23, inset.
6.5.24e Maleatis is probably Malea (Map 6.5.23, inset) in southern Arcadia, mentioned by Pausanias (8.27.4).

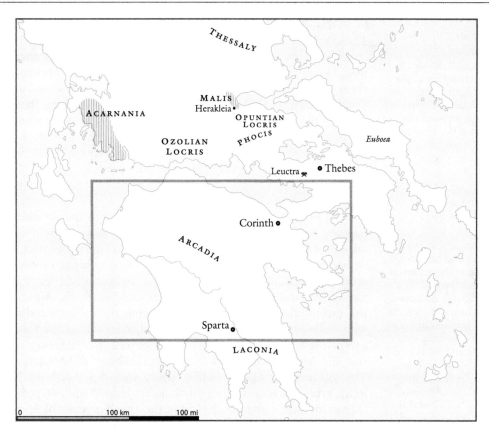

Map 6.5.23

257

6.5.25
370
MANTINEIA
The Thebans decide to invade when the people of Karyai tell them of the lack of Spartan manpower and some *perioikoi* offer to revolt if the Thebans come.

6.5.26–27
370–369
OION-KARYAI-SPARTA
Ischolaos and his troops fail to meet the enemy in the narrow part of the pass. After the Arcadians ascend the mountain, the Spartan garrison fights well but are finally overwhelmed and annihilated. The Arcadians join the Thebans at Karyai and the Thebans advance, pillaging Sellasia and the environs of Sparta itself.

6.5.28–29
370–369
SPARTA
The Thebans do not attack, although they see that the Spartans are few in number. The Spartans arm six thousand helots, promising them freedom, but are frightened by their numbers until reassured by the presence of loyal mercenaries and allies.

of all this, therefore, they were in no way eager to advance on Sparta. [25] Then, however, some men of Karyai[a] arrived and told the Thebans that the countryside was in fact deserted,[b] and they promised that they themselves would serve as guides for the Thebans, adding that the Thebans should slay them if their report proved false. Also present were some citizens of the *perioikic* towns, asking for Theban assistance and claiming that they would revolt if the Thebans should but show themselves in their territory. They added that even now, although the Spartiates were calling upon their neighboring communities to bring assistance, these requests were being refused. Hearing all this and hearing the same from every source, the Thebans were finally won over, and they themselves advanced via Karyai,[c] while the Arcadians invaded via Oion in Skiritan territory.

[26] Now if Ischolaos had gone forward into the difficult part of the pass and had made his stand there, no one, it was said, could have ascended via that route. But as it was, he remained in the village itself, because he wished to take advantage of the men of Oion as his allies. So then a large number of Arcadians ascended the pass. Ischolaos and his men met them face-to-face and were gaining the upper hand when the Arcadians attacked them in the flank and rear, leaping up onto the rooftops and pelting them with stones and javelins. They killed Ischolaos and all the rest of his men, except for a few who escaped unrecognized. [27] Having accomplished this, the Arcadians marched to join the Thebans[a] at Karyai;[b] and when the Thebans learned of the Arcadian victory, they descended into Laconia with much greater boldness. They immediately burned and pillaged Sellasia[c] and then made their camp in the plain in the sacred precinct of Apollo.[d]

On the next day they set out again and arrived at Sparta, where they did not attempt to cross via the bridge[e] into the city, because they could see the hoplites in the temple of Athena Alea[f] ready to engage them. Instead, keeping the Eurotas River on their right, they marched along, burning and pillaging houses that were full of many fine things.

[28] Back in the city, the women could not bear to see the smoke rising from the fires—indeed, Spartan women had never before even laid eyes on an enemy. And since Sparta was not encircled by a wall, the Spartiates were posted in separate detachments around the city and kept guard in this way; they were very few in number, and that was indeed apparent.[a]

6.5.25a　Karyai (two possible locations according to the *Barrington Atlas*): Map 6.5.23, inset.
6.5.25b　They were apparently referring to the road between Sparta and Thyrea (Map 6.5.23, inset). See Pausanias 3.10.7.
6.5.25c　For another version of the decision to invade, see Diodorus (Appendix O, 15.62.3–4).
6.5.27a　Thebes: Map 6.5.31, AY.
6.5.27b　Diodorus writes that the allies divided their forces into four divisions, each to invade Laconia by a different route (Appendix O, 15.63.4).

6.5.27c　Sellasia: Map 6.5.31, BX.
6.5.27d　The sacred precinct of Apollo was on the left (east) bank of the Eurotas River (Map 6.5.31, BX). See Pausanias 3.14.6 for the temple. Sparta lay on the right (west) bank.
6.5.27e　The exact location of the bridge is not known.
6.5.27f　The temple of Athena Alea was on the road from Sparta to Therapne (Map 6.5.31, BX); see Pausanias 3.19.7.
6.5.28a　Plutarch says that Agesilaos was in charge of these arrangements (Plutarch, *Parallel Lives*, "Agesilaos" 31.2–5, 32).

Those in charge of the city decided to offer a promise of freedom to any helot who would willingly take up arms, be marshaled among the forces, and fight together with the Spartans; [29] and it was said that altogether more than six thousand helots were enrolled, a number so large that at first they caused fear among the Spartans when they were arrayed together[a] (there seemed to be too many of them), but when the mercenaries from Orchomenos[b] remained faithful and the Spartans received help from the Phleiasians,[c] Corinthians,[d] Epidaurians,[e] Pelleneians,[f] and a few other cities,[g] they grew less fearful of the helots they had enrolled.

[30] As the Theban army advanced they came opposite to Amyklai,[a] and here they crossed the Eurotas River. Now wherever the Thebans camped, they would immediately cut down as many trees as they could and throw them down in front of their lines, intending in this way to protect themselves. The Arcadians,[b] however, took no such precautions but, leaving behind their weapons, busied themselves with plundering the nearby houses. On the third or fourth day after this, the Theban cavalry advanced by divisions into the racecourse in the precinct of Poseidon the Earth-holder;[c] the Thebans were there in full force, as were the Eleians,[d] along with those cavalrymen from the Phocians,[e] Thessalians,[f] and Locrians[g] who were serving on the expedition.

[31] The Spartan cavalry formed up against them, but they appeared to be very few in number. The Spartans, however, had laid an ambush with about three hundred of the younger hoplites hidden in the temple of the sons of Tyndareus;[a] these men now rushed out as the Spartan cavalry simultaneously charged. The enemy did not await them but immediately gave way, and many of the infantry turned to flee when they saw the cavalry retreat. When the Spartan pursuit ended, the Theban army stopped and camped again. [32] It now seemed rather more certain that they would not make another assault on the city, and in fact the army soon struck camp and departed, taking the road that leads to Helos[a] and Gytheion.[b] They burned any unwalled cities that they came upon, and for three days they besieged Gytheion, where the Spartans had their dockyards. Some of the *perioikoi*

6.5.30–32
370–369
AMYKLAI
The Thebans cross the Eurotas River by Amyklai. The Spartans ambush their cavalry but are not successful. After the skirmish, the Thebans stand firm for several days and then march against Gytheion and Helos, burning and pillaging as they go. They are assisted by some of the *perioikoi*.

6.5.29a The Spartans feared, as they always did with the helots (serfs), that a great number of them together might attack the Spartans or, in this case, make common cause with the enemy in exchange for their freedom. Indeed, according to Plutarch (*Parallel Lives*, "Agesilaos" 32.7), many of the helots had already defected to the enemy.
6.5.29b Orchomenos (in Arcadia): Map 6.5.31, BX.
6.5.29c Phleious: Map 6.5.31, BY.
6.5.29d Corinth: Map 6.5.31, BY.
6.5.29e Epidauros: Map 6.5.31, BY.
6.5.29f Pellene: Map 6.5.31, AX.
6.5.29g These cities were Troizen, Hermione, and Halieis (Map 6.5.31, BY) and Sicyon (Map 6.5.31, AY).
6.5.30a Amyklai: Map 6.5.31, BX. A village

about 3 miles south of Sparta.
6.5.30b Arcadia: Map 6.5.31, BX.
6.5.30c The precise location of this sanctuary to Poseidon Gaiaochos is unknown, but Pausanias (3.20.2) says that it was between Therapne and Amyklai.
6.5.30d Elis: Map 6.5.31, BX.
6.5.30e Phocis: Map 6.5.31, AX.
6.5.30f Thessaly: Map 6.5.31, AX.
6.5.30g Locris, Ozolian and Opuntian: Map 6.5.31, AX.
6.5.31d Sons of Tyndareus: the Dioskouroi, Kastor and Polydeukes, also mentioned at 6.3.6. Pausanias 3.16.2 mentions the temple at Amyklai and the supposed house of the Dioskouroi.
6.5.32a Helos, possible location: Map 6.5.31, BY.
6.5.32b Gytheion: Map 6.5.31, BX.

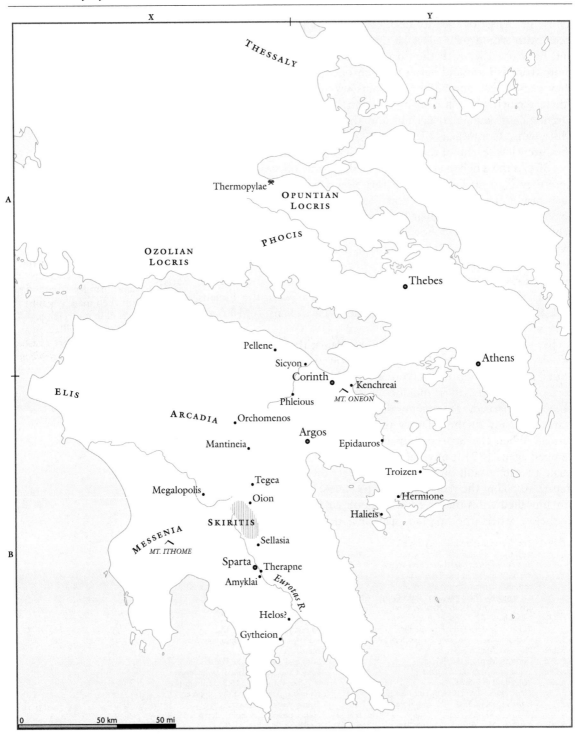

THESSALY

Thermopylae ✳   OPUNTIAN LOCRIS

PHOCIS

OZOLIAN LOCRIS

Thebes

Pellene

Sicyon

Corinth   Kenchreai

Athens

Phleious   MT. ONEON

ELIS

ARCADIA   Orchomenos

Argos

Epidauros

Mantineia

Troizen

Tegea

Megalopolis   Oion

Hermione

SKIRITIS

Halieis

Sellasia

MESSENIA

MT. ITHOME

Sparta   Therapne

Amyklai   *Eurotas R.*

Helos?

Gytheion

0   50 km   50 mi

MAP 6.5.31

now not only participated in the attacks but also served together with the Theban allies.[c]

[33] When the Athenians[a] learned what had happened, they determined that they must now do something about the situation in Sparta, and in accordance with a resolution of the Council, they called an Assembly.[b] It so happened that ambassadors from Sparta and those allies still faithful to Sparta were present in Athens, and the Spartans Arakos, Okyllos, Pharax,[c] Etymokles, and Olontheus addressed the Assembly, all of them saying much the same thing. They reminded the Athenians that the Spartans had always been present with them in their greatest crises, and always to their benefit. They said that the Spartans had joined in driving the tyrants from Athens[d] and that the Athenians had eagerly helped the Spartans when they were being besieged by the Messenians.[e] [34] They spoke too of all the successes that had been achieved when they had acted in concert, reminding them first of how they both beat back the Persian,[a] then recalling for them how the Greeks chose the Athenians as leaders of the naval force and guardians of the common funds—all with Spartan support[b]—and how the Athenians in their turn approved of Sparta's being selected by all the Greeks to be leaders on land.[c] [35] One of them even said something like this: "If, gentlemen, you and we see things eye to eye, we can expect that a thing long spoken of—the decimation[a] of the Thebans—will be accomplished."

6.5.33–35
370–369
ATHENS
Upon hearing of the events in the Peloponnese, the Athenians call an Assembly, which is addressed by several Spartan envoys. They recall the many occasions when Sparta and Athens worked together to their mutual benefit and how often one had come to the aid of the other in numerous crises. The Spartans call on Athens to help them now, but many Athenians are skeptical.

6.5.32c A most striking indication of Xenophon's pro-Spartan feeling (see the Introduction, §12.5–10) is found in the fact that he here omits all reference to the greatest of the humiliations that Sparta suffered at this time: the reestablishment by Epaminondas, the Theban general, of the independence of Messenia (Map 6.5.31, BX), which for centuries had been subject to the Spartans. Xenophon also ignores Sparta's second great humiliation at the hands of Epaminondas: the founding in those years of "the great city," Megalopolis (Map 6.5.31, BX), as the capital of an independent Arcadia. Nevertheless, he does allude several times in Book 7 to the accomplished fact of Messenian independence (7.1.29, 7.4.9, 7.4.27, 7.5.5), and to the existence of Megalopolis at 7.5.5.

6.5.33a Athens: Map 6.5.31, AY.

6.5.33b On the operating rules of the Athenian Council and Assembly, see Appendix B, §5, 8–11. The speaker's platform from the Assembly survives; see Figure 6.5.33.

6.5.33c Arakos might be the admiral mentioned at 2.1.7 and 3.2.6. For an earlier reference to Okyllos, see 5.4.22. Pharax is possibly the same man as the admiral mentioned in 3.2.12. Etymokles, who was mentioned as a friend of Agesilaos at 5.4.22, also appears at 5.4.32.

6.5.33d This refers to the expulsion of the Peisistratids in 511; see Herodotus, *Histories* 5.64–65.

6.5.33e The reference is to the so-called Third Messenian War, whose dates are controversial but which *The Cambridge Ancient*

History places at 465–456. The Athenian assistance to the Spartans—who, according to Thucydides 1.102, were besieging the Messenians on Mount Ithome (Map 6.5.31, BX) and not themselves being besieged, as Xenophon or his Spartan speaker has it here—took place in 462. The whole affair did not end well, because the Spartans became suspicious that the Athenians might sympathize with the helots and rudely sent them home.

6.5.34a This refers to the defeat of the Persian invasion of Greece in 480–479.

6.5.34b This refers to the foundation of the Delian League in 477 and the first assessment of funds; see Thucydides 1.96. This version of Spartan support for Athens agrees with Thucydides 1.95; but the Aristotelian *Constitution of the Athenians* 23.2 and Isocrates 12.52 say that the Spartans were unwilling for the Athenians to take the leadership. Delos: Map 7.1.34, BY.

6.5.34c This argument is fallacious. In 480, the Greeks chose Sparta to lead them on both land and sea. Thereafter there was no occasion on which "all" the Greeks made such a choice of commander.

6.5.35a The word *decimate* used here, as at 6.3.20, means literally to "tithe at a tenth" of one's property, but here it means that Thebes would be taken down a peg, punished, put in her rightful place. It has no connection with the Roman military punishment called decimation, in which every tenth man in a unit was executed.

FIGURE 6.5.33. THE ATHENIAN ASSEMBLY SPEAKER'S PLATFORM (BEMA) ON THE PNYX HILL, WHERE THE ASSEMBLY MET AND DELIBERATED.

6.5.36
370–369
ATHENS
Arguments arise about the oaths that the Athenians had made requiring them to assist all injured parties. There is no consensus, and the Assembly is disrupted by turmoil.

But the Athenians by no means accepted these arguments; a murmur went through the people to the effect that "this is what they say now, but when their affairs were going well, they waged war on us." The most powerful remark of the Spartans was thought to be the reminder that when they defeated Athens in war, they had prevented the city from being wiped out, although the Thebans had advocated just that course.[b] [36] The point that the Spartans especially pressed, however, was that the Athenians had to bring help now to the Spartans to fulfill the oaths they had sworn;[a] for the Arcadians and their allies had marched against the Spartans even though the Spartans had committed no wrong but were instead aiding the Tegeans,[b] who had been the victim of Mantineian[c] aggression in violation of the oaths. This argument, however, provoked another uproar in the Assembly, since some said that the Mantineians were right to have avenged the murder of Proxenos and his men by the party of Stasippos,[d] while others said they were wrong because they took up arms against the Tegeans.

6.5.35b   For the Theban advocacy and the Spartan refusal to destroy Athens, see 2.2.19.
6.5.36a   For the oaths referred to here, see 6.5.2.
6.5.36b   Tegea: Map 6.5.31, BX.

6.5.36c   Mantineia: Map 6.5.31, BX.
6.5.36d   For the murder of Proxenos and his men, see 6.5.6ff.

[37] While these matters were being debated in the Assembly, Kleiteles, a Corinthian,[a] rose and spoke as follows: "Men of Athens, it is perhaps a matter of debate who began the wrongs. But as for us Corinthians, has anyone accused us, since the peace came into effect, of campaigning against another city or of seizing anyone's property or of ravaging someone's land? Yet the Thebans have come into our territory and cut down our trees, burned our houses, and seized our cattle and property. How can you be acting in accordance with your oaths if you will not bring us assistance when we have so openly been wronged? You yourselves were the ones who took great care that all of us[b] should swear our oaths to all of you." This speech led to a further commotion, to the effect that Kleiteles had spoken rightly and to the point.

[38] After Kleiteles, Prokles of Phleious[a] rose and spoke. "Men of Athens, I think it must be clear to all of you that had the Spartans not stood in the way, the Thebans would have marched against you before anyone else, for they believe that it is you who are preventing them from ruling over the Greeks. [39] Since matters stand so, I think that in marching out and bringing help to the Spartans, you are equally helping yourselves. You would have a much harder time of it if the Thebans, who dwell on your borders, became rulers of Greece than when your main opponents lived far off. And you would be of much greater help to yourselves when there are still men who will be your allies than you would if those allies were destroyed and you were compelled to fight alone against the Thebans.

[40] "If, nevertheless, you are afraid that the Spartans might again cause you trouble in the future should they escape harm this time, bear in mind that one does not normally fear the rise to power of those whom one has benefited but, rather, those whom one has injured. Consider this, too: it makes sense for both individuals and states to acquire some goodwill while they are strong, so that if they ever become weak, they may obtain the assistance of those for whose benefit they labored previously. [41] If you help the Spartans now when they need you, you will take advantage of a heaven-sent opportunity to acquire them as unhesitating friends for all time. And I think that they will receive benefits from you not in the presence of a few people only: for the gods, who see all things both now and in the future, will know what has happened here, as will your allies, your enemies, and even the rest of the world, Greek as well as non-Greek, since these matters are of concern to all. [42] And if the Spartans in return should be seen as behaving wickedly toward you, who in the world would ever be eager to take their side? Therefore you can expect them to behave as good men, not bad ones, for they, if anyone, seem to have constantly endeavored to win praise and to shun shameful deeds. [43] Think, too, that if Greece should

6.5.37
370–369
ATHENS
Kleiteles of Corinth addresses the Assembly, calling the Thebans aggressors who have injured the Corinthians and demanding that the Athenians fulfill their oaths to assist them.

6.5.38–39
370–369
ATHENS
Prokles of Phleious addresses the Assembly, arguing that if the Athenians march, they will not be so much assisting Sparta as helping themselves against Theban hegemony.

6.5.40–43
370–369
ATHENS
Prokles continues, listing further reasons why Athens should now come to the assistance of Sparta and how she will benefit from such a course.

6.5.37a   Corinth: Map 6.5.31, BY.
6.5.37b   The "all of us" in this gathering might well include the Spartans and has been used by scholars to advance the argument that the Spartans were party to the peace instituted after the battle of Leuctra.

6.5.38a   Phleious: Map 6.5.31, BY. This Prokles was a friend of Agesilaos. He was mentioned earlier (5.3.13); for a later speech of his, see 7.1.2–11.

ever again be endangered by the Persians, whom would you trust more than the Spartans? Is there anyone you would be happier to have by your side than those whose countrymen, when they were stationed at Thermopylae,[a] chose one and all to die in battle rather than live and allow the Persian into Greece? Is it not just, therefore, that you and we should provide help to them, since they were brave men when they fought with you and there is reason to hope that they will be so again?

6.5.44–48
370–369
ATHENS
Prokles concludes his speech with a long recitation of points that should persuade the Athenians to come to the aid of the Spartans.

[44] "It is also worth your while to show eagerness to help them for the sake of their allies who are present here with them. For you can be certain that these very men who have been faithful to the treaty and loyal to the Spartans would likewise be ashamed if they did not show gratitude to you. And if we who are willing to share Sparta's danger seem to be small cities, consider that if your city joins us, we who aid the Spartans will no longer be small. [45] Let me tell you, men of Athens, that even in days gone by I often envied your city, because I had heard that all who fled to you— whether they had been wronged or were fearful for some other reason— found assistance here. Now I no longer need to rely on hearsay but am present here, and I see the Spartans, those most famous of men, along with their most faithful allies here before you and needing your assistance. [46] I also see the Thebans,[a] who once failed to persuade the Spartans to enslave you,[b] now asking you to allow the men who preserved you to be destroyed.

"There is a fine account told of your ancestors, that they did not allow those Argives who had died at the Kadmeia to remain unburied.[c] Well, it would be a much finer accomplishment for you to prevent the Spartans here, while they are still alive, from being outraged and destroyed. [47] And there is another noble deed told of your ancestors, that they restrained the violence of Eurystheus and preserved the sons of Herakles:[a] would it not now be a finer deed if you preserved not just the founders of Sparta but the entire city of Sparta? It would in fact be the most splendid of deeds if you were to bring assistance to these Spartans, who once saved you with a vote that brought them no danger,[b] by taking up arms and undergoing dangers for their sake now.

6.5.43a   Thermopylae: Map 6.5.31, AX. Scene of the heroic stand of a small Spartan force against the Persians in 480. On Thermopylae, see Herodotus, *Histories* 7.223.

6.5.46a   This statement does indicate that the Thebans were present at this Assembly. But some scholars do not believe they were actually there, because no other passage supports their presence; they believe that Prokles is just using vivid rhetorical language here.

6.5.46b   In 404; see 2.2.19.

6.5.46c   According to the legend known as the Seven against Thebes, King Adrastus of Argos (Map 6.5.31, BY) led six other champions against Thebes (Map 6.5.31, AY) in the disputes that followed the disgrace of King Oedipus. However, the Argive army was totally defeated, and the

other six champions were killed. The Thebans refused to let the enemy dead be buried, and Adrastus successfully appealed to King Theseus of Athens to intervene and force the Thebans to comply with Greek norms. The story was a frequent theme of Athenian propaganda, for example, Isocrates 4.55.

6.5.47a   When Eurystheus expelled the sons of Herakles from the Peloponnese, they fled to Athens, where they received refuge. They later returned with an Athenian force and defeated Eurytheus. See Herodotus, *Histories* 9.27, and Diodorus 4.57, for this story.

6.5.47b   Because at the end of the Peloponnesian War the Spartans were far stronger than any of their allies, so they had nothing to fear from Thebes.

[48] "We who are asking you to aid these brave men are proud to be here; but as for you, who can actually bring them some concrete assistance, it would seem the height of nobility to remember not the occasions when they harmed you but, rather, those when they benefited you, and to render them thanks not only on your own behalf but also on that of all Greece, since they proved themselves brave men on her behalf."

[49] After he had finished speaking, the Athenians made their deliberations. They voted to assist the Spartans with all their forces and would not even listen to anyone who attempted to express a contrary view. They chose Iphikrates[a] as general and after the sacrifices proved favorable, he ordered his troops to take their evening meal in the Academy[b] where many of them, it is said, had arrived even before Iphikrates himself. After this, Iphikrates led them out and they followed, believing that he was leading them to some noble task. But once he arrived at Corinth, he wasted time and for several days took no action, which caused the soldiers for the first time to find fault with him. He did lead them out finally, and they followed eagerly attacking all the fortified places against which he directed them.

[50] As for the enemy back in Sparta,[a] many Arcadians,[b] Argives,[c] and Eleians[d] had already departed, since they lived just over the Spartan border, and as they departed they led or carried off whatever they had seized as plunder. The Thebans[e] and the rest of their allies also decided to leave Spartan territory, partly because they saw the army growing smaller each day and partly because their supplies were now dwindling, having been used up, stolen, wasted, or burned. To top it off, it was now winter,[f] and so all of them decided to depart.

[51] While these troops were retiring from Sparta,[a] Iphikrates was leading his troops back from Arcadia into Corinth. Now Iphikrates was certainly a good general, and I do not fault his conduct on other occasions, but I find that his actions on this campaign were completely incompetent and ineffectual. For although he tried to put a guard at Oneon[b] to prevent the Boeotians from returning home, he left the best road for this purpose, the one that leads past Kenchreai,[c] completely unguarded. [52] And when he wished to learn whether the Thebans had passed by Oneon, he sent the entire Athenian and Corinthian cavalry to serve as scouts, and yet a small

6.5.49
370–369
ATHENS-CORINTH-ARCADIA
The Athenians vote to send a full force to assist Sparta and choose Iphikrates to lead it. When he delays at Corinth, his troops censure him for that until he resumes the advance.

6.5.50
370–369
SPARTA
Many Theban allies have gone home by now, and the Thebans decide to leave, too.

6.5.51–52
369
PELOPONNESE
When the Thebans begin to leave, Iphikrates leads his men back from Arcadia to Corinth, leaving the best pass unguarded so that the Thebans can march home. Xenophon criticizes his lackluster generalship on this campaign.

6.5.49a   Iphikrates was last mentioned at 6.4.1.
6.5.49b   For the location of the Academy, see Map 2.4.30, inset.
6.5.50a   Sparta: Map 6.5.31, BX.
6.5.50b   Arcadia: Map 6.5.31, BX.
6.5.50c   Argos: Map 6.5.31, BY.
6.5.50d   Elis: Map 6.5.31, BX.
6.5.50e   Thebes: Map 6.5.31, AY.
6.5.50f   According to Diodorus (Appendix O, 15.67), the invasion lasted eighty-five days. Plutarch (*Parallel Lives*) gives the length variously as three ("Agesilaos" 32.8) or four ("Pelopidas" 25.1) months.
6.5.51a   The troops were in fact in Messenia

(Map 6.5.31, BX). See Figure 7.1.27, of the substantial remains today of the formidable fortifications that Epaminondas built at the restored capital city on Mount Ithome (Map 6.5.31, BX) in order to assure the independence of Messenia.
6.5.51b   Mount Oneon: Map 6.5.31, BY. This mountain, about 1,600 feet high, is about 3 miles southwest of Corinth.
6.5.51c   Kenchreai: Map 6.5.31, BY. This was Corinth's seaport on the eastern side of the Isthmus.

force is as effective as a large one when it come to scouting, not to mention that it is much easier for a few men rather than many men to retire if the need for that arises, both in terms of finding a good road and for retiring without haste. Was it anything other than the height of folly to send out so many troops who were still in fact inferior in number to those of the enemy? And in the event, the horsemen were spread out over such a large territory due to their number that when it was necessary to retire, they encountered so much difficult terrain that more than twenty of them perished. The Thebans, for their part, returned home at the time and via the route of their own choosing.

BOOK SEVEN

In the next year,[a] ambassadors with full powers came to Athens[b] from the Spartans[c] and their allies in order to discuss the terms of an alliance between the Spartans and Athenians. Many foreigners and many Athenians spoke to the effect that the alliance needed to be on fair and equal terms. Prokles the Phleiasian[d] spoke the following:

[2] "Men of Athens, since it now has seemed good to you to have the Spartans as friends, I think that we must examine what will make such a friendship as long-lasting as possible. It is probable that the treaty will last longest if it is made in accordance with what is most beneficial for both sides. Now pretty much everything else has been agreed upon, but we must still examine the question of how to arrange the command. Your Council[a] has proposed that you Athenians would have the leadership of the naval forces while the Spartans would command the infantry and cavalry, and indeed I myself think such a division arises not so much by human as by divine nature and fortune. [3] First of all, you occupy a position that is most appropriate for this command, since the majority of the cities that have need of the sea dwell around your city, and all of them are weaker than you are. In addition to this, you have harbors, without which one cannot exploit naval power. You also possess many triremes, and it is your custom of old to systematically construct additional ones. [4] And you have also mastered all the skills that are required for these pursuits. Moreover, you have far greater experience of naval matters than the rest of mankind, since the majority of you draw your livelihood from the sea, and so while attending to your own private affairs, you simultaneously become skilled in naval warfare. Here is yet another point: more triremes could sail out together

7.1.1
369
ATHENS
Athens and Sparta discuss the terms of an alliance.

7.1.2–4
369
ATHENS
The speech of Prokles of Phleious to the Athenians. He argues that there are many political, historical, geographical, and cultural reasons why Athens should claim leadership of the alliance at sea.

7.1.1a "The next year" does not refer to the next calendar year. Xenophon means here the campaign year (roughly corresponding to our 369) that, in the system used by his predecessor Thucydides, would begin a few days after the events at the end of Book 6. Some scholars think Xenophon means to look a full twelve months forward, to the spring of 368, and there is even a third view that he is referring to the next Athenian archon year, which would begin roughly in our July 369.
7.1.1b Athens: Map 7.1.22, AY.
7.1.1c Sparta: Map 7.1.22, BX.
7.1.1d Phleious: Map 7.1.22, AY.
7.1.2a The Athenian Council of Five Hundred, whose regular function was to prepare the agenda for Assembly meetings, including formulating many of the motions to be put to the people. See Appendix B, The Athenian Government and the Oligarchy of the Thirty, §5, 8.

from Athens than from anywhere else, and this is not a minor consideration when one is talking about naval leadership, since people are happiest to join the power that has first displayed its strength.

[5] "Furthermore, the gods have given you success in this field. For you have participated in the greatest and most numerous sea battles, and you have won the most successes and suffered the fewest misfortunes. It is likely, therefore, that the allies would be happiest to share in these dangers if you were in command. [6] You can see that this naval experience is necessary and appropriate from the following: the Spartans once fought against you for many years, and although they controlled your territory, they made no progress in conquering you; but when God granted them victory at sea, you found yourself immediately and completely in their power.[a] It is thus perfectly clear that your security depends entirely on the sea. [7] Since it is nature that has made this your situation, how could it be sensible for you to hand the command at sea over to the Spartan? For they themselves admit that they are less skilled than you in naval matters in the first place and, second, that the risk would not be equal in a naval battle, since for the Spartans the contest would concern only their men in the triremes, while for you Athenians it would concern not only the men fighting but also your wives and children, and indeed your entire city.

[8] "That is your situation; now let us look at how things stand with the Spartans. First, they dwell inland, and so as long as they control the land, they can live well, even if they are kept from the sea. They too recognize this situation, so from their very youth they train for land warfare. And in the most important aspect—obedience to commanders—they are best by land, just as you are best by sea. [9] And just as you can embark large forces swiftly by sea, so they can march out quickly and in the greatest number by land, which increases the probability that allies will eagerly join the Spartans. And just as God has granted you success at sea, so he has granted them success on land. For they have waged the most numerous land wars and have suffered the fewest defeats and gained the most victories. [10] One can safely infer from past deeds that their experience on land is no less necessary than yours by sea. For you fought with them for many years[a] and often defeated them at sea, but you had no success in gaining the victory in the war. But as soon as the Spartans incurred just one defeat on land,[b] then their wives and children, together with their entire city, were threatened with peril. [11] So then it would likewise be dreadful for the Spartans to relinquish the leadership on land, since they are the most skilled at this type of warfare.

7.1.6a   Prokles refers to the Peloponnesian War (431–404) and to the annual Spartan invasions of Athenian territory in Attica (Map 7.1.22, AY). The naval victory mentioned is that of Aigospotamoi; see 2.1.28. Aigospotamoi (Aigospotamos): Map 7.1.22, locator.
7.1.10a   The speaker refers again to the Pelopon-

nesian War, which lasted twenty-seven years.
7.1.10b   The Thebans defeated the Spartans sharply at Leuctra (Map 7.1.22, AY); see 6.4.1–15.

"I have now given the reasons for my support of your Council's proposals, which I consider to be the most beneficial course for both sides. May good fortune attend you Athenians in deciding in a way that is best for us all."

[12] In this way Prokles ended his speech, and after he was vigorously praised by both the Athenians and the Spartans who were present, Kephisodotos[a] came forward to speak: "Men of Athens, are you not ashamed to be so completely deceived? If you will listen to me, I will immediately reveal to you how this is the case. It is being proposed that you will have the leadership by sea. But if the Spartans become your allies, it is obvious that they will send trireme commanders and perhaps some marines who will be Spartan citizens, but the sailors themselves will be helots[b] or mercenaries. [13] These are the sorts of men you will command. But it is likewise clear that when the Spartans summon you to a joint campaign on land, you will send Athenian hoplites and cavalry. In this way they will command Athenian citizens, while you will command their slaves and men of the least worth. Now tell me, Timokrates of Sparta, did you not just say that you came to Athens in order to make a treaty that is fair and equal?"

"That is what I said," said Timokrates.

[14] "Would it not, then, be fairer for each side to hold the joint command by land and sea in turn, and for you to share in whatever advantage might be derived from the naval command and us to share in whatever advantage might accrue from the command on land?"

When they heard this, the Athenians changed their minds and voted that each side should hold the joint command for a rotating period of five days.

[15] Both sides and their allies now mobilized for a campaign, and they decided that they would march to Corinth[a] and guard Oneon[b] jointly. And so while the Thebans[c] and their allies were still on the march, they arranged their forces so that various units guarded specific parts of Oneon, with the Spartans and Pelleneians[d] stationed at the spot that was easiest to attack. The Thebans and their allies marched to a location thirty stades[e] from the defenders and camped in the plain. During the night they marched out against the Spartan guardpost, having previously calculated the hour at which they needed to depart in order to arrive at their destination by dawn. [16] They had calculated perfectly, and they fell upon the Spartans and Pelleneians just when the night watches were finishing and the rest of the men were rising, each one going about his task. The Thebans attacked and struck their opponents: they were prepared and in good order, their oppo-

7.1.12–14
369
ATHENS
Kephisodotos argues that this division is unfair and that the cities should share command on land and sea. The Athenians vote for this scheme.

7.1.15–17
369
MOUNT ONEON
The Thebans launch a dawn attack on the Spartan camp and rout them from their position. The Spartan commander concludes a truce (which was considered to be to the advantage of the Thebans) and leads his troops away.

7.1.12a	Kephisodotos was last mentioned at 6.3.2.		into the Peloponnese (Map 7.1.22, AX).
7.1.12b	Helots: see Appendix E, Spartan Government and Society, §11–12.	7.1.15c	Thebes: Map 7.1.22, AY.
		7.1.15d	Pellene: Map 7.1.22, AX.
7.1.15a	Corinth: Map 7.1.22, AY.	7.1.15e	Thirty Attic stades of 583 feet would
7.1.15b	Mount Oneon: Map 7.1.22, AY. The road from northern Greece passed through this mountain range southeast of Corinth		convert to a modern distance of 3.33 miles. See Appendix I, Units of Distance, Currency, and Capacity in Xenophon's *Hellenika*, §4–5, 13.

nents unprepared and in disorder. [17] Some of the defenders broke away and fled to the nearest hill, where their commander could have held their position, since he might have obtained as many hoplites and peltasts[a] from the allies as he needed and supplies could have been safely brought in from Kenchreai;[b] but he did not do this. And even though the Thebans were at a loss as to how to descend the hill on the side facing Sicyon[c] and were even considering a retreat, he made a truce with them, which seemed to a majority of people at the time to have been made more to the advantage of the Thebans than of the Spartans. And having done this, the Spartan commander[d] departed and led away his troops.

[18] The Thebans then safely descended into the plain, and joining up with their allies, the Arcadians,[a] Argives,[b] and Eleians,[c] immediately attacked Sicyon and Pellene. They also made an attack on Epidauros[d] and devastated all its territory. Then they marched back from this campaign in a manner that showed their utter contempt for all their foes, for as soon as they came near the city proper of Corinth, they began to run toward the gates, the ones that lead to Phleious, intending to burst into the city if they happened to find the gates open. [19] Some light-armed forces advanced from the city and met the picked men from the Theban forces[a] when they were a little less than four plethra[b] from the wall. The Corinthian troops leapt up onto burial monuments[c] and any other high places that were located in front of the city and, by throwing missiles and javelins, managed to kill a large number of the Thebans in the front ranks; having routed them, they pursued them for a distance of three or four stades.[d] After this, the Corinthians dragged the corpses to the wall, gave them back under truce, and set up a trophy.[e] This incident helped to raise the morale of the Spartan allies.[f]

7.1.18–19
369
CORINTH
The Thebans unite with their Peloponnesian allies and attack Sicyon, Pellene, and Epidaurus. Their surprise attack on Corinth is defeated and driven off. They suffer many casualties.

7.1.17a   Peltasts: lightly armored infantry.
7.1.17b   Kenchreai: Map 7.1.22, AY.
7.1.17c   Sicyon: Map 7.1.22, AY.
7.1.17d   It is noteworthy that Xenophon does not name this commander. See Appendix O, Selections from the *Histories* of Diodorus Siculus Relevant to Xenophon's *Hellenika*, 15.68.4–5, for a different account of this battle.
7.1.18a   Arcadia: Map 7.1.22, AX.
7.1.18b   Argos: Map 7.1.22, AY.
7.1.18c   Elis: Map 7.1.22, AX.
7.1.18d   Epidauros: Map 7.1.22, AY. Diodorus (Appendix O, 15.69.1) says that the Theban general Epaminondas first attacked Troizen (Map 7.1.22, BY) and Epidauros unsuccessfully and then went against Sicyon.
7.1.19a   This group of "picked men from the Theban forces" is Xenophon's first and only reference to the famous Theban Sacred Band, an elite military unit comprising 150 pairs of lovers sworn to fight to the death. First organized by Gorgidas in 378, it remained undefeated

until it was annihilated by Philip of Macedon at the battle of Chaeronea (Map 7.1.22, AY) in 338.
7.1.19b   The ancient unit called a plethra equaled 100 feet. Assuming that Xenophon meant the Attic foot of 11.65 modern inches, 4 plethra would equal something less than 388 feet. See Appendix I, §4, 13.
7.1.19c   Since no one (other than founding heroes) was allowed to be buried within the walls of ancient Greek cities, the roads leading out from a city near its walls were often lined with cemeteries, many of whose graves were furnished with large burial monuments.
7.1.19d   If these were Attic stades, the distance would have been 600–800 yards.
7.1.19e   After a hoplite battle in ancient Greece, the victors would gather up their dead, strip those of the enemy, and raise a trophy, usually a set of captured armor raised on a pole.
7.1.19f   For another account of the battle, see Diodorus (Appendix O, 15.69.1–4).

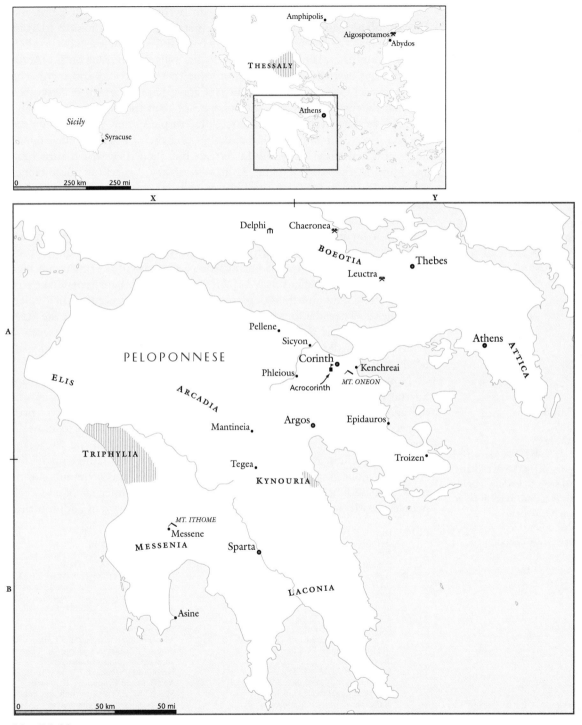

MAP 7.1.22

7.1.20–22
369
CORINTH
Reinforcements for the allies arrive from Dionysios, including some cavalry. Although the Athenian and Corinthian cavalry hang back, the horsemen from Dionysios successfully harass the plundering parties of the Thebans and their allies. The Thebans soon leave, and the Sicilian reinforcements, after defeating the Sicyonians and capturing a fortress, sail back to Syracuse.

[20] Just after these events, more than twenty triremes with Celtic and Iberian infantry and about fifty horsemen arrived[a] from Dionysios[b] to assist the Spartans. On the next day the Thebans and their allies drew up their forces, filling the plain[c] from the sea to the hills that border on the Acrocorinth[d] and destroying everything of value that they could find there. The Athenian and Corinthian cavalry did not approach the enemy, because they saw that they were numerous and strong. [21] But the cavalry from Dionysios, few as they were, scattered into different places and ran alongside the Theban forces, throwing javelins and attacking them; whenever their opponents attacked them, they would retreat, but then they would turn back again and throw more javelins. And even as they carried out these tactics they would dismount from their horses and rest; but if someone attacked them when they were not on their horses, they would leap up onto them with ease and ride away. Moreover, if anyone pursued them far from the Theban main body, they would counterattack as soon as their pursuers turned back to join their own forces, throwing their javelins and, by so doing, wreaking havoc on the enemy, compelling his entire army to advance or retreat by their maneuvers. [22] After this, the Thebans remained there for just a few days and then departed for home, as did each of their allied contingents. Then the forces from Dionysios invaded Sicyon,[a] met the Sicyonians in battle in the plain, and defeated them, killing around seventy. They also took the stronghold of Deras[b] by force. Having performed such deeds, this first force sent by Dionysios sailed back to Syracuse.

Now up to this time the Thebans[c] and the others who had revolted from Sparta[d] had been conducting their activities and making their campaigns in full agreement under the leadership of the Thebans. [23] But now a man named Lykomedes from Mantineia[a] appeared: he was second to none in birth and was very wealthy and ambitious. This man filled the Arcadians with pride, telling them that the Peloponnese[b] was the fatherland of the Arcadians alone, inasmuch as they alone of its inhabitants were autochthonous,[c] and adding that the Arcadians were the most numerous of all Greek peoples and had the strongest physiques as well. To prove in addition that

7.1.23–24
369
ARCADIA
Lykomedes of Mantineia persuades the Arcadians to stop following Theban orders and to form their own independent command. The Arcadians, thus encouraged, appoint new leaders selected by Lykomedes.

7.1.20a   Diodorus 15.70.1 (see Appendix O) says that the Celtic and Iberian troops did fight well and numbered two thousand.
7.1.20b   Dionysios the tyrant of Syracuse, Sicily (Map 7.1.22, locator); see 2.2.24.
7.1.20c   The plain between Corinth, Sicyon, and the sea.
7.1.20d   Acrocorinth: Map 7.1.22, AY. A steep, flat-topped hill near the city of Corinth on which was situated an ancient walled citadel. See Figure 4.4.5 for two views of the Acrocorinth.
7.1.22a   Sicyon: Map 7.1.22, AY. This passage suggests, though Xenophon does not say so explicitly, that the Sicyonians must have in the meantime taken the Theban side.
7.1.22b   Deras: site unknown.

7.1.22c   Thebes: Map 7.1.22, AY.
7.1.22d   Sparta: Map 7.1.22, BX.
7.1.23a   Mantineia: Map 7.1.22, AX. Diodorus 15.59.1 (see Appendix O) says Lykomedes was from Tegea (Map 7.1.22, BX), not Mantineia. This is certainly an error on his part, and elsewhere (15.62.1, see Appendix O) he calls him Lykomedes from Mantineia.
7.1.23b   Peloponnese: Map 7.1.22, AX.
7.1.23c   Autochthonous, that is, the Arcadians believed that they as a people had never immigrated from somewhere else. Herodotus (*Histories* 8.73) says that the Arcadians and Kynourians (Kynouria: Map 7.1.22, BX) were the only autochthonous peoples of the Peloponnese.

they were the bravest of people, he cited as evidence the fact that people who needed military assistance turned first to the Arcadians, noting, too, that the Spartans had never invaded Athens without the Arcadians, just as now the Thebans did not attack Sparta without them. [24] "If, then, you are sensible," he said, "you will stop following wherever someone else leads you. In earlier times you followed the Spartans and helped them grow stronger; so now, if you continue to follow the Thebans blindly and do not demand a share of the leadership, you will perhaps discover that you will have done for the Thebans exactly what you did for the Spartans." When the Arcadians heard this, they were elated, and they became enamored of Lykomedes, considering him to be the only true man, and selecting as their leaders the men whom Lykomedes told them to appoint.[a]

But at the same time, it is true, there were real achievements about which the Arcadians could justifiably feel proud. [25] For example, when the Argives invaded Epidauros and the Epidaurians were prevented from escaping by the mercenaries with Chabrias[a] and by Athenian and Corinthian[b] forces, the Arcadians went to their assistance and released the Argives who were being besieged, even though they had to contend not only with enemy forces but with difficult terrain.[c] And on another occasion, they made an expedition against Asine in Laconia,[d] where they defeated the Spartan garrison, killed Geranor, the Spartiate serving as commander, and laid waste the suburbs of Asine.[e] Indeed, once the Arcadians decided to march somewhere, nothing could prevent them: not nightfall, not storms, not distance, not even mountains difficult to cross. And so at that moment they thought themselves much the strongest of the Greeks.

[26] This led the Thebans to become somewhat jealous and no longer treat them as friends. The Eleians, too, now became hostile to the Arcadians, because they had demanded from the Arcadians those cities that had been taken from them by the Spartans;[a] the Arcadians, however, took no account of the Eleians but instead paid a great deal of attention to the Triphylians[b] and the other cities that had revolted from Elis, holding these in high regard because they claimed to be Arcadians.

7.1.25–26
369–368
ARCADIA
The Arcadians are also heartened by their military achievements at Epidauros and Asine. Thus challenged, Thebes ceases to be friendly to them, and the Eleians, resenting the Arcadians' refusal to return certain cities to them, also become hostile.

7.1.24a   Here for the first time Xenophon describes the Arcadians as though united in an Arcadian Federation. See Appendix H, Political Leagues (Other Than Sparta's) in Xenophon's *Hellenika*, §8. For more on Lykomedes, see 7.1.39, 7.4.2–3, and Appendix O, 15.59.1, 15.62.2.
7.1.25a   Chabrias, Athenian general: see Appendix M, Brief Biographies of Important Characters in Xenophon's *Hellenika*, §6.
7.1.25b   Corinth: Map 7.1.22, AY.
7.1.25c   This incident is not narrated or explained further by Xenophon.
7.1.25d   Xenophon says Asine is in Laconia, but this stretches the latter's boundaries into what we would call Messenia (all locations: Map 7.1.22, BX), on the western side of the Taygetos mountain range.

This is probably a geographic error on his part, but it may represent a prevailing Spartan characterization of Asine as a Laconic city.
7.1.25e   Again, no further details of these incidents are known.
7.1.26a   These cities and peoples are listed at 3.2.30–31 as Phrixa, Epitalion, the Letrinoi, the Amphidolians, the Marganeis, the Akroreians (for all previous: Map 3.2.26, inset), and Lasion (Map 3.2.26). In 6.5.2, the city of Skillous (Map 6.4.27, BX) is added to that list.
7.1.26b   Triphylia: Map 7.1.22, BX.

7.1.27
368
DELPHI
Philiskos of Abydos arrives with funds from Ariobarzanes. He assembles all at Delphi to negotiate a peace, but the negotiations fail, given the conflicting demands.

7.1.28
368
ARCADIA
A second expedition arrives from Syracuse and is sent to Sparta. From there they go with Archidamos against Arcadia.

7.1.29–31
368
ARCADIA
When the Syracusans seek to return, the Messenians attempt to block their route. Coming to their aid, Archidamos meets and attacks the Arcadians and Argives. His forces rout them, inflicting many casualties without losing a man. Sparta rejoices, and the Thebans and Eleians are not unhappy with this result.

[27] It was in these circumstances, with each of the parties proudly confident of their own abilities, that a man from Abydos[a] named Philiskos came bearing a large amount of money from Ariobarzanes.[b] First he gathered together at Delphi[c] the Thebans and their allies, along with the Spartans, to negotiate a peace. When they had assembled there, however, they did not consult the god at all about how to make peace but instead discussed it among themselves. The Spartans demanded that they should control Messene,[d] but the Thebans refused to allow this, and so Philiskos began to gather a large army of mercenaries so that he might wage war on Sparta's side.[e]

[28] While these events were going on, a second armed force arrived from Dionysios. The Athenians argued that this force should be sent to Thessaly[a] to oppose the Thebans there, while the Spartans wanted it to go to Laconia, and the allies decided in favor of the latter course. When the expeditionary force from Dionysios had sailed around to Sparta,[b] Archidamos[c] took them along with his citizen army when he began his campaign. He conquered Karyai[d] by force and slaughtered all those whom he took alive there. Then he marched immediately from there against the Parrasians[e] in Arcadia and with his reinforcements laid waste their countryside.

When the Arcadians and Argives[f] came to their assistance, Archidamos retreated and camped in the hills above Melea.[g] While they were there, Kissides, the commander of the forces sent by Dionysios, said that their appointed time had expired, and he no sooner said this than he departed, taking the road that leads to Sparta. [29] But the Messenians cut him off when he reached a narrow defile in the road, and Kissides then sent to Archidamos requesting help. Archidamos did indeed go to his aid, but as the Spartans arrived at the branch road leading to Eutresia,[a] the Arcadians and Argives were at the same time marching toward Laconia, their intention being to cut Archidamos off and prevent him from returning home. But Archidamos turned aside to a spot where the ground is level, just at the

---

7.1.27a Abydos: Map 7.1.22, locator.
7.1.27b Ariobarzanes, the Persian satrap, had last been mentioned at 5.1.28.
7.1.27c Delphi: Map 7.1.22, AX.
7.1.27d Messene: Map 7.1.22, BX. This is Xenophon's first mention of the foundation and fortification of Messene, the capital city of a now independent Messenia. The city had been established and fortified by Epaminondas on Mount Ithome (Map 7.1.22, BX) after the first Theban invasion of the Peloponnese, a fact that is completely ignored in Xenophon's narrative of that invasion at 6.5.51–52. See the Introduction, §3.5, 12.9, 15.7. See also Figure 7.1.27, showing remains of city walls that Epaminondas' army helped build.
7.1.27e See Appendix O, 15.70.2, for Diodorus' account of Philiskos' mission, which asserts that it was the Thebans' demand for control of the cities of Boeotia (Map 7.1.22, AY), not the Spartan demand for

7.1.28a Thessaly: Map 7.1.22, locator. For more about the activities of Thebes in Thessaly and northern Greece, see "Pelopidas" in Appendix M, 20.
7.1.28b Of course Xenophon means they sailed to Spartan territory, as Sparta itself lies far inland.
7.1.28c Archidamos son of Agesilaos was last mentioned at 6.4.18–26. Although exactly when Agesilaos died and his son (also known as Archidamos III) became king is controversial, the date most often favored is early 360, about a year and a half after the end of the *Hellenika*. For more on Archidamos III, see Appendix M, §5.
7.1.28d Karyai, possible locations: Map 7.1.34, BX.
7.1.28e Parrasia: Map 7.1.34, BX.
7.1.28f Argos: Map 7.1.34, AX.
7.1.28g Reading Mueller's conjecture for the manuscripts' impossible "Medea." There is no known location for Melea. (John Marincola)
7.1.29a Eutresia, possible location: Map 7.1.34, BX.

Messene, that caused him to fail.

FIGURE 7.1.27. REMAINS OF THE FOURTH-CENTURY FORTIFICATIONS ON MOUNT ITHOME, MESSENIA, PRESUMABLY BUILT BY EPAMINONDAS. THE FALLEN LINTEL (ABOVE) IS A MASSIVE BLOCK OF STONE SOME SEVENTEEN FEET LONG, FOUR FEET HIGH, AND THREE FEET WIDE. THE WALLS (BELOW) WERE TWENTY-NINE FEET HIGH IN PLACES AND SPANNED 5.5 MILES, PROTECTING MESSENE'S AGRICULTURAL LAND AS WELL AS ITS ACROPOLIS IN TIME OF SIEGE.

junction of the roads to Eutresia and Melea, and here he drew up his men for battle. [30] It is said that he went along in front of the regiments and exhorted them as follows: "Fellow citizens, let us now show ourselves to be brave men and so to be able to look people in the eye. Let us hand over to our descendants the same kind of country that we inherited from our fathers. Let us no longer feel shame before our children and wives, elders and foreigners, those very people in whose eyes we were in past time the most renowned of all Greeks." [31] They say that after he made this speech, lightning and thunder appeared out of a clear sky as favorable omens to him. And by chance it also happened that a sacred precinct and statue of Herakles[a] was situated on the right wing of the army. As a result, they say, the soldiers were so full of strength and boldness that the leaders' real task was to prevent them from pushing forward in their eagerness.[b] When Archidamos advanced against the enemy, only a few of them waited until the Spartans were within spear range, and these were killed. The rest fled, and many of them fell at the hands of the pursuing cavalry and Celts.

[32] When the battle was over, Archidamos set up a trophy and immediately dispatched Demoteles to Sparta to announce there the magnitude of the victory and the fact that not a single Spartan had died in the battle, while very many of the enemy had been slain.[a] It is said that when those back in Sparta heard the news, they all began to weep, beginning with Agesilaos, and then on to the old men and the ephors, and finally everyone. So it is indeed the case that tears are common to both joy and grief. No less pleased at the Arcadian defeat were the Thebans and Eleians, since they had by now become thoroughly annoyed with Arcadian pride.

[33] The Thebans had been constantly scheming about how they might become the leaders of all of Greece, and they now decided that they might secure some advantage with the Persian King if they sent ambassadors to him. They accordingly called together their allies and, on the pretext that Euthykles the Spartan was at the Persian court,[a] dispatched Pelopidas of Thebes,[b] Antiochos of Arcadia (the pancratist),[c] and Archidamos the Eleian to the Persian court and Argeios[d] went with them; and when the Athenians learned of this, they sent Timagoras and Leon.

7.1.32
368
ARCADIA
The people of Sparta weep at news of the "Tearless Battle." Xenophon says tears are common to both joy and grief. The Thebans and Eleians are not unhappy.

7.1.33–35
367
SUSA
In an attempt to gain the leadership of Greece, the Thebans send Pelopidas with envoys from other cities to the Persian King. Pelopidas is favored by the Persians because Thebes fought on Xerxes' side and has never attacked Persian territories. Moreover, the Thebans defeated the Spartans at Leuctra and plundered Spartan territory.

7.1.31a A phrase that follows in the manuscript ("whose descendant he [Archidamos III] is said to be") is not included in the translation here, since it was originally probably an explanatory note that later crept into Xenophon's text. (John Marincola)

7.1.31b Pushing forward would have broken and disrupted the phalanx lines, a dangerous error.

7.1.32a This battle became known, at least among Spartans and their allies, as the "Tearless Battle." See Appendix O, 15.72.3–4, for Diodorus' account of the battle.

7.1.33a No details of Euthykles' mission are known, but it is probably related to Philiskos' support of the Spartans in the previous year.

7.1.33b This is the first time Xenophon mentions Pelopidas, the great Theban leader who had played a leading role in freeing the Kadmeia (the acropolis of the city of Thebes: Map 7.1.34, AY) from Spartan control. See 5.4.2–12 for these events, though Xenophon suppresses Pelopidas' name in connection with them. See "Pelopidas" in Plutarch's *Parallel Lives* and Appendix M, §20.

7.1.33c The *pankration*, an Olympic sporting event, combined boxing and wrestling.

7.1.33d Perhaps the same man as mentioned at 7.4.15, in which case he is from Elis (Map 7.1.34, AX). But some scholars think that Argeios is the adjective Argive and that the proper name has fallen out.

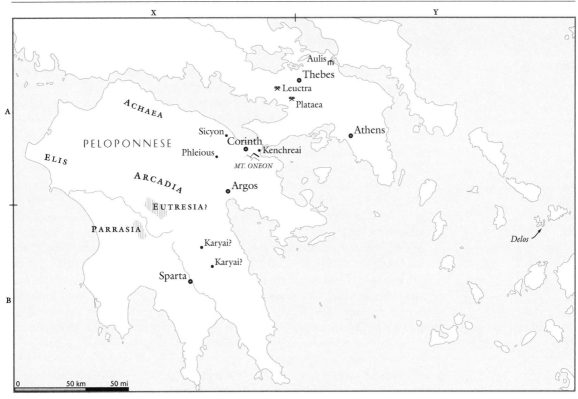

MAP 7.1.34

[34] When they were all together there, Pelopidas had a great advantage with the Persian King, for he could claim that the Thebans, alone of all the Greeks, had fought side by side with the Persians at Plataea[a] and that they had never thereafter campaigned against the King. He added that the Thebans were hated by the Spartans because they had refused to march with Agesilaos against the King[b] and because they had not allowed Agesilaos to sacrifice to Artemis at Aulis,[c] the very place from which Agamemnon had set out when he campaigned against Asia and destroyed Troy.[d] [35] What also greatly contributed to Pelopidas' standing in the eyes of the King was that the Thebans had been victorious at Leuctra[a] and that they had openly ravaged Sparta's territory. Pelopidas also said that the Argives[b] and Arcadians[c] had been defeated in battle by the Spartans because the Thebans had not been present. The Athenian[d] Timagoras verified that everything

7.1.34a Plataea: Map 7.1.34, AY. Pelopidas is
         referring to the last great battle on Greek
         soil between the Persians and their allies
         and the combined Greek forces, which
         took place in 479.
7.1.34b See 3.5.5.
7.1.34c Aulis: Map 7.1.34, AY. For the Theban
         refusal to allow Agesilaos to sacrifice at

         Aulis in 396, see 3.4.3.
7.1.34d Troy: Map 3.4.12, AY.
7.1.35a Leuctra: Map 7.1.34, AX. For a descrip-
         tion of the battle of Leuctra in 371, see
         6.4.4–15.
7.1.35b Argos: Map 7.1.34, AX.
7.1.35c Arcadia: Map 7.1.34, AX.
7.1.35d Athens: Map 7.1.34, AY.

Pelopidas had said was true, and so he was held in the second place of honor after Pelopidas.

[36] The King then asked Pelopidas what terms he wished him to establish, and Pelopidas replied that he wanted Messenia to be autonomous and free from Spartan rule; the Athenians to draw up their ships onto the land;[a] and the King to wage war on Athens and Sparta if they failed to obey these orders, and to first attack any city that failed to join in the campaign. [37] When the King had written these stipulations and they had been read out to the ambassadors, Leon said in the hearing of the King, "By Zeus, Athenians, it seems the time has come for you to seek a friend other than the King." This remark was reported to the King by his interpreter, after which the King added a rider to his proclamation that "if the Athenians know more just arrangements, they should come to the King and inform him."

[38] When the ambassadors returned to their home countries, the Athenians put Timagoras to death, because Leon had brought formal charges that Timagoras had failed to share quarters with him and had taken counsel with Pelopidas in all matters.[a] At Elis[b] Archidamos praised the King because he had honored the Eleians in preference to the Arcadians. In Arcadia, meanwhile, Antiochos, who had refused to accept the King's gifts because the Arcadians had been slighted, told the Ten Thousand[c] that he had seen in Persia numerous bakers and cooks, wine stewards and doorkeepers, but although he looked hard, he could see nowhere men of the sort that could fight with Greeks. In addition, he said that the abundance of the King's money seemed to him nothing more than boasting, since even the golden plane tree[d] about which so much had been made was not even big enough to give shade to a grasshopper.

[39] At Thebes, the Thebans had called together representatives from all the allied cities to hear the King's letter, and the Persian who brought the letter showed everyone the King's seal and then read out its contents. The Thebans thereupon ordered all those who wished to be a friend to both the King and themselves to swear to the provisions of the King's decree, but the representatives of the cities said they had not been sent to swear to any oaths but only to listen, and if the Thebans needed the cities to agree to certain terms, they would have to send round to the cities to obtain sworn guarantees. Lykomedes the Arcadian added that they ought not to have this meeting in Thebes but, rather, in the place where they would actually be campaigning. The Thebans became angry with him and accused him of

7.1.36a   Pelopidas is insisting that the Athenians immobilize their fleet, which is in reference to Athens' current campaign against Amphipolis (Map 7.1.22, locator), largely ignored by Xenophon. See a brief mention at 4.3.1 and the Introduction, §3.6.

7.1.38a   For more on Timagoras' fate, see Demosthenes 19.191. Plutarch (*Parallel Lives*, "Artaxerxes" 22.6) says

that Timagoras was condemned because he took bribes from the King.

7.1.38b   Elis: Map 7.1.34, AX.

7.1.38c   This Ten Thousand was what the Arcadian Assembly was called. Xenophon describes its formation at 6.5.6. See also Appendix H, §8.

7.1.38d   This famous "treasure" of the Persian King was mentioned by Herodotus in his *Histories* at 7.27.2.

trying to destroy the alliance; Lykomedes responded by refusing even to take his seat at the congress; instead, he departed for home, and all the Arcadian ambassadors went with him.

[40] Since those who had gathered together in Thebes refused to take any oath, the Thebans sent messengers to the various cities, ordering them to swear to abide by what the King had stipulated, thinking that each city individually would be reluctant to disobey them and thereby incur their hostility and that of the King as well. They came first to Corinth,[a] but the Corinthians told them that they had no need of agreements with the King, and they refused to take the oath. Other cities answered in the same way, following the Corinthian lead, and so this attempt by Pelopidas and the Thebans to rule over Greece fell apart.

[41] Epaminondas,[a] on the other hand, decided that the Thebans had to make an expedition against Achaea;[b] he thought that bringing the Achaeans over to the Theban side would induce the Arcadians and the rest of the allies to respect the wishes of the Thebans. He therefore persuaded Peisias, the Argive general, to seize Mount Oneon[c] in advance. Peisias learned that those responsible for defending Oneon—a man named Naukles, who commanded the Spartan mercenaries, and Timomachos the Athenian—were carrying out their duties carelessly, and so, taking along provisions for seven days, he set out with two thousand hoplites and captured the hill above Kenchreai[d] during the night. [42] The Thebans arrived within the seven days and marched unopposed over Oneon, and all the allies joined in the campaign against Achaea, which was commanded by Epaminondas.

Now in response to the entreaties of the aristocrats of Achaea, Epaminondas managed by his own authority to prevent the democratic faction from exiling the aristocrats or altering the constitution. He received pledges from the Achaeans that they would be allies of the Thebans and would follow wherever the Thebans commanded them; having made these arrangements, he then returned home.

[43] The Arcadians, however, and the opposition faction[a] in Achaea accused Epaminondas of having arranged a settlement that was beneficial to the Spartans,[b] and so the Thebans decided to send governors to the Achaean cities. These governors, then, with the assistance of the common people, drove out the aristocrats and established democracies throughout Achaea. Those who had been driven out, however, quickly banded together and marched against each city in turn; since they were numerous, they were able to accomplish their restoration and once again take control of the

7.1.41–43
366?
ACHAEA
Epaminondas attempts to coerce Achaea to accept Theban hegemony, and he finally succeeds, establishing democracies in the Achaean cities, installing Theban governors in them, and expelling the aristocrats. But the aristocrats band together and retake their cities one by one and now, instead of resuming their former neutral policy, ally themselves firmly with Sparta. Arcadia is thereby pressed by Achaeans from the north and Spartans from the south.

7.1.40a Corinth: Map 7.1.34, AX.
7.1.41a This is the first mention by Xenophon of the great Theban general Epaminondas, who had already been active for some years and whose participation was vitally important to Thebes' recent successes: see the Introduction, §3.4–6 and 13.3, for Xenophon's omissions of this sort. For more information on Epaminondas, see Appendix M, §9.

7.1.41b Achaea: Map 7.1.34, AX.
7.1.41c Mount Oneon: Map 7.1.34, AX. A strategic post through which passed a main route south from Corinth to the rest of the Peloponnese.
7.1.41d Kenchreai: Map 7.1.34, AX.
7.1.43a In this case, the democratic faction now opposed the agreement the Achaeans had made with the Thebans.
7.1.43b Sparta: Map 7.1.34, BX.

cities. And now, having returned, they no longer steered a middle course in foreign affairs but fought eagerly on the side of the Spartans. So the Arcadians now found themselves hard-pressed on one side by the Spartans and on the other by the Achaeans.

[44] Up to this time, Sicyon[a] had followed its ancestral laws. This was to change, however, when a man named Euphron, who enjoyed the greatest influence with the Spartans, now decided that he wanted a similar status with Sparta's foes.[b] He therefore told the Argives and Arcadians that if the wealthiest men gained control of Sicyon, the city would again take the side of Sparta whenever a suitable opportunity arose. "But," he said, "if the city becomes a democracy, you can be certain that it will remain loyal to you. If, then, you will support me, I will call the commons together and I will thereby simultaneously give you evidence of my good faith and make the city firm in its alliance with you. Know that I will do this because, like you, I have long resented Spartan arrogance and would happily escape from being their slave."

[45] Upon hearing this, the Argives and Arcadians happily agreed to assist him. With the Argives and Arcadians present, he immediately called together the people of Sicyon, telling them that a government was now going to be established with equal rights for all. Once they had gathered, he told them to choose whichever men seemed best to them to serve as generals. They elected Euphron himself, Hippodamos, Kleandros, Akrisios, and Lysandros. After this was done, Euphron appointed his son Adeas to command the mercenaries, removing their former leader, Lysimenes. [46] Euphron immediately won over some of these mercenaries by buying their loyalty with favors, and he acquired additional mercenaries, sparing neither public nor sacred moneys.[a] He also appropriated the property of all those whom he expelled on a charge of being pro-Spartan. Some of his fellow officeholders he put to death by treachery, others he banished, and in this way he came to control everything and ruled manifestly as a tyrant. He contrived that the allies should support him in all this partly by bribing some of them with money and partly by assisting others with his mercenary force whenever they went on their campaigns.

[1] While these events were progressing, the Argives erected a fort in the territory of Phleious[a] at Mount Trikaranon[b] above the Heraion,[c] and the Sicyonians were fortifying Thyamia[d] on their borders; and as the situation progressed, the Phleiasians became very hard-pressed and began to run short of necessities. They nevertheless remained faithful to their alliance with the Spartans. Now if a great city does some fine deed, all the historians

---

7.1.44–46
368
SICYON
Euphron of Sicyon tells the Arcadians and Argives that if they will support him, he will establish an anti-Spartan democracy in his city and be a steadfast ally of theirs. When they provide the requested support, he overthrows the existing regime and supposedly sets up a democracy. In fact, he takes control over everything and establishes himself as a tyrant, buying the acquiescence of the allies with money and mercenaries.

7.2.1
368–365
PHLEIOUS
The Phleiasians are hard-pressed but remain loyal to Sparta. Xenophon is determined to describe their noble deeds.

7.1.44a	Sicyon: Map 7.1.34, AX.	7.2.1b	Mount Trikaranon: Map 7.2.5; a hill with
7.1.44b	Diodorus (15.70.3) dates this event to		three low summits, forming the northeast
	369/8. Some scholars think Xenophon		boundary of the Phleiasian plain. See
	did not mean to suggest that Euphron's		Figure 7.2.1.
	coup at 7.1.44 came after the events at	7.2.1c	This temple of Hera is said by Pausanias
	7.1.43.		(2.13.3–4) to be on the slope of Phleious'
7.1.46a	See 7.3.8.		acropolis.
7.2.1a	Phleious: Map 7.1.34, AX.	7.2.1d	Thyamia: precise location unknown.

FIGURE 7.2.1. TEMPLE FOUNDATION AT PHLEIOUS WITH MOUNT TRIKARANON IN THE BACKGROUND (TOP). BUILD-
ING FOUNDATION AT THE FOOT OF MOUNT TRIKARANON, ON THE RIGHT (BOTTOM).

record it; but I think that if a small city has accomplished many fine deeds, it is even more fitting to make them known.[c]

7.2.2–3
370–369
PHLEIOUS-SPARTA
Xenophon tells of Phleiasian loyalty to Sparta, of how the Phleiasians hired their own guide to join the army at Prasiai and were rewarded by the Spartans with a special gift of an ox.

7.2.4
369
PHLEIOUS
Another anecdote of Phleiasian bravery is their feat of attacking and routing a more numerous Argive rear guard.

7.2.5–6
369
PHLEIOUS
Phleiasian exiles plot a surprise attack on Phleious with an invading force of Arcadians and Argives. The attack succeeds, and they occupy the acropolis of the city without a struggle.

[2] The Phleiasians[a] had become friends of Sparta when it was at the peak of its power.[b] And yet, when the Spartans were defeated at Leuctra,[c] many of the *perioikic*[d] towns and all the helots revolted, as did the Spartan allies, with only a few exceptions. And when all the Greeks, so to speak, were at war against Sparta, the Phleiasians remained faithful, even though this meant that they incurred the enmity of Arcadia[e] and Argos,[f] the most powerful states in the Peloponnese.[g] Nevertheless, they continued to support the Spartans:[h] it once happened that they were serving in the allied forces with Corinth, Epidauros, Troizen, Hermione, Halieis, Sicyon, and Pellene[i] (the last-named had not yet revolted),[j] [3] and by lot they were the last of all the troops slated to cross over to Prasiai.[a] Now the Spartan officer accompanied those crossing first and went on ahead, leaving the Phleiasians behind. But even so they did not turn back; instead, they hired a guide from Prasiai, and although their enemies were in the neighborhood of Amyklai,[b] they got through as best they could and arrived at Sparta.[c] On account of this, the Spartans gave them many honors, and as a special gift of hospitality they sent them an ox.[d]

[4] Again, when the enemy had retired from Sparta[a] and the Argives, angry at the loyalty of the Phleiasians to the Spartans, had invaded the territory of Phleious in full force and were laying waste their land, even then they did not yield. But when the Argives were withdrawing after having destroyed as much as they could, the Phleiasian horsemen rode out and followed after them, and although all the Argive horsemen and the companies posted behind them were employed to guard their rear, nevertheless the Phleiasians, who were but sixty in number, attacked these troops and turned the entire rearguard to flight. To be sure, they killed only a few of them, yet they set up a trophy, with the Argives looking on, precisely as if they had killed them all.

[5] At another time the Spartans and their allies were guarding Mount Oneon,[a] and the Thebans[b] approached, intending to march over it.[c] The

7.2.1e	The rest of chapter 7.2 is taken up with examples of Phleiasian loyalty to Sparta and resistance to Sparta's enemies.		Diodorus (Appendix O, 15.69.1) tells us that other cities besides Sicyon were brought over to the Thebans at this point. At any rate, they had defected by 367, when Xenophon says expressly that they were on the side of the Thebans (7.2.11).
7.2.2a	Phleious: Map 7.2.5.		
7.2.2b	Sparta: Map 7.2.5. Sparta's power could be said to have reached its peak in 379.		
7.2.2c	The battle of Leuctra (Map 7.2.5) of 371; see 6.4.4–14.	7.2.3a	Prasiai: Map 7.2.5.
7.2.2d	*Perioikoi*: see Appendix E, §10.	7.2.3b	Amyklai: Map 7.2.5.
7.2.2e	Arcadia: Map 7.2.5.	7.2.3c	The occasion for Phleiasian help to Sparta was during the first Theban invasion of the Peloponnese, when most of the Spartan allies revolted; see 6.5.24ff. For mention of Phleiasian help arriving at Sparta, see 6.5.29.
7.2.2f	Argos: Map 7.2.5.		
7.2.2g	Peloponnese: Map 7.2.5.		
7.2.2h	The Phleiasian support for Sparta referred to here (see 6.5.29) took place in 370.		
7.2.2i	Corinth, Epidauros, Troizen, Hermione, Halieis, Sicyon, Pellene: Map 7.2.5.	7.2.3d	Xenophon mentions a similar special gift in *Anabasis* (4.8.24).
7.2.2j	The date of this collective action is 370/69. Pellene defected sometime after this, probably when the Thebans invaded its territory later in 369 (7.1.18), for	7.2.4a	In the year 369.
		7.2.5a	Mount Oneon: Map 7.2.5.
		7.2.5b	Thebes: Map 7.2.5.
		7.2.5c	See 7.1.15.

284

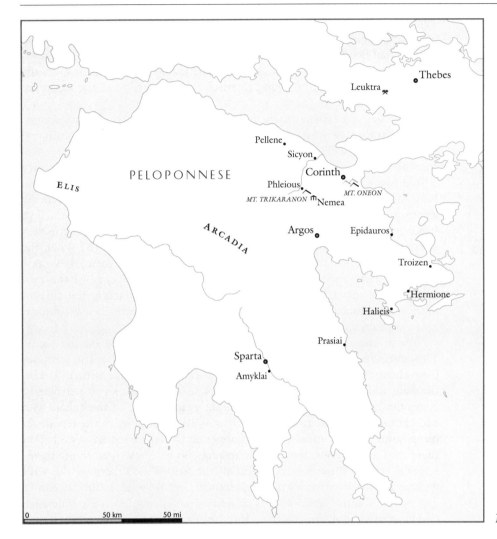

MAP 7.2.5

Arcadians and the Eleians were making their way through Nemea[d] in order
to join up with the Thebans when some Phleiasian exiles told them that if
they would appear in the city on their behalf, they could capture Phleious.
An agreement was made, and the exiles, with about six hundred other men,
took ladders and went during the night to lie in ambush beneath the very
wall of Phleious. At the moment when the scouts signaled from Mount
Trikaranon[e] that enemies were approaching the town, and the people in the
city were giving all their attention to this threat, the traitors inside gave the
signal to those lying in ambush that it was time to begin climbing the wall.
[6] They did so and found that the guards were not at their posts, so they

7.2.5d   Elis and Nemea: Map 7.2.5.   7.2.5e   Mount Trikaranon: Map 7.2.5.

went after the day guards (who numbered ten, one from each group of five being left behind as a day guard);[a] they killed one in his sleep and another after he had fled for refuge to the Heraion.[b] The rest of the guards ran away and jumped down from the wall on the side facing the city. In this way the men who had climbed up found themselves in possession of the acropolis[c] without a struggle.

[7] When the alarm reached the city, the citizens of Phleious came running to the rescue. At first the enemy came out from the acropolis and fought in the space in front of the gates leading to the city. But then, overwhelmed by the number of citizens who had come against them, they retired toward the acropolis, the citizens streaming in together with them. Now the space inside the acropolis[a] was immediately cleared, but the enemy leapt up onto the wall and the towers and from those heights continued to strike and pelt those below. The men on the ground defended themselves and fought the enemy on the stairs that led up to the wall. [8] When the citizens gained possession of some of the towers here and there, they came to close quarters with the enemy and fought desperately against the men that had mounted their walls. By their daring and courage, the citizens pushed back their opponents, who soon found themselves being confined into a smaller and smaller space.

Just at this moment the Arcadians and Argives arrived on the scene. They encircled the city and began to dig through the wall of the acropolis from above.[a] Some of the citizens within continued to strike at their foes on the wall, and others attacked the men outside the city as they were trying to climb the ladders, while yet others fought against those of the enemy who had climbed up to the towers. The citizens also found fire in the tents and, using some sheaves of wheat that happened to have been harvested right there on the acropolis, they set the towers ablaze. Some then threw themselves down from the towers in fear of the fire, while others on the walls were struck by the citizens and toppled off. [9] As soon as they began to give way, the entire acropolis was cleared of the enemy. Then the Phleiasian cavalry charged out from the city, and the enemy, upon seeing them, hastily retreated, leaving behind the ladders, the corpses, and even some of their own men who were badly wounded but still alive. Not less than eighty of the enemy perished either in the fighting inside the city or in their attempt to escape by jumping down from the walls. When it was over, one could see men grasping one another by the hand in joy at their deliverance and

7.2.6a Apparently fifty men, organized into ten groups of five, were posted as night guards on the wall of the acropolis. One from each group served as a day guard.
7.2.6b Heraion at Phleious: precise location unknown.
7.2.6c The precise location of the acropolis of Phleious is unknown. It was probably on the slopes of Mount Trikaranon, which lies adjacent to the city. See Figure 7.2.6 (bottom) for a view of the remains of a

temple (perhaps the Heraion) situated below Mount Trikaranon.
7.2.7a Pausanias (2.13.3–5) suggests that it was a very large space.
7.2.8a The meaning of this phrase is not quite clear. Evidently part of the walls of the Phleiasian acropolis faced inward and separated the acropolis from the city, while the higher part, where the Arcadians and Argives were fighting, faced outward.

women bringing them drink, weeping in their joy. At that time "tearful smiles,"[a] as the saying goes, held them all.

[10] In the next year, the Argives and all the Arcadians invaded Phleiasian territory again. Their reasons for the continuous attacks on Phleious were that they were angry with them and that their territory lay between Argos and Arcadia; they thus hoped that by cutting off the Phleiasians' access to necessities, they could bring them to terms. But on this occasion too the cavalry and picked troops of the Phleiasians, aided this time by some Athenian cavalry that were present, attacked the enemy as they were crossing a river. Having defeated the enemy force, they compelled it to spend the rest of the day beneath the high ground, appearing to all the world as though they were troops friendly to the Phleiasians, who were keeping watch so that their grain would not be trampled down.

[11] On yet another occasion, the Theban commander at Sicyon campaigned against Phleious, taking with him his own garrison troops and some Sicyonians and Pelleneians (the latter were by this time following Thebes); Euphron also participated in this campaign in command of around two thousand mercenaries. The majority of the troops marched over Mount Trikaranon and down to the Heraion, intending to lay waste the plain. The general left the Sicyonians and Pelleneians behind on the heights opposite the gates that lead toward Corinth[a] in order to prevent the Phleiasians from coming around by that way in an attempt to gain higher ground above his men at the Heraion. [12] But when the men in the city realized that the enemy was marching toward the plain, the Phleiasian cavalry and the picked men charged out against them, and in the ensuing fighting they prevented the enemy from entering the plain. They spent most the day in skirmishes, with Euphron and his men pursuing as far as the ground was suitable for cavalry, while the men from the city chased their opponents as far as the Heraion.

[13] When the time seemed right, the enemy departed, taking a roundabout way over Trikaranon, because the ravine[a] in front of the wall prevented them from joining up with the Pelleneians by the most direct route. The Phleiasians followed them a short way up the hill but then turned back and, taking the road that led alongside the wall, they charged directly against the Pelleneians and those troops who were with them. [14] The troops with the Theban commander, seeing the haste of the Phleiasians, put forth every effort to reach the Pelleneians so as to support them, but the Phleiasian cavalry got there first and assaulted the Pelleneians. They withstood the onslaught at first, and the Phleiasians had to give way, but when the infantry arrived to assist them, the Phleiasians attacked again and fought hand-to-hand with the enemy, who now, in turn, gave way. Some of the Sicyonians were killed, as were many of the Pelleneians, who were good fighters.

7.2.10
368
PHLEIOUS
The Phleiasians, aided by Athenians, repel another invasion attempt by the Arcadians and Argives.

7.2.11–15
367
PHLEIOUS
Another Theban-led invasion of Phleious is successfully defeated when the Phleiasians use their interior lines to attack and inflict serious losses on an isolated portion of the invading force.

7.2.9a   "Tearful smiles": in the *Iliad* (6.484), when Andromache meets Hektor, she smiles through her tears.
7.2.11a   Corinth: Map 7.2.5. These gates must have stood on the northeast side of the city.
7.2.13a   This ravine was formed by a stream that flowed from east to west just south of the city.

[15] After the struggle, the Phleiasians set up a trophy, singing their *paean* loudly, as you would expect.[a] And the men with the Theban general and with Euphron just stood there and watched them, as if they had raced up to see a spectacle. When the Phleiasians had finished, they returned home while the others went back to Sicyon.

[16] The Phleiasians accomplished another noble deed when they captured a Pelleneian named Proxenos[a] alive and then released him without demanding a ransom, even though at the time they were in great need of all kinds of supplies. Who could deny that those who did such things were noble men and brave fighters?

[17] It is also quite evident that they kept faith with their friends by patient endurance. For when they were prevented from gathering the crops from their own territory, they survived partly by getting what they could from the enemy and partly by purchasing necessities from Corinth. This was a difficult task, because they could get to the marketplace only by exposing themselves to great dangers: it was difficult to afford what they needed, difficult likewise to escort those who went to procure and transport the goods through enemy lines, and likewise extremely difficult to find sureties for the pack animals that would carry back the goods. [18] When they were reduced to utter desperation, they managed to have Chares[a] send them an escort. While he was[b] in Phleious, they asked him to convey their noncombatants into Pellene.[c] Having left these men at Pellene, they went to the market, made their purchases, and loaded up as many of the animals as they could. Then they departed by night, realizing that they would be ambushed by the enemy but feeling that the lack of food was worse than facing the enemy in battle. [19] The Phleiasians with Chares went ahead, and when they fell in with the enemy, they immediately went to work and attacked them, cheering one another on and at the same time calling out to Chares to come to their assistance. After they had won the victory and driven the enemy from the road, they made it safely home, together with the provisions they were transporting. When the men arrived home, they slept until late the next day, since they had been up the whole previous night.

7.2.16
367
PHLEIOUS
Another noble deed of the Phleiasians.

7.2.17–19
366
PHLEIOUS
Xenophon praises the endurance and patience of the Phleiasians and describes the dangerous manner in which they brought supplies in to their hard-pressed city.

7.2.15a After a hoplite battle in ancient Greece, the victors would gather up their dead, strip those of the enemy, and raise a trophy, usually a set of captured armor attached to a pole. The *paean* was a ritual chant that classical Greek soldiers and sailors sang as they advanced into battle, rallied, or celebrated victory.

7.2.16a This translation accepts the emendation of Schneider, reading Proxenos as the name of a person. Several other translations, including the Oxford Classical Text, render the phrase as "captured their *proxenos* in Pellene"—that is, a Pelleneian citizen who looks after the affairs of the Phleiasians in Pellene, somewhat like a modern consul. However, it is difficult to see what would be generous or brave

about the Phleiasians' forgoing a ransom for setting free their own *proxenos*, whereas doing so for a captured Pelleneian named Proxenos would make sense. (John Marincola) For the Greek, see Translator's Notes.

7.2.18a Chares: a famous Athenian general. See Diodorus 15.75.3.

7.2.18b "He was": reading Hartman's *egeneto* for the manuscripts' *egenonto*. (John Marincola) For the Greek, see Translator's Notes.

7.2.18c This must have occurred when Pellene was friendly to the alliance of Corinth, Athens, Sparta, and Phleious, among others. Presumably Pellene had reverted to the Spartan side when Achaea as a whole did so (7.1.43).

[20] When Chares awoke, the cavalry and the best of the hoplites came to him and said, "Today, Chares, you can accomplish an exceptional deed. The Sicyonians[a] are building a fort[b] on our border, and they have many builders at work on it but not many hoplites to guard them. We, the cavalry and the strongest hoplites, will lead, and if you and your mercenaries will follow us, you might find matters already accomplished for you, or perhaps just by appearing you will turn the tide, as happened at Pellene. Now if you think there is something hard to accomplish in our plan, we urge you to consult the god with sacrifices, for we think the gods will encourage you to do this even more than we have done. You must realize, Chares, that if you accomplish this feat, you will have established a stronghold from which to attack the enemy; you will have saved an allied city; you will be most renowned in your own city; and you will be most famous among both allies and enemies."

[21] Chares was persuaded and thereupon sacrificed to the gods. The Phleiasian cavalry immediately donned their breastplates and put the bridles on their horses, while the hoplites made the necessary preparations for infantry. They took up their gear and went to the place where Chares was sacrificing; he and the seer came to meet them and announced that the omens were favorable.[a] "Wait a moment," they said, "for we will now join you on the march." As soon as the herald made the proclamation, the mercenaries swiftly rushed out in a kind of divine enthusiasm. [22] Chares then began his advance, preceded by the cavalry and infantry. They marched swiftly at first and then began to run, until finally the horsemen were riding at full gallop and the infantry were running as fast as they could while maintaining their formation, and Chares hurried along after them. The time was a little before sunset when they arrived at the fortification: some of the enemy were variously washing, cooking, making bread, or getting ready for bed. [23] When they saw the vehemence of the attack, they were struck with panic and immediately fled, leaving behind all their supplies for those brave men, who feasted on the goods that had been abandoned. Other provisions were brought to them from the city, and after pouring libations for their good fortune, singing the *paean*, and setting guards on the fort, they went to sleep. During the night a messenger informed the Corinthians about what had happened at the fort at Thyamia and, in a most friendly manner, they made a proclamation in their city ordering that all their teams and pack animals should be brought out; they then loaded them with food and sent them off to Phleious. And the Corinthians continued to send a convoy out every day for as long as the fortifications were being built.[a]

7.2.20–23
366
PHLEIOUS-THYAMIA
The next day, the Phleiasians persuade Chares to join them in raiding the fort that the Sicyonians are building at Thyamia. In a fit of zeal, they attack the fort so vigorously that the enemy flees, and they feast on the supplies left behind. Corinth sends them provisions while the Phleiasians take possession of the fort and complete its construction.

7.2.20a Sicyon: Map 7.2.5.
7.2.20b The fort at Thyamia, whose location is unknown. Its construction by the Sicyonians was mentioned at 7.2.1.

7.2.21a For the role of sacrifices, augury, and omens before battle, see the Introduction, §8.5, 10.9, 13.5.
7.2.23a The Phleiasians now took over and completed the construction of this fort.

[1] I have now narrated the actions of the Phleiasians and shown how they were continually loyal to their friends, brave in battle, and firm in their alliances, even when they were in sore need of the necessities of life.

Just about this time, Aeneas the Stymphalian[a] (who had become general of the Arcadians[b]), thinking that what was happening at Sicyon was unbearable,[c] went with his army up to the acropolis,[d] called together the leading Sicyonian aristocrats still in the city, and sent for those who had been exiled without a decree of the people.[e] [2] This frightened Euphron so much that he fled to the Sicyonian harbor[a] and summoned Pasimelos from Corinth.[b] Using Pasimelos as his intermediary, Euphron handed over the harbor to the Spartans,[c] returning to an alliance with them and saying that he would remain faithful to Sparta. He claimed that when Sicyon had voted whether or not to revolt from their alliance with Sparta, he and a few others had been against it; [3] afterward, he added, he had set up a democracy because he wished to have vengeance on those who had betrayed him. "And now, Spartans," he said, "all those who betrayed you have been sent into exile by me. If I could, I would have taken my whole city with me in going over to your side; but as it is, I control only this harbor, which I now hand over to you." Many heard him say these words, but it is not at all clear how many actually believed him.

[4] Since I have now started to tell the story of Euphron and his affairs, I wish to follow it through to the end. When the aristocrats and the commons at Sicyon were at war with each other, Euphron obtained a mercenary force from Athens[a] and, upon returning home, won control of the town[b] with the help of the commons. But a Theban governor still controlled the acropolis, and Euphron saw that he could not be master of the whole city if the Thebans possessed the acropolis. He therefore obtained money and went off to Thebes,[c] intending to persuade the Thebans to expel the aristocratic faction at Sicyon and hand control of the city back over to himself. [5] The former exiles, however, learned of his journey and of the preparations he had made, so they likewise made their way to Thebes. When they saw Euphron in friendly association with the magistrates in Thebes, they feared that he might accomplish his objective,

7.3.1a Stymphalos: Map 7.4.11, AX. Some scholars think that this Aeneas is Aeneas Taci-
tus, the military writer whose *How to
Survive Under Siege*, the first work in
antiquity devoted exclusively to military
strategy, has come down to us.
7.3.1b Arcadia: Map 7.4.11, AX.
7.3.1c Sicyon: Map 7.4.11, AX. Xenophon is
apparently implying that Aeneas was angry
with Euphron's actions as tyrant and with
his threat to set up a democracy and abandon the ancestral laws of Sicyon.
7.3.1d The acropolis of Sicyon. This was
controlled at the time by a Theban
commander, who may have approved of
Aeneas' actions or at least regarded the
squabblings of his Peloponnesian allies

and the ideology of their regimes with
indifference, provided they toed his line
militarily. That appears to have been
Epaminondas' own attitude.
7.3.1e Those who had been expelled by
Euphron's tyrannical behavior; see 7.1.46.
7.3.2a Sicyon's harbor: precise location unknown.
7.3.2b This Pasimelos of Corinth is probably the
same one mentioned at 4.4.4. Corinth:
Map 7.4.11, AY.
7.3.2c Sparta: Map 7.4.11, BX.
7.3.4a Athens: Map 7.4.11, AY.
7.3.4b He won control of the *astu*, the city
center within the walls but not including
the acropolis.
7.3.4c Thebes: Map 7.4.11, AY.

and some of them therefore took the risk of assassinating him right then and there on the acropolis while the magistrates and the council[a] were in session. The magistrates brought the men who had done this before their council and spoke as follows:

[6] "Fellow citizens, we demand the penalty of death for these men who have killed Euphron. We realize that sensible men do nothing unjust or unholy, while wicked men do such things but in secret so as not to be observed; yet these men before you so exceed all in daring and brutality that they decided on their own to kill Euphron in the presence of the very magistrates and you, the members of the council, who have the authority here to say who should and should not be put to death. If these men do not pay the ultimate penalty, who will ever be brave enough to visit our city? And what will the city suffer if we allow anyone who wishes to do so to kill another person even before that person has explained why he has come here? We charge these people with being the most unholy, most unjust, and most lawless of men and with having shown the greatest contempt for our city. When you have heard the evidence, you must assign to them whatever penalty you think they deserve." [7] This was the speech of the magistrates.

All the men accused of killing Euphron denied that they had done so except one, who confessed that he had done the deed, and his defense was something like this:

"Surely, men of the council, anyone who knows that he is completely in your power cannot possibly have contempt for you. In what, then, did I trust when I killed this man? I assure you that first of all I believed that I was acting justly, and second that you would evaluate the situation correctly. I knew how you had dealt with the supporters of Archias and Hypates:[a] they had behaved very much like Euphron, and when you captured them, you did not wait to take a vote but instead took vengeance at your first opportunity, believing that those who are plainly evil, who are clearly traitors, or who aim at tyranny are thought by all mankind to be worthy of death. [8] Now wasn't Euphron guilty of all these transgressions? He found sanctuaries full of gold and silver dedications and left them completely empty.[a] Who was a more obvious traitor than Euphron, a man who, though on the friendliest terms with the Spartans, suddenly chose you in their place? And who, after giving and receiving pledges, betrayed you in turn and handed over the harbor to your enemies? Was he not without question a tyrant, he who not only liberated slaves but also gave them citi-

7.3.7–11
366
THEBES
Only one of the accused admits to having killed Euphron, but he defends himself as having acted justly, since Euphron was such a two-faced, traitorous wretch.

7.3.5a The magistrates were the Boeotarchs. For more on them and the Boeotian council, see Appendix H, §6, and Appendix P, Selected Fragments of the *Hellenica Oxyrhynchia* Relevant to Xenophon's *Hellenika*, 19.2–4, which describes the Boeotian government of the fourth century.

7.3.7a Archias and Hypates were the pro-Spartan polemarchs (chief magistrates of Thebes) who in 383 had supported Leontiades in his

treacherous plot to bring the Spartans into the Theban acropolis and who were assassinated by the band of seven Theban patriots at the infamous banquet in 379. See 5.2.25–31. The assassin is referring here to the deaths of the supporters of Archias and Hypates, who were seized as they left the Kadmeia under truce and lynched (5.4.12).

7.3.8a For the appropriation of sacred moneys, see 7.1.46.

zenship, and who killed, drove into exile, and took the property of not men who had committed crimes but, rather, those whom he wished simply to treat thus?[b] And these were men of the higher class.

[9] "Moreover, he returned to the city of Sicyon with the Athenians, who are your worst enemies; he set himself in arms against your governor there, and when he could not drive him from the acropolis, he procured money and came here in hope of accomplishing that goal. Now if he had been caught in the act of gathering arms against you, you would be thanking me for having killed him. And yet he came here with money intending to corrupt you with it and to persuade you to allow him to become the master of Sicyon again: how would it be just for you to have me executed when I gave such a man his just deserts? When people are compelled to certain actions by force of arms, they may suffer injury, but they are not revealed as unjust. But those corrupted by money to do something that is ignoble simultaneously come to harm and incur public disgrace.

[10] "If Euphron had been my enemy and your friend, I agree that it would not have been right for me to kill him in your presence. But he was the man who betrayed you, so how could he possibly be more of an enemy to me than to you? 'Well,' someone might counter, 'he came to our city of his own free will.'[a] To this I would reply that if someone had killed him when he was away from your city, his killer would have been praised; but as it is, since he came here to do you harm in addition to all the injury he has done you before, will anyone, then, deny that it was just to put him to death? Where can anyone point to agreements between Greeks and traitors, two-time deserters, or tyrants? [11] Remember also the decree you passed that exiles should be liable to arrest in any of the allied cities.[a] So how could anyone say that it was unjust to kill an exile who had returned to his home town without a joint decree of the allies? If you execute me, gentlemen, I contend that you will be avenging the death of a man who was your greatest enemy, but if you judge that I have acted justly, you will be seen as avenging both yourselves and all your allies."

[12] After listening to this speech, the Thebans decided that Euphron had suffered a just fate. His fellow citizens, however, believing that he had been a good man, escorted his body home and buried him in the marketplace, where they honor him as if he were the founder of the city. It seems that most people define "good men" as those who are their benefactors.

7.3.12
366
THEBES
The Thebans decide that
Euphron was killed justly.

7.3.8b   An interesting list of some of the attributes of a tyrant.

7.3.10a The logic seems to be that, since Euphron came of his own free will, he could not have considered himself our enemy; if he thought he was our enemy, he would have kept away from the city. But it must be admitted that the logic here is roundabout.

7.3.11a The argument here is as follows: according to the decree, the exiles from any state in the Theban alliance were not to be harbored by other alliance members but were to be expelled altogether from the territory controlled by the alliance. If they returned to their home city, they should be given a worse punishment than mere return to exile and further expulsion: that is, death. Euphron did return to Sicyon without due process; therefore, he should be put to death when apprehended anywhere within the alliance territories.

[1] Euphron's story has now been told, and I return to the point from which I began my digression.[a] While the Phleiasians[b] were fortifying Thyamia[c] and Chares was still with them, Oropos[d] was seized by the exiles. When the Athenians marched out in full force to Oropos and summoned Chares from Thyamia, the harbor of Sicyon[e] was in turn recaptured by the citizens of Sicyon and the Arcadians. No allies came forth to help the Athenians, so they marched home, leaving the Thebans in control of Oropos until there could be arbitration to settle the dispute.[f]

[2] Now Lykomedes[a] had learned that the Athenians were finding fault with their allies because, although they themselves had endured much hardship for their allies, none of the allies in turn gave assistance to them. He therefore persuaded the Ten Thousand[b] to try to make an alliance with the Athenians. At first some of the Athenians were displeased at the thought of becoming allies with men who were enemies of the Spartans, since Athens was on friendly terms with Sparta. But afterward they considered the situation and came to the conclusion that it would be a good thing for the Spartans no less than for themselves if the Arcadians did not look to Thebes for assistance; and so they accepted the alliance with the Arcadians. [3] Having made these arrangements, Lykomedes departed from Athens and thereupon met his death in a way that most showed the hand of heaven: for although he had many ships at his disposal, and although he selected the one he wished to use and indeed even made an agreement with the crew to bring him to the spot that he chose, yet he disembarked exactly where the Arcadian exiles[a] happened to be, and in this way, then, he met his death. But the alliance between Athens and Arcadia was nonetheless established.

[4] Demotion[a] then made a speech in the Athenian[b] Assembly, in which he said that he thought the treaty of friendship with the Arcadians[c] had been made well, and he added that the generals ought now to take some action to make Corinth[d] safe for the Athenian people. When the Corinthians heard of this, they swiftly dispatched guards of their own to all those places where the Athenians had stationed troops, and they ordered the Athenians to depart, saying that they no longer needed their garrisons. The

7.4.1
366
SICYON-OROPOS
Oropos is seized by exiles, and the Athenians try but fail to oust them. Sicyon recovers its harbor.

7.4.2–3
366
ATHENS-ARCADIA
The Arcadian Lykomedes persuades the Athenians to establish an alliance with the Arcadians. On his way home he is killed by exiles.

7.4.4–7
366/5
ATHENS-CORINTH
The Athenians wish to maintain their positions in Corinthian territory, but the Corinthians send them away with thanks and decide to try to make peace with the Thebans. With the permission of the Thebans, they send envoys to Sparta to explore whether the Spartans too could accept a peace now.

7.4.1a	The Euphron digression began at 7.3.2.	
7.4.1b	Phleious: Map 7.4.11, AX.	
7.4.1c	Thyamia: precise location unknown.	
7.4.1d	Oropos: Map 7.4.11, AY. Oropos was a seaport on the Gulf of Euboea between Attica and Euboea (Map 7.4.11, AY), in an area that had long been claimed by both Athenians and Thebans. According to Diodorus (Appendix O, 14.17), the Boeotians moved the town about a mile from the sea and incorporated it into Boeotia (Map 7.4.11, AY) in 402, but the city again became independent later and now favored Athens. It is not clear whether it was independent or under Athenian control at the time of its seizure by the exiles. For a version of these events that asserts that Oropos belonged to Athens,	

	see Diodorus (Appendix O, 15.76.1).	
7.4.1e	Sicyon: Map 7.4.11, AY.	
7.4.1f	It is unclear whether this arbitration ever took place, but in any case, the Thebans remained in control of Oropos.	
7.4.2a	For Lykomedes, see 7.1.23. He was from Arcadia.	
7.4.2b	The Ten Thousand here refers to the Arcadian Federation's assembly. See Appendix H, §8.	
7.4.3a	These were probably Arcadian oligarchs, but Xenophon's brevity here leaves much unclear.	
7.4.4a	Aside from this reference, Demotion is otherwise unknown.	
7.4.4b	Athens: Map 7.4.11, AY.	
7.4.4c	Arcadia: Map 7.4.11, AX.	
7.4.4d	Corinth: Map 7.4.11, AY.	

Athenians obeyed, and when they came together from their garrison posts into the city of Corinth, the Corinthians made a proclamation that if any of the Athenians had been wronged, their names should be written down so that they might obtain justice.

[5] As this was going on, Chares arrived with his navy at Kenchreai.[a] When he heard what had been done, he said that he had learned there was a plot against the city and that he had come to give assistance to Corinth. The Corinthians praised his action but were not at all willing to receive his ships into their harbor, and they told him to depart. They also sent the hoplites away after giving them their due. Thus the Athenians departed from Corinth. [6] They were now compelled, in accordance with their alliance, to send cavalry to the Arcadians in case anyone should attack them, but they did not set foot in Laconia[a] for the purpose of war.

The Corinthians now thought that it would be difficult for them to ensure their own safety, since even before this they had been defeated on land,[b] and the Athenians were now added to those people unfriendly to them; and so they resolved to gather together a mercenary force of infantry and cavalry. Once they had assembled such a force, they used them simultaneously to guard their city and to do a great deal of damage to their nearby enemies. They sent to Thebes[c] to ask whether they might obtain peace if they were to dispatch men specifically to ask for it. [7] When the Thebans replied that peace could be obtained and told them to send a delegation, the Corinthians asked if in addition they could canvass their allies so that a peace might be made with all those who wished it, while those choosing war could be left to continue the fighting. The Thebans conceded this too, and so the Corinthians went to Sparta,[a] where they gave the following speech:

[8] "Men of Sparta, we have come to you as your friends, and we ask if you see any safety for us in prolonging the war, tell us why and how this is so. On the other hand, if you recognize that our situation is desperate, we ask that you make peace along with us, if it is also to your advantage. We would be happier to enjoy security with you than with anyone else. If, however, you find that a continuation of war is to your advantage, we ask that you allow us to conclude a separate peace. For with our safety assured, we might still at some point in the future be useful to you, whereas we shall never again be of use if we are now destroyed."[a] [9] When the Spartans heard these words, they advised the Corinthians to make peace for them-

7.4.8–9
365
SPARTA
The Corinthians ask the Spartans to make peace along with them or to allow them to make peace separately. Sparta permits them and any other allies who wish to do so to seek peace for themselves, but they say they cannot accept the loss of Messenia, and will fight on.

7.4.5a   Kenchreai: Map 7.4.11, AY.
7.4.6a   Laconia (that is, Spartan territory): Map 7.4.11, BX.
7.4.6b   This "defeat" refers to the Theban incursion into Corinthian territory in 370; see 6.5.37.
7.4.6c   Thebes: Map 7.4.11, AY.
7.4.7a   Sparta: Map 7.4.11, BX.
7.4.8a   The destruction feared by the Corinthians

may come not only from the Theban enemy but also from their own mercenaries, just referred to at 7.4.6. Around this time the mercenary leader, Timophanes, was assassinated for becoming tyrant (Plutarch, *Parallel Lives*, "Timoleon" 4) or, perhaps more accurately, for aiming to become tyrant; see Diodorus (16.65.3–4, though wrongly dated) and n. L.10e.

selves, and they counseled the other allies who did not wish to continue the war along with the Spartans to cease from all hostile activity. The Spartans also said that they themselves would continue fighting and would accomplish whatever God wished, but they would never accept being deprived of Messenia,[a] which they had inherited from their fathers.

[10] After the Corinthians received this reply, they went to Thebes to make peace. The Thebans, however, demanded that they also swear to an alliance, to which the Corinthians responded that an alliance was not peace but, rather, hostilities against different people, whereas they were present to conclude a just peace if the Thebans were willing. Now the Thebans admired the Corinthians for refusing to wage war against their benefactors, even though they found themselves in danger; and so they agreed to make peace with the Corinthians, the Phleiasians,[a] and those who had come with them to Thebes, on the principle that each city should keep its own territory. And on these terms the oaths were duly sworn.[b]

[11] As a result of this agreement, the Phleiasians immediately evacuated Thyamia. The Argives[a] had also sworn to observe the peace on the same terms, but when they found out that they were unable to bring it about that the Phleiasian exiles should remain in Trikaranon[b] (pretending in this way that they would be holding it as a part of Argive territory), they simply took the place over and garrisoned it themselves, claiming that it was their territory, although just before this they had been laying it waste on the grounds that it was enemy land. The Phleiasians called for arbitration on the matter, but the Argives refused.

[12] At just about this time, and after the death of the elder Dionysios,[a] his son, the younger Dionysios, sent a force of twelve triremes to the assistance of the Spartans. Timokrates commanded this force, and with it he assisted the Spartans in capturing Sellasia,[b] after which he sailed back to

7.4.10
365
THEBES
After a Theban demand for alliance in return for peace is refused, the Thebans relent and grant a separate peace to Corinth, Phleious, and others.

7.4.11
365
MOUNT TRIKARANON
The Phleiasians evacuate Thyamia, but the Argives occupy Mount Trikaranon on behalf of the Phleiasian exiles.

7.4.12
365
SICILY
Dionysios the Younger sends twelve triremes to help Sparta. Elis captures Lasion.

7.4.9a   Messenia: Map 7.4.11, BX.
7.4.10a Phleious: Map 7.4.11, AY.
7.4.10b Xenophon has often been taken to imply that this treaty was one of a series of bilateral treaties between the Thebans and their north Peloponnesian opponents, rather than a common peace initiated by the Great King, which is how Diodorus (Appendix O, 15.76.3) describes it. Scholars have recently been more prepared to accept that the peace was open to all, as indeed Xenophon himself appears to imply at 7.4.7. But there continues to be controversy on two main points. Did the Great King send a new rescript revising what he had said in 367 (7.1.36), for example now siding with the Arcadians rather than with the Eleians as he had previously? Did the Athenians take part, thus making their peace temporarily with the Thebans? Those who believe in Persian/Athenian involvement rely espe-

cially on Demosthenes 9.16, which maintains that both the King and the Greeks as a whole accepted Athens' claim to the Thracian Chersonese (Map 7.4.11, locator), a claim Athens seems first to have exploited in earnest in 365. If true, 366/5 is the date that fits best, though other dates have been suggested. Other scholars think Demosthenes was being tendentious. If the Persians and Athenians were involved, Xenophon has been gravely misleading; for a possible reason why, see the Introduction, §9.4.
7.4.11a Argos: Map 7.4.11, AY.
7.4.11b Mount Trikaranon: Map 7.4.11, AY.
7.4.12a Dionysios, tyrant of Syracuse in Sicily: Map 7.4.11, locator. He died in 367 and was succeeded in that year by his son, Dionysios the Younger (Dionysios II).
7.4.12b Sellasia: Map 7.4.11, BX. For the capture of Sellasia, see 6.5.27.

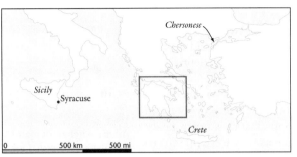

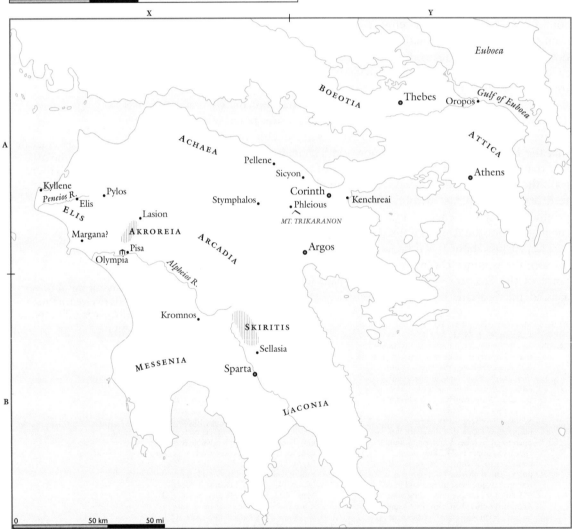

MAP 7.4.11

Sicily. Shortly after this, the Eleians[c] captured Lasion,[d] which long ago had been theirs but at the present time was a member of the Arcadian Federation.

[13] The Arcadians took this matter seriously, calling up their troops and dispatching help to the city. Coming to the assistance of the Eleians were the Three Hundred and the Four Hundred.[a] The Eleians camped on a somewhat level area during the day. When night came, the Arcadians ascended to the peak of a mountain above the Eleian position, and they charged down upon the Eleians at dawn. The Eleians, seeing them coming from above and noting their great number, were nevertheless ashamed to flee, at least while the enemy was at a distance, so they waited until they came to close quarters. At that point, however, the Eleians fled, and they lost many men and much armor, since they had to retreat over difficult ground.[b]

[14] After the Arcadians had won this success, they marched against the cities of the Akroreians.[a] They captured all of them except Thraustos,[b] and then went to Olympia,[c] where they made a stockade around the hill of Kronos and thus made themselves masters of the Olympian mountain.[d] They also captured Margana,[e] which was betrayed to them. The Eleians, with matters having reached this point and the Arcadians now approaching their city, were thoroughly disheartened. Indeed, the Arcadians advanced even into the Eleian marketplace, but the cavalry and the rest of the Eleians took their stand there and drove them out, killing some of them, and thereafter setting up a trophy.

[15] Even before this there had been dissension at Elis.[a] One party, that of Charopos, Thrasonidas, and Argeios,[b] was trying to make the city a democracy, while the other party, that of Stalkas,[c] Hippias, and Stratolas, was urging the establishment of an oligarchy. The Arcadians, who had a large force at their disposal, seemed to be allied with those favoring democracy, and this led Charopos and his party to feel a little emboldened; he obtained the agreement of the Arcadians to assist them in seizing the acropolis. [16] No sooner had they done so, however, than the cavalry and the Three Hundred immediately marched up and expelled them, with the result that around three hundred men went into exile with Argeios and

7.4.13
365
LASION
The Arcadians march against the Eleians and rout them in a dawn attack from a high position taken up during the night.

7.4.14
365/4
ELIS
The Arcadians march toward Elis, conquering many Akroreian cities, advancing to the Eleian marketplace before the Eleians rally and repulse them.

7.4.15–18
365/4
ELIS
Pro-democratic and pro-oligarchic factions contend for control in Elis. The democratic faction, supported by the Arcadians, seizes the acropolis of the city but is driven out and flees into exile. A second Arcadian attempt to invade Elis is thwarted by Achaean assistance to Elis.

7.4.12c   Elis: Map 7.4.11, AX.
7.4.12d   Lasion: Map 7.4.11. For more on Lasion, see 3.2.30.
7.4.13a   Apparently the Three Hundred and the Four Hundred were elite bands of Eleian troops, the Four Hundred being cavalry.
7.4.13b   See Diodorus' account of the initial stages of this Arcadian-Eleian war in Appendix O, 15.77.1–4.
7.4.14a   Akroreia: Map 7.4.11, AX.
7.4.14b   Thraustos: precise location unknown, said to be near the source of the Peneios River (Map 7.4.11, AX), not far from Lasion.
7.4.14c   Olympia: Map 7.4.11, AX.
7.4.14d   It is unclear from Xenophon's words whether he means the entire range of mountains that stretch from the Alpheios River (Map 7.4.11, AX) valley to the valley of the Peneios River, or more specifically the great mountain that dominates the city of Pisa (Map 7.4.11, AX).
7.4.14e   Margana (Marganeis), possible location: Map 7.4.11, AX. See 3.2.25, when the Marganeis joined Agis against the Eleians.
7.4.15a   For a description of the earlier trouble, see 3.2.27.
7.4.15b   For Argeios, see 7.1.33.
7.4.15c   The name is corrupted in the text; suggestions for emendation have included Sitalkas and Eualkas. (John Marincola)

Charopos. Not much later these exiles, assisted by some Arcadians, captured Pylos,[a] and many of the popular party from Elis then left their city and joined the exiles, since they now possessed a fine territory and were allied with the great strength of the Arcadians.

Somewhat later the Arcadians again invaded the territory of Elis, having at that time been persuaded by the exiles that the city would now go over to them. [17] But in the meantime the Achaeans[a] had become friendly with the Eleians and assisted them in defending their city. This prevented the Arcadians from doing anything more than ravaging their land. As soon as they left Eleian territory, however, they learned that the Pelleneians[b] were at Elis, and they made an extremely long march by night and seized the Pelleneian border town of Olouros.[c] The Pelleneians had already returned to their alliance with the Spartans,[d] [18] and so when they learned about the events at Olouros, they likewise made a roundabout journey to a point at which they could enter their own city. After this, though they were very few in number, they fought with the Arcadians in Olouros and with the entire democratic party of their own state, and they did not cease their efforts until they had captured Olouros by siege.

[19] The Arcadians then made another campaign against Elis. The Eleians attacked them when they were camped between Kyllene[a] and the city,[b] but the Arcadians held their ground and defeated them. Andromachos, the Eleian cavalry commander who was thought to be responsible for the decision to attack, committed suicide. The rest of them returned to Elis. Sokleides the Spartiate, who was present, also died in this battle (by this time the Spartans were allies of the Eleians).[c] [20] The Eleians were now hard-pressed in their own city, and so they sent heralds to the Spartans requesting them to campaign against the Arcadians, thinking that the Arcadians would cease their activity if they were attacked from both sides. Archidamos[a] then made an expedition with his citizen forces and captured Kromnos.[b] He left behind three of the twelve battalions[c] to guard it and then returned to Sparta. [21] The Arcadians, however, who happened to have their forces concentrated for the attack they had made on Elis, came to the rescue. They encircled Kromnos with a double palisade and from this position of safety proceeded to besiege those inside Kromnos. The Spartans were vexed that their own citizens were under siege, so they dispatched a force under the command again of Archidamos. When he

7.4.19–21
365/4
KROMNOS
The Eleians request Spartan aid after being defeated by the Arcadians, and in response a Spartan force captures the city of Kromnos. The Spartan garrison of that city is besieged by the Arcadians, who resist Spartan efforts to divert them from the siege.

7.4.16a Pylos of Elis, not Messenia: Map 7.4.11, AX.
7.4.17a Achaea: Map 7.4.11, AX.
7.4.17b Pellene: Map 7.4.11, BX.
7.4.17c Olouros: site unknown.
7.4.17d Sparta: Map 7.4.11, BX. See 7.2.18 and n. 7.2.18c.
7.4.19a Kyllene: Map 7.4.11, AX.
7.4.19b Elis (the city): Map 7.4.11, AX.
7.4.19c In the aftermath of Leuctra they had joined the Thebans and were still pro-Theban in late 367 (7.1.38), but at some point between then and now they obviously came back to the Spartan side, prob-

ably because of their hostility toward the Arcadians.
7.4.20a This Archidamos (who was later to reign as Archidamos III) was the son of Agesilaos; see 7.1.28. He first appears at 5.4.25 and later, after Leuctra, at 6.4.18.
7.4.20b Kromnos: Map 7.4.11, BX.
7.4.20c Three *lokhoi* (battalions) of the twelve Spartan battalions: two *lokhoi* equaled a *mora* (regiment) of which there were six in the Spartan army. On Spartan battalions see Appendix F, The Spartan Army (and the Battle of Leuctra), §3–5.

arrived, he began to lay waste as much of Arcadia[a] and Skiritis[b] as possible, and he devised everything he could in the hope that he might be able to lure back to Arcadia those men besieging Kromnos. The Arcadians, however, were not at all inclined to leave, and they disregarded everything that Archidamos did.

[22] Archidamos now noticed that the Arcadians had carried the outer wall of their stockade over a certain hill, which he thought could be captured and, once taken, would render the position of the besiegers at the foot of the hill untenable. As he was leading his men up by a circular route to this hill, the peltasts running in front of his main force saw the Eparitoi[a] outside the palisade and attacked them, and the Spartan cavalry attempted to support their attack.

The Eparitoi did not give way, however; they massed together for the moment but otherwise took no action. When the Spartans renewed the attack, the Eparitoi responded not by retiring but by themselves advancing and launching an attack, and now, as the shouting grew great, Archidamos himself came up to help, having turned off along the wagon road that goes to Kromnos. He led his men in double file, as he happened to have them formed up for the march. [23] Thus, when they came near each other, the troops of Archidamos were in column, since they had been marching along the road, while the Arcadians were in close formation with their shields tightly massed together. In such a situation the Spartans could not hold out for long against the multitude of Arcadians. Archidamos received a wound right away—a blow straight through his thigh—and some of the men in front of him were almost immediately killed: Polyainidas perished, as did Chilon, who was married to Archidamos' sister. More than thirty of them fell in that encounter.

[24] Then, when the Spartans retired from the road onto open ground and formed themselves up in battle order there, the Arcadians remained in their formation, just as they were. Though the Arcadians were fewer in number, they were in much higher spirits, since they had forced their enemy to retreat and had attacked and killed a number of them. The Spartans, on their side, were very disheartened, seeing that Archidamos was wounded and hearing the names of the dead men, who were good fighters and practically the most renowned men in Sparta. [25] When the two armies drew near again to close quarters, one of the older men shouted out and said, "Why, men, should we fight rather than make a truce and be reconciled?" Both sides were glad to hear this and made a truce.[a] The Spartans took up the bodies of the dead and departed, while the Arcadians went back to where the attack had begun and there erected a trophy.

7.4.22–25
365/4
KROMNOS
Archidamos leads the Spartans against the Arcadians, but the Spartans get the worst of it. Archidamos is wounded, and other distinguished Spartans are killed. A truce is declared, and as the Spartans recover their dead the Arcadians erect a trophy.

7.4.21a   Arcadia: Map 7.4.11, AX.
7.4.21b   Skiritis: Map 7.4.11, BX.
7.4.22a   Eparitoi: a *corps d'élite* five thousand strong, according to Diodorus (Appendix O, 15.62.2), and an Arcadian attempt to copy the Theban Sacred Band; see

Appendix H, §8.
7.4.25a   This sounds as if the Spartans asked for a truce to recover their dead, thus admitting defeat, an interpretation also supported by the fact that the Arcadians erected a trophy at the battle site.

[26] While the Arcadians were occupied at Kromnos, the Eleians from the city marched first against Pylos,[a] and on the way they encountered those Pylians who had been expelled from Thalamai.[b] The Eleian cavalry were riding forward, caught sight of these men, and immediately attacked them. Some were killed, while others fled to a hill. When the Eleian infantry arrived, they assaulted the hill, killing some there and capturing about two hundred of them alive. They sold the foreigners among them and executed all who were Eleian exiles. After this the Eleians captured Pylos along with its inhabitants (since no one came to the Pylians' aid), and they also recaptured Margana.[c]

[27] After this the Spartans[a] once again made an expedition against Kromnos,[b] this time by night. They gained control of that part of the palisade that was opposite the Argives[c] and immediately called out to those Spartans who were besieged within. All those who happened to be closest and who acted quickly managed to get out, but a large force of Arcadians,[d] which came to the rescue, prevented many of the Spartans from escaping. Those who did not get out were shut up within the palisade. They were then captured and distributed among the allies in groups, one each going to the Argives, Thebans,[e] Arcadians, and Messenians.[f] More than a hundred Spartiates and *perioikoi* were captured.[g]

[28] Since the Arcadians were now free from the burden of besieging Kromnos, they once again turned their attention to Elis,[a] and they now placed a stronger guard over Olympia.[b] As an Olympic year was coming on,[c] they prepared to celebrate the Olympic Games together with the men of Pisa,[d] who claim to have been the first people to have been in charge of the holy site. But when the month for the games arrived and it was the days on which the festal assembly gathers, the Eleians, who had made their preparations openly and had called upon the Achaeans[e] for assistance, now appeared, making their way along the road that leads to Olympia. [29] The Arcadians had never thought that the Eleians would come against them, and they themselves were organizing the festivities with the Pisans. They had in fact already conducted the horse race and had finished with the first four events of the pentathlon;[a] because of this, those who were taking part

7.4.26a This refers to a Pylos in Elis, not the one in Messenia: both, Map 7.4.29. The exiled democratic faction of Elis had earlier taken Pylos with Arcadian help; see 7.4.16.

7.4.26b Thalamai: a strong fortress in Elis whose location is not known.

7.4.26c Margana (Marganeis), possible location: Map 7.4.29. See 7.4.14.

7.4.27a Sparta: Map 7.4.29.
7.4.27b Kromnos: Map 7.4.29.
7.4.27c Argos: Map 7.4.29.
7.4.27d Arcadia: Map 7.4.29.
7.4.27e Thebes: Map 7.4.29.
7.4.27f Messenia: Map 7.4.29.
7.4.27g Spartiates and *perioikoi*: Spartiates were citizens of Sparta—the ruling group. *Perioikoi* were full citizens of towns in Laconia that the Spartans had left in possession of

their territories. They enjoyed some freedom to conduct their own internal affairs but were without a voice in foreign affairs and were compelled to follow the Spartiate lead in war. See Appendix E, §10.

7.4.28a Elis: Map 7.4.29.
7.4.28b Olympia: Map 7.4.29.
7.4.28c The 104th Olympiad, in the year 364. For more on the ancient Olympic festival, see Appendix J, Ancient Greek Religion in the Time of Xenophon, §10.
7.4.28d Pisa: Map 7.4.29.
7.4.28e Achaea: Map 7.4.29.
7.4.29a The five contests of the pentathlon were running, jumping, throwing the discus, hurling the javelin, and wrestling. Wrestling was always the last of the five events.

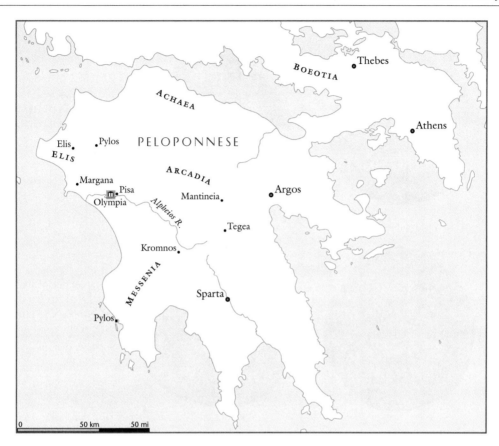

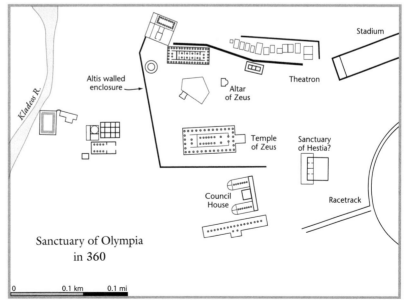

Sanctuary of Olympia
in 360

MAP 7.4.29

FIGURE 7.4.30.
COIN OF ELIS: HEADS OF
ZEUS AND OLYMPIA.

COIN OF PISA: HEAD OF
ZEUS AND HIS WINGLESS
THUNDERBOLT. THE LETTER-
ING SPELLS THE NAME PISA.

in the wrestling were no longer at the Racetrack[b] but in the space between the Racetrack and the altar.[c]

The Eleians, who had now reached the sacred precinct, were under arms. The Arcadians for their part did not advance to meet them but deployed themselves along the Kladeos River,[d] which flows by the Altis[e] and empties into the Alpheios.[f] They had about two thousand Argive hoplites and about four hundred Athenian[g] horse with them as allies.

[30] The Eleians formed up on the other side of the Kladeos and, after sacrificing, immediately marched against their enemy.[a] Now in the past the

7.4.30–31
364
OLYMPIA
The Eleians are especially courageous and initially drive their enemies back but soon find themselves in a position where they take losses and have to withdraw to their camp.

7.4.29b The Racetrack (Map 7.4.29, inset) was apparently where the first four events were conducted.
7.4.29c The great Altar of Zeus: Map 7.4.29, inset.
7.4.29d Kladeos River: Map 7.4.29, inset.
7.4.29e The Altis was the most sacred part of the precinct at Olympia, bounded on the south and west by a natural right-angled terrace (now enclosed by a wall) and to the north by the Hill of Kronos. The Olympic Racetrack and stadium lay to its east and extended into it. In the seventh century it was a meadow with open-air

altars, and it still retained much of that character, but beginning in the early sixth century various temples and other buildings were erected in it.
7.4.29f Alpheios River: Map 7.4.29.
7.4.29g Athens: Map 7.4.29.
7.4.30a Diodorus' account of a battle at Olympia during what is presumably the 104th Olympiad has the same antagonists, but the roles are reversed: the Eleians are conducting the games and are attacked by the Pisans and their allies the Arcadians, who then proceed to celebrate the games. See Appendix O, 15.78.2–3.

Eleians' military skill had been scorned by the Arcadians and Argives, as well as by the Achaeans and Athenians. On this day, however, the Eleians led their allies into battle as if they were the bravest men ever: they clashed with the Arcadians first and immediately routed them. Then they withstood the attack of the Argives who were coming to the Arcadians' assistance and finally mastered them also. [31] The Eleians then pursued their foes as far as the space between the Council House[a] and the Sanctuary of Hestia[b] and the viewing area[c] adjoining these buildings, and although they fought bravely here too and were pushing their enemy back toward the altar, they then came under fire from those on the porticoes and the Council House and the great temple,[d] who were pelting them with missiles, and since they were fighting at ground level, many of them were killed, including not least Stratolas himself, the commander of the Three Hundred. After these things happened, the Eleians withdrew to their own camp.

[32] The Arcadians and their followers, however, were so petrified of what might happen the next day that they did not sleep at all during the night but broke down the buildings that had been beautifully assembled[a] and used their wood to make a palisade. When the Eleians advanced the next day, they saw the strong fortification that had been built, and they saw too that many men were standing on top of the temples, so they went back home to Elis. They had revealed themselves to be brave men, and their bravery was such as could, of course, be inspired and produced by a god in a day, but human beings could not do it even over a long period for men who were not actually courageous.

[33] Now up to this time the magistrates of the Arcadian Federation had been using sacred funds[a] to pay the Eparitoi, but the Mantineians[b] now became the first to pass a resolution not to use these funds any longer for this purpose. They themselves instead raised the portion of money that was their share of the expenses for the Eparitoi, and they sent it to the Arcadian magistrates. The magistrates, however, charged the Mantineians with harming the federation, and they summoned the Mantineian leaders to appear before the Assembly of Ten Thousand.[c] When the Mantineians ignored the summons, the Arcadian magistrates condemned them, and they even sent the Eparitoi to seize those who had been convicted and bring them into custody. The Mantineians, however, closed their gates and would not admit

7.4.32
364
OLYMPIA-ELIS
The Arcadians fortify their position so well that the Eleians decide to return home, having proved their bravery.

7.4.33
364–363
ARCADIA
When the Mantineians vote to cease using sacred treasures to fund the Eparitoi, the Arcadian magistrates at first condemn them and even threaten them with Theban force.

7.4.31a   Council House: Map 7.4.29, inset.
7.4.31b   Sanctuary of Hestia?: Map 7.4.29, inset. The map shows what the site probably looked like in 364, but scholars do not agree on its precise location.
7.4.31c   The Theatron, or "viewing area," was an unbuilt sloping space from which spectators at Olympia could watch the ceremonies.
7.4.31d   The temple of Olympian Zeus: Map 7.4.29, inset.
7.4.32a   These were built for the crowds of visitors who came to participate in the religious ceremonies and to watch the

athletic contests at Olympia.
7.4.33a   In this case, Xenophon refers to the sacred treasures of Olympia. Many ancient Greek shrines contained great wealth accumulated from offerings and dedications to their gods from worshipers over the years. Converting sacred offerings for military or other profane purposes invited charges of sacrilege, especially in the case of an international shrine like Olympia.
7.4.33b   Mantineia: Map 7.4.29.
7.4.33c   "Ten Thousand" here refers to the Arcadian Assembly; see Appendix H, §8.

7.4.34–35
364–363
ARCADIA
Others come to agree with Mantineia, and the Arcadian Federation votes not to use sacred funds to support the elite armed force This creates problems also, and they finally agree that it would be best to give custody of the temple and its treasures back to the Eleians. This pleases the Eleians, and both sides now conclude an armistice.

7.4.36–37
363
TEGEA
All the Arcadians celebrate the peace except those magistrates who fear condemnation. They and the Theban governor arrest members of the aristocratic party. Many are taken, but many others escape or are let go, and the Thebans capture very few Mantineians—the ones they wanted most—because they had gone home, since Mantineia was close to Tegea.

the soldiers into the city. [34] Because of all this, there were some others in the Assembly of Ten Thousand who quickly began to say that it was not right to use sacred funds and thus leave to their children for all future time this offense against the gods. The Assembly then likewise passed a resolution to use sacred funds no longer. As a result, those who could not afford to belong to the Eparitoi without pay swiftly melted away, while those who had the capability urged one another to join the force, so that the men of means would no longer be beholden to the poorer element, but instead the poor would now be under the control of the wealthy.[a]

Because of this, those magistrates who had in their term used the sacred funds now realized that they might incur the death penalty when they had to render their accounts at the end of their term in office. So they sent to the Thebans[b] and informed them that unless they sent out an army, the Arcadians[c] would probably return to their alliance with Sparta.[d] [35] The Thebans were preparing to send out such a force when those who wanted what was best for the Peloponnese[a] persuaded the Arcadian Federation to send envoys to Thebes to tell them not to send an armed force against Arcadia unless the Arcadians should summon them.

And while they were saying this to the Thebans, they decided that there was no need for war. They concluded that they really did not need to be in charge of the temple of Zeus and thought that if they gave that office back to the Eleians,[b] they would be acting more justly and piously, and that such a course of action would be pleasing to the god. Since the Eleians were of the same mind, both sides decided on peace, and an armistice was concluded.

[36] The oaths were administered, and all swore to observe them, including the Tegeans[a] and the Theban governor, who happened to be in Tegea with three hundred Boeotian[b] hoplites. All the other Arcadians who were staying in Tegea feasted and celebrated, offering libations and singing *paeans* because peace had been established. The Theban governor, however, and those magistrates afraid of submitting their accounts went with the Boeotians and those of the Eparitoi who shared their views, and closed the gates of the Tegeans' wall. They then summoned the members of the aristocratic faction who were feasting and started to arrest them. Since Arcadians from all the cities of the federation were there and since all of them wanted peace, it was necessary to arrest a great many men; and so both the prison and the town hall quickly became full. [37] Many thus were kept in custody, yet many too leapt down from the walls, and some

7.4.34a Xenophon's point here is that the Eparitoi had been dominated by the poorer classes, who were pro-Theban; with the elimination of pay for this body, those of means would now predominate among its members, and the wealthy tended to be pro-Spartan. The result of the elimination of pay, therefore, was that the pro-Spartan party could now gain the upper hand. It is clear, however, from 7.4.36 that a pro-Theban element
remained in the corps.
7.4.34b Thebes: Map 7.4.29.
7.4.34c Arcadia: Map 7.4.29.
7.4.34d Sparta: Map 7.4.29.
7.4.35a For Xenophon this would, of course, be the oligarchical party. Peloponnese: Map 7.4.29.
7.4.35b Elis: Map 7.4.29.
7.4.36a Tegea: Map 7.4.29.
7.4.36b Boeotia: Map 7.4.29.

even had been allowed to escape through the gates, since there was no general anger among the people there, except for those magistrates who feared that they would be put to death. The Theban governor and his accomplices were particularly at a loss, because they had seized only a few of those Mantineians whom they most wanted to apprehend. This was because Mantineia was close by[a] and nearly all the Mantineians had already gone home.

[38] When day came and the Mantineians learned what had happened, they immediately dispatched messages to the rest of the Arcadian cities telling them to take up arms and to guard all the passes. They themselves did the same while simultaneously sending to Tegea and demanding that all the Mantineians in custody there be released. They also insisted that none of the other Arcadians should be held in prison or executed without trial. Finally they said that if anyone was charged with some crime, the city of Mantineia would serve as surety for him, and they swore that they would produce anyone who was summoned before the Ten Thousand.

[39] When the Theban governer heard these demands, he was uncertain how to deal with the situation, so he released all the men in custody. The next day he summoned any Arcadians who were willing to attend, and he defended his actions, claiming that he had been deceived and that he had heard that the Spartans were under arms at the frontier and that some of the Arcadians were intending to betray the city to them. Those who were there exonerated him, even though they knew he was lying about these matters. At the same time, however, they sent ambassadors to Thebes to denounce him and to demand the death penalty.

[40] Epaminondas[a] happened at that time to be general at Thebes, and his response, so it is said, was that the Theban commander had acted more properly when he arrested the men than when he let them go.[b] "For we went to war on account of you, and you then concluded peace without even asking our opinion. Couldn't someone accuse you with full justice of having betrayed us? In any case, rest assured that we will march into Arcadia, and we shall fight there together with those who are on our side."

[1] When these doings were reported to the Arcadian Federation and to the individual cities, the Mantineians and all the rest of the Arcadians who cared for the Peloponnese,[a] and likewise the Eleians and the Achaeans,[b] concluded that the Thebans clearly wanted the Peloponnese be in the very weakest state, so that its enslavement would be as easy as possible. [2] "For why else do they want us to fight with one another, except that we may harm each other and so that both sides might need Theban assistance? Why else would they be preparing now to invade Arcadia when we have told

---

7.4.38–40
363/2
ARCADIA-THEBES
The Mantineians demand the release of all those imprisoned, promising to stand surety for any who are charged with a crime. The Theban governor releases all of them and is exonerated in a local hearing, although his audience knows he is lying. Envoys to Thebes ask for his condemnation. Epaminondas, the Theban general, says that the Arcadians are at fault for making peace without advising or consulting with their allies, the Boeotians.

7.5.1–3
362
PELOPONNESE
The Mantineians and some other Arcadians, fearing a Theban plot to keep the Peloponnesians weak so as to more easily enslave them, send envoys to both Athens and Sparta to request assistance against Thebes.

7.4.37a   Mantineia is about 12 miles from Tegea.
7.4.40a   This is the first mention of Epaminondas since 7.1.43.
7.4.40b   For the strained relations between the Thebans and the Arcadians, see 7.1.22–23, 7.1.32, 7.1.39.

7.5.1a   Peloponnese: Map 7.5.6, BX. Again Xenophon refers to the aristocratic faction; see 7.4.35.
7.5.1b   By this time the oligarchs were again in control of Achaea.

them that we do not need them at present? Is it not clear that their expedition is being planned with a view toward harming us?" [3] Whereupon they sent to Athens[a] to request assistance, and ambassadors from the Eparitoi[b] also made their way to Sparta and called on the Spartans to join with them in preventing the attempt by anyone to march against the Peloponnese with the goal of enslaving it. As to the matter of command, they arranged at once that each state would be the leader in its own territory.

[4] While they were making these preparations Epaminondas started out from Thebes. Accompanying him[a] were all the Boeotians,[b] the Euboeans,[c] and many Thessalians,[d] both from Alexander and from Alexander's opponents.[e] The Phocians,[f] however, did not march with Epaminondas, saying that their treaty with Thebes called for them to assist if someone attacked the Thebans, but there was no provision to assist in a campaign against other cities. [5] Epaminondas calculated that he would receive support in the Peloponnese from the Argives,[a] the Messenians,[b] and those Arcadians who favored the Theban cause, namely the people of Tegea,[c] Megalopolis,[d] Asea,[e] and Pallantion,[f] as well as any others that would be forced to take this side because they were small towns and were located between the cities just named.

[6] Now Epaminondas had departed quickly from Thebes, but when he arrived at Nemea,[a] he delayed there, hoping to catch the Athenians as they were coming into the Peloponnese and thinking this would be a great achievement, one that would both encourage his own allies and bring despair to his enemies: in short, defeating the Athenians would bring nothing but benefit to Thebes. [7] But while Epaminondas delayed there in Nemea, all the coalition forces were concentrating at Mantineia, and when he heard that the Athenians had abandoned their decision to march by land and were instead preparing to go by sea and march through Spartan territory to aid the Arcadians, he left Nemea and marched to Tegea.

7.5.4–7
362
NEMEA
Epaminondas marches to Nemea, where he delays, hoping to catch the Athenians while on their march into the Peloponnese. But when he learns that the Athenians have decided to go by sea, he advances to Tegea, not far from Mantineia, where the forces hostile to Thebes are assembling.

7.5.3a Athens: Map 7.5.6, BY. For the alliance between Sparta and Athens, see 6.5.49.
7.5.3b The Eparitoi sent envoys to Sparta because this military unit now had a strong oligarchical element. Pausanias (8.8.10) says that this embassy was the idea of the Mantineians but that the Arcadian Federation did not consent to it.
7.5.4a Xenophon has not mentioned the activities of Epaminondas in the north; for these see Diodorus (Appendix O, 15.78–79).
7.5.4b Boeotia: Map 7.5.6, AY.
7.5.4c Euboea: Map 7.5.6, AY.
7.5.4d Thessaly: Map 7.5.6, AX.
7.5.4e This Alexander was the tyrant of Pherai (Map 7.5.6, AX); see 6.4.35–37. He is included, without being named, in the reference to anti-Theban Thessalians at 7.1.28; see also Diodorus 15.71.2–4. He had been forced to join the Thebans after losing the battle at Mount Cynoscephalae (Map 7.5.6, AX) in late summer 364.
7.5.4f Phocis: Map 7.5.6, AX.
7.5.5a Argos: Map 7.5.6, BX.

7.5.5b Messenia: Map 7.5.6, BX.
7.5.5c Tegea: Map 7.5.6, BX.
7.5.5d Megalopolis: Map 7.5.6, BX. This is the only place where Xenophon mentions Megalopolis, a city that had been founded during these years by the Arcadians as the center of their new confederation. Xenophon's failure to tell us about its foundation is another of his major omissions. The precise date is debated by modern scholars, but one plausible view is that it was a long, drawn-out business. The idea may have been agreed on shortly after Leuctra in 371, but the main building works, perhaps started in early 369 on Epaminondas' first expedition to the Peloponnese, were not finished until late 368, shortly after the Tearless Battle (7.1.32). For a brief narration of the city's foundation, see Diodorus (Appendix O, 15.72.4).
7.5.5e Asea: Map 7.5.6, BX.
7.5.5f Pallantion: Map 7.5.6, BX.
7.5.6a Nemea: Map 7.5.6, BX.

FIGURE 7.5.6. REMAINS OF THE TEMPLE OF ZEUS IN THE SANCTUARY AT NEMEA.

[8] Now I would not claim that this campaign of Epaminondas' was fortunate, but in terms of preparation and boldness, the man was second to none. I praise him first of all for making his camp inside the wall of Tegea: here he had greater security than if he had camped outside the walls, and his enemies were less certain of what his plans might be. In addition, if he needed to make any preparations, there was a greater supply of provisions within the city walls. Finally, when the enemy camped outside the city, Epaminondas could see whether they were doing things correctly or making mistakes. Moreover, although he thought that his forces were superior to those of the enemy,[a] he nonetheless refused to lead his army out from the city when he saw his opponents taking superior positions. [9] Finally, however, when he saw that as time passed no more cities were coming to join him, he decided that he had to take some action; otherwise he would utterly lose his reputation, which previously had been so glorious.

Therefore, when he learned that his opponents had occupied a strong fortified position around Mantineia and had sent for Agesilaos and the entire Spartan force, and also that Agesilaos was on the march and already

7.5.8–10
362
TEGEA-SPARTA
Xenophon praises Epaminondas' generalship and tells how, when he learned of Agesilaos' advance to Mantineia, he ordered an immediate march directly to Sparta and would have taken the undefended city had not Agesilaos chanced to learn of his march and returned to his city in time to organize a defense of it.

7.5.8a   According to Diodorus (Appendix O, 15.84.4), Epaminondas had 30,000   infantry and 3,000 cavalry; his enemies, 20,000 infantry and 2,000 cavalry.

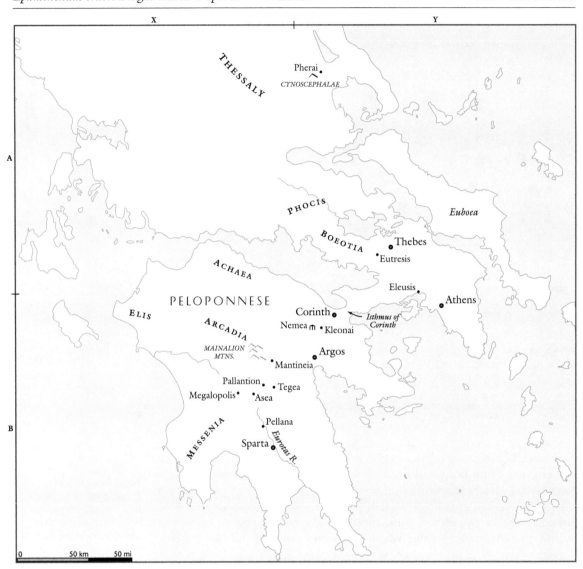

MAP 7.5.6

at Pellana,[a] he ordered his men to take their dinner and then immediately
led them on toward Sparta.[b] [10] And if a Cretan[a] had not by some divine
chance met up with Agesilaos and informed him that the Theban army was
on the march, Epaminondas would have taken the city like a nest emptied
of defenders. But because of the advance word that he thus received, Agesi-

7.5.9a   Pellana: Map 7.5.6, BX.
7.5.9b   Sparta: Map 7.5.6, BX.
7.5.10a Crete: Map 7.4.11, locator. Diodorus
         (Appendix O, 15.82.5–83.4) says that the
         Spartan king (whom he misstates as Agis)

sent some Cretan runners to warn Agesilaos back in Sparta of the approach of the
Boeotians just in time for Agesilaos to
organize a defense of the city.

laos was able to arrive back at Sparta first and to deploy the Spartiates at their positions of defense, even though his numbers were small indeed, since all of his cavalry, his entire force of mercenaries, and three of the twelve battalions[b] were away in Arcadia.[c]

[11] When Epaminondas arrived at the very city of Sparta, he did not enter at the place where he would have to fight on level ground and where his troops would be pelted from the roofs of the houses—that is, where, though superior in numbers, they would find themselves with no advantage against their opponents, who were few.[a] Rather, he chose a spot that he thought would be favorable and where he could descend rather than go up into the city.[b] [12] For what happened next, one can say either that the divinity was responsible or that no one can withstand desperate men.[a] For when Archidamos, with not even a hundred men, led the way from the city and crossed over difficult ground that some might have thought would give him trouble, and when he even marched straight uphill[b] against his enemies, then his opponents—those breathers of fire, those soldiers who had already defeated the Spartans, who had a vast superiority in forces, and who were occupying the favorable ground—did not withstand Archidamos and his men but gave way to them. [13] Those in the first ranks of Epaminondas' army were killed; but when the Spartans from the city, elated at their victory, pursued the enemy farther than was appropriate, the Spartans in turn began to be killed. It seemed as if the divinity had foreordained the extent of the victory they were to gain. Archidamos then set up a trophy on the site of the Spartan victory and gave back the enemy dead under truce.

[14] Epaminondas now realized that the Arcadians would soon be coming to assist the Spartans,[a] and he had no wish to fight against a united Lacedaemonian force, especially as they had just won a victory, while his own troops had been defeated. So he marched back to Tegea[b] as quickly as he could, and there rested his hoplites while he sent the cavalry to Mantineia,[c] entreating them to make a special effort and pointing out that it was likely that Mantineia's livestock and its entire population were

7.5.11–13
362
SPARTA
Epaminondas arrives at Sparta and avoids an attack over level ground inside the city. Instead he finds a place where his troops can descend into the city. Nonetheless, his army is routed by a small force of desperate Spartans led by Archidamos.

7.5.14
362
SPARTA
Realizing that the Arcadians would soon reinforce the Spartans, Epaminondas withdraws his army to Tegea.

7.5.10b On Spartan battalions see Appendix F, §3–5.
7.5.10c Arcadia: Map 7.5.6, AX.
7.5.11a The text is corrupt, but the meaning is fairly certain. (John Marincola)
7.5.11b Sparta lies in the plain of the Eurotas River (Map 7.5.6, BX), but the plain is not level. It descends gently from west to east until, just before it reaches the Eurotas, it rises to higher ground on the eastern edge of the city. It descends again to the river and rises sharply to even higher ground on the eastern bank. So it is thought that Xenophon here says that Epaminondas chose not to approach Sparta on the gentle ascent from the west but, rather, from the higher, steeper ground on the east, which makes Archidamos' successful uphill attack with small numbers all

the more remarkable.
7.5.12a For another example of this view of divinity, see 6.4.23.
7.5.12b For hoplites to attack uphill, even in superior numbers, was notoriously risky and almost always unsuccessful. See Thrasyboulos' speech at Mounichia at 2.4.15 and Appendix L, Land Warfare in Xenophon's *Hellenika*, §7–8.
7.5.14a One might deduce from the peril of the Mantineians working outside the walls (7.5.15–17) that the entire Arcadian army was marching south. Certainly the Spartan cavalry and the three regiments (*lokhoi*) with the Arcadians must have been on their way to Sparta at that time.
7.5.14b Tegea: Map 7.5.6, BX.
7.5.14c Mantineia: Map 7.5.6, BX.

7.5.15–17
362
MANTINEIA
The Athenian cavalry arrives at Mantineia just in time to attack the approaching enemy forces. This brave attack permits the Mantineians to save everything they had outside the walls. Xenophon praises the Athenians, who give a good account of themselves.

7.5.18
362
MANTINEIA
Epaminondas decides that he must save his reputation by giving battle once more before leaving the Peloponnese.

outside the walls, particularly since it was harvest time.[d] [15] So they set forth.

The Athenian[a] cavalry, meanwhile, having set out from Eleusis,[b] took their dinner at the Isthmus;[c] they then passed through Kleonai[d] and were at the point of arriving at Mantineia and camping in some of the houses inside the wall when the Mantineians, clearly seeing the enemy approaching, asked them to give assistance if they could. For they said that all their cattle and their slaves, as well as many of their children and old men, were outside the walls. The Athenians listened to their request, and even though they themselves and their horses had not yet had anything to eat that morning, they went out to bring assistance to the Mantineians. [16] Who could fail to admire their bravery? For though they saw that the enemy coming against them were numerous, and though the cavalry had already suffered misfortune in Corinth,[a] they gave no thought to this, nor to the fact that they were about to fight Thebans and Thessalians, men who had the highest reputation for horsemanship.[b] Instead, they felt a sense of shame at the thought of being on the spot but failing to assist their allies. So as soon as they caught sight of the enemy, they charged them, feeling a deep desire to win back their ancestral reputation.[c] [17] And by engaging the enemy there, they were responsible for saving everything that the Mantineians had outside their walls. Brave were the men among them who died,[a] and it is clear that the men they killed were equally brave. For no one had a weapon so short that he did not reach his enemy with it. And the Athenians did not abandon the corpses of their own men but, rather, gave back some of the enemy dead under truce.[b]

[18] Epaminondas now considered that within a few days he would have to depart, because the time for the campaign was running out,[a] and that if he were to abandon those to whom he had come as an ally, they would be left under siege from their enemies and his reputation would be completely

7.5.14d Harvest time would be around July. That so many people and farm animals were in the fields meant that they were an easy target for attack.

7.5.15a Athens: Map 7.5.6, BY.

7.5.15b Eleusis: Map 7.5.6, BY.

7.5.15c Isthmus of Corinth: Map 7.5.6, BY. It is about 50 miles from Mantineia.

7.5.15d Kleonai: Map 7.5.6, BY.

7.5.16a The misfortune may refer to the events narrated at 6.5.52 or perhaps 7.1.20–21, but it is not certain.

7.5.16b See Figure 7.5.18 for two images of Theban horsemen on pottery.

7.5.16c This part of the battle seems to have been fought just outside the gates of Mantineia; see Plutarch, *Moralia* 346.

7.5.17a Xenophon here refers to, but does not actually name, his own son, Gryllos, who was among the dead and who was regarded as having fought particularly heroically. Gryllos received a public burial at Mantineia (Pausanias 8.11.6) and other

honors, including being depicted in the picture of the battle commissioned by the Athenians for one of their public buildings. Xenophon's other son, Diodorus, also took part.

7.5.17b Diodorus also has Mantineia saved from Epaminondas by the timely arrival of Athenian forces, but in his version (Appendix O, 15.84.2), the Athenians man the defenses of the city. He does not mention a cavalry action as part of the "rescue." But he does mention one that opened the main battle at Mantineia (Appendix O, 15.85.3–8).

7.5.18a Since the Boeotarchs entered office around the winter solstice, this cannot refer to an imminent expiration of Epaminondas' own command. The campaign may have had a time fixed either by the Theban government or by the allies, or the troops under Epaminondas would have been eager to return home for their own harvests.

7.5.18. TWO EARLY-FOURTH-CENTURY VASES SHOWING THEBAN HORSEMEN, ONE HEAVILY ARMED (ABOVE) AND THE OTHER LIGHTLY ARMED (RIGHT).

destroyed: for he had been defeated at Sparta by just a few troops, although he himself had commanded a large force; then he had lost the recent cavalry engagement at Mantineia; and his entire invasion of the Peloponnese had had the effect of uniting the Spartans, Arcadians, Achaeans, Eleians, and Athenians against Thebes. And so it did not seem possible for him to withdraw from the region without another engagement, and he thought that if he were victorious this time, it would make up for all his previous mistakes, while if he were to die in battle, such a death would be glorious inasmuch as he was attempting to win dominion over the Peloponnese for his own country.

[19] And it does not seem to me unusual that he should have calculated in this way: for such are the thoughts of ambitious men. What I find more remarkable is how well he prepared his army, how they shrank from no labor night or day, nor did they flinch from any danger; and although provisions were in short supply, his men were nevertheless ready to obey his every command. [20] And when at last he gave the order to his men to prepare themselves—for the battle was now imminent—the cavalry were eagerly whitening their helmets (as Epaminondas had commanded them to do), and the Arcadian hoplites were painting the Theban clubs[a] on their shields, just as if they were Thebans, and they were all sharpening their spears and stabbing swords[b] and polishing their shields.

[21] And when he led them out to battle so prepared, it is also worthwhile here to consider the actions that he took. First, as might be expected, he deployed them in battle order, which made it seem as if he were preparing for battle. But when he had arranged the army as he wished, he did not lead them by the most direct route against the enemy; rather, he led them to the mountains that face Tegea from the west.[a] This move gave his enemy the impression that there would be no battle that day. [22] Moreover, when they arrived at the mountain and he had reviewed the phalanx, he had them ground arms at the foot of the hills, so that it would appear that he intended to set up camp there. By doing this, he caused the majority of his enemy to relax, which not only diminished their fighting spirit but also made them negligent in their preparations for battle. Epaminondas then brought the regiments that were marching in column into line and thus strengthened the beaklike formation around himself.[a] At that point, ordering his men to take up their arms, he led them forward, and they followed. When the enemy saw the men unexpectedly coming upon them, not a one of them was able to remain still, but some ran to their posts or lined themselves up or bridled their horses or put on

7.5.20a The club was the symbol of Herakles, the patron of Thebes.

7.5.20b Sharpening their spears and swords because hoplites went into battle with two spears and one sword.

7.5.21a The Mainalion Mountains: Map 7.5.6, BX.

7.5.22a It is not entirely clear what kind of maneu-vers Xenophon is here describing, but the purpose will have been, as at Leuctra, to increase the strength of the left wing by vastly increasing its depth. Diodorus (Appendix O, 15.85.2) gives the order in which the various contingents were arrayed.

their breastplates: all resembled men who were about to suffer some hurt rather than inflict it.

[23] Epaminondas then led his army forward like a trireme, with the "ram" foremost, thinking that if he could strike and break through the enemy line anywhere, he could destroy the enemy's entire force.[a] He was preparing to fight with the strongest part of his army, and he had placed the weakest units far away from him, for he knew that if they were defeated, it would cause despondency in the rest of his forces while encouraging the enemy. Now the enemy had drawn up their cavalry in rows to a depth similar to a hoplite phalanx but without any infantry intermingled among them.[b] [24] Epaminondas, however, arrayed his cavalry in a wedge formation, and he stationed infantry among them, believing that when his cavalry broke through, he would have achieved total victory, since it is very difficult to find men who are willing to stand their ground when they see their own forces in flight. And in order to prevent the Athenians from bringing assistance from the left wing to the right, he stationed a group of cavalry and hoplites on some hills opposite them, knowing that by so doing, he would make the Athenians fear that if they went to the rescue, the troops on the hills would attack them from behind. And thus he made his charge, and he was not disappointed in his hope. By defeating the troops where he had concentrated his attack, he managed to put the entire enemy force to flight.[a] [25] But when Epaminondas himself fell,[a] the rest of his forces could not properly exploit their victory, so that although the troops of the enemy phalanx were in flight, the hoplites failed to kill a single one of them, and did not advance one step from the place where they fought the battle. The enemy cavalry was also put to flight, but here too Epaminondas' cavalry did not pursue them, and so they killed neither cavalry nor infantry but timidly slipped away through the lines of the fleeing enemy, just as if they had been defeated. Both the hoplites and the peltasts that had been stationed among the cavalry shared in the cavalry's victory, and they acted as if they had won, but upon coming to the enemy's left wing, the majority of them were slain by the Athenians.

[26] When the battle was over, the result was the opposite of what everyone had expected. Given that nearly all of Greece was gathered there

Epaminondas cleverly plans his attack to exploit the enemy's deployment. His tactics succeed brilliantly, but after he is killed in the fighting, his forces do not exploit the victory.

When the battle is over, everyone is surprised that it has not settled anything. Both sides act like winners and losers. Xenophon ends his history here.

7.5.23a   The wedge formation, although similar to that used against the Spartans at Leuctra (6.4.10–12), represents a relatively new development in hoplite warfare. See Appendix L, §6.

7.5.23b   Some scholars adopt the conjecture of Ruestow and Koechly *eph' hex* (for the manuscripts' *ephexes,* "in a row"), which would mean "six deep." (John Marincola) Often in ancient warfare, cavalry units were strengthened by deploying infantry intermingled with the horsemen. See Appendix L, §9, and Figure 7.5.25b, a fragment depicting a *hamippos* assisting a cavalryman.

7.5.24a   Diodorus' account of this battle at Mantineia is quite different from that of Xenophon; see Appendix O, 15.86–89.2.

7.5.25a   Many claimed the achievement of killing Epaminondas. According to Pausanias (8.11.5), the Mantineians said it was one of their own named Machairon, the Spartans said it was a Spartiate, and the Athenians said it was Gryllos, son of Xenophon. Diodorus (Appendix O, 15.87.2) and Plutarch (*Parallel Lives,* "Agesilaos" 35.1) say it was a Spartan named Antikrates. The variant traditions suggest that no one knew who had actually done the deed.

FIGURE 7.5.25A. VIEW OF THE VALLEY OF MANTINEIA, WHERE THE BATTLE TOOK PLACE.

FIGURE 7.5.25B. FRAGMENT OF
AN ATHENIAN FRIEZE SHOWING A
HAMIPPOS RUNNING WITH THE
CAVALRY. *HAMIPPOI* WERE TRAINED TO
RUN WITH THE HORSEMEN, HOLDING
ON TO THE TAILS OF THE HORSES AND
THE HEMS OF THE RIDERS' CLOAKS.

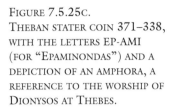

FIGURE 7.5.25C.
THEBAN STATER COIN 371–338,
WITH THE LETTERS EP-AMI
(FOR "EPAMINONDAS") AND A
DEPICTION OF AN AMPHORA, A
REFERENCE TO THE WORSHIP OF
DIONYSOS AT THEBES.

and had stood with one side or the other, everyone thought that if a battle occurred, the victor would rule over the defeated and the defeated would be subject to the victor.ᵃ But the god so arranged it that each side set up a trophy as if victorious, and each was not prevented by the enemy; each gave back the dead under truce as if victorious, and both received back their dead under truce as if defeated. [27] And although each side claimed the victory, neither side was seen to have gained anything—no city, territory or increased rule—that they did not have prior to the battle.ᵃ In Greece as a whole there was more uncertainty and disturbance after the battle than there had been before.

To this point, then, let it be written by me. Perhaps someone else will be concerned with what happened after this.

7.5.26a   There are no casualty numbers recorded
           for this battle.
7.5.27a   A general peace was concluded after the
           battle. The Messenians (Map 7.5.6, BX)
           were allowed to partake in this peace as a

separate state, and because of this, the
Spartans alone refused to swear to it. See
Diodorus (Appendix O, 15.89), Polybius
4.33, and Plutarch, *Parallel Lives*, "Agesilaos" 35.3.

APPENDIX A

The Arginousai Affair

§1. Athenian democracy reached perhaps its most extreme moment at a meeting of the Assembly in 406, when people flatly asserted that "it was a terrible thing if someone did not allow the people to do whatever they wished" (1.7.12). What they wished at the moment, it turned out, was to execute the generals who had won a desperate naval battle off the Arginousai Islands,[a] between the island of Lesbos and the coast of Asia. Xenophon devotes considerable space to the episode, including the first extended direct speech in the *Hellenika*. He finds in what happened a paradigm for reversals suffered by individuals and cities that act unjustly. Vivid though his narrative is, however, it omits or contradicts details in Diodorus,[b] an account that scholars generally find preferable. Readers will find some background on Athenian generals and the usual procedures for accountability helpful in trying to understand these events.

§2. Though the Athenians selected most of their government officials by lot, they elected ten military commanders annually, one from each of the ten tribes into which the Athenians were divided. These generals could be reelected without interruption. They commanded on sea as well as on land, and the Assembly could send more than one of them on an expedition. Eight participated in the battle of Arginousai (1.6.29–30), all apparently equal in rank, as was normal. The recent experiment naming Alcibiades commander in chief (1.4.20) had not turned out well.

§3. Like other magistrates, generals could be removed from office. They could be impeached by a procedure known as *eisangelia*, and they each had to have a performance review (*euthyna*) at the end of their term. An individual would lodge an *eisangelia* with the Council of Five Hundred, the central executive body in Athens, which met daily except for festival days, or about three hundred times a year. The five hundred men of the Council comprised fifty men from each of the ten Athenian tribes, chosen by an annual lottery among male citizens over thirty years old. (The Athenians considered lotteries more democratic than elections.) The Council could

---

NOTE: Important locations cited within Appendices A through N are keyed to a series of Reference Maps at the end of this volume, called Ref. Map 1, Ref. Map 2, etc.

A.1a Arginousai Islands: Ref. Map 2, BY.
A.1b See Appendix O, Selections from the *Histories* of Diodorus Siculus Relevant to Xenophon's *Hellenika*, 13.101–2.

dismiss the complaint, send the case on to a jury court, or ask the Assembly to decide whether to hear the case itself or refer it to a jury court. (The Council prepared the agenda for Assembly meetings and frequently proposed resolutions to the Assembly.) Meetings of the Assembly were run by a presiding committee (the *prytaneis*) consisting of one of the ten tribal groups in the Council; the tribal groups each presided for one-tenth of the year, thirty-five or thirty-six days, in an order determined by lot. Each day a new individual was chosen by lot as chair (*epistates*) of this presiding committee. The Assembly could not consider anything the Council had not placed on the agenda, but it could amend or reject motions or pass substitutes. Any adult male Athenian citizen could attend, speak at, and vote in the Assembly. A decision by simple majority vote was final, unless the people themselves reversed their decision or unless the proposer of the motion was prosecuted successfully for making an illegal proposal (see 1.7.12). Men voted by raising their hands (a famous example occurs at 1.7.7).

§4. In the Athenian law courts, citizens over the age of thirty served on large jury panels numbering in the hundreds or even thousands, representing the people as a whole. A citizen initiated a case by serving the defendant with a summons, requiring him to appear before a designated magistrate. Magistrates probably resolved most disputes; major cases went to a jury. Magistrates could compel the defendant to present sureties (*enguetai*) who would pledge to pay the sum at issue if the defendant did not appear for the trial. In front of the jury, the plaintiff and the defendant spoke for themselves. They received equal time, measured by a simple water clock. The flow of water was stopped for the reading of a law or a witness' testimony. When the water ran out, time was up. All trials finished within one day. The jurors received no instructions and conducted no deliberations; unlike in the Assembly, they voted by secret ballot. The laws specified a penalty in some cases. In others, after a vote for conviction, the speakers each proposed a penalty, and the jury voted again to choose between the two.

§5. Indictments of generals following annual performance reviews (*euthynai*) were apparently less common, probably because serious complaints tended to lead to an *eisangelia* indictment before their term expired. We do not know how the Athenians conducted these performance reviews for generals in the fifth century. Perhaps a subcommittee of the Council was responsible and turned serious charges over to a jury court.

§6. The Athenians were not slow to prosecute their generals. The list of defendants includes such famous names as Miltiades, Themistokles, Pericles, and Alcibiades. During the twenty-five years after the Peloponnesian War began in 431, at least three generals were fined, one was exiled, three were condemned to death in absentia, and one was executed; another committed suicide during his trial. We know for certain of only one who was acquitted, and he was said to have bribed the jury.[a] The standard form of execution, *apotumpanismos*, involved fastening the con-

A.6a See Diodorus in Appendix O, 13.64.6.

demned man to a wooden board with tight iron collars around his neck, wrists, and ankles and leaving him to die.

§7. What, then, happened after the battle of Arginousai? The following reconstruction draws on the accounts of both Xenophon and Diodorus. After winning the battle, the eight Athenian generals met to decide whether to rescue their shipwrecked men or to chase the fleeing Peloponnesian ships. They opted to do both, delegating the rescue mission to Theramenes and Thrasyboulos—both experienced men, former generals, who were commanding individual triremes at Arginousai—while the generals led the pursuit themselves. But a storm soon prevented any further activity at sea, and all but a few of the men from twenty-five ships (1.6.34)—almost five thousand men,[a] including slaves but also more of the wealthy than were usually found on Athenian ships (1.6.24)—were lost. The generals sent a letter home reporting their victory and blaming only the storm for their failure to pick up the shipwrecked men. The Athenians were happy to hear of the victory but angry that men had died in the water without any attempt to rescue them and that their bodies had not been recovered (Diodorus, curiously, mentions only the corpses, omitting the living men who were abandoned in the water.)[b] Generals were expected to recover their dead. For example, after winning a battle near Corinth in 424, the Athenian general Nikias was about to sail off when he discovered he was missing the bodies of two of his men who had died in the fighting. Since enemy reinforcements had arrived, he had to ask for a truce to recover the dead, a request that normally amounted to an admission of defeat.[c] He apparently felt he had no choice.

§8. When the generals heard about the reaction in Athens, they incorrectly deduced that Theramenes and Thrasyboulos, who had already returned home, must have accused them. They sent a second letter to the Assembly, blaming Theramenes and Thrasyboulos for failing to carry out the assigned rescue. But when Theramenes and Thrasyboulos told their side of the story, the Assembly relieved all eight generals of their commands. Two of them went into self-imposed exile and did not return to Athens.

§9. When the other six did return, it was not immediately clear what would happen. Archidamos[a] imposed an administrative fine on one of the generals and accused him (whether at a trial contesting the fine or at his performance review we do not know) not only of financial misconduct but also of misconduct as a general. The jury court decided that the charges merited a prosecution and ordered him held pending trial. The Council then met to hear what the generals had to say. It voted to imprison them all and ask the Assembly to determine how to proceed. What Xenophon describes in 1.7.4–7 is not a meeting of the Assembly acting as a law court but a meeting for the Assembly to decide what to do next. Theramenes and some others urged that the generals should undergo a performance review (that is, that the normal procedure be followed). Each of the generals defended himself briefly, but because the meeting was not a judicial session, they could not make for-

---

A.7a Each trireme was crewed by two hundred men. See Appendix K, Trireme Warfare in Xenophon's *Hellenika*, §2.
A.7b For Diodorus' comment, see Appendix O, 13.100.1.
A.7c Thucydides 4.44.5–6.

A.9a Archidamos, whom Xenophon calls the leader of the people in Athens, was in charge of the two-obol allowance, a fund established to relieve wartime poverty and hardship (1.7.2).

mal speeches in their own defense. The Assembly failed to reach a decision about what to do and asked the Council to bring in a recommendation. Some days later, the Council proposed that the Assembly vote on whether the generals were guilty of failing to rescue the men; and if they were found guilty, that they be executed and their property confiscated. Euryptolemos and others promptly served a summons to Kallixenos, who had drafted the Council's motion, for introducing an illegal proposal, but Euryptolemos was shouted down, and he dropped the charge. Xenophon says that shouts similarly intimidated the presiding committee, with the exception of Socrates, into allowing the vote. In his *Memorabilia*,[b] Xenophon makes Socrates not only a member of the committee, but also the chair for the day. If that is right, how did the proposal come to a vote? We cannot be certain. Perhaps Socrates capitulated; perhaps the presiding committee outvoted him; perhaps the Assembly met again on another day, with a new chair, and Xenophon has condensed two meetings into one, strengthening the impression that the Athenians rushed to condemn the generals.

§10. The centerpiece of Xenophon's account is Euryptolemos' long speech (1.7.16–33) urging that the generals be tried individually, either by the Assembly for harming the people or by a jury court for betraying the city. The speech repays close reading, for Euryptolemos' description of what occurred is not entirely consistent with Xenophon's earlier narrative. In the end Euryptolemos argued for the Assembly to try the generals individually and to do so according to the obscure decree of Kannonos, which is otherwise mentioned only in an Aristophanes play (*Ekklēsiazousai* 1090). When the Assembly chose between Euryptolemos' proposal and that of the Council, Xenophon says it first voted for that of Euryptolemos, but after a sworn objection (alleging a miscount?), it voted for the Council's motion. The Assembly then found the generals guilty, and the six of them who had returned to Athens were executed.

§11. Was the Assembly's action illegal? Since Euryptolemos dropped his prosecution of Kallixenos for making an illegal motion, and since Kallixenos escaped before his trial when later charged with deceiving the people (1.7.35), no court ever ruled. Euryptolemos would have had a hard time showing that the motion violated a particular law. No law said, "If a general fails to rescue men in the water, he shall be tried by the following procedure." He would have had to argue that the motion was inconsistent with a legal principle embodied in the laws. But the laws did not require a trial for every defendant. *Kakourgoi* ("wrongdoers") caught in the act, for instance, were subject to arrest and execution without trial unless they claimed innocence. The generals admitted that they had sailed off to discuss the situation, rather than immediately going to the rescue (Theramenes emphasizes the point at 2.3.35). So the majority of Athenians might have thought a trial unnecessary because the generals admitted what they had done. Xenophon felt differently, and the two votes and the subsequent indictment of Kallixenos suggest that many Athenians agreed with him. It is also true that, while the Athenians continued to execute generals on

A.9b Xenophon, *Memorabilia* 1.1.18, 4.4.2.

occasion (eleven more were sentenced to death before 322), they never again adopted anything like the process after Arginousai. On the other hand, the Arginousai executions sent a clear message to future commanders. Diodorus says that Chabrias specifically remembered Arginousai after his victory at Naxos[a] in 376 and stopped his pursuit in order to pick up the shipwrecked Athenians (15.35.1).[b]

Peter Krentz
W. R. Grey Professor of Classics and Professor of History
Chair, Department of Classics
Davidson College
Davidson, North Carolina

A.11a   Naxos: Ref. Map 2, DY.   A.11b   See Appendix O, 15.35.1.

APPENDIX B

The Athenian Government
and the Oligarchy of the Thirty

§1. Sparta's attempt at regime change in Athens after defeating the Athenians in the Peloponnesian War was the second time the Athenian democracy had been overthrown in less than ten years. Comparing Xenophon's eyewitness account with other sources, especially the Aristotelian *Constitution of Athens*, raises some provocative questions. A brief account of the development of Athenian democracy and the short-lived revolution in 411 will help readers understand the dramatic events in 404/3.[a]

§2. After disturbances in the sixth century, the Athenians turned to a reformer named Solon, who divided the population into four classes based on income. Eligibility for public offices was determined by class: the treasurers came from the top class, for example, and the archons from the top two. Members of the lowest class were eligible only for the Assembly and the jury courts (probably the Assembly meeting as a court). Solon also created a Council of Four Hundred, one hundred from each of the four traditional tribes, but it is not clear how active it was. The Council of the Areopagus, comprising former archons, continued to supervise the laws and the officials.

§3. In spite of Solon's efforts, Peisistratos managed to seize power in 561/60. He and his sons ruled Athens, with some interruptions, for half a century. After the expulsion of the tyrants in 511/10, an aristocrat named Kleisthenes replaced the old system of four tribes with one based on ten new tribes, each consisting of a number of geographically defined administrative districts (demes). After Kleisthenes, an Athenian's civic identity was fixed in his deme, one of 139 in Attica.[a] Upon turning eighteen, a young Athenian was registered as a citizen after a formal vote of his deme members. An Athenian's full official name included his own name, his father's name, and his deme name (for example, Xenophon son of Gryllos, of the deme Erchia).

§4. The tribes were the basis of civic administration in classical Athens. Kleis-

B.1a   The fullest ancient account of Athenian political
developments is the Aristotelian *Constitution of
Athens*, on which see P. J. Rhodes' magisterial
A Commentary on the Aristotelian Athenaion

Politeia, rev. ed. (Oxford: Oxford University
Press, 1993).
B.3a   Attica: Ref. Map 2, CX.

thenes established a Council of Five Hundred, fifty men from each tribe, chosen annually by lot from the demes in proportion to their population. They served for one year and could not serve more than twice. For one-tenth of the civic year—each of these bodies of fifty acted as the city's standing executive committee (the *prytaneis*) in an order determined by lot. In Xenophon's day, the *prytaneis* ate together in the Tholos, a round building on the west side of the agora just south of the Council House,[a] where the Council normally met. An individual selected by lot served as chair for one day. He kept the keys to the sacred treasuries and public records buildings, and even slept in the Tholos with one-third of his committee. Heralds, envoys, and letters all went first to this standing committee, which prepared the agenda for the Council.

§5. By the middle of the fifth century, Athens had become still more democratic, and public officials were paid for their service. The Council of the Areopagus lost power in 462/1, being restricted to dealing only with intentional homicide and arson, while the Council of Five Hundred became the central executive body in the city. The Council met daily except for festival days, or perhaps about three hundred times a year. About sixty percent of the counselors chaired a meeting of the Council. The Council prepared the agenda for Assembly meetings and frequently proposed resolutions to the Assembly. As the central executive body in Athens, it also conducted a formal check on the qualifications of the future council members, the archons, and even the cavalry's horses; it supervised the public buildings and the fleet; it tried officials accused of misconduct in office, especially financial misconduct; it approved the design for the new dress presented to the statue of Athena every four years; and it worked with other officials to carry out their administrative duties.

§6. The Athenians had some seven hundred magistrates in all, most chosen annually by lot and serving on committees. The chief administrative officers were the nine archons (the eponymous archon, who gave his name to the year;[a] the *basileus*, or king; the polemarch, or war leader; and six *thesmothetai*, or lawgivers) and their secretary. In 457/6, members of the third class became eligible for the archonship. The Eleven,[b] who served as Athens' jailers and executioners, were also chosen by lot; their unusual number probably indicates that they preceded Kleisthenes' creation of the ten tribes. Athenians believed that selection by a random lottery was more democratic than by election, and they assumed that every citizen—at least every citizen in one of the top three property classes—could do these jobs. Anyone could denounce an official by a procedure known as *eisangelia*, which would lead to a trial. At the end of their term officials underwent a performance review (*euthyna*).

§7. Military officers and treasurers, however, were elected. Ten generals, one from each tribe, were elected every year for annual terms, and they could be reelected without interruption. Ten taxiarchs—one for each *taxis*, or tribal regiment—were also elected, as were two cavalry commanders and ten squadron commanders, one for each squadron of the cavalry. The generals commanded on sea as well as on land,

B.4a Tholos, agora, Prytaneion (Council House):   B.6b See 2.3.54, 2.4.8, 2.4.38.
      Ref. Map 5.
B.6a See 1.2.1, 1.3.1, 1.6.1, 2.1.10, 2.3.1.

and the Assembly could send more than one general on an expedition. At the battle of Arginousai, there were eight (1.6.29–30), all equal in rank. A general could convene extraordinary meetings of the Assembly, and on campaign he had the authority to arrest, expel, fine, and perhaps even execute soldiers. Like other magistrates, generals could be prosecuted by *eisangelia* while in office and were subject to a *euthyna* at the end of their term.

§8. The Assembly usually met on a hillside called the Pnyx,ᵃ a little west of the agora. All adult male citizens could attend, speak, and vote; six thousand was considered a good turnout. The Assembly had the final authority on whatever business it considered, and it debated all major decisions of state, such as whether to go to war, sign a treaty, embark on a new campaign, send an embassy, receive envoys, raise and assign forces, raise or spend money, or honor a citizen or foreigner. In addition to the forty regular meetings each year, the Assembly could meet as often as necessary. A different member of the *prytaneis* chaired the meeting every day, and he and his fellow prytaneis served as the presiding committee, responsible for maintaining order, keeping to the agenda, determining the results of the voting, and ending the meeting.ᵇ The Assembly considered items in the order set by the Council. Motions were introduced, and speakers advocated, contested, or modified what was proposed. While anyone could speak, the people often allowed a *prostates tou demous* (1.7.2, an unofficial "leader of the people") to speak for them. By law the Assembly could not consider anything the Council had not placed on the agenda, but it could amend or reject motions or pass substitutes. The people voted by raising their hands (a famous example occurs at 1.7.7). A decision by simple majority vote was final, unless the people themselves reversed their decision or unless the proposer of the motion was prosecuted successfully for making an illegal proposal (see 1.7.12).

§9. Magistrates probably handled most disputes; they could serve as arbitrators between contending parties and could hand out small fines. Bigger cases went to the jury courts. The increasing volume of business led to the creation of a sophisticated system by the 450s, when jurors began to be paid. They had to be at least thirty years old. Each year a pool of six thousand potential jurors was selected by lot from citizens who volunteered, and juries for the individual cases were chosen by lot from this pool. Juries ranged in size from two hundred to six thousand, depending on the nature of the case.

§10. Athenian law provided many possible procedures. They fall generally into two types: private cases (*dikai*), in which the victim (or a member of his family in the case of homicide) brought the charges, and public cases (*graphai*), in which anyone could prosecute. Athens had no public prosecutor, depending instead on individual citizens to step forward. Individuals who prosecuted too often earned a nasty reputation as *sukophantai*,ᵃ men who were thought to prosecute for profit, either by receiving a share of the fine if they won their case or by reaching an out-of-court settlement. As a brake on this sort of behavior, prosecutors in *graphai* had to

B.8a Pnyx Hill, Athens: Ref. Map 5. See Figure 6.5.33, a view of the Bema, the speaker's platform for the Athenian Assembly on Pnyx Hill.

B.8b *Prytaneis*: see their role (and that of Socrates) in

the Assembly that dealt with the generals of Arginousai at 1.7.14–15.

B.10a *Sukophantai*: see 2.3.12, 2.3.22, 2.3.38.

pay a thousand drachmas[b] if they received less than one-fifth of the votes; prosecutors in *dikai* risked no penalties for losing a case and received most of any financial penalty. A potential prosecutor began by summoning his opponent to appear before a magistrate to answer his charge. The magistrate collected court fees and arranged for a preliminary hearing. Magistrates may have decided small private cases, but larger ones, and all *graphai*, proceeded to trial. The magistrate could compel the defendant to present sureties (*enguetai*) who would pledge to pay the sum at issue if he did not show up for the trial (1.7.7).

§11. In front of the jury, litigants spoke for themselves (though they could give some of their time to a supporting speaker) and had a limited amount of time to speak, timed by a simple water clock. The flow of water was stopped for the reading of a law or a witness' testimony. When the water ran out, time was up. More important cases got more time, but all trials finished within one day. The jury received no instructions and did not deliberate. Jurors voted by placing a pebble in one of two baskets and could keep their vote secret by placing a clenched fist into each basket, concealing the actual release of the pebble. The laws specified a penalty in some cases. In others, the speakers each proposed a penalty, and the jury voted again to choose between the two. Penalties included fines (sometimes including imprisonment until the fine was paid), confiscations, public humiliation in the stocks, limited or total loss of political rights, exile, and death. The standard form of execution, *apotumpanismos*, involved fastening a person to a wooden board with tight iron collars around the neck, wrists, and ankles and leaving him to die. In the fourth century, men sentenced to death were allowed to drink poisonous hemlock if they could afford to pay for it, another form of bloodless execution, though much more unpleasant than Socrates' death scene in Plato's *Phaedo* makes it seem. Theramenes' death in 404 is one of the earliest recorded uses of hemlock for execution (2.3.56). The Athenians normally seem to have been willing to let condemned men escape into exile.

§12. After the Athenian expedition to Sicily[a] was annihilated in 413—a turning point in the Peloponnesian War—the Athenian exile Alcibiades, who had become an advisor to the Persian satrap Tissaphernes but hoped to return to Athens, suggested to Athenians serving in the fleet based at Samos[b] that if only Athens had an oligarchy instead of a democracy, he could bring the Persians over to the Athenian side. Once that seed was planted, the idea took on a life of its own. Even after it became clear that Alcibiades could not deliver on his promises, oligarchic plotters murdered some of their political opponents and pushed a vote through the Assembly that dissolved the democracy in the summer of 411. "It was," comments Thucydides,[c] "no easy matter to deprive the Athenian people of their freedom, almost a hundred years after the deposition of the tyrants, when they had not only not been subject to any during the whole of that period, but were accustomed during more than half of it to rule over subjects of their own." The Assembly voted to

---

B.10b One thousand drachmas was a huge amount in the fourth century. A laborer at Athens could hope to earn one drachma a day at the end of the fifth century.

B.12a Sicily: Ref. Map 1.
B.12b Samos: Ref. Map 2, CY.
B.12c Thucydides 8.68.4.

establish a Council of Four Hundred, with full powers to govern. The Four Hundred promptly abolished all pay for public service.[d] They were to convene an Assembly of either no more than or no fewer than five thousand (sources differ), those best able to serve the state with their financial resources or in person. This they did not do. They did try, without success, to negotiate peace with Sparta.[e] They had no more success in establishing their control over their own fleet at Samos, where the men rejected the oligarchy, took an oath to continue the war, and elected Alcibiades general. The Four Hundred began fortifying Eetioneia, a breakwater at the entrance to Athens' port, the Peiraieus.[f] When the Athenians heard that a Peloponnesian fleet had assembled in response to an invitation from Euboea,[g] Theramenes, then a member of the Four Hundred, raised an alarm, claiming that oligarchic extremists among the Four Hundred planned to use Eetioneia to admit the Peloponnesian fleet into the Peiraieus. (Thucydides says this plot really existed.)[h] The infuriated Athenian hoplites then demolished the fortification. When the enemy fleet sailed around Attica, defeated an Athenian fleet off Eretria,[i] and caused all of Euboea to revolt, Theramenes prompted the Athenians to depose the Four Hundred and entrust the government to the Five Thousand, now defined as all Athenian hoplites. The Four Hundred had ruled only four months.

§13. Thucydides praised the rule of the Five Thousand as the best government the Athenians had during his lifetime,[a] but he says little about the details. The orator Lysias claims that the Five Thousand actually numbered nine thousand.[b] In addition to the hoplite Assembly, there was probably an elected Council of Five Hundred and a continued prohibition of state pay. Under this form of government, the Athenians revoked Alcibiades' exile and won a major naval battle at Kynossema.[c] In the following winter and spring, they won the further victories at Abydos[d] and Cyzicus[e] described by Xenophon (1.1.5–7, 1.1.11–18). By the summer of 410, when they passed a resolution prohibiting the overthrow of the democracy, the Athenians had evidently gone back to full democracy. Neither Xenophon nor any other source mentions the change.

§14. The restored democracy continued the process of revising the laws begun by the Four Hundred and continued by the Five Thousand. Other actions vigorously reasserted the power of the people. The earliest known new law made death and confiscation of property the penalty for overthrowing the democracy or holding office after an overthrow. Prosecutors went after former supporters of the Four Hundred in the courts. Soldiers who had remained in town during the oligarchy lost the right to serve on the Council or speak in the Assembly, because they were suspected of at least tacitly supporting the oligarchy. Kleophon introduced a new two-obol payment, either a subsistence allowance paid to citizens impoverished by

B.12d   Abolishing pay for public service effectively barred poor citizens from holding office.
B.12e   Sparta: Ref. Map 2, DX.
B.12f   Eetioneia and Peiraieus: Ref. Map 5.
B.12g   Euboea: Ref. Map 2, CX.
B.12h   See Thucydides 8.91.3.
B.12i   Eretria (on Euboea): Ref. Map 3, BZ.
B.13a   See Thucydides 8.97.2.
B.13b   See Lysias 20.13.
B.13c   Kynossema: Map 2.1.16. Site of an Athenian

naval victory in the Hellespont in 411; see Thucydides 8.104–6.
B.13d   Abydos: Ref. Map 2, AY.
B.13e   Cyzicus: Ref. Map 2, AY.

the war or a resumption of the payment for public service suspended in 411. The source of the money is not clear. Prior to 413, the Athenians had levied an annual tribute on their empire, assessed for each city according roughly to its perceived means. This was replaced in 413 by an import and export duty of five percent in all the harbors of the empire, but it is not clear how long that continued as a general levy (though it was still in force in 405 on Aegina),[a] and it would have been very difficult to collect during the last decade of the war. In 410 the Athenians levied a ten percent duty on goods passing through Chalcedon[b] (1.1.22), whose relation to the five percent duty is unclear (five percent as the goods entered the port and five percent as they left it?). It is possible that tribute was formally reimposed: a fragmentary inscription might be a tribute reassessment from 410, but the date is uncertain. Not long after the events of 1.1.22, Chalcedon agreed to pay its customary tribute again (1.3.8), but this is perhaps an exceptional case. Generals certainly resorted to extorting money from allies when they could,[d] but Athens was in no position to rely on regular collection of assessed tribute. A property tax on capital was levied on Athenian citizens twice during the last period of the war (Lysias 21.3), but the Athenians finally had to turn precious dedications to Athena into coins: silver starting in 409/8 and gold in 407/6. Pericles had listed such objects among Athens' resources in 431, but it is a sign of how financially strapped they were that the Athenians actually melted down these sacred gifts.

§15. Athenian democracy reached perhaps its most extreme moment at a meeting of the Assembly in 406, when people flatly asserted that "it was a terrible thing if someone did not allow the people to do whatever they wished" (1.7.12). The Athenians then condemned and executed six of the eight generals who had won the battle of Arginousai.[a] Under the command of less experienced generals in the following year, the Athenians lost the final great battle of the war at Aigospotamoi and, eight months later, were forced to surrender (2.1.20–2.2.23).

§16. Scholars debate whether the peace treaty that ended the Peloponnesian War called for the "ancestral constitution" in Athens and what the phrase would have meant. Xenophon does not include such a clause, though the Aristotelian *Constitution of Athens*[a] and Diodorus[b] do. Nor does Xenophon mention the Spartan admiral Lysander's presence at the Assembly meeting in September 404 that voted to turn Athens over to the Thirty.[c] Lysander began by advising the Athenians to choose thirty men to govern, but when Theramenes objected, Lysander accused the Athenians of breaking the peace treaty by failing to destroy their Long Walls and the Peiraieus fortifications within the allotted time. He then threatened to execute Theramenes if he did not cease his opposition. Theramenes capitulated and was himself elected a member of the Thirty as a moderating influence.[d]

B.14a   On the five percent tax, see Thucydides 7.28.4 and Aristophanes, *Frogs* 363.. Aegina: Ref. Map 3, CY.

B.14b   Chalcedon: Ref. Map. 2, AZ.

B.14d   See *Hellenika* 1.1.8, 1.1.12, 1.4.9; compare with Thucydides 2.69, 3.19, 4.50, 4.75.

B.15a   Arginousai Islands: Ref. Map 2, BY. For a more detailed treatment of this episode, see Appendix A, The Arginousai Affair.

B.16a   Aristotelian *Constitution of Athens* 34.3.

B.16b   See Appendix O, Selections from the *Histories* of Diodorus Siculus Relevant to Xenophon's *Hellenika*, 14.32.

B.16c   For the dates followed here, see P. Krentz, *The Thirty at Athens* (Ithaca: Cornell University Press, 1982), pp. 147–52. *The Cambridge Ancient History* prefers a slightly earlier chronology, with the Thirty installed in July.

B.16d   See Appendix O, 14.3.5–7 and 14.4.1, and Lysias 12.71–76.

§17. Xenophon's account of the oligarchy (2.3.11–2.4.43) explains why later sources dubbed the oligarchs the Thirty Tyrants. Not only does he connect the word *tyrant* with them three times,[a] but he also describes them as acting as quintessential tyrants: acquiring a bodyguard, removing prominent citizens, confiscating property, disarming the people, expelling a number of them from the city, and even executing some without just cause. In his later prosecution of Eratosthenes, a member of the Thirty, the resident foreigner (metic) Lysias describes his own arrest and escape. His brother Polemarchos failed to get away and was executed by hemlock.[b] According to Xenophon, only after the Thirty executed Theramenes did Thrasyboulos, a former general, begin an insurrection that led to the restoration of the democracy. The Aristotelian *Constitution of Athens* has an interesting alternative sequence of events: Thrasyboulos occupies Phyle[c] before the Thirty execute Theramenes, disarm everyone excluded from full citizenship, and bring in troops from Sparta. This version, while not turning the Thirty into saints, makes them less tyrannical. Is the *Constitution of Athens* whitewashing Theramenes, or is Xenophon excusing himself for having supported the Thirty by suggesting that he had little choice, given the presence of the Spartan garrison?[d]

§18. Whichever chronology is correct, it is clear that the Thirty were not of one mind. They began by appointing a Council of Five Hundred but did not produce all the new laws they were empowered to write. After complaints by Theramenes, the Thirty produced a list of Three Thousand who were to be the full citizens. The ideologues led by Kritias, a famous admirer of Sparta, hoped to make Athens more like Sparta, with a Gerousia, or Council of Elders (the Thirty); a body of *homoioi*, or "similars" (the Three Thousand); and *perioikoi*, or neighbors without full citizenship, in this case, the men excluded from the Three Thousand who were forced to leave Athens and live outside the city. Their Athens also gave harsh treatment to foreigners, although not the outright expulsion (*xenelasia*) practiced in Sparta. Theramenes wanted a broader franchise, something like the government of the Five Thousand so admired by Thucydides. In the event, we hear of only one meeting of the Three Thousand (2.4.23). The ideologues, with the experience of 411 behind them, had no intention of letting Theramenes once again turn an oligarchy into a moderate democracy. According to Xenophon, when the Council balked at condemning Theramenes to death, Kritias had him removed from the list of the Three Thousand and condemned to death, using a new law that granted the Thirty the power to execute anyone outside the Three Thousand (2.3.51). In the Aristotelian *Constitution of Athens*, the Council of Five Hundred approves a law excluding anyone from the Three Thousand who had helped to demolish the fortification at Eetioneia or acted against the Four Hundred in any way.[a] That definition included

B.17a   See 2.3.16, 2.4.1, 6.3.8.
B.17b   Lysias 12.4–19.
B.17c   Phyle: Ref. Map 3, BY.
B.17d   See the Introduction, §15.2, where Xenophon's
        account is preferred.
B.18a   Aristotelian *Constitution of Athens* 37.1.

Theramenes, and if it did not condemn him to death, it made him vulnerable. Is this law a fiction, or did Xenophon suppress it to excuse the members of the Council of Five Hundred from any responsibility for Theramenes' death?

§19. The revolt launched by Thrasyboulos from exile started slowly. In January 403 he seized Phyle, later the site of a fourth-century Athenian fort, with only seventy men (2.4.2). A snowstorm ruined the Thirty's first attempt to capture the resistance fighters (2.4.3), and Thrasyboulos' numbers began to grow. By April or May he had about seven hundred men and successfully attacked the soldiers that the Thirty had sent out against him (2.4.4–7). Becoming more desperate, the Thirty secured the fortification at Eleusis,ᵃ executing most of the Eleusinians (2.4.8–10). When Thrasyboulos' numbers reached one thousand, he led the resisters on a night march to the Peiraieusᵇ and defeated the Thirty's troops in a battle at the Hill of Mounichiaᶜ (2.4.10–19). Xenophon does not reveal the extent of foreign involvement in the insurgency: an incomplete inscription rewarding foreigners who fought for democracy has been restored with about seventy to ninety names of men "who joined in the return from Phyle" and about 290 more "who joined in fighting the battle at Mounichia." Most of these foreigners probably fought as light-armed troops (see 2.4.12).

§20. Despite the loss of their leader Kritias in the fighting, and even after they were deposed by the Three Thousand, the Thirty were not ready to give up. They moved to Eleusis and sent to Sparta for help (2.4.23–28). Lysander, who thought of the Thirty as similar to the dekarchiesᵃ he had installed at Samos and elsewhere (2.3.7; see also 3.4.2), managed to get himself sent out in June or July with fresh land forces, together with his brother Libys in command of a fleet (2.3.28). The brothers besieged the insurgents in the Peiraieus and soon began to turn the tide (2.3.29). But the Spartans did not all support Lysander's policy, or Lysander himself. Jealous of Lysander, Pausanias, one of the two Spartan kings, led out a larger army, including contingents from most of Sparta's Peloponnesian allies. After fighting briefly with the men in the Peiraieus, Pausanias brokered a reconciliation agreement in October calling for the return of the democratic exiles, the restoration of the democracy, and the independence of Eleusis, where anyone afraid to live in Athens was free to go (2.4.28–42). Xenophon notes that the Athenians later marched against Eleusis, killed the oligarchs' generals when they came out for a conference, and agreed to an amnesty. He ends the story of the Thirty with a highly positive comment on the success of the amnesty, which he says the Athenians still abide by (2.4.43). From the fuller version of the reconciliation agreement in the Aristotelian *Constitution of Athens* (39.1–6), we know that the amnesty was part of the original agreement in 403. Since the reincorporation of Eleusis took place in

B.19a   Eleusis: Ref. Map 3, BY.
B.19b   Peiraieus: Ref. Map 5.
B.19c   Hill of Mounichia: Ref. Map 5. P. J. Rhodes and Robin Osborne, eds., *Greek Historical Inscriptions 404–323 B.C.* (Oxford: Oxford University Press, 2003), No. 4. Note that the granting of citizenship for foreigners in the first category is entirely restored; more probably, they received the "equality of obligations"

(*isoteleia*) promised by Thrasyboulos in 2.4.25.
B.20a   Dekarchies: when Lysander and the Peloponnesian fleet liberated the cities of the Aegean from Athenian rule in 405–404, he set up new governments (dekarchies) ruled by ten men—local, pro-oligarchic citizens—usually selected by Lysander. Later these governments proved unpopular, and Sparta abolished them.

401/400,[b] Xenophon postdates the amnesty to follow the treacherous slaughter of the oligarchs' generals, which might otherwise appear as a blot on the democrats' record. (Smaller blots may be noted at 1.7.35 and 3.1.4.) The thrust of Xenophon's narrative, though, is consistent with what Athenian orators have to say in the fourth century. To rebuild their community, the Athenians allowed former oligarchic sympathizers to think of themselves as victims and therefore to share in the people's victory when the exiles returned.

§21. The restored democracy emphasized its commitment to law by drawing a distinction between laws (*nomoi*) and decrees (*psephismata*). When the revised law code was finally completed, it was ratified not by the Assembly but by an ad hoc body consisting of the five hundred Council members chosen by lot, together with five hundred lawgivers (*nomothetai*) elected by the demes. In the fourth century, the Assembly passed decrees but not laws. New laws had to be approved by lawgivers selected from the jury pool and therefore at least thirty years old. Anyone proposing a decree was subject to prosecution if the decree was inconsistent with the laws. The restored democracy lasted three-quarters of a century, until it was put down by the Macedonians in 322, but Xenophon says no more about constitutional changes at Athens after the reconciliation of 403.

Peter Krentz
W. R. Grey Professor of Classics and Professor of History
Chair, Department of Classics
Davidson College
Davidson, North Carolina

B.20b Aristotelian *Constitution of Athens* 40.4.

APPENDIX C
Chronological Problems in the Continuation
(1.1.1–2.3.10) of Xenophon's *Hellenika*

§1. Xenophon did not expect his readers to be interested in chronology, and consequently he does not provide as much chronological information as historians today would like.[a] Many chronological problems have been identified throughout the *Hellenika*, some of which are briefly mentioned in the Introduction and footnotes to this edition. However, in the first section of the work (1.1.1–2.3.10), often referred to as "the Continuation" (that is, of Thucydides' narrative of the Peloponnesian War), the chronological problems are more deep-seated and interconnected and thus need to be set out in an appendix rather than in separate footnotes on each affected passage.

The Join between Thucydides and Xenophon

§2. Thucydides' history comes abruptly to an end with the satrap Tissaphernes in Ephesus[a] on his way to the Hellespont.[b] Xenophon takes up the story shortly after Thucydides' account ends, and in a place that is not a natural starting point, but he does not begin quite where Thucydides ended; he does not mention Ephesus or Tissaphernes here, and in fact, he leaves a gap of a month or so, passing over a major Spartan shipwreck off Mount Athos.[c] This is not in dispute today, though some people explain it by suggesting that either the very end of Thucydides' text or the very beginning of Xenophon's has been lost.

§3. Some scholars think that some of the events that Xenophon proceeds to tell actually belong to the earlier period. They say, for example, that his account of how and why the Spartans sent their man Klearchos to Byzantium[a] recounts the exact same events as Thucydides had.[b] As Thucydides shows, Klearchos certainly went to Byzantium with a small fleet in 411, and Xenophon has not written here as though he is now going back a second time. However, the reason he gives for the dispatch

---

C.1a For general comments on Xenophon as a chronologist, see the Introduction, §9.4.
C.2a Ephesus: Ref. Map 2, CY.
C.2b Hellespont: Ref. Map 2, BY.
C.2c Mount Athos: Ref. Map 2, AX. See Diodorus'

account of the shipwreck disaster, Appendix O, Selections from the *Histories* of Diodorus Siculus Relevant to Xenophon's *Hellenika*, 13.41.1.
C.3a Byzantium: Ref. Map 2, AZ.
C.3b See *Hellenika* 1.1.35–36, Thucydides 8.80.3.

of Klearchos is quite different from that given by Thucydides, the number of ships is different, and the details about what happened are different. So it is easier to see this as an example of Xenophon not dovetailing his narrative with that of Thucydides than as his putting an incident in the wrong place. Another example of a possibly misplaced event is the exile of the Syracusan[c] Hermokrates: this is recounted at *Hellenika* 1.1.27 as occurring in the summer of 410, but according to some modern scholars, it actually fell a year earlier, in the context in which Thucydides mentions it at 8.85.3. However, Thucydides is looking forward, at least to some extent, from his current narrative context when he mentions Hermokrates' exile, and he could be looking forward to the following year. But it is true that if Hermokrates was in fact exiled in 411 and Xenophon has muddled the order of events, that would explain another puzzle as well: although at *Hellenika* 1.1.26, undoubtedly to be put in 410, the Syracusan ships are at Antandros[d] with the rest of the Peloponnesian fleet, shortly afterward in his narrative, at 1.1.31, when the new Syracusan commanders take them over, we find them at Miletus,[e] well over one hundred miles to the south. That is puzzling not only because Xenophon does not describe the move but also because in 410 the Peloponnesians were on much better terms with Pharnabazos, the northern satrap, than they were with Tissaphernes, so it is a bit odd if they moved some or all of their ships well into the latter's sphere of influence. But the Peloponnesian fleet, including these Syracusan ships, had undoubtedly been based on Miletus in 411,[f] so possibly the Milesian events of 1.1.31 really belong in 411. Still, a return to Miletus in 410 is not downright impossible—nobody doubts that the Syracusans were with Tissaphernes at Ephesus a little later, as Xenophon says at 1.2.8—or perhaps there is a mere slip by Xenophon or even by a copyist in the name of the city at 1.1.31, into which nothing more should be read.

§4. Thus each individual problem can be explained away. But the conjunction of problems means that doubts continue as to whether piecemeal explanations are right. It has even been suggested that Xenophon had not actually read Thucydides' Book 8. At any rate, he has certainly not made it clear what we are supposed to make of the links with it.

The Interpolations in the Continuation (1.1.1–2.3.10)

§5. Thucydides was careful about chronology in his account of the Peloponnesian War, which he divided into campaign years, themselves divided between summer and winter seasons; but he included only one express statement about the absolute date of the war (at 2.1–2). The Athenians could identify a year by the name of the person who held the office of eponymous archon during that year; the similar annual office at Sparta was that of the eponymous ephor; and at 2.1–2 Thucydides names the holders of these offices at the start of the war. At first sight, Xenophon seems even more concerned than Thucydides with establishing a reliable chronology for the events he describes. Xenophon's text divides the narrative into years, which are identified not only as campaign years but also as archon years and ephor years,

C.3c　Syracuse: Ref. Map 1.
C.3d　Antandros: Ref. Map 2, BY.
C.3e　Miletus: Ref. Map 2, CY.
C.3f　See Thucydides 8.85.3.

and sometimes by reference to contemporary Olympic Games and to astronomical events as well.

§6. Unfortunately, there is no doubt that the identifications of the various years in Xenophon's text have generally been done incorrectly. The running indications of the length of the war add up to twenty-six and a half campaign years, but the correct total is twenty-seven and a bit;[a] just to confuse matters further, 2.3.9 gives it as twenty-eight and a half years. The person given as Athenian archon in the first of the chronological notices, at 1.2.1, was archon in 408/7, but the context in 1.2.1 is an earlier year (whether it is 410 or 409 is discussed in §10 below, but no modern scholar thinks it belongs in 408). There is a similar mistake with the next notice, at 1.3.1. The spring noted at 1.4.2 should logically have received a chronological notice, but it is missing (though the change of year is taken into account in the numeration of campaign years).

§7. However, these difficulties are almost certainly not the fault of Xenophon himself. The great majority of scholars agree that these notices of campaign years, archon years, ephor years (including the full list of ephors at 2.3.10), and Olympiads are interpolations in the text made by others, using chronological handbooks, in the third century at the earliest. Because the main interpolator failed to notice the change of year at 1.4.2 but the numeration of campaign years does recognize that change, and also because, as stated above, the running indications of campaign years are inconsistent with the final reckoning at 2.3.10, we can deduce that there were at least two interpolators at work: the first one interpolating the archon years, the Olympic references, and the final count of war years, and the second one the running campaign-year references. Most scholars who accept that the text has been interpolated (but not the editor of the Oxford Classical Text[a]) also think that the three notices about Sicilian affairs at 1.1.37, 1.5.21, and 2.2.24 are interpolations, especially as the first two are chronologically misplaced; and that it is also probable that the two notices about Persian affairs at 1.2.19 and 2.1.8–9 are not from Xenophon, since the first starts with the same formula as the interpolated Syracusan notices and the second contains inconsistencies in diction and substance with the main narrative. The list of the junta of the Thirty at 2.3.2 is also most likely interpolated, as is, on balance, the notice about a battle in Thessaly at 2.3.4.

§8. But it is not clear exactly how extensive the interpolations are. Many different views have been expressed as to how much of 2.3.1–10 is due to the interpolators (the only part that nobody seems to doubt is 2.3.6–8). Scholars have generally accepted the indications of change of season in the narrative (though a few have doubted even some of these), but there are scholars who think that some or all the phrases indicating a change of year are also interpolated. However, it seems that at least the notice about an eclipse of the moon at 1.6.1 is genuine: the eclipse is in the correct place for the main narrative but in the wrong place for the interpolators' indicated dates, and that notice grammatically requires the year-change marker preceding it. Therefore, most scholars accept the year-change markers not only here but also at 1.2.1, 1.3.1, 2.1.10, and 2.3.1 (though there are some arguments against the last).

C.7a   E. C. Marchant, ed., *Historia Graeca*, Oxford Classical Texts (Oxford: Oxford University Press, 1900).

§9. Thus, unfortunately, in trying to assess Xenophon as a historian, we are unclear whether he made any systematic attempt in the Continuation to indicate changes of year, though no one doubts he did give several indications of the change of seasons.

The Missing Spring:
The Chronology of the Peloponnesian War from 410 to 406

§10. Even if Xenophon was trying to be systematic in indicating year changes during the phase of the Peloponnesian War that he covers, there is no dispute that one year change is missing from his text. Thucydides ends in the autumn of 411, and all our ancient evidence (including the interpolated text of Xenophon) agrees that the battle of Aigospotamoi[a] was fought in the year in which Archytas was Athenian archon, that is, 405/4. Therefore, there should be six indications of the coming of spring or the beginning of a campaign year between the beginning of *Hellenika* and the account of the Aigospotamoi campaign at 2.1.15, but unfortunately there are only five (1.2.1, 1.3.1, 1.4.1, 1.6.1 and 2.1.10). There is no modern consensus as to where the missing change should be placed: all solutions produce an uncomfortably large gap between events in one period and squeeze an uncomfortably large number of events into another, and thus they all produce different ideas of what actually happened. The problem is made more difficult to solve because, as explained in §5–9, we are not sure how many of Xenophon's year-change markers and seasonal indicators we can trust to be authentic.

§11. The early modern scholars who first systematically investigated the chronology suggested that the year whose start has not been expressly flagged by Xenophon begins in spring 410, and that the year marker and summer mentioned at 1.2.1 is, therefore, that of 409. The spring he failed to mark would come at 1.1.11, around the time of the battle of Cyzicus[a] (which all scholars agree was in 410). Diodorus says the preliminaries of the battle took place "winter now being nearly over,"[b] so spring could come either just before the battle (at 1.1.11) or just after it (at 1.1.22). This placement of "the Missing Spring" in 410 establishes a chronological scheme for the remaining years that is known as the "low" chronology, and this is the scheme that creates the fewest problems with Xenophon's narrative when considered without reference to other evidence. However, it has a number of difficulties, of which the following seem the greatest cause for concern.

§12. In the low chronology, the Athenians stay largely inactive for well over a year after their considerable victory at Cyzicus in early 410. Furthermore, Thrasyllos, one of the commanders of the Hellespont fleet, was sent to Athens at that point for reinforcements (1.1.8), but in the low chronology he did not return to the east Aegean[a] until summer 409, which is the low chronology's date for his campaign to Miletus and Ephesus (1.2.1–13). The most plausible explanation given by supporters of the low chronology is that this delay was because Athens was extremely short of money in 410.

C.10a   Aigospotamoi (Aigospotamos): Ref. Map 2, AY.
C.11a   Cyzicus: Ref. Map 2, AY.
C.11b   See Appendix O, 13.49.2.
C.12a   Aegean Sea: Ref. Map 2, BX.

§13. At the other end of this disputed period, the low chronology crowds the campaign year 406, into which it puts both the victory of the Spartan admiral Lysander at Notion[a] and the whole of the campaign of his successor Kallikratidas, which ended with his death at the battle of Arginousai.[b] Notion cannot be placed right at the outset of the year, as Alcibiades and others would not be sailing around the Aegean in the depth of winter except in dire necessity; thus Kallikratidas cannot have succeeded Lysander until around the start of the second quarter. Kallikratidas' term of office began with various comings and goings between Ephesus and Sardis,[c] and we learn from Diodorus (13.76)[d] that he then took Delphinion[e] and Teos[f] before his victory at Methymna and the siege of Konon in Mytilene.[g] All this will more than fill the second quarter. Still, if we can put the battle of Arginousai in the late summer of 406, this may be a squeeze but one not too difficult to accept. However, there is a piece of evidence placing the battle in the second quarter of 406. The Athenians enrolled slaves as rowers for their fleet in this battle and subsequently freed them, and according to an ancient commentator on Aristophanes' play *Frogs* (line 694), the slaves were freed in the archon year 407/6. But to put the battle before the change of archon year around midsummer, at the end of the second quarter of 406, means we can't fit in before it all the preceding events that are required to take place in 406 by the low chronology. This can be countered by saying that the rest of the evidence does suggest, though not conclusively, that the battle of Arginousai was actually fought in the third quarter of 406; it is quite credible that the ancient commentator or his source made the small slip of giving as the date of the actual freeing of the slaves the date that really belonged to the prebattle decree promising them freedom if they fought for Athens.

§14. According to the most natural interpretation of the transmitted text of *Hellenika* 1.4.7, the Persian satrap Pharnabazos held an Athenian embassy to Persia incommunicado for three years after Cyrus arrived in the west to head the redoubled Persian war effort, and only after that long delay were the ambassadors released, whereupon they went to the Athenian camp. This is impossible in the low chronology, in which there is only a little more than two years between its earliest possible date for the arrest of the ambassadors (407) and the destruction of the Athenian camp as a result of the battle of Aigospotamoi (405). The best answer seems to be to emend the text from "three years" to "three months," which in fact makes more sense in the context anyway and provides the bonus of allowing Xenophon's references to Euryptolemos the ambassador appointed by Alcibiades (1.3.12) to be one and the same person as Euryptolemos the friend who both welcomed Alcibiades to Athens (1.4.19) and spoke in the great debate on punishing the generals after the battle of Arginousai (1.7.12, 1.7.16–33).

§15. Lastly, a number of points in Diodorus create difficulties for the low chronology. At 13.52.1 and 13.64.1–2 Diodorus implies, contrary to the low chronology (see §11 above), that there was only a short gap between the battle of

C.13a Notion: Ref. Map 2, CY.
C.13b Arginousai Islands: Ref. Map 2, BY.
C.13c Sardis: Ref. Map 2, CY.
C.13d For all Diodorus passages cited in this appendix, see Appendix O.

C.13e Delphinion: Ref. Map 4, BX.
C.13f Teos: Ref. Map 4, BX.
C.13g Methymna and Mytilene, Lesbos: Ref. Map 2, CY.

Cyzicus and Thrasyllos' campaign near Ephesus; but these could be blunders by Diodorus in abridging Ephoros, his main source for these years. A third passage is more tricky to explain away. Diodorus at 13.64.7 says that Athens occupied Pylos[b] for fifteen years. We know from Thucydides 4.2–6 that the Athenians had taken Pylos in early summer 425, so its recapture fifteen years later should be in 410. But Xenophon mentions the recapture at 2.18, and according to the low chronology, at this point in Xenophon's narrative we should be in late 409. Some say this is simply another blunder by Diodorus, who is prone to blunders, but that does not seem likely in this case, because the Diodorus 13 passage in fact does not place the recapture in 410 but in 409/8. If he had made his own calculation, he should have reckoned the period of occupation as at least sixteen years, rather than fifteen. It seems therefore that the calculation comes from his source, presumably Ephoros; most likely it will have come indirectly from the main source probably used by Ephoros for these years, the redoubtable "P," the Oxyrhynchus Historian.[c] This seems the strongest argument against the low chronology. There are ways of getting out of it, such as emending Diodorus' number here, but no one can feel comfortable with such devices.

§16. For one, several, or all of these reasons, different scholars have proposed various chronological schemes to identify the summer referred to at *Hellenika* 1.2.1 as the summer of 410 (rather than that of 409 as in the low chronology)[a] and locate the "Missing Spring" at some later point. The first scholars to put forward a "high" chronology of this sort suggested that the Missing Spring is that of 407 and located it in the text around 1.5.11, just before the battle of Notion. But two other versions have been proposed more recently: one in which the Missing Spring (again of 407) would be found around 1.4.8, just as Xenophon has Alcibiades off in Caria[b] collecting tribute; and a second in which the Missing Spring is that of 408 and should be placed around 1.3.14, where Xenophon is describing how Euryptolemos' embassy set out from the Athenian army as it besieged Byzantium.

§17. These high or mixed chronologies also suffer major difficulties. The nature of the problem, of course, requires all solutions to involve a year in which not much happens. Thus it is not too damaging to those solutions that place the Missing Spring in 407 that they either involve curious inactivity by Lysander after his victory at Notion (if we put the omission at 1.5.11) or have Alcibiades spending a whole year collecting tribute in poor and strategically unimportant Caria (if we put the omission at 1.4.8). But the delays required by all three high chronologies in relation to Persian affairs are more serious. Putting the Missing Spring in 407 means there must have been a long delay (at least ten months if spring 407 should come at 1.5.11, almost two years if it should come at 1.4.8) between Cyrus' appointment as Persian overlord in the west and his getting to his appointed sphere of operations, or at least to when he began operating effectively in his new position. This does not seem likely: everything we know about him shows him to have been an ambitious

C.15b   Pylos (in Messenia): Ref. Map 3, DX.
C.15c   For an explanation of the relationship among the works of Diodorus, Ephoros, and P, the Oxyrhynchus Historian, see the Introduction, §7.1–8.
C.16a   See the Table of Rival Theories of the Chronology of the Ionian War at the end of this appen-

dix, where the Missing Spring is clearly identified as the spring of 410 in the low chronology and variously as the spring of 407, 407, and 408 in the high chronologies.
C.16b   Caria: Ref. Map 2, CZ.

young man eager to make his mark on events. Making the Missing Spring that of 408 and putting it at 1.3.14 requires Pharnabazos to delay Euryptolemos' embassy for a year before Cyrus appears on the scene, a delay for which no motivation is given (unlike the further delay after Cyrus arrives). These Persian-related delays seem much more difficult to explain than the Athenians' comparative inaction in 410–09 on the low chronology (explained by lack of funds) and constitute the chief problem with the high chronologies.

§18. According to all three high chronologies, the early summer of 1.2.1 in which Thrasyllos took an Athenian fleet to Ionia[a] is the summer of 410, the last quarter of the Athenian archon year 411/10. But the usually accurate late-first-century scholar Dionysius of Halicarnassus puts Thrasyllos' departure for Ionia in the year in which Glaukippos was archon at Athens, and that is the next year, 410/9.[b] However, it has been suggested that the mention of early summer in 1.2.1 is yet another interpolation. If so, Thrasyllos could have set out in late summer 410, and there would be no contradiction between the high chronology and Dionysius. But this theory involves the invention of facts by the interpolator and not just the addition and misplacement of material from handbooks, so it is not attractive. Still, the idea of some kind of slip by Dionysius, though uncomfortable, is not impossible.

§19. It is something of a squeeze to fit in before the early summer of 410 all the events that Xenophon says or implies happened before Thrasyllos arrived in Ionia. Xenophon says that the Syracusans burned their ships (1.1.18) after the battle of Cyzicus, which seems to have been right at the end of the winter, and shortly afterward (1.1.24–25) began to build new ones. It seems from 1.2.8 that they had completed the task and moved on to Ephesus by the time Thrasyllos arrived there, and they must have worked hard to get them done then, if that was in early summer of the same year. But admittedly Xenophon implies that they did indeed work hard.

§20. Of the board of Athenian generals elected after the battle of Notion (1.5.16), one died in summer 406,[a] and another was captured; the remaining eight generals are attested as being in command at the time of Arginousai (1.7.1–2) For the low chronology and two of the high chronologies, this is no surprise, since according to them we are talking of one and the same board. But on the high chronology that puts the Missing Spring at 1.5.11, just after the battle of Notion, there is a gap of over a year between 1.5.16 and the battle of Arginousai, and so it requires that two boards of generals were elected in successive years with an overlap of at least eight names. Such a degree of overlap in successive elections is not attested elsewhere and is sometimes said to be impossible. But that is to put the matter too strongly: quite a few of the Athenian elite were in exile at this point, and if the Athenians were still angry with Alcibiades and his closest supporters, the pool of acceptable candidates was not as large as usual.

§21. At first sight, it looks as though we could be helped with our chronological problem by the fact that Xenophon seems to tell us about six different Spartan

C.18a   Ionia: Ref. Map 2, CY.
C.18b   Dionysius of Halicarnassus, *Hypothesis to Lysias'*
          Speech 32.
C.20a   Lysias 21.8.

navarchs (admirals of the fleet) over these years (Mindaros, Pasippidas, Kratesippidas, Lysander, Kallikratidas, and Arakos). We know that each navarch's term of office in principle lasted no longer than a year, and we further know from Thucydides[a] that earlier in the Peloponnesian War their term of office started in the autumn. From this one might think that where Xenophon mentions a navarch, that reference could be used to place the surrounding narrative in its correct year. However, this turns out to be a further area of difficulty. There is some doubt as to whether Pasippidas actually held the office of navarch; even if he did, since at some point he was disgraced, it could be that his navarchy was brought to a premature conclusion and the term of his successor started early. To add to the confusion, it has been suggested that after 410 navarchs' terms of office as a rule started in the spring so as to correlate with the start of the sailing season (though there is some evidence, which in my view has not been adequately explained away, that at least in 400 the changeover was in the autumn).

§22. It is chilling to note that the ancient commentator on Aristophanes' play *Frogs* (line 1422) tells us of a disagreement between Xenophon and a near contemporary Athenian annalist, Androtion, regarding a chronological point during this phase of the war (the archon year of "Alcibiades' return," a phrase that is itself arguably ambiguous between his "return to Athens" and his "return to exile," and therefore slippery to use to support one or other of the competing chronologies). Although the likeliest explanation is that the ancient commentator has been confused by the chronological interpolations into Xenophon's narrative, there remains the grim possibility that the chronology of this period was being contested even within the lifetime of eyewitnesses. The problem is insoluble and will remain so unless further evidence is found, such as a passage of P for this period that comments on or fills in one or other of the odd gaps in activity that each theory at present has to posit. If a choice has to be made, the low chronology seems the better bet, on the basis that the period of inactivity it calls for is less problematic than any of those associated with the various high or mixed theories. This is the choice made by *The Cambridge Ancient History*, whose chronology is taken as the standard in the side notes to this volume.

§23. The four rival theories discussed in this appendix are set out diagrammatically in the table that follows, each as expounded by a particular modern scholar. On some points, the modern discussion does not specify the precise placing of each component in the table, and I have inferred where the component should fit in under the theory in question, so as to make comparison between the four theories easier.

David H. Thomas
Hertfordshire, UK

C.21a   Thucydides 3.16.3, 3.18.5.

Table of Rival Theories of the Chronology of the Ionian War

Date	Low Chronology *CAH/Landmark* *Xenophon's* Hellenika	High Chronology 1 (e.g., Munn)	High Chronology 2 (Robertson)	High Chronology 3 (Pierart)
411	Battle of Abydos	Battle of Abydos	Battle of Abydos	Battle of Abydos
410	Battle of Cyzicus	Battle of Cyzicus	Battle of Cyzicus	Battle of Cyzicus
	Missing Spring (1.1.22)	Spring 1.2.1	Spring 1.2.1	Spring 1.2.1
	Thrasyllos in Athens	Thrasyllos in Athens	Thrasyllos in Athens	Thrasyllos in Athens
	Alcibiades inactive★	Thrasyllos in Ionia	Thrasyllos in Ionia	Thrasyllos in Ionia
409	Spring of 1.2.1	Spring of 1.3.1	Spring of 1.3.1	Spring of 1.3.1
	Alcibiades inactive	Capture of Chalcedon	Capture of Chalcedon	Capture of Chalcedon
		Siege of Byzantium begins	Siege of Byzantium begins	Siege of Byzantium begins
	Thrasyllos in Ionia	Athenian embassy sets out	Athenian embassy sets out	Athenian embassy sets out
	Recapture of Pylos	Capture of Byzantium	Capture of Byzantium	
408	Spring of 1.3.1	Cyrus appointed	Cyrus appointed	
		Spring of 1.4.1	Spring of 1.4.1	**Missing Spring** (1.3.14)
	Capture of Chalcedon	Athenian embassy arrested	Athenian embassy arrested	Athenian embassy held back
	Siege of Byzantium begins	Alcibiades in Caria	Alcibiades in Caria	
Summer		Alcibiades in Athens		
	Athenian embassy sets out	*Slow progress of Cyrus*	*Slow progress of Cyrus*	
	Capture of Byzantium	Alcibiades on Andros		
407	Spring of 1.4.1	**Missing Spring** (1.5.11)	**Missing Spring** (1.4.11)	Spring of 1.4.1
	Cyrus appointed			Cyrus appointed
	Athenian embassy arrested			Capture of Byzantium
	Cyrus arrives	Cyrus arrives	*Slow progress of Cyrus*	Cyrus arrives
	Alcibiades in Caria	Battle of Notion		Alcibiades in Caria
Summer	Alcibiades in Athens		Alcibiades in Athens	Alcibiades in Athens
	Alcibiades on Andros	*Lysander inactive*	Alcibiades on Andros	Alcibiades on Andros
406	Battle of Notion		Battle of Notion	Battle of Notion
	Alcibiades retires		Alcibiades retires	Alcibiades retires
	Spring of 1.6.1	Spring of 1.6.1	Spring of 1.6.1	Spring of 1.6.1
	Kallikratidas campaigns	Kallikratidas campaigns	Kallikratidas campaigns	Kallikratidas campaigns
	Battle of Arginousai	Battle of Arginousai	Battle of Arginousai	Battle of Arginousai
405	Spring of 2.1.10	Spring of 2.1.10	Spring of 2.1.10	Spring of 2.1.10
	Battle of Aigospotamoi	Battle of Aigospotamoi	Battle of Aigospotamoi	Battle of Aigospotamoi

★Italics indicate what is difficult to accept in the various chronological schemes.

Sources for Table

Andrewes, A., in *The Cambridge Ancient History*, vol. 5, 2nd edition (Cambridge: Cambridge University Press, 1992), pp. 503–5.

Munn, M. H., *The School of History* (Berkeley: University of California Press, 2000), pp. 335–9.

Robertson, N., "The Sequence of Events in the Aegean in 408 and 407 B.C.," *Historia* 29 (1980): 282–301.

Pierart, M., *Chios entre Athènes et Sparte. La Contribution des exilés de Chios a l'effort de guerre lacédémonien pendant la Guerre du Péloponnèse. Inscriptiones Graecae* V 1, 1+ (*Supplementum Epigraphicum Graecum* XXXIX 370★), *Bulletin de Correspondance Hellénique* 119 (1995): 253–82, on pp. 276–7.

APPENDIX D

Persia in Xenophon's *Hellenika*

§1. The Persian empire was created in a period of rather more than a half-century during the reigns of Cyrus (c. 557–530), Cambyses (530–522), and Darius I (522–486). The founder, Cyrus, was originally ruler of Anshan, a small kingdom located physically in southwestern Persia and culturally at an intersection of Elamite and Iranian traditions. A succession of campaigns, notably those against Astyages (Media), Croesus (Lydia), and Nabonidus (Babylon)[a] but also others whose details are now lost, gave him control of Anatolia, the Levant, Mesopotamia, and the Iranian plateau. This vast imperial state (already well beyond the scope of any Near Eastern predecessor) was further extended by Cambyses' conquest of Egypt[b] in 525 and Darius' assertions of sovereignty in the Indus Valley and in Thrace and Macedonia[c] during the penultimate decade of the sixth century. From his heartland imperial capitals at Susa,[d] Persepolis, and Ecbatana, the self-styled Great King and King of Kings presided over the *dahyāva* ("lands" or "peoples") listed in various royal inscriptions—a collection of geo-ethnic entities that reflects the pre-Persian political divisions of the landmass and partly (but only partly) corresponds to the system of *nomoi* (tribute-provinces) described in Herodotus' *Histories*, Book 3. From these he extracted tribute and demanded obedience, but in return (at least in the royal representation of things in texts and iconography) he offered protection and enjoyed the cooperative support of his subjects. In the real world, the burden of taxes and the affront to historical identity and independence could provoke rebellion and invite firm and violent repression (notably in Egypt, Babylonia, and even Media)—and that is quite apart from the brief but intense period of instability that surrounded the death of Cambyses and Darius' eventual succession. Between the spin of royal propaganda and the occasional violent disturbance caused by nationalist insurrection or dissidence in the royal family or the wider elite, the empire is most readily characterized by bureaucracy (reflected in documentary archives from various locations) and an absence of active cultural imperialism: against an administrative background whose lower echelons were necessarily ethnically diverse, Persians remain

D.1a   Media and Babylon: Ref. Map 1. Lydia: Ref.
Map 2, CZ.

D.1b   Egypt: Ref. Map 1.

D.1c   Thrace: Ref. Map 2, AY. Macedonia: Ref.
Map 2, AX.

D.1d   Susa: Ref. Map 1.

the dominant group, but they were more interested in enjoying the fruits of empire and jockeying for position among themselves than in pursuing any proactive agenda of changing the character of subject areas.

§2. At least as seen through the lens of Greek historiography, the era of conquest came to an end with the attempts to extend Persian rule to central and southern Greece in the early fifth century. (There is no other comparable lens through which to look—the Greek narrative of Persian imperial history is the only one to survive, and perhaps the only one ever to have been written—but such other sources as we have do nothing at all to contradict this impression.) What we know as the Persian Wars were definitive for the Greek historical experience in the fifth and fourth centuries. They created the conditions for the Athenian empire (which removed Persians from Europe and reclaimed the western fringe of Anatolia), for that empire's eventual demise—a process in which Persian resources played a crucial and probably indispensable role—and for the eventual upshot in the shape of the so-called King's Peace of 387/6:[a] this was a diplomatic instrument that reaffirmed the Great King's control of Asia (thereby reclaiming the disputed western fringe of Anatolia) and confined the hegemonic aspirations of mainland Greek states to the Aegean[b] and the Balkans. This was a remarkable achievement, one secured more by money and manipulation than by deployment of huge military resources. If one is assessing the strength of the fourth-century empire, the achievement does have to be set against the prolonged failure to recover Egypt, which was free of Persian control from c. 404 to 343 and frequently received help from Greeks (albeit mercenary ones) in maintaining that freedom. Nonetheless, the world in which Xenophon wrote *Hellenika* was, for a Greek, one defined by the existence to the east of a great and wealthy power that actually controlled a small part of the Hellenic world and could call some of the shots in the rest of it; and although Panhellenists professed to believe otherwise, few seriously believed that any significant change in this state of affairs was likely to occur anytime soon.

§3. Persia appears in *Hellenika* as a component of Greek history (and Greek history seen in a distinctive focus), not in its own right. Interaction—variously confrontational, collusive, or deceptive—between high-ranking Persian officials and major Greek city-states (and indeed between the officials themselves, some of it hostile[a]) is of central importance to the events covered between the start of the work and 5.1.36. Even so, less than half of that stretch of text (itself only just over half of *Hellenika*) has a Persian component, and in the rest of the work, although the King's Peace (see n. D.5d) defines the context for Greek power politics, Persia almost entirely disappears from the narrative. One exceptional passage (7.1.33–38) takes us to the Persian court, but in general what we see of the empire in *Hellenika* is confined to its northwestern extremity in Asia Minor. Persia's repeated failure to regain control of Egypt (which seceded in the late 400s) is ignored, her troubles with Cyprus[b] are barely mentioned (4.8.24, 5.1.10), and reference to rebellion in Media (1.2.19) and

---

D.2a   In the appendices, dating of events may vary by author from the chronology used in the text of this volume, which follows that of *The Cambridge Ancient History.*

D.2b   Aegean Sea: Ref. Map 2, BX.
D.3a   See 1.5.8, 3.1.3, 3.1.9, 3.2.13, 3.4.26, 4.1.37.
D.3b   Cyprus: Ref. Map 1.

neighboring Kadousia[c] (2.1.13) is entirely incidental.[d] Whatever value *Hellenika* has as a source for Persian history lies primarily in memorable vignettes such as the depiction of the Aeolian satrapy[e] at 3.1.10–28 or the meeting of Pharnabazos, the Persian satrap of Hellespontine Phrygia,[f] and the Spartan king Agesilaos at 4.1.29–40—both of which are part of a sympathetic presentation of Pharnabazos that begins at 1.1.6 and only finally ends with his journey east to marry one of the Persian King's daughters (5.1.28). This presentation may not be wholly objective: the hostility that Xenophon (and others) felt to the neighboring satrap Tissaphernes no doubt contributes to friendly treatment of his rival. But—bearing in mind that there is some ambivalence even in the generally favorable portrayals of two much higher-ranking Persians, Cyrus the Elder in *Cyropaedia* and Cyrus the Younger in *Anabasis*[g]—it may nonetheless be Xenophon's least problematic attempt to convey the idea that the Persians were not necessarily a bad lot; and this does have something, however intangible, to contribute to our understanding of the Achaemenid[h] world order.

§4. The first part of *Hellenika* (down to 2.3.9) deals with the final six years of the Peloponnesian War. Tissaphernes successfully defends Ephesus[a] against Athenian attack (1.2.6–9) but in general cuts the same mysteriously devious figure already familiar from Thucydides' Book 8: we are not invited to take seriously his alternative to Cyrus' strategy[b] for dealing with Athens and Sparta (1.5.8–9). Pharnabazos, by contrast, is a well-intentioned and energetic supporter of Sparta,[c] until forced by Alcibiades' military success to allow the Athenians an opportunity to negotiate directly with the King (1.3.8–14, 1.4.1). This initiative is thwarted by the arrival of Cyrus and the discovery that Spartan diplomats have already made a new accommodation with the King (1.4.2–3). We sense here how difficult it was to fight a conflict far from the center of imperial power. Neither here nor elsewhere does Xenophon provide much support for the view that the King was largely detached from events on the distant periphery of his territory, though he cannot, of course, have managed affairs there on a hands-on basis.[d] We also note that, typically, Xenophon does not describe the precise terms—in particular, those concerning the status of Greeks in Asia Minor—upon which the new accommodation was based. Pharnabazos disappears from the narrative, Tissaphernes is sidelined (1.5.8–9), and Sparta's war with Athens is reinvigorated by the wealth at Cyrus' disposal.[e] The Spartan navarch

D.3c Kadousians: Ref. Map 1.
D.3d In any case, 2.19 may be an interpolation (for interpolations, see Appendix C, Chronological Problems in the Continuation [1.1.1–2.3.10] of Xenophon's *Hellenika*, §5–9). Another interesting probable interpolation is 2.1.8–9, reporting Cyrus' arrogant execution of two of his cousins for breaching a rule of etiquette that properly could only be applied in the presence of the King.
D.3e Aeolis: Ref. Map 2, BY. Xenophon pictures Mania as a "satrap" and calls her province a "satrapy," but he knew that she was a subordinate appointee of Pharnabazos, and the passage provides particularly clear evidence that the terminology (satrap/satrapy) was not confined to the high-ranking viceroys (like Pharnabazos himself) who were responsible for extensive territories and were directly appointed by the Persian King.
D.3f Hellespontine Phrygia: Ref. Map 2, AY.

D.3g Xenophon's *Cyropaedia* and *Anabasis*. See the Introduction, §4.2–3, 5.2, 7, 10.12.
D.3h "Achaemenid" refers to the dynastic family of the Kings of Persia. To learn more about Cyrus the Younger, Pharnabazos, and Tissaphernes, see Appendix M, Brief Biographies of Important Characters in Xenophon's *Hellenika*, §7, 21, and 29, respectively.
D.4a Ephesus: Ref. Map 2, CY.
D.4b Tissaphernes' strategy—supposedly drawn from the advice of Alcibiades—was to keep the Greek states fighting among themselves and prevent any one state from achieving decisive victory (Thucydides 8.46).
D.4c See 1.1.6, 1.1.14, 1.1.24–26, 1.3.5–7.
D.4d On the King's role, see 3.2.20, 3.4.5, 4.8.16, 5.1.31.
D.4e On Cyrus' financial support for Sparta, see 1.5.3–7, 2.1.11, 2.1.14, 2.3.8.

Kallikratidas chafes at the Persian protocol that keeps him hanging around at the door of Cyrus' residence (1.6.6, 1.6.10) and more generally chafes at Sparta's dependence on barbarian help. (Xenophon devotes a lot of space to this theme, though scholars disagree about the extent of his approval of Kallikratidas' stance.) Lysander, by contrast, has no such problems during two tours of duty (the second, at 2.1.7, a legal fiction urged on the Spartans by Cyrus, among others) and in due course inflicts the decisive defeat on the Athenians at Aigospotamoi.[f]

§5. The next phase of Persian involvement in Greek affairs begins with the aftermath of Cyrus' abortive attempt in 401 to dethrone Artaxerxes II (3.1.1–2). Apart from his receipt of Spartan support, nothing is said about the background. Cyrus left Anatolia in 405 because of Darius' illness (2.1.13–14), but the circumstances of his return are unstated (see instead *Anabasis* 1.1.1–8); as a result, no local context is provided for Tissaphernes' crucial demand that the Ionian cities of Asia Minor acknowledge his authority over them, a demand that led to Spartan intervention in defense of Asiatic Greek liberty (3.1.3). Xenophon's version of what followed is indispensable but quirky; a notable example of this quirkiness is that he mentions the failed Spartan-Persian negotiations of 393/2 (4.8.12–16) but not the subsequent abortive diplomatic process of 392/1.[a] The attempt by successive Spartan commanders to neutralize the Persians in western Anatolia[b] was compromised by the outbreak of the Corinthian War in 395 (facilitated by Persian money[c] but not in truth caused by it) and by Sparta's naval defeat at Cnidus[d] in 394. A direct consequence of the defeat at sea was that a Persian (or Greco-Phoenician: see 4.3.12) war fleet visited the waters around Greece for the first time since 480 (4.8.7–11) and Pharnabazos set foot on Peloponnesian soil. Eventually, however, resurgent Athenian ambitions prompted King Artaxerxes to cut a deal with Sparta and underwrite what came to be known as the King's Peace (5.1.31).[e] An important consequence of the peace was the definitive reincorporation of the Asiatic Greeks into the Persian empire. *Hellenika*, however, concentrates on its consequences in mainland Greece, and Persia thereafter appears only in political rhetoric (6.1.22) or in diplomatic negotiations[f] that were effectively part of that mainland narrative and, even so, more rarely than other sources suggest might have been appropriate.

§6. Although Persian material occupies only a quarter of *Hellenika* as a whole, some light is nonetheless thrown on the Persian imperial landscape, both literally and metaphorically.

§7. Sardis[a] and Daskyleion[b] emerge as major centers. The latter's palace, teeming river, well-stocked villages, and so-called "paradises" (a term that embraces not only

D.4f Aigospotamoi (Aigospotamos): Ref. Map 2, AY.
D.5a We know of these negotiations because they are reflected in Andocides 3.33 (*On the Peace with Sparta*).
D.5b See 3.1.3–2.20, 3.4.1–29, 4.1.1–2.8, 4.8.1–22, 4.8.31–39.
D.5c See 3.5.1–2.
D.5d Cnidus: Ref. Map 2, DY. On Sparta's naval defeat, see 4.3.10–12, 4.8.1.
D.5e The King's Peace (387/6) ended the Corinthian War between the Spartans (who had gotten the upper hand thanks to Persian subvention) and her mainland Greek enemies, notably Athens. It was

based on the principle that Asia—including Klazomenai (Ref. Map 2, CY) and Cyprus—belonged to the King, while other Greek cities were to be "autonomous." This suited the King (for obvious reasons) as well as the Spartans, who believed that "autonomy" would weaken their enemies by denying them the chance to create a power base through federal or alliance systems, without compromising Sparta's ability to dominate them.
D.5f See 6.3.12, 7.1.27, 7.1.33–40.
D.7a Sardis: Ref. Map 2, CY. See 1.1.9–10, 1.5.1, 3.4.25, 4.1.27, 4.8.21.
D.7b Daskyleion: Ref. Map 2, AY. See 3.4.13, 4.1.15.

enclosed hunting grounds but also collections of cultivated trees) are evoked (4.1.15, 4.1.33), but Sardis is not described, although the area around the city does provide copious booty for an unopposed Spartan army (3.4.21). Gordion[c] is on the route from Pharnabazos' satrapy (Hellespontine Phrygia) to the center of the empire, but we do not learn exactly where Pharnabazos' party met the Spartan ambassadors in 408/7 nor, therefore, how the route ran beyond Gordion. The route taken by another set of ambassadors at 7.1.33 is also unspecified, as is that of Agesilaos to somewhere in Paphlagonia.[d] (By contrast, at 2.1.13 Xenophon mentions an otherwise unknown place in Media called Thamneria. He seems to lack a consistent interest in geographical exactitude.) Away from the city-states bordering on the Aegean, the empire (alias the "King's territory")[e] can be seen as composed of *ethnē*,[f] some of which are ripe for secession (Paphlagonia: 4.1.3–15), while others have an ambiguous relation to the imperial power (Mysians[g]; Bithynians[h]). The empire also contains "cities" (3.4.12, 4.1.1). A rhetorical claim by Derkylidas (4.8.5) that small Greek communities can maintain independence (against a background of generally effective royal authority) is hard to validate. Other small Greek cities are in the control of descendants of Spartan and Eretrian[i] beneficiaries of the Great King's favor (3.1.6).

§8. Xenophon is not punctilious about administrative geography. We assume that Pharnabazos was the satrap of Hellespontine Phrygia. Translating the Greek literally, Xenophon merely speaks in terms of "Pharnabazos' Phrygia" (3.4.26; see also 3.2.1) or his "land and sphere-of-rule" (3.4.10; see also 4.8.3). Cyrus' position is more fully described in *Anabasis* (1.1.2) than in *Hellenika* (1.4.2–3), though it is *Hellenika* that uses an Iranian term, *karanon*, for one of Cyrus' roles: commander of those who muster at Kastolos. (The *Hellenika* passage glosses the word as *kurios*, or "master." *Anabasis* simply replaces it with *stratēgos*, or "general.") Tissaphernes loses influence when Cyrus arrives (1.5.2, 1.5.8–9), but changes in his official status are not clarified. When he recovers and becomes "satrap of those he previously ruled and of those whom Cyrus ruled as well" (3.1.3), the reader of *Hellenika* cannot quite tell what this means, though as supreme commander (3.2.13)—*stratēgos tōn pantōn* (literally "general of all")—he outranks Pharnabazos.[a] The precise implications of his possession of an estate (*oikos*) in Caria[b] for official authority in that region are a matter of debate. Individuals like Tithraustes, Tiribazos, Ariobarzanes, and Strouthas[c] are mentioned in the narrative and play important roles, but there is no clear identification of their rank or official post. At a lower level Zenis and his wife Mania (Greeks from Dardanos[d]) have "satrapal" authority in Troadic Aeolis,[e]

D.7c Gordion: Ref. Map 1. See 1.4.1.
D.7d Paphlagonia: Ref. Map 1. See 4.1.1–3.
D.7e See 1.1.24, 1.2.17, 3.1.13.
D.7f *Ethnē*: roughly, "nations." Persian royal inscriptions describe the empire as composed of *dahyāva*, a word variously translated as "lands" or "peoples." See 4.1.2, 4.1.21.
D.7g Mysia: Ref. Map 2, BZ. See 3.1.13, 4.1.24.
D.7h Bithynia: Ref. Map 2, AZ. See 3.2.2.
D.7i Eretria: Ref. Map 3, BZ. See 3.1.6.
D.8a Compare 4.1.37, where, after Tissaphernes' death,

Pharnabazos fears that someone else may be appointed "general" over him.
D.8b Caria: Ref. Map 2, CZ. See 3.2.12, 4.12.
D.8c See for Tithraustes, 3.4.25, 3.5.1; for Tiribazos, 4.8.12, 5.1.6, 5.1.28, 5.1.30; for Ariobarzanes, 5.1.28, 7.1.27; for Strouthas, 4.8.17–19.
D.8d Dardanos: Map 3.1.13, AX.
D.8e Troadic Aeolis is Aeolis in the vicinity of Troy (Ilion): Ref. Map 2, BY.

supplying military resources, tribute, and political advice to Pharnabazos, the master (3.1.26) who appointed them (3.1.10–12) and holds them in esteem (3.1.11, 3.1.13). But Spithridates, an exceptionally noble Persian (4.1.6) with two hundred cavalrymen at his disposal (3.4.10), whose quarrel with Pharnabazos is only explained in Xenophon's *Agesilaos*,[f] occupies an unlabeled position within Pharnabazos' satrapy, as do Rathine and the satrap's bastard brother Bagaios (3.4.13). Ariaios, a figure with an interesting past,[g] pops up unexplained at Sardis (4.1.28).

§9. We hear of Persian wealth and luxury;[a] an Arcadian politician describes the King's famous golden plane tree as not big enough to provide shade for a grasshopper (7.1.38), but Cyrus' silver-and-gold throne must have been impressive (1.5.3). In a famous scene Pharnabazos experiences some embarrassment in the presence of Agesilaos' simple dress and behavior (4.1.30). Gifts or acts of generosity are a normal feature of royal and satrapal behavior.[b] Sometimes they shade into bribery or political manipulation; sometimes they fit a context of Greek *xenia*,[c] for personal ties of that sort are possible between Greek and Persian. But even the generally sympathetic Pharnabazos has an entourage of concubines and other influential figures to whom it is prudent to pay court (3.1.10), and it is taken for granted that everyone is equally the king's slave and owes obeisance (*proskunēsis*) to his superiors (4.1.35–36, 6.1.12).

§10. Persian officials sometimes choose to divert or defer fighting,[a] but enough combat occurs to provide an opportunity to learn something of the military aspect of the empire. Unfortunately we get a fairly bland picture, in which the most distinctive feature is repeated reference to cavalry,[b] evidently present in larger numbers than are to be expected in purely Greek contexts—and armed with better weapons (3.4.14). Even so, when unsupported by infantry, the Persian cavalry is vulnerable to a combination of Greek cavalry and hoplites (3.4.23–24). We also hear of scythe-chariots (4.1.17), the use of Greek mercenaries (3.1.13, 3.2.15), and the ad hoc posting of garrison troops in Carian fortresses (3.2.14)—implying the normal absence of such defenses. (Compare the temporary use of armed sailors by Pharnabazos at 1.1.24.) But we are given no clues about how to imagine what the Persian infantry who happened to be present might have looked like, or how they might have been recruited: although they are distinguished from Carian White-Shields and Greek mercenaries, one can hardly even be sure whether the label "Persian" guarantees they are ethnic Iranians. The same goes for other unspecific bodies of infantry[b] and for the "allies" whom Tissaphernes summons up for the defense of Ephesus at 1.2.8. Agesilaos had "barbarians" captured by freebooters

---

D.8f   Pharnabazos had sought to take Spithridates' daughter as a concubine (*Agesilaos* 3.3).

D.8g   Xenophon knew Ariaios well as the lieutenant of Cyrus the Younger during his campaign against his brother Artaxerxes, which Xenophon described in his *Anabasis*. After Cyrus' death, Ariaios gained a pardon from the King, broke his oath of fidelity to the Greeks in the army, and helped Tissaphernes accomplish the arrest of the Greek generals.

D.9a   Persian wealth: 1.1.14, 1.5.3, 2.1.13–14, 6.1.12.

Luxury: 1.5.3, 4.1.30, 7.1.38.

D.9b   See 1.1.9, 1.31, 1.5.6, 2.1.14, 3.1.6, 3.1.10, 3.1.15, 3.4.26, 3.5.1, 4.1.39, 7.1.38.

D.9c   *Xenia*: the formalized relationship between individuals sometimes translated as "guest-friendship." For examples of *xenia* between Greeks and Persians, see 2.1.14, 4.1.29–39.

D.10a   See 1.2.4, 1.2.6, 1.2.16, 3.2.1, 3.2.15, 3.4.12–15, 3.4.21–24, 4.1.18–19, 4.8.18.

D.10b   See 1.1.14, 1.2.6, 3.4.21, 3.4.23.

sold naked to show that they were white-skinned because they never undressed and physically feeble because they spent all their time on vehicles (3.4.19): the message was that Sparta was at war with women, but we are bound to wonder what the actual connection was between these unfortunates and the military forces of the Achaemenid empire.

Christopher Tuplin
Department of Classics and Ancient History
School of Archaeology, Classics and Egyptology
University of Liverpool
Liverpool, UK

APPENDIX E
Spartan Government and Society

Xenophon as Ethnographer of the Spartans

§1. Herodotus visited Sparta (*Histories* 3.55), as Thucydides possibly did too (Thucydides 1.10 seems to presume autopsy). Xenophon not only lived in Sparta for some time but even became a kind of honorary Spartan, thanks to his enduring relationship with Agesilaos.[a] The extent of the resulting pro-Spartan bias in Xenophon's writings is still a matter of some dispute, but there can be no doubting that he wrote as an insider and participant observer. In particular, he wrote as one of those who, in his telling phrase, "wanted what was best for the Peloponnese."[b] It could have been said of him, as it was of the Athenian Kimon,[c] that his very soul was Peloponnesian. With his generally conservative, pro-oligarchic political attitudes he combined a specific virulent distaste for Thebes:[d] that is, for the moderately democratic and anti-Spartan Thebes that undid all Sparta's and Agesilaos' good work (as Xenophon saw it) by defeating Sparta at Leuctra[e] and establishing a hegemony of mainland Greece between 370 and 362 during which Thebes oversaw the liberation of the Messenian helots[f] and the establishment of an Arcadian[g] Federation with a brand-new, anti-Spartan capital city of Megalopolis.[h]

§2. Xenophon's account—or, rather, his several reinforcing but not quite identical accounts—of Sparta and Spartans may be found in the *Hellenika*, his general history of Greece from 411 to 362 (best translated as "A History of My Times," since it is not in fact a general Hellenic history), and in two specialist essays, the *Constitution of the Lacedaemonians* (*Lakedaimoniōn Politeia*) and the quasi-biographical encomium the *Agesilaos*, the twin fruits of his privileged inside information. Xenophon was not as great a master of narrative exposition as either Herodotus or Thucydides, but the limpidity of his style masks a sophistication that requires his text to be read between as well as on the lines. He was not afraid to criticize Sparta when he felt that criticism was obligatory, especially in matters of religion. On the other hand, his devotion to the aristocratic ideal of *philetairia*[a] clouded his

E.1a See the Introduction, §4.3, and Appendix G, Agesilaos, §1.
E.1b Peloponnese: Ref. Map 2, CW. See 7.4.35, 7.5.1.
E.1c Stesimbrotus, quoted in Plutarch, *Parallel Lives*, "Kimon" 4.4–5.
E.1d Thebes: Ref. Map 2, CX.
E.1e Leuctra: Ref. Map 3, BY. See Appendix F, The Spartan Army (and the Battle of Leuctra), §11–12.
E.1f Messenia: Ref. Map 3, DX. Messenian helots: see §11–12 below.
E.1g Arcadia: Ref. Map 3, CX.
E.1h Megalopolis: Ref. Map 3, CX.
E.2a *Philetairia*: love of one's comrades.

judgment of Agesilaos, and hence, since Agesilaos was the most powerful Spartan of his day, of Sparta, too.

§3. At 5.4.1 Xenophon illustrates his own religious "hand of god" interpretation of human history—so much closer to Herodotus than to Thucydides—with a Spartan exemplum. In 382, by invading, occupying, and garrisoning Thebes, the Spartans had broken the oath they had sworn, under the terms of the first Common Peace of 386,[a] to respect the autonomy of all states great and small. Sparta's defeat by Thebes at Leuctra in 371 is interpreted by Xenophon, writing prospectively in a context of 379, as divine retribution for that sacrilege. That, for him, was a sufficient explanation of Sparta's consequent decline and fall as a great power.

§4. Occasionally, it is possible to set side by side Xenophon's accounts of Spartan history in the *Hellenika*, where Agesilaos is its protagonist, and the relevant narrative portions in the opening chapters of the *Agesilaos*. In one instance, Agesilaos' coercion of Sparta's recalcitrant Peloponnesian League ally Phleious[a] in 381–379, the comparison is peculiarly revealing. In the *Hellenika* (5.3.16) Xenophon honestly relates that "many" Spartans openly complained that for the sake of a few men they were making themselves hated by a city—actually, a democratically governed city—of more than five thousand (more than twice the size of the Spartan citizen body). But in the *Agesilaos* (2.21), an encomium, the grounds for the unhappy Spartans' complaint against Agesilaos are tacitly suppressed, and instead Xenophon praises Agesilaos for his *philetairia*, that is, his devotion to his (oligarchic) comrades in Phleious. There seems indeed to be something of a schizophrenic dichotomy in Xenophon's approach: even where Agesilaos is manifestly responsible for impolitic or even sacrilegious acts, he is shielded by his faithful friend from explicit blame for them.

§5. There is no good reason to disbelieve that Xenophon admired Sparta in principle, both as a polity and as a society. If we may trust a much later biographical source,[a] Xenophon so far endorsed the Spartan educational system that, at the suggestion of Agesilaos, he put his own two sons through the grueling Spartan system of state education (§20). Yet the real Sparta, as opposed to the idealized Sparta of his dreams, in the end disappointed him dreadfully. Toward the close of the *Constitution of the Lacedaemonians* comes a sad chapter (Chapter 14) that was probably intended as the work's conclusion (it is misplaced in the manuscript tradition). This dwells on the perceived gap between the "Lykurgan" Sparta (see §6) that he has hitherto lovingly described and the Sparta of "the present time," which is most easily taken to be the post-Leuctra 360s or early 350s.[b] After detailing a number of the present-day Spartans' grosser delicts, the chapter concludes: "Plainly they obey neither Heaven nor the laws of Lykurgos."

E.3a Also known as the King's Peace (see 5.1.31–36) and called by some the Peace of Antalkidas. For Antalkidas, see Appendix M, Brief Biographies of Important Characters in Xenophon's *Hellenika*, §4.

E.4a Phleious: Ref. Map 3, CY.

E.5a Diogenes Laertius (third century C.E.), *Lives and Opinions of the Eminent Philosophers* 2.54.

E.5b There is a wide range of opinions about the date of the *Constitution of the Lacedaemonians*; a different view is taken in the Introduction, §5.2.

Lykurgos

§6. Xenophon has no occasion to mention Lykurgos in the *Hellenika*. But in the *Constitution of the Lacedaemonians* he places all Sparta's laws and customs under the sign of reforms proposed by Lykurgos and religiously sanctioned by Apollo of Delphi. Herodotus, too, ascribes most of Sparta's basic political and military institutions to the reforms of the famed lawgiver (*Histories* 1.65). But he, like Thucydides (1.18), believes that before achieving stable reforms Sparta endured a period of extreme instability, lawlessness, and civil strife. Xenophon, however, places Lykurgos' reforms much earlier, contemporary with the very foundation of Sparta by the returning descendants of Herakles. Nor would Xenophon have countenanced the critical line later taken by Aristotle, who, in his *Politics* (1269–71), found the very basis (*hupothesis*) of the constitution (*politeia*) as laid down by "the lawgiver" to be fundamentally flawed. Aristotle indeed seems to have aimed his several major criticisms of Sparta against precisely the sort of encomium that Xenophon's *Constitution of the Lacedaemonians* for the most part delivers.

The Names for the Spartans, the City of Sparta, and Its Territory

§7. The strict technical term for Spartan citizens of full status was Spartiatai,[a] or Spartiates. They were also known as *homoioi*,[b] which literally means "same-ish," that is, identical in one or more respects but not in all; the English *peers* best captures the nuance of a term that is classically Spartan in both being and not being egalitarian. Xenophon uniquely (at *Hellenika* 3.3.6) preserves the correlative term *hypomeiones* ("inferiors") for those Spartans who were of sub-*homoioi* status. But Xenophon, like other authors, more usually calls them Lakedaimōnioi, which could have either a geographical or a political connotation. In the political sense (for example, at 5.3.16) it meant the full citizens of Sparta—as did Spartiatai and *homoioi*. In the geographical sense it meant the inhabitants of Lakedaimōn, denoting the entire territory of the Spartan state, for which both Lakonikē (Herodotus, *Histories* 1.69, 6.58, 7.235) and "*gē* of the Lakedaimōnioi" (*gē* meaning "land"; *Histories* 7.158.2) were alternative usages. Rather confusingly, Lakedaimōn could also be used when referring to events in the city (or, more accurately, "town")[c] of Sparta, which was properly called Spartē.[d] (Lakōn, feminine Lakaina, was an alternative form. It is from *lakōnikos*, the adjectival form of *lakōn*, that we get our word *laconic*.)

§8. The civic territory of Sparta consisted of pretty much all the southern portion of the Peloponnese, some 8,000 square kilometers (3,000 square miles) altogether; this made Sparta easily the largest city-state in the entire ancient Greek world, more than double the size of the next biggest, that of Syracuse in Sicily.[a] It

E.7a The term is found in *Hellenika* at 3.3.5–6, 3.4.2, 4.3.23, 5.1.11, 5.3.8, 5.4.39, 6.4.15, 6.5.21, 6.5.25, 7.4.27, 7.5.10. See also Herodotus, *Histories* 1.65.2, among many other mentions, and Thucydides 1.128.3.

E.7b *Homoioi* is found in *Hellenika* only at 3.3.5; it is used also in Xenophon's *Constitution of the Lacedaemonians* (10.7, 13.1, 13.7) and *Anabasis* (4.6.14).

E.7c Lakedaimōn as "town" of Sparta: 2.2.12, 3.2.20, 3.3.1, 4.2.12, 6.1.3, 6.4.16, 6.5.23.

E.7d *Spartē*: 2.3.1, 7.1.28, 7.1.32, 7.2.3, 7.5.9. The corresponding anglicized terms used in this Landmark edition are Spartiate (for full-status citizens); Laconia, Laconian, Laconians; Lacedaemon, Lacedaemonian, Lacedaemonians; and Sparta, Spartan, Spartans.

E.8a Syracuse (in Sicily): Ref. Map 1.

may be divided into two roughly equal halves separated by the Taygetos mountain range[b] (rising to 2,404 meters, or more than 8,000 feet). To the west lies Messenia,[ᵉ] the ancient as well as modern term. To the east, where the town of Sparta lies in the valley of the Eurotas River,[c] is the region known for convenience as Laconia[d] (in origin a late Roman, not a classical Greek, name).

Other Inhabitants of Lakedaimōn:
Sub-Spartiates, *Perioikoi*, and Helots

§9. The problem with the term Lakedaimōnioi, for us rather than for the ancients, is that it could also encompass inhabitants of Lakedaimōn who were not full citizens of Sparta. One passage of the *Hellenika* (3.3.3–11), describing the alleged conspiracy of Kinadon in c. 400, presents in unique detail a conspectus of all these sub-Spartiate Lacedaemonians: *hypomeiones, perioikoi,* helots, and *neodamōdeis.* We shall deal below with *perioikoi* (§10), helots (§11–12), and *neodamōdeis* (§12). The *hypomeiones,* uniquely named by Xenophon (3.3.6), remain a bit of a puzzle. Kinadon, the alleged conspiratorial ringleader, seems to have been an ex-Spartiate, demoted for economic rather than military or other political reasons. He appears to have been born and brought up a Spartiate but presumably found himself unable to pay his mess dues (§20) and, though perhaps initially willing as well as able to be a good citizen, was thereby technically disqualified from the benefits as well as burdens of full Spartiate status. One further category of—temporary—residents is worth noticing here, that of the *trophimoi xenoi* (5.3.9). These were literally "nurtured foreigners," that is, sons sent by their pro-Spartan fathers from other communities (who "wanted what was best for the Peloponnese," §1) to Sparta to be raised with the sons of Spartiates and go through the Spartan educational system, as Xenophon's own two sons may have (§5).

§10. There were perhaps as many as eighty communities of *perioikoi*, situated on the periphery of the two great riverine valleys of Laconia and Messenia and all around the very long, indented coastline. Referred to as *poleis,* they enjoyed some form of local autonomy but had no rights or privileges at Sparta. The *perioikoi* performed crucial economic and military functions for their Spartan overlords. Since the Spartans themselves were debarred from economic enterprise, the *perioikoi* were the Spartans' traders and manufacturers. Militarily, the *perioikoi* both functioned as Sparta's first line of defense along the city's extensive borders against any attack from outside and increasingly made up for the dwindling numbers of Spartiates in the hoplite ranks (§19); from about the mid-fifth century they were actually brigaded in the same regiments with the Spartiates. Internally, they acted as Sparta's early-warning system and on-the-spot defense forces against domestic helot rebellion.[ᵃ] The Kinadon-conspiracy passage (§9) alleges that (all) *perioikoi* could not conceal their desire to eat the Spartiates raw,[b] but that is surely a huge exaggeration. Most *perioikoi* most of the time were contented with their lot: as free, though not

E.8b   Mount Taygetos, the north-south mountain range lying just to the west of Sparta: Ref. Map 3, DX.
E.8c   Eurotas River: Ref. Map 3, DX.
E.8d   Laconia: Ref. Map 2, DX.
E.10a See Appendix F, §4.
E.10b For this fierce statement, see 3.3.6.

enfranchised, members of the most powerful state in the Greek world, some of whom might even rise to positions of responsibility and eminence. However, during the winter of discontent in 370/69, when the Thebans and their allies invaded Laconia in massive force, it was not only the helots of Messenia but also "many of the *perioikoi*" (especially those of northern Laconia) who revolted from Sparta (7.2.2).

§11. Apart from the status and behavior of women (§22), the other great social oddity of Sparta was the helots (*heilōtai*, probably meaning "captives"). These were local Greek natives inhabiting both Laconia and Messenia on either side of the Taygetos range. The Spartans eventually reduced them over a period of perhaps a century or more (c. 735–600) to a serflike status, to which the usual Greek word meaning "slave" (*doulos*) was somewhat inexactly applied. For example, in the treaty of alliance between Sparta and Athens concluded in 421 and supposed to last for fifty years, the helots are specifically referred to collectively as "the slave class."[a] The helots, especially those of Messenia, were always a hot property, hard either to suppress or to incorporate smoothly into the Spartan machine. Annually, the ephors (§16) declared war on the helots, thus transforming the enemy within into enemies of state who might be killed with impunity and without incurring the ritual pollution of murder; it was under the auspices of this declaration that the Krypteia (§20) operated. The development of Sparta as a peculiarly military society was necessitated as much as anything by the helots. The Spartans exploited the helots' forced labor for a number of purposes, above all for agriculture in the exceptionally fertile riverine plains of the Eurotas and Pamisos[b] valleys. The annual produce was delivered to the individual Spartiates to whose land the helots were specifically and presumably hereditarily attached, and it was from this produce that the Spartiates paid their mess dues.[c]

§12. Xenophon treats the helots in a number of ways. They, too, feature in his Kinadon story as cannibalistically inclined enemies of the Spartiate class. This is much more historically plausible. In the 460s both the Messenian and the Laconian helots had revolted, exploiting the great earthquake of c. 464. It had taken at least five years to suppress that revolt (in which two Messenian *perioikic poleis* also participated), and even then the Spartans were forced to allow a certain number of the helot rebels to go free from Messenia, whereafter they established themselves in a new settlement just across the Corinthian Gulf from the Peloponnese at Naupactus.[a] Understandably, therefore, the clause of the treaty with Athens of 421 in which the helots were specifically mentioned (§11) provided that the Athenians must come to the aid of the Spartans "should the slave class revolt." Actually, the Athenians promoted helot defection in both Laconia and Messenia by holding on to a fortified position at Pylos (Koryphasion)[b] until 409 (1.2.18). It is a telling comment on Xenophon's lack of objectivity that when the helots of Messenia did again revolt en masse in 370/69, and with total success, he could not bring himself to record that revolt in its proper chronological place (that would have been at 6.5.28, but it is not

E.11a *Douleia*: see Thucydides 5.23.3.
E.11b Pamisos River: Ref. Map 3, DX.
E.11c See Appendix F, §3, for the importance of paying
       mess dues.

E.12a Naupactus: Ref. Map 3, BX.
E.12b Pylos (Koryphasion), Messenia: Ref. Map 3, DX.
       Koryphasion was the Spartan name for Pylos.

referred to until 7.2.2), any more than he could bear to refer to the newly founded—or resurrected, as the ex-helots saw it—*polis* of Messene on Mount Ithome[c] until well after the event (7.4.27). That was a form of autonomy that Xenophon could abide no more than could his hero Agesilaos. Being a helot was a hereditary status, but it was not necessarily a life sentence, even for nonrebels. Beginning in the 420s, during the first phase of the Peloponnesian War, the Spartans dangled the carrot by liberating some thousands of helots (but at the same time wielded the big stick by carrying out an exemplary massacre of two thousand of the most spirited who applied for freedom and so were considered most likely to revolt in the future).[d] The most favored category of these liberated ex-helots was called *neodamōdeis*—not quite "new citizens," but new men with some of the privileges of full members of the Spartan *damos* ("people").[e] It is therefore highly implausible that, as Xenophon's Kinadon-conspiracy passage alleges, (all) *neodamōdeis* could not conceal their desire to eat the Spartiates raw.

Political System

§13. As a military society,[a] Sparta predictably ordered its political arrangements from the top down. At the very pinnacle of the hierarchy were the two kings, each from a different aristocratic house and claiming divine descent ultimately from Zeus via Herakles and his descendants Agis and Eurypon.[b] (For their religious functions, see §21.) The kings' special privileges included lavish funeral rituals that were the very opposite of the austerely restrained burial practices prescribed for nonroyal Spartans. For Herodotus,[c] they recalled "barbarian" (Egyptian, Scythian) rather than normal Greek funerary customs, but Xenophon went further, describing the funeral rites of Agis II in c. 400 as "greater than could have been expected for an ordinary mortal human" (3.3.1). The importance and the oddity of the Spartan kingship are further brought out by Xenophon's dwelling on the succession crisis that followed Agis' death (3.3.1–4). In Herodotus, rivalry and antagonism between the two kings are presented as a normal state of affairs. That was certainly the case with first Pausanias and Agis II (3.5.25), then Pausanias and Agesilaos (5.2.3), and finally Agesilaos and Kleombrotos (5.4.25); but Xenophon also reveals how in exceptional cases, as between Agesilaos and his much younger co-king Agesipolis, the relationship might be one of relative amity (5.3.20). The two kings automatically shared the elite dining mess known as the public tent (*damosia*); the literal translation of the phrase at 4.5.8 that appears as "headquarters staff" is "the men around the public tent."[d]

§14. Not all the details of the kings' powers are absolutely clear. For example, Thucydides (1.20.3) perhaps unfairly accused Herodotus (without actually naming him) of foolishly believing that kings had two votes each in the Gerousia (§15), whereas in fact they had only one. It is anomalous that the kings allegedly appointed

E.12c Messene and Mount Ithome: Ref. Map 3, DX.
E.12d Thucydides 4.80.
E.12e See Appendix F, §6.
E.13a See Appendix F, §3, for the importance of paying mess dues.
E.13b After these ancestors the kings from one family

(including Agesilaos) were called Eurypontids, and those from the other family were called Agiads.
E.13c Herodotus, *Histories* 6.52.
E.13d See also 5.4.28, where *philition* is translated as "mess hall."

the citizens of Sparta who would act as the diplomatic representatives (*proxenoi*) of other Greek cities, whereas normally it was the prerogative of the partner city itself to make the choice.[a] Moreover, when Herodotus says that it was the kings' prerogative to declare and wage war on whomever they wished,[b] he may perhaps be preserving an older state of affairs, for it is clear from Thucydides and Xenophon that in practice the Spartan Assembly (§17) would have to vote affirmatively for war for it to become official. Besides, the law permitting only one king at a time to command any Spartan or allied army or force (for example, Agis at Dekeleia[c]) was passed as recently c. 505 and is mentioned by Herodotus himself.[d] Technically, formally, the powers of the kings were circumscribed: in his *Constitution of the Lacedaemonians* (15.7) Xenophon describes the monthly exchange of oaths (presumably sworn at the monthly meeting of the Assembly) whereby the ephors (§16) swore on behalf of the city of Sparta to keep the position of the kings unshaken so long as the kings abided by their oath to rule according to the city's established laws. Even when commanding an army abroad, a king had to be accompanied by two ephors (2.4.36) and might have a special supervisory board attached to him, too (3.4.2, 3.4.8), like the board of thirty attached to Agesilaos in Asia. But in practice, as the career of the nonpareil Agesilaos shows, it was possible for an astute king to exploit his charisma, wealth, and connections (see especially 5.4.28 for the stream of petitioners, foreigners, and slaves, as well as Spartan citizens, that Agesilaos might regularly deal with) to become the leading man in the state.

§15. The Gerousia (3.3.5) was a tiny permanent body of thirty senior citizens. Besides the two kings, who were members by birthright, the other twenty-eight were elected by the Spartan citizenry as a whole, and elected for life. The odd election procedure, of competitive shouts by the Assembly, is described by Plutarch (*Parallel Lives*, "Lykurgos" 26.2); Aristotle considered it "childish" (*Politics* 2, 1270b, 1271a). Candidates had to be over sixty, that is, beyond the age of military service, and probably also had to be members of those aristocratic families, including those of the two kings, that called themselves collectively "descendants of Herakles" (Herakleidai). This political empowerment of the old reflected the Spartans' general reverence for the principle of seniority (see, for example, 5.3.20). The Gerousia acted as a probouleutic (predeliberative) body for the Assembly and also functioned as Sparta's supreme court of justice. Even Spartan kings might be tried before the Gerousia (3.5.25), on which occasions it would probably be joined by the members of the Board of Ephors (§16). Voting in such cases was open, each judge having one vote, but trials took place in camera. There were no truly popular courts in Sparta, as there were in democratic Athens. Presumably, except in the cases where it acted as a supreme court, the Gerousia would aim to operate by consensus rather than by formally registering votes. Thanks to the authority of the Gerousia, Sparta may properly be labeled a gerontocracy.

§16. The Board of Five Ephors (*ephor* means "overseer" or "supervisor") was

E.14a   Herodotus, *Histories* 6.57.
E.14b   Ibid. 6.56.
E.14c   Dekeleia: Ref. Map 3, BZ. Agis commanded a
            Spartan army that occupied and fortified
            Dekeleia in Attica during the final years of the
            Peloponnesian War (see Thucydides 7.19; see also

Hellenika 2.2.7, 5.3.10).
E.14d   Herodotus, *Histories* 5.75.

elected by the Assembly (§17). All Spartan citizens were eligible for election, which was conducted according to the same "childish" procedure as elections for the Gerousia (§15). Even quite poor Spartans might stand and be elected. But election was for one year only, and reelection was banned, so ephors might be very powerful for their year in office but unheard of before or after. The board constituted the effective day-to-day government of Sparta (implied by Kritias at 2.3.34). One of the five, the so-called eponymous ephor, gave his name to the Spartan civil year (for example, see 1.3.1, 1.6.1). Among their many powers, the ephors supervised a king's behavior (§14), even in the most intimate matter of dynastic marriage,[a] and it was their responsibility to make a preliminary decision (*anakrisis*) by majority agreement as to whether or not a king should be required to stand trial. Internal factionalism, which was endemic, might encourage or require them to take sides, as a majority did in favor of King Pausanias in 403 (2.4.28–29) and as most boards did in favor of Agesilaos during his exceptionally long reign (see, for example, 5.2.9, 5.4.14). Besides supervising the kings, ephors were also responsible in wartime for military mobilization[b] and for transmitting instructions to both army and naval commanders in the field,[c] and in peacetime for the conduct of the unique state education system known as the Agōgē (§20).

§17. The Assembly (Ekklēsia) consisted of all Spartiates, or *homoioi* (§7): citizens in good standing, that is, adult males of legitimate Spartan birth on both sides aged twenty or over who had passed successfully through the compulsory educational system and been duly elected members of a mess (§20). The name Ekklēsia is confirmed by implication by the unique reference at 3.3.8 to "the so-called Little Ekklēsia"; there is no point in titling one kind of assembly a "little" one "so-called" unless there exists a big one (but not so called). This principal, regular Spartan Assembly met statutorily once a month on the feast day of Apollo but could be summoned when needed to extraordinary sessions (as at Herodotus, *Histories* 7.134.2, where the Assembly is given the generic name *haliē*, or "gathering"). Meetings were presided over by the eponymous ephor, who would invite only selected individuals to speak—members of the Gerousia, the four other current ephors, and perhaps other senior officeholders or ex-officeholders. The matter would then be put to the popular vote of the Assembly, which would be registered in the usual Spartan way by shouting (Thucydides 1.87.2). The result depended on the presiding ephor's judgment as to which shout—for or against the motion—had been the louder, or, in the case of uncertainty, a formal division could be held (Thucydides 1.87); but scope for manipulation seems blatant. The Assembly decided mainly matters of peace and war (for example, war against the Acarnanians[a] on behalf of the Achaeans[b] in 389; 4.6.3). Occasionally, legislation was required (Herodotus, *Histories* 5.75; §14), by a complicated procedure whose details are again hugely disputed among scholars. According to what I consider the most probable reconstruction, any such new legis-

E.16a   Herodotus, *Histories* 5.39–41.
E.16b   See 4.6.3, 4.8.32, 5.1.33, 5.2.24, 5.4.14.
E.16c   See 3.2.6, 5.1.1.
E.17a   Acarnania: Ref. Map 3, AW.
E.17b   Achaea: Ref. Map 3, BX.

lation would have had to originate within the elite Gerousia and/or the Board of Ephors. If a proposal commanded majority support in the Gerousia, a motion would then be put by the presiding ephor before a meeting of the Assembly for its final decision.

The Peloponnesian League and the Spartan Empire

§18. Herodotus (*Histories* 1.68) believed anachronistically that as early as 550 the Spartans had already brought most of the Peloponnese under their control. In fact, that degree of control was achieved only by the establishment of Sparta's Peloponnesian League alliance around 500.[a] Yet, despite this modern term, the league never included all Peloponnesian cities—most notably not Argos,[b] always a rival for Peloponnesian hegemony (see 4.7). On the other hand, the alliance also extended well outside the Peloponnese, eventually as far as Olynthos.[c] The alliance was devised and led by Sparta as a privileged system of separate offensive and defensive military treaties between itself and the other member states. Allies swore to have the same friends and enemies as the Spartans and to follow wherever the Spartans might lead them. In return, the allies were granted a formal right of approval or collective veto of Spartan wishes, to be exercised at congresses held in Sparta (5.2.11–24, in 382). But the alliance mainly benefited Sparta, which gained for itself protection against hostile invasion and whose relatively few citizen hoplites were enlarged into an allied army of formidable proportions. One propaganda claim that Sparta seems regularly to have used in order to legitimate her leadership was an alleged principled opposition to tyrannies or one-man dictatorships,[d] but in the fifth and fourth centuries the alliance was more often used against democracies, such as those of Mantineia[e] and Phleious,[f] and in favor of narrow regimes of pro-Spartan oligarchs, such as the dekarchies (ten-man juntas) favored especially by Lysander (3.5.13, n. 3.15.13a). As such, the Peloponnesian League became a key instrument of Spartan imperialism, though not without putting such strain on the alliance's resources of manpower and goodwill that in 382 Sparta was forced to allow allies who wished to commute their required contribution of troops to a payment in cash (5.2.21).

§19. "Thus it appeared that now at last Sparta's empire [*arkhē*] had been firmly established."[a] Thus does Xenophon comment, with great dramatic irony, on Sparta's position of power in mainland Greece generally in 379, just before it began to unravel, thanks to the Thebans en route to its demise on the field of Leuctra in 371 (5.4.1, 5.4.46). The point about "now at last" is that Sparta had showed grand imperialist ambition since defeating the Athenians in 404 and then attempting to step into their shoes as the great imperial power of the eastern Mediterranean.[b] At the peak of their ambition they had dispatched governors called harmosts far and

E.18a In *Hellenika*, the Peloponnesian League alliance is mentioned at 4.5.18, 5.2.7, 5.2.11, 5.2.20, 5.2.32, 5.3.26, 5.4.36–7, 5.4.46, 5.4.60.
E.18b Argos: Ref. Map 2, CX.
E.18c Olynthos: Ref. Map 2, AX. See 5.3.26, 5.2.11–24.
E.18d Herodotus, *Histories* 5.92α.2.
E.18e Mantineia: Ref. Map 3, CX. See 5.2.7, 4.5.18.

E.18f Phleious: Ref. Map 3, CY. See 5.3.8–17.
E.19a This is Paul Cartledge's own translation of the passage at 5.3.27. John Marincola's translation of it in *The Landmark Xenophon's Hellenika* reads: "In every way it seemed that Sparta had arranged her rule to be strong and secure."
E.19b Mediterranean Sea: Ref. Map 1.

wide in the Aegean[c] (4.2.5) and had even attacked the forces of the Persian empire[d] in pursuit of their declared aim of "liberating" the Greeks of Asia[e] from Persian control. But they had stirred against themselves a powerful coalition of Greek enemies, and by 386 they had decided that discretion was the better part of valor. In return for Persian support of their rule in mainland Greece, the Spartans abandoned the Asiatic Greeks to Persian suzerainty. They made a desert and called it peace, the King's Peace (5.1.36).[f] As early as 376, discontent with Sparta was being expressed by significant numbers of allies (5.4.60), and after Leuctra "some were even pleased at what had happened" (6.4.15). Xenophon wrote despairingly in his *Constitution of the Lacedaemonians* (Chapter 14): "At one time the Spartans would have taken care to ensure that they deserved to occupy the leading position. Nowadays their main preoccupation is just to exercise authority rather than to be worthy of so doing."

Social and Educational System

§20. The civic virtue Xenophon believed the Spartans to have lost was instilled through a unique system of universal and compulsory public education called the Agōgē, or "Upbringing." Xenophon gives a quite detailed account of it in his *Constitution of the Lacedaemonians.*[a] In the *Hellenika* Xenophon refers to it just once, obliquely, as literally "the fine things in the city" (*ta en tēi polei kala,* 5.3.9).[b] Through its carefully defined stages all Spartan boys, except the two heirs-apparent, were required to pass successfully between the ages of seven and eighteen. The military character and purposes of this education (*paideia*) were explicit: above all else, it aimed to instill disciplined obedience to orders, a corporate rather than an individual or even a family identity, and a devotion to the communal good. Aristotle, however, criticized it for turning out men more like wild beasts than civilized human beings. One element that outsiders found particularly odd or even shocking was institutionalized pederasty. After graduating from the Agōgē, at eighteen, a select few adolescents (*paidiskoi,* "boy-ish," between boys and men) embarked on the Krypteia, or "Secret Service"; for up to two years they lived off the land in the wild as isolated individuals, stealing their food and learning extreme survival techniques, including murdering at night with their sole permitted implement, a dagger, any particularly dangerous helots they encountered. At the age of twenty they reentered normal Spartan community and society by being elected to a mess, or small dining group. Full adult Spartan citizenship depended on maintaining one's mess membership by payment of the required monthly dues in agricultural produce. When Agesilaos wanted to support some pro-Spartan oligarchic exiles from democratic Phleious, he encouraged them to form themselves into Spartan-style messes (*sussi-*

E.19c Aegean Sea: Ref. Map 2, BX.
E.19d Persian empire: Map 1.4.9, locator.
E.19e Asia (Asia Minor): Ref. Map 1.
E.19f The King's Peace (The Persian King's Peace), also known as the Peace of Antalkidas (5.1.36).
E.20a See Chapters 2–3; see also in greater detail Plutarch's *Parallel Lives,* "Lykurgos" 16–21,

though there are problems of anachronism there.
E.20b See *Constitution of the Lacedaemonians* 3.3–4.4.

tia, 5.3.17). Competition between Spartiates did not cease with the end of the Agōgē; it was at its fiercest for election to the elite royal bodyguard known as *hippeis*.[c] *Oliganthrōpia* (shortage of manpower), however, increasingly afflicted the Spartan citizen body.[d]

Religion

§21. The Spartans were, as a people and a community, quite exceptionally pious, even superstitious. As Herodotus had put it, they "considered the things of the gods more weighty than the things of men."[a] Xenophon too was highly pious, which was one major reason he admired and valued Spartan society so much, and Agesilaos' piety was one of the supreme virtues for which he eulogized the king.[b] The Spartans earned from Xenophon in his *Constitution of the Lacedaemonians* (13.7, 13.5) the title of "craftsmen of war" not because of their skill in other military departments but because of the minute attention they paid to the conduct of pre-battle sacrifices and other divinatory signs. One peculiarity of the Spartans' general military devotions was the conduct of sacrifices at the crossing of rivers, which seem to have had a special magical potency for them.[c] Spartan kings were themselves priests (and so conducted the *diabatēria* when commanding an army); they maintained close connections with the holiest of all Greek shrines, that of Apollo at Delphi.[d] The perceived importance to Sparta both of Delphi and of military divination is apparent not least from the special grant of Spartan citizenship to the seer Teisamenos of Elis and his brother in order to enable the Spartans (as they saw it) to win five major victories, beginning with Plataea.[e] Regent Pausanias refused to order the Greek advance at Plataea until the sacrificial omens were right.[f] Derkylidas, when commanding in Asia Minor in 399/8, sacrificed again and again on four days running until he got the message he wanted (3.1.17). On several other major occasions—not least the battles of Marathon[g] and Thermopylae[h]—the Spartans put religious obligations before any others. In 390 the Spartans from the village of Amyklai[i] (one of the five villages constituting Sparta town) were sent home from Corinth[j] so they could celebrate the major Hyakinthia festival in honor of Apollo and Hyakinthos (4.5.11).

Women

§22. Last but very much not least, some mention must be made of the women of Sparta, though it has to be said that they are almost as invisible in Xenophon's account as they are visible in that of Herodotus. We do not find in Xenophon the

---

E.20c See 3.35, 3.39, 6.4.14, n. 6.4.14c. For further, see Appendix F, §7.
E.20d See Appendix F, §3.
E.21a Herodotus, *Histories* 5.63.2, 9.7.
E.21b See Appendix G, §4.
E.21c River-crossing sacrifices (*diabatēria*): 5.4.37, 5.4.47, 6.4.19, 6.5.12.

E.21d Herodotus, *Histories* 6.56–7.
E.21e Ibid. 9.35–7, 9.33–5. Plataea: Ref. Map 3, BY.
E.21f Ibid. 9.61–2.
E.21g Marathon: Ref. Map 3, BZ.
E.21h Thermopylae: Ref. Map 3, AX.
E.21i Amyklai: Ref. Map 3, DX.
E.21j Corinth: Ref. Map 3, BY.

sort of historically prominent individuals mentioned by Theopompos,[a] nor the apophthegms attributed to them by Plutarch, nor, on the other side, the grave criticism leveled at the Spartan women collectively by Aristotle (*Politics* 2, 1269b) for their cowardly and confusing conduct in the face (literally) of the invading Thebans in 370/69. The one Spartan woman who is mentioned individually by Xenophon is Kyniska, sister of Agesilaos, but that is in the *Agesilaos* (9.6), not the *Hellenika*, and the point of the mention is to draw an unfavorable contrast between her breeding of racehorses—a sign merely of wealth rather than manly virtue—and her brother's breeding of warhorses. On the other hand, by implication Xenophon praises to the skies the female relatives both of those Spartans who died at Leuctra and of those who did not: the former went about in public with properly cheerful countenances, whereas the latter equally properly skulked away out of sight, mired in shame and humiliation (6.4.16).

> Paul Cartledge
> A. G. Leventis Professor of Greek Culture
> Faculty of Classics
> University of Cambridge
> Cambridge, UK

E.22a Theopompos of Chios (born c. 380) wrote a history of Greece thematically centered on the life of Philip of Macedon, in which two prominent Spartan women (Xenopeitheia and Chryse) who flourished around 370 were executed on the orders of King Agesilaos. The work doesn't survive, but this anecdote is cited by Athenaios (fl. beginning of the third century) in his *Deipnosophistai*, Book XIII.

APPENDIX F
The Spartan Army
(and the Battle of Leuctra)

Army Organization

§1. In his account of the battle of Plataea[a] (479), Herodotus mentions a "Pitanate *lokhos*," or "regiment of Pitana."[b] This is a detail he could have learned from the distinguished Archias,[c] whom he had met in that Spartan village (Herodotus calls it a *dēmos*, but in technical Spartan language it was an *ōba*). Thucydides,[d] however, pours scorn on an unnamed predecessor (meaning Herodotus) who was naive enough to believe that there had once been a Pitanate *lokhos* when in fact none had ever existed. This is most likely because by Thucydides' day there had been a change in Spartan army organization and such a regiment no longer existed. Yet Thucydides, for all his skepticism about uncritically received oral tradition and hearsay testimony, and despite his immense historiographical acumen, seems to have been deceived by the widespread but false view that all Sparta's political and military institutions were of hoary antiquity.[e]

§2. The likeliest historical inference is that a major military reform was enacted sometime between the battle of Plataea and Thucydides' Peloponnesian War (431–404). According to this scenario, the Spartan army of the early fifth century described by Herodotus and based on regiments called *lokhoi* would have been replaced by one based on regiments called *morai* ("divisions"), as described by Xenophon, both in the *Hellenika* and in the *Constitution of the Lacedaemonians*. Xenophon should have known what he was talking about, as he fought as a mercenary with a Spartan army at Coronea[a] in the early fourth century (*Hellenika* 4.3) and clearly spent a great deal of time at Sparta.

§3. The chief reason for such a major organizational reform is not hard to find: namely, the growing shortage or shrinkage of adult Spartan military manpower (what Aristotle was to call *oliganthrōpia*). In 480 there were reportedly some eight thousand Spartan citizens of military age and capacity,[a] but by 371 there were only about one thousand. A major loss of life among young as well as mature Spartans

F.1a Plataea: Ref. Map 3, BY.
F.1b Herodotus, *Histories* 9.53.2.
F.1c Ibid. 3.55.2.
F.1d Thucydides 1.20.3

F.1e Ibid. 1.18.
F.2a Coronea: Ref. Map 3, BY.
F.3a Herodotus, *Histories* 7.234.2.

had been caused in c. 464 by a massive earthquake whose epicenter was near Sparta itself. The Peloponnesian War had also taken its toll of lives. But to these natural and military causes must be added certain social factors, including the increasing concentration of privately owned land in ever fewer and ever richer hands. Spartiate citizen-soldiers were required to feed themselves in their messes from foodstuffs produced by helots on land they themselves owned. Thus the concentration of land ownership directly reduced the number of men able to contribute food to the common messes that were at the basis of the political and military systems.

§4. One vital purpose of the postulated army reform (which I would date to the later 440s, during a brief interlude of peace with Athens) was therefore to compensate for the decrease in the number of frontline citizen-status hoplites. This was achieved by several means, but above all by incorporating selected *perioikoi* into the new mixed "divisions." Within the *perioikic* communities there was clear class differentiation: the wealthier *perioikoi* served the Spartans as either hoplites (3.5.7, 5.2.24, 7.4.27) or cavalrymen (5.4.39), and some even rose to hold positions of command in the fleet. Such service was normally compulsory, but in 380 some of the upper classes (literally *kaloikagathoi*, "fine and good," 5.3.9) among the *perioikoi* volunteered to serve with King Agesipolis at Olynthos,[a] in the far north. It was when *perioikoi* served in Spartan or larger allied armies together with Spartan citizens that they were most naturally called Lacedaemonians. There is no sign that the inclusion of *perioikic* hoplites in what had formerly been exclusively Spartiate regiments had any deleterious effect on Sparta's military capacity or efficiency—rather the opposite, as the battle of Mantineia in 418 proved.[b] *Perioikoi* had been regarded as a necessary complement to Spartan citizen troops since at least the Plataea campaign of 479,[c] when an equal number (five thousand) of *perioikic* hoplites was sent out alongside the Spartiate contingent. But at Mantineia they fought alongside Spartiates in the same divisions, an innovation that eluded Thucydides, who seems to have precisely halved the actual number of Lakedaimōnioi, both Spartiates and *perioikoi* together, who fought there. *Morai* are arguably present on Sphakteria[d] in 425 and turn up at Athens in 403 (2.4.31), at Lechaion[e] in 390, where one is decimated (4.5.11–17); and at Orchomenus in Boeotia,[f] also in 390 (5.1.29).

§5. In both the old army based on *lokhoi* and the new army based on *morai*, regimental commanders were known as polemarchs,[a] which may be part of the explanation for Thucydides' confusion. Polemarchs were automatic members of the kings' "public tent."[b] After the battle of Leuctra[c] (§11–12), however, Xenophon ceases to speak of *morai* and speaks only of *lokhoi* ("battalions": at 7.4.20, "three of the twelve battalions" in Arcadia[d] in 365/4; at 7.5.10, "three of the twelve battalions," again in Arcadia, in 362). So it has been inferred that a further army reform occurred in or after 371 to

F.4a   Olynthos: Ref. Map 2, AX.
F.4b   See Thucydides 5.65–74. Mantineia: Ref. Map 3, CX.
F.4c   Herodotus, *Histories* 9.11.3.
F.4d   Sphakteria, an island off Pylos (Messenia): Ref. Map 3, DX. See Thucydides 4.8.9.
F.4e   Lechaion: Ref. Map 3, BY.
F.4f   Orchomenus (in Boeotia): Ref. Map 3, CX.
F.5a   Two Spartan polemarchs, named Chairon and Thibrakos, were buried honorifically in the

Athenian Kerameikos cemetery (2.4.33; see Figure 2.4.33); one named Praxitas enters the walls of Corinth (4.4.7–9); another, called Gylis, is killed by Locrians after the battle of Coronea (4.3.20–23); and another, who is not named, is mentioned at the Nemea River battle (4.2.22).
F.5b   Xenophon, *Constitution of the Lacedaemonians* 13.1.
F.5c   Leuctra: Ref. Map 3, BY.
F.5d   Arcadia: Ref. Map 3, CX.

take account of the Leuctra losses and of the changed situation of Sparta in relation to the *perioikoi* following the defection and independence of those of Messenia and northern Laconia.[e] This is a possible, but not in my view a necessary, inference.

§6. Helots served individually on campaign as body servants (4.5.14), as light-armed skirmishers (at Plataea),[a] and on two occasions as heavily armed fighters, first in northern Greece under Brasidas in 424[b] and then in Sicily in 413.[c] Another means of increasing Spartan troop numbers was to liberate helots specifically for military service. The ex-helot *neodamōdeis*, above all, were used as garrison troops either on the Spartans' frontiers at home or abroad, as for example at Athens between 404 and 403 (2.3.13–14, 3.4.2).[d] However, *neodamōdeis* troops from Brasidas' expedition served in the line at Mantineia in 418.[e]

Hoplites

§7. Full Spartan citizen soldiers were the crack hoplite (heavily armed infantry) force of the entire Greek world. Their key item of equipment was their heavy, basically wooden round shield, which protected only one side of them (4.5.13), so that it had to be wielded in dense phalanx formation, usually eight ranks deep. The elite of the elite were organized in a unit three hundred strong called the Horsemen (*hippeis*). This name was a vestige of a time when the socially privileged had indeed been mounted troops, but by the late fifth century (some would say as early as the Battle of the Champions,[a] c. 544), they fought on foot and their title had acquired a new, specialized meaning: the Horsemen were the royal bodyguards, selected from those aged twenty to twenty-nine by a rigorously competitive process.[b] They make an appearance on the battlefield at Mantineia[c] in 418 and at Leuctra (6.4.14)[d] and could also be used for special operations, as during the Kinadon conspiracy of c. 400 (3.3.9). A force of three hundred is also mentioned as defending Laconia at the time of the 370/69 Theban-led invasion (6.5.31), but we cannot be certain that they are the *hippeis*.

§8. Sparta also had a true cavalry, raised since 424,[a] but this was very much the inferior service. Agesilaos bred warhorses, but these were strictly for others to ride. At the time of Leuctra, so Xenophon states explicitly, Spartan cavalry was in very bad shape (6.4.10–11). It gets several further mentions (6.5.31, 7.5.10) but never in a remotely starring role.

§9. Besides hoplites and cavalry, Sparta employed lighter-armed troops as skirmishers and scouts—for example, the specialist Skiritai, from the *perioikic* border region of Skiritis[a] in northern Laconia (5.2.24).

§10. In common with all other Greek states as the fourth century wore on, Sparta increasingly recruited mercenaries. Mnasippos on Corcyra[a] in 373 had a well-

F.5e   Messenia and Laconia: Ref. Map 3, DX.
F.6a   Herodotus, *Histories* 9.29.
F.6b   Thucydides 4.78.1, 5.34.1.
F.6c   Ibid. 7.19.3, 7.50.1, 7.58.3.
F.6d   *Neodamōdeis* troops were first mentioned in Thucydides at 5.34.
F.6e   Ibid. 5.67.1
F.7a   Herodotus, *Histories* 1.82.
F.7b   Xenophon, *Constitution of the Lacedaemonians* 4.3–4.

F.7c   Thucydides 5.72.4.
F.7d   This translation accepts Estienne's emendation of *hippeis* (the Horsemen). See n. 6.4.14c for further.
F.8a   Thucydides 4.55.2.
F.9a   See Xenophon, *Cyropaedia* 4.2.1–4, and Thucydides 5.67. Skiritis: Ref. Map 3, DX.
F.10a   Corcyra: Ref. Map 2, BW.

organized force with divisional and regimental commanders (*lokhagoi* and taxiarchs, 6.2.18). At the time of Leuctra, Xenophon's mention of the Spartans' mercenaries is meaningful (6.4.9), as is his reference to the entire mercenary force as being in Arcadia in 362 (7.5.10): the good old days of self-reliant hoplite eminence were gone.

The Battle of Leuctra

§11. Xenophon's *Constitution of the Lacedaemonians* is full of praise for the Spartans' drill, perfected on the parade ground at home but capable of being deployed to powerful effect in the field. For example, Agesilaos skillfully carried out the maneuver known as *anastrophē* when he withdrew his army from the valley at Mantineia (6.5.18–19), and Mnasippos on Corcyra in 373 intelligently attempted the same maneuver, although the enemy's attack prevented its successful implementation (6.2.21). Like their ancestors at Thermopylae,[a] the Spartans knew how to fight in relays, sending out to the fray first their fittest and most eager hoplites, those in the youngest ten-year classes, aged twenty to twenty-nine (4.5.14), precisely the age group from which the *hippeis* (§7) were recruited. The Spartans were careful to conduct a prebattle sacrifice actually in the field and advanced to battle with measured and unison step to the sound of the *aulos*.[b] Yet all this preparation and centuries of almost unbrokenly successful tradition went for naught at Leuctra in 371. The world had changed, and the Spartans had failed to keep up, though they were unlucky to have to come up against two of the greatest Greek generals of all time: Pelopidas and, above all, Epaminondas. Instead of the conventional eight ranks deep, Epaminondas drew up his troops fifty deep. Instead of putting his crack force on the right wing, as was usual in hoplite battle, he stationed the Sacred Band, as they were known (150 couples of lovers), under Pelopidas on his left flank. And instead of advancing with all units lined up so as to attack the enemy everywhere, head-on and simultaneously, he held back his right so that his infantry advanced at an oblique angle to the Spartans and their allies. Moreover, he began the attack not with infantry but with cavalry, and Theban cavalry were excellent, second in quality only to the Thessalians.[c]

§12. Xenophon suggests that the Spartan commander, King Kleombrotos, was both less than fully competent and less than wholly sober. But to his credit as a historian he does not disguise the loss of morale among Sparta's Peloponnesian League allies. Sparta contributed only seven hundred full-citizen troops, including the three hundred *hippeis*. More than half of the seven hundred were killed, bringing the total citizen body down below one thousand. The defeat was total. And within a year defeat abroad, well beyond the Peloponnese,[a] had been compounded manifold by defeat at home, actually within the borders of the Spartan state, which were violated for the first time ever. Though the unwalled town of Sparta was not actually penetrated, the surrounding territory was ravaged and looted, and Epaminondas' huge force of perhaps as many as seventy thousand made their way right through Laconia and down to the coast at *perioikic* Gytheion,[b] Sparta's port, where the dockyards were set aflame and destroyed. The *perioikoi* of northern Laconia had already revolted. Now, far more dis-

F.11a Thermopylae: Ref. Map 2, BX.
F.11b *Aulos*: see Thucydides 5.70.
F.11c Thessaly: Ref. Map 2, BX.

F.12a Peloponnese: Ref. Map 2, CW.
F.12b Gytheion: Ref. Map 2, DX.

astrously, their example was followed by the helots of Messenia. When Epaminondas helped establish the new cities of Messene[c] and Megalopolis[d] (in Arcadia), Sparta's fate as a great power was sealed. Thereafter Sparta was condemned to be no better than a local Peloponnesian wrangler rather than a big player in the main game.

The Spartan Fleet

§13. Sparta, partly for geographical reasons, was not naturally cut out to be a major sea power. The Spartan Eurybiadas was merely the token Admiral of the Fleet in supreme command at the battle of Salamis[a] in 480; and King Leotychidas, who had command of the (mainly Athenian) joint Hellenic fleet in 479, showed himself singularly timorous. That was still the pattern in the first phase of the Peloponnesian War, as exemplified by the irresolute and timid maneuvers of Alkidas, commander of the Peloponnesian fleet in 428–427.[b] But after 413, when Sparta entered into a treaty relationship with Persia and received bucketfuls of Persian money, the situation was transformed, so that by the time of the battle of Arginousai[c] in 406, the Spartans' ships were more seaworthy and their sailors more skilful than those of their Athenian opponents. A key part of this transformation was to turn the old military rank of navarch, or Admiral of the Fleet, to which appointments had previously been made only from time to time and without definite term, into a new annual post, with a second in command called an *epistoleus* (literally, "secretary"). The powers of the navarch rivaled those of a king commanding a land army, and Lysander showed how they could be translated into political power. Lysander was appointed first in 407, but his willingness to collaborate with Persia and his un-Spartan cult of personality earned him the enmity of his successor Kallikratidas (1.6.2). Reappointment as navarch was illegal, so when Lysander was sent out again in 405, it was technically as *epistoleus*; but it was he, in fact, who won the war for Sparta at Aigospotamoi[d] and sought to capitalize on it for personal and ideological ends (2.4.28). Agesilaos was both ideologically and pragmatically opposed to this enhancement of naval authority, but his appointment (3.4.29) of an inexperienced and incompetent relative as navarch in 394 backfired on him spectacularly (4.3.13). It was as navarch, significantly, that Antalkidas brought about the end of the Corinthian War in 387, with Persian financial aid (5.1.25–28). But the peace named after him, more usually called the King's Peace, left no role for a Spartan navy, which, as was contemptuously observed (7.1.12–13), was in any case rowed merely by helots; and it was on land that Sparta's fate as a great Greek power was determined negatively, first at Leuctra in 371 (§11–12) and then again at Mantineia in 362 (7.5).

Paul Cartledge
A. G. Leventis Professor of Greek Culture
Faculty of Classics
University of Cambridge
Cambridge, UK

F.12c   Messene: Ref. Map 3, DX.
F.12d   Megalopolis: Ref. Map 3, CX.
F.13a   Salamis: Ref. Map 3, BY.
F.13b   See Thucydides 3.16ff. This fifth-century Alkidas

is not to be confused with the fourth-century Spartan statesman of the same name.
F.13c   Arginousai Islands: Ref. Map 2, BY.
F.13d   Aigospotamoi (Aigospotamos): Ref. Map 2, AY.

APPENDIX G

Agesilaos

Xenophon's Special Relationship

§1. Xenophon was a wealthy, highly intelligent (he was a former pupil of Socrates), and oligarchic Athenian who in 401 signed up as a mercenary under the banner of the Persian pretender Cyrus the Younger, who had been instrumental in Athens' defeat in the Peloponnesian War. Sparta covertly supported Cyrus (but he was killed at Cunaxa[a] in Mesopotamia) and in 399 incorporated the remnant of the so-called Cyreians or Ten Thousand mercenaries into its own anti-Persian army in Asia.[b] By then Xenophon was their commander, and as such he fought with the Spartans under Agesilaos against his own city of Athens at the battle of Coronea[c] in 394. Either for such treasonable support of Sparta or for joining up with Cyrus earlier, Xenophon was exiled; but through the good offices of his new friend and patron Agesilaos, he was granted an estate at Skillous,[d] not far from Olympia.[e] He lived there for more than twenty years,[f] during which period he is said to have sent his two sons at the invitation of Agesilaos to be educated at Sparta in the Agōgē.[g]

§2. Exactly when Xenophon composed and/or published his various works is a matter of scholarly controversy. At any rate, his encomium of Agesilaos was not published until after the king's death in 360/59, and it is my own view that most of his works were composed or finished during the 360s and 350s, in Corinth[a] and Athens. Apart from the *Agesilaos*, Xenophon wrote a second work specifically on Spartan matters, the *Constitution of the Lacedaemonians*, and the *Hellenika* is both full of Spartan references and informed by a deep personal engagement with the city's fortunes (for example, 5.4.1). Some details reveal that Agesilaos was a special source of both information and interpretation for Xenophon.

G.1a Cunaxa: Ref. Map 1.
G.1b Asia (Asia Minor): Ref. Map 1.
G.1c Coronea: Ref. Map 3, BY.
G.1d Skillous: Ref. Map 3, CX.
G.1e Olympia: Ref. Map 3, CX.
G.1f See *Anabasis* 5.3.
G.1g Agōgē: Spartan education system for males. See

Appendix E, Spartan Government and Society, §20.
G.2a Corinth: Ref. Map 2, CX.

Agesilaos' Birth and Upbringing

§3. Agesilaos was born lame, and this was used as an argument against him when he competed with his older half brother Agis II's son for the succession to the Eurypontid throne[a] in about 400 (3.3.3). But the gammy leg had not prevented his passing through the Agōgē with distinction and attracting as his older lover the ambitious Lysander. Lysander's metaphorical interpretation of an oracle warning Sparta against a "lame" kingship was crucial in securing the succession for his former beloved in 400 (3.3.4), though in 396 Agesilaos made it clear that he was no one's poodle, and certainly not Lysander's.[b]

Agesilaos as King

§4. Agesilaos ruled as king for more than forty years, one of the longest Spartan reigns on record, and he was also one of the two most powerful Spartan kings we know about (the other being the Agiad king Kleomenes I, ruled c. 520–490). Normally, he was careful to present himself as a "citizen king," always obedient to and usually upholding both the laws[a] and the appointed officials and standing up for the virtues that characterized equally all Spartans who, like himself, had gone through the Agōgē. Conspicuously, for example, he refused to accept the divine honors that Lysander, no less conspicuously, had agreed—and perhaps sought—to receive. However, in 396 Agesilaos set himself up as a heroic second Agamemnon, sacrificing at Aulis[b] on behalf of all Greeks as he prepared to embark on an anti-Persian expedition in Asia, only to be foiled not by nature but by the local power of Boeotia,[c] formerly an ally of Sparta's but by then a deadly foe (3.4.3–4). Xenophon's posthumously published encomium enumerated Agesilaos' many virtues, not least among them his piety (for example, after the battle of Coronea he "did not forget the divine power," 4.3.20).

Agesilaos as General

§5. Agesilaos was never a great general, though he was a cunning one. Before Agesilaos, no Spartan king had campaigned on the continent of Asia. In 396, at the urging of Lysander, Agesilaos assumed command of a large anti-Persian campaign for the "liberation" of the Greeks of Asia that had been going on since 399 (3.4.3–6). But Lysander was soon swept aside as a rival for supreme influence, and in 395 Agesilaos, again unprecedentedly, assumed command of both the land and the naval forces. But his campaign by land was only moderately successful;

G.3a   Two dynastic lines shared the heriditary dual Spartan kingship: the Eurypontids, descended from Eurypon, and the Agiads, descended from Agis. Both claimed descent from Herakles. See Appendix E, §13.
G.3b   See *Hellenika* 3.4.7–9.
G.4a   Plutarch, *Parallel Lives*, "Agesilaos" 30.4, cites a

conspicuous exception to Agesilaos' upholding of the laws after the Spartans heard the news of the defeat at Leuctra. Equally noteworthy is Xenophon's failure to mention it at 6.4.16.
G.4b   Aulis: Ref. Map 3, BY.
G.4c   Boeotia: Ref. Map 2, CX.

Xenophon tries to make a lot of the battle of Sardis[a] in 395 (3.4.20–25), but the more objective Oxyrhynchus Historian[b] puts that modest achievement in true perspective. The campaign at sea was a total disaster. Agesilaos was guilty of a gross act of nepotism by entrusting the navy to the incompetent command of Peisander, a relative by marriage. At the battle of Cnidus[c] in 394, Peisander was utterly defeated by a Persian fleet commanded by the Athenian Konon and lost his life, while the Spartans lost such control as they had exercised along the Asiatic coast (3.4.29, 4.3.10–14). Worse still, back home in Greece, Sparta found itself faced by a menacing, Persian-funded coalition. Agesilaos, supported by Xenophon, boasted of a new planned march (*anabasis*) to the heart of the Persian empire, but the sordid reality was that he had to be ordered back home by the ephors in spring 394 (4.1.41).[d] He won the battle of Coronea in 394 but failed to make major impact in the rest of the Corinthian War (for example, 4.5.1–2), which was decided in the Spartans' favor essentially at sea, again with Persian aid, as in the latter portion of the Peloponnesian War, in 413–404. In the early 370s, although he had led forces three times into Boeotia,[e] he failed seriously to dent the growing power of his nemesis, Thebes.[f] He defended Sparta as best he could in 370/69 against a Theban-led invasion that his own mistaken policies had provoked and enabled, but by then he was in his midseventies, and he never again held a major command in Greece. It is a telling comment on his ultimate failure that he died in North Africa aged eighty-four during his return from serving as a mercenary commander in support of anti-Persian rebellion in Egypt.[g]

Foreign Policy

§6. Agesilaos' conduct of relations toward two Greek cities neatly encapsulated his foreign policy as a whole. Ever since the Thebans contemptuously disrupted his sacrifice at Aulis in 396, he felt and expressed an unreasoning hatred toward Thebes (5.1.33), a feeling that Xenophon entirely shared. In 386 he insisted that the Thebans must not be allowed to swear to the King's Peace in the name of "the Boeotians" but, rather, that all Boeotians must swear separately, city by city, to comply with the peace's clause prescribing that all Greek cities great and small should be "autonomous"—that is, independent of any superior power, such as Thebes (5.1.32). He thereby broke up the Boeotian federal state. In 382 he supported Phoibidas' illegal and indeed sacrilegious occupation of Thebes (5.4.1, 6.3.9; see also §9); but in 379/8 Thebes was liberated and reestablished the Boeotian federal state on new, democratic lines and grew immensely in military power, despite Agesilaos' best efforts to curb it (5.4.46). In 371 Epaminondas turned Agesilaos' own interpretation of the autonomy clause against him by demanding that the *perioikic*

G.5a Sardis: Ref. Map 2, CY.
G.5b See the Introduction, §5, and Appendix P,
      Selected Fragments of the *Hellenica Oxyrhynchia*
      Relevant to Xenophonn's *Hellenika*, Fragment 14.
G.5c Cnidus: Ref. Map 2, DY.
G.5d See Appendix P, Fragment 24.4.
G.5e Although the expedition described at 4.58, which

presumably took place in 377, had to be aborted at Megara (Ref. Map 3, BY) when Agesilaos was struck down by a burst blood vessel, which almost killed him. See 5.4.38–41, 5.4.47–55, 5.4.58.

G.5f Thebes: Ref. Map 2, CX.
G.5g Egypt: Ref. Map 1.

poleis be treated as autonomous;[a] Agesilaos would have none of it (6.3.18–19), and war with Thebes and defeat at Leuctra were the result. Agesilaos' insensate hostility to Thebes was not shared by his co-king Kleombrotos (5.4.16), though it was he who was in—rather ineffectual—command of the Spartan and allied army at Leuctra, where he died.

§7. Phleious[a] was a long-standing member of the Peloponnesian League, occupying as it did a key geopolitical position in the northeast Peloponnese.[b] At some time before the late 380s it had become a democracy, and for this as well as its alleged disloyalty during the Corinthian War Agesilaos decided to intervene forcibly in its internal affairs (5.3.10–17). His goal was to restore a small group of fanatically pro-Spartan oligarchic exiles, who would then rule Phleious in the manner approved by both Agesilaos and Xenophon as "wanting what was best for the Peloponnese" (7.4.35; see also 7.5.1). But the protracted siege this required (381–379) had a most unwelcome side effect: even a number of Spartans began to criticize Agesilaos openly for weakening Sparta's hold on the affections of its alliance as a whole, saying that for the sake of a few individuals they were making themselves hated by a city of more than five thousand citizens. Xenophon in his *Agesilaos* (2.21) tried to make the best of things by saying that this was a striking demonstration of Agesilaos' virtue of *philetairia* (love of his comrades); but even he was compelled to admit that Agesilaos' behavior could be criticized on "other grounds," the very ones spelled out in the more objective *Hellenika* (5.3.16).

§8. Vis-à-vis Persia, Agesilaos' attitude was much more complex. Both at the beginning and at the end of his career he was an avowed "Persia hater" (as he is labeled favorably in Xenophon's *Agesilaos* 7.7), leading military campaigns of liberation and reprisal in first a public and latterly a private capacity. But in 395 he concluded a pact of ritualized guest-friendship (*xenia*) with a son of the Persian satrap Pharnabazos (4.1.39–40), and in 386 he embraced the King's Peace (5.1.36) with a will, not least because it enabled him to dismantle the power of Thebes. An anecdote preserved by Plutarch[a] is telling: when asked why the Spartans had "medized" (taken the Persians' side), Agesilaos is said anecdotally to have rejoined: "It is not the Spartans who have medized but the Persians who have laconized [taken the Spartans' part]."

Domestic Politics

§9. Two episodes, the trials of Phoibidas (5.3.32–4, in 382) and Sphodrias (5.4.28–31, in 378), are peculiarly revealing of the nature and extent of Agesilaos' domestic power and influence. Phoibidas issued from a high Spartan political family with royal connections. But his proverbial fifteen minutes of fame came in 382,

G.6a   Plutarch, *Parallel Lives,* "Agesilaos" 28.1–2.
G.7a   Phleious: Ref. Map 3, CY.
G.7b   Peloponnese: Ref. Map 2, CW.
G.8a   Plutarch, *Parallel Lives,* "Agesilaos" 23.2.

when he sacrilegiously occupied the acropolis of Thebes (the Kadmeia) in peacetime. He was quite properly put on trial for his life at Sparta; but the influence of Agesilaos, who defended the outcome (control of Thebes) as good for Sparta and studiously ignored the illegal and impious means whereby that result was obtained, was sufficient to ensure that Phoibidas received only a fine.[a] A few years later, Agesilaos appointed him governor of the key town of Thespiai[b] as part of his strategy for total imperial control of Boeotia, but Phoibidas overreached and got himself killed (5.4.41–5).

§10. Not unlike Phoibidas, Sphodrias was a high-ranking Spartiate who committed a gross international illegality (an attack on Athens in peacetime in 378) but was defended by Agesilaos and prospered as a result. But there were significant and revealing differences between the two cases. Sphodrias, too, was tried on a capital charge but was actually acquitted although he had in effect admitted his guilt and condemned himself by refusing to return to Sparta for the trial; many (as even Xenophon reports) considered this the most unjust verdict ever passed by a Spartan court (5.4.15–16, 5.4.20–34). Sphodrias' action, moreover had scuppered and sabotaged Agesilaos' own, nonaggressive policy toward Athens.[a] So why did Agesilaos support Sphodrias? First, he was a member of the circle around the Agiad king Kleombrotos, so here Agesilaos was seeking to win over a political opponent to his anti-Theban cause. There was also a personal dimension: Sphodrias' son Kleonymos was the beloved of Agesilaos' son Archidamos. Publicly, however, Agesilaos stated that Sparta needed fine soldiers like Sphodrias—an oblique reference to Sparta's growing manpower shortage. Agesilaos' domestic political strategy was a total success: Sphodrias died on the battlefield of Leuctra (6.4.14), fighting under Kleombrotos' command. But his foreign policy did Sparta nothing but harm: Sphodrias was carrying out Agesilaos' (disastrous) policy toward Thebes.

Paul Cartledge
A. G. Leventis Professor of Greek Culture
Faculty of Classics
University of Cambridge
Cambridge, UK

G.9a See *Hellenika* 5.2.24–32; Diodorus (Appendix O, Selections from the *Histories* of Diodorus Siculus Relevant to Xenophon's *Hellenika*, 15.20.2); Plutarch, *Parallel Lives*, "Agesilaos" 23–24.
G.9b Thespiai: Ref. Map 3, BY.
G.10a Agesilaos' nonaggressive policy toward Athens is revealed at 5.4.22 and 5.4.32; its failure in Theban actions is described at 5.4.63.

APPENDIX H

Political Leagues (Other Than Sparta's)
in Xenophon's *Hellenika*

§1. Although Greek writers thought of the *polis* ("city-state") as the characteristic Greek political unit, some Greeks lived in villages that had less of a civic personality than a full-fledged *polis*. These villages commonly formed part of a larger-scale regional body (an example from the *Hellenika* is Aetolia[a]). Similarly, some regions that did have full-fledged *poleis* also combined their *poleis* in a larger body, from either an early time or later, by conscious decision (an example is Boeotia[b]). Finally, a powerful city could attach to itself for the purpose of pursuing a joint foreign policy a body of allies in which that powerful city played the leading role (Sparta's Peloponnesian League[c] was of that kind, as were Athens' Delian League[d] in the fifth century and Second Athenian League[e] in the fourth). Greek writers can apply the term *koinon* ("community") to any of these larger bodies, though more often they refer simply to the Aetolians or the Boeotians or the Peloponnesians[f] (or, in the last case, "the Spartans and their allies"). Modern writers may apply the term *league* to any of them, but other terms, such as *federation*, are used also, particularly in the case of the regional bodies.

§2. The Acarnanian league (Arcania[a] is on the west coast of Greece, north of the Corinthina Gulf[b]) is the only one of which Xenophon uses the term *koinon*. References to the Acarnanians in Thucydides show that foreign policy was the concern of the league as a whole rather than of individual cities or villages. Xenophon regularly refers to the Acarnanians as a single entity, and at 4.6.4 the Spartan king Agesilaos, on reaching their frontier, sends a message to their authorities at Stratos[c] to threaten that unless they change sides and join him, he will lay their country waste—which he then does.

H.1a   Aetolia: Ref. Map 3, AX.
H.1b   Boeotia: Ref. Map 2, CX.
H.1c   The Peloponnesian League is discussed in Appendix E, §18–19.
H.1d   Delian League, originally based on the island of Delos: Ref. Map 2, CY.
H.1e   The Second Athenian League is referred to by other names by other writers and authorities. For instance, *The Cambridge Ancient History* and *The*

Oxford Classical Dictionary call it the Second Athenian Confederacy. Peter Green, the translator of the selections of Diodorus that appear in this volume in Appendix O, prefers to call it the Second Athenian Sea-League.
H.1f   Peloponnese: Ref. Map 2, CW.
H.2a   Acarnania: Ref. Map 3, AW.
H.2b   Corinthian Gulf: Ref. Map 3, BX.
H.2c   Stratos (capital city of Acarnania): Ref. Map 3, AW.

§3. There were other such leagues in this part of Greece. The Aetolians, still a primitive people in the time of Thucydides[a] and even in the late fourth century,[b] appear in the *Hellenika* only in connection with Agesilaos' raid on the Acarnanians: after that he returned to the Corinthian Gulf through Aetolia, which he could not have done without the consent of the Aetolians (4.6.14). An inscription of 367 records a protest by Athens to the *koinon* (using that word) against the imprisonment of its sacred envoys by one of the Aetolian cities.[c] Regional federations existed also in Phocis[d] and in both Opuntian (northern) and Ozolian (western) Locris;[e] the existence of an Opuntian (or "Hypocnemidian") federation is attested in an inscription of the early fifth century.[f]

§4. On the south side of the Corinthian Gulf were the Achaeans,[a] separated from the rest of the Peloponnese by mountains and more involved with central Greece. In the fifth century Herodotus wrote of them as divided into twelve "parts," to which he gave the names of twelve cities;[b] by the early fourth century there was a federal organization that incorporated Calydon[c] (4.6.1) and Naupactus,[d] on the north side of the gulf. In the *Hellenika* the Achaeans regularly function as a single unit. However, we read at 7.1.41–3 that in 366 Epaminondas won over the Achaeans to the Theban side,[e] promising not to impose constitutional changes; but after Thebes had succumbed to pressure, sent governors to the cities, and set up democracies in them, the exiled aristocrats regained control and aligned their cities with Sparta.

§5. Thessaly[a] is more complicated. From an early date there was some kind of federal organization, with federal officials and a mechanism for making decisions on behalf of the whole of Thessaly.[b] Thucydides writes of military contingents from the individual cities[c] but also of tension between oligarchic cliques that could act on their own and men who claimed that an important decision ought to be approved by the *koinon* of all the Thessalians.[d] In the *Hellenika*, Lykophron of the city of Pherai,[e] "wanting to rule the whole of Thessaly," in 404 won a battle against Larissa[f] and other cities (2.3.4). In 375, Polydamas of Pharsalus[g] appealed for Spartan support against Jason of Pherai, who already controlled much of Thessaly and neighboring regions and hoped to become *tagos* (an old military office that he was reviving for his own purposes) of all Thessaly; Sparta could not provide sufficient support, so Polydamas joined Jason, and Jason became *tagos* and levied tribute (6.1.2–19). Jason planned to preside over the Pythian Games at Delphi[h] in 370 but

H.3a Thucydides 3.94.4–5.
H.3b Diodorus 18.24.2
H.3c P. J. Rhodes and Robin Osborne, eds. *Greek Historical Inscriptions 404–323 B.C.* (Oxford: Oxford University Press, 2003), No. 35.
H.3d Phocis: Ref. Map 3, AY. For regional federations there, see, for example, 3.5.3–4; and for the mention of individual cities, see 6.4.21, 8.4.27.
H.3e See, for example, 4.2.17. Opuntian Locris: Ref. Map 3, AY. Ozolian Locris: Ref. Map 3, AX. On a regional federation for these, see, for example, 4.2.17.
H.3f Russell Meiggs and David M. Lewis, *A Selection of Greek Historical Inscriptions to the End of the Fifth Century B.C.* (Oxford: Clarendon Press, 2004), No. 20. Translated in C. W. Fornara, *Archaic Times to the End of the Peloponnesian War* (Cambridge: Cambridge University Press, 1977), No. 47.

H.4a Achaea: Ref. Map 2, CW.
H.4b Herodotus, *Histories* 1.145.
H.4c Calydon: Ref. Map 3, BX.
H.4d Naupactus: Ref. Map 3, BX.
H.4e David Thomas in the Introduction (n. Intro.9.3a) cites 367 for this development, but he makes clear that his view on this is a minority one. *The Cambridge Ancient History* uses the date 366. Thebes: Ref. Map 2, CX.
H.5a Thessaly: Ref. Map 2, BW.
H.5b See, for example, Herodotus, *Histories* 5.63.
H.5c Thucydides 2.22.
H.5d Ibid. 4.78.
H.5e Pherai: Ref. Map 2, BX.
H.5f Larissa (in Thessaly): Ref. Map 2, BX.
H.5g Pharsalus: Ref. Map 2, BX.
H.5h Delphi: Ref. Map 2, CX.

was assassinated, and various of his relatives succeeded him as rulers of Pherai and *tagoi* of Thessaly.[i] Xenophon has only two passing allusions to what happened in the 360s (7.1.28, 7.5.4). Opponents of Pherai appealed first to Macedon[j] and then to Thebes, and organized themselves in a *koinon* headed by an archon. Eventually, in 364, Alexander of Pherai was defeated, to survive as a subordinate ally of Thebes with his power limited to Pherai.[k] He then turned against Athens, which had previously supported him, and Athens reacted by ending its alliance with him and making an alliance with the *koinon*.[l] Soon, however, Athens and Pherai were supporting Phocis in the Third Sacred War for the control of Delphi, while the *koinon* was prominent among the opponents of Phocis. In 352 the last rulers of Pherai were expelled by Philip of Macedon, and the *koinon* made Philip archon of Thessaly, so that Thessaly became a dependency of Macedon.

§6. We first hear of a Boeotian Federation in 519, when Plataea[a] successfully resisted pressure from Thebes to join it.[b] The federation was perhaps dissolved in the mid-fifth century, when Athens controlled Boeotia, and revived afterward. An account of its organization in the 390s, based on eleven local units, is given in the *Hellenica Oxyrhynchia*.[c] Thebes controlled four of the units, and was the seat of the federal authorities. The next-strongest city, Orchomenus,[d] was won over by the Spartan Lysander in 395, at the beginning of the Corinthian War (3.5.6). When Sparta sought a diplomatic end to the war, its proposals for the autonomy of all cities at first included the dismantling of the federation (4.8.15). Later it was willing to spare the federation if Orchomenus could secede,[e] but in 386 through the King's Peace[f] it did insist on the dismantling of the federation (5.1.32–3). (However, Sparta did not require the dismantling of the other federations mentioned above.) After a period in which Thebes was occupied by Sparta (382–379), the federation was revived by Thebes, in a new form not based on regional units and having a federal assembly; some Boeotian cities were resistant to Theban domination (for example, Plataea and Thespiai,[g] 6.3.1). The unsympathetic Xenophon writes more often of the Thebans than of the Boeotians.

§7. In 432, to resist Athenian pressure, some cities in the neighborhood of Olynthos[a] abandoned their separate sites and migrated to Olynthos; this enlarged city came to refer to itself as "the Chalcidians."[b] An inscription of the 390s or 380s records an alliance between the Chalcidians and Amyntas III of Macedon and uses the term *koinon*.[c] The Chalcidians supported the Thebans in the Corinthian War, though not as major participants.[d] We do not know whether they and their neighbors swore to the King's Peace, or whether the *koinon* was dissolved, but if it was, it

H.5i See 6.4.28–37. See also Appendix O, Selections from the *Histories* of Diodorus Siculus Relevant to Xenophon's *Hellenika*, 15.60.

H.5j Macedon: Ref. Map 2, AX.

H.5k See Appendix O, 15.61, 15.67, 15.72.3–4 (and Diodorus 15.71, 15.72.1–2, 15.75, which do not appear in Appendix O); and Plutarch, *Parallel Lives*, "Pelopidas" 26–35.

H.5l Rhodes and Osborne, *Greek Historical Inscriptions* 44.

H.6a Plataea: Ref. Map 3, BY.

H.6b Herodotus, *Histories* 6.108.

H.6c See Appendix P, Selected Fragments of the *Hellenica Oxyrhynchia* Relevant to Xenophon's *Hellenika*, Fragment 19.2–4.

H.6d Orchomenus (in Boeotia): Ref. Map 3, AY.

H.6e Andocides 3.13. See also 3.20.

H.6f See 5.1.31 for the terms of the King's Peace. A most important provision required that all Greek cities, "both large and small, should be autonomous."

H.6g Thespiai: Ref. Map 3, BY.

H.7a Olynthos: Ref. Map 2, AX.

H.7b Chalcidice: Ref. Map 2, AX. See Thucydides 1.58.2, 2.29.6.

H.7c Rhodes and Osborne, *Greek Historical Inscriptions* 12.

H.7d See Appendix O, 14.82.3.

was soon revived. In 382 Sparta was asked by cities not wanting to be absorbed into the *koinon* (5.2.11–19: Xenophon always writes of "Olynthos") and by Amyntas[e] to intervene, and presumably represented this as enforcement of the autonomy principle of the King's Peace. In 379 the Chalcidians surrendered (5.3.26), and presumably the *koinon* was dissolved—but c. 375 whatever remained of the state joined the Second Athenian League as "Chalcidians from Thrace,"[f] and that name was still used on the coins.

§8. In 385 Sparta had split the Arcadian city of Mantineia[a] into its component villages (5.2.1–7). In 370, after Sparta's defeat at Leuctra,[b] Mantineia reunited and then supported a party in Tegea[c] that wanted an Arcadian Federation (6.5.3–11). The federation had an Assembly of Ten Thousand (perhaps based on a low property qualification), a council, and a body of officials entitled *damiorgoi*;[d] it also had a force of Eparitoi[e] (copying the Theban Sacred Band) to provide a professional nucleus for the army.[f] Members of many communities in southwest Arcadia were drafted into a new "great city," Megalopolis[g] (mentioned once in passing by Xenophon: 7.5.5). After 364 the use of sacred funds from Olympia[h] provoked a split in the federation, which led to the campaign culminating in the battle of Mantineia in 362 (7.4.33–7.5.27). The two factions continued after that, each claiming to be the Arcadian Federation.

§9. The Second Athenian League was a league of a totally different kind. In 478/7 Athens had founded the Delian League (referred to in 6.5.34) to continue fighting against Persia; it began as a free alliance but developed into an empire over which Athens exercised unprecedented control. Sparta embarked on the Peloponnesian War in 431 in order to destroy it, and in 404, thanks to Persian support, succeeded in doing so. After the King's Peace of 386, Sparta's interpretation of the terms in its own interests caused widespread disquiet. The raid on Athenian territory by Sphodrias in 378 was the last straw for Athens (5.4.20–34), and in 378/7 the Second League was founded to uphold the King's Peace and defend the Greeks against the Spartans.[a] The nearest Xenophon comes to mentioning this league is his remarks that Athens built gates for the Peiraieus,[b] fitted out ships, and supported the Boeotians (5.4.34), and that Athens and its allies swore individually to the Peace of spring 371 (6.3.19); but there is an account in Diodorus that is supported by a series of inscriptions.[c] The league was popular at first, but it never brought as much power and wealth to Athens as the Delian League. As the Delian League became simply an instrument of Athenian policy when regular fighting against Persia ended

H.7e See Appendix O, 15.19.2–3.
H.7f Rhodes and Osborne, *Greek Historical Inscriptions* 22.101–2. Thrace: Ref. Map 2, AY.
H.8a Arcadia and Mantineia: Ref. Map 3, CX.
H.8b Leuctra: Ref. Map 3, BY.
H.8c Tegea: Ref. Map 3, CX.
H.8d Rhodes and Osborne, *Greek Historical Inscriptions* 32.
H.8e The Eparitoi, according to Diodorus (15.62.2, 15.67.2), was an elite force of Arcadians five thousand strong.
H.8f See 7.1.38, 7.4.2, 7.4.33–4.
H.8g Megalopolis: Ref. Map 3, CX.
H.8h Olympia: Ref. Map 2, CW.

H.9a Professor Rhodes' dating of the foundation of the league to 378/7, as well as its derivation from Sphodrias' raid on Attica, is controversial. *The Cambridge Ancient History*, whose chronology is used as the base for this edition, places the foundation of the Athenian League in 379/8, just before Sphodrias' raid, in which case outrage caused by the raid could not have led to the formation of the league.
H.9b Peiraieus: Ref. Map 5.
H.9c See Appendix O, 15.28–9. See in particular a prospectus for the league and a list of members recruited to c. 375 in Rhodes and Osborne, *Greek Historical Inscriptions* 22.

(c. 450), the Second Athenian League became simply an instrument of Athenian policy when after Leuctra the Athenians supported Sparta against Thebes (one of the founding members). The league was crippled by warfare between Athens and some of its major allies from 357 to 355, known as the Social War.[d] But it survived until Athens and all the mainland Greek states except Sparta were enrolled by Philip of Macedon in his League of Corinth in 338/7.

P. J. Rhodes
Department of Classics
University of Durham
Durham, North Carolina

H.9d   See the Introduction, §3.9, 12.12.

APPENDIX I
Units of Distance, Currency, and Capacity in Xenophon's *Hellenika*

§1. No universal standards for units of distance, currency, or capacity existed in Xenophon's time. Ancient Greeks in different locales used different-sized units. At the same time, they understood the importance of maintaining standard units of measurement, especially weights, measures, and capacities necessary to ensure fair and reliable commercial and official transactions. We have ample evidence of the lengths to which communities such as ancient Athens went to maintain such standards, by appointing officials to oversee their use and by making available publicly accessible specimens of relevant units.[a]

§2. Units of distance were probably the most difficult standards to establish and publicize. Units of currency, which indicated weights, and of capacity (liquid and dry) were easier to standardize. It is essential to recognize that all modern equivalences for ancient units of measurement, which existed in a bewildering diversity, can only be approximations and that precision is impossible to attain. For this reason, different modern reference works often give somewhat different absolute values for the same ancient units; the table of equivalences at the end of this appendix should be consulted with this limitation in mind.

§3. Greek (and other Mediterranean and Near Eastern) units for measuring distance were originally based on notional lengths of parts of the human body, as the famous Roman architect and engineer Vitruvius says.[a] The length of units varied according to the local standard in use, but there seems to have been an effort to publicize the ratios existing between the more widely recognized standards. Scholars have calculated absolute values for Greek units by studying the dimensions and construction marks of surviving buildings, the length of the distance between the start and finish lines in running tracks in ancient Greek athletic stadiums, two wooden measuring instruments found in a shipwreck of about 400,[b] and the depiction of length standards

I.1a On classical Athens' officials, see Aristotle, *Athenaion Politeia* 10.1–2, 51.1–2. For a long third-century Athenian inscription specifying procedures for overseeing weights and measures, see *Inscriptiones Graecae*, vol. 2, 2nd ed. (Berlin: Reimer, then De Gruyter, 1873–), no. 1013 (translated in Austin 2006, p. 129). For a discussion of

two relief sculptures displaying standard units of length, see Wilson Jones 2000. Official weights and measures found in the agora of ancient Athens are cataloged in Lang and Crosby 1964 and illustrated on plates 102–6 in Camp 1986.

I.3a Vitruvius, *On Architecture* 3.1.5.

I.3b Shown in Steiglitz 2006.

FIGURE I.1. THIS METROLOGICAL TRIANGULAR STONE SLAB CARVED IN RELIEF SHOWS STANDARD DIMENSIONS FOR MEASUREMENT OF THE FOOT, THE PALM, THE FINGER (INCH), A FATHOM (OUTSTRETCHED ARMS), AND A CUBIT (ELBOW TO FINGERTIP). SCHOLARS AGREE THAT IT WAS PROBABLY CARVED SOMETIME BETWEEN 460 AND 430. ITS PROVENANCE IS UNKNOWN.

related to the male body carved on two surviving metrological relief sculptures, one preserved in the Ashmolean Museum in Oxford and the other, the so-called Salamis Relief, in the Archaeological Museum at Peiraieus.[a]

§4. Greek measures of distance were originally based on notional lengths of parts of the human body, with the foot as the basic unit. The length of a Greek foot varied according to the standard being used. A foot on the Attic (that is, Athenian) standard equaled approximately 11.65 inches (29.6 centimeters), while on the Olympic standard a foot equaled approximately 12.60 inches and on the Doric standard approximately 12.87 inches. Longer units were multiples of feet; the unit measuring 100 feet long was called a plethron (plural, plethra; see 4.3.17, 7.1.19). The unit measuring 600 feet was called a stade (from the Greek *stadion*, "racetrack"; see 2.2.15, for example). The absolute length of a plethron or a stade therefore depends on which standard is being used. Xenophon does not indicate which one he means, but it is most likely the Attic or the Olympic. On the former standard, a stade would measure approximately 583 modern ("English") feet, while on the latter it would measure approximately 630.

§5. In this edition of Xenophon's *Hellenika*, the editor has always quoted the ancient Greek units cited by Xenophon and converted them, in accompanying foot-

I.3a   See Wilson Jones 2000 and Vickers 2006. The relief in the Ashmolean Museum (Figure I.1) can also be viewed at www.ashmolean.org/ash/faqs/q002/q002001.html. A list of questions on the relief is at www.ashmolean.org/ash/faqs/q002. For the so-called Salamis Relief in the Archaeological Museum at Piraeus, the port of Athens, see Wilson Jones 2000, Vickers 2006, and www.ajaonline.org/archive/104.1/wilson_jones_mark.html.

notes, into modern units based on certain explicit assumptions. For example, when Xenophon cites a distance as 100 stades, a footnote states that if he means the Attic stade of 583 feet, the distance would be 58,300 feet, or a bit more than 11 miles. Attic units of distance were generally shorter than other ancient Greek units, so the conversion distances are probably at the lower end of the possible scale. Most distances cited by Xenophon were surely the result of estimation rather than precise measurements, so our inability to be precise in specifying the distances referred to in his text is therefore perhaps less significant than it might otherwise be.

§6. When Xenophon refers to money, it seems reasonable to assume that he is referring to the standards of measurement in common use in his hometown of Athens, unless his text gives us a clear indication that he is referring to some other standard. Athenian coins were one of the very few Greek currencies that circulated internationally and that people around the Mediterranean world were readily willing to accept in payment.

§7. In Xenophon's time currency meant coins (there were no bills), minted in bronze, silver, or (more rarely) gold. The standard of measurement for coins minted at Athens is also called Attic.[a] Greek mints identified their coinages by designs and inscriptions, but they did not usually include an indication of a coin's value as money. Consumers were expected to know how much a particular coin was worth. Greek silver and gold coinages derived perhaps as much as ninety-five percent of their monetary value from the intrinsic bullion value of the precious metal in each coin; the remaining value was added by the implicit guarantee that the authority issuing an official coinage, which was identified by the pictures and (sometimes) words stamped onto the coins, would enforce its acceptance as legal tender in its homeland. For ordinary transactions, Greeks assumed that the purity of the precious metal in coins from different mints was essentially the same.

Since the value of silver and gold currency depended primarily on the amount of precious metal in the coins, the weight of the coins mattered. (Bronze coins, the small change of the ancient Greek world, were much less valuable and circulated at agreed-upon values.) A small denomination commonly mentioned is the obol, which on the Attic standard weighed 0.72 grams on average. Six obols equaled 1 drachma (see 1.5.4), which weighed about 4.3 grams on average on the Attic standard. The largest Attic-standard coin in usual circulation was a 4-drachma piece (tetradrachma), although on rare occasions 10-drachma coins (dekadrachmas) could be produced. The term *stater* ("weight") designated the largest denomination in each currency standard and represented different multiples of the drachma in different weight standards.

§8. For calculating large amounts of money, Greeks used units of accounting that are most easily understood for our purposes as numbers of drachmas. A mina (see 1.5.5) was a unit of 100 drachmas, which on the Attic standard would amount

I.7a   Attica: Ref. Map 2, CX.

to about 15 ounces (approximately 430 grams). A talent (see 1.3.8) was a unit of 6,000 drachmas, which on the Attic standard would amount to about 57 pounds (a little less than 26 kilograms). Since the terms *talent* and *mina*, strictly speaking, referred only to weight (there was no talent or mina coin), they could also be used to indicate amounts of precious metal still in bullion form (or the weight of substantial amounts of other materials).

§9. Another well-known currency standard was named after the mint on the island of Aegina,[a] not far from Athens. According to Xenophon (5.2.21–22), the Peloponnesian[b] Greeks referred to this Aeginetan standard in designating amounts of money for pay and fines in a military pact. Coins minted on the Aeginetan standard weighed about forty percent more than on the Attic standard and were correspondingly more valuable in each denomination. The exchange rate between the two standards was seven Aeginetan coins to ten Athenian. At 5.2.21 Xenophon mentions one of the multiples of the obol that some city-states minted, a triobol (worth three obols, or half a drachma, weighing about 3 grams on average) on the Aeginetan standard. The stater mentioned by Xenophon at 5.2.22 is presumably also on the Aeginetan standard, which would make it a double drachma (didrachma) weighing about 12.2 grams.

§10. The only meaningful way to measure the value of ancient money in its own time is to study wages and prices. Since wages and prices in antiquity were as variable as they are today, generalizations about them cannot be authoritative.[a] There was no standard or mandatory wage scale; before the inflation that came during the Peloponnesian War (431–404), a laborer at Athens could perhaps hope to earn a third of a drachma per day. Toward the end of the fifth century, that amount had risen to a drachma a day, which is what a rower on a warship in the Athenian navy earned. A talent (equal to 6,000 drachmas) was therefore a huge sum, enough to pay the wages of a crew of a two-hundred-man warship for a month, or twenty years' wages for an individual worker making a drachma per day for three hundred days each year.

§11. By about 425 an Athenian citizen received half a drachma for each day spent on jury duty. This payment seems to have been enough to make jury service attractive for men who could use the money to supplement other income, but it was not enough to replace a day's pay for most workers. Food and clothing could be expensive by modern Western standards. Enough barley to provide a day's porridge, the dietary staple, for a family of five cost only one forty-eighth of a drachma, but a gallon of olive oil, another staple, cost 3 drachmas. A woolen cloak cost from 5 to 20 drachmas, while a pair of shoes could cost from 6 to 8 drachmas.

§12. At 3.2.27 Xenophon refers to the unit of capacity known as the medimnos, often translated as "bushel." This held about 47.22 U.S. dry-measure quarts (about 52 liters) on the Attic standard.

I.9a   Aegina: Ref. Map 3, CY.
I.9b   Peloponnese: Ref. Map 2, CW.

I.10a   Loomis 1998, pp. 261–320, conveniently tabulates the specific evidence from classical Athens.

§13. Table of Units of Distance, Currency, and Capacity in Xenophon's *Hellenika*

Distance

Foot = 11.65 inches (Attic standard)

Plethron (100 feet) = 97 "English" feet (Attic standard)

Stade (600 feet) = 583 "English" feet (Attic standard)

Currency

Obol = 0.72 grams (Attic standard)

Triobol = 3 grams (Aeginetan standard)

Drachma (6 obols) = 4.3 grams (Attic standard)

Stater (2 drachmas) = 12.2 grams (Aeginetan standard)

Mina (100 drachmas) = 430 grams (Attic standard)

Talent (6,000 drachmas) = about 26 kilograms (Attic standard)

Capacity

medimnos = 47.22 U.S. dry-measure quarts (Attic standard)

Thomas R. Martin
Department of Classics
College of the Holy Cross
Worcester, Massachusetts

Bibliography

Austin, M. M., ed. *The Hellenistic World from Alexander to the Roman Conquest: A Selection of Ancient Sources in Translation.* Cambridge: Cambridge University Press, 1981, 2nd ed., 2006.

Ben-Menahem, H., and N. S. Hecht. "A Modest Addendum to 'The Greek Metrological Relief in Oxford.'" *Antiquaries Journal* 65 (1985): 139–40.

Camp, John M. *The Athenian Agora: Excavations in the Heart of Classical Athens.* London: Thames and Hudson, 1986.

Chantraine, H. "Gewichte." In *Der Kleine Pauly: Lexikon der Antike in fünf Bänden*, edited by K. Ziegler and W. Sontheimer, vol. 2, cols. 791–3. Munich: Deutscher Taschenbuch Verlag, 1979.

———. "Talent." In ibid., vol. 5, cols. 502–3.

Fernie, Eric. "The Greek Metrological Relief in Oxford." *Antiquaries Journal* 61 (1981): 256–63.

Hitzel, Konrad. "Gewichte. III. Griechenland." In *Der Neue Pauly*, vol. 4, cols. 1050–53. Stuttgart and Weimar: Verlag J. B. Metzler, 1998.

Hultsch, Friedrich. *Griechische und Römische Metrologie.* 2nd ed. Berlin: Weidmannsche Buchhandlung, 1882.

Lang, Mabel, and Margaret Crosby. *Weights, Measures, and Tokens.* Vol. 10 of *Athenian Agora.* Princeton, NJ: The American School of Classical Studies at Athens, 1964.

Loomis, William T. *Wages, Welfare Costs and Inflation in Classical Athens.* Ann Arbor: University of Michigan Press, 1998.

Lorenzen, Eivind. *Technological Studies in Ancient Metrology.* Copenhaven: Nyt Nordisk Forlag, 1966.

Morrison, John. "Ancient Greek Measures of Length in Nautical Contexts." *Antiquity* 65 (1991): 298–305.

Neal, John. *All Done with Mirrors: An Exploration of Measure, Proportion, Ratio and Number.* London: The Secret Academy, 2000.

Oxé, A. "Das spartanisch-dorische Hohlmasssystem," *Rheinisches Museum* 90 (1941): 334–41.

Rhodes, P. J. *A Commentary on the Aristotelian Athenaion Politeia.* Oxford: Clarendon Press, 1981.

Schulzki, Heinz-Joachim. "Hohlmasse. III. Griechenland." In *Der Neue Pauly*, vol. 5, cols. 673–4. Stuttgart and Weimar: Verlag J. B. Metzler, 1998.

———. "Masse. II. Klassische Antike." In ibid., vol. 7 (1999), cols. 988–9.

Stieglitz, Robert R. "Classical Greek Measures and the Builder's Instruments from the Ma'agan Mikhael Shipwreck." *American Journal of Archaeology* 110.2 (2006): 195–203.

Vickers, Michael. *The Arundel and Pomfret Marbles in Oxford.* Ashmolean Handbooks. Oxford: Ashmolean Museum, 2006.

Wilson Jones, Mark. "Doric Measure and Architectural Design 1: The Evidence of the Relief from Salamis." *American Journal of Archaeology* 104 (2000): 73–93.

APPENDIX J

Ancient Greek Religion in the
Time of Xenophon

§1. Greeks of the classical period related to their gods as they related to each other, by means of conversation, commerce, and competition. The Greeks went to the gods for advice, attempted to make deals with the gods, and saw the gods as acutely interested in the various kinds of competition that figured so large in their own lives: artistic and athletic competition, political rivalry, and war.

§2. The future, the success or failure of various undertakings, was in the hands of the gods, and humans could hope to know it. The most passive means of determining divine will was to observe and interpret the natural world. The gift of access to divine will was given by Apollo to the *theopropos* ("he to whom the gods are evident").[a] The appearance of the organs and entrails of sacrificial victims could bode well or ill, and an army might wait to march or to attack until a well-shaped liver might appear in the body of a sacrificed animal (3.4.15, 4.7.7). Unconscious acts or thoughts of human beings, like natural phenomena, could reveal the gods' will. Xenophon interprets a chance sneeze as a sign from the gods in the *Anabasis*.[b] Earthquakes usually signified displeasure from the gods (3.2.24, 3.3.2), but at 4.4.7, Xenophon shows that they could be interpreted in other ways.

§3. The gods communicated with the Greeks directly, if often obscurely, at particular sacred places, the oracles. There were many oracles (Apollo spoke from an oracle at Abai in Phocaea, Zeus from an oracle at Dodona, Amphiaraos from Oropos, Trophonios from Lebadeia),[a] but by far the most famous was the oracle of Apollo at Delphi.[b] When Greek writers mention "the oracle," they mean Apollo at Delphi. There the god's priestess, the Pythia, answered requests with utterances expressed in poetic verse, which were passed along to suppliants by attending priests.[c] Individuals and cities brought questions to the Delphic oracle on subjects ranging from matters of petty curiosity to matters of vital political importance. The oracular responses that figure most largely in historical sources, though, are the ones

---

J.2a In Homer, *Iliad* 1.69, the seer Chalcis is defined by his ability to intepret the flights of birds.

J.2b Xenophon, *Anabasis* 3.29.

J.3a Oracles at Abai, Dodona, Oropos, and Lebadeia: see Herodotus, *Histories* 1.46, and Pausanias 4.32.5. Abai and Lebadeia: Ref. Map 3, AY.

Dodona: Ref. Map 2, BW. Oropos: Ref. Map 3, BZ.

J.3b Delphi: Ref. Map 2, CX.

J.3c See Michael Flower, *The Seer in Ancient Greece* (Berkeley: University of California Press, 2008), pp. 211–39.

on matters of war, beginning with the famously equivocal answer to the Lydian[d] king Croesus, who asked if he should go to war with Persia: "Do so and you will destroy a great empire" was the answer, which he interpreted in his own favor, to his later regret.[e] The Athenians consulted the oracle before the Persian Wars but did not heed the answer, which seemed to council submission.[f] Xenophon consulted the oracle before undertaking the expedition into Persia as a mercenary, but did not ask about the success of the war, only for advice on what sacrifices to offer.[g]

§4. While seers observed the world for signs of divine thought and oracles provided answers, prayer was a conversation with the gods, often assuming a reciprocal relationship. In this way prayer and sacrifice were closely related. In the *Euthyphro* (14c), Plato has Socrates ask, "So sacrifice is us giving a gift to the gods, and prayer is us asking a favor of them?" to which Euthyphro, representing an orthodox view of religious practice, agrees. Greeks offered prayers, sometimes supplemented by more concrete gifts, in gratitude for divine favors already received; an Athenian gave a statue to Hermes around 500 and wrote on it: "Oenobius the herald gives this statue in commemoration to Hermes, returning a favor."[a] Other prayers and offerings seemed to put the gods under an obligation; a common phrase from inscriptions on offerings is "now you give a favor in return!" (*su charin antidido*).[b]

§5. Few undertakings of any significance took place without at least a prayer, and often a sacrifice, to ask for divine favor, and prayers were very often accompanied by sacrifices, which could be offerings of grain, fruits, or vegetables or meat from a slain animal.[a] Pausanias, the second-century C.E. travel writer, gives this description of a large, public sacrifice at Athens: "They set barley mixed with wheat on the altar of Zeus of the City and leave it unprotected. They have an ox prepared for the sacrifice. The ox is permitted to go up to the altar and eat the grain. One of the priests, named the Ox Killer, cuts down the ox, throws away the axe as the ritual requires, and flees. The rest put the axe on trial as if they did not know the human being who was responsible."[b]

§6. The expectation of reciprocity applied to requests of oracles. Croesus of Lydia sent lavish gifts to Delphi before asking about his war against Persia.[a] In fact, most of the cities of Greece gave rich offerings to Apollo at Delphi, either in expectation of future beneficence or in thanks for victories or other favors; these treasures, although they belonged to the god and were controlled by the priests of Apollo, were collected in treasuries "owned" by various cities: Athens and Thebes[b] had treasuries filled with spoils of war, and that of Syracuse[c] was filled with spoils from the disastrous Athenian expedition of 415–413 against Sicily; Cnidus[d] sent gifts after Apollo ended a plague, and the Siphnian treasury, into which Siphnos[e] paid a tithe of the proceeds of their gold mines, was particularly rich.

J.3d   Lydia: Ref. Map 2, CZ.
J.3e   Herodotus, *Histories* 1.52.
J.3f   It is possible that the Athenians never consulted Delphi again after 479 on a political matter.
J.3g   Xenophon, *Anabasis* 3.1.6
J.4a   *Inscriptiones Graecae* I³ 776.
J.4b   *Inscriptiones Graecae* I 1014, I³ 791.
J.5a   Vegetable sacrifice: see Xenophon, *Anabasis* 5.3.9, and Pausanias 8.42.11. Meat sacrifice: the most basic form of this, before a simple meal in a swine-

herd's hut, appears at Homer, *Odyssey* 14.414–453.
J.5b   Pausanias 1.24.4
J.6a   Herodotus, *Histories* 1.50–51.
J.6b   Thebes: Ref. Map 2, CX.
J.6c   Syracuse (in Sicily): Ref. Map 1.
J.6d   Cnidus: Ref. Map 2, DY. For a description of that expedition, see Thucydides Books 6 and 7.
J.6e   Siphnos: Ref. Map 3, DZ. See Pausanias 10.11.2.

§7. The sanctity of Delphi gave it privileged status. Although Delphi was in the territory of Phocis,[a] it was not ruled by the Phocians but by the Amphiktyonic Council, an assembly of representatives from twelve Greek cities who set policy for the shrine;[b] this council was responsible for maintaining the temples and managing finances but had broader powers, which included punishing those states that were deemed to have committed sacrilege.[c] But the vast wealth contained in the various treasuries at Delphi made the site an attractive target for aggression, particularly during the fourth century, as wars among Greeks were increasingly fought by mercenary armies. The middle of that century saw a possible threat by Jason of Pherai[d] to seize the treasuries of Delphi (6.4.30), and a succession of Phocian mercenary commanders actually did convert the treasures of Apollo into currency to pay their armies.[e]

§8. Prayer and sacrifice were regular events, marking an ongoing interaction between humans and gods. Festivals were outside the normal course of life, times set aside for celebrating and honoring the gods; they were also a gift from the gods.[a] The oldest of the Greek festivals seem to have been based on the agricultural year, marking times of planting and harvesting: the Anthesteria, associated with the "blossoming" in spring, was at Athens called the Older Dionysia, the older festival to the god Dionysus.[b] Diodorus says that when the women of Syracuse were celebrating the Thesmophoria, a women's festival in honor of Demeter, "they were imitating the old way of life."[c] This festival, the most widely attested in the Greek world, shows most clearly the ability of festivals to provide a break from normal routine: at the Thesmophoria, women came together without men for several days, and their husbands were obliged not only to allow their wives leave to attend but also to pay the costs.[d]

§9. The most important, solemn, and ancient festivals allowed Greeks to be initiated into mystery cults; they provided not only a break from daily life but an entry into new spiritual life. Of these, the Mysteries of Demeter and Kore at Eleusis[a] were the most ancient and widely known. Their celebrations originated in the myth recounted in the Homeric Hymn to Demeter, and their focus was on issues of life and death, birth and rebirth. Although no ancient writer violated the sanctity of the rites by describing them in detail, we see plenty of evidence for their profoundly moving impact. In the first century the Roman Cicero has a character in one of his dialogues say to a friend, "Your city of Athens has clearly made many divine and extraordinary contributions to human life, but none of them are better than those of the Mysteries. They educated us out of a life of rude barbarism into true humanity. The ceremonies are called initiations, and we recognize in them the first principles of living. We have gained from them the way of living in happiness and dying with a

J.7a   Phocis: Ref. Map 3, AY.
J.7b   Aeschines 3.116. Aeschines was a prominent Athenian orator of the fourth century.
J.7c   Aeschines 3.119, 3.122.
J.7d   Pherai (in Thessaly): Ref. Map 2, BX.
J.7e   Diodorus 16.56.3–8
J.8a   Plato, *Laws* 2.653d.
J.8b   Thucydides 2.15.4.
J.8c   Diodorus 5.4.7, 5.5.2.
J.8d   Isaios 3.80. Isaios was an Athenian orator who

lived c. 420–350.
J.9a   Eleusis: Ref. Map 3, BY.

better hope."[b] Other prominent cults in honor of feminine deities seem to have been extremely ancient. The cult whose center was the temple of Artemis in Ephesus,[c] managed by priestesses who were dedicated to sexual chastity, was said by Pausanias (7.2.6) to have predated the coming of Greeks to the Ionian coast.

§10. A common feature of festivals was competition, and they provided a more wholesome, or at least less costly, outlet for competitive spirit than warfare. Competitive sports appear in Homeric epic, when the Greeks conduct games in honor of the dead hero Patroclus.[a] By the sixth century, there was a "circuit" (*periodos*) of athletic festivals that included the Pythian Games (at Delphi), the Nemean Games (at Nemea),[b] the Isthmian Games (at Corinth),[c] and of course the most famous of the ancient games, the festival in honor of Zeus at Olympia.[d] Iphitus, king of Elis,[e] is traditionally said to have founded the Olympic Games in 776, and they were conducted from then on every four years. At first, the games consisted of just a single footrace, to which other contests were added over time: horse races, chariot races, boxing, wrestling, special events for boys, and finally nonathletic competitions for heralds and trumpeters.[f] Prizes were symbolic—an olive crown—rather than monetary, a fact that astonished non-Greeks.[g] But Olympic victors often earned rich rewards upon returning home, such as the competitor from Akragas[h] who was escorted into his city by three hundred chariots.[i] Olympic victors might assume a degree of divine favor that would lead them into trouble, as happened to the Athenian Cylon when he assumed that his Olympic victory in the 630s might lead him to become a tyrant of Athens.[j]

§11. Other festivals included different kinds of competitions, from beauty contests (at a festival to Hera on Lesbos)[a] to the great drama festivals of Athens—the Dionysia and the Lenaea—which were the occasion for presenting the dramas of Aristophanes, Aeschylus, Sophocles, Euripides, and the countless poets whose comedies and tragedies do not survive. All these competitions honored the gods and fostered a sense of community, both among citizens of a *polis* and between citizens of different cities. Because these festivals honored the gods, and were indeed established by the gods, the Greeks believed that the gods insisted on efforts to ensure that Greeks could attend them without fear. According to tradition, when asked how to save Greece from wars and pestilence, the Delphic oracle (speaking for Apollo) urged Iphitus of Elis to institute a universal period of truce for the duration of each Olympic festival.[b] This is perhaps the oldest example of a "festival truce," but by the fourth century there were others, most notably the annual truce whereby even states at war allowed safe passage of Greeks traveling to Eleusis in Attica for the Eleusinian Mysteries.[c] At the festivals, too, participants were supposed to be safe from violence. Xenophon (4.4.2) mentions the shocking sacrilege of a massacre of

J.9b　Cicero, *Laws* 2.14.36.
J.9c　Ephesus: Ref. Map 2, CY.
J.10a　Homer, *Iliad* 23.
J.10b　Nemea: Ref. Map 3, CY.
J.10c　Corinth: Ref. Map 3, BY. The games were held at the Isthmus of Corinth, hence the name.
J.10d　Olympia: Ref. Map 2, CW.
J.10e　Elis: Ref. Map 2, CW.
J.10f　Pausanias 5.8.
J.10g　Herodotus, *Histories* 8.26.3.

J.10h　Akragas (in Sicily): Ref. Map 1.
J.10i　Diodorus 13.34.1.
J.10j　Thucydides 1.126.
J.11a　See Alkaios, Fragment 30 (Lobel, Edgar, Sappho, Alcaeus, and Denys Lionel Page. *Poetarum Lesbiorum fragmenta*. Oxford: Clarendon Press, 1955.). Lesbos: Ref. Map 2, BY.
J.11b　Pausanias 5.4.6.
J.11c　Aeschines 2.133.

citizens at Corinth that the perpetrators planned and executed during the festival of Artemis Eucleia at Corinth.

§12. Read in their context, many of the passages that provide our evidence for religious practices and beliefs also call them into question. We know, for example, that Greeks could seek divine protection by making themselves suppliants at altars mainly because of the instances when suppliants were dragged away from altars and killed;[a] we know that murder during a religious festival was a terrible sacrilege from accounts of murders at festivals. We also know that some oracles, in their ambiguity of meaning, did their recipients no good, and that prayers and sacrifices before battle inevitably failed to secure victory for the soldiers on one side. In their hour of need during the great plague of the 420s, Thucydides (2.47.4) says of the Athenians that "as many prayers as they offered at the temples, or no matter what oracles and the like they employed, none provided any help at all." Nevertheless, with the possible exception of a few intellectuals, the traditions of reverence toward the gods, competition in their presence (and for their favor), and vigorous negotiations with them are richly attested from the Homeric world into the Hellenistic Age, practiced across the Greek world by people at all levels of society, from the provincial and barely literate to the most widely traveled, sophisticated aristocrats, like the philosopher, historian, and soldier Xenophon.

Christopher Blackwell
Department of Classics
Furman University
Greenville, South Carolina

J.12a   Thucydides 1.126.

APPENDIX K

Trireme Warfare in Xenophon's *Hellenika*

§1. The disaster at Syracuse[a] (415–413) marked the effective end of Athenian naval supremacy. She would rebuild her fleets and continue to be a force, but Xenophon's account of the following half century tells of a hard-fought struggle among many contenders to dominate the Aegean Sea.[b] Although in the ancient Mediterranean world geography and tradition favored islands and coastal cities as emergent sea powers, dominance could not be achieved without also having access to the vital resources of timber, manpower, and plenty of revenue.[c] Thus the Persian king Artaxerxes and Jason of Pherai[d] posed alarming threats to the traditional masters of the Aegean. Athens, Sparta, and reportedly the Phoenicians managed on occasion to raise fleets of two or even three hundred warships,[e] but mostly the seas were dotted with much smaller flotillas that nevertheless effectively patrolled, threatened, or deterred.

§2. The standard ship of the line in all these navies was the trireme, a seaborne projectile armed with a bronze ram and powered by three banks of rowers.[a] Triremes patrolled coasts, blockaded harbors,[b] guarded sea-lanes (especially those from the grain-rich Black Sea),[c] enforced the collection of tribute and tolls,[d] and transported armies,[e] important people,[f] and news. But most essentially triremes were designed for battle on the open seas. Speed and ramming were their primary offensive weapons. Only a small complement of fighting men—ten marines and four archers—was traditionally stationed on a trireme. The number and nature of armed men on board could vary,[g] but the ram remained the primary weapon. Unlike those of tubby merchant ships, built for capacity, trireme hulls were long and narrow,[h] probably able to slice through the water as fast as any oar-powered ship before or since, propelled by the coordinated strokes of 170 oarsmen. A crew of sixteen sailors and officers operated the sails, and they, together with the normal complement of armed men and the rowers, brought the total number of men on a trireme to 200. Triremes could also be equipped with sails, so wind had to be taken into account as

K.1a Syracuse (in Sicily): Ref. Map 1.
K.1b Aegean Sea: Ref. Map 2, BX.
K.1c See 5.2.16, 6.1.11, 7.1.3–7.
K.1d Pherai (in Thessaly): Ref. Map 2, BX.
K.1e Large Phoenician fleets: 2.1.20, 2.2.7, 3.4.1.
　　　 Phoenicia: Ref. Map 1.
K.2a See Figure K.2.
K.2b See 2.2.9, 4.8.6, 5.1.2, 5.1.7, 6.2.7–8.

K.2c See 1.1.22, 2.1.17, 4.6.14, 5.4.61.
K.2d See 1.1.8, 1.1.12, 1.1.22, 4.8.27, 4.8.31, 5.1.6,
　　　 6.2.38.
K.2e See 6.4.18.
K.2f See 1.1.9, 4.1.15.
K.2g See 1.2.1, 6.2.37.
K.2h Approximately 120 by 15 feet.

FIGURE K.1. THE TRIREME *OLYMPIAS* UNDER SAIL.

a factor in strategy, but battle tactics were based entirely on rowing maneuvers. In preparation for battle, every care was taken to gain the advantage of superior speed. Sails and all items extraneous to the battle at hand (masts, tackle, spares, supplies) were removed from the ship.[i] The hulls themselves were dry-docked as often as possible in order to keep them from becoming waterlogged and thus from sitting heavily and moving slowly in the water.[j] Not all triremes were in equal condition or could attain equal speeds.[k] Trireme crews took pride in crewing the fastest ship in a fleet, and captains selected the most experienced men to complete their crews.[l] The tip of this giant water-arrow was a bronze ram that splintered enemy hulls or oars upon contact. The force of impact was as destructive as the pronged tip of the

K.2i This would explain how the Athenian general Konon, in flight from Aigospotamoi (Aigospotamos) (Ref. Map 2, AY), was able to capture the main sails of the Peloponnesian fleet (2.1.29), which had been left in camp before the battle. This capture may well have hindered, if not prevented, the Peloponnesians from pursuing his ships. See also 6.2.27.

K.2j See 1.5.10.
K.2k See 2.1.24, 5.1.27.
K.2l See 1.6.19.

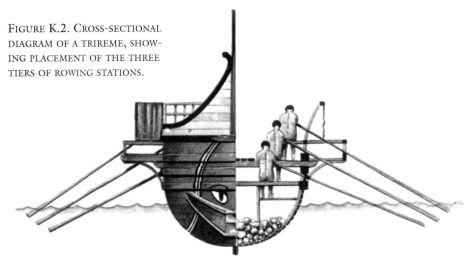

FIGURE K.2. CROSS-SECTIONAL DIAGRAM OF A TRIREME, SHOWING PLACEMENT OF THE THREE TIERS OF ROWING STATIONS.

weapon; the head of the ram was designed to strike a broad area and split as many seams of the enemy hull as possible without actually penetrating (and thus getting stuck in) the foreign wood.

§3. Conventional sea battles began with a face-off: the two opposing navies lined up against each other.[a] Each line was extended as far as possible in order to prevent the enemy from sailing around the ends of the line and attacking the unprotected sterns from behind (*periplous*). At the same time, the line could not be over-extended; ships had to be spaced closely enough to prevent the enemy from sailing through gaps (*diekplous*) and either smashing through one's own oars or wheeling about and attacking from behind.[b] And commanders had to consider yet a third factor: ships could not be so closely packed that their oars interfered with those of the adjacent ship in their own line. If a commander did not trust his single line to hold out against a superior opponent, he might form a second line behind the first, to cover the point(s) of weakness.[c] A fleet whose line had been outflanked or breached had few defensive options. A commander with skilled crews could pull his ships into a circle, prows bristling outward, and hope to stave off his opponents until exhaustion or nightfall prompted them to give up the attack. Or he could order a tactical retreat to a nearby beach from which his ships could be similarly defended.[d]

§4. It was extremely difficult to achieve any of these offensive or defensive formations. Ancient accounts of naval encounters frequently describe how winds, currents, the crews' varying levels of skill and commitment, and the unpredictable fortunes of war[a] altered the blueprints of battles. Drills on the *Olympias*,[b] a modern reconstruction

K.3a See 1.6.31, 2.1.23.
K.3b The Athenian formation at Arginousai was designed to prevent this; see 1.6.31.
K.3c See 1.6.29–32 for the deployments of the two opposing fleets at the battle of the Arginousai Islands (Ref. Map 2, BY).
K.3d See 1.1.7.
K.4a For example, Kallikratidas' unfortunate tumble at 1.6.33.

K.4b The *Olympias* was designed by scholars and marine architects and commissioned in 1987. The ship is on permanent display at the Hellenic Navy Museum, near the Peiraieus. See Figures K.1, K.2, K.3, and 2.2.7; see also J. S. Morrison, J. F. Coates, and N. B. Rankov, *The Athenian Trireme: The History and Reconstruction of an Ancient Greek Warship*, 2nd ed. (Cambridge: Cambridge University Press, 2000), esp. pp. 231–75.

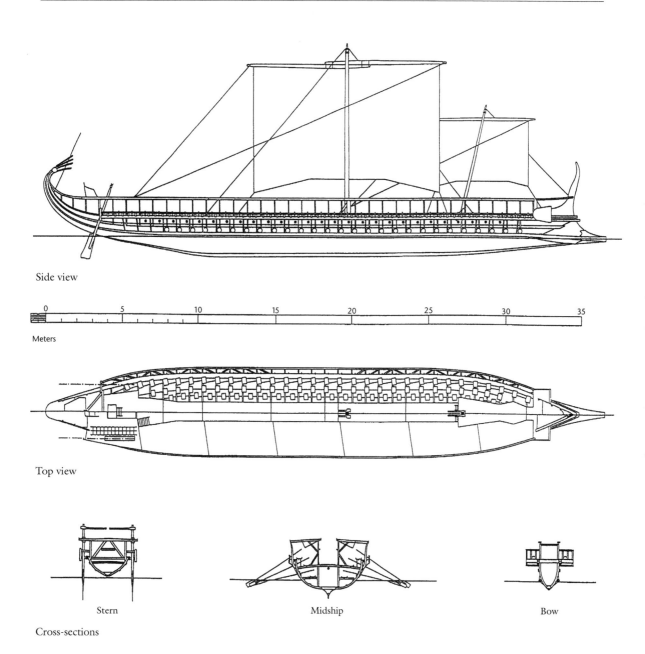

Side view

Meters

Top view

Stern   Midship   Bow

Cross-sections

FIGURE K.3. DIAGRAM OF THE MODERN TRIREME *OLYMPIAS.*

of a trireme, have demonstrated the difficulties that a crew would have in hearing and executing orders in quiet, controlled conditions, much less in the tumult of battle.

§5. It is no wonder, then, that commanders frequently resorted to trickery and unorthodox measures to increase their chance of success. The outcomes of many of the sea battles recounted by Xenophon hinged on the element of surprise. One favored technique was the attack or escape under cover of night.[a] Landmarks were the primary means of navigation in Greek antiquity, and so sailing was mainly a daylight activity. Even battles ceased at sundown. Perhaps because it was so unusual, Xenophon vividly describes the extraordinary nature of the Spartan vice-admiral Gorgopas' nighttime pursuit of an Athenian squadron and the ensuing moonlight battle.[b] Experience on the *Olympias* indicates that rowing triremes is always a noisy process and sound carries great distances over water. Night escapades could only have been successful because they exploited what the enemy reasonably expected. Other tricks succeeded for the same reason. Whatever the exact purpose of Konon's sidescreens,[c] his escape plan worked because repetition lulled the enemy into complacent inattention. Those tables were famously turned on Konon at Aigospotamoi,[d] where the Athenians were defeated not by fast ships or skilled crews but by hungry bellies and each side's expectation that the other would follow precedent.

§6. A rammed ship, even if severely damaged, did not sink immediately. There were no significant obstacles to bar the crews from jumping overboard; the empty wooden hull would swamp and become completely unmaneuverable but would float on the surface for some time until it became completely waterlogged and finally sank. It was the victor's prerogative to sail out among the debris of the battlefield and collect the drifting hulls and men. Captured enemy were enslaved (or worse);[a] captured hulls were refitted or salvaged for parts and material.[b] Rams, which were made of bronze and could weigh more than half a ton, were salvaged where possible for the value of the metal or perhaps for reuse on other ships. Sometimes captured rams were sawn off by the victors and erected as trophies on land nearest to the battle site.[c]

§7. The Achilles' heel of the ancient navy was its crew. The need to feed, finance, occupy, and sometimes even inspire the rowers was a crucial element of any naval campaign. First and foremost was the need to feed and rest the rowers. Rowing was a cramped, stifling, sweaty, smelly job. The long, narrow warships had limited space for provisions or preparing meals and no place at all for rowers to stretch out and sleep. One of the extraordinary aspects of the Spartan admiral Teleutias' night raid into the Peiraieus harbor was that the ships were rowed continuously, with oarsman resting (presumably at their benches) at alternating turns.[a] Every trireme captain had to think daily about where he would be able to stop for the night and how his sailors would get fed. Sailors could bring some food on board and eat "on the run," but more often mealtimes meant putting in to shore to allow sailors to forage in town or countryside. These midday breaks, when ships were beached and troops dispersed,

K.5a   For instances in the *Hellenika* where forces maneu-vered at night in order to surprise their opponent, see 1.1.13, 1.6.28, 4.8.35, 5.1.8–9, 5.1.19, 5.1.25, 6.2.11.
K.5b   See 5.1.8–9.
K.5c   See 1.6.19 and n. 1.6.19a.
K.5d   See 2.1.20–29. Lysander's trickery exploited the poor decision made by the Athenian leaders to locate their base camp far away from city markets that could supply food to the fleet's crews.
K.6a   See 2.1.31.
K.6b   See 1.1.18, where Syracusans burn ships rather than leave them to their victorious opponents.
K.6c   See 2.3.8, 6.2.36.
K.7a   See 5.1.19.

were moments of great vulnerability. Lysander based his winning strategy at Aigospotamoi on his enemies' need to forage for meals far from their ships.[b] The Athenian Iphikrates, whom Xenophon praises as the naval commander par excellence,[c] forestalled this danger by training his men simultaneously to eat and to maintain lookouts and be at the ready for immediate redeployment.[d] Logistics forced fleets to hug the coasts—a factor that had to be planned for defensively and could be aggressively exploited.

§8. A trireme captain also had to keep his crew paid. The crew could consist of all or a mixture of slaves, lower-class citizens, resident aliens (metics), or mercenaries.[a] All had to be paid to row, as they needed to purchase food and other necessities with their own funds.[b] Oarsmen, especially noncitizens, might change ships for better pay. Lysander, for example, urged Artaxerxes to fix the pay at one Attic drachma per day on the grounds that "if this was the wage offered, the Athenian crews would desert their ships."[c] Lysander, Kallikratidas, Konon, and Teleutias all struggled to fund their fleets,[d] and Xenophon's account is peppered with references to the need to pay rowers.[e]

§9. Idle crews were a potential source of trouble and were certainly a waste of money. Thus we hear of Syracusan sailors helping the city of Antandros finish fortifications while their fleet was being rebuilt, of Konon's sailors rebuilding the Long Walls, and of Iphikrates "maintaining" his sailors by letting them work on the land for the Corcyraeans.[a] The task of keeping sailors employed was particularly troublesome when the fleets remained stationed abroad over the winter. The sailing and fighting season regularly lasted from May through September; cold temperatures, storms, and contrary winds and currents reduced sea traffic to a minimum in the intervening months, although some instances of voyages and even battles during winter are known.[b]

§10. Maintaining crew cohesiveness was paramount to the effective functioning of the trireme. Trials on the *Olympias* demonstrated that even very experienced rowers need extensive group practice in order to coordinate their strokes sufficiently to achieve the speeds and perform the maneuvers ascribed to triremes. First, each individual had to became proficient at rowing on a specific level: oar mechanics and visibility varied significantly depending on one's position relative to the waterline and the ends of the ship. Second, close cooperation was vital to keeping all those oars working in tandem; the consequences of blades clashing like a row of falling dominoes could easily wreak havoc along the entire line. The need for constant training was no different in antiquity.[a] One unexpected discovery of the modern experiment was that the dense wooden environment absorbed sound within the confines of the

K.7b   See 2.1.25, 2.1.27.

K.7c   See 6.2.32.

K.7d   See 6.2.28–29.

K.8a   For use of mercenaries at sea, see 7.1.12; for slaves, see 1.6.24 and 5.1.11; for metics, see Thucydides 7.63.3.

K.8b   See 2.1.27.

K.8c   See 1.5.4.

K.8d   See 1.1.24–25, 1.5.3–8, 1.6.6, 1.6.18, 2.1.11, 2.1.14, 4.8.10, 4.8.12, 5.1.24. See also 2.3.40, 6.2.1.

K.8e   See 1.5.4–7, 1.6.12, 2.1.5, 2.1.12, 5.1.13, 5.1.24.

K.9a   For Syracusans at Antandros (Ref. Map 2, AY), see 1.1.26; for rebuilding the Long Walls of Athens (Ref. Map 5), see 4.8.10; for Iphikrates' sailors

working the land at Corcyra (Ref. Map 2, BW), see 6.2.37.

K.9b   All locations in this note can be found on Ref. Map 2 at the coordinates indicated. See Thucydides 8.30–44 for naval operations in the winter of 412/11 in the Aegean (BX), Samos (CY), Chios (CY), Rhodos (DY), Ionia (CY), and Caria (CZ). At 1.1.12 the battle of Abydos (AY) is thought by some to have been fought as late as November, and others believe that the battle of Cyzicus (AY), 1.1.14–19, took place earlier than May 410.

K.10a Mindaros' fleet was out practicing maneuvers at 1.1.16. Iphikrates had his fleet train and practice maneuvers as it sailed toward Corcyra, 6.2.30, 6.2.32.

hull, making it very difficult for the rowers to hear signals. As a result, each oarsman relied heavily on the body language of those sitting directly in front of or above him. The crew became an integrated network, and holes or substitutions in the rowing arrangement threw a wrench in the gears of the rowing machine. Rowers were not randomly replaceable.

§11. It was the responsibility of the captain (trierarch) to keep his crew trained and intact.[a] In the Athenian system, captaincy was a one-year public service, undertaken by only the wealthiest citizens as a sort of patriotic burden or tax. The state supplied a ship, the minimum necessary equipment, and the basic rate of pay for a crew; the captain was responsible for hiring the crew and outfitting and maintaining (and returning) the ship. The amateur captain probably relied heavily on his paid staff. The most important member (and the only one who is ever named) was the helmsman (*kybernetes*). Alcibiades trusted his helmsman, Antiochos, enough to give him command of the fleet during Alcibiades' absence, and it is the helmsmen who are called as witnesses in the trial of the Arginousai generals.[b] Ultimate command of a fleet lay in the hands of one or several of the generals (*strategoi*) elected by the citizens to lead the army or the fleet. Sparta had a specific office of admiral (navarch), but men appointed to this position might or might not have much experience on the water,[c] and the assignment of a commander perceived as incompetent was another potential source of grumbling among the crews.[d]

§12. Xenophon's predecessor, Thucydides, had chronicled the glory days of classical sea power. Control of the water serves as a focus and a metaphor in his story of Athenian imperialism. He gives us, also, a glimpse of the beginning of the end. We see the Athenians lose their edge in naval technology; the Peloponnesian allies develop new warship designs and strategies that the Athenians emulate too late. Xenophon is by comparison a landlubber; the sea is an element, but not a centerpiece, in his account of Athens' and Sparta's final bitter decline. His story of the sea and its ships is not nearly as detailed or coherent. But in his narrative we can see the human dimension of naval warfare and the pivotal role of the anonymous rowers in the struggle for command of the Aegean. Two generations later, Alexander the Great circumvented the need for rowers and gained control of the seas by conquering the coasts and ports on which the fleets of the eastern Mediterranean relied for manpower, provisions, and timber.

Nicolle Hirschfeld
Assistant Professor
Department of Classical Studies
Trinity University
San Antonio, Texas

K.11a For difficulties in keeping triremes fully manned, see 1.5.20, 5.1.27, 6.2.12.

K.11b Alcibiades leaves Antiochos in charge at 1.5.11–12, and the generals furnish a helmsman as a witness in the Arginousai trial at 1.7.6. Another instance in the *Hellenika* that shows the importance of the helmsman is at 1.6.32, when Hermon the Megarian advises the Spartan admiral Kallikratidas.

K.11c Agesilaos appointed his inexperienced brother-in-law Peisander to command the Spartan fleet (3.4.29).

K.11d Spartan sailors complained of Kallikratides' qualifications when he replaced Lysander (1.6.4).

APPENDIX L
Land Warfare in Xenophon's *Hellenika*

§1. Greece in the late fifth and early fourth centuries was in a period of military ferment. Traditional Greek warfare had been limited and formalized: heavily armored citizen infantrymen called hoplites predominated, leaving little place for light infantry or cavalry. Most wars were border conflicts, in which battlefield maneuver and pursuit were rare. The long years of the Peloponnesian War (431–404), and the decades of struggle for hegemony that ensued, overturned the old ways of fighting. Instead, as armies grew in complexity and capability, commanders experimented with innovative tactics and strategies, and cities evolved new expectations about war.

§2. The *Hellenika* provides an insider's perspective on these developments. Xenophon probably first saw battle as a teenager with the Athenian cavalry in the last decade of the Peloponnesian War. In his twenties he gained extensive experience leading mercenaries in Mesopotamia and Asia Minor, and subsequently he accompanied the Spartan army on many of its campaigns. A skilled cavalryman and an able general, Xenophon trained a veteran's eye on the warfare of the period. He pays close attention to tactical innovations and records details of ordinary soldiers' lives that others ignore. At the same time, he did not intend the *Hellenika* as a handbook on warfare: he mentions many military terms without explanation, and his battle accounts are often compressed or distorted to fit his narrative purposes.[a]

§3. Hoplites remained the mainstay of Greek armies in Xenophon's age. The hoplite's trademark was his concave round shield of bronze-faced wood, about three feet in diameter. Weighing some twelve to sixteen pounds, the shield was supported on its bearer's left arm by a distinctive double grip. For armor, men wore hammered-bronze breastplates or less-expensive corselets of leather or laminated cloth. These were supplemented by bronze helmets and greaves (shin guards). During the late fifth century, hoplites began to trade protection for mobility, with some eventually discarding all body armor and relying on shields and helmets for defense.

L.2a The Introduction, §10, on Xenophon's manipulative use of pointed anecdotes, discusses the example of the battle of Sardis.

Offensive gear changed less. The primary hoplite weapon of the era, a seven- or eight-foot-long thrusting spear with bronze point and end-spike, differed little from that of the Persian Wars a century before. The *machaira*, a curved single-edged saber, became an increasingly popular secondary weapon but never entirely replaced the traditional double-edged short sword.

§4. Most hoplites were citizen militia who furnished their own equipment and had little formal training. Well into the fourth century, only Sparta possessed systematic military instruction for its entire citizen body.[a] Some cities did form elite units of *epilektoi* (7.2.10), picked troops who trained full-time at public expense. Most famous of these was the Theban Sacred Band (7.1.19), comprising 150 pairs of lovers sworn to fight to the death. Outside Sparta, military organization, too, was rudimentary. Many armies grouped their hoplites into *lokhoi*, or companies, probably of several hundred men apiece.[b] The Athenians usually deployed their hoplites in ten *phylai*, or regiments (4.2.19), one for each of Athens' ten civic tribes. Xenophon also mentions a smaller unit called the *lokhos*, or company (1.2.3, 4.2.5), used by both citizen and mercenary forces.

§5. Hoplites fought in a densely packed phalanx formation, typically eight ranks deep (3.2.16). Each man required about three feet of lateral space, meaning that a phalanx of ten thousand hoplites in battle array could stretch three-quarters of a mile. Because the left edge of each hoplite's shield overlapped his neighbor's exposed right shoulder, advancing phalanxes often drifted to the right as men edged further behind their comrades' shields (4.2.18). Generals therefore tended to station themselves and their best troops on the right wing, hoping to overwhelm the enemy left before their own inferior left flank collapsed.

§6. While traditional hoplite-on-hoplite clashes had involved little maneuver, the commanders of Xenophon's era exploited this emphasis on the right wing to develop more complex tactics. The highly trained Spartans could extend their right wing beyond an enemy army's left, then wheel inward to assail its flank or rear (4.2.20). They could also wheel in reverse to retract a threatened flank (6.2.20–21). The Thebans relied on increasingly deep formations (4.2.18) to overwhelm opponents. This approach was perfected by Epaminondas and Pelopidas in the 370s. At the battle of Leuctra[a] in 371, the Thebans added another twist by concentrating a massive force more than fifty ranks deep not on their right but on their left wing, where the Spartans least expected it (6.4.12). A further refinement appeared at the battle of Mantineia[b] (362), where Epaminondas led his infantry, arrayed in a deep wedge or column, directly against the opposing Peloponnesian right-center before the enemy could engage Thebes'[c] weaker allies (7.5.22–25).

§7. Though supreme in pitched battle, hoplites on hills or in built-up areas were vulnerable to archers, slingers, and peltasts. Peltasts were unarmored foot soldiers whose primary weapon was the javelin.[a] They attacked at a run, throwing their missiles before turning to escape. Smart commanders learned how to counter such attacks by dispatching their youngest, swiftest hoplites in pursuit (4.4.16), by using cavalry (5.4.54), or by deploying peltasts of their own, but these techniques did not

L.4a   See Appendix F, §1–6.
L.4b   Military companies: see 3.4.16, 6.4.13, 7.2.4, 7.5.22.
L.6a   Leuctra: Ref. Map 3, BY.

L.6b   Mantineia: Ref. Map 3, CX.
L.6c   Thebes: Ref. Map 2, CX.
L.7a   See 2.4.15–16, 3.2.3–4, 4.3.22–23, 4.6.7.

always work. In 390, Athenian peltasts ambushed a Spartan hoplite regiment at Lechaion, near Corinth,[b] killing almost half the regiment (4.5.7–18).

§8. Both hoplites and light infantry increasingly found themselves involved in urban combat. There was extensive street fighting in Athens' port of Peiraieus[a] during the struggle against the regime of the Thirty[b] and in Laconia[c] during the Theban invasion of 370–369 (6.5.26–32). Much fighting also took place on and near city walls.[d] Urban combat was especially brutal during revolutions and civil strife.[e]

§9. Greek cavalrymen of the period were lightly armored and generally preferred throwing javelins to shock combat. During his campaigns in Asia Minor[a] and Thessaly,[b] the Spartan king Agesilaos had some success in creating an effective cavalry.[c] By the 370s, though, Spartan horsemen were of poor quality (6.4.10–11). Thessaly and Boeotia,[d] in contrast, developed increasingly good cavalry forces. Although cavalry was not yet the decisive arm on the battlefield, preliminary mounted skirmishes could influence the course of a hoplite clash (6.4.13). When properly handled, cavalry could also drive away peltasts (4.5.13) and was extremely useful for scouting, raiding, and pursuit. Some cities deployed units of light infantrymen specially trained to fight together with horsemen (7.2.4, 7.5.23).

§10. Mercenaries had long been part of the fabric of Aegean[a] life, but the late fifth century witnessed a dramatic increase in the numbers of Greeks going abroad for hire. Political exiles and gentlemen adventurers figure prominently in accounts of mercenary life, but most ordinary soldiers simply sought pay and booty. The region of Arcadia in the Peloponnese[b] earned renown for the quality of its hoplite mercenaries (7.1.23), as did Crete[c] for its archers. The Persian satraps (governors) of Asia Minor became major employers of Greek mercenaries. Indeed, in 401 the Persian prince Cyrus recruited more than ten thousand of them to support his bid to usurp the Achaemenid throne.[d] Although Xenophon records the widespread use of hired professionals (6.2.16), he says little about the challenges they posed to the traditional ethos of the citizen soldier or of the dangers of mercenary-backed tyranny (7.4.8).[e]

§11. The role of commanders, too, was changing as constant war gave rise to a new class of experienced professionals. Some, like Agesilaos, headed citizen armies, while others, among them Xenophon himself, made their mark leading mercenaries. Successful generalship now required much more than personal bravery and charisma. Strategic deceptiveness,[a] organizational skill,[b] and effective use of terrain,[c] along with knowledge of field fortifications and urban fighting,[d] all became essential. The Macedonians[e] usually get the credit for inventing combined-arms warfare,

L.7b   Lechaion and Corinth: Ref. Map 3, BY.
L.8a   Peiraieus: Ref. Map 5.
L.8b   See 2.4.11–19, 2.4.33–34.
L.8c   Laconia: Ref. Map 2, DX.
L.8d   See 3.5.19, 4.4.12, 4.7.6, 7.1.19.
L.8e   See 3.2.28, 5.4.8–12, 6.5.9.
L.9a   Asia (Minor): Ref. Map 1.
L.9b   Thessaly: Ref. Map 2, BX.
L.9c   See 3.4.15, 3.4.22–24, 4.3.6.
L.9d   Boeotia: Ref. Map 2, CX.
L.10a Aegean Sea: Ref. Map 2, BX.
L.10b Arcadia, Peloponnese: Ref. Map 3, CX.
L.10c Crete: Ref. Map 1.

L.10d Xenophon's *Anabasis* describes his own participation in this expedition. See the Introduction, §4.2, 5.2.
L.10e As the note to the text on this passage at 7.4.8 explains further, Xenophon obliquely refers to an attempted coup in Corinth c. 365 by the mercenary leader Timophanes.
L.11a See 4.5.3, 5.4.48, 7.5.21.
L.11b See 3.4.16–19.
L.11c See 4.2.19, 7.1.29.
L.11d See 1.3.4, 6.4.14.
L.11e Macedon: Ref. Map 2, AX.

but it was the leaders of Xenophon's day who first understood the potential of hoplites, cavalry, and light infantry working together.[f]

§12. Professional leadership also meant better logistical support, although in this area developments moved slowly. Men generally started from home carrying several days' rations (7.1.41). When that ran out, they purchased food from local markets (3.4.11, 5.4.48) or from traveling sutlers (6.4.9). Troops without money or those operating in hostile territory foraged, plundered, or requisitioned, although dispersed foragers were vulnerable to surprise attack (3.4.22, 4.1.17–19). Failing to provide timely pay, especially to mercenaries, could also lead to demoralization and mutiny (6.2.16–19). In extraordinary circumstances supply convoys could be arranged (7.2.17–19), but only the Spartans possessed organized transport and medical services. Wealthier citizen soldiers brought along slave attendants to help carry baggage, but poorer men shouldered the load themselves. Noncombatant boys and women became valued adjuncts, especially in mercenary forces (6.2.23).

§13. For all these changes, certain time-honored rituals of war persisted. Religious sacrifices before battle were a must;[a] sometimes generals also delivered speeches.[b] As they advanced, rallied, or celebrated soldiers sang their native *paeans*, or war hymns (4.2.19). Afterward, victors customarily erected on the field a trophy (from *tropaion*, the turning point of the battle), consisting at least partly of arms and armor stripped from enemy dead.[c] Losers for their part requested, and were granted, a truce in which to recover their dead.[d] These rules were followed even in the midst of bitter civil strife (2.4.19). As Xenophon saw it, religious piety and good leadership were inseparable,[e] and woe betide the officer who neglected the proper rites or ignored the omens (3.1.18).

§14. Just as warfare defined Xenophon's life, so did it shape the history of his era. Fifty years of near-constant conflict saw the failure of three successive attempts, by Athens, Sparta, and Thebes, to exert hegemony over Greece. These wars sapped populations and treasuries across Greece. The professionalism in military affairs they engendered also posed a severe threat to the traditional social order of the *polis*. Exhausted and confused, the Greek cities in the mid-fourth century prepared for yet another round of struggle, little knowing that within a generation military hegemony would be imposed from outside, by the Macedonians.

John W. I. Lee
Associate Professor
Department of History
University of California at Santa Barbara
Santa Barbara, California

L.11f   See 2.4.25, 3.4.13–15, 3.4.23, 4.1.20, 4.2.20, 4.2.23, 4.3.15, 4.6.10, 7.2.10, 7.5.23–24.
L.13a   See 3.4.23, 4.1.22, 4.2.20.
L.13b   See 2.4.13–17, 7.1.30–31.
L.13c   See 1.2.3, 3.5.19, 4.3.21, 4.5.10, 4.6.12.

L.13d   Although the Thebans on at least two occasions, at Delium (Thucydides 4.97–101) and at Haliartos (3.4.23–24), refused to grant a truce in the normal manner but made it conditional.
L.13e   See 3.2.16, 3.4.15, 4.1.22.

APPENDIX M

Brief Biographies of Important Characters
in Xenophon's *Hellenika*

Agesilaos: see Appendix G
1. Agesipolis
2. Agis II
3. Alcibiades
4. Antalkidas
5. Archidamos III
6. Chabrias
7. Cyrus the Younger
8. Derkylidas
9. Epaminondas

10. Eteonikos
11. Herippidas
12. Iphikrates
13. Jason of Pherai
14. Kallistratos
15. Kleombrotos
16. Konon
17. Kritias
18. Lysander
19. Pausanias

20. Pelopidas
21. Pharnabazos
22. Sphodrias
23. Teleutias
24. Theramenes
25. Thibron
26. Thrasyboulos (of Steiria)
27 Thrasyllos
28. Timotheos
29. Tissaphernes

Agesipolis

§1. Agesipolis ruled as the Agiad[a] king of Sparta from 394 to 380. He was the son of King Pausanias (§19), who outlived him but for many years resided in Tegea[b] (3.5.25) as an exile after he was convicted for failure in the Corinthian War but also—and perhaps mainly—for being too soft on Athenian and possibly other democrats. Because Agesipolis was underage at the beginning of his reign, his relative (and guardian) Aristodemos initially ruled as regent for him (4.2.9). Agesipolis' first command was to lead an expedition against Argos.[c] The Argives tried to turn religion against the Spartans by declaring a sacred truce, but Agesipolis brilliantly thwarted them. He had previously received the approval of Zeus' oracle at Olympia[d] for an invasion of Argive territory and then had it confirmed by the oracle of Zeus' son Apollo at Delphi[e] (4.7.2–6). The relationship of Agesipolis and his contemporary Eurypontid king Agesilaos constituted a shining exception to the rule that Spartan co-kings did not get on with each other; in the joint royal mess they reportedly enjoyed discussing their youth, hunting exploits, horsemanship, and love of boys (5.3.20). That need not mean that they agreed with each other about policy, and Diodorus (15.19.4) says that after the King's Peace in 386 Agesipolis was opposed to Agesilaos' hard-line imperialism against other Greek states; but scholars disagree

M.1a Two dynastic lines shared the hereditary dual Spartan kingship: the Eurypontids, descended from Eurypon, and the Agiads, descended from Agis. Both claimed descent from Herakles.

M.1b Tegea: Ref. Map 3, CX.
M.1c Argos: Ref. Map 2, CX.
M.1d Olympia: Ref. Map 2, CW.
M.1e Delphi: Ref. Map 2, CX.

about how far to believe Diodorus. However that may be, in 385 he certainly executed an aggressive imperialist policy of which Agesilaos no doubt approved, by leading Spartan forces against Mantineia.[f] (Agesilaos had declined the command on specious grounds, perhaps wanting to ensure that Agesipolis would subsequently have difficulty in attacking his policy.) Agesipolis captured the town by damming a river, causing it to flood, which threatened to undermine Mantineia's walls. He permitted his father to intercede for the Mantineian democrats and allowed them to go into exile, but he still insisted that the city's people would be dispersed to the four villages they had originally occupied (5.2.1–7). He led a Spartan expedition against Olynthos[g] in 380[h] but died there of a fever (5.3.9, 5.3.18–19), and his body, embalmed in honey, was returned to Sparta for the characteristic royal funeral.

Agis II

§2. Agis II, king of Sparta, son of Archidamos III, reigned from 427 to 400. He achieved little in Spartan military operation in the Archidamian War[a] (431–421) and in 418 initially had further problems when he led Spartan forces against Argos and its allies. Although he skillfully outmaneuvered the Argives, he did not achieve a decisive military victory but agreed to a four-month truce, for which he was criticized. However, when the Argives did not honor the truce and, still in 418, threatened to march with their allies on Tegea, Agis gained renown by leading the Spartans and their allies to a decisive victory over them at Mantineia. This victory reestablished Spartan authority in the Peloponnese[b] and prestige in Greece generally. In 413, Agis' forces occupied and fortified the Attic town of Dekeleia[c] and remained there until the siege of Athens in 405–404, cooperating with the naval forces under Lysander (§18) until Athens surrendered. His final campaign was a successful invasion of Elis.[d] He died in 400, having acknowledged Leotychidas as his son and successor; but because of a liaison between Agis' wife Timeaea and Alcibiades (§3), Leotychidas was not recognized as legitimate, so Agis was succeeded by his younger half brother, Agesilaos.

Alcibiades

§3. Alcibiades (c. 452–404/3) was the son of Cleinias, an Athenian politician and general, and Deinomache, of the ancient aristocratic family of the Alkmeonidai. After being brought up by his guardian, Pericles (the most powerful politician in Athens of his day), he became a pupil of the philosopher Socrates. In his *Memorabilia*, Xenophon tries to make out that this relationship did not last long, but Plato, our principal source of information about Socrates, emphasizes its length and intimacy. He was spoiled as an adolescent because of his great beauty, and his flamboyant, arrogant, and sometimes petulant behavior became notorious. In 421/20 he was

M.1f Mantineia: Ref. Map 3, CX.
M.1g Olynthos: Ref. Map 2, AX.
M.1h Our text, which follows *The Cambridge Ancient History* chronology, says this took place in 381 (5.3.1–7). Many other scholars give 380 as the date of the fighting at Olynthos, as Paul Cartledge does here. This is an example of scholars reaching diverse con-

clusions about chronology in Xenophon's *Hellenika*.
M.2a The Archidamian War is the modern name for the first phase of the Peloponnesian War between Athens and Sparta.
M.2b Peloponnese: Ref. Map 2, CW.
M.2c Dekeleia: Ref. Map 3, BZ.
M.2d Elis: Ref. Map 2, CW.

responsible for drawing Athens into a coalition with Argos and other enemies of Sparta, though this policy was discredited after the Spartan victory at Mantineia (418). During this period, Alcibiades' principal political adversary was the more established and pacific statesman Nikias, although they temporarily cooperated with each other to avoid ostracism in 416. Despite this rivalry, the Athenians appointed both of them to command the Sicilian[a] expedition in 415, which Alcibiades had promoted, even though Nikias had opposed it. On the eve of the expedition, many herms, stylized statues of the god Hermes that stood as boundary markers throughout Athens, were found to have been mutilated. Alcibiades was accused of involvement in this (no doubt wrongly) and with blasphemously imitating the Eleusinian Mysteries (quite possibly correctly). Although he tried to make his accusers bring him to trial immediately, he was compelled to sail to Sicily; but, shortly after his arrival there, he was recalled to Athens for trial. He escaped to Sparta and encouraged the Spartans both to provide assistance to the Syracusans[b] and to reopen their war with Athens and establish a permanent Spartan fort at Dekeleia in Attica[c] (413). He convinced the Spartans to focus on the Aegean[d] rather than the Hellespont[e] in 412, but his influence at Sparta dwindled after that, partly because of a personal quarrel with King Agis (§2), and he finally had to seek refuge with the Persian satrap Tissaphernes (§29), who initially welcomed him. Alcibiades is said to have advised Tissaphernes to keep both Athens and Sparta weak by alternately giving and withholding his support from the Spartans. He also attempted to bring about an oligarchic revolution in Athens, which did occur in 411, but its leaders were, or had become by then, strongly opposed to him. He therefore backed the Athenian fleet at Samos,[f] which had remained loyal to democratic principles. The men of the fleet appointed him general and he proceeded to conduct successful military operations in the Hellespont, achieving a great victory at Cyzicus[g] in 410. All outstanding charges against him were dropped upon his return to Athens in 407, and he was even elected to an extraordinary command. But a subordinate he had left in command during a temporary absence from the main fleet was defeated by Lysander (§18) at Notion[h] in early 406. Alcibiades' enemies in Athens then secured his dismissal from command, and he withdrew to Thrace.[i] The following year, after his attempt to offer good advice to the Athenian generals at Aigospotamoi[j] failed and their fleet was annihilated, he took refuge in Phrygia,[k] the territory of the Persian satrap Pharnabazos (§21). He was attacked and murdered somewhere in Phrygia in 404/3 while on his way to visit the Persian King at Susa.[l] There were various ancient theories as to those responsible. Some said it was on the orders of Pharnabazos, instigated by the Spartans (who in turn had been stirred up by their Athenian junta, the Thirty); others, that Pharnabazos arranged it for his own reasons; and yet others, that it was carried out by the brothers of a Persian woman Alcibiades had seduced. Although presented in the ancient sources as rival views, these theories are not necessarily incompatible.

M.3a   Sicily: Ref. Map 1.
M.3b   Syracuse: Ref. Map 1.
M.3c   Attica: Ref. Map 2, CX.
M.3d   Aegean Sea: Ref. Map 2, BX.
M.3e   Hellespont: Ref. Map 2, BY.
M.3f   Samos: Ref. Map 2, CY.
M.3g   Cyzicus: Ref. Map 2, AY.

M.3h   Notion: Ref. Map 2, CY.
M.3i   Thrace: Ref. Map 2, AY.
M.3j   Aigospotamoi (Aigosopotamos): Ref. Map 2, AY.
M.3k   In this case, Phrygia probably means Hellespontine Phrygia: Ref. Map 2, BZ.
M.3l   Susa: Ref. Map 1.

Antalkidas

§4. Antalkidas was a Spartan politician and general, the son of Leon, probably the Leon who was one of the ephors of Sparta in 419/18. In 392, he was appointed as ambassador to Tiribazos, the satrap of western Asia. Together, the two planned to negotiate peace for Sparta with the Persian King Artaxerxes II. Fearing Athenian opposition to the peace, Tiribazos covertly gave Antalkidas funds to revive a Peloponnesian navy (which had been destroyed at Cnidus[a] in 394), whereby he could harass the Athenians and thereby persuade them to support the peace. However, the Great King preferred to stick with Athens, so when Tiribazos was superseded by Strouthas in 391, these negotiations came to a halt. In 388, Antalkidas was again sent to Asia as Spartan admiral and ambassador, and this trip was successful. He was able to convince Artaxerxes to decree a peace dictated by Persia under Spartan influence, and his naval strength in the Hellespont then forced Athens to accept it. The Peace of Antalkidas, or the King's Peace, as it was also called, was promulgated in 387/6. By its terms, Persian control was extended to all cities in Asia Minor and to the islands of Klazomenai[b] and Cyprus,[c] while all other Greek cities were to be independent, except for the islands of Lemnos,[d] Imbros,[e] and Skyros,[f] which would come under Athenian rule. This treaty ended the Corinthian War and revived Spartan hegemony in mainland Greece, promoted by various self-serving interpretations of "independence" on Sparta's part. Ancient sources allege that Antalkidas disapproved of Sparta's hostile policy toward Thebes as promoted by King Agesilaos. Whether or not this is true, Antalkidas continued to act as a specialist in Persian diplomacy. He served on an embassy to Susa in 372/1 that helped lay the ground for Sparta's diplomatic victory in the peace of that year; and when in 368 Philiskos, the envoy of the then satrap of Phrygia, Ariobarzanes, was persuaded to remain loyal to Sparta despite its defeat at the battle of Leuctra,[g] it seems likely that Antalkidas was responsible, since he is recorded as being a personal friend of Ariobarzanes. Nevertheless, in 367 Artaxerxes changed sides, and it is said that, following the failure of his last embassy as a very old man, Antalkidas committed suicide. This is problematic, as the Spartan ambassador in 367 is named as Euthykles, but those who accept that Xenophon has suppressed Persian involvement in the peace negotiations of 366 can believe that Antalkidas came out of retirement to conduct them on Sparta's behalf.

Archidamos III

§5. Archidamos III son of Agesilaos was king of Sparta from 360 (or 359) to 338. As heir apparent to the Eurypontid throne, he was excused from going through the

M.4a   Cnidus: Ref. Map 2, DY.
M.4b   Klazomenai: Ref. Map 4, BX.
M.4c   Cyprus: Ref. Map 1.
M.4d   Lemnos: Ref. Map 2, BX.
M.4e   Imbros: Ref. Map 2, AY.
M.4f   Skyros: Ref. Map 3, AZ.
M.4g   Leuctra: Ref. Map 3, BY.

Agōgē[a] but participated in it vicariously by becoming the senior lover of a young man who was going through it, Kleonymos son of Sphodrias (§22). When in 378 Sphodrias was indicted on a capital charge for his abortive raid on the Peiraieus[b] in peacetime, Archidamos interceded with Agesilaos for the life of his beloved's father (5.4.25–6). Xenophon's narrative terminates in 362, before Archidamos became king (in 360), but the several passages that mention him show that he was carefully prepared to assume his father's role by being entrusted with serious military responsibilities.[c] He led the force sent to aid the Spartan army after its defeat by the Thebans at Leuctra in 371, and he commanded Spartan forces when they defeated the Arcadians[d] and Argives at the so-called Tearless Battle in 368. He courageously defended Sparta against the forces of Epaminondas (§9) in 362 and supported the Phocians[e] against Thebes[f] in the Sacred War of 355–346. Shortly after that war's disastrous close, he led a Spartan mercenary force to Crete[g] to support the city of Lyktos against Knossos; and sometime later, when the Spartan colony of Taras[h] in southern Italy requested help against the local Lucanians, he was sent there with a fleet and an army. He was killed in southern Italy in battle at Manduria in 338.

Chabrias

§6. Chabrias (c. 420–357) was a very distinguished Athenian general whose contribution is deliberately underplayed by Xenophon. During the Corinthian War, he is found in service in Thrace and as the principal Athenian commander before Corinth[a] in 389 in succession to Iphikrates (§12). In 388, he sailed to Cyprus to assist Athens' ally Evagoras, on the way intervening on Spartan-held Aegina.[b] After the King's Peace of 387/6 he became a mercenary commander in the service of King Acoris of Egypt,[c] who was in rebellion against the Persians; but perhaps in 380 Pharnabazos (§21), charged by the Persian Great King with recovering Egypt, strong-armed the Athenians into recalling Chabrias. In 378 a body of troops under his command kept the Spartans from invading Attica when King Kleombrotos (§15) moved to deal with Thebes after its liberation from Spartan control by Pelopidas (§20) and others. Subsequently Chabrias played a major part in helping the Thebans resist Agesilaos' invasions of Boeotia[d] (probably it was for this reason that Xenophon denigrates him). He brought many Aegean[e] islands and cities into the newly formed Second Athenian League in the course of 377 and 376. In 376 he won a major naval victory at the battle of Naxos,[f] which restored Athens' position as the leading Greek state in the Aegean, a status Athens retained for more than fifty years. In 372 his rival Iphikrates took him, along with the senior politician Kallistratos (§14), who seems to have been a key ally, on a naval expedition to relieve Cor-

M.5a   Agōgē: the rigorous Spartan education system for males.
M.5b   Peiraieus: Ref. Map 5.
M.5c   See 6.4.18, 6.4.19, 6.4.26, 6.5.1, 7.1.28–9, 7.1.31, 7.4.20–21, 7.5.12–13.
M.5d   Arcadia: Ref. Map 3, CX.
M.5e   Phocis: Ref. Map 3, AY.
M.5f   Thebes: Ref. Map 3, BY.

M.5g   Crete: Ref. Map 1.
M.5h   Taras (Taranto), Italy: Ref. Map 1.
M.6a   Corinth: Ref. Map 2, CX.
M.6b   Aegina: Ref. Map 3, CY.
M.6c   Egypt: Ref. Map 1.
M.6d   Boeotia: Ref. Map 2, CX.
M.6e   Aegean Sea: Ref. Map 2, BX.
M.6f   Naxos: Ref. Map 2, DY.

cyra.[g] Chabrias replaced Iphikrates as Athenian general in the Peloponnese in 369/8, at the time of the second invasion by Epaminondas (§9), whom he successfully repelled from the gates of Corinth. He was prosecuted, along with Kallistratos, after the fall of Oropos[h] in 366; despite his acquittal, he was briefly out of favor, though he is attested as general again in 363/2. Subsequently, he commanded mercenaries in Egypt alongside Agesilaos in 361–360, served unsuccessfully as Athenian general in the Hellespont in 358/7, and was killed in action at the battle of Chios[i] in 357/6, fighting for Athens against her rebellious allies.

Cyrus the Younger

§7. Cyrus the Younger, or Cyrus II (424/3?–401), was the second son of Persian King Darius II and Queen Parysatis, and apparently her favorite. In 408/7, at a very early age, he was sent by the king to take command of Persian forces in western Asia and to assist the Spartans in their war against the Athenians. A close relationship with Lysander (§18), commander of the Spartan fleet, was soon established, and with the steady support of Cyrus, the Spartans were able to recover from defeats at sea until Lysander finally achieved a decisive victory over the Athenians at Aigospotamoi. Cyrus was recalled to the Persian court in 405/4 because of his father's fatal illness, but when Darius died, Cyrus lost the argument that as a son born after his father became Great King, he should be preferred to his elder brother for the succession. Shortly after the latter's coronation as Artaxerxes II, Tissaphernes (§29) accused Cyrus of plotting against the King, and only the intercession of his mother saved Cyrus from execution. Ultimately, he was sent back to Asia Minor as the satrap of Lydia[a] and Phrygia, where, over the next three years, he covertly amassed a large force of native troops and Greek hoplite mercenaries (of whom Xenophon was one). In the spring of 401 he began to advance this force eastward against Artaxerxes, but he did not officially announce that his objective was to defeat the King and to take the throne himself until his army reached the Euphrates River.[b] As he marched down the river toward Babylon,[c] his forces were intercepted by Artaxerxes at the head of a large army at Cunaxa.[d] In the ensuing battle (401), the Greeks defeated the forces opposed to them, but elsewhere Cyrus was killed. The Greek soldiers thus found themselves without leaders in the center of hostile Persian-controlled Mesopotamia. A description of their long, arduous, and perilous march north to the Black Sea[e] and back to Greece is the subject of Xenophon's book *Anabasis*.[f]

Derkylidas

§8. A Spartan general who was active from 411 to 389, Derkylidas emerged as one of the leading Spartan commanders in Asia. In 411, he was sent to the Hellespont to procure the revolt of Abydos[a] and Lampsacus[b] from Athens, which he

M.6g Corcyra: Ref. Map 2, BW.
M.6h Oropos: Ref. Map 3, BZ.
M.6i Chios: Ref. Map 2, CY.
M.7a Lydia: Ref. Map 2, CZ.
M.7b Euphrates River: Ref. Map 1.
M.7c Babylon: Ref. Map 1.

M.7d Cunaxa: Ref. Map 1.
M.7e Black Sea (Pontus): Ref. Map 1.
M.7f On *Anabasis.*, see the Introduction, §4.2–3.
M.8a Abydos: Ref. Map 2, AY.
M.8b Lampsacus: Ref. Map 4, AX.

accomplished, and he was appointed harmost of Abydos. Slandered by Pharnabazos (§21), he was publicly disgraced in 407, but in 399 he was sent back to Asia to succeed Thibron (§25) as commander of Spartan forces. From 399 to 397, he waged war skillfully against Pharnabazos, having secured a truce from Tissaphernes (§29), and conquered a number of small cities. During one truce in 398, he crossed over to the Thracian Chersonese[c] and built a wall across the isthmus to keep the Thracians from attacking the Greek cities there. In 397, when he was ordered to attack Tissaphernes, he obtained an offer of peace terms, but he was replaced in 396 by King Agesilaos. Derkylidas appears to have returned to Sparta, because in 394 he was sent to Agesilaos at Amphipolis[d] to inform him of a Spartan victory near Corinth. Derkylidas was sent on to the Hellespont to carry the news there and to again assume the duties of harmost at Abydos. After the Spartan fleet's defeat at Cnidus in 394, Derkylidas continued to hold Abydos and Sestos[e] loyal to Sparta, despite Persian efforts to secure their alliance, until he was succeeded in his post in 389. It is not known how or where he died.

Epaminondas

§9. Epaminondas (d. 362) was a great Theban general and politician. In winter 379/8 he participated, under the leadership of Pelopidas (§20), in liberating his city from Spartan occupation. In 371 he was elected Boeotarch from Thebes and attended the peace conference at Sparta. There he insisted that the restored Boeotian Federation be recognized, and for that reason Sparta excluded Thebes from the peace and immediately invaded Theban territory. Epaminondas was the main commander who led the Theban forces against the Spartans at Leuctra; by employing novel tactics, he so utterly defeated them that Sparta's military power and reputation was permanently diminished. In 370/69, after his forces invaded and pillaged Laconia,[a] he liberated the Messenians[b] and, by building and fortifying their city at Mount Ithome,[c] deprived the Spartans of many of the helots on whom their power depended. He was also instrumental in the foundation of Megalopolis,[d] the fortified city built for the newly created Arcadian Federation. He thus established, in just a few years, two independent powers on Sparta's northern and western borders that, by their tenacious resistance to Spartan attempts at reconquest, effectively reduced Sparta from a global to a local power. Epaminondas led a further invasion of the Peloponnese in 369, was out of office in 368, rescued Pelopidas from captivity in Thessaly[e] in early 367, and invaded the Peloponnese for the third time in 366.[f] He is reported to have proposed building a Theban fleet of one hundred ships, and he certainly sailed to the Hellespontine area in 364 with a fleet, perhaps smaller than this, to make trouble for Athens. He was killed in the hour of victory, during his fourth invasion of the Peloponnese, at the battle of Mantineia in 362.

M.8c Chersonese: Ref. Map 2, AY.
M.8d Amphipolis: Ref. Map 2, AX.
M.8e Sestos: Ref. Map 2, AY.
M.9a Laconia: Ref. Map 3, DX.
M.9b Messenia: Ref. Map 3, DX.
M.9c Mount Ithome: Ref. Map 3, DX.

M.9d Megalopolis: Ref. Map 3, CX.
M.9e Thessaly: Ref. Map 2, BX.
M.9f David Thomas in the Introduction (§9.3) dates this third invasion to mid-367.

Eteonikos

§10. Eteonikos was a Spartan senior officer who in 412 aided the Spartan admiral Astyochos in his unsuccessful operations against Lesbos.[a] He was appointed harmost in Thasos[b] but was expelled, along with the pro-Spartan faction, by the Thasians in 409. Three years later, in 406, he served under Kallikratidas, the Spartan admiral that year, at the blockade of Mytilene.[c] After the battle of the Arginousai Islands, Eteonikos cleverly extricated his ships from Mytilene and escaped to Chios, where he shortly afterward thwarted a dangerous plot among his hungry men to sack the city of Chios. He commanded flotillas under Lysander (§18) and led the Spartan forces who were landed on the Athenian-held beach in the course of the battle of Aigospotamoi in 405. After that battle Lysander sent him with ten ships to bring all the lands in the vicinity of Thasos over to the Spartan side. He is probably the same Eteonikos whom Xenophon mentions in his *Anabasis* as serving at Byzantium[d] in late summer 400. At some point unknown he served as harmost of Aegina, to which he returned in 389. The last we hear about him is in 388, when Spartan sailors refuse to sail under him because he has not paid them; their morale, though not their pay, was restored by Teleutias (§23).

Herippidas

§11. Herippidas was a Spartan officer, active from 399 or earlier to 378. He is first heard of restoring "order" to Herakleia-in-Trachis[a] by slaughtering five hundred malcontents and then expelling the Oetaeans from their lands. In 396 he was one of the Spartiates who accompanied Agesilaos to Asia Minor; there he was used as an ambassador to Tissaphernes (§29), and the following year he took over from Xenophon the command of the remnants of the Ten Thousand who had campaigned with Cyrus (§7). Xenophon blames Herippidas' tactlessness for the defection of the Persian noble Spithridates and, in his account of the battle of Coronea[b] (394), insinuates that he did not keep very good order among the Ten Thousand. Many years later, in 382, after Phoibidas had seized the Kadmeia at Thebes on Sparta's behalf and been recalled for so doing, Herippidas was one of the three Spartan officers sent to continue the occupation. During this period, he is probably the Spartan officer who intervened on Histiaia in Euboea[c] against Jason of Pherai (§13). When the Thebans under Pelopidas (§20) liberated the Kadmeia at the end of 379, Herippidas was put on trial by the Spartan authorities for surrendering without permission and put to death. Xenophon suppresses the names of the three Spartan officers concerned, as he routinely fails to give the names of Spartans who in his eyes disgrace Sparta in land conflicts.

M.10a	Lesbos: Ref. Map 2, BY.		M.11a	Herakleia-in-Trachis: Ref. Map 3, AX.
M.10b	Thasos: Ref. Map 2, AX.		M.11b	Coronea: Ref. Map 3, BY.
M.10c	Mytilene: Ref. Map 2, BY.		M.11c	Histiaia and Euboea: Ref. Map 3, AY.
M.10d	Byzantium: Ref. Map 2, AZ.			

Iphikrates

§12. Iphikrates was an Athenian general, active from 394 (or possibly a little earlier) to 353. The self-made son of a cobbler, he came to the attention of the Athenian general Konon (§16) for his courage and enterprise as a marine, possibly at the battle of Cnidus in 394; while still a very young man, he became a captain of peltasts (light-armed infantry). He first came into prominence in 390 when the force of peltasts he commanded severely mauled a Spartan battalion at Lechaion,[a] near Corinth. Afterward, he was redeployed to the Hellespont, where in 389 he ambushed and defeated a force commanded by the Spartan general Anaxibios. He also conducted naval operations in that theater. After the King's Peace in 386, Iphikrates entered the service of the Thracian king Seuthes and subsequently of his son and successor Cotys; around this time, he married one of Seuthes' (or, less likely, Cotys') daughters. He served Cotys for several years, including being sent to help King Amyntas of Macedon[b] before joining Pharnabazos (§21) in his preparations for a Persian invasion of Egypt, which ultimately failed in 373. Iphikrates returned to Athens after having quarreled with Pharnabazos, and the Athenians sent him in command of a fleet to Corcyra. The Spartan force besieging Corcyra was defeated before Iphikrates arrived, but he did ambush and capture nine of ten Syracusan triremes that had come to assist the Spartans. When Epaminondas (§9) invaded the Peloponnese in winter 370/69, Iphikrates was instructed to help Sparta but was later criticized for failing to hinder Epaminondas' operations or exit from the Peloponnese. Probably in 368 he returned to the northern Aegean, where he intervened successfully in Macedon on the side of the Dowager Queen Eurydike, but in three years of campaigning he achieved little toward the main Athenian objective: the recovery of Amphipolis. He was replaced as principal Athenian commander in the North Aegean by Timotheos (§28) in 365 and returned to the service of Cotys for several years until the hostility between Cotys and Athens became too much for him. Iphikrates' last known command of Athenian forces took place in 356 at the naval battle of Embata,[c] where he refused to engage the enemy because of a storm. Subsequently (probably in 353), he was prosecuted at Athens for this by his fellow general Chares, but he made such a compelling speech (now lost) in his own defense that he was acquitted.

Jason of Pherai

§13. Jason ruled as tyrant of Pherai[a] in Thessaly from the 380s or earlier until his assassination in 370. From the name of his daughter Thebe, it appears he was friendly toward Thebes as early as 385; he had clashed with the Spartans at Histiaia in Euboea well before 379. He amassed an impressive mercenary force. Jason's sole

M.12a Lechaion: Ref. Map 3, BY.
M.12b Macedon: Ref. Map 2, AX.
M.12c Embata: an unknown site lying in the strait

between Chios and the mainland.
M.13a Pherai (in Thessaly): Ref. Map 2, BX.

rival in Thessaly, Polydamas of Pharsalus,[b] was forced to capitulate to Jason in 375/4 after having solicited and failed to secure assistance from his Spartan allies. With Polydamas' submission, Jason gained control of all of Thessaly and was elected *tagos*.[c] Although he cooperated with his friend Timotheos (§28) in Athens in 373, he seems to have preferred the friendship of Thebes. He did not fight in the battle of Leuctra in 371, but he did come right away when he was summoned by his Theban allies. However, when the Thebans asked him to attack the defeated Spartans, he refused to do so; instead, he negotiated an armistice between the two parties, arguing that that was in the best interests of Thebes. In the following months, Jason extended his power significantly, securing Perraibia[d] and the surrounding territories and establishing an alliance with Amyntas, king of Macedon. In 370, Jason alarmed Greece by mobilizing the entire Thessalian army around the time of the Pythian Games at Delphi.[e] Various motivations have been surmised for this act, but his true purpose will never be known, as he was assassinated before he had completed preparations for whatever move he intended.

Kallistratos

§14. Kallistratos (fl. 392–c. 355) was a major Athenian politician for almost forty years. He is first recorded by the third-century Athenian local historian Philochoros as having in 392/1 successfully prosecuted the Athenian ambassadors to the Congress of Sparta in that year (a congress unrecorded by Xenophon) for provisionally agreeing to peace terms that included formally accepting Persian control over the Greeks of mainland Asia Minor. His uncle Agyrrios is subsequently recorded as having succeeded Thrasyboulos (§26) in command in the Aegean. Despite Kallistratos' desire to continue the war against Sparta in 392/1, it seems that he was not perceived as a diehard anti-Spartan, since, according to Plutarch, it was by using his name that Pelopidas (§20) sought, during the Liberation of Thebes from Spartan rule in winter 379/8, to gain access to the house of the head of the pro-Spartan faction in Thebes, Leontiades. Kallistratos was elected a general immediately after the break with Sparta in 378, actively supported the vigorous expansion of the Second Athenian League thereafter, and assisted Iphikrates (§12) in his expedition to relieve Corcyra in 372. Xenophon shows him as making the most conciliatory and persuasive speech of the Athenian ambassadors to the Congress of Sparta of 371, where Sparta succeeded in isolating Thebes but, despite a strong position secured by rumors of Persian backing, did not insist on Athens' joining in the military alliance that was supposed to crush Thebes once and for all. Although probably out of office in the immediate aftermath of the Spartan defeat at Leuctra, Kallistratos was responsible (despite Xenophon's silence) for the later Athenian decision to support Sparta's

M.13b   Pharsalus: Ref. Map 2, BX.
M.13c   The Thessalian *tagos* was neither king nor tyrant but a leader who seems to have been selected by a unanimous vote of the rulers of the four ancestral Thessalian tribal territories, which may

explain why the office was only intermittently filled. See n. 6.1.8a.
M.13d   Perraibia: Ref. Map 2, BW.
M.13e   Delphi: Ref. Map 2, CX.

continued existence militarily, but he was discredited in 366 by the failure of Athens' Peloponnesian allies to come to Athens' aid at the siege of Oropos. It seems likely that he was back in favor in 362, when Athens supported Sparta in the campaign that climaxed with the battle of Mantineia, and probably around this time he is recorded as an ambassador to Arcadia and Messene.[a] However, he fled into exile in 361 having been condemned to death for reasons that are not clear. Among other North Aegean ventures, he assisted the Thasians in creating a new colony at Krenides[b] on the mainland nearby, but the inhabitants subsequently handed it over to Philip of Macedon. Shortly thereafter, perhaps in 355, he tried to return to Athens, which was once again hostile to Thebes and Persia and sympathetic to Sparta, but he was arrested and put to death in accordance with the sentence passed on him in 361.

Kleombrotos

§15. Kleombrotos son of Pausanias (§19) was the twenty-third Spartan Agiad king, who ruled from 380 to 371. Although he was sent to Boeotia in early 378 to regain control of Thebes, he failed to accomplish this objective and returned home, leaving Sphodrias (§22) in command. Because of this initial failure, the next two Theban expeditions were led by the other Spartan king, Agesilaos. In 376, after Agesilaos had become unfit for campaign through a leg injury, Kleombrotos again led out the army via the Megarid[a] but did not penetrate into Boeotia. The following year, he was sent to Phocis to invade Boeotia from the northwest. The sources do not expressly say whether he marched home again when the Peace of 375/4 was made, but this seems the better view. In 371 he was again ordered to march via Phocis to Boeotia. He captured Kreusis[b] and met the Theban army at the plains of Leuctra. In the resulting battle, he was mortally wounded, and he died shortly after being carried from the battlefield. He was succeeded by his son, Agesipolis II.

Konon

§16. Konon (c. 445–392) was an Athenian general who commanded Athenian naval forces in the last years of the Peloponnesian War. He led the squadron based on Naupactus[a] in 414 and probably also in 411 (perhaps the years in between as well) and commanded major Athenian fleets in the Hellespont and Aegean from 407 to 405. In 406, the Spartans bottled him up in Mytilene, and the battle of Arginousai was fought to relieve him, but as he was not himself present at the battle, the Athenians did not include him in their anger at the other generals, who failed to pick up shipwrecked sailors and corpses. At Aigospotamoi, where in 405 Lysander

---

M.14a   Messene: Ref. Map 3, DX.
M.14b   Krenides: Ref. Map 2, AX.
M.15a   Megarid: territory of the city of Megara (Ref. Map 3, BY) through which one had to march when traveling between the Peloponnese and the

northern mainland.
M.15b   Kreusis: Ref. Map 3, BY.
M.16a   Naupactus: Ref. Map 3, BX.

annihilated the Athenian navy, Konon was the only Athenian general alert enough to escape destruction. Either afraid to return to Athens after suffering such a great loss or realizing that Athenian defeat and the end of democracy were now inevitable, he fled with his squadron of eight ships to his friend King Evagoras in Cyprian Salamis.[b] By 397, the Persian satrap Pharnabazos (§21) had chosen him to act as Persian admiral in the Aegean, initially based at Caunus[c] in Caria[d] and subsequently at Rhodos,[e] where he brought about a revolution. So by 394, Konon had been operating in the Persian interest for some time. Diodorus reports that Konon traveled to Babylon[f] to the Persian king Artaxerxes (probably in winter 395/4) to present plans for the defeat of the Spartans. The King granted him money and supplies and told him to pick his preferred Persian general. Konon chose to work with Pharnabazos, and in summer 394 they put to sea with a combined fleet of more than ninety ships[g] and crushed the Spartan fleet in a naval battle off Cnidus. Thus in 393 he returned to Athens at the head of a Persian fleet, with funds that allowed the Athenians to finish restoring the Long Walls that the Spartans had forced them to dismantle. In 392, Konon was sent as part of an Athenian delegation to Sardis[h] to protest against the new rapport between Persia and Sparta, but the satrap Tiribazos, suspicious that Athens intended to restore her empire, had the entire delegation imprisoned. Konon escaped to Cyprus but died there shortly afterward.

Kritias

§17. Kritias (c. 460–403), the son of Kallaischros and great-uncle of the philosopher Plato, is best known as the violent and cruel leader of the junta at Athens subsequently known as the Thirty Tyrants. Born into a wealthy and aristocratic family that traced its lineage back to the mid-seventh century, he was, like his younger contemporary Alcibiades (§3), an associate of Socrates. He was accused of taking part in the mutilation of the herms (stylized statues of the god Hermes that marked many boundaries in Athens) in 415 but was released on the testimony of his kinsman Andocides, who confessed to the outrage and named other accomplices, not including Kritias. It is not known what part, if any, he may have played in the Athenian oligarchic revolution of 411. Although one fourth-century orator claimed that all the Thirty had been members of the Four Hundred (the oligarchic regime) and another identifies Kritias as a leader of the extremist faction within the Four Hundred, these are quite likely to be caricatures in view of the undoubted fact that he remained in Athens after the return of democracy; but it is probable that he had not actively opposed the Four Hundred, since it seems that in 404/3 he made that a charge in his attack on Theramenes (§24). He proposed the recall of Alcibiades (perhaps in 408) and was exiled to Thessaly around the time of Alcibiades' disgrace in early

M.16b Salamis (on Cyprus): Ref. Map 1.
M.16c Caunus: Ref. Map 2, DZ.
M.16d Caria: Ref. Map 2, CZ.
M.16e Rhodos: Ref. Map 2, DZ. For Konon's activities at Caunus and Rhodos in 395, see Diodorus in Appendix O, Selections from the *Histories* of Diodorus Siculus Relevant to Xenophon's *Hel-*

lenika, 14.79.4–8, and Appendix P, Selected Fragments of the *Hellenica Oxyrhynchia* Relevant to Xenophon's *Hellenika*, Fragments 22 and 23.
M.16f See Appendix O, 14.81.4–6.
M.16g See Appendix O, 14.83.4.
M.16h Sardis: Ref. Map 2, CY.

406. His activities there are mysterious to us; they seem to have involved arming some of the *penestai* (the Thessalian serf class), but this seems more likely to have been in the course of factional maneuvers among Thessalian aristocrats than a genuinely democratic move. After Sparta defeated Athens in 404, he returned from exile to help establish the oligarchic rule of the Thirty. Xenophon and other sources present him as being at this time a sinister, ruthless, and bloodthirsty politician and a pro-Spartan fanatic. He was killed in the Peiraieus, fighting against the pro-democratic forces led by Thrasyboulos (§26) in 403. No trace of this, however, appears in the depiction of him by his great-nephew Plato in various dialogues, in two of which (*Timaeus* and *Kritias*) he recounts the myth of Atlantis.

Lysander

§18. Lysander (d. 395), Spartan general and statesman. Xenophon did not like Lysander but did not disguise his power and influence. He was of possibly mixed aristocratic-helot parentage but nevertheless gained admission to royal circles as the lover of the then king's brother Agesilaos within the Agōgē (the system of Spartan education and military training). He was made admiral in 407/6, in which capacity he became a friend of the Persian prince Cyrus the Younger (§7) and secured his unstinting support. This enabled him greatly to improve the Peloponnesian fleet, and he won a victory against Athens at Notion that caused the second disgrace of Alcibiades (§3). In 405 he again took command of the Spartan fleet and, moving it to the Hellespont, decisively destroyed the Athenian fleet at Aigospotamoi. He blockaded Athens and in 404 imposed upon it the oligarchic regime of the Thirty.[a] He also established oligarchic dekarchies (selected committees of ten) to rule many of the former cities of the Athenian empire and supported them with harmosts (Spartan military governors or commanders). In 403, King Pausanias (§19) and the Spartan government grew suspicious of Lysander's increasing power. They reversed his support for narrow juntas, in Athens and elsewhere, and as he fell out with them, he looked to Agesilaos—whom he helped to the kingship, probably in 400—to restore his position. Agesilaos supported him at first, and followed Lysander's advice to campaign in Asia in 396; but then Agesilaos, too, grew wary of Lysander's power and popularity and snubbed and dishonored him. The following year Lysander overreached himself and attacked the Thebans before Pausanias' forces had joined up with him. He was killed in battle at Haliartos[b] in Boeotia while Agesilaos was still in Asia. His arrogance and ambition made him unpopular, but he was one of the most competent Spartan commanders. Xenophon is silent about the divine honors that were accepted by Lysander in his lifetime from the restored oligarchs of Samos—a silence that should be taken to signal severe disapproval.

M.18a Xenophon has deliberately suppressed mention
       of Lysander at the key assembly, for which one
       needs to refer to Lysias 12.71–76; Plutarch,
       Parallel Lives, "Lysander" 15.5; and Diodorus,
       Appendix O, 14.3.
M.18e Haliartos: Ref. Map 3, BY.

Pausanias

§19. Pausanias, an Agiad king of Sparta, reigned as a minor from 445 to 426 (during the temporary exile of his father Pleistoanax) and again from 408 to 394. In 405 he led the Spartan army into Attica after the crushing defeat of the Athenian navy at the battle of Aigospotamoi, but his co-king Agis (§2) appears then to have taken charge of the siege of Athens. In 403 he was sent to replace Lysander (§18) at the head of Spartan forces besieging the Athenian democrats under Thrasyboulos (§26) at the Peiraieus. Revoking Lysander's policy, he secured a truce between the democrats and the junta of the Thirty, restoring the democrats to Athens and allowing the remaining members of the Thirty to live in Eleusis.[a] On his return to Sparta, Pausanias was put on trial for this before the Spartan Gerousia[b] and was very nearly convicted. Although Xenophon does not mention it, Pausanias led one of Sparta's campaign armies against Elis[c] in the war waged between 402 and 400. In 395 Pausanias was sent with an army to Haliartos to join forces with Lysander, but he arrived after Lysander's defeat and death in battle. Rather than renew the fighting, Pausanias asked for a truce to collect the dead at Haliartos, and agreed to withdraw his forces from Boeotia. For this and also for his previous lenience toward the Athenian democrats, he was tried, convicted, and sentenced to death at Sparta; but he escaped to Tegea, where he lived in exile for the rest of his life. He interceded at Mantineia in 385/4, persuading his son, King Agesipolis (§1), to spare the lives of the leading democrats and to merely exile them. Pausanias also wrote a political pamphlet while in exile, advocating reform of several features of the Spartan constitution.

Pelopidas

§20. Pelopidas (born c. 410–364) was a Theban general and politician who became a military and political partner of Epaminondas (§9); the two together designed and led Thebes to a brief period of hegemony in Greece. When the Spartans occupied the Theban Kadmeia (acropolis) in 382, Pelopidas took refuge in Athens, from where, three years later (379/8), he led the coup that overthrew the pro-Spartan oligarchs of Thebes and drove the Spartans out of the Kadmeia. He was then elected Boeotarch, the first of thirteen times that he held that office. He gained fame from Theban victories against the Spartans at Tegyra[a] (375) and Leuctra (371). He commanded an elite, highly trained Theban batallion made up of 150 pairs of homosexual lovers, which was called the Sacred Band. Pelopidas accompanied Epaminondas on his first invasion of the Peloponnese (370/69) but thereafter turned his attention to northern Greece. In 369 he intervened in Thessaly to limit the ambitions of Alexander of Pherai, the successor of Jason (§13), and to expel King Alexander II of Macedon from Larissa,[b] following up by establishing a protectorate over Macedon. He intervened again in Macedon the following year, after

---

M.19a Eleusis: Ref. Map 3, BY.
M.19b See Appendix E, Spartan Government and Society, §15.

M.19c Elis (city): Ref. Map 3, BW.
M.20a Tegyra: Ref. Map 3, AY.
M.20b Larissa (in Thessaly): Ref. Map 2, BX.

King Alexander's death, but on his way home was captured and imprisoned by Alexander of Pherai being subsequently rescued by Epaminondas. On a diplomatic mission to the Great King in 367, he persuaded the Persians to withdraw their support from Sparta. Finally, in a third intervention against the tyrant Alexander of Pherai, Pelopidas died in 364 in battle at Cynoscephalae[c] in the hour of victory.

Pharnabazos

§21. Pharnabazos (fl. 413–370?) son of Pharnaces succeeded his father and grandfather as satrap of Phrygia in 413, governing from the city of Daskyleion.[a] When in that year he and his rival and colleague Tissaphernes (§29) the satrap of Lydia and Caria were instructed by Darius II to recover tribute from the Greek cities of Asia, they both opened negotiations with Sparta and began to cooperate with Peloponnesian forces to defeat Athens. Pharnabazos fought alongside the Spartans in the battles at Abydos (411), Cyzicus (410), and Chalcedon[b] (408), but in 408 he successfully encouraged the Athenians to negotiate with King Darius. However, the arrival of pro-Spartan Cyrus (§7) aborted these negotiations. It is thought that Pharnabazos, perhaps acting at the request of Lysander (§18) or the junta of the Thirty at Athens, or perhaps for his own reasons (or for both), stood behind the assassination of Alcibiades (§3), which took place in Phrygian territory in 404. Once the Spartans initiated hostilities against Persia, they invaded Phrygia in 399, 396, and 395; Pharnabazos was forced to defend his territory against them, and in the third campaign his own country houses and game parks were ravaged. The famous meeting (395) between Pharnabazos and Agesilaos ended in a truce, under which Agesilaos promised to leave Pharnabazos' province and attack the Persians elsewhere. The next year, a Persian fleet under the joint leadership of Konon (§16) and Pharnabazos won a decisive victory at Cnidus. The Persian fleet then sailed to Athens, where Pharnabazos provided Konon with money to help the Athenians complete the rebuilding of their fortifications. In 388/7 Pharnabazos was recalled to Susa, where he was rewarded by being given one of the King's daughters in marriage. At some point—according to *The Cambridge Ancient History,* in 385–383— he unsuccessfully attempted to put down a rebellion in Egypt; in 373, after a long period of planning, he commanded a second attempt against Egypt, this time with the support of the Athenian commander Iphikrates (§12), but this attempt also failed. He is thought to have died shortly thereafter.

Sphodrias

§22. Sphodrias (c. 425–371) first appears as a Spartan officer who was appointed harmost at Thespiai,[a] in Boeotia, by King Kleombrotos (§15) in early 378. In the following year, although Sparta and Athens were at peace, he was persuaded to

---

M.20c Cynoscephalae: Map 5.3.14.
M.21a Daskyleion: Ref. Map 2, AY.
M.21b Chalcedon: Ref. Map 2, AZ.

M.22a Thespiai: Ref. Map 3, BY.

lead—or perhaps outwitted into leading—his troops on an expedition into Attica unauthorized by the Spartan government. It was said that he was trying to seize Athens' port, the Peiraieus, by night but that he had miscalculated, and when day broke, he discovered that his troops had merely reached Thria[b] (near Eleusis), still miles away from the Peiraieus. So he turned back, driving off cattle and plundering houses along the way. The Athenians protested vigorously and were promised that Sphodrias would be punished. Fearing execution, Sphodrias did not return to Sparta, where he was in fact indicted and tried in absentia, but he was acquitted through the influence of Agesilaos. Xenophon implies that this was because Agesilaos' son Archidamos (§5) was the lover of Sphodrias' son Kleonymos. But what Sphodrias was really intending in his raid, whether the entire Spartan government (specifically, King Kleombrotos) was quite as ignorant about it as was made out, and exactly why Agesilaos had him acquitted are all matters of controversy. In 371 Sphodrias served at the battle of Leuctra, in the immediate escort of King Kleombrotos, and he was killed while defending the king.

Teleutias

§23. Teleutias (c. 425–381) son of Theodoros was the younger half brother of King Agesilaos on the mother's side. Appointed to the command of the Spartan fleet in 392 perhaps as admiral, he regained control of the Corinthian Gulf[a] and in 391 captured the Corinthian dockyards at Lechaion in a joint operation with Agesilaos. In 390 he was sent to Cnidus to command the fleet there, and from there he traveled to Rhodos, capturing ten Athenian triremes along the way. The Athenians dispatched Thrasyboulos (§26) to assist the Rhodian democrats, but he preferred to campaign in the Hellespont, and so the Spartans managed to capture Rhodos. In 389 Teleutias assisted the Aeginetans against an Athenian invasion and succeeded in driving away the Athenian ships, but he was relieved from the command before he was able to conquer their nearby fort. He commanded the fleet again in 387 when he successfully raided the Peiraieus. A few years later, in 382, he was appointed general in the campaign against the Olynthians, and although he received substantial assistance from Amyntas II of Macedon and Derdas of Elimeia,[b] he was unable to gain victory over the enemy that year. In an action at Olynthos in 381, he became angry at the audacity of the enemy and carelessly allowed his troops to approach too close to the enemy's walls. This position led to a successful enemy counterattack in which Teleutias himself died fighting.

Theramenes

§24. Theramenes (d. 404) was an Athenian politician, son of Hagnon, who was an important political figure in Athens and the founder of Amphipolis[a] in 437/6. In

M.22b Thria: Ref. Map 3, BY.   M.23b Elimeia: Ref. Map 2, AW.
M.23a Corinthian Gulf: Ref. Map 3, BX.   M.24a Amphipolis: Ref. Map 2, AX.

411 Theramenes played a large part in the oligarchic coup at Athens that established the government of the Four Hundred; but later, disturbed by the extreme oligarchs among the Four Hundred, he opposed that regime and roused soldiers at the Peiraieus to demolish a mole the regime was building that could have been used to facilitate a Spartan capture of the port. Elected to the post of general after the establishment of the more moderate and democratic government of the Five Thousand, he campaigned in the West Aegean and on the Macedonian coast before commanding a squadron of warships under Alcibiades (§3) at the successful battle of Cyzicus (410). Subsequently, he instituted sieges of Chalcedon and Byzantium that restored both cities to Athenian allegiance (Chalcedon by treaty; Byzantium in 408, when it was betrayed to Alcibiades by insiders). It is not clear for how long he acted as general thereafter under the restored democracy, but he was at any rate not elected for 406/5 and so was only a trierarch (ship captain) at Arginousai in 406. When that battle ended, he and others were instructed to rescue survivors and to retrieve the corpses of the dead. They were, however, prevented from doing so by a fierce storm that came up. Although the generals involved in the battle were prosecuted and condemned en masse by the Athenian Assembly, Theramenes managed to avoid responsibility for the disaster, and Xenophon accuses him of promoting the prosecution. In 404, after the Spartan Lysander (§18) won the battle of Aigospotamoi and while Lysander's fleet was blockading Athens, Theramenes was sent to negotiate peace terms. After some delay he brought back from Sparta the harsh but ultimately accepted terms that marked the end of the Peloponnesian War. Theramenes was then selected to join the junta of the Thirty, which was imposed by Lysander a few months later. The Thirty were ostensibly supposed to establish a new constitution based on the "ancient" Constitution of Athens, but instead they ruled as a tiny group of autocrats. Ignoring Theramenes' advice, they carried out enough judicial murders and confiscations for posterity to give them the title the Thirty Tyrants. By objecting to these policies, Theramenes came into conflict with Kritias (§17), one of the most extreme leaders of the Thirty. It was not long before Kritias, supported by thugs and the Spartan garrison, had Theramenes summarily expelled from the government and executed.

Thibron

§25. Thibron (fl. 400, d. 391) was a Spartan general who led an expedition to Ionia in 400/399 with the aim of protecting the Asiatic Greeks from the Persian satrap Tissaphernes. Thibron had only mixed success until later in 399, when, having enlisted into his army the six thousand survivors of Cyrus' Greek mercenaries (led, at this point, by Xenophon), he succeeded in bringing Pergamum[a] over to his side and much of Aeolis,[b] although he besieged but was unable to take Larissa.[c] When he was ordered to attack Caria, he allowed his troops to plunder allied Greek

M.25a Pergamum: Ref. Map 2, BY.   M.25c Laris(s)a (in Aeolis): Ref. Map 4, BX.
M.25b Aeolis: Ref. Map 2, BY.

cities, and after he was replaced by Derkylidas, he was tried for this at Sparta and exiled. However, he was recalled in 391 and again sent to Asia Minor to battle the new Persian satrap Strouthas. According to Xenophon, Thibron proved to be an incompetent military commander, accomplishing little besides plundering raids. On one of these expeditions, his disorganized troops were surprised by enemy cavalry and he himself was killed. Xenophon seems to have a personal animus against Thibron—presumably Thibron treated him arrogantly in 399. It is slightly odd, since, unlike Derkylidas and Agesilaos, whom Xenophon admired, Thibron had some pretensions to literary culture, as he is recorded as having written a work on the Spartan constitution.

Thrasyboulos (of Steiria)

§26. Thrasyboulos of Steiria[a] (d. 389) son of Lykos was an Athenian general and politician. In 411, he commanded a ship at Samos and aided in the suppression of an oligarchical conspiracy there. While in Samos, word came of the establishment of the government of the Four Hundred in Athens, and both Thrasyboulos and Thrasyllos (§27) announced their resistance to this oligarchic regime. The fleet removed from office the current generals as suspected of supporting the oligarchy. Thrasyboulos was one of the replacements chosen by the fleet. He then instigated the recall of Alcibiades (§3) and went personally to retrieve him from his refuge with the Persian satrap Tissaphernes (§29). Thrasyboulos commanded the right wing of the fleet that won the Athenian victories at Kynossema[b] (411) and Abydos (winter 411/10) and was also one of the commanders at the even greater victory over the Spartan fleet at Cyzicus (410). Some modern scholars see him as contributing even more than Alcibiades to this run of Athenian successes. He was then sent to Thrace, where he campaigned successfully, and was elected general by the restored home democracy in Athens along with Alcibiades for 407/6. After the battle of Notion in early 407, Thrasyboulos was not reelected, even though, as he was besieging Phocaea[c] at the time, he was not to blame for the defeat: no doubt he was regarded as too close to the disgraced Alcibiades. Consequently, he served as a trierarch alongside Theramenes (§24) at the battle of Arginousai (406), where he was one of those who were tasked with recovering the shipwrecked crews and corpses after the battle. The recovery was abandoned because of a storm. However, his part in the subsequent miscarriage of justice in which six of the generals were executed because of this seems to have been relatively small.

When Lysander (§18) imposed the rule of the Thirty in 404, Thrasyboulos, a staunch democrat, left Athens and went into exile at Thebes, where he was welcomed. While there, he gathered a small body of men with which he seized the Athenian border fortress of Phyle[d] and defeated a large force that the Thirty sent

M.26a   Steiria (Attic deme): Ref. Map 3, BZ. Xenophon   M.26b   Kynossema: Map 2.1.16.
        calls him just Thrasyboulos up to 4.8.25, then   M.26c   Phocaea: Ref. Map 2, BY.
        adds "of Steiria" in order to avoid confusion   M.26d   Phyle: Ref. Map 3, BY.
        with Thrasyboulos of Kollytos (Ref. Map 5). See
        n. 1.1.12a for further.

out against him. Growing stronger, he proceeded to march to the Peiraieus, where the Thirty's forces attacked him, but he once again defeated them, killing their leader, Kritias (§17). The Athenian oligarchs applied to Sparta for aid and were joined by the Spartan king Pausanias (§19), whose forces were able to gain a victory over Thrasyboulos and his troops. But after that battle, Pausanias organized an armistice and a reconciliation between Thrasyboulos and the "men of the city," who were now separate from the Thirty, who had taken refuge in Eleusis. Once the reconciliation was established, Thrasyboulos and his fellow exiles were welcomed back to Athens. He achieved prominence in the restored democracy and is credited with having avoided a renewal of the civil war by granting amnesty to the "men of the city" and subsequently to almost all the oligarchs in Eleusis.

Though in 397/6 he had opposed attempts to ally Athens with the Persians for the purpose of resisting Spartan hegemony, in 395 he supported an alliance between Thebes and Athens for the same objective and led an army to aid the Thebans after their lands were ravaged by Spartan troops. The following year he commanded Athenian troops in the allied army when it was defeated by the Spartans at Nemea[c] and he generally believed to have again been in command of the Athenian contingent at the battle of Coronea. In 390 he was sent to aid the Rhodians against Teleutias (§23), but he sailed instead to Thrace, where he succeeded in obtaining an alliance with the Odrysian Thracians[f] for Athens. He continued to promote democracy and Athenian alliances in Byzantium, Chalcedon, and, despite losing twenty-three ships in a storm, Lesbos. He then set out again for Rhodos but, perhaps as a consequence of news of a decisive Spartan victory there, allowed himself to be diverted to the mainland of Asia Minor, where, in a series of highly provocative acts, considering that the Great King was still supporting Athens against Sparta, he interfered in Klazomenai, exacted money from Halicarnassus[g] and finally raided Aspendos,[h] far to the southeast, near the Eurymedon River,[i] where the citizens, outraged by the depredations of his soldiers, attacked him in his tent at night and killed him.

Thrasyllos

§27. Thrasyllos was an Athenian politician and soldier whose political career is first noted in 411, when he is found organizing democratic opposition in the fleet stationed at Samos to an oligarchic coup at Samos and also to one that had taken place at Athens. Because of his role in that cause, he was elected general for 411/10 by the Samian fleet. Later in 411, he and Thrasyboulos (§26) led the Athenian fleet to victory at the battles of Kynossema and Abydos; he was then sent back to Athens to obtain further troops. In 410 he successfully repelled an advance on the walls of Athens by the Spartan king Agis (§2), and in 409 he led a largely unsuccessful cam-

M.26e   Nemea: Ref. Map 3, CY.
M.26f   Odrysian Thrace: Ref. Map 2, AY.
M.26g   Halicarnassus: Ref. Map 2, DY.
M.26h   Aspendos: Map 4.8.27.
M.26i   Eurymedon River: Map 4.8.27.

paign in Ionia.[a] He was again elected general for 406/5 after Alcibiades (§3) fell from favor; however, in 406 he was executed by the Athenians with five other Athenian generals after the battle of Arginousai for having failed to rescue their sailors who were shipwrecked or to retrieve the bodies of their dead comrades.

Timotheos

§28. Timotheos of Anaphlystos[a] (?–353), the son of Konon (§16), studied in his youth with Isocrates and commanded Athenian fleets from 378 to 356. He was clearly one of Athens' most able military commanders in the second quarter of the fourth century, and Athens had several able generals in that period. Timotheos is first attested as general in 378, with Chabrias (§6) and Kallistratos (§14). In 375 he was sent on a voyage around the Peloponnese, raiding Laconia on the way, and on arrival in northwest Greece he gained the adherence of Corcyra and other states in the region to Athens' cause (though it is disputed whether Corcyra joined the Second Athenian League). At the battle of Alyzeia,[b] he defeated the Spartan admiral Nikolochos, who had been sent out to check his progress, a victory that contributed to the favorable terms Athens gained in the Peace of 375/4. Recalled as a result of that peace, he stopped on his way home to land some exiles on Zacynthus,[c] an act that Sparta considered a breach of the peace and for which she renewed the war, although initially only in a desultory manner.

In 373 Timotheos was put in command of a fleet to aid the Corcyraeans against a Spartan invasion force, but a lack of funds and men prevented him from sailing there. Instead he cruised the Aegean seeking sailors and money, but because of his delay, the Athenians recalled him to Athens, where he was accused by fellow generals Iphikrates (§12) and Kallistratos. Supported at his trial by powerful friends, including Jason of Pherai (§13), he gained an acquittal but was not reinstated in command. Instead, allegedly wishing to avoid submitting to the ordinary audit of his generalship, he left Athens to take a command in Persian service in their continuing attempt to bring Egypt back under control, staying abroad for perhaps two years or so.

Xenophon does not mention him after 373, but Timotheos had another period of glory in the late 360s. He first reappears as an Athenian general in 366. Some scholars consider that his return to favor is the consequence of the disgrace of his old enemy Kallistratos following the Theban capture of Oropos in that year. However that may be, he was sent to help Ariobarzanes, satrap of Hellespontine Phrygia in succession to Pharnabazos (§21), but he found that Ariobarzanes was in open revolt against King Artaxerxes, and since the Athenians had instructed him to refrain from any action against the King, he left the region. His instructions, however, do not seem to have prevented him from sailing instead to Samos, driving out the Persian garrison there, and subjecting the island to Athens, which proceeded to expel

M.27a Ionia: Ref. Map 2, CY.   M.28c Zacynthus: Ref. Map 3, CW.
M.28a Anaphlystos (Attic deme): Ref. Map 3, CZ.
M.28b Alyz(e)ia: Ref. 3, AW.

the Samians and confiscate their land. This success was followed by vigorous military campaigns in the Hellespont and North Aegean regions over the years 365–362, during which he captured or brought over many cities to Athens. But he never succeeded in taking Amphipolis, the main preoccupation of Athens in this area, and finally in 360/59 he failed in a direct assault on it.

In 356, during the Social War, he shared command of the Athenian fleet with Iphikrates and Chares; at the battle of Embata he and Iphikrates held back their forces because of a gale, while Chares attacked alone and suffered heavy losses. When Chares complained of their failure to support him, the two generals were recalled and subsequently brought to trial. Iphikrates was acquitted, supposedly because he had fewer enemies. Timotheos, however, was found guilty and fined the huge sum of one hundred talents. Since he could not pay the fine, he fled to exile in Chalcis on Euboea[d] where he died a short time later (by 353). It was said that his conviction resulted from his arrogant and aristocratic nature. Later the Athenians repented of their harsh treatment. They forgave most of the fine, gave him an honored burial in the Kerameikos,[e] and put up statues to his memory.

Tissaphernes

§29. Tissaphernes (fl. 416–395) was appointed Persian satrap of the coastal provinces (Lydia, Ionia, Caria) after having suppressed the rebel Pissuthnes, perhaps in 416. When ordered to collect tribute from the Greek cities in Asia in 413, he opened negotiations with the Spartans to defeat Athens, and in 412 he succeeded in establishing an alliance with them. Although he initially gave Sparta support against Athens, his assistance dwindled and became erratic. The policy he was following— clearly designed to prolong the war and to weaken, if not exhaust, both antagonists— had been urged upon him by the renegade Alcibiades (§3), in flight from both Athens and Sparta (though it may well be that Tissaphernes would have done just the same without Alcibiades' advice). When Darius II decided in 408 to tilt more definitely in Sparta's favor, he reduced Tissaphernes' rule to just the province of Caria and sent his own son Cyrus (§7) to the region with greater authority and funds. Consequently, the Spartans accomplished a decisive victory at the battle of Aigospotamoi in 405. Tissaphernes warned Darius' successor, Artaxerxes II, that Cyrus would prove dangerous to him; by 401, when Cyrus began to mobilize his army and advance eastward, Tissaphernes had already joined the royal forces. He fought in the battle of Cunaxa (401), where his role there seems to have been decisive in producing a victory for Artaxerxes. Cyrus was killed in that battle, and it was Tissaphernes' cavalry that later drove and harassed Cyrus' Greek mercenaries (now led by Xenophon and others) north out of Persian territory. Artaxerxes restored Tissaphernes to his former position as satrap of the coastal provinces, and in that office his renewed demand for tribute from the Greek cities in Asia prompted Spartan mil-

M.28d Chalcis and Euboea: Ref. Map 3, AY.

M.28e Kerameikos: Ref. Map 5. The Kerameikos was a district of Athens (where the clay for noted Athenian pottery came from). It had workshops and a famous gate and cemetery.

itary intervention (400/399). He responded to the Spartan threat with some effective military action, but he also managed to divert most Spartan attacks to the territory of his neighbor Pharnabazos (§21). In 395, however, he was severely defeated by Agesilaos at Sardis, and shortly after this failure, his enemies, who included the Queen Mother Parysatis, succeeded in having him arrested and executed.

Skyler Balbus
Bard College at Simon's Rock
Great Barrington, Massachusetts

Paul Cartledge
A. G. Leventis Professor of Greek Culture
Faculty of Classics
University of Cambridge
Cambridge, UK

Robert B. Strassler
Brookline, Massachusetts

David Thomas
Hertfordshire, UK

NOTE: Paul Cartledge wrote the biographies of Agesipolis, Archidamos III, and Lysander. The rest of the biographies in Appendix M are the result of the combined efforts of Skyler Balbus, Robert B. Strassler, and David Thomas.

APPENDIX N

Compositional Theories of Xenophon's *Hellenika*

§1. Many different theories of how Xenophon might have composed his *Hellenika* have been put forward, though only two are discussed at length in the Introduction (§8.5–8, the first two theories listed below). In order that the reader of this book does not get the wrong impression that these two theories exhaust what scholars have seen as the possibilities, this appendix outlines the principal variants.

§2. The simplest view, and one that has become increasingly popular in recent years, is that the work was composed as a unity in the 350s. The chief weakness of this unitarian position, discussed more fully in the Introduction (§8.6), is that there is a break at 2.3.10 in Xenophon's handling of one particular point of style (usage of so-called particles), and unitarians have not satisfactorily explained this. This stylistic break is also associated with other differences in approach and attitude (an example is given in the Introduction, §8.5).

§3. Accordingly, others have proposed the theory that the work was composed in two parts. The so-called Continuation (of Thucydides) down to the end of the Peloponnesian War is put in the 380s and the rest in the 350s. This binary theory is adopted in the Introduction. Some put the break at 2.2.23 and others at 2.3.10.

§4. A variant binary theory is to put the Continuation in the late 400s, before Xenophon went on Cyrus' expedition. The best argument for this alternative date is that the obituary of Cyrus at *Anabasis* 1.9 suggests that Xenophon regarded him as a hero. As this is not the impression given by *Hellenika*, it is tempting to say Xenophon changed his mind about Cyrus when he met him in 401. The main difficulty with putting the Continuation in 403–402 is that no one doubts that Xenophon wrote to continue Thucydides' work after it broke off, but the evidence (although not absolutely conclusive) suggests strongly that Thucydides was still alive and writing after Xenophon left for the East in 401. Some scholars imagine a more active collaboration between the two of them, which would make it easier to see Xenophon working on *Hellenika* in the late 400s, for there is some evidence from late antiquity pointing in this direction: Diogenes Laertius (*Lives of the Philosophers* 2.6.57) says Xenophon edited and published Thucydides' papers, and Marcellinus (*Life of Thucydides* 43) reports a view that Xenophon wrote what has been transmitted to us as Thucydides Book 8. But most scholars regard these ancient reports as fantasies, based merely on the facts that even before its sudden ending, Thucydides' Book 8 has not received the author's final polish and that Xenophon's work picks up more or less where Thucydides left off. Even if one believed the ancient reports, it wouldn't follow that Xenophon wrote and edited his Continuation as early as the 400s.

§5. Some people who see Xenophon as writing *Hellenika* at two different times place the dividing line not at the end of the Peloponnesian War but a few pages later, usually at the end of Book 2, after the account of the Thirty. There is a clear break in the structure of *Hellenika* at this point, as what precedes focuses largely on Athens and what follows is more clearly written from a Spartan or Spartan supporter's perspective; the narrative also hurries forward over two and a half years at the beginning of Book 3. However, this theory has to ignore the stylistic evidence that puts the break before the account of the Thirty.

§6. Fundamentally at variance with unitarian or binary theories are theories that see Xenophon as composing *Hellenika* over many years, either continuously as a journal or in stops and starts. Diogenes Laertius (*Lives of the Philosophers* 2.6.52) provides ancient support for the idea that Xenophon worked on *Hellenika* through the Skillous[a] years (the 380s and 370s), and obviously Xenophon must also have been at work after leaving Skillous to produce the account of the 360s. Proponents of theories of long-running composition have sometimes pointed to particular passages that, it is argued, must have been written before the 350s; a favorite has been Xenophon's description of the battle of Coronea[b] at 4.3.16 as "quite unlike any other of our time," which some claim to be incompatible with a date after Leuctra[c] (371) or Mantineia[d] (362). Yet, claiming that the battle of Coronea took a unique course is quite different from stating that it involved the most soldiers or deaths or was the most important or decisive battle of the period. More generally, theories of long-running composition are supported by the anecdotal and episodic nature of the book; conversely, they are weakened by tracing underlying unities of theme and attitude, but this is not conclusive evidence against a long period of composition, since these unities pervade the whole of Xenophon's writings.

§7. The stylistic evidence of a break in writing around 2.3.10 is a difficulty for theories of long-running composition, though less so if the work before the break is dated to the 400s rather than the 380s. The theory of truly continuous composition is difficult to believe; it is hard to see how the account of the 370s can be contemporary with the events it describes, since Xenophon makes chronological errors over the war in those years in the west that suggest he was writing about it a good time afterward, while his comments on events of the year 379 at 5.4.1 presuppose the

N.6a   Skillous: Ref. Map 3, CX. Xenophon lived at Skillous, near Olympia, for about twenty years while exiled from Athens. See the Introduction, §4.3.

N.6b   Coronea: Ref. Map 3, BY.
N.6c   Leuctra: Ref. Map 3, BY.
N.6d   Mantineia: Ref. Map 3, CX.

battle of Leuctra, which occurred in 371. However, it is more difficult to rule out a view putting possibly some part of Book 2, Books 3 and 4, and perhaps Book 5 in the 360s and only Books 6 and 7 in the 350s. Some of those who put it all (after 2.3.10) in the 350s ultimately rely less on specific argument and more on general, and admittedly only impressionistic, feelings about the work's literary unity.

§8. One element in the controversy is the comparison between the account of Agesilaos' campaigns in Asia and in the Corinthian War in *Hellenika* Books 3–4 and the very closely parallel account in Xenophon's *Agesilaos*. The latter must have been written as it stands in the 350s, as the work is a postmortem eulogy of Agesilaos, who died in early 360 at the earliest. The Introduction to this edition of *Hellenika* (§5.5) makes a claim that only one point of comparison allows a safe inference as to the sequential order of the works. If the argument set out very briefly there is correct, *Hellenika* 4.6.4–12 comes after *Agesilaos* 2.20. If that is so, it obviously adds weight to the view that *Hellenika* Books 3–5, as well as Books 6 and 7, belong in the 350s; but it is possible that Xenophon wrote *Hellenika* Book 3 and even some of Book 4 in the 360s before hearing of Agesilaos' death, then wrote *Agesilaos*, and then turned back to *Hellenika* Book 4.

§9. It seems safe to say that scholarly agreement is unlikely ever to be reached on this issue, unless perhaps yet more papyri are found with hitherto unknown texts from fourth-century historians to give us more context within which to place Xenophon's work.

David Thomas
Hertfordshire, UK

APPENDIX O

Selections from the *Histories* of Diodorus Siculus Relevant to Xenophon's *Hellenika*

Translated by Peter Green*

BOOK XIII SELECTIONS

The Aftermath of Kynossema
13.41–42

13.41. [1] After his defeat the Lacedaemonian admiral Mindaros retreated to Abydos, where he repaired those of his ships that had suffered damage. He also sent Epikles the Spartan to the triremes located in Euboea with orders to fetch them over posthaste. [2] When Epikles got there, he assembled the ships, fifty in all, and hurriedly put to sea. When they were off Mount Athos, so huge a storm arose that every ship went down, and of their crews only twelve men survived. [3] These facts are set out on a dedication that, as Ephoros tells us, stands in the temple at Coronea and carries the following inscription:

> These from fifty vessels, escaping death,
>   Brought their bodies ashore by Athos' reefs—
> Twelve only; all others the sea's great gulf destroyed
>   With their ships, hit by fearful gales.

[4] At about the same time Alcibiades, in command of thirteen triremes, reached the fleet stationed at Samos. Those there had already heard about his persuading Pharnabazos not to send the three hundred [Phoenician] triremes as reinforcements for the Lacedaemonians. [5] Since he got a friendly reception on Samos, he initiated discussions about the matter of his return home, with many promises about how he

---

NOTE: The sites mentioned in the texts of Appendices O and P are not referred to any maps of this volume as the maps were prepared to support Xenophon's text and not the texts of other historians.

O* These selections are drawn from Peter Green's new translation, *Diodorus Siculus, The Persian Wars to the Fall of Athens: Books 11–14.34 (480–401 B.C.E.).* Green's translation is based chiefly on the Budé edi-

tion, as well as on the Teubner and Loeb editions. See the Bibliography for details on all these works. Certain place-name spellings have been changed here to conform with this volume, which adheres to those in the *Barrington Atlas*. In the appendices to this volume, certain spellings of proper names may vary from author to author.

could be of service to his country. He also defended his own previous conduct, shedding many tears over his personal misfortunes, in that he had been compelled by his enemies to demonstrate his valor at the expense of his native city.

13.42. [1] Since the troops enthusiastically welcomed what he said and reported it all back to Athens, the *demos* voted to dismiss the charges outstanding against him and to let him participate in the command. Observation of the practically effective aspects of his daring, coupled with his renown among the Greeks, led them to the plausible assumption that if he joined them, this would be no small factor in the recovery of their position. [2] What was more, Theramenes—a leading figure in the government of the day, who, if anyone, was seen as a man of good sense—advised the *demos* to recall Alcibiades. When news of these matters reached Samos, Alcibiades added nine ships to his own thirteen and took them to Halicarnassus. After getting a cash payment from that city, [3] he proceeded to sack Meropis [Cos] and then returned to Samos with a great deal of booty. Since the accumulated spoils were so large, he divided the proceeds between the troops on Samos and his own men, thus very quickly ensuring that those who enjoyed his bounty would be well-disposed toward him.

[4] About the same time the citizens of Antandros, who were controlled by a garrison, sent to the Lacedaemonians asking for troops, with whose help they threw out their guards, thus making Antandros a free city. The reason they got help from the Lacedaemonians is that the latter were furious with Pharnabazos for sending the three hundred ships back to Phoenicia.

[5] Of the [historical] writers, Thucydides ended his history [during this year], having covered a period of twenty-two years in eight—or, as some divide it, nine—books: both Xenophon and Theopompos begin at the point where Thucydides leaves off. Xenophon covers a period of forty-eight years, while Theopompos deals with a seventeen-year segment of Greek history, bringing his narrative to a close, in twelve books, with the sea battle off Cnidus.

[6] These, then, were the events that took place in Greece and Asia [Minor]. . . .

The Battle of Abydos
13.45–47.2

13.45. [1] In Greece Dorieus the Rhodian, the admiral in command of the triremes from Italy, once he had put down the disturbance on Rhodos, set sail for the Hellespont. He was eager to join Mindaros, who had stationed himself at Abydos and was collecting from every quarter ships belonging to the Peloponnesian alliance. [2] When Dorieus was already near Sigeion in the Troad, the Athenians at Sestos, having heard about his progress along the coast, put out against him with their entire fleet, some seventy-four ships in all. [3] For a while Dorieus held course, having no notion what was happening; but when he perceived the size of the [Athenian] fleet, he took fright and, seeing no other way of escape, sought refuge at Dardanos. [4] He disembarked his troops, took over the city garrison, and speedily fetched in a massive supply of missiles. He then divided his forces, stationing part on the prows [of the ships] and part in well-chosen positions ashore. [5] The Athenians came sailing in at full tilt and set about hauling the ships off; and since they out-flanked and outnumbered their opponents all around, they began to wear them down. [6] As soon as the Peloponnesian admiral Mindaros heard about this, he at once put out to sea from Abydos with his entire fleet and set course for the Darda-nian promontory, bringing eighty-four vessels to reinforce those under Dorieus. The ground forces of Pharnabazos were also in the vicinity, as support for the Lacedaemonians.

[7] When the two fleets approached each other, both sides ranged their triremes in battle order: Mindaros, with ninety-seven ships, posted the Syracusans on his left wing, while he himself commanded the right; on the Athenian side, Thrasyboulos commanded the right wing and Thrasyllos the other. [8] After they had disposed their forces in this manner, the commanders raised the signal for battle, and their trumpeters, at the one command, began to sound the attack; and since the rowers evinced no lack of enthusiasm, while the steersmen handled their helms most skill-fully, the struggle that ensued was breathtaking. [9] Whenever the triremes surged forward to ram, then the steersmen, at just the right instant, would turn their ships at the precise angle to force a head-on collision. [10] Thus the marines, seeing their ves-sels borne broadside on toward the enemy's triremes, would be in high alarm and despair for their lives; but then, when the steersmen, through their seasoned exper-tise, would foil the attack, they would once more become cheerful and optimistic.

13.46. [1] Nor did those men who had been posted on the decks fail to convert their zeal into action. Some, from long range, shot arrow after arrow, till soon the air was full of missiles; others, every time they moved in close, would throw their javelins, aiming either at the defending marines or else at the steersmen themselves. Whenever ships collided, they would keep up the fight with their spears and then, at the moment of impact, jump aboard the enemy's triremes and engage in hand-to-hand combat with swords. [2] At every setback the victors would start whooping and yelling, while the other side would be shouting as they charged to the rescue, so that over the entire battle scene a huge confused uproar prevailed.

For a long time the battle hung in the balance because of the high degree of rivalry animating both sides; but somewhat later Alcibiades unexpectedly showed up from Samos with twenty ships, by pure chance being on a voyage to the Hellespont. [3] While these vessels were still far off, each side, hoping that it was for them that reinforcements had come, were buoyed up in their hopes and fought with even greater passion and daring. However, when the squadron drew close, no signal was displayed for the Lacedaemonians; instead Alcibiades ran up a purple ensign from his own ship for the Athenians, this being the signal he and they had arranged beforehand. At this the Lacedaemonians, in some alarm, turned and fled; and the Athenians, elated by their advantage, pressed on in pursuit of the retreating vessels. [4] They quickly captured ten of them; but after this a storm and strong winds arose, which greatly hampered them in their pursuit. With the waves running so high, ships would not answer their helms, and ramming proved impracticable, since the [target] vessels were receding at the moment of impact. [5] The Lacedaemonians finally got to shore and took refuge with the land forces of Pharnabazos. The Athenians at first tried to drag [their opponents'] vessels out to sea and fought savagely to this end; but they were cut up by Persian troops and so withdrew to Sestos. [6] This was because Pharnabazos, in his desire to rebut the charges the Lacedaemonians were making against him, attacked the Athenians with more than ordinary violence. At the same time, regarding the three hundred ships sent back to Phoenicia, he informed them that he had done this on learning that the kings of Arabia and Egypt were hatching plots together against that country.

13.47. [1] After the sea battle had ended in this manner, the Athenians, it being already dark, sailed off to Sestos; but when day dawned, they came back to pick up their wrecks and set up a second trophy beside the first one. [2] About the first watch of the night, Mindaros made for Abydos: here he repaired his damaged vessels and sent a request to the Lacedaemonians for both naval and infantry support, since he planned, while the fleet was being readied, and with the help of Pharnabazos, to lay siege to such cities as were allied with the Athenians.

The Euboean Revolt: Chalcis
13.47.3–8

[3] The citizens of Chalcis, together with most of the other inhabitants of Euboea, had revolted from Athens and because of this were extremely worried that, as islanders, they might be reduced by the Athenians, who had control of the seas. They therefore invited the Boeotians to join them in constructing a double mole across the Euripos, thus linking Euboea to Boeotia. [4] The Boeotians agreed, it being to their advantage too that Euboea should remain an island for all others but become mainland for them. All the cities then embarked energetically, vying one with another, on the building of this mole, since it was not only all citizens who were required to turn out but also the resident foreigners. Thus, by reason of the great number who presented themselves for work, the undertaking was very soon completed. [5] On the Euboean side the mole was lined up in the direction of Chalcis, and in Boeotia toward Aulis, since it was here that the gap was narrowest. As it happened, there had always been a tidal current at that point, with the sea regularly reversing its flow; and now the force of the current became greatly intensified, since the sea was forced into an excessively narrow channel, with clear passage left for one

vessel only. They also built high towers at the end of each arm and set up wooden bridges across the channel.

[6] Theramenes, who had been sent out by the Athenians with thirty ships, at first endeavored to hinder those engaged on these works, but since the mole builders were protected by a strong military guard, he gave up that idea and instead set course for the islands. [7] Being anxious to afford both [Athenian] citizens and their allies relief from the levies they paid, he went ravaging enemy territory and amassed considerable spoils. He also went around the cities of the allies and extracted cash payments from any persons in them advocating political change. [8] When he put in at Paros, he found an oligarchy [established] in the city: he thereupon restored freedom to the people, and on those who had been involved with the oligarchy he imposed heavy fines.

Corcyra and Pydna
13.48–49.2

13.48. [1] About this same time it so happened that violent civil dissention, with some butchery, took place on Corcyra. Several reasons have been alleged for this, above all, the rancorous mutual hatred that existed between its inhabitants. [2] Never in any other city did so great a slaughter of citizens occur, nor sharper strife and contentiousness leading to such destruction. Before this particular conflict, indeed, the number of those killed by their own fellows had already, it would seem, reached about fifteen hundred, and every one of them was a prominent citizen. [3] Despite these previous misfortunes, however, Fortune laid yet another calamity on them by once more heightening the differences that divided them. The Corcyraeans of the highest rank, being bent on introducing an oligarchy, were in sympathy with the Lacedaemonian cause, whereas the radical masses were all for an Athenian alliance. [4] Indeed, the peoples now struggling for the leadership embraced quite different principles: the Lacedaemonians made the most prominent citizens in the cities allied to them responsible for the conduct of public affairs, whereas the Athenians established democracies in such cities. [5] The Corcyraeans, then, seeing their most powerful citizens inclining toward a handover of their city to the Lacedaemonians, sent word to the Athenians requesting a body of troops as a protective garrison. [6] Konon, the Athenian general, sailed to Corcyra and left there six hundred of the Messenians from Naupactus; he himself coasted on with his ships and anchored close to the precinct of Hera. [7] The six hundred, together with the [local] populists, waited till the marketplace had filled up and then made a sudden attack on the Lacedaemonians' supporters, arresting some, killing others, and driving more than a thousand into exile. They also freed the slaves and enfranchised the resident aliens as a counter measure against the numbers and influence of those who had fled the country. [8] The latter had sought refuge on the mainland opposite; and after a few days certain persons in the city who supported the exiles' cause took over the marketplace, recalled the exiles, and launched an all-out struggle to settle this matter once and for all. When darkness fell and the fighting broke off, they came to an agreement with each other, abandoned their cutthroat rivalry, and thenceforward shared their native city as a single people.

Such was the conclusion of the massacre on Corcyra.

13.49. [1] King Archelaös of Macedon, finding that the citizens of Pydna would not submit to his authority, brought up a strong force and put their city under siege. He received assistance also from Theramenes, with his fleet; but after the siege had gone on for some while, the latter sailed on to Thrace to join Thrasyboulos, the commander in chief of the entire expeditionary force. [2] Archelaös now continued the siege of Pydna with increased determination, and when he had finally reduced the city, he shifted it about twenty stades [two to three miles] inland.

The Battle of Cyzicus
13.49.2–52.1

13.49. [2] Winter now being nearly over, Mindaros began assembling his triremes from all quarters, including many from the Peloponnese as well as from other allies. When the Athenian generals in Sestos discovered the size of the fleet being put together by the enemy, they were highly worried by the possibility of an attack in strength that might capture their ships. [3] They therefore hauled down the vessels they had ashore at Sestos, cruised around the Chersonese, and dropped anchor at Kardia. From here they sent triremes to Thrasyboulos and Theramenes in Thrace, requesting them to bring their fleet there as speedily as possible; they also summoned Alcibiades from Lesbos with such ships as he had. The entire armada thus converged on one spot, the commanders being eager for a finally decisive engagement.

[4] Meanwhile Mindaros, the Lacedaemonian admiral, sailed to Cyzicus, put his entire force ashore, and invested the city. Pharnabazos also appeared there with a large army, and the two of them together laid siege to Cyzicus and took it by storm.

[5] The Athenian generals took the decision to sail to Cyzicus, stood out to sea with their entire fleet, and sailed around the Chersonese [into the Hellespont]. Their first landfall was at Elaious; but after that they were careful to sail past Abydos at night, to avoid revealing the great number of their ships to the enemy. [6] When they reached Proconnesus, they bivouacked there for the night; the next day they disembarked the troops they had transported on Cyzicene territory, with orders to Chaireas, their commander, to lead his army against the city.

13.50. [1] The generals meanwhile divided the fleet into three squadrons, of which Alcibiades commanded one, Theramenes another, and Thrasyboulos the third. Alcibiades and his squadron sailed well ahead of the others, with the intention of provoking the Lacedaemonians into a battle, while Theramenes and Thrasyboulos planned to [outflank and] encircle the enemy and cut off their retreat to the city once they had sailed out. [2] Mindaros, seeing only the twenty ships of Alcibiades bearing down on him and knowing nothing of the rest, regarded them with contempt and boldly set out against them from the city with a fleet eighty strong. When he got close to Alcibiades' squadron, the Athenians, as they had been instructed, feigned flight, and the Peloponnesians, in great excitement, followed hard after them, convinced they were winning. [3] But when Alcibiades had drawn them on a good way farther from the city, he gave the signal, and instantly, at one and the same time, his own triremes went about to confront the enemy, and Theramenes and Thrasyboulos sailed toward the city and cut off the Lacedaemonians' line of retreat. [4] Mindaros and his officers, now aware of the great size of the enemy fleet and realizing that they had been outgeneraled, became considerably alarmed. In the end, with Athenians appearing from all directions and the Peloponnesians' way back to the city already barred, Mindaros was forced to seek refuge ashore at the place known as Kleroi, which was where Pharnabazos and his army were stationed. [5] Alcibiades pursued him energetically, sank some of his ships, and disabled and captured others; most of them had been moored along the shore, and these he seized, throwing grappling irons onto them and attempting by means of these to drag the ships clear of land. [6] When the ground forces from ashore came to the aid of the Peloponnesians, a great slaughter took place: the Athenians, because of the edge they held, were fighting with greater daring than was prudent, while the Peloponnesians had a great advantage in numbers, since Pharnabazos' army was backing up the Lacedaemonians and fighting from the land, which gave its position greater security. [7] Thrasyboulos, seeing these ground troops assisting the enemy, disembarked the rest of his own marines, with the intention of providing relief for Alcibiades; he also sent word to Theramenes to link up with Chaireas and his infantry and come with all speed to continue the fight on land.

13.51. [1] While the Athenians were thus occupied, Mindaros, the Lacedaemonian commander, was engaged in a struggle with Alcibiades for the ships that were being dragged off, and dispatched Klearchos the Spartan with part of the Peloponnesian contingent, as well as the mercenary corps from Pharnabazos' army, against the troops under Thrasyboulos. [2] Thrasyboulos, with the marines and archers, at first put up a vigorous defense against the enemy; but though he inflicted heavy casualties on them, he saw not a few of his own men fall as well. However, just when the mercenaries serving Pharnabazos had the Athenians encircled and were crowding in on them from all sides, Theramenes showed up, bringing both his own troops and Chaireas' infantry. [3] Though Thrasyboulos' troops were exhausted and had given up hope of rescue, their spirits suddenly soared once more with the arrival of such powerful reinforcements. [4] A long and hard-fought battle ensued. First Pharnabazos' mercenaries began to retreat, so that the continuity of their battle line was broken; and finally the Peloponnesians left behind with Klearchos, after both inflicting and suffering heavy casualties, were forced out.

[5] Once these were overcome, Theramenes and his men hurried to relieve Alcibiades' embattled troops. Even when their forces were combined, however, Mindaros did not let Theramenes' attack trouble him. He simply divided the Peloponnesians and used half of them to hold this advance; with the remaining half, which he commanded in person, he drew up his battle line against Alcibiades' troops, adjuring each of his own soldiers not to bring Sparta's renown into disrepute—and in an infantry battle, at that. [6] He put up a heroic struggle for the ships, fighting in the very forefront of the battle, but though he slew many of his opponents, in the end he was cut down by Alcibiades' men as he contended honorably for his fatherland. When he fell, the Peloponnesians and all the allies flocked together and broke into panic-stricken flight. [7] The Athenians pursued their enemies for a while, but on learning that Pharnabazos was approaching at great speed with a large cavalry force, they changed direction and made for the ships. They secured the city and then set up two trophies, one for each victory: the first, on the island known as Polydoros, for the sea battle, and the second for the infantry engagement, at the spot where they first turned the enemy to flight. [8] Both the Peloponnesians in the city and all survivors from the battle fled to Pharnabazos' camp; and the Athenian generals, having simultaneously vanquished two such substantial forces, captured all their ships, besides rounding up numerous prisoners and an incalculable amount of booty.

13.52. [1] When word of this victory reached Athens, the people, faced with the good fortune that had befallen the city on the heels of earlier disasters, were exultant over their successes and together made sacrifice to the gods and held various festivities. They also selected for the campaign a thousand of their most physically robust hoplites, together with a hundred cavalry; in addition to these they sent out thirty triremes to Alcibiades and his force, so that, now that they had the mastery at sea, they might with impunity despoil those cities that supported the Lacedaemonians.

Peace Offer
13.52.2–53

13.52. [2] The Lacedaemonians themselves, however, when they heard about the disaster that had befallen them at Cyzicus, sent ambassadors to Athens to negotiate for peace, their ambassador in chief being Endios. On being granted permission, he came forward and spoke in a succinct, "laconic" manner: this is why I decided not to omit his speech just as it was delivered:

[3] "Men of Athens, we want to make peace with you, [on these terms]: that

each of us keep what cities we now possess; that the strongholds we maintain in each other's territories be abandoned; and that our prisoners of war be ransomed by exchange, one Laconian for one Athenian. We are not unaware that this war is harmful to us both, though far more so to you. [4] Don't bother with my arguments, though: just look at the facts. We have the whole of the Peloponnese to cultivate, but you, [now], only a small part of Attica. The war has brought us Laconians many allies but from you Athenians has taken as many as it has presented to your enemies. We have the wealthiest of all monarchs in the known world to meet our expenses in this war, whereas you are dependent on its most indigent inhabitants. [5] Thus our troops, in view of their ample pay, serve with enthusiasm; whereas yours, who have to meet war taxes from their own resources, have no stomach either for war's hardships or for its high costs. [6] Furthermore, when we carry on the war at sea, the only state resources we risk losing are hulls, while most of the personnel you have aboard are citizens. Most important of all, even if we are defeated in a naval campaign, we still retain our acknowledged supremacy on land, since a Spartan infantryman doesn't even know what flight means. But once you're driven from the sea, it's not for supremacy that you contend on land but to stave off destruction.

[7] "It remains for me to show you why, when we have so many substantial advantages in this war, we still call on you to make peace. I'm not saying that Sparta is benefiting from hostilities, simply that she's suffering less damage than Athens. Only madmen would feel good about sharing their enemy's misfortunes when it was open to them to have no experience of misfortune whatsoever. Destruction of the enemy brings no joy so great that it can match the wretchedness of one's own people. [8] Nor are these the only reasons why we wish to come to terms with you: it is also because we cherish our ancestral customs. When we contemplate the bitter rivalries inherent in warfare and the varieties of awful suffering to which they give rise, we feel we should make it clear to all, to both gods and mortals, that of all men we are least to blame for such things."

13.53. [1] After the Laconian had advanced these and other similar arguments, the most reasonable-minded among the Athenians were leaning in their opinions toward the idea of peace; but the habitual warmongers, who made a practice of turning civic disturbances to their own profit, wanted hostilities [to continue]. [2] One adherent of this attitude was Kleophon, the most prominent populist leader of the day. He now came forward and addressed the issue at length in his own peculiar manner. By stressing the magnitude of their [recent military] successes—as though Fortune were not in the habit of handing out prizes for primacy to all sides in turn—he whipped up public excitement. [3] So the Athenians were talked into a flawed decision, of which they repented too late for any good it might do them, and were deceived by mere flattery into so thoroughgoing a blunder that never thereafter at any time could they really recover from its effects. [4] However, these events, which took place somewhat later, will be discussed in the period to which they belong. At the time, the Athenians—being elated by their successes and cherishing many grandiose hopes because of having Alcibiades as their commander in chief—imagined they had already recovered their supremacy.

The Aftermath of Cyzicus; Sparta Recaptures Pylos
13.64

[1] In Greece [Thrasyllos],[a] who had been sent out by the Athenians with thirty ships, a large number of hoplites, and a hundred cavalrymen, made landfall at Ephesus. After disembarking his troops at two separate landing points, he launched assaults on the city. Those within the walls came out against them, and a hard-fought battle took place. Since the Ephesians were engaged in full force, four hundred Athenians lost their lives: the remainder Thrasyboulos got aboard his ships and then set sail for Lesbos. [2] The Athenian generals [operating] in the Cyzicus area now sailed to Chalcedon, where they set up the fortress of Chrysopolis and left a sufficient force there to garrison it. Those in command they instructed to impose a ten percent tariff on all traffic from the Black Sea. [3] After this they split their forces. Theramenes was left behind with fifty vessels to besiege Chalcedon and Byzantium. Thrasyboulos was dispatched to the Thrace-ward regions, where he set about bringing over the local cities. [4] Alcibiades now sent [Thrasyllos] and his thirty-five ships on separately and sailed to the territory held by Pharnabazos. Working together, they laid waste a great deal of it: as a result, they glutted their troops with plunder but also themselves amassed money from the spoils, since they were anxious to relieve the [Athenian] people of the burden of war taxes.

[5] When the Lacedaemonians realized that all Athenian forces were now deployed in the Hellespontine area, they made an expedition against Pylos, held with a garrison by the Messenians. They did this by sea with eleven ships (five from Sicily, six crewed by their own citizens), while they had also assembled ground forces in adequate numbers. After investing the fortress, they [enforced their siege][a] by both land and sea. [6] The moment the Athenian *demos* got the news, they sent out thirty ships under Anytos son of Anthemion to relieve the besieged. Anytos duly sailed but, because of storms, was unable to round Cape Malea and so returned to Athens. This so angered the *demos* that they charged him with treason and put him on trial. In this perilous situation Anytos saved his neck by laying out cash, and appears to have been the first Athenian actually to bribe a jury. [7] For quite a while the Messenians in Pylos continued to hold out in the expectation of relief from the Athenians; but what with the enemy's endless round of assaults and the fact that, of their own number, those who were not dying from their wounds had been reduced

O.13.64.1a   Here, as at 13.64.4, 13.66.1, 13.74.1, and
13.97.6, I read Palmerius' emendation
[Thrasyllos], which has Oldfather's clear
approval, for the manuscripts' "Thrasyboulos." (Peter Green)

O.13.64.5a   "Enforced their siege" translates Post's
plausible emendation. (Peter Green)

to desperate straits through lack of food, they finally evacuated the position under truce. This, then, was how the Lacedaemonians regained control of Pylos after a fifteen-year occupation by the Athenians, beginning with Demosthenes' fortification of the site.

Nisaia, Chios
13.65

[1] While these events were taking place, the Megarians seized [their port of] Nisaia, which at the time was in Athenian hands, and the Athenians sent out against them Leotrophides and Timarchos, with a thousand infantry and four hundred cavalry. The Megarians came out to confront them under arms and in full force, and after augmenting their numbers with some of the forces from Sicily, they formed their battle line near the hills known as the Horns. [2] The Athenians fought brilliantly and routed an enemy who greatly outnumbered them. Large numbers of Megarians perished but no more than twenty Lacedaemonians, since the Athenians, who had been infuriated by the seizure of Nisaia, did not pursue the Lacedaemonians but inflicted heavy casualties on the Megarians out of pure resentment.

[3] The Lacedaemonians now appointed Kratesippidas admiral, manned twenty-five of their own vessels with allied crews, and ordered them out to the assistance of their allies [in the eastern Aegean]. Kratesippidas spent some while off the Ionian coast without accomplishing anything worthy of note; later, however, in return for a cash payment furnished by the exiles from Chios, he reinstated them and captured the Chian acropolis. [4] These Chian returnees now in their turn banished the political opponents who had been responsible for exiling them, to a total of about six hundred. The latter seized a place called Atarneus on the mainland opposite, a stronghold of extreme natural ruggedness, and from then on used it as a base for conducting guerrilla warfare against those in power on Chios.

The Recapture of Byzantium
13.66–67

13.66. [1] While these events were taking place, Alcibiades and [Thrasyllos] fortified Lampsacus, left a sufficient garrison there, and themselves sailed with their forces to join Theramenes, who with seventy ships and five thousand troops was ravaging [the territory of] Chalcedon. When their fleets and armies were united in the one location, they invested the city from sea to sea with a wooden stockade. [2] Hippokrates, the man stationed in the city by the Lacedaemonians as commander (what Laconians referred to as a "harmost"), led out against them both his own troops and all the Chalcedonians. A fierce battle ensued, in which Alcibiades' troops fought with great bravery. Hippokrates himself was killed. Of his troops some perished, while the severely wounded all sought refuge inside the city. [3] After this Alcibiades sailed down to the Hellespont and the Chersonese, his object being to collect cash payments, while Theramenes made an agreement with the citizens of Chalcedon that they should pay the same amount of tribute [to Athens] as they had done previously. From there he took his forces across to Byzantium and laid that city under siege, beginning the investment with great speed and energy. [4] Alcibiades, after collecting his payments, persuaded a good number of the Thracians to join the campaign under him and also attracted a mass enlistment from the Chersonese. He then set out with his entire force. First he captured Selymbria by betrayal, mulcted the Selymbrians of a large sum of money, and imposed a garrison on them. He then moved on fast to join Theramenes at Byzantium. [5] When their forces were united, they began making preparations for a siege, [in the knowledge that] they intended to conquer a city of great substance that was crammed with defenders: apart from the Byzantines themselves, of whom there were many, the Lacedaemonian harmost Klearchos had numerous Peloponnesians and mercenaries on hand. [6] Thus, though they continued to make assaults for some while, during this period they did no serious damage to the defenders. But as soon as the governor left to get funds from Pharnabazos, certain Byzantines who detested the severity with which he exercised his office (Klearchos was indeed a stern authoritarian) betrayed the city to Alcibiades and his colleagues.

13.67. [1] These sailed out that afternoon with their entire fleet and also marched their ground forces some distance away, as though they meant to raise the siege and remove their armaments to Ionia; but as soon as it got dark they returned, reaching the city about midnight. They then sent the triremes with orders to start hauling away the [Byzantines'] merchantmen and to make as much noise as possible, as though the entire force were there. They themselves meanwhile stood ready with their land forces before the walls, watching for the agreed-on signal from those who were to surrender the city. [2] So the men aboard the triremes carried out their instructions, slamming into some of the vessels with their rams, trying to tear others loose by means of grappling irons, and all the time keeping up a tremendous hullabaloo. At this the Peloponnesians in the city—and everyone else unaware of the deception—rushed down to the harbors to save the situation. [3] Those betraying the city now raised their signal from the wall and let Alcibiades and his men in by means of ladders—a completely safe move, since everyone was off harborward. [4] But when the Peloponnesians discovered what had happened, to begin with, they left half their number at the harbor and then with the rest came running back to recover the captured walls; [5] and although almost the entire Athenian force was now inside the city, the Peloponnesians were not dismayed but kept up their resistance for a long time, they and the Byzantines battling the Athenians together. Indeed, in the end the Athenians would never have reduced the city by force of arms had not Alcibiades, seeing his chance, proclaimed that the Byzantines were to suffer no improper treatment: this was what made the citizen body change sides and turn against the Peloponnesians. [6] Most of the latter, as a result, fell fighting gallantly, while the survivors, about five hundred of them, sought refuge at the altars in the temples. [7] The Athenians returned the city to the Byzantines after first making them allies and then came to an agreement with the suppliants at the altars: they would remove their arms, convey their persons to Athens, and turn them over to the *demos* for a decision regarding them.

Alcibiades Returns to Athens
13.68–69

13.68. [1] When the year had run its course, the Athenians conferred the archonship upon Euktemon, . . . and the Ninety-Third Olympiad was celebrated, in which Eubatos of Cyrene won the *stadion*. About this time the Athenian generals, now that they were masters of Byzantium, made for the Hellespont and took every city along it except for Abydos. [2] Then, leaving Diodoros and Mantitheos in charge there with a sufficient force, they themselves sailed to Athens with the ships and the spoils, having accomplished many notable deeds for their country. When they were nearly there, the whole populace came out to meet them, overjoyed at their successes; and great numbers of aliens, too, as well as women and children, all thronged down to Peiraieus. [3] For this return of the generals gave ample scope for astonishment, seeing that they brought with them no less than two hundred captured ships, together with a vast quantity of prisoners and spoils of war. Their own triremes they had taken much trouble to decorate with gilded arms and wreaths, as well as with items of booty and every other kind of adornment.

But most people had hastened down to the harbor to catch a glimpse of Alcibiades, slaves and free vying with one another, so that the city was completely deserted. [4] For by now this man had come to be so admired that the more prominent Athenians thought they had finally found a strong character who could oppose the people openly and boldly, while the indigent figured they would have in him a first-rate champion who would heedlessly throw the city into turmoil in order to relieve their penury. [5] In boldness he far outstripped all others; he was an immensely clever speaker, unrivaled as a general, his daring marked by practical success. Over and above this he was quite extraordinarily handsome in appearance, with a brilliant mind and a spirit bent on high endeavors. [6] In short, almost everyone nursed such lofty assumptions concerning him as to be convinced that, with his return, good fortune in their public affairs had likewise come back to the city. In addition, just as the Lacedaemonians had been ahead of the game while he was on their side, so [the Athenians] expected that they, too, would enjoy success with this man as an ally.

13.69. [1] So when the fleet came into the harbor, the crowd turned toward Alcibiades' ship, and as he stepped from it everyone welcomed him, congratulating him on his successes but also on his return from exile. He greeted the crowds warmly and [later] called a meeting of the Assembly, at which he made a lengthy defense of his personal actions. This generated such goodwill toward him among the masses that all agreed it was the city that had been at fault as regards the decrees voted against him. [2] As a result, his property, which had been impounded by the state, was returned to him, and in addition they threw into the sea the stelae on which his sentence and the other verdicts against him had been inscribed. They also passed a vote that the Eumolpidae should revoke the curse they pronounced against him at the time when he was believed to have profaned the [Eleusinian] Mysteries. [3] Finally, they appointed him supreme commander on land and at sea, entrusting all their armaments to him. They also elected as his fellow generals those whom he wanted, Adeimantos and Thrasyboulos.

[4] Alcibiades manned a hundred ships and sailed to Andros, where he seized a stronghold called [Gaurion][a] and fortified it. When the Andrians came out against him in full force, together with the Peloponnesians guarding the city, a battle took place, which the Athenians won. Of those from the city, many were killed; and of those who survived, some scattered across the countryside, while others sought refuge within the walls. [5] Alcibiades made some attacks on the city but then left a sufficient garrison in the position he had fortified, appointed Thrasyboulos its commander, and then himself sailed on to Cos and Rhodos, both of which he plundered, collecting ample booty for the maintenance of his troops.

Notion
13.70–72.2

13.70. [1] Though the Lacedaemonians had lost their entire naval force, together with its commander, Mindaros, they nevertheless did not sink into despair. They now chose as admiral Lysander, reputed to surpass all others in strategical skill and possessed of a daring that could deal successfully with any situation. On assuming the command, he set about enrolling an adequate number of troops from the Peloponnese and manned as many ships as he could. [2] He then sailed to Rhodos, where he augmented his squadron with all the ships available from the various Rhodian cities. From there he moved on to Ephesus and Miletus. After fitting out the triremes in these cities, he requisitioned those from Chios and thus made ready at Ephesus a fleet consisting of some seventy vessels. [3] On hearing that King Darius' son Cyrus had been dispatched by his father to support the Lacedaemonian war effort, he traveled to Sardis to meet him. To such an extent did he sharpen the young man's enthusiasm for the war against the Athenians that he got ten thousand darics from him, there and then, as pay for his troops; and for the future Cyrus bade him make his requests without reserve, since he had instructions from his father to furnish the Lacedaemonians with anything they might require. [4] Lysander then

O.13.69.4a   "Gaurion" is Rhodomanus's emendation,   the otherwise unknown "Katrion" of
              based on Xenophon's *Hellenika* 1.4.22,   Diodorus' manuscripts. (Peter Green)
              and accepted by Vogel and Oldfather, of

returned to Ephesus and summoned the wealthiest men from the cities [of Ionia], with whom he set up political groups, promising them that if his plans were successful, he would place them in charge of their several cities. As a result, these men competed with one another to provide greater aid than had been demanded of them; and so very soon, against all expectations, Lysander came to have an abundance of every kind of supply useful for warfare.

13.71. [1] When Alcibiades heard that Lysander was fitting out his fleet in Ephesus, he set sail thither with his entire fleet. He cruised in close to the harbors, but when no one came out against him, he brought most of his ships to Notion and left them anchored there, entrusting the command of them to his personal steersman Antiochos, with orders not to risk a sea battle during his absence; he himself meanwhile took the troop transports and sailed with all speed to Klazomenai, since this city, an ally of Athens, was suffering from incursions by some of its exiles. [2] Antiochos, however, being impetuous by nature and eager to bring off some brilliant coup on his own account, ignored what Alcibiades had told him. Manning ten of the best ships and ordering the captains of the remainder to keep them ready for action should there be need for them to join in, he sailed up close to the enemy and challenged them to battle. [3] Lysander, who had learned, from some deserters, about Alcibiades' departure with the best of his troops, figured that this was a good moment to accomplish something worthy of Sparta. He therefore put out in response to the challenge with all his ships. The leading [Athenian] ship, on which Antiochos had stationed himself for the engagement, he sank; the rest he put to flight and pursued, till the Athenian captains manned the rest of their vessels and rallied in support, though in no kind of ordered formation. [4] A sea battle developed close inshore between this crowded mass of ships, in which the Athenians, because of their disorder, got the worst of it and lost twenty-two vessels. However, very few of their crew members were taken prisoner: for the most part they swam safely ashore. When Alcibiades heard what had happened, he hastened back to Notion, manned all his triremes, and sailed up to the enemy-held harbors; but Lysander would not venture out against him, so Alcibiades [gave up and] set course for Samos.

13.72. [1] While these events were taking place, the Athenian general Thrasyboulos sailed against Thasos with fifteen ships. He fought and defeated those who made a sally from the city, killing about two hundred of them; he then laid siege to the city itself, boxing in its inhabitants. [In this way] he forced them to take back their exiles (who were those supporting the Athenians), to accept a garrison, and to become allies of Athens. [2] After this he sailed to Abdera, at that time one of the most powerful cities in Thrace, and brought it over [to the Athenian side]. These, then, were the accomplishments of the Athenian generals after setting out from home.

The Dismissal of Alcibiades
13.73.3–74

13.73. [3] Alcibiades put to sea with all his ships and made for Cyme. He then proceeded to bring false accusations against the Cymaians, since he wanted an excuse for despoiling their territory. To begin with, he rounded up large numbers of prisoners and was taking them back to his ships; [4] but those in the city came out to the rescue in full force and fell on him unexpectedly. For a while he and his troops resisted firmly, but then large numbers from city and countryside alike flocked to the support of the Cymaians, so that they were forced to abandon their prisoners and run for it to the ships. [5] Alcibiades, much distressed by these setbacks, sent to Mytilene for his hoplites, drew up his forces before the city, and challenged the Cymaians to battle. When no one came out, he laid waste [Cyme's] territory and then set sail for Mytilene. [6] The Cymaians now dispatched an embassy to Athens, accusing Alcibiades of having laid waste an allied city that had done no wrong. There were also many other charges brought against him. Some of the troops at Samos, who had their own differences with Alcibiades, sailed to Athens and denounced him in the Assembly as pro-Lacedaemonian—and for cultivating the friendship of Pharnabazos with an eye to getting mastery over his fellow citizens once the war had ended.

13.74. [1] Alcibiades' reputation was badly enough damaged by the reverse he had suffered in the sea battle and the offenses he had committed with regard to Cyme; but since these [other] accusations had very soon come to be generally believed, the Athenian *demos*, viewing the man's brashness [now] with some suspicion, elected as their ten generals Konon, Lysias, Diomedon, and Pericles, together with Erasinides, Aristokrates, Archestratos, Protomachos, [Thrasyllos],[a] and Aristogenes. Of these their first choice was Konon, and they at once sent him out to take over the fleet from Alcibiades. [2] Alcibiades duly ceded the command to Konon and handed over his forces. After this he dismissed the idea of returning to Athens and, taking one trireme only, withdrew to Paktyë in Thrace, since, in addition to the anger of the public, he was worried by the lawsuits that had been filed against him. [3] Many individuals, observing how powerfully he was resented, had made him the object of numerous charges; the most serious of these was the one to do with horses, the sum involved being estimated at eight talents. Diomedes, a friend of his, had sent a four-horse team with him to Olympia. Alcibiades, however, when recording the entry in the usual way, listed the horses as his own. Having won the four-horse race, he then took all the prestige of the victory for himself and did not [even] return the horses to the man who had trusted him with them. [4] Reflecting on all these matters, Alcibiades was afraid that the Athenians would pick a good opportunity to exact retribution from him for all the wrongs he had done them. He therefore of his own accord imposed upon himself the penalty of exile.

O.13.74.1a   Again, there is confusion in Diodorus or at least in the manuscripts of his work between Thrasyboulos (who was a general) and Thrasyllos. Diodorus names the general correctly at 13.97.6, 13.98.3, 13.101.5.

Kallikratidas
13.76–79.7

13.76. [1] When this year's events drew to a close, in Athens Antigenes succeeded to the archonship. About this time the Athenian general Konon, after taking over the forces based on Samos, fitted out all vessels there present and, in addition, called in those of the allies, being determined to make his fleet a match for that of the enemy. [2] The Spartans, meanwhile, since Lysander's term as admiral had expired, sent out Kallikratidas to succeed him: a very young man of unblemished and straightforward character, as yet lacking experience in foreign ways, and of all the Spartans the most law-abiding. (It is generally agreed that during his period of command he committed no injustices against either cities or individuals and indeed dealt severely with those who attempted to bribe him, taking punitive action against them.) [3] He it was who now sailed to Ephesus and took over the fleet. After he had called in the allied contingents, his total command, including the ships he took over from Lysander, numbered 140 vessels. Since the Athenians controlled Delphinion, in Chian territory, he sailed against them with his entire fleet and set about besieging the place. [4] The Athenian [garrison], about five hundred in number, took fright at the great size of his force and abandoned their position, passing through the enemy lines under a truce. Kallikratidas took over the fortress and demolished it. Then he sailed against the Teïans, got inside the walls of their city by night, and stripped it of spoils. [5] After this he sailed to Lesbos with his armada and attacked Methymna, which had an Athenian garrison. He organized continuous assaults, yet to begin with got nowhere. But not long afterward certain individuals betrayed the city to him, and he slipped [his troops] inside the walls. Though he despoiled the city of its possessions, he spared its men and returned it to the Methymnaians. [6] This done, he made for Mytilene, turning over the hoplites to Thorax the Lacedaemonian, with orders to force-march thither as fast as might be while he himself sailed down the coast.

13.77. [1] The Athenian general Konon had seventy ships, fitted out for naval warfare in a manner that no earlier general had ever equaled as regards preparation. He took all these ships when he sailed to the relief of Methymna. [2] However, on learning that the city had already fallen, he then bivouacked on one of the so-called Hundred Islands. At daybreak, seeing the enemy squadrons approaching, he decided it would be dangerous to risk a full-scale engagement there, against double his own number of triremes. Instead he planned to avoid battle by sailing outside [the islands] and then to draw some of the enemy triremes after him toward Mytilene, where he would engage them. In this way, he reckoned, if he won, he could put about for the pursuit, but if defeated, seek refuge in the harbor. [3] So after embarking his troops, he put to sea, setting a leisurely pace for his oarsmen so as to give the Peloponnesian ships time to get near him. As the Lacedaemonians approached they kept pushing their craft faster and faster in the hope of overtaking the rearmost enemy vessels. [4] As Konon continued to retreat, those with the best of the Peloponnesian ships stepped up their pursuit, exhausting their rowers through this sustained labor at the oars and getting a very considerable distance ahead of the rest. Konon duly observed this, and when his ships were close to Mytilene, he ran up a purple pennant from his own vessel: this was the signal to his captains. [5] In response, just as the enemy was close-hauling them, they suddenly and simultaneously put about: the rank and file raised the battle *paean*, and the trumpeters sounded the attack. The Peloponnesians, dumbfounded by this new move, made a hasty attempt to get their ships into defensive line; but as they had no time to put about and the slower ships behind them had abandoned their usual formation, they fell into a state of noisy disorder.

13.78. [1] Konon exploited his opportunity with some skill, closing in on them promptly and making it impossible for them to establish a battle line. Some of their vessels he holed [by ramming] while shearing off the oar banks of others. Of those ships facing Konon not one turned to flight: they all continued to back water while waiting for their own stragglers. [2] The Athenians on the left wing, however, did put their opponents to flight, pressing ever harder on their heels and pursuing them for a considerable time. But when the Peloponnesians finally got all their ships together, Konon, in concern at the enemy's numbers, broke off the chase and set course for Mytilene with forty vessels. [3] The Athenians who had been in pursuit now found themselves, to their great alarm, completely surrounded by the entire Peloponnesian fleet. Their retreat to the city thus cut off, they were forced to run their ships ashore. The Peloponnesians pressed them hard with every trireme they had, so that the Athenians, seeing no other way of escape open to them, made for dry land, abandoned their vessels, and fled for refuge to Mytilene.

[4] By thus capturing thirty of their ships, Kallikratidas had, as he realized, dealt a crippling blow to the Athenians' naval power; but he foresaw that the struggle on land still remained to be resolved. He therefore sailed on to Mytilene himself. Meanwhile Konon, who, the moment he got there, took steps to anticipate the siege he saw coming, set about preparatory defenses at the harbor entrance. In the shallows he sank small boats weighted down with rocks; where the water was deeper he anchored stone-carrying merchantmen. [5] So the Athenians—together with a large crowd of Mytilenaians who, because of the war, had come into the city from the fields—quickly completed their preparations for the siege. Kallikratidas now disembarked his troops on the beach near the city, made a camp, and set up a trophy for the sea battle. Next day he picked the best of his ships and (after instructing them not to get separated from his own vessel) put to sea, determined to smash through the enemy's barrier and force his way into the harbor. [6] Konon meanwhile put some of his troops aboard the triremes (which he stationed with prows facing the open entrance) and others on the big merchantmen; others again he posted to the harbor breakwaters to ensure that the harbor was protected on all

sides, by both land and sea. [7] Konon himself, with his triremes, then got ready for battle, blocking the open space between the barriers. The men stationed on the merchantmen dropped their great stones from the yardarms on the enemy's ships, while those lining the breakwaters stood off any bold attempts to force a landing.

13.79. [1] The Peloponnesians, however, were in no way outdone by the Athenians when it came to competitive zeal. They advanced [on the harbor] in close formation, with their best fighting men stationed on the quarterdecks, and thus made this naval engagement also an infantry battle. When [their ships] crashed into those of their opponents, they boldly jumped aboard the latter's prows, confident that men who had just been defeated would not hold firm against terrifying violence. [2] The Athenians and Mytilenaians, however, seeing that their only hope of survival lay in victory, were determined to meet a gallant death rather than break ranks. With this unsurpassable emulation possessing both sides, a huge death toll resulted, since everyone exposed their bodies unstintingly to the perils of combat. [3] Those on the quarterdecks suffered continual hurt from the mass of missiles coming at them: some fell into the sea, mortally wounded, while others, so long as their wounds were still fresh, fought on without being conscious of them. Large numbers were finished off by the bombardment from the yardarms, since the Athenians up aloft kept lobbing down these huge stones. [4] The fighting nevertheless went on for a long time, with heavy casualties on both sides, till Kallikratidas, wanting to give his troops some respite, had the trumpeters sound the recall. [5] After a while he manned his ships once more and renewed the struggle. Finally, after a protracted struggle, he just managed, through the great number of his ships and the physical toughness of his marines, to force the Athenians back from their position. When the latter fled for safety to the inner basin, Kallikratidas brought his ships through the barriers and dropped anchor close in to the city. [6] (The entrance for the control of which they had fought had a good harbor, which was nevertheless outside the city; for the ancient city is a small island, and the later foundation lies opposite it on Lesbos itself, while between the two runs a narrow strait that increases the city's strength.) [7] Kallikratidas now disembarked his forces, invested Mytilene, and made assaults on it from all quarters.

This, then, was the situation at Mytilene.

Arginousai
13.97–100

13.97. [1] While these events were going on, the Athenians, who had suffered a continuous series of reverses, made citizens of the metics and any other foreigners willing to join their struggle. In this way a great crowd of new citizens was rapidly put on the rolls, and the generals kept calling up for active service all of them who were fit. They put sixty ships into commission, fitting them out at great expense, and then sailed for Samos. Here they found the other generals, who had collected eighty triremes from the surrounding islands. [2] They had also asked the Samians to man ten additional triremes. It was thus with one hundred and fifty ships in all that they put to sea and dropped anchor at the Arginousai Islands, with the firm intention of raising the siege of Mytilene. [3] When Kallikratidas, the Lacedaemonian admiral, learned that these ships were approaching, he left Eteonikos and the ground forces to take care of the siege, while he himself manned one hundred and forty ships and hastily put to sea on the other side of the Arginousai. These islands (which were then inhabited, with a small Aeolian township) lie between Mytilene and Cyme, close in to the mainland by the Kane promontory.

[4] The Athenians immediately took note of the enemy's approach, since they were anchored at no great distance from them. However, on account of the strong winds they refused battle, instead making preparations for an engagement on the following day. The Lacedaemonians did likewise, though the seers on both sides were against it. [5] On the Lacedaemonian side, the head of the victim, which was lying on the beach, vanished from sight when a wave broke over it, and this led the seer to forecast the death of the admiral in action. It is said that when Kallikratidas heard his prophecy, he remarked that if he did die during the battle, he would do nothing to lessen Sparta's good name. [6] As for the Athenians, their general [Thrasyllos], who held the supreme command for that day, had the following dream the night before. He seemed to be in Athens, at the theater, which was crowded, and he, with six of the other generals, was acting in Euripides' tragedy *The Phoenician Women*, while their competitors were performing *The Suppliants*. The result, in his dream, was a "Kadmeian victory"[a] for them, and they all died, thus repeating the fate of those who marched against Thebes. [7] On hearing this, the seer revealed that seven of the generals would lose their lives. Since the sacrificial omens indicated victory, the generals banned any public reference to their own demise but had the victory announced by the omens proclaimed throughout their entire force.

13.98. [1] The admiral Kallikratidas assembled his rank and file and encouraged them with words appropriate to the occasion, concluding as follows: "I am so eager to face this challenge for my country that even with the seer foretelling, from the sacrificial victims, victory for you but death for me, I am nevertheless ready to die. So, aware as I am that after a commander's death his forces are prone to confusion, I now hereby designate as admiral, should I meet with some mishap, Klearchos, a man of proven experience in the business of warfare." [2] By speaking thus, Kallikratidas caused not a few to emulate his valor and themselves become more eager for the battle. So the Lacedaemonians, with words of encouragement one to another, went aboard their ships. Meanwhile the Athenians (after being exhorted by their generals to go [bravely] into the conflict ahead of them) hastily manned the triremes, after which all of them took up their positions. [3] The right wing was commanded by Thrasyllos, together with Pericles (the son of that other Pericles

O.13.97.6a   A Kadmeian victory was one in which the victor suffered crushing losses (later called a Pyrrhic victory). The term derives from the story of the Seven Against Thebes, in which
the two sons of Oedipus (a descendant of Theban founder Kadmos), warring over the throne of Thebes, end up killing each other.

who, because of his authority, was known as "the Olympian"). Thrasyllos also co-opted Theramenes—who was serving on this campaign in the ranks—into joint leadership of the right wing, since previously he had often commanded armaments. The remaining generals he stationed at intervals along his entire battle line. This line covered the whole extent of the Arginousai Islands, since he was anxious to spread out his ships as widely as possible. [4] Kallikratidas now put to sea. He himself was in command of his right wing, while the left he had allotted to the Boeotians, under the Theban Thrasondas. Being unable to equal the enemy's line in length (the islands extended a very considerable distance), he instead divided his fleet, forming it into two separate squadrons, and fought a double engagement, one on each wing. [5] His move caused considerable amazement all around to those watching, since there were in effect four fleets battling one another and the total number of ships gathered into the one area was not far short of three hundred. This is the largest sea battle on record fought by Greeks against Greeks.

13.99. [1] The admirals gave the order for the trumpeters to sound [the attack]; and at the same moment the war cry was raised in turn by the entire force on either side, making a quite extraordinary din. All the rowers drove at the waves zestfully, vying one with another, each eager to be the first to begin the battle. [2] Most of them, indeed, because of the length of the war, had considerable battle experience; and they brought to the occasion unsurpassed enthusiasm, since it was the cream of the forces [on both sides] that had come together for this decisive conflict, and all of them assumed that those who won the battle would finish off the war. [3] Kallikratidas in particular, having heard from the seer the end that would be his, was determined to claim for himself the most glorious death possible. He was thus the first to attack the ship of Lysias the general, which he, along with the triremes accompanying him, stove in at the initial onset and sank. Of the remaining vessels [opposed to him] he rammed some, rendering them unseaworthy, and sheared off the oar banks of others, which incapacitated them for combat. [4] Finally he rammed Pericles' trireme with great violence, opening up a great hole in its side; but the beak of the ram jammed in the gap, so that [the crew] were unable to back away again. At this Pericles threw a grappling iron onto Kallikratidas' vessel, and once it had a firm hold, the Athenians crowded around and sprang aboard, overwhelming the crew and butchering them all. [5] It was at this point, they say, that Kallikratidas, after fighting brilliantly and holding his own for a long while, was finally worn down by the number of his attackers, who dealt him wounds from all quarters. When their admiral's defeat became generally known, the Peloponnesians panicked and gave way. [6] But although the Peloponnesian right wing was routed, the Boeotians on their left continued to put up a vigorous fight for a considerable time, since not only they but also the Euboeans alongside them—and indeed all those who had defected from Athens—were scared that the Athenians, should they recover their position of authority, would exact retribution from them for their revolt. However, on seeing that most of their ships had sustained damage and that the bulk of the victorious fleet was now coming about to deal with them, they were forced to flee. Of the Peloponnesians some got safely to Chios and others to Cyme.

13.100. [1] The Athenians pursued their beaten opponents for a good distance, littering the entire adjacent area of the sea with corpses and wrecked ships. After this some of the generals thought that they should pick up the dead, since the Athenians took an extremely harsh view of those who left corpses unburied; others, however, said they should sail to Mytilene and raise the siege as quickly as possible. [2] But then a huge storm developed, so that the triremes were tossed about; and the rank and file, both as a result of their grueling experience in the battle and because of the size of the waves, were against picking up the dead. [3] Finally, as the storm grew more violent, they neither sailed to Mytilene nor stopped to pick up the dead but were forced by the winds to put in at the Arginousai. In this battle the Athenians lost twenty-five ships, together with most of their crews, and the Peloponnesians seventy-seven; [4] and because so many vessels had gone down, along with those who manned them, the whole coast from Cyme to Phocaea was strewn with corpses and wreckage.

[5] When Eteonikos, still besieging Mytilene, heard from someone about the Peloponnesian defeat, he sent his ships to Chios but himself, with his ground forces, withdrew to the city of Pyrrha, which was an ally; for he was afraid that if the Athenians brought up their fleet against him and the besieged then made a sortie from the city, he risked losing his entire force. [6] In fact, the Athenian generals, after sailing to Mytilene and collecting Konon and his forty ships, put in at Samos, from where they carried out damaging raids on enemy territory. [7] After this those dwelling in the Aeolid and Ionia and such islands as were allied with the Lacedaemonians met in Ephesus and, as a result of their deliberations, resolved to send to Sparta and ask for Lysander as admiral; for during his term as supreme naval commander he had accomplished a great deal and was thought to surpass all others in strategic skill. [8] The Lacedaemonians, however, had a law against sending the same man out twice and were not ready to break with ancestral custom. They therefore chose Arakos as admiral but sent Lysander with him as a private citizen, instructing Arakos to take his advice in all matters. So these two, on being sent out to assume command, began to assemble as many triremes as they could, both from the Peloponnese and from their allies.

The Trial of the Generals
13.101–103.2

13.101. [1] When the Athenians heard of their success off the Arginousai, they congratulated the generals on the victory but took it ill that men who died fighting for Athenian supremacy should have been left unburied. [2] Now since Theramenes and Thrasyboulos had returned to Athens ahead of the rest, the generals assumed it was they who had brought charges before the populace regarding the dead, and therefore sent letters against them to the *demos*, explaining that it was in fact they who had been ordered to pick up corpses. This, however, became the main cause of their undoing. [3] They could have had the powerful assistance in their trial of Theramenes and his group: men who were skilled speakers, who had numerous friends, and, best of all, had participated with them in the events surrounding the battle. But now, on the contrary, they had them as adversaries and bitter accusers. [4] Now when the letters were read before the *demos*, the immediate reaction of that body was anger at Theramenes and his friends; but after these had spoken on their own behalf, this anger was redirected against the generals. [5] As a result, the *demos* notified them that they would be required to stand trial and instructed them to turn over command of their forces to Konon, whom they cleared of responsibility in the matter. The rest of them, they decreed, were to return as soon as possible. Of these, Aristogenes and Protomachos, fearing the wrath of the masses, fled; but Thrasyllos and Calliades, as well as Lysias, Pericles, and Aristokrates, sailed back to Athens with the bulk of their ships, hoping that they would have the help of their crews—a sizable body—during their trial. [6] However, when the populace gathered in assembly, they listened to the charge and those whose words were calculated to please them, but the defendants they shouted down and would not let speak. Also, no little damage was done the latter by the relatives of the deceased, who appeared before the Assembly in mourning and begged the *demos* to punish the men guilty of leaving unburied those who had been happy to die for their country. [7] Finally, then, the friends of the bereaved, together with Theramenes' partisans (of whom there were many), got their way, and the upshot was that the generals were condemned to death, with the forfeiture of their property to the state.

13.102. [1] When the matter had been thus decided and they were about to be led off to death by the public executioners, Diomedon, one of the generals, stepped forward: a man both active in the prosecution of the war and regarded as a paragon of righteousness and every other virtue. [2] Everyone fell silent. He said: "Men of Athens: may the decision taken concerning us turn out auspiciously for the city. Regarding the vows we made for victory: since Fortune has preventing our discharging them—and it would be well that you give them your consideration—do you pay [what is due] to Zeus the Savior and Apollo and the Hallowed Goddesses, since it was to them we made our vows before we won our victory at sea." [3] After Diomedon made this statement, he was led away with the other generals to the execution decreed for them, though among all decent citizens he had aroused tears and much compassion. That a man about to meet an unjust end should make no mention at all of his own misfortune but, rather, on behalf of the city that was doing him wrong, should ask for his vows to the gods to be paid—this seemed the act of a pious and high-minded man, one who little merited the fate awaiting him. [4] So these [officers] were put to death by the eleven magistrates legally appointed for that purpose, though they not only had committed no offense against the city but had won the greatest naval engagement ever fought by Greeks against Greeks, besides distinguishing themselves brilliantly in other battles and, because of their personal acts of valor, setting up trophies over their [defeated] enemies. [5] To such a degree at this time were the people out of their right minds, and unjustly spurred on by their populist leaders, that they took out their anger on men who deserved not punishment but much praise and many decorations.

13.103. [1] Very soon, however, persuaders and persuaded alike had cause to be sorry for what they had done, since it was as though heaven itself had decided to exact retribution from them. Those who had been gulled were paid out for their ignorance not all that long afterward, when they were subjected to the power not of one despot but of thirty; [2] and their deceiver, Kallixenos, being also the motion's proposer, was brought to trial, as soon as the commons repented, on a charge of deceiving the *demos*. Without being allowed a defense, he was pinioned and thrown into the public prison. However, he managed, without being observed, and in the company of several others, to dig his way out of prison and make his way to the enemy at Dekeleia. As a result, he escaped death; but for the rest of his natural life, the shameful thing he had done meant that not in Athens alone but among Greeks everywhere he always had to face the pointing fingers of contempt.

Aigospotamoi, Gylippos
13.105–106

13.105. [1] When the Athenian generals heard that the Lacedaemonians were besieging Lampsacus in full force, they got their triremes together from all quarters and hastily put out to sea against them with 180 vessels. [2] Finding the city already taken, they instead dropped anchor at Aigospotamoi and from this base sailed out daily against the enemy, challenging them to a battle. But the Peloponnesians steadfastly refused to come out and face them, and this left the Athenians at a loss as to what to do in the circumstances, since they were running out of rations with no prospect of further supplies on-site. [3] It was now that Alcibiades came to them with a proposition. Medokos and Seuthes, he said, the kings of the Thracians, were his friends and had agreed to provide him with a large force if he wanted to finish off the war against the Lacedaemonians. He therefore invited [the Athenians] to give him a share of the command, promising them one of two things: he would either force the enemy to fight them at sea or else fight them himself on land along with the Thracians. [4] This proposal Alcibiades made because of the longing he had to achieve, through his personal efforts, some major success for his country and thus, by his benefactions, to bring the people back to their former friendly regard for him. The Athenian generals, however, figuring that they would incur the blame for a defeat, whereas everyone would attribute any success to Alcibiades, told him to take himself off double-quick and never come near the camp again.

13.106. [1] Since the enemy continued to refuse a naval engagement and the troops were on the verge of starvation, Philokles (who held the command that day) ordered the other captains to man their triremes and follow while he, with thirty ships that were then ready, set out ahead of them. [2] Lysander, who had learned about this [plan] from some deserters, now stood out to sea with his entire fleet, put Philokles to flight, and chased him back in the direction of the other ships. [3] These Athenian triremes had not yet been manned, and everyone was thrown into confusion by the unexpected appearance of the enemy. [4] Lysander, perceiving the hullabaloo and disorder among the enemy, promptly disembarked Eteonikos and those troops of his who were used to fighting on dry land. Eteonikos, losing no time, seized his chance and overran part of the [Athenian] camp. Lysander himself meanwhile sailed up with all his triremes ready for battle and, by throwing out grappling irons, began to drag off the ships that were moored inshore. [5] The Athenians were dumbfounded by this unexpected [maneuver]: they had no chance to get their vessels afloat, and they were unable to fight it out ashore. After a brief resistance they were routed. Immediately—some deserting the ships, and the rest the camp—they took to flight, in whatever direction each individual hoped escape might lie. [6] Of the triremes ten only got away. One of these belonged to Konon the general, who, fearing the fury of the *demos*, abandoned any thought of returning to Athens: instead he fled to Cyprus and sought refuge with its ruler Evagoras, with whom he was on terms of friendship. Most of the troops retreated overland and got safely to Sestos. [7] The rest of the ships Lysander captured; and having taken Philokles the general prisoner, he conveyed him to Lampsacus and there executed him.

After this he put messengers aboard his fastest trireme and sent them to Lacedaemon to bring news of the victory, decorating the vessel with the most valuable arms and spoils. [8] He then moved against the Athenians who had taken refuge in Sestos, capturing the city but allowing the Athenians to withdraw under truce. Immediately thereafter he embarked his troops and made for Samos. He himself embarked on the siege of the city but dispatched to Sparta Gylippos (the same man who had taken a squadron to fight alongside the Syracusans in Sicily) as escort for the booty, and with it fifteen hundred talents of silver. [9] The money was in small sacks, each of which also contained a tally stick with a note of the amount. Gylippos, unaware of this [precaution], secretly opened up the sacks and skimmed off three hundred talents. The notes gave him away to the ephors; he fled the country and was condemned to death. [10] Something very similar had happened to Gylippos' father Cleandridas, who at an earlier time also went into exile, when he was suspected of having been bribed by Pericles not to carry out a raid into Attica. He too was condemned to death, fled to Thurii in Italy, and stayed there. So these men, who were otherwise thought well of, by acting in such a manner, clouded the remainder of their lives with shame.

Book XIV Selections

Lysander and the Thirty
14.3–4

[1] There being no archon in Athens because of the city's defeat as an independent power,[a] the year was the 780th after the capture of Troy, . . . and during this year the Ninety-Fourth Olympiad was held, in which Korkinas of Larisa won [the *stadion*]. [2] About this time the Athenians, finally worsted, made a treaty with the Lacedaemonians, by the terms of which they were required to demolish their city walls and to adopt their "ancestral constitution" [*patrios politeia*]. The walls they removed, but differences of opinion arose concerning the form of government. [3] For those who inclined toward oligarchy argued for undertaking between them that former system under which a very small group represented the whole citizen body; on the other hand, the majority, as committed democrats, recommended the government of their fathers, asserting that this, as all agreed, was true democracy. [4] When the dispute on this point had continued for some days, those favoring oligarchy dispatched envoys to Lysander the Spartan—since after the war he had been sent out to organize the administration of the cities, and in most of them oligarchies had been established—hoping as a result, very plausibly, that he would support their scheme. They therefore crossed over to Samos, since Lysander, after his recent capture of the city, was still in residence there. [5] When they solicited his aid, he agreed to cooperate with them. He appointed the Spartan Thorax as governor of Samos, and himself, with a hundred ships, sailed into Peiraieus. He then summoned an assembly and advised the Athenians to choose thirty men to run the government and manage all the city's affairs. [6] When Theramenes spoke against this and read out the clause in the treaty agreeing to the adoption of the ancestral constitution, saying that it would be an outrage if they were robbed of their freedom in contravention of a sworn agreement, Lysander retorted that it was the Athenians who had broken the terms of the armistice by pulling down their walls later than the agreed date. He also threatened Theramenes with the direst consequences, saying that if he did not stop his opposition to the Lacedaemonians, he would be put to death. [7] As a result, Theramenes and those assembled with him were forced, out of sheer terror, into abolishing the democracy on a show of hands. Thirty men were then chosen to direct the city's public business: officially as "governors," in fact as tyrants.

14.4. [1] The people, aware of Theramenes' reasonable nature and convinced that his high principles would act to some degree as a brake on the cupidity of their new leaders, included him in their vote as one of the Thirty. Those elected were required to appoint a Council and the various other officials and to draft the laws by which they would govern. [2] The business of lawmaking they continually put off, always proffering plausible excuses, while the Council and other official vacancies they filled from the ranks of their personal friends, so that while these had the name

---

O.14.3.1a   The archon for 404/3, Pythodoros, was not
             democratically elected, and his appointment
             was voided subsequently by the *demos*, which

determined (Xenophon, *Hellenika* 2.3.1)
that the year was one without an archon
(*anarchia*). (Peter Green)

of magistrates, they were in fact mere lackeys of the Thirty. To begin with, they brought to trial the city's most notorious malefactors and condemned them to death; and so far what was going on met with even the most reasonable citizens' approval. [3] But after this, since they were planning more violent (and illegal) activities, they requested a garrison from the Lacedaemonians, promising to establish a regime in Sparta's best interests. This was because they knew that without foreign arms they would be unable to carry out any murders, since all citizens would combine to ensure their own common security. [4] When the Lacedaemonians sent them a garrison, with Kallibios as its commander, the Thirty first won over the garrison commander with bribes and various other favors; then, picking out from among the wealthy citizens those who suited their plans, they proceeded to arrest them as revolutionaries, put them to death, and confiscate their possessions. [5] When Theramenes opposed his fellow officials and threatened to join the resistance group insisting on general security, the Thirty called a meeting of the Council. Kritias, as their spokesman, brought numerous charges against Theramenes, accusing him of betraying this government in which he himself had chosen to serve; but Theramenes then took the floor, rebutted the charges in detail, and got the entire Council on his side. [6] Kritias and his supporters, scared that this was a man who might, in time to come, overthrow the oligarchy, threw a cordon of soldiers with drawn swords around him and set about his arrest. [7] But Theramenes, anticipating this, sprang up toward the altar of Hestia of the Council, exclaiming that he was taking refuge with the gods, not because he thought this would save him but in his determination to make his killers also involve themselves in an act of impiety against the gods.

Socrates' Intervention, Theramenes' Death
14.5.1–4

[1] When the officers came up and dragged him away, Theramenes bore his ill fortune nobly, since he had partaken of philosophy to no small degree in the company of Socrates; but the crowd as a whole, though feeling pity for Theramenes' distress, dared not come to his rescue because of the strong armed guard surrounding him. [2] Socrates the philosopher and two of his close friends rushed forward and attempted to check the officers. Theramenes, however, urged them to do no such thing. While he had only praise (he said) for their friendship and courage, it would be the greatest misfortune for him should he prove the cause of death to such intimate associates. [3] Socrates and his companions, since they had no support from anyone else and saw that the threatening attitude of those in authority was intensifying, kept quiet. Then those who had been so ordered tore Theramenes away from the altar and dragged him through the middle of the marketplace to his death. [4] The populace, cowed by the arms of the garrison, felt a common pity for him in his distress and wept, not only for his sorry fate but for their own enslavement, since

every one of these wretches, on seeing the high virtues of a Theramenes thus contemptuously treated, realized that they themselves, given their lesser status, would be sacrificed without a moment's thought.

The Thirty's Excesses
14.5.5–6.3

14.5. [5] After Theramenes' death the Thirty continued to pick off wealthy citizens, bring false charges against them, put them to death, and plunder their estates. Those they executed included Nikeratos, son of that Nikias who had been a general at Syracuse: a man of moderate and kindly behavior to everyone and for wealth and reputation first, or nearly so, among all Athenians. [6] In consequence every household joined in lamenting the fate of this fine man, and the recollection of his decency brought tears to their eyes. Nor did the tyrants abate their lawless conduct; on the contrary, their madness so increased that they slaughtered the sixty wealthiest foreign residents in order to get possession of their property. With citizens being executed daily, almost all the well-to-do fled the city. [7] Among others they did away with Autolykos, a notably outspoken man, and in general they concentrated on the most distinguished individuals. To such an extent did they wreak destruction on the city that over half the Athenian population fled.

14.6. [1] The Lacedaemonians, observing the city of Athens and determined that the Athenians should never regain their old power, were very pleased and made their attitude quite clear by voting that Athenian exiles anywhere in Greece should be compulsorily returned to the Thirty and that anyone who sought to prevent this should be liable to a fine of five talents. [2] Though this was an outrageous decree, the other cities, terrified by the solid power of the Spartans, complied with it. The sole exception was Argos, whose citizens were the first to offer these fugitives compassionate asylum—moved by hatred of Lacedaemonian cruelty as well as by pity for the fate of the unfortunate. [3] The Thebans, too, voted that anyone who witnessed an exile being arrested and did not offer him all possible assistance should incur a fine.

Dekarchies*
14.10.1–2

[1] In Greece the Lacedaemonians, having successfully concluded the Peloponnesian War, were by common consent agreed to hold supreme power both on land and at sea. They now appointed Lysander admiral[a] and commissioned him to make a tour of the cities, setting up in each of them the officials they call harmosts; for the Lacedaemonians, being opposed to democracies, wanted the cities to be governed by oligarchs. [2] They also imposed tribute on those they had defeated; and

O.14.10.1–2* See Xenophon's *Hellenika* 3.4.2.   *Nauarchos* is perhaps best translated
O.14.10.1a   Lysander was indeed de facto commander;   "naval commander" here. (Peter Green)
           his actual title was *epistoleus* ("secretary").

although prior to this they had not used coined money, from now on they collected more than a thousand talents annually in the form of tribute.[a]

The Death of Alcibiades
14.11.1–4

14.11. [1] At the same time as these events, Pharnabazos, Darius the [Great] King's satrap, out of a desire to build credit with the Lacedaemonians, arrested Alcibiades the Athenian and put him to death. However, since Ephoros' account states that he was plotted against for other reasons, I think it may not be unprofitable to set down here the plot against Alcibiades as presented by this historian. [2] In his seventeenth book he says that Cyrus and the Lacedaemonians were planning secretly to make war together against Cyrus' brother Artaxerxes and that Alcibiades, having learned of Cyrus' intentions from certain informants, went to Pharnabazos and gave him a detailed account of them. He then asked him for safe conduct to Artaxerxes, eager to be the first to reveal this conspiracy to the King. [3] Pharnabazos, however, on hearing his story, appropriated the report himself and dispatched confidants of his own to inform the King of the matter. So when Pharnabazos would not give him an escort to the King, Ephoros says, Alcibiades set off to the satrap of Paphlagonia in the hope of journeying up-country with his help instead. But Pharnabazos, scared lest the King should get wind of the truth about this business, sent men to kill Alcibiades on the road. [4] They caught up with him at a village in Phrygia where he had found shelter for the night and stacked kindling all around [the house]. When they set it ablaze, Alcibiades tried to defend himself but was overcome by the flames and the javelins cast at him and so met his end.

Thebes Captures Oropos
14.17.1–3

14.17. [1] When the year had run its course, Mikion became archon in Athens.[a] . . . After [he] had entered on [his] term of office, the inhabitants of Oropos, torn by civil factionalism, exiled a number of their citizens. [2] For a while the exiles worked to secure their return by their own efforts; but when in the end they proved unable to carry out their plan, they persuaded the Thebans to send a force to help them. [3] The Thebans then marched against Oropos, took control of the city, and resettled its inhabitants seven stades [a little under a mile] from the sea. For a while they let them govern themselves but then gave them [Theban] citizenship and annexed their territory to Boeotia.

O.14.10.2a The figure given for Spartan tribute is wildly exaggerated, as are many figures given by ancient authors. (Peter Green)

O.14.17.1a Diodorus dates his years by citing those who served as archon in Athens and those who were elected to office, such as consuls, in Rome. I have deleted the citations of Roman officers because they are more often than not wrong and in any case provide no useful information to readers of Xenophon's *Hellenika*—the focus of this volume. These deletions often, as here, require a change of pronoun or verb, which is set off in brackets. (R.B.S.)

Sparta's Attack on Elis
14.17.4–12

[4] At the same time as these events, the Lacedaemonians lodged numerous complaints against the Eleians, chief among them the fact that they had stopped the [Spartan] king Pausanias from sacrificing to the god, and also because they had not allowed the Lacedaemonians to compete in the Olympic Games. [5] As a result, they decided to go to war with [the Eleians] and sent them ten ambassadors, who were to order them to grant their dependent townships autonomy and require of them their agreed contribution to the cost of the war against the Athenians. [6] They acted thus in pursuit of pretexts that put them in a good light, and convincing reasons for going to war. But when the Eleians not only took no notice but actually accused them of enslaving the Greeks, they sent out Pausanias, one of their two kings, against them, with four thousand soldiers. [7] There accompanied him also numerous troops from almost all the allies, except the Boeotians and the Corinthians: they, out of disgust at the Lacedaemonians' behavior, would not take part in this campaign against Elis. [8] So Pausanias, invading Elis by way of Arcadia, quickly overran the frontier post of Lasion. Then he led his troops through [the district of] Acroreia, where he won over four cities: Thraistos, Halion, Epitalion, and Opous. [9] From here he marched on Pylos. This position, too, which was about seventy stades [just under nine miles] from Elis, he captured in short order. He then advanced on Elis itself and encamped on the hills across the river. Shortly before this the Eleians had received allied support in the shape of a thousand picked troops from the Aetolians, and had assigned them the area around the public gymnasium to guard. [10] Now this was the point at which Pausanias had begun to establish his siege, with contemptuous indifference [to his opponents], convinced that the Eleians would never dare make a sortie against him. But suddenly the Aetolians, together with a mass of citizens, came charging out from the city, terrifying the Lacedaemonians and killing about thirty of them. [11] At this point Pausanias raised the siege. Then, realizing that the city itself would be hard work to capture, he made his way through Eleian territory, ravaging and looting as he went—consecrated land though it was—and amassed vast amounts of booty. [12] With winter now imminent, he built fortified guardposts in Elis, left adequate forces to man them, and himself with the remainder of his army went into winter quarters at Dyme.

The Fall of the Thirty
14.32–33

14.32. [1] The Thirty Tyrants, now in control of affairs in Athens, never let up on their daily round of exilings and executions. The Thebans, angered by what was going on, made the exiles welcome; and Thrasyboulos, known as "the Steirian," an Athenian who had been banished by the Thirty, succeeded—with the covert assistance of the Thebans—in capturing a place in Attica called Phyle. This outpost was both strongly fortified and only a hundred stades [twelve and a half miles] from Athens, thus offering them numerous opportunities for attacks. [2] The Thirty Tyrants, on learning what had happened, first led out their forces against them with the intention of besieging the place; but while they were encamped near Phyle a heavy snowfall took place. [3] When some of the troops set about shifting their tents, the main body got the impression that this was a retreat and that some hostile force was nearby. A wave of so-called panic fear swept through the army, and they struck camp and moved to another site.

[4] The Thirty, perceiving that those citizens in Athens who had no part in the regime of the Three Thousand were elated by the possibility of overthrowing the current government, relocated them to Peiraieus and maintained their control of the city by means of armed mercenaries. They also accused the inhabitants of Eleusis and Salamis of abetting the exiles and slaughtered them all. [5] While this was going on, many of the exiles flocked in to join Thrasyboulos. [The Thirty also dispatched an embassy to him,]ᵃ ostensibly to discuss the fate of certain prisoners but privately to urge him to break up the group of exiles and instead to join them, the Thirty, in the running of the city as the elected replacement for Theramenes. He would, they added, have the authority to bring back into the country any ten exiles he chose. [6] Thrasyboulos replied that he preferred his current exile to power with the Thirty and, further, that he would not stop fighting until every citizen was repatriated and the people got back their ancestral constitution. The Thirty—conscious that many were rebelling against them out of hatred, while the exiles' numbers continued to grow—sent envoys to Sparta soliciting aid, and themselves, after mustering all the troops they could raise, pitched camp in open country near the deme known as Acharnae.

14.33. [1] Thrasyboulos, leaving behind a sufficient guard for his base [at Phyle], led out the exiles, some twelve hundred in number, and made a surprise night attack on the enemy's camp. He killed large numbers of them, spread terror through the rest by this unforeseen move, and forced them to retreat to Athens. [2] After the battle Thrasyboulos at once force-marched to Peiraieus and occupied Mounichia, a bare, easily defendable hilltop. The tyrants, under the command of Kritias, then descended on Peiraieus with their full force and assaulted Mounichia. The battle lasted a long time and was sharply contested, with the Thirty having the advantage of numbers, and the exiles that of the natural strength of their position. [3] But finally, after Kritias fell, the troops with the Thirty, terror-struck, backed off to more level ground, where the exiles dared not venture down against them. Subsequently large numbers [of the Thirty's forces] deserted and joined the exiles: Thrasyboulos and his men then launched a sudden attack on the enemy, won the ensuing battle, and thus gained control of Peiraieus. [4] Straight away many up in Athens, eager to be rid of the tyranny, flocked down to Peiraieus from every quarter; and all the

---

O.14.32.5a   The words in brackets are not in the manuscripts, but something along these lines is needed to make sense of the text. Peter   Green here translates a supplement by Rhodomanus reported by Wesseling.

exiles, then dispersed among various cities, on hearing of Thrasyboulos' successes, made for Peiraieus too, so that from now on the exiles' forces were far superior, and as a result, they embarked on a siege of the city.

[5] Those still in Athens now deposed the Thirty from power and expelled them from the city. They then appointed ten men with full authority to bring the war, if they could, to an amicable conclusion. But on assuming power, these men ignored their commission, revealed themselves as tyrants, and sent a request to Lacedaemon for forty ships and a thousand troops, under the command of Lysander. [6] But Pausanias, the king of the Lacedaemonians, who was envious of Lysander and saw that Sparta had become highly unpopular in the Greek world, marched out at the head of a large army and, on arriving in Athens, successfully reconciled those in the city with the exiles. Thus the Athenians regained their own country and from now on governed it in accordance with their own laws; and those who feared retribution for their endless series of crimes they allowed to take up residence in Eleusis.

Sparta and Elis
14.34.1

[1] The men of Elis, scared by the Lacedaemonians' superior power, terminated their war against them, the conditions being that they should surrender their triremes to the Lacedaemonians and leave their outlying cities independent.

Tissaphernes, Thibron, Xenophon
14.35.6–37.1

14.35. [6] The Greek communities of Asia, on learning of Tissaphernes' imminent arrival, and being deeply concerned for their own safety, sent ambassadors to the Lacedaemonians, begging them not to stand by and let their cities be laid waste by the barbarians. The Lacedaemonians promised them support and sent ambassadors to Tissaphernes with a request that he not take any hostile military action against the Greek cities. [7] But Tissaphernes and his army, on arrival at the nearest city, that of the Cymaeans, laid waste all the surrounding countryside and took large numbers of prisoners. He then corraled the Cymaeans in their city and laid siege to it. However, since by the time winter was approaching he had still not managed to reduce it, he ransomed his prisoners at a stiff price and raised the siege.

14.36. [1] The Lacedaemonians appointed Thibron commander of the war against the King, gave him a thousand men from their own citizen body, and instructed him to recruit such troops from their allies as he should consider expedient. [2] Thibron marched to Corinth and there issued his requests for allied troops. He then sailed to Ephesus with a total force of not more than five thousand. On arrival he enlisted some two thousand men, from both the above-mentioned cities and other ones, so that when he set out his total forces numbered more than seven thousand. A march of about 120 stades [fifteen miles] brought him to Magnesia, which was governed by Tissaphernes. He took this city at the first assault and then made straight for Tralles in Ionia, where he set about besieging the citadel; but when he failed to make any headway because of its strong defenses, he returned to Magnesia. [3] Now this city was unwalled, and Thibron feared that once he was gone, Tissaphernes would, as a result, regain control of it. He therefore relocated it to a nearby hill, known as Thorax. He then made a sortie into enemy territory, thus procuring his troops a glut of every sort of booty. However, when Tissaphernes appeared with a strong cavalry force, he felt it prudent to return to Ephesus.

14.37. [1] About the same time, of those men who had campaigned with Cyrus and managed to get back safely to Greece, some now returned to their own countries, but the majority of them, who had grown accustomed to a soldier's life, chose Xenophon as their general.

Derkylidas
14.38.2–3, 14.38.6–7

[2] After these men had assumed office, the Lacedaemonians, on being informed that Thibron was proving incompetent in his management of the campaign, sent out Derkylidas as general to Asia. On taking over command, he marched against the cities of the Troad. [3] Now Hamaxiton, Kolonai, and Arisbe[a] he took at the first assault, followed by Ilion, Kebrenia, and the rest of the cities throughout the Troad, capturing some by trickery and reducing others by force. He then concluded an eight-month truce with Pharnabazos and made an expedition against a group of Thracians then dwelling in Bithynia. After ravaging their territory, he led his army back into winter quarters. . . .

[6] During these events the Thracians launched a mass invasion of the Chersonese, ravaged the entire region, and put its cities under siege. Being thus hard-pressed by the war, the inhabitants of the Chersonese begged Derkylidas to come over from Asia and help them. [7] He made the crossing with his army, drove the Thracians out of the Chersonese, and sealed the area off with a wall he built from sea to sea. By this act he forestalled any future Thracian incursions and was honored with lavish gifts as a result. He then took his troops back to Asia.

Konon
14.39.1–3

[1] When the truce with the Lacedaemonians was ratified, Pharnabazos went up-country to the King and persuaded him to make ready a fleet and appoint Konon the Athenian as its admiral, he being a skilled veteran who had seen much active service, especially at sea. This military expert was currently resident on Cyprus, at the

---

O.14.38.3a Arisbe is much farther north, on the coast of the Hellespont; for the third town Xenophon (*Hellenika* 3.1.13) has Larisa, a more geographically plausible suggestion.

However, there is another Kolonai near Arisbe, and it is not impossible that Derkylidas' campaign took in this area as well. (Peter Green)

court of King Evagoras. Once the King had been won over, Pharnabazos got five hundred talents of silver and made preparations for commissioning a fleet. [2] To that end he embarked for Cyprus, requested the kings there to fit out a hundred triremes, and, after discussions with Konon about the command of a fleet, appointed him high admiral, hinting at great benefits to come from the King. [3] Konon, who hoped both to recover the leadership for his country should the Lacedaemonians be defeated and at the same time to win great renown for himself, accepted the command at sea.

The Arrival of Agesilaos
14.79.1–3

[1] In Greece the Lacedaemonians, anticipating the magnitude of their war against the Persians, put Agesilaos, one of their two kings, in command. He mustered six thousand troops and formed a Council of Thirty from Sparta's most distinguished citizens; he then transported his forces from [Euboea][a] to Ephesus. [2] Here he recruited four thousand more. When he took the field, his army consisted of ten thousand foot soldiers and four hundred cavalry and was followed by as large a crowd again of sutlers, drawn by the prospect of plunder. [3] He made his way across the Caÿster plain, ravaging the territory in Persian possession as he went, until he reached Cyme. Here he spent most of the summer, raiding and plundering Phrygia and the surrounding regions, after which, having given his troops their fill of booty, he returned to Ephesus during the autumn.

Konon and Rhodos
14.79.4–8

[4] During the course of these events the Lacedaemonians sent ambassadors to Nephereus, king of Egypt, regarding an alliance, but in lieu of men he presented the Spartans with gear for one hundred triremes, and five hundred thousand measures of grain. Pharax, the Lacedaemonian naval commander, put to sea from Rhodos with 120 vessels and made for Sasanda in Caria, a stronghold 150 stades [almost nineteen miles] from Caunus. [5] From here he made a sortie and blockaded Caunus, together with Konon, the commander of the King's fleet, who was in harbor there with forty ships. However, when Artaphernes and Pharnabazos appeared with a strong force to rescue the Caunians, Pharax raised the siege and withdrew, with his entire fleet, to Rhodos. [6] After this Konon assembled eighty triremes and sailed to the Chersonese. The Rhodians expelled the Peloponnesian fleet, abandoned their Lacedaemonian alliance, and admitted Konon, with his entire fleet, into their city [harbor]. [7] Now those Lacedaemonians who were convoying the gift of grain from Egypt knew nothing of the Rhodians' defection and therefore

O.14.79.1a   "Euboea" (more specifically, the port of   manuscripts, based on Xenophon's *Hel-*
             Geraistos) is Knoepfler's emendation—   *lenika* 3.1.4. (Peter Green)
             accepted by Bennett for the Budé edition—
             for the nonsensical "Asias" of the

approached the island in complete confidence, so that the Rhodians, and Konon the Persians' admiral, escorted their ships into harbor and stocked the whole city with grain. [8] There also joined Konon ninety more triremes, ten from Cilicia and eighty from Phoenicia, commanded by the ruler of Sidon.

The Battle of Sardis
14.80

[1] After this Agesilaos led his forces into the Caÿster plain and the neighborhood of Sipylos, where he laid waste the holdings of the inhabitants; but Tissaphernes mustered ten thousand cavalry and fifty thousand foot, with whom he followed close behind the Lacedaemonians, killing those who became detached from the main body while foraging. Agesilaos drew up his troops in square formation and kept close to the lower slopes of Mount Sipylos, watching for a favorable moment at which to attack the enemy. [2] On reaching the region around Sardis, he ravaged Tissaphernes' gardens and pleasure park, which had been laid out with consummate art and at great expense, containing plants and everything else designed for the peaceful enjoyment of the good things of life. After this he turned back, and when he was halfway between Sardis and Thybarnai, he sent out Xenokles the Spartan by night to a wooded area, with fourteen hundred troops, to set up an ambush for the barbarians. [3] At daybreak he himself moved on with his main force. When he had got past the site of the ambush and the barbarians were making a disordered attack on his rearguard, he suddenly turned about and faced the Persians. A sharp engagement ensued. He gave the signal to the troops in ambush, and they charged the enemy, chanting their victory song. The Persians, seeing themselves caught between two fronts, panicked and fled on the spot. [4] Agesilaos and his men pursued them for some distance, slew more than six thousand of them, rounded up a whole mass of prisoners, and plundered their camp, which was full of a variety of good things. [5] Tissaphernes escaped from this battle to Sardis, dumbfounded at the daring of the Lacedaemonians. Agesilaos set out for the upper satrapies but failed to obtain good omens from his sacrifices, and because of this took his forces back to the coast.

[6] Artaxerxes, the Great King of Asia, was already apprehensive about the war with the Greeks; when he learned of these defeats, he became furious with Tissaphernes, whom he regarded as responsible for the outbreak of war in the first place. He was also under pressure from his mother Parysatis to take revenge on Tissaphernes, since she had never forgiven him for betraying her son Cyrus when he launched his campaign against his brother. [7] The King therefore appointed Tithraustes commander, with instructions to arrest Tissaphernes, and dispatched letters to the cities and satraps ordering them to do whatever he required of them. [8] On arrival at Kolossai in Phrygia, Tithraustes, through the cooperation of a satrap named Ariaios, arrested Tissaphernes while he was in his bath, cut off his head, and

sent it to the King. He then personally persuaded Agesilaos to discuss terms and concluded a six months' truce with him.

Alliance Against Sparta
14.82

[1] When this year ended, in Athens Diophantos became archon. . . . [The] Boeotians and Athenians, and the Corinthians and Argives besides, made a collective alliance. [2] Since the Lacedaemonians were detested because of their oppressive domination, it would, they thought, be easy to break their rule if there was general agreement between the principal cities. So first they established a general council in Corinth, to which they sent representatives to work out policy, and made general provision for the conduct of the war. After this they dispatched ambassadors to the cities and induced many of the Lacedaemonians' allies to defect. [3] The whole of Euboea came over to them immediately, as did the Leucadians, followed by the Acarnanians, the Ambraciots, and the Chalcidians from the Thrace-ward regions. [4] They also attempted to persuade the inhabitants of the Peloponnese to secede from the Lacedaemonians, but there no one listened to them, since Sparta lay directly on their flank and formed a kind of citadel and fortress for the entire Peloponnese.

[5] Medios, prince of Larissa in Thessaly, who was at war with Lykophron, the tyrant of Pherai, appealed to the council for support, and they sent him two thousand troops. [6] When this reinforcement arrived, Medios captured Pharsalus, which was garrisoned by Lacedaemonians, and sold the inhabitants as booty. After this the Boeotians and Argives, operating independently of Medios, seized Herakleia-in-Trachis. Let into the city at night by certain individuals, they proceeded to slaughter every Lacedaemonian they caught but permitted other Peloponnesians to leave with their possessions. [7] They then recalled those Trachinians who had been exiled by the Lacedaemonians and turned the city over to them as their residence, they indeed being the most ancient occupants of this region. Afterward Ismenias, the leader of the Boeotians, left the Argives in the city as a garrison, while he himself persuaded the Ainianians and the Athamanians to abandon their Lacedaemonian alliance and recruited troops from them and their allies. With the force of just under six thousand that he raised in this manner, he launched an attack on the Phocians. [8] While he was setting up his camp near Naryx in Locris (where they say Ajax was born), the citizen militia of Phocis came out against him, led by Alkisthenes the Laconian. [9] A lengthy and hard-fought battle ensued, which the Boeotians won. They then pursued the fugitives till nightfall, killing not far short of a thousand of them, though during the battle itself they lost about five hundred of their own men. [10] After this engagement both sides dismissed their troops and sent them back to their various homes. The members of the council, meeting in Corinth and finding everything going the way they had anticipated, mustered troops to Corinth from all the cities to the number of more than fifteen thousand infantry and about five hundred cavalry.

The Battles of the Nemea River and Cnidus
14.83

[1] The Lacedaemonians, seeing that the greatest cities in Greece were making common cause against them, voted to recall Agesilaos and his expeditionary force from Asia. Meanwhile they themselves enlisted, from their own resources and those of their allies, twenty-three thousand foot soldiers and five hundred cavalry and marched against the enemy. [2] The engagement took place by the Nemea River and went on till nightfall. There were partial successes on both sides; but while of the Lacedaemonians and their allies eleven hundred men fell, for the Boeotians and their allies the number was two thousand eight hundred.

[3] The first opposition Agesilaos encountered after shipping his forces across to Europe came from certain Thracians, who came against him with a large horde: these barbarians he defeated in a pitched battle, killing most of them. After this he marched his army through Macedonia, following the same route that Xerxes took on the occasion of his expedition against the Greeks. [4] So Agesilaos, after traversing Macedonia and Thessaly, proceeded through the pass of Thermopylae and made his way through Phocis to Boeotia.[a]

Konon the Athenian and Pharnabazos, joint commanders of the [Persian] royal fleet, were stationed at Loryma in the [Carian] Chersonese with more than ninety triremes. [5] On learning that the enemy's naval forces were at Cnidus, they prepared to engage them. Peisander, the Lacedaemonian admiral, sailed from Cnidus with eighty-five triremes and anchored at Physkos in the [Carian] Chersonese. [6] From here he put out again and engaged the royal fleet, attacking its leading vessels and getting the better of the exchange. But when the Persians came to the rescue with their triremes in close formation and all his allies fled landward, Peisander turned his own vessel and confronted them, considering such ignoble flight shameful and unworthy of Sparta. [7] After putting up a brilliant struggle and killing many of the enemy, he finally died fighting, in a manner worthy of his country. Konon's forces drove the Lacedaemonians ashore and captured fifty of their triremes, but most of the crew members jumped overboard, swam ashore, and got away by land. However, some five hundred were taken prisoner. The remaining triremes escaped safely to Cnidus.

The Battle of Haliartos; The Death of Lysander
14.84

[1] When Agesilaos, who had received reinforcements from the Peloponnese, marched his army into Boeotia, the Boeotians and their allies at once set out to meet them at Coronea. In the engagement that followed, the Thebans routed the division facing them and chased them back to their camp, but the rest, after a brief show of resistance, were turned to flight by Agesilaos and those with him. [2] The

O.14.83.4a   See also Plutarch, *Parallel Lives*, "Agesilaos" 17.3 (Teubner), 17.2 (Loeb);
            Xenophon, *Hellenika* 4.3.9. (Peter Green)

Boeotians got the Athenians to agree to join them in this war but for the moment took the field alone, marching to Haliartos, which was under siege by Lysander and the Lacedaemonians. A battle ensued, in which Lysander and many of the Lacedaemonians and their allies fell [summer 395]. The Boeotian phalanx as a whole quickly backed off from their pursuit, but about two hundred Thebans charged overconfidently into rough terrain and got themselves killed. [3] This was known as the Boeotian War. On learning of the defeat, Pausanias, the Lacedaemonian king, made a truce with the Boeotians and led his forces back to the Peloponnese. [4] In these circumstances, a kind of fever spread through the cities: some regained their independence by expelling their Lacedaemonian garrisons, while others joined Konon and his supporters. It was from this point that the Lacedaemonians lost their supremacy at sea. Konon's group decided to take their entire fleet to Attica. After putting to sea, they won over the islands of the Cyclades and then sailed to Cythera. [5] They took this island at the first assault, sent the Cytherans under truce to Laconia, and then, leaving behind an adequate garrison for the city, sailed to Corinth, where they disembarked. After discussing their agenda with representatives of the council, they struck up an alliance with them, supplied them with funds, and then set sail for Asia.

[6] During the same period Aîropos, the king of the Macedonians, died of an illness after a reign of six years and was succeeded by his son Pausanias, who ruled for one year. [7] Theopompos of Chios brought his twelve-book *History of Greece* down to this year, ending with the naval battle of Cnidus. This historian began at the sea battle of Kynossema, [which is where Thucydides left off his account[a]], covering an overall period of seventeen years.

Konon's Rebuilding of Athens' Long Walls
14.85

[1] When the year had run its course, Euboulides became archon in Athens. . . . [2] At this time Konon, commandant of the royal fleet, made landfall in Peiraieus with eighty triremes and promised the citizens that he would rebuild their city walls (both the fortifications of Peiraieus and the Long Walls had been dismantled in accordance with the terms of the Lacedaemonian armistice after the Athenian defeat in the Peloponnesian War). [3] So Konon engaged a large number of skilled artisans, gave them the bulk of his rowers as laborers, and in this way quickly got the larger part of the walls restored. The Thebans likewise provided five hundred skilled artisans and stonemasons, while various other cities also lent their support. [4] Tiribazos, however, the commander of land forces in Asia, jealous of Konon's successes, and on the pretext that he was employing the King's forces to win over cities to Athens, summoned him to Sardis, where he had him arrested, put in shackles, and jailed.

O.14.84.7a   Thucydides' narrative breaks off after, not
             before, the battle of Kynossema.

Massacre at Corinth
14.86

[1] In Corinth, a group of violent hotheads got together while contests were being held in the theater, carried out a massacre, and filled the city with factional strife. When they got Argive support for this reckless coup, they slaughtered 120 of their fellow citizens and sent 500 into exile. [2] While the Lacedaemonians were getting ready to bring back the exiles and raising a force with which to do it, the Athenians and Boeotians came to the assistance of the butchers, in order to secure the city's allegiance. [3] The exiles, together with the Lacedaemonians and their allies, made a night attack on Lechaion and the naval station and captured them by assault. The next day those in the city made a sortie, led by Iphikrates, and a battle took place, which the Lacedaemonians won, killing not a few of the enemy. [4] After this the Boeotians and Athenians, together with the Argives and Corinthians, advanced in full strength on Lechaion and began by investing it, forcing a passage inside the outer defenses; but afterward the Lacedaemonians and the exiles, by dint of some brilliant fighting, managed to force out both the Boeotians themselves and everyone else with them. They then withdrew to the city, with the loss of about a thousand men. [5] The Isthmian Games were now imminent, and disagreement arose as to who should run them. After much acrimonious debate, the Lacedaemonians got their way and ensured that the exiles organized the festival. [6] Since during this war almost all the severe fighting occurred in the neighborhood of Corinth, it came to be known as the Corinthian War. It lasted for eight years.

Pausanias Banished
14.89

[1] Pausanias, the king of the Lacedaemonians, as a result of charges brought by his fellow citizens, was exiled after a reign of fourteen years. His son Agesipolis succeeded him and reigned for the same length of time as his father. [2] That other Pausanias, the king of the Macedonians, also died, treacherously murdered by Amyntas after a reign of one year, having thus usurped the throne Amyntas held for twenty-four years.

Iphikrates at Corinth
14.91.2–92.2

14.91. [2] The exiles occupying Lechaion in the territory of Corinth, after being admitted by certain individuals at night, attempted to get control of the city walls; but when Iphikrates' forces made a sally against them, they lost three hundred of their men and fell back on the naval station. A few days later, as a battalion of the Lacedaemonian army was passing through Corinthian territory, Iphikrates and some of the allied forces in Corinth made a surprise attack on them and wiped them out almost to a man. [3] Iphikrates and his light-armed troops now invaded the territory of Phleious, where he fought an engagement with the city's militia, killing more than three hundred of them. He next marched against Sicyon. The Sicyonians met him outside their walls but lost about five hundred men and retreated into the city.

14.92. [1] After these incidents the Argives launched a full-scale military expedition against Corinth. They captured the acropolis, occupied the city, and brought all Corinthian territory under Argive control. [2] Iphikrates the Athenian likewise had designs on the region, since to hold it was advantageous for the domination of Greece; but when this plan met with public opposition, he resigned his command. The Athenians thereupon dispatched Chabrias to Corinth as general in his place.

Thrasyboulos in the Eastern Aegean
14.94

[1] When the year had run its course, in Athens Philokles became archon. During this year there also was held the Ninety-Seventh Olympiad, in which Terires was the victor [in the *stadion*]. [2] At this time the Athenians named Thrasyboulos as general and sent him out in command of forty triremes. He first sailed to Ionia, where he collected funds from the allies, and then put to sea again. He next spent some time in the Chersonese and made alliances there with Medokos and Seuthes, the kings of the Thracians. [3] Somewhat later he made his way from the Hellespont to Lesbos and anchored offshore from Eresos. But with the onset of gale-force winds, twenty-three of his triremes were lost. Escaping with the rest, he made a tour of the cities of Lesbos in an attempt to bring them over, since with the exception of Mytilene they had all defected. [4] His first port of call was Methymna, where he engaged the city militia, commanded by the Spartan Therimachos. Fighting brilliantly, he killed both Therimachos and not a few of the Methymnaians, driving the rest back inside their walls. He laid waste the territory of Methymna and received the surrender of Eresos and Antissa. After this he collected ships from his allies in Chios and Mytilene and set sail for Rhodos.

Stasis on Rhodos
14.97.1–4

[1] When this year had run its course, in Athens Nikoteles became archon. . . . After [his] assumption of office, the pro-Spartan faction in Rhodos rose up against the *demos* and drove the partisans of Athens out of the city. [2] When these got together, armed themselves, and endeavored to regain control of affairs, those allied with the Lacedaemonians outfought them, killed a good many, and pro-

nounced an official sentence of banishment on those who escaped. They also, in the fear that certain citizens might start a revolution, immediately sent ambassadors to Lacedaemon asking for support. [3] The Lacedaemonians sent them seven triremes, together with three men, Ekdikos, Philodokos, and Diphridas,[a] to take charge of their affairs. This team first put in at Samos, where they persuaded the city to defect from the Athenians, after which they sailed to Rhodos and assumed responsibility for affairs there. [4] Now that things were going their way, the Lacedaemonians determined to recover their dominance at sea. They assembled a naval force and, little by little, began to reestablish control over their allies. To this end they sailed to Samos and Cnidus and Rhodos, and by signing up ships and the best marines wherever they went, they managed, at great expense, to fit out twenty-seven triremes.

Thibron and Thrasyboulos in Asia
14.99

[1] When this year had run its course, in Athens Demostratos became archon. . . . During this period Artaxerxes dispatched Strouthas as general to the seaboard, with a strong force, to make war on the Lacedaemonians. When the Spartans learned of his presence, they sent out Thibron to Asia as general. Thibron captured the stronghold of [Isinda] and a high mountain called Koressos,[a] forty stades [five miles] distant from Ephesus. [2] With a force, including the troops recruited in Asia, now eight thousand strong, he advanced through the royal domains, laying them waste as he went. Strouthas, leading a large contingent of barbarian cavalry, together with five thousand heavy-armed infantrymen and more than twenty thousand light-armed troops, pitched camp not far from the Lacedaemonians. [3] Finally, after Thibron had set out with a detachment only of his troops and was encumbered with a great deal of booty, Strouthas attacked, killed him in single combat, slaughtered most of his men, and took others prisoner. A few only got safely away to the fort of Knidinion.

[4] Thrasyboulos, the Athenian general, quit Lesbos with his fleet and made for Aspendos, mooring his triremes in the Eurymedon River. Although he had received payment from the Aspendians, nevertheless some of his troops proceeded to ravage their territory. When night came, the Aspendians, infuriated by this outrageous

O.14.97.3a The manuscripts have the names of two of these men as Eudokimos and Diphilas. Peter Green has chosen to follow Xenophon's *Hellenika* 4.8.22, which has them as Ekdikos and Diphridas. Xenophon is unlikely to have gotten Spartan names wrong.

O.14.99.1a The manuscripts read "Ionda" and (with one significant exception) "Kornissos." My translation adopts the emendation "Isinda" given by B. D. Meritt for "Ilonda" in *The Athenian Tribute Lists*, vol. 1 (Cambridge, Mass.: American School of Classical Studies, 1939), p. 493. For "Kornissos" Meritt proposed "Solmissos." An older suggestion for "Kornissos" was "Koressos," the reading of one

manuscript, but there is serious doubt as to whether Koressos was a mountain (it is referred to as a harbor by the Oxyrhynchus Historian; McKechnie and Kern 31, 118). However, "Koressos" remains a strong possibility on the view of the topography of Ephesus taken by the *Barrington Atlas* (it may also have been the name of the mountain above the harbor) and does have manuscript support. I therefore print it in my translation while acknowledging that radical changes (mostly due to silting) in the coastal terrain around Ephesus from antiquity onward make all topographical speculation highly uncertain. (Peter Green)

behavior, set upon the Athenians, killing Thrasyboulos and some others. At this the Athenian trireme captains panicked, quickly manned their vessels, and made course for Rhodos. [5] But since the city had defected, they joined the exiles who had got possession of a fort in their fight against the men of the city. When the Athenians heard about the death of their general Thrasyboulos, they sent out Agyrios as general in his place. This, then, was the situation in Asia.

The King's Peace
14.110

[1] After these events the year ran its course, and in Athens Theodotos became archon. . . . [2] During [his] term of office the Lacedaemonians, who were under heavy pressure because of the war they were fighting against both the Greeks and the Persians, sent their naval commander Antalkidas to Artaxerxes to negotiate peace terms. [3] After he had debated the subject of his mission to the best of his ability, the King declared that he would make peace on the following terms: The Greek cities of Asia were to be subject to the King, but all the other Greek cities were to be autonomous; and against those who refused to abide by the terms of this treaty he would wage war through the agency of those who accepted it. [4] Now the Lacedaemonians approved the treaty and raised no objections to it, but the Athenians, the Thebans, and some others took it very hard that the cities of Asia should be thus abandoned. However, since they were incapable of fighting a war on their own, they were compelled perforce to yield and accepted the treaty.

[5] Now that he had settled his differences with the Greeks, the King began readying his forces for the campaign against Cyprus, since while Artaxerxes had been distracted by his war against the Greeks, Evagoras[a] had won control over almost the whole of the island and mustered very substantial armed forces.

BOOK XV SELECTIONS

Proem
15.1.1–5

[1] Throughout this entire study we have made it a rule to adopt that freedom of expression customary in the writing of history while adding the praise appropriate to men of virtue for their excellent deeds and pronouncing just censure on the unworthy when they do wrong. By such means, we are convinced, we shall encourage those naturally inclined toward excellence, drawn by the lure of immortal renown, to undertake the finest actions, and by fitting reproofs dissuade those of a contrary nature from plunging into vice. [2] Therefore, since our narrative has reached the period when the Lacedaemonians first suffered a major setback through their improbable defeat at Leuctra and then, after a second failure at Mantineia, unex-

O.14.110.5a   Evagoras, king of the city of Salamis on
              Cyprus, provided a refuge for Konon after
              his flight from Aigospotamoi.

pectedly lost their hegemony over the Greeks, we think we should maintain the basic principle underlying our narrative and put on record an appropriate censure of the Lacedaemonians. [3] For who would not regard as worthy of condemnation men who, after inheriting from their ancestors a most solidly based hegemony—one that indeed, through those ancestral virtues, lasted more than five hundred years— then saw it (as the Lacedaemonians of that time did) destroyed by their own thoughtlessness? Nor was this accidental. For it was with much toil and at great risk to themselves that those who preceded them achieved their high renown, and by treating those subordinate to them humanely and with moderation; whereas this later generation not only subjected the allies to harsh and violent abuse but arrogantly and without just cause warred against the Greeks and thus, quite understandably, lost their dominion through their own imprudence. [4] For it was in their misfortunes that the hatred of those they had wronged found the opportunity for revenge against their oppressors, and those who from ancestral times had never suffered defeat now fell victims to the kind of intense contempt that predictably targets those who wipe out the achievements of their forefathers. [5] This is why the Thebans, who previously for many generations had remained subject to their superior power, were transformed by their unlooked-for victory over the Lacedaemonians into the leading power in Greece, while the Lacedaemonians, after the loss of their hegemony, were never able to recover their ancestral prestige.

Sparta Attacks Mantineia
15.5

[1] At the same time as these events, the Lacedaemonians determined to march upon Mantineia—disregarding the treaty then in force—for the following reasons. The Greeks were benefiting from the common Peace of Antalkidas, under the terms of which all the cities had been relieved of their garrisons and had had their autonomy restored. The Lacedaemonians, however—rulers by nature and warmongers by choice—found this peace an intolerable burden and, in their urge to recover the absolute power with which they had once dominated Greece, were eager for any venture that held promise of a new beginning. [2] So they began by stirring up trouble in the cities, using their private friends to provoke civil disorder there. Some cities, indeed, offered plausible excuses for such rabble-rousing, since, on regaining their independence, they demanded a reckoning from those in authority under the Lacedaemonian regime. Because of the recollection of past wrongs by the populace, these inquisitions were conducted with great severity, and large numbers found themselves exiled. The Lacedaemonians therefore came forward as the rescuers of the defeated faction. [3] By taking these men in and then forcibly returning them to their homes, they first subjugated the weaker cities and subsequently also made war on the more considerable ones, forcing them into subjection, too. They had maintained the common peace for rather less than two years.

Seeing that the city of Mantineia was located close to their frontier and abounded in valiant men, they found its growth as a result of the peace disturbing and were eager to humble the pride of its citizens. [4] So first they sent ambassadors to the Mantineians, ordering them to demolish their city walls and relocate the entire population back to those five original villages from which in ancient times they had come together to establish Mantineia. When no one paid the slightest attention to this, they sent out an expeditionary force and put the city under siege. [5] The Mantineians dispatched ambassadors to Athens seeking aid, but the Athenians decided not to contravene the terms of the common peace. Despite this, the Mantineians chose to resist the siege on their own and put up a vigorous defense against the enemy. This, then, was the way that affairs in Greece became embroiled in a new round of wars.

Sparta's Reduction of Mantineia
15.12

[1] In Greece, the Lacedaemonians kept up their siege of Mantineia, and all summer the Mantineians maintained their stubborn resistance against the enemy. They had a reputation as the most valiant of all the Arcadians, and this was why in the past the Lacedaemonians had always stationed them on their flank, as the most reliable of their allies. But with the onset of winter the river that runs by Mantineia became swollen as a result of the rains, and the Lacedaemonians diverted its course by means of great earthworks so that it now flowed directly into the city, turning the entire area into a marsh. [2] As a result, houses began to collapse, and the Mantineians, in consternation, were forced to surrender their city to the Lacedaemonians. Once the latter had it in their hands, they inflicted no further suffering on the Mantineians except to order their dispersal to their original villages. But as a result, they were obliged to demolish their own city before moving out.

Amyntas of Macedon and Sparta
15.19.2–3

[2] In Macedon King Amyntas, after a defeat at the hands of the Illyrians, renounced his right to rule, and furthermore, as a result of this renunciation of authority, made over a large tract of his frontier territory as a gift to the people of Olynthos. At first the Olynthian *demos* got the revenues from the land thus granted to them, but later, on the king's unexpectedly regaining confidence and indeed recovering his entire kingdom, the Olynthians felt unable, when asked for it, to return the territory in their possession. [3] Amyntas therefore both mustered troops of his own and, after concluding an alliance with the Lacedaemonians, persuaded them to send him a general and a strong expeditionary force to fight the Olynthians. The Lacedaemonians, now determined to extend their power into the Thrace-ward regions,

enlisted troops both from their own citizens and from their allies, to a total of more than ten thousand. This body they placed under the command of Phoibidas the Spartan, who was ordered to reinforce Amyntas and with him to conduct joint operations against the Olynthians. They also sent out another force against the people of Phleious, defeated them in battle, and made them subject to the Lacedaemonians.

Sparta Occupies the Theban Kadmeia
15.20.1–3

15.20. [1] When Euandros was archon in Athens, during [his] term of office the Lacedaemonians got control of the Kadmeia in Thebes. This is how it came about. Seeing that Boeotia had a great number of cities and that its inhabitants were men of outstanding valor, while Thebes still retained its ancient reputation and was, in short, a kind of acropolis for all Boeotia, they were afraid that, should a suitable opportunity present itself, this city might make a bid for the leadership of Greece. [2] On that account the Spartans gave secret instructions to their leaders that if they ever got the chance, they should occupy the Kadmeia. Since these were his orders, the Spartan Phoibidas, who had been appointed to a command and was leading an expeditionary force against the Olynthians, proceeded to seize the Kadmeia. When the Thebans, infuriated by this act, mustered under arms, he brought them to battle and defeated them. He then banished three hundred of Thebes' most distinguished citizens. Having thus thoroughly cowed the rest, he installed a strong garrison and left to resume his prior mission. As a result of this episode, the Lacedaemonians were in very ill repute among the Greeks. They therefore slapped Phoibidas with a public fine—but made no move to withdraw his garrison from Thebes. [3] This was how the Thebans lost their independence and were forcibly made subject to the Lacedaemonians. . . .

Sparta Defeats Olynthos
15.20.3–23.5

Since the Olynthians continued to war against King Amyntas of Macedon, the Lacedaemonians relieved Phoibidas of his command but replaced him as general with his own brother, Eudamidas. They then gave Eudamidas three thousand hoplites and sent him off to prosecute the war against the Olynthians.

15.21. [1] So he marched into Olynthian territory, joined forces with Amyntas, and went on fighting Olynthos. At this stage the Olynthians, who had mustered a considerable force, got the better of their encounters, since they had more troops than the enemy. However, the Lacedaemonians now made ready a considerable force of their own and appointed Teleutias as the general in command of it. This Teleutias was brother to King Agesilaos and had a high reputation for valor among his fellow citizens. [2] Setting out with this force from the Peloponnese, he took up a position close to the Olynthians and reinforced his own troops with those of Eudamidas. This put him on equal terms with the enemy. To begin with, he laid waste the territory of Olynthos and acquired a great mass of booty, which he shared out among his soldiers. But when the Olynthians, together with their allies, took the field in full strength, he met them in battle. At the onset neither side could prevail, and so they abandoned the struggle; but there followed a sharp encounter during which Teleutias himself fell, fighting bravely, and the Lacedaemonians lost more than twelve hundred men. [3] After the Olynthians brought off so striking an achievement, the Lacedaemonians, eager to make good their setback, busied themselves with rounding up more solid reinforcements, while the Olynthians, convinced that the Spartans would indeed come against them in greater strength and that the war would drag on for years, laid in massive stores of grain and recruited additional troops from their allies.

15.22. [1] When Demophilos was archon in Athens . . . [2] . . . the Lacedaemonians appointed King Agesipolis general, provided him with an ample expeditionary force, and voted for war against the Olynthians. On moving into Olynthian territory, Agesipolis took over the forces already encamped there and continued the war against the local inhabitants. The Olynthians, alarmed by the size of the king's army, engaged in no major battles during the course of the year but from start to finish restricted themselves to slingers' exchanges and the briefest of skirmishes.

15.23. [1] When the year had run its course, in Athens Pytheas became archon. . . . In Elis the One Hundredth Olympiad was celebrated, during which Dionysodoros of Taras won the *stadion*. [2] While these men were in office Agesipolis, the Lacedaemonian king, died of an illness after a reign of fourteen years; his brother Kleombrotos succeeded to the throne and reigned for nine. The Lacedaemonians appointed Polybiadas general and sent him out to the war against the Olynthians. [3] He took over command and, by conducting the war both aggressively and with professional skill, scored a number of victories. With this increasingly successful record and after winning several pitched battles, he drove the Olynthians back into their city and put them under siege. Finally he so broke his opponents' morale that he forced them into subjection to the Lacedaemonians. After this cooption of the Olynthians into the Spartan alliance, many of the other cities hastened to get themselves enrolled under Lacedaemonian leadership. The result was that during this period the Lacedaemonians reached the apogee of their power and won hegemony over Greece by both land and sea. [4] For the Thebans were under a garrison, the Corinthians and Argives had been weakened by their recent wars, while the Athenians were in bad odor among the Greeks because of the colonists they settled in conquered territories. The Lacedaemonians themselves had devoted particular attention to maintaining a large population well versed in the use of arms, so that the power of their leadership made them feared by all. [5] As a result, the greatest dynasts of those days—that is, the King of Persia and Dionysius, the ruler of Sicily—paid court to Sparta's leaders and sought to secure their alliance for themselves.

The Liberation of Thebes
15.25–27.3

15.25. [1] When Nausinikos was archon in Athens . . . the so-called Boeotian War, fought by the Lacedaemonians against the Boeotians, broke out for the following reasons. Since the Lacedaemonians were illegally garrisoning the Kadmeia and had exiled many [of Thebes'] most distinguished citizens, the exiles banded together and, with Athenian backing, returned by night to the city of their birth. [2] First they killed all those who supported the Lacedaemonians, catching them unawares in their own houses while they were asleep. They then called on the citizens to rally to the cause of freedom and thus got the support of every Theban. The entire citizen body assembled under arms and at daybreak set about blockading the Kadmeia. [3] The Lacedaemonian garrison of the citadel, fifteen hundred strong including the allied contingent, dispatched messengers to Sparta to report the Theban uprising and ask for immediate reinforcements. Meanwhile, helped by their commanding position, they killed large numbers of their assailants and put not a few out of action with severe wounds. [4] The Thebans—in expectation of the arrival of a large army from Greece to aid the Lacedaemonians—sent ambassadors to Athens, reminding them that the Thebans had once helped restore Athenian democratic rule, at the time when Athens was enslaved by the Thirty Tyrants.

15.26. [1] The Athenian people, after hearing the ambassadors out, voted to send as large a force as possible for the immediate liberation of Thebes, thus at one and the same time both repaying the earlier benefit and acting in the hope of winning over the Boeotians as powerful allies against Lacedaemonian preeminence; for by common report this people was second to none in Greece as regards both the number of its men and their valor as warriors. [2] Finally, Demophon was appointed general and raised an emergency levy of five thousand hoplites and five hundred cavalry. At dawn the following day he led this body out from the city, pressing on at full speed in his determination to forestall the Lacedaemonians. The Athenians, nonetheless, went ahead with preparations for an expedition into Boeotia in full force, should the need arise. [3] By taking shortcuts, Demophon showed up at Thebes before he was expected; and since numerous troops were likewise hastily flocking in from the other cities in Boeotia, a huge support force very quickly gathered to help the Thebans. [4] The number of foot soldiers thus assembled was twelve thousand, and of cavalry more than two thousand. Since all of them were eager to prosecute the siege, they divided their forces and assaulted the citadel in relays, keeping up a nonstop attack by day and night.

15.27. [1] The troops in the Kadmeia, with the encouragement of their leaders, maintained a vigorous defense against the enemy, confident that the Lacedaemonians would arrive at any moment with a large army. So long as they had adequate provisions, they met trouble with stubborn courage, killing and disabling many of their assailants, abetted by the naturally strong position of the citadel. But when the lack of food became acute and the Lacedaemonians kept taking endless time over their preparations, they split into two factions. [2] The Lacedaemonians thought they should hold out till death, whereas the troops from the allied cities fighting with them (who outnumbered them considerably) argued that they should surrender the Kadmeia. Under this pressure even those from Sparta itself, being in the minority, felt compelled to abandon the citadel. They therefore agreed to a truce and, under its terms, withdrew to the Peloponnese. [3] The Lacedaemonians, however, were on their way to Thebes with a sizable force and got there just too late for their attack to be successful. They court-martialed the three officers commanding the garrison, condemned two of them to death, and imposed such a heavy fine on the third that his resources were insufficient to pay it.

The Foundation of the Second Athenian Sea-League
15.28

[1] When Kallias was archon in Athens[a] . . . the Boeotians, gaining confidence from the Lacedaemonian setback at Thebes, got together, established a common alliance, and raised a very sizable army, anticipating that the Lacedaemonians would now march on Boeotia in full force. [2] The Athenians chose as ambassadors their most distinguished citizens and sent them out to those cities under Lacedaemonian authority with an invitation to join the cause of common freedom. This was because the Lacedaemonians, by means of the vastly superior forces they kept deployed, ruled those under their control with arrogant severity, and as a result, many of the latter were now inclining toward Athens. [3] The first to listen favorably to this appeal were the people of Chios and Byzantium, followed by the Rhodians, the Mytilenaians, and some of the other islanders; and with the steady and continuous growth of this movement among the Greeks, more and more cities defected to the Athenians. The Athenian people, elated by the goodwill of these allies, established a federal council including them all and assigned representatives for each city. [4] It was determined, by general agreement, that the council should meet in Athens; that the cities, whether great or small, should enjoy equal standing, each having one vote; and that all, while accepting the Athenians as leaders, should remain independent. The Lacedaemonians, realizing that this secessionary trend of the cities was uncontrollable, nevertheless—by means of diplomacy, declarations of benevolence, and generous promises—strove hard to counter the hostility with which they were now regarded. [5] At the same time they also devoted much

O.15.28.1a Kallias was archon in Athens in 377/6. This passage is generally regarded as valuable evidence for a process that stretched over several years, but unfortunately, scholars generally think, 377/6 is a misleading, if not downright mistaken, date to which to assign the key events. The inscription that gives the prospectus for the Second Athenian League (Rhodes and Osborne 22 [see Bibliography]), as it was commonly called, says it was voted in in the year in which Nausinikos was archon, in the seventh *prytaneia* (the seventh of the ten divisions of the Athenian civic year). It therefore dates from 378/7 (more exactly, from around February 377). In this prospectus, the central institution of the league, the federal council, is already in existence, about four months before 377/6. So although the precise chronology of the events covered by this passage is disputed, scholars generally think that the principal ones must have taken place earlier than summer 377, and perhaps much earlier. Scholarly consensus assigns the raid of Sphodrias (15.29.5–6) to spring 378, so if Diodorus is right in his relative chronology in which the federal council was founded before the raid, this key event belongs in early spring 378.

thought to their preparations for war, in the anticipation that this Boeotian war would be a serious and lengthy business for them, given that the Thebans had as allies both the Athenians and all the other Greeks who were members of their federal council.

Chabrias in Egypt
15.29.1–4

[1] At the same time as these events, the king of Egypt, Akoris, who was unfavorably disposed toward the king of Persia, recruited a considerable mercenary army: for by offering high pay to those who enlisted and handing out frequent bonuses, he very soon had many of the Greeks in his service for the campaign he was planning. [2] But since he lacked a competent general, he sent for Chabrias the Athenian, a man of exceptional military judgment and intelligence, who also enjoyed a high reputation for personal valor. Chabrias, then, without obtaining Athenian official approval, accepted the offer, took command of the forces in Egypt, and embarked on vigorous preparations for a campaign against the Persians.[a] [3] Now Pharnabazos, who had been designated by the Great King as commander in chief of the Persian armed forces, likewise made great preparations of military armaments; but he also sent ambassadors to Athens, first to denounce Chabrias, who by accepting this Egyptian command had alienated the Great King's goodwill toward the Athenian people, and second, to ask for the loan of Iphikrates as a general. [4] The Athenians, eager to win back the Great King's favor and to conciliate Pharnabazos, at once both recalled Chabrias from Egypt and sent out Iphikrates as a general to collaborate with the Persians.

Sphodrias' Raid on Peiraieus
15.29.5–7, 15.30.1–2

[5] The truce concluded at an earlier time between the Lacedaemonians and the Athenians had sufficed to keep the peace up to this point. But then Sphodrias the Spartan, who had been appointed to high command and was by nature an impulsive and reckless individual, was persuaded by the Lacedaemonian king Kleombrotos— without the authorization of the ephors—that he should occupy Peiraieus. [6] Sphodrias, leading a force of more than ten thousand men, duly made an attempt on Peiraieus by night; but when his presence became known to the Athenians, he was forced to abort the attack and withdrew without achieving anything. Indicted before the Spartan council, he was, most improperly, acquitted through having the kings active on his behalf. [7] Accordingly the Athenians, who took this episode very hard, decreed by vote that the Lacedaemonians had broken the truce and formally declared war on them, appointing as generals three of their most distinguished

O.15.29.2a   Chabrias was at Athens in winter 379/8 (Xenophon's *Hellenika* 5.4.14), so the events in this paragraph did not literally take place "at the same time" as those in the preceding section. This is a regular phrase of Diodorus' and indicates a very loose and generalized simultaneity. In this instance, almost all scholars believe that Chabrias' sojourn in Egypt was a few years earlier. (Peter Green)

citizens, Timotheos, Chabrias, and Kallistratos. They voted a levy of twenty thousand hoplites, five hundred cavalry, and crews for two hundred ships. They also admitted the Thebans to the federal council on terms of absolute equality. [8] Furthermore, they voted to restore to their former owners the land requisitioned as cleruchies,[a] and they passed a law that no Athenian could farm land outside Attica. By this generous act they regained the goodwill of the Greeks and made their own position of leadership stronger.

15.30. [1] So many of the other cities, for the reasons stated above, were encouraged to defect to the Athenians; and the first and most enthusiastic new allies were the cities of Euboea, with the sole exception of Histiaia. Now Histiaia had received substantial benefits from the Lacedaemonians but had been ruthlessly treated in wartime by the Athenians, so it was understandable that she should maintain both her undiminished hatred for the Athenians and her unshakable loyalty to the Spartans. [2] Be that as it may, seventy cities entered into alliance with the Athenians and took part, on a basis of equality, in the federal council. So with the power of the Athenians continually on the rise, while that of the Lacedaemonians diminished, a point was reached where the two cities were about evenly matched.

Chabrias and Agesilaos in the Boeotian War
15.32–34.2

15.32. [1] Agesilaos entered Boeotia at the head of his army. The total forces under his command amounted to more than eighteen thousand men, including the five Lacedaemonian regiments [*morai*], each with a full complement of five hundred. (What the Spartans call the "Skiritan company" is not drawn up with the rest but has its own special position with the king and goes to the assistance of any hardpressed division; consisting as it does of specially picked men,[a] it is a major factor in shifting the balance of a pitched battle and more often than not is directly responsible for victory.) Agesilaos also had fifteen hundred cavalry. [2] He pressed on as far as the city of Thespiai, which was garrisoned by the Lacedaemonians, pitched camp near it, and gave his troops a few days' rest from what had been a tough march. When the Athenians learned of the Lacedaemonians' arrival in Boeotia, they at once sent a relief force to Thebes, consisting of five thousand foot and two hundred horse. [3] After these troops had been concentrated into a single position, the Thebans occupied an oval hilltop some twenty stades [two and a half miles] distant from

O.15.29.8a Cleruchies were special colonial settlements established by Athens during the fifth century on land confiscated from conquered states. This land was allotted to poor Athenians who, even if they moved to it, did not lose their Athenian citizenship. Many cleruchies were punitive in nature and were bitterly resented by those on whom they had been imposed.

O.15.32.1a The Skiritan company was a specialist unit o six hundred from the northern Laconian district of Skiritis. Some scholars think that Diodorus confused the Skiritans company

here with the king's bodyguard, known as the *hippeis*; others are convinced that they were scouts or peltasts. Both theories are possible but speculative. The exact nature of Spartan military units is one of the most vexing problems in all of Greek history. Peter Green and other scholars think that Diodorus may well be right, on the ground that the Skiritan company was an elite force of hoplites who enjoyed a position of privilege on the left wing in the battle line.

the city, utilizing the difficult terrain as a bastion of defense. It was here that they awaited the enemy's attack, since they were so in awe of Agesilaos' reputation that they dared not face him on equal terms down in the plain. [4] Agesilaos now led his army in battle order against the Boeotians. As soon as he got within range, he began by sending his light-armed troops up against his opponents as a test of their attitude to battle. When the Thebans, thanks to their commanding position, repulsed this attack without trouble, he then led his entire force against them, in close array, as a scare tactic. [5] But Chabrias the Athenian, who was in command of the mercenaries, instructed his troops to await the enemy in a contemptuous fashion, holding their battle line, shields propped against their knees, spears upraised. [6] This order they obeyed as one man at the word of command. Agesilaos, much impressed by the enemy's good discipline and contemptuous posture, rejected the idea of making an assault against higher ground and of forcing his opponents to show their mettle in a hand-to-hand conflict. Having learned by experience that they would indeed, if so compelled, dare to fight for victory, he offered them battle in the plain. But when the Thebans refused to be drawn, he withdrew his infantry phalanx and sent out the cavalry and light-armed units to plunder the countryside, which they did unopposed. In this way he acquired a great mass of booty.

15.33. [1] Both the Spartan counselors who accompanied Agesilaos and his staff officers expressed surprise that Agesilaos, a man with a reputation for vigorous action, who also had the larger and more powerful army, should have chosen not to engage the enemy in a decisive battle. To this Agesilaos replied that in the present instance the Lacedaemonians had been victorious without any risk, since when they were plundering the countryside, the Boeotians had not dared to come out and protect it. But if, when the enemy had themselves conceded the victory, he had nevertheless forced them to fight it out, the Lacedaemonians might even—granted the capriciousness of fortune—have suffered an upset in the venture. [2] At the time it was thought that this reply of his represented a reasonable guess at how things might turn out; but considered in the light of later events, his utterance was regarded not so much as a merely human response but, rather, as a divinely inspired oracle. For when the Lacedaemonians did campaign against the Thebans with a vast army and forced them to fight for their freedom, the result was sheer disaster. [3] First they were defeated at Leuctra, in which battle there perished large numbers of their citizens, including their king Kleombrotos. Later, when they fought at Mantineia, they were utterly routed, thus in an unlooked-for manner losing their hegemony. For good fortune has a way of unexpectedly tripping up the overambitious and teaching them not to hope for anything in excess. Agesilaos, at any rate, was sensibly satisfied with his initial success and thus kept his expeditionary force unharmed.

[4] After this Agesilaos and his army returned to the Peloponnese. The Thebans, who had been saved by the generalship of Chabrias, were astounded at the man's

tactical brilliance. Though Chabrias had many fine exploits to his credit in war, he was especially proud of this stratagem, and he insisted on having the statues granted him by the *demos* modeled in the same posture. [5] When Agesilaos was gone, the Thebans marched against Thespiai. They destroyed the city's frontier outpost, with its garrison of two hundred men, but after making numerous assaults on Thespiai itself without accomplishing anything of note, they took their troops back to Thebes. [6] Phoibidas the Lacedaemonian, who had a considerable garrison in Thespiai, made a sortie from the city and launched a headlong attack on the retreating Thebans. By so doing, he lost more than five hundred soldiers. However, he himself, after putting up a most valiant fight and receiving many wounds in front, ended his life heroically.

15.34. [1] Not long afterward the Lacedaemonians once more marched against Thebes, with the same force as previously. The Thebans occupied certain new strong positions, which enabled them to prevent the enemy from despoiling the countryside, but still did not venture out to meet the whole Lacedaemonian army face-to-face and fight it out down in the plain. [2] But when Agesilaos offered battle, they moved down gradually to engage him. A bitter and drawn-out struggle ensued. To begin with, Agesilaos and his men had the better of it, but then the Thebans came pouring out of the city in full force, and Agesilaos, seeing this tide of men rushing down on them, had his trumpeter sound the retreat and withdrew his troops from the battle. This was the first occasion on which the Thebans did not regard themselves as inferior to the Lacedaemonians: they set up a trophy and from then on faced Spartan troops with confidence.

The Battle of Naxos
15.34.3–35.2

15.34. [3] As regards the land forces, this was how the situation developed; at sea, about the same time, a great naval battle was fought between Naxos and Paros, in the following circumstances. Pollis, the Lacedaemonian admiral, on being informed that a large shipment of grain was being delivered to the Athenians in a number of merchantmen, lay in wait, watching out for the arrival of this grain consignment, with the intention of attacking the merchantmen. Getting wind of this, the Athenian government dispatched a squadron to protect the grain while in transit, and the convoy was thus escorted safely to Peiraieus. [4] Subsequently Chabrias, the Athenian admiral, sailed for Naxos with his entire fleet and put it under siege. Bringing up his siege engines, he proceeded to batter away at the walls with them and made a concerted effort to take the city by direct assault. While all this was going on, Pollis, the Lacedaemonian admiral, sailed in to rescue the Naxians. Spurred on by ambitious rivalry, both sides readied themselves for a naval engagement, lining up their ships in battle order and advancing directly against each other. [5] Pollis had sixty-five triremes and Chabrias eighty-three. As the lines closed, Pollis, in command of the right wing, was the first to attack the opposing triremes on the left, commanded by Kedon the Athenian: with consummate skill Pollis both killed Kedon himself and sank his ship. In similar fashion he went on to attack the remaining vessels, ramming and crippling them, putting some out of action and forcing others to retreat. When Chabrias saw this, he detached a squadron of his own ships and sent them to the relief of the hard-pressed [left wing], thus retrieving a near-defeat. He himself, with the strongest part of the fleet at his disposal, put up a splendid fight, disabled a number of triremes, and captured a good many others.

15.35. [1] Though he had thus gained the victory and indeed had turned all the enemy vessels to flight, he held off altogether from pursuit, remembering the sea battle of Arginousai, when the *demos* rewarded the great public service of the victorious commanders by condemning them to death, the charge being that they had failed to bury those who had died during the engagement. Since the circumstances were much the same, he was anxious to avoid the possibility of suffering a similar fate. As a result, he abandoned the idea of pursuit in favor of retrieving the floating bodies of his fellow citizens, rescuing those who were still alive and taking up the dead for burial. Had he not devoted his attention to this matter, he could easily have destroyed the entire enemy fleet. [2] During this battle eighteen Athenian triremes were destroyed; the Lacedaemonians lost twenty-four, and eight more were captured with their crews. After winning this notable victory, Chabrias sailed back to Peiraieus with a rich haul of booty and received a rapturous welcome from his fellow citizens. This was the first naval victory that the Athenians had won since the Peloponnesian War, since the successful engagement off Cnidus had not been achieved with their own ships but by the use of the [Persian] royal fleet.

The Battle of Tegyra
15.37.1–2

[1] At the same time as these events the Thebans marched against Orchomenus with five hundred elite warriors and accomplished a most noteworthy exploit. The Lacedaemonians kept a strong garrison in Orchomenus, and when it came out to meet the Thebans and a tough battle took place, the Thebans—who were taking on a force double their number—defeated the Lacedaemonians. Never before in their past history had this happened: they considered themselves lucky if they scored a victory against a heavily outnumbered [Spartan] adversary. [2] As a result, the Thebans were filled with pride, their reputation as warriors continued to grow, and they had clearly reached a position where they could compete for the leadership of the Greek states.

The Peace of 375/4
15.38

[1] When Hippodamas was archon in Athens . . . Artaxerxes, the Great King of Persia—who was planning a campaign against the Egyptians and, to that end, exerting every effort to recruit a substantial mercenary army—determined to put an end to the various wars in Greece. His particular hope in so doing was that once the Greeks were rid of their domestic conflicts, they would be all the readier to enlist as mercenaries. He therefore sent ambassadors to Greece, inviting the cities to conclude a common peace. [2] The Greeks, who were weary of these never-ending wars, welcomed his proposals, and all accepted a peace that left every city independent and ungarrisoned. The Greeks therefore appointed commissioners to go from city to city and evacuate all the garrisons.

[3] Only the Thebans refused to accept the implementation of the treaty city by city, treating all Boeotia as part of the Theban confederacy.[a] The Athenians strongly opposed this, their spokesman being the popular leader Kallistratos, while Epaminondas eloquently presented the case in the federal council on behalf of the Thebans. The upshot was that the peace was unanimously ratified by all the other Greeks, the Thebans alone being excluded from it.[b] Epaminondas, by virtue of his personal prestige, inspired his fellow citizens with confidence and encouraged them to hold out against the collective decision of the rest. [4] For the Lacedaemonians and the Athenians, who had been rivals for the leadership through thick and thin, now began to make mutual concessions, deciding between them that the first was most worthy of rule by land and the second by sea. As a result, they did not take kindly to a third party advancing claims on the leadership and set about detaching the cities of Boeotia from the Theban confederacy.

Corcyra, Timotheos, Plataea
15.45–47.7

15.45. [1] Throughout Greece disorder reigned in the cities as a result of the unaccustomed form of government, and conditions of general anarchy encouraged numerous uprisings, with those who aimed to establish oligarchies getting support from the Lacedaemonians, while the partisans of democracy had the Athenians on their side. [2] Both these cities observed the agreement for a short period, but then action in support of their dependent communities led them to renew the war, in total disregard of the common peace that had been concluded. On Zacynthus, for example, the populists, who nursed considerable resentment against those who had controlled the city under the Lacedaemonian regime, exiled every one of them. . . . These "populists"[a] sought refuge with Timotheos, the commander of the Athenian

O.15.38.3a The Theban confederacy here is the same organization called the Boeotian Federation in the text of *Hellenika* and Appendix H.

O.15.38.3b The contemporary evidence from inscriptions and the pamphleteer Isocrates (14.41) shows that Thebes was not excluded from the Peace of 375/4.

O.15.45.2a As is generally recognized, there must be a lacuna here, since it is not the Spartan-backed exiles who would have turned for aid to Timotheos but their opponents. Clearly the Lacedaemonians had restored the exiled oligarchs, who then in turn proceeded to exile the populists. (Peter Green)

fleet, serving him as naval allies. [3] Having thus secured his collaboration, they got him to ship them across to the island, where they seized a coastal stronghold known to them as Arcadia. Making sorties from this base with the support of Timotheos, they did considerable damage to those in the city. [4] When the Zacynthians asked the Lacedaemonians for assistance, they first sent ambassadors to Athens to denounce Timotheos; but when they saw that the Athenian people were in sympathy with the exiles, they put together a fleet, manned twenty-five triremes, placed Aristokrates in command, and sent them off to the relief of the Zacynthians.

15.46. [1] At the same time as these activities, certain friends of the Lacedaemonians on Corcyra rebelled against the democracy there and called upon the Spartans to send them a fleet, promising to deliver Corcyra into their hands. The Lacedaemonians, well aware of Corcyra's critical importance for anyone aiming at sea power, were eager to get control of this city. [2] So they at once dispatched twenty-two triremes to Corcyra under the command of Alkidas. To ensure that they were received as friends by the Corcyraeans and could then take over the city along with the exiles, they pretended that this expedition's destination was Sicily. [3] The Corcyraeans, however, detected this Spartan plot, kept their city under close guard, and sent ambassadors to Athens asking for support. The Athenians voted to help the Corcyraeans and exiled Zacynthians, sent out Ktesikles as general commanding the exiles, and made preparations for dispatching a naval squadron to Corcyra.

[4] At the same time as these events, in Boeotia the Plataeans actively pursued the Athenian alliance and sent to ask [Athens] for military support, since they were determined to turn their city over to the Athenians. At this the Boetarchs, who were ill disposed toward the Plataeans and anxious to forestall the arrival of a relief force from Athens, immediately led out a strong force against them. [5] They reached the neighborhood of Plataea before any attack was expected, so that most of the Plataeans were out in the fields, where they were picked up and carried off by the cavalry. The remainder, who had fled to the city and now found themselves without allies, were forced to accept terms agreeable to their enemies: they had to take their movable property, abandon the city and never again set foot in Boeotia. [6] After this the Thebans demolished Plataea and also sacked Thespiai, which was on unfriendly terms with them. The Plataeans, together with their wives and children, found refuge in Athens, where through the generosity of the *demos* they were granted full civic rights [*isopoliteia*]. This, then, was the situation in Boeotia at that time.

15.47. [1] The Lacedaemonians appointed Mnasippos general and sent him out to Corcyra with sixty-five triremes and fifteen hundred soldiers under his command. He sailed to the island, took aboard the exiles, and then penetrated the harbor, where he seized four ships. The remaining three vessels had run ashore, where they were set on fire by the Corcyraeans to prevent their falling into enemy hands. His infantry also landed and wiped out a group that had occupied a certain hill: one way and another, he seriously scared the Corcyraeans. [2] The Athenians had, some time before, sent out Timotheos, Konon's son, with sixty ships as reinforcements for Corcyra. Before carrying out this commission, however, he sailed off to Thrace, where he called on a number of cities to join the alliance and acquired thirty more triremes. [3] For his delay in bringing aid to Corcyra he was at first removed from his command, since the *demos* was extremely angry with him. However, when he coasted home to Athens with a large number of envoys from cities joining the alliance, after adding those thirty extra triremes and putting the entire fleet in excellent condition for active service, then the *demos* had second thoughts and reappointed him general.[a] [4] They had also previously equipped forty further triremes, so that his total fleet now numbered one hundred and thirty; they also stockpiled adequate supplies of grain, missiles, and every other necessity for warfare. To meet immediate needs, they chose Ktesikles as general and dispatched him with five hundred troops to assist the Corcyraeans. [5] He landed on Corcyra secretly, at night, unnoticed by the besiegers. Finding the citizens split into hostile factions and managing the conduct of the war very poorly, he proceeded to reconcile the factions and, by careful attention to the city's affairs, improved the morale of the besieged. [6] At first, in a surprise attack on the besiegers, he killed some two hundred of them, and subsequently in a major battle he slew Mnasippos himself and a good many others besides. Finally he surrounded the besiegers and put them under siege, a feat for which he won high praise. [7] With the Corcyraean war now virtually over, the Athenian fleet, commanded by Timotheos and Iphikrates, reached Corcyra.[a] They had arrived too late to be of use and achieved nothing worthy of note, except for their encounter with some Sicilian triremes that Dionysios had sent out, under the command of Kissides and Krinippos, to honor his alliance with the Lacedaemonians. There were nine of these, and they captured them all, complete with their crews. By selling off these prisoners as booty, they collected more than sixty talents, with which they paid their troops.

The Ratification of the Peace of 372/1
15.50.4

[4] It was now that the Great King, Artaxerxes, seeing that Greece was once more in a turmoil, sent ambassadors calling for an end to these fratricidal wars and the establishment of a common peace in accordance with the agreements they had made earlier. The Greeks unanimously welcomed his proposal, and all the cities, Thebes alone excepted, ratified a common peace. Only the Thebans, on the grounds that they were keeping Boeotia as a united confederacy, failed to win admission from the other Greeks, since it was generally agreed that the treaty was to

O.15.47.3a A virtually contemporary speech, preserved as No. 49 in the corpus attributed to Demosthenes though in fact by another Athenian politician, Apollodoros, proves that Timotheos was not reappointed general immediately afterward.

O.15.47.7a Diodorus is in error in saying that Timotheos accompanied Iphikrates to Corcyra. In fact, he was prosecuted by Iphikrates for dereliction of duty; though acquitted, he went abroad to serve Artaxerxes II as a mercenary (372). He did not regain his position in Athens for several years. Thus Diodorus' assertion here that he was joint naval commander with Iphikrates in spring 372 is patently impossible. (Peter Green)

be ratified under oath city by city. As a result, they remained, as before, excluded from the peace and still kept Boeotia as a separate league tributary to themselves.

Leuctra
15.51–56.4

15.51. [1] When Phrasikleides was archon in Athens . . . the Thebans, being excluded from the treaty, were obliged to carry on the war against the Lacedaemonians alone: no city could ally itself with them, since all had sworn to keep the common peace. [2] With the Thebans thus isolated, the Lacedaemonians were resolved to make war on them and reduce Thebes to utter slavery. Since the Lacedaemonians made no secret of their plans and the Thebans were destitute of allies, everyone believed that Thebes would be easily vanquished by the Spartans. [3] Thus any goodwill that the Greeks had for the Thebans found expression as sympathy for the disasters awaiting them, while those who disliked them were overjoyed at the prospect of Thebes' imminent reduction to slavery.

Finally the Lacedaemonians completed the preparation of their great army and entrusted the command of it to King Kleombrotos. Then, first of all, they dispatched ambassadors to Thebes, with orders that all cities in Boeotia were to be autonomous, Plataea and Thespiai were to be repopulated and their territories restored to the original occupants. [4] The Thebans replied that, as they never meddled with the affairs of Laconia, the Spartans had no business interfering in Boeotia. This being their response, the Lacedaemonians at once dispatched Kleombrotos and his army against Thebes. The Lacedaemonians' allies were highly enthusiastic about the war, since they confidently assumed that there would be no conflict or battle but that the Boeotians would surrender without fighting.

15.52. [1] So they [the Spartans] advanced as far as Coronea, where they pitched camp and waited for the latecomers among their allies. On the appearance of the enemy, the Thebans voted to evacuate their women and children to Athens. They then chose Epaminondas as their general and entrusted him with the overall command in the forthcoming campaign, with six Boeotarchs as his advisers. [2] Epaminondas called up for active service all Thebans of military age, enlisted the best trained of the other Boeotians, and marched from Thebes at the head of a force that numbered no more than six thousand all told. [3] During the troops' exodus from the city, many of them observed what they took to be unfavorable omens for the expedition. At the city gates Epaminondas and his men encountered a town crier, giving notice in the prescribed fashion of a runaway blind slave and warning people not to hide him or smuggle him out of Thebes but, rather, to lay hands on him and bring him back. [4] The older men among those who heard this town crier regarded his words as an omen for the future, whereas the younger ones kept quiet, in case they should be thought to be dissuading Epaminondas from the campaign out of cowardice.

To those telling him he should pay heed to such omens Epaminondas replied: "One omen is best, to fight to defend your country."ᵃ [5] This forthright response by Epaminondas took the pious aback. But then a second omen appeared, more unfavorable than the first. When the staff orderly came forward, holding a spear with a ribbon attached to it, and began to announce the orders from headquarters, a gust of wind detached the ribbon and wrapped it around a gravestone. Now it was here that lay buried certain Lacedaemonians and Peloponnesians who had died while on campaign with Agesilaos. [6] Some of the older men, again, who happened to be present made a solemn protest against the army taking the field when the gods were so obviously opposed to it. Epaminondas made no reply to them but led his army on regardless, convinced that a reasoned decision in favor of what was right and a firm regard for what was just offered a preferable choice to these present signs. [7] At the time, then, Epaminondas—who had been trained in philosophy and made sensible use of the arguments he had absorbed as part of his education—incurred severe criticism from a number of people; but later, as a result of his successes, he was regarded as a man of outstanding military skill, and indeed rendered the greatest services to his country. So he at once led out his forces, occupied the pass at Coronea in advance of the enemy, and set up his camp there.

15.53. [1] Kleombrotos, on learning that the enemy had got to the pass before him, decided against an attempt to force his way through there and instead marched through Phocis. He then followed the rough coastal road, from where he made his way into Boeotia without encountering any resistance. Along the way he overran some of the outposts and seized ten triremes. [2] He then moved on to the place called Leuctra, where he pitched camp and rested his troops after their march. Meanwhile the Boeotians were advancing toward the enemy and within close range of them. When they came to the top of a line of low hills, they suddenly caught sight of the Lacedaemonians, spread out over the entire plain of Leuctra, and the spectacle of so vast an army took them aback. [3] The Boeotarchs met to decide whether they should stay put and try conclusions with an army that so greatly outnumbered them or pull back and establish a battlefront on higher ground. As it turned out, their votes were evenly divided, three of the six Boeotarchs thinking that they should retreat and three—including Epaminondas—that they should stay where they were and fight. This serious and baffling impasse was resolved by the seventh Boeotarch, whom Epaminondas talked into voting with him and thus made his opinion prevail. This is how the decision was taken to risk everything on a direct confrontation.

[4] Epaminondas, noting the superstitious fear affecting his troops on account of the portents that had occurred, deployed all his personal resourcefulness and military guile in a determined effort to counter the nervous piety of the rank and file. A number of men had lately arrived from Thebes, and he persuaded them to say that the arms in the temple of Herakles had mysteriously vanished and that a rumor had

O.15.52.4a Epaminondas is quoting Homer, *Iliad*
        12.243.

gone around in Thebes that the heroes of ancient times had taken them and departed to help the Boeotians. He also produced another man who had supposedly just come back from a descent to the oracular cave of Trophonios, who claimed that the god instructed them, when they were victorious at Leuctra, to establish a contest in honor of Zeus the king, with garlands as prizes. This is the origin of the festival celebrated by the Boeotians at Lebadeia.

15.54. [1] Another contributor to the success of such trickery was the Spartan Leandrias, an exile from Lacedaemon then on active service with the Thebans. He was brought forward in the Assembly and asserted that there was an ancient saying among the Spartans that they would lose their hegemony when they were defeated by the Thebans at Leuctra. [2] Epaminondas was also approached by certain local oracle-mongers, claiming that the Lacedaemonians were fated to suffer a major disaster near the tomb of the daughters of Leuktros and Skedasos. [3] Leuktros was the person from whom the plain derived its name. His daughters, together with those of one Skedasos, had been raped by some Lacedaemonian ambassadors: the victims, unable to endure this outrage, called down curses on the country that had sent out their violators and then took their own lives. [4] Many other such tales were reported. When Epaminondas then called an assembly and in his own words rallied the troops to face the struggle ahead, they all had a change of heart, shook off their superstitious fears, and looked forward to the coming battle in high spirits. [5] At this juncture there also reached the Thebans an allied contingent from Thessaly, fifteen hundred foot and five hundred horse, commanded by Jason. He persuaded both Boeotians and Lacedaemonians to make a truce and thus arm themselves against the incalculable quirks of fortune. [6] When the truce came into effect, Kleombrotos marched his army out of Boeotia and was met by a second large force of Lacedaemonians and allied troops, under the command of Agesilaos' son Archidamos. The Spartans, seeing how well prepared the Boeotians were and being anxious to counter their desperate boldness, had dispatched this second force to ensure that by sheer number of combatants they would eclipse the enemy's audacity. [7] Once these two armies had united, the Lacedaemonians dismissed any fear of Boeotian mettle as mere cowardice. As a result, they took no notice of the truce but set off back to Leuctra in a highly confident mood. The Boeotians likewise were ready for battle, and both sides now deployed their forces.

15.55. [1] On the Lacedaemonian side it was the descendants of Herakles, King Kleombrotos and Archidamos son of King Agesilaos, who were stationed as commanders on the wings, while on the Boeotian side Epaminondas set up that personal and extraordinary order of battle which, through his own sheer strategic flair, enabled him to achieve his famous victory.[a] [2] What he did was select the very best

---

O.15.55.1a The differences between Xenophon's and Diodorus' account of the events just prior to the battle of Leuctra are noteworthy. According to Xenophon, the truce brokered by Jason took place after, not before, the battle. Archidamos was not present at the battle and thus could not have commanded a wing of the Spartan army, and Archi-

damos' junction with Spartan forces in Boeotia belongs after the battle, when Kleombrotos was dead. Peter Green believes that Diodorus' account is so specific and so greatly at variance with that of Xenophon that it must depend on an alternate source. He thinks, however, that Jason's truce is equally plausible in either scenario.

of his soldiers and pack them all in the same wing in which he himself planned to fight. The weakest he posted on the other wing, with instructions to refuse battle and to retreat slowly as the enemy's attack developed. By thus deploying his phalanx in echelon, he intended to use the wing composed of his elite troops to decide the battle. [3] When the trumpets on both sides sounded the charge and at this onset the armies raised their battle cry, the Lacedaemonians advanced on both wings with their phalanx in crescent formation. On the Boeotian side, while one wing retreated, the other advanced on the double to engage. [4] When the lines met in a hand-to-hand melee, at first both sides fought furiously and the battle was evenly balanced, but after a while Epaminondas' men, through their valor and the massive solidity of their ranks, began to get the upper hand. Large numbers of Peloponnesians were now slaughtered, unable to stand against the sheer weight of these elite warriors. Of those who resisted, some were killed, while the rest were cut down, taking all their wounds in front. [5] Now so long as the Lacedaemonian king Kleombrotos was alive and had about him numerous comrades in arms ready and willing to die on his behalf, victory continued to hang in the balance; but when, despite boldly tackling every danger, he still could make no headway against his opponents but died fighting heroically, covered with wounds, then a great mass of corpses piled up as a desperate battle developed over his body.

15.56. [1] With this wing now bereft of its commander, Epaminondas' heavyweights pressed the Lacedaemonians hard and at first, by sheer force, thrust the enemy a short way back out of line; but the Lacedaemonians put up a gallant struggle over their king and managed to get possession of his body, even though they lacked the strength to make it to victory. [2] For the *corps d'élite* surpassed them in feats of valor, to which the courage and exhortations of Epaminondas greatly contributed, so that with huge effort the Lacedaemonians were forced back. At first they would not break ranks as they gave ground, but finally, as many of them fell, and with no leader alive to give them orders, a total rout of the entire army ensued. [3] Epaminondas' men, pressing hard on the heels of the fugitives, cut down large numbers of their opponents, scoring a most notable victory. Because they had measured themselves against the finest warriors in Greece, and with a handful of men had, against all expectation, triumphed over a numerically far superior force, they now established for themselves a formidable reputation as warriors. Epaminondas, as general, won the highest plaudits: in large part through his personal courage and strategical insight he had fought and beaten the hitherto invincible masters of Greece. [4] There fell in the battle not less than four thousand Lacedaemonians, and of the Boeotians some three hundred. A truce was then arranged for collecting the bodies of the dead and for the return of the Lacedaemonians to the Peloponnese. Such was the outcome of matters to do with the battle at Leuctra.

Arcadia, Jason of Pherai, Alexander
15.59–61.2

15.59. [1] About the same time Lykomedes of Tegea[a] persuaded the Arcadians to unite in a single confederacy and to have a federal assembly consisting of ten thousand men, with the authority to decide matters of war and peace. [2] But the result was major civic dissension among the Arcadians, with the opposing factions determining the issue by force of arms. Many were killed, and more than fourteen hundred fled the country, some to Sparta, others to Pallantion. [3] Now the latter were returned by the Pallantians to the victorious faction, who put them to death; but those who had taken refuge at Sparta persuaded the Spartans to invade Arcadia. So King Agesilaos, with an expeditionary force plus the fugitives, marched into the territory of the Tegeans, since they were held responsible for the civil war and the fate of the refugees. By despoiling the countryside and making assaults on the city, he thoroughly scared the Arcadians of the hostile faction.

15.60. [1] At the same time as these events, Jason, the tyrant of Pherai—a man of exceptional military intelligence, who had attracted many neighboring states into an alliance—persuaded the Thessalians to lay claim to hegemony over the Greeks, this being, as it were, a prize for excellence open to those strong enough to contend for it. [2] Now it so happened that the Lacedaemonians had suffered a crushing defeat at Leuctra, that the Athenians were only interested in achieving supremacy at sea, that the Thebans were not worthy of the highest rank, and that the Argives had been seriously weakened by factional discord and fratricidal mayhem. The Thessalians therefore made Jason their overall leader and military commander in chief. On assuming power, Jason won over some of the neighboring peoples and made an alliance with King Amyntas of Macedon.

[3] An odd thing happened this year: no less than three heads of state died at about the same time. Amyntas son of Arrhidaios, king of Macedon, died after a reign of twenty-four years, leaving three sons, Alexander, Perdiccas, and Philip. His son Alexander inherited the throne and ruled for one year.[a] [4] Similarly, the Lacedaemonian king Agesipolis passed away, after a year's reign, and was succeeded by his brother Kleomenes, who reigned for thirty-four years. [5] The third member of this trio, Jason of Pherai—who had been chosen as ruler of all Thessaly and was reputed to govern his subjects fairly—was assassinated: either, as Ephoros writes, by seven youths who conspired together in pursuit of fame or, according to some other writers, by his brother Polydoros, who succeeded him in the leadership and ruled for one year.

[6] Douris of Samos,[a] the historian, began his history of Greece at this point. These, then, were the events that took place during this year.

O.15.59.1a Lykomedes came from Mantineia, not Tegea, as Diodorus recognizes later at 15.62.2. Mantineia is also cited by Xenophon (*Hellenika* 7.1.23) and Pausanias 8.27.2. (Peter Green)

O.15.60.3a The Marmor Parium, a famous inscription dating from 264/3 (F. Jacoby, *Die Fragmente der griechischen Historiker* 239, F 72), plausibly dates Amyntas' death to 371/70 (archonship of Phrasikleides) and that of Alexander II to 368/7 (archonship of Nausigenes) which agrees with Diodorus Siculus. Alexander's one-year reign should thus probably be emended to two. (Peter Green)

O.15.60.6a Douris of Samos, c. 340–260, Greek historian (and tyrant of Samos) who wrote an annalistic history of Samos, and an account of Greece (Macedonia) from the battle of Leuctra (371) to the death of Lysimachus (281).

15.61. [1] When Lysistratos was archon in Athens . . . [2] . . . Polydoros of Pherai, who had been ruler of Thessaly, was poisoned at a drinking party to which he had been invited by his nephew Alexander.[a] This same nephew, Alexander, then assumed the leadership and held it for eleven years. Having acquired power illegally and by violence, he governed in accordance with this original mode of action. Whereas the dynasts before him had treated the common people reasonably and as a result were popular, his rule, being both harsh and violent, made him an object of hatred.

The Arcadian Appeal to Athens
15.62

[1] In the Peloponnese, the Lacedaemonians sent Polytropos as general to Arcadia, with a citizen levy of a thousand hoplites, together with five hundred Argive and Boeotian refugees. In Arcadia he made his way to Orchomenos and put this city under close guard, since it was well disposed toward the Spartans. [2] Lykomedes of Mantineia, the Arcadians' general, took command of their special *corps d'élite*, five thousand strong, and brought them to Orchomenos. As the Lacedaemonians led their forces out of the city, a violent battle took place, in which there perished about two hundred Lacedaemonians, their general included, while the remainder were chased back into the city. [3] Though the Arcadians had scored a victory, they still retained a nervous respect for Sparta's power and doubted whether they would be able to carry on a war with the Lacedaemonians single-handed. Accordingly, in association with the Argives and Eleians, they first sent an embassy to Athens, soliciting their alliance against the Spartans. When no one took up this request, they made diplomatic approaches to the Thebans and prevailed on them to set up an alliance against the Lacedaemonians. [4] So the Boeotians led out their forces at once, along with some Locrian and Phocian allies, and made for the Peloponnese. The Boeotarchs in command were Epaminondas and Pelopidas; the other Boeotarchs had readily ceded the command to them in recognition of their bravery and intelligence. [5] When they reached Arcadia, the Arcadians, Eleians, Argives, and other allies all came out in full force to join them. After more than fifty thousand had gathered, their leaders, meeting in council, decided to march on Sparta itself and to lay waste the whole of Laconia.

The First Theban Invasion of the Peloponnese
15.63–65.6

15.63. [1] The Lacedaemonians had seen many of their young men destroyed in the catastrophe at Leuctra, had lost not a few in their other defeats, and were, in

---

O.15.61.2a   Alexander of Pherai did not kill his uncle
                  Polydoros. He killed his uncle Polyphron in
                  revenge for Polyphron's murder of Alexander's father Polydoros.

short, reduced by misfortune to a mere handful of citizen soldiers. Since on top of this some of their allies had defected, while others were, for similar reasons, short of manpower, they were sinking into a state of chronic weakness. Because of this they were compelled to turn for help to the Athenians—the same people on whom, in days gone by, they had imposed the Thirty Tyrants, whose walls they had forbidden them to rebuild, whose city they had once planned to destroy utterly, leaving Attica as nothing but grazing land for sheep. [2] Yet nothing is stronger than necessity and fate, by which the Lacedaemonians were forced to beg help from their worst enemies. However, they were not disappointed in their hopes; for the Athenian people, with magnanimous generosity and unfazed by the power of Thebes, voted to come out in full force to the aid of the Lacedaemonians now that the latter were in danger of enslavement. They at once appointed Iphikrates general and sent him out that same day with a body of young draftees, twelve thousand strong. His troops were full of enthusiasm, and Iphikrates marched them at a cracking pace. [3] The Lacedaemonians, with the enemy moving into position on the Laconian frontier, set out from Sparta, likewise in full force, and advanced to meet their opponents, much reduced in military strength but resolutely courageous in spirit. [4] Epaminondas and his staff, realizing that the country of the Lacedaemonians was difficult terrain to penetrate, figured it would not be to their advantage to make their invasion with so large a force all in one body, and so decided to split it into four divisions, each of which would enter the country at a different point.

15.64. [1] The first division, that of the Boeotians, took the direct route to the city called Sellasia and induced its inhabitants to secede from the Lacedaemonians. [2] The Argives came in by the marches of Tegea, fought a battle with the garrison guarding the passes, and killed about two hundred of them, including the garrison commander, Alexander the Spartan, and the Boeotian refugees. [3] The third division, consisting of the Arcadians and containing the largest number of troops, struck into the region known as Skiritis. This was heavily guarded by a large garrison under one Ischolas, a man of outstanding courage and intelligence. A highly distinguished soldier himself, he now performed a heroic and memorable exploit. [4] He saw that, because of the enemy's vast numbers, all who engaged them in battle were going to be killed. To abandon his position in the pass would, he decided, be unworthy of Sparta; but at the same time to save soldiers would be useful to his country. In an unexpected manner he managed to achieve both ends, thus emulating the earlier courageous exploit of King Leonidas at Thermopylae. [5] For he picked out the young men and sent them back to Sparta to serve their country when its very survival was at stake; but he himself, together with the veterans, stayed on to guard his position. After slaying many of the enemy, they were encircled by the Arcadians and perished to the last man. [6] The Eleians, who formed the fourth division, made their way by other tracts of open country to Sellasia, this being the designated rendezvous for all of them. When the entire invasion force was assembled at Sellasia, they set out for Sparta itself, sacking and burning the countryside as they went.

15.65. [1] The Lacedaemonians, who for five hundred years had kept Laconia free from despoliation, on seeing it thus laid waste by the enemy, could not restrain themselves but were on the point of rushing out of the city in a transport of fury. However, they were stopped by the elders (who pointed out that if they rushed off into the outback, that left Sparta vulnerable to attack) and were persuaded to stay where they were and maintain the city's security. [2] Meanwhile Epaminondas and his troops crossed Taygetos,[a] came down into the Eurotas Valley, and began crossing the river, which was swollen and fast-flowing, it being the winter season. When the Lacedaemonians saw their adversaries in some disorder because of the difficulty of the crossing, they seized this propitious opportunity for an attack. Leaving the women and children, together with the elderly, to guard Sparta, they mustered every man of military age in battle order and rushed out en masse against the enemy. Falling upon them suddenly while they were still crossing, they slaughtered large numbers of them. [3] However, the Boeotians and the Arcadians defended themselves well and began to encircle their opponents by dint of superior numbers. At this point the Spartans—having given clear proof of their manly courage in the form of all the deaths they inflicted—returned to the city. [4] After this Epaminondas, with his entire force, launched a terrifying attack on the city. The Spartans, aided in their defense by the natural strength of the terrain, killed large numbers of their assailants as they rushed precipitately forward; but finally the besiegers, by bringing tremendous pressure to bear, for a little while convinced themselves that they had indeed conquered Sparta by main force. However, the losses sustained by the attackers in dead and wounded led Epaminondas to have his trumpeter sound the retreat. Even then individuals would approach the city and challenge the Spartans to meet them in a set battle or demand that they admit their inferiority to their enemies. [5] When the Spartans replied that, on finding the right moment, they would indeed fight a decisive battle, their challengers retired from the city. After ravaging the whole of Laconia and collecting a vast amount of booty, they went back to Arcadia.

[6] At this point the Athenians, who had shown up too late to help, returned to Attica without accomplishing anything noteworthy, but as many as four thousand troops came to the assistance of the Lacedaemonians from their various other allies. In addition to these they enlisted a thousand recently emancipated helots and two hundred of the Boeotian refugees. They also called on not a few of the neighboring cities and thus began to assemble a force that was a match for that of their enemies. They kept and trained this as a single corps, steadily gaining confidence and readying themselves for the decisive struggle.

O.15.65.2a   The idea that Epaminondas and his army, after fighting an engagement at Sellasia, in the foothills of the Parnon mountain range north of Sparta, would then descend into the Eurotas Valley by crossing the Taygetos mountain range is topographical nonsense, since Taygetos lies directly west of the valley. (Peter Green)

The Theban Establishment of Messene
15.66.1

[1] Epaminondas—whose nature drove him to lofty endeavors and the pursuit of eternal fame—advised the Arcadians and his other allies to resettle Messene, for many years left in ruins by the Lacedaemonians, and a site admirably placed for attacks on Sparta. When they all agreed, he hunted out the surviving Messenians, enrolled as citizens any others who volunteered, and refounded Messene, by these methods providing it with numerous colonists. He divided the land up between them, restored the buildings, and thus recovered a notable Greek city from oblivion. By this act he won universal approbation.

Epaminondas' Second Invasion
15.68–70.2

15.68. [1] It was after these events that the Arcadians, the Argives, and the Eleians, by common accord, determined to make an expedition against the Lacedaemonians. They then sent an embassy to the Boeotians and persuaded them take part in this campaign. They appointed Epaminondas commander, along with some other Boeotarchs, and fielded an army of seven thousand foot and six hundred horse. The Athenians, on learning that the Boeotian army was on its way to the Peloponnese, dispatched a force against them, under the command of Chabrias. [2] He made his way to Corinth, where he enlisted more troops from Megara and Pellene, as well as Corinthians, thus bringing his numbers up to ten thousand. When, after this, the Lacedaemonians and the rest of the allies gathered in Corinth, the total count was not less than twenty thousand. [3] They therefore decided to fortify all points of access and deny the Boeotians entry to the Peloponnese. From Kenchreai to Lechaion they cut off the region with palisades and deep ditches; and since the number of enthusiastic workers available enabled them to complete this project in short order, they had the entire region fortified before the Boeotians got there.

[4] When Epaminondas arrived with his force, he made an inspection and noted that the easiest point of access was that where the Lacedaemonians were on guard. So to begin with, he challenged the enemy to a pitched battle, though they were almost three times his number. When none of the enemy were bold enough to advance beyond the line of defense but all sat tight behind their palisades, he launched an all-out attack on them. [5] Violent assaults were carried out all along the line, against the Lacedaemonians in particular, since their section was easy to get at and hard to defend. Both sides manifested intense rivalry. Epaminondas, accompanied by Thebes' bravest warriors, finally managed to drive the Lacedaemonians back. He then broke their defense line, led his forces through the gap, and so entered the Peloponnese, an achievement no whit inferior to any of his previous exploits.

15.69. [1] He made straight for Troizen and Epidauros, where he laid waste the countryside but failed to reduce the cities themselves, since they were strongly garrisoned. Nevertheless, Sicyon and Phleious and some other cities he scared into transferring their allegiance to him. He then marched against Corinth. When the Corinthians came out against him, he defeated them in battle and drove them back inside their walls. The Boeotians were so elated by their success that some of them recklessly forced their way through the gates and into the city. The Corinthians, in alarm, took refuge in their houses. Chabrias, the Athenian general, however, in a counterattack as clever as it was courageous, forced these Boeotians back out of the city, killing large numbers of them. [2] A fiercely disputed conflict ensued. The Boeotians, mustering all their resources, launched a terrifying assault on Corinth; but Chabrias brought his Athenians out of the city, took up a position on high ground, and resisted the enemy's attack. [3] The Boeotians, relying on their physical strength and the experience gained in a series of campaigns, counted on overcoming the Athenians by main force, while Chabrias and his men—the higher terrain giving them an edge in the struggle, and helped by abundant supplies from the city—killed some of their assailants and incapacitated others. [4] After suffering heavy losses and having failed to accomplish anything, the Boeotians beat a retreat. In this way Chabrias wore down his opponents and won a great reputation for courage and military acumen.

15.70. [1] Two thousand Celts and Iberians sailed from Sicily to Corinth, sent by the tyrant Dionysios, with five months' pay, to fight as allies of the Lacedaemonians. The Greeks, wanting to test their abilities, sent them into action. In both individual combat and pitched battles they performed valiantly, and many of the Boeotians and their allies were killed by them. So they acquired a reputation for outstanding swordsmanship and courage, carried out many useful services, and at the end of the summer were duly rewarded by the Lacedaemonians and sent back to Sicily. [2] Afterward Philiskos sailed to Greece on a mission for King Artaxerxes, calling on the Greeks to put an end to their wars and conclude a common peace. Everyone gladly agreed to this proposal except for the Thebans, who, in accordance with their own plan, had brought all Boeotia into one private tributary league subject to them and were therefore excluded. With the common peace thus failing to win general acceptance, Philiskos left the Lacedaemonians two thousand top-class mercenaries, paid in advance, and went back to Asia.

The Tearless Battle and the Foundation of Megalopolis
15.72.3–4

[3] Shortly afterward a great battle was fought between the Lacedaemonians and the Arcadians, in which the Lacedaemonians scored a notable victory. This was their first success after the defeat at Leuctra, and a surprising one, since there fell more than ten thousand Arcadians but of the Lacedaemonians not a single man. The priestesses at Dodona had predicted to the latter that this would be a "tearless war" for the Lacedaemonians. [4] After the battle the Arcadians, scared by the prospect

of Lacedaemonian invasions, picked a good location and there founded the so-called Great City [Megalopolis]. To create it, they amalgamated [the populations of] twenty villages from the Arcadian regions of Mainalia and Parrasia.

Oropos and the Peace of 366/5
15.76.1, 15.76.3

[1] When the year had run its course, in Athens Kephisodoros became archon.... While [he was] in office, Themesion, tyrant of Eretria, seized Oropos. This city, a dependency of Athens, he then lost in an improbable manner: for when the Athenians marched against him with a greatly superior force, the Thebans came to his assistance and took over the city in trust, but failed to give it back. . . .

[3] At the same time the Persian King sent a mission that persuaded the Greeks to put an end to their wars and conclude a common peace among themselves. In this way the so-called Spartan-Boeotian War was finally terminated, having lasted more than five years from its beginning at the battle of Leuctra.

The Arcadia-Elis War
15.77.1–4, 15.78.1–3

15.77. [1] When Chion was archon in Athens . . . peace did indeed prevail throughout Greece, though in some cities the first excuses for war once more appeared, as did surprising new forms of revolutionary activity. The Arcadian exiles, for example, starting out from their base in Elis, took over a stronghold called Lasion in the district of Triphylia. [2] For many years now the Arcadians and Eleians had been laying rival claim to Triphylia, and as each in turn got the upper hand, they ruled the district alternately. At the time in question it was the Arcadians who had control over Triphylia; but the Eleians, using the refugees as their excuse, now wrested it from them. [3] The Arcadians were furious. They first sent ambassadors to demand the return of the district. When no one took any notice, they sent for allied support from Athens and, when they got it, marched against Lasion. The Eleians came to the aid of the refugees, and a battle took place near Lasion. Since the Arcadians had a far larger force, the Eleians were defeated, losing more than two hundred men. [4] This was how the war started, but the dissension between Arcadians and Eleians soon became more serious. Elated by their success, the Arcadians at once launched a campaign against Elis and took the cities of Margana and Kronion,[a] followed by Kyparissia and Koryphasion. . . .

15.78. [1] When Timokrates was archon in Athens . . . the 104th Olympiad, at which an Athenian, Phocides, won the *stadion*, was celebrated by the Pisans and Arcadians. [2] While he was in office, the Pisans, by recalling their country's high reputation in ancient times and presenting evidence from mythic tradition, tried to prove that the privilege of holding the Olympic festival belonged to them. In the belief that

O.15.77.4a   Kronion is not a city but the hill of Kronos
                 above Olympia, as it is identified by
                 Xenophon at 7.4.14.

they now had an excellent opportunity to assert their rights in this matter, they struck up an alliance with the Arcadians, who were the Eleians' enemies. With these as their fellow combatants, they marched against the Eleians, then actually holding the games.[a] [3] The Eleians put all their forces in the field to resist them, and a fierce battle took place, witnessed by all the Greeks who were at the games as spectators. There they sat, comfortably out of danger, wreaths on their heads, applauding both sides' feats of bravery. In the end the Pisans won and proceeded with the celebration of the games. Later, however, the Eleians left this Olympiad out of the official record, on the grounds that it had been held illegally and by force.

Epaminondas and Sea Power; The Reduction of Orchomenos 15.78.4–79.6

15.78. [4] At the same time as these events, Epaminondas the Theban, whose reputation among his fellow citizens was of the highest, made a speech at a meeting of the Assembly in which he urged them to make a serious bid for supremacy at sea. In the course of his argument (which he had pondered over a long period) he tried to show that such a project was both advantageous and attainable, alleging, among other things, that it was easy for those in power on land also to establish their mastery at sea. The Athenians, for instance, in the war against Xerxes, had manned two hundred triremes from their own resources, yet were under the command of the Lacedaemonians, who furnished ten only. By presenting this and many other arguments germane to his theme in his speech, he persuaded the Thebans to strive for naval supremacy.

15.79. [1] So the people voted on the spot to build one hundred triremes and a corresponding number of ship sheds[a] and to urge the citizens of Rhodos, Chios, and Byzantium to collaborate with them in their plans. Epaminondas himself was sent out with a force to these aforementioned cities. Meanwhile Laches, the Athenian general, had been dispatched with a considerable fleet to obstruct Theban activity. Epaminondas scared him into sailing away and brought the cities over to the side of Thebes. [2] If this man had lived longer, it is generally agreed, the Thebans would certainly have acquired supremacy at sea in addition to their hegemony on land. But it was not to be long before he died heroically, after securing a most brilliant victory for his country at Mantineia; and with his death the affairs of Thebes likewise suffered instant eclipse. But these matters we shall discuss more fully a little later, in their proper place.

[3] It was also now that the Thebans determined, for the following reasons, to

O.15.78.2a Almost all scholars think that this is the wrong way around: that, as Xenophon has it (7.4.28–32), the Pisans were conducting the games with Arcadian support when the Eleians attacked them and were eventually beaten off. Most scholars think it is an error by Diodorus himself rather than a rival tradition to Xenophon, as Diodorus 15.77.4 shows that the Arcadians were in occupation of Kronion at Olympia.

O.15.79.1a "Ship sheds" is an emendation (*neōsoikous*)

for "dockyards/naval bases" (*neōria*) of Diodorus' manuscripts. Since we know (Lionel Casson, *Ships and Seamanship in the Ancient World*, Princeton University Press, 1971, p. 363; Demosthenes 14.22) the exact distinction between the two, and that one *neōrion* could normally accommodate thirty triremes, the setting up of an equal number of *neōria* and ships is evident nonsense. What Diodorus had in mind was *neōsoikous*: one ship, one ship shed. (Peter Green)

make an expedition against Orchomenus. A group of refugees who wanted to change Thebes' political system to an aristocracy persuaded the cavaliers of Orchomenus, three hundred in number, to join their plot. [4] These men, alone among the Thebans, were in the habit, on a regular appointed day, of meeting for an armed exercise, and they agreed to use this occasion to carry out the attack. So, along with many others who had hastened to join the undertaking, they kept the rendezvous at the appointed time. [5] Now the originators of the scheme had had a change of heart and revealed their plot to the Boeotarchs, thus betraying their fellow conspirators and, by this public service, contriving to save their own skins. The authorities arrested these cavaliers of Orchomenus and brought them before the Assembly, where the people voted to execute them, to reduce the population of Orchomenus to slavery, and to demolish their city. For ever since ancient times the Thebans had been on bad terms with them, paying tribute to the Minyans in the heroic age till they were liberated later by Herakles. [6] The Thebans, then, regarded this as a fine opportunity. Now that they had a plausible excuse for exacting retribution, they marched against Orchomenus, captured the city, killed all the men, and sold the women and children into slavery.

The Campaign and Battle of Mantineia
15.82–89.2

15.82. [1] When this year had run its course, in Athens Charikleides became archon. . . . While [he was] in office, the Arcadians, in conjunction with the Pisans, ran the Olympic Games; they also had control of the sanctuary and the treasures in it.[a] Since the Mantineians had abstracted not a few of the offerings for their personal use, they were eager—being criminally liable—for the war against Elis to drag on, in order to avoid having to give an accounting of their expenditures with the return of peace.[b] [2] But peace was what the rest of the Arcadians wanted, so the Mantineians raised a faction against their fellow countrymen. Two rival groups came into being, one headed by Tegea, the other by Mantineia. [3] Their differences became so intense that they resorted to a decision by arms. The Tegeans sent ambassadors to the Boeotians and prevailed on them to send Tegea assistance: the Boeotians appointed Epaminondas general, gave him a sizable force, and sent him to reinforce the Tegeans. [4] The Mantineians, intimidated by this force from Boeotia—and by Epaminondas' reputation—sent ambassadors to the Boeotians' worst enemies, the Athenians and Lacedaemonians, and persuaded them to join the fight on their side. Both peoples quickly sent them large contingents, and as a result, a number of major engagements were fought in the Peloponnese.

[5] Thus the Lacedaemonians, being near neighbors, immediately marched into Arcadia. At the same time Epaminondas, advancing with his army, was not far from Mantineia. The local inhabitants informed him that the Lacedaemonians were out in

O.15.82.1a Peter Green argues that it is not impossible, given the chaos and turmoil of 364, the 104th Olympiad year, that the Pisans and Arcadians did indeed try to celebrate the games illegally in the following year, 363/2.
O.15.82.1b By contrast, Xenophon (7.4.33–35) says the

Mantineians *objected* to the misappropriation of temple funds by other Arcadians who were, therefore, desperate for the war against Elis to continue.

full force, ravaging the territory of Tegea. [6] Deducing from this that Sparta had been left without troops, he planned a major coup. Luck, however, was working against him. He set out by night on a fast march to Sparta; but the Lacedaemonian king Agis[a] was on his guard against Epaminondas' clever tricks and shrewdly figured out what he meant to do. He therefore dispatched some Cretan runners, by means of whom he stole a march on Epaminondas, alerting those left in Sparta to the imminent arrival of the Boeotians in Lacedaemon to sack the city and promising that he himself and his army would get there as fast as he possibly could to succor his country in this crisis. His instructions to those in Sparta were to keep watchful guard over the city and not to panic, since he would very soon be there to reinforce them.

15.83. [1] The Cretans carried out their orders with due dispatch, and so the Lacedaemonians, most improbably, managed to avert the occupation of their country: for had his plan of attack not been revealed in advance, Epaminondas' raid on Sparta would have come as a complete surprise. So while both generals deserve praise for their ingenuity, we should rate the Lacedaemonian's military acumen higher. [2] We may concede the fact that Epaminondas, by staying up all night and force-marching the entire way, reached Sparta by daybreak. But Agesilaos, who had been left behind on guard and had been alerted by the Cretan runners only a short while previously, had at once, with great energy, set about organizing the city's defenses. [3] He placed the oldest children and the elderly on the rooftops, with instructions to use their position to repulse the attackers if they forced their way into the city. The men of military age he assembled and distributed among the various natural strongholds and approaches. After thus barricading every possible way of access, he awaited the enemy's attack.

[4] Epaminondas divided his troops into several assault groups and began a simultaneous coordinated attack at all points; but when he saw the disposition of the Spartans, he knew at once that his plan of action had been discovered. Nevertheless, though he encountered a vigorous defense at every position and was at a disadvantage because of the site's natural strengths, he still launched his direct assault. [5] He took some hard knocks, gave as good as he got, and refused to abandon his daring scheme until the Lacedaemonian army returned to Sparta. Then, however, the size of the relief force and the approach of night compelled him to give up the attack.

15.84. [1] On learning from his prisoners that the Mantineians had arrived in full force to help the Lacedaemonians, he promptly retired a short distance from the city, pitched camp, and arranged dinner for his troops. Then, leaving behind a small cavalry detachment with orders to keep campfires burning till the morning watch, he himself set out with the rest of the army, in a hurry to make a surprise attack on those left to guard Mantineia. [2] Next day, after a lengthy march, he made a sudden, and unexpected, descent on the Mantineians. Yet although his plan had made allowance for every possibility, he did not achieve his aim. Fate was working against

O.15.82.6a Diodorus (or his manuscripts' tradition) is in error here. He substitutes a nonexistent Agis for Agesilaos at 15.82.6 and has Agesilaos himself left behind as Sparta's defender. But from other sources we know that it was Agesilaos who commanded the Lacedaemonian army and that he had already left Sparta with it, though he had not gone far when he learned of Epaminondas' plan and so got back to Sparta in time to save the city. It was his son Archidamos (Xenophon's *Hellenika* 7.5.12) who had stayed behind as garrison commander. (Peter Green)

him, and so, unexpectedly, victory eluded his grasp. Just as he was approaching the nearly defenseless city, there arrived on the far side of Mantineia the relief force sent by the Athenians, six thousand men under the command of Hegelochos, a man well thought of by his fellow citizens. He brought this strong force into the city and drew up the rest of the defense force with a view to determining the issue by force of arms. [3] At this point the Lacedaemonians and the Mantineians showed up, too, and everyone readied themselves for a decisive conflict, summoning their allies from all around. [4] The Mantineians had the support of the Eleians, the Lacedaemonians, the Athenians, and some others, their total complement being more than twenty thousand foot and about two thousand horse. There fought beside the Tegeans the larger part (and those the best) of the Arcadians, as well as the Achaeans, the Boeotians, the Argives, and some others, allies from the Peloponnese and elsewhere. The full number assembled consisted of more than thirty thousand foot and not less than three thousand horse.

15.85. [1] Both sides immediately tried to move into an advantageous position for this decisive struggle. When they were drawn up in battle formation, the seers on both sides, after making sacrifice, declared that victory had been foretold by the gods. [2] The order of battle was as follows. The Mantineians and the other Arcadians formed the right wing, with the Lacedaemonians stationed beside them as their fellow combatants. Next to the Lacedaemonians were the Eleians and Achaeans, while the weaker of the remaining forces occupied the rest of the line. The left wing was held by the Athenians. [On the other side,] the Thebans themselves were drawn up on the left wing, with the Arcadians stationed beside them. The right wing they entrusted to the Argives, while the center was filled en masse by all the other contingents—Euboeans, Locrians, Sicyonians, Messenians, Malians, Ainianians, Thessalians, and the rest of the allies. Both sides divided their cavalry, placing squadrons on each wing. [3] This was the order of battle for the two armies. As they drew near each other trumpets sounded the charge and both sides raised their war cry, trying to outshout each other as a guarantee of victory. The battle began with a hotly contested engagement between the cavalry on either flank. [4] The Athenian horsemen attacked those of Thebes and got the worst of it. This was not because of the quality of their mounts, nor through any personal failure of morale or lack of experience as riders, in none of which areas was the Athenian cavalry deficient. Where the Athenians were far inferior to their adversaries was in the numbers and equipment—not to mention the tactical expertise—of their light-armed troops. They themselves had only a few javelin-men, whereas the Thebans had three times as many, slingers as well as javelin-men, recruited from various regions of Thessaly. [5] These men trained assiduously from boyhood in their special type of warfare, so that their skilled experience more often than not played a decisive role in battles. Thus it was that the Athenians, because of the numerous wounds they suffered at the hands of these light-armed troops, were overwhelmed by their opponents and all turned and fled. [6] Nevertheless, after retreating beyond the two wings, they managed to retrieve their setback, since even in retreat their formation remained unbroken. Thus when they encountered some Euboeans and mercenaries who had been sent to occupy a nearby line of hills, they joined battle with them and killed them all. [7] The Theban cavalry did not pursue the fugitives but instead attacked the infantry phalanx opposite them, making a heroic effort to outflank it. A close-fought engagement took place, in which the Athenians were overwhelmed and took to flight; but then the Eleian cavalry commander, who was stationed at the rear, came to the aid of the fugitives, killed large numbers of Boeotians, and turned the tide of battle. [8] In this way, then, the appearance on the left wing of the Eleian cavalry reversed the setback their allies had suffered. On the other wing, however, there was a violent clash between cavalry units, and for a short while the battle hung in the balance; but then, because of the numbers and prowess of the Boeotian and Thessalian horsemen, the Mantineians and their supporters were forced to retreat, with heavy losses, and fell back on their own [infantry] phalanx.

15.86. [1] Such, then, was the result for each side of the cavalry engagement. But when the infantry met their opponents in hand-to-hand conflict, they embarked on a titanic and astounding struggle. Never before in a battle of Greeks against Greeks were such vast numbers of men involved, nor did leaders in higher esteem or more powerful warriors ever display such bravery in action. [2] It was the very finest infantrymen of those days—those of the Boeotians and Lacedaemonians, whose lines were opposite each other—who first joined battle, with utter disregard for their own lives. They began by using their spears on each other, and the blows fell so thick and fast that most of them were broken, after which they fought on with swords. [3] Body hard against body, they inflicted all manner of wounds on one another, yet their proud spirit would not let them give up. Thus for a long time the supreme courage displayed on both sides made them persist in this frightful struggle, with the result that the battle continued to hang in the balance, for each man was indifferent to personal risk and desperate to perform some brilliant deed of valor, nobly accepting death for the sake of glory.

[4] After the battle had raged for a long while without either side gaining a clear advantage, Epaminondas, suspecting that victory would require a personal display of courage on his part, made up his mind to force the issue. He therefore immediately assembled the pick of his troops, drew them up in close formation, and charged with them into the midst of the enemy. He not only led the charge but was the first to throw his javelin, hitting the Lacedaemonian commander. [5] Then, as the rest of his men quickly joined in the hand-to-hand fighting, by killing some and spreading panic among others he cut his way through the enemy phalanx. The Lacedaemonians, intimidated by Epaminondas' great prestige and the sheer impact of the contingent surrounding him, withdrew from the battle. The Boeotians, however, pressed hard on their heels, killing those in the rearguard, so that a great mass of corpses piled up.

15.87. [1] But when the Lacedaemonians saw Epaminondas, transported by passion, pressing his attack too rashly, they made a concerted attack on him. The target of dense volleys of missiles, he dodged some, caught others on his shield, even plucked some from his body and used them to defend himself against his attackers. But while thus engaged in a heroic struggle for victory, he took a fatal wound in his chest. The spear broke off short, leaving its iron head in his body; the wound robbed him of all strength, and he at once collapsed. A violent struggle took place over his body, with many casualties on both sides. Finally, with a huge effort, and by dint of their superior physical strength, the Thebans overwhelmed the Lacedaemonians. [2] A rout took place, but after pursuing the fugitives for a short while, the Boeotians turned back, in the belief that recovering the bodies of the dead had top priority. So trumpeters sounded the retreat, and both sides, abandoning the struggle, proceeded to set up trophies claiming victory. [3] Now the Athenians had indeed defeated the Euboeans and mercenaries guarding the hills and remained in possession of the dead, while the Boeotians, similarly, awarded themselves the victory after having overpowered the Lacedaemonians and being left as masters of the fallen. [4] For some time, then, neither side sent representatives to discuss the recovery of the dead, to avoid giving the impression of conceding defeat. But eventually the Lacedaemonians made the first move and sent a herald to ask for the recovery of their dead; and after that both sides buried their own fallen.

[5] Epaminondas was carried back to camp still alive, and doctors were summoned. When they gave it as their opinion that the moment the spearhead was extracted from his chest, death would undoubtedly ensue, he ended his life in the most courageous fashion. [6] First he sent for his squire and asked him if he had saved his shield. When the squire said he had, and placed it where he could see it, Epaminondas asked him another question: which side had won? On the boy's responding that the Boeotians were the victors, he said, "Then it's time to die," and ordered the spearhead to be pulled out. At this the friends gathered around him cried out in protest, and one of them exclaimed, in tears, "You're dying childless, Epaminondas." "Not so, by Zeus," said he. "I leave behind two daughters named Victoria—one for Leuctra, the other for Mantineia." Then the spearhead was removed, and quietly, without any fuss, he breathed his last.

15.88. [1] We have always made a practice, at the demise of great men, of bestowing on them such praise as is proper in each case. Thus we feel it would be most inappropriate to leave the death of such a man as this unnoticed. For in my opinion Epaminondas excelled his contemporaries not only in military acumen and experience but also in decency and magnanimity. [2] The generation of Epaminondas included many other famous men: Pelopidas the Theban; Timotheos, Konon,[a]

O.15.88.2a Konon is of course of the earlier generation
            (coeval with Agesilaos), as Diodorus
            knows perfectly well. Peter Green thinks
            that the Greek could very easily be cor-
            rected (reflecting scribal eye slippage) to
            read, in translation: "Timotheos, Chabrias,
            and Iphikrates from Athens, not to men-
            tion (at a slightly earlier period) Agesilaos
            the Spartan and Konon the Athenian."

Chabrias, and Iphikrates from Athens; not to mention (in a slightly earlier period) Agesilaos the Spartan. From a previous generation, in the critical days of the Medes and Persians, we may single out, among the Athenians, Solon, Themistokles, and Miltiades, followed by Kimon, Myronides, Perikles, and some others, and in Sicily a group including Gelon son of Deinomenes. [3] Nevertheless, if one were to compare these men's merits with the prestige and military expertise of Epaminondas, one would find the latter's achievements far superior. In each of the others one would discover a single talent only to justify their reputation, whereas in him all talents were combined. For in physical strength and subtlety of argument, not to mention brilliance of mind, contempt for money, decent moderation, and—most important of all—military courage and skill, he far outstripped all of them. [4] Consequently, his country achieved hegemony over Greece while he lived but lost it after his death, when things went steadily from bad to worse, till finally, because of the folly of its leaders, it came to experience enslavement and annihilation. This, then, was how Epaminondas, a man of universally recognized achievement, ended his life.

15.89. [1] After this battle the Greeks—who all claimed a disputed victory and had proved themselves evenly matched in prowess, but at the same time were exhausted by the succession of battles they had fought—ended the conflict and made peace with one another. They established a common peace and alliance, and in this alliance included the Messenians. [2] The Lacedaemonians, however, on account of their irreconcilable differences with these last, refused, because of the Messenians, to be a signatory to the treaty and were the only Greeks to remain excluded from it.

BOOK XVI SELECTIONS

Philip of Macedon Battles the Phocians
16.35

[1] After this Philip went into Thessaly with his army, at the invitation of the Thessalians.[a] His first action taken in support of them was to carry on the campaign against Lykophron, tyrant of Pherai. Thereupon Lykophron appealed for aid to his allies the Phocians, who sent him seven thousand men under Phaÿllos, the brother of Onomarchos. Philip, however, defeated these Phocians and drove them out of Thessaly. [2] Onomarchos himself now mustered his entire military strength and—in the belief that he would become master of all Thessaly—hurried to the assistance of Lykophron and his supporters. Philip and the Thessalians together met the Pho-

O.16.35.1a The statement by Diodorus that Philip was invited by the Thessalians to attack Lykophron, the tyrant of Pherai, provides significant information by which we can date the completion of Xenophon's *Hellenika*. This is so because at 6.4.37, Xenophon wrote that Tisiphonus succeeded Jason as tyrant of Pherai and that he remained in power *"up to the time that this narrative was written" (italics added)*. Thus, whenever Lykophron (who succeeded Tisiphonus) became tyrant, the *Hellenika* narrative must have been complete and in final form. There is some disagreement about the date of Diodorus' statement; in *The Cambridge Ancient History*, the Thessalian invitation to Philip occurred in the spring of 353, but the translator here, Peter Green, prefers August 353, as Diodorus recounts these events under the archon year 353/2. Whichever is correct, we can be confident that the *Hellenika* was finished sometime in the first half of the year 353 or earlier, but not later. (R.B.S.)

cians in battle. Onomarchos, with the numerical advantage, beat them twice and inflicted heavy casualties on the Macedonians. As a result, Philip found himself reduced to desperate straits. His troops' morale was so low that they had begun to desert him, and he barely managed to restore order among them by a fighting speech to the rank and file. [3] After this Philip withdrew into Macedonia, while Onomarchos invaded Boeotia, fought and defeated the Boeotians, and captured the city of Coronea. Soon after returning from Macedonia to Thessaly with his army, Philip marched against Lykophron, tyrant of Pherai. [4] Lykophron, being no match for him, appealed for support to his allies the Phocians, promising that he and they would share the running of affairs in Thessaly. This brought Onomarchos hurrying to his aid with twenty thousand foot and five hundred horse. Philip, meanwhile, having persuaded the Thessalians to fight this campaign at his side, mustered a combined force of more than twenty thousand foot and three thousand horse. [5] A hard-fought battle took place, which—through the greater numbers and courage of the Thessalian cavalry—Philip won. Onomarchos and his men fled toward the sea, where, by pure chance, Chares the Athenian was sailing by with a large fleet of triremes. The result was a massacre of the Phocians, since the fugitives, Onomarchos among them, stripped off their armor and tried to swim out to the triremes. [6] In the end more than six thousand Phocians and mercenaries were killed, the general among them, and at least three thousand taken prisoner. Philip hanged Onomarchos and shot the rest as temple robbers.

APPENDIX P

Selected Fragments of the *Hellenica Oxyrhynchia* Relevant to Xenophon's *Hellenika*

Translated by John Marincola*

Thrasyllos' Attack on Ephesus,* 410 or 409
Fragment 1

[1] . . . to attack the walls . . . the majority of the triremes . . . the rest, a place in the territory of Ephesus. . . . Having disembarked his entire force, he led them toward the city. . . . But the Ephesians and those of the Spartans[a] . . . did not see the Athenian forces commanded by Pasion,[b] since they happened to be still far off and taking a longer way on their march than the others. They did see, however, those commanded by Thrasyllos who were now nearly upon them. They met them at the harbor that is known as Koressos, and they had with them as allies those who had brought assistance . . . and . . . the most trustworthy . . . and those who live in the Kilbian [?][c] plain.

[2] After this, Thrasyllos,[a] the Athenian general, came to the city and left some of the soldiers to prosecute the siege, while he himself led others to the hill, which is high and difficult to climb. And some within the city and some outside were compelled to flee. Timarchos[b] and Possikrates were in command of the Ephesians. . . .

Fragment 2

[1] . . . toward strong places . . . and fled toward them, and he led the army forward. And since the enemy were fleeing, the Athenians eagerly pursued, in order that they

P* These selected passages have been translated by John Marincola from the papyrus fragments published in M. Chambers, ed., *Hellenica Oxyrhynchia* (Stuttgart and Leipzig: Teubner, 1993). See the Introduction, §7.1–8. The many ellipses in the text reflect the torn and ragged condition of the two-thousand-year-old papyrus. Some words have to be extrapolated from a few letters, the context, and the size of the spaces between extant words. See Figure Intro. 7.2 for an example.

P.1* See 1.2.6–11 and Appendix O, Selections from the

Histories of Diodorus Siculus Relevant to Xenophon's *Hellenika*, 13.64.1.
P.1.1a Neither Xenophon nor Diodorus mentions the presence of Spartans at this battle.
P.1.1b Pasion is not otherwise known. It has been suggested that the text should read "Pasiphon," as a man by that name in 409 was general at Samos.
P.1.1c "Kilbian" is a proposed modern emendation.
P.1.2a See 1.1.33–34.
P.1.2b Diodorus mentions Timarchos as an Athenian commander; see Appendix O, 13.65.1.

might take the city by force. But Timarchos and Possikrates, the commanders of the Ephesians, summoned their own hoplites. When the Athenians were at hand. . . . [fourteen lines follow, only partially readable.]

[2] Now all those who retreated by the road leading to the sea were transported safely away, while many of those who took the upper road were destroyed. . . .

The Battle between the Athenians
and the Megarians at "the Horns,"* 409
Fragment 4

[1] . . . The Spartans . . . immediately retreated in formation to the hills. The Athenian soldiers did not pursue these, but following after the Megarians . . . of the road that leads to the city, and they struck down a great number of them. After this they ravaged the land, gave back under truce the corpses of the Megarians and of the twenty or so Spartans who had also been killed, and set up a trophy. Having taken these actions, they went home.

[2] When the Athenians learned what had happened in the battle, they grew angry with the generals[a] and they were annoyed because they thought that the generals had rashly incurred danger and risked the safety of the city on a throw of the dice; but they were greatly delighted with the victory, for, as it happened, this was the first time they had defeated the Spartans since the battle at Pylos.[b] . . .

The Battle of Notion,* 406
Fragment 8

[1] . . . having manned the ten best-sailing triremes, he[a] ordered the other triremes to lie in wait for these, until the enemy's ships had sailed out far from the land. He himself with the ten ships made for Ephesus . . . intending to draw them on. [2] As soon as Lysander spied them . . . three ships . . . the very ones that formerly . . . they sunk Antiochos . . . and they destroy. . . . Those of the Athenians . . . immediately . . . toward the. . . .

Lysander, however, taking up all his triremes, pursued the enemy. [3] When the rest of the Athenians saw that the Spartans had gone off and were pursuing their contingent of ten ships, they immediately went onboard their ships and hastened to bring help to the ships that were being pursued. But they could not man all their triremes before the enemy were swiftly upon them; the majority of the ships, however, managed to sail a short way out from the harbor of Colophon . . . and those

P.4*   "The Horns" (*ta kerata*) were the hills opposite the island of Salamis on the border between Athens and Megara. This incident is not reported by Xenophon; but see Diodorus 13.65.1–2 (Appendix O), which is most likely dependent on the Oxyrhynchus Historian.
P.4.2a   The generals were Leotrophides and Timarchos.
P.4.2b   "Pylos" is a restoration, though a likely one; the battle of Pylos, a great Athenian success in the

Archidamian War, occurred in 425: see Thucydides 4.3ff. Since the Athenians had defeated the Spartans at sea, the author is clearly referring to the first land victory of the Athenians over the Spartans since Pylos.
P.8*   For descriptions of this battle, see 1.5.12–14, and Appendix O, 13.71.2–4.
P.8.1a   "He" refers to Antiochos, who had been left in charge by Alcibiades: see 1.5.11.

ships sailing by . . . while they themselves, being thrown into disarray, . . . and because of their lack of formation, they fled before the enemy.

The Spartans, seeing the Athenians in flight, turned to the attack and destroyed [number missing] of them and captured twenty-two; the rest they towed to Notion. [4] When they had done this and set up a trophy by the harbor of the city, they sailed back to Ephesus.[a] The Athenians for the present did nothing, but when two or three days had passed, they attended to. . . .

The Expedition of Demainetos *
Fragment 9

[1] Around this same time, a trireme sailed out from Athens without the authorization of the people. Demainetos was in command of it;[a] he had revealed his plan in a secret meeting of the Council (so it is said), and when some of the citizens supported his plan, he brought them down to the Peiraieus, took a ship from the dockyards, and put to sea, intending to sail to Konon.[b] [2] Thereafter a commotion arose; the wealthy and educated classes were greatly vexed and claimed that the Athenians would destroy their city by beginning a war with the Spartans. The members of the Council were frightened by the commotion and summoned the people, pretending that they had had no share in Demainetos' business. When the multitude was gathered together,[a] the followers of Thrasyboulos, Aisimos, and Anytos[b] arose and told the citizens that they would be incurring a great danger if they did not absolve the city of responsibility for Demainetos' actions.

[3] Now those Athenians who were moderate and had property[a] were pleased with the present political situation. The masses and the popular leaders at this particular time were afraid and therefore obeyed those who had given advice; they sent to Milon, the harmost of Aegina,[b] and told him to take whatever vengeance he could on Demainetos, since the latter had acted without authorization from the city. Yet in nearly all the time before this event, those same elements were trying to disturb the present state of affairs and had often worked against the Spartans.

P.8.4a   "Ephesus" is conjectured by Chambers.
P.9*   This secret mission of Demainetos is not treated by Xenophon or any other historian; the date could be either winter 397/6 or spring 396.
P.9.1a   Demainetos' official capacity when he sails to Konon in 396/5 is not known. He is mentioned by Xenophon (*Hellenika* 5.1.10, 5.1.26) as an Athenian general in 388/7 and in 387/6 (generals could be reelected each year).
P.9.1b   Konon had been one of the Athenian commanders in the final battle of the Peloponnesian War at Aigospotamoi, but had escaped when the Athenians were defeated (2.1.28) and fled to King Evagoras of Cyprus. He hoped to revive Persian naval power and defeat the Spartans, and he accomplished this three years after the current events, in 394, at Cnidus. At the present time he was based in Caunus.

P.9.2a   That is, when an assembly of the Athenians had been called.
P.9.2b   Moderate democrats, all three men were prominent opponents of the Thirty at Athens in 404/3. Thrasyboulos is often mentioned in *Hellenika*, beginning at 1.1.12. Aisimos may have been general in 403 when he led the men of the Peiraieus back to Athens at the conclusion of the armistice (he is not mentioned in the *Hellenika*). Anytos was general in 409/8 and later exiled by the Thirty (2.3.42).
P.9.3a   Probably the same people described at Fragment 9.2 as the "wealthy and educated."
P.9.3b   Aeschines 2.78 speaks of a sea battle in which Demainetos defeated a Spartan admiral (not harmost) named Cheilon. Despite the different name, he may be the same person as Milon, as might the Chilon of *Hellenika* 7.4.23.

Fragment 10

[1] They had, for example, dispatched arms and crews to the ships with Konon, and embassies had been sent to the King . . . and the supporters of . . . krates, Hagnias and Telesegoros.[a] Those ambassadors had been seized by Pharax, the former admiral,[b] who sent them to Sparta, where the Spartans put them to death.

[2] These men were being spurred on by the supporters of Epikrates and Kephalos,[a] who happened to be very keen to entangle the city in a war. Now they did not maintain this viewpoint, because they had spoken with Timokrates and had taken his money;[b] rather, they had wanted to do this from long before. And yet some maintain that Timokrates' bribes were responsible for the Athenians' banding together with the Boeotians and those others in the aforementioned cities. The people who say this, however, are unaware that all these cities were hostile to the Spartans from long before and had been looking for ways to involve themselves in a war. The Argives and Boeotians . . . hated the Spartans because the Spartans were treating their political opponents as friends, while those in Athens were eager to have the Athenians give up their peace and quiet and instead turn to war and meddlesomeness, so that they might make money from the public funds.

[3] Those of the Corinthians who wanted a change in the present state of affairs were, like the Argives and the Boeotians, similarly hostile to the Spartans; only Timolaos[a] was opposed to the Spartans on private grounds, although he had formerly been very well-disposed toward them and had very much supported Sparta, as can be learned from the events that occurred during the Dekeleian War.[b] [4] For as the commander of five ships, Timolaos had ravaged some of the islands belonging to the Athenians; and when in command of two ships, he sailed to Amphipolis, fitted out from there four more ships, and with all these together he conquered Sichios,[a] the general of the Athenians, in a sea battle (as I have mentioned previously) and captured five enemy triremes and thirty ships that had been dispatched there. And after this, commanding . . . triremes, he sailed to Thasos and caused that island to revolt from its alliance with Athens. [5] So then it was for these reasons, and not because they were induced by the gold of Pharnabazos, that those in the aforementioned cities hated the Spartans.

P.10.1a   The broken name might be Hippokrates, Autokrates, or Aristokrates (though the last might be too long for the space); it is not likely to be Epikrates, mentioned just after. Hagnias is mentioned by the orator Isaios (11.8) and the historian Philochorus (F. Jacoby, *Die Fragmente der griechischen Historiker* 328, Fr 147). Telesegoros is unknown.

P.10.1b   Pharax had most likely served as a Spartan admiral in 398/7.

P.10.2a   Epikrates was one of the men of the Peiraieus and had great influence with the people, according to Lysias 27.5–6. Kephalos was another democratic leader, with much influence, according to Demosthenes 18.219.

P.10.2b   More than one source claims he received money from Timokrates. On Timokrates' bribes of Persian gold see 3.5.2, where Xenophon explicitly denies that any Athenians took the money.

P.10.3a   See 3.5.1.

P.10.3b   The last phase of the Peloponnesian War, lasting from 413 to 404; so called because during this period the Spartans had fortified and occupied Dekeleia, a township in Attica.

P.10.4a   The text is likely corrupt here, since no Sichios is known. Some emend to Simichos, who is mentioned by another ancient source, though the only information there is that he was an Athenian commander at Amphipolis.

Fragment 11

[1] When Milon, the harmost of Aegina, had heard what the Athenians had to say,[a] he speedily manned a trireme and set out in pursuit of Demainetos, who happened at that time to be around Thorikos in Attica. [2] When Milon sailed against . . . attempted to . . . made an onslaught. . . . And getting possession of one of their ships, he left behind his own, because the hull was in rather bad shape; he put his own sailors onto the ship and sailed on to join the force with Konon. . . .

Fragment 12

[1] This, then . . . the most important events . . . in this winter. At the beginning of summer it was the eighth year.[a] . . . [about eight mutilated lines follow] [2] . . . and Pollis[a] now arrived at the ships of the Spartans and their allies, having been sent out from Sparta to take over the command from Archelaïdas. And around this same time ninety ships of the Phoenicians and Cilicians came to Caunus, from which ten sailed from Cilicia and the rest . . . of them the Sidonian ruler . . . [3] And Konon, learning of it and taking up . . . and manning the triremes . . . as swiftly as possible sailed up the river called the Caunian and into the Caunian Lake . . . of Pharnabazos and Konon . . . . . . phernes, a Persian man, . . . he sent them back to the King. . . .

The Battle of Sardis, 395
Fragment 14.3–6

[3] . . . always . . . similarly . . . closer . . . nothing other than the river[a] . . . [4] . . . hoplites and . . . hundred[a] light-armed troops, and he [Agesilaos] put the Spartiate Xenokles in charge of them, ordering that whenever the enemy should march against them, . . . to array themselves for battle. . . . And rousing the army at dawn, he again led them forward. The barbarians, as was their custom, followed; some attacked the Greeks, some rode around them, while yet others pursued in no order throughout the plain. [5] Xenokles, when he judged it to be the right moment to attack, brought the Spartans out from their ambush and attacked the enemy at a run. As each of the barbarians saw the Greeks coming on against them, they fled throughout the whole plain. When Agesilaos saw that the enemy were petrified, he sent from his army the light-armed troops and the cavalry to pursue them, and these, together with the forces from the ambush, attacked the barbarians.

[6] They did not pursue the enemy for a very long time, because they could not catch them, the majority being cavalry and troops without heavy armor, but they managed to kill around six hundred of them. Drawing back the pursuit, they went

P.11.1a   That is, their encouragement to punish Demainetos (see Fragment 9.3).

P.12.1a   It seems clear that this historian, like Thucydides, is narrating events according to winters and summers. To what year the "eighth" refers has been much discussed; it cannot refer to 397/6, and so most scholars divide between 396/5 and 395/4.

P.12.2a   This is a conjecture based on Fragment 22.1, where Pollis is named as Cheirikrates' predecessor.

P.14.3a   For the possible importance of these apparently stray words in the damaged papyrus, see the Introduction, §10.7.

P.14.4a   There is a number missing before "hundred."

up to the very camp of the enemy, and since no serious guard had been put on it, they quickly captured it, taking many provisions, many men, and much equipment and money, some belonging to Tissaphernes himself, some belonging to others.

Fragment 15

[1] Since the battle turned out this way, the barbarians, in fear of the Greeks, retreated with Tissaphernes to Sardis. Agesilaos remained there three days, during which time he gave the bodies back to the enemy under truce, set up a trophy, and plundered all the countryside; then he led his army into Greater Phrygia. [2] On the march he did not keep the soldiers in a square formation but allowed them to go out and attack any portion of the land that they wished, as well as to do harm to the enemy. Tissaphernes, learning that the Greeks were marching forward, took up the Persian troops in turn and followed behind, keeping many stades back. [3] Agesilaos went through the plain of Lydia and led the army back through the mountains that lie between Lydia and Phrygia. When they had crossed over these, he marched the Greeks down to Phrygia until he came to the Maeander River, which . . . from the Kelainai,[a] which is the greatest city in Phrygia, and empties into the sea near Priene. . . . [4] . . . after the Spartans and their allies had made camp, he sacrificed to discover whether he should cross the river or not and march against Kelainai or lead his army back. And when the omens failed to prove favorable for him, he waited around that day (the day on which he had arrived) and the following, and then led the army back. . . . Agesilaos then . . . the plain called Maeandrian . . . inhabited by Lydians and Mysians, Carians and Ionians.

The Boeotian Constitution
Fragment 19

[1] In this summer,[a] the Boeotians and the Phocians went to war with each other. Most responsible for this enmity were certain men in Thebes.[b] A few years before this[c] there had been civil strife in Thebes, [2] and at that time the political arrangement in Boeotia was as follows. In each of the cities there were four councils; political participation was not open to all but only to those who had a certain level of wealth. Each of these councils sat in turn; after they had discussed the business before them,[a] they referred it to the other three, and what was approved by all four was considered valid.

[3] The cities continued to maintain these arrangements, whereas the Boeotian Federation[a] was organized in the following way. All those who dwelt in Boeotia were divided into eleven divisions, and each furnished a Boeotarch[b] according to the follow-

---

P.15.3a   Kelainai in western Phrygia, at a later date the site of Apamea. Many scholars assume that in the lacuna it was stated that the source of the Maeander was at Kelainai (see Herodotus, *Histories* 7.26; Xenophon, *Anabasis* 1.2.7).

P.19.1a   The year is 395.

P.19.1b   The Oxyrhynchus Historian names these men (in the chapter following this excerpt) as Ismenias, Antitheus, and Androkleidas.

P.19.1c   Sometime between the year 404, when the Peloponnesian War ended, and the year 395.

P.19.2a   In view of what is said in the following paragraph about federal arrangements in Boeotia, it seems likely that these individual councils took up only local matters.

P.19.3a   The author, having described the situation in the individual cities, now turns to the Boeotian Federation as a whole.

P.19.3b   The term means "Boeotian magistrate" (as opposed to the magistrate of an individual city).

ing scheme. The Thebans contributed four, two for their own city and two for Plataea, Skolos, Erythrai, Scaphae, and the rest of the places that had formerly been united politically with Thebes but at that time were subjects[c] of Thebes. Orchomenus and Hyettos furnished two Boeotarchs; Thespiai with Eutresis and Thisbe furnished two; Tanagra furnished one; and one was also supplied by Haliartos, Lebadeia, and Coronea. In this last case, each of the cities took turns in sending their single Boeotarch, and this was also the arrangement with Akraiphiai, Kopai, and Chaeronea.[d]

[4] In this way, then, each of the divisions supplied the magistrates.

Each division also provided sixty counselors for each Boeotarch and paid the cost of their daily expenses. Each district had been assessed to provide approximately a thousand hoplites and a hundred cavalry for the army. Put in general terms, each division, in accordance with the number of Boeotarchs it supplied, shared in the public treasury, paid taxes, supplied jurors, and likewise had a share in everything both good and bad. Boeotia as a whole was arranged, then, in this way, and the Council and the federal assemblies met on the Kadmeia.[a]

The Boeotian Invasion of Phocis*
Fragment 21

[1] The party of Androkleidas and Ismenias[a] were eager to urge their people to war against the Spartans. They wanted to destroy Spartan rule so that they themselves would not be destroyed on account of the pro-Spartan party, and they thought it would be easy to do this because they supposed that the King would provide money, the very thing that the messenger sent by the King[b] had announced; and they thought too that the Corinthians, Argives, and Athenians would take part in such a war, for inasmuch as those were enemies of the Spartans, they would provide them with the assistance of their citizens.

[2] Although these were their intentions in regard to the situation, they thought that it would be difficult to openly attack the Spartans, since they could never persuade the Boeotians or the rest of the Thebans to make war against the Spartans, who were the rulers of Greece. They therefore attempted the following deception to lead them into war. They persuaded some men of Phocis to invade the territory of the so-called Western Locrians. Now the cause of the enmity between these two peoples was as follows. [3] There is a piece of land around Mount Parnassus that is constantly in dispute between these two peoples, and indeed they had previously

---

P.19.3c The term used by the author (*syntelountōn*) might indicate as well that these cities paid tribute money to Thebes.

P.19.3d The arrangement in which Thebes was the most powerful partner by number of Boeotarchs is thus:

Thebes (2) + Plataea-Skolos-Erythrai-etc. (2)	4
Orchomenus-Hyettos	2
Thespiai + Eutresis-Thisbe	2
Tanagra	1
Haliartos-Lebadeia-Coronea*	1
Akraiphiai-Kopai-Chaeronea*	1

*yearly alternation among the cities

All these cities can be found on Ref. Map 3, AY and BY, except Scaphae (site unknown).

P.19.4a The Kadmeia was the Theban acropolis.

P.21* The date is late summer 395. The events are told from a different perspective in *Hellenika* (3.5.3–5).

P.21.1a Theban factional leaders, the Spartans held them responsible for all the trouble in Greece: see 5.2.35

P.21.1b This messenger is usually assumed to be Timokrates.

gone to war over it. Often the two sides, Phocians and Locrians, use the territory to graze their flocks, and whenever one of the sides happens to perceive the other doing this, they gather together many strong men and steal their livestock. Now although this had happened on both sides many times before, they were for the most part reconciled to each other by means of arbitration and negotiations. But at that time, when the Locrians seized some livestock in retaliation for the Phocians' actions, the Phocians invaded Locris, spurred on by some men who had been put up to it by Ismenias and Androkleidas.

[4] Since their land was being ravaged, the Locrians sent ambassadors to the Boeotians, accusing the Phocians and demanding that the Boeotians bring assistance. (The Thebans had always been well-disposed toward the Locrians.) Gladly seizing their opportunity, the party of Ismenias and Androkleidas persuaded the Boeotians to bring assistance to the Locrians. The Phocians, when they heard what had been decided at Thebes, then withdrew from Locris and immediately sent ambassadors to Sparta, demanding that the Spartans forbid the Boeotians from entering their territory. Although the Spartans found the report unbelievable, they nevertheless sent men to forbid the Boeotians from making war upon the Phocians, saying that if the Boeotians felt that they had been wronged in any way, they should obtain justice from the Spartans in a meeting of the allies. But the Boeotians had been spurred on by the deceitful state of affairs that had been set in motion, and they dismissed the Spartan ambassadors with nothing accomplished and themselves took up arms and marched against the Phocians.

[5] They swiftly invaded Phocis, and having ravaged the territory of the Parapotamioi, the Daulians, and the Phanotians, they attempted to attack the cities. In the case of Daulis their attack accomplished nothing and they had to retreat, even sustaining a few losses; but they captured the suburb of Phanotis by force. Having accomplished this, they marched further into Phocis, overrunning a part of the plain around Elateia, the Pedieis, and others living in that area and then departing. As they were making their way back past Hyampolis, they thought they would make an attempt on this city, a place that is quite strong. They attacked the walls, and although there was no lack of enthusiasm, they accomplished nothing other than the loss of about eighty of their men, and so they retreated. Having done such damage to the Phocians, the Boeotians then departed for their own country.

Konon and the Mutiny in Caunus*
Fragment 22

[1] When Cheirikrates,[a] who had come as admiral succeeding Pollis, had taken over command of the Spartan and allied ships, Konon filled out twenty ships, set out from Rhodos, and sailed to Caunus. Wishing to meet with Pharnabazos and

P.22*   These events follow immediately on those of the
            previous fragment, although the scene now
            shifts to Asia Minor. The date is late summer
            and autumn of 395.
P.22.1a Cheirikrates is known only from the
            Oxyrhynchus Historian.

Tithraustes and obtain funds from them,[b] he went up from Caunus to them. [2] It happened that at this time he owed the soldiers many months' pay,[c] for they had been poorly paid by the generals. This is consistently the case with those who fight on behalf of the King: even in the Dekeleian War, when the Persians were allied with the Spartans, they sent quite paltry and stingy amounts of money, and the allies' triremes would have often been disbanded had it not been for Cyrus' eagerness. It is the King who is responsible for this state of affairs: whenever he decides on war, he sends a little money at the beginning to those in charge, but for the rest of the time he takes no thought for the matter, and those who are in charge of affairs, not being able to pay the soldiers out of their own funds, often have to look on as their forces are disbanded. [3] This, then, is customarily what happens.

Now when Konon was in the presence of Tithraustes and telling him that their affairs were in danger of being ruined because of the lack of funds, and that it was not seemly that these men fighting for the King would fail because of this, Tithraustes dispatched some of the barbarians in his retinue to give the soldiers their pay, drawing from a sum of 220 talents of silver. This money had been taken from Tissaphernes' personal property.

Tithraustes then waited a short while in Sardis and then went up to the King, after appointing Ariaios and Pasiphernes as generals in charge of affairs and giving them the silver and gold that was still left for the prosecution of the war; they say that this amount appeared to be about 700 talents.

Fragment 23

[1] Those of the Cypriots with Konon[a] sailed to Caunus, because they had trusted the word of some men who were spreading false stories that they were not about to receive the money owed to them but that instead discharges only were being prepared for the crews and marines. They were angry at this and gathered together in an assembly and chose as their commander a man of Karpasian nationality,[b] and they gave him a bodyguard of two soldiers from each company . . . Konon . . . as it happened . . . when Konon returned . . . there was a discussion about their actions. . . . [2] Konon . . . forbade . . . to trust their words . . . of the Greeks . . . to escort, and making this response, he claimed that he wished . . . and for the rest. But the Karpasian who was general of the Cypriots followed him toward the multitude of the soldiers. [3] He set out together with Konon, and when they were at the gates, Konon happened to be in front and had come out first from the wall; some of the Messenians who customarily accompanied Konon, without the latter's knowledge, seized the Karpasian man as he was exiting from the gates, because they were eager to keep him in the city so that he might pay the penalty for the wrongs he had done. Those of the Cypriots who were accompanying him grabbed hold of the

P.22.1b Diodorus (14.81.4–6) says that Konon visited the Persian King Artaxerxes in this year in an attempt to get money; presumably this was in addition to his meeting with Tithraustes.

P.22.1c Isocrates, *Panegyricus* 142, says they went without pay for fifteen months.

P.23.1a These men had probably been provided for Konon by Evagoras, the leader of Cyprus: see Isocrates, *Evagoras* 56.

P.23.1b Karpasia was a city in Cyprus. Commentators point out the deliberate omission of the man's name.

Karpasian man in turn and prevented the Messenians from leading him away, and the multitude of Cypriots outside the gate, perceiving what was happening, came up and gave assistance to the general. But Konon . . . running into the midst of the men . . . into the city. The Cypriots, striking the Messenians who had laid hold of the Karpasian, drove them off, and since they were persuaded that Konon had made all the arrangements for the distribution of pay in an unfair manner, they themselves boarded the triremes after these actions, intending, so some were saying, to take the men from Rhodos on board and sail to Cyprus, [4] and attacking Salamis,[a] they would then urge on those of the Cypriots who wished to march with them to the acropolis, so that they might straightaway destroy this power,[b] on the grounds that it alone was responsible for all their sufferings. . . . [5] When they[a] had landed, Konon went to Leonymos, the commander of the infantry,[b] and said to him that he alone was capable of saving the King's expedition: for if he gave Konon the Greek garrison that was watching over Caunus and as many Carians as he could, Konon could put an end to the disorder in the army. Leonymos told him to take as many soldiers as he wished. Konon allowed that day to pass—the sun was already setting—but on the next day before dawn he collected from Leonymos a great number of Carians and all the Greeks and led them out from the city. He then placed some of them around the outside of the camp, while others . . . he stationed at the ships and the shore. When he had done this, he ordered the herald to proclaim that each one of the soldiers should go to his post. From the Cypriots he arrested the Karpasian and sixty others, killing them and crucifying their general.

[6] When those who had been left behind in Rhodos heard what had happened, they became angry, and they treated the commanders appointed by Konon roughly, striking them and driving them from the camp, and they left the harbor, causing much commotion and disarray among the Rhodians. But Konon, coming from Caunus, arrested the leaders and put them to death, while he distributed to the rest their pay. So then the army of the King, which had in this way incurred great danger, put an end to its disorder, thanks to Konon and his energetic resolve.

Agesilaos' Army in Asia*
Fragment 24

[1] Agesilaos, while he was on his way to the Hellespont with the army of Sparta and the allies, did the inhabitants no harm all the time that he was on the march, for he wished to abide by the treaty that had been made with Tithraustes.[a] But when he had come down into the territory of Pharnabazos, he led the army forward, plundering and devastating the land. Leaving the Plain of Thebe and the so-called Plain of Apia, he invaded Mysia and attacked the Mysians, ordering them to join his expedition. (Most of the Mysians are autonomous and not subject to the King.)[b] He did

---

P.23.4a   Salamis, the city on Cyprus, not the island off Attica.

P.23.4b   It seems that the men intended to overthrow Evagoras, but from what follows it appears that they never made it to Cyprus.

P.23.5a   The Cypriots, presumably.

P.23.5b   He commanded the Greek and Carian contin-gent of the King's army and, as is clear here, was not subordinate to Konon.

P.24*   The date is autumn 395.

P.24.1a   Diodorus (Appendix O, 14.80.8) says the truce was for six months.

P.24.1b   This probably means that Persian rule over the Mysians was intermittent.

no harm to all those Mysians who chose to join him, but he destroyed the territory of the rest. [2] When, in his progress, he arrived at what is called Mysian Olympos, he noticed that the way through was difficult and narrow; wishing to pass through it safely, he sent some men to the Mysians and, having made an agreement with them, led his army through their territory. Although the Mysians allowed many of the Peloponnesians and their allies to go through, they attacked the hindmost troops and killed quite a lot of them, since those troops were not marching in good order because of the narrowness of the land. Agesilaos, halting the army, took no further action that day, tending instead to the proper rites for the dead, who numbered about fifty.

On the next day, he again began to march forward after having put many of Derkylidas' mercenaries[a] (as they were called) in position for an ambush. Each of the Mysians, thinking that Agesilaos was departing on account of the attack received on the previous day, went out from their villages and pursued the army, intending to attack the rearguard in the same way as before. The men set in ambush, however, when the Mysians were at hand, leapt up from their hiding places and came to close quarters with the enemy. The Mysian leaders and their men in the first lines were suddenly fighting with the Greeks and were killed; seeing their first men entangled, the majority of the Mysians fled back to their villages. When the news of this action reached Agesilaos, he led the army back along the same route, until he joined up with the men in the ambush. He camped in the very same place where he had done so on the previous day. [3] After this the relatives of the Mysians who had died . . . sending heralds . . . took up their dead under truce; more than 130 of them had been killed.

Agesilaos, taking some guides from the villages and waiting . . . days, then led his army forward and marched down into the territory of the Phrygians, though not the place where he had attacked the previous summer[a] but, rather, into another area, which was still unravaged and which he now proceeded to attack, using Spithridates and his son as guides. [4] Now Spithridates was Persian by birth and had spent time at the court of Pharnabazos and attending him. Thereafter, becoming his enemy, he began to fear that he might be arrested and harmed, and so he fled immediately to Cyzicus, and later he came to Agesilaos, bringing with him his son Megabates, who was young and handsome. Agesilaos received them, most of all because of the young man (since it is said that he was very passionately attached to him) but secondarily thinking that Spithridates could be a guide for his army and useful in other matters as well. [5] For these reasons, then, he received them both eagerly.

Agesilaos himself then led the army forward and, having ravaged the territory of Pharnabazos, he came to a place called Leonton Kephalai[a] and attacked it. But the attacks were unsuccessful, so he gathered up the army and marched forward, devas-

P.24.2a   These are the men who had fought with
          Cyrus and whom Xenophon had led back
          to the Black Sea from before Babylon. They
          joined Thibron's forces (Xenophon, *Anabasis*
          7.8.24) but seem to have taken their name
          from his successor, Derkylidas (*Hellenika*,
          3.1.8).

P.24.3a   Summer 396, mentioned by Diodorus (Appen-
          dix O, 14.79.3).
P.24.5a   The name means "Lions' Heads."

tating and laying waste that part of the country that was unravaged. [6] Coming in turn to Gordion, a place well fortified and built upon a hill, he had his army set up camp there, and he remained for six days, making attacks on the enemy but maintaining the army with many provisions. But when he could not capture Gordion, owing to the efforts of Rhathanes[a] (a Persian who was in charge of the place), he struck camp and led the soldiers onward, with Spithridates telling him to make his way to Paphlagonia.[b]

Fragment 25

[1] After this, leading the Peloponnesians and their allies forward, he came to the mountains of Phrygia and Paphlagonia, and there he camped, sending Spithridates to Gyes.[a] Spithridates made the journey to Gyes and brought the king back with him to Agesilaos. [2] Agesilaos, making a truce with the Paphlagonians,[a] swiftly brought his army to the sea, because he was afraid that they would lack provisions for the winter. He did not go by the same road by which he had come previously but took a different one, reckoning that it would be more . . . for the soldiers if they had to . . . the Saggarios[b] River. And he dispatched . . . and Gyes had sent to him [?] . . . [number lost] cavalry and more than two thousand infantry. [3] Leading the army down to Kion, which is in Mysian territory, he at first remained there for ten days, devastating Mysian territory in retaliation for their attacking him around Olympos; thereafter, he led the Greeks through coastal Phrygia and attacked a place called Miletou Teichos.[a] Failing to capture it, he led the soldiers back and continued his journey alongside the Rhyndakos River, and he came to Lake Daskyleitis, beneath which lies the Daskyleion,[b] an extremely strong site that had been fortified by the King and where it was said that Pharnabazos had stored all the gold and silver in his possession.

[4] Agesilaos had the army camp there and sent for Pagkalos,[a] who was *epibates*[b] to the admiral Cheirikrates and was watching over the Hellespont with five triremes. Pagkalos came speedily, sailing into the lake with his triremes, and Agesilaos ordered him to place on board all the booty of greater value and to take it to . . . around Cyzicus, so that it might be used to pay the army. He discharged the Mysian soldiers and ordered them to return in the spring, for he was planning after[c] the coming winter to make an incursion into Cappadocia,[d] because he had heard that this land stretched, like a thin ribbon, from the Pontic Sea as far as Cilicia and Phoenicia, and its measure was so great that those who traveled on foot could make the journey from Sinope[e] to Soloi in five days. . . .

P.24.6a	Rhathanes is mentioned by Xenophon at *Anabasis* 6.5.7 and *Hellenika* 3.4.13.	P.25.3a	The name means "Wall of Miletus."
P.24.6b	See 4.1.2 for Spithridates' promise to make the Paphlagonian king Agesilaos' ally.	P.25.3b	Xenophon's *Hellenika* 4.1.15–16 notes this as the location of Pharnabazos' palace.
P.25.1a	This is the Otys of Xenophon: see *Hellenika* 4.1.3.	P.25.4a	Pagkalos is otherwise unknown.
		P.25.4b	Probably a Spartan title for the commander of a small, separable detachment.
P.25.2a	See *Hellenika* 4.1.3–15 for a more detailed account of these events.	P.25.4c	Reading *meta*, as added by some scholars.
		P.25.4d	Agesilaos was recalled to Greece before he could do this.
P.25.2b	This is a conjecture; the Saggarios is the largest river in northwest Anatolia.	P.25.4e	The place-name is a conjecture.

TRANSLATOR'S NOTES

John Marincola

In making this translation, I have benefited greatly from the standard commentaries on the *Hellenika* as well as from previous translations. I am grateful to Robert Strassler, who helped me at times to state things more clearly, and especially to David Thomas, whose keen eye detected and corrected a host of ambiguities and errors. The responsibility for any errors and omissions that remain is entirely my own.

The translation is based on the Oxford Classical Text of E. C. Marchant.[a] Exceptions are noted below, in the ancient Greek, along with the emendations this translation has accepted and (in parentheses) the sources of those emendations.

Passage	*Oxford Classical Text*	Landmark *Hellenika* translation
1.1.37	ἐν ᾧ... Ἰμέραν	[ἐν ᾧ... Ἰμέραν] (Sievers)
1.2.1	[ὡς ἅμα καὶ πελτασταῖς ἐσομένοις,]	ὡς ἅμα καὶ πελτασταῖς ἐσομένοις,
1.2.8	†σφίσιν	Ἐφέσιοι (Sauppe)
1.2.10	†οἰκεῖν	οἰκεῖν
1.3.1	Παντακλέους ...παρεληλυθότων	[Παντακλέους...παρεληλυθότων] (Marsham)
1.4.16	†τοιούτοις δοκεῖν εἶναι οἷοισπερ πρότερον†	τοιούτοις δοκεῖν εἶναι οἷοισπερ πρότερον
1.5.11	†τειχίζειν	τειχίζειν
1.5.21	ἐν ᾧ... μῆνας	[ἐν ᾧ... μῆνας] (Unger)
1.6.4	γιγνωσκόντων †ἀπείρους ... τοῦτο†	γιγνωσκόντων, καὶ ἀπείρους ... τοῦτο

† Text the translator/editor believes is corrupt

[ ] Words that appear in the manuscripts but that modern editors believe to be later additions and not by Xenophon himself

< > Material taken from supplements by modern scholars

* Lacuna in text

TN.a E. C. Marchant, *Historia Graeca*, Oxford Classical Texts (Oxford: Oxford University Press, 1900).

Passage	*Oxford Classical Text*	Landmark *Hellenika* translation
1.6.17	ὑπὸ τῶν πολεμίων κατακωλυθείς,	* ὑπὸ τῶν πολιτῶν κατακωλυθείς *
1.6.21	ἐγειρόμενοι	ἐπειγόμενοι (Göller)
1.6.32	†οὐδὲν μὴ κακίον οἰκεῖται†	οὐδὲν μὴ κακίον οἰκήσει (Breitenbach)
1.7.24	†ἀδικοῦντες	ἀδίκως (Leonclavius)
1.7.27	†ἀποκτείναιτε†	ἀποκτείνητε
1.7.27	μεταμελήσει δὲ ὕστερον· †ἀναμνήσθητε†	μεταμελήσει· <μεταμελῆσαι> δὲ ὕστερον ἀναμνήσθητε (Hatzfeld)
1.7.33	[οὐχ ἱκανοὺς … προσταχθέντα]	οὐχ ἱκανοὺς … προσταχθέντα
2.1.12	†πρὸς τὸ ναυτικόν	<τὰ> πρὸς τὸ ναυτικόν (Marchant)
2.2.10	†εἰ	[εἰ] (Dindorf)
2.3.20	κελεύσαντες ἐπὶ τὰ ὅπλα	κελεύσαντες * ἐπὶ τὰ ὅπλα
2.3.31	[καὶ γὰρ ὁ κόθορνος … ἀμφοτέρων]	καὶ γὰρ ὁ κόθορνος … ἀμφοτέρων
2.3.36	†παρανενομηκέναι	παρανενοηκέναι (F. A. Wolf)
2.3.48	†δραχμῆς	ἀρχῆς (Wyttenbach)
2.4.8	ἱππεῦσιν	Ἐλευσινίοις (Classen)
2.4.34	πρὸ τῶν ἄλλων	πρὸ τῶν Ἁλῶν (Madvig)
2.4.39	κατέβησαν †	κατέβησαν, ἐκκλησίαν ἐποίησαν (Cobet)
3.2.27	†δι' αὐτῶν†	τὴν πόλιν δι' αὐτῶν (Leonclavius)
3.4.5	ἦ μὴν ἀδόλως … σοῦ πράττοντος	ἦ μὴν ἀδόλως ἐμὲ ταῦτα πράξειν. Καὶ σοι δέ, ἔφη, ἔξεστι παρ' ἐμοῦ πίστιν λαβεῖν ἦ μὴν ἀδόλως σοῦ πράττοντος (Cobet)
3.4.22	εἶπε	εἶπε<ν ὁ ἡγεμὼν> (Xenophon, *Agesilaos* 1.30)
3.5.2	†τε αὐτῶν ἄρχεσθαι†	αὐτῶν τὴν ἀρχὴν ἔσεσθαι (Liebhold)
4.1.6	μὲν	μέντοι (Denniston)
4.4.17	ἐπεκδραμόντας πελτασταῖς	ἐπ' ἐκδραμόντας πελταστὰς (Madvig)
4.5.18	ὄρθρου	πρὸ ὄρθρου (Büchsenschütz)

† Text the translator/editor believes is corrupt

[ ] Words that appear in the manuscripts but that modern editors believe to be later additions and not by Xenophon himself

< > Material taken from supplements by modern scholars

* Lacuna in text

Passage	*Oxford Classical Text*	Landmark *Hellenika* translation
4.6.4	τοὺς συμμάχους	τοὺς Ἀχαιοὺς συμμάχους (Simon)
4.7.5	οὐ πόρρω	αὖ πόρρω (Tillmanns)
5.1.13	αὖ †ἐπὶ ταύτῃ	αὐτεπιτάκτην (Desrousseaux)
5.1.13	†ἐπὶ ταύτας τας ναυς ναύαρχον	ἐπὶ ταύτας τὰς ναυς [ναύαρχον] (Hatzfeld)
5.1.27	καὶ †τῶν βραδυτέρων	καὶ ὑπὸ τῶν βραδυτέρων (Breitenbach)
5.4.36	<προσ> γένοιτο (Rinkes)	γένοιτο
6.1.14	† δοκεῖν εἶναι†	δοκοῦσαν εἶναι (Estienne)
6.2.32	†ὅπως	ὅπως
6.3.11	†ὧς	ἅς (Breitenbach)
6.3.13	Everything from τί μήν ἐστιν to ἀρεστά obelized.	εὔδηλον ὅτι * εἰ (Hatzfeld)
6.3.13	ἃ ὀρθῶς ἔγνωμεν	ὡς ὀρθῶς ἔγνωτε (Hartman)
6.4.3	[ὡς...αὐτούς]	ὡς...αὑτούς
6.4.14	μὲν ἵπποι	μὲν ἱππεῖς (Estienne)
6.4.23	ἀναγκάζοιντο †ἐκγενέσθαι τοῦ ζῆν	ἀναγκάζοιντο, ἐκγενέσθαι τοῦ ζῆν
6.5.35	†σφίσιν	σφίσιν
7.2.1	[ἐν] τῷ Φλειοῦντι	ἐν τῷ Φλειοῦντι
7.2.8	†ἐπὶ τὸ τεῖχος...ἐμάχοντο†	τοὺς ἐπὶ τὸ τεῖχος (Leonclavius)...ἐμάχοντο.
7.2.16	πρόξενον	Πρόξενον (Schneider)
7.2.18	ἐγένοντο	ἐγένετο (Hartman)

† Text the translator/editor believes is corrupt

[ ] Words that appear in the manuscripts but that modern editors believe to be later additions and not by Xenophon himself

< > Material taken from supplements by modern scholars

* Lacuna in text

CROSS-REFERENCE TABLE

of Related Passages in Xenophon's *Hellenika*, Diodorus' *Histories*, and the *Hellenica Oxyrhynchia*

Xenophon's *Hellenika* Bk./Chap./Sect.	Event Described	Date[a]	Diodorus' *Histories*[b] Bk./Chap./Sect.	*Hellenica Oxyrhynchia*[c] Frag./Sect.
1.1.1	Aftermath of Kynossema	411	13.41–42	
1.1.2–7	Battle of Abydos	411	13.45–47.2	
	Euboean revolt, Chalcis	411	13.47.3–8	
	Corcyra, Pydna	411	13.48	
1.1.11–22	Battle of Cyzicus	410	13.49.2–52.1	
	Peace offer	410	13.52.2–53	
1.1.32	Kratesippidas at Chios	409	13.65.3–4	
1.2.6–11	Thrasyllos at Ephesus	409	13.64.1	Fr 1–2
	Spartans take Pylos	409	13.64.5–7	
	Battle at the Horns of Megara	409	13.65.1–2	Fr 4
1.3.14–22	Recapture of Byzantium	408	13.66–67	
1.4.8–9	Thrasyboulos at Thasos	407	13.72.1–2	
1.4.11–13	Alcibiades returns to Athens	407	13.68–69	
1.5.10–14	Battle of Notion	406	13.70–71.4	Fr 8
1.5.16–17	Alcibiades dismissed	406	13.73.3–74	
1.6.1–14	Kallikratidas takes command	406	13.76	
1.6.15–23	Kallikratidas and Konon at Mytilene	406	13.77–79.7	
1.6.24–38	Battle of Arginousai	406	13.97–100	
1.7.1–35	"Trial" of the generals	406	13.101–103.2	

CRT.a All dates given are according to *The Cambridge Ancient History*, vol. 5, 2nd ed. (Cambridge: Cambridge University Press, 1992), unless otherwise noted.

CRT.b See Peter Green's translation in Appendix O and n. O*.
CRT.c See John Marincola's translation in Appendix P and n. P*.

Xenophon's *Hellenika* Bk./Chap./Sect.	Event Described	Date	Diodorus' *Histories* Bk./Chap./Sect.	*Hellenica Oxyrhynchia* Frag./Sect.
1.7.14–15	Socrates at the "trial" of the generals[d]	406		
2.1.21–30	Battle of Aigospotamoi	405	13.105–106.1–7	
	Disgrace of Gylippos	405[e]	13.106.8–10	
2.3.11–14	The Thirty installed by Lysander	404	14.3–4.1	
2.3.20–23	Excesses of the Thirty and Spartans	404	14.4.2–4	
2.3.22–56	Theramenes condemned and executed	404	14.4.5–5.4	
	Socrates at the trial of Theramenes[f]	404	14.5.1–3	
2.4.1	Further excesses of the Thirty and Spartans	404	14.5.5–6.3	
	Dekarchies	404–403	14.10.1–2	
	Death of Alcibiades	404	14.11.1–4	
2.4.2–43	Fall of the Thirty; democracy restored	403	14.32–33	
	Oropos taken by Thebes	402[g]	14.17.1–3	
3.1.3	Tissaphernes presses Ionian Greeks	400	14.35.6–7	
3.1.4–7	Thibron to Asia; Xenophon joins him	400/399	14.36–37	
3.1.8–9, 3.16–28, 3.2.1	Derkylidas' truce with Pharnabazos	399	14.38.2–3	
3.2.2–10	Derkylidas and Thracians	399–398	14.38.6–7	
3.2.21–31	Sparta and Elis	402?–400	14.17.4–12, 14.34.1	
	Konon appointed admiral by the King	397	14.39.1–3	
3.4.3–19	Agesilaos in Asia	396	14.79.1–3	
	Konon at Rhodos	396	14.79.4–8	
3.4.10	Spithridates comes to Agesilaos	396		Fr 24.3–4
	Demainetos sails to Konon	396/5		Fr 9
3.4.20–24	Battle of Sardis	395	14.80.1–5	Fr 14.4–15.3
3.4.25–26	Execution of Tissaphernes	395	14.80.6–8	Fr 16[h]
3.5.3–5	Boeotian invasion of Phocis	395	14.82.7–10	Fr 21
3.5.25	King Pausanias of Sparta flees trial	395–394	14.89.1	
	Konon and mutiny at Caunus	395		Fr 22–23

CRT.d Readers may also wish to compare Xenophon's mention of Socrates' objection to the collective "trial" of the generals (1.7.14–15) with Diodorus' report that Socrates objected to the condemnation of Theramenes (14.5.1–3), though, of course, the two passages are not strictly parallel.

CRT.e The date 405 for this event does not appear in *The Cambridge Ancient History*.

CRT.f See n. CRT.d.

CRT.g The date 402 for this event derives from Diodorus' text. It does not appear in *The Cambridge Ancient History*.

CRT.h Papyrus No. 16 is too fragmentary at this point for it to be translated in Appendix P, but from the proper names that occur in it we can tell it is dealing with Tissaphernes' execution.

Xenophon's *Hellenika* Bk./Chap./Sect.	Event Described	Date	Diodorus' *Histories* Bk./Chap./Sect.	*Hellenica Oxyrhynchia* Frag./Sect.
4.1.1	Agesilaos campaigns in Phrygia, Paphlagonia	395		Fr 24
4.1.2–15	Agesilaos and Otys (Gyes)	395		Fr 25.1–2
4.1.15–28	Agesilaos at Daskyleion	395		Fr 25.3–4
	Anti-Spartan Alliance	395–394	14.82.1–4	
4.2.1–8	Agesilaos recalled	394	14.83.1	
4.2.14–23	Battle at Nemea River	394	14.83.1–2	
4.3.1–9	Agesilaos marches to Boeotia	394	14.83.3–4	
4.3.10–14	Battle of Cnidus	394	14.83.4–7	
4.3.15–21	Battle of Coronea	394	14.84.1	
	Death of King Aîropos of Macedon	394	14.84.6	
4.4.1–4.5.2	Massacre at Corinth; war around Corinth	393–390	14.86	
4.5.11–19	Iphikrates at and around Corinth	390–389	14.91.2–92.2	
4.8.1–8	Pharnabazos and Konon cruise Aegean	394–393	14.84.4–5	
4.8.9–10	Konon rebuilds Athens' walls	393	14.85.2–3	
	Konon is arrested by Tiribazos	392	14.85.4	
4.8.17–19	Death of Thibron	391	14.99.1–3	
4.8.20–24	Stasis on Rhodos	391–389	14.97.1–4	
4.8.25–29	Thrasyboulos at the Hellespont, Lesbos	390–389	14.94	
4.8.30–31	Death of Thrasyboulos	389	14.99.4–5	
	Proem		15.1.1–5	
5.2.1–7	Sparta forces Mantineia to surrender	385/4	15.5, 15.12	
5.2.11–24	Olynthos' neighbors ask for Spartan help	382	15.19.2–3	
5.2.25–31	Spartans occupy the Kadmeia of Thebes	382	15.20.1–2	
5.2.37–5.3.6	Teleutias commands and dies at Olynthos	382	15.21.1–2	
5.3.8–9, 5.3.18–19	Agesipolis dies at Olynthos	381	15.22–23.2	
5.3.26	Sparta defeats Olynthos	379	15.23.2–3	
5.3.27	Sparta's power at apogee	379	15.23.3–5	
	Chabrias in Egypt	379	15.29.1–4	

Xenophon's *Hellenika* Bk./Chap./Sect.	Event Described	Date	Diodorus' *Histories* Bk./Chap./Sect.	*Hellenica Oxyrhynchia* Frag./Sect.
5.4.2–12	Liberation of Thebes	379/8	15.25–28.1	
	Foundation of Second Athenian League	378	15.28.2–5	
5.4.20–34	Sphodrias' abortive raid on Peiraieus	378	15.29.5–7	
	Expansion of Second Athenian League	378–377	15.29.7–30.2	
5.4.35–46	Agesilaos' first invasion of Boeotia	378	15.32–33.6	
5.4.47–55	Agesilaos' second invasion of Boeotia	377	15.34.1–2	
5.4.61	Naval battle off Naxos	376	15.34.3–35.2	
	Battle of Tegyra, Boeotia	375	15.37.1–2	
6.2.1	Peace of 375/4	375/4	15.38	
6.2.2–14	Operations in the west	375–374	15.45–46.3	
6.2.15–39	The Spartan Mnasippos at Corcyra	373–372	15.47.1–7	
6.3.1	Thebans expel Plataeans	373	15.46.4–6	
6.3.18–20	Thebes excluded from Peace of 372/1	371	15.50.4	
6.4.1–16	Battle of Leuctra	371	15.51–56.4	
6.5.6–21	Tegean stasis; Aegesilaos invades Arcadia	370	15.59	
6.4.28–35	Jason and Alexander of Pherai	370–369	15.60–61.2	
6.5.22–25	Arcadians persuade Thebans to invade Sparta	370	15.62	
6.5.26–52	First Theban invasion of the Peloponnese	370–369	15.63–65.6	
	Theban establishment of Messene	369	15.66.1	
7.1.15–26	Second invasion by Epaminondas	369	15.68–70.1	
7.1.27	Philiskos' intervention to settle conflict	368	15.70.2	
	Megalopolis founded	368	15.72.4	
7.4.1	Thebans sieze Oropos	366	15.76.1	
7.4.10	Peace of 366/5	365	15.76.3	
7.4.12–27	Arcadia-Elis War	365–364	15.77.1–4	
7.4.28–32	Eleians battle Arcadians at Olympia	364	15.78.1–3	
	Epaminondas' naval expedition	364	15.78.4–79.2	
	Thebes destroys Orchomenus	364	15.79.3–6	
7.4.33–40	Factions at Mantinea, Tegea, Thebes	364–363/2	15.82.1–4	
7.5.3–14	Agesilaos prevents the sack of Sparta	362	15.82.5–83.4	
7.5.15–17	Mantineia campaign, cavalry battle	362	15.84.1–2	
7.5.18–27	Mantineia campaign; Epaminondas dies	362	15.84.2–89.2	

GLOSSARY

Agiads and Eurypontids: the two Spartan royal families, each of which contributed one of the two reigning kings. The Agiads descended from Agis, the Eurypontids from Eurypon, and both claimed descent from Herakles.

Agōgē: the harsh, military-oriented system of compulsory public education for Spartan boys ages seven through eighteen.

agora: an ancient Greek city's marketplace, its center for commercial, social, and political activity.

Amphiktyonic Council: representatives from twelve cities who set policy for the shrine of Apollo at Delphi. The council also maintained the temples, managed the shrine's finances, and punished states that committed sacrilege.

anabasis: a march up-country (into the interior). The name of a book by Xenophon describing the march from western Asia Minor to Cunaxa near Babylon in 401 by the army of Cyrus the Younger.

anakrisis: the power exercizable by the ephors to make a preliminary decision by majority agreement as to whether or not a king should be required to stand trial.

apotumpanismos: an Athenian form of execution, in use prior to hemlock poisoning, which involved fastening the condemned man to a wooden board with tight iron collars around his neck, wrists, and ankles and leaving him to die.

astu: the city center within the walls but not including the acropolis.

aulos: a flute of some kind to the music of which the Spartan troops kept time while advancing into battle.

Bouleuterion: the building in which meetings of the Council took place.

damiorgoi: a body of officials of the Arcadian League.

Deigma: an area on the quai at the Peiraieus where merchants displayed their goods.

dekarchies: new governments, ruled by ten men, that Lysander imposed on the Aegean cities that he and the Peloponnesian fleet liberated from Athenian rule in 405/4. These governments were made up of pro-oligarchic local citizens, usually selected by Lysander. They later proved unpopular, and Sparta abolished them.

dekateutērion: literally, "tithed at a tenth," a Greek term used when ten percent of someone's confiscated property is dedicated to the god. It is often translated into English as "decimate," but the Greek term has nothing to do with the Roman military punishment of executing one tenth of the men in a disgraced unit.

deme: originally just "district" but at Athens, after the reforms of Kleisthenes in 508/7, demes became formal political units of the state. Every citizen's name included the deme where he had been officially enrolled.

demos (*damos* **in the Doric dialect**): originally those Greeks who lived in the villages (demes) of the land. In Athens and other states the term came to mean the common people, the most numerous body of citizens in the state.

diekplous: naval tactic of sailing between the enemy's ships and turning to attack from the rear.

eisangelia: impeachment process for an Athenian general, magistrate, or other officeholder.

Ekklēsia: the Assembly, a gathering of citizens of a Greek city for purposes of deciding important matters of state.

enguetai: guarantors a defendant could be compelled to present to the courts, who would pledge to pay the sums at issue if the defendant did not show up for his trial.

enomōtia: the Spartan half-unit that consisted of thirty-two to thirty-six men.

Eparitoi: an elite Arcadian corps of highly trained professional soldiers (similar to the Theban Sacred Band) that formed the nucleus of the army.

ephors (Ephorate): a powerful board of five officials who were elected annually, for one year only, to oversee the day-to-day governance of Sparta. They could and at times did rule on the kings' behavior.

epilektoi: picked elite troops, usually hoplites, who trained full-time at public expense and served as a city's standing army—for example, Thebes' Sacred Band and Arcadia's Eparitoi.

epistates: chairman for the day of Athens' *prytaneis* (presiding committee of the Council).

epistoleus: secretary to the navarch, commander of the Spartan fleet. A low office held by Lysander so that he could lawfully serve consecutive terms with the fleet and unofficially command it.

eponymous archon/ephor/magistrate: the official whose name was used to identify the year (the year when so and so was archon).

ethne: peoples or states.

Eurypontids and Agiads: Spartan royal houses. See **Agiads and Eurypontids**.

euthyna (plural *euthynai*): performance review that all Athenian magistrates, officials, and generals had to undergo upon completion of their term.

fillet: a ribbon that was customarily placed on the head of a victorious athlete.

Gerousia: Spartan Council of Elders. Consisting of the two kings plus twenty-eight men over age sixty who were elected for life, the Gerousia served as a predeliberative body for the Assembly and as Sparta's supreme court.

guest-friendship (*xenia*): a formal relationship, usually formed between eminent citizens of different states but sometimes between an individual and a whole state. The parties committed themselves to profound mutual obligations, including hospitality, advice, and support, which were not taken lightly. These commitments could pass to succeeding generations.

hamippos (plural *hamippoi*): lightly armed infantry trained to fight alongside the cavalry. They were trained to run with the horsemen, holding on to the tails of the horses and the hems of the riders' cloaks.

harmost: Spartan-appointed governor of an allied or captured city and/or commander of Sparta's garrison there.

helot: Laconian or Messenian native reduced to a serflike status by the Spartans and forced to cultivate the land for them.

hippagretai: three Spartan officers whose special duties included selecting the three hundred *hippeis*, the Horsemen, who performed special tasks and served as the king's bodyguard.

hipparch: a commander of cavalry.

hippeis: literally, "cavalrymen," but at Sparta this was the name of the Horsemen, the elite royal bodyguard of three hundred picked men. Despite their name, they actually fought with the king on foot.

homoioi: "Equals," literally, "same-ish," a name for full citizens of Sparta, also called Spartiates.

hoplite: armored foot soldier, carrying a large round shield, a thrusting spear, and a short sword; the standard heavy infantry type of the classical Greek world.

Horsemen, the: see *hippeis*.

hypomeiones: Spartan citizens who were disqualified from the rights and burdens of full citizenship, perhaps because they were unable to pay their communal mess dues.

kakourgoi: wrongdoers caught in the act who could be arrested and executed without trial unless they claimed innocence.

kaloikagathoi [*kaloi k'agathoi*]: the "fine and good," the aristocratic upper classes.

karanon: a Persian military term for "commander."

Knight: the second rank of Athenian citizens. Knights' income was great enough to support a horse, so they often served in the cavalry.

koinon: Greek term (meaning "community") for a large political association or league of states.

korē: a Persian garment whose sleeves were longer than normal. As a mark of respect for the King when in his presence, a Persian thrusts his hands into the garment in order to render them harmless in the sense that they cannot then hold or reach for weapons.

kothornos: a boot (literally, "slipper"), used in the theater, that could be worn on either foot.

kottabos: a game played at drinking parties by throwing the dregs of one's wine at a target to see if one might be successful in love.

Krypteia: a Spartan "Secret Service" in which select eighteen-year-olds, after graduating from the Agōgē, lived alone in the wild for up to two years, learning extreme survival techniques and carrying out covert activities, which might include the murder of selected helots.

kybernetes: the helmsman of a ship, of a trireme.

Lacedaemon, Lacedaemonian(s): a name for the region and people of Sparta.

lokhos (plural *lokhoi*): a company of soldiers, varying in size but often of several hundred men, commanded by *lokhagoi*.

metic: resident alien living in a city of which he is not a citizen. At Athens metics could not own land and were subject to special taxes and military service. Many were involved in commerce.

mora (plural *morai*): later Spartan military units, or "divisions."

navarch (*nauarch/nauarchos*): commander of the Spartan fleet.

neodamōdeis: a class of newly made citizens (literally, "newly put in the *damos*"), though their precise status is dubitable and their rights and/or privileges are unknown. The first mention of them is at Thucydides 4.21, when they are settled on the border of Elis, alongside the helots whom Brasidas took to Thrace and liberated on their return.

nomoi: laws, as distinct at Athens in the fourth century from decrees (*psephismata*).

nomothetai: after the restoration of the democracy at Athens, these five hundred elected lawgivers ratified the revised law code with a committee of the Council and, in the fourth century, approved all laws.

odeion: a building designed for musical performances.

oliganthrōpia: what Aristotle called the decline in number of Spartan military manpower.

paean: a ritual chant to honor and thank the gods that classical Greek soldiers and sailors sang as they advanced into battle, rallied, or celebrated victory.

palton: a light spear used by the Persian cavalry.

pankration: an Olympic sporting event that combined boxing and wrestling.

Paralos: one of two special Athenian state triremes used on sacred embassies and other official business. (The other was the *Salaminia*.)

peltast: an unarmored, missile-throwing infantryman, usually equipped only with a javelin and a small wicker shield.

penestai: a poor (*penēs* means "poor man") and landless hereditary serf class of Thessaly, similar to Spartan helots.

perioikoi: a class of citizens from towns around Sparta (literally, "the dwellers around") who did not have full Spartan citizenship rights and privileges but were compelled to serve in the army and follow the Spartan lead in war. They were also Sparta's traders and manufacturers, since Spartans were barred from economic enterprise.

periplous: naval tactic of sailing around the flank of an enemy fleet's line and then attacking it from the side or rear.

philetairia: love of one's comrades.

phylai: tribes. The Athenians usually deployed their hoplites in ten phylai, or regiments, each one drawn from of Athens' ten civic tribes.

Pnyx: hill in Athens where the Assembly met to conduct its deliberations.

polemarch: title used for a high-ranking regimental commander of Sparta or for the chief magistrates of Thebes. There was a polemarch at Athens, too, but he did not have military duties.

polis (plural *poleis*): a Greek city or city-state.

proskunēsis: Persian practice of prostrating oneself before the King, as everyone was equally the King's slave. Many Greeks were offended by this custom.

proxenos: a man who, although a citizen and resident of his own state, served as a "friend or representative" (much like a modern honorary consul) of a foreign state.

prytaneis: the presiding committee of the Council at Athens, which was responsible for running the meetings of the Assembly. They resided in the Prytaneion.

psephismata: decrees as distinct from laws (*nomoi*) at Athens in the fourth century.

Pythia: priestess of Apollo at Delphi who transmitted the god's words in oracles.

resident foreigner/alien: see **metic**.

satrap: Persian governor of one or more provinces, appointed by the King.

Skiritai: a company of special picked troops from the region of Skiritis in northern Laconia.

Spartiates: full citizens of Sparta.

stadion: the two-hundred-yard footrace.

stoa: a shedlike structure with one open side whose roof is supported by columns.

stratēgos (plural *stratēgoi*): general or military commander.

sukophantai: men who were thought to prosecute for profit, either by receiving a share of the fine if they won their case or by reaching an out-of-court settlement.

sussitia: the system whereby Spartiates did not dine at home but ate together in small military-style messes. Full adult citizenship depended on maintaining one's mess membership by payment of the monthly dues in agricultural produce, supplied by one's helots.

tagos (plural *tagoi*): the ruler of Thessaly, neither king nor tyrant but a leader who seems to have been selected by a unanimous vote of the rulers of the four ancestral Thessalian tribal territories, which may explain why the office was only intermittently filled.

taxiarch: Greek military unit commander.

theopropos: a seer, "he to whom the gods are evident."

Thesmophoria: a women's festival in honor of Demeter.

trierarch: captain of a trireme.

trireme: the standard Greek warship in the fifth and fourth centuries, armed with a bronze ram at the front and powered by three banks of rowers.

tropaion (**trophy**): a battlefield monument erected by the victors in thanks to the gods who had given them the victory. Usually consisted of a set of armor taken from the enemy dead and erected on a post at the site of the battle.

trophimoi xenoi: literally, "nurtured foreigners," sons sent by their pro-Spartan fathers from other communities to be educated at Sparta.

xenagoi: Spartan citizens who were responsible for gathering the allies from the other Peloponnesian states.

xenia: see **guest-friendship**.

ANCIENT SOURCES
Cited in This Edition of Xenophon's *Hellenika*

Aeneas Tacticus, fourth-century writer of treatises on military tactics, only one of which, *How to Survive Under Siege*, is extant. Some scholars think he is the Aeneas of Stymphalos cited in *Hellenika* at 7.3.1.

Aeschines (c. 397–c. 322), prominent Athenian orator. Three of his speeches survive.

Agatharchides, second-century grammarian, historian, and geographer from Cnidus who wrote a history and geography of Europe, one of Asia, and *On the Erythraean Sea.*

Alkaios (c. 620–580), Greek lyric poet whose works are known from fragments and quotations.

Andocides (c. 440–390), Athenian orator. Became an informer when arrested after the mutilation of the herms in 415. At least three of his speeches survive.

Androtion, fourth-century Athenian annalist and orator; pupil of Isocrates.

Aristophanes (second half of the fifth century), most famous Athenian playwright of Old Attic Comedy. Eleven of whose comedies survive.

Aristotle (384–322), philosopher, pupil of Plato, teacher of Alexander the Great, and founder of the Lyceum (Lykeion) at Athens c. 335. Much of his work survives, on subjects including logic, natural sciences, politics, and poetics.

Athenaios (fl. beginning of the third century C.E.), Greek writer from Naucratis, Egypt. His only extant work, *Deipnosophistae* (*Banquet of the Sophists*), a collection of excerpts from some eight hundred ancient authors (many of whose works are now lost) provides information on many aspects of the ancient world.

Cornelius Nepos (c. 100–24), Roman author of the earliest surviving set of biographies in Latin.

Deinarchos (c. 360–290), Greek orator from Corinth who lived in Athens. Wrote legal speeches for others to deliver, two of which survive.

Demosthenes (384–322), Athenian statesman and the most famous of ancient Greek orators. Many of his speeches survive. He was an active Athenian politician and committed suicide rather than be taken prisoner by his enemies, the Macedonians.

Diodorus Siculus, first-century Greek author of a universal history, of which large sections survive. (Excerpts are included in Appendix O.)

Diogenes Laertius (dates uncertain but probably early third century C.E.), Greek author of *Lives and Opinions of Eminent Philosophers.*

Dionysius of Halicarnassus (c. 60 B.C.E.–10 C.E.), Greek scholar who lived many years in Rome. He wrote a history of Rome in Greek (ten of its twenty books survive), as well as rhetorical treatises.

Ephoros (fl. c. 360–c. 330), fourth-century Greek historian who wrote the first universal history, of which only fragments survive. Diodorus Siculus says he used him as the main source for his treatment of the events of the mid-fourth century in his *Histories*, which overlaps with Xenophon's narrative in the *Hellenika*.

Euripides (c. 485–406), great Athenian tragedian. Eighteen (possibly nineteen) of his plays survive.

Herodotus (c. 485–425), Greek historian originally from Halicarnassus, Asia Minor. Traveled extensively. Wrote a history of the Persian War of 480–479, which survives today.

Isaios (c. 420–350), Athenian speechwriter. Eleven of his speeches survive. He was an expert on inheritance law in Athens.

Isocrates (436–338), prominent Athenian orator, speechwriter, and educator. He may have been a student of Socrates; at the school he founded in Athens, he taught Ephoros, Theopompos of Chios, and Isaios. He is famous for having argued that Greeks should stop warring among themselves and instead unite and attack Persia.

Ktesias (late fifth century), Greek who spent many years as physician to the Persian court and wrote a book derived from his experiences and researches there. Only fragments of this work survive.

Lucian (second century C.E.), Greek satirist and traveling lecturer. His surviving dialogues include *How to Write History*.

Lysias (c. 445–385), speechwriter for participants in Athenian court cases, though he himself was not an Athenian but a resident alien. More than thirty of his speeches survive, providing us with some historical details. Especially noteworthy is the oration he wrote when, after the expulsion of the Thirty Tyrants, he returned from exile and prosecuted Eratosthenes (one of the Thirty) for having had his brother Polemarchos put to death.

Oxyrhynchus Historian or "P," unknown author of the *Hellenica Oxyrhynchia* (he may have been an Athenian named Cratippus). Of this Greek history of the 400s and 390s, written in the first half of the fourth century and excerpted in Appendix P, only fragments have come down to us.

Pausanias (c. 150 C.E.), geographer who, in his work *Periegesis of Greece* wrote detailed travel descriptions of topography, monuments, art, history, customs, and more. Archaeological work has revealed that many of his descriptions were accurate.

Philochoros (c. 340–261), Athenian politician and historian who wrote a history of Athens, of which only fragments survive. He was executed by the Macedonians.

Plato (427–347), Athenian philosopher and writer, student of Socrates, and teacher of Aristotle. Founded the Academy c. 385. Many of his works survive.

Pliny the Elder (23–79 C.E.), writer of the encyclopaedic *Natural History*, which survives. He died while observing the eruption of Mount Vesuvius in 79 C.E.

Plutarch (46–120 C.E.), prolific writer from Chaeronea, Boeotia, many of whose biographies and essays survive.

Polyainos (fl. second century C.E.), Macedonian author of *Stratagems*, a wide-ranging collection of military maxims and strategies.

Strabo (64 or 63 B.C.E.–c. 21 C.E.), Greek geographer, historian, and traveler. His *Geography* is a series of sketches, based on his travels and the works of predecessors, describing the known world of his day.

Thucydides (c. 460–390s), Athenian historian of and general in the Peloponnesian War.

Xenophon (c. 430–late 350s), Greek historian, author of several surviving works, including the *Hellenika* (the present volume) and the *Anabasis*, an account of Cyrus the Younger's expedition against his brother Artaxerxes, in which Xenophon participated.

BIBLIOGRAPHY
for the General Reader

INSCRIPTIONS AND FRAGMENTS

Inscriptiones Graecae. Berlin: Reimer, then De Gruyter, 1873–.

Jacoby, Felix. *Die Fragmente der griechischen Historiker*. 15 vols. Berlin, 1923–30; Leipzig, 1940–58.

Meiggs, Russell, and David M. Lewis. *A Selection of Greek Historical Inscriptions to the End of the Fifth Century B.C.* Oxford: Clarendon Press, 1975.

Rhodes, P. J., and Robin Osborne, eds. *Greek Historical Inscriptions 404–323 B.C.* Oxford: Oxford University Press, 2003.

XENOPHON AND THE XENOPHONTIC PERIOD

Anderson, J. K. *Xenophon*. London: Duckworth, 1974.

Buckler, John. *Aegean Greece in the Fourth Century B.C.* Leiden: Brill, 2003.

———. *The Theban Hegemony, 371–362 B.C.* Cambridge, MA: Harvard University Press, 1980.

Cambridge Ancient History, The. 2nd ed. Cambridge: Cambridge University Press. Vol. 5: *The Fifth Century B.C.*, 1992. Vol. 6: *The Fourth Century B.C.*, 1994.

Cartledge, Paul. *Agesilaos and the Crisis of Sparta*. London: Duckworth, 1987.

Cawkwell, George. Introduction to *Xenophon: A History of My Times*, translated by Rex Warner. 2nd ed. Harmondsworth: Penguin, 1979.

Dillery, John. *Xenophon and the History of His Times*. London: Routledge, 1995.

Gray, Vivienne. *The Character of Xenophon's* Hellenica. London: Duckworth, 1989.

———. "Xenophon and Isocrates." In *The Cambridge History of Greek and Roman Political Thought*, edited by C. Rowe and M. Schofield. Cambridge: Cambridge University Press, 2000.

Hamilton, C. D. *Agesilaus and the Failure of Spartan Hegemony*. Ithaca: Cornell University Press, 1991.

———. *Sparta's Bitter Victories: Politics and Diplomacy in the Corinthian War*. Ithaca: Cornell University Press, 1979.

Higgins, W. E. *Xenophon the Athenian: The Problem of the Individual and the Society of the Polis*. Albany: State University of New York Press, 1977.

Hornblower, Simon, and Antony Spawforth, eds. *The Oxford Classical Dictionary*. 3rd ed. Oxford: Oxford University Press, 2003.

Kagan, Donald. *The Fall of the Athenian Empire*. Ithaca: Cornell University Press, 1987.

Krentz, P. *The Thirty at Athens*. Ithaca: Cornell University Press, 1982.

Lane Fox, Robin, ed. *The Long March: Xenophon and the Ten Thousand*. New Haven: Yale University Press, 2004.

Lee, John W. I. *A Greek Army on the March: Soldiers and Survival in Xenophon's* Anabasis. Cambridge: Cambridge University Press, 2007.

Pownall, Frances. *Lessons from the Past: The Moral Use of History in Fourth-Century Prose*. Ann Arbor: University of Michigan Press, 2004.

Tuplin, Christopher. *The Failings of Empire: A Reading of Xenophon* Hellenica *2.3.11–7.5.27*. Stuttgart: Franz Steiner Verlag, 1993, Historia, Einzelschriften 76.

———, ed. *Xenophon and His World: Papers from a Conference Held in Liverpool in July 1999*. Stuttgart: Franz Steiner Verlag, 2004, Historia, Einzelschriften 172.

HELLENIKA EDITIONS AND COMMENTARIES

Brownson, Carleton L., trans. *Xenophon in Seven Volumes, 1 and 2*. Loeb Classical Library. Cambridge, MA: Harvard University Press. Vol. 1, 1918. Vol. 2, 1921. Available online through Tuft University's Perseus Digital Library Project. Gregory R. Crane, ed. www.perseus.tufts.edu.

Krentz, P., ed. and trans. *Hellenika I–II.3.10*. With Introduction and commentary. Warminster: Aris & Phillips, 1989.

———. *Hellenika II.3.11–IV.2.8*. With Introduction and commentary. Warminster: Aris & Phillips, 1995.

Marchant, E. C., ed. *Historia Graeca*. Text only. Oxford Classical Texts. Oxford: Oxford University Press, 1900.

Underhill, G. E. *A Commentary on the Hellenica of Xenophon*. Oxford: Oxford University Press, 1900. Reprinted Salem, NH, 1984.

TRANSLATIONS OF OTHER WORKS BY XENOPHON

Ambler, Wayne, trans. *The Education of Cyrus*. Ithaca: Cornell University Press, 2001.

Lipka, Michael, trans. *Xenophon's* Spartan Constitution: *Introduction, Text, Commentary*. Berlin: Walter de Gruyter, 2002.

Tredennick, Hugh, trans., and Robin H. Waterfield, ed. and trans. *Conversations of Socrates*. London: Penguin, 1990.

Waterfield, Robin, trans. *The Expedition of Cyrus*. With Introduction by Tim Rood. Oxford: Oxford University Press, 2005.

———. *Hiero the Tyrant and Other Treatises*. With Introduction by Paul Cartledge. London: Penguin, 1997.

HELLENICA OXYRHYNCHIA EDITIONS AND COMMENTARY

Chambers, M., ed. *Hellenica Oxyrhynchia*. Text only. Stuttgart: Teubner, 1993.

McKechnie, P. R., and S. J. Kern, eds. *Hellenica Oxyrhynchia*. With translation and commentary. Warminster: Aris & Phillips, 1988.

DIODORUS SICULUS EDITIONS AND COMMENTARY

Bonnet, M., and E. R. Bennett, eds., trans. into French. *Diodore de Sicile Bibliothèque Historique Livre XIV*. Paris: Les Belles Lettres, 1997, Budé edition.

Green, Peter, trans. *Diodorus Siculus, The Persian Wars to the Fall of Athens, Books 11–14.34 (480–401 B.C.E.)*. With Introduction and commentary. Austin: University of Texas, forthcoming.

Oldfather, C. H., trans. *Diodorus of Sicily Volume V (Books XII.41–XIII)*. Loeb Classical Library. Cambridge, MA: Harvard University Press, 1962.

———. *Diodorus of Sicily Volume VI (Books XIV–XV.19)*. Loeb Classical Library. Cambridge, MA: Harvard University Press, 1963.

———. *Diodorus of Sicily Volume VII (Books XV.20–XVI.65)*. Loeb Classical Library. Cambridge, MA: Harvard University Press, 1963.

Stylianou, P. J. *A Historical Commentary on Diodorus Siculus Book 15*. Introduction and commentary only. Oxford: Oxford University Press, 1998.

Vial, C., ed., trans. into French. *Diodore de Sicile Bibliothèque Historique Livre XV*. Paris: Les Belles Lettres, 1977, Budé edition.

Vogel, F., ed. *Diodori Bibliotheca Historica*. Vol. III. Text only. Leipzig: Teubner, 1893. Reprinted Stuttgart, 1964.

OTHER WORKS CITED

Andrewes, A. "Notion and Kyzikos: The Sources Compared." *Journal of Hellenic Studies* 102 (1982): 15–25.

Camp, John McK. *The Athenian Agora: Excavations in the Heart of Classical Athens*. New York: Thames and Hudson, 1986.

Casson, Lionel. *Ships and Seamanship in the Ancient World*. Rev. ed. Baltimore: Johns Hopkins University Press, 1995.

Develin, R. *Athenian Officials 684–321 B.C.* Cambridge: Cambridge University Press, 1989.

Morrison, J. S., J. F. Coates, and N. B. Rankov. *The Athenian Trireme: The History and Reconstruction of an Ancient Greek Warship*. 2nd ed. Cambridge: Cambridge University Press, 2000.

Rhodes, P. J. *The Athenian Boule*. Oxford: Oxford University Press, 1972.

———. *A Commentary on the Aristotelian Athenaion Politeia*. Rev. ed. Oxford: Oxford University Press, 1993.

Figure Credits

INDEX

Abydos, Athenians capture 30 Peloponnesian ships,
1.1.5–7; Alcibiades defeats Pharnabazos, 1.2.16;
Derkylidas exhorts it to remain loyal to Sparta, 4.8.4;
when Spartans and Athenians contest control of the
city, Iphikrates ambushes Anaxibios, who dies
fighting, 4.8.34–39; Athenians blockade Spartan
force, 5.1.6–7; Antalkidas captures 8 Athenian
triremes, 5.1.6–27;

Acarnania/Acarnanians, join allied forces at Nemea River,
4.2.17; attack Calydon, 4.6.1; Spartan force invades
and captures their livestock, 4.6.3–7; peltasts harass
Spartans from heights, 4.6.7; suffer heavy losses before
Spartans withdraw, 4.6.7–12; make peace with Spartans
to forestall another attack, 4.7.1

Acarnanian League, Agesilaos demands that it withdraw
from its alliance with Athens and Boeotia, 4.6.4

Achaea/Achaeans, of Peloponnese, appeal to Sparta for
help against Acarnanians and their allies, 4.6.1–2;
Acarnanians make peace with them to forestall
further Spartan attack, 4.7.1; help Eleians repel Arcadian invasion, 7.4.17–18; Epaminondas succeeds in
establishing democracies in, but aristocratic factions
regain power and ally Achaean cities with Sparta,
7.1.41–43

Achaea/Achaeans, of Phthiotis, betray colonists of Herakleia
to Oetaeans, 1.2.18

Acrocorinth, younger men of Corinth escape Argive attack
by running to, 4.4.4–5; Agesilaos withdraws toward,
making Corinthians think the city has been betrayed to
him, 4.5.3; Thebans and their forces fill hills bordering
on, 7.1.20

acropolis

    Athens, *see* **Athens/Athenians**

    Elis, democratic faction seizes but is driven into exile,
7.4.15–18

    Gergis, Derkylidas takes control of, 3.1.23

    Oreos, sailors from grain ships imprisoned by Alketas seize,
and the city revolts against the Spartans, 5.4.56–7

    Pharsalus: Polydamas is entrusted with, during civil strife,
as mark of citizens' respect, 6.1.2–3; he refuses to hand
it over to Jason but gives him his children as hostages,
6.1.18

Phleious: Spartans are allowed to occupy to help in
defense against Athenians, 4.4.15, 5.3.15; exiles seize
but are driven out by citizens, 7.2.6–9

Sicyon: Aeneas the Stymphalian takes his army to and calls
on aristocrats to overthrow Euphron, 7.3.1; Euphron
cannot dislodge Theban harmost from, after winning
control of the city, 7.3.4

Skepsis, Derkylidas sacrifices to Athena at, 3.1.21

Spartan occupation of Thebes' is unjust, 5.4,1

Thebes: Spartan army commander occupies in plot with
Leontiades, 5.2.29, 5.2.35; Xenophon describes
occupation as unjust, 5.4.1; Spartans forced to
withdraw from after overthrow of polemarchs,
5.4.10–12; Euphron of Sicyon is assassinated while
magistrates and Council are in session on, 7.3.5–12;
see also **Kadmeia**

Adeimantos son of Leukolophides, sent to Andros as general to help Alcibiades suppress revolt, 1.4.21; retains
his command when other generals are deposed, 1.7.1;
captured at Aigospotamoi, 2.1.30; Spartans spare
because he had voted against decree to cut off captives'
right hands, 2.1.32

Aegina, Lysander restores to Aeginetans, 2.2.9; Spartan fleet
drives away Athenian naval squadron from, 5.1.1–2,
5.1.5; Athenian hoplites fortify a post on, 5.1.2;
Chabrias leads Athenian force and ambushes Spartans
on, 5.1.10–12; Teleutias resumes command of Spartan
fleet at, 5.1.13–18; raiders from harass Athenians,
5.1.29, 6.2.14

Aeolis/Aeolians, Pharnabazos gives subsatrapy of to Mania
wife of Zenis, 3.1.11–12; Derkylidas exhorts cities of to
free themselves, 3.1.16

Agamemnon, Agesilaos invokes memory of before sailing to
Asia, 3.4.3

Agesandridas, commands Spartans in naval victory over
Athenians, 1.1.1

Agesilaos king of Sparta, disputes succession with Leotychidas and is chosen as king, 3.3.1–4; persuaded by
Lysander to lead campaign in Asia against Persians,
3.4.2; attempts to sacrifice at Aulis but is interrupted
by Thebans, 3.4.3–4, 7.1.34; agrees to a truce with
Tissaphernes at Ephesus, knowing that the Persian is

enemy, 5.3.5–6; attack Theban rear as they retreat to their city, 5.4.52; at Leuctra, poorly trained and in poor physical shape, 6.4.11, fall back on their own hoplites, 6.4.13; after failed ambush at Amyklai, charge Thebans, who withdraw, 6.5.31; *see also* Agesilaos; Derkylidas; Pausanias, *above*

tactics, overcome infantry when going up a slope that is easy for horses to ascend, 5.4.54

Thebans: march on Haliartos, 3.5.19, 3.5.23; send contingent to join Teleutias' attack on Olynthos, 5.2.37; Phillidas summons from their houses after killing polemarchs, 5.4.9; make surprise attack on Spartans but throw their spears before the enemy is in range, 5.4.38–41; attack Phoibidas, 5.4.42; at Thespiai, retreat to an impassable ravine and counterattack, 5.4.44; forces at Leuctra, 6.4.10; cross into Laconia but give way to Spartan charge, 6.5.30–32; high reputation, 7.5.16; whiten their helmets in accordance with Epaminondas' orders, 7.5.20; *see also* Epaminondas, *above*

Thessalian cavalrymen join Agesipolis' force as they wish to become known to him, 5.3.9

Celtic and Iberian infantry, sent to Corinth by Dionysios of Syracuse to help Spartans against Thebans, 7.1.20–22; help Archidamos rout Arcadians, 7.1.31

Chabrias, sails to Aegina and successfully ambushes Spartan force, 5.1.10–12; commands peltasts guarding the road through Eleutherai, 5.4.14; Theban mercenaries appeal to for assistance, 5.4.54; commands an Athenian fleet that defeats the Spartan fleet, 5.4.61; Iphikrates asks him to serve as his colleague, 6.2.39; his mercenaries prevent the Epidaurians from escaping, 7.1.25

Chalcedon/Chalcedonians, Athenians fortify nearby Chrysopolis, establish a counting house to collect tax on vessels coming from Black Sea, 1.1.22; Pharnabazos sets out to assist, 1.1.26; Spartans send Klearchos to guard, 1.1.35; deposit all their movable property with Bithynian Thracians, but Alcibiades obtains it with threats, 1.3.2–3; Alcibiades besieges and defeats Spartan garrison and Persians, 1.3.4–7; Alcibiades and Pharnabazos agree terms under which Chalcedonians will continue paying tribute to Athenians, 1.3.8–12; open their gates to Lysander, who allows Athenian guards to leave under a truce and leaves a Spartan harmost and garrison, 2.2.1–3; Thrasyboulos makes them allies of Athenians once more, 4.8.28

Chalcis (Euboea), 100 citizens of in allied cavalry at Nemea River, 4.2.17

Chares, 7.4.1, 7.4.5; helps Phleiasians escort food supplies, attacking Sicyonian fort, 7.2.18–23; Athenians summon to lead their force against Oropos, 7.4.1

chariots, scythed, Pharnabazos attacks Greek foragers near Daskyleion, 4.1.17–19

Charmides son of Glaucon, one of the Ten who ruled Peiraieus, killed in battle, 2.4.19

Chersonese, Alcibiades goes to to collect money, 1.3.8, retires to his castle in, 1.5.17, observes Athenian ships' maneuvers from, 2.1.25; Derkylidas builds wall across to stop Thracian raids, 3.2.8–10

children, Byzantium's women and children perishing through famine, 1.3.19; Thrasyboulos promises his men that victory will restore them to their wives and children,

2.4.17; Spithridates leaves the King's service, taking his, 3.4.10; Spartans say allies fear peltasts as children fear the bogeyman, 4.4.17; Thebans kill their factional enemies and their enemies' children, 5.4.12; Polydamas gave his to Jason as hostages, 6.1.18; Eutaia had only old men, women, and children, 6.5.12; some in Arcadian Federation argue that theirs will suffer for offense against the gods if Eparitoi are funded from sacred monies, 7.4.34; Mantineians ask Athenians for help since many old men and children were outside the walls, 7.5.15

Chios/Chians, Kallikratidas fits out 50 additional ships with men of Chios and Rhodos, 1.6.3; Chians contribute funds to Kallikratidas when Cyrus delays payment, 1.6.12; Eteonikos' men conspire to attack Chios to relieve their poverty, 2.1.1; Eteonikos demands payment to deter his rebellious soldiers from attacking the city, 2.1.5; Chians join allies in demanding that Lysander be reappointed commander of the fleet, 2.1.6; Atarneus is seized by exiles from, 3.2.11

Chrysopolis, Athenians fortify and establish customs house, 1.1.22

Cilicia, with help of Spartan fleet, Cyrus suppresses Syenessis' revolt, 3.1.1

citizenship

Abydos, Derkylidas persuades citizens to remain loyal to Sparta, 4.8.3–4

Aeolis, Mania's son-in-law is stirred up by men who say it is shameful for a woman to rule while he is merely a private citizen, 3.1.14

Alcibiades, on his return to Peiraieus, is said by some to be the ablest of the citizens, 1.4.13

Antandros, Syracusans are awarded citizenship for their role in defending the city, 1.1.26

Archidamos: commands citizen army, 7.1.28, 7.1.30; captures Kromnos with his citizen forces, 7.4.20

Athenians: many private citizens offer themselves as sureties for the generals, 1.7.7; some citizens praise Euryptolemos for serving a summons against Kallixenos, 1.7.12; grant citizenship to Byzantines who opened city gates to Alcibiades when they are expelled by Lysander, 2.2.1; restore citizenship to those deprived of it in attempt to strengthen the city, 2.2.11; Kritias recognizes that a large number of citizens will always be hostile to oligarchy, 2.3.24; Theramenes deplores the hiring of foreign troops when a similar force could have been formed from Athens' own citizens, 2.3.42; laws of the oligarchy allow the Thirty to put to death any citizen not on the list of Three Thousand, 2.3.51; the Thirty decree that citizens not on the list will be forbidden to enter the city and evicted from their estates, 2.4.1; only those citizens who think solely of their own gain welcome the Thirty's condemnation to death of Eleusinian prisoners, 2.4.9; Thrasyboulos addresses his fellow citizens, 2.4.13; after their victory over the Thirty, the men of Phyle do not remove the tunic of a single fallen citizen, 2.4.19; Kleokritos the herald emphasizes common experience of Athenian citizens under unholy rule of the Thirty, 2.4.20–22; men of Peiraieus offer citizenship and equal taxation to any man who fights with them, 2.4.25; after the flight of the Thirty, the Ten grapple with mutual distrust among the citizens, 2.4.27; after democratic government is

Tegean, are taken in by Spartans, who assist them against Thebans, 6.5.10, 6.5.24

Thebans: exiles plan and carry out coup against polemarchs, 5.4.2–9; those who were in exile prefer to do battle at Leuctra than repeat that experience, 6.4.6; Thebans decree that exiles should be liable to arrest in any allied city, 7.3.11

Thessaly: all those who are not in exile join Agesilaos, 4.3.3; Polydoros exiles men from Larissa accused of complicity in murder of Jason, 6.4.34

Thibron exiled from Sparta for allowing his army to plunder friends, 3.1.8

Thrasyboulos: exiled from Athens by the Thirty, 2.2.42–43; promises Lesbian exiles restitution if they help him against Methymna, 4.8.28

Timotheos: takes Corcyra but does not enslave or exile the people, 5.4.64; lands some Zacynthian exiles on their island, arousing Spartan attack, 6.2.2

faction, *see* **aristocracy/aristocrats; commons, popular faction; democracy; people; oligarchy/oligarchs**

famine, Byzantine conspirators open gates to Athenians to prevent women and children perishing from hunger, 1.3.19; Thasos suffering from, due to wars and civil strife, 1.4.9; Olynthians are forced to submit to Spartans since no food can reach their city, 5.3.26; Thebans are greatly distressed by lack of grain since unable to reap crops from their land for 2 years, 5.4.56; Corcyraeans suffer so greatly from hunger that some defect to the enemy, 6.2.15; Phleiasians' take great risks to bring supplies into the city since lack of food was worse than facing the enemy, 7.2.17–19

festivals

Apatouria, Theramenes and his followers wear black clothes and have their hair shorn as if they were mourning relatives, 1.7.8

Aphrodite, feast of, Phillidas, in charge of celebrations, lures Theban polemarchs to their assassination, 5.4.2

Corinth: impious massacre is plotted during a festival, when all men refrain from killing, 4.4.2; the massacre takes place during the festival of Eucleia, 4.4.3–5

Hyakinthia, Amyklaians always return home to celebrate and sing the *paean* to Apollo, 4.5.11

Mysteries, Kleokritos invokes beauties of, 2.4.20

Naked Youths, festival of, news of defeat at Leuctra reaches Sparta on day of, 6.4.16

Olympic, Eleians attack Arcadians, 7.4.28–31

Plynteria (Athens), Alcibiades returns on day of, 1.4.12

Pythian, Jason prepares magnificent celebration of, 6.4.29–30

Thesmophoria, women of Thebes celebrate, 5.2.29

fire

Agesilaos sends men with fire in pots to sustain his troops on heights of Peiraion, 4.5.4; he leads his soldiers away quickly so that they do not even see the fires of the enemy and it could not said he let them back in fear, 6.5.21

Athena: temple of in Phocaea is set on fire by lightning, 1.3.1; ancient temple of at Ephesus catches fire, 1.6.1

Athenians set fire to Lydian villages, 1.2.4

Iphikrates allows no fires in camp apart from one in front so no one could approach unobserved, 6.2.29

Kallikratidas sees campfires of the enemy at night, 1.6.28

Larisaeans set wooden cover on fire to prevent Thibron's shaft from cutting off their water supply, 3.1.7

Phleiasians find fire in the tents and set the towers ablaze, 7.2.8

Poseidon, temple of catches fire, 4.5.4

Spartan women cannot bear to see smoke from enemy fires in Spartan territory, 6.5.28

Thebans, Xenophon sarcastically calls them "these breathers of fire," 7.5.12

wasps' hive must be set on fire to avoid retaliation, 4.2.12

flutes, music of flute girls accompanies demolition of Athens' Long Walls, 2.2.23; Agesilaos orders that all the flute players should play at celebration of victory at Coronea, 4.3.21; Thersander, a great imitator of Spartan ways, was a fine flute player, 4.8.18

fort/fortress, Athenians fortify Chrysopolis to tax Pontus shipping, 1.1.22

friendship, ancestral, Agesilaos is ancestral friend of Mantineians, 6.5.4; *see also* **guest-friendship**

gambling, Kallistratos observes that the majority of gamblers who make a winning roll and immediately double their bet become completely impoverished, 6.3.16

games, Theramenes plays symposium game with dregs of hemlock, 2.3.56; *see also* **Isthmian Games; Olympic Games; Pythian festival**

garlands, Eteonikos orders garlands be worn as pretense that Spartans have won sea battle, 1.6.36; Lysander hands the Spartans those he received as gifts, 2.3.8; Agesilaos' victorious soldiers dedicate their garlands to Artemis, 3.4.18; after victory at Coronea, Spartans honor god with, 4.3.21; Argives send garlanded heralds to Agesipolis claiming holy truce is in force, 4.7.3; Teleutias' troops laud him with, 5.1.3–4; Thebans send garlanded herald to Athens after Leuctra, 6.4.24

garrison(s), *see also* **harmosts**

Achaeans establish to protect Calydon, 4.6.1

Argive, not dismissed by Corinthians, 5.1.34

Athenian: at Methymna on Lesbos, 1.6.24; of Chalcedon and Byzantium sent by Lysander to Athens, 2.2.1–2; withdrawn from the cities and Iphikrates recalled, 6.4.1; at request of Corinthians, withdrawn from Corinthian territory, 7.4.4

Greek: of Aeolian cities were mistreated by Meidias, go over to Derkylidas, 3.1.16; both sides send to protect Corinth and Sicyon, otherwise prosecuted the war with mercenaries, 4.4.14

Persian: of the other cities refuse rule of Meidias and stay faithful to Pharnabazos, 3.1.15; commander of Kebren holds out for reward from Pharnabazos, 3.1.17; satraps agree to establish in the strongholds of Caria, 3.2.14; Pharnabazos leaves garrison at Cythera commanded by Nikophemos, an Athenian, 4.8.8

Spartan: commander Eteonikos expelled from Thasos, 1.1.32; commander Labotes killed at Herakleia, 1.2.18; commander Hippokrates killed at Chalcedon, 1.3.6; Klearchos is commander at Byzantium, 1.3.15–17; Lysander sends to Athens to protect the Thirty, 2.1.13; threatens the Council at Athens to facilitate arrest of Theramenes, 2.3.55; occupies half of the Odeion at Athens, 2.4.10; Derkylidas establishes at Kebren, 3.1.19; Agesilaos leaves 4,000 men in Asia as, 4.2.5; Praxitas establishes at Sidous and Krommyon, 4.4.13;

bringing grain into the city because Spartan commander dallies with a boy, 5.4.56–57

Thessaly, unlike Athens, has such abundant supplies that they export it, 6.1.11

grain ships, Agis confounded by the many grain boats sailing into Peiraieus, 1.1.35; Athenian ships always stationed at Hellespont to watch over merchantmen, 1.1.36; Teleutias sails down coast of Attica, capturing boats and grain ships, 5.1.22–24; Antalkidas, with fleet of 80 triremes, is master of the sea, preventing grain ships' sailing to Athens, 5.1.28; sailors from grain ships imprisoned by Alketas seize Oreos' acropolis, and the city revolts against the Spartans, 5.4.56–57; those going to Athens stop at Geraistos because of enemy ships at Aegina, Keos, and Andros, 5.4.61

greed, Theramenes refers to those who betray others for a shameless love of gain, 2.3.43; Thebans call rule of Spartans greedy, 3.5.1

Gryllos, Xenophon's son (though not named by Xenophon), dies in cavalry action at Mantineia, 7.5.17

guest-friendship, of Apollophanes with both Pharnabazos and Agesilaos, 4.1.29; Agesilaos pledges with Pharnabazos' son and honors in later years by helping Eualces' son enter *stadion* at Olympic Games, 4.1.39–40; of Ariobarzanes and Antalkidas, 5.1.28; Ismenias is accused by Spartans of having become guest-friend of Persia, 5.2.35

Gylis, Spartan polemarch, invades Locris and is killed, 4.3.21–22

gymnasia, hoplites and cavalry train to win Agesilaos' prizes, 3.4.16

Halieus, hoplites from in Spartan force at Nemea River, 4.2.16

Hannibal, invades Sicily with 100,000 men and captures 2 Greek cities, 1.1.37

harmost(s)

Agesilaos leaves Euxenos in command of Spartan garrison in Asia, 4.2.5

Agis leaves Lysippos at Epitalion as, 3.2.29

Derkylidas was harmost of Abydos, 3.1.9; did not withdraw from Abydos when others fled from their cities, 4.8.3; gathers all harmosts fleeing from European cities to Sestos, 4.8.5

Lysander leaves Sthenelaos as garrison commander of Byzantium, 2.2.2; has himself appointed as, to lead force supporting the Thirty against men of Peiraieus, 2.4.29

Persians demand that Spartans remove their harmosts from the cities, 3.2.20

Pharnabazos and Konon expel from coastal cities, 4.8.1

Theban envoys complain that Spartans appointed helots as harmosts and that harmosts tyrannized cities that came over to them from Athenians, 3.5.12, 3.5.13

Theban harmost controls acropolis of Sicyon, 7.3.4

Thibron appointed to lead Greek force supporting Ionian cities against Tissaphernes, 3.1.4

Hellespont, likely site of sea battle between Athenians and Spartans, 1.1.1; Dorieus sails into from Rhodos and repulses Athenian attack, 1.1.2–3; Athenians sail from, to collect money, 1.1.8; Alcibiades concentrates his ships at Sestos, 1.1.11; Athenian generals sail to after taking Cyzicus, 1.1.22; Athenians destroy 3 allied ships,

which are attacked by the 9 ships they keep on constant watch, 1.1.36; Athenians sail to after defeat at Ephesus, 1.2.11; Alcibiades marshals his forces at Lampsacus, 1.2.15–17; Athenians attack Chalcedon and Byzantium, 1.3.1–3; Alcibiades demands money from, 1.3.8; Byzantium opens its gates to Athenians, 1.3.14–22; Thrasyboulos sails to Phocaea from, 1.5.11; one of Konon's ships avoids blockade by sailing to and warns Athenians of siege of fleet at Lesbos, 1.6.20, 1.6.22; Erasinides is accused of appropriating public funds from, 1.7.2; Lysander attacks and plunders Lampsacus, harassing Athenians who land to forage for food, 2.1.17–21, 2.1.27; he sails from, with 200 triremes, to besiege Peiraieus, 2.2.5; Derkylidas crosses over after truce with Pharnabazos, 3.2.9; Agesilaos sends Lysander to from Ephesus, 3.4.10; Agesilaos marches his army to from Asia and awards prizes for best soldiers, 4.2.6; Derkylidas sets out for, to announce Spartan victory at Nemea River to Asian cities, 4.3.3; force from fights with Athenians at Coronea, 4.3.17; Pharnabazos orders Konon to win over cities of, 4.8.6; Thrasyboulos imposes a tax on ships coming in from the Black Sea and changes government of Byzantium to a democracy, 4.8.27; Spartans attempt to reduce Athenian influence and send Anaxibios to Abydos, 4.8.31–32; Athenians send Iphikrates to reinforce Thrasyboulos' arrangements, 4.8.34

helmets, Epaminondas orders his cavalry to whiten, 7.5.18

helots, who rebelled at Malea released by treaty, 1.2.18; Theban envoy accuses Sparta of establishing as harmosts, 3.5.12; in Spartan army, 4.3.15, 5.2.24, 6.1.14, 6.5.24, 6.5.28; regarded by Polydamas as second best force, 6.1.14; as inadequate fighters, 6.1.14, 7.1.12; Spartans arm 6,000 with promise of their freedom and are alarmed at large number when they are arrayed together, 6.5.28–29; Prokles regards as inadequate sailors in proposed joint fleet, 7.1.12; Spartans accused of planning to send as sailors to a joint force commanded by Athenians, 7.1.12; revolt after Spartan defeat at Leuctra, 7.2.2; *see also* ***neodamōdeis***

Hera, Corinthians flee to temple of in Peiraion, 4.5.5; Phleious, temple of (Heraion), 7.2.1, 7.2.6, 7.2.11

Herakleidai, 3.3.3

Herakles, Thebans are encouraged to hear that the weapons from the temple of Herakles has vanished, 6.4.7; Spartans encouraged by statue of as they attack Arcadians, 7.1.31

Herippidas, commissioned to witness oath by Tissaphernes, 3.4.6; Agesilaos appoints to command the men who served with Cyrus, 3.4.20; a leading member of the thirty Spartiates, asked to obtain Spithridates' consent for his daughter's marriage to Otys, 4.1.11–13; attacks Pharnabazos' camp and seizes booty and pack animals, 4.1.21–25; intercepts Spithridates and the Paphlagonians, stripping them of their share of the booty, 4.1.26; chosen as one of 3 to judge Agesilaos' competitions, 4.2.8; commands allied contingents at Coronea, 4.3.15; his troops advance to battle on the run, 4.3.17; commands Spartan ships, 4.8.11; one of the commanders who surrender the Theban acropolis (but not named by Xenophon), n. 5.4.13a

Malians, join allied force at Nemea River, 4.2.17

Mania, wife of Zenis, persuades Pharnabazos to appoint her subsatrap of Aeolis, 3.1.11–12; is strangled by her son-in-law Meidias, 3.1.14

Mantineia/Mantineians, join Spartans against Corinthians and their allies, 4.2.13; Spartans' contempt for, 4.4.17; Agesilaos avoids so that his men will not see Mantineians rejoicing over Spartan defeat at Lechaion, 4.5.18; ordered by Spartans to tear down their city wall, 5.2.1–2; Agesilaos asks to be relieved of command against because of past service of Mantineians to his father during the Messenian wars, 5.2.3; Spartans subdue the city by flooding it and resettle the population in 4 villages, where they establish aristocratic rule, 5.2.3–7; leaders of the popular party allowed to depart without harm, 5.2.6; villages enthusiastically support Spartan mobilization against Thebans, 6.4.18; vote to unite and encircle city with a wall, refusing Spartan request to delay, 6.5.4–5; intervene in faction fighting in Tegea, 6.5.6–9; attack Orchomenos and drive off mercenaries, 6.5.13–14; gather their allies but do not attack Spartan force outside the city, 6.5.15–17; oppose use of sacred treasure to pay Arcadian Eparitoi, 7.4.33–34; evade capture by Thebans at Tegea and secure release of captives, 7.4.37–38; vulnerable to attack at harvest time, are rescued by Athenian cavalry, who gain time for them to bring livestock and people within the walls, 7.5.14–17; battle of Mantineia, 7.5.18–27

Margana/Marganeis, peltasts leave Eleians to join Spartan side, 3.2.25; Eleians agree with Spartans to leave autonomous, 3.2.30; slingers in Spartan force at Nemea River, 4.2.16; betrayed to Arcadians, 7.4.14; recaptured by Eleians, 7.4.26

Medes, Darius resumes rule over, 1.2.19

Media, the King summons Cyrus to Thamneria, where he lies ill, 2.1.13

Megabates son of Spithridates, referred to but not named, 3.4.10; joins Spithridates in leaving Daskyleion for Sardis, 4.1.27

Megalopolis, supported Epaminondas, 7.5.5

Meidias, strangles his mother-in-law Mania in Aeolis and seizes power, 3.1.14–15; makes peace with Derkylidas and allows him to take Skepsis and Gergis, 3.1.20–24; Derkylidas strips of the wealth he had stolen from Mania, 3.1.23–28

Melos, Lysander restores to Melians, 2.2.9; Konon and Pharnabazos sail to Spartan territory via, 4.8.7

mercenaries

Agesilaos: offers prizes to mercenaries who best fit out company of hoplites, archers, and peltasts, 4.2.5; gives Kleitorian force a month's pay and orders them to gain control of Mount Cithaeron, 5.4.37; returns to command defense of Sparta though all his cavalry and mercenaries are still in Arcadia, 7.5.10

Chares, commands force that attacks Sicyonians at Thyamia with divine enthusiasm, 7.2.20–21

Corcyra, Mnasippos orders company commanders to lead out the mercenaries, 6.2.18

Corinthians: continue to prosecute the war with after disbanding their citizen armies, 4.4.14; Iphikrates' force fights at Corinth, 4.4.9; employ against Sicyonians, 4.4.14; gather force after rejecting Athenian alliance, 7.4.6

Derkylidas orders Meidias' bodyguard to ground their arms as they will now be his mercenaries, 3.1.25

Diphridas uses ransom for Strouthas' daughter and son-in-law to pay, 4.8.21

Euphron: bribes to gain support, 7.1.46; commands force of around 2,000, 7.2.11; obtains force from Athens and goes to Thebes, where he is assassinated, 7.3.4–6

Hermokrates recruits to restore generals exiled from Syracuse by the people, 1.1.31

Iphikrates commands force of at Corinth, 4.4.9

Kephisodotos points out to Athenians that command at sea means command over Spartan slaves or mercenaries, 7.1.12

Kleitorians: agree to make unit recruited for war with Orchomenos available to Agesilaos, 5.4.36; Jason of Pherai threatens to seize control of Pharsalus with his well-trained force, 6.1.5–6; trains to high level, 6.4.28

Kleombrotos orders Sphodrias to hire to strengthen Spartan garrison at Thebes, 5.4.15

Lysander besieges Peiraieus with force of, 2.4.30

Mania uses Greek mercenaries to conquer cities of the Troad, 3.1.13

Mantineians defeat Polytropos' force of, 6.5.14

Mnasippos attacks Corcyra with 1,500; fails to pay or feed them, and they become dispirited, 6.2.5, 6.2.16

Orchomenians take in Corinthian mercenaries against Mantineian threat but are driven back, 6.5.11, 6.5.13–14

Pharnabazos hires to attack Spartans, 4.8.7

Philiskos of Abydos raises on Spartan side, using Persian gold, 7.1.27

Sicyonians, employ against Corinthians, 4.4.14; Euphron bribes to gain their support, 7.1.46

Spartans: ephors give Anaxibios enough money to hire 1,000 to attack Abydos, 4.8.32, 4.8.35; mercenaries flee when Thebans counterattack at Thespiai, 5.4.45; Orchomenian mercenaries help in defense of Sparta, 6.5.29; alleged to be prepared to send as sailors to a joint force commanded by Athenians, 7.1.12; join inept Spartan defense at Oneon, 7.1.41; *see also* Agesilaos, *above*

Teleutias tells Amyntas to hire if he wants to regain his kingdom, 5.2.38

Theban, pursue Agesilaos at walls of Thebes, 5.4.54

merchant vessels, *see also* **grain ships; troop transport ships**

Athenians maintain 9 ships at Hellespont to keep watch over merchantmen, 1.1.36

Eteonikos, on learning of Peloponnesian fleet's defeat at Arginousai Islands, orders traders at Lesbos to quietly load their ships and sail to Chios, 1.6.37

Lysander attacks merchant vessels sailing from Hellespont and cities that have revolted from Spartan alliance, 2.1.17

Teleutias: raids Peiraieus, dragging off merchant ships and ferries, 5.1.20–21; raids merchant ships at Sounion and gives his soldiers one month's advance pay, 5.1.22–23

messengers, Boeotarchs send horsemen to prevent Agesilaos from sacrificing at Aulis, 3.4.4; Tissaphernes sends a messenger to Agesilaos at Ephesus, 3.4.5; Agesilaos is informed that he commands the fleet as well as the army, 3.4.27; Archidamos sends Demotoles to Sparta to announce victory, 7.1.32

Messenia/Messenians, Agesilaos says Mantineians helped his

supplies *(cont'd)*

a ransom although they are in great need of supplies, 7.2.16; take great risks to bring in supplies to their beleaguered city, 7.2.17–19

Spartans: give Agesilaos a 6-month supply of grain for Asia expedition, 3.4.3; pack animals are blown off cliff by high winds, 5.4.17; leave behind in Corcyra much grain, wine, and slaves when fleet escapes, 6.2.26; commander makes peace with Thebans though he could have held his position and obtained supplies, 7.1.17

Thebans: succeed in bringing grain into the city because Spartan commander dallies with a boy, 5.4.56–57; they and their allies leave Spartan territory because their supplies are dwindling, having been used up, stolen, wasted, or burned, 6.5.50

Thessaly, unlike Athens, has such abundant supplies of grain that they export it, 6.1.11

Thibron attempts to take Laris(s)a by cutting off its water supply, 3.1.7

the Thirty's attempt to prevent men at Phyle from obtaining supplies is thwarted by a snowstorm, 2.4.3

surprise attacks, *see also* **ambushes**

Agesilaos: surprised by allied attack, quickly deploys for battle, 4.2.19; makes on Thessalians and routs them, 4.3.4–8; lays an ambush of 300 hoplites in the temple of the sons of Tyndareus to stop Theban advance, 6.5.31

Antalkidas surprises flotillas under Thrasyboulos of Kollytos in the Hellespont, 5.1.27

Chabrias ambushes Gorgopas on Aegina, 5.1.10–12

Derkylidas' forces are surprised on the Maeander plain, 3.2.14–17

Epaminondas deceives the enemy so that his attack is a surprise, 7.5.21–22

Lysander's on the Athenians at Aigospotamoi, 2.1.27

Persian cavalry defeat Greek cavalry in surprise engagement, 3.4.13–14

Pharnabazos makes a surprise attack on foragers at Daskyleion, 4.1.17–19

Phleiasians: exiles plot with Arcadians and Eleians, 7.2.5; attack Sicyonian fort at sunset, 7.2.22

Teleutias makes on Peiraieus, 5.1.19–22

Thebans: cavalry makes on Spartans, 5.4.38; launch dawn assault on Spartans near Oneon, 7.1.15–17

Thrasyboulos routs the Thirty at Phyle with a dawn attack, 2.4.6–7

Spartans: attacked by Athenian allies at Nemea River, 4.2.19; follow Athenians unseen and launch surprise attack on those landing at Cape Zoster, 5.1.9

Syracuse/Syracusans, burn their ships at Cyzicus to save them from Athenians, 1.1.18; build wall at Antandros and are given the title of benefactors and the priveleges of citizenship, 1.1.26; generals exiled by the people insist their sailors must obey the state, 1.1.27–29; Ephesians reward those who fought most bravely to repel Athenian attack, 1.2.10; Thrasyllos captures 4 of their ships at Methymna, 1.2.12; prisoners sent to Athens escape by tunneling, 1.2.14; Dionysios becomes tyrant and defeats Carthaginians, 2.2.24; ships join Spartans under Antalkidas, 5.1.28; ships setting out to support Spartans in Corcyra are captured by Iphikrates; the commander takes his own life, 6.2.33–36; Dionysios

sends troops to assist Spartans, 7.1.20–21; a second armed force from Dionysios arrives, 7.1.28; after the death of his father, the younger Dionysios sends another force to assist the Spartans, 7.4.12

taxation, *see also* **tribute**

Athenians: establish a custom house at Chrysopolis in Chalcedon to collect 10 percent tax on vessels coming from the Black Sea, 1.6.22; gathering at Peiraieus, exchange oaths that all who fight for them against the Thirty will have same taxation rights as citizens, 2.4.25; contract let for the one-tenth tax on ships coming from the Black Sea, 4.8.27, 4.8.30; worn out by war taxes, 6.2.1

Syracusans and Selinuntians are granted right to live in Ephesus tax-free, 1.2.10

Thebans persuade Opuntian Locrians to levy a tax on land disputed with Phocians, 3.5.3

taxiarchs, 1.6.30, 1.6.34, 4.1.26, 6.2.18–19

Tearless Battle, Archidamos routs Argives and Acadians, 7.1.29–31

Tegea/Tegeans, Pausanias crosses the border and waits for allied troops to join him there, 3.5.7; he flees to and dies there, 3.5.25; join Spartans against Corinthians and their allies, 4.2.13; opposed in battle line at Nemea River by 4 tribes of Athenians, 4.2.19; Athenians suffer losses at hands of, 4.4.21; Agesilaos arrives at and mobilizes forces against Thebans, 5.1.33; enthusiastically join Spartan force, especially the followers of Stasippos, 6.4.18; factions dispute pan-Arcadian unity in Council of the Thearoi, 6.5.6–7; after losing vote in Council of the Thearoi, anti-Spartan faction calls on Mantineians, and Stasippos' force is defeated after opponents climb on the roof and pelt men below with roof tiles, 6.5.6–9; Spartans mobilize against Mantineia to help Tegean exiles, 6.5.10; Arcadians from Tegea join Mantineians, 6.5.16; exiles join Spartan garrison at Oion, 6.5.24; Spartans maintain that they are defending Tegeans against Mantineian aggression, 6.5.36–37; Arcadians celebrate peace at, 7.4.36–37; Mantineians demand release of prisoners, 7.4.38; Epaminondas marches toward, making his camp within the city, 7.5.7–8; withdraws back to the city after his army is defeated by Spartans, 7.5.14

Teisamenos the seer, arrested for supporting Kinadon's conspiracy, 3.3.11

Teleutias brother of Agesilaos, supports Agesilaos' attack on harbor of Corinth, 4.4.19; takes command of Herippidas' ships and controls the gulf again, 4.8.11; ordered eastward, he sails to Rhodos, captures 10 Athenian ships, 4.8.23–24; drives off Athenian squadron attempting to build fortification on Aegina, 5.1.1–2; relieved of his command, is lauded and garlanded by his troops, 5.1.3–4; sent to command fleet again (since sailors refuse to row for Eteonikos, who has withheld their pay), he promises them honor and booty, 5.1.14–18; raids Peiraieus and seizes merchant ships and ferries, 5.1.19–21; raids merchant ships at Sounion and gives his soldiers one month's advance pay, 5.1.22–23; dispatched against Olynthos as governor, 5.2.37; orders Amyntas to recruit mercenaries and reaches Poteidaia without plundering allies' lands, 5.2.37–39; wins battle before Olynthos, 5.2.40–43;

attempt to use peltasts against Olynthian cavalry fails, and he is killed in battle, 5.3.3–6

temples, *see also* **Delphi; shrines**

Agesilaos: camps around temple of Artemis Astyrene on the Plain of Thebe, 4.1.41; after battle of Coronea, protects enemy soldiers who have taken refuge in a temple, 4.3.20; at Peiraion, decides that of those who have taken refuge in the temple, only those who took part in the slaughter at the Eucleia festival should be handed to Corinthian exiles, 4.5.5; after recovering bodies of the dead, leads his army back to the temple of Hera, 4.5.7; at Megara, suffers from a burst blood vessel as he goes up from the temple of Aphrodite to the magistrates' residence, 5.4.58

Agesipolis dies of fever before the temple of Dionysos at Aphytis, before he can revisit its shady buildings and bright, cold waters, 5.3.18

Athena: temple of at Phocaea struck by lightning, 1.3.1; ancient temple of caught fire, 1.6.1

Athens: the Thirty order soldiers to deposit confiscated weapons in the temple on the Acropolis, 2.3.20; troops sent to Peiraieus by the Thirty fill the road that leads to the temple of Mounichian Athena, 2.4.11

Derkylidas orders Meidias to open the gates of city of Geris and accompany him to the temple to sacrifice to Athena, 3.1.22

Ephesus, temple of Artemis, 1.2.6

Leuctra, Thebans are heartened by reports that doors of the temples opened of their own accord and arms of Herakles statue have disappeared from his temple, 6.4.7

Leukophrys, very sacred temple of Artemis, 3.2.19

Olympia, Eleians withdrawn under fire from those on the porticoes and the Council House and the great temple, 7.4.31

Spartans: allow Eleians to continue to supervise temple of Olympian Zeus as the other claimants are considered boors, 3.2.31; lay an ambush of 300 hoplites in temple of sons of Tyndareus to stop Theban advance, 6.5.31

Tegea, some of Stasippos' men take refuge in temple of Artemis but surrender after being pelted with roof tiles, 6.5.9

Thebans advancing on Sparta do not attempt to cross the bridge into the city because they can see hoplites in temple of Athena Alea ready to engage them, 6.5.27

Thasos, Thrasyboulos sails out with 20 ships from, 1.1.12; civil strife drives out Spartan governor, 1.1.32; suffers from war, civil strife, and famine when Thrasyboulos subdues, 1.4.9; among cities where Athenian generals gather to bring help to Tenedos, 5.1.7

Thearoi, Council of (in Tegea), 6.5.6

theater, Spartans pursue enemy to theater in Peiraieus, from where light-armed men rush out and attack them, 2.4.32–33; Corinthians are slain in, 4.4.3; Spartans announce names of dead of Leuctra at close of men's chorus' performance, 6.4.16

Thebes/Thebans, Eleians prevent Agis from praying for victory, asserting that Greeks should not consult oracles about war with Greeks, and Agis leaves without sacrificing, 3.2.22; prevent Agesilaos from sacrificing at Aulis, 3.4.3–4; Androkleidas, Ismenias, and Galaxidoros accept Persian bribes to make war on Spartans, 3.5.1; persuade Opuntian Locrians to levy a tax on land disputed with Phocians, thus provoking Phocian attack,

3.5.3; Spartans use Locrian invasion of Phocis as excuse to attack Thebes, 3.5.5;

Agesilaos camps at temple of Artemis Astyrene, 4.1.41; initiate battle at Coronea by raising their war cry and charging, 4.3.17; rout Orchomenians but then suffer losses fighting through the Spartan line, 4.3.18–19; Agesilaos allows to collect their dead, 4.3.21; Agesilaos defeats at Coronea, 4.3.15–19; are alarmed at Persian proposal for autonomy to Greek cities for fear of losing control of Boeotia, 4.8.15;

threaten King's Peace by demanding right to sign on behalf of all Boeotians but finally grant autonomy to Boeotia in face of Spartan threats, 5.1.32–33; Leontiades persuades Phoibidas to use Spartan force to seize acropolis and arrests his rival, Ismenias, 5.2.25–31; Spartans agree to support Leontiades, and 3 judges sentence Ismenias to death, 5.2.35–36; Spartans continue to occupy acropolis of Thebes although they had promised autonomy to all cities, 5.4.1; Phillidas and Melon plot assassination of polemarchs, disguising the young male assassins as women, 5.4.2–7; the conspirators open the prison and call for a popular rising, 5.4.8–9; they allow Spartan governor to leave the acropolis under safe conduct but murder their enemies and even their enemies' children, 5.4.10–12; Spartans declare war, dispatching army under Kleombrotos, 5.4.13–18; Thebans bribe Sphodrias, Spartan governor at Thespiai, to attack Attica to bring Athenians into the war, 5.4.20–21; repulse Spartans, 5.4.38–46; Agesilaos attacks, 5.4.47–55; succeed in bringing grain into the city because Spartan commander dallies with a boy, 5.4.56–57;

conquer cities in Boeotia and attack Phocis, 6.1.1; Theban attacks on Athens' allies lead Athens to leave war with Sparta, 6.3.1; Athens invites to join in sending emissaries to Sparta to negotiate peace, 6.3.2; Athens invites to join in sending emissaries to Sparta to negotiate peace, 6.3.2; reluctantly agree to swear to peace, then wish to retract, 6.3.19–20; determine to resist Kleombrotos, 6.4.6–7; victory over Spartans at Leuctra, 6.4.8–15; Athenians ignore their herald, so they appeal to Jason of Pherai, 6.4.19–20; Jason advises them to seek a truce with Spartans, which he negotiates, 6.4.21–23; allies beg them to invade Spartan territory, and they decide to advance, 6.5.23–24; lay waste towns around Sparta, 6.5.30–32; withdraw with their plunder, 6.5.50;

launch dawn attack on Spartans and Pelleneians near Oneon and agree to a truce, 7.1.15–17; join their allies in attacking Sicyon and Epidauros but are driven off at gates of Corinth, 7.1.18–19; draw up their forces on plain of Corinth but suffer attacks from horsemen sent to reinforce the allies by Dionysios, and leave for home, 7.1.20–22; Lykomedes persuades Arcadians to throw off their leadership, 7.1.23–24; welcome Spartan victory over Arcadians, 7.1.32; wishing to gain leadership of Greece, send Pelopidas and other ambassadors to seek Persian support, 7.1.33; Pelopidas invokes Thebes' support of Persia at Plataea and its victory over Sparta at Leuctra, then asks Persia to demand that Sparta give up Messenia and that Athens immobilize its fleet, threatens to go to war against them if they do not agree, 7.1.34–36; the King includes these terms in a written proclamation, 7.1.37; aristocrats, 7.1.42; Theban governors succeed in establishing democracies in

REFERENCE MAPS
Directory

Sites that are listed in this directory but, due to inappropriate scale or crowding of map labels, could not be placed on the Reference Maps are identified as located on the text map on which they appear.

Abai, Ref.3, AY
Abydos, Ref.4, AX
Academy (Athens), Ref.5
Acarnania, Ref.3, AW
Achaea, Ref.2, CW
Achaea Phthiotis, Ref.2, BX
Achilleion, Ref.4, AX
Acrocorinth, 4.4.12, inset
Acropolis (Athens), Ref.5
Aegae, Ref.4, BY
Aegean Sea, Ref.2, BX
Aegina, Ref.3, CY
Aeolis, Ref.4, BY
Aetolia, Ref.3, AX
Agora (Athens), Ref.5
Agora (Peiraieus), Ref.5
Aigospotamoi (Aigospota-
  mos), Ref.4, AX
Aigosthena, Ref.3, BY
Ainis (Ainiania), Ref.3, AX
Aixone (deme), Ref.3, BZ
Akanthos, Ref.2, AX
Akroreia, Ref.3, CX
Alpheios River, Ref.3, CX
Altis (Olympia), 7.4.29, inset
Alyz(e)ia, Ref.3, AW
Ambracia, Ref.2, BW
Amphidolia, Ref.3, CX
Amphipolis, Ref.2, AX
Amyklai, Ref.3, DX

Anaphlystos (deme), Ref.3,
  CZ
Andros, Ref.2, CX
Antandros, Ref.4, AX
Aphytis, Ref.2, BX
Apollonia, Ref.2, AX
Arcadia, Ref.3, CX
Arginousai Islands, Ref.4,
  BX
Argos, Ref.2, CX
Artemis, Temple of
  (Peiraieus), Ref.5
Asea, Ref.3, CX
Asia, Ref.1
Asine, Ref.2, DW
Asopos River, Ref.3, BY
Aspendos, 4.8.27
Astyra?, Ref.4, AY
Atarneus, Ref.4, AX
Athens, Ref.2, CX
Athos, Mount, Ref.2, AX
Attica, Ref.2, CX
Aulis, Ref.3, AY
Aulon, Ref.3, CX

Babylon, Ref.1
Bendis, Shrine of (Peiraieus),
  Ref.5
Bithynia, Ref.2, AZ
Bithynian Thrace, Ref.2, AZ
Black Sea (Pontus), Ref.1

Boeotia, Ref.2, CX
Bosporus, Ref.2, AZ
Byzantium, Ref.2, AZ

Calydon, Ref.3, BX
Camarina, 2.3.4, inset
Caria, Ref.2, CZ
Carthage, Ref.1
Caunus, Ref.2, DZ
Cephallania, Ref.3, BW
Cephisus River, Ref.3, AY
Chaeronea, Ref.3, AY
Chalcedon, Ref.2, AZ
Chalcidice, Ref.2, AX
Chalcis, Ref.3, AY
Chersonese, Ref.4, AX
Chios, Ref.4, BX
Chios (island), Ref.4, BX
Chrysopolis, Ref.2, AZ
Cilicia, Ref.1
Cithaeron, Mount, Ref.3, BY
Cnidus, Ref.2, DY
Colophon, Ref.4, BY
Corcyra, Ref.2, BW
Corcyra (island), Ref.2, BW
Corinth, Ref.2, CX
Corinth, Isthmus of,
  Ref.3, BY
Corinthian Gulf, Ref.3, BX
Coronea, Ref.3, BY
Cos, Ref.2, DY

Council House (Prytaneion)
  (Athens), Ref.5
Council House (Olympia),
  7.4.29, inset
Crete, Ref.1
Cunaxa, Ref.1
Cyme, Ref.4, BX
Cynoscephalae (Thessaly),
  5.3.14
Cyprus, Ref.1
Cyrene, Ref.1
Cythera, Ref.2, DX
Cyzicus, Ref.4, AY

Dardanos, 3.1.13, AX
Daskyleion, Ref.4, AY
Deigma (Peiraieus), Ref.5
Dekeleia, Ref.3, BZ
Delos, Ref.2, CY
Delphi, Ref.2, CX
Delphinion, Ref.4, BX
Dionysus, Theater of
  (Peiraieus), Ref.5
Dodona, Ref.2, BW
Dolopia, Ref.2, BW

Eetioneia (Peiraieus), Ref.5
Egypt, Ref.1
Eion, Ref.2, AX
Elaious, Ref.4, AX
Eleusis, Ref.3, BY

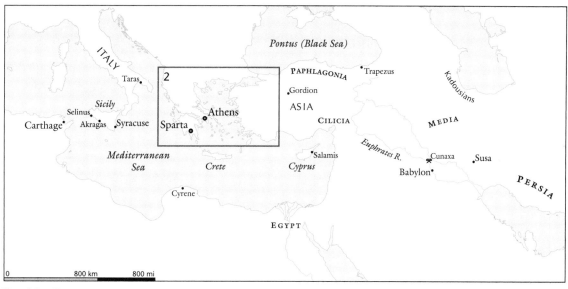

REF. MAP 1

Pharsalus, Ref.2, BX
Pheia, Ref.3, CW
Pherai (Laconia), Ref.3, DX
Pherai (Thessaly), Ref.2, BX
Phleious, Ref.3, CY
Phocaea, Ref.4, BX
Phocis, Ref.3, AY
Phoenicia, 3.4.12, locator
Phrixa, Ref.3, CX
Phrygia, Ref.2, BZ
Phyle, Ref.3, BY
Pisa, Ref.3, CX
Pisidia, Ref.2, CZ
Plataea, Ref.3, BY
Pnyx Hill (Athens), Ref.5
Pontus (Black Sea), Ref.1
Poteidaia, Ref.2, AX
Potniai, 5.4.50, AX
Prasiai, Ref.3, DY
Priene, Ref.4, BY
Proconnesus (city), Ref.2, AY
Proconnesus (island), 5.1.17, AY
Propontis, Ref.2, AY
Pygela, 1.2.10, BY
Pylos (Elis), Ref.3, BX
Pylos (Messenia), Ref.3, DX

Racetrack (Olympia), 7.4.29, inset
Rhion, Cape, Ref.3, BX
Rhodios River, 4.8.27, inset
Rhodos, Ref.2, DZ
Rhoiteion, 1.1.22, inset

Salamis (Cyprus), Ref.1
Salamis (island), Ref.3, BY
Samos, Ref.4, BX
Samos (island), Ref.4, BX
Samothrace, Ref.2, AY
Sardis, Ref.2, CZ
Saronic Gulf, Ref.3, BY
Selinus, Ref.1
Sellasia, Ref.3, DX
Selymbria, Ref.2, AY
Sestos, Ref.4, AX
Sicily, Ref.1
Sicyon, Ref.3, BY
Sidous, Ref.3, BY
Siphnos, Ref.2, DX
Skepsis, Ref.4, AX
Skillous, Ref.3, CX
Skione, Ref.2, BX
Skiritis, Ref.3, DX
Skolos, Ref.3, BY
Skotoussa, 4.3.9, AX
Skyros, Ref.3, AZ

Sounion, Cape, Ref.3, CZ
Sparta, Ref.2, DX
Spartolos, Ref.2, AX
Stadium (Olympia), 7.4.29, inset
Steiria (deme), Ref.3, BZ
Stratos, Ref.3, AW
Strymon River, Ref.2, AX
Stymphalos, Ref.3, CX
Susa, Ref.1
Syracuse, Ref.1

Tanagra, Ref.3, BY
Taras (Taranto), Italy, Ref.1
Taygetos, Mount, Ref.3, DX
Tegea, Ref.3, CX
Tegyra, Ref.3, AY
Temnos, Ref.4, BY
Tenea, Ref.3, CY
Tenedos, Ref.4, AX
Teos, Ref.4, BX
Teuthrania, 3.1.13, AX
Thasos, Ref.2, AX
Theater of Dionysus (Peiraieus), Ref.5
Theatron (Olympia), 7.4.29, inset
Thebe, Plain of, 4.1.31

Thebes, Ref.2, CX
Therapne, 6.5.31, BX
Thermopylae, Ref.2, BX
Thespiai, Ref.3, BY
Thessaly, Ref.2, BX
Thisbe, Ref.3, BY
Tholos (Athens), Ref.5
Thorikos, Ref.3, CZ
Thrace, Ref.2, AY
Thria, Ref.3, BY
Thurii, 1.5.13, locator
Thyrea, 6.5.23, inset
Thyrreion, Ref.3, AW
Torone, Ref.2, BX
Tralles, Ref.4, BY
Trapezus, Ref.1
Trikaranon, Mount, Ref.3, CY
Triphylia, Ref.3, CX
Troad, Ref.4, AX
Troizen, Ref.3, CY
Troy (Ilion), Ref.2, BY

Zacynthus, Ref.3, CW
Zeus, Altar of (Olympia), 7.4.29, inset
Zeus, Temple of (Olympia), 7.4.29, inset
Zoster, Cape, Ref.3, CZ

579

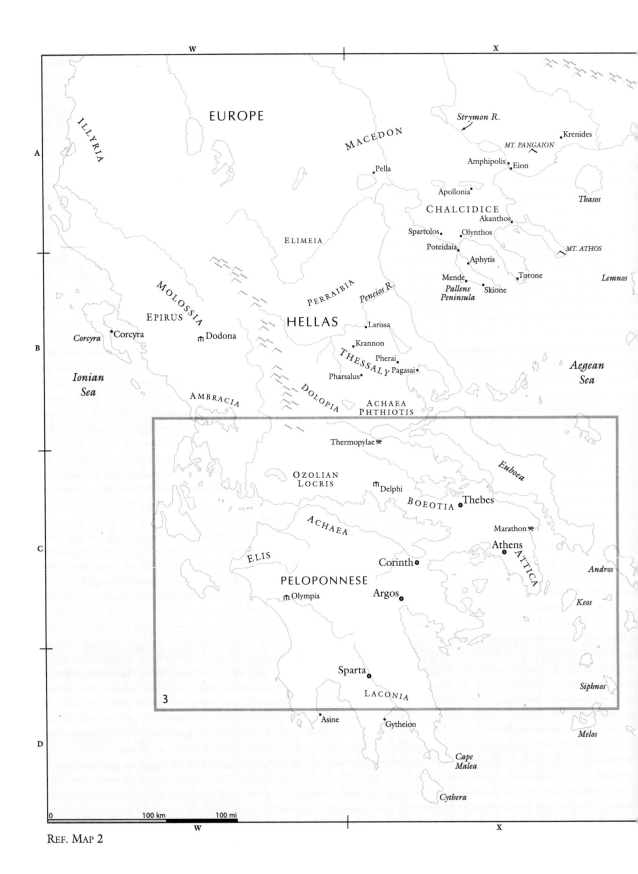

W   X

EUROPE

ILLYRIA

MACEDON

Strymon R.

MT. PANGAION   • Krenides

A   Amphipolis • Eion

•Pella   Apollonia •

Thasos

CHALCIDICE
                                                     Akanthos•

ELIMEIA   Spartolos•   •Olynthos
                                                   Poteidaia•
                                                              Aphytis•   *MT. ATHOS*

B   Mende•   *Lemnos*
                                                   Pallene   Skione
MOLOSSIA   *Peninsula*
                PERRAIBIA   *Peneios R.*   Torone•
EPIRUS   ⌂ Dodona
Corcyra •Corcyra   HELLAS   •Larissa   *Aegean*
                                                                              Sea
                                      •Krannon
Ionian   THESSALY   •Pherai
Sea   Pharsalus• Pagasai

AMBRACIA   DOLOPIA
                                              ACHAEA
                                              PHTHIOTIS

                Thermopylae ✳

                OZOLIAN   *Euboea*
                LOCRIS   ⌂ Delphi

C   BOEOTIA •Thebes

            ACHAEA   Marathon ✳

        ELIS   Athens•   *Andros*
                                    Corinth ⊙   ATTICA
        PELOPONNESE   *Keos*
            ⌂ Olympia   Argos •

                                                              Siphnos

            Sparta •
                    LACONIA

    3   *Melos*
            •Asine   •Gytheion

                        Cape
                        Malea

D

                        Cythera

0   100 km   100 mi
W   X

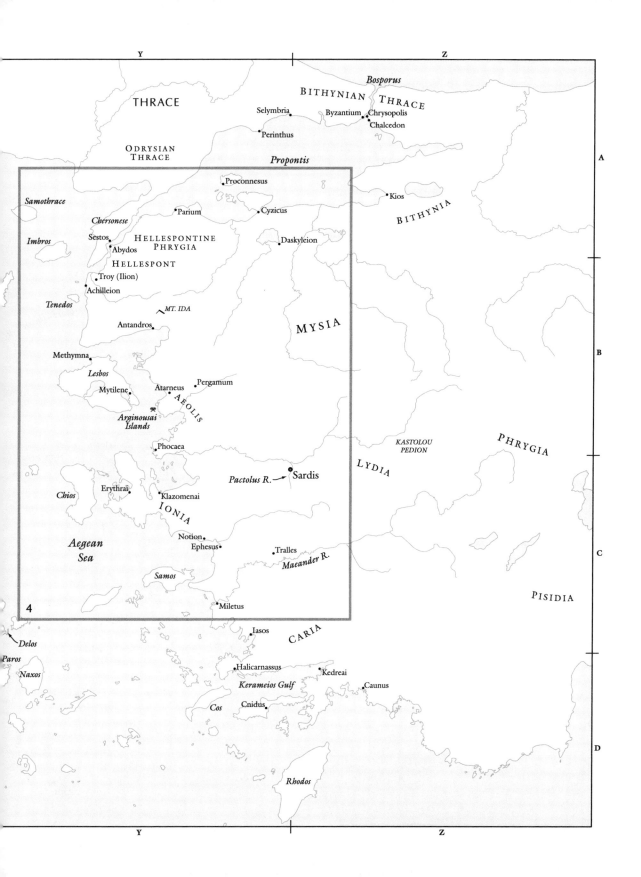

Y
Z

Bosporus

THRACE

BITHYNIAN THRACE

Selymbria
Byzantium • Chrysopolis
Chalcedon

Perinthus

ODRYSIAN
THRACE

Propontis

A

Proconnesus

Kios

BITHYNIA

Samothrace

Parium
Cyzicus

Chersonese

Sestos
Abydos

HELLESPONTINE
PHRYGIA

Daskyleion

Imbros

HELLESPONT

Troy (Ilion)
Achilleion

MYSIA

Tenedos

MT. IDA

Antandros

B

Methymna

Lesbos

Atarneus
Pergamum

Mytilene

AEOLIS

*KASTOLOU
PEDION*

PHRYGIA

*Arginousai
Islands*

Phocaea

Sardis
Pactolus R.

LYDIA

Chios

Erythrai

Klazomenai

IONIA

*Aegean
Sea*

Notion
Ephesus

Tralles

C

Samos

Maeander R.

Miletus

PISIDIA

4

Iasos

CARIA

Delos

Paros

Naxos

Halicarnassus
Kedreai

Kerameios Gulf

Caunus

Cos

Cnidus

D

Rhodos

Y
Z

W   X

Narthakion

AINIS   MALIS

Thyrreion

Herakleia-
in-Trachis
MT. OETA   Thermopylae

A   *Leucas*   ACARNANIA

Alyz(e)ia   Stratos   AETOLIA

OZOLIAN
LOCRIS

Delphi

Oiniadai   Calydon   Naupactus

*Cape
Rhion*

Corinthian Gulf

ACHAEA

B   *Cephallania*

Pellen

Kyllene   ELIS   Kleitor

Peneios R.   Elis   Pylos   Stymphalos

PELOPONNESE

Zacynthus   Lasion   ARCADIA   Orchomenos

AMPHIDOLIA   AKROREIA

Margana?   *Kladeos R.*   Mantineia

Pheia   Letrinoi   Olympia   Pisa   Heraia

*Ichthys
Peninsula*   Skillous   Phrixa   EUTRESIA?

C   TRIPHYLIA   *Alpheios R.*   Pallantion   Tegea

Lepreon   Megalopolis   Asea

Oion

Aulon   Kromnos   Malea   SKIRITIS
Leuktron

MT. ITHOME   Pellana   Sellasi

Messene   *Pamisos R.*   Sparta   *Eurotas R.*

D   MESSENIA   Pherai   Amyklai

LACONIA

Pylos   *MT. TAYGETOS*

0   50 km
        50 mi

W   X

REF. MAP 3

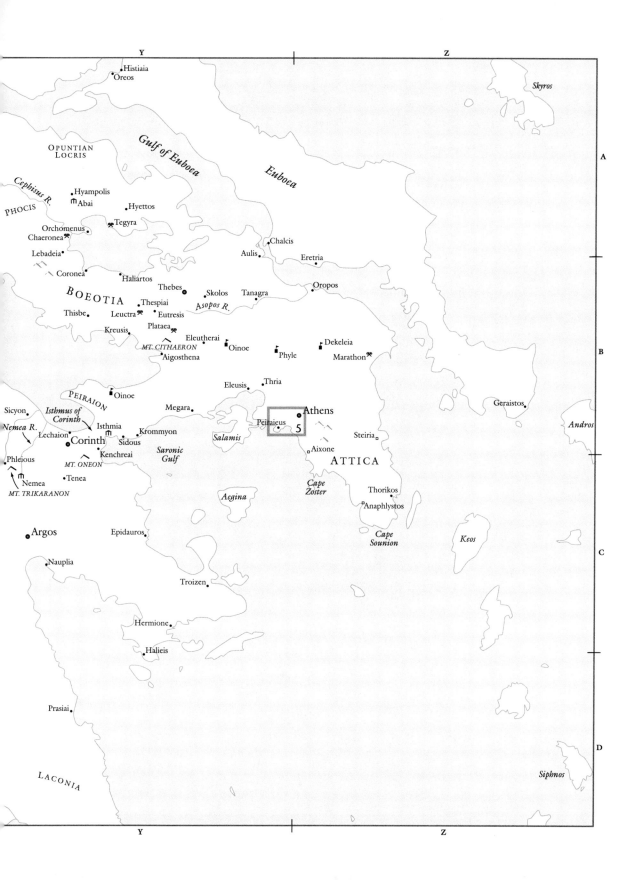

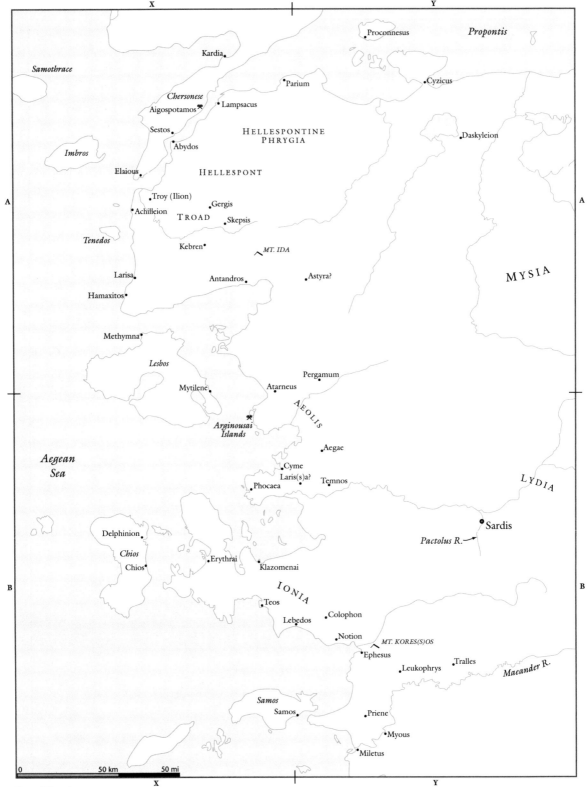

X   Y

Propontis

Proconnesus

Kardia

Parium

Samothrace

Cyzicus

Chersonese
Aigospotamos ✳   Lampsacus

Daskyleion

Sestos
Abydos

HELLESPONTINE
PHRYGIA

Imbros

Elaious

HELLESPONT

A   A

Troy (Ilion)
Gergis
Achilleion
TROAD
Skepsis

MYSIA

Tenedos

Kebren

MT. IDA

Larisa
Antandros
Astyra?

Hamaxitos

Methymna

Lesbos

Pergamum

Mytilene
Atarneus

AEOLIS

✳
*Arginousai
Islands*

Aegae

*Aegean
Sea*

Cyme
Laris(s)a?
Phocaea

Temnos

LYDIA

Delphinion

Chios

Chios

Erythrai
Klazomenai

Sardis

Pactolus R.

B   B

IONIA

Teos

Colophon
Lebedos
Notion

MT. KORES(S)OS

Ephesus
Leukophrys
Tralles

Maeander R.

Samos

Samos

Priene

Myous

Miletus

0   50 km   50 mi

X   Y

REF. MAP 4

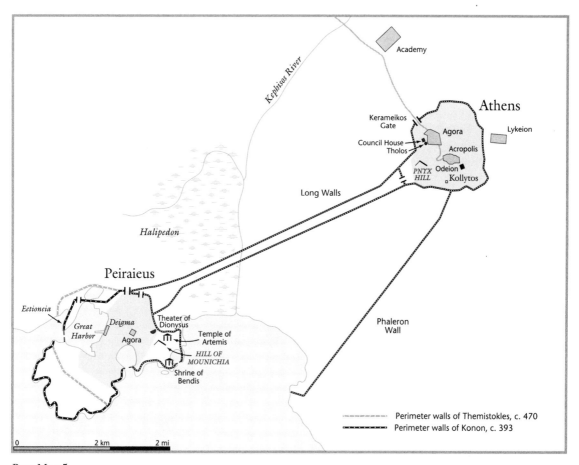

Kephisos River

Academy

Athens

Kerameikos
Gate

Agora

Lykeion

Council House
Tholos

Acropolis

Long Walls

PNYX
HILL

Odeion

Kollytos

Halipedon

Peiraieus

Phaleron
Wall

Eetioneia

Theater of
Dionysus

Great
Harbor

Deigma

Temple of
Artemis

Agora

HILL OF
MOUNICHIA

Shrine of
Bendis

0   2 km   2 mi

Perimeter walls of Themistokles, c. 470
Perimeter walls of Konon, c. 393

REF. MAP 5

Gerestus

Leon Pr.

Salamis

Athenæ

a

Cynosura Pr.

Andros I.

Hydrusa

Andrus

Dium

nis I.

Piraus
Portus

Sinus

Aegina I.
& U.

Suni
um
Pr.

Helena I.

Mare Myrtoum

Plinio

urus

Saro

Belbina I.

& Pausaniæ

olis

nicus

Polyegos I.

Cia
hodie Zea

I.

Delos
I.
Ptolemeo

Tenos I.

ione

Traezen

Longa et
Macre I.

Cythnus

Seri
phus
I.

Rhena hod
Suda I.

Cythnus quæ et
Ophiusa et Driopis
I.

CYCLADES I.

Artemisium

Albona I.

Thera I. quæ et
Calliste

Oea
Eleu
sin

Siph
nus I.

rgolicus

Epidaurus
Limera

Antimelus I.

oniæ
s

Melus I.

Cimolis I.

Malea Pr.

Amorgus I

Philocandr

Sicymus I.

era

a I.

LATÈ SUM

The

MARE MEDI